*"A child, more than all other gifts . . .
brings hope with it and forward-looking thoughts."*—GEORGE ELIOT

The Bookshelf
for Boys and Girls

Prepared under the Supervision of

THE EDITORIAL BOARD
OF THE UNIVERSITY SOCIETY

The Manual of Child Development

THE UNIVERSITY SOCIETY, INC.

Educational Publishers since 1897

NEW YORK

In addition to its wealth of new material THE BOOKSHELF FOR BOYS AND GIRLS combines the very best features of its highly successful predecessors: namely, Boys and Girls Bookshelf, copyright 1912, 1915, 1920; Young Folks Treasury, copyright 1909, 1917, 1919; Father and Son Library, copyright 1921; Modern Boy Activity, copyright 1921, 1923; The Mother's Book, copyright 1919; The Child Welfare Manual, copyright 1916; The Home Kindergarten Manual, copyright 1921; Bible Stories and Character Building, copyright 1915; The Home University Bookshelf, copyright 1927, 1938, 1945; The Bookshelf For Boys and Girls, copyright 1948.

Manufactured in the U.S.A.

iv

SMILEY BLANTON, M.D.
Psychiatrist; Assistant Professor, Cornell
University Medical College

FLORENCE BREWER BOECKEL
Education Director of the National Council for
Prevention of War

GELETT BURGESS
Author and Illustrator

FRIDA DAVIDSON
Social Worker and Author

MRS. DOROTHY CANFIELD FISHER
Author of "A Montessori Mother," etc.

EDWARD HOWE FORBUSH
State Ornithologist, Massachusetts

SIDONIE MATSNER GRUENBERG
Director, Child Study Association of America

A. NEELY HALL
Author of "The Boy Craftsman,"
"The Handy Boy," etc.

EDNA E. HARRIS
Teacher, Public Schools, City of New York

ELIZABETH HARRISON
President of the National Kindergarten College,
Chicago, Ill.

WILLIAM J. HEALY
Provincial Librarian, Winnipeg, Manitoba, Canada

FLORENCE HOLBROOK
Author of " 'Round the Year in Myth and Song"

FRANCES CARPENTER HUNTINGTON
Author of "Tales of a Chinese Grandmother"

ESTELLE MARGUERITE KENZEL
Teacher of Special Subjects, Public Schools,
City of New York

MILTON I. LEVINE, M.D.
Assistant Professor of Pediatrics, Cornell University
Medical College
Assistant Attending Pediatrician, New York Hospital
Pediatrician for City and Country School and
Bank Street Schools, New York City

MIRIAM T. LOWENBERG
Assistant Professor of Foods, Nutrition and Child
Development, Iowa State College; Author
of "Food for the Young Child"

MAX McCONN, M.A., Litt.D.
Dean, Lehigh University
Author of "Planning for College"

LUCILLE MARSH
Educational Editor, "The American Dancer"
Author of "The Dance in Education"

ROWLAND L. MINDLIN, M.D.
Pediatrician, Assistant in Pediatrics
Cornell University Medical College

HARRIS W. MOORE
Supervisor of Manual Training, Public Schools,
Watertown, Mass.; Author of "Manual Training
Toys for the Boy's Workshop"

MRS. BERTHA PAYNE NEWELL
Formerly Head of the Department of Kindergarten
Education, University of Chicago; Mother

FREDERICK BOGUE NOYES, M.D.
Professor of Orthodontia, University of Illinois
College of Dentistry

JOHNSON O'CONNOR, A.B., A.M.
Director of the Human Engineering Laboratories,
The Stevens Institute of Technology

MICHAEL VINCENT O'SHEA
Former Professor of Education
University of Wisconsin

GEORGE TRUMAN PALMER, Ph.D.
Former Director of the Division of Research,
American Child Health Association, New York

EMILIE POULSSON
Author of "Love and Law in Child Training,"
"Nursery Finger Plays," etc.

ELIZABETH PRICE
National Recreation Association

LYDIA J. ROBERTS
Assistant Professor of Home Economics,
University of Chicago

MARY D. SWARTZ ROSE
Nutrition Expert

MANDEL SHERMAN, Ph.D.
Professor of Education, The University of Chicago
Author of "Mental Hygiene and Education"

ALICE CORBIN SIES
Former Associate Professor of Childhood Education,
University of Pittsburgh; Mother

ELVA S. SMITH
Children's Librarian, Carnegie Library, Pittsbugh, Pa.

FRED C. SMITH, A.B., B.S., A.M., Ed.M., LL.D.
Dean of Graduate School and Academic Dean of The University of Tennessee; Editor of *Occupations, The Vocational Guidance Magazine*; Author

VILHJALMUR STEFANSSON
Explorer and Writer

FRANCES BRUCE STRAIN
Educator, Lecturer, Psychologist; Associate Educa tional Director of the Cincinnati Social Hygiene Society; Author of "Being Born" and "New Patterns in Sex Training"

DILLON WALLACE
Author and Explorer

THOMAS D. WOOD, M.D.
Professor of Physical Education, Columbia University

PARTIAL LIST OF ILLUSTRATORS
Examples of whose work appear in THE BOOKSHELF

HAROLD ADES	WALTER CRANE	MAXFIELD PARRISH
ANNE ANDERSON	EDMUND DULAC	MALCOLM PATTERSON
FLORENCE ANDERSON	JOAN ESLEY	E. C. PEIXOTTO
CULMER BARNES	NAT FALK	VICTOR PÉRARD
FRANK L. BAUM	JOSEPH FRANKÉ	LUCY FITCH PERKINS
ANNA WHELAN BETTS	MARGUERITE GAYER	HOWARD PYLE
R. B. BIRCH	ROBERT A. GRAEF	ARTHUR RACKHAM
E. H. BLASHFIELD	T. VICTOR HALL	HAZEL ROCHESTER
R. I. BRASHER	RUTH HALLOCK	HARRY ROUNTREE
PAMELA VINTON BROWN	R. BRUCE HORSFALL	COBB SHINN
GELETT BURGESS	EMILIE BENSON KNIPE	HAROLD SICHEL
HARRISON CADY	CHARLES F. LESTER	HUGH SPENCER
BESS BRUCE CLEVELAND	J. C. LEYENDECKER	ALBERTINE R. WHEELAN
F. Y. CORY	RALPH NELSON	
PALMER COX	H. A. OGDEN	

For a more extensive list of illustrators see "Index to Artists," Volume 9.

A Word to Parents about this Manual of Child Development

"**E**DUCATION, if it is to mean anything, must teach us how to live." Thus, with profound truth, spoke one of America's greatest educators, Horace Mann.

The basis for living richly and fully, with lasting satisfaction, is good character. Education without character is "as sounding brass or a tinkling cymbal." Good character is the rock upon which good living is built.

Like a rock, however, character grows slowly. Children must not be expected to develop it overnight. It must be nurtured by parents who themselves have character and who know that it is not something one can "teach," like arithmetic or geography, but something which grows out of a child's many-sided development plus a sense of emotional security.

To help parents foster this development, we have divided it into a four-fold plan: (1) PHYSICAL; (2) MENTAL; (3) SOCIAL and EMOTIONAL; and (4) MORAL and SPIRITUAL aspects of growth. Within the framework of these four aspects, this Manual of Child Development presents parents with (1) A Chart of Child Development, which is an outline of the average child's growth, arrived at by studies of thousands of children; (2) A section devoted to essential traits to be developed in order to form good character and personality; and (3) The four-fold plan and how to apply its physical, mental, social and emotional, and moral or spiritual aspects of your child.

The Chart is the key to the entire Manual. It tells you what to expect of an *average* child at each successive stage of his or her development in each of the four aspects of that development. It refers you to the pages which you will want to read in the rest of the Manual telling you exactly why and how to apply its precepts to your child, that is, what to do and what not to do.

For convenience the Chart is arranged by chronological periods — from birth to first birthday, from first to second birthday, and so on. But this is in no sense to be taken to mean that there is a sharp line of division or that any two babies develop according to a set pattern or at a set rate. Periods shade into each other, often imperceptibly. Some babies develop faster than the average, some more slowly. Some are far ahead of the average in one respect and far behind in another. This is as natural and as normal as that every face is different from every other. But just as faces, for all their differences, have a basic fundamental structure, so is there a general average for babies.

If your baby is ahead of schedule, it does not necessarily mean that he is a genius, any more than it necessarily means that he is backward just because he is slower than average in some things.

Boys and girls differ in their rate of development too, as we have indicated in the Chart; and racial, cultural, and regional differences in families have their effect as well. So be sure to look upon the Chart merely as a series of guide-posts, *not* as a rigid yardstick.

Beginning on page 3 is a series of informative short articles on each of the characteristics desirable for your child to have, with, in each case, the reasons for their desirability and suggestions for developing them. After each trait are lists—some for the pre-school and some for the school-age child—of stories, poems, and articles, all to be found in the nine other volumes of THE BOOK-SHELF, each illustrating the trait under discussion.

One word of warning: Be very careful, in reading these stories, etc. to your child or in giving them to him to read, *not* to do so in the spirit of moralizing. This can and often does more harm than good for it may give the child a sense of guilt and therefore of resentment and defiance toward you. Let your child read for *pleasure,* not for punishment. If he comes upon a pertinent point in a story *of his own accord,* he will be quick enough to apply it to himself.

Most parents come to their jobs without special preparation and do not know what is best for their children to read. Nor would it be obtainable if they *did* know, except at enormous cost and superhuman diligence. That is why THE BOOKSHELF and its Manual of Child Development are so valuable. THE BOOKSHELF is a priceless treasure-house of what a child will want to and ought to read. The Manual tells you how to use it for the growth and development of your own child.

In presenting this *new* edition of THE BOOKSHELF with the revised up-to-date Manual of Child Development we acknowledge with gratitude the practical suggestions of countless mothers, educators, doctors, child-study specialists, and interested friends.

THE PUBLISHERS

CONCERNING PROFESSIONAL DIFFERENCES OF OPINION IN THIS MANUAL

IN THIS MANUAL the most diligent editorial effort has been made to present to parents the best of present-day thinking on the subject of infant and child care. Where modern opinion is *unanimous* in abandoning an outmoded belief in favor of a new one, we have advocated the new view. Where there is an authoritative difference of opinion on any specific subject, we have usually given preference to the one which seemed most sensible to us. We have presented *both* points of view when both seemed to have merit.

NEW LIGHT ON PSYCHOLOGICAL AND EMOTIONAL FACTORS

Today's top-ranking pediatricians, child psychologists, and other child-study experts seem agreed that more attention should be paid than has formerly been done to the emotional and psychological development of children. They realize that many so-called "bad habits" are the result *not* of either physical or moral infirmities but of emotional disturbances such as fear, a sense of insecurity, nervous tension, loneliness, and, above all, too little "mothering"—not enough warmth and love.

The practice of pediatrics has made great strides in the past few years, and as a result, the physical aspects of a baby's development have become easier for mothers to understand and to cope with. Mothers must, of course, pay adequate attention to all physiological symptoms; but it is now pretty generally understood that psychological factors may and often do profoundly affect a child's physical development and behavior patterns.

BABIES ADVANCE WHEN THEY ARE READY

It is no longer considered wise to expect all babies to develop at set rates of speed or at pre-determined times. "Go by the individual baby's rhythm rather than by the clock or the calendar" is the generally accepted theory today, and the reader will find this theory advocated in many of the articles in this Manual.

Important emphasis is also given in this book, to the related belief that babies will go on, of their own accord, from one stage of development to another *when they are physically, mentally and emotionally ready to do so*. Urging them to advance to the next step when *you* think it is time, or at an age when some other baby advances, is a great mistake and may damage the child's nervous and emotional system as he grows older.

APPROXIMATELY WHEN TO EXPECT CHANGES

There are, however, mothers who want to have *some* sort of expectancy program and *some* sort of approved schedule to be guided by. We have therefore included several *suggested* schedules for daily routines as well as *approximate* times of expectancy for successive stages of development. These are merely guides, however, and individual deviations from them should not be considered "abnormal" unless there are serious contributing factors.

THE BASIS OF CHARACTER

Another important new aspect of child-rearing is the changed attitude toward character-building. We know now that trying to build character by habit-training *alone* will not work. Neither will "pointing a moral and adorning a tale" do the trick. Nor is "setting a good example" the whole story. A child will imitate what he sees at home, it is true. But he must *love* the person who has the characteristics he is imitating; otherwise they will become superficial or insincere in the child. Real character traits spring not from what parents *tell* their children to do but from the genuine feelings and attitudes the parents have (and practice) and the degree to which these attitudes are admired and respected by the children. Thus a frank, relaxed, loving, outgoing, secure relationship between good parents and their children is the *essential* basis for the development of the best a child is capable of in character and personality.

THE HOME COMES INTO ITS OWN ONCE MORE

Finally, there has recently been a decided trend toward a return to the home and the family as the rightful center of a child's life. This had for some years been considered an "old-fashioned" concept. We are glad to note the modern return to the home. It is, and in our opinion always has been and will always be, the natural, normal pivot on which all of society must turn if it is to be strong from the core.

ALLOW FOR DIFFERENCES OF OPINION

Thus, if there are occasional discrepancies of point of view in the pages that follow, they will be the result of honest and wholly to-be-respected differences of opinion. Even the best of doctors disagree about details, and since this Manual has been written by many eminent doctors, child psychologists and educators, it is only natural that their differences should be reflected in their writings. Besides, different family set-ups sometimes require different routines and different procedures. So choose what best suits your particular situation and, above all, your particular baby. You can have complete confidence that there is competent authority for every difference of opinion you may encounter here.

CONTENTS

EDITORIAL BOARD v
LIST OF ILLUSTRATORS vii
INTRODUCTION ix
CONCERNING PROFESSIONAL DIFFERENCES OF
  OPINION IN THIS MANUAL xi
CHART OF CHILD DEVELOPMENT . xix
  Prepared by the Editorial Board of
    The University Society
BIBLIOGRAPHY
  PARTIAL LIST OF BOOKS AND PAMPHLETS
    CONSULTED xx
IMPORTANT NOTE FOR MOTHERS OF CHIL-
  DREN OF ANY AGE xxi
CHART:
  FROM BIRTH TO ONE YEAR . . xxii
  FROM ONE YEAR TO TWO YEARS xxviii

FROM TWO TO THREE YEARS . . xxxiv
FROM THREE TO SIX YEARS . . xlii
FROM SIX TO NINE YEARS . . . liv
FROM NINE YEARS THROUGH
  PRE-ADOLESCENCE lxxii
FROM PUBERTY THROUGH
  ADOLESCENCE (THE TEENS) . lxxxviii

SUGGESTED READING GUIDE . . ciii
INTRODUCTION TO TRAITS TO BE DISCOURAGED,
  CORRECTED OR LEFT TO BE OUTGROWN . cx
TRAITS TO BE DISCOURAGED, COR-
  RECTED OR LEFT TO BE OUT-
  GROWN cxi
INTRODUCTION TO ESSENTIALS OF GOOD CHAR-
  ACTER AND PERSONALITY 1

ESSENTIALS OF GOOD CHARACTER AND PERSONALITY

ACCURACY 3
ADAPTABILITY AND ADJUSTABILITY . . . 4
AFFECTION AND LOVE 5
ALERTNESS AND ATTENTIVENESS . . . 6
APPLICATION AND CONCENTRATION . . . 7
APPRECIATION AND GRATITUDE 8
ASPIRATION 9
CAUTION AND PRUDENCE 10
CHEERFULNESS AND OPTIMISM 11
CLEANLINESS AND HEALTH 12
CONFIDENCE 13
CONSCIENCE 14
CONTENTMENT 15
COOPERATION AND TEAMWORK 16
COURAGE 17
COURTESY, POLITENESS AND MANNERS . . 18
DEMOCRATIC SPIRIT 19
DIGNITY AND RESERVE 20
EMOTIONAL MATURITY AND STABILITY . . 21
FAIRNESS AND JUSTICE 22
FRIENDLINESS 23
GENEROSITY 24
GOOD SPORTSMANSHIP 25
GOOD TEMPER 26
HELPFULNESS 27
HONESTY AND HONOR 28
IDEALISM AND LIFE PURPOSE 29
IMAGINATION 30
INDEPENDENCE, SELF-RELIANCE AND SELF-HELP . 31
INDIVIDUALITY AND ORIGINALITY 32

INDUSTRY AND DILIGENCE 33
INITIATIVE AND AMBITION 34
INVESTIGATION, JUDGMENT AND DECISION . . 35
KINDNESS 36
LEADERSHIP 37
LOYALTY 38
MODESTY AND SIMPLICITY 39
NATURALNESS AND UNAFFECTEDNESS . . . 40
OBEDIENCE 41
OPEN-MINDEDNESS AND REASONABLENESS . . 42
ORDERLINESS AND NEATNESS 43
PATIENCE 44
PATRIOTISM AND CIVIC RESPONSIBILITY . . . 45
PERSEVERANCE AND PERSISTENCE 46
PUNCTUALITY AND PROMPTNESS 47
RESPECT, REVERENCE AND FAITH 48
RESOURCEFULNESS AND INGENUITY . . . 49
RESPONSIBILITY 50
SELF-AMUSEMENT AND SELF-DIRECTION . . . 51
SELF-CONTROL 52
SELF-RESPECT 53
SELF-SACRIFICE AND SERVICE TO OTHERS . . . 54
SENSE OF HUMOR 55
SINCERITY 56
SYMPATHY AND CONSIDERATION FOR OTHERS . 57
SYSTEM AND EFFICIENCY 58
TACT 59
THINKING AND REASONING 60
THOROUGHNESS 61
THRIFT 62

TOLERANCE 63
TRUSTWORTHINESS AND DEPENDABILITY . . . 64
TRUTHFULNESS 65

UNSELFISHNESS 66
WILL POWER AND DETERMINATION 67

PHYSICAL DEVELOPMENT

BABY CARE AND FEEDING

SO YOU'RE EXPECTING A BABY 71
    From U. S. Children's Bureau Publication

BIRTH REGISTRATION 76
MOTHER'S MILK THE BEST FOOD FOR BABY . . 77
HYGIENE OF THE NURSING MOTHER 77
THE PREMATURE, SMALL OR DELICATE BABY . 79
    From U. S. Children's Bureau Publication

DIFFICULTIES OF THE NURSING PERIOD . . . 85
WEANING 87
    From U. S. Children's Bureau Publication

THE CHOICE OF MILK 88
    From U. S. Children's Bureau Publication

WATER FOR THE BABY TO DRINK 97
DIFFICULTIES OF THE BOTTLE-FED BABY . . . 98
FOODS BESIDES MILK 99
    From U. S. Children's Bureau Publication

FEEDING THE AVERAGE BABY 103
SUGGESTED DAILY FEEDINGS FOR AVERAGE WELL
    BABIES WITH SAMPLE MILK MIXTURES FOR
    DIFFERENT WEIGHTS AND AGES 104
CIRCUMCISION 106
WHY THE BABY CRIES 106
THE BABY'S CARETAKERS 107
SPECIAL SUMMER RULES 108
    By L. Emmett Holt, M.D., and Henry
    L. K. Shaw, M.D.
    Revised by Rowland L. Mindlin, M.D.

THE BABY'S CLOTHES 109
    From U. S. Children's Bureau Publication

THE DAILY BATH 114
CARE OF SPECIAL ORGANS 115
SUNSHINE AND FRESH AIR 116
    From U. S. Children's Bureau Publication
SITTING UP 117
BABY'S EXERCISES 117
THE BABY'S DAY 118
    From U. S. Children's Bureau Publication

HABITS AND HABIT TRAINING

FORMING GOOD HABITS 121
    From U. S. Children's Bureau Publication

LEARNING TO EAT 122
    By Miriam E. Lowenberg

LEARNING TO WASH AND DRESS 123
    By Ethel B. Waring

TOILET HABITS 125
    From U. S. Children's Bureau Publication
BED WETTING 126
    By Rowland L. Mindlin, M.D.
THUMB SUCKING 128
    By Rowland L. Mindlin, M.D.
NAIL BITING 128
MASTURBATION 129

HEALTH AND HYGIENE

PRESERVING HEALTH 130
    From U. S. Children's Bureau Publication
BATHING 132
THE CHILD'S TEETH 133
    From U. S. Children's Bureau Publication
CARE OF THE EYES 134
CARE OF THE EARS 136
DO YOUR EARS HEAR? 136
    By Harold Hays
CARE OF THE CHILD'S HAIR 137
CARE OF THE NOSE AND THROAT 138
CHILD POSTURE 138
    By Milton I. Levine, M.D.

REST

SLEEP 141
FATIGUE AND NAUGHTINESS 143

EXERCISE

SPORTS FOR EXERCISE 145
    By Rowland L. Mindlin, M.D.
DANCING FOR YOUR CHILDREN 146
    By Lucille Marsh

GROWTH AND DEVELOPMENT

WHAT HEIGHT AND WEIGHT TABLES MEAN . 151
    By George Truman Palmer, Ph.D.
HOW TO USE HEIGHT AND WEIGHT TABLES . . 152
HEIGHT AND WEIGHT TABLES 153
    By Robert Morse Woodbury, M.D.
        Bird T. Baldwin, Ph.D., and
        Thomas D. Wood, M.D.
WEIGHT CHART 158
HEIGHT CHART 158
PERIODIC HEALTH EXAMINATIONS 159

FOOD FOR THE FAMILY

NUTRITIONAL REQUIREMENTS OF GROWING
   CHILDREN 161
     By Mary E. Sweeny and
     Dorothy Curts Buck

PLANNING THE YOUNG CHILD'S MENU . . . 166
     By Miriam E. Lowenberg

FOOD PLAN FOR THE GROWING CHILD 168

SUGGESTED MENUS FOR CHILDREN
   FROM TWO TO SIX 169
     By S. Josephine Baker, M.D.

FOOD FOR SCHOOL BOYS AND GIRLS 170
     By Mary Swartz Rose

THE SCHOOL LUNCH-BOX 171
     By Mary Swartz Rose

LUNCH TIME AT SCHOOL 171
FOOD BETWEEN MEALS 172
GOOD FOOD HABITS 172
     By Lucy H. Gillett

SUMMER DRINKS FOR CHILDREN 173
     By Alice Irwin

TEACHING CHILDREN TO LIKE WHOLESOME
   FOODS 175
     By Lydia J. Roberts

HOUSING

A HOME FOR THE CHILDREN 179
THE BABY'S ROOM 179
PLAY PLACES IN THE HOUSE 181
     By Katherine Beebe

THE LITTLE CHILD'S ROOM 182
     By Ellen Creelman

THE PORCH AS A PLAYGROUND 182
     By William Byron Forbush

THE GIRL'S OWN ROOM 183
     By Allen L. Churchill

THE BOY'S OWN ROOM 184
     By Frank H. Cheley

THE BACKYARD 186
     By Allen L. Churchill

VACATIONS

THE BABY'S VACATION 189
     By Mrs. Max West

HOW TO GIVE CHILDREN A GOOD TIME DURING
   VACATION 190
     By Nena Wilson Badenoch

SEA BATHING 192
     By Guy Hinsdale, M.D.

TAKING ADVANTAGE OF THE SUMMER CAMP FOR
   YOUR BOY 193
     By Frank H. Cheley

SUMMER CAMPS FOR GIRLS 195
     By Allen L. Churchill

HOME NURSING

SYMPTOMS OF ACUTE ILLNESS 199
CARING FOR THE SICK CHILD 200
     By Mrs. Max West

HOME NURSING 201
     By Mary E. Carter, R.N.

POULTICES AND THE LIKE 205
     By Harry Roberts, M.D.

USE OF ENEMAS AND SUPPOSITORIES 207
CAUTION 207
PRESCRIBING BY MAIL 208
INTRODUCTION TO HEALTH REQUIREMENTS . . 209
     By Ella Oppenheimer, M.D.

NEW YORK STATE DEPARTMENT OF HEALTH
   REQUIREMENTS FOR COMMUNICABLE DISEASES 210

THE IMPORTANCE OF QUARANTINE 214
AGAINST WHAT SHOULD WE BE IMMUNIZED? . 215
WHILE THE CHILDREN ARE GETTING WELL . . 218
     By Abraham Levinson, M.D.

AMUSEMENTS FOR CONVALESCENT CHILDREN . 220
     By William Byron Forbush

TEACH CHILDREN THAT THE DOCTOR IS
   THEIR FRIEND 222

MAKE FRIENDS WITH THE DENTIST 222
INDEX TO DISEASES OF CHILDHOOD 223

DISEASES OF CHILDHOOD

By Rowland L. Mindlin, M.D.

THE COMMON CONTAGIOUS DISEASES 225
LESS COMMON CONTAGIOUS DISEASES . . . 231
DISEASES OF THE SKIN 236
DISEASES OF THE RESPIRATORY TRACT 238
DISEASES IN THE ABDOMEN 240
DISEASES OF THE KIDNEY 245
DISEASES DUE TO ALLERGY 246
DISEASES OF THE EYE 248
DISEASES OF NUTRITION 249
PHYSICAL INJURIES 250

BASIC MEDICAL AND SICKROOM SUPPLIES . . 253
POISONS AND THEIR ANTIDOTES 254
     By The American Red Cross
POISONOUS PLANTS 256
     By Theodore Tieken, M.D.

MENTAL DEVELOPMENT

THE LEARNING PROCESS

How Children Learn 259
  From U. S. Children's Bureau Publication

Learning Self-Reliance 261
  By Dorothy Canfield Fisher

Play a Way of Learning 262

Reasoning in Early Childhood 265
  By John Dewey

Curiosity 266
  By Elizabeth J. Woodward

When the Children Ask Questions . . . 268

Observation 269
  By Mrs. Elizabeth Hubbard Bonsall

Imitative Play 271
  By Alice Corbin Sies

Dramatics in the Home 273

SPEECH AND LANGUAGE

Your Child's Speech 275
  By James Sonnett Green, M.D.

Stuttering 277
  By Smiley Blanton, M.D.

Teaching a Child to Talk 279
  By Michael Vincent O'Shea

Enlarging the Child's Vocabulary . . . 280
  By Ann Roe-Anderson

Learning to Use Language 281

Home Opportunities in English 283

Work and Play in English 287
  By Edna E. Harris

The Reading Mother (verse) 296
  By Strickland Gillilan

READING AND STORY TELLING

The Baby's Story Hour 297
  By Mary Adair

The Use of Mother Goose 299

Literature for Pre-School Children . . . 301

The Poetry Habit 303
  By Clara Whitehill Hunt

Fairy Tales for Children 306

How to Tell Stories 307
  By Mary L. Read

Good Taste Needs Cultivation 307
  By Margaret Ernst

Six Tests 309

Child Culture 309
  By Lena E. Bliss

PICTURES AND DRAWING

How to Interest Children in Pictures . . 311
  By Estelle M. Hurll

Pictures for Children 313
  By Edith Riland Cross

Drawing and Coloring by Little Children . 314
  By Mrs. Bertha Payne Newell

Self-Discovery Through Painting and
  Drawing 315
  By Helmut Hungerland

MUSIC

Music and Rhythm 317
  By Mrs. Bertha Payne Newell

Mothers and Practicing 319
  By J. Lillian Vandevere

Children's Singing in the Home 321
  By Myrtle Douglas Keener

Making Music Together 322
  By Frances M. Andrews

NATURE STUDY

The Heritage of Childhood 325
  By Augusta M. Swan

Animal Friends 325
  By Mrs. Helen Y. Campbell

Nature Study for Young Children . . . 326
  By Rhoda Bacmeister

Nature Study for Older Boys and Girls . . 328
  By E. W. Butterfield

LEISURE TIME ACTIVITIES

Selecting Toys Wisely 331

Special Requisites for Outdoor Playthings 334

Your Family's Leisure 334

Adventuring in Handcraft 335
  By Elizabeth Price

Hobbies 337
  By Elizabeth Price

HOME AND SCHOOL

Will You Send Your Child to a Nursery
  School? 341
  By Winifred E. Bain, Ph.D.

WILL YOU SEND YOUR CHILD TO A
KINDERGARTEN? 343
By Winifred E. Bain, Ph.D.

YOUR CHILD'S PROGRESS IN THE ELEMENTARY
SCHOOL 345
By Winifred E. Bain, Ph.D.

HOW THE HOME CAN COOPERATE WITH THE
SCHOOL 347

WHO SHALL GO TO COLLEGE? 350
By Max McConn

VOCATIONAL GUIDANCE

VOCATIONAL GUIDANCE IN HOME AND SCHOOL . 355
By Fred C. Smith

HOW TO RECOGNIZE YOUR CHILD'S SPECIAL
ABILITY 358
By Clarence C. Robinson

VOCATIONAL APTITUDES THAT AFFECT SCHOOL
SUCCESS 360
By Johnson O'Connor

SOCIAL AND EMOTIONAL DEVELOPMENT

HOME LIFE

A HAPPY FAMILY—IF 367
By Dr. Mary Fisher Langmuir

THE HOME ATMOSPHERE 370
THE COOPERATIVE FAMILY 372
TRAINING IN HOUSEHOLD TASKS 373
By Mrs. Bertha Payne Newell

SHARING THE LIFE OF THE FAMILY CIRCLE . . 374
By Mrs. V. Oma Grace Oliver

THE CHILD NEEDS SOLITUDE 374
FAMILY DIFFERENCES 375
THE FAMILY LODGE 377
SPECIAL NOTE TO FATHERS 379

MANNERS

MANNERS RIGHT FROM THE START 381
By Eva Von B. Hansl

FRIENDSHIPS

LEARNING SOCIAL BEHAVIOR 389
By Marguerite Wilker

THE LITTLE CHILD NEEDS FRIENDS 391
By Alice Corbin Sies

FINDING FRIENDS FOR THE PRE-SCHOOL CHILD . 392
By Mrs. Preston F. Gass

IMAGINARY COMPANIONS 393
WHEN FRIENDS SEEM TO BE DOING HARM . . 394

SEX EDUCATION

BEGINNING SEX EDUCATION 395
By Edith D. Dixon

PREPARING FOR MATURITY 397
By Frances Bruce Strain

THE QUESTION OF PETTING 399
By Max J. Exner, M.D.

COMMUNITY LIFE AND CITIZENSHIP

PREPARING OUR CHILDREN FOR CITIZENSHIP . . 403
APPRECIATING OUR PUBLIC SERVANTS 404
CHILDREN AND THE WORLD TODAY 405
BOYS' CLUBS AS A HELP TO THE HOME . . . 407
BOY SCOUTS 408
By the Editorial Board of the Boy Scouts
of America

GIRL SCOUTS 409
By Mrs. Jane Deeter Rippin

CAMP FIRE GIRLS 410
By Rowe Wright

THE YMCA AND YWCA 412
THE JEWISH CENTER 413
By the Jewish Welfare Board

COLUMBIAN SQUIRES 414
THE AMERICAN YOUTH FOUNDATION 416
By John L. Alexander

A DEED AND A WORD (VERSE) 416
By Charles Mackay

MORAL AND SPIRITUAL DEVELOPMENT

'THE BROTHERHOOD OF MAN" 418
By Henry F. Cope, D.D.

DISCIPLINE

WHEN PUNISHMENT IS NECESSARY 419
By Helen K. Champlin

WHAT ARE GOOD CHARACTER HABITS AND HOW
ARE THEY DEVELOPED? 422
By Corinna Marsh

MOTIVES TO WHICH YOUTH RESPONDS . . . 423
By Henry Neumann, Ph.D.

THE FEAR-PUNISHMENT 425
By Edith Lochridge Reid

THE FAMILY OF JUDGES 426
By E. M. Megraw

USE PRAISE INSTEAD OF BLAME 427
By Helen K. Champlin

HOW TO TELL STORIES FOR CHARACTER-BUILDING 429

PERSONALITY PROBLEMS

How Personality Grows 431
    By Mandel Sherman, Ph.D.
The Timid Child 433
    By Mandel Sherman, Ph.D.
The Hysterical Child 434
    By Mandel Sherman, Ph.D.
The Self-Centered Child 435
The Cross Child 435
The Contrary Child 436
The Child Who Sulks 436
The Child Who Has Temper Tantrums . . 437
The Quarrelsome Child 437
The Child Who Teases 439
The Impudent Child 439
    By William Byron Forbush
The Forgetful Child 440
    By Michael Vincent O'Shea
The Lazy Child 441
    By Sidonie Matsner Gruenberg
The Child Who Is Jealous 443
    By Minerva Hunter
The Child Who Lies 443
The Vain Child 445
    By Christine Terhune Herrick

The Child Who Steals 446
Personality in the Making 447

RELIGIOUS TRAINING

The Importance of Religious Training . . 451
    By Mary Collins Terry
The Beginnings of Religious Training . . 451
    By Mary E. Rankin
Family Prayers and Saying Grace . . . 458
    By Mary Collins Terry
Some Simple Prayers 459
The Religious Education of a Catholic
    Child 460
    By Josephine Brownson
The Religious Training of a Jewish Child 463
    By Mrs. Rose Barlow Weinman
Making the Bible Real to the Child . . . 470
    By Rev. Theodore G. Soares
The Aim of Religious Education 475
    By George R. Dodson
Religious Training of Older Children . . 478
    By Frank H. Cheley
Sunday in the Home 480
How to Keep the Poison of Racial and Re-
    ligious Prejudice from Our Children . . 481
    By Corinna Marsh

ADOLESCENCE

From U. S. Children's Bureau Publication *Guiding the Adolescent*

INTRODUCTION TO SECTION ON
    ADOLESCENCE 484
What Is Adolescence? 485
PHYSICAL GROWTH AND DEVELOP-
    MENT 485
Maturing of the Reproductive System . . 485
Physical Hygiene 486
Problems Incidental to Physical Growth
    and Development 487
ATTITUDES TOWARD SEX 488
Sex Instruction 488
Sex Talk and Reading 489
Masturbation 490
ADOLESCENCE AND MENTAL
    DEVELOPMENT 491
Measurement of Intelligence 491
The Slow Mind 492
The Average Mind 492
The Superior Mind 492
Special Abilities and Disabilities . . . 493
THE INDIVIDUAL AS A WHOLE . . . 493
Some Educational Pitfalls 495

The Question of Work 498
LEARNING TO USE LEISURE 500
Present Complaints 500
Education in the Use of Leisure 501
Adolescents at Leisure 503
ASOCIAL CONDUCT 504
Stealing 506
Incorrigibility 507
Evading Reality 508
Daydreaming and Romancing 508
Cheating 509
Truancy 509
Drinking 510
THE ADOLESCENT AND HIS
    COMPANIONS 510
The Importance of Friends 510
"Crushes" 511
Boy and Girl Relations 512
THE NEEDS OF THE PARENT . . . 514
Graded and Classified Index to Contents of
    The Bookshelf 518
Index to Manual of Child Development . . 537

The CHART *of*
CHILD DEVELOPMENT

Prepared by

The EDITORIAL BOARD of the UNIVERSITY SOCIETY, INC.

With the Advice of
Outstanding Specialists in

PEDIATRICS, MEDICINE, PSYCHIATRY,

NUTRITION, HYGIENE,

CHILD STUDY, CHILD PSYCHOLOGY,

CHILD GUIDANCE, FAMILY LIFE,

HOME COUNSELLING, EDUCATION,

VOCATIONAL GUIDANCE, AND RELIGION

BIBLIOGRAPHY

PARTIAL LIST OF BOOKS AND PAMPHLETS CONSULTED IN THE MAKING OF THE CHART OF CHILD DEVELOPMENT

Common Sense Book of Baby and Child Care
By Benjamin Spock, M.D.
(Duell, Sloan and Pearce)

Infant and Child in the Culture of Today
By Arnold Gesell, M.D and
Frances L. Ilg., M.D.
(Harpers)

The Child from Five to Ten
By Arnold Gesell, M.D. and
Frances L. Ilg., M D.
(Harpers)

Babies Are Human Beings
By C. Anderson Aldrich, M.D. and
Mary M. Aldrich
(Macmillan)

Off to a Good Start
By Irma S. Black
(Harcourt, Brace)

The Parents' Manual
By Anna W. M. Wolf
(Simon and Schuster)

Infant Care
U. S. Children's Bureau Publication

Your Child from One to Six
U. S. Children's Bureau Publication

Parents' Questions
By Child Study Association of America Staff
(Harpers)

The Doctor's Job
By Carl Binger, M.D.
(Norton)

Being Born
By Frances Bruce Strain
(Appleton-Century)

What Books for Children?
By Josette Frank
(Doubleday)

Play: A Yardstick of Growth
By Clara Lambert
(Play Schools Association)

Emotional Problems of Living
By O. Spurgeon English, M.D. and
Gerald H. J. Pearson, M.D.
(Norton)

Growing Together
By Rhoda W. Bacmeister
(Appleton-Century)

SOME OF THE OTHER AUTHORITIES CONSULTED

In addition to the books and pamphlets listed above and many others on allied subjects, we have kept informed on the latest developments in child care by constant consultation of the current publications of such excellent sources of material as:

THE UNITED STATES CHILDREN'S BUREAU

These publications, put out by our Government for the benefit of mothers and children throughout the nation, offer sound, sensible, up-to-date advice on practically every phase of maternity and child care from the pre-natal months on.

THE CHILD STUDY ASSOCIATION OF AMERICA

CHILD STUDY, the Quarterly Journal of Parent Education, presents new challenges and new approaches to the problems of parent-child relationships and provides both illumination and stimulation for parents interested in understanding what motivates behavior.

THE BANK STREET SCHOOLS

The Bureau of Educational Experiments publishes the findings of its research in child growth as applied to child education. These studies are of especial interest to parents and teachers of children of nursery school age.

NATIONAL PARENT-TEACHER

This is the official magazine of the National Congress of Parents and Teachers whose object is to bring into closer relationship the home and the school, to raise the standards of home life, and to promote the welfare of children in home, school, church and community.

PARENTS' MAGAZINE

This magazine, written exclusively for parents, provides them with authoritative guidance on every phase of child development in every age-range from infancy through adolescence.

IMPORTANT NOTE

FOR MOTHERS OF CHILDREN OF ANY AGE

THE following approved CHART OF CHILD DEVELOPMENT presents, in outline form, a summary of "What to Expect of Average Children," "What to Do for Your Child," and "What to Avoid" at each of seven successive stages of a child's development from birth through adolescence.

We have considered each of the seven stages from four points of view: (1) Physical, (2) Mental, (3) Social and Emotional, and (4) Moral and Spiritual.

There is, of course, no rigid dividing-line to mark off any of these aspects of growth from the others. They are all essential parts of a well-integrated personality, and any one of them may be affected by any or all of the others.

We all want our children to develop evenly so as to become well-balanced people. But we know that boys and girls often develop unevenly. We hope that in time they will catch up where they seem to have fallen behind—and they usually do. But there is much we can do to help in the process.

These four classifications of growth, then, are intended to make it easy to recognize any marked lack of balance in your child's development. That is, the CHART should help you to see whether your child is essentially stronger or weaker in any one aspect of growth than in the others.

In the matter of "What to Expect" at any specified age, the CHART can give you only general averages to go by. This does not mean that many perfectly normal children do not develop more quickly or more slowly—sometimes by many weeks or even months. They do—many of them. The directions in "What to Do for Your Child" and in "What to Avoid" are also merely guides.

A great many of the subjects mentioned in the CHART are given fuller treatment in the body of the MANUAL.

Specific subjects in the MANUAL (alphabetically listed in the Index) should be consulted when specific problems arise. But many procedures contributing to the welfare of any child are profitably begun in the early years and are to be continued throughout childhood. And some—such as caring for your child when he is ill, to name only one of many—do not belong to any one age. Such measures must be applied at whatever age the need arises. We suggest, therefore, that *the entire CHART be studied from the beginning, no matter what the present age of your child may be.*

One final word—a word of apology to parents of girls. We have referred to all children, throughout the CHART, as *he.* This is obviously because it would be wasteful of time and space to say *he or she* every time, not because we don't think girl babies are every bit as important as boy babies.

—The Editors

At some time during this period most children are ready to be encouraged in:

AFFECTION and LOVE

CONTENTMENT

PHYSICAL DEVELOPMENT

A newborn baby unfolds like a flower. Day by day the mother can see tiny wrinkles disappear, little hollows fill out. Babies are born able to suck and to swallow. But for the first month of life they spend most of their time sleeping. Their comparatively few waking hours are devoted mainly to growing accustomed to their new environment.

The reactions of babies to this environment vary with the individual child. In general, they will advance only when their own individual rate of growth makes them ready to do so, but almost any mother can tell, by many understandable signs, when her baby is thriving and when something is wrong. It does not mean that your child will be a genius if he is ahead of schedule or that he will be backward if he develops more slowly. So, if the baby balks, don't be too rigid about following time schedules. Remember that children who were too strictly brought up as babies are far more likely to be unhappy and maladjusted in later life than those who were brought up in an atmosphere of security, loving warmth, happy laughter, and common sense.

Easy-going tolerance is more valuable in bringing up a baby than any number of rigid rules and regulations. But a good, up-to-date book on child care is better than any hit-or-miss information, and it is most important to have a wise, sympathetic physician who understands babies.

Your own instincts, if you are the "natural mother" type, are likely to be right for your baby on the whole. If you think you are not naturally that type of woman, the chances are that you will soon learn to be if you take care of your own baby. If you do it happily and conscientiously, you will find it the most rewarding job in the world.

Love your baby for what he is, not for something you would like him to be; smile at him often; be as relaxed as you can when you are with him; and don't be afraid to cuddle him. Showing him that you are glad he belongs to you will be the best thing you can do for him all along the line. Experience and interest will bring you confidence and skill.

FROM BIRTH TO ONE YEAR

WHAT TO EXPECT OF AVERAGE CHILDREN

At One Month:

Most babies can move head and eyes
Open and close fists
Cry
Gain steadily in weight and strength
Some may look cross-eyed

At Four Months:

See many things
Can hold up head
May tremble or be easily startled
May roll or bang head
Usually begin to eat some solid foods
Can be held in a sitting position
Coo, gurgle, smile and laugh
Begin drooling and fretting because of teething
May suck thumb

At Nine Months:

Creep or roll
Can usually sit steadily, stand, and take a few steps if they hold on

Still put things in mouth
Reach for toys and can hold them
Can usually sleep through the night
Can feed themselves a cracker, bread, etc.
Probably have two lower front and two upper front teeth. (The first tooth usually appears at about seventh month)

At One Year:

Can feed themselves with fingers
Bowel movements are generally regular
Can stand alone; a few can walk a little at this age. Some need help sitting down once they are on their feet
Have six teeth, four above and two below
Can eat most simple foods
Are usually willing to drink out of a cup
Get more fussy about food and less hungry
Still need frequent attention
Soft spot on top of head may close any time between nine months and two years. Average is between twelve and eighteen months.

WHAT TO DO FOR YOUR CHILD

Register baby's birth.

Get household help for at least the first few weeks if possible.

Guard your own health by proper diet, sufficient rest and relaxation.

Nurse your baby, and enjoy it, if you possibly can. This is most important, physically and psychologically, for both of you.

Supplement your own milk with a formula when necessary or desirable.

If nursing is impossible (and don't give up trying until you are sure) feed according to doctor's directions.

Have boy babies circumcised at about the second week if doctor approves.

Keep your baby's clothes simple and washable—and try to distract his attention while you are dressing him.

Bathe and sunbathe baby carefully; make bathtime pleasant for him.

See that baby gets plenty of fresh air and sunshine but keep him out of drafts, strong winds, and too-hot sun.

Let the rhythm of your baby's particular digestive system, not the clock, set the schedule of his feedings.

Give baby a night feeding if and when he wakes and cries for it.

Begin giving baby an occasional sip of milk from a cup at about five months.

Begin to wean breast-fed baby to the cup, if he is ready, between eight and ten months.

Wean bottle-fed baby when he is ready. (This is sometimes after the twelfth month.)

If necessary to wean from breast to bottle, do so *gradually,* in first six months.

Let baby stop eating when he wants to. It is of the greatest importance to make all mealtimes pleasant for him.

Be sure your baby gets vitamin D (the sunshine vitamin) in cod liver oil or some other form.

Be sure baby gets enough vitamin C in orange juice or some other form.

If baby shows signs of *wanting* to suck thumb or other fingers, give him more opportunity to suck at breast or bottle instead.

As soon as baby is regularly finishing all his bottles, gradually increase the amount of his formula—but do not urge him to take more than he wants.

Consult doctor promptly about any change in baby's digestion, and about when to give him solid foods—usually by four months.

Consult doctor about rash on baby's body.

Be sure baby gets enough sleep. If he is restless, look for the cause. Help him to get more sleep by making him more comfortable. Change his diapers when he is wet or soiled.

Keep track of baby's height and weight, and consult doctor if gains are not fairly regular.

Give baby his own room if possible, especially to sleep in.

Learn to recognize symptoms of various childhood illnesses.

If baby is really sick, call the doctor at once and keep baby by himself.

Even if baby is well, take him to the doctor or a health station once a month for the first six months or, to be on the safe side, for the first year.

Put baby in play pen before he gets used to more freedom.

When baby teethes, realize that he must put things in his mouth to chew on. The best you can do is to provide him with things that are clean and safe.

Have baby vaccinated before he is a year old—unless the doctor objects.

Have him inoculated against diphtheria at around nine months.

When he cries try to discover why he is crying—then try to remove the cause.

Above all, take it easy, keep a sense of balance, and enjoy your baby *as he is* at each stage of his development.

WHAT TO AVOID

Try not to be interrupted during nursing.

Avoid giving baby soothing syrups.

It is important not to let worry or tension, fatigue or depression keep you from being cheerful and relaxed with your baby.

Under no circumstances allow anyone with a cold or other illness to come near baby.

It is not wise to let baby cry for long periods if you can help or comfort him. (Continuous crying is always a sign that *something* is wrong. Don't worry about "spoiling" the baby if you pick him up when he cries.)

There is no need to worry about the rate of baby's gains in weight, size, achievements, etc., as long as there are any gains at all. Remember no two babies develop alike.

Be sure not to try to train your baby in bowel or bladder functions until you are sure he is physically as well as psychologically ready. (This is usually after the first year and seldom before.)

Postpone having baby vaccinated if he has eczema, if he has been frail or sickly, during a hot spell, or if there are colds around.

SUGGESTED READING

Recommendations for further reading on the subjects outlined above may be found by referring to the *Suggested Reading Guide* at the end of this CHART.

MENTAL DEVELOPMENT

It is impossible, of course, during the first few months of a baby's life, to see day-by-day mental development as we see physical development. But it is there just the same, noticeable in his increasing alertness, interest in the world around him, and sensitiveness to sounds, shapes, textures, and personalities.

Physically healthy babies who feel secure in their mother's love usually show signs of healthy development both mentally and emotionally. Once the world about them gains their attention, its impressions crowd into their receptive minds. For the first few years of life, their world is the home they were born into. Fortunate is the child whose home is one of contentment, simplicity and security—a home in which he feels the happiness of those around him and knows that he belongs to them and is loved and wanted by them.

WHAT TO EXPECT OF AVERAGE CHILDREN

At Four Months:
   Most babies recognize mother and other familiar people
   Can grasp objects; enjoy dangling toys

At Nine Months:
   Can make many sounds and can sometimes speak a few actual words
   Respond to name and understand many of mothers' attitudes and remarks
   Imitate sounds, gestures, facial expressions

Can do simple nursery plays
Enjoy being taken out, looking around

At One Year:
   Listen intently to words and understand a few familiar sentences
   Can usually say four or five words
   Repeat performances that seem to please
   Respond to repetition, rhythm, music
   Play well with simple toys
   Can usually recognize themselves in mirror

WHAT TO DO FOR YOUR CHILD

Respond to baby's smiles.
Talk to your baby in the simple, rhythmic way he loves, and sing to him.
Give him a few simple washable toys.

Take him outdoors as often as possible, weather permitting, and let him look around.
Indoors give him a chance, at some time, to move about freely and safely.

WHAT TO AVOID

Stop talking baby talk as soon as or, better, before baby begins to imitate what you say.
Keep baby from getting over-stimulated.
It is unwise to force or to try to train him beyond his capacity in anything.
Remember that he understands at least the attitudes, if not the actual meaning, expressed in your remarks, facial expressions, and gestures—so be careful not to express yourself in ways which you do not wish to see your child imitate. Never let him feel that taking care of him is a nuisance or a chore.

SUGGESTED READING

Recommendations for further reading on the subjects outlined above may be found by referring to the *Suggested Reading Guide* at the end of this CHART.

SOCIAL AND EMOTIONAL DEVELOPMENT.

The term "social," as it is used here, refers to that very important aspect of a child's development, his responses to and relationships with other people, as well as his ability to become an emotionally mature, well-adjusted, independent human being on his own.

A baby's social development begins as soon as he recognizes his mother. His joyousness in the company of those he loves is rooted in his emotions—that is, in his affection for and confidence in his family. It is up to the family to nurture that confidence and to see that it is justified, especially throughout the child's formative early years.

WHAT TO EXPECT OF AVERAGE CHILDREN

At Four Months:

Most babies smile at mother and other familiar people

At Nine Months:

Can play happily alone for an hour or more
Like to have familiar people around
May be shy with strangers

At One Year:

Try to attract attention
Are capable of fear, anger, affection, sympathy, frustration, anxiety, and jealousy
Cry when restrained or thwarted
Enjoy carriage rides, playing with familiar people, being chased and caught, hiding, being found, waving "bye-bye"

WHAT TO DO FOR YOUR CHILD

Be as friendly and companionable with your baby as possible. Show him that you enjoy being with him.

Cuddle him, love him, surround him with the feeling of warmth and comfort he needs for his whole future emotional well-being.

Let him play by himself as long as he is happy doing so. Stay with him when he seems to need you.

Respond to his moods and emotions by showing him that you are sympathetic and interested. This will not "spoil" him.

Reassure him, when he is frightened or lonely, by a calm, gentle, warm tone of voice.

WHAT TO AVOID

You cannot successfully force him to be sociable with strangers.

Stern indifference to his demands will only increase his sense of insecurity.

Battling with your child about anything is foolish, partly because you can't win, partly because battles only make him more resistant, not less.

Fussing over him when he doesn't need it is almost as bad as ignoring him when he needs comfort.

Show no concern over his babyish eating habits, bowel and bladder functions, or other seeming lags in development. Doing so will only give him a sense of his failure to live up to what you expect of him and give him less confidence in himself. Be patient and wait for these abilities to develop.

SUGGESTED READING

Recommendations for further reading on the subjects outlined above may be found by referring to the *Suggested Reading Guide* at the end of this CHART.

MORAL AND SPIRITUAL DEVELOPMENT

Infants, of course, have no idea of the difference between right and wrong, good and bad. Their standard is only the approval or disapproval of the other members of the family. It is obviously desirable, therefore, for their own protection, that those they love and depend on show approval of what is good in their behavior and vice versa.

Between birth and the first birthday a baby is not capable of moral or spiritual understanding and he can therefore not be trained in anything that comes properly under that heading. But the seeds of personality are within him from the moment of his birth. These can be made ripe for good constructive development by surrounding the baby with an atmosphere of genuine warmth of feeling, sincere affection, peace, gentleness, kindness, and understanding. In such an atmosphere his moral and spiritual development will blossom and flower naturally as he becomes ready and able to understand its implications. His conscience develops as he begins to understand what the people he loves think is good or bad, what they expect of him.

WHAT TO EXPECT OF AVERAGE CHILDREN

At One Year:

Most babies are trustful, loving, responsive to parental approval or disapproval

Understand mild correction if uniformly repeated when necessary, and realize that obedience is expected of them

Are not old enough to understand moral and spiritual values or abstract ideas

WHAT TO DO FOR YOUR CHILD

Teach kindness by surrounding your child with an atmosphere of kindness.

Be friendly and tolerant, but assume that obedience to simple routines is expected.

Let your child feel that there is a certain rhythm and order in his daily routine.

WHAT TO AVOID

Try not to subject him to abrupt changes, sudden noises, or anything else which might instill fear in him.

Be careful not to expect your child to understand more than he is able to.

Try your best not to be unfriendly, ungentle, unkind, or intolerant yourself.

At all costs keep your child from being exposed to friction in family life or to confusion and disorder in his early surroundings.

SUGGESTED READING

Recommendations for further reading on the subjects outlined above may be found by referring to the *Suggested Reading Guide* at the end of this CHART.

FROM ONE YEAR TO TWO YEARS

(For Development from Birth to One Year, See Pages xxii to xxvii)

Continue to encourage your child in the good traits he has already begun to develop. Try again with those previously mentioned for which he may not have been ready earlier. And begin now to encourage him in the following traits for which most children are ready at some time during this period:

CONFIDENCE, COURAGE and FORTITUDE (Physical)
OBEDIENCE, SELF-AMUSEMENT

PHYSICAL DEVELOPMENT

During the second year healthy babies continue their gains in height and weight and add walking and talking to their abilities. They are still dependent on grown-ups to care for their needs. Their rapidly developing muscles urge them to intense activity and they must be allowed to play freely in safe surroundings. Some babies become feeding problems at this age. For those who show any tendency in this direction it is essential that mothers show no concern, in the child's presence, about the subject. This is one of many instances where a child's physical development depends largely on his emotions. If you suspect any physical condition as a basis for poor appetite, consult a doctor. But keeping calm is essential for the child and therefore, first of all, for the mother.

WHAT TO EXPECT OF AVERAGE CHILDREN

Between Twelve and Eighteen Months:

Most children between one and one-and-a-half sleep about thirteen hours, usually with one nap

Can eat from a spoon, hold a glass or cup to drink from

Walk in a wobbly, toddling gait

May walk upstairs with help; can sometimes climb downstairs without help

Like to run around doing "errands"

Are often balky about food, toilet, etc.

Soft spot on top of head should be closed

At Two Years:

Can sometimes run or at least trot

Can walk up and downstairs alone

Can build blocks, push and pull objects

Delight in rough and tumble play

Can cooperate in dressing and undressing

Have about sixteen teeth

Should be dry daytimes and often at night

WHAT TO DO FOR YOUR CHILD

When baby has learned to walk, get him shoes with soles, and let him get out of his carriage or play pen when he wants to.

Let him get dirty; he should at this stage.

When he begins to wander around the house, the only sensible way to keep him from hurting himself and wrecking the house is to put valuable, breakable, and dangerous things away.

Take every possible precaution to minimize the danger of baby's hurting himself. Have broad-based chairs, harness on baby carriage, gates at top and bottom of stairs, window guards. Keep hot things, sharp knives, matches, needles, poisons, etc. out of reach.

If one nap a day seems not enough but two seems too many, try giving baby his supper and putting him to bed a bit earlier.

If his appetite seems variable, let him eat as much of what he likes as he wants and give him a vacation from what he does not like for a while. If you don't make a fuss about it, he'll soon strike his own proper balance.

If he balks at drinking milk, try giving him his milk in the form of milk soups, puddings, etc. for a while. It won't hurt him to cut down a bit on milk if he is getting a balanced diet.

If he throws food on the floor, casually remove his plate. He has probably had all he wants by the time he begins that trick anyway. Try giving him smaller portions.

When your baby shows signs of wanting to feed himself with a spoon (usually between fifteen and eighteen months), let him try. He will do it clumsily, but it is better to put a bib on baby and a big piece of oilcloth on the floor under his chair than to be impatient with him and his mussiness.

Start new foods gradually, especially fats which baby can digest only in small quantities.

Be cheerful about letting your child have fruit juice or a snack between meals if he is cross because of hunger. If it is only a snack, it will not spoil his appetite, and even if it does, a temporarily spoiled appetite is better than a spoiled disposition. The important thing is to keep the idea of food always pleasant for him.

WHAT TO AVOID

If baby is sucking his thumb, be sure not to try to stop him in *any* way except by offering him more to eat or something interesting to do and by making his life generally happier.

Under no circumstances shame your baby if he is still having bowel or bladder accidents at two. Just keep on taking him to the bathroom at regular intervals. Give him more time and be patient.

Scolding him for getting into everything won't help and neither will constantly saying "No, no!" to everything he does. Instead, keep dangerous things out of his reach as far as possible, and when he does try to get into something he shouldn't, distract his attention to something he *can* do.

When baby drops or throws his toys, neither make a game of it by picking them up nor scold him. Tie a few toys to his pen or crib, and just remove those he has thrown down.

It is foolish to try to make baby sleep if he doesn't want to; but let him sleep, even if it isn't his regular nap-time when he does want to.

Avoid feeding problems by *never* forcing him to eat more than he wants or seeming concerned about his eating behavior. If you offer him regular, well-balanced meals and are entirely casual and cheerful about his food at all times, baby will eventually strike a diet that is good for him. If he doesn't, or if you have already prejudiced him, consult a doctor or, if necessary, a guidance counsellor. On the other hand, let him have food when he wants it even if it isn't his regular mealtime.

It is better not to keep on feeding baby after he shows signs of wanting to feed himself. (This takes great patience, but it is worth it.)

It is not good to force baby in any direction, but be sure to take advantage of the time when he is ready to advance.

Most doctors today advise against trying to teach a child to walk. Most children begin to do it by themselves, some time between the ninth and eighteenth month.

If your child is left-handed, refrain from doing anything about it. Above all, don't try to make him right-handed, which may have psychological consequences far more serious than left-handedness.

SUGGESTED READING

Recommendations for further reading on the subjects outlined above may be found by referring to the *Suggested Reading Guide* at the end of this CHART.

MENTAL DEVELOPMENT

The first years of a child's life are the years of his most rapid mental growth. When we consider the multitude of impressions, taken for granted by adults, which babies experience for the first time, we must see how unwise it would be to urge them to go faster than their own natural pace. We must realize how miraculously fast that pace is, regardless of how slow it may seem to us.

WHAT TO EXPECT OF AVERAGE CHILDREN

Between Twelve and Eighteen Months:

Some children may be able to speak as many as ten words and the use of words increases even when most of them are not accurately pronounced

May begin to put words together into short phrases, often in the wrong order

Cannot yet, however, understand the verbal meaning of scolding, persuasion, etc. although they may have for some time recognized the significance of various tones of voice, such as approval, disapproval, etc.

Still need constant repetition of an idea for it to make a lasting impression

Begin to be able to foretell the result of actions (This shows improving memory and is the beginning of reasoning)

Imitate the actions, gestures, and sounds of those around them, thus gaining understanding and skill

Pretend to do things they are not able to do, such as reading a paper or book

Take noticeable pleasure in musical tones and often chant rhythmically if more or less tunelessly at this time

Wave good-bye and seem to understand what it means

Memory improves perceptibly; can recall events of yesterday

Can tell the difference between black and white, between one and many; between bowel and bladder functions

Can build with as many as six blocks

Like to talk, may use dozens of words

Like simple rhymes and stories about themselves

Like exploring drawers, boxes, etc.

WHAT TO DO FOR YOUR CHILD

Be careful of what you say and how you say it because your child will pattern his speech after yours.

Correct his speech if necessary now and then, but be sure to do it in a friendly way without nagging.

Credit your baby with the beginning of an ability to reason.

Remember that most babies need occasional variety in food, toys, outings, etc.

Simple playthings are best, for babies of this age are both imaginative and destructive. They prefer playing at the things their parents do—cooking, sweeping, reading, etc.

Let your child do as much of such tasks as dressing himself, feeding himself, etc. as he can, even if he is slow and clumsy.

Let him explore his own small world as far as safety permits.

Read Mother Goose and similar, simple rhymes to him.

Let him hear simple songs. Sing them to him yourself if you can.

Choose pictures for his room that are appropriate and that he likes.

Give him sheets of paper and soft crayons to play with occasionally.

Encourage his attempts to help you and to amuse himself.

Choose playthings he can do something with himself—not too complicated or too perishable.

Begin to consider a nursery school.

WHAT TO AVOID

When there is something the child must do, instead of asking him whether he wants to, simply lead him where you want him to go— cheerfully and without argument about it.

Avoid interrupting him suddenly when he is absorbed in something.

It is not good to give a small child too many reasons, warnings, or other occasions for worry. Make any necessary explanations as brief and simple as possible.

If you make suggestions, try not to make more than one at a time.

Remember that scolding, nagging, slapping, etc. are not good ways of teaching anything.

SUGGESTED READING

Recommendations for further reading on the subjects outlined above may be found by referring to the *Suggested Reading Guide* at the end of this CHART.

SOCIAL AND EMOTIONAL DEVELOPMENT

Some of the child's most important developments as a social creature occur during the second year of his life. Children who feel happy and secure in their home environment learn at this time to live happily with the members of their families and to meet strangers, perhaps shyly at first but with increasing trust.

WHAT TO EXPECT OF AVERAGE CHILDREN

Between One and Two Years:

Most children show affection spontaneously

Express joyful emotions with dancing, clapping hands, and laughing

Express anger and frustration when restrained from doing what they want to do

Love companionship but may be shy

Are sympathetic toward hurt members of the family, pets, toys, etc.

Sense of self, self-ownership, self-importance, etc., shows in self-assertion

Many show signs of balkiness, contrariness

Often say "No!" to almost everything

Are likely to show signs of jealousy if there is a new baby

WHAT TO DO FOR YOUR CHILD

Remember that the atmosphere of your home is the greatest influence in your child's life. Make it as wholesome and pleasant as possible.

Let your child feel the security of your presence, but let him have freedom, too, in order to develop a healthy outgoing spirit.

Let him get used to strangers gradually.

Let him see other children play as often as possible so he gets used to them.

Make playing with other children and sharing toys *fun,* not an unpleasant duty.

Remember that naughty words and aggressive behavior are normal at this age and can best be handled not by threats and scoldings but by good-humored understanding.

Encourage comradely relationship between the children and their father. This is just as important for girls as for boys.

When your child dawdles, remember that he is feeling his way to many skills and that time doesn't mean to him what it does to you.

Remember that a child must like people spontaneously before he can be naturally polite to them.

The best way to teach a child good manners is to have him grow up in a family whose members are naturally courteous to and considerate of each other.

Try to prevent temper tantrums before they occur.

If there is another baby in the family by now, let the older baby feel that the new baby belongs to him too. Pay extra attention to the older baby at this time and make him feel that you love him as much as ever.

If he shows jealousy of the new baby, let him know that you love him anyway. At the same time guard against opportunities for him to hurt the new baby by trying to avoid situations that bring such opportunities about.

WHAT TO AVOID

Never tease the child or allow him to be teased by anyone.

Try not to discuss his problems in his presence, especially before strangers.

Never encourage him to show off.

It is unwise to force strangers on him if he is shy of them.

Don't worry about babies' poor table manners or try to make "little ladies" and "little gentlemen" out of them at this age.

Instead of appearing shocked by his efforts to shock you with naughty words, take it in your stride. This phase will pass if you refuse to be impressed.

Keep his bedtime activities from stimulating him too much. Keep him as calm as you can.

It is foolish to ask your child unnecessary questions. Remember that his natural response, at this age, is "No!"

Refrain from punishing your child in any way that will not teach him what you really want him to learn. Breaking his spirit or his heart will do nothing but harm. An occasional quick spank, if you can't find a better way, may be less harmful than lengthy disapproval or withdrawal of affection.

If you want your child to *like* his room and his bed, it is obviously unwise to put him there for punishment.

Above all, avoid getting into arguments with him. It cannot do either of you any good.

SUGGESTED READING

Recommendations for further reading on the subjects outlined above may be found by referring to the *Suggested Reading Guide* at the end of this CHART.

MORAL AND SPIRITUAL DEVELOPMENT

A two-year old is still too immature to understand abstract differences between right and wrong. He is, however, well aware of the difference between approval and disapproval from those he loves. He wants their approval and will do all he can to gain it. When he is being "naughty," he is doing so not because he is "bad" but because he is not yet mature enough to control his behavior. This is true even when he seems to be deliberately bad; so punishing him is not much use.

What parents *can* do, however, even at this early age, is to surround their children with an atmosphere of goodness and mercy, that it may follow them all the days of their lives. No amount of Sunday School or other moral teaching in later years can take the place of those important impressions made by the spirit of a child's first world—his home. Moral teaching, to be effective at any time, must fall on fertile ground. It is up to all parents to prepare their children to receive spiritual grace at such time as they may be mature enough to do so. This preparation comes not by any attempt to *instruct* a baby at this tender age but by giving him the certain feeling that a life of loving kindness is valued and practiced by his parents.

WHAT TO EXPECT OF AVERAGE CHILDREN

Between One and Two Years:

Children may exhibit fear, anger, jealousy, and temper but they may also show kindness and affection toward those who appeal to their sympathies

Children reflect the moods of those around them, meeting cheerfulness with cheerfulness, good temper with good temper.

WHAT TO DO FOR YOUR CHILD

Let him gain self-confidence by helping him to do for himself what he wants to try.

Let him get the feeling of order by showing him where his things belong and helping him to put them there.

Be affirmative, not negative, in your suggestions, and keep them kindly.

Let him see acts of kindness.

Make generosity a pleasure to him rather than a virtue, since he is not ready yet to know what virtue is.

Be prepared for balky behavior and deal with it in a firm but always friendly way.

Praise small successes and encourage any step in the right direction.

A child may now be taught a simple prayer.

WHAT TO AVOID

Try not to expect or ask too much of your child in the control of his behavior.

Refrain from anger, irritability, impatience, etc. in yourself and from arousing jealousy, anxiety, insecurity, or fear in your child.

It will only confuse your child if you try to instill in him any ideas or concepts which are beyond his ability to understand or to act upon.

SUGGESTED READING

Recommendations for further reading on the subjects outlined above may be found by referring to the *Suggested Reading Guide* at the end of this CHART.

FROM TWO TO THREE YEARS

(For Development from One to Two Years, See Pages xxviii to xxxiii)

Continue to encourage your child in the good traits he has already begun to develop. Try again with those previously mentioned for which he may not have been ready earlier. And begin now to encourage him in the following traits for which most children are ready at some time during this period:

CHEERFULNESS and OPTIMISM, CLEANLINESS and GOOD HEALTH HABITS, FRIENDLINESS, HELPFULNESS, INDEPENDENCE, SELF-RELIANCE and SELF-HELP, INVESTIGATION, DECISION, KINDNESS

PHYSICAL DEVELOPMENT

Children between two and three often present new problems to their parents. This is especially so with a first child. At this age children grow fast in all directions. Many of the seemingly "naughty" things they do are really perfectly normal manifestations of growth at this period, a sort of over-exuberance caused by a realization of new physical powers. Who wouldn't want to try hitting, kicking, banging, exploring, balking, etc. if he had just learned how? If you keep this in mind, you will find it easier to be patient with your child's behavior. Try not to thwart him any more than you have to for his own safety or that of others. The calmer you are about it the better for all concerned—and the sooner he will grow through this phase.

WHAT TO EXPECT OF AVERAGE CHILDREN

Between Two and Two-and-a-Half Years:

Children are very active; grab everything and don't easily let go

Want to investigate and handle everything

May resist sleep or sleep too long

May resist bowel and bladder elimination

May go suddenly from intense activity to long passivity, sometimes accompanied by thumb-sucking

Are restless; may climb out of bed and explore at nap-time

Appetite may be uneven—sometimes very good, sometimes very poor, with more interest in between-meal snacks than in regular meals

Girls find it easier to stay dry than boys

Usually enjoy bath-time at this age

May still find dressing difficult, but can usually manage undressing alone if not too tired

Usually have all twenty first teeth by two-and-a-half

At Three Years:

Can run, jump, climb, ride a tricycle, etc.

Can do many things with hands and feet

Can button and unbutton, hang clothes on hooks, etc. (Girls are generally better and quicker than boys at things like this)

Like to drink from a cup
Can eat quite neatly, spilling very little
Can put away toys
Have increased control over muscles and motions

Can feed, dress, and toilet themselves with very little help
Appetite grows more stable
Dressing is still difficult but there are some improvements

WHAT TO DO FOR YOUR CHILD

When it becomes necessary to control the child's wild activity, find other channels for it rather than trying to make him stop.

See that your child rests in bed every day after lunch even if he doesn't sleep.

If your child hurts himself and comes to you for sympathy, give him the comfort he wants and bind up his wounds. As long as you don't emphasize his misery but calmly distract him to other activities, it is of greater help to give him the security of your sympathy than to make him feel he ought to "be brave."

Let him feed himself when he wants to and let him eat what he prefers, assuming that all he has to choose from is good for him.

Give him small between-meal snacks if he needs them, but keep candy and other sweets for special treats—after meals, not before.

Let him have all the fun he wants in his bath.

Help him to dress himself if and when he needs help, but try not to hurry him or change his routine if he objects.

Realize that such seemingly physical manifestations as stuttering, nail-biting, excessive handling of genitals, etc. are almost always signs of mental or emotional tension or unhappiness. Find out what is causing the tension and try to remove or treat the cause. But refrain from *all* nagging, punishing, or superficial correcting, none of which do any permanent good, but on the contrary, merely increase the tension.

Give him enough interesting things to do, plenty of chance to play with other children and alone, and get routine things done without making issues of them.

WHAT TO AVOID

Try not to hurry the child.

Do not interfere with his moods and activities unless absolutely necessary.

Show no anxiety about his habits of elimination, eating, sleeping, etc.

If your child becomes interested in the various parts of his body and in the bodies of those of the opposite sex, one of the worst things you can do is to be shocked or to behave as though he had done something wicked. This kind of curiosity is perfectly natural— and the child should be reassured on the subject. And never give a child the idea that there is anything bad about any part of his body.

SUGGESTED READING

Recommendations for further reading on the subjects outlined above may be found by referring to the *Suggested Reading Guide* at the end of this CHART.

MENTAL DEVELOPMENT

As he nears the age of three, a child's mental curiosity knows no bounds. He drives you mad asking questions. Nothing escapes him. His imagination takes him everywhere. Being sometimes unable to distinguish between real life and events of the imagination, he loves stories of all kinds and often tells them with a combination of truth and fiction which adults are apt to label lies. Sometimes he makes up these stories out of fear or anxiety but more often out of innocence of the meaning of truth. He relates everything to himself, not because of egotism in the adult sense but because he has just come to the realization that he is a functioning human being in his own right.

Three-year-olds change their minds constantly and without any seeming reason. They try to decide things for themselves but are usually unable to do so without parental help, and this is exasperating to them. The best thing parents can do about this is to lead them along into doing necessary things without raising issues that call for any decision.

WHAT TO EXPECT OF AVERAGE CHILDREN

Between Two and Two-and-a-Half Years:

Children are not yet ready to respond to direct questions or direct commands

Don't seem to know what they want

Say "No!" to almost everything but don't necessarily mean it

Like repetition of familiar stories and rhymes day after day

Like stories about themselves, familiar people, animals, children and vehicles

Enjoy looking at books by themselves

Enjoy listening to strongly rhythmic music on the radio, etc.

Can sing a few familiar tunes

Experiment at drawing and coloring

Especially enjoy finger-painting

Like to make pies with mud, sand, clay

Improve in block-building ability

Begin to know where they are going and how to get there

Have no sense of time

Do not like changes, new routines, etc.

Have stubborn sense of possession

At Three Years:

Have more patience; can listen longer

Love being read to; prefer repetition of familiar stories but show interest in new stories of imagination, as well as those concerning familiar experiences

Have a vocabulary of anywhere from 100 to 1,000 words; talk in sentences; improve fast in language ability

Pay attention to what adults say, accept their suggestions and act on them

Are curious and eager to learn

Understand simple humor

Are willing to sacrifice some immediate satisfaction for future gratification

Can sing, though generally not on pitch, and recognize familiar melodies

Like to use crayons and are beginning to form designs

Can build long trains and high towers with blocks

Can fold paper lengthwise and crosswise but not diagonally

Enjoy excursions, have destination in mind, and are fascinated by all they see

Have little sense of time but can tell night from day

Too much must not be expected of them; occasional relapses are normal

Are likely to become so absorbed in one occupation that stopping is difficult.

WHAT TO DO FOR YOUR CHILD

Read your child stories he likes, but don't let his mind get over-stimulated by them especially before bedtime, which should be kept as peaceful and pleasant as possible. Regular bedtime stories, soothing in effect, are excellent at this time.

Give him plenty of crayons, blocks, toys, etc. with which to occupy his creative impulses.

Let him look at picture books of his own choosing and listen to music he likes.

Treat his contrariness with occasional gentle humor, not sarcasm.

Take him on excursions and let him learn about his world by observing it

Let him learn to do things by doing them.

If he asks you questions about where babies come from, answer as simply and as truthfully as possible. There is no need to give him more than the briefest explanation, but it is far better that what you *do* tell him is the truth rather than some fairy or stork story that you will have to deny later.

Answer any questions he asks about sex differences in the same way—calmly, unemotionally, and truthfully.

Let him go to nursery school if feasible, when he seems ready—usually between two and three years. If there is none available, consider getting a few children together in an informal play group.

WHAT TO AVOID

It is unwise to force a child beyond his ability or to worry about lapses in progress.

Try not to interfere with his absorption in books, play, or other occupations.

Do not expect too much of him even if he

seems bright and quick. Do not be satisfied with too little either. If you are, he may become dependent instead of self-reliant

Never compare him, in his presence, with other children.

SUGGESTED READING

Recommendations for further reading on the subjects outlined above may be found by referring to the *Suggested Reading Guide* at the end of this CHART.

SOCIAL AND EMOTIONAL DEVELOPMENT

Children between two and three are often hard to get along with. They are apt to be balky and contrary; bossy and fussy; yet they hate to be bossed or interfered with themselves. They are on the rush one minute, dawdling exasperatingly the next. They are likely to be affectionate at this period and may become intensely jealous, especially if there is another baby. They begin to play with other children, forming attachments to others and cooperating in group activities. They may be easily frightened, unhappy, or lonely—all signs that something is amiss in their emotional lives. No matter what the provocation may be, avoid nagging or battling with your child at this time. He needs patience, affection, and understanding.

WHAT TO EXPECT OF AVERAGE CHILDREN

Between Two and Two-and-a-Half Years:
Children at this age sometimes go to extremes of contrariness
Like to be helpful to adults
Capacity for choice is weak
Tension and fatigue may make them stutter or show other temporary signs of emotional strain
Are very imitative
Insist on having things as they are accustomed to have them
May show preference for one parents
Love to be with other children but are likely to snatch and grab at their things
At Three Years:
Don't like to be alone, especially at bedtime
Will be especially affectionate; think mother and father are wonderful; want to imitate everything they say and do
Want to assert themselves even if it means defying parents whom they love
Are often obstinate and contrary
Usually have worries about themselves
Are often quite sociable
Are ready to accept suggestions
Can be quite helpful around the house
Like playing with other children, especially out of doors
Still need play supervision after half an hour or so of playing without it
May have difficulty adjusting to people
Sometimes slip back to babyish ways, even wetting or thumb-sucking
May invent imaginary companions

WHAT TO DO FOR YOUR CHILD

This is a trying time, but patience is especially necessary now that the child is trying to live in a world of many frustrations.

Use your best brand of tact at this stage. If you feel you have to overcome his resistance to something, do it gently by leading, not by pushing. Base your discipline on friendly firmness, not on anger or punishment.

If he is cross, go about the necessary tasks cheerfully but without unnecessary talk.

Respond warmly to all signs of affection and friendliness.

See that your child has congenial companions to play with. Supervise play when necessary and be ready to help when there is friction.

Let him follow his own desires about joining others in play. Trying to force him will only make him shyer if he is shy to begin with. Call his attention to what the other children are doing and show him ways of cooperating.

Understand that if he tells lies, takes things that belong to others, or shows undependability according to adult standards, he is doing so because he doesn't yet understand what is wrong about such behavior.

Protect his rights to his own things.

Caution him for safety without making him afraid or timid.

Encourage adaptability by expecting him to accept other people and household routines as a matter of course.

Set good examples in politeness, table manners, gentleness, etc., and expect them to be followed—at least to some extent.

Occasionally suggest kind, thoughtful, courteous, and generous acts for the child to do— but do not persist if he resists. If he does, wait till later before you try again.

WHAT TO AVOID

Try not to make your child feel too guilty about his misbehavior. Guilt feelings may be more damaging than the behavior.

Never let him feel that you don't love him or are disappointed in him even when you disapprove of some things he does.

Scolding, punishing, or nagging him for childish behavior he has not yet learned to control can do only harm. (These need understanding and removal of causes.)

Never laugh at, ridicule, or ignore his attempts to express affection, sympathy, or any other emotion regardless of how inept, awkward, or ridiculous his attempts may seem.

Never encourage your child to show off and don't let other adults coax or tease him to do so.

Try not to confuse him by too many directions, warnings, etc.

Comparing him (favorably or unfavorably) to other members of the family can result only in hurt feelings for someone.

Be sure not to discourage him from developing his own individuality or to squelch his development by exercising autocratic authority over him. (Remember that he is being brought up to live as a self-governing person in a democracy, not in a totalitarian state of unquestioning obedience to orders.)

Never instill fear in him or let anyone else do so. (There is a difference between caution and fear.) Be sure to find out whether fears are causing any of his so-called misbehavior. If so, reassure him until you have banished the fears and their causes.

SUGGESTED READING

Recommendations for further reading on the subjects outlined above may be found by referring to the *Suggested Reading Guide* at the end of this CHART.

MORAL AND SPIRITUAL DEVELOPMENT

The standards of right and wrong are set by the home. Most children by the time they are three are so loyal to the standards of their home that they will defend those standards to outsiders, however rebelliously they may behave in their own family circle. This is the time for mothers to resolve not to say "No!" continuously but instead to make it as easy as possible for the child to do the right things and keep him from being tempted to do the wrong ones. What you do will speak louder than what you say.

WHAT TO EXPECT OF AVERAGE CHILDREN

Between Two and Two-and-a-Half Years:

Children usually appear self-reliant and want to be good, but are not yet mature enough to be able to carry out most of their promises

Need a great deal of adult help but sometimes resist it in an effort to be self-reliant

Are not yet able to respond to direct questions or direct commands

Will try to be cooperative and helpful but often fail

At Three Years:

May be disobedient but can understand that obedience is one way to a happier life

Confuse make-believe with fact, causing them to tell stories when the truth is called for; but they can begin to understand the difference if it is explained gently, calmly, and without punishment

Begin to understand the meaning of trustworthiness

Begin to understand the need of order

WHAT TO DO FOR YOUR CHILD

Expect obedience and gain it not by demands but by firm friendly requests. Make only reasonable requests and not too many of them. Be prepared to drop some for the time being if necessary and repeat them at a later time.

Forestall fears where you can, but be understanding of them when they appear and try to reassure the child about them.

Build up a child's sense of security and self-confidence between make-believe and fact.

Be orderly and thus encourage a sense of order in the child.

Develop a sense of justice by making a point of being fair and just yourself.

Begin to establish habits of industry and helpfulness by letting your child help you with your work.

Encourage the child to play contentedly by himself and wholeheartedly with other children.

Praise him for any evidence of trustworthiness, kindness, generosity, etc.

Let him feel you are always available for help when he needs it.

Know how to deal with expected behavior problems so that you will not make disciplinary mistakes when they occur.

Before bed-time hear your child say the simple prayer he knows by now.

Merit his trust in you and show him in an understandable way, your own trust in God.

You may, perhaps, begin telling him a few simple Bible stories in words that he can understand.

WHAT TO AVOID

If you show discontent or disappointment with your child, you cannot expect him to show opposite qualities.

It never helps the essential problem to punish a child for his misdeeds, especially if you do it in anger.

Be careful not to set standards too high for his age and ability so that he feels foredoomed to failure. This may have lasting effects.

You cannot expect him to understand the significance of character-building at this age; but you can help him find satisfaction and success in doing those things which he knows will please you. Be sure you are pleased by things which are really good, not by those which are merely convenient to you.

SUGGESTED READING

Recommendations for further reading on the subjects outlined above may be found by referring to the *Suggested Reading Guide* at the end of this CHART.

MEMORANDA

(For Development from Two to Three Years, See Pages xxxiv to xl)

Continue to encourage your child in the good traits he has already begun to develop. Try again with those previously mentioned for which he may not have been ready earlier. And begin now to encourage him in the following traits for which most children are ready at some time during this period:

INITIATIVE, CAUTION and PRUDENCE, COOPERATION, COURTESY, POLITENESS, MANNERS, DEMOCRATIC SPIRIT, GENEROSITY, HONESTY, IMAGINATION, INDIVIDUALITY and ORIGINALITY, LOYALTY (to FAMILY), ORDERLINESS and NEATNESS, RESPECT, SELF-DIRECTION, SELF-CONTROL, SELF-RESPECT, SERVICE to OTHERS, SENSE of HUMOR, SYMPATHY, CONSIDERATION of OTHERS, TRUTHFULNESS, UNSELFISHNESS

PHYSICAL DEVELOPMENT

The year between three and four is in many ways the most delightful age of childhood for it is during these months that the child definitely begins to become "a person." He can do a great many new things by now and he tries to do them all with gusto. He gains every day in physical strength, coordination, and control. He is likely to be an affectionate little creature, too, at this age. He is really beginning to grow up now, and he is endearing indeed.

From three to six physical abilities develop at a fairly steady pace, increasing in skill rather than changing in character. For the sake of convenience and brevity, therefore, we are considering this three-year period as a unit. Not that this period, any more than any other, can be rigidly set off from the years that precede or those that follow it. Throughout life one age merges imperceptibly into another, regardless of birthdays; and, as we cannot stress too often, each individual child progresses, too, at his own pace. There is, however, in general, a rapid growth in height and weight, and an increase in strength, as well as intense muscular activity, during this three-to-six period. The rate of growth may vary but it will be decidedly noticeable and very gratifying.

WHAT TO EXPECT OF AVERAGE CHILDREN

From Three to Four Years:
Most children gain in poise and control
Can run, jump, climb, and skip, but not yet skillfully
Can button and unbutton most clothes and some can lace shoes, but do it clumsily
Cannot tie a bow
Can comb hair, brush teeth
Can throw a ball, but not accurately
Can build a whole house with blocks
Can go to the toilet without help daytimes
Eat and sleep well if healthy and happy

Appetite is generally good, but at this age children often lose interest in feeding themselves

Can't sit still for more than a minute or so at a time

May have frequent colds and stomachaches

From Four to Five Years:

Are very active—love to hop, jump, skip, climb, and race

Tend to go out of bounds

Can do things with their hands with increasing accuracy (cutting, lacing, etc.)

May have difficulty getting back to sleep if they wake at night

Improve in appetite

Can help set the table; usually enjoy being in the kitchen when meal is being prepared; like to ring dinner bell and help in other small ways

Have very few accidents — can usually manage themselves alone in bathroom

Dress themselves poorly in general but like to try on adult clothes

From Five to Six Years:

Can skip and jump well

Like dancing and physical exercise

Can hop on one foot

Can turn somersaults

Can handle wagon and sled easily

Can completely undress themselves but dressing still presents a few difficulties

Can wash themselves but sometimes dawdle and forget

Like to do all the things they know how to do

Usually have fewer colds than at four but are subject to whooping cough, measles, chickenpox, etc.

Usually cut the first permanent tooth during the year before or the year after six

WHAT TO DO FOR YOUR CHILD

See that your child has a rest period, if not an actual nap, in the middle of every day, at least up to the age of five or six.

Give him enough pure water to drink daily.

See that he has at least three regular meals a day, consisting of plenty of well-planned, well-balanced foods, including a minimum of three quarters of a quart of milk in some form.

If possible, let him sleep in a room by himself, certainly in a bed by himself, in a room with good circulation of air.

Keep to a fairly regular schedule about baths, meals, bedtime, etc., but allow occasional deviations so that the child does not become too dependent on routine.

Let him out of doors as much as possible, dressed for the weather.

Allow him all the freedom of activity possible, in appropriate clothes that fit comfortably and can stand rough use.

Supply him with play equipment appropriate for his age and ability.

Note his gains in height and weight.

Teach him to brush his teeth twice every day and take him to the dentist regularly. (The care of a child's teeth is very important.)

Consult doctor about vaccination, inoculation, and other health precautions before child goes to school.

Learn what to do for a sick child and know how to keep him contented while convalescent.

Respect quarantine laws.

See that your child thinks of doctor, dentist, etc. as friends.

Try to find out which of your child's symptoms, illnesses, etc. are purely physical and which may be partly or wholly psychological or emotional in origin. If you can't be sure, consult a doctor who understands psychosomatic symptoms.

Take him to the doctor or health station for periodic health examinations.

Plan vacations, outings, parties, etc. ahead of time so that they may yield the most in health and wholesome recreation. Include the whole family in at least some of them.

WHAT TO AVOID

Keep your child away from crowds to protect him from exposure to contagion.

Keep him from getting overtired.

No symptom of illness—such as a cold, upset stomach, fever, etc.—should ever be neglected. But avoid passing on to your child any anxiety you may feel. Once you are sure a symptom is nothing serious, try not to make a fuss about it. If you do so, the child may find that being sick is a good way to gain your concern or attention. That is something you will want to guard against.

It is not wise to dress him too warmly when he is playing vigorously or to cover him too heavily in bed.

Don't let him wear ill-fitting hand-me-down clothing.

If your child must share his room, let it be with another child, not an adult.

Never make an issue of your child's eating habits. If they are bad, they may very well be so because you have shown the child that you are worried or concerned about them.

If you make unfavorable comments about the food when your child is at the table, he will be sure to adopt every prejudice he hears expressed, especially at this age.

Never laugh at, make fun of, or in any way comment unfavorably on any physical defect or backwardness in your child. Don't worry if he is shorter or taller, or thinner or fatter, than other children in the family—as long as you know he is healthy.

SUGGESTED READING

Recommendations for further reading on the subjects outlined above may be found by referring to the *Suggested Reading Guide* at the end of this CHART.

MENTAL DEVELOPMENT

From three on, children learn many things by doing them. At four they begin to learn, also, in a more mental way—by consciously trying to find out about things. They want to know how and why about everything. They not only talk a blue streak but can hold conversations. Between the ages of three and six they may add as many as five hundred or more words a year to their vocabularies. By five they not only love to hear stories but like to tell them as well. By six they are ready for school. This is a period of great mental receptivity. It is, moreover, a period in which children identify themselves with their parents. They imitate them not blindly but because of admiration and real affection. This is not the time for parents to shift the responsibility for their children's education to the school and the church. The home is still the most important school in the world.

Children have intense curiosity at this period and their incessant questions are often trying to parents who cannot or will not be bothered by incessant answering. But do the best you can. If you do not answer their questions honestly and intelligently, you are depriving them of a vital part of their education. Sometimes, to be sure, their constant "Why?" is not a desire to know but a technique to keep you talking to them. You have to know the difference. But patience, intelligence, and truth-telling will reap handsome rewards for you in the greater enrichment of your children's minds and general outlook on life.

WHAT TO EXPECT OF AVERAGE CHILDREN

From Three to Four Years:

Mental growth is rapid; children have definite ideas about everything

The mental process changes from an imitative to an original one

Children's words often outrun their knowledge at this age; they talk so well that they sometimes seem to know more than they actually do

Like new, different, and rhythmic words, stories, etc.; no longer insist on constant repetition but want more variety

Ask questions endlessly

May become curious about death

Can pay attention longer, and, as a result, memory improves

Love to dramatize experiences

Imagination makes them tell tall tales and produce ingenious alibis

Are very versatile—can be serious, humorous, truthful, fanciful, etc. from one minute to the next

Can be trusted with many minor responsibilities

Like to try new chores and projects

Like to draw pictures and listen to stories and music

Are aware of others' opinions

Can count to about ten

Have only a vague idea of time

Reason logically but often make mistakes because of limited experience and information

From Four to Five Years:

Children have very lively minds at this age

Can talk and eat at the same time

Love to talk and ask "Why?" and "How?" constantly

Hop from one interest to another; seldom stay at one thing long

Want to be more grown-up than they are

Use silly words to make up stories they consider funny

Like to show off talking and thinking ability

Love rhymes

Enjoy simple singing games

Can identify simple melodies

Improve in ability to explain things

In drawing, usually draw largest the things they like best regardless of actual proportions

Begin to criticize their own efforts

From Five to Six Years:

Are much more reliable than at four

Ask questions for information; want to know what things are for, how they work, etc.

Become intensely interested in helping with home chores

Like to finish what they have started and then go on to something else

Can usually draw a recognizable if crude human figure, remember a simple plot, and carry a melody

Have a greatly increased vocabulary of words and will use them without baby talk if encouraged to do so by parents

Answer questions intelligently

Understand that printed words are symbols of objects and ideas

Like to act out favorite stories

Can distinguish their own right and left hand, but not others'

Are conscious of and interested in sex differences

Develop an intense interest in the origin of things—among them babies

Become less imaginative, more literal and factual

WHAT TO DO FOR YOUR CHILD

Answer your child's questions in terms that he can understand and see that the information you have given him satisfies him for the time being.

Be prepared for the question "What shall I do now?"

Help him to learn how to count (to 10), to tell time, to distinguish between left and right, to do simple household chores.

Encourage his attempts at dramatizing stories by a sympathetic and interested attitude.

Hold simple conversation with him, extending to him the same courtesy and attention you would give an adult.

If you can speak another language, now is a splendid time to teach it to your child in conversation.

Call his attention to the funny side of things. Laugh at them with him.

Read and tell him stories about animals, vehicles, and children.

Encourage him to express himself in stories, songs, drawings, scrapbooks, etc.

Give him plenty of pencils, crayons, paper, picture and story books, etc.

Have good pictures on the walls of your home and discuss them with him. Make him picture-conscious.

Sing with him. Play the piano for him if you can. Listen with him to music he enjoys on the radio or phonograph.

Help him to plant some large seeds, and as they grow tell or read him stories of plant life.

Give him constructive toys that do not break easily.

Work with his creative instincts by encouraging handicrafts.

If he is not already in nursery school, try to let him attend for at least a year before he goes to regular school.

Accept the help a modern kindergarten offers you.

WHAT TO AVOID

It is unwise to make a child feel that he is doing something bad if he tells you whoppers occasionally. He is indulging his growing imagination, and that is, in general, a good thing. But if he does it too consistently, help him understand the difference between make-believe and fact.

When he asks about the difference between boys and girls, how babies come, etc., it is better not to begin with the stork story or any other untruths, because he will lose confidence in you when he finds out later that you have deceived him. The elementary truth, a step at

a time, is the best way. And don't make a solemn occasion of it. Take it in your stride; give it to him in his.

Don't be shocked by his interest in sex differences or make him feel that there is anything wrong about it.

Instead of overstimulating his already active mind, see that it has enough outgoing interests to satisfy him.

Trying to force your child's taste to agree with yours is foolish and useless. Surround him with good things and he will choose them of his own accord when he is ready to understand them. But if you try to ram them down his throat he may turn against them forever.

See that you do not use the kind of speech you do not want him to use. If you give him a good example to follow, you will not need to worry if he hears poor speech elsewhere.

SUGGESTED READING

Recommendations for further reading on the subjects outlined above may be found by referring to the *Suggested Reading Guide* at the end of this CHART.

SOCIAL AND EMOTIONAL DEVELOPMENT

At three years of age most children begin to be more outgoing, less emotionally turned in on themselves. They are more at home with people than they have been, both in the family and outside. It doesn't last, however. It is a definite maturing over the balkiness of the two-and-a-half period, but before the child is four it is very likely that he will have acquired new insecurities and other unsettling emotions. He lives an inner life of fantasy, which may result in fears, anxieties, doubts, and tensions. He often makes a show of being brave but this is just a front to cover his fears. This is the age when he should be given many wholesome activities to occupy him.

By five, however, he begins to grow up for good, emotionally speaking. At six he is more reliable than he has ever been before and, feeling independent, he can generally be depended on to do what is expected of him—assuming that not too much is expected. He plays well with other children by now and is also able to amuse himself for a time when he is alone.

Altogether, during these years, he is becoming a human being with a distinct social personality of his own.

WHAT TO EXPECT OF AVERAGE CHILDREN

From Three to Four Years:

Most children begin to be independent

Have a constant desire to talk and be sociable

Begin to have new fears intensified by imagination—perhaps fear of the dark, of animals, of death, of deformed persons, and of many unfamiliar things.

May invent imaginary companions who seem real to them

Have strong, intense emotions concerning those they love

Enjoy simple dramatic play, such as being doctor, mother, etc.

Crave companionship of other children, yet may have difficulty in adjusting to them

May occasionally sink back into the behavior of babyhood

Show many evidences of aggressiveness and self-interest

From Four to Five Years:

Love to be with other children

Prefer play to anything else

Are given to quoting mother or father as final authority on any question

Love their own home unless it has been made specifically distasteful to them

Love to act out home scenes

Can usually fight their own battles unless there are too many of them to fight

Love going out alone with father

Are less likely than at three to invent imaginary playmates

Still need to be prepared for new social contacts

Are generally cooperative in social projects

From Five to Six Years:

Are so sure of themselves that they want to be protective of younger children

Are proud of their possessions, clothes, accomplishments

Mother is the adored center of their universe

Like to talk about what they used to be like when they were tiny babies—thus detaching themselves from babyhood

Become more competent and more stable, have more confidence in people

Get along well with playmates in small groups, preferably one at a time

Seek affection and applause

May be shy but slowly begin to build steady relationships with people

May still have frightening dreams or nightmares about wild anmials, bad people, etc.; but in general have fewer fears than they have had.

Do not very often go off into temper tantrums, and when they do, return to normal sooner than formerly

Tend to monopolize conversation at table, which may interfere with eating behavior

No longer like to show off before company

Take very little responsibility about clothes

Like to prepare and plan for things

Like to finish what they have started but cannot always do so without help

Become more interested in mothering a new baby than in the sex aspects of birth

Become quite modest about exposing body

Girls usually love dolls at this time, but some do not. Boys may suddenly refuse to play with dolls or other girlish toys, though some like dolls at this age. Both boys and girls may still want a soft toy to take to bed with them.

WHAT TO DO FOR YOUR CHILD

Let the child be alone when he wants to be, but listen, with as much interest as possible, to everything he has to say, which ,at this age, will probably be a great deal.

Encourage him to play with other children of his own age.

Try to make him see the value of good sportsmanship. When you are acting as referee, be scrupulously fair in your decisions. Show your child, and the other children too, that they must learn to accept defeat gamely and play fair at all times.

Do everything you can to help your child to be interested in things and people outside himself. (This is especially important with a first child or an only child.)

Encourage the child and his father to have a friendly, chummy relationship and to go off on excursions together occasionally without you. (Girls as well as boys need the companionship of their fathers.)

If you have a child who tends to be shy and unsociable, especially with strangers, be as friendly and easy-going as possible with people yourself so that the child has a chance to absorb the friendliness of the atmosphere you create.

Most children like to be helpful and it is

likely that your child will perform at least some of his duties with enthusiasm if you let him *enjoy* them. Make the daily routines as pleasant as you can so that he will find some satisfaction in getting them done. Encourage him, or lend a hand, to get the necessarily dull things done quickly.

Lead your child, don't push him. He'll go where you want him to far more willingly.

Let him get as dirty as he likes when he is playing; then he will take far more kindly to cleaning up when it is necessary.

Encourage your child to *like* people and trust them. Out of this attitude will grow kindness and consideration—the best basis for the kind of good manners that really count.

If your child exhibits undue aggressiveness or hostility, make allowances for him because these are emotions to be expected at this age, but do your best to channel them for socially constructive purposes through play, tools, etc.

You can reason with a child of three or four, but try not to get into long explanations and arguments. It is better to steer him gently, but firmly, in a friendly, happy, self-confident way, through the routines of the day.

Remember that what makes a child behave well is not a threat or a punishment but a genuine feeling that you are glad you have him and a knowledge that he can rely on you for justice and consideration. Show him that you love *him* even though you may have to stop some of the things he does.

If there is to be a new baby in the family, discuss it freely and frankly with the older child. He will be far more receptive and less likely to be jealous if he has been prepared and feels that he has a share in the event.

Jealousy of a new baby may take various forms such as worry about other things, a return to babyish behavior, sulking, or some childish attempts to hurt the baby or get rid of it. Your two jobs are (1) to protect the safety of the new baby and (2) to assure the elder child that you still love him as much as ever, maybe more, *no matter what he may do.*

If your child is nervous or shows new fears, try to give him an increased feeling of security. Make all necessary explanations as simple and matter-of-fact as possible. Give him an extra hug or two occasionally. Find new things for him to do, especially helping you.

Remember that a child's later attitude toward sex, marriage, etc. is largely formed by his sense of how his mother and father get along together. Be sure you have given your child the elementary facts about where babies come from before he goes to school.

Make your child feel that he is a partner in the home and that it belongs to him too. That will deepen his roots there.

Let your child have a pet to love, but do not expect him to be entirely or even largely responsible for its care at this age.

Begin to give him a sense of belonging to the community in which he lives as well as to his home.

Encourage him to be cooperative and responsible in his relations with other people, both children and adults, and to join in any community projects appropriate to his age, interests, and abilities.

WHAT TO AVOID

Try not to let him feel that you choose his friends for him or that you do not let him choose his own.

Too much adult companionship is not good for children.

It is foolish to try to teach a child manners—or anything else for that matter—without giving him a sense of the basic meaning behind what you are trying to teach.

Never make a child feel unduly guilty for his mistakes. Help him rather, to get a feeling of enjoyment from doing the right thing.

Never make explanations scary, and never put deep fears of *any* kind into a child's mind.

(Caution against common dangers can be given without creating fear.)

Remember that a child's seeming conceit and boastfulness, which usually show themselves at about four, are normal ways of trying out his new powers. Belittling him or making fun of his attitude will only make him worse. Let him outgrow this stage as he will if you don't tease him.

Forcing a shy child to be sociable to a guest will do no good. Give him a chance to take the initiative himself. If he doesn't, just go ahead and be sociable yourself. He will catch on in time if you don't make him self-conscious about it.

You can spoil a child by fussing over him or giving him too much attention *when he doesn't need it*. Reserve your attention for the times when he *does* need it. Be friendly and firm—not unfriendly and wavering.

It is better to keep a child from getting into trouble than to punish him after he has got into it.

Spanking is not to be recommended, but it sometimes clears the air and is preferable to a long-drawn-out punishment or atmosphere of hostility. If you must spank, get it over with quickly so that you can both soon go back to feeling friendly.

It is better not to threaten a child—certainly not with something that can't or won't be carried out.

Do your best to forestall and avoid jealousy between two children. Minimize it as well as you can if it crops up. Don't increase it by making comparisons. Let both children feel that you love them as they are.

Never force an older child to share his toys with the younger. Generosity has no meaning unless it comes spontaneously because of genuine feeling. Forcing generosity on a child who seems selfish does only harm, no real good.

Making a little boy feel self-conscious if he likes dolls or a little girl if she prefers boyish toys and activities can do only harm. Never shame your child about any behavior. Either let time take care of it or, if *necessary*, get professional help in handling it.

SUGGESTED READING

Recommendations for further reading on the subjects outlined above may be found by referring to the *Suggested Reading Guide* at the end of this CHART.

MORAL AND SPIRITUAL DEVELOPMENT

The child from three to six who has been handled sensibly during his early years is usually truthful. If his parents have been wise and he trusts them, he never needs to lie through fear. But his imagination begins to expand richly at this time. At first fact and fancy are confused in his mind. Later he may tell tall tales to enjoy the sensation he creates. In neither case should he be made to feel guilty. The difference between fact and fancy and the desirability of telling the truth about real happenings should be pointed out to him as occasions arise, in terms he can understand. And it goes without saying that he should be able to trust his parents to tell *him* the truth when he asks questions or when they give him any information.

1

WHAT TO EXPECT OF AVERAGE CHILDREN

From Three to Four Years:

Children are interested in everything

Have a deep inner desire to be happy

Love approval and will do a good deal to gain it if not interfered with

Praise themselves if they do not get enough praise from others

Like showing kindness (sometimes alternating with cruelty) to a younger, shyer, or less competent child, or to a pet

Begin to be cooperative and constructive

From Four to Five Years:

Become aware of others' opinions and care about them

Appreciate receiving new privileges

Are inclined to wander out of bounds

Are usually less eager to help around the house than at three

Develop strong sense of home and family

May be able to sit through a short part of church service

Usually enjoy Sunday School

May like to say prayers

From Five to Six Years:

Want to do things independently and become more and more responsible and self-reliant in doing them

Show quite remarkable ability to endure hardships

Can often distinguish between truth and falsehood

Are interested in natural beauty

Begin to have a sense of goodness—may sometimes be "a little angel" but not consistently

May blame others for their own wrongdoing

Begin to have an understanding that there is a vast creative force called God; ask frequent questions about Him

Are interested in now and here—still have little understanding of past and future

WHAT TO DO FOR YOUR CHILD

Learn what to do constructively in place of punishment.

Make the best possible use of praise. Emphasize the child's successes, not his failures.

Give him as much independence as you think he is ready for, keeping it within bounds by your approval and, when necessary, disapproval. Try to keep a good balance between freedom and restraint.

Be consistent, fair and truthful with your child.

Build self-reliance by showing him what the consequences of his actions will be and by guiding him toward success. (Do not do this, however, until he is mature enough to understand consequences. Above all, do not make him anxious about them.)

Teach your child to be trustworthy by showing him that what he does, either at home or away from home, means more to you than whether he is caught doing it.

Understand the new techniques of handling personality problems.

Realize that character is caught rather than taught. What you are is more effective than what you say.

Control what you say about other people. Make it good whenever you sincerely can.

Teach all the virtues by example—and try to be the kind of person whose example your child will want to imitate because he loves and admires you.

Continue simple prayers both morning and evening. The morning prayers are the more important because they give the child the whole day in which to think of and act on them. The evening prayer should be a reassuring and comforting one. Stay with him while he says it.

Have a clear picture, in your own mind, of your aim in religious training.

Bring the child up in his own faith but

teach him tolerance toward the faiths, beliefs, and customs of others.

Enter him in Sunday School and have him attend as often as possible. Make sure he enjoys it by giving him a simple inspirational background of religious meaning—geared to his understanding.

Be kind and trustworthy yourself.

WHAT TO AVOID

If you try to teach religion to a child before he is ready to appreciate its meaning, you run the risk of setting him against it.

Remember that young children do not understand abstract terms like goodness, mercy, justice, etc.

If you yourself lack appreciation of the value of beauty, art, music, character, religion, etc., you cannot expect such appreciation of your child, although he may come to it later through outside influences.

If you do not want your child's values of life to be based on material considerations, be sure your own are not either.

Never invoke fear or anxiety in your child.

Never laugh at his questions about birth, death, heaven, God, church, etc. No matter how confused they may be or how ridiculous they may seem.

Do not expect him, at this age, to sit quietly through a long church church service.

If you have a superior or snobbish attitude toward other people you have no right to expect forbearance or consideration or kindness from your child.

You should not try to force your child to love someone he really doesn't like. Love and respect are not the same.

SUGGESTED READING

Recommendations for further reading on the subjects outlined above may be found by referring to the *Suggested Reading Guide* at the end of this CHART.

MEMORANDA

(For Development from Three to Six Years See Pages xlii to liii)

Continue to encourage your child in the good traits he has already begun to develop. Try again with those previously mentioned for which he may not have been ready earlier. And begin now to encourage him in the following traits for which most children are ready at some time during this period:

ADAPTABILITY and ADJUSTABILITY, ALERTNESS and ATTENTIVENESS, APPRECIATION and GRATITUDE, CONSCIENCE, FAIRNESS, LEADERSHIP, LOYALTY (to FRIENDS), MODESTY and SIMPLICITY, OPENMINDEDNESS and REASONABLENESS, PATIENCE, PUNCTUALITY and PROMPTNESS, RESOURCEFULNESS and INGENUITY, RESPONSIBILITY, REVERENCE, SINCERITY, THINKING and REASONING, THRIFT, TOLERANCE, TRUSTWORTHINESS and DEPENDABILITY

PHYSICAL DEVELOPMENT

After six most children change in many ways, both physical and psychological—so much so, in fact, that child specialists are likely to refer to "six-year-oldness" as though it were a recognizable trait in itself.

Although six-year-oldness is quite different from five-year-oldness, it is likely to begin at about five-and-a-half. Children of this age, having acquired many new powers, tend to go to extremes in trying them out. They are eager and excitable because they find themselves full of so many newly acquired skills. But growth is not steady between six and nine. Periods of rapid growth are often followed by times of almost no noticeable growth at all. The framework of the body seems to enlarge almost from day to day even though the weight may change very little at certain times.

There is usually a kind of quieting down at seven. At eight there is another spurt of activity, better health (in a generally healthy child), and a great speeding up of activity. Nine-year-olds begin to show greater physical skill and greater control of motions. They are rapidly growing from what we think of as childhood to the stage which we think of as youth.

WHAT TO EXPECT OF AVERAGE CHILDREN

At Six to Seven Years:

Children grow at an erratic, not a steady pace

Their muscles grow heavier and coordinate better; framework of body enlarges

Indulge in almost constant activity and enjoy it hugely

Like rough-and-tumble play and often overdo it to the point of fatigue

Like to do things with their hands but usually do them awkwardly

Tend to wriggle and squirm

May have tremendous appetites but eyes may be bigger than stomachs

Are likely to slight breakfast but eat hugely all the rest of the day

Like to use fingers rather than knives, forks, and spoons for eating

Usually have very positive likes and dislikes in food. Almost invariably refuse lumpy or stringy foods

Six-year-olds usually have control of their functions of elimination but are often too busy playing to think of them. As a result they may not get to the bathroom in time and accidents may occur. They are usually very much ashamed when this happens

Still need help in bathing and often resist the idea of a bath at all (This is especially true of boys)

Are usually interested in new clothes but usually do little or nothing about taking care of them

May have frequent colds

Often have complaints about hurts, muscular pains, being too hot, too cold, etc.

Subject to chickenpox, measles, whooping cough, mumps, diphtheria or scarlet fever. In general, more susceptible to infectious diseases than at five, but do not necessarily have any of them

Tire easily, yet hate to stop activity

May complain of frequent stomachache, which may or may not be logical in origin (such as the kind, signifying a desire not to go to school, which is entirely cured as soon as it is too late to go)

Are headlong and clumsy

At Seven to Eight Years:

Are usually less brisk, more cautious, and sometimes more tense in activity than at six

Carpentry is often favorite occupation at this age, especially with boys

May sometimes be persuaded to try disliked foods

Generally willing to go to bed and usually sleep well

Begin to take functions of elimination for granted

Can bathe and get ready for bed alone but like company of mother or father

Dawdle and dream in bathtub and need checking up afterwards to see whether they are really clean

Are still not interested in neatness or care of clothes

May still have some typically six-year-old childhood diseases

Usually have fewer colds than at six

May have headaches, especially after too much excitement

May appear deaf, but this is often due to absorption in activity and lack of attention (Real deafness is easily detected)

May return, temporarily, to nose-picking, nail-biting, or even thumb-sucking

Tend to fidget

Are aware of body and do not like to expose it

At Eight to Nine Years:

Become healthier, speedier, and noticeably more mature in appearance

Change from the awkwardness and clumsiness of seven to postures of poise and grace

Are always on the go; like to perform feats of daring and courage

Still leave many things uncompleted; like to dash from one activity to another

Are almost always ravenously hungry

Can usually manage knife and fork fairly well, but revert to fingers now and then

Eat with great speed—often bolt food; will belch quite unashamedly after overeating

Like to stay up longer at night

Usually sleep very well, for about ten hours

Can usually be persuaded to have about three baths a week

Can now tie shoelaces so that they stay tied

Do not tire as quickly as at seven

Lose sense of caution—tend to have accidents for this reason

Excitement, emotional tension, intense laughter, etc. may produce involuntary release of urine

Thumb-sucking may recur at this age, usually for the last time, and more often in boys than in girls

Twelve permanent teeth usually come in between 5 or 6 and 9

WHAT TO DO FOR YOUR CHILD

Encourage improved habits of eating, sleeping, elimination, washing, etc. Expect to have to remind him of these, but do not nag.

Interest child in cleaning up after work, play, etc. Make the job pleasurable to him. Once he has the hang of it, let him do it his own way without interruption. (Do not expect perfect results.)

Without appearing anxious, call his attention occasionally to lapses in his eating habits. (If you can't do it without appearing anxious, it is better not to do it at all.)

Think up devices for saving his feelings when he is unable to live up to his declarations, remembering that at six he often bites off more than he can chew.

Remember that at six and seven a child still needs reminding about going to the bathroom. Remind him calmly at strategic times, but never emphasize it or insist on it. Anything is better than giving him an anxiety about bathroom functions. It is best to let children go to the bathroom one at a time.

"I forgot to remind you to wash" (or dress or whatever) is a better way to phrase it than "*You* forgot to—," etc. (In other words, be tactful.)

It is sometimes beneficial to help your child plan a washing and dressing schedule for himself.

Realizing that young children like nice clothes but don't like to keep them nice, get your child a few in-between clothes good enough for school but not too good to play in.

See that your child thinks of bed as a pleasant place—one he likes to go to for relaxation and rest.

Feed a school child the kind of food suited to his activities, but also indulge his preferences if they are reasonable. Find suitable substitutes for or other ways of preparing foods he doesn't like (milk in puddings, eggs in drinks, etc.). Encourage your child to try new or previously disliked foods, but don't force them on him.

If your child's posture is not all it should be, look into possible reasons. If you suspect that his vision is defective or that there is any other physical cause, take him to a doctor. But remember that many a child droops, slouches, stands or sits round-shouldered because of fatigue, or sometimes loneliness, unhappiness, jealousy, or for some other psychological reason. Build up his self-confidence and his relationship with others, and the chances are that his posture will improve. (It certainly won't if you nag him about it.)

See that the child understands the essential rules of good hygiene. Cooperate with the school doctor and nurse. They can help you keep your child on the road to good health.

Know the signs of overfatigue and of illness in your child.

Help your child to exercise ordinary caution. (Accidents are frequent at this period due to overabundance of energy coupled with heedlessness.)

Encourage exercises and sports which develop poise, balance, and physical skill—such as swimming, rowing, running, jumping, climbing, ball-playing etc.

If your child shows any interest in dancing, let him go to dancing school or join a dance-group of his own choosing.

Keep track of your child's growth in weight, height, and physical abilities, but remember that "normal" weight and height are not the same for all children.

If you have no yard or other convenient outdoor play place, do all you can to get your child to a park or public playground.

Plan to take at least some vacations with your child or children if possible.

Remember that, in matters of health (mental and emotional as well as physical), prevention is better than a need to cure. Use common sense about watching your child's diet, rest, and exercise routines.

Teach your child to cooperate with health authorities in preventing the spread of coughs, colds, and other illnesses.

Know how to treat, care for, and entertain your child when he is sick and convalescent— and be careful to keep him quiet and unexcited.

WHAT TO AVOID

Try not to let your child overtax his strength or his abilities.

Keep him from sudden changes, such as overheating, chilling, etc.

Try not to let him be exposed to illness.

Avoid overexcitement—on your part or the child's.

Try not to nag your child about his clumsiness, noise, wriggling, jerking, nail-biting, or other manifestations of tension or rapid growth. The less you comment on them, the sooner they are likely to disappear. One constructive suggestion is worth a dozen naggings or scoldings.

Guard against tension or fatigue before mealtime. Flexibility in the matter of meals and bedtime is far better than too rigid adherence to routines.

Never make going to bed a punishment or do anything to keep mealtime and bedtime from seeming pleasant occasions for your child.

Avoid comparing your child's size or physical prowess with other children's. If your child is "out of step" physically (smaller than other boys of the same age, or taller than other girls) try to suggest activities in which skill is more important than size.

SUGGESTED READING

Recommendations for further reading on the subjects outlined above may be found by referring to the *Suggested Reading Guide* at the end of this CHART.

MENTAL DEVELOPMENT

In purely mental pursuits like reading and writing, as well as in those dictated by the mind but performed by the hand — such as handcrafts, drawing, sewing, carpentry, piano-playing, and construction in general—new skills develop in profusion between the ages of six and nine. School enters the picture at this time and so there is opened to these children an exciting new world of mental activity. The imagination is given every chance to flower and the mind develops richly under the stimulus of a good teacher. This is not to say that children outgrow all their childishness when they go to school. They are as much interested in play as ever. Indeed they may crave it more than ever at this time as an escape from too much pressure. But they usually play more purposefully at this age, with a more specific goal in mind than formerly.

Many children like to make and construct things at this age. They like collecting objects and arranging them. They want to win at games. They love to keep count of how many and how much, how long and how far.

At this age children often read voraciously. The wonderful, richly peopled world of books, coupled with the newly acquired privilege of living in that world through the ability to read, is nothing short of thrilling to them. It is at this period that a life-long interest in good literature can be either made or marred.

To be sure, they will probably read the comics too. This may be because it is a sort of fashion, among children of this age, to read them, or it may be that the oversimplified pictures and action-stories provided by the comics appeal to their immature tastes and undeveloped reading skills. At any rate, children will be pretty sure to resist your efforts to get them to stop reading the comics if you nag or ridicule them about it. The antidote is to make good books easily accessible to your child—not *adult* good books but books which are appropriate for and essentially interesting to a child of his age. If you don't make an issue of his absorption in the comics, and if you do have other inviting children's books around the house, he will come to them of his own accord when he is mentally and emotionally ready.

Children are usually interested in rhythmic music at this age too. You may find, also, that your child can scarcely be pried loose from the dramatic programs he likes on the radio, however horrible or boring some of them may seem to you.

It is during this time that the teacher takes over from the mother some of the responsibility for the child's mental development. This does not mean, however, that the mother's job is over in this respect. On the contrary experience has shown over and over again that children who come from homes where culture is valued almost invariably do better in school and have a better foundation for intellectual competence throughout life than those who come from homes where there is no interest in or concern for education.

So go along with your child as his mind develops. Keep ahead of him if you can, not forgetting that times, methods, events, and knowledge have advanced since *you* went to school. Keep your mind interested, well-informed, and open to new ideas. Be prepared to give your child the information he expects of you or help him find it, and give it to him as patiently, as accurately, and as understandably as you can. That will keep *you* on your mental toes—an exercise which will do both you and your child a world of good.

FROM SIX TO NINE YEARS

WHAT TO EXPECT OF AVERAGE CHILDREN

At Six to Seven Years:

Some children may have difficulty in adjusting to school disciplines; some, on the other hand, may get an added sense of security from an understanding teacher or from learning new skills

Many like to report the day's events to mother or father

Begin to store their minds with factual information

Are learning to reason more correctly and more logically as memory improves

Have a great capacity to pretend—a capacity which enriches their play, their reading, and their imagination (But by now they know the difference between fancy and reality)

Girls usually show more interest in reading, writing, drawing and spelling of simple words, boys in number work

Both boys and girls usually like stories about animals, people, trains, etc., and comics

Like listening to radio, but some prefer outdoor play

In general, like to work and are interested in seeing results of activities; may go to extremes

Begin to print letters but may print them backwards

Are learning to read combinations of words but usually make many mistakes

Are often too intense (wriggle, make faces, etc.) when they try to read

Begin to be interested in money—as an allowance and as reward for doing chores, etc., but don't understand saving for some remote purpose

Begin to understand time, the past, and the future; but live chiefly in the present; appeals or threats regarding what they will become when they are grown up make little or no impression

At Seven to Eight Years:

Like to reflect about things, and may therefore brood, sulk, be shy, sad, and sometimes heedless of surroundings

Like to act on their ideas

Are interested in concrete things only; abstract ideas (justice, mercy, equality, etc.) do not appeal to them

Are generally critical of themselves and argumentative with others

Begin to be intelligently aware of the world and of the people who inhabit it, especially those they know or have heard about

Still need to be reminded of time, tasks to be done, etc.

Interest in magic, supermen, etc. gives way, somewhat, to simple scientific inquiry

Begin to be skeptical of childish beliefs such as Santa Claus, etc.

Boys usually like to make and invent things; girls enjoy coloring and cutting things out; both like games, puzzles, tricks, etc.

Begin to enjoy movies, but may be frightened by them (Most boys and many girls definitely dislike love stories)

Are likely to keep school work and home activities in separate mental compartments

Are likely to be forgetful

Improve rapidly in the mechanics of reading

Love to write and to erase

Enjoy being members of a group but want to be free to wander off alone if they feel like it

At Eight to Nine Years:

Are actively curious about everything, especially origin of things

Are speedier in all responses

Like to listen to adult conversation

Like to swap and barter

Are increasingly aware of money, property, ownership, and possessions

Are interested in the insides of things—the earth, the human body, mechanisms, etc.; like to know what makes things work

Want to explore the unfamiliar

Love to talk, to exaggerate, to dramatize

Begin to make fundamental distinctions between real and unreal

Like to make collections, and begin to appreciate quality as well as quantity

Like indoor table games and are usually very good at them

Love to receive mail especially if they can read it themselves

Spend less time reading than they did at seven, and again like to be read to, the novelty of being able to read to themselves having somewhat worn off

Comic books are still favorites, but most children also like childhood classics, books of far away times and places, humor, fairy tales, and blood-and-thunder

Love to look at pictures in magazines and cut them out

Usually have a crude sense of humor

Develop a sense of ownership and money

Enjoy the radio; listen to their favorite programs with rapt attention

Often want to go to the movies but still dislike romantic films

Usually enjoy school

Enjoy learning through others' mistakes

Make transition from home to school and from school to home more easily

Can work more independently than at seven

Read with greater regard for meaning

Favor exciting and humorous stories; scorn "babyish" stories

May be careless in writing but want to write neatly

Have an increasing sense of time and punctuality; may even telephone home if they are going to be late

Like taking trips to new places

Now know left from right in others as well as in themselves

WHAT TO DO FOR YOUR CHILD

Be interested in matters of interest to your child.

Make the most of the child's interest in collecting things by showing him the desirability of perseverance and orderliness in arranging his collection.

Encourage him to think for himself by letting him make decisions whenever he is able.

Help him develop good taste in literature by having around the house, easily accessible to him, good books which are well selected for appropriateness and interest to a child of his age and tastes.

Put table talk to good use by making it interesting and stimulating to the child and by including him in it.

Let your own conversation be worth listening to.

Encourage the child's love of poetry and rhythm.

Have good pictures in your home and help your child appreciate them. (If you are not sure of your own knowledge about art, read a good book on the subject or have someone who understands good art explain it to you.)

Be interested in and appreciative of the child's efforts to draw, paint, read, and write; but do not push him beyond his capacity or interest.

Let your child take piano lessons (or learn to play on some other instrument) if he shows any interest in doing so. If possible, choose a teacher who makes it interesting to him as he goes along so that he will want to practice. You won't get anywhere by nagging and you may make the whole idea of music distasteful to him. Be interested, yourself, in his progress. Help him over the difficult places. Play for him if you know how or practice with him. You might consider taking lessons yourself. However you accomplish it, the important thing is to keep your child interested in his progress so that he will *want* to make an effort. Sometimes taking lessons with a class or a group helps.

Provide your child with play materials which he likes and which will at the same time give him creative interests and physical activity.

Encourage his efforts to express himself through handcrafts, scrapbooks, clay, carpentry, or construction of any kind which interests him.

Let him have a pet and give him as much responsibility about caring for it as he is willing to assume without making this a burden or a bone of contention.

Take an interest in his hobbies and collections, and give him a place to keep them.

Help him in making a weather map, a bird calendar, or in any other nature project which interests him.

Begin to give him some understanding of money by letting him have a small regular allowance and then letting him spend it as he likes. Show him the value of spending his allowance wisely and of saving some of it for something he wants later, but not in the too far distant future. Help him decide, but do not decide for him, the purpose or the rate of saving. Let him learn by his own mistakes while the amount he controls is small.

Give him experience in counting money by trusting him with small sums, sending him on occasional errands, and expecting him to bring back the correct change. Show him the value of money but also teach him the limitations of money—what kinds of values money cannot buy (the values of the mind and spirit). Teach him to judge things by value rather than by price.

Understand the advantages of a good modern progressive school. Remember that the world your child must be prepared to cope with is a very different place from the one you lived in as a child. But remember, too, that there are certain eternal verities as valid for today and tomorrow as they ever were. Do not, therefore, be deflected by fads and fancies; but do keep an open mind concerning real improvements in methods and techniques and especially in the goals toward which modern education is striving.

Cooperate with the school you send your child to.

Encourage your child to finish necessary projects by keeping up his interest in the desirable results he is aiming at.

Praise accuracy whenever he displays it; but remember that his imagination needs scope and enrichment too.

Help to develop his sense of humor by laughing with him at his jokes and by telling him jokes and stories (appropriate to his understanding, of course) which *you* consider funny. Show him that there is really nothing amusing about teasing, practical jokes, name-calling, remarks which hurt people or meanness in any form. Examine your own ideas of humor, remembering that a well-developed wholesome sense of humor is a desirable quality and a great asset for coping with daily problems, especially in bringing up children.

WHAT TO AVOID

This is not the time to wash your hands of all interest in your child's mental activities just because he goes to school. Grow along with him and try to understand his problems.

Never make fun of his taste, his sense of humor, or his interests. You must expect them to be crude at this period. Instead of ridiculing them, give him sufficient evidence of your own good taste, etc., and the chances are that he will come to appreciate the better things when he is mentally mature enough to do so.

It is not good to allow a child to live too

much in a world of make-believe. He does occasionally need to pretend and to boast; but if he does so too much, see that his real life is neither too dull nor too exacting but richer in opportunities to feel successful and approved.

Refrain from censoring his preferences in radio, movies, comics, etc. He will outgrow them if he isn't nagged about them and if he has plenty of opportunity to see that the people he admires prefer better things.

Try not to be impatient with his many mistakes, and when you correct him, do so with as much tolerance as you can.

Letting him make money the most important value in life is wrong, but so is letting him disregard it entirely. If possible give him a general understanding of the family's financial status and aims, and let him have his say in some of the family's discussions of what to spend money for and what to save it for.

Try not to be impatient of his moods of reflection, brooding, and intense absorption. Remember that his mind is receiving and trying to digest an enormous number of new impressions.

Never force your child beyond his mental capacity, but try not to keep him a baby either. Rejoice in his development and help him along the way—at his own pace.

Making him do things differently from the way his friends or schoolmates do them is sometimes very embarrassing to a child. The herd instinct is very strong at this age. Most children want to conform in every particular and should be allowed to within reason.

It is not sensible to thwart his curiosity or to seem shocked at any of his interests and probings. Just answer him as informatively as you can and get dependable books to answer questions where you can't.

Remember not to take his exaggerations too seriously. They are normal at this age.

Don't let occasional backsliding and lapsing into childishness worry you.

It is unwise to let a child go to the movies at all before he is about seven or too often after that. Most current movies are not suitable for young children as they are apt to be overstimulating. Give your child plenty of other interesting things to do—but be sure they are really interesting to him.

If his enthusiasm leads him into so many interests at one time that he becomes discouraged or fatigued, try to cut them down.

Remember that he frequently forgets and still needs supervision. But try not to make it obtrusive or unpleasant. Just see that really necessary things are not left undone.

Never allow any adult to make fun of him, no matter how much ignorance he may display. His playmates will do it, but that may be helpful. At least he can give *them* tit for tat.

SUGGESTED READING

Recommendations for further reading on the subjects outlined above may be found by referring to the *Suggested Reading Guide* at the end of this CHART.

SOCIAL AND EMOTIONAL DEVELOPMENT

In the years between six and nine children begin to be far more influenced by the world outside the home than by the home itself. They begin to imitate teachers and friends as formerly they imitated members of the family. Many parents become alarmed over situations arising from this tendency; but those who have laid a good foundation in the first six years need have no fear. Children continue, at this age, to use home standards as yardsticks for measuring new ideas and acquaintances, even if new standards seem to become temporarily more alluring.

Children, in these years, learning new customs and new modes of behavior, may become impatient with their parents and are sometimes severely critical of them. But that is part of their social and emotional growing-up process. Parents should be glad to see that their children are striving toward independence, eager to acquire their own standards, getting ready to assume responsibility for themselves and grow into citizens of the world. Even though they seem not to know their own minds and may behave in a rebellious, balky, and impertinent manner (to try out their newly-envisioned independence), they are usually quite aware of what their behavior should be, and in a normal, wholesome family they will settle down as soon as they get a little more accustomed to their freedom. The chances are that they still love their parents very deeply underneath; but it is up to the parents, from now on, to *earn* their children's love. The days of "my parents right or wrong" are over. Henceforth the parents have to be right in their children's eyes. Of such is the essence of growth!

WHAT TO EXPECT OF AVERAGE CHILDREN

At Six to Seven Years:

Children change radically from six on; they go from one extreme to another, are exasperatingly inconsistent

Always want to win, to be first, to be best-loved, etc.; yet will be quarrelsome and bossy and then enraged because their behavior has frustrated their desire to come out on top

Play better with one companion than with two or more

At a party for six-year-olds every child will want the first prize and will scramble wildly to get it—and the losers will take it hard.

Emotions, at this age, take on more individual patterns

Many try to break away from parental domination, but are often lost and confused without certain familiar routines to guide them

May find difficulty in making adjustments to either home or school or to the necessity of alternating between them (Some children suffer severe emotional or physical reactions to this divided authority)

Are usually impulsive, excitable, and very set in their ways

Generally have compulsions like having to touch every lamp-post, step over cracks, skip every other stone, etc.

Are usually proud of losing their baby teeth—a sign of pleasure in growing up

Begin to show a few small evidences of common sense

May have violent temper tantrums as outlet for the inner conflict of growing up

Want their own way just for the sake of finding out whether they can get it, but are usually ready to listen to reason

May be stubborn or possessive

Are often defiant, rude, haughty, boisterous, "fresh," domineering, and argumentative—usual reaction to all requests being "No!" or "I won't!"; but are usually sorry afterwards

Six-year-olds frequently laugh or talk in their sleep, but their dreams are usually less frightening than formerly

Are utterly absorbed in themselves and will resent any interference unless it is in the form of praise

Often return to babyish behavior and make-believe play—especially when the transition from five-year-old to seven-year-old behavior seems too difficult

Try to free themselves from mother and may go from extreme affection one minute to extreme antagonism the next—but in general like to do things with her

Seem to want to fight and argue all the time

Are often rude and insulting to relatives, guests, etc.

Want affection, especially when they are on their worst behavior

Become much more demanding of their fathers' time, attention, and affection

Like to teach younger children but are pretty sure to bully them

At Seven to Eight Years:

Children usually begin to quiet down at seven, but often their seeming tranquillity

means that they are too intensely absorbed with themselves

Live a rich inner life and tend to mull over their feelings

Become more sensitive to others' feelings

Often long for baby brother or sister

Become more interested in older playmates and adults; may go in for hero-worship, but hero changes frequently; often "adore" their teachers

Are still variable and unstable in mood, but are more anxious to please than they were at six

Tend to tattle; are not good losers

Tend to have their feelings easily hurt

Have a strong sense of self-righteousness

Are likely to have moods of sullenness rather than temper tantrums; may go in for slamming doors behind them in a huff

Become more reasonable and sensible as they approach eight

Begin to teach themselves by repeating satisfactory behavior

If they cry, they do so, usually, because their feelings have been wounded, and they are ashamed to be caught at it; may try very hard to control themselves

Worry a good deal about themselves

May inwardly blame themselves for everything that goes wrong while outwardly blaming someone else

May become very excited at evidences of what they consider unfair

Want to be perfect in everything, and are self-conscious about mistakes

Need people to talk to at times

Are instinctively democratic; if not under group pressure will choose companions they like regardless of race, creed, color, or social status

Still have fears, but are usually better at handling them than at six; try hard to be brave

Are often afraid to begin new things; but once started, hate to stop

Like to sit quietly planning things; very likely to withdraw to one room for this purpose

Become real members of family group, assuming some responsibility for chores, etc.

Usually outgrow six-year-old impertinence, rudeness, etc.; may even be particularly polite, but still resent being interrupted at work or play

Want more companionship from fathers, but are increasingly willing to be alone

Like to go visiting and generally behave better with strangers

Become more realistic, less given to inner fantasy

Like games, tricks, etc.; enjoy "putting one over" on adults

At Eight to Nine Years:

Become quicker in adjusting themselves to people and situations

Are generally more outgoing and friendly than at seven

Still want to be praised for everything they do

May be very jealous

Pay more attention to adult conversation and behavior; want not so much to imitate them as to be included

May still be quarrelsome with playmates and schoolmates

Are learning how to be good sports when they lose but are still not too good about it

Become more cooperative in group projects

Like to trade and swap and are becoming fairer at it

Begin to be acutely aware of distinctions between the interests and activities of boys and girls

Are increasingly curious about human relationships of all kinds

Begin to be interested in people outside their personal kin as well as in foreign manners, customs, ways, etc.

Love to talk enthusiastically, extravagantly, and dramatically, demanding complete attention

Are ready to tackle new things and usually show considerable courage

Can shift rapidly from one interest to another—are, in fact, impatient to do so

Cry easily, but less often through self-pity, more often through sympathy real or imagined

Are critical of others, and also of themselves, but can't stand criticism from others

May still have childish fears, but in new effort to conquer them sometimes refuse to admit that they have them

Are usually very ambitious but may be caught between their ambitions and their capacities

Usually behave better away from home than at home, due to desire to make a grown-up impression

Are less helpful at home than at seven, probably for the same reason

Like to be rewarded for good behavior

Are more and more demanding and exacting of mothers

Are likely to be very exacting with all members of family, including themselves

Begin to form intense friendships, usually with children of same sex, often with older ones

Begin to improve in manners, and are often very polite especially to strangers

Hate to play alone; demand playmates who will cooperate fully

Begin to organize and join clubs, though interest in them may lag

Are increasingly aware of the peculiarity of their particular likes and dislikes

Become more responsive both at home and in school

Begin to enjoy taking turns showing a growing sense of fairness

Become generally more self-reliant though still dependent on opinion of others in their circle

WHAT TO DO FOR YOUR CHILD

Give your child a party for his sixth birthday if you can, but plan it carefully and keep it simple, short, and small in numbers, for although children love parties at this age, they are likely to be boisterous and wildly competitive if not supervised.

Remember that when your child rebels against good manners and good habits you thought you had taught him, it is a sign that he really knows them and will settle down to accepting them at seven or eight. He has to rebel at six because he is in a period of transition from the babyhood of five to the grownupness of seven.

Be willing to compromise with him, at least to the extent of sounding friendly when you ask him to do something. Showing great irritation or nagging him will accomplish nothing except further rebellion

Respect his right to his own secrets, of which there will probably be many at this age.

Understand that "compulsive" behavior (stepping over cracks, etc.) is a normal emotional manifestation. Ease up a bit in your demands on a child who behaves this way to excess. He needs *less* discipline, not more. It is a good thing, in fact, to relax home pressures on the child if he seems to be nervous or tense in *any* way.

Help him to get along well with other children by letting him dress, act, and behave as much like his companions as possible. Encourage him to bring his friends home by being hospitable to them whether or not *you* would have chosen them.

The important thing is to make sure your child gets along comfortably with friends of his own choosing. The kind of companions he prefers will change with the years if you don't insist on doing the choosing for him. The standards and ideals of his early home environment will come through in the end if you allow for a bit of crudity and eccentricity in these formative years.

Remember that radio programs, movies, comics, etc., which seem to appeal to almost all children at this age, must have some values to them or they wouldn't be so popular. It is probably best to let this mania run its course, as it will in time if not too much of an issue is made of it and if, at the same time, the child is provided with enough other real interests and wholesome activities. Keep the amount of his radio-listening, movie-going, and comics-reading under enough control to allow him time for more desirable interests. Also, take him to *suitable* movies, if you can find any, and to other entertainments which you think he will enjoy. Of course it is only common sense, however, to keep your child away from radio programs and movies which really scare or otherwise upset him. Try to do this without a battle by substituting other enjoyable interests.

Be careful not to hurt your child's feelings. Be tolerant of his mistakes. Try to make him see the humor of humorous situations, but never ridicule him.

Try to make games of such necessary routines as keeping clothes and other belongings orderly. Remember that this is not a natural instinct with most children. Help your child to realize the value of orderliness in terms of making life easier.

Try to give him the feeling that people are, in general, friendly and that he need feel no hesitation in returning their friendliness in a natural, spontaneous way.

Do your best to prevent outbursts and rebellions before they happen by phrasing your requests in as acceptable a way as possible— that is, so that they cannot be answered by "No!" For instance, instead of "Will you put your toys away now?" say "Let's put the toys away now," and go about it cheerfully. The child will, in all likelihood, join you in a few minutes and may even finish the job alone.

If your child behaves in a withdrawn, sullen, or impetuous way, you can suspect that fears or insecure feelings of some kind are behind his behavior. Consult his teacher for possible clues and be on the lookout for them yourself—without trying to pry the cause out of the child who may not, himself, understand what the trouble is. If you cannot root out the exact reason for the behavior, you are safe in doing everything you can to help your child feel more secure. Remember that childish fears may manifest themselves in seemingly unrelated behavior and can cause serious emotional disturbances.

If your child greets you with a burst of violent hostility, count ten before replying, and when you do, try not to scold him, for he probably already feels guilty. Instead try to understand what it is all about. Approach the problem indirectly if you can, and give him some opportunity to make amends. Try, too, to give him a constructive outlet for his natural aggressiveness.

Encourage friendship between the child and his father, and encourage the father to assume more parental responsibility while this friendship is strong.

Have family get-togethers whenever the spirit moves. Have fun with your children. Make your home a place they like because the whole family can enjoy doing things together there. Holding regular "Family Lodge" meetings may prove a good and enjoyable way of doing this.

Try to prevent jealousy by guarding against favoritism or discrimination in your relationships with your children.

Try not to feel jealousy yourself when your child begins to think that pleasing his teacher or his friends is more important than pleasing you.

If your child is having difficulties of any kind at school, find out why. The trouble may be emotional, mental, or physical. There are tests available which can throw light on where the difficulty lies. Inquire about these tests.

Praise your child whenever possible. He thrives on praise at this age and cannot endure disapproval, however much he may deserve it.

Whether he is the kind of child who is over-anxious about getting to school on time or the kind who pays no attention to punctuality, it may be wise to get him an alarm clock either to remind him of the time or to keep him from feeling nervous about it. A gift of an inexpensive wrist-watch (if you think he is able to take care of it) may help too.

Try to include your child in adult conversation occasionally—certainly in family affairs like meals, holidays, plans for vacations, etc.

Take occasion to discuss such subjects as loyalty, cooperation, good sportsmanship, etc. with your child, not as abstract virtues (which he can't understand) but when a concrete example of them (or their opposites) crop up in his behavior or in the behavior of someone he knows or reads about. Praise him when he practices any of them of his own accord.

This is a good time to strengthen his own natural instincts for tolerance, fair play, and democratic living in general.

If your child is characteristically disorderly and messy, expect him to clean up, but give him a helping hand. Help him to plan and schedule his activities too. That will encourage him to get things done more responsibly and with less friction.

Protect the rights of your child and of other children too. Be scrupulously fair in your judgments and decisions.

Protect your child against incorrect or upsetting sex talk by giving him the right information in the right way at home.

Let your own good manners, good taste, good temper, tolerance, etc. set his standards of behavior (which he will probably brag about away from home even if he seems to ignore them when he is with his own family).

Help him become acquainted with the community he lives in and try to interest him and his companions in working for worthy community projects within their understanding and ability.

Allow for individual differences in children. Appreciate their special qualities.

WHAT TO AVOID

It is cruel to scold or punish a child for behavior caused by fear, loneliness, unhappiness, insecurity, etc. or to moralize about the "bad" things he does due to emotional disturbances which he himself may not understand.

Prying into a child's secrets or private affairs may set up a serious resistance against you in him. (Make it easy for him to give him your confidence and then bide your time.)

Try to keep your child from listening to frightening radio programs and from going to unselected movies which you think will overstimulate him. Remember, however, that most children, if they are not oversensitive, get satisfaction out of blood and thunder.

Try not to spoil his tolerance and democratic attitudes by adult discrimination based on social snobbery or racial or religious prejudices.

Try not to expect too much of your child or too little either. Let him try to do things alone as much as he wants to and thinks he can; but remember that he may really need help if he is too embarrassed to ask for it.

Discourage him from making unkind or unfair criticisms of teachers, neighbors, playmates, etc. But if you know that one of them is unkind or unfair to your child, assure him that you are on his side and will do all you can to help him weather his difficulties.

SUGGESTED READING

Recommendations for further reading on the subjects outlined above may be found by referring to the *Suggested Reading Guide* at the end of this CHART.

MORAL AND SPIRITUAL DEVELOPMENT

During this period the child begins, for the first time, to have an inkling that the choice between right and wrong is a quality of character. The choice is his own, regardless of others' approval or disapproval. He can't always make the grade, but he wants to be good, and there is kindled in his heart "that little spark of celestial fire called conscience." This, therefore, is the time for parents to live up to their own highest standards so that they may never disappoint the child whose faith in them will no longer be blind but will henceforth have to be deserved and reinforced by performance.

WHAT TO EXPECT OF AVERAGE CHILDREN

At Six to Seven Years:
Children at this age usually like to hear about God and are often interested in

looking up verses in the Bible
Take a deeper interest in prayers; many become devoutly religious at six or seven

Do things with joy and love

Often resolve to be good of their own accord.

May be too absorbed in the thought of death and frightened by it

Try to get rid of their own fears by trying to help another child get rid of his

Some children are frightened by the idea of God—fear He may punish them for misdeeds—but they should never be allowed to be emotionally upset by this idea. Some have other fears causing them to lie, steal, etc.; but these acts must not be considered as moral issues at this age, even when children who commit them know they are wrong (In such cases, it is generally a problem of disturbed emotions)

May overdo generosity at this age

At Seven to Eight Years:

Begin to have a sense of righteousness and of conscientiousness

Try harder to do the right thing

Begin to lose fear of death; are more interested in *causes* of it

Become more unselfish; are better able to share and to give

Are generally proud and boastful of their families when away from home

Become more responsible, more amenable to reason

Are pleased with themselves when they behave well, displeased when they behave badly

Become a little more orderly

At Eight to Nine Years:

Begin to have an ethical sense, feel ashamed of their mistakes

Become better losers

Have feelings of modesty about their bodies and functions

Want to know more about God, Heaven, the Bible, etc.

Are likely to be wonderfully tolerant, sympathetic, and kind, although they may vary this with occasional disrespect, etc.

Want to be good and do what is expected of them, but may blame others for their own errors

Are apt to be acquisitive, but are, in general, more honorable and trustworthy than at seven

May be charmingly generous

Become more aware of time and the demands of punctuality

Begin to lose childish fears and acquire the beginnings of moral courage

Have ambitions and aspirations but are easily discouraged by failure

Become increasingly self-confident, but are easily shaken by mistakes

Are sensitive to ridicule, thrive on praise

Begin to develop a sense of fair play

Appreciate goodness in others

WHAT TO DO FOR YOUR CHILD

When you read him stories and biographies of fine people whom you would like him to emulate, be very careful not to stress the moral involved. That may have just the opposite effect from the one you intended. If he is old enough to understand the story, he will get the point himself.

Learn how to tell stories so that the child will be interested in them. Remember that a child is born with the seed of character in him.

Nurture it so that it grows and flowers under the influence of a good environment.

Remember that disobedience may have various motives. Find out the cause before you take any action. Never forget that blind obedience to the will of an adult has no value (except in a totalitarian country). Obedience, to be of real value, must be motivated by the child himself so that it can be built up into self-discipline.

Teach your child the importance of responsibility. Give him a few tasks, beginning with very simple ones, for which you expect him to be responsible. Help him if and when he needs help, and praise him for trustworthiness, perseverance, accuracy, etc. as he shows these qualities.

Remember that the home is the foundation of the child's religious feeling. His experience with his earthly parents gives value and meaning to his acceptance of God as his heavenly Father.

Listen with sympathy and understanding to his prayers, no matter how childish some of his ideas may seem to you.

Be patient with his lapses in behavior. Instead of scolding him for them, try to help him find ways back into grace.

Encourage him to join you in acts of helpfulness toward others.

Protect him from influences you know to be spiritually destructive.

Show your child (if he is mature enough to accept this idea without feeling threatened by it) that in the final analysis he will feel the effects of his own acts.

Remember that generosity is a trait of character, not a lesson which can be taught. To be of value, it must be genuinely felt, not practiced for ulterior motives.

Make the Sabbath a day of deep inner happiness in the home—a day whose memory your child will cherish all his life. And try to give *every* day some spiritual meaning.

WHAT TO AVOID

Be careful not to ask too much of your child by imposing on his good nature.

Never make careless promises or threats. Make as few of both as you can, but be sure you keep your word when you do.

Never put a child in a situation where he must lie to save himself.

Try to overlook some of the child's especially irritating habits, remembering that most of them are necessary in the process of growing up and that they will disappear in time if you keep the home atmosphere sweet, calm, affectionate, and happy.

If a child of six or over lies, cheats, or steals (as many do), don't make the mistake of appealing to his "honor" (which he is not yet able to understand in the adult sense) and don't make him feel frightened or worried about himself. Usually a child who does these things at this age knows he has done wrong. But he has in all likelihood done so because of some deep inner need, such as the need for attention, affection, or success and recognition. If your child lies, cheats, or steals for any of these reasons, look into the whole matter of his basic needs. Make sure he has enough love, enough friends, and a feeling of success and confidence and security. If you cannot fathom the cause and his misdemeanors continue, seek the help of your minister or a guidance counsellor or a mental hygiene clinic if your town has one.

SUGGESTED READING

Recommendations for further reading on the subjects outlined above may be found by referring to the *Suggested Reading Guide* at the end of this CHART.

MEMORANDA

(For Development from Six to Nine Years See Pages liv to lxx)

Continue to encourage your child in the good traits he has already begun to develop. Try again with those previously mentioned for which he may not have been ready earlier. And begin now to encourage him in the following traits for which most children are ready at some time during this period:

ACCURACY, AMBITION, APPLICATION and CONCENTRATION, ASPIRATION, TEAMWORK, COURAGE and FORTITUDE (MORAL) JUSTICE, GOOD SPORTSMANSHIP, HONOR, INDUSTRY and DILIGENCE, JUDGMENT, PATRIOTISM, LOYALTY (to COUNTRY), PERSEVERANCE and PERSISTENCE, SELF-SACRIFICE, SYSTEM and EFFICIENCY, TACT, THOROUGHNESS, WILL POWER and DETERMINATION

PHYSICAL DEVELOPMENT

At about nine boys and girls begin to leave childhood behind and move into the age of pre-adolescence known as puberty. Girls do this earlier and faster, as a rule, than boys, but each individual chil⅃ ⅃as his own pace and rate of development. Most children, as a matter of fact, ⅃ecome so markedly individual during this period that there are few rules whic⅃ can be laid down specifically for any single year. We are therefore conside⅃ing these pre-adolescent years as a unit.

It is during this period that individual physical be⅃avior patterns begin to shape toward adulthood. That is, each child is in the process of becoming his permanent self — either good with his hands or clumsy, either a good eater (often voraciously so) or a poor one, either physically strong or physically weak.

This process is often painful for both children and parents. It is painful for parents because the children seem to have forgotten every good habit they have learned. Even the best behaved children usually become frantically restless at this period. They will twitch, scratch, pull and pick at themselves, and find it practically impossible to sit or stand still for a minute. The children find their own behavior painful because they don't understand what is happening to them. Some of them, no matter how well-trained they may have seemed at eight, begin to revert, at nine, to behavior which can only be described as infantile. Some go so far back as to chew their fingers, wet their beds, etc.

This kind of behavior in a child of nine or ten is naturally alarming. But it is quite a normal if difficult phase of pre-adolescent development. It is almost as though the child's body had to go backward before it could make the great jump forward which it will have to make in the adolescent years.

FROM NINE YEARS THROUGH PRE-ADOLESCENCE

Girls and boys develop at different rates during this time. The average girl *begins* her puberty development at about eleven and completes it with the onset of menstruation at about thirteen. The average boy gets started toward puberty two years later and is therefore two years later, or more, in reaching adolescence. But there is no rule about it. Many perfectly normal boys and girls mature either earlier or later than the average by as much as several years.

The health of children whose health has been generally good up to this time usually continues good or improves. Gains in height and weight, however, seem to slow up almost to a standstill. For all his characteristic restlessness and fidgeting, there is, just before puberty, something akin to a pause in a child's physical expansion, as though nature were giving the body mechanism a rest in preparation for the revolutionary change to maturity which is to come.

WHAT TO EXPECT OF AVERAGE CHILDREN

Nine-year-olds play and work harder, are likely to overdo

General health of normally healthy children tends to be very good, but there are often complaints about aches and pains when disliked tasks have to be done.

Physical strength improves in both girls and boys, more in the latter

Head approaches final adult size

Lungs increase greatly in capacity

Both boys and girls become more speedy in their bodily activities

Both are extremely restless—may fidget, squirm, wriggle, etc.

Posture may be awkward and slouchy

Appetite is usually enormous

Voices are often shrill and piercing

Manual skills improve greatly at nine, are taken for granted at ten

By ten children can usually talk and do something else at the same time

Boys often like to wrestle and fight; girls usually prefer dramatic play, often with paper dolls, costumes, etc.

Boys usually become intensely interested in and skillful at construction games, work with tools, etc.

Both boys and girls are careless about clothes and cleanliness

Can, if they want to, manage dressing, bathing, washing, tooth-brushing, hair-combing, etc. completely by themselves, but may not do it

Boys are more daring and reckless than girls; therefore have more accidents

At nine the rate of growth in girls usually slows down to something less than two inches a year for two years; at eleven and twelve girls may gain in height at the rate of three or three-and-a-half inches a year

At eleven and twelve many girls suddenly gain between ten and twenty pounds a year, instead of five to eight as formerly; they do not usually, however, become fatter in spite of this great gain (Their internal processes account for this)

Boys usually follow this procedure two years later or whenever they begin their puberty development

Some children, especially girls, reach adult proportions very rapidly once they begin puberty development

At about eleven most girls *begin* to develop secondary sex characteristics such as enlarged breast area, the appearance of pubic hair and then, in the next two years, hair in armpits, widening hips, coarsened skin textures, etc. Boys usually begin to show secondary sex characteristics two years later, and when they do, their voices crack and change from very high to very low; their genitals develop rapidly; pubic hair develops early, then hair in the armpits and later on the face

In spite of this maturing, children do not get their complete set of permanent teeth until somewhere around twelve or thirteen, sometimes not until fifteen

Boys are usually stronger than girls from this age on

It is not at all unusual for both boys and girls to revert to infantile habits such as nail-biting, thumb-sucking, bed-wetting, scratching, and body-fingering at this age

This is a period when nature apparently finds it necessary to disorganize and even to destroy some of what the child has been so that future growth can begin on a new basis

WHAT TO DO FOR YOUR CHILD

Chiefly, bear with the irritating fidgeting, fussing, and restlessness, realizing that this behavior of pre-adolescents is normal and will pass in due time.

Within reason, cater to your child's appetite. His very positive likes and dislikes indicate his individual needs in the way of food at this time. Plain, good food and plenty of it is what he usually wants.

Let him bathe himself. (He may suddenly become very modest about letting you or anyone else see him undressed.) If necessary, supervise for cleanliness, but remember that a little dirt is preferable to a battle or an unhappy child.

Point out to him occasionally (not so often as to make it ineffective) the sanitary necessity of taking daily care of his teeth, ears, eyes, hair, skin, etc. (Don't be discouraged if he temporarily disregards your advice.)

Keep up his periodic health examinations, and have his vision, hearing, etc. tested if he seems to be having any difficulty at school. Try to get him to rest adequately.

Let him exercise his muscles as much as he wants to, short of overfatigue.

Let him dance for pleasure and grace. (Boys of this age will probably scorn to do so, but girls usually enjoy it.)

If remedial exercises for posture have been recommended by a doctor, encourage (but do not nag) him to persist in them. Above all, understand the nature of his difficulties which may be psychological as well as physical.

Give him his own room and his own place to play in the house, and, if you have no yard for him to play in, try to make some other play place available to him. He needs a lot of space, at this time, for rough-and-tumble play, for "goings on" with his "gang," for making and concocting things, and for letting off steam.

Let him go to a summer camp if you can.

Show him the importance of reporting to you any signs of a cold or other illness such as chill, fever, headache, constipation, etc., but do not make him anxious about his health.

Teach him the value of community health measures such as quarantine, inoculation etc.

WHAT TO AVOID

Do not let his life become too strenuous and exacting. It is almost certain to have a bad reaction if you do.

Avoid serving rich and indigestible food.

Make your meals plentiful but simple so that whatever your child chooses to eat (even if he occasionally wants a lot of only one thing) it will be wholesome food.

Try to keep from having too many chocolate candies or other rich sweets around the house. Satisfy the child's craving for sweets by simple hard candy, honey, occasional simple chocolates (after meals only), and by an abundance of fruit.

Providing too many activities for him will only confuse him. He will find plenty of his own and will usually get a great deal more benefit from them if he has chosen them for himself than if an adult has suggested them.

Never let him be exposed to contagion if you can help it.

Punishing him or otherwise stirring him up about his nervous habits and "compulsions" like face-twitching (tics), wriggling, fidgeting, etc. will accomplish nothing except to aggravate the condition. These are almost always the result of too much tension caused by parents who are themselves too tense and unrelaxed or too demanding and insistent on obedience to adult standards of behavior. (Be as relaxed and outgoing as possible. Create a calm, cheerful, and happy atmosphere around the child. Take it easy!)

Above all, try to avoid nagging, scolding and worrying. None of those things will accomplish anything constructive. Be patient and good-humored. This phase won't last forever, but there is very little you can do about it until nature makes the child ready for the next stage of really growing up.

SUGGESTED READING

Recommendations for further reading on the subjects outlined above may be found by referring to the *Suggested Reading Guide* at the end of this CHART.

MENTAL DEVELOPMENT

Nine, ten, and eleven are the years when most children's interests are predominantly mental. Pre-adolescent youngsters usually have a lively curiosity about everything, and they are constantly seeking facts and information on the ever-widening variety of subjects which interest them. By nine they are able to use their minds for reflection—a trait of real mental maturity—and they are able to motivate their own behavior as well as to evaluate it.

Furthermore, nine-year-olds are beginning to understand values. They can make mature mental comparisons based on well thought-out practical considerations. They become reasonable, sometimes to a point of pure logic difficult for their elders to live up to. They are realistic in the extreme, fair-minded, and usually very practical. In short, they are rapidly becoming mentally mature boys and girls—so much so, indeed, that mental development, at this age, usually far surpasses development in other directions.

The years from nine through pre-adolescence are sometimes spoken of as the "memory period" because the average brain seems to acquire and retain information more readily at this time than at any other. This characteristic thirst for facts coupled with a growing interest in reading (on the part of most children) makes this the ideal age for supplying them with an abundance of good literature, in both books and magazines, suited to their interests.

As in their physical development, girls are usually a year or two ahead of boys in mental maturity during this period. But the boys will catch up in their own good time, and when they do, if they are the mental type, there will be no stopping them!

WHAT TO EXPECT OF AVERAGE CHILDREN

Children become very critical of themselves at about nine, and soon thereafter become equally critical of others

Many are absorbed in reading—will read anything available; some (and these may be girls but are more likely to be boys with other types of interests) do not read at all

Some will read practically nothing but comics at nine; others, who have formerly been absorbed by comics, will begin to take more interest in junior classics, mysteries, biographies, and stories

Both boys and girls love to go to the movies but, at nine, ten, and eleven, still usually dislike love-stories. Girls tend to prefer musicals; boys like action-pictures

Most children of both sexes have a passion for the radio and want to listen to their favorite programs from late afternoon to bedtime regardless of anything else they may have to do (Most of them insist they can do homework and listen to the radio at the same time, and, surprisingly, many of them can)

Musically-minded children begin to take real interest in music even to the point of liking to practice, wanting to know about composers, etc.

Most children *like* to use their minds for all mental projects that interest them at this age; they may, however, sit staring into space seemingly thinking of nothing at all for awhile

Begin to use language as a tool

Write better and usually enjoy the idea of writing notes, letters, stories, notices, compositions, etc.

Become less absorbed in fantasy, more in realistic stories; may be more easily directed toward poetry and science

Begin to be greatly interested in industry and trade as well as science

Are tremendously interested in solving practical problems by means of mathematics, logic, invention, and general resourcefulness

Are fascinated by transportation, especially aviation

Learn many vital things through experience and through interest in pets, wild life, woodcraft, etc.

Have more purpose in their thinking and planning

Begin to organize information they have acquired

Concentrate better

Increased desire to memorize causes memories to improve

Some children, sometimes even the bright ones, have difficulty with their school work at this time, seeming unwilling or unable to learn, to concentrate, to study, or to cooperate. These difficulties are not necessarily of mental inability but may be due *either* to physical defects of vision, hearing, fatigue, or illness, *or* to emotional problems which may block learning processes, and they should, of course, be treated accordingly

WHAT TO DO FOR YOUR CHILD

Help him to think and reason for himself. This is much harder than doing his thinking for him and requires great patience, but it is abundantly worth while.

Make the most of his interest in having a goal. Show him how to work toward it efficiently—how to accomplish the most with the least effort and in the shortest time. But don't expect his goal to remain constant.

Encourage resourcefulness by giving him opportunities to use his knowledge and experience in many ways.

Make use of opportunities to improve his speech habits by pointing out examples of especially good diction on the radio or wherever else the child hears it. (Do not be too dismayed, however, if he temporarily relishes using the sloppy diction, current slang, or strange jargon of his favorite comics character, or even the low language of his "gang." This, too, is a passing phase.)

You can help him to value really good literature only if your own appreciation of it is genuine, discriminating, and varied enough to include some of his interests. The same is true of good taste in any other cultural activities—art, music, etc.

Encourage his creative efforts in any direction and praise his good results (without belittling him for the poor ones). Call his attention to beauty wherever you find it. When he reaches a point of understanding art and beauty beyond your own education in these matters, go along with him. Keep on educating yourself too.

Encourage his interests in handcrafts, hobbies, and all mental and cultural activities, but never force these on him or hold him to standards beyond his individual capacities.

Try to make music so interesting to him that he will want to improve himself in some kind of musical performance. If he simply will not become interested in spite of your best efforts, stop his lessons. One good way to interest a child in music at this time is to let him study with a class or group for ensemble playing.

Give him specific household tasks for which he will be responsible. Try to enlist his interest in them instead of making them a chore. See that they don't conflict with his own interests.

Make the most of his interest in money by giving him an adequate allowance and letting him learn (by his own trials and errors) how to handle both the spending and the saving of money. Let him have an increasing share in family budgeting and help make decisions concerning some of the family's financial projects.

Encourage his spirit of curiosity and adventure by allowing him to go on group excursions to industrial expositions, manufacturing plants, engineering projects, stores, shipyards, markets, farms, slums and other places where he will learn more about how the world works and how its people live.

Look for signs of individual ability in your child and give him every opportunity to pursue and exercise his special talents.

Take increased, rather than decreased interest in his school. Select a good progressive school for him on the basis of his particlular needs, remembering that the chief thing he has to learn there is how to get along well in *his* world of today and tomorrow, not in *your* world.

Remember that the world's most successful people are those who love their work. Therefore see that your child's work is made as interesting to him as possible. His enthusiasm for the work he enjoys will make it easier for him to work at the necessary studies he does not enjoy.

Coöperate with your child's school by joining the Parent-Teacher Association, by friendly interest in and tactful praise of a good teacher's work, and by consultation with the principal, if necessary, concerning the child's program.

If your child says he "hates school" or if he is unhappy or doing poorly there, or if he feels he has to show off in a "smarty" way, realize that it is probably because he feels inadequate in some way. Consult the teacher about giving him more opportunity to shine in the things he does well. See that he has a chance to merit—and that he gets—recognition and praise for what he *can* do and that he is not held up to ridicule or blame for what he cannot or does not do well. If his maladjustment continues in spite of all your efforts, try a child guidance or mental hygiene clinic.

Let your child and his friends have as much part as possible in understanding the purpose and working out the details of their projects. The more planning they do themselves, the more interest they will take in completing their jobs efficiently.

Help your child over the difficult places in his homework, if you can, when he asks you to, but not to the extent of doing it for him. And if he needs private tutoring, it is better for an accredited outsider to do it than for a parent, because the parent, being himself too concerned or insufficiently equipped, may only increase the child's tension or confusion.

Finally, use your influence to improve your community schools in every way you can—by showing your interest, cooperating with progressive methods, voting for honest and intelligent local officials, and by working for better-paid teachers and better education for all.

WHAT TO AVOID

Refrain from acting or thinking for your child. (Help him to *understand* but let him think and act for himself from there on.)

Holding a child to a too difficult schedule, a too rigid program, or any other standards he feels he cannot live up to is bound to have a bad effect on him in later life.

If he does poor work at school or is unable to adjust to the school's demands, he should never be blamed, ridiculed, or scolded. He needs help, not censure.

Making disparaging remarks in his presence about his teacher or the school discipline or making unfavorable comparisons between his school and the "old-fashioned school" will merely decrease his respect for school in general and make him feel his efforts are not worth while.

Try not to confuse your own hopes and ambitions with the child's interests—not to be so eager for your child to excel that you push him faster than he wants to or can go.

Try to keep from putting too much pressure on him to study, practice, etc.

Adding your own fears, worries, anxieties, and tensions to any your child may have can only aggravate his.

Above all, never do anything about your child's reading difficulties, if he has them, which may develop a lasting fear or distaste of reading. Find out what is causing his difficulty. Be sure you have good advice on the subject, then follow the advice even if the recommendation is to let him read the comics or picture books or nothing at all for awhile.

SUGGESTED READING

Recommendations for further reading on the subjects outlined above may be found by referring to the *Suggested Reading Guide* at the end of this CHART.

SOCIAL AND EMOTIONAL DEVELOPMENT

The period between childhood and adolescence is one in which even the best brought up children are likely to behave in ways which alarm and shock their elders. Not only do they tend to defy all adult authority but, to make matters worse, they foregather in groups and gangs of their contemporaries, usually composed entirely of members of their own sex and often of the least desirable of them from the parental point of view.

Something is definitely happening to the child's personality structure, and it is perhaps not surprising that child guidance clinics are most often called on for help during this period. For it would seem that between nine and approximately thirteen children's previous personality patterns have to be disorganized and destroyed so that new ones may be formed on a more adult basis.

Girls, being in general two years ahead of boys in their emotional and sexual development, are scornful and disdainful of boys of their own age and at the same time resentful of the fact that they are too immature for them. The boys, meanwhile, usually have nothing but contempt for the girls and their incessant giggling and whispering.

The result is that girls band themselves into groups whose chief object seems to be to talk about the inferiority of boys while boys go about in gangs and resent the very existence of girls whom they consider unmitigated nuisances. Of two things we can be certain: (1) that there is bitter rivalry between the sexes—with its attendant intense friendships between members of the same sex, and (2) that no adult can, at this stage, hope to wield the influence that a friend or member of the gang wields.

The fervent and loyal alliance of our children with their contemporaries is apparently a necessary step toward adulthood. This may be difficult for parents to accept especially as it so often seems to be accompanied by defiance of them and all their standards. But we must realize that an emotional upheaval is taking place in these pre-adolescent children in which their childhood personality patterns are breaking down so that the new patterns of adulthood can be built up.

Parents must have understanding, patience, and forbearance a-plenty in order to live through this period without being driven to distraction and discouragement. Most of the disciplinary techniques which have previously worked with the children will not suffice at this period. It is hard to show friendliness, good temper, and affection to youngsters who may not only fail to respond to friendly overtures but actually scorn any sign of intimacy from adults, even their own parents. But it must be remembered that their revolt is not really against adults but against their own childishness. They are growing up.

In order to get along with their difficult pre-adolescents, parents have to do some adjusting themselves. They must know how to treat the child like a baby when he needs to be treated like a baby and like an adult when that is what he wants. They must be flexible enough to change with the child's changing demands, ingenious enough to think up new techniques and new responses to new challenges. That will help, if anything can, to show the child that, after all, his parents may be pretty good too!

WHAT TO EXPECT OF AVERAGE CHILDREN

Not all children behave badly at this age, but some time between nine and thirteen most of them do

Girls are likely to form or join clubs composed entirely of girls; boys belong to "gangs" of boys exclusively; both talk of how they "despise" members of opposite sex, yet may tease each other about interest in one of them or brag about their own sophistication in the matter

Some girls wish they were boys and behave as much like them as possible

Both boys and girls like group adventure and excitement

Often form deep attachments to some other child of same age and sex

Tend to choose as their best friends the very children most disapproved of by their parents (This is one way of asserting their independence)

Have great curiosity about the secrets of adult life and relationships, especially about the more out-of-the-ordinary aspects

Boys may talk and joke about their bodies; girls usually do not—are likely to be very modest

Boys are usually noisier, rougher, dirtier, and more daring than girls; consider neatness and obedience signs of sissiness

Both boys and girls admire achievement in skills and winners in games and contests

Many actually seem to enjoy the distress they are causing their elders

Most refuse to discuss their problems, worries, and fears, or even to admit (to an adult) that they have any

Are likely to be ungrateful, unappreciative, suspicious, and irritable

Are easily offended

Are usually fascinated by vulgarity, especially vulgar language

May be quite shameless about some things, over-modest about others

Cry very seldom in public (If they do, it is likely to be because of emotional rather than physical hurts)

Would usually rather die than show affection publicly

May lose a good deal of self-control

Sometimes find that wanting to be admired by their parents and their companions too involves painful conflicts

Will behave according to the code their gang approves—which *may* be a fairly decent and honorable one but may also include smoking, swearing, defying adults, and, in general, experimenting with being an independent person

WHAT TO DO FOR YOUR CHILD

Realize that if your child suddenly exhibits incredibly bad behavior at this time, defies parental authority, forgets his manners, forsakes his family for chums of his own age and sex (preferably those you especially disapprove of), these are all manifestations of normal pre-adolescence.

Analyze your child's behavior on this basis and see what you can do toward his eventual good. That is, decide which things you can afford to ignore because he will probably outgrow them and which you must take firmly in hand for direction and regulation.

Try new techniques of discipline, such as offering to give your child more responsibility in disciplining himself, showing willingness to compromise, including him in adult activites, etc.

Learn how to interpret various kinds of behavior in your child; find out what lies behind each kind.

Give him the opportunity of proving to himself that he is now a "regular guy."

Realize that he needs more space, both figuratively and literally, and wider horizons.

Ignore some of his relatively mild digressions from your standards.

Treat him as much like a grown-up as possible. Use words and expressions better suited to his age than you have used heretofore. Be sure that when you praise him you do it for his maturer achievements, not for childish ones.

Remember that the *way* you make requests of your child is more important now than what you request.

Encourage his natural abilities and skills and praise him when he exhibits them.

Reassure him about any fears or worries he may have.

Try to make your home and your yard so attractive that the boy's gang or the girl's club will enjoy meeting there. Welcome your child's friends when he invites them to your home regardless of what you may think of them.

Make use of your child's desire to grow up by showing him that loyalty, usefulness, responsibility, fairness, etc. are desirable adult qualities.

Do what you can to encourage those friendships which seem to you desirable. (But don't expect your child to prefer friends of your choosing.) If his chosen companions are undesirable from your point of view, remember that they may be desirable from the point of view of his needs at this time. And remember, too, that in a few years he will choose his friends by standards more likely to reflect his home training.

Toward the end of this period tell your child how to prepare for the emotional as well as physical changes he or she can expect with the onset of puberty and adolescence.

Become acquainted with the other parents in your neighborhood and especially with the parents of your child's friends. Take part in or organize plans for a better community life. Do what you can to make it possible for *all* children to have better opportunities to become decent, honorable, well-educated citizens.

Point out really good leadership to your child wherever you find it, since leadership is a quality he admires at this age.

Cooperate with the child's interest in group life by approving of teamwork among his friends for such ends as promoting community health, safety, and general welfare, even if you don't approve of all of the members of his group.

As soon as they reach the age of admittance, allow your boy or girl to join the Boy Scouts, Girl Scouts, Campfire Girls, the "Y" or whatever similar organizations are appropriate to his or her religious or ethical interests.

Show your willingness to be companionable with your child on *his* level of interests. This is the time for fathers to go fishing, hiking, etc. with their boys and for mothers and daughters to get together on feminine projects.

Finally, realize that although poor manners, wild antics, and unreliable behavior are to be expected at this age, your child may also be carrying emotional problems which are unresolved hold-overs from previous years. If these seem to be increased or intensified at this time, recognize them and get professional guidance before the child's unhappiness becomes too deeply rooted and damaging. Remember, however, that every child who occasionally lies, steals, runs away, or otherwise behaves in a typically pre-adolescent manner at this time is not necessarily headed for serious trouble. But consult an expert counsellor, at least for a psychological check-up, if you are in any doubt at all.

WHAT TO AVOID

Choosing your child's friends for him or trying to arrange his social life, especially if you include members of the other sex, almost never works out well at this time.

Your child really doesn't want to lose your approval, however little he may do to merit it, but if there is a conflict between your approval and the gang's, the gang is pretty sure to win at this time. This is normal and often necessary—so try not to resent it or to fight it. Just be available and make your influence as good as possible. It will probably win out in the end if you can make the child feel that you are now approaching him in a new, more adult way.

Don't try to teach him "manners" at this time. It may set him against the whole idea of courtesy. Wait until he is more receptive to the idea of being polite.

Avoid these common mistakes that many parents are tempted to make at this time: (1) trying to fight the child by getting as tough as he is, (2) feeling defeated by your parental ineffectiveness. (*You* may need a psychiatrist if you feel that way), (3) prying into his secrets or talking to him about his emotions when he doesn't want to discuss them with you, (4) showing him that you are shocked by his language or his behavior, (5) trying to compete with him or with his friends, (6) expecting him to do things which *you* approve of but which would make him less popular with his gang or less loyal to the gang's code, (7) trying to protect him from the world in which he is trying to fit himself to live on his own.

Avoid, if possible, making a serious problem out of a trivial one. Prevent the child's behavior from becoming a problem at all, if you can, by treating it calmly, firmly, and realistically. You are lost if you become overemotional or hysterical about it. But don't make light of a problem which calls for serious concern.

Try not to get excited or overemotional about your child. (You won't be able to hide it from him if you do for the pre-adolescent is very adept at sizing up his parents.)

Avoid reminding the child that he is behaving like a baby. That is the last thing he wants to hear even if it is true. Surprise him by telling him you know he is having a difficult time growing up (but don't discuss it any further), and try new ways of helping him to meet new challenges.

SUGGESTED READING

Recommendations for further reading on the subjects outlined above may be found by referring to the *Suggested Reading Guide* at the end of this CHART.

MORAL AND SPIRITUAL DEVELOPMENT

By the time they are nine or ten children usually have a highly developed ethical sense. They are well aware of the difference between right and wrong, and, although their behavior would seem to deny it, the fact is that most of them are desperately eager to be good at this age—or at least to do what seems right to them by their own standards.

Paradoxical as it may sound, it is often this very desire to be good which makes them behave badly. The explanation of that is that their own consciences are now developing into strict monitors. They no longer leave it to their parents to tell them whether they are good or bad; they know it themselves. And they are very self-critical. They may even begin to think sometimes that they are wicked and evil when their developmental changes impel them to act wildly or defiantly in spite of themselves.

Thus, being too inexperienced to realize that everyone has hostile feelings at times, they think that they alone are evil and wicked. The voice of their own conscience nags at them like a too strict parent, sometimes setting up a sense of guilt and sometimes one of defiance.

Research has shown that the children whose behavior is most troublesome at this period are those whose parents have held them to standards which were too strict, thus setting up destructive feelings of guilt anxiety. Shrinking under their parents' disapproval, such children come to think they can never be good no matter how hard they try. So they don't try. In their pre-puberty years their own consciences may have this effect on them. But they will be able to work it out if their parents don't reinforce these feelings by telling them they are "bad."

The best thing for parents to do at this time, therefore, is to keep and show their faith in at least the *potential* goodness of their children. Help them out of their feelings of guilt or worry by making it as easy as possible for them to be good and by assuring them that you love *them* even though you may disapprove of the things they do. Let them know that you consider their present behavior, if it is bad, a temporary and understandable way of getting rid of bad feelings —something you confidently expect them to outgrow in time. Keep your own standards high, but be tolerant of the questing attitude of your children at this period in their lives for it is a time when they may be expected to doubt and question all faith and all authority, even religion.

Unless your child is seriously disturbed at this time, either mentally or emotionally (in which case you may need professional help), the chances are that his own happy earlier experiences will tide him over his difficulties now.

Be sure not to make your standards too high or too rigid for him at this age. Relax a bit, don't take life too seriously. Meet each situation with good sense, understanding, patience, and tolerance. These and the element of time itself work wondrous changes!

WHAT TO EXPECT OF AVERAGE CHILDREN

Pre-adolescents are usually scrupulously fair; they mostly *want* to be truthful, honorable, trustworthy, dependable, etc., but often fail to live up to their own standards, and usually don't know why

Conscience and self-criticism are very strong though often not articulate

Ten- or eleven-year-olds tend to lose interest in church and Sunday School, doubt the faith of their elders, and demand rational explanations of God, heaven, religion, and everything else

Are usually sorry after they have behaved badly but may not admit it

Gain in courage, independence, and teamwork

Respect for their own groups' rules, laws, and codes are more important to them than personal demands or requests of adults

May have sudden urges to reform—to put things in order, have better manners, do what they know they should (Do not be discouraged, however, if these reforms are short lived and if there are lapses and back-slidings)

May have hostile feelings toward certain adults or adults in general (These, if undeserved, will subside or disappear in time if the child is helped to feel that the adults are not hostile to him)

May be antagonistic toward home and its members, seemingly ungrateful, unappreciative, etc. and correspondingly worshipful of outside friends and acquaintances (This will disappear too, in time, but the home folks will have to *merit* respect and admiration from now on)

Have few, if any, natural prejudices against racial, religious or social groups as such, unless they have been implanted by others

Are gaining, in spite of possible appearances to the contrary, in self-control, self-dependence, and courage; are learning to govern themselves, to be responsible for their words, thoughts, and acts

WHAT TO DO FOR YOUR CHILD

Recognize that your ideas of good and bad behavior are no longer your child's only criterion—that he is forming his own ideas of right and wrong too. Help him to evaluate and to combine his ideas and yours.

Be tolerant of his evidences of lack of faith, realizing that, at this time, mental investigation is more dominant than spiritual belief.

Let the child discipline himself whenever he tries to do so, remembering that self-discipline must be the basis of his future moral behavior.

Accept any indication of regret for poor behavior or of determination to do better, but be careful not to add to the child's feeling that he is wicked. If you think he is too heavily burdened with a feeling of guilt, examine your own disciplinary behavior in the light of whether it has been too strict, too wishy-washy, too tense, confusing, unrelenting, or in any other way to blame.

Encourage every effort the child makes to improve, but be patient with lapses and back-slidings.

Expect your child to question, if not to defy, your set of behavior standards and to try out those of his companions. Keep your own code flexible. Examine it now and then to make sure it is valid and tolerant of changing ideas. But keep your faith in the eternal verities of right and wrong and know that your child, if he loves and respects you, will, in time, come to accept and adopt them as his guiding ethics.

Listen without censure to your child's new views on moral problems but be sure he knows where you stand on them. Respect his search for reason.

If you think he has made a wrong decision, ask him his reasons and show him,, rationally, where you think he was mistaken. Also be willing, at all times, to give him your reasons for your decisions, making sure they *are* reasons, carefully considered, not mere whims.

Be as receptive as possible to anything he wants to tell you; but trying to get information out of him if he wants to keep it to himself will be futile and may only make him resentful.

Remember that your continued example of service, sympathy, kindness, thoughtfulness, appreciation of others, etc., will in time win your child's admiration, even though he may seem not to notice or value these qualities.

Make the most of the desirable qualities he does have now, such as fairness, good sportsmanship, honor, resourcefulness, perseverance, etc. by praising him for them when he shows them and by directing them into good channels whenever possible.

Give your child the spiritual and moral guidance he needs to stand firm under the pressures of life. He needs faith in his religion and in his own ideals.

Create in your home an atmosphere of love for one another and of faith in a Supreme being, remembering that for every child religion is based on the quality of home relationships.

Teach your child to know God through using the Bible and through the family's reverence and worship of the good, the true, and the beautiful.

Make worship a joyous family occasion and include your child in it. See that it is never allowed to become boring or meaningless to him. Show him the beauty of its substance, not merely its outward form.

Bring up your child in an atmosphere of faith, hope, and love—and remember that "the greatest of these is love."

WHAT TO AVOID

Never make promises you do not intend to or cannot keep or give your child arbitrary commands.

Never belittle his investigations or ridicule his ideas, questions, or behavior.

Having your feelings hurt by his seeming defiance of your moral or spiritual code would be childish on your part.

Holding the child too strictly to your standards will do him no good. (Remember that being too strict with your child may make him feel he is too wicked ever to try to be good. Be firm but flexible.)

Never give your child a sense of guilt or allow anyone else to do so. (If he is already over-burdened with a sense of guilt and manifests it by stealing, lying, disobedience, defiance, etc., realize that he needs not more pressure but less. He should have more appreciation and a more relaxed, understanding, happy, loving atmosphere at home, without fear of parental anger or punishment.)

Forcing the child to do things which will make him unpopular or disliked or ridiculed by his friends is cruel and should never be indulged in by any mother.

Never scare your child with threats of punishment, especially the loss of your love.

SUGGESTED READING

Recommendations for further reading on the subjects outlined above may be found by referring to the *Suggested Reading Guide* at the end of this CHART.

MEMORANDA

FROM PUBERTY THROUGH ADOLESCENCE

(THE 'TEENS)

(For Development from Nine Years to Adolescence See Pages lxxii to lxxxvi)

Continue to encourage your child in the good traits he has already begun to develop. Try again with those previously mentioned for which he may not have been ready earlier. And begin now to encourage him in the following traits for which most children are ready at some time during this period:

**CLEANLINESS (MORAL), DIGNITY and RESERVE,
EMOTIONAL MATURITY and STABILITY,
IDEALISM and LIFE PURPOSE, LOYALTY (to IDEALS),
NATURALNESS and UNAFFECTEDNESS, CIVIC RESPONSIBILITY,
FAITH, PHYSICAL DEVELOPMENT**

PHYSICAL DEVELOPMENT

The word adolescence has two meanings. It refers to the growing-up process that takes place in boys and girls between childhood and adulthood, and it is also used to denote the time when this process takes place—roughly, the 'teens.

As in the previous period of development, from nine through puberty, girls usually reach adolescence approximately two years earlier than boys and continue to develop earlier all along the line until full maturity is reached.

Adolescence, which lasts about eight years, is a time of conflicts and paradoxes. During these years, beginning at approximately twelve or thirteen, boys and girls are too big or too old to be children and still not quite big enough or old enough to be adults. As a result, adolescents are likely to be problems to themselves and to their parents. If parents will remember, however, that the essence of the problem lies in the perfectly normal see-sawing back and forth between childhood and adulthood, they will be spared a great deal of needless worry.

Adolescence manifests itself visibly by a sudden, rapid, and rather amazing increase in height, weight, and general size. This growth, beginning at about twelve for the average girl and about fourteen for the average boy (though it may be earlier or later by several years in both sexes), slows down a bit after the first two years or so, but generally continues steadily, if somewhat more slowly, until about nineteen in girls, twenty-one or two in boys.

The most important physical development during adolescence is, of course, the maturing of the reproductive organs. This process causes such profound changes in a child's physical functioning that certain modifications of routine must be made, and attention must be given to new procedures of personal hygiene.

In general, however, the child in whom a parent has already established good habits of personal hygiene needs chiefly to be made to realize the increased importance of continuing these habits.

Adolescence may be a trying time for the adolescents themselves as well as for all those concerned in their welfare. But it is, after all, an inevitable stage in the process of growing up. If it is so considered, its sudden spurts and surprising lapses will be no more disturbing than the more gradual processes of other years.

WHAT TO EXPECT OF AVERAGE ADOLESCENTS

The onset of adolescence is usually accompanied by sudden and rapid increases in height, weight, and size

Continuous growth, slowing down somewhat after the first two years of extraordinarily rapid growth, can be expected throughout adolescence, though many girls reach their full adult height before sixteen, many boys before eighteen

Physical strength increases greatly during early 'teens

Reproductive organs come to maturity during adolescence, sometimes early, sometimes late

Most girls in the United States have their first monthly period (which is likely to be quite irregular for some time thereafter) at about thirteen and most boys begin to have nocturnal emissions at about fifteen (But variations of as much as two years in either direction are normal)

Breast development is usually the first sign of sexual maturing in girls, occurring, generally, well before the appearance of pubic hair (Boys, as well as girls, sometimes have a slight breast development at puberty)

Besides developing breasts, other maturity traits preceding or accompanying the onset of adolescence are: Growth of hair in armpits and pubic regions, further development of genitals in both boys and girls; in boys a break in the voice, broadening shoulders, hair on the face; in girls broadening hips and generally less angular contours

Acne (pimply complexion) is common in both boys and girls in early adolescence. This may be due partly to overactive sweat glands, carelessness in keeping the skin scrupulously clean, or possible digestive disturbances caused by rich or otherwise unsuitable foods; but it may be due merely to natural bodily changes

Adolescents often become self-conscious, moody, or unhappy over poor complexion, ungainly growth, etc.

Many become slouchy, round-shouldered, awkward in their motions

Developing sex glands may cause immature sexual behavior such as self-stimulation of genitals, physical awkwardness, experimentation with "petting," etc.

Growth may use up much reserve energy, causing spurts of overactivity alternating with spells of inertia (which are not necessarily laziness or any health defect but merely normal manifestations of adolescent growth)

Wisdom teeth appear after seventeen

WHAT TO DO FOR YOUR ADOLESCENT

First and most important, be sure you yourself understand what is happening to your adolescent. Treat all adolescent manifestations in an adult way as the natural and normal processes of growth which they are.

Prepare your adolescent (preferably during

pre-adolescent years, but at this time if it has not previously been done) for the changes to come by giving the child all necessary instructions for proper hygiene and care of the body.

Regard menstruation as the natural and normal process it is. If your daughter has been frail or ill or if she experiences any unusual discomfort for any reason, take her to a physician. Otherwise encourage her to go about her ordinary activities in the usual way, warning her merely against overexertion and overexposure to wet or cold during her periods.

For your son, encourage his father to discuss with him, in as helpful a way as possible, the changes which are occurring in his body.

If your adolescent's posture has become poorer, first find out whether it is because of the difficulty of carrying a body which is growing so rapidly or whether it is wholly or largely due to self-consciousness. In either case, explain the importance of good posture for health. Encourage wholesome and moderate exercise, participation in games and other activities that will build up self-confidence as well as muscular control. If your child is a girl, advise her (tactfully) in the matter of choosing appropriate clothes and show her, in general, how to look more attractive. It may help her to overcome at least some of her self-consciousness. In a boy encourage hobbies and interests that help him overcome his shyness.

If your adolescent's face breaks out in unsightly pimples, first assure him or her that skin eruptions are fairly common during adolescence. Point out, however, that it is essential during this time to keep the digestive system in good working order by a wholesome diet of plain (not rich) foods, free elimination, plenty of rest, sunshine, and outdoor exercise —and that it is of the utmost importance to give the face a thorough twice-daily washing with soap and warm water. If the skin fails to respond to this routine, a physician should be consulted, but most complexions will improve somewhat if this regimen is habitually followed. It may take some time, however, to clear up entirely.

Tell your adolescent (to clear up any confusing ideas he may have picked up from others) exactly what the sexual and reproductive functions are for which the body is getting ready. If you feel you cannot do this adequately or comfortably, consult your family physician about it.

Explain that the maturing process may prove sexually disturbing at times but that hard work and play, comfortable and regular sleep, cold baths or showers, and an absorbing interest in wholesome activities will help toward diverting the mind and calming the body.

Do everything you can to see that your children's attitude toward sex is sane and healthy. (This will be possible only if your own attitude on the subject is sane and healthy.)

Both boys and girls should understand the functions of reproduction of both sexes.

Encourage both boys and girls to keep their bodies clean and to wear comfortable clothing.

If your adolescent needs an outlet for all that superfluous growing energy, it may be helpful to encourage him or her to take a part-time job (particularly an outdoor job) in spare hours, if the schedule permits. (A confining indoor job may be unwise if sunshine, fresh air, and exercise are more needed.)

Realize that most adolescents are incapable of long-sustained physical effort.

Try to train them for the wise use of leisure as well as of working hours.

WHAT TO AVOID

You cannot expect all aspects of a child's growth to balance during adolescence.

It is unwise to have meals too rich in sweets and starches. (Coffee, tea, and of course alcohol, are unsuitable for adolescents. Whole-grain bread and cereals, milk, and an abundance of fresh vegetables and fruit are essential in the daily diet.)

It is no longer considered healthy to coddle petty illnesses or to treat menstrual periods as an illness.

Never make fun of any of the physiological

changes and rapid physical developments of adolescence.

Don't fail to recognize the importance of sane, healthy, and realistic sex instruction for adolescent boys and girls.

Keep yourself from becoming emotionally upset about your child's possible tendencies to self-examination and from making him feel wicked or guilty about them.

Neither ignore nor condemn immature sexual attitude or behavior. (Be frank and honest about it.)

SUGGESTED READING

Recommendations for further reading on the subjects outlined above may be found by referring to the *Suggested Reading Guide* at the end of this CHART.

MENTAL DEVELOPMENT

Although the normal adolescent's mental activities increase during adolescence, they often do so somewhat more slowly than they did in the period of important mental development prior to adolescence. In some, indeed, there is a definite decrease in mental growth during adolescence. Mental growth is, in either case, less easy to observe than physical growth and very much more difficult to measures. Some parents find this especially so because they take a really active interest in their children's mental activities only when they (the children) enter high school and begin to make plans for the future. A really conscientious parent, however, will have been interested in the child's mental development long before this time—from babyhood on, in fact—and will realize that it is a continuous process throughout life and comprises the sum total of an individual's accumulated experience, knowledge, and insight, not merely "book learning."

There have been devised in recent years, a number of tests for measuring various mental processes. Of these the best-known and probably the most useful is the so-called I.Q. (or Intelligence Quotient) test. This is a device for comparing an individual's mental age with his actual age in years. It is very useful in determining whether a child's mental ability is average, above average, or below average, for his age.

There are other tests too, of varying usefulness, and although no single test can give an absolute and final verdict regarding anyone's abilities, many of them can tell a great deal. They are particularly important in pointing out what an individual child's relation to other children in his age group may be and they furnish valuable clues to the child's abilities, aptitudes, and handicaps. These clues are often important in gauging a child's mental capacities, measuring his achievements, and for setting him on the road he would probably do best to follow vocationally. Tests of various kinds are excellent guides to follow in planning the child's further education.

WHAT TO EXPECT OF AVERAGE ADOLESCENTS

Ability to memorize usually increases but is accompanied by extreme distaste for rote memorizing unless for a much-desired purpose

There is usually a steady, if sometimes imperceptible, gain in mental and mechanical abilities, though there may be lapses when they seem to stand still or decrease

Imaginative powers usually show great increase; so do the abilities to reason, to judge, and to apply experience

Girls tend to excel in verbal studies, boys in mathematical subjects—but this is not invariably true

Boys are generally superior to girls in manual precision and steadiness

Although adolescents are able to do advanced school work and may have a relatively mature attitude toward life in general, mental growth usually slows down during adolescence and sometimes stops toward the end of it

As children advance in years, competition becomes keener and failures in school consequently more frequent

Some fail because of poor preparation, others because they are emotionally upset or unhappy, some because their parents do not encourage them to a real interest in their school work or allow them enough time or privacy to prepare it

Interest in activities outside of school rather than in academic subjects does not necessarily indicate lack of intelligence

Mental confusion may increase at this age, but so may mental keenness

WHAT TO DO FOR YOUR ADOLESCENT

Encourage your child to take tests for general intelligence, learning ability, special aptitudes, etc. (If his school does not give such tests, take him to someone qualified to give and to interpret them.)

Cooperate by telling the tester any pertinent factors in the child's personality, environment, or home life.

Be sure you understand the nature and purpose, as well as the limitations, of mental tests, aptitude tests, etc.

Realize that adding to his experience, understanding, knowledge, and insight outside of school may be just as enriching to his mental growth as what he learns in school.

If tests (and experience) show that your child's mental processes or academic abilities are lower, accept this limitation and try to place him in a school where he will not be made to feel a sense of discouragement or failure. Plan for *his* happiness rather than for your ambitions for him. Plan to make the most of the abilities he has and develop them to full capacity.

If he is about average, recognize his attainments for what they are, put him in a school where the competition is not too keen, and encourage him to fulfill his own ambitions to the best of his ability.

If his tests and record show superior intelligence or abilities, it will probably be better to enrich his interests than to push him ahead in grade. That is, it may be wiser to encourage him to read more widely and undertake more projects than to promote him to a grade where his classmates may be far beyond him in physical and emotional maturity.

Recognize your child's superior mental endowment, if he has it, and appreciate it. But give him plenty of opportunities, also, for physical and emotional maturing on his own age level. If possible send such a child to a school where he is not bored by lack of stimulation and where there are other superior children. And emphasize his becoming a well-adjusted, happy adult rather than merely an intellectual giant.

Take any special abilities, as well as special disabilities, into account in guiding his education. Encourage the special abilities, but not at the expense of a well-balanced education. Help him to overcome or to compensate for any disabilities he may have by special instruction, remedial assistance, or any other help which may be indicated.

If your boy or girl is falling behind in school work, find out why. If failure is caused by poor preparation, worry, too many interruptions in school work, inability to adjust to school, lack of interest in academic achievement in general, or in certain subjects, immaturity due to overprotection, emotional insecurity, or any other factor, recognize the cause

and do everything you can to remedy it.

Above all, remember that an overambitious parent (one who goads the child to fulfill the parent's ambitions rather than the child's own) is selfishly gratifying personal pride and can greatly damage the child's development. Let your child feel free to develop his own ambitions, not yours.

Have a wholesome attitude about your own work so as to inspire your child to have the same attitude about his.

Encourage him to use his leisure time, as well as his working time, to good advantage.

Remember that "all work and no play makes Jack a dull boy." Give your adolescent the opportunity to play—to relax and have fun—for the sake of his mental as well as physical and emotional health.

Encourage his interest in things and people he is unfamiliar with and give him a chance to learn about them.

WHAT TO AVOID

It is unwise to push a child beyond his mental capacity.

It is important to know just where your child stands in relation to other children in his age group. But it is not wise to urge him to do or be like some other child you may know.

It is foolish to allow a child to develop his

intellect to the exclusion of other faculties.

It would obviously be unwise to put him with children whose minds are either greatly superior or greatly inferior to his. (Boredom and lack of mental stimulation are bad for a child, but so is too keen competition and a feeling of failure.)

SUGGESTED READING

Recommendations for further reading on the subjects outlined above may be found by referring to the *Suggested Reading Guide* at the end of this CHART.

SOCIAL AND EMOTIONAL DEVELOPMENT

Because social and emotional maturity are today recognized as assets of vital importance to any well-adjusted adult, and because such maturity has been found sadly lacking in too many, its cultivation is of especial significance in the formative years of adolescence.

Social and emotional immaturity is seen in individuals (including adults who are full-grown in the physical sense) who refuse to submit to any authority, who are excessively selfish, and who meet all of life's difficulties or responsibilities by running away or by "escaping" into one or another emotional retreat.

The object of all education, both in and out of school, is, or should be, the well-rounded development of the individual into a harmoniously balanced whole. And it is during adolescence that such development may often go awry. Social and emotional problems harass the boy or girl who is desperately trying to adjust to them with, often, pitifully inadequate equipment.

It is, unfortunately, very difficult, at this point to undo emotional maladjustments carried over from early childhood which may cause severe unhappiness or frustration. Where a child is so burdened, obviously psychiatric or other professional help is needed.

But the chief problem of parents, during their children's adolescence, is to keep them running along on an even keel, to help them learn to handle new and unfamiliar emotions, to encourage them to independence and still offer them the guidance they often need and want.

The greatest hazard many adolescents have to contend with is that one or both of their parents may themselves be emotionally immature. Where this is so, the children carry a double burden and they will be far less likely to achieve the social stability and emotional security they will need to become well-integrated, independent, and responsible adults.

Chiefly, then, your job is first to become as adult yourself as it is in your power to do, even if it means that you need psychiatric help, and then to do all you can to help your adolescent boy or girl to achieve the same desirable state. Help him or her enter into adulthood not with fear and shirking but with a joyous, confident assuming of its responsibilities as well as its fulfillments.

WHAT TO EXPECT OF AVERAGE ADOLESCENTS

May still show some pre-adolescent fears and worries, chiefly concerning social matters and customs

Girls may have intensely emotional attachments or "crushes" on an older girl or woman, especially on a teacher

Falling in and out of love frequently is entirely normal and serves, in the long run, as a sort of emotional stabilizer

May have fits of violent anger, often behaving in a manner reminiscent of a babyish temper tantrum or a childish case of the sulks

Are usually very self-conscious about changing appearance and puberty development

Girls are often embarrassed and upset by the fear that others will detect their menstrual difficulties; boys are often disturbed, frightened, or embarrassed by their dreams, by nocturnal emissions, changing voices, enlarging organs

Both boys and girls worry, are shy, or otherwise manifest self-consciousness concerning social behavior

Sensitiveness to what others think about

them (or to what they imagine others think) may cause extreme reserve on some occasions, recklessness on others

Vanity, showing off, affectation, and self-assertion (sometimes alternated by extreme reticence) are common

A growing sense of chivalry sometimes follows apparent indifference and even hostility to members of the opposite sex

Adolescents, especially girls, sometimes begin to take interest in being immaculately clean, well-groomed, etc.

The "crowd" (meaning boys and girls) begins to supersede the all-boy or all-girl "gang"

Are extremely unhappy if not popular

Generally have one intimate "best friend"

There is, sometimes, a new urge to be original or individual

Feel (rightly) that they must achieve independence from parental control and therefore spend a great deal of time away from home, but also need to feel that they can return to the home for help and reassurance if and when they want it

Boys may tease girls but want to be popular with them

Girls often giggle, rave, act silly, etc. but at the same time they probably want so much to be popular with boys that they may disclaim all interest in them

Begin to criticize others for being immature

Become concerned about their families and compare them to other families

Often accuse parents of having misled them by being unrealistic about "life"

Will do practically anything to gain social acceptance where they want it

WHAT TO DO FOR YOUR ADOLESCENT

Do everything you can to help your child develop emotional stability and maturity. Make the home as harmonious as possible to him and as attractive as possible to his friends.

Drop all unnecessary rules and regulations and encourage your child to assume responsibility for manly or womanly conduct.

Help him grow in independence.

Give him an allowance in accordance with his needs and with his companions'. Let him learn, by experience, all he can about the earning, saving, spending, and giving of money.

Teach him that there is real satisfaction in work and let him have the financial as well as the emotional rewards of the work he does.

Instead of giving him all the disagreeable jobs to do, do some of them yourself or at least share them with him, and give him some of the interesting ones, too.

Try to help the child's father understand the adolescent's problems and to be patient with his or her rebelliousness, moodiness, etc.

If your child is having difficulty in adjusting to school, companions, or situations in general, find out what his problems are and do all you

can to help him. Know your child's companions and something about their home environment. Be hospitable to his friends.

Teach him the duties of a host and give him opportunities to practice them in entertaining not only his own friends but occasionally yours.

Encourage all efforts at self-reliance and help the child to use time wisely for play, work, and social contacts.

Equip your child with both the information and the confidence he needs to meet life as it actually exists.

Understand that the anti-social conduct of some adolescents is caused by their inability to handle the complex problems of their own maturing.

Let your adolescent take a job in his spare time (if his health, school work, and disposition allow), realizing that that is one of the best ways for young people to learn how to get along with other people. Responsible work is also an excellent antidote for worry, dissatisfaction, moodiness, etc.

Give your adolescent every opportunity to make intelligent use of his leisure time. Suggest ways to him if he cannot easily think of them himself, and help him get the necessary materials for his hobbies and activities.

Continue to get up occasions for family good times—but make them more on an adult level than you did when your boy or girl was a young child. Have family get-togethers for fun and for interesting projects. Have family jokes, family customs, celebrations, etc. that the boy or girl can enjoy and be proud of. Remember that leisurely, comfortable, spontaneous companionship between young people and their parents is far more valuable than set occasions where companionship is enforced.

Encourage your child to have afternoon parties for his friends and an occasional evening one. Let the child plan and prepare these parties and help him if he wants your help at the same time. Make allowance for the fact that normal adolescents want to spend much of their time away from home with their own friends. They need experience in making their own choices and becoming independent.

Help your boy or girl to realize his responsibilities by encouraging him to join such organizations as the Y.M.C.A., Y.W.C.A., etc. and by pointing out their duties as a citizen.

Understand that all conduct is motivated by inner forces of which the young people are often not aware. Find out what is motivating your adolescent's conduct. Then treat the cause, not the conduct.

Discourage trends toward delinquency not by threats or punishment but by seeing that your adolescent's emotional strivings are understood and, if possible, satisfied.

Face reality, and help your child find satisfactions in real achievements rather than in escape from reality into daydreaming, romancing, running away, etc.

If your child has not already learned to meet both failure and success, find ways to help him learn how to do so not just as a good sport but by strengthening his self-confidence and belief in himself.

Keep the home atmosphere as happy, stable, realistic, and dependable as possible in order to give your adolescent boy or girl that sense of security which is so all-important for wholesome emotional and social development.

WHAT TO AVOID

There is nothing to be gained in keeping your young people in ignorance about themselves, their bodies, their emotions, or any other aspect of life, in subjecting them to rigid disciplinary measures for misconduct, or in keeping them emotionally starved or secluded.

"Babying" them when they are trying to become adults; bribing them to behave well—or to do anything else, resenting their efforts at independence, keeping them overdependent or overprotecting them, or shielding them from the life with which they will have to deal in adulthood are all faults to be avoided.

Try to understand that the subconscious motives which account for adolescents' social and emotional behavior must not be ignored but should be seriously considered and taken into account.

It makes no sense to push, prod, or generally harass adolescents for being shy, jealous, or unhappy, or to make them feel conspicuous, awkward, or ridiculous in any way.

Try not to dominate your child with your own preferences, tastes, or ambitions.

Avoid being overcritical. (Try patience and understanding instead.)

Above all, don't fail to realize the importance of getting psychiatric or other professional help when family conflicts and adolescent maladjustments get out of hand.

SUGGESTED READING

Recommendations for further reading on the subjects outlined above may be found by referring to the *Suggested Reading Guide* at the end of this CHART.

MORAL AND SPIRITUAL DEVELOPMENT

The moral fiber of a child is usually fairly well established by the time he reaches adolescence. If he is rebellious at this time, as most normal adolescents are, he is usually rebelling against the outward forms rather than the inward meaning of morality. As a matter of fact, adolescents generally have very high ideals of morality, and their consciences are likely to be strong and keen. They will almost always respond to an appeal to their sense of what is right and fair.

While some adolescents are intensely spiritual, others often fail to realize the importance of the spiritual aspect of morality.

Actually, the spiritual side of life should appeal particularly to boys and girls at the time when they are making the transition from childhood to manhood or womanhood. It illuminates and clarifies the essential reasons and aims of their lives, helping them to direct both their bodies and their minds and giving purpose to what they do and how they do it. Establishing their relation with the Infinite enriches their relation with other people and enhances their understanding of life. It is through spiritual development that they acquire an appreciation of the Creator, come to realize that they are part of His creation and as such His partners and co-workers in making the universe a better place for all of us to live in.

Wise parents will have shown their children, long before adolescence, the beauty of living by faith in the Fatherhood of God and the brotherhood of man. But it is at this age, when most children are groping for a way to happiness, that they will be especially grateful for having such a faith, for realizing its value as a fine foundation on which to build their lives.

As parents we must ourselves realize the superiority of spiritual over material considerations. We must appreciate the fact that whether or not we can give our children all we might like to in a material way, we can all give them a heritage of spiritual values which are of so much greater importance.

The Golden Rule—"Whatsoever you would that men should do unto you, do ye even so unto them"—is still a splendid rule for anyone to live by, and parents would do well to stress its value to their adolescents who are, at this time, so particularly responsive to its spirit of fairness and justice, of thoughtfulness and kindness.

A story in point is that of a boy who, coming home from school one day, noticed that an old Negro woman walking ahead of him with a heavy basket of wash suddenly dropped the basket and the newly-washed clothes spilled out onto the street. The handle of the basket had broken and the old woman was distressed. The boy helped her gather the clothes together, fixed the basket as well as he could, and then courteously helped the old woman and her basket on to the next bus that came along.

That night at dinner the boy said to his father, "It does make you feel good when you do something to help somebody else, doesn't it?" The boy had discovered one of the great spiritual truths of life—that there is a wonderful sense of joy in the giving of unselfish service to others.

Not all adolescents, however, discover this truth for themselves, and it is these who present a problem to their parents, for adolescence is primarily an age of self-assertion and rebellion. The chief thing to remember, if you are the parent of such a child, is that what you *do* speaks louder and means infinitely more than what you *say*. Indeed, what you *do,* if it is good, will probably be eventually adopted by the child as his own, whereas what you merely *say* is very likely to be flouted even if it is good.

Putting the pressure of authority on an adolescent who is doing all he can to break away from it is certainly unwise. It is, indeed, interesting to note that those children who have been the most strictly brought up, with too many or too rigid prohibitions and repressions, are almost invariably the ones least able to assume responsibility for their own moral choices when they reach adulthood. And no wonder. They have not been given enough opportunity to decide for themselves what is right and what is wrong, and they are therefore so frightened by the prospect of making their own moral choices that they fail.

Children who have always been brought up to assume as much responsibility for their own acts as they were able to, however, usually welcome the freedom of choice which adulthood offers them and they are therefore likely to make wise choices. It is a foolish parent indeed who bravely leads a child to the brink of this freedom and then, when the reins should be slackened and finally let go, tightens them in a last desperate effort to hold on to parental control.

The young adolescent is bent on sloughing off his parents' ideas and on forming principles for guiding his own conduct. He does things because *he* thinks they are right, not because someone else says so. Or, if he does things which are wrong, as he may occasionally do even if he knows they are wrong, he is coming into the realization that he will be held responsible for them.

He may still be immature enough to resent this and to try to put the blame on someone else or on the conditions of his life or on the world in general. ("I didn't ask to be born!" is a common expression of resentment at this age.) He must be shown, however, that if he does not like the world as he finds it, it is up to him either to fish or cut bait—that is, either to make his adjustment to the world as he finds it or to try to change the world for the better. He can do the latter by using his influence for good through societies in his school, his church, and his community.

During late adolescence boys and girls whose parents have intelligently helped them to become morally acceptable human beings begin to reward their parents' efforts. They become young adults of integrity, principle, and character. The world has always been, and will continue to be, in need of young men and women with high ideals and constructive principles. The parent who has nurtured such ideals and principles in a son or a daughter has made a priceless contribution to the welfare of mankind.

WHAT TO EXPECT OF AVERAGE ADOLESCENTS

Most adolescents are harrassed by doubts, indecisions, and perplexities

Are often very sensitive to the beauty and idealism of religion but at the same time may not want to go to church (Some become deeply religious and find great comfort in church and other religious observances)

Have keen consciences and like to make moral judgments

Are extremely responsive to generous actions and sentiments, kindness, sympathy, idealistic ideas, self-sacrifice, etc.

Greatly admire people with fine characters and attractive personal qualities, are loyal to them, and try to be like them

Develop their own moral code of principles and conduct, and may be very intolerant of those whose ideals and actions do not measure up to their standards

Resent keenly any attempt on the part of adults to influence their religious or ethical beliefs

May turn against their parents' teachings and beliefs if they find, through education and experience, that people they have reason to admire hold religious,

educational, social, or other views quite different from those held by their parents; may ardently espouse one or more of these different views as an expression of resentment against parental authority

For the same reason they may work hard and happily outside the home, making a real effort to please teachers and employers while appearing irritable, sulky, lazy, and resentful of being asked to do the smallest task at home

May behave badly, vulgarly, affectedly, or rebelliously on the surface, but are often serious, generous, courageous and unselfish at heart and are often desperately eager to express these good qualities; but often they do not know how or are afraid of ridicule

Normal adolescents have a need to live their own lives, and will in all likelihood be able to do so happily and well if they have been prepared by their parents to assume the responsibilities and obligations that go with independence and maturity

Want, above all else, to find the meaning of life and to feel secure in it

WHAT TO DO FOR YOUR ADOLESCENT

As far as is practical and ethical, let your adolescent live his own life according to *his* standards; but don't be afraid to maintain your own moral and spiritual values and live up to them to the best of your ability and to let your child know what you believe, think, and feel. Remember that children are proud of parents who keep high standards even when they (the children) rebel against them.

Continue building your family's spiritual life on the firm foundation of faith in the fatherhood of God and the brotherhood of man.

Base your spiritual teachings on the assumption that parents and children are co-workers with God in doing the world's work.

Link up your lives with the religious organization of your choice in your community and give it your cooperation and support.

Remember that to give your child the opportunity to make his life a success in the spiritual rather than the material meaning of that word, you must add to his "three R's" that most important fourth R—religion.

If you wish your child to carry the spirit of his religion into his daily life, a good way to remind him of it is to make family prayers a twice-daily ritual. This can become a program of sincere devotion if every member of the family observes it. In the morning pray for guidance in meeting problems and in the evening offer appreciation for help received.

Try to get your child to join or keep up membership in his church clubs and societies unless he gets no satisfaction from them. In that case, try to get him to join one which he really enjoys.

Encourage your boy to join the Boy Scouts and your girl the Girl Scouts if they have not already done so. Cooperate in their purpose of doing at least one good deed every day by doing so yourself, and by having it a general family custom for all members, whether they belong to the Scouts or not.

Continue trying to inspire your adolescent to do the right thing, but do not insist upon having your way about it. Let him learn from the consequences of what he does.

Encourage his pride; discourage vanity, pretentiousness, vulgarity. (Do this with simple dignity, by example, not by preaching.)

Learn what influences his attitudes, what motivates his behavior. Be willing to admit that you may be (or may have been) narrow, bigoted, unprogressive, possessive, intolerant, etc., and that others who are now influencing your boy or girl may know more, be more intelligent, or have a better view of life than you. If this is so, do everything you can to improve your own point of view.

In any case, hold before him constantly (by example) the ideals of fairness, kindness, human dignity, integrity. Do and be what you want him to do and be.

Praise his expressions of generosity, sympathy, self-sacrifice, etc. If he carries them to extremes, however, so that he makes an emotional burden of them, teach him to use good judgment about them. Try to understand and ease his conflicts.

Without expecting perfection or in any way goading him beyond his capacities, encourage him to live up to his own best standards, to be satisfied with himself only when he does his best.

Be patient when he misunderstands your attitude and tolerant when he disagrees with it. Try to understand his.

Let him share in the fun and joy of family life as well as in its duties and devotions.

Be appreciative of all his endeavors to be a good citizen, a good friend, and a good human being *according to his own lights.*

Provide opportunities for him, if he lacks them, to render helpful service to others and in general to express his good impulses.

Do everything you can to prevent him from having unhealthy feelings of guilt about himself. (Helping him to overcome his mistakes and weaknesses is another matter and is often necessary and desirable; but at all costs make him feel that you have faith in *him* and in his potentialities for good.)

Realize that *all* of life's experiences are potential forces for character building. Let your child experience life as it comes (within the limits of safety, of course) and learn as much as possible from it.

Try to give your child a sense of the satisfaction and inspiration of work well done—any kind of work.

Realize that young people today are as fine, courageous, and idealistic, as they ever were—maybe more so. (If they do not seem so, isn't it because the life we are asking them to adjust to is a more materialistic, more complicated and confused one than that of *our* younger days?)

Point out to your adolescent that even though the vocabulary for certain things may have changed (for example, *spooning, necking, petting*), and even though the present generation is able to be franker than ours was about the facts of life, there are still things (like using too much make-up, dressing too provocatively, petting, promiscuity, etc.) which are always cheapening and which defeat their seeming purpose in the end.

If you think your adolescent is using his leisure time unprofitably or unwisely, examine your own use of *your* leisure time. (Are you sure you are setting a good example in this regard? And if so, are you sure you are not being priggish and prudish in your attitude?)

Show your child the wisdom of getting satisfaction from inner resources of feeling and appreciation without regard to social status or financial considerations.

If your child shows delinquent tendencies (cheating, lying, stealing, truancy, drinking, sex practices, etc.) try to find out why. Has your early training been too strict? Too lax?

Lacking in understanding? Overprotective? Self-righteous? Impatient? Neurotic? Over-ambitious? If you find you cannot get to the core of the matter, by all means take the child to a competent counsellor or guidance service. In any case, do your best to be understanding, sympathetic, and dependable.

Be willing to face facts squarely, as they really exist, even if they are unpleasant.

Be aware that practically all human conduct is dominated by motives that have their roots in earlier experiences and lie below the surface of conscious reasoning.

See that your child never gets the idea that deception can work to his ultimate advantage—and show him that such temporary advantages as it may bring him are never worth the cost in self-respect.

Remember that it is no longer considered desirable for children of this age to view their parents with blind respect or to endow them with virtues which they do not possess. **Try to be the kind of person your child can *honestly* admire and be proud of.**

Help your adolescent, if you can, to acquire a philosophy of life which will make his burdens bearable and his rewards enjoyable to him.

Remember that from this age on, the ideal relation between parents and their children is one of *mutual* effort to understand their differing interests, problems, and needs.

Do your best at all times to make your home the dependable, happy, welcoming place your child will always enjoy coming back to.

Remember that the best kind of family life is founded on spiritual values and therefore one of inner contentment.

WHAT TO AVOID

Try not to make any of your requests or suggestions in the form either of preachments or peremptory demands.

Don't expect perfection—or anything near it. (No one ever achieves it, though one of the best things in life is aiming at it.)

Refuse to accept racial, religious, or social intolerance—in yourself or in your child. (Remember that equality of opportunity is a fine American ideal unfortunately not always practiced.)

Do not allow your own insecurities and inferiorities to interfere with your appreciation of any superior qualities your child may have or with your acceptance of his handicaps.

Never ridicule your child's ideals, no matter how "impractical" they may seem to a more practical mind.

Try not to let yourself become angry, tearful, hurt, or shocked by any manifestation of normal adolescent behavior.

Never make your child feel abnormal, wicked, or unduly guilty. (Be understanding and constructive instead.)

Do not try to get confessions from him about his private life if he does not give them willingly.

Be sure you do not try to argue down his knowledge with irrational beliefs.

See that you do not allow mistakes and conflicts in your own life to damage his happiness and security.

Don't fail to recognize the value of leisure, as well as work, for building character.

Be sure you aren't competing with your child in matters relating to his needs and satisfactions. (Be morally as well as practically generous.)

Above all, don't try to keep your child or children dependent on you by selfish, demanding, or possessive attitudes. Send them out into the world equipped with the best moral and spiritual armor you can give them. Then let them go—with your blessing and your love!

SUGGESTED READING

Recommendations for further reading on the subjects outlined above may be found **by referring** to the *Suggested Reading Guide* at the end of this **CHART.**

SUGGESTED READING GUIDE
With Page-References to Articles in This
MANUAL OF CHILD DEVELOPMENT
For Those Who Wish Further Information
on the Important Topics Outlined in the Foregoing CHART

THE BABY
(Up to Three)

BEFORE THE BABY IS BORN

So You're Expecting a Baby 71

WHEN THE BABY IS BORN

Birth Regstration 76

FEEDING THE BABY

Mother's Milk the Best Food for Baby . . 77
Hygiene of the Nursing Mother 77
The Choice of Milk 88
Water for the Baby to Drink 97
Foods Besides Milk 99
Feeding the Average Baby 103
Sample Milk Mixtures for Different Weights
   and Ages 104
Training the Child from Birth to Like
   Wholesome Foods 177
The Baby's Day 118

SPECIAL PROBLEMS IN FEEDING AND CARE

Difficulties of the Nursing Period . . . 85
Wet Nurses 86
The Premature, Small or Delicate Baby . 79
Difficulties of the Bottle-Fed Baby . . . 98
Special Summer Rules 108

WEANING THE BABY

Weaning 87

CIRCUMCISING BOY BABIES

Circumcision 106

CRYING

Why the Baby Cries 106

BATHING AND CLEANLINESS

The Daily Bath 114
Care of Baby's Eyes 115
Care of Baby's Ears 115
Care of Baby's Mouth 115
Care of Baby's Nose 115
Care of Genital Organs 115
The Baby's Room 179

TEETHING

The Child's Teeth 133

CLOTHING THE BABY

The Baby's Clothes 109
Diapers 110
Bands, Shirts, and Baby Pants 112
Socks, Stockings, and Shoes 112
Nightgowns, Dresses, and Suits 113
Outer Garments 114
Bibs 114

SLEEP AND REST

Sleep 141

SUN AND AIR

Sunshine and Fresh Air 116

DAILY SCHEDULE

The Baby's Day 118

EXERCISE AND WALKING

Baby's Exercises 117
Beginning to Crawl 118
Baby Pen 118
Sitting Up 117
Standing and Walking 118
Helping a Baby to Exercise 118

HABITS TO BE ENCOURAGED

(See also CHARACTER, PERSONALITY,
AND DISPOSITION DEVELOPMENT)

Forming Good Habits 121
Learning to Eat 122
Training the Child from Birth to Like
    Wholesome Foods 177
Learning to Wash and Dress 123
Toilet Habits 125

HABITS TO BE OVERCOME

Thumb Sucking 128
Bet Wetting 126
Masturbation 129

TOILET TRAINING

Bowel Training 125
Bladder Training 125
Toilet Conveniences 126
Teaching the Child to Use the Right Words 126
Constipation 126

BABY-SITTERS AND NURSES

The Baby's Caretakers 107

SUMMER CARE

Special Summer Rules 108
The Baby's Vacation 189

BABY CARE IN HEALTH AND SICKNESS

Preserving Health 130
The Doctor 131
A Home for the Children 179
The Baby's Room 179
Symptoms of Acute Illness 199
Health Department Requirements . . . 209
Against What Should We Be Immunized? . 215
Diseases of Childhood 225
    (For Specific Ailments, Consult INDEX
    at the Back of this MANUAL)
The Common Contagious Diseases . . . 225
Less Common Contagious Diseases . . . 231

Diseases of the Skin 236
Diseases of the Respiratory Tract . . . 236
Diseases in the Abdomen 240
Diseases of the Kidney 245
Diseases Due to Allergy 246
Diseases of the Eye 248
Diseases of Nutrition 249
Physical Injuries 250
Poisons and Their Antidotes 254
Poisonous Plants 256
Caring for the Sick Child 200
Medical and Sickroom Supplies 253
Home Nursing 201
Poultices 205
Enemas and Suppositories 208
How to Prevent Contagion 215
The Importance of Quarantine 214
Amusements for Convalescent Babies . . 220

HOME INFLUENCES

The Home Atmosphere 370
Personality in the Making 447
Special Note to Fathers 379

LEARNING PROCESS IN BABIES

How Children Learn 259
Learning Self-Reliance 261
Play a Way of Learning 262
Imitative Play 271

TALKING

Your Child's Speech 275
Teaching a Child to Talk 279
Stuttering 277

PLAY AND GAMES FOR BABY

Riding-Games 297
Knee-Games 298
Foot-Plays 298
Ear-Game 298
Nose-Games 298
Finger-and-Hand Plays 298
Face-Plays 298
Play a Way of Learning 262
Imitative Play 271
Selecting Toys Wisely 331
Where to Play 331
Toys for the Baby 332

STORIES AND VERSES FOR BABY

The Baby's Story-Hour 297
The Lullaby 297
Hand-and-Finger Stories 298

Egoistic Stories 299
The Use of Mother Goose 299
Rhythm 299
Rhymes That Please the Senses 300
Baby's Sense of Humor 300
First Animal Stories 300
Grandmother Stories 300
Poetry in Earliest Babyhood 304
Use of Lullabies and Finger-Plays . . . 304
How to Tell Stories 307
The Poetry Habit 303

PETS
Animal Friends 325

DISCIPLINE
When Punishment is Necessary 419
Learn What to Expect at Different Ages . 420
Corporal Punishment Usually Valueless . 421

RELIGIOUS BEGINNINGS
What Children Bring into the World . . 453
The Family the Child's First Religious
   World 453

CHARACTER, PERSONALITY, AND DISPOSITION DEVELOPMENT
Affection and Love 5
Contentment 15
Confidence 13
Courage (Physical) 17
Good Temper 26
Obedience 41
Self-Amusement 51
Cheerfulness and Optimism 11
Cleanliness and Health 12
Friendliness 23
Helpfulness 27
Independence, Self-Reliance and Self-Help 31
Investigation 35
Kindness 36
Personality in the Making 447
Forming Good Habits 121
What are Good Character Habits? . . . 422

THE CHILD
(From Four to Adolescence)

HOME AND FAMILY
A Happy Family—If 367
The Home Atmosphere 370
The Cooperative Family 372
Training in Household Tasks 373
Sharing the Life of the Family Circle . . 374
The Child Needs Solitude 374
Family Differences 375
The Family Lodge 377
Special Note to Fathers 379

HABITS TO BE ENCOURAGED
(See also CHARACTER, PERSONALITY,
   AND DISPOSITION DEVELOPMENT)
Good Food Habits 172
Learning to Like Wholesome Foods . . . 175
Learning to Wash and Dress 123
What are Good Character Habits? . . . 422
Manners 381

HABITS TO BE OVERCOME
Bed Wetting 126
Thumb Sucking 128
Nail Biting 128

Masturbation 129
Stuttering 277

CHILD CARE IN HEALTH AND IN SICKNESS
Preserving Health 130
Child Posture 138
The Child's Teeth 133
Care of the Eyes 134
Do Your Ears Hear? 136
Deafness 136
Care of the Child's Hair 137
Care of Nose and Throat 138
Keeping the Child Well 130
Home Nursing 201
Teach Children Doctor is Their Friend . 222
Poultices 205
Enemas and Suppositories 208
How to Prevent Contagion 210
Importance of Quarantine 214
Diseases of Childhood 225
(For Specific Ailments, Consult INDEX
   at the Back of This MANUAL)
The Common Contagious Diseases . . . 225
Less Common Contagious Diseases . . 231

Diseases of the Skin 236
Diseases of the Respiratory Tract . . . 238
Diseases in the Abdomen 240
Diseases of the Kidney 245
Diseases Due to Allergy 246
Diseases of the Eye 248
Diseases of Nutrition 249
Physical Injuries 250
Poisons and Their Antidotes 254
Poisonous Plants 256

CONVALESCENCE

While the Children are Getting Well . . 218
Amusements for Convalescent Children . 220

CLEANLINESS

Bathing 132
Learning to Wash and Dress 123
Care of the Child's Hair 137

FOOD, DIET, AND NUTRITION

Nutritional Requirements of Growing
    Children 161
Planning the Young Child's Menu . . . 166
Food Plan for the Growing Child . . . 168
The School Lunch Box 171
Lunch Time at School 171
Food Between Meals 172
Good Food Habits 172
Summer Drinks for Children 173
Teaching Children to Like Wholesome Foods 175

SLEEP AND REST

Sleep 141
Fatigue and Naughtiness 143

POSTURE

Child Posture 138

HEIGHT AND WEIGHT

What Height-Weight Tables Mean . . . 151
How to Use Height and Weight Tables . 152
Height and Weight Tables 153

PLAY, PLAY-TIMES, PLAY-THINGS AND PLAY-PLACES

Play-Places in the House 181
The Little Child's Room 182
The Porch as a Playground 182
The Backyard 186

How to Give the Children a Good Time
    During Vacation 190
Play a Way of Learning 262
Imitative Play 271
Dramatics in the Home 273
Selecting Toys Wisely 331
Special Requisites for Outdoor Playthings . 334
Amusements for Convalescent Children . 220

LEISURE-TIME ACTIVITIES

Your Family's Leisure 334
Adventuring in Handcraft 335
Hobbies 337
Taking Advantage of the Summer Camp for
    Your Boy 193
Summer Camps for Girls 195
How to Give the Children a Good Time
    During Vacation 190

FRIENDSHIPS

The Little Child Needs Friends 391
Finding Friends for the Pre-School Child 392
Imaginary Companions 393
When Friends Seem to be Doing Harm . 394

EXERCISE AND SPORTS

Sports for Exercise 145
Dancing for Your Children 146
Sea Bathing 192

NATURE STUDY

Animal Friends 325
Nature Study for Young Children . . . 326
Nature Study for Older Boys and Girls . 328

THE LEARNING PROCESS

How Children Learn 259
Play a Way of Learning 262
Reasoning in Early Childhood 265
Curiosity 266
When the Children Ask Questions . . . 268
Observation 269

SPEECH AND LANGUAGE

Your Child's Speech 275
Stuttering 277
Enlarging the Child's Vocabulary . . . 280
Learning to Use Language 281

READING AND LITERATURE

Literature for Pre-School Children . . .	301
The Poetry Habit	303
Fairy Tales for Children	306
How to Tell Stories	307
How to Tell Stories for Character-Building	429
Home Opportunities in English	283
Work and Play in English	287

PICTURES AND DRAWING (ART)

How to Interest Children in Pictures . .	311
Pictures for Children	313
Drawing and Coloring by Little Children .	314
Self-Discovery Through Painting and Drawing	315

MUSIC

Music and Rhythm	317
Mothers and Practicing	319
Children's Singing in the Home	321
Making Music Together	322

CULTIVATING GOOD TASTE

Good Taste Needs Cultivation	307
The Comic Strips	308
The Movies	308
The Radio	308

BEHAVIOR AND MANNERS

Manners Right from the Start	381
Learning Social Behavior	389

SCHOOLS

Will You Send Your Child to Nursery School?	341
Will You Send Your Child to Kindergarten?	343
Your Child's Progress in the Elementary School	345
How the Home Can Cooperate with the School	347
How to Recognize Your Child's Special Ability	358

SEX EDUCATION

Beginning Sex Education	395
Preparing for Maturity	397

DISCIPLINE

When Punishment is Necessary	419
Motives to Which Youth Responds . . .	423
The Fear-Punishment	425
The Family of Judges	426
Use Praise Instead of Blame	427

PREPARING FOR CITIZENSHIP AND COMMUNITY LIFE

Preparing Our Children for Citizenship .	403
Appreciating Our Public Servants	404
Children and the World Today . . .	405
Boys' Clubs as a Help to the Home . . .	407
Boy Scouts	408
Girl Scouts	409
Camp Fire Girls	410
YMCA and YWCA	412
Jewish Center	413
Columbian Squires	414
American Youth Foundation	416
How to Keep the Poison of Racial and Religious Prejudice from Our Children .	481

RELIGIOUS EDUCATION

Brotherhood of Man	418
Importance of Religious Training . . .	451
Beginnings of Religious Training . . .	451
Family Prayers and Saying Grace . . .	458
Simple Family Prayers	459
Religious Education of a Catholic Child .	460
Religious Educaton of a Jewish Child . .	463
Making the Bible Real to the Child . . .	470
The Aim of Religious Education	475
Sunday in the Home	480

PROBLEMS OF PERSONALITY

How Personality Grows	431
Timid Child	433
Hysterical Child	434
Self-Centered Child	435
Cross Child	435
Contrary Child	436
Child Who Sulks	436
Child Who Has Temper Tantrums . . .	437
Quarrelsome Child	437
Child Who Teases	439
Impudent Child	439
Forgetful Child	440
Lazy Child	441
Child Who is Jealous	443
Child Who Lies	443
Vain Child	445
Child Who Steals	446

CHARACTER, PERSONALITY, AND DISPOSITION DEVELOPMENT

Accuracy	3
Adaptability and Adjustability	4
Affection and Love	5

Alertness and Attentiveness 6
Application and Concentration 7
Appreciation and Gratitude 8
Aspiration 9
Caution and Prudence 10
Cheerfulness and Optimism 11
Cleanliness and Health 12
Confidence 13
Conscience 14
Contentment 15
Cooperation and Teamwork 16
Courage 17
Courtesy, Politeness and Manners . . . 18
Democratic Spirit 19
Fairness and Justice 22
Friendliness 23
Generosity 24
Good Sportsmanship 25
Good Temper 26
Helpfulness 27
Honesty and Honor 28
Imagination 30
Independence, Self-Reliance, and Self-Help 31
Individuality and Originality 32
Industry and Diligence 33
Initiative and Ambition 34
Investigation, Judgment and Decision . . 35
Kindness 36
Leadership 37
Loyalty (to family and country) . . . 38
Modesty and Simplicity 39

Obedience 41
Open-Mindedness and Reasonableness . . 42
Orderliness and Neatness 43
Patience 44
Patriotism and Civic Responsibility . . . 45
Perseverance and Persistence 46
Punctuality and Promptness 47
Respect, Reverence and Faith 48
Resourcefulness and Ingenuity 49
Responsibility 50
Self-Amusement and Self-Direction . . . 51
Self-Control 52
Self-Respect 53
Self-Sacrifice and Service to Others . . . 54
Sense of Humor 55
Sincerity 56
Sympathy and Consideration for Others . 57
System and Efficiency 58
Tact 59
Thinking and Reasoning 60
Thoroughness 61
Thrift 62
Tolerance 63
Trustworthiness and Dependability . . . 64
Truthfulness 65
Unselfishness 66
Will Power and Determination 67
How to Tell Stories for Character Building 429
Personality in the Making 447
Motives to Which Youth Responds . . . 423
What are Good Character-Habits? . . . 422

THE ADOLESCENT

PHYSICAL GROWTH

Height and Weight Tables 153
Maturing of the Reproductive System . . 485
Problems Incidental to Physical Growth and
  Development 487

PHYSICAL HEALTH AND HYGIENE

Sports for Exercise 145
Physical Hygiene 486

INTELLIGENCE AND MENTAL DEVELOPMENT

Adolescence and Mental Development . . 491
Measurement of Intelligence 491
The Slow Mind 492
The Average Mind 492
The Superior Mind 492
Special Abilities and Disabilities . . . 493

EDUCATIONAL PROBLEMS

Some Educational Pitfalls 495
Who Shall Go to College? 350

VOCATIONAL GUIDANCE AND JOBS

The Question of Work 498
Vocational Guidance in Home and School . 355
How to Recognize Your Child's Special
  Ability 358
Vocational Aptitudes That Affect School
  Success 360

HOME LIFE

A Happy Family—If 367
The Family Lodge 377
Adolescents at Leisure 503
The Girl's Own Room 183
The Boy's Own Room 184

LEISURE-TIME PURSUITS

Learning to Use Leisure 500
Present Complaints 500
Education in the Use of Leisure 500
Adolescents at Leisure 503

COMPANIONS AND FRIENDS

The Importance of Friends 510
"Crushes" 511
Boy and Girl Relations 512

MANNERS

Why Manners? 381
Maturity and Independence in Manners . . 387

PROBLEMS OF ADJUSTMENT

The Individual as a Whole 493

PROBLEMS OF CONDUCT, BEHAVIOR AND DELINQUENCY

Stealing 506
Incorrigibility 507
Evading Reality 508
Daydreaming and Romancing 508
Cheating 509
Truancy 509
Drinking 510

SEX PROBLEMS AND INSTRUCTION

Attitudes Toward Sex 488
Sex Instruction 488
Sex Talk and Reading 489

Masturbation 490
The Question of Petting 399
Boy and Girl Relations 512

CLUBS AND OTHER ORGANIZATIONS THAT PREPARE BOYS AND GIRLS FOR BETTER CITIZENSHIP

Boys' Clubs as a Help in the Home . . . 407
Boy Scouts 408
Girl Scouts 409
Camp Fire Girls 410
The YMCA and the YWCA 412
The Jewish Center 413
The Columbian Squires 414
The American Youth Foundation . . . 416

RELIGIOUS EDUCATION

Making the Bible Real to the Child . . . 470
Religious Training of Older Children . . 478
How to Keep the Poison of Racial and Religious Prejudice from Our Children . 481

CHARACTER, PERSONALITY, AND DISPOSITION DEVELOPMENT

Civic Responsibility 45
Dignity and Reserve 20
Emotional Maturity and Stability . . . 21
Faith 48
Idealism and Life Purpose 29
Naturalness and Unaffectedness 40

PARENTS' NEEDS, BLUNDERS, AND ATTITUDES

The Needs of the Parent 514

HOW TO USE
The Following List of
TRAITS TO BE DISCOURAGED, CORRECTED, OR LEFT TO BE OUTGROWN

ON the eight pages immediately following is an alphabetically arranged list of undesirable traits, some of which most children exhibit at one time or another and which may present problems to parents. All such traits are printed in heavy black type, as **ADJUSTMENT DIFFICULTIES, AFFECTATION,** etc.

To make it as easy as possible for the reader to find a particular trait, we sometimes list it under more than one heading. For instance, the trait which we call **HOSTILITY** is also listed under **AGGRESSIVENESS, HATRED,** and **RESENTMENT** as well as **HOSTILITY.** If you look under any of these headings, you will be directed: Look under **HOSTILITY**

When you look up a problem-trait in this list, you already know that it is to be discouraged or corrected or left to be outgrown. But you also want to know how to go about whatever is to be done about it and also how to encourage your child to develop desirable traits in place of undesirable ones.

Under *each undesirable* trait, therefore, you will find a list of *desirable* traits (headed by the word **See:**). All the desirable traits listed here are described and discussed, one to a page, on pages 3 to 67, in the section called ESSENTIALS OF GOOD CHARACTER AND PERSONALITY. You will find them arranged in alphabetical order and it is to be hoped that the discussions of them will prove helpful in each specific case.

TRAITS TO BE DISCOURAGED, CORRECTED, OR LEFT TO BE OUTGROWN

To MAKE IT EASIER for a mother to get help on any particular problems which her child may be presenting at any time, we have assembled, below, a list of TRAITS TO BE DISCOURAGED, CORRECTED, OR LEFT TO BE OUTGROWN.

This list, alphabetically arranged, gives you, under each problem-trait, references (under See) to the series of articles on ESSENTIALS OF GOOD CHARACTER AND PERSONALITY beginning on page 3. These articles, it is hoped, will throw constructive light on the problem under consideration.

Do *not* think that there is anything unusual about your child if he seems to have developed some or even many of these problem-traits. Almost all children develop most of them at one stage or another. If manifested for temporary periods, they are perfectly normal phases of child-life. Any child who had none of them would be abnormal indeed. Most children outgrow them, if allowed to, as time goes on. The trouble with too many parents is that they interfere too much. In their very efforts to correct their children's faults, they may set up resistances, rebellions, and inhibitions which hinder rather than help natural development.

If your child manifests a long-standing behavior problem which seems to be getting worse instead of better, consult a doctor or psychiatrist or anyone professionally trained in child-guidance problems. Otherwise, remember that doing nothing is better than doing the wrong thing. Doing the *right* thing—which is often merely letting nature take its course—is best of all.

ADJUSTMENT DIFFICULTIES

See:
ADAPTABILITY AND ADJUSTABILITY
AFFECTION AND LOVE
CHEERFULNESS AND OPTIMISM
COOPERATION AND TEAMWORK
EMOTIONAL MATURITY AND STABILITY
FRIENDLINESS
GOOD SPORTSMANSHIP
GOOD TEMPER
INDEPENDENCE, SELF-RELIANCE, AND SELF-HELP
INITIATIVE AND AMBITION
LOYALTY
NATURALNESS AND UNAFFECTEDNESS
OBEDIENCE
OPEN-MINDEDNESS AND REASONABLE-NESS
RESOURCEFULNESS AND INGENUITY
SELF-CONTROL
SELF-RESPECT
SYMPATHY AND CONSIDERATION FOR OTHERS

AFFECTATION

See:
COURTESY, POLITENESS, AND MANNERS
MODESTY AND SIMPLICITY
NATURALNESS AND UNAFFECTEDNESS
SENSE OF HUMOR

AGGRESSIVENESS Look under HOSTILITY

AMBITION, LACK OF

See:
APPLICATION AND CONCENTRATION

ASPIRATION
CHEERFULNESS AND OPTIMISM
CONFIDENCE
COOPERATION AND TEAMWORK
IDEALISM AND LIFE PURPOSE
INDEPENDENCE, SELF-RELIANCE, AND
   SELF-HELP
INDUSTRY AND DILIGENCE
INITIATIVE AND AMBITION
PERSEVERANCE AND PERSISTENCE
WILL POWER AND DETERMINATION

ANXIETY Look under **FEAR** and
ADJUSTMENT DIFFICULTIES

BAD MANNERS Look under
  UNKINDNESS

BEHAVIOR PROBLEMS
See:
ADAPTABILITY AND ADJUSTABILITY
AFFECTION AND LOVE
CONFIDENCE
CONSCIENCE
CONTENTMENT
COOPERATION AND TEAMWORK
COURTESY, POLITENESS, AND MANNERS
DIGNITY AND RESERVE
EMOTIONAL MATURITY AND STABILITY
GOOD SPORTSMANSHIP
GOOD TEMPER
KINDNESS
OBEDIENCE
OPEN-MINDEDNESS AND REASONABLE-
   NESS
PATIENCE
RESPONSIBILITY
SELF-RESPECT
SELF-CONTROL
SYMPATHY AND CONSIDERATION FOR
   OTHERS
TACT
UNSELFISHNESS

BOREDOM Look under **MOODINESS**

CARELESSNESS
See:
ACCURACY
ALERTNESS AND ATTENTIVENESS
APPLICATION AND CONCENTRATION
CAUTION AND PRUDENCE
CLEANLINESS AND HEALTH
COOPERATION AND TEAMWORK
COURTESY, POLITENESS, AND MANNERS

HONESTY AND HONOR
INDUSTRY AND DILIGENCE
INDEPENDENCE, SELF-RELIANCE, AND
   SELF-HELP
ORDERLINESS AND NEATNESS
PERSEVERANCE AND PERSISTENCE
PUNCTUALITY AND PROMPTNESS
RESPONSIBILITY
SYSTEM AND EFFICIENCY
THOROUGHNESS
TRUSTWORTHINESS AND DEPENDABILITY
WILL POWER AND DETERMINATION

CONCEIT
See:
DIGNITY AND RESERVE
MODESTY AND SIMPLICITY
SELF-RESPECT

DAWDLING
See:
ALERTNESS AND ATTENTIVENESS
APPLICATION AND CONCENTRATION
EMOTIONAL MATURITY AND STABILITY
INDUSTRY AND DILIGENCE
INITIATIVE AND AMBITION
PERSEVERANCE AND PERSISTENCE
PUNCTUALITY AND PROMPTNESS
WILL POWER AND DETERMINATION

DIRTINESS
See:
CLEANLINESS AND HEALTH
NEATNESS AND ORDERLINESS
SELF-RESPECT

DISCIPLINARY DIFFICULTIES Look
under **ADJUSTMENT DIFFICULTIES**
  and **BEHAVIOR PROBLEMS—**

DISCOURTESY Look under
  UNKINDNESS

DISHONESTY
See:
ACCURACY
CONSCIENCE
COURAGE AND FORTITUDE
EMOTIONAL MATURITY AND STABILITY
HONESTY AND HONOR
IMAGINATION
SINCERITY

TRUSTWORTHINESS AND DEPEND-
ABILITY
TRUTHFULNESS

DISLOYALTY
See:
AFFECTION AND LOVE
CONSCIENCE
COOPERATION AND TEAMWORK
FAIRNESS AND JUSTICE
FRIENDLINESS
LOYALTY
PATRIOTISM AND CIVIC RESPONSIBILITY
RESPECT, REVERENCE, AND FAITH

DISOBEDIENCE Look under **ADJUST-MENT DIFFICULTIES** and **BEHAVIOR PROBLEMS**

DISORDERLINESS
See:
CLEANLINESS AND HEALTH
INDUSTRY AND DILIGENCE
ORDERLINESS AND NEATNESS
RESPONSIBILITY
SYSTEM AND EFFICIENCY

DISRESPECT
See:
APPRECIATION AND GRATITUDE
CONFIDENCE
DEMOCRATIC SPIRIT
FAIRNESS AND JUSTICE
LOYALTY
PATRIOTISM AND CIVIC RESPONSIBILITY
RESPECT, REVERENCE, AND FAITH
TOLERANCE

EGOTISM Look under **SELFISHNESS**

ENVY Look under **JEALOUSY**

EXTRAVAGANCE
See:
CAUTION AND PRUDENCE
CONTENTMENT
MODESTY AND SIMPLICITY
SELF-SACRIFICE AND SERVICE TO OTHERS
SYSTEM AND EFFICIENCY
THRIFT

FEAR
See:
AFFECTION AND LOVE
ALERTNESS AND ATTENTIVENESS
CONFIDENCE
COURAGE AND FORTITUDE
EMOTIONAL MATURITY AND STABILITY
FRIENDLINESS
INDEPENDENCE, SELF-RELIANCE, AND
SELF-HELP
LEADERSHIP
SELF-RESPECT
TRUTHFULNESS

GREEDINESS
See:
COOPERATION AND TEAMWORK
DEMOCRATIC SPIRIT
FAIRNESS AND JUSTICE
GENEROSITY
GOOD SPORTSMANSHIP
HELPFULNESS
KINDNESS
MODESTY AND SIMPLICITY
SYMPATHY AND CONSIDERATION FOR
OTHERS

GROUCHINESS Look under **MOODINESS**

HATRED Look under **HOSTILITY**
—below

HOSTILITY
See:
ADAPTABILITY AND ADJUSTABILITY
AFFECTION AND LOVE
APPRECIATION AND GRATITUDE
COOPERATION AND TEAMWORK
DEMOCRATIC SPIRIT
FRIENDLINESS
GENEROSITY
HELPFULNESS
JUSTICE AND FAIRNESS
OBEDIENCE
OPEN-MINDEDNESS AND REASONABLE-
NESS
RESPECT, REVERENCE, AND FAITH
SELF-SACRIFICE AND SERVICE TO OTHERS
TOLERANCE

IMITATIVENESS
See:
AFFECTION AND LOVE
CHEERFULNESS AND OPTIMISM
COOPERATION AND TEAMWORK

COURTESY, POLITENESS, AND MANNERS
FAIRNESS AND JUSTICE
FRIENDLINESS
HELPFULNESS
INDIVIDUALITY AND ORIGINALITY
KINDNESS
ORDERLINESS AND NEATNESS
PATIENCE
PATRIOTISM AND CIVIC RESPONSIBILITY
RESPECT, REVERENCE, AND FAITH
SYMPATHY AND CONSIDERATION FOR
    OTHERS
TRUSTWORTHINESS AND DEPENDABILITY

IMMATURITY
See:
ADAPTABILITY AND ADJUSTABILITY
CONFIDENCE
DIGNITY AND RESERVE
EMOTIONAL MATURITY AND STABILITY
GOOD SPORTSMANSHIP
IDEALISM AND LIFE PURPOSE
INDEPENDENCE, SELF-RELIANCE, AND
    SELF-HELP
OPEN-MINDEDNESS AND REASONABLE-
    NESS
SELF-CONTROL
SELF-RESPECT
TRUSTWORTHINESS AND DEPENDABILITY

IMMODESTY
See:
COURTESY, POLITENESS, AND MANNERS
DIGNITY AND RESERVE
MODESTY AND SIMPLICITY
SELF-RESPECT

IMPATIENCE
See:
PATIENCE
PERSEVERANCE AND PERSISTENCE

IMPOLITENESS Look under
UNKINDNESS

INACCURACY
See:
ACCURACY
HONESTY AND HONOR
TRUTHFULNESS

INDECISIVENESS Look under POOR
JUDGMENT

INDIFFERENCE
See:
AFFECTION AND LOVE
APPRECIATION AND GRATITUDE
CONSCIENCE
IDEALISM AND LIFE PURPOSE
KINDNESS
LOYALTY
PATRIOTISM AND CIVIC RESPONSIBILITY
RESPONSIBILITY
SELF-SACRIFICE AND SERVICE TO OTHERS
SYMPATHY AND CONSIDERATION FOR
    OTHERS

INEFFICIENCY
See:
ACCURACY
APPLICATION AND CONCENTRATION
CAUTION AND PRUDENCE
DILIGENCE AND INDUSTRY
INDEPENDENCE, SELF-RELIANCE, AND
    SELF-HELP
LEADERSHIP
ORDERLINESS AND NEATNESS
PERSEVERANCE AND PERSISTENCE
PUNCTUALITY AND PROMPTNESS
RESOURCEFULNESS AND INGENUITY
RESPONSIBILITY
SELF-AMUSEMENT AND SELF-DIRECTION
SYSTEM AND EFFICIENCY
THINKING AND REASONING
THOROUGHNESS
THRIFT

INFERIORITY, SENSE OF
See:
AFFECTION AND LOVE
CONFIDENCE
COOPERATION AND TEAMWORK
EMOTIONAL MATURITY AND STABILITY
FRIENDLINESS
HELPFULNESS
INDIVIDUALITY AND ORIGINALITY
INITIATIVE AND AMBITION
SELF-RESPECT

INGRATITUDE
See:
APPRECIATION AND GRATITUDE
FRIENDLINESS
GENEROSITY
HELPFULNESS
KINDNESS
LOYALTY

INSECURITY Look under **FEAR** and **ADJUSTMENT DIFFICULTIES**

INSINCERITY Look under **DISHONESTY**

INTOLERANCE

See:
COOPERATION AND TEAMWORK
DEMOCRATIC SPIRIT
FAIRNESS AND JUSTICE
LEADERSHIP
MODESTY AND SIMPLICITY
SYMPATHY AND CONSIDERATION FOR
    OTHERS
TOLERANCE

INTROSPECTION

See:
COOPERATION AND TEAMWORK
FRIENDLINESS
HELPFULNESS
SENSE OF HUMOR

IRRESPONSIBILITY

See:
CONSCIENCE
COOPERATION AND TEAMWORK
EMOTIONAL MATURITY AND STABILITY
HELPFULNESS
INDEPENDENCE, SELF-RELIANCE AND
    SELF-HELP
INVESTIGATION, JUDGMENT AND
    DECISION
PATRIOTISM AND CIVIC RESPONSIBILITY
PUNCTUALITY AND PROMPTNESS
RESPONSIBILITY
SELF-AMUSEMENT AND SELF-DIRECTION
SELF-CONTROL
THINKING AND REASONING
TRUSTWORTHINESS AND DEPEND-
    ABILITY

JEALOUSY

See:
AFFECTION AND LOVE
CONTENTMENT
COOPERATION AND TEAMWORK
FAIRNESS AND JUSTICE
GOOD SPORTSMANSHIP
MODESTY AND SIMPLICITY
UNSELFISHNESS

LAZINESS

See:
ALERTNESS AND ATTENTIVENESS
APPLICATION AND CONCENTRATION
COOPERATION AND TEAMWORK
HELPFULNESS
INDEPENDENCE, SELF-RELIANCE AND
    SELF-HELP
INDUSTRY AND DILIGENCE
INITIATIVE AND AMBITION
PERSEVERANCE AND PERSISTENCE
RESOURCEFULNESS AND INGENUITY
RESPONSIBILITY
SYSTEM AND EFFICIENCY

LYING Look under **DISHONESTY—**

MEANNESS

See:
AFFECTION AND LOVE
APPRECIATION AND GRATITUDE
CONSCIENCE
KINDNESS
SYMPATHY AND CONSIDERATION FOR
    OTHERS

MIND-WANDERING

See:
ALERTNESS AND ATTENTIVENESS
APPLICATION AND CONCENTRATION
INDUSTRY AND DILIGENCE
PERSEVERANCE AND PERSISTENCE
RESOURCEFULNESS AND INGENUITY
SYSTEM AND EFFICIENCY
THINKING AND REASONING
WILL POWER AND DETERMINATION

MOODINESS

See:
CHEERFULNESS AND OPTIMISM
COOPERATION AND TEAMWORK
COURTESY, POLITENESS AND MANNERS
FRIENDLINESS
HELPFULNESS
INITIATIVE AND AMBITION
SELF-SACRIFICE AND SERVICE TO OTHERS
SENSE OF HUMOR

"NAUGHTINESS" Look under **BEHAVIOR PROBLEMS** and **ADJUSTMENT DIFFICULTIES—**

NOISINESS

See:

COURTESY, POLITENESS AND MANNERS
DIGNITY AND RESERVE
MODESTY AND SIMPLICITY
PERSONAL WORTH AND PRIDE
SELF-CONTROL
SYMPATHY AND CONSIDERATION FOR
    OTHERS

OBSTINACY Look under **STUBBORN-
    NESS**

OVERDEPENDENCY

See:

CONFIDENCE
COOPERATION AND TEAMWORK
COURAGE AND FORTITUDE
EMOTIONAL MATURITY AND STABILITY
INDEPENDENCE, SELF-RELIANCE AND
    SELF-HELP
INDIVIDUALITY AND ORIGINALITY
SELF-AMUSEMENT AND SELF-DIRECTION
SELF-CONTROL

OVERSERIOUSNESS Look under
    PESSIMISM—below

PESSIMISM

See:

CHEERFULNESS AND OPTIMISM
CONFIDENCE
FRIENDLINESS
GOOD TEMPER
IDEALISM AND LIFE PURPOSE
PERSEVERANCE AND PERSISTENCE
RESOURCEFULNESS AND INGENUITY
RESPECT, REVERENCE, AND FAITH
SENSE OF HUMOR

POOR JUDGMENT

See:

ALERTNESS AND ATTENTIVENESS
CAUTION AND PRUDENCE
CONSCIENCE
FAIRNESS AND DECISION
INVESTIGATION, JUDGMENT, AND
    DECISION
LEADERSHIP
RESOURCEFULNESS AND INGENUITY
SYSTEM AND EFFICIENCY
THINKING AND REASONING

PREJUDICE Look under **INTOL-
    ERANCE**

PURPOSELESSNESS Look under
    AMBITION, LACK OF

REBELLIOUSNESS Look under
BEHAVIOR PROBLEMS and **ADJUST-
MENT DIFFICULTIES**

RECKLESSNESS

See:

CAUTION AND PRUDENCE
INVESTIGATION, JUDGMENT, AND
    DECISION
RESPONSIBILITY
SELF-CONTROL
TRUSTWORTHINESS AND DEPEND-
    ABILITY

RESENTMENT Look under
    HOSTILITY

RUDENESS Look under **UNKIND-
    NESS**

SELF-CONSCIOUSNESS

See:

ADAPTABILITY AND ADJUSTABILITY
AFFECTION AND LOVE
CHEERFULNESS AND OPTIMISM
CONFIDENCE
CONTENTMENT
COOPERATION AND TEAMWORK
COURAGE AND FORTITUDE
EMOTIONAL MATURITY AND STABILITY
FRIENDLINESS
HELPFULNESS
INDEPENDENCE, SELF-RELIANCE, AND
    SELF-HELP
INDIVIDUALITY AND ORIGINALITY
LEADERSHIP
NATURALNESS AND UNAFFECTEDNESS
RESPONSIBILITY
SENSE OF HUMOR

SELFISHNESS

See:

APPRECIATION AND GRATITUDE
CONTENTMENT
COOPERATION AND TEAMWORK

COURTESY, POLITENESS AND MANNERS
DEMOCRATIC SPIRIT
FAIRNESS AND JUSTICE
FRIENDLINESS
GENEROSITY
GOOD SPORTSMANSHIP
HELPFULNESS
KINDNESS
SELF-SACRIFICE AND SERVICE TO OTHERS
SYMPATHY AND CONSIDERATION FOR
    OTHERS
UNSELFISHNESS

SENSITIVENESS Look under SELF-CONSCIOUSNESS

SHYNESS Look under SELF-CONSCIOUSNESS

SLOPPINESS Look under CARELESSNESS

SLOWNESS Look under DAWDLING

SNOBBERY
See:
COOPERATION AND TEAMWORK
COURTESY, POLITENESS AND MANNERS
DEMOCRATIC SPIRIT
DIGNITY AND RESERVE
FRIENDLINESS
LOYALTY
MODESTY AND SIMPLICITY
SYMPATHY AND CONSIDERATION FOR
    OTHERS
TOLERANCE

STEALING Look under DISHONESTY

STUBBORNNESS
See:
ADAPTABILITY AND ADJUSTABILITY
FAIRNESS AND JUSTICE
GOOD SPORTSMANSHIP
GOOD TEMPER
INVESTIGATION, JUDGMENT, AND
    DECISION
OPEN-MINDEDNESS AND REASONABLE-
    NESS
TOLERANCE

SUSPICIOUSNESS
See:
AFFECTION AND LOVE
CONFIDENCE
FAIRNESS AND JUSTICE
FRIENDLINESS
GENEROSITY
LOYALTY
OPEN-MINDEDNESS AND REASONABLE-
    NESS
RESPECT, REVERENCE AND FAITH
TRUSTWORTHINESS AND DEPEND-
    ABILITY

TACTLESSNESS
See:
APPRECIATION AND GRATITUDE
COURTESY, POLITENESS, AND MANNERS

TEMPER TANTRUMS (Look under ADJUSTMENT DIFFICULTIES and BEHAVIOR PROBLEMS

THOUGHTLESSNESS Look under CARELESSNESS

TIMIDITY Look under SELF-CONSCIOUSNESS

UNDEPENDABILITY
See:
ACCURACY
HONOR AND HONESTY
IMAGINATION
INVESTIGATION, JUDGMENT, AND
    DECISION
LEADERSHIP
LOYALTY
PUNCTUALITY AND PROMPTNESS
RESPONSIBILITY
SINCERITY
TRUSTWORTHINESS AND DEPEND-
    ABILITY
TRUTHFULNESS

UNFAIRNESS
See:
DEMOCRATIC SPIRIT
FAIRNESS AND JUSTICE
GOOD SPORTSMANSHIP
HONESTY AND HONOR
LEADERSHIP
OPEN-MINDEDNESS AND REASONABLE-
    NESS
SYMPATHY AND CONSIDERATION FOR
    OTHERS

TOLERANCE
TRUSTWORTHINESS AND DEPEND-
  ABILITY

UNFRIENDLINESS
See:
ADAPTABILITY AND ADJUSTABILITY
AFFECTION AND LOVE
CHEERFULNESS AND OPTIMISM
COOPERATION AND TEAMWORK
DEMOCRATIC SPIRIT
FRIENDLINESS
GOOD TEMPER
NATURALNESS AND UNAFFECTEDNESS
TACT

UNIMAGINATIVENESS
See:
ASPIRATION
IMAGINATION
INDIVIDUALITY AND ORIGINALITY
RESOURCEFULNESS AND INGENUITY
RESPECT, REVERENCE AND FAITH
SENSE OF HUMOR
TACT

UNKINDNESS
See:
COURTESY, POLITENESS AND MANNERS
KINDNESS
SYMPATHY AND CONSIDERATION FOR
  OTHERS
TACT

UNREASONABLENESS Look under **STUBBORNNESS**

UNTIDINESS Look under **DISORDERLINESS**

UNTRUSTWORTHINESS Look under **DISHONESTY**

WILFULNESS Look under **STUBBORNNESS**

WORRISOMENESS Look under **FEAR and ADJUSTMENT DIFFICULTIES**

ESSENTIALS OF
GOOD CHARACTER AND
PERSONALITY

THE DESIRABLE TRAITS described and discussed in the following pages comprise what we consider to be ESSENTIALS OF GOOD CHARACTER AND PERSONALITY. They are the characteristics to be encouraged in children at appropriate stages of their growth as indicated in the CHART OF CHILD DEVELOPMENT at the beginning of each of its seven age-divisions.

It is to be hoped, too, that mothers will find, in the following discussions of desirable traits, suggestions for overcoming the undesirable characteristics listed under TRAITS TO BE DISCOURAGED, CORRECTED, OR LEFT TO BE OUTGROWN on the immediately foregoing eight pages.

For practical usefulness in this important task of parenthood, we have followed the discussion of each trait with a list of stories and articles to be found in the first nine volumes of the BOOKSHELF exemplifying the particular trait under discussion. References are given to the volume and page where the selected stories are to be found.

Thus you will have a handy, carefully selected guide to just what you will want your child to read (or to read to him if he is not yet of school age) in order to exemplify the trait or traits you would like him to develop.

It will be neither necessary nor desirable for you to labor the moral or stress the point. If you let your child read these stories for enjoyment rather than for obvious correction he will be far more likely to accept the story and to make his own application of it to himself. Letting him do this his own way is the most effective thing you can do to help him build his character and personality.

All the traits named in the CHART are listed, in the following pages, in alphabetical order. Their place and value are carefully explained and practical suggestions are given for their development. But the principal purpose of this division is to show, by references to the nine volumes of THE BOOKSHELF FOR BOYS AND GIRLS, which stories, articles, etc., may best help the children to love and seek these essentials of good character and personality in their personal lives.

✤ ✤ ✤

The heavier numbers refer to the volume and the lighter ones to the page number in the nine volumes of BOOKSHELF.

ACCURACY

Freedom from mistake or error; precision; exactness.

MANY of life's richest rewards go to those who have developed a high degree of accuracy. That includes accuracy of thought, of craftsmanship, and, last but not by any means least, accuracy of statement—truthfulness.

Accuracy is not some priceless gift of the gods nor is it an inherited trait. It comes from long, systematic effort. One has to keep trying to observe carefully and to understand what one sees. One has to learn to use words exactly and to act with precision.

To understand the importance of accuracy you have only to think about its opposite—inaccuracy. Think of the endless confusion, hardships, and heartaches caused by people who never learned to be careful and accurate. Each year billions of dollars and thousands of lives are lost through their collective inaccuracy.

From the beginning, it is wise to train your child in accuracy in the ways suited to his stage of development. This does not mean that we should always limit a child to facts. Fantasy, imagination, and much delightful nonsense are important parts of a child's world, too. Indeed, young children cannot be accurate (in the adult sense) in speech or action. But you can start training them by play that encourages alert observation, and by teaching them the meaning of words. They can learn *exactly* where toys belong, and so on.

As they grow older, they should be able to give facts more and more accurately when facts are called for. One way to teach them is to question guesswork and vague information. "Let's look it up" may well be a home watchword. As your child gets old enough, you can begin helping him to look up such everyday matters as the spelling and meaning of words, dates, places and persons. Have a good dictionary, atlas, encyclopedia, an information almanac, and other reference books where the child can easily get at them. Use them often yourself, and help him to find things he wants to know. When he asks questions, answer accurately if you can. Otherwise, look up the answers together.

Help your child to see when accuracy is called for and when it is not. Show him its importance when it *is* called for—not only in such fields as science, engineering, mechanics, business, etc., but in work and study of all kinds. Many stories he will read can be counted on to teach him the penalties one has to pay in life for inaccuracies of one kind and another. He will see the moral himself. You will not need to point it out.

Suggested Reading

Arranged in Order of Interest to Children, from the Younger to the Older Age-Groups

	VOL.	PAGE		VOL.	PAGE
Ten Little Blackbirds	1	262	Pictures and Painting	5	27
Ten Little Kittens	1	263	Modeling Small Sculptures in White		
Over in the Meadow	1	266	Soap	5	75
How Many Donkeys	2	74	An Alphabet to be Cut from Paper	5	96
The Squire's Bride	3	201	The Little Mother's Work-Basket	5	213
To Your Good Health	3	212	Handicraft for Girls	5	249
Miss Jennia Jones	4	307	Woodwork for Older Children	5	269
The Farmer in the Dell	4	308	Stamp Collecting	5	349
Here We Go 'Round the Mulberry Bush	4	309	Indoor Games	7	259
Fun with Drawing	5	1	Washington Crossing the Delaware	9	149
Fun with Crayons	5	21			

Knowledge without accuracy is a diamond unpolished and without setting. It is therefore of the greatest importance that the young should early acquire the habit of accuracy. —D. G. MITCHELL.

ADAPTABILITY AND ADJUSTABILITY

The ability to conform readily to new situations, changed circumstances, and unfamiliar environments; to be sufficiently comfortable with oneself to be able to establish satisfactory relationships with other people.

SUPPOSE you were shipwrecked on a desert island. What would you do? Could you adapt yourself to it as ingeniously as Robinson Crusoe did? That was a famous example of meeting the requirements of an outstandingly difficult situation. The same ability can help any of us in the more ordinary situations that arise in life.

Being adaptable helps us to face sudden misfortune and conquer it. It makes us able to change our plans quickly when necessary, to grasp opportunities when they arise, to meet troubles constructively and enjoy good times to the full when and as they come.

Adults are often less adaptable than children. We must be careful not to get into ruts, not to let the family routine get too rigid. It is good to vary the schedule now and then.

When there is a family emergency, let everybody help, children included. Let them make suggestions. They will be learning to meet the unexpected.

Take your children to unfamiliar places and get them into new situations. They will like the adventures and will grow more able to meet and deal with them.

Growing accustomed to changes will make children more adaptable to new situations. But teaching them to adjust to *people* is a more difficult problem because it involves fundamentals of personality development.

The ability to get along harmoniously with other people is probably the most valuable trait of maturity and therefore very much worth developing in your children.

It will help to make family friends of many different kinds of people. Visit them and ask them to your home. The children will enjoy learning that there are many different good ways of doing things—many different good kinds of people.

But no child can become well adjusted to other people if he is not, from the beginning, well adjusted to himself. That is, a baby must be made to feel utterly secure in his parents' love in order to develop happily as a well-integrated human being. His relation to his parents must be one of mutual acceptance and love. If it is, and if it continues to be, the child will have the best possible foundation for making a good adjustment to other people.

One of the most useful things parents can do for their children is to take stock, every so often, of the relationship that develops between them. Build that relationship on a good, solid foundation of security for the child. Love him, enjoy him, and try to understand the motives which underlie all adjustment and behavior problems. That will be the best thing you can do for him.

Suggested Reading

Arranged in Order of Interest to Children, from the Younger to the Older Age-Groups

	VOL.	PAGE		VOL.	PAGE
The Land of Counterpane	1	190	The Boy Who Was Helped	9	13
Susan and the Rain	1	214	The Childhood of a Singer	9	50
Mary Ellen's Birthday Party	2	239	A Courageous Boy Who Became President	9	72
No Room	2	42			
The Happy Cure	2	60	Helen Keller	9	110
Caleb's Luck	2	257	Daniel Boone	9	226
Elizabeth Ann Fails in an Examination	2	304	The Western Pioneer	9	240
Mother Makes Christmas	2	352	Abraham Lincoln, Who Saved the Union	9	244
When the Mail Came Through	2	376	Alfred E. Smith	9	284
Robinson Crusoe	6	89	Radisson, "The Canadian Ulysses"	9	323
Peary, Discover of the North Pole	8	210			

"A child's relationship to his parents . . . profoundly affects all his later relationships and his whole personality."
—THE CHILD STUDY ASSOCIATION OF AMERICA.

AFFECTION AND LOVE

Feelings of strong personal attachment; emotional sympathy and its expression.

THE feelings between parent and child, brothers and sisters, friend and friend, or husband and wife are all different kinds of love. Without love, life would be dreary indeed. None of us can be happy and emotionally secure unless we feel that we are loved. Children need this feeling especially. They are far from sure of themselves and without the support of loving adults the strangeness of the world frightens them, sometimes terrifies them.

A child who does not feel entirely secure in the love of his parents is bound to suffer from this lack not only at the time but in later life. Many of the adult neurotics who fill psychiatrists' offices are there for this very reason. The child who feels secure and happy in his parents' love, however, is most likely to develop an affectionate nature himself. He knows the joys of both giving and receiving affection.

It is possible, of course, to "spoil" a child by giving him everything and expecting nothing of him in return. It is possible, too, to embarrass him by too ardent and demonstrative show of affection, especially in public. But you can do him far greater harm by loving him too little or by giving him too little assurance of your love. It is almost impossible to show a baby or young child too much love, though they can easily be "smothered" by continual petting and coddling. Then they may become peevish and over-dependent, losing their alert interest in other things. Show your love by sympathetic understanding, care for the child's needs, and interest in his achievements more often than through actual caresses.

Give your child an abundance of love, so that he may never doubt your feelings for him. Then he, in turn, will be able to express, naturally and whole-heartedly, this outgoing emotion which will mean much to his happiness throughout life.

Suggested Reading

Arranged in Order of Interest to Children, from the Younger to the Older Age-Groups

	VOL.	PAGE		VOL.	PAGE
The Story of a Little White Teddy Bear	1	10	Caleb's Luck	2	257
The Shy Little Horse	1	110	Blue Rocking Chair Tells a Story	2	280
Only One Mother	1	197	Beauty and the Beast	3	116
Here Comes Daddy	1	220	Cradle Song	4	225
The Puppy Who Wanted a Boy	1	345	The Christmas Carol	6	165
Little Fox Lost	2	91	The Little Red Princess of the Forest	8	186
Answer to a Child's Question	2	100	The Wanderings of Odysseus	8	229
The Seventh Pup	2	103	Roland	8	319
Karoo, the Kangaroo	2	119	William Tell	8	337
How Bambi Found the Meadow	2	148	The Child of Urbino	9	27

"Affection is the broadest base of good in life."
—GEORGE ELIOT.

ALERTNESS AND ATTENTIVENESS

Alertness: Vigilance; watchfulness; wide-awakeness.
Attentiveness: The state of being observant, heedful; of paying careful attention.

ATTENTIVENESS and alertness help a child to take care of himself in this fast, competitive world. They help him to win at games, to get ahead in school, and to win the battles of later life as well. Whatever your child's future work may be, he will need to be alert and attentive to it, and ready to seize opportunities, to make quick decisions. The race is to the swift, the mental as well as physically fit.

Alertness and attentiveness are necessary for a child's very safety. If a child is inattentive he may not see danger coming. Then when he suddenly wakes up to find himself in a dangerous spot, he may get confused and frightened. One who gets dreamy or absent-minded in traffic, for instance, is in great danger.

A healthy, happy child is usually bright-eyed and alert. If he is imaginative he may day-dream at times, but in action he is interested and observant. Excessive day-dreaming often results from poor health, emotional unhappiness, or lack of mental stimulation. A child needs an interesting world about him to keep him alert and attentive.

Give him love and encouragement. Show him that you are genuinely interested in his affairs—his block-building or his plans for a club. Make a point of taking him to see interesting places and things, of showing him the fascinations of common things. Broaden his interests and keep the spirit of adventure alive.

Some mothers, by a constant stream of directions, actually teach their children to be inattentive. "Do this,—do that,—wash your hands,—come here,—stop that,—etc." In self-defense the child soon learns to ignore it all.

Many a child is accused of inattentiveness, too, because he is very attentive—to his own affairs. He is concentrating deeply. Do not break such concentration unnecessarily if you value attentiveness. If you must interrupt, go to the child, see what he is doing, and share his interest for a moment before you ask him to share yours.

❧ ❧ ❧

Suggested Reading

Arranged in Order of Interest to Children, from the Younger to the Older Age-Groups

	VOL.	PAGE		VOL.	PAGE
The Story of a Little White Dog	1	144	The Farmer in the Dell	4	308
Sneezer	1	154	We'll All Go A-Singing	4	311
The Little Red Lighthouse and The			I'm Very, Very Tall	4	315
Great Gray Bridge	1	165	English Harvesters' Dance	4	320
Champion Fire 'n Feather	2	142	What's Wrong with This Picture?	5	159
Almost an Ambush	2	158	Paul Revere's Ride	6	291
Number 9, the Little Fire Engine	2	173	Learning to Look About You	7	169
Rococo Skates	2	314	The Army of Two	9	119
High Water in Arkansas	2	319	Daniel Boone	9	226
The Tiger, the Brahman, and the Jackal	3	331	Radisson, "The Canadian Ulysses"	9	323
The Melon Eaters	4	48			

"The power of applying attention, alert and steady, to a single object is the sure mark of superior genius." LORD CHESTERFIELD.

APPLICATION AND CONCENTRATION

Application: Careful attention to a task or project.
Concentration: Close mental application and continued exclusive attention.

THE ability to apply himself to his jobs and to concentrate on them will be of the greatest value to any child in his school work and all his subsequent problems. A few minutes of concentration does the work of hours required when the attention falters.

Learning concentration is difficult for young children. Their minds, just awakening to a world of new impressions, are easily diverted. A two-year-old normally attends to one thing for an average of less than a minute. For a five-year-old, five minutes is satisfactory. Yet much development in concentration can occur in these early years.

Help your child develop it by giving him play materials with many possible uses. Show him an interesting new possibility when he is about to throw the toy down. Thus his attention is held a moment longer each time. He learns that it is fun to investigate thoroughly. Use his interest in imitation and in helping you to show him the satisfactions of a job well done—and appreciated.

These are the steps in teaching a child to work at a task and finish it:

First, choose a task that will give him satisfaction, one that he really wants to do.

Second, choose something that will not be too hard or too long for him.

Third, choose a time when he is wide awake, alert, eager, not at all tired.

When he has finished, join him in admiring what he has done. Praise his effort and his persistence. Then, as he tackles harder tasks, encourage him to finish what he starts.

Do not be discouraged if he does not always do so. Do you always persevere? Are there not, in fact, some jobs that turn out differently from what we expect, and *ought* to be abandoned? The point is not chiefly to finish everything—that might be just stubbornness. It is rather to work hard and concentrate while you are working.

So see that when he studies or works at any enterprise he has as few distractions as possible. One can concentrate in the midst of distractions after he has learned how, but it is much easier when there are no distractions such as the radio, other children at play, noises, or other interests.

Suggested Reading

Arranged in Order of Interest to Children, from the Younger to the Older Age-Groups

	VOL.	PAGE
How Doth the Busy Little Bee	1	192
Try Again	1	206
Kentucky Birthday	2	97
The Seventh Pup	2	103
Caleb's Luck	2	257
The Brownies	3	226
The Maid in the Mirror	3	307
The Blue Boy	4	55
Cross Word Puzzles	5	171
The Little Mother's Work Basket	5	213

	VOL.	PAGE
Good Pictures and How They Are Made	5	337
Bible Curiosities and Memory Tests	7	323
An Inventor's Boyhood	9	10
The Child of Urbino	9	27
The Boyhood of a President	9	56
Madame Curie	9	107
Patrick Henry	9	170
Sir John A. MacDonald	9	342

"Application and concentration are essential for success in any undertaking."
—ANDREW CARNEGIE.

APPRECIATION AND GRATITUDE

Appreciation: A favorable critical estimate; esteem and the expression thereof.

Gratitude: Thankfulness; appreciation of benefits, favors, etc.

ONE who feels truly appreciative of other people's qualities and of what is done for him, and who expresses that feeling with sincerity and charm, is certain to be popular throughout his life. People will *like* to do things for him because they know that their kindnesses are truly appreciated. The appreciation must, of course, be genuine. A parrot-like "thank you" may be mere habit. But a real feeling brightens the character and wins friends.

We all recognize the pure pleasure to be had from the appreciation of art and music. We try to be sure that our children learn to enjoy them. But the field is far wider than that. All beauty, all goodness, all lovely things, are to be appreciated, enjoyed, and loved. A spirit sensitive to beauty has the inner joys of the poet or artist even if they are never expressed in works of art. "As a man thinketh in his heart, so is he," and one cannot do better than to follow the Biblical injunction:

"Whatsoever things are true, whatsoever things are honest, whatsoever things are just, whatsoever things are pure, whatsoever things are lovely, whatsoever things are of good report; if there be any virtue, and if there be any praise, *think on these things.*"

Children respond easily to pretty things: a shining pebble or a friendly smile. Call their attention to pleasant things. There is no need to be sentimental about it! It is enough to say, "Oh look!", "Listen to that!", "How good this tastes!" or "How kind of her to do that!"

When we appreciate what someone has done for us, we feel gratitude. Children can easily be taught to express it not only in words, but in returning the kindness. Let this be done not as a duty or obligation, but for the pleasure of giving pleasure.

Teach your child appreciation and gratitude for all the kind and lovely things of life, the simple and common as well as the great. Having a "thankful heart" will come as near guaranteeing his happiness as any one thing can.

Suggested Reading

Arranged in Order of Interest to Children, from the Younger to the Older Age-Groups

	VOL.	PAGE		VOL.	PAGE
The Barnyard	1	126	My Lord Bag of Rice	3	310
My Scottie	1	136	Horatius at the Bridge	6	107
How Spot Found a Home	1	141	Decoration Day Ode	6	304
I'm Glad	1	203	The First Thanksgiving Day	6	305
The Wonderful World	1	203	Beowulf	8	273
The Tongue-cut Sparrow	1	324	The Boy Who Was Helped	9	13
The Goose That Laid the Golden Egg	2	10	Clara Barton	9	113
The Lion and the Mouse	2	13	Lafayette, Friend of America	9	209
Such a Kind World	2	137	The Mayo Brothers	9	282
Waukewa's Eagle	2	244	Grenfell's Sermon in Deeds	9	377
How the Good Gifts Were Used by Two	3	282			

"A thankful heart is not only the greatest virtue, but the parent of all other virtues."
—CICERO.

ASPIRATION

Longing or desire to attain something lofty, great, or noble.

"HIGH AIMS form high characters," said Tryon Edwards. Robert Browning had the same idea when he said, " 'Tis not what man does which exalts him, but what he would do."

A person's aspirations are the guiding stars of his life. Never cloud these stars for your child by either scorn of their worth or doubt of their attainability. By steadfast devotion to his aspirations and by faith in their possibility many a man has lifted himself to seemingly impossible heights.

Ambition may have a cheap or vulgar objective, but aspiration always has a high goal. Yet the two are closely related. Most boys at one time or another want to be firemen, aviators, detectives, or sailors. Most girls think of being actresses or nurses. To them these are lofty ideals. *Never* make fun of your child's aspirations, whether he declares he will be a cowboy or a famous painter. Never mind if his objective seems to you unworthy or fantastically impossible.

Instead of laughing, comment on the fine qualities involved, the courage, devotion, insight, and skill. To these he may well *aspire*. Your admiration of them will help him to set them as goals for himself. He will still want to be brave, long after he has outgrown wanting to be a fireman.

All children have their aspirations. Like most of their other attitudes, they are strongly influenced by parents and home. They admire what they see admired. Often children want to be just like a beloved parent. Later they choose models from a wider field, some man or woman they know and admire, a famous person, living or dead, a national hero, or even some noble fictional character.

Take your child's aspirations seriously. Encourage them and show your faith in him. Talk cheerfully but seriously with him about the qualities he will need in achieving them. Discuss simple things he can begin to do at once to prepare himself. Praise progress. Aspirations that never get into action are weak things.

Above all, do not try to impose your own aspirations on your child. Every man must choose his own. A child's will usually change often as he grows. Join him in admiring and working toward the best qualities of each as it appears. He will learn much, including how to choose ever more worthy purposes to which to aspire.

Suggested Reading

Arranged in Order of Interest to Children, from the Younger to the Older Age-Groups

	VOL.	PAGE		VOL.	PAGE
Little by Little	1	199	The Great Stone Face	6	105
A Child's Letter to God	1	379	Pilgrim's Progress	6	134
What Do We Plant?	2	85	King Arthur and His Knights	6	265
The Christmas Apple	2	333	A Vision of the Future	6	300
The Ugly Duckling	3	77	A Psalm of Life	6	326
Princess Finola and the Dwarf	3	181	The New Year	6	330
The Princess on the Glass Hill	3	205	The Story of Bede	8	369
The Boyhood of Sir Walter Raleigh	4	18	The Boyhood of a Musician	9	48
St. Elizabeth	4	105	Joan of Arc	9	93
Beethoven and Mozart	4	199	William Penn	9	178

"The very fruit of the gospel is aspiration. It is to the heart what spring is to the earth, making every root and bud and bough desire to be more."
                                                              —HENRY WARD BEECHER.

CAUTION AND PRUDENCE

Attention to warnings and safeguards against danger. Examination of possible consequences of words and deeds. Care and skill in the management of practical affairs.

MANY unfortunate, even tragic, incidents could have been avoided. They would not have happened except for someone's ignorance, carelessness or recklessness. How many lives and how much damage could be spared by everyone's being habitually cautious and prudent!

Most children are neither cautious or prudent, partly through ignorance of danger, partly through the optimism natural to healthy youth. There are cautious children, of course, timid and fearful ones whose need is chiefly more faith in the world and in themselves. When we think of both types we see that what we need to teach is caution without fear, prudence without mean suspicion. It is not an easy line to draw.

Of course when the child is very small, it is the mother's business to protect him from danger. She needs to know and use good safety practices in the home. But the child is unconscious of this. His education in caution begins when he does encounter things which may hurt him.

Many mothers teach cowardice by their continual warnings of danger or else the children find out that they are *not* hurt by the threatened danger and thenceforth disregard warnings. They become reckless. Don't keep your child out of the water. Teach him to swim. Don't forbid him to climb. Teach him to do it safely. He must learn to rely on himself to recognize danger and to meet it. You will not always be there to warn or protect him. He will take pride in knowing where risks lie and how to guard against them.

In discussing dangers, do so in a matter-of-fact way with no warnings of horrible possibilities, especially in talking to a sensitive child. It is enough to warn of immediate pain or discomfort. That influences a child much more than the fear of future handicaps. Gruesome details make bad dreams, but not caution.

A child can be taught not only to keep safe in his common activities, but to have the habit of approaching the unfamiliar with reasonable caution. It really is a dangerous world we live in, yet it is better for a child to be hurt occasionally than to become timid. The thing to do is not to shrink back, but to go ahead slowly and "watch your step" with senses alert. It can have all the charm of playing scouts and Indians!

Then there are habits which the children can learn and practice for the safety of others as well as themselves. What importance they feel when they can demonstrate them, perhaps protect a younger child or teach him "the right way"! That applies to crossing streets, picking up things which might otherwise be "booby traps" to trip over, carrying knives and scissors with the points down, and endless similar matters.

Caution can be developed without undue fear by making the child competent to recognize and deal with hazard. He will rejoice in his competence. "It's smart to play safe!"

Keen senses, muscles well under control, inquiring mind, thoughtfulness, and habitual caution and prudence are the best safety devices.

Suggested Reading

Arranged in Order of Interest to Children, from the Younger to the Older Age-Groups

	VOL.	PAGE		VOL.	PAGE
The Story of a Little White Teddy Bear	1	10	Almost an Ambush	2	158
The Three Bears	1	67	Indians in the House	2	274
Little Red Riding Hood	1	77	Snow White and the Seven Dwarfs	3	33
The Tale of Peter Rabbit	1	97	The Sweet Porridge	3	49
Timid Timothy	1	104	The Tiger, the Brahman, and the Jackal	3	331
The Ant and the Grasshopper	2	3	Woodwork for Older Children	5	269
The Country Maid and Her Milk Pail	2	4	Pinocchio	6	55
The City Mouse and the Country Mouse	2	12	The Wanderings of Odysseus	8	229
How Bambi Found the Meadow	2	48	The Adventures of Jacques Cartier	9	315

"Fortunate is he whom the dangers of others have rendered cautious."
—LATIN PROVERB.

CHEERFULNESS AND OPTIMISM

Cheerfulness: The quality of being joyous, ungrudging, hearty.
Optimism: An inclination to put the most favorable construction upon happenings, to anticipate the best possible outcome.

A CHEERFUL and optimistic disposition is so obviously a desirable trait that it scarcely needs emphasis. Optimism routs many groundless fears and worries. A firm belief that things will turn out for the best dispels many unwarranted fears. Cheerful people are popular because they brighten the lives of others and make their burdens seem lighter. They are truly like rays of sunshine because of the lift and cheer they bring into a drab scene.

Cheerfulness and optimism are much to be desired in our children. But you cannot make a child cheerful or optimistic by telling him to be so. Nor can you do it by showing the false and foolish "Pollyanna" type of cheerfulness yourself.

A child's natural cheerfulness rests upon good health and faith in his parents' love. Give your child smiles and sympathetic understanding. Be cheerful and fundamentally optimistic yourself. Then, if you keep the child healthy in body and spirit, he will probably fall into the family pattern.

Children like to laugh and be happy. See that they have something to be really happy about. It takes little to delight them, a word of praise, a little joke or a bit of nonsense, a game, a song, a pretty shell, or a simple toy.

Naturally, you cannot expect a hurt, worried, or frightened child to be cheerful without help. When there is pain or disappointment to bear, show sympathy but not discouragement. Help the child to look beyond his troubles. It will not last forever. "Tomorrow we shall be having fun again." Even at the moment there is a silver lining to be found somewhere, something pleasant that one can still do or think about. Find it for him. Call on imagination, or even a little nonsense, to lift you both right over the hurt. He will soon learn the trick himself.

Anyone can be cheerful when everything is going well, but real optimism goes deeper than that. Your love, courage, and ingenuity can build it in your child. He will enjoy the good times wholeheartedly and will know how to face bad ones with courage for the present and faith in the future. That is optimism.

Suggested Reading

Arranged in Order of Interest to Children, from the Younger to the Older Age-Groups

	VOL.	PAGE		VOL.	PAGE
Johnny Chuck Finds the Best Thing in the World	1	138	What the Old Man Does is Always Right	3	110
Singing	1	181	The Old Woman and the Tramp	3	190
Happy Thought	1	184	The Light-Hearted Fairy	3	224
Laughing Song	1	198	The Magic Fishbone	3	242
I'm Glad	1	203	Jingle Bells	4	298
Who Likes the Rain?	1	212	The Story of Pippa	6	74
The Ice-Cream Man	1	238	Robin Hood	8	282
The First Day at School	1	248	A Jest of Little John	8	290
Mr. Scrunch	2	36	The Girlhood of a Singer	9	50
The Peterkin Papers	2	180	Johnny Appleseed	9	136
			Captain Robert A. Bartlett	9	293

"Wondrous is the strength of cheerfulness and its power of endurance. The cheerful man will do more in the same time, will do it better, will persevere in it longer, than the sad or sullen." —THOMAS CARLYLE.

CLEANLINESS AND HEALTH

Cleanliness: Freedom from dirt; purity.
Health: State of being sound in body, mind, and spirit; wholesome, energetic, and free of disease or pain.

CLEANLINESS is not only next to godliness; it is also an important factor in general health, physical, mental, and emotional. "A sound mind in a sound body" is as good a prescription today as it ever was.

Cleanliness, however, is something children have to learn, for most young children seem to love to get thoroughly dirty. This is perfectly natural and nothing to be in the least worried about. They equally enjoy dabbling in water, however, and this is a pleasure which mothers can make much of in teaching cleanliness.

Many of our attitudes toward things in later life depend on how they were introduced to us in childhood. So it is important to have the child enjoy his introduction to necessary habits. Let him dabble his hands in a basin of water. To him that is fun. Let him do all he can about washing himself. These things help him take kindly to cleanliness. If we want to keep his attitude toward getting clean pleasant, we must be patient, no matter how clumsy or slow he is at first. If we keep on making cleanliness a pleasure, he will enjoy cleaning up the bowl and tub, as well as himself, by the time he is about five years old.

You must expect his habit of cleanliness to have lapses later. It bores most school-age children to make themselves clean and neat, to wash before meals, brush teeth, comb hair, and so on. This is natural, too. Do not undo the good work you have done in early childhood by nagging your child about cleanliness when he gets to the older "don't care" stage. A certain amount of dirt is far healthier than a neurosis about cleanliness.

Habits of cleanliness, firmly but casually enforced, will finally have their effect. Many children considered "incurably careless" suddenly show interest in keeping clean and neat. This often happens at the "teen age" when they become very eager to make a good impression.

Parents should show a clean, healthy attitude toward life and its functions, toward people and ideas, and a frank approach to all the child's problems in growing up. Thus they may give the child an all-around attitude of wholesome cleanliness. That is one of the bases of mental and emotional as well as physical good health.

⚘ ⚘ ⚘

Suggested Reading

Arranged in Order of Interest to Children, from the Younger to the Older Age-Groups

	VOL.	PAGE		VOL.	PAGE
Little Bear Takes His Nap	1	4	Outdoor Games and Sports	7	241
Before a Bath	1	219	Physical Fitness	7	343
After a Bath	1	219	Gymnastic Plays	7	336
The Good Little Bad Little Pig	1	233	First Aid	7	362
The Happy Cure	2	60	A Little Dutch Boy and Girl of Old		
The Family Who Never Had Roller			New York	8	198
Skates	2	271	Clara Barton	9	113
Five Peas in a Pod	3	82	Theodore Roosevelt	9	268
An Interior	4	88	The Mayo Brothers	9	282
Mother's Cooking School	5	195			

"Health is the most admirable manifestation of clean living."
—F. H. A. HUMBOLDT.

CONFIDENCE

Assurance, the state of feeling sure.

CONFIDENCE in himself and in others is a great emotional stabilizer in a child's development. It improves his chances of success in whatever he undertakes and removes one of the greatest causes of failure—the very fear of failure.

In this unpredictable world, confidence is a most useful asset. There are inevitably many situations and undertakings which we face with alarm, especially in childhood. In such cases, a timid child may give up and run away. A vain and egotistical child may bluff and bluster. But a confident child will size up the situation, prepare himself as well as possible, and then tackle it with a determination to succeed, or at least to make a good try. If he fails, he can be helped to understand why, so that his basic faith in himself is not shaken. He is then better prepared to succeed the next time.

A child needs not only self-confidence but confidence in other people. This should not be a blind idea that there is no cruelty, dishonesty, or selfishness in the world. It should rather be faith that most people are, on the whole, pretty decent and will justify the trust you put in them.

Confidence breeds loyalty as surely as suspicion breeds deceit and fear.

Parents should help their children to have confidence in their school and their teachers. Neither may be perfect. The parents may be working for improvements. But meantime the children, if filled with distrust, will fail to make gains as they should. In the same way, confidence is the basis of successful relations with neighbors.

Cultivate reasonable self-confidence in your children beginning at a very early age. Their confidence springs from your faith in them and their ability, and from successful achievement. Do not expect too much of them. A child should succeed most of the time, and he can if his undertakings are on the right level. They should be things he feels are important and worth-while, yet should be within his abilities. Even so, he will, and *should,* fail occasionally. Thus he will know his limitations and learn constructive ways of facing failure.

So confidence grows gradually, along with strength and skill. The child has confidence because he knows what he can do. It is not vanity, but reasonable, justified self-confidence.

❧ ❧ ❧

Suggested Reading

Arranged in Order of Interest to Children, from the Younger to the Older Age-Groups

	VOL.	PAGE		VOL.	PAGE
Timid Timothy	1	104	A Nurse's Childhood	9	6
How the Little Kite Learned To Fly	1	206	An Inventor's Boyhood	9	10
Pino and Paint	2	109	The Boyhood of a Statesman	9	10
How Bambi Found the Meadow	2	148	The Boyhood of a Sculptor	9	23
His First Bronc	2	155	The Boyhood of a President	9	56
Be Strong	6	325	Susan B. Anthony	9	102
The New World	8	170	George Washington	9	191
Perseus	8	221	Andrew Jackson	9	230
Siegfried	8	308	Theodore Roosevelt	9	268
Bonnie Prince Charlie	8	389	Lord Nelson, Admiral of the Seas	9	304

"Self-confidence is the first requisite to great undertakings."
—SAMUEL JOHNSON.

"Confidence begets confidence."
—PROVERB.

CONSCIENCE

Sense of the moral goodness or blameworthiness of one's own conduct, intentions, or character, together with a feeling of obligation to do right or be good.

O F THAT "still, small voice" within us which we call conscience, a great writer once said, "It is so delicate that it is easy to stifle it, but it is also so clear that is is impossible to mistake it," and another adds, "A good conscience is to the soul what health is to the body."

Those two quotations express what, in our hearts, we all know; that no rewards or punishments from outside can ever have the meaning or force of what our own consciences tell us about ourselves. A well-disciplined conscience, therefore, is the best friend we can have throughout life. Without it we shall find neither tranquillity of mind nor peace of soul.

But how teach this to our children? A baby has no sense of right or wrong and consequently no conscience. He knows merely, as he grows, that some of his actions are pleasing to his mother and others displeasing. Thus he forms a standard by which he tests whatever he wants to do.

First, then, a mother must be sure to show pleasure at the truly good things her child does or tries to do, not merely at those which happen to suit her convenience. Babies often cause trouble when they are only trying to help.

Gradually, however, as the child is ready for the responsibility, she should let him be his own judge of the rightness of his actions and desires.

It must be only in matters where he already has an accepted standard to measure by: "Is that kind?" "Is it fair?"

Above all, do not make him feel guilty if he fails. Judging and controlling our own acts is difficult enough for adults; remember always how much harder it must be for a child. Be patient and forgiving. Do not expect perfection.

Be the best example you possibly can to your child. Point out to him what is right, and see that you conform to it in your own actions. Remember that before adolescence the child's ability to distinguish between right and wrong is just forming and needs guidance—but gentle guidance, please!

With adolescene, conscience becomes very keen. The child already has his standards of truth, honesty, and so on, though he may need tactful help in developing those related to his new problems. On the whole it is a time of high ideals and lofty purposes. Go on setting the best example you can, but do not try any longer to force your standards on your children. During this time they will develop the conscience to go forth and battle for their own ideas of what is right. Encourage them, help them, and strengthen their moral fiber by the example of your integrity. And wish them Godspeed. That will be the best you can do.

Suggested Reading

Arranged in Order of Interest to Children, from the Younger to the Older Age-Groups

	VOL.	PAGE		VOL.	PAGE
Prayer for Children Everywhere	1	380	The Recessional	6	297
Indians in the House	2	274	The Story of Frithiof	8	297
The Selfish Giant	3	150	The Iliad of Homer	8	353
How Indian Corn Came to the World	3	354	Edwin and the King of the North	8	366
Moses	4	150	The Child of Urbino	9	27
The Two Natures	4	160	The Pilgrims and the Puritans	9	157
The Story of Pippa	6	74	William Penn	9	178
The Pilgrim's Progress	6	134	Abraham Lincoln, Who Saved the Union	9	244
Dorigen	6	150	Robert E. Lee	9	250
The Christmas Carol	6	165	A Black-Robed Voyageur	9	336

"We cannot live better than in seeking to become better, nor more agreeably than in having a clear conscience." —SENECA.

CONTENTMENT

The state of being satisfied with what one has.

THE real spirit of contentment, in adulthood, comes from a deeply satisfied emotional and spiritual life. It is a quality all too rarely seen in a generation where everybody seems to be striving for more and more of the world's goods, more money, more luxury, more power. Blest indeed are the rare few who find contentment in the satisfaction of emotional fulfillment and spiritual peace.

Children often become discontented because they have too much—too many toys, too great and too luxurious a variety of diversions, too many and too stimulating forms of entertainment. these are confusing to a child and tend only to make him want still more, partly in bewilderment, partly in tyranny. That is, a child who gets a new toy "to quiet him" every time he tires of an old one soon learns that throwing away toys is a good way of getting attention. Childlike, he will use this means of tyrannizing over his parents as long as it works.

Wise parents will try to keep a child's toys few and simple. A baby will enjoy an old or homemade toy quite as much as an expensive new one.

If a child grows up discontented, it is usually because the spirit of the home is one of worldly ambition and dissatisfaction. A mother who is constantly saying "I wish we had this" or "I wish we could afford that" or "I wish your father had a better position or made more money" is certain to have this attitude reflected in discontented children.

In other homes children learn to enjoy and be thankful for beautiful, common things like a sunny morning, a starry night, or a colorful flower garden. The beauty of great music, art, and literature, too, is now available to everyone as never before. But still deeper contentment arises from the love and devotion which bind all members of the group together into a happy family. In homes where these things are emphasized, the children are likely to grow up joyously contented with what they have.

Contentment, after all, comes from within. No amount of external luxuries can give it to us. If we do not find it within ourselves, we shall never find it anywhere else. We shall do well to prove this to our children by our own spirit.

❧ ❧ ❧

Suggested Reading

Arranged in Order of Interest to Children, from the Younger to the Older Age-Groups

	VOL.	PAGE		VOL.	PAGE
The Bear Who Wanted to Be a Bird	1	102	How the Good Gifts Were Used by Two	2	282
The Land of Counterpane	1	190	The Fisherman and His Wife	3	20
The House the Pecks Built	1	270	What the Old Man Does is Always		
900 Buckets of Paint	1	302	Right	3	110
A Little Fish Story	1	328	The Apple of Contentment	3	271
The Goose That Laid the Golden Egg	2	10	The Wishing Ring	3	279
The City Mouse and the Country Mouse	2	12	Hashnu, the Stonecutter	3	315
No Room	2	42	The Story of the Bluebird	6	122
Never Worked and Never Will	2	76	The Mountain and the Squirrel	6	324
Johnny Chuck Finds the Best Thing in			The Barefoot Boy	6	335
the World	2	138	The Girlhood of a Singer	9	50

"The contented man is never poor; the discontented never rich."
—GEORGE ELIOT.

COOPERATION AND TEAMWORK

Acting jointly with another or others for a common purpose.

ALL MEMBERS of the family must work together for the good of all to make a harmonious, smoothly running household. It takes only one uncooperative member to weaken the whole seriously. The same is true of other undertakings, from games to industry and the professions—from a small club meeting to the great United Nations.

Because cooperation is so important, children should learn early to share in the family routines. This does not mean merely giving them tasks to do, for no one likes to do work without understanding why. Explain the goal to your child and get him interested in it. Show him that everybody needs to pull together to reach it. Make him see that his part is important, that the rest of the family is depending on his help.

Children love to feel wanted, to know that they are an important and necessary part of the group. Use this fact to encourage cooperation. Like so many other good habits, cooperation and teamwork should begin in the home.

Be careful not to expect more of your child than he is both able and willing to do. He will do more if he can take part in the planning as well as the carrying out of any project. He himself will see where he can help.

He must learn, too, that in a good, democratic team, or family, no one person stars all the time or always "bosses the job." Other children will help to teach him this with their scorn of a "grandstand player." They demand that a player should pass on an opportunity to the team-mate who can best use it for the good of the team. This is hard for an eager, self-confident child to do, but recognition of his good sportsmanship helps. And it helps when others do the same for him. So be sure that you yourself "pass him the ball" at times and do not dominate the group too constantly.

When your children are very young they are so eager to help that they will usually take directions easily. They accept you naturally as the leader, and their reward is your appreciation.

As they grow older and more self-assertive, you must be more tactful to get cooperation. Ask, suggest, and consult them rather than directing or commanding. Sometimes get the whole family working on things the children want done. In this way they see the benefits of cooperation.

In adolescence children often cooperate better outside the family than in. Do not be alarmed or resentful. The main problem of this period is learning to get along with their contemporaries, and that is very important. The boy or girl who "has no time" to help at home, is probably cooperating feverishly with the football team or the dramatics club. He is learning a valuable kind of teamwork. By and by he will be able to cooperate in both kinds of situations.

Suggested Reading

Arranged in Order of Interest to Children, from the Younger to the Older Age-Groups

	VOL.	PAGE
The Little Red Hen and the Grain of Wheat	1	84
Belling the Cat	2	6
The Bundle of Sticks	2	19
Mr. A and Mr. P	2	196
When the Mail Came Through	2	376
The Musicians of Bremen	3	45
The Husband Who Minded the House	3	174
The Brownies	3	226
The Five Queer Brothers	3	318
The Farmer in the Dell	4	308

	VOL.	PAGE
German Clap Dance	4	322
Swedish Clap Dance	4	323
I See You	4	325
The Three Little Kittens	4	331
The Wishing Carpet	6	19
Outdoor Games and Sports	7	241
Amundsen, Discoverer of the South Pole	8	213
Madame Curie	9	107
The Story of the Boston Tea Party	9	121
The Signers of the Declaration of Independence	9	181

"United we stand; divided we fall."
—JOHN DICKINSON.

COURAGE
(Physical and Moral)

That strength of character which equips one to meet and endure danger, adversity and suffering resolutely.

COURAGE being among the most admired of human characteristics, we all want our children to have it.

There are two kinds of courage, physical and moral. Physical bravery comes first. A child can begin quite early to learn to bear his small bumps and scratches bravely. Mother helps if she makes no undue fuss about them. Too much sympathy is alarming, for it convinces him that he is badly hurt.

It is hard for a child to cooperate in having his hurts cleaned and dressed. He cannot understand the necessity and he knows it will be painful. Be gentle, patient, and quick about it. Tell him honestly whether it will hurt; but encourage him that the pain will soon be over and by assurance that he is a brave child who can bear it. Praise every evidence of courage.

Physical courage involves also the ability to face physical danger. Some children are afraid to climb, to venture into the water, afraid of the dark, and so on. It may be because of over-cautious parents, native timidity, or other reasons. At any rate they must get over it if they are to be respected by their fellows. Courage cannot be forced. It must be learned by very gradually increasing *happy* contacts with the thing feared. Parents can use much ingenuity in making pleasant associations.

Some other children are courageous to the point of recklessness. They need to be protected while being taught caution. Do not try to keep such a child from adventures. Rather teach him how to do safely the things he wants to do. Make him proud of his "know-how."

Moral courage develops later than physical. It is the resolution to do and say what one considers right regardless of consequent unpopularity or even suffering. It springs from a strong sense of right and justice and faith in one's own ability to endure hardships. It will operate as soon as the voice of conscience means more to the child than public approval or the avoidance of pain. It needs to be tempered by cooperation, tact, and tolerance, lest it develop into self-righteousness.

The question of fighting is closely tied up with courage, at least in the popular mind. We want neither cowardice nor over-aggressiveness in our children. But we might as well recognize that all normal children do a certain amount of fighting, and certain ages seem to be naturally more aggressive than others. One can see that children fight fairly, use no dangerous weapons, and do not bully weaker children. And at each step, one can show them a little better way to settle differences. It is even possible, as they grow older, to help them understand when it is right to fight and when not. Finally they will understand exchanges, compromises, arbitration, and obedience to established law or justice.

If a child develops physical courage and prowess backed by moral courage, he will have a fine double-barreled weapon for winning the battles of life.

Suggested Reading

Arranged in Order of Interest to Children, from the Younger to the Older Age-Groups

	VOL.	PAGE		VOL.	PAGE
Timid Timothy	1	104	The Friends of the Indians	8	206
The Story of a Little White Dog	1	144	William Tell	8	337
The Horse That Came from Heaven	2	125	A Courageous Boy Who Became President	9	72
Pony Penning Day	2	172	Joan of Arc	9	93
Waukewa's Eagle	2	244	Helen Keller	9	110
Elizabeth Ann Fails in an Examination	2	304	The Story of Molly Pitcher	9	133
High Water in Arkansas	2	319	The Western Pioneer	9	240
To Your Good Health	3	212	Marguerite de Roberval	9	320
Horatius at the Bridge	6	107	The Story of Madeleine de Verchères	9	325
Wee Willie Winkie	6	179			
The New World	8	170			

"True courage is not the brutal force of vulgar heroes, but the firm resolve of virtue and reason." —ALFRED N. WHITEHEAD.

COURTESY, POLITENESS AND MANNERS

Behavior marked by good breeding, tact, and consideration for others.

COURTESY, politeness, and manners, and the greatest of these is courtesy! Courtesy is, essentially, simple consideration for the comforts and convenience of others. Politeness and manners are the practice of special little courteous customs which have become traditional. Manners without courtesy are insincere and empty. Courtesy without manners is sincere and kind, but may be clumsy. The three together are like good oil in the social machinery. They make things run smoothly and pleasantly.

Every mother wants her child to show courtesy and good manners because she knows they will win him friends and make his life more pleasant and gracious.

Politeness and manners are matters of information and habit. They are the garments in which courtesy is suitably clothed. These little forms which generations of people have found pleasant to use all originated in true courtesy. they are not to be scorned. Any child, or adult, will be the more welcome, and will feel the more at ease for the habit of using them.

Like most habits, they are learned largely by imitation. Baby picks up "thank you" as he does any other word, and he soon finds that it brings special smiles. Help your children to make politeness habitual so that it seems as natural as eating with a fork. They will often forget, yet when they particularly want to be gracious they will not feel clumsy or inept. And when they forget, do not nag. That brings resentment and so destroys true courtesy, the incentive to good manners.

Courtesy is a matter of the heart. To teach it you must set a consistent example of consideration, thoughtfulness, and kindness. It must be the expected standard of living in the family and outside. If a child has grown up in such a home, impoliteness seems obviously ugly to him.

It will probably take many years for your child to outgrow occasional outbursts of rebellion, bad temper, and uncivilized behavior. All of them are natural, and it requires adult control fully to overcome them at all times. Do not expect too much of him for his age and stage of development. Just surround him with an atmosphere of natural, everyday courtesy and consideration. The child who develops a friendly, loving spirit will have the basis for the best forms of courtesy.

❊ ❊ ❊

Suggested Reading

Arranged in Order of Interest to Children, from the Younger to the Older Age-Groups

	VOL.	PAGE		VOL.	PAGE
The Three Bears	1	67	The Princess Whom Nobody Could Silence	3	178
The Barnyard	1	126	How the Good Gifts Were Used by Two	3	282
Child's Grace	1	377	The Barmecide's Feast	6	26
Let Our Home be a Friendly Home	1	380	Getting Up a Party	7	235
The Golden Rule	1	383	The Fine Art of Living Together	7	237
The Country Maid and Her Milk Pail	2	4	The Boyhood of a Patriot	9	15
The Fox and the Stork	2	9	The Boyhood of a President	9	56
The Dog in the Manger	2	16	The Story of Nathan Hale	9	126
The Baker's Daughter	2	192	William Penn	9	178
Toads and Diamonds	3	147	Sir Walter Raleigh	9	297

"All doors are open to courtesy."
—THOMAS FULLER.

DEMOCRATIC SPIRIT

Tolerance of and respect for the rights and opinions of others.
Belief in and practice of equality of opportunity for all.
Opposition to snobbery and social exclusiveness.

ANYONE with a truly democratic spirit feels sure of his own worth and integrity while respecting the rights of others. Therefore he can meet everyone on terms of equality without either patronizing or fawning. That is the spirit of a free and kindly person, the spirit on which our American way of life is based. If we want that way of life to survive, we must cultivate the democratic spirit in our children.

It is not hard to do, for children, if left to themselves, are far more democratic than their elders. What people wear, what they know or have, where they live, what their race, creed, or color may be—these things matter little if at all to children. We must be careful that we do not ourselves *give* them prejudices, for most of us, try as we may, do have some. Children are so sensitive and alert that no open criticism is needed. They can catch prejudice from the tone of voice in speaking of some class of people, from a subtle dig, or even a raised eyebrow.

We must remember to teach our children that people are to be judged as individuals, never as members of a particular race, religious group, and so on. There are fine, honest, intelligent people (and some dishonest and unworthy ones) in *every* group.

Parents who do not let their children associate with some supposedly inferior group do them no kindness. On the contrary, they are depriving them of the great American privilege of choosing their companions on the sensible basis of congeniality of interests. A child should meet "all kinds" on terms of equality so that he will not consider himself either inferior or superior.

Your child will probably choose some friends who seem undesirable to you, perhaps rough or vulgar. Do not forbid them. Show that you appreciate their good qualities, their loyalty to a friend, humor, initiative, or whatever it may be. Make them welcome in your home. There you can supervise the play tactfully and win their friendship. In that setting your own child will realize when manners are lacking. The other child will see the difference, too, and may learn things that will help him. Thus, you solve your problem and give another child a helping hand too.

If you try to separate your child from what you consider undesirable friends they will have all the lure of forbidden fruit to him. If he is allowed to learn by experience, while you protect him from serious consequences in his mistakes, unworthy friends will be dropped when he sees through them. In the end he will choose companions like him in character and interests.

The home is the strongest influence in a child's life. Make your home the kind where everyone is equally important and where all are consulted on family matters. That lays the foundation for a democratic spirit.

Suggested Reading

Arranged in Order of Interest to Children, from the Younger to the Older Age-Groups

	VOL.	PAGE		VOL.	PAGE
The Camel and the Pig	2	21	William Penn	9	178
All Mutt	2	129	Benjamin Franklin	9	198
The 500 Hats of Bartholomew Cubbins	2	210	Lafayette	9	209
Fung's Fourth	2	298	Thomas Jefferson, Writer of the Declaration of Independence	9	217
Willie's Good Recess	2	301			
Hiawatha's Childhood	3	352	Abraham Lincoln, Who Saved the Union	9	244
The Peace Pipe	3	353	Woodrow Wilson	9	272
For A' That and A' That	6	326	Alfred E. Smith	9	284
How Cincinnatus Saved Rome	8	271	Wendell L. Willkie	9	286
Susan B. Anthony	9	102	Sir John A. MacDonald	9	342
Jane Addams	9	105			

"By the law of God, given by Him to humanity, all men are free, are equal, and are brothers."
—GIUSEPPI MAZZINI.

DIGNITY AND RESERVE

Self-restraint in one's speech and bearing. Quiet and natural observance of the proprieties of conduct. A quality of character which permits warmth and friendliness but not over-effusiveness.

DIGNITY AND RESERVE are qualities associated with good breeding everywhere. Natural dignity and reserve spring from a sense of one's own and other people's worth, and so are found in people of all ranks. True dignity means behavior that is appropriate and in good taste. Stiffness and formality do not make dignity; they are often only ridiculous. One may be dignified and reserved and at the same time warm and friendly. People who gush and chatter, gossip, and behave conspicuously in public are not respected or genuinely popular with any but their own kind, and not always with them.

Now of course one of the most delightful things about babies is their complete lack of dignity and reserve. Like little animals, they go directly after what they need or want with no thought of accepted codes of behavior. Charming as this may be in a baby, undignified behavior is anything but charming in an adult.

Reserve must be learned gradually as the child grows up. He must be taught that one does not say everything he thinks, and that many things are discussed only with the family.

As your children grow into adolescence you may be startled by their noisy, conspicuous behavior. It is merely a clumsy attempt to win the approval of their fellows, and it will pass as they learn better ways. At this same time, in fact, there is an opposite tendency,—one to reserve, a sort of shyness caused by their awakening interest in their own personalities. They have new problems of growth and development to solve. They may want to think them out without talking much about them.

Do not prod or pry or intrude. Let them have the dignity of privacy, if they want it. You keep yours. This should not in any way imply unfriendliness. On the contrary, it is at this time in their lives that they most need parental warmth and emotional dependability. But they are coming to understand the meaning of reserve and may respect, admire, and imitate it in their parents.

Try to help them steer a center course between too much dignity and too little. Never let the emotional atmosphere get chilly. It is far better to sacrifice dignity and reserve than friendship and love. But it is quite possible to have both. This is the ideal toward which to strive.

Suggested Reading

Arranged in Order of Interest to Children, from the Younger to the Older Age-Groups

	VOL.	PAGE		VOL.	PAGE
The Shy Little Horse	1	110	Going to Work	4	131
The Talkative Tortoise	1	331	Ploughing in Acadia	4	142
The Dog Who Chose a Prince	2	114	Tennyson Calls on Carlyle	4	207
The Cloth Merchants	4	27	The Village Blacksmith	6	96
Marie de' Medici	4	41	Patrick Henry	9	170
The Blue Boy	4	54	William Penn	9	178
The Trousseau	4	111	George Washington	9	191
Mona Lisa	4	116	Lafayette, Friend of America	9	209
Joanna of Aragon	4	126	Abraham Lincoln, Who Saved the Union	9	244

"The simplest way to dignity is humility."—PROVERB.

EMOTIONAL MATURITY AND STABILITY

(Manliness — Womanliness)

The ability to adjust to successive stages of growth and development. Readiness for human relationships on a basis of physical, mental, and emotional adulthood.

ONE OF THE MOST important and valuable things that modern psychology has taught us is that a child must become mature emotionally and mentally, not only physically, in order to be happily adjusted to adult life. It is no more "cute" or appealing for an adult to behave like a child emotionally than it would be to suck his thumb. Adults must be able to adjust themselves to people and situations with self-reliance and independence. If we cannot do that, we are imperfectly developed, mere overgrown children.

Maturity and independence cannot descend suddenly on anyone on his twenty-first birthday! They must be achieved over the years, through carefully guided experience. First of all, the parents must learn to keep growing themselves in self-control, understanding, patience, and the other qualities that constitute emotional maturity. They must set an increasingly good example of poise and serenity. Next, they must be unselfish enough to *want* their children to become increasingly independent of them, and must encourage evidences of such independence.

But good intentions are not enough. Good intentions must be reinforced by an understanding of the *causes* behind the symptoms in children's behavior. Without this understanding, the eminent child-psychologist, Dr. Nina Ridenour, tells us, "more problems are created by parents out of their desire to improve their children than from any amount of negligence, indifference, or just pure cussedness."

These are the essentials a mother must bear in mind to help her children become emotionally mature and stable men and women:

1. She must help her children learn how to live more and more independently. Life is a continual process of growth and development. At every stage they need new freedoms in order to make new adjustments.

2. Children grow and learn at their own rate and in their own rhythm. Forcing, nagging, scolding, or punishing them can do only harm. They must not be expected to stop crying, control the bladder, or "grow up" in any way *until they show readiness to do so*. Likewise, freedom and responsibilities must be given faster to keep pace with development. The timing of these things varies in each individual child.

3. The *causes* of children's "misbehavior" may be hidden anxieties, jealousies, or fears. We must prevent or cure these *causes*, not the symptoms. Those will go of themselves when the cause is removed.

4. The best way to avoid these causes of trouble is to give the child the security of a happy home with well-adjusted parents who love each other and their children. Parents should encourage but not force development, *enjoy* their children and show it, but not overindulge them. Above all they should let the children behave independently as soon as they are able to, all along the line.

Suggested Reading

Arranged in Order of Interest to Children, from the Younger to the Older Age-Groups

	VOL.	PAGE		VOL.	PAGE
Susan and the Rain	1	214	The Great Stone Face	6	105
P-Penny and His Little Red Cart	1	243	Una and the Lion	6	118
The Country Maid and Her Milk Pail	2	4	Hans Brinker	6	202
Elizabeth Ann Fails in an Examination	2	304	Prince Gareth	6	277
A Miserable Merry Christmas	2	346	The Little Red Princess of the Forest	8	186
Christmas Every Day	2	370	The Boyhood of a Statesman	9	19
When the Mail Came Through	2	376	The Boyhood of a Sculptor	9	23
The Magic Fishbone	3	242	The Girlhood of a Singer	9	50
The Maid in the Mirror	3	304	Marguerite de Roberval	9	320
Hiawatha's Childhood	3	352	The Story of Madeleine de Verchères	9	325

"Psychologically, there is an insistent need for a condition of at-homeness. It is needed to make one's life stable and to give a mature purpose to life."
—DR. ARTHUR H. COMPTON.

FAIRNESS AND JUSTICE

Reasonable, right, honest, upright, and impartial judgment and behavior.

FAIRNESS AND JUSTICE are essential in anyone who hopes to gain the respect of his fellow-men or to have the peace of mind which comes from self-respect. A large part of the ills of the world arise from injustice—from "man's inhumanity to man." It is most important that children should develop ideas and standards of fairness and justice and learn to put them into practice.

Small children have little if any sense of the rights of others. But as they play together and see that all are treated with equal consideration and affection they begin to understand that the others have rights. They learn that there are things one may not do; that if Alice may not snatch your doll, neither may you snatch hers.

This appreciation that there are rules that apply equally to all is the basis of a sense of justice. As children begin to play organized games together they become very conscious of what is fair, and scornful of those who cheat. Children learn much from each other about fair dealing, but their impulses are strong and often selfish. They incline to "give themselves the benefit of the doubt." They need also the example, advice and guidance of adults.

Parents must be scrupulously fair and just. Be careful to show no favoritism toward one of your children, or towards your own children when in a group with others. Be absolutely impartial when settling disputes or quarrels. Never penalize a whole group for a fault only one is responsible for. That is so clearly unjust that children rightly resent it.

Beware, too, of punishing children arbitrarily. That looks like revenge for their having displeased you, not like justice. Try, instead, to arrange things so that they will learn that uncomfortable consequences are the *natural result* of wrong doing.

Show them at all times that you have high standards of fairness and justice and live up to them in your dealings, personal, business and social. Do not be afraid to let them see that you are quite "smart enough" to take unfair advantages, but that you would scorn to do so.

Expect them to play fair. If they take mean advantages, as they will at times, remind them of the necessity of fairness and justice. Call their attention to advantages they gain through the fairness of others so that they will appreciate such things. Then they are more likely to want to do the same for others. Experience will help them to understand the esteem that fairness brings, and the distrust and contempt that are the reward of unjust behavior.

Suggested Reading

Arranged in Order of Interest to Children, from the Younger to the Older Age-Groups

	VOL.	PAGE		VOL.	PAGE
The Three Little Pigs	1	89	The Child of Urbino	9	27
Why Jimmy Skunk Wears Stripes	1	122	Carrie Chapman Catt	9	103
The Golden Rule	1	383	The Walking Purchase	9	142
The Fox and the Stork	2	9	Patrick Henry	9	170
The Wolf in Sheep's Clothing	2	18	Thomas Jefferson	9	217
The Jackal and the Camel	2	323	Theodore Roosevelt	9	268
The Tongue-Cut Sparrow	2	324	Oliver Wendell Holmes	9	279
The Ghost of the Great White Stag	3	345	Sir Walter Raleigh	9	297
The Story of the Wonderful Tar Baby	3	359	Marguerite de Roberval	9	320
William Tell	8	337	A Black-Robed Voyageur	9	336

"Justice is the rightful sovereign of the world."

—PINDAR.

FRIENDLINESS

Feeling of affection, esteem, and sympathetic understanding toward other persons.

Next to a loving family, a man's friends are his most valuable possession. Nothing gives more fundamental human satisfaction than the sense of being liked, of having friends. We all want that. What situation can be sadder than when a man "has not a friend in the world?" Yet the recipe for making them is simple. "To make a friend, be a friend." Children can learn that by guided experience.

As he grows, there are two opposite and equally natural impulses at work in the child. He has a natural interest in other people and a desire for affection. But he has also a natural fear of the unfamiliar and a feeling of personal reticence. This may express itself in shyness.

Sometimes one impulse dominates, sometimes the other. Do not be worried. A shy child is not unfriendly. He merely needs to be protected from unsuitable advances from people he has not yet accepted as friends. With shyness one must "make haste slowly." Some of the most loyal people never do have a large group of casual intimates. They choose fewer friends, usually more slowly, and develop a deeper relationship.

A child who is actively and persistently hostile to people, or who cannot be drawn into gradually making friends, has some deeper difficulty. It may be jealousy, guilt-feelings, fear, or worry caused by a family situation. The mother should make every effort to find and correct the cause.

Meantime she should make extra efforts to give the child security through her own dependable affection. She should continue seeing that he has pleasant contacts with both children and adults, though they may be slight.

Sometimes a friendly child becomes suddenly unfriendly when he goes to school. This is because he is involved in new problems of social adjustment for which he is unprepared. This is particularly likely to happen if he has had little previous experience with group play. He may meet—or be guilty of—ridicule, bullying, and other forms of hostility.

Young children are pretty selfish and there are many clashes of will. They waver between friendliness and quarrels in the process of learning how to get along together. Parents can try to encourage the happy sharing of interests but should not be alarmed by occasional fighting.

By eight, a child usually has close friends to whom he is very loyal, and fighting is more often group against group. The friendliness should be encouraged, whether or not the companions are those the mother would choose. The important thing, at this age, is the friendliness, not the choice of friends.

Above all, make the friends of any member of the family welcome in your home. A home made gay and cheerful by the visits of friends is the best propaganda for and practice in friendliness.

❧ ❧ ❧

Suggested Reading

Arranged in Order of Interest to Children, from the Younger to the Older Age-Groups

	VOL.	PAGE		VOL.	PAGE
There Was Tammie!	1	118	Jan of the Windmill	6	38
The Cat Who Thought He Was a Mouse	1	127	Hans Brinker	6	202
The Lion and the Mosquitoes	1	316	The Arrow and the Song	6	325
The Christmas Tree in the Woods	1	362	The Fine Art of Living Together	7	237
Let Our Home Be a Friendly Home	1	369	The Story of Myles Standish	8	190
Under the Little Fir	1	380	The Friends of the Indians	8	206
Willie's Good Recess	2	250	Robin Hood	8	282
Thumbelina	3	85	Captain Robert A. Bartlett	9	293
Auld Lang Syne	4	355	Sir Isaac Brock, Hero of Queenstown	9	334

"Life has no pleasure nobler than that of friendship."
—Dr. Samuel Johnson.

GENEROSITY

The desire to share and to give. Liberality in deed, in thought and in spirit.

A TRULY GENEROUS person knows that "What you keep is lost; what you give is forever yours." He has learned what lasting satisfaction generosity gives. Selfish people, on the contrary, are never happy for long. They are suspicious and stingy, small-minded and small-souled.

But the mere giving of favors or presents is not necessarily generous. It may be an attempt to buy good-will or favors in return. At best, that is business; at worst, bribery.

True generosity does not look for rewards. It is not an "Indian giver." It gives for keeps. Its object is unselfish service and nothing else. Things generously given are offered with a truly heartfelt desire to give someone else help or pleasure. As James Russell Lowell so well expressed it, "The gift without the giver is bare."

Teaching a child to be generous involves a good deal more than insisting that he share or give away his possessions. If you *make* a child do this, he may be resentful and actually hate you or the people you are trying to make him be generous to. So when you want him to give up some selfish advantage, try to create a situation where he can be persuaded to consent willingly, and where he will in the end gain much satisfaction from the sacrifice.

He can learn, for instance, that he really has more fun with his wagon when he shares it with another child. Tell him how fine that was, that he not only had a better time himself, but made his playmate happy. Encourage him to appreciate other people's fine qualities generously, not to make ungenerous comparisons.

Give generously, thoughtfully, and graciously yourself. Let your child see that you feel that the worth of a gift lies in the affection that prompts it and the thoughtful understanding that chooses something appropriate to the recipient. When you receive gifts or kindnesses, express your thanks in terms that show the same thing. Show your child how to accept thanks or praise for generosity graciously and modestly, if it happens to be given, placing the emphasis on pleasure that the gift turned out to be well selected.

And never let your child measure generosity by money value. Show him that it is a matter of the spirit—the spirit of service. A well chosen though trifling gift given with a loving heart is worth a thousand times more than money given grudgingly. Live, yourself, by this tenet, and your child will be sure to follow suit.

❧ ❧ ❧

Suggested Reading

Arranged in Order of Interest to Children, from the Younger to the Older Age-Groups

	VOL.	PAGE		VOL.	PAGE
My Scottie	1	138	The Shoemaker and the Elves	3	218
How Old Mr. Long-Tail Became a Santa			How the Good Gifts Were Used by Two	3	282
Claus	1	353	The Wonderful Pear Tree	3	304
Katie Meets Buffalo Bill	2	263	The King of the Golden River	6	62
A Tree of Apples	2	284	A Christmas Carol	6	165
The Gift	2	332	The Boy Who Was Helped	9	13
The Christmas Apple	2	333	Johnny Appleseed	9	136
When Christmas is Over	2	384			

"It is the will, and not the gift, that makes the giver."
—LESSING.

GOOD SPORTSMANSHIP

Being a good loser and a gracious winner. Conduct becoming
to one who, in honest rivalry, accepts the results graciously.

BEING a "good sport" is one of the most enthusiastically admired of all traits. Everyone likes a person who is cheerful when he loses and gracious when he wins. A poor sport, on the other hand, makes himself unpopular through his conceit and bragging in success and his blaming of anything and anyone but himself when he fails.

The spirit of fair play is not inborn. It is one, however, which not only adults but other children start to teach a child very young. That is a great help for all through middle and later childhood the opinion of his playmates is paramount with the child.

At first a child is unabashedly selfish. He wants to win all the time. Yet he can see that others want to, too. He doesn't like it when they brag or crow in success or complain in defeat. They make it clear that they do not like him when he does it. To be accepted, he must be at least a reasonably good sport.

A great deal can be learned at home, too, especially in playing together. Every player should sometimes win and sometimes lose. Always letting a child win makes him selfish and unable to accept defeat. Letting him lose too often tempts him to cheat. Handicaps will level the differences in strength and skill. Parents and older children must set the example of fair play and good sportsmanship. They should approve the child when he lives up to these ideals and check him when he does not.

If home life is guided by the spirit of the Golden Rule, "Do unto others as ye would that they should do unto you," it seems fair also in contests. Presently the child learns that there is no fun in contests without uncertainty of the results. He will demand well matched sides and will expect and enjoy fluctuation of "the luck." Even a child can see that all sorts of unexpected things influence the results of a game, helping one side or another. One side "gets the breaks" today. Tomorrow it may be the other way. Presently the child's reaction to defeat will be a challenge to a return bout.

As the child grows, he learns to apply the spirit of good sportsmanship to contests other than games. He tries hard to win but is not discouraged or embittered by failure. Neither is he conceited over success. Children can learn high standards of sportsmanship on the athletic field. It is there that they learn to play fair, not to give up while the faintest chance remains, not to be discouraged by set-backs, and not to become cocky, overconfident, or overbearing in success.

Those are the lessons of good sportsmanship. They are learned in childhood at play, and they stand us in good stead all our lives.

❧ ❧ ❧

Suggested Reading

Arranged in Order of Interest to Children, from the Younger to the Older Age-Groups

	VOL.	PAGE		VOL.	PAGE
The Rooster and the Sun	2	26	Indoor Games	7	259
The Seventh Pup	2	103	Paper and Pencil Games	7	269
All Mutt	2	129	Robin Hood	8	282
The Baker's Daughter	2	192	A Jest of Little John	8	290
Hans Brinker	6	202	Theodore Roosevelt	9	268
Outdoor Games and Sports	7	241	Wendell L. Willkie	9	286

"They who lose today may win tomorrow."
—DEMOSTHENES.

25

GOOD TEMPER

Pleasant frame of mind. Agreeable disposition.

GOOD TEMPER is a characteristic which includes many other desirable traits: cheerfulness, consideration, helpfulness, humor, kindness, patience, reasonableness, self control, sympathy, to mention only a few. All these traits should be cultivated in a child from his earliest days. Yet a pleasant frame of mind comes fundamentally from good health and faith that the world is a pretty decent place to live in.

That makes it clear what we should do to develop good temper in a child. He should be kept healthy and happy and should find his world just, kind, and affectionate. If that is consistently true, the child will be fundamentally good-tempered.

Nevertheless he will certainly learn that the world is not all sunshine. He may be sick, and is sure to meet difficulties, unfairness and thwarting. Then he will need help in keeping his good temper. It is not to be expected that he will do so at first. He will probably lose his temper completely a good many times. He may very likely have violent tantrums until he learns better ways of meeting opposition.

Even in the most violent tantrums, however, children seldom hurt themselves if you let them alone. Three things will help: Be as casual and indifferent as possible about the demonstration of temper; when the child is happy, teach him other ways of getting what he wants; give him every possible chance for independent action and decisions.

Sulking is another form of bad temper more difficult to handle. Here the child feels unfairly treated and so retreats into himself. Sometimes ignoring the sulks and being persistently good natured and affectionate yourself helps. Sometimes a bit of sympathy with his disappointment followed by a tactful humorous twist is the answer. Sometimes distraction to another interest is successful. It depends on the child, but a background attitude of affection is always helpful.

All the training you give the child in keeping his temper, added to the cultivation of other good traits, will put him on the road to the good mental and emotional health which means a pleasant disposition and good temper. A handy motto for everyone to keep in mind is "Keep your temper; nobody else wants it!"

✤ ✤ ✤

Suggested Reading

Arranged in Order of Interest to Children, from the Younger to the Older Age-Groups

	VOL.	PAGE
The Story of a Little White Teddy Bear	1	10
Singing	1	181
The Land of Counterpane	1	190
The Blowaway Hat	1	224
The Lion and the Mosquitoes	1	316
The Wind and the Sun	2	5
The Peterkin Papers	2	180
Mr. A and Mr. P	2	196

	VOL.	PAGE
Young Lucretia	2	262
Cinderella	3	123
Toads and Diamonds	3	147
The Husband Who Minded the House	3	174
The Story of Pippa	6	74
The Christmas Carol	6	165
Some Simple Rules for Conversation	7	240
The Boyhood of a Story-Teller	9	1

"Good nature is one of the most precious gifts ... spreading itself like oil over the troubled sea of thought and keeping the mind smooth and equable in the roughest weather."
—WASHINGTON IRVING.

HELPFULNESS

The desire to give aid and to be of assistance where assistance is needed and wanted.

NO ONE of us is so strong that we do not sometimes need help, or so weak that we cannot sometimes help another. The spirit of helpfulness is strong in little children; but it is too often discouraged by adults.

A child of two loves to do things to help mother, though what he actually does often hinders more than it helps. Yet if the mother doesn't allow him to help because she hasn't time for his bungling efforts, he will become discouraged. He will give up trying to help. It is better to encourage the spirit of helpfulness, even if the child is clumsy. He will become increasingly efficient, and will still enjoy helping as he grows older.

If parents, from the beginning, share things with their children — work together, play together, and plan together — the children will feel that their help is important.

Duties should be suited to the capacities of the child. The idea that they are working for mother, for those they love, will inspire them. They will rejoice in recognition of their contributions. At three or four they can make stabs at dusting, brushing up, helping with dishes. At four or five they can make little gifts. From six to nine they can begin to do regular chores, to weed and dig in the garden, wash dishes, care for pets, etc. From nine to fourteen they can do many of the regular household tasks both indoors and out.

Both boys and girls can be taught to be helpful about the home. Make their work as pleasant as possible, introducing game ideas or contests frequently. Be generous with praise and appreciation.

But helpfulness is not confined to doing chores, or to family life. Children can learn the satisfactions of helping a smaller child, of returning the lost baby bird to its nest, of guiding a blind or handicapped person through traffic. Such little acts both express and increase his spirit of helpfulness toward every one.

꙰ ꙰ ꙰

Suggested Reading

Arranged in Order of Interest to Children, from the Younger to the Older Age-Groups

	VOL.	PAGE		VOL.	PAGE
The Little Red Hen and the Grain of Wheat	1	84	The Shoemaker and the Elves	3	218
			The Brownies	3	226
The Story of a Little White Dog	1	144	The Magic Fishbone	3	242
Sneezer	1	154	Wee Willie Winkie	6	179
The Little Red Lighthouse and the Great Gray Bridge	1	165	The Child of Urbino	9	27
			Jane Addams	9	105
The Lion and the Mouse	2	13	Evangeline Booth	9	116
Casperl and the Princess	3	194			

"Light is the task where many share the toil."
—HOMER.

HONESTY AND HONOR

Honesty: Straightforwardness in thought, speech and conduct. Truthfulness. Freedom from fraud.

Honor: Excellence of character, rightfully deserving esteem. Integrity, uprightness. Practice of what is right, just, and true.

THE MAN who has been scrupulously honest all his life, not because it is the best policy but because of his own conscience, is the one on whom the world can and does rely. He is also the man who can rely on *himself,* for "Oh, what a tangled web we weave, when first we practice to deceive!"

The advantages of honesty and the disadvantages of dishonesty are too obvious to have to be "sold" to any mother. What does need explaining, perhaps, is (1) why children are sometimes dishonest; and (2) how to teach a child to be honest.

(1) Before a child is old enough to understand the meaning and virtue of honesty, he may do dishonest things because he doesn't know any better. He may indulge in petty thievery, for example, out of greed, curiosity, or to get attention. As he grows older, he may behave dishonestly to get security or power because he is lonely or unhappy; to show defiance or anger; or because he never seems to win without cheating.

(2) Honesty comes slowly in children; the conception of honor even more slowly. Neither can be taught as "habits." But both can and will come as a result of their parents' example. As Dorothy Canfield Fisher has so wisely put it, "There is no moral instruction that can be compared with the training children can get from their parents without a single mention of the words right and wrong. What parents actually do day after day . . . is the best textbook available. I'd almost say that it is the only one that reaches their subconscious selves, that deep subsoil of personality in which all moral standards are rooted."

If you are honest and truthful, if your child sees that his parents have high standards of honor and behave accordingly, he will do the same. If, however, he steals or cheats, look first into the causes. Find out why he does it. Never make him feel wicked. That will only scare him and make things worse. Probably he needs more emotional security at home and help in making friends outside. Give him all the love and understanding you can.

Don't try to shame him into honesty. Just be honorable yourself and make yourself the kind of person he will want to be like.

❧ ❧ ❧

Suggested Reading

Arranged in Order of Interest to Children, from the Younger to the Older Age-Groups

	VOL.	PAGE
Why Jimmy Skunk Wears Stripes	1	122
The Wolf in Sheep's Clothing	2	18
Barnum's First Circus	2	290
Young Lucretia	2	362
Beauty and the Beast	3	116
Why the Sea Is Salt	3	129
Dick Whittington and His Cat	3	154
The Wishing Ring	3	279
The Round Table of King Arthur	4	100

	VOL.	PAGE
The Pied Piper of Hamelin	6	52
How Cincinnatus Saved Rome	8	271
The Story of Frithiof	8	297
Roland	8	319
The Spartans	8	351
The Child of Urbino	9	27
The Walking Purchase	9	142
Abraham Lincoln, Who Saved the Union	9	244
Oliver Wendell Holmes	9	279
Sir Walter Raleigh	9	297

"Nothing will bring you more honor than to do what right you may."
—FRANCIS BACON.

IDEALISM AND LIFE PURPOSE

The desire to rise above material considerations for the pursuit of a loftier, more meaningful goal.

"**A**S A MAN THINKETH in his heart, so is he," the Bible tells us. Teach your child to build his life's purpose on an ideal and you will have given him the best possible moral weapon for achieving a worthwhile goal.

"Where there is no vision the people perish." Where there is no idealism the individual falls easily into despair, for a life built exclusively on material values can bring no peace of mind, no genuine satisfaction to any soul. "Money can buy medicine but not health," as Ibsen reminds us, "food but not appetite, servants but not friendship or peace and happiness."

It will not be difficult to give your child a sense of idealism. Most children are idealists at heart, naturally. They worship heroism as well as heroes. They want to have lofty goals, and they will work hard to "follow the gleam." The trouble is that sometimes their goals and their ideals are not yours. It is then that your worth as a parent and as a human being will be put to the test. If you insist upon submitting your goals for the child's own, he will become discouraged and indifferent, and in all likelihood he will lose his sense of idealism entirely.

Your role is to praise and encourage constructive idealism in your child when he manifests it. The goal will change with the years or the months, sometimes from day to day. Be patient and understanding about that. Guide and direct him, if you must, tactfully and gently. Never try to impose your goals on him. Your child's life purpose must come from his own interests and experiences. All you can do is to show him that idealism includes ideals of character and service as well as of achievement.

Help him to drop old ideals for new ones as his interests change and grow. Talk to him, using idealistic terms to which he can respond emotionally, about future possibilities for his life-to-be. But give him clearly to understand that the choice will be his own, and that there is no need for a hurried decision. Let life train him in living. Let his own ideals inspire him. Point out to him others' achievements but not to the disparagement of his own. Don't impose your will on his. Don't rush him. Instead, encourage him to experience life and to savor it. Give him the opportunity to meet his fellows and become an all-around human being.

Suggested Reading

Arranged in Order of Interest to Children, from the Younger to the Older Age-Groups

	VOL.	PAGE
The Council of Animals	2	23
The Advantage of Knowledge	2	24
Ring Around the World	2	93
Moses	4	150
"With Malice Toward None"	4	187
The Great Stone Face	6	105
The Pilgrim's Progress	6	134
A Psalm of Life	6	326
Gradatim	6	327
The New Year	6	330

	VOL.	PAGE
The Story of Garibaldi's Boyhood	9	82
Jane Addams	9	105
Clara Barton	9	113
Patrick Henry	9	170
William Penn	9	178
George Washington, Father of Our Country	9	191
Woodrow Wilson	9	277
A Black-Robed Voyageur	9	336

"Be not simply good; be good for something."—HENRY DAVID THOREAU.

IMAGINATION

The capacity to form mental concepts or pictures beyond factual realities. The quality which enables one to project or to create ideas in the realms of literature, art, music, science, etc.

WITHOUT imagination no creative work is possible and no long-range planning can be done. Out of imagination come the songs of musicians and poets, great works of art and literature. It is necessary, too, for the making of inventions, for bold advances in science, commerce or exploration. Imagination is the mother of idealism, purpose, ambition, and achievement.

But the use of imagination is not limited to serious creative achievement. It can also be a source of happiness, gaiety, and good spirits. It is the frosting on the cake. It can sprinkle the dullest day with stardust.

From about three years of age, children begin to become imaginative. They waver between the worlds of reality and "pretending." Often they confuse the two. They may tell fanciful tales instead of plain fact. The mother who has some imagination herself will not scold or punish her child for such stories. She will enter into his world of "pretend." If he is playing soldier, she will tell him this is "mess call" and he should get his "rations." Without spoiling the fun she will help him little by little to be sure of the differences between fact and fancy,—to enjoy and use each in the right place.

As he gets a little older the child shows more purposeful and constructive imagination. He undertakes to build, paint, do, or otherwise realize what he has imagined. He learns how much hard work it takes. If he does accomplish something satisfactory to him (no matter how poorly it meets adult standards) his success is the best guarantee that he will try creative imagination again.

Sometimes children get to using the magic carpet of imagination to get away from real problems or real unhappiness, instead of facing them and trying to solve them. They live more and more in a world of fancy. When that happens the mother should find out what it is about the child's real life that is so hard to face. She must try to make his adjustment to the real world easier and happier. This is the time to give him extra assurances of love and of being wanted, to see that his life is full of interesting real experiences and activities.

If he gets those from the world about him, he will use his imagination not for escape but for constructive thinking.

Suggested Reading

Arranged in Order of Interest to Children, from the Younger to the Older Age-Groups

	VOL.	PAGE		VOL.	PAGE
Wynken, Blynken and Nod	1	2	Paul Bunyan Stories	3	372
The Rockaby Lady	1	17	Pictures and Painting	5	27
The Gingerbread Boy	1	73	Aladdin and the Wonderful Lamp	6	5
The Owl and the Pussy Cat	1	94	The Water Babies	6	41
Pooh Goes Visiting	1	276	The Story of Peter Pan	6	70
The Elephant's Child	1	286	Gulliver's Travels	6	77
The Sugar-Plum Tree	2	96	The Story of the Bluebird	6	122
Silver	2	99	The Tempest	6	128
The 500 Hats of Bartholomew Cubbins	2	210	King Arthur and His Knights	6	265
The Sleeping Beauty	3	2	The Argonauts	8	241

"Imagination rules the world."
—NAPOLEON BONAPARTE.

INDEPENDENCE, SELF-RELIANCE AND SELF-HELP

Independence: The ability to live one's own life by governing and disciplining oneself, without subservience to others.

Self-Reliance: Confidence in oneself, one's own efforts and powers.

Self-Help: Knowing how to provide for oneself without the aid of others.

THE TEST of whether a person is really adult is whether he is actually able to take care of himself in an independent and self-reliant way. No amount of book learning or of habit training will take the place of the simple ability to take charge of one's own life. Without it, anyone is still a child, regardless of his age.

Our chief job as parents is, of course, to help our children reach a full, useful, and happy maturity. In doing so they will become more and more independent of us, until they are at last able to start out entirely on their own.

Training in independence and self-reliance should begin while the child is still a baby. This is not unkind, but kind. Babies long to do things for themselves; they grab at the spoon when you feed them, at their shoes when you dress them. Allow them to try helping themselves, and as soon as possible show them how.

It takes patience to let the clumsy, dawdling two-year-old button his own coat, hold his cup, or turn on the water faucet for his own drink of water. But we must restrain ourselves. We must let him do what he can. That does not mean only what he can do *well*. He will make many mistakes as part of the process of learning. But we must let him try, and encourage him.

The mother who likes to do everything for her children and wants "to keep them babies" is in reality selfish. She cares more for her own importance to the child than for his development.

A child wants to be active, to tackle the problems that come his way; but sometimes they are too much for him. Then he needs to know that you are not only *for* him in his efforts, but willing to assist with suggestions or a helping hand when necessary. Whenever possible let your help be the kind that assists him to find his own solution, rather than the kind that takes the whole problem off his hands.

As children grow older, they can be trusted in more and more ways to direct themselves. They have learned more about what is safe, possible, and socially permissible. Don't forbid their "crazy ideas" unless they are actually dangerous. Let them learn by trying. Let them use many kinds of tools and learn to do all sorts of things. "Handy hands" give one a feeling of competence.

Let the children explore on their own. Show your faith in them by leaving them, more and more, as they grow, to make their own decisions and learn to accept the consequences. Only so can they become self-reliant, independent adults able to cope with life on their own.

Suggested Reading

Arranged in Order of Interest to Children, from the Younger to the Older Age-Groups

	VOL.	PAGE
The Little Red Hen and the Grain of Wheat	1	84
The Three Little Pigs	1	89
Timid Timothy	1	104
Mike Mulligan and His Steam Shovel	1	160
P-Penny and His Little Red Cart	1	243
The Magic Fishbone	3	242
The Wishing Ring	3	279
Self-Directed Work and Play	5	114
Robinson Crusoe	6	89
Hans Brinker	6	202

	VOL.	PAGE
Be Strong	6	325
Gymnastics for Little Folks	7	339
Gymnastic Plays	7	344
Roland	8	319
William Wallace	8	383
The Boy Who Was Helped	9	13
The Boyhood of a Statesman	9	19
The Boyhood of a President	9	56
Daniel Boone, Indian Fighter and Pioneer	9	226
The Story of Madeleine de Verchères	9	325

"The best lightning rod for your protection is your own spine."
—RALPH WALDO EMERSON.

INDIVIDUALITY AND ORIGINALITY

Individuality: Distinctive character.

Originality: The ability to be independently inventive or creative in thought or action.

ONE of the blessings of living in a democracy is that we respect the dignity of the individual person. We encourage our children to think for themselves, to create according to their own original ideas, to cultivate their individual tastes, and to respect the individual differences of others. Under a totalitarian dictatorship we should have to make them as much alike as possible and teach them blind obedience to authority.

Any mother of as many as three children can tell you that they are all born different and that distinct personalities are obvious at a very early age. Although there are many stages (like learning to talk) through which they all pass, they do it at different times and in different ways. In the early years they are very imitative, too, but what they select to imitate and the manner of doing it is highly individual.

Every mother should look for the unique characteristics of her child and try to encourage the development of all good or harmless traits that seem marked in his character. Give him the full scope he needs for trying out his own ideas. In order to help your child to flourish in his own best way you must have three important attitudes toward him:

First, you must consider him a person in his own right, not a copy of some ancestor, or the *property* of his parents. Treat him with courtesy and consideration. Prize his individuality.

Second, you must be flexible in your demands and regulations. Don't make hard and fast rules, except when it is really necessary. There are many good ways to do most things. Keep your sense of proportion and your sense of humor. Learn to *enjoy* novel things, differences, the unexpected. Let the schedule go occasionally in the interests of fun or a special treat. Let the family feel free to propose any kind of enterprise or excursion which will give refreshment or enrichment of the spirit.

Third, you must try to understand your child's individual growth. It will not be regular or even in all respects, but let him grow in his own way. Neither force nor hold him back. Give him his head wherever possible. Encourage him to follow his spontaneous interests, to think, work, play, experiment and create in the ways that are natural to him. And in order that latent abilities may be aroused, see that your child has a varied experience and broad opportunities to find his natural interests.

❧ ❧ ❧

Suggested Reading

Arranged in Order of Interest to Children, from the Younger to the Older Age-Groups

	VOL.	PAGE		VOL.	PAGE
Madonna of the Rocks	4	73	Patrick Henry	9	170
The Poet Shakespeare at Stratford	4	171	George Washington	9	191
The Story of Columbus	4	178	Benjamin Franklin	9	198
Beethoven and Mozart	4	199	Daniel Boone, Indian Fighter and Pioneer	9	226
How Cincinnatus Saved Rome	8	271			
An Inventor's Boyhood	9	10	Andrew Jackson, Soldier and Seventh President	9	230
Boyhood of a Sculptor	9	23			
The Child of Urbino	9	27	Theodore Roosevelt	9	268
The Boyhood of a President	9	56	Oliver Wendell Holmes	9	279
Madame Curie	9	107	Sir John A. MacDonald	9	342
Clara Barton	9	113	Grenfell's Sermon in Deeds	9	377

"Every human being is intended to have a character of his own; to be what no other is and to do what no other can do."

—WILLIAM HENRY CHANNING.

INDUSTRY AND DILIGENCE

Habitual steady attention to and painstaking persistence in any task, project or pursuit.

"NEVER DEPEND upon your genius," said John Ruskin. "If you have talent, industry will improve it; if you have none, industry will supply the deficiency."

How true this is! So often children use their general quickness of mind, their talent or their "genius" as an excuse not to work at their tasks or studies. The truth is, however, that even the most talented of the world's great men and women have achieved success by hard work.

The foundations of America were laid by industrious people. "No drones in our hive" is as good a family slogan today as ever, for without useful activity no one can succeed in any worthwhile undertaking.

Children will *start* working to imitate their elders; but, once learned, tasks like washing dishes, sweeping, or mowing the lawn lose their glamor. What the children really want is a sense of power from knowing that they can do them. So just about the time they get good at something, they get bored doing it. I you *require* them to continue, the emotional drive is yours, not theirs. They may learn obedience, but not diligence.

So how are we to teach this priceless quality of going at a project with energy and sticking to it? The answer is before us if we watch children. They do work furiously and long *at the things that interest them.* Interest is the best spur to industry. Others are the satisfaction of achievement, and the possession and use of the product.

There is no true distinction between work and play in childhood. Children work hard at their play. The boys working at a "shack" are industrious. They will *drive themselves* to work in the face of fatigue and distractions. Play projects like that are among the best for developing diligence.

So a good way to cultivate industry is to make sure that the children are challenged by fascinating projects which gradually increase in difficulty. You will sometimes need to give special encouragement or even a little help, so that they may reap the rewards of success. As they grow older, the purposes that drive them will be broader and less immediate. A boy may works months to earn money for a bicycle.

Cultivate respect for good work and pride in doing it. Show your admiration for the patience, skill, and integrity that go into a good job, no matter how humble. The carpenter, the garage man, and the cleaning woman, as well as the engineer or scientist, have a "know how" about their own jobs that is to be respected. Show concern about doing your own work well, and encourage your child to do the same. Praise a good job. Interest in and respect for the job, plus joy in accomplishment, result in industry.

Suggested Reading

Arranged in Order of Interest to Children, from the Younger to the Older Age-Groups

	VOL.	PAGE
The Little Red Hen and the Grain of Wheat	1	84
How to Get Breakfast	1	114
How Doth the Little Busy Bee	1	192
The Ant and the Grasshopper	2	3
Never Worked and Never Will	2	76
The Seventh Pup	2	103
Pony Penning Day	2	172
Caleb's Luck	2	257
Casperl and the Princess	3	194
The Shoemaker and the Elves	3	218
The Brownies	3	226

	VOL.	PAGE
The Maid and the Mirror	3	307
Modeling Small Sculptures in White Soap	5	75
Wonderful Uses of Colored Paper	5	92
Labor	6	327
The Boy Who Was Helped	9	13
The Child of Urbino	9	27
The Boyhood of an Engineer Who Became President	9	68
Young Days of John Milton	9	76
Benjamin Franklin	9	198

"A man who gives his children habits of industry provides for them better than by giving them a fortune." —RICHARD WHATELY.

INITIATIVE AND AMBITION

Initiative: Self-reliant enterprise; the ability to be a self-starter.
Ambition: Eager desire for superiority of attainment.

ENTERPRISE and ambition are essential to making a success in a competitive society. If people are not to be herded like sheep, they must show initiative, choose their own purposes and work toward them. No one admires a man or woman who always has to be told what to do and prodded into doing it.

A healthy, happy, young child is full of initiative and ambition, always "starting something," always trying to do something or other. A dull, inert child is a sick child, physically, mentally, or emotionally. Perhaps he has met so many "don'ts" that he is discouraged. He gives up trying. This can happen with a baby or with an older child whose parents reject his ideas and substitute their own. If he does not give up, he may become rebellious or develop other behavior difficulties.

Respect your child's ambitions and projects, whether for the present or the future. Just what he may want to undertake now or to become in the future is not the important point. Both will probably change. What is important is that he is showing initiative and ambition. Encourage his undertakings and give him a little help if it is necessary to his success. The less you need give, the more self-reliant he becomes. Initiative grows with self-confidence, and success breeds ambition to try yet greater things.

Children are natural hero-worshipers. They find their heroes and heroines in their parents, a beloved aunt or uncle, a gay and charming girl, the local football hero, people of whom they read in newspapers and magazines, and the great figures of history and literature. These they want to imitate, often quite superficially at first. Do not ridicule their clumsy efforts. They are attempts at self-improvement, however artificial or misguided they may seem. As the child's character and understanding develop, he will choose more and more worthy models and goals for his ambition.

In closing, let us give you this Recipe for Initiative and Ambition:

(Quantity sufficient to satisfy two parents)
One or more good healthy children
Add: self-confidence and
    past successful achievement.
Expose to plenty of interesting experiences, situations and materials.
Allow a generous measure of freedom, and mix all well.
Brush over lightly with understanding and loving guidance.

Suggested Reading

Arranged in Order of Interest to Children, from the Younger to the Older Age-Groups

	VOL.	PAGE
The Little Red Hen and the Grain of Wheat	1	84
How To Get Breakfast	1	114
How Spot Found a Home	1	141
Mike Mulligan and His Steam Shovel	1	160
Number 9, the Little Fire Engine	1	172
How Doth the Little Busy Bee	1	192
Dick Whittington and His Cat	3	154
The Maid in the Mirror	3	307
Gutenberg, Inventor of Printing	4	165
Daniel Webster	4	188

	VOL.	PAGE
James Watt	4	190
The Porcelain Stove	6	237
Marco Polo	8	168
The New World	8	170
Peary, Discoverer of the North Pole	8	210
An Inventor's Boyhood	9	10
A Courageous Boy Who Became President	9	72
Susan B. Anthony	9	102
Paul Jones	9	213
Andrew Jackson	9	230

"Initiative is doing the right thing without being told."
—ELBERT HUBBARD.

INVESTIGATION JUDGMENT AND DECISION

Investigation: The habit of following up or making research by patient inquiry, observation, and examination of facts.

Judgment: The exercise of comparison and discrimination for the mental formulation of values and relations.

Decision: Quality of being able to come to a conclusion on the basis of evidence and judgment.

GOOD JUDGMENT and the ability to come to wise decisions are such valuable traits that we hope all children will have them. Happiness and success may depend upon them, and many good jobs and other benefits are lost by the lack of them.

These abilities are not born in a child but must be learned as he grows up. Many parents give their children continual directions on what to do and how to do it, leaving them no opportunity to decide for themselves. They feel that the children are not yet old enough to decide wisely. What they do not realize is that they never will be unless they are allowed to make decisions, including some mistaken ones. Learning requires practice.

From babyhood a child should be encouraged to investigate and to decide things, small ones at first, and then see what happens as a result. Without preaching, parents can help him to understand why some decisions turn out better than others. That improves his ability to judge the next time.

As he gets to be a big child, capable of logical and impersonal thought, a more formal system may be encouraged. Benjamin Franklin had a good system which many intelligent and successful men have since used for making wise and considered decisions.

The idea is to make two lists—one of all the good reasons one can think of *for* the proposed course of action, the other of those *against* it. This must be done thoughtfully, fairly, and without prejudice. Then one balances the importance of one list against that of the other and decides accordingly. What results is no "snap judgment" but one reached on the basis of investigating and then carefully considering all the available evidence. It may still turn out to have been wrong, because we cannot always understand all the factors involved. We all make mistakes and always shall. However, this system is an excellent basis for reasonable judgment.

Your older children may easily be interested in this system. It has some of the elements of a game. We cannot expect very skillful evaluations from them at first, but we can try to show them what is admissible as evidence and what is not. Preconceived prejudices and personal wishes look pretty weak in cold black and white.

If your children will accept this method and practice it, they will have a good basis for deciding wisely. Maturity and experience should do the rest.

Suggested Reading

Arranged in Order of Interest to Children, from the Younger to the Older Age-Groups

	VOL.	PAGE		VOL.	PAGE
Better Than Television	1	242	Robinson Crusoe	6	89
The Lion and the Mosquitoes	1	316	Wee Willie Winkie	6	179
The Miller, His Son, and Their Donkey	2	7	Your Friends	7	238
The City Mouse and the Country Mouse	2	12	Peary, Discoverer of the North Pole	8	210
Clever Elsie	3	56	The Boyhood of a Patriot	9	15
Woman's Wit	3	292	Susan B. Anthony	9	102
James Watt	4	190	Madame Curie	9	107
Woodwork for Older Children	5	269	How a Woman Saved an Army	9	130
Good Pictures: How They Are Made	5	337	Oliver Wendell Holmes	9	279
Pinocchio	6	55	Radisson, "The Canadian Ulysses"	9	323

"How little do they see what really is who frame their hasty judgment upon that which seems."
—ROBERT SOUTHEY.

KINDNESS

The expression of understanding, sympathy, and love of humanity. Benevolence.

"THAT BEST PORTION of a good man's life," the poet Wordsworth tells us, "is made up of his little, nameless, unremembered acts of kindness and of love."

If any one characteristic could cure the world of its ills, kindness would be the one. Think of a world ruled by kindness. Think of every person in the world guiding his life by the lovely, simple dictum, "Be ye kind to one another." What a beautiful world it would be, without any of the evidences of "man's unhumanity to man."

Unfortunately, although we all agree to this in theory, many of us do not guide our lives by it. Wars and certain other kinds of murder, cruelty, and greed are not only sanctioned by society but, in some instances, actually encouraged on moral grounds.

Perhaps mothers can do more than anyone else to change this, though it is not easy. Little children, like little animals, have many savage instincts. They must be taught kindness. But how? Not by merely telling them about the value of kindness and expecting them to be kind because you tell them to. They must learn in three ways— by example, by explanation and by experience.

In the first place, bring your child up in an atmosphere of kindness. Then it will seem natural, familiar and right to him. Guide and direct him with kindness and affection. See that the home is ruled by kindness. See that kindness is offered to all you meet, not only to friends, but to people who serve you in stores and shops, and even to strangers whom you may be able to help.

Explain. Without preaching, help your child to see *how* to be kind, and why it is so satisfying. Do it casually and briefly in connection with particular situations. Let him see how everyone likes a kind person. Let him learn thoughtfulness by being shown many simple ways to be kind. And let him see how happy it makes you to have been able to help someone.

The deepest conviction comes, however, from experience. The experience of receiving kindness helps, because it makes clear how pleasant a thing kindness is. But the experience of being kind is more important still. The child who is kind to some little animal and feels its gratitude and devotion, learns the true satisfaction of kindness. To be able to help another, to make him happy, makes one feel stronger, more important and worth-while. We all love that.

Remember that what a child does *with satisfying results* he will repeat. So when your child does some small favor or shows consideration, show him that you appreciate his kindness. Encourage him to think of pleasant little services or surprises for others. Let him see that you expect kindness in his acts, that it is *like him* to be kind.

If he is unkind do not scold. Admit that it was not good, not like his best self, and that you feel sorry about it. But remember that we all do wrong sometimes and show that you have faith that he can do better next time.

Fundamentally, the basis for a better, kinder, and more peaceful world lies in better and kinder people. You can help form them.

❧ ❧ ❧

Suggested Reading

Arranged in Order of Interest to Children, from the Younger to the Older Age-Groups

	VOL.	PAGE		VOL.	PAGE
My Scottie	1	136	Why the Sea Is Salt	3	129
The Puppy Who Wanted a Boy	1	345	Toads and Diamonds	3	147
Under the Little Fir	1	369	The Selfish Giant	3	150
The Golden Rule	1	383	Dick Whittington and His Cat	3	154
No Room	2	42	How the Good Gifts Were Used by Two	3	282
Hurt No Living Thing	2	86	Hiawatha's Childhood	3	352
The Dog Who Chose a Prince	2	114	The King of the Golden River	6	62
Such a Kind World	2	137	Where Love Is, God is	6	262
The Stork and the Holy Babe	2	360	A Jest of Little John	8	290
The Friendly Beasts	2	361	A Nurse's Girlhood	9	6

"What do we live for if it is not to make life less difficult for each other?"
—GEORGE ELIOT.

LEADERSHIP

Qualities fitting one to guide or direct others in action, thought, or opinion.

IN A DEMOCRATIC society we have no caste of leaders, no group who are always leaders while others follow. We expect any responsible citizen to be able both to follow and to lead upon occasion. Each one of us finds himself, at times, in a position where others look to us for leadership. It may be at a club, or committee meeting, an office get-together, a situation where a policy or problem is to be decided upon, or any social or personal discussion. None of us can shirk responsibility for leadership in such matters, if he happens to be the one best fitted, or the one chosen to lead for the time being.

The ability to be a good leader is a most valuable trait. It implies responsibility, since a leader is, temporarily at least, directing the power of the whole group. He must remember that the strength he guides is not his own but that of the group, and must be used for the benefit of all. He must be decisive, but open-minded, willing to listen to the suggestions of others and to accept good ones without fear for his own prestige. He must know how to stand on his own feet without stepping on anyone else's.

One could go on almost indefinitely listing the qualities of a good leader, for the better human being anyone is, the better leader he can become. Everything you do to help your child become more friendly, respectful of others, capable, enthusiastic, resourceful, independent, and so on, will make him a better leader as well as follower.

But is there nothing more specific you can do? Yes. You can give him guided experience in leadership. There are endless opportunities for leadership in every family. See that they are passed around. Today Alice is in charge of the picnic lunch, and she will assign everyone his job. Tomorrow Bert is "captain" of the group that washes the car. Mother or father might organize things better, but if they always lead, the children can learn only to follow.

Let your child get accustomed to leadership of increasingly important and complicated undertakings. Teach him by example and by tactful guidance how to handle the difficulties every leader meets. Show him how to lead fairly. Such training is the best help you can give your child toward developing leadership.

❧ ❧ ❧

Suggested Reading

Arranged in Order of Interest to Children, from the Younger to the Older Age-Groups

	VOL.	PAGE		VOL.	PAGE
Horatius at the Bridge	6	107	Benjamin Franklin	9	198
The New World	8	170	Lafayette, Friend of America	9	209
The Wanderings of Odysseus	8	229	Paul Jones, Naval Hero	9	213
Roland	8	319	Daniel Boone, Indian Fighter, and Pioneer	9	226
William Wallace	8	383			
The Story of Garibaldi's Boyhood	9	82	Andrew Jackson, Soldier and Seventh President	9	230
Joan of Arc, Maid of Orleans	9	93			
Susan B. Anthony	9	102	Abraham Lincoln, Who Saved the Union	9	244
Clara Barton	9	113	Theodore Roosevelt	9	263
Patrick Henry	9	170	Twelve National Heroes	9	307
George Washington, Father of Our Country	9	191	Sir Wilfrid Laurier	9	348

"Be all the things that are big and fine and worth-while and the world will welcome you as a leader."
—FRANK H. CHELEY

LOYALTY

Faithfulness. The quality of being constant and true to any
person, state, or idea to whom or which one owes allegiance.

Loyalty is a virtue so necessary to social life that it is prized in all kinds of society from the primitive tribe to the most civilized nation. Even criminals consider nothing so low as the "double-crosser," the person without loyalty to his friends or group. We must, then, teach our children loyalty, first to people, then to groups, and finally to abstract ideals.

Loyalty is like the ripples made by a stone thrown into water. It begins at the center, the home. Let an outsider attack any member of it and even a child defends him with whole-hearted loyalty, though he may disagree with him at home. The same holds true in the later, wider loyalties of life—loyalty to friends, school, community and country. We are even now trying, in the United Nations, to set up an organization through which our loyalty to all men, as brothers, may act.

Loyalty means standing firmly by what one believes in, even in the face of argument, disbelief, or attack. It implies honesty, courage, and sometimes self-sacrifice. It is not a mere refusal to criticise or to listen to criticism. It may require active defense of what one holds dear. And true loyalty is not blind. It recognizes faults in the loved person and strives to overcome them, while remaining loyally devoted to the best that is in him.

Loyalty within the family group is the beginning. If a child hears his mother criticize his father his own loyalty is injured. But a mother must not only avoid being disloyal. She must praise the members of the family generously and work to strengthen family unity. She must build family loyalty by making the home an attractive place, spiritually as well as physically.

Family loyalty is the first step, but a wise mother will help actively in developing wider loyalties. She will show by example and explanation that one should support the various groups with which he is associated. As a child becomes loyal to these other groups, he accepts from each its common ideals and is loyal to them also. Thus he adds to his own set of abstract ideals of courage, honesty, and so on, and these become a part of his character. In the final analysis these loyalties to things within himself keep him true.

As Shakespeare has so well said, "This first: to thine own self be true, and it must follow as the night the day, thou canst not then be false to any man."

❧ ❧ ❧

Suggested Reading

Arranged in Order of Interest to Children, from the Younger to the Older Age-Groups

	VOL.	PAGE		VOL.	PAGE
Fung's Fourth	2	298	The Child of Urbino	9	27
A Family in the Land of Von Winkelried	4	202	Joan of Arc	9	93
			How a Woman Saved an Army	9	130
The Man Without a Country	6	216	The Story of Molly Pitcher	9	133
O Captain! My Captain!	6	296	Abraham Lincoln, Who Saved the Union	9	244
Concord Hymn	6	303	Robert E. Lee	9	250
The Story of Myles Standish	8	190	Twelve National Heroes	9	307
Beowulf	8	273	Marguerite de Roberval	9	320
The Story of Frithiof	8	297	The Story of Laura Secord	9	339
Roland	8	319	The Story of the Men Who Settled		
William Tell	8	337	Canada	9	356

"Nothing is more noble, more venerable, than loyalty."
—Cicero.

MODESTY AND SIMPLICITY

Modesty: The quality of estimating oneself moderately, without forwardness or boastfulness. Unassuming character.

Simplicity: Preference for being plain in manner and mode of life, free of elaborateness or complexity.

MODESTY and simplicity are really matters of good taste. Modesty and directness bespeak the lady and the gentleman everywhere. Boasting, immodesty, and over adornment show only bad taste and win scorn rather than admiration.

However, young children have very little sense of quality. Their developing nervous systems are such that they enjoy strong colors, loud, fast music, and in general things that are blatant and obvious rather than in quiet good taste. Therefore children often behave in ways that seem cheap, immodest, or even shocking to their parents. Sometimes they do it in a mood of rebellion. Sometimes the fault lies with parents who are over-refined "nice Nellies," too easily shocked by perfectly natural things.

Children will probably outgrow these things if you give them a chance,—that is, if you yourself set standards of natural, not artificial modesty and simple good taste and if you are the kind of person they want to be like.

Naturally, you can never nag a child into having a taste for the simple amenities of life any more than you can nag him out of his preference for the comics, cheap radio programs and movies, or immodest or vain behavior. Nor can you hurry him out of this phase. The best you can do is to surround him with good books, good music, and entertainment in good taste, and show him your preference for these things.

Show him that people who behave with becoming modesty and natural simplicity are happier and better liked than those who do not. And show him, too, that the really durable satisfactions in life are simple and unassuming things. The fancy ones are not as satisfactory, in the end, as they look.

Suggested Reading

Arranged in Order of Interest to Children, from the Younger to the Older Age-Groups

	VOL.	PAGE		VOL.	PAGE
The Lion and the Mosquitoes	1	316	Toads and Diamonds	3	147
The Little Fish Story	1	328	Casperl and the Princess	3	194
The Oak and the Reed	2	22	The Great Stone Face	6	105
The Rooster and the Sun	2	26	King Robert of Sicily	6	357
The Christmas Apple	2	333	How Cincinnatus Saved Rome	8	271
The Fisherman and His Wife	3	20	King Charles XII of Sweden	9	79
The Emperor's New Clothes	3	74	George Washington	9	191
The Nightingale	3	89	Benjamin Franklin	9	198
The Fir Tree	3	104	A Man Like a Stone Wall	9	260

"The greatest truths are the simplest; and so are the greatest men."
—J. C. HALE.

NATURALNESS AND UNAFFECTEDNESS

Simple straightforward manners and behavior, representing one's true nature, appearance, or sentiments without anything artificial, false or synthetic about them.

ONE OF THE REASONS we find babies so delightful is that they are so utterly natural and spontaneous. Yet we often go busily to work to cure them of these qualities and teach them insincerity, although we know that the finest people are simple and natural. They feel at home in the world and dare to be themselves. The person with unnatural and affected manners advertises to the world that he is ashamed of something within himself and trying to cover it up.

Yet we have many thoughts, emotions, and impulses which it would not do to express freely and naturally. Society demands certain standards of behavior, of adults at least, and these standards children must gradually come to accept. The trouble comes when we demand that children express feelings they have not yet learned to have. The child who is required to say "I'm sorry" when he is not, learns not courtesy but insincerity and untruthfulness.

It requires patience and skill to teach the child to feel friendly, to be thoughtful and considerate, but when it is done his expression of those feelings will be natural and unaffected. If we can only resist the temptation to urge children to act more civilized than they feel, we can keep them sincere and natural all the while that we are gradually civilizing them.

The real crux of daring to be natural is the faith that both you and other people are worthwhile and likable without any pretenses. If you feel that way, there is nothing you need to hide behind affected mannerisms. Make your child know that he is loved for himself and cultivate respect and affection for others.

Good manners and thoughtfulness seem natural to children when every member of the family practices them habitually. Then there is no need for "company manners."

"I don't see why my children always act their worst when we have guests," a mother said. "I'm sure I've instructed them to behave properly." But would she expect them to learn to play the piano by being "instructed," unless they practiced daily?

Children who are given special directions for behavior before guests feel strain and nervous tension. They are confused and lose sight of the simple, natural desire to please the company. It is a good idea to use the best dishes and silver occasionally, just for the home folks, so that the children will feel at ease in using them. Just so, simple good manners used daily in the home become natural to the children.

If they are taught to think more of *being* worth while, and less often reminded of "what people may think," children may be awkward at times, but never affected. They will have the simple charm of naturalness which is so appealing in a growing child.

Suggested Reading

Arranged in Order of Interest to Children, from the Younger to the Older Age-Groups

	VOL.	PAGE
The Shy Little Horse	1	110
The Ugly Duckling	3	77
Cinderella	3	123
The Blue Boy	4	54
The Story of Pippa	6	74
Hans Brinker	6	202
A Nurse's Girlhood	9	6
The Boy Who Was Helped	9	13
The Boyhood of a Sculptor	9	23
The Child of Urbino	9	27

	VOL.	PAGE
The Girlhood of a Singer	9	50
The Boyhood of an American Author	9	64
A Courageous Boy Who Became President	9	72
Patrick Henry	9	170
Lafayette, Friend of America	9	209
Thomas Jefferson	9	217
The Wife Who Taught Her Husband To Be President	9	229
Abraham Lincoln, Who Saved the Union	9	244

"The wisest man could ask no more of Fate than to be simple, modest, manly, true."
—JAMES RUSSELL LOWELL.

OBEDIENCE

The practice of obeying; compliance with requests or orders; willingness to submit to authority; submission to restraint.

WHENEVER people live together it is necessary for the welfare of all that they should obey laws and regulations, also that some should take directions from others. Otherwise, we should have not a social system but chaos. There are natural laws, divine laws, and man-made ordinances which must be obeyed. Each carries a penalty for infringement. People who break them fill the hospitals and jails.

There is no arguing about natural law. If the child does not build stably, his block house will fall. (Such laws enforce themselves.) Of course parents should protect the child when necessary. He must not learn the need of wraps by catching pneumonia.

There are man-made laws which are to be learned and obeyed in much the same way. If the speed limit is 50, we do not drive 60. If Tommy sees father do so, his sense of obedience to law is injured.

As he grows older, the child can learn how such laws are made in a democracy. He can understand that their real source is the people themselves. A law is like a promise given—something we have all agreed to do—and common honesty demands that we keep it.

How many times we have said that a good home is a little democracy! Very early children learn to understand the making of laws and they cheerfully obey—and enforce—rules they have helped to make. Participation in clubs and other democratic groups also helps them to become law-abiding citizens of the home and community.

To teach obedience:

1. Start early to teach the child to accept reasonable controls willingly.
2. DO NOT GIVE *UNNECESSARY* DIRECTIONS. That builds resentment.
3. Be as courteous and tactful in giving necessary directions to a child as to an adult.
4. Allow plenty of time for the child to respond.
5. Explain the reasons for your request if he asks or if you doubt his willingness to comply.
6. Listen to his opinions respectfully and compromise if it seems wise.
7. Be kind but firm about carrying through whatever decision is made.
8. Give the child experience in directing the group when possible, so that he appreciates the value of obedience.

There are, of course, times when a child must obey his parents immediately without question, for example, when danger threatens. A child who has found by experience that his parents are wise, kind and reasonable will trust them enough to obey at once when they demand it. This is a mutual trust. After all, his mother obeys *his* call for help, doesn't she? This is obedience based on intelligence, not on blind habit or fear. Intelligent obedience will not have to be discarded when the child is grown, but will form the best basis for obeying community laws.

Suggested Reading

Arranged in Order of Interest to Children, from the Younger to the Older Age-Groups

	VOL.	PAGE		VOL.	PAGE
The Three Bears	1	67	Indians in the House	2	274
Three Little Kittens	1	82	A Tree of Apples	2	284
The Story of Peter Rabbit	1	97	Barnum's First Circus	2	290
Peppi and the Custard	1	113	Pilgrim's Progress	6	134
Watch Me!	1	115	The Boyhood of a President	9	56
The Train That Would Not Stay on the Track	1	148	The Boy Who Braved the Duke of Wellington	9	76
The Good Little Bad Little Pig	1	233	King Louis XIV of France	9	78
Katie Meets Buffalo Bill	2	263	U. S. Grant, Soldier and President	9	255

"We are unfit for any trust till we can and do obey."
—GEORGE MACDONALD.

OPEN-MINDEDNESS AND REASONABLENESS

Willingness to listen to others' opinions impartially; to attack
a problem fairly, and to judge and decide on the basis of
relevant facts.

OPEN-MINDEDNESS AND REASONABLENESS are indeed noble attributes of the mind. They make for a better, happier world for everybody. They substitute fairness for unfairness, facts for irrational beliefs, thought for prejudice, truth for untruth.

Their opposite is prejudice. Most of us are prejudiced to some degree. We have attitudes not founded on facts. If allowed to become habitual, these prejudices do great harm. They narrow the vision and thwart the wholesome development of the person holding them. They may be unjust to others. They delay progress, for prejudiced people are not willing to learn.

It is easy for the unscrupulous to exploit prejudiced people by setting them against one another.

Children are usually quite open-minded. That is, they are willing to consider any point of view presented to them. They have not yet caught prejudices from older people. Parents must make every effort to "be as little children" in this respect. If they are tolerant and open-minded and fight against prejudice wherever they meet it, their children will remain open-minded.

Reasonableness is a little different. It implies the ability to reason backed by the ability to guide one's actions by reason rather than by impulse. A baby has neither of these abilities, but both begin developing early, and should increase throughout life.

Be patient and reasonable with your children. Explain to them the things they are able to understand. Help them to learn to think things out logically. Help to cultivate their self-control —and your own.

Suggested Reading

Arranged in Order of Interest to Children, from the Younger to the Older Age-Groups

	VOL.	PAGE		VOL.	PAGE
The Horse Who Lived Upstairs	1	132	Where Love Is, God Is	6	262
Susan and the Rain	1	216	Traveling in Many Countries	8	59
Mary Ellen's Birthday Party	1	239	The Boyhood of a Statesman	9	19
900 Buckets of Paint	1	302	A Pig That Nearly Caused a War	9	139
The Lion and the Mosquitoes	1	316	Honors to the Flag	9	150
The Council of Animals	2	23	William Penn	9	178
Mr. Scrunch	2	36	George Washington, Father of Our		
The Happy Cure	2	60	Country	9	191
Mr. A and Mr. P	2	196	Benjamin Franklin	9	198
			Theodore Roosevelt	9	268

"To approach a problem with prejudice is to close the door of knowledge."
—RALPH WALDO EMERSON.

ORDERLINESS AND NEATNESS

The habit of having a proper place for everything and of keeping everything in its place. Method, system, tidiness.

ORDER AND NEATNESS can, of course, be carried to excess, but when practiced with reason they make life more comfortable, efficient and gracious. A neat personal appearance is an important factor in making people like us. Orderliness makes for a pleasant appearance and for convenience in use. Neatness and orderliness are therefore very valuable traits to cultivate.

We shall understand the problem better if we can realize what an enormous confusion of lights, colors, shapes, sounds, and motions the world is to a young child. He sees, feels, and hears hundreds of things that he cannot understand. He is not yet able to organize or order them in his mind.

Naturally he takes great joy in the things he does know well. Things that look familiar and "like home" make him feel secure and happy. There is the key to the beginning of orderliness! Make order the natural, familiar thing in the home. Then he will enjoy it and will gradually do more and more to maintain it. Be systematic and orderly yourself. Keep things in their places and encourage the child to do so.

Do not expect too much, and do all you can to make tidying up easy and pleasant. See that there are low hangers and drawers for the child's clothes, low shelves for his toys, and arrangements in the bathroom such that he can help himself easily. Don't expect him to pick up his toys when he is tired. Don't let the floor get strewn with so many toys that putting them away seems endless. Encourage him to put things away when he is through with them, and pick up a few for him casually as you pass by. At the end of playtime see that the room is left neat, helping with the picking up if necessary.

The two-year-old is proud to know where Daddy's slippers belong, and the ten-year-old wants to be able to find his skates quickly. The older child can even understand the natural penalties of loss and delay which he pays for disorder. And all children like the social approval they get for neatness. Mention it favorably when children look particularly neat or have tidied things up well.

Do not limit them to keeping themselves and their possessions neat. Ask for and give them help. Make orderliness a family project. It is more friendly and gracious that way.

As the child grows older he can assume more responsibilities for order at home. He deserves family appreciation of these services. In his own room let him arrange things as he likes, even to moving the furniture. He must practice creating as well as maintaining order.

Mothers often despair at the untidiness of their children. It is usually worst when the child's growth has brought him to a point of great interest in other matters. If the home is kept orderly and happy, and if patient, gentle training is continued, the children will in all probability grow up orderly and neat.

Suggested Reading

Arranged in Order of Interest to Children, from the Younger to the Older Age-Groups

	VOL.	PAGE
Mrs. Goose's Rubbers	1	294
The Zigzag Boy	1	301
Mr. Nobody	1	301
The Lost Key	1	308
Snow-White and Rose-Red	3	9
Snow-White and the Seven Dwarfs	3	33
The Brownies	3	226
Color—Design—Drawing	5	33
Week-Days in Dolly's House	5	79
The Wonderful Uses of Colored Paper	5	92
Mother's Cooking School	5	195
	VOL.	PAGE
Woodwork for Older Children	5	269
Good Pictures: How They are Made	5	337
Stamp Collecting	5	349
A Little Dutch Boy and Girl of Old New York	8	198
Life in Old New York	8	201
Amundsen, Discoverer of the South Pole	8	213
Boyhood of a Patriot	9	15
George Washington, Father of Our Country	9	191

"Set all thy things in their peculiar place, and know that order is the greatest grace."
—JOHN DRYDEN.

PATIENCE

The quality of being expectant without haste, discontent, or complaint. Endurance with equanimity: forbearance of obstacles, delays failures pain, trials and tribulations.

WE HAVE all grown up with the admonition that patience is a virtue. But it is even more: it is a necessity. "God moves in a mysterious way His wonders to perform," and many of these ways seem unfair, unreasonable, and agonizingly slow of fulfilment. But it is no use to try to hurry them. They must come to bud, and blossom, and fruition in their own good time. There is nothing we can do about it but wait,— and we might as well wait patiently.

Mr. Walter Pitkin says, "In this atomic age . . . patience is more useful than ever before . . . Those who practice it succeed and grow happy. Those who flout it come to early grief.

"Life grows more and more complex. We have to deal with more and more people and things . . .

"So master patience more thoroughly than ever before. Teach the young to be patient. Then we shall have around us fewer failures and fewer frustrated souls who have overlooked the best experiences of life in their haste to win some short-lived and trifling pleasure."

Patience is a quality which only life can really teach. Most children are naturally impatient because they are full of energy and eagerness and their desires are for immediate gratifications. You cannot expect a young child to be patient very long. But he is practicing patience when he waits even a minute for what he wants. If his patience is recognized and rewarded, he will be able to wait a little longer next time.

As he grows older and can think in terms of longer periods of time, he will make plans and have hopes and ambitions for the future, be it next week or "when I'm grown up." He will learn that the bigger and more worth-while the project, the longer one must work and wait to achieve it. He will learn that growth in nature is slow and bides its time. He will see that the seasons, Christmas, and his birthday, arrive at their proper times and nothing can hurry them. By implication, then, he will learn the virtue of waiting for the many worth-while fruits of labor and planning, of growth and maturing, of the fulfilment of hopes and dreams and ambitions.

Being a good mother requires so much patience that in your own efforts to be one you will set your child a wonderful example in this great and important quality.

Suggested Reading

Arranged in Order of Interest to Children, from the Younger to the Older Age-Groups

	VOL.	PAGE		VOL.	PAGE
Try Again	1	206	The Wanderings of Odysseus	8	229
The Steadfast Tin Soldier	3	97	Childe Horne	8	278
Fun With Crayons	5	21	The Boyhood of a Story-Teller	9	1
Color—Design—Drawing	5	33	Joan of Arc	9	93
The Wonderful Uses of Colored Papers	5	92	Madame Curie	9	107
Cross Word Puzzles	5	171	Helen Keller	9	110
The Little Mother's Work Basket	5	213	The Pilgrims and the Puritans	9	157
Pilgrim's Progress	6	134	Sir Walter Raleigh	9	297
Griselda	6	160	Marguerite de Roberval	9	320
Champlain, Explorer of the St. Lawrence	8	203	Mackenzie, the Great Explorer	9	330

"The most useful virtue is patience."—JOHN DEWEY.

PATRIOTISM AND CIVIC RESPONSIBILITY

Love of country; devotion to the welfare of the country, city, or community of which one is a citizen.

LET US FIRST get over the old-fashioned idea that patriotism mean flag-waving or "my country right or wrong" or "might makes right." Truly right-minded people in America are strongly opposed to any such narrow idea of patriotism.

We are, however, fortunate in that we have a country of whose ideals we can be justly proud. The American ideal is freedom for all people so long as they live according to laws essential to the welfare of all. True, we do not always live up to the best of our ideals. But we are quick to admit our own mistakes and quick to expose injustice where we see it. We are free to express our opinions on any and every subject under the sun. This is a blessing which we enjoy more than any other country in the world, and it is of the utmost importance that our children realize it and understand it.

As opposed to our democratic form of government there are totalitarian forces abroad in the world today, both fascistic and communistic. They seek to undermine democracy and our children's faith in it. We must combat these forces with all the moral means at our command, by assuming our own civic responsibilities and using them to strengthen and improve our own system of government. We must enlist our children's interest in civic matters and show them that they too must do their part in understanding issues and in helping to better conditions. The time is past when they, or we, can "let George do it."

Our government represents those of us who express ourselves by assuming our civic responsibilities. We *are* the government. Let us teach this to our children so that they may appreciate what a great privilege it is to be an American. Let us encourage them to study what is going on, to question facts and sources, to attend town meetings, to write to constituted authorities protesting abuses and encouraging honest government. Let us help them to prepare themselves to be well-informed citizens and intelligent voters. Let them realize that "the noblest motive is the public good."

❧ ❧ ❧

Suggested Reading

Arranged in Order of Interest to Children, from the Younger to the Older Age-Groups

	VOL.	PAGE		VOL.	PAGE
High Water in Arkansas	2	319	Joan of Arc, Maid of Orleans	9	93
When the Mail Came Through	2	376	The Story of Nathan Hale	9	126
The Liberty Bell	4	169	Patrick Henry	9	170
America the Beautiful	4	364	The Signers of the Declaration of Independence	9	181
The Man Without a Country	6	216			
The American Flag	6	291	George Washington, Father of Our Country	9	191
Paul Revere's Ride	6	291			
Concord Hymn	6	303	Abraham Lincoln, Who Saved the Union	9	244
How Cincinnatus Saved Rome	8	271	Lord Nelson, Admiral of the Seas	9	304
William Tell	8	337	Twelve National Heroes	9	307
Robert the Bruce	8	385	Sir John A. MacDonald	9	342

"Now is our time for putting our house in good order and for joining ourselves together in a strong brotherhood for the management of our rich estate. Now is our time to take up our duty that goes with these riches, to stand as a strong rock of defense for free men everywhere, and to be the true friend of all men of good will throughout the world."
—DAVID CUSHMAN COYLE.

45

PERSEVERANCE AND PERSISTENCE

Accomplishment through continuous trying.
Steadfastness in effort.

PERSEVERENCE AND PERSISTENCE are probably responsible for more of life's successes than any other traits. Even genius has been described as "an infinite capacity for taking pains."

Children vary greatly in natural persistence. Some give up easily in the face of difficulties and get blamed for flightiness. Others persist doggedly in spite of repeated failures. Their very persistence may be annoying to the adults around them and they are often called obstinate. Their persistent effort should be recognized.

Children can be taught persistence by keeping up their interest in things just a little longer than it would spontaneously last, and by success. When necessary give them a little help, but don't take charge. The problem is still theirs. Urge them to try again. Say you will help. Success achieved is the best assurance of persistent effort next time.

Lack of persistence comes from repeated failure and doubt of one's own ability. Success seems impossible, so the child makes only half an effort. Obviously what is needed is self-confidence and successes. When a child chooses his own activities, he wants to succeed and will work for it if he thinks he has a chance.

Failures come to all of us, of course. We may become over-confident and attempt too much, or too much may be demanded of us. It requires judgment and experience to estimate correctly.

Children naturally make many mistakes, and so do adults in their estimates of a child's ability.

If a child fails in a task, that is sufficient proof that in some way it was too hard for him, physically, mentally, or emotionally. He is not to be blamed. Tomorrow he will be stronger and may succeed. The important thing is to see that he is not discouraged but feels that with a better plan or a more earnest effort he may succeed next time. Individual failures do not matter much. One can use them to learn from. It is the habit of failure and the resulting discouragement that destroy persistence.

The old adage, "If at first you don't succeed, try, try again" is a good one for both you and your children. The famous story of Bruce and the spider (to be found in Volume IV of this Bookshelf) has long been one of the best-known object-lessons in this important habit. Reading it to your children may impress them with the King's patience and the lesson he learned from the spider's persistence.

Help your children to persevere in their tasks. Get them into the habit of finishing what they start. Let them learn by their own experience of success. Give them projects of gradually increasing length and difficulty. Their pride in one successful project will develop perseverance for the next.

Suggested Reading

Arranged in Order of Interest to Children, from the Younger to the Older Age-Groups

	VOL.	PAGE
There Was Tammie!	1	118
How the Little Kite Learned to Fly	1	206
Try Again	1	206
The Hare and the Tortoise	2	15
The Seventh Pup	2	103
The Horse That Came From Heaven	2	125
Caleb's Luck	2	257
The Ugly Duckling	3	77
The Princess on the Glass Hill	3	205
Little Mother's Work Basket	5	213
Handicraft for Girls	5	249

	VOL.	PAGE
The Pilgrim's Progress	6	134
Riddles, Puzzles, Tricks, and Stunts	7	297
Champlain, Explorer of the St. Lawrence	8	203
Peary, Discoverer of the North Pole	8	210
An Inventor's Boyhood	9	10
Madame Curie	9	107
Adventures of Lewis and Clark	9	234
Marcus Whitman's Ride	9	238
A Man Like a Stone Wall	9	260

"We have only begun to fight."
—JOHN PAUL JONES.

PUNCTUALITY AND PROMPTNESS

The characteristic of keeping engagements and obligations on time.

FOR MANY REASONS, punctuality and promptness are good habits to acquire early in life. First of all, meeting appointments promptly saves yourself and others both time and annoyance. People tend to keep appointments with you punctually, too, if you are habitually on time. Dates of occasions which mean something to others, time for doing things in the daily routine, payment of bills, dues, etc. should be attended to promptly, too. If so handled they help to keep the mechanics of life running smoothly.

People who have no sense of time are forever rushing—and never getting things done. They are always in a state of anxiety, and are constantly missing out on things they would like to do, just because they do not plan their time properly.

It is difficult to teach the value of punctuality to a child, especially to an imaginative one given to dawdling and day-dreaming. Over-fussiness about punctuality on the part of mothers accounts for a good deal of their children's rebellion against it. A child often concentrates with all his might on what he is doing or thinking and time does not exist for him. We should not keep breaking in on him with demands that he stop immediately to do this or that.

If he is absorbed in his play or work, a young child should be warned ahead of time that it will soon be supper-time or whatever time you want him to be ready for. He will come more readily, too, if you usually have something pleasant for him at the appointed time. Say "It is time to—" at least as often about things he enjoys as about those that bore him.

Little children enjoy the sense of security and power that it gives them to know "what comes next" in the daily routine. Ask them that, and let *them* tell *you*. They can come to take pleasure in the smooth, peaceful progress of the day when things are done promptly and there is plenty of time left for play.

If needless delays cause a child to miss things he enjoys, he will finally learn to be more prompt. He will see that some things just won't wait for him, and gradually he will be able to readjust himself quickly enough to be on time. It won't come easily or fast, for to a child the shining, living moment is far more real than the future.

But keep the family schedule running as smoothly as possible. Let the child see that you consider it worth a maximum effort to get things done on time, to meet appointments promptly, to catch trains or busses, and to waste neither your time or that of others. In time he will learn that one gets the most value from time by using it according to a well-laid plan. Then one can manage work and other duties and still have time for recreation, social pleasures, or even just to "loaf and invite your soul."

Suggested Reading

Arranged in Order of Interest to Children, from the Younger to the Older Age-Groups

	VOL.	PAGE
Little Boy Blue	1	35
A Diller, a Dollar	1	35
The Three Little Pigs	1	89
Number 9, the Little Fire Engine	1	172
Frogs at School	1	193
Time to Rise	1	210
Champion Fire 'n Feather	2	142
Cinderella	3	123
O Hana San of Japan	8	99
The Little Red Princess of the Forest	8	186

"Know the true value of time. Never put off until tomorrow what you can do today."
—CHESTERFIELD.

RESPECT, REVERENCE AND FAITH

The gracious offering of esteem, tribute, deference, and honor
to that which one admires and believes in. Worship of what
is sacred.

RESPECT, REVERENCE AND FAITH, although
each different from the other two, all imply a lift of the spirit above the material values
of life. They are all emotions in praise of noble,
lofty, or sacred things. We respect those personal qualities, laws, conventions, and ideals
which seem to us good. We revere persons of
noble character, feeling both love and awe for
them. We have faith in God, in our religion, in
the sacred beliefs we live by.

Present day children too often seem lacking in
veneration. Afraid of being considered soft or
sentimental, they scoff at such feelings. These
children are not necessarily insensitive. Children
who try to act "hard-boiled," who treat everything noble with ridicule, often feel deeply. Perhaps they have been ridiculed for showing their
deeper and finer feelings, and have therefore become ashamed of them. Or they may have been
required to pretend such feelings before they were
mature enough to have them or understand them.

Man cannot exist, spiritually, unless he can
believe in something nobler and higher than himself, some power above and beyond the material
and human. Children, "trailing clouds of glory"
as they come, realize this almost instinctively. It
is in their natures to love, and as they grow older
they are full of idealism and admiration for what
seems noble and good to them. The child who
giggles at what we find sacred does so through
embarrassment at his own emotions, not through
a desire to mock.

We must take our children's ideals seriously,
all of them. A child can be shown the wonder and
mystery, the beauties and exactitudes of nature—
of night and day, sun and moon, blossoms and
fruit, tides, seasons, stars, births, deaths. From
an understanding that there is a Creator of these,
the child can come to respect what is decent and
admirable; to revere what is worthy of awe and
reverence; to have faith in what is good, true,
and noble; and to worship what is sacred. Your
own sincere expression of these emotions will be
a guiding light for your child to follow.

※   ※   ※

Suggested Reading

Arranged in Order of Interest to Children, from the Younger to the Older Age-Groups

	VOL.	PAGE		VOL.	PAGE
The Cherry-Tree Carol	1	360	Moses	4	150
God is Great and God is Good	1	381	Pilgrim's Progress	6	134
All Things Bright and Beautiful	1	382	Where Love Is, God Is	6	262
Do You Know How Many Stars?	1	384	Battle Hymn of the Republic	6	299
The Sandpiper	2	87	To a Waterfowl	6	317
The Lamb	2	92	Lead, Kindly Light	6	328
The Gift	2	332	Abou Ben Adhem	6	330
The Christmas Apple	2	333	King Robert of Sicily	6	357
The Angelus	4	32	Honors to the Flag	9	150
Children of the Shell	4	43	Russell H. Conwell	9	289

*"The more I study nature, the more I stand amazed at the work of
the Creator."*
—LOUIS PASTEUR.

RESOURCEFULNESS AND INGENUITY

Resourcefulness: The ability to find ways and means of planning, making, and doing things, and of solving problems.

Ingenuity: Inventiveness. Skill in devising and contriving.

ONE OF THE BEST traits a child can have is the ability to meet new situations successfully. Life often puts us into strange environments and unfamiliar situations. A resourceful person finds zest and enjoyment in novelty. He gets thrills and satisfaction out of adventure, for he knows his own ability to meet the demands of the occasion. Anyone who has not developed these qualities of ingenuity and resourcefulness is more likely to be frightened in the same circumstances. He may be unable to think quickly or act with decision, just when it is imperative to do so.

Children enjoy mental activity just as they do physical activity. They are always thinking, planning, investigating, experimenting. Encourage them to think for themselves just as you encourage them to help themselves in other ways. Too many parents over-direct their children in an attempt to protect or to train them. Thus they stifle the children's natural resourcefulness and ingenuity.

Let your child think things out for himself. Let him use his toys as he thinks best. Let him try to make, do, and mend things, even if the results are far from perfect. Encourage him to think up makeshifts when proper equipment is not available. Use leading questions to help him work out ways and means of doing things. Encourage his ingenuity in thinking them out. Do a lot of wondering—"I wonder how we could do this. What do you think?"

Dealing with people often requires resourcefulness and ingenuity. A child can learn to enjoy the ingenuity involved in answering any remark both truthfully and kindly. Many quarrels and misunderstandings can be avoided by this social resourcefulness, which we commonly call tact.

When your child faces a difficult problem, do not solve it for him except as a last resort. Let him work out some sort of solution by himself if possible. Encourage him all you can in this. Give hints or suggestions that may help him to think more clearly, if it seems necessary. Offer a solution only if he is completely stopped.

Children brought up in this way will have had so much experience in inventing and devising ways to meet new situations that they will accept the challenge of each new adventure cheerfully and with self-confidence.

❧ ❧ ❧

Suggested Reading

Arranged in Order of Interest to Children, from the Younger to the Older Age-Groups

	VOL.	PAGE		VOL.	PAGE
Mike Mulligan and His Steam Shovel	1	160	Gutenberg, Inventor of Printing	4	165
The Fox and the Little Red Hen	1	331	Fun With Crayons	5	21
The Lion and the Goat	2	25	Self-Directed Work and Play	5	114
Almost an Ambush	2	158	Ali Baba and the Forty Thieves	6	14
The Doughnuts	2	201	Robinson Crusoe	6	89
Barnum's First Circus	2	290	Toys and Toy Games	7	271
High Water in Arkansas	2	319	How a Woman Saved an Army	9	130
Young Lucretia	2	362	Benjamin Franklin	9	198
The Musicians of Bremen	3	45	Marguerite de Roberval	9	320
Hansel and Gretel	3	65	Madeleine de Verchères	9	325

"Resourcefulness is applied experience."
—JENNIE ELLIS BURDICK,

RESPONSIBILITY

Moral accountability. Reliability of character.

FEW CHARACTERISTICS are more widely and justly appreciated than responsibility. If a man or woman dependably carries through whatever he undertakes he will be universally respected. Many interesting and worthwhile opportunities will be open to him in business, social, and civic life. He will have the satisfaction of knowing that he really is accomplishing important things. Thus, responsibility is one of the most valuable characteristics with which we can hope to endow our children.

People who have not developed their ability to take responsibility often "go to pieces" when circumstances suddenly put new responsibilities upon their shoulders. Young men may fail of advancement for lack of the ability to carry responsibility. Women may be unable to keep their homes orderly and to be good wives and mothers for the same reason. Yet they could have learned, during childhood, how to manage and enjoy greater and greater responsibilities.

Give your child a chance to be responsible in small matters at first, and let his responsibilities increase as fast as his growth and development warrant it. Young children *want* to do things by themselves. Who has not heard the cry, "ME do!" from a child who wants to open the car door or turn on the faucet himself? Show him how, and then let him do it.

If he likes to bring in the morning paper, encourage his doing it regularly. Let him feel important because the family counts on him for that and appreciates his dependable service. If he forgets, remind him tactfully. If he tires of it after a while, do not nag or insist. He may need a new and perhaps more important responsibility by then.

There are all kinds of responsibilities around any home which children can assume as they develop. They need not always be duties that recur daily or weekly. At certain stages of development those become hated drudgery. Give children occasionally the thrill of a *big* responsibility. Let the half-grown child take a deposit down to the bank for you, or let the budding cook plan, buy, and prepare the family food for a whole day.

There is no other training for responsibility which can compare with the actual experience of responsibilities successfully carried. When your child cries, "*I* can do it!" let him try if possible. Sometimes give him the happy surprise of showing that you trust him to do some "grown-up" thing he has not even thought of undertaking. Most of us tend to underestimate what our children are capable of. Give them increasing responsibilities, adapted to their development. Show them that you make a point of meeting your own responsibilities. Then have faith in their responsibility and reliability, and let them see that you do.

※ ※ ※

Suggested Reading

Arranged in Order of Interest to Children, from the Younger to the Older Age-Groups

	VOL.	PAGE		VOL.	PAGE
The Seventh Pup	2	103	Clara Barton	9	113
Caleb's Luck	2	257	Evangeline Booth	9	116
Indians in the House	2	274	The Story of Nathan Hale	9	126
Elizabeth Ann Fails in an Examination	2	304	George Washington	9	191
The Magic Fishbone	3	242	Abraham Lincoln	9	244
The Apple of Contentment	3	271	Dewey, Hero of Manila	9	264
The Maid in the Mirror	3	307	Woodrow Wilson	9	272
The Boyhood of a President	9	56	The Story of Madeleine de Verchères	9	325
A Courageous Boy Who Became President	9	72	Sir Wilfrid Laurier	9	348

"Responsibility educates."—WENDELL PHILLIPS.

SELF-AMUSEMENT AND SELF-DIRECTION

The ability to keep oneself occupied and entertained by one's own devices, authority, and management.

THE ABILITY to be responsible for one's own decisions and acts should be the goal of self-discipline. Adults who remain dependent upon others to tell them what to think and do are not mature human beings but remain emotionally infantile. They are not really happy because they have no faith in themselves. They are, in fact, likely victims of totalitarian dictatorships. They will accept a dictator to direct them, as a child does his father, because they cannot take the responsibility for self-direction.

Young children can be taught the elements of self-direction in their play activities. Allow them to investigate and experiment; do not constantly interrupt and direct. Thus they learn to play contentedly by themselves.

Any little child is, when his mother leaves him, likely to whimper or yell for her return. If your child does so, play with him a little, so that his desire for affection and society are satisfied, then hand him some new or interesting object, and slip quietly away. Come back in a few moments, before he gets lonesome. Next time you can stay a bit longer and so, very gradually, baby learns to be happy without you for a considerable time. He learns to amuse himself.

Sometimes older children keep asking "What can we do now?" This is usually the result of having had others amuse them too much, or of having had so many ill chosen toys that they expect novelties continually. A wise choice of toys is very important. Good constructive toys stimulate the child's ingenuity as they can be put to dozens of different uses. Good stories are helpful, and new experiences that broaden a child's ideas of the world give him something in his own head to fall back on for play ideas.

If your child is too dependent on others for play ideas, work on the matter gradually. You have probably over-directed him in the past and you must learn not to hover, direct, or manage. Withdraw your support little by little. Get him started on something if necessary, and then become "too busy" with your own affairs, so that he must carry on alone. Get him to take a larger and larger part in planning his own activities. Encourage play with other children (and *not* with those older than he); then he will be expected to do his part.

If he is old enough to read, the volume "Things to Make and Things to Do" will help him. He will soon take pleasure in directing himself—and very probably others! He will be growing toward maturity, and you will have more free time.

✵ ✵ ✵

Suggested Reading

Arranged in Order of Interest to Children, from the Younger to the Older Age-Groups

	VOL.	PAGE		VOL.	PAGE
Playgrounds	1	184	The Melon-Eaters	4	48
The Land of Counterpane	1	190	James Watt	4	190
Where Go the Boats?	1	209	Self-Directed Work and Play	5	114
What's in the Mail-Box?	1	232	Stamp Collecting	5	349
Some Things to Guess	1	256	Playing with Nature's Toys	7	227
Some More Things to Guess	1	257	Outdoor Sports and Games	7	241
Fun With Crayons	5	21	Pencil and Paper Games	7	269
Modeling	5	31	An Inventor's Boyhood	9	10
The Wonderful Uses of Colored Papers	5	92	The Boyhood of a President	9	56
Gymnastic Plays	7	343	Theodore Roosevelt	9	268

"The sooner you get a child to be a law unto himself, the sooner you make a man of him."
—DR. N. McLEOD

SELF-CONTROL

The ability to exercise directing, guiding, and restraining
power over one's emotions, words, and actions.

MOST THOUGHTFUL PEOPLE will agree that the object of discipline should be to make the child a responsible, adaptable, self-controlled human being. Self-control as opposed to the need for control by others is the essence of maturity. Solomon's proverb "He that ruleth his own spirit is greater than he that taketh a city" shows that the value of self-control has long been recognized.

Self-control involves denying a momentary impulse in order to achieve a greater good. Baby shows dawning self-control when he says "Please" instead of grabbing. He is guiding his actions by what he has learned of the ways that work best in the world. That is self-control.

Of course he is trying to get the most out of life, but he has found that following every impulse is not the best way to do it. As he grows older, he will find that approval for being a brave boy means more than the relief of tears when he skins his knee. So he controls his sobs.

This is a sort of secondary control from outside rather than true self-control, for his eye is on what others demand of him. Still it is a legitimate step in arriving at the time when his own ideal of himself as a brave boy would prevent his howling even if he were all alone. When that happens, he has arrived at true *self*-control about skinned knees. He wants to be brave more than he wants to cry and he is able to control his actions to conform with his deeper desires. One step is taken on the road to self-control.

Most of us are still struggling along somewhere on that road ourselves. Don't we yield to impulses occasionally and do things that "we know we'll be sorry for"? Or we do things which we know are not very wise or noble, but which give us so much satisfaction that we are never really sorry that we did them. It's nothing to be particularly ashamed of. We are all human and we can't live all the time by ultimates and shouldn't try. Certainly we mustn't expect it of children.

Some people work so hard for self-control that they try to deny all their spontaneous impulses on principle, as though being impulsive must be bad. They become cold, solemn, and puritanical. They lack all spontaneity as well as real sympathy and understanding. They are not very lovable. Heaven pity a child who has to live with them! It would be small wonder if he hated the very idea of self-control.

A child needs a family where everyone practices reasonable self-control in order that he and others may get the best out of life, yet makes no fetish of it. He needs a *chance* to practice self-control—which he cannot do if he is constantly controlled by others. He needs encouragement to try for the greater satisfactions that self-control brings. He must know that his family has faith in his growing self-control and expects progress. He will be rewarded by the pleasures he gains for himself and the happiness he gives others.

But they must not expect too much too soon. It is a long, slow process, which can be helped but not forced.

❧ ❧ ❧

Suggested Reading

Arranged in Order of Interest to Children, from the Younger to the Older Age-Groups

	VOL.	PAGE
Timid Timothy	1	104
Watch Me!	1	115
Sneezer	1	154
The Talkative Tortoise	1	332
The Magic Fishbone	2	242
The Maid in the Mirror	2	307
The Five Queer Brothers	2	318
Why Mr. Possum Loves Peace	2	359
Pilgrim's Progress	6	134
Some Simple Rules for Conversation	7	240

	VOL.	PAGE
Perseus	8	221
William Tell	8	337
The Boyhood of a Patriot	9	15
King Louis XIV of France	9	78
Daniel Boone, Indian Fighter and Pioneer	9	226
A Man Like a Stone Wall	9	260
Radisson, "The Canadian Ulysses"	9	323
Joseph Howe of Nova Scotia	9	345

"No man is free who cannot govern himself."—PYTHAGORAS.

SELF-RESPECT

A reasonable pleasure in one's best qualities.

SELF-RESPECT is one of the most necessary parts of a balanced and wholesome character. It is unendurable to live with a person you can't respect, yet you will have to live with yourself twenty-four hours a day as long as you live at all. How vital it is that we help our children to be worthy of respect and to know that they are!

Self-respect grows from two main sources, the opinions of others, and the evidence of our own experience. A child needs to know that he is accepted and loved for what he is. If everyone thinks he's pretty nice, he feels that he must be.

You can't love your child too much, but you *can* love him foolishly, selfishly, or blindly. That will hurt him. You should estimate his good and bad points as fairly as you possibly can and *be honest with him* about them. Lavish and indiscriminate praise, or making excuses for weakness may produce conceit or teach deceitfulness; they do not build self-respect. Children know honesty, and only honest praise means anything. *That* is priceless in building self-esteem.

Praise your child's achievements, but do not ignore or cover up his failures, mistakes, and wrong-doing. Admit them and the need of correcting them when possible and of doing better next time. Let him know that you are sure he *can* do better, that your love and faith are unshaken.

This means that you must use great wisdom and judgment in knowing what it is fair to expect of your child as he grows. If you expect too much, he is under a strain and may feel worried and hopelessly incompetent. If you expect too little, he may grow insincere or lazy. Try to base your judgment on what he seems able to do without strain, and when in doubt lean toward the side of charity.

Stronger even than the opinion of others is the testimony of experience. A child respects himself for what he knows he can do. If he laces his shoes, makes a home-run, or builds a model plane—there is the fact to testify to his ability.

Let children do things for themselves as fast as they are able. Let them do things for others, too. That has the wonderful advantage of implying superior power. Mother used to have to do everything for him; now he is big and strong enough to do things for her.

Give children every possible opportunity to develop new skills. That is a fine way to realize their own competence.

Praise good qualities and achievements in others, including those which your child knows are also his own. Commend progress in what he can do and in what he can be. Let him know that there speaks his best self, his true self, of which you are proud. Then he, too, will come to expect well of himself. He will hold himself up to his own standards and take "reasonable pleasure in his own best qualities."

❧ ❧ ❧

Suggested Reading

Arranged in Order of Interest to Children, from the Younger to the Older Age-Groups

	VOL.	PAGE		VOL.	PAGE
The Advantage of Knowledge	2	24	The Mountain and the Squirrel	6	324
The Skunk in Tante Odette's Oven	2	65	For A' That and A' That	6	326
Never Worked and Never Will	2	76	Elegy in a Country Churchyard	6	359
The 500 Hats of Bartholomew Cubbins	2	210	Clara Barton	9	113
Fung's Fourth	2	298	Benjamin Franklin	9	198
Willie's Good Recess	2	301	Andrew Jackson, Soldier and Seventh		
The Ugly Duckling	3	77	President	9	230
Dick Whittington and His Cat	3	154	Abraham Lincoln, Who Saved the Union	9	244
Alexander Visits Diogenes	4	162	Alfred E. Smith	9	284
The Village Blacksmith	6	96			

"Never esteem anything of advantage to you that shall make you forsake your word or lose your self-respect." —MARCUS AURELIUS.

SELF-SACRIFICE AND SERVICE TO OTHERS

Forfeit of one's own interests for the sake of helping others.

THE SPIRIT of genuine self-sacrifice and willing service to others springs from a love of people so deep that it makes one feel himself an integral part of a greater unity. Most people have it in regard to the family, many extend it to larger groups, and a few to all humanity. It speaks through kind and thoughtful service. The desire to help is not dependent on thanks or return favors. It is as natural as the way a leaf manufactures food for the whole tree or a mother nurses her baby. Like all the greatest wonders, it is natural and common.

Anyone enjoys doing things for those he loves. Children begin to "want to help" as soon as they can toddle, and this impulse lays the foundation for broader service. Make the spirit of the family one of helpfulness and happy service. Encourage the child to do small things for members of the family and later for friends and neighbors. Let there be many "surprises" to please both adults and children, and let the children help to prepare them. They will soon appreciate the joys of service.

Above all, teach your child to *like people*. Speak of the good qualities of friends and neighbors and show your affection for them. Take it for granted that it would be pleasant to help them out when you can. Show sympathy and interest, too, in the problems and activities of people you do not know personally. Help wherever you can and let your child know that you like to do so. Allow him to help when he can.

He will soon learn of the many groups that devote themselves to service of one sort or another, and will probably like to help. Community drives are likely to find willing workers among the children if the services required are simple.

Any mother can find dozens of projects in the community, beginning with the home, at which the child can lend helpful service contributing something of his own. Beginning this habit early will do wonders at building his character.

❧ ❧ ❧

Suggested Reading

Arranged in Order of Interest to Children, from the Younger to the Older Age-Groups

	VOL.	PAGE
The Banyan Deer	1	314
God's Helpers	1	380
Black Stallion and Red Mare	2	165
The Christmas Apple	2	333
Princess Finola and the Dwarf	3	181
Casperl and the Princess	3	194
The Shoemaker and the Elves	3	218
The Brownies	3	226
The Fire Bringer	3	338
How Indian Corn Came to the World	3	354
St. Elizabeth	4	105

	VOL.	PAGE
Moses	4	150
A Family in the Land of Von Winkelried	4	202
Horatius at the Bridge	6	107
Roland	8	319
Joan of Arc	9	93
Madame Curie	9	107
The Story of Nathan Hale	9	126
Abraham Lincoln, Who Saved the Union	9	244
The Mayo Brothers	9	282

" 'Tis nobleness to serve." —RALPH WALDO EMERSON.

SENSE OF HUMOR

The faculty of being able to laugh at laughable things; to adapt oneself to the ludicrous side of life and not to take it too seriously.

THE GENIAL Chinese philosopher, Dr. Lin Yutang, says: "Modern man takes life far too seriously, and because ne is too serious, his world is full of troubles. The importance of humor should never be forgotten . . . There is a purifying power in laughter . . . If you have a sense of humor, you have the key to good sense, to simple thinking, to a peaceable temper, and to a cultured outlook on the world."

What wise words these are! All of us would do well to live by them. Life doesn't take *us* seriously. It frequently pokes us in the ribs and laughs at us. Why not laugh back?

A sense of humor helps in many ways. It helps us dismiss the petty annoyances which beset us all. It is a splendid nerve tonic and adds zest to daily tasks. It is a saving grace in distress and adversity,—a precious thing not to be lost in coping with the practical and prosaic considerations of adult life.

Children begin early to see the funny side of life. They may laugh at things we do not think funny, but that is not important. What matters is that they laugh at what seems funny to them.

Keep up this spirit! See that smiles, fun, and laughter accompany family life, everyone taking part. Play games with the children. Keep life gay and amusing. Don't let it sag.

Humor has its pitfalls. Because children laugh so easily, they may laugh cruelly, over teasing or the discomfiture of others. They should be shown that such laughter not only seems mean and in poor taste, but adds to the hurt of one already in trouble.

If you expect a child to understand this attitude, you must be very careful never to laugh at him in his childish difficulties. There may be a very funny side to such episodes. If so, show your sympathy for his trouble, but try also to get him to see the amusing aspect of it. If you can laugh together over it, he will learn the healing power of humor. Such laughter will drive away many a quarrel, grudge, or fit of ill temper.

If the home is full of gaiety, nonsense, and jokes, happiness flourishes in it. Laughter is always there just under the surface, and a sense of humor can be called on at any time to make dull days or dreary jobs fun.

❧ ❧ ❧

Suggested Reading

Arranged in Order of Interest to Children, from the Younger to the Older Age-Groups

	VOL.	PAGE
The Owl and the Pussy-Cat	1	94
The Blowaway Hat	1	224
Fun and Nonsense (whole section)	1	269
The Table and the Chair	1	274
Cheerful Tales and Verse (whole section)	2	27
Fun and laughter (whole section)	2	179
The Real Princess	3	102
What the Old Man Does Is Always Right	3	110
The Husband Who Minded the House	3	174

	VOL.	PAGE
The Squire's Bride	3	201
The Dragon's Story	3	290
The Five Queer Brothers	3	318
How Pecos Bill Won His Bouncing Bride	3	357
Uncle Remus Stories	3	359
Paul Bunyan Stories	3	372
Don Quixote	6	96
A Mad Tea-Party	6	110
Tartarin of Tarascon	6	226

"There is certainly no defense against adverse fortune which is, on the whole, so effectual as an habitual sense of humor."—T. W. HIGGINSON.

SINCERITY

Honesty of mind and genuineness of intention.
Candor. Freedom from hypocrisy and falseness.

A PERSON who is sincere at heart and in spirit, and who has fundamental honor and integrity, has assets of good will greater than money in the bank. His word is his bond; people gladly extend credit to him; they trust him. This is of inestimable value to him.

Sincerity, however, is not a trait which should stand alone. One can be perfectly sincere in an unworthy purpose. Hitler, for example, probably was. Sincerity needs to be backed by a well informed mind and a fine character. Therefore the foundation for sincerity which you must lay in your child is mental, emotional, and spiritual integrity. If he has these, he can dare to be sincere.

Insincerity is a trait which children learn from adults; not the other way around. In the beginning, children are innocent of any desire to be insincere. They see no reason for it. In adult life, however, social conventions make tactful remarks, occasional white lies, and other small insincerities necessary. One must sometimes resort to them if one would get along with a minimum of friction. It is a pity that it should be so, for small, superficial insincerities can easily grow into larger and more fundamental ones.

Children need an explanation of the insincerities adults use to smooth out casual relationships. They will be less confused by them if they know that they are merely social conventions, a sort of code-language that we all understand.

Naturally, the fewer of them there are, the better. Let parents be fundamentally sincere. Let their sincerity be intelligent and directed toward worthy ends. Let them guard their actions as well as their speech against insincerity. Let them, so far as possible, live a simple life in which there are few reasons for insincerity. Let them keep silent rather than say an insincere thing, either pleasant or unpleasant. And let them learn to find many pleasant things to talk of with genuine sincerity. Their children will be only too happy to follow suit.

ℐ ℐ ℐ

Suggested Reading

Arranged in Order of Interest to Children, from the Younger to the Older Age-Groups

	VOL.	PAGE		VOL.	PAGE
The Wolf in Sheep's Clothing	2	18	Helen Keller	9	110
The Emperor's New Clothes	3	74	Patrick Henry	9	170
The Nightingale	3	89	William Penn	9	178
Ploughing in the Nivernais	4	136	Lafayette, Friend of America	9	209
The Story of Myles Standish	8	190	Theodore Roosevelt	9	268
The Friends of the Indians	8	206	Oliver Wendell Holmes	9	279
Joan of Arc	9	93	A Black-Robed Voyageur	9	336
Susan B. Anthony	9	102	Sir John A. MacDonald	9	342
Carrie Chapman Catt	9	103	Grenfell's Sermon in Deeds	9	377

"Inward sincerity will of course influence the outward deportment; where the one is wanting, there is great reason to suspect the absence of the other."
—LAURENCE STERNE.

SYMPATHY AND CONSIDERATION
FOR OTHERS

The ability to understand and enter into the feelings and interests of others, to condole with their difficulties, and to do what one can to be of help and comfort to them.

GENUINE SYMPATHY for others and true consideration for them come from an "understanding heart," that most precious gift. Of it a wise man once said, "An understanding heart is worth more than a dozen college diplomas." So it is; for an understanding heart can often do for a friend what all the brains in the world cannot.

Of course an understanding heart is richer and acts more effectively when combined with intelligence. But the truly understanding heart has wisdom of its own. It understands but does not intrude. It sympathizes but does not pry. It knows when and how to act and when and how to heal by silence. It deepens affection and adds warmth to every human relationship.

Babies and young children naturally respond to affection. Mother's smile brings an answering smile. That is one of their charms. But the little one needs response to his overtures, too. He may be clumsy, and get in the way of a busy mother, but "Go away and don't bother me" is one of the surest ways to kill his desire to be helpful.

Try to remember that a child needs sympathy and understanding *all* the time, even when—perhaps especially when—he has been "naughty."

"You are a good child, but you have made a mistake" is a much more constructive way of dealing with "naughtiness" than to say "You are a bad, naughty child." Keep your sympathy and understanding consistent throughout childhood, adolescence, indeed throughout your child's life.

Mark the small successes of any member of the family with a family celebration, however simple. Let any misfortune be the signal for extra consideration for everyone. In that way children learn how sympathetic sharing can double pleasure and halve sorrow. Show your child how much his consideration for you and for other members of the family is appreciated. See that he has plenty of things and people to love,—dolls, toys, pets, friends, and loving relatives. Help him to find little ways to make them happy.

But don't let sympathy be limited to the family and personal friends. If a child sees that his parents are considerate of everyone and help the needy whenever they can, he will want to do the same.

It takes time and patience to cultivate sympathy and consideration in a child; but no other job in parenthood is so well worth the effort. A child with a truly understanding heart is the richest reward a parent can have.

❦ ❦ ❦

Suggested Reading

Arranged in Order of Interest to Children, from the Younger to the Older Age-Groups

	VOL.	PAGE		VOL.	PAGE
The Story of a Little White Teddy Bear	1	10	A Miserable Merry Christmas	2	346
My Scottie	1	136	Young Lucretia	2	362
Under the Little Fir	1	369	Beauty and the Beast	3	116
Prayer for Children Everywhere	1	380	The Jackal and the Camel	3	323
The Golden Rule	1	383	The Princes in the Tower	4	68
The Fox and the Stork	2	9	A Christmas Carol	6	165
Pino and Paint	2	109	The Little Red Princess of the Forest	8	186
Karoo, the Kangaroo	2	119	Cato, the Younger	8	365
Such a Kind World	2	137	Clara Barton	9	113
How Bambi Found the Meadow	2	148	William Penn	9	178

"Sympathy is the golden key that unlocks the hearts of others."
—SAMUEL SMILES.

SYSTEM AND EFFICIENCY

Orderly organization of a project planned and executed so as to yield the most effective result measured against the necessary output of time, energy, money, etc.

ANYONE who has tried it knows how a system straightens out the maddening confusion and myriad details of a difficult job. Some women seem to keep their homes looking nice, their families well clothed, well fed and happy, and still always have time left for rest or relaxation. Others struggle along, always behind with their work, tired and irritable. The difference is largely a matter of system and efficiency.

A system, of course, is simply a carefully made plan. It clears away indecision and waste motion, bringing order and purpose into any project. What a lot of time, money, and energy we waste through inefficiency and lack of system! Instead, "Plan your work and then work your plan."

An orderly home, where things are kept in their places and family routines run smoothly, begins to train a child for system while he is yet a baby. He *likes* it, because it seems familiar and homelike. He does not yet make the plan, but he enjoys helping to carry it out.

If he has always known where to find things, he will be annoyed by the delays that confusion brings. As he gradually assumes responsibility for his own things he will assign them definite places,—though he may not always remember to put them there.

Whenever you do things with your child, let him see your habit of planning, of thoughtful action. "I wonder what would be the best way to—" or "Would it be quicker if we—." He will soon respond with his own plans.

Between eight and twelve or fourteen many children are very disorderly at home. It seems as though early training had been wasted. But at this time they are probably elaborating a constitution and by laws for their club, or working out intricate team plays for some game. They are still using system, but in a new area.

The blessed thing about a good system is that *it works!* It provides its own reward in terms of fun and accomplishment. Praise it. "That's a good system you figured out,—saves time and effort." Or, if the child is discouraged in his work, "Perhaps you need to get a system."

As he grows older he will be able to plan more wisely and for longer periods as to what he will do with his time, his money, and his energy. He will learn, too, that not all aspects of life lend themselves to organization and efficiency. You don't make love that way, or paint a sunset, or write a great poem. Impulse, emotion, and even whimsy, have their places in a full life. He will come to allow for that without giving up his conviction that, when there is a serious job to do, system and efficiency are in order.

❧ ❧ ❧

Suggested Reading

Arranged in Order of Interest to Children, from the Younger to the Older Age-Groups

	VOL.	PAGE
P-Penny and His Little Red Cart	1	243
Fun With Drawing	5	1
Fun With Crayons	5	21
Color—Design—Drawing	5	33
The Wonderful Uses of Colored Paper	5	92
Cross Word Puzzles	5	171
Mother's Cooking School	5	195
Woodwork for Older Children	5	269
Good Pictures: How They Are Made	5	337
Stamp Collecting	5	349
Robinson Crusoe	6	89

	VOL.	PAGE
Amundsen, Discoverer of the South Pole	8	213
How Cincinnatus Saved Rome	8	271
William Tell	8	337
Olaf the Brave	8	372
A Nurse's Girlhood	9	6
Madame Curie	9	107
George Washington, Father of Our Country	9	191
Benjamin Franklin	9	193
The Mayo Brothers	9	282

"There is always a best way of doing everything, if it be to boil an egg."
—RALPH WALDO EMERSON.

TACT

Delicate and sympathetic perception of what is appropriate and considerate in dealing with others.

TACT has been called "the unsaid portion of what we think." Actually the word does come from a Latin one meaning "to be silent." Often, however, tact is more than that. It may involve doing or saying things. Tact is a gracious way of relieving tensions, of avoiding or curing embarrassments. It eases situations, and makes people feel happier.

This is obviously a valuable trait. It gives charm to the personality and shows sensitiveness to and consideration for the feelings of others. The following story is an illustration of what tact can accomplish:

Two boys went up to a house and sat down on the steps, shuffling their muddy feet and dragging a heavy cart back and forth on the path. It was not their house or even their own neighborhood; yet they had taken noisy possession. Presently a man opened the door, watched them quietly a moment and then said pleasantly, "How do you do? Won't you come in?"

The boys looked up in abashed surprise, sheepishly got up and hurried away without a word. The man smiled and closed the door. The man could have shouted, scolded, threatened, or abused the trespassers, doubtless with unpleasant re-

sults before the boys went away. Because he was pleasant and tactful the annoyance ceased at once, and no one's feelings were hurt.

People who "rub us the wrong way" often do so unintentionally merely because they are insensitive to our feelings. Many of us are more or less tactful with adults but amazingly *tactless* with children. Children have keen ears, alert eyes, and tender sensibilities. Yet people say things about children as though they were deaf, laugh at their mistakes, and makes them feel ridiculous, stupid, or guilty. This is not only tactless but downright cruel. Children need affectionate understanding and courteous respect even more than adults do.

Be tactful with your children and teach them how to be so themselves. Teach them that tact is just an ingenious way of being kind and pleasant. By middle childhood they enjoy ingenuity. They like to learn the "how" of doing things with "no fuss, no muss," no hard feelings, —but neatly and prettily. Commend their attempts at tact. Remind them sometimes by a smile or a wink that "this is one of the times when we won't say all that we think." They will love the shared secret, and tact will develop.

❧ ❧ ❧

Suggested Reading

Arranged in Order of Interest to Children, from the Younger to the Older Age-Groups

	VOL.	PAGE		VOL.	PAGE
The Lion and the Mosquitoes	1	316	Hans Brinker	6	202
The Wind and the Sun	2	5	Getting Up a Party	7	235
The Fox and the Stork	2	9	The Fine Art of Living Together	7	237
Mr. A and Mr. P	2	196	Your Friends	7	238
Willie's Good Recess	2	301	The Child of Urbino	9	27
What the Old Man Does Is Always Right	3	110	William Penn	9	178
Toads and Diamonds	3	147	Benjamin Franklin	9	198
The Old Woman and the Tramp	3	190	The Wife Who Taught Her Husband to Be President	9	229
How the Good Gifts Were Used by Two	3	282	Dewey, the Hero of Manila	9	264

"The nearer you come into relation with a person, the more necessary do tact and courtesy become." —OLIVER WENDELL HOLMES.

THINKING AND REASONING

The ability to exercise powers of judgment, conception, or inference, to reflect for the purpose of reaching a logical conclusion.

THE ABILITY to think is one of the great differences that sets men apart from the rest of the animal kingdom. Thinking is natural to human beings. Thought and reasoning have formed all the cultures of mankind. They have been necessary for the creation not only of art, science, and literature, but for the great bridges that span our rivers, the cars and planes we ride in, and all the everyday conveniences among which we live.

We all think—we can't help it—but some think clearly and logically, others in confused, disorganized ways. Yet, although some of us can never be mental giants, any child can learn to use well the mentality he has.

The foundations of thought are experience and observation. Then comes language, the tool of thought. First the child understands what is said to him. Soon he speaks himself, forming and sharing thoughts. Speak clearly and simply to your child. You will be laying foundations for clear thinking later. Play little games of memory and imagination with them. Such "fun" is mental training. Encourage alert interest and observation and broaden the child's range of experiences as fast as he is able to accept them.

Children are full of curiosity, a sort of mental hunger. They reach out for information to feed their minds just as they do for food for their bodies. They ask what, why and how. Their ability to reason is still very elementary, but they want to learn.

We can help children to think straight in these ways:

1. Answer their questions as truthfully and accurately as you can, taking into consideration what they can understand.

2. Talk with them about what they see, do, and read. Make a family habit of intelligent discussion and accurate recounting of experiences.

3. Never ridicule them for mistakes in reasoning. Show them, pleasantly but seriously, how to get the matter straight.

4. As they get older, help them to analyze their problems and think them out logically. Do not try to do their thinking for them. Let them try things out. Let them put their judgment and decisions to the test of trial and experience. They will learn by both success and mistakes.

5. When they show good, logical reasoning, commend them.

6. Above all, watch your own reasoning to be sure that it sets a clear example of logic and impartiality for them to follow.

*   *   *

Suggested Reading

Arranged in Order of Interest to Children, from the Younger to the Older Age-Groups

	VOL.	PAGE		VOL.	PAGE
Mother Goose Riddles	1	66	Cross Word Puzzles	5	171
The Three Pigs	1	89	Robinson Crusoe	6	89
The Fox and the Little Red Hen	1	331	Wee Willie Winkie	6	179
Elizabeth Ann Fails in an Examination	2	304	Paper and Pencil Games	7	269
Space Ship to the Moon	2	325	Riddles, Puzzles, Tricks and Stunts	7	297
Rococo Skates	2	314	How Cincinnatus Saved Rome	8	271
Woman's Wit	3	294	The Child of Urbino	9	27
The Tiger, the Brahman, and the Jackal	3	331	The Army of Two	9	119
Listening to the Sphinx	4	108	How We Bought Louisiana	9	220
Story of Columbus	4	178	The Story of Laura Secord	9	339

"He that will not reason is a bigot; he that cannot reason is a fool; and he that dares not reason is a slave." —SIR W. DRUMMOND.

THOROUGHNESS

Habitual care and exactness about details in carrying things through to completion.

THERE ARE FEW satisfactions in life more wholesome and thoroughly gratifying than the glow that comes from knowing that one has done a good job. There is a self-respecting integrity about a competent and conscientious workman that demands respect.

It is easy for any of us, of course, to slight the difficult parts of a project or ignore those we dislike or find boring. But slipshod habits of workmanship can lead only to poorly done jobs. Superficial habits of study are sure to produce holes in one's grasp of a subject. Either habit can be responsible for serious failures in life.

In teaching thoroughness to children there are several things to remember. In the first place, children must not be judged by adult standards. Their nervous systems and muscular coordinations are very different from ours. Too great an insistence on fine detail or on working for a long time may be injurious. Gone are the days when the eyes and nerves of young girls were "trained" (or rather *strained*) by fine needlework.

It requires considerable judgment to know what degree of thoroughness is appropriate to a child's development, as regards either time or detail. The best guide is what he seems able to do without strain. If his persistence and attention to standards in any kind of work improves over a period of a few months, progress may be considered satisfactory.

For physiological reasons, there are periods in a child's life when he is less thorough than at others. Development is not steady. Up to seven, standards are very slap-dash indeed. Then comes a period of increasing understanding and muscular control, and by about ten the child shows spontaneous interest in methods and detail. From then on until adolescence skill increases rapidly. But during early adolescence the child usually becomes careless and slap-dash again. He may show lots of spirit, but is not persistent or careful. Put up with it as bravely as you can and he will steady down again later.

Don't expect your child to be as thorough in something he dislikes but *has* to do as he is in something he enjoys. Sometimes we expect thoroughness of our children in matters which do not seem to them worth doing at all. But anyone who respect his job will do his best at it.

So see that your child has many opportunities to undertake ambitious projects that he enjoys.

And finally, make your own attitude helpful. Encourage him to try to meet whatever seem *to him,* at this particular stage of development, good standards. Let him see that you consider it important to "do a nice job" in your own work. Comment on the details of his achievements that show care and thoroughness. A child loves to feel that he knows how to do things well, and he will be proud to do them better and better.

※ ※ ※

Suggested Reading

Arranged in Order of Interest to Children, from the Younger to the Older Age-Groups

	VOL.	PAGE
The Maid in the Mirror	3	307
The Gleaners	4	6
The Melon-Eaters	4	48
Modeling Small Sculptures in White Soap	5	75
Making Things Out of Paper	5	81
Cross Word Puzzles	5	171
Little Mother's Work Basket	5	213
Handicrafts for Girls	5	249
Woodwork for Older Children	5	269
Good Pictures: How They Are Made	5	337

	VOL.	PAGE
The Child of Urbino	9	27
The Boyhood of an Engineer Who Became President	9	68
Susan B. Anthony	9	102
Helen Keller	9	110
Johnny Appleseed	9	136
Patrick Henry	9	170
A Man Like a Stone Wall	9	260
Dewey, Hero of Manila	9	264
Theodore Roosevelt	9	268
The Story of Madeleine de Verchères	9	325

"Whatever is worth doing at all is worth doing well."
—LORD CHESTERFIELD.

THRIFT

Management of one's money by the practice of habitual economy and providence, by industry, frugal spending and systematic saving.

MONEY is something we all have to use for better or for worse. It no longer plays the minor role in family security that it did when most of the food, clothing, and shelter was provided by the work of the family on the farm. Today money affects not only family buying power but various relationships with other people inside and outside the family. Since money is such an important and ever present problem, children need to start learning about it early.

Most parents find an allowance one of the best ways of teaching children the value of money. The size of the allowance should depend upon the child's age and development and upon family resources. To a lesser degree it may be influenced by the allowances current among his friends. Once given, the allowance should be the child's to spend as he pleases. You may suggest or advise, but not control. Do not reproach or punish him for spending it foolishly. Let him learn by experience. If he needs more money—for gifts, replacements, or special needs—help him find ways to earn it.

Do not require him to put all, or any, of his money in a bank. But if there is anything he especially wants which costs more than his week's allowance, show him that he may be able to get it by saving a little every week. Begin with concrete, little things which require small savings on his part. Little by little he will learn to save for larger necessities and desires, and for a more distant future.

As soon as they are able to understand it, children should learn that money is a measure of certain material values, and also that there are other values, spiritual and emotional, beyond the monetary one.

They should have a realistic notion of the family's resources and goals. As they grow older they should be parties to the budgeting of the family's money. They should understand that it must be used for the good of the family as a whole. Speak of "our money" at these times. Thus they will see the need for everyone to help by work or self-sacrifice, and will appreciate the benefits they receive.

Try, by your own example, and with explanations when necessary, to show the children both the uses and the abuses of money. Show them how to spend wisely and how important for security it is to save systematically. Above all, teach them *values*. Teach them to be good judges of value in the things money can buy; and to understand and prize the things it cannot.

❧ ❧ ❧

Suggested Reading

Arranged in Order of Interest to Children, from the Younger to the Older Age-Groups

	VOL.	PAGE
The Ant and the Grasshopper	2	3
The Wishing Ring	3	279
The Gleaners	4	6
Two Squirrels	4	12
A Frugal Meal	4	139
A Hungarian Village	4	180
Hans Brinker	6	202

	VOL.	PAGE
The Boyhood of a Statesman	9	19
A Courageous Boy Who Became President	9	72
How People Lived in Colonial New England	9	162
Benjamin Franklin	9	198

"Make all you can, save all you can, give all you can."
—JOHN WESLEY.

TOLERANCE

The disposition to understand and to respect others' rights to beliefs, practices, or habits differing from one's own.

TOLERANCE is one of the most basic and necessary virtues of our time. Unless all mankind can learn to live together in mutual respect and kindness, we shall soon not live at all. Tolerance rests upon the recognition that each individual is different from every other and has a right to his own ideas, preferences, and goals, as long as he grants others the same right.

Differences can be the basis for fear and suspicion, or they can add interest and variety to life. Animals, children, and many adults, are afraid of what they do not understand. "This man looks different from me and my friends. Should I keep away from him, or should I show him that I am more powerful than he so that he will not dare to attack me?"

That is the natural history of intolerance. Strangeness breeds suspicion and fear. Fear breeds hate and persecution.

If this sequence is so natural, how can it be broken? We fear *what we do not understand.* Once it was practically impossible to understand the man whose home was in a far country, but that is no longer true. And in the United States we are particularly lucky in having fellow-citizens who represent most of the races, religions, and great thought-groups of the world. We *can* understand if we will make the effort. Kindly, sympathetic understanding, is our greatest weapon against intolerance and cruelty.

Let your home radiate kindliness toward all people. Examine your own heart to see if there is any class or group that you feel is inferior or less worthy than others. Then learn about them; work until you can feel how it would be to be one of them. If possible, make friends among them. You will find that under all the differences human hearts are still human.

Although children may be troubled by very obvious differences, they are usually quite indifferent to the ones that bother adults—until adults or older children teach them intolerance, perhaps only by a shrug, a tone of voice, or some little cutting remark. To the natural child, if John will share his candy, play fair, and can sock out a fast ball, well he's a swell guy, regardless of race, nationality, religion, or special or economic position. The children are right. Help your children to stand firm in the belief that character is what counts.

And always make it clear that each individual is to be judged on his own merits, not *pre*-judged Have friends, and encourage your children to have friends, among as wide a range of people as possible.

You will find many ways to teach tolerance if your heart is really in the task of helping your children to practice human brotherhood. If the next generation can approach that goal, we **can** yet enslave the atoms instead of each other.

❧ ❧ ❧

Suggested Reading

Arranged in Order of Interest to Children, from the Younger to the Older Age-Groups

	VOL.	PAGE		VOL.	PAGE
All God's Children .	1	381	Benjamin Franklin	9	198
Ring Around the World	2	93	Abraham Lincoln, Who Saved the Union	9	244
Fung's Fourth	2	298	Theodore Roosevelt	9	268
Willie's Good Recess	2	301	The Mayo Brothers	9	282
The Mountain and the Squirrel . . .	6	324	Alfred E. Smith	9	284
The Pilgrims and the Puritans . . .	9	157	A Black-Robed Voyageur	9	336
William Penn	9	178	Sir Wilfrid Laurier	9	348

"It is not a merit to tolerate but rather a crime to be intolerant."
—PERCY BYSSHE SHELLEY.

TRUSTWORTHINESS AND DEPENDABILITY

Quality of being worthy of confidence and trust; reliability.

THE VALUES of trustworthiness and reliability are so well known that few better compliments can be given than the simple, "You can always depend on him." People prize a friend like that above all others. An unreliable boy or girl, on the other hand, will find that it gets harder and harder to win people's confidence. The good jobs, the honors and rewards of life, go to those who prove themselves trustworthy and dependable.

An old proverb tells us that "trust begets trust." That is, the best way to make a person trustworthy is to trust him. This is particularly true of a child.

Give your child certain tasks to do. If possible, let him choose for himself the ways in which he will help. Be sure they are tasks he is well able to do. Setting the table, cleaning the silver, putting away toys after use, or hanging up his clothes are a few of the chores children can usually be trusted with. Make it clear to the child that, once he has accepted it, his task is his responsibility. Show him that you trust him to do it without further prodding from you.

If you keep entirely out of it after that, he will usually feel that it is up to him to do what is expected of him. Praise him when he succeeds.

He may forget, or he may be defiant and wilfully neglect his task. He may fail to do it because of any number of childish distractions. If this happens, be careful not to make him feel guilty about it. Do not, in any circumstances, let him think you have lost faith in him. Just begin over. Give him something else to do, and tell him that you trust him to do it. Make no reference to his earlier failure. Don't let him feel that he is untrustworthy. Give him every chance to prove to you than he *can* be depended on.

And, of course, *never* fail him by betraying his trust in *you*. "A promise is a promise" be it good or bad, so make none that you may not keep. Let the child know how important this is.

If you keep trying patiently, you can usually make your child trustworthy by being absolutely trustworthy yourself and by having unshakeable faith in the child's desire and ability to make good. Show him that you depend upon him to keep his word, to be faithful to his trust.

If he still betrays your confidence in him, there must be deep psychological reasons for it. Take him to a good psychiatrist or child guidance clinic. But if you are truly patient about his early lapses, you will probably need no further help.

❧ ❧ ❧

Suggested Reading

Arranged in Order of Interest to Children, from the Younger to the Older Age-Groups

	VOL.	PAGE		VOL.	PAGE
Corkie	1	156	Wee Willie Winkie	6	179
Number 9, the Little Fire Engine	1	172	Where Love Is, God Is	6	262
The Dog Who Chose a Prince	2	114	Casabianca	6	340
The Horse That Came From Heaven	2	125	The Friends of the Indians	8	206
Indians in the House	2	274	How Cincinnatus Saved Rome	8	271
Elizabeth Ann Fails in an Examination	2	304	Roland	8	319
High Water in Arkansas	2	319	William Penn	9	178
Beauty and the Beast	3	116	Lafayette, Friend of America	9	209
Scarface	3	342	Sir Isaac Brock, Hero of Queenstown	9	334
The Pied Piper of Hamelin	6	52	Joseph Howe of Nova Scotia	9	345

"It is happier to be sometimes cheated than not to trust."
—JOSEPH ADDISON.

TRUTHFULNESS

The character of recognizing what is true and rendering it accurately.

TRUTHFULNESS is basic to good human relationships. The man whose word can be believed is trusted and honored, while the confirmed liar rarely has a friend in the world.

It is not always easy to tell the truth even if one wants to. One must observe well and accurately and then be able to put what one has observed into clear language. All this is too much to expect of small children. In the first place why should they see any importance in trying to match the words with the facts? Besides, they are so imaginative and playful that they have the most confused ideas of fact and fancy.

As they grow older, however, they can learn to distinguish truth from falsehood. They will come to know the difference between "let's pretend about this" and "we must tell the truth about that." Take the child's imaginary stories calmly and don't make him feel guilty about them. Enjoy them with him. But with some tall tale you may say, "That's a very pretty make-believe story: but now let's hear what really happened." By the time the child is four or five, he should have a pretty good idea of the difference between fact and fancy.

Older children learn that as they assume responsibility for their own deeds and words, those deeds and words must be reliable. At this time children may lie for various reasons. The sensible mother will look for causes and try to correct those as well as the lies themselves.

Sometimes they are following a bad example. Sometimes they are careless and forgetful, or observe inaccurately. Those faults are relatively easy to deal with. More often, however, a child will lie for deeper reasons. It may be that he is afraid of what will happen if he tells the truth, or because he has other fears and anxieties. Or he may be living too much in a world of his own imagination because he is not satisfied in the world of reality. He may not be getting enough love and security from real people.

If the child lives in a world of fancy and lies too often after he starts going to school, try to find out what is behind it. You may be sure that something is lacking that he needs, or that he is afraid or under undue pressure of some kind. Never punish him for a lie. Try to find the cause and remove it. If you cannot find any reason, you may want to consult a guidance clinic. Meantime, be as affectionate and understanding as you can, and praise the child if he makes an effort to tell the truth.

Be truthful yourself, and of course *never* lie to a child. Hold before your child the fine ideal of honor of those who will face a penalty rather than lie. Give him reason to feel confidence in your understanding and forgiveness, so that he will not lie through fear. His standards of truthfulness will gradually improve.

❧ ❧ ❧

Suggested Reading

Arranged in Order of Interest to Children, from the Younger to the Older Age-Groups

	VOL.	PAGE		VOL.	PAGE
Why Jimmy Skunk Wears Stripes	1	122	The Jackal and the Camel	3	323
The Lambikin	1	322	The Ghost of the Great White Stag	3	345
The Shepherd Boy Who Cried "Wolf"	2	20	Aladdin and the Wonderful Lamp	6	5
A Boy Hero	2	281	Dorigen	6	150
One Eye, Two Eyes, Three Eyes	3	60	Some Simple Rules for Conversation	7	240
The Emperor's New Clothes	3	74	Sohrab and Rustam	8	345
The Nightingale	3	89	The Boyhood of a President	9	56
The Apple of Contentment	3	271	Benjamin Franklin	9	198

"Keep one thing forever in view—the truth."
—HORACE MANN.

UNSELFISHNESS

Willingness to sacrifice one's own possessions, comforts, or advantages in order to make others happier or more comfortable.

UNSELFISHNESS brings rich rewards of joy and contentment. But selfishness has many forms, all of them self-defeating in the long run. Emerson knew this well when he said, "The selfish man suffers more from his selfishness than he from whom that selfishness withholds some important benefit." But children cannot understand that.

Children up to the age of two or three are naturally quite selfish. They hang onto their things tenaciously, and grab others' as well. If they are told to give things away or share them to be unselfish, they do not know what you are talking about. If they comply, it is not through unselfishness, nor should they be blamed if they refuse.

A child expected to do unselfish things before he can understand the reasons may react by being extra greedy. We must realize that the child goes through a stage of being absorbed in himself before he reaches the unselfish stage.

The change will not come about suddenly, either. A child is able to be unselfish only after he himself feels secure. See that his possessions are really *his* to control, so that he can learn the meaning of "mine." Soon comes an understanding of "not mine" and then of "yours" or "his." The idea behind sharing is still more difficult, for it is "sometimes mine, sometimes yours," or "ours." Naturally, he can't be expected to operate on that basis until he has some idea of time.

As he gets older and plays with other children he will see that some things give more fun when shared. From this time on he can be induced to care more and more for the social satisfactions of giving and of sharing. Finally he will come to put them ahead of more selfish pleasures.

Some children do not make this progress. They continue to be selfish and grasping. This may be because of a bad example, because of fears, jealousy or other unhappiness, or because they were forced to act unselfish before they felt secure.

On the other hand some become too unselfish, allowing themselves to be imposed upon, and seeming to have no sense of their own rights. Such children are usually afraid in some way or are trying desperately to win approval or acceptance in this way. This behavior shows unsatisfied emotional needs which must be met before the child dares "stand up for himself."

If a child over six or seven shows poor adjustment in either of these ways, look for the causes. Make him feel thoroughly loved and fully accepted. Help him toward self-confidence. Then he will be *able* to be normally unselfish. Then you will see him enjoy giving up some things in order to make another happier. In time he will learn how much more blessed it is to give than to receive.

❧ ❧ ❧

Suggested Reading

Arranged in Order of Interest to Children, from the Younger to the Older Age-Groups

	VOL.	PAGE
The Story of a Little White Dog	1	144
Bread and Milk	1	185
How Old Mr. Long-Tail Became a Santa Claus	1	353
Under the Little Fir	1	369
The Dog in the Manger	2	16
Why the Sea is Salt	3	129
The Selfish Giant	3	150
The Old Woman and the Tramp	3	190

	VOL.	PAGE
The Brownies	3	226
The Wonderful Pear Tree	3	304
Children of the Shell	4	43
St. Elizabeth	4	105
The King of the Golden River	6	62
The Great Stone Face	6	105
A Christmas Carol	6	165
Johnny Appleseed	9	136
Grenfell's Sermon in Deeds	9	377

"One must be poor to know the luxury of giving."
—GEORGE ELIOT.

WILL POWER AND DETERMINATION

Mental drive and strength of character enabling one to carry through what one has decided to accomplish.

WITHOUT will power and determination no long-range project can ever be accomplished. This is true of all kinds of ambitions, from such a comparatively simple desire as to reduce one's weight all the way to a coveted position in the world. Obviously, therefore, will power and determination are characteristics to be developed in the child.

In helping him to develop these qualities, there are several things to remember:

First, unless a person is heartily interested in achieving a goal, he is unlikely to use much will-power to reach it. There are plenty of times when your child is determined to do something or other and can develop will-power by earnest and successful effort. When *you* choose what he shall attempt, it is usually *your* will power or power of persuasion that drives it through to completion.

Second, if a child fails too often in what he undertakes, it tends to decrease his will-power. Therefore, it may be wise to discourage him from undertaking things obviously beyond him, or from starting big projects when he is in poor mental or physical condition. But be cautious about this. A few experiences of failure are wholesome lessons. Furthermore, our children are very often capable of much more than we suppose.

It is all right to talk over the proposed project with your child, cheerfully discussing advantages, difficulties, and problems, to help him see the probabilities more clearly. But do not expect him to realize everything involved. That he can do only through experience.

As he gets into the thing and encounters unexpected difficulties, help to renew his will-power by an occasional mention of the happy ending to come. Teach him the great secret of "little by little." When today's achievement seems nothing to him, look back with him over a week and see how *much* has been accomplished by small daily progress.

Teach him to stop and rest when he is tired. What seems impossible today may seem easy tomorrow when he is rested. Teach him to set a near-by goal, a partial goal, so that he can often have the satisfaction of reaching it. "Today our job is half done" gives new determination. Confidence in one's ability to succeed is fundamental to determination; so do all that you can to help your child to a reasonable self-confidence and an optimistic estimate of his own abilities.

Two mistakes about will-power are common. Some people resent it in a child (when it is inconvenient for them) calling it stubbornness, and trying to destroy it. Others expect to develop it by forcing a child to finish whatever he undertakes. That does not develop the child's will-power. What if he does make a mistake and finds later that what he wanted is really not worth the effort to him? He will be the better able to count costs the next time.

⚜ ⚜ ⚜

Suggested Reading

Arranged in Order of Interest to Children, from the Younger to the Older Age-Groups

	VOL.	PAGE
The Maid in the Mirror	3	307
Moses	4	150
David	4	150
Horatius at the Bridge	6	107
The Porcelain Stove	6	237
A Psalm of Life	6	326
Roland	8	319
The March of the Ten Thousand	8	363
Robert the Bruce	8	385
A Courageous Boy Who Became President	9	72

	VOL.	PAGE
The Boy Who Braved the Duke of Wellington	9	76
Joan of Arc	9	93
George Washington, Father of Our Country	9	191
Andrew Jackson, Soldier and President	9	230
The Western Pioneer	9	240
Theodore Roosevelt	9	268
Twelve National Heroes	9	307
Sir John A. MacDonald	9	342
Grenfell's Sermon in Deeds	9	377

"Great souls have wills; feeble ones have only wishes."
—CHINESE PROVERB.

HEALTHY ATTITUDES TOWARD HEALTH

IT IS no longer possible to think of good health in terms of physical development only. We have long known that healthy babies are usually happy babies. What we have more recently discovered is that happy babies have a better chance of being healthy.

There are, of course, certain general rules for the physical care and feeding of children. These are set forth in the section of this MANUAL immediately following. No mother can or should follow them slavishly. Every mother should be flexible enough to break them when her common sense and judgment, based on her baby's individual needs, would make a change seem more desirable.

If you can manage to show no anxiety or worry about your child's eating and other health habits—understand that physical health or the lack of it may depend on emotional and psychological factors—make your basic relationship with your child as free from fuss, as easy, pleasant and loving as possible—nature will be pretty sure to take the healthiest possible course.

PHYSICAL DEVELOPMENT

"A babe in a house is a well-spring of pleasure."
                                        —*M. F. Tupper*

"A child, more than all other gifts that earth can offer ...
brings hope with it and forward-looking thoughts."
                                        —*George Eliot*

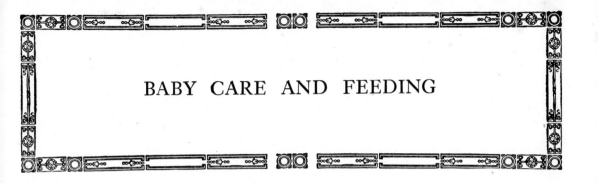

BABY CARE AND FEEDING

SO YOU'RE EXPECTING A BABY *

So you're going to have a baby! How lucky you are to be having your child at a time when the care an expectant mother now gets makes pregnancy safer. That matter of your care before the baby's birth makes all the difference. You'll be careful enough of that baby once he's here! Well, he needs to be taken care of before he's born, too, and the best way to do that is to take care of *yourself.*

WHEN SHALL I GO TO THE DOCTOR?

It's easy to put off going to the doctor, but it doesn't pay. In the first place, he often charges a lump sum for your complete care, so you might as well start your visits early and take advantage of his skill and experience from the very beginning. The public-health nurse in your community can be consulted too. Perhaps she will hold mothers' classes for the purpose of answering questions between your visits to the doctor or the clinic. You can write all your questions down as they pop into your mind and take them with you when you go to your doctor or to the clinic, and not have to fall back on friends or relatives whose information may be out of date, or at least is based on their own very limited experience.

Starting out the right way, too, lessens the chances for complications. For when your physician examines you early and follows through carefully month by month the likelihood of your having a normal baby is increased.

HOW SHALL I CHOOSE HIM?

Pick out a doctor who has had good training, one you like and have confidence in, too. You'll want to talk very intimately with him (or her),

*From U. S. Children's Bureau Publication.

and it's easier to do this with some one you trust. If you are uncertain about whom to go to, ask your local health department or hospital for a list of competent physicians.

The first visit is the hurdle to get over, isn't it? But don't be nervous. Your doctor will be sympathetic and understanding. Think of the years of training he had just in order to acquire all the special knowledge that helps to make child-bearing safer.

HOW CAN I BE SURE I'M PREGNANT?

Probably the first thing that made you think you were pregnant was a skipped menstrual period. There are other signs, though, that more surely confirm your suspicions. The breasts begin to undergo some changes, becoming somewhat larger, tender to the touch, and with some darkening around the nipples. Other signs of pregnancy are the greater frequency of urination for a time, and a change in the way things taste, with an increase in the activity of the salivary glands. Your physician will by vaginal examination determine the size of the uterus and give the final answer.

At first he will want you to see him once a month, in order that he may check up on your blood pressure and make an examination of your urine. As pregnancy progresses, it becomes important to do this oftener, so after the sixth month he'll probably want you to come in every 2 weeks, and during the last month, every week. By this careful check he will recognize any early abnormal symptoms or signs that require care, and will be able to plan treatment if this is needed.

Your last visit to the doctor will be after the baby is born when he will want to check up to see that all is well.

WHEN SHALL I EXPECT THE BABY?

The date of your baby's birth cannot be exactly determined, but it will probably take place about 280 days after the first day of your last monthly period. An easy way of fixing the date is to count back 3 months from the first day of the last period and add 7 days. Some babies are born several days earlier than expected, some a little later. When birth takes place 2 or 3 weeks later than anticipated, pregnancy probably occurred in connection with the skipped period rather than the one before. Most babies, though, come within a week of the expected date.

Does 9 months seem a long time to wait? If you were going to feel as uncomfortable all along as you may during a very short part of the early period, that 9 months' stretch might look endless. But you'll probably get to feeling better and better as the time goes on. Many women look and feel their best during the latter months of pregnancy.

"Look their best!" you say. Yes, their skin is clear and bright, their appetite good, they sleep well, and their happy frame of mind contributes to their appearance. Your figure won't exactly please you, but a lot can be done about that, too. If you have a well-fitted foundation garment, and plan your clothes well you won't feel so awkward. If you have never worn a girdle you probably will not need to use one now. Be sure to wear the right shoes; they can be pretty, but to help you look your best they must be comfortable. Your increased weight makes it advisable to wear shoes that give you real support. If you have been wearing high heels, make the change to low heels gradual or they may cause you discomfort.

HOW CAN MY HUSBAND SHARE IN THE PLANNING?

After the baby comes you and your husband will find it surprisingly natural always to think first of the baby's needs. Before his arrival, make the most of the time when you don't have to think of the baby's schedule or arrange for a "sitter" every time you want to go out. Have a lot of fun together. Take plenty of rest during the day so that you'll be ready to go out in the evening when occasion arises. Plan your Sundays to be as free as possible of cooking and housework, so that you can relax and enjoy together activities time can't be found for during the week. It is jollier to go out of doors for walks, or gardening, or sight-seeing if you have some one to do these things with. By taking advantage of these months you can cement a firm and close companionship that your necessary absorption with the baby later on won't damage. Many husbands feel a little hurt and neglected when the baby makes such insistent demands on their wives' time and attention. If they have been prepared for this, and realize that love is perfectly capable of expanding to include two, they are going to be amused by their jealous twinges, if any. These are far less likely to occur if husbands are made to feel, before the baby is born, that getting ready to be a father is just as important as preparing to be a mother.

Read with your husband about how the baby is developing. He will be in no danger of feeling that he is a "forgotten man" if he keeps up to date on what is happening. Men are usually much interested in the fascinating story of human growth, as told in a book like *The Story of a Baby* by Marie Hall Ets (Viking— New York).

HOW CAN I INSURE MY HEALTH?

But no matter how much your husband's interest and help around the house may contribute during pregnancy, it is you who have the main responsibility of making and following a plan of living that will keep you happy and well.

For one thing, your food becomes a vastly important matter. Now nature takes what she wants out of your body for the baby—it's up to you to look after your own nourishment! It's not necessarily that you need to eat much more, but that you need to eat more wisely than you perhaps have before. Your diet must be varied enough so that there is an ample supply of all the body-building and regulating foods as well as the energy-giving foods.

Your doctor will advise about your food needs. He will certainly want you to have plenty of the "protective" foods such as milk, eggs, fruits, and vegetables. He may want you to have more meat than you have been eating.

Your baby should be storing up iron. Everytime you eat such things as eggs, lean meats, liver, and whole-grain or enriched cereals or bread, you help him out. Leafy vegetables, especially turnip tops and kale, are also rich in iron. Potatoes are another reliable source.

Those vitamins that supply the spark so necessary to keep the body working on all cylinders are needed in generous quantities. Oranges, grapefruit, and tomatoes are year-around stand-bys for vitamin C. In season good big servings of raw salad greens, berries, and melons, also supply vitamin C. Eat such foods right along. Green and deep-yellow vegetables like carrots and sweet potatoes supply generous quantities of vitamin A. Your doctor probably will pre-scribe some form of vitamin D, such as fish-liver oil.

Fruits like apples, prunes, dates, and raisins will satisfy your desire for sweet things, which you might otherwise fill by eating too many foods like cookies and sweet desserts. Of course there's no objection to pie, cake, and candy in moderation if you're getting all the protective foods you need, but foods rich in sugar, fat, or both may add to your weight, and may upset your digestion, too, so go slow, very slow on them.

Have lean meat, fish, or poultry every day if you can, and liver once a week. These, with eggs, cheese, and milk, furnish the building ma-terials for your baby's body and keep yours in good repair. Whole-grain or enriched bread and cereals, with their valuable minerals, vita-mins, and protein, should be on your list every day.

IS MILK REALLY SO IMPORTANT?

Nothing can take the place of milk as a "quality" food. There are many ways to get the daily quart in addition to drinking it. How-ever, in many foods prepared with milk you get only a relatively small amount. If you drink 2 or 3 glasses a day, and use milk gen-erously in cooking, your intake should easily be a quart a day. A 1¼ inch of cheese yields as much body-building material as a cup of milk Cook your whole-grain or enriched cereal in milk instead of water and see how much it adds to the flavor. Often serve desserts made with milk—sherbets, ice-cream, rice pudding. Just remember that milk is an invaluable food at this time. Whether you use dried or canned milk, or fresh pasteurized milk, it will be well worth whatever it may cost. Skim milk has all the elements of whole milk that make it so valuable for building muscles, bones, and teeth, but less fat and vitamin A, both of which you can get from butter or fortified margarine.

The milk you use will add to your intake of fluids, too. Because your body must get rid of the baby's waste products, as well as your own,

liquids are an absolute "must." Part of this requirement can be in the form of tea and coffee and fruit juices, but having a quart of milk a day will make it less necessary for you to have it on your mind to down all those glasses of water that used to be recommended. Drink as much water as you like, of course, but don't make a sacred duty of it. To keep bowels open is very necessary, and water helps there.

IS IT TRUE I MUST LOSE "A TOOTH FOR EVERY CHILD"?

No! This statement is an old wives' tale. No harm should come to the mother's teeth be-cause of pregnancy alone. Having a baby does not cause decay; neither does it prevent it. You will be liable to have those dental diseases which are common to women of your age. A visit to your dentist early in pregnancy is another one of the "musts." It will give him a chance to find and fill any cavities, or make any ex-tractions necessary, so that no infections can interfere with good digestion. Good chewing sur-faces are necessary if you are to eat the wide variety of foods essential to your good health.

HOW ABOUT THIS UP-CHUCKING?

Most girls think of morning-sickness as one of the things to dread during the early months of pregnancy, but actually it needn't be the bugbear those Job's comforters you'll run into would have you believe. You can usually out-wit nausea by having something brought you to eat before you stir out of bed in the morn-ing, and by nibbling at crackers if it begins to rear its head between meals. A great many women aren't bothered at all, and the chances are if you make up your mind you're going to be one of them, your mind will influence your body in the right direction. The more cheerful and happy you are about your pregnancy, the less you'll be annoyed by all sorts of symptoms, imaginary or otherwise.

HOW CAN I KEEP FROM BEING AFRAID?

Why is it that women don't dread facing the birth of their second child the way they did their first? Because they've found childbirth isn't as bad as it's painted. If we didn't use the term "labor pains," but spoke instead of the contrac tions of the muscles which make childbirth possible, perhaps we wouldn't put it into our heads that pain is the big feature of the occasion. (The big feature is the baby.) While giving birth isn't an easy performance, it has been made so much safer and easier by modern medical skill that fear should be tossed out the window.

Worry is so futile, and so unnecessary. You can nourish a whole crop of fears while you're pregnant, or you can choose to be serene and carefree. If it's ignorance that's making you fearful, ask your doctor the questions that bother you. Don't be timid about it—he's met up with all kinds of problems, and he will be able to give you answers that will take a big load off your mind.

Any big new experience carries with it some fear. Mankind has always feared the unknown. But this curiosity has always pushed him ahead into that unknown, and so has yours! You wouldn't miss this experience for a million dollars, would you?

Some people are afraid their child will be feeble-minded. Some are afraid because they've never faced a big responsibility before, and don't feel sure they can take it. Are you bothered by someone's gloomy prediction that your baby may be "marked" by disagreeable things you chance to see or experience? Such old notions have absolutely no basis, for the fetus has no connection whatever with your nervous system through which any such shocks would have to be transmitted. Its only connection with your body is indirectly through your bloodstream. Others have more trivial fears, such as that childbirth will spoil their figure, or that they'll miss out on a lot of fun because they'll be tied down.

You needn't be ashamed of your fears. Every one has 'em. But don't *keep* them. Pack them up and put them on your doctor's shoulders. He can reassure you about the extreme rarity of feeble-mindedness or other abnormality. He can comfort you no matter what your worry, for he's dealt with them all.

Why leave any time for worry? You need all your time for other things, like getting out-of-doors every single day for as long as you can, visiting friends and having lots of good laughs with them, reading good books, and listening to the radio while you sew or knit.

HOW ACTIVE CAN I BE WITH SAFETY?

You should work enough to keep your body functioning well, but not at hard, heavy work. Heavy lifting, scrubbing, or standing for long hours are not for you. No amount of indoor exercise at housework, though, will do for you what getting out in the sunshine does. If you have a job that's not too strenuous or confining, there's no need of stopping work (unless on your doctor's orders) before the eighth month. You may be a lot better off because you have to get out every day.

Nowadays when it's fashionable to be pregnant, there's no need to get "cabin fever" by hiding yourself indoors because your figure "ain't what she used to be." If you wear shoes that take account of your changed center of gravity you'll look better than if you are tilted up on the higher heels you may have worn when you could get about more nimbly.

Unless your sports were of the violently active sort, such as tennis or basket-ball, you can continue them as long as you feel like it. Simply modify them to suit—for instance, swim, but not dive. Of course, follow your doctor's say-so.

As your weight increases it will become more and more important to rest frequently, so that the blood vessels in your feet and legs don't become congested. Varicose veins are really something to steer clear of. You can help by lying down several times a day for short periods, flat on your back with a pillow under your knees, and by stretching out on an easy chair or couch, with your feet up, whenever you have a few minutes to read or sew. Sit down while you fix vegetables, pare apples, or iron. It will pay, and keep you from looking or feeling fagged and dragged-out.

ARE THERE ANY DANGER SIGNALS TO WATCH FOR?

If you are going to the doctor right along he will be in a position to prevent most complications. To be on the safe side, however, it is a good thing to know the signs or symptoms that should be reported to your doctor immediately, if any of them should occur. They are these:

Any sort of illness with or without a fever
Persistent headaches or dizziness
Swelling of the feet, hands, or face
Pain in the abdomen
Bleeding from the vagina
Any vomiting occurring late in pregnancy (this is not to be confused with the slight amount of regurgitation that happens often in early pregnancy and is of no consequence)
Breaking of the bag of waters or amniotic sac

that surrounds the baby (this last usually means that labor is under way, in which case it is not a danger warning, in the sense that the others are, but rather a signal of the approach of birth).

Let your doctor know immediately if any of the above things occur. Don't be afraid that your doctor will think you are "silly" or worrying about imaginary ailments in reporting any such symptoms to him.

He wants to save you any unnecessary pain or danger, and he can do this only if you co-operate by letting him know of any unusual happenings.

To go to bed and stay there until the doctor has seen you is a good rule to follow if any of the above signs appear.

WHAT ABOUT MISCARRIAGE?

A miscarriage is the loss of a baby before it is able to live outside its mother's body, which is during the first six months of pregnancy. The causes are too involved to go into here, but such things as falls, popularly associated with miscarriage, usually have little or nothing to do with such loss. Your best precaution will be to lead a healthy, sensible life, and during the early months refrain from intercourse during the times when the monthly periods would normally occur, as miscarriage is more likely at these times. Intercourse should be discontinued by about the seventh month and should not be resumed until about 6 weeks after the baby's birth. But you ask your doctor about this.

HOW ABOUT MY CLOTHES?

Pregnancy isn't a synonym for dowdiness any more. A lot can be done by cleverly cut clothes, and a lot more by careful grooming. Take extra pains with your hair, your nails, and your make-up, and you'll draw attention away from the temporary bulge. Have at least one good, but not necessarily expensive dress, for wear when you go out. If it's a becoming color, and has some eye-catching, fresh, frilly accessories you'll feel well-dressed even though you wear it often.

It's hard to find anything more comfortable, convenient and deceptive than slacks (or shorts in summer) with shirts worn with the tails outside. Suspenders will prevent any binding at the waistline. Whatever kind of girdle and brassiere you select, be sure they act as real supports, without constriction.

WHAT SHALL I GET READY FOR THE BABY?

Your preparations before the baby's coming may be very simple. Young infants do not need an elaborate outfit of clothes, for the less they are handled in being dressed and undressed the better they like it. You will scarcely ever put a dress on the baby, as he is more comfortable in shirt, diaper, and nightgown. Here are the essentials. You can, of course, provide as many "extras" as you care to; but it is going to be more important to spend time with your baby than it is to spend it washing and ironing for him.

Shirts—4 (long or short sleeved according to the season)
Diapers—3 to 4 dozen
Nightgowns—5 or 6 (opening down the back, preferably)
Blankets—3 or 4 (small, lightweight)
Bunting—1 (or knit or flannel squares to wrap him in when going out)
Mattress—1 (may be homemade, of soft, old blanket, folded to fit crib or basket)
Rubber sheet—1 (big enough to tuck under the mattress on both sides)
Quilted cotton pads—5 or 6 (about 18 inches square to be placed under the baby)
Sheets—3 to 6 (may be made by cutting down partly-worn household sheets)

"THE TIME HAS COME," THE WALRUS SAID

Are your nightgowns and toilet articles packed for that momentous trip to the hospital? It will give you a comfortable feeling to know you're ready to start off at a moment's notice. After the first 2 to 3 days of hospital gowns you'll be able to wear the pretty ones you've got ready, and the dainty bed-jacket that was a present.

You'll want to make good use of your days in the hospital. Those days of rest not only help you get back to normal, but they also give you a chance to get acquainted with your baby, and to learn how to take care of him while you have some one to teach and help you. If you are relaxed, instead of impatient to go home, the baby will have a better start at the business of nursing, too. By beginning to have some responsibility for his care while you are in the hospital, you'll not find the transition to caring for him at home so sudden.

Many a mother who thinks she may be unable to nurse her baby will find that it is surprisingly pleasant and easy thing to do provided she follows her doctor's instructions in the care of her breasts before her baby is born and if she does not give up trying in the early stages of the nursing period.

Not only do distinct advantages and benefits come to a baby from being breast-fed, but there are advantages to his mother, too. Breast-feeding brings about a very satisfying intimacy between you and your baby that contributes to the happiness of you both. The relaxed feeling that comes from knowing that you are able to nourish your baby yourself is good psychologically, too. It means that you will be freed from the time-consuming business of making up a formula and boiling bottles. If you nurse your baby you get valuable rest periods several times a day. Of course the bottle-fed baby should be held while he is being fed until he is old enough to hold the bottle himself.

And from the very start, accept the help of your husband in the baby's care. He will enjoy the baby a great deal more if he is intimately associated with him from the very start. Only by daily contacts will he get the thrill that you do from seeing the baby's accomplishments appear: when his eyes begin to follow a moving object, when he turns his head in response to a voice, when he first smiles, and when he holds his wobbly head up. By jointly sharing in the everyday, intimate experience of learning to know the baby, as you watch his amazingly fast development, you will take first steps into a partnership of parenthood, a partnership more satisfying than any money-based partnership ever formed.

BIRTH REGISTRATION

A STORY is told of a young woman who, in order to get a farm that was willed to her, had to prove the date of her birth. She finally succeeded, but only by proving that she was born on the same day that a high-bred calf was born in her father's barn! The calf had a birth certificate, but the girl had none!

It may sometimes be of the utmost importance to your child that there be in existence an accurate, legal record of his birth and parentage. It would be well to ask the doctor to make sure that your baby's birth is properly registered, or go to the registrar's office yourself.

The birth certificate is filed with a local clerk or registrar who is usually connected in the large centers with a Bureau of Vital Statistics under the Department of Health.

Birth registration is important for the following reasons:

To identify the child

To prove the child's age and place of birth

To prove legitimacy

To establish right to enter school

To prove the right to take up employment

To prove right to inherit property

To establish legal age for voting, marriage, or liability for military service

To establish right to enter the professions or to hold public offices

To prove mother's right, when a widow, to a widow's pension

To establish right to obtain passport for travel abroad

To help health officers in making complete, accurate, important statistics about babies

The form usually contains the following items:

Baby's name

Sex of Baby

Place of Birth and Registration Number

Date of Birth. Day, month, and year

If twin or triplet, number in order of birth

Name of Father

Birthplace of Father

Maiden name of Mother

Birthplace of Mother

Attendant at Birth; Physician, Midwife, or other

Address of Attendant

MOTHER'S MILK THE BEST FOOD FOR BABY

MOTHER's milk is the best food for the baby. It is suited to his needs, just as cow's milk is suited to the needs of the calf. The best method of feeding a baby for his first six or seven months is at his mother's breast. Until the end of this time no baby should be taken entirely off the breast unless there is a very good reason. No mother should wean her baby except on the advice of her doctor.

Breast milk is easily digested, cheap, clean, and convenient. Breast feeding gives a baby a better chance in life for steady, normal growth. It also helps to start him off with that sense of security which is so important.

Almost every mother can nurse her baby. She should take for granted that she can do so. With this in mind, she should learn to care properly for her health and to avoid fatigue. She should nurse the baby at regular intervals. The breasts should be completely emptied to stimulate them.

HYGIENE OF THE NURSING MOTHER

SUCCESSFUL nursing depends largely on the mother's health and on her attitude toward nursing. If her breast milk is to be of the greatest benefit to the baby, the mother should follow the plan here suggested:

1. Try to avoid worry and emotional upsets. The calm, unworried mother is likely to nurse her baby more successfully than the anxious, excitable mother.

2. Sleep at least 8 hours every night and take an hour's rest in the daytime. After the first month or so, the baby should sleep through the night without any feeding after 10 P.M., and the mother's sleep will not be broken.

3. Plan your diet with your baby's growth and health in mind, as well as your own health. (Suggestions for a satisfactory diet are given on this page and the following one.)

4. Guard against constipation. Make every effort to regulate the bowels naturally by means of food, exercise, and regular habits. Do not take a cathartic unless the doctor orders one. Some medicines are secreted into the milk and may affect the baby.

5. Bathe often.

6. Take pleasant exercise in the open air and sunshine, but avoid overtiring yourself. Your daily work may give you enough exercise, but you should spend some time outdoors in the sun daily, preferably at midday in winter and before noon and after 3 P.M. in summer. You should get so much sunlight that your skin becomes tanned. Your milk will be better for the baby if you get plenty of sunlight.

7. Care for the breasts only with very clean hands. Wash the nipples with boiled water before and after each nursing and cover them with clean cloth between nursings. Consult the doctor if the nipples are cracked or sore, if the breasts are caked or tender, or if for any reason the baby does not nurse well. A cracked nipple, if neglected, may result in an abscess of the breast. Upon the care of the breasts, in many cases, depends the success of breast feeding.

DIET OF THE NURSING MOTHER

The mother's daily diet should be planned so as to provide the baby with the best possible food and at the same time to keep up her own strength. It should include plenty of the "protective foods"—milk, eggs, vegetables, fruit and, if ordered by the doctor, a vitamin D preparation.

1. A quart of milk a day should be taken. If a full quart is not used with the meals, either as a drink or in cooking, a glass should be taken in the mid-morning, in the mid-afternoon, or before going to bed. If good fresh milk cannot be had, evaporated or dried milk may be used. Milk is the most important single food in the nursing mother's diet, but not more than a quart a day need be taken. The diet should be varied.

2. Vegetables, raw or cooked, should be eaten two or three times daily. Fresh vegetables of every kind should be used, especially dark-green, leafy ones. Canned vegetables may be used when the fresh ones are not available.

3. Fruit, especially oranges or grapefruit, should be eaten daily. Fresh fruit is best, but when it is too expensive dried or canned fruit

may be used. Tomatoes, fresh or canned, may be substituted for oranges or grapefruit.

4. An egg should be eaten every day.

5. At least a quart of water a day should be taken. Coffee or tea in moderation are allowable, but should not replace milk, which is essential. Beer and other alcoholic beverages do not increase the supply of breast milk, but in small amounts do not affect either the milk or the baby.

6. Vitamin D in some form will be ordered by the doctor if it is required. It is usually given to nursing mothers who do not have an opportunity to spend much time in the sun. Cod liver oil or a more concentrated preparation in liquid or capsule form may be prescribed.

7. Laxative foods. To regulate the bowels, green, leafy vegetables should be eaten and also fruit, especially figs and prunes. Whole-grain bread and cereal may help to correct constipation. A glass of water taken the first thing in the morning may help.

A DAY'S FOOD PLAN FOR THE NURSING MOTHER

A quart of milk, a leafy vegetable, a citrus fruit (orange or half grapefruit), and an egg are essential in the nursing mother's daily diet. The following plan for the whole day's food may be helpful:

BREAKFAST

Fruit: Half grapefruit, whole orange, or whole banana.

Cereal (well cooked): Oatmeal, farina, or corn meal with whole milk and sugar.

Bread and butter: Two slices of bread, with two pats of butter.

Milk: One cup, or one cup of cocoa made with whole milk.

An egg, or bacon and egg, may be added to this meal. (The egg should be boiled, coddled, or poached.) Coffee in moderation may be taken in additon to the milk if desired.

10 A.M. LUNCHEON

Milk: One glass of whole milk (if this does not interfere with the appetite for dinner).

DINNER

Meat, fish or egg.

Salad: Lettuce, romaine, endive, cress, raw cabbage, tomato, celery and nut, fruit with mayonnaise or French dressing.

Vegetables: Baked potato with butter, tomatoes, carrots, peas, or string beans; properly cooked cabbage, spinach, or other greens, creamed.

Bread and butter: Two slices of bread, with one pat of butter.

Dessert: Custard, gelatin, canned or raw fruit, milk pudding.

Milk: One glass of whole milk.

SUPPER

Soup or other hot dish (made with whole milk): Creamed pea, tomato, or other vegetable soup, or a scalloped vegetable, or macaroni and tomatoes, or rice and cheese.

Bread and butter: Bran or graham muffins or toasted raisin bread, with two pats of butter.

Dessert: Stewed fruit and cake or baked apple with top milk or cream.

Milk: One glass of whole milk.

Tea in moderation may be taken in addition to the milk. A glass of milk may be taken at 10 P.M.

HOW TO NURSE THE BABY

As soon as the baby is born and once a month thereafter, if possible, a physician should be consulted in regard to feeding, and his advice followed.

Twelve to twenty-four hours after birth the baby is usually put to the breast for a few minutes. At this time the breasts secrete a thick yellowish fluid called colostrum, which the baby needs. The true milk comes into the breasts later. After the first nursing follow a fairly regular schedule of feeding—about every four hours by the clock unless the doctor advises shorter intervals. The usual hours for feeding are: 6 A.M., 10 A.M., 2 P.M., 6 P.M., 2 A.M. But these hours need not be followed exactly. If the baby awakens half an hour, or even an hour early, and cries for his feeding, let him nurse ahead of time. If he sleeps through the scheduled hour you can wake him up for the feeding if you want. But there is no harm in letting the baby sleep as long as he likes. When he needs the milk he will cry for it.

Nurse the baby in a comfortable and restful position. The busy mother may add to her rest period by lying down while nursing. Do not encourage the baby to play nor allow him to sleep at the breast. Before and after each feeding hold him up to help him get rid of the air that he may have swallowed.

The usual length of nursing should be 10 to 15 minutes—seldom more than 20. A strong baby may get enough milk in 5 minutes, and a weak baby may take the full 20 minutes to get enough. And sometimes a baby may want just to suck for that length of time. If the baby does not get enough milk, the doctor may advise giving a bottle feeding after nursing.

Emptying the breast completely by regular nursing helps to produce milk. For this reason, if the milk is plentiful, it is advisable to give only one breast at a feeding, so that the baby will empty it completely, and to give the other breast at the next feeding. If the milk is not plentiful, both breasts may need to be given to satisfy the baby, but one breast should be emptied before the other is given, and the breast that is given last at one nursing should be given first at the next one, so that at each nursing one breast is completely emptied.

If for any reason the baby does not empty the breast completely, emptying it by hand helps to maintain the supply of milk.

Nursing should be enjoyed by both mother and baby.

THE PREMATURE, SMALL, OR DELICATE BABY *

A PREMATURE BABY is a baby born more than 2 weeks before the end of 9 months of pregnancy. Such a baby is usually not so well developed at birth as a full-term baby.

The successful rearing of a premature baby requires not only the advice of a doctor and the assistance and guidance of a nurse, but also intelligent and earnest cooperation by the mother, the father, and all the other members of the family. All these should work together from the baby's birth to provide for his welfare.

The doctor's directions will be aimed at keeping the baby warm, properly nourished, and protected from infection, and they should be carried out carefully. The instructions given here are intended to help the mother care for her baby in whatever way her own doctor directs. If these instructons differ from those of her doctor, the mother should realize that her doctor's instructions, based on his examination of her baby and his observation of that baby's behavior, growth, and development, are planned to meet her baby's individual needs.

Because a premature baby always excites special interest, the mother will receive much well-meant advice from neighbors and other persons, but she should disregard this advice and take that of the doctor. She should also be very strict in refusing to let visitors go near the baby, because even if they appear to be healthy they may carry infection to the baby that may be fatal to him.

It is well for the mother of a premature baby to realize that if her baby keeps well he has as good a chance as a full-term baby to develop normally. After he grows up he is likely to be as strong as if he had been born at the normal time.

A mother who, during pregnancy, places herself under a physician's care will be more likely to have a full-term baby than one who goes without such care. Some causes of premature birth are unavoidable, however, and, in spite of every effort, a certain number of babies are born prematurely.

Most premature babies are born unexpectedly, and it is wise for every expectant mother to have all equipment ready about 2 months before the baby is due.

The earlier a baby is born, the more difficult it is to care for him. A baby born 2 or 3 weeks before the expected date of his birth may be quite strong and little different from a full-term baby, but a baby born 4 or more weeks early may be very small and difficult to save. Occasionally a baby born at full term is exceptionally small and feeble and must be cared for like a premature baby. *All babies weighing less than 5½ pounds at birth should be treated as if premature.*

CARE IMMEDIATELY AFTER BIRTH

It is of the utmost importance to give a premature baby proper care during and *immediately after* birth. He needs care by a doctor and a nurse who know what to do and who have the equipment needed.

* From *Infant Care*, U. S. Children's Bureau Publication.

As soon as the baby is born he should be placed in a soft, warm blanket wrapped loosely about him. The doctor or the nurse will, if necessary, remove mucus or other fluid from his mouth and throat by means of a rubber suction bulb (ear syringe) or by a small catheter attached to a glass syringe. When it is certain that the baby is breathing well he may be placed, with the blanket still wrapped loosely around him, in an incubator or some kind of heated bed that can be kept at a temperature of about 80° to 90° F. The cord can then be dressed and drops put into the eyes to prevent infection.

If the baby is born at home the decision must be made whether he is to be cared for at home or taken to a hospital.

Premature babies that weigh more than 4 pounds and are vigorous can usually be taken care of satisfactorily at home if the home conditions are favorable and certain precautions are taken. Some smaller babies also do well at home; in fact, they are often cared for best at home unless a hospital suitably equipped for the care of such babies is available. If, however, the baby is feeble and it is difficult to make him breathe, very special care is needed, which usually can best be had in a hospital.

It is best to have the doctor or the nurse who has seen the baby advise the family whether his condition is good enough to permit the journey to the hospital and how he should be transported. A public-health nurse or a visiting nurse may be available to stay with the baby during the trip.

The baby should not be taken to the hospital until his breathing is well enough established for such a trip to be safe. Great care should be taken to keep him warm during the trip, as chilling at this time decreases the chances of saving his life. To prevent him from losing any of his body heat he should be wrapped in a soft, clean blanket which has been warmed, and he should be carried in a basket lined with warm water bottles (115°F.) To prevent burns, a folded blanket or towel should be placed between the baby and the bottles. The doctor or nurse may be able to provide as a carrier a special bag that is easier and safer to use than a basket.

GENERAL CARE

A doctor, preferably one trained in care of babies, should see the baby *at birth and at regular and frequent intervals thereafter,* and his directions should be followed carefully. If the services of a nurse, preferably one who has had training in the care of premature infants, can be obtained, it will be a great help to the mother. Skilled nursing care can usually be obtained from a Public-health nurse. If more hours of nursing care are needed than this nurse can give, she can advise the mother how to get in touch with another nurse.

In caring for a premature baby three main aims must be kept in mind:

1. To keep the baby warm.
2. To protect him from infections.
3. To feed him properly.

Keeping the Baby Warm

At birth a baby loses the protection that he has had inside his mother's body (in the uterus) where he is surrounded by fluid that is kept at an even temperature by the mother's body. A baby born at term is better prepared to become adjusted readily to living outside his mother's body than is the premature baby. The baby that is prematurely born must be protected from changes in the environment, even slight changes in temperature. The amount of heat necessary to keep the premature baby warm will depend upon his size, development, and vigor. The more premature and the smaller he is the more difficult it will be to regulate his body temperature properly. The baby's body temperature, taken by rectum two or three times a day, should be about 97° to 99° F. An even temperature as low as 97° F. is probably better for the baby than an uneven temperature that goes higher. The temperature of the room and of the bed should be kept as constant as possible.

The Premature Baby's Room

It is easier to keep the premature baby's room warm and at an even temperature if it is a small room. One window, or preferably two, will allow for sunlight, and for ventilation by opening at the top. The baby's bed should be so placed that the air from the window will not blow on the baby. A thermometer should be hung on the wall over the baby's bed but not near a radiator or a window. Frequent readings of the thermometer should be made and recorded on a chart so placed that it is easy to read. The temperature of the room should be maintained evenly at a point between 75° and 80° F. day and night.

Heated Beds

In addition to a warm room some type of heated bed is usually needed by a premature baby. A thermometer should be placed on the mattress, beside the baby and under the covering if any covering is used. The temperature of the air inside the bed, at the mattress level, should be kept as even as possible at a point to be decided on by the doctor (usually from 80° to 90° F.), depending on the size, vigor, and body temperature of the baby. It may be well to increase the moisture in the air by placing a shallow pan of water inside the bed near the source of heat.

A simple type of heated bed is a box with a basket inside that is placed on blocks. The box has a sliding cover with a window in it. An asbestos pad, the size of the bottom of the basket, is placed under the basket, over the source of heat, so that there will be no danger of burning the baby. Heat is obtained from hot-water bottles of rubber or metal, or heated bricks or bags of heated sand, placed in pans on the floor of the box and under the basket. Bricks or bags of sand or hot-water bottles should not be too hot to hold in the bare hands. The temperature inside the bed should be kept constant and it is best therefore to change one hot bag or brick at a time, so as not to cool the bed.

If the house is wired for electricity an electrically heated incubator, so constructed that the temperature can be regulated automatically, can be used. The moisture (relative humidity) inside such a bed can be increased by placing a pan of water near the source of heat (an electric-light bulb). Many State health departments have such incubators to lend.

If an *electrically heated* incubator is to be used the doctor will advise you with regard to the type to be selected, and the doctor and nurse will teach you how to use it. The following precautions should be taken:

1. A baby in an incubator should be observed often to see that he is all right.

2. The thermometer inside the incubator should be looked at often to see that the temperature of the incubator is properly regulated.

3. The amount of heat should be regulated by a thermostat so that the bed cannot get too hot (above 90° F.) and so that the temperature at the mattress level will vary as little as possible, preferably not more than 2° F.

4. Electric-light bulbs should be protected by wire guards and should be so placed that the baby cannot come in contact with the guards.

5. The incubator must be large enough for the baby to move his arms and legs freely without touching any heating unit or other mechanism. It should be at least 13 inches wide, 23 inches long, and 9 inches high (above the mattress level).

6. Never exclude air completely from an incubator.

In warm weather it may not be necessary to heat the incubator; but there is an advantage in keeping the baby in it, for it protects him from drafts and from infection due to contact with persons who may come into the room.

Clothing

The premature baby's clothing should be light and loose, as it is especially important that such a baby have plenty of opportunity to move his arms and legs freely. Immediately after birth the baby should be placed in a soft, warm blanket and the blanket folded loosely about him. He should be kept in the blanket while the care necessary at his time is given. For temporary use a wadded jacket made of gauze, lined with cotton batting, may be used. Later a one-piece light-weight flannel gown may be substituted for the jacket.

The usual type of diaper is not suitable for the premature baby. A small square of absorbent cotton covered with gauze, or some other type of disposable pad, can be laid under the baby to serve as a diaper—*not folded between the legs.* These pads can be easily changed when they become soiled.

Care of the Skin

The premature baby's skin is very tender. After birth the folds of the skin may be wiped gently with soft, dry gauze or cotton. It is best not to bathe the baby with water or even with oil during the first 12 to 24 hours after birth. He need not be bathed even for a week or 10 days or longer. After the first day the folds under the arms and between the legs may be patted or wiped very gently with soft gauze or cotton moistened with a little warm mineral oil. When using the oil pour a small amount into a clean dish or cup; if any is left over it should be thrown away. When the pad used for a diaper is changed the parts of the body that are soiled may be wiped with oil.

When the baby is older and more vigorous and when he no longer needs to be kept in an incubator he may be bathed just as any young baby is.

Protection From Infection

Premature babies are very susceptible to infection, especially skin infections and colds. They have very little resistance to infection, and a cold may be very serious—even fatal—to a premature baby.

Infection is carried to a premature baby from the hands of the person caring for him or from the nose and throat of persons coming near him, or from unboiled milk or water. Infection is also carried by flies and other insects.

To protect the baby from infection observe the following rules carefully:

Only one person in the household should care for a premature baby, and no one except the person who cares for the baby regularly should go near him.

While caring for a premature baby the mother or nurse should wear a gown that she keeps especially for this purpose.

The person who cares for the premature baby should wash the hands before handling the baby each time; it is very important to wash the hands *before* and *after* changing the diaper pad and just before feeding the baby.

No one with any infectious condition, even a slight cold, should be allowed to take care of, or go near, a premature baby. Visitors, especially young children, should never be permitted in a premature baby's room.

Flies and other insects should be kept away from a premature baby. If the house is not well screened a netting should be kept over the baby's bed.

The premature baby's tender skin may become infected if rubbed. The parts of his body that become soiled should be cleaned by gentle wiping with soft gauze or cotton moistened with oil.

Just as soon as the premature baby's bedding and clothing become wet or soiled they should be changed without taking the baby out of the bed.

Sleep

The premature baby in the early weeks of life will sleep most of the day and night and will usually have to be wakened for feeding. It is important that he be kept awake for the feeding so that he will swallow well. If he cannot be roused the doctor should be notified immediately.

Bowel Movements

The premature baby passes dark, sticky, green material called meconium on the first 2 days of life, just as does the full-term baby. During the next few days the movements will become brown, then yellow. Most premature babies have four to six bowel movements a day, which are small and pasty. If the baby has frequent movements (more than six a day) or loose movements, even if not frequent, or if a bowel movement contains blood, the doctor should be notified immediately. Blood in a bowel movement may be red or dark brown.

FEEDING

The doctor will advise the mother in regard to the baby's feeding. The instructions given here are to guide the mother before the doctor comes and to help her in following his directions.

The premature baby does not need food or water for about 12 hours after birth, but after this a sufficient supply of fluid is essential. The amount given daily will at first be small; it may be increased gradually until he can take daily a total amount of fluid (milk and water) equal to about one-eighth or one-sixth of his body weight (about 2 ounces for each pound of body weight).

The milk and the water should be given in the way best suited to the baby's condition. Most premature babies are not able to suck well, and therefore they are fed with a medicine dropper. Some babies are so weak that feeding must be given with a stomach tube (so-called catheter feeding). Only a trained person should be allowed to do this.

It is wise to delay putting a premature baby to the breast until his breathing and swallowing are well established and until he is strong enough not to be overtired by nursing. If the baby cannot nurse at the breast, or is too weak to draw milk from the nipple of a bottle, the mother's milk should be expressed by hand or by means of a breast pump and fed to the baby slowly with a medicine dropper. Water also may be given, slowly, by medicine dropper. The end of the glass medicine dropper should be covered with a piece of soft-rubber tubing to prevent injury to the baby's mouth. The rubber tubing should extend about a quarter of an inch beyond the end of the glass tube.

Any utensil that is to touch the baby's food or water must be sterilized by boiling for 5 minutes before it is used, and carefully washed with soap and water after it is used. This includes not only the medicine dropper and rubber tip but also such things as the breast pump, the cup or glass used to hold milk or water, the funnel and strainer, and all nursing bottles, bottle caps, and rubber nipples.

To give water or milk raise the baby's head and shoulders and squeeze the water or milk slowly from the dropper while watching to be sure that the baby is able to swallow. Gentle pulls on the dropper will often stimulate him to suck and swallow. Care must be taken not to give the milk or water faster than he is able to swallow it.

Care should be taken not to overtire the baby during feeding. The feeding should require no more than 20 minutes. Very small premature babies, because they can take only small amounts of milk at any one feeding, may have to be fed every 2 hours. Larger infants may be fed at 3-hour or even at 4-hour intervals.

Water

The premature baby should not be given water until he is about 12 hours old. The water that the baby will need during each 24 hours should be boiled and cooled and should be kept in a covered glass jar that has been boiled for 5 minutes to make it sterile.

It is best to begin with very small amounts of water, about one-half to 1 teaspoonful, given with a medicine dropper every 2 to 3 hours, alternating with the feedings. A record should be kept of the amount of water taken. If the baby is too weak to take the necessary amount of fluid by mouth the doctor may inject fluid, such as salt solution, under the skin as often as he considers necessary.

During the period when the baby is receiving very small feedings of breast milk, special care must be taken to give him enough boiled water. As he takes more milk he may take less water, but it is well to offer water to him between feedings even when he is strong enough to take an adequate amount of milk.

Milk

Milk feedings may usually be begun after the baby is 18 hours old.

Breast Milk

Breast milk is the best food for the premature baby. At the end of 12 hours the first efforts should be made to empty the mother's breasts. The colostrum—and the milk when it comes—should be expressed at regular intervals and given to the baby. As it may be some weeks before the baby is able to draw even small amounts of milk from the breast, it will be necessary for the mother to empty her breasts at regular intervals, not only to obtain milk for the baby during the early weeks of life but to keep up the milk flow until the baby is strong enough to nurse.

Cow's Milk

If breast milk cannot be obtained, cow's-milk feeding will become necessary. Various milk mixtures have been given to premature babies with success. The doctor will order the mixture best suited to the baby's individual needs.

If it is not possible to get a doctor' advice at once, one of the following milk mixtures may be used temporarily:

Evaporated milk, 3 ounces.
Water, 6 ounces.
Granulated sugar or corn sirup, 1 level tablespoonful.
or
Half-skimmed cow's milk, 8 ounces.
Water, 2 ounces
Granulated sugar or corn sirup, 1 level tablespoonful.
The mixture should be boiled.

Half-skimmed cow's milk is obtained by removing half the cream from the top of the bottle. The milk and remaining cream should be thoroughly mixed.

The doctor may order that some form of sugar be used other than granulated sugar or corn sirup.

Vitamins

The premature baby needs, in addition to milk, whether breast milk or cow's milk, vitamins that are important for growth and development.

A premature baby needs vitamin D even more than a full-term baby because he is growing more rapidly. For promotion of normal growth and prevention of rickets he should receive about two or three times as much vitamin D as the full-term baby, or about 1,600 to 2,400 international units a day. Vitamin D is contained in fish-liver oils such as cod-liver oil, but *cod-liver oil should not be given to premature infants who are small and do not swallow well.* Vitamin D should be given to the premature baby in a concentrated form and one that contains vitamin A also. It should be begun before the end of the first week of life.

A premature baby needs to have vitamin C also. This is the vitamin contained in orange juice. In order to give the proper amount to meet the needs of the premature baby a concentrated form of vitamin C, ascorbic acid, should be given (one 25-mg. tablet a day, dissolved in water), beginning when the baby is 2 weeks old. As the premature baby grows larger and more vigorous, the amount of ascorbic acid may be increased, or orange juice may be given in place of it. The amount of orange juice will be the same as for the full-term baby.

Iron

When the premature baby is about a month old the doctor will prescribe some preparation of iron to prevent him from becoming anemic.

As the premature baby grows older the same foods should be added to his diet as are added to the diet of the full-term baby.

GAIN IN WEIGHT

The premature baby, like the full-term baby, usually loses some weight in the first 2 or 3 days after birth. He begins to take food when he is about 18 hours old, and when he is 4 or 5 days old he will usually be able to take enough food to prevent further loss of weight. Premature babies usually regain the birth weight by the second or third week.

The baby should be weighed at least twice a week. The weighings should be at about the same time of day, and the weight should be written down and shown to the doctor. Great care should be taken not to chill the baby during the weighing. He can be weighed in his jacket or gown or wrapped in a warmed blanket. Then the covering can be weighed separately and its weight subtracted from the total weight of the baby and the covering.

The baby may not gain weight every day, and some days he may lose weight, but week by week he should gain steadily if he is well and is properly fed.

OUTDOOR LIFE

Since changes in temperature are to be avoided for the premature baby, he should not be taken outdoors while very small. The age at which he may be taken outdoors varies with the size and degree of prematurity of the baby and with the weather and the season of the year. After he has attained the size and vigor of a 2-month-old full-term baby, he may be taken outdoors just as a full-term baby of this size would be.

Sun baths cannot be given to small premature babies. Special effort must be made to give them some form of tested vitamin D. When they grow larger and more vigorous, sun baths can be given just as to full-term babies.

HEALTH EXAMINATIONS

The mother should make arrangements to have the baby seen by a doctor at regular intervals. The doctor will examine the baby and advise the mother in regard to his feeding and general care. The examination will include an appraisal of the baby's physical and mental development.

LATER DEVELOPMENT

As the premature infant grows older he should gradually become more and more like a full-term baby. Though small, he should have good color, his muscles should be firm, and he should gradually become active and alert. He may be slower than a full-term baby in learning to do some things like holding up his head and sitting up. If he is protected from infection and gets the proper food and care he will catch up to the full-term baby in course of time. The time that this will take will depend on how many weeks before term he was born.

DIFFICULTIES OF THE NURSING PERIOD

DURING the early period of nursing there may be minor digestive disturbances in the baby which may cause mothers some anxiety. These are usually a matter of adjustment of the baby's digestive tract to a new function and should never be considered an excuse for weaning from the breast.

STOOLS

The first passages from a newborn baby's bowels are known as meconium. The excretion is very dark green, thick and sticky, with little or no odor. This soon changes to the normal yellow stool of the healthy infant as the baby begins to feed at his mother's breast.

Ordinarily a breast-fed infant should have one to four stools a day, bright orange-yellow in color (though occasionally greenish), soft and mealy, often rather loose in character.

Occasionally a breast-fed baby, who is apparently perfectly well, with a normal temperature, comfortable and thriving, continues to have loose greenish stools containing small curds or some mucus. Such stools in an artificially fed baby would be reason for changing the food, but in a nursing baby who is well and gaining they may be largely disregarded.

A sudden increase in the number of stools in a day, especially if they are watery or green, should not be disregarded. This is a danger sign and usually means that the baby has caught a cold or some other infection. In very young infants such a diarrhea can be very serious and the doctor should be consulted promptly.

Occasionally the breast-fed baby may be constipated. When this happens it is most often because there is not enough breast milk. Or it may be that the baby's anal muscle is tightly contracted and he has not learned how to relax it. When this is the case, a suppository or a soap stick about as big around as a lead pencil and an inch and a half long gently passed into the baby's rectum when he is uncomfortable will relieve the condition. It is usually outgrown in a few weeks. Under no circumstances should any laxative medicines be given.

UNDERFEEDING

It happens sometimes that a breast-fed baby is underfed. Such an infant shows no gain in weight or more often shows a loss in weight. The baby either nurses for a brief interval and then gives up and falls asleep or shows great distress after an exhausting attempt to obtain food. The stools are scanty, often only brown stains. The child seems weak and may feel flabby and look pale, but he usually cries very little and sleeps much.

The fact that a baby does not gain in weight or actually loses in weight immediately suggests that he is not getting enough food. Weighing the baby for several days before and after each feeding will prove this. If the baby is not getting enough food, artificial food must be temporarily supplied as a part of the diet.

It may be that the mother has not enough milk or it may be that the baby is not vigorous enough to nurse properly or has a deformed mouth.

If the trouble is due to real lack of milk supply more attention should be paid to the hygiene of the mother. She must have plenty of rest and sleep and she must take the proper amount of food and liquid. Under any circumstances it is most important that the breasts be emptied thoroughly at regular intervals in order to stimulate the production. Persistent efforts to increase the amount of milk will usually be successful.

Weak babies or those with deformed mouths should be fed the milk which has been drawn from the breast.

METHOD OF EMPTYING THE BREAST

Fortunately there are very satisfactory methods of emptying the breast on which a weak or physically defective child fails. This matter is especially important because the weak child needs breast milk, and his very condition tends to diminish not only the amount he takes but also the amount of milk available.

The electric breast pump is the most effective means for emptying the breast. The principle upon which it works is that of intermittent suction. The breasts are compressed coincidentally with the applied suction. This type of breast pump actually promotes a better flow of milk when the supply is poor.

The water breast pump, which can be attached to a water faucet, is also very effective.

Hand breast pumps do not completely evacuate the breasts and they may therefore become a source of infection. For this reason the hand breast pump is not being used very much today.

Hand expression of the milk is the least desirable method; but directions are given for use in an emergency when a breast pump is not available.

Wash the hands thoroughly and dry on a clean towel. Wash the nipple with fresh absorbent cotton and boiled water. Have a sterilized glass tumbler or large-mouthed bottle to receive the milk.

Grasp the breast gently but firmly with the thumb placed in front and the fingers on the under surface of the breast. The thumb in front and the first finger beneath should rest just outside of the pigmented area of the breast.

With the thumb a downward pressing motion is made on the front against the fingers on the back of the breast, then the thumb in front and fingers behind are carried downward to the base of the nipple.

This second act should end with a slight forward pull with gentle pressure at the base of the nipple, which causes the milk to flow out.

The combination of these three movements may be described as "Back-down-out."

It is not necessary to touch the nipple.

This act may be repeated 30 to 60 times a minute after some practice.

If after such methods the mother's milk still is insufficient, mixed feeding—part breast feeding and part bottle feeding—may be given for weeks or even months. One bottle feeding a day may be given in place of the breast or the bottle may be given after each breast feeding to make up the necessary amount.

OVERFEEDING

Overfeeding is rare in the breast-fed baby. When it occurs it usually means that the nursing periods are too frequent or that the quantity taken at one time is too large, or occasionally that the milk is too rich in fat. Under such circumstances the baby usually spits up after nursing and is fussy.

To remedy this, the time at the breast should be decreased and the interval between feedings increased to four hours. A few spoonfuls of warm water given the baby from a nursing bottle just before nursing will dilute the milk.

ILLNESS

Nursing mothers should be warned against removing the baby from the breast merely because the mother has a slight disorder or sickness. During most cases of brief illness of the mother, the infant may be safely nursed.

A sudden, severe illness of the mother, especially an acute infectious disease with fever, may make it necessary to remove the baby from the breast temporarily. This may mean for only a few feedings, but if the mother's illness is longer and more serious, the baby may be deprived of the breast for a week or two. In any case it is wise to make every effort to keep up the supply of breast milk by emptying the breasts completely at regular intervals, and the baby should return to breast feeding at the first possible moment.

While the mother is acutely ill, put the baby on artificial feeding only under a doctor's advice.

WET NURSES

In some cases if the mother cannot nurse the baby it is necessary to engage the services of a wet nurse. Some new-born babies, especially those prematurely born, and some very delicate babies, or those suffering from chronic digestive disturbance, can only with difficulty be made to thrive on artificial food. For such babies it is wise to provide a wet nurse. In some large cities there are agencies where breast milk can be bought, or wet nurses can be obtained. In small towns or in the country wet nurses or breast milk can be secured by advertising, or by inquiry at a maternity hospital in some near-by city. Frequently breast milk may be obtained by expression from another mother and not infrequently a friend will nurse another baby than her own.

When a wet nurse is secured it is not necessary that her baby should be the same age as the baby to be nursed. It is best to engage a nurse whose baby is old enough and whose condition is such as to indicate that she can produce an abundant milk supply. Also, the wet nurse should not be too near the weaning period.

Every wet nurse should nurse her own baby. Her peace of mind will insure better breast milk. In addition, if the baby to be wet-nursed is small and weak, it may be an advantage to have the wet nurse's breasts emptied afterwards by a more vigorous child. Professional wet nurses in hopitals often furnish enough milk for several babies at a time, so there need be no fear that a wet nurse cannot supply milk for two if she has good breasts, if her life is properly regulated, and if her diet is ample and nutritious.

The general appearance of the wet nurse and her child should be considered before she is engaged. The healthy appearance of her child is a guaranty of her ability to nurse. Also it is absolutely necessary that the nurse herself be given a complete physical examination by a physician. She must be perfectly healthy and must not have any disease which she could transmit to her nurseling.

Acute tuberculosis, gonorrhea, and syphilis are the diseases most to be looked for. The complete physical examination which should be given her by a physician before she is engaged should include an X-ray of the chest, the blood test for syphilis, and examination for gonorrhea, whether or not she shows any symptoms of these diseases.

WEANING*

BECAUSE breast feeding is so good for the baby a mother should plan to nurse her baby at least 7 or 8 months unless there is a very good reason not to.

There are only a few good reasons for permanently weaning a baby under 6 months. Among them are the following conditions in the mother: Another pregnancy; any chronic illness of a weakening nature, such as cancer, chronic Bright's disease, chronic heart disease, or severe anemia; severe prolonged infectious diseases, such as typhoid fever and lung tuberculosis; diseases in which the mother may not be responsible for her actions, such as epilepsy or dementia.

A mother with active tuberculosis of the lungs is almost sure to give the disease to her baby if she is near him, and therefore she should never nurse the baby, not even take care of him.

Sometimes the mother's return to employment may make early weaning necessary. Sometimes careful planning by both father and mother will make it possible for the mother to remain at home and nurse their baby, especially when they realize what a good start in life breast feeding will give the baby.

It may be necessary for the mother temporarily to discontinue feeding the baby from the breast if mother and baby have to be separated for a short time, or if the mother contracts a disease which the baby may catch, or if the mother herself becomes extremely ill. If the mother is not too ill it is wise to make every effort to keep up the supply of breast milk by emptying the breasts completely by hand or by breast pump at regular intervals. During the mother's illness, while the baby is not getting breast milk, regular feedings of cow's-milk mixture must be given, prepared according to a formula given by the doctor. Breast feeding should be resumed at the first possible moment.

*From *Infant Care*, U. S. Children's Bureau Publication.

Some of the reasons often given for weaning are really not sufficient to make weaning necessary. Some babies are weaned unnecessarily because the mother discovers that her breast milk looks blue and thinks it is "too thin." Breast milk is always bluer and thinner than cow's milk. Its quality cannot be determined by looking at a few drops, nor can it be satisfactorily told even by laboratory examination. Difficulties that arise during the breast-feeding period, such as colic, spitting up, increase in number of stools, and green stools, are much more likely to be caused by shortage of milk than by poor quality. A baby with these symptoms should be seen by a doctor. Even if the supply of breast milk decreases to the point where the baby is not gaining weight, weaning may not be necessary. Before weaning is considered, every effort should be made to increase the supply of breast milk by attention to the mother's diet and general hygiene. When the amount of breast milk is insufficient the baby may be given a cow's-milk mixture after each breast feeding.

Menstruation may return during the nursing period. It is not a reason for weaning the baby.

How To Wean the Baby

Weaning should be made as easy as possible for the baby. Before the baby is weaned consult the doctor with regard to the cow's-milk mixture to be used. A boiled mixture of cow's milk, water, and sugar or corn sirup usually is satisfactory. This plan can be used for most babies:

For a week give one feeding of cow's milk a day and three breast feedings. Then for 4 or 5 days give two feedings of cow's milk a day and two breast feedings. For the next 4 or 5 days give three feedings of cow's milk a day and one breast feeding. After that (between 2 and 3 weeks after the beginning of weaning) the baby gets no breast feedings but gets four feedings of cow's milk a day, as well as the additional foods mentioned on pages

Rapid weaning may occasionally be necessary. Additional substitutions of bottle feedings for breast feedings may have to be made at shorter intervals. The rapid method of weaning should not be used except for some very urgent reason. Sudden weaning is frequently very difficult, especially with young babies, and of course should be done only in an emergency. It is also painful for the mother.

Many babies at 8 or 9 months can learn at once to drink from a cup and thus will not need to learn to give up the bottle a few months later.

When a bottle feeding is to be given a breast-fed baby the milk mixture can be selected as described on page 104. The feedings can be prepared according to the suggestions on page 120.

During the first 6 months of life no baby should be taken off the breast unless there is very good reason. After the baby is 6 months old cow's-milk feeding may be begun, but it is best that a baby should be at least partly breast-fed until he is 7 or 8 months old.

The baby who is old enough to be weaned, or the younger baby who cannot be breast fed, is usually given a boiled cow's-milk mixture.[1] Boiling the milk makes it safe and also more digestible. Even boiled milk, however, is not readily digested by all babies, and it is therefore often necessary to add water. Adding water to the milk, of course, makes it weaker, and sugar is added in order that the baby may be nourished adequately.

The cow's milk used for babies may be fresh, evaporated, or dried, and there are several varieties of sugar that may be used. Your doctor will help you decide which milk and which sugar to use for your baby's milk mixture.

---

[1] Goat's milk may be used for babies in the same way as cow's milk, provided the same precautions are taken in the production and care of the milk and the preparation of the feeding.

THE CHOICE OF MILK *

Fresh Milk

FRESH MILK should be obtained from a dependable source. It should be kept cool and clean. If you cannot get fresh milk from a dependable source or do not have a cool place in which to keep the milk, it is better not to use fresh milk for baby feeding. Fresh milk should be pasteurized before it is sold.

All fresh milk should be boiled before it is given to the baby.

Evaporated Milk

Evaporated milk is whole milk from which some of the water has been removed. As put into the can it has less than half the original bulk of the fresh milk from which it was made. It is sterilized in the can, and no sugar is added. All brands of evaporated milk now sold in the United States meet the Government standards and are suitable for infant feeding.

Evaporated milk will keep without refrigeration until the can is opened. When the can has been opened the milk must be kept covered and in a cold place, just like fresh milk. It may be kept in the can.

When evaporated milk is diluted with an equal amount of boiled cooled water it has practically the same food value as fresh whole milk that has been boiled. It may be used in the same proportions as fresh whole milk in preparing the milk mixture for the baby. It is not necessary to boil a milk mixture made with evaporated milk and boiled water as the milk has already been heated and sterilized. Evaporated milk is a safe and inexpensive milk for babies.

Evaporated milk must not be confused with condensed milk, which contains a large amount of sugar and therefore is not a suitable food for babies.

Dried Milk

Dried milk, or milk powder, is manufactured by removing practically all the water from fluid milk; no sugar is added. Dried milk may be made from whole milk, skimmed milk, or partly skimmed milk, and from sweet or sour milk. Be sure to read the label before buying dried milk so as to get the kind you want.

Canned dried milk will keep without refrigeration until the can is opened. After the can is opened and the powder has been exposed to the air the can must be kept tightly covered and

---

* From *Infant Care*, U. S. Children's Bureau Publication.

cold, damp or soiled utensils should never be used to dip out the powder, as this may contaminate what is left in the can. Since a can of dried milk may not be used up for some time, dried milk should not be used unless the opened can of powder can be kept cold.

If dried whole sweet milk is mixed with water according to the directions on the can (usually 4 level tablespoonfuls of milk powder to 8 ounces of water), it may be used in the same way as fresh whole milk in preparing the mixture. The mixture should be boiled.

Other types of dried milk may be used according to the doctor's directions.

Special Forms of Milk

Various kinds of evaporated, fresh, and dried milk are on the market. Whatever kind of milk is used, remember that all milk except evaporated milk must be boiled before being given to the baby.

Lactic-Acid Milk

Lactic-acid milk is usually made for babies by adding lactic acid to boiled milk, although it may be made by adding a culture to the milk. The boiled milk must be cold before the lactic acid is added. Otherwise the milk is likely to form curds that will not pass through the holes in the nipple.

Vitamin D Milk

Vitamin D milk is milk—fresh, evaporated, or dried—that has had its vitamin D value increased by some special process. The amount of vitamin D that these fortified milks contain varies but most of them have a vitamin D value of 400 international units per quart of fresh milk or of evaporated or dried milk after sufficient water has been added to make a quart.

Patent Milks for Infants

There are on the market a number of proprietary, or patent, milk mixtures. They should be used only under the direction of a doctor.

IMPORTANCE OF BOILING

It is of utmost importance to any baby who must be bottle-fed that the milk be boiled to make it safe. Boiling milk kills any disease germs that the milk may contain. It also makes milk more digestible.

The curds formed in the baby's stomach in the process of digestion of raw cow's milk are apt to be large and tough. They are frequently found undigested in the baby's stool. Such undigested raw-milk curds found in stools look very much like white or yellowish lima beans.

When milk has been boiled for 5 minutes it is more digestible. The curds that are formed in a baby's stomach from boiled milk are small and soft and are more like the curds from breast milk.

Because boiling milk makes it both safe and more digestible, many of the digestive disturbances and other difficulties of bottle feeding do not appear when only boiled milk is given to the baby. It is perhaps the one rule that can be laid down for all bottle fed babies.

The milk must be boiled as part of the home preparation of the baby's milk mixture unless evaporated milk is used, which has been sterilized in the process of manufacture. The curds formed in the baby's stomach by evaporated milk are even softer than those formed by boiled fresh milk.

Constipation does not result from the use of boiled milk except in very rare cases. Even if it does develop, it can usually be corrected by making other changes in the food according to the doctor's directions and it is unimportant in comparison with the serious disorders that may follow the use of raw milk.

THE CHOICE OF SUGAR

Your doctor will decide what kind of sugar is best for your baby's milk mixture. The kinds commonly used are: Corn sirup, granulated sugar, a mixture of malt sugar and dextrin, milk sugar, and even honey. There are also proprietary or patent sugars for infant feeding.

Either granulated sugar or corn sirup is satisfactory for most babies, and both are inexpensive. The dark kind of corn sirup is usually preferable to the light because it is likely to contain more minerals, especially iron. Sirup should be kept covered and cool.

Proprietary or patent sugars for infants.—Many infant foods on the market contain no milk but are intended to be added to the milk; they consist largely of sugars. This type of patent food should be added to milk in place of other sugar only as directed by the doctor.

PLANNING A FORMULA

The milk mixture that is best for **your baby** should be planned by the doctor.

The amount and kind of milk and sugar and the amount of water that should be used in the mixture vary according to the individual needs of the baby. Even though the doctor has planned a formula for the baby, it may be necessary for him to change that formula, perhaps more than once, before a mixture suited to the baby's individual needs is found. After the right mixture has been found it will need to be changed from time to time.

Babies, even at the same age, vary a good deal in the amount of food they require. For example, very active babies need more food than babies that are less active. After observing a great many babies, doctors have found that, on the average, they can predict about how much food a baby will need at different ages.

Quantity of Milk

On his first day of life a baby is usually given no milk—only water, sweetened or unsweetened.

On the second day of life, if it is not possible to feed the baby at his mother's breast, cow's milk is begun (with water and sugar added as described on page 104); that is, 1 ounce of milk for each pound of the baby's weight. A 7-pound baby at this age usually needs 7 ounces of milk in 24 hours.

From the fourth to the seventh day a baby needs as a rule 1¼ to 1½ ounces of milk daily for each pound of his weight.

During the second, third, and fourth weeks the baby usually needs not less than 1½ ounces of milk daily for each pound of his weight, and he may need more.

From the beginning of the second month to the end of the ninth month most babies need 1½ to 2 ounces of milk daily for each pound of their weight.

When the baby is 9 months old he will be taking a variety of other foods, so that it is seldom necessary to increase the amount of milk further.

After the baby is about 9 months old, whether he has been breast fed or bottle fed, he may be given daily about 32 ounces (1 quart) of cow's milk (boiled) unmixed with water or sugar. Some of this milk may be used in cooking the baby's cereal or may be poured over it.

Quantity of Sugar

During the first week of life a 7-pound baby, as a rule, will need 1 tablespoonful of corn sirup or granulated sugar added to the whole day's allowance of milk mixture. During the first month this may be gradually increased to 2 tablespoonfuls, during the second month to 2½ tablespoonfuls, and during the third or fourth month to 3 tablespoonfuls. Most babies will not require more than 3 tablespoonfuls a day of sirup or granulated sugar at any time.

At the beginning of the seventh month begin to decrease this amount of sugar gradually, until at the beginning of the ninth month no sugar is added to the milk.

One level tablespoonful of corn sirup or granulated sugar weighs the same as 1½ tablespoonfuls of milk sugar or of a mixture of malt sugar and dextrin; therefore if either of these is used, one and one-half times as many tablespoonfuls will be needed as of corn sirup or granulated sugar.

Quantity of Water

As a rule during the first week of life a baby's milk is diluted about half and half with water; gradually less of the water needed is put into the milk mixture, more being given as drinking water. Some doctors prefer that the baby get all the water that he needs between feedings rather than in the milk mixture.

Throughout the first year of life a baby needs 2 to 2½ ounces of fluid daily for each pound of his body weight. If he does not obtain this much fluid in his milk mixture and fruit juices, the rest may be supplied as drinking water.

In hot weather a baby will need more fluid than in cold weather.

NUMBER OF FEEDINGS

Most babies do well if fed every 4 hours. The very young baby fed every 4 hours will have six feedings in 24 hours, usually at 6 a.m., 10 a.m., 2 p.m., 6 p.m., 10 p.m., and 2 a.m.

As soon as the baby will sleep through the 2 a.m. feeding—usually by the second month, but sometimes earlier—he will need only five feedings in 24 hours. Later, as a rule some time after he is 4 or 5 months old, he will also sleep through the 10 p.m. feeding. Four feedings in 24 hours will then be sufficient.

Some babies need to be fed at shorter intervals than every 4 hours. The baby fed every 3 hours will need eight feedings in 24 hours, or seven feedings if during the night the intervals can be longer than 3 hours.

The exact hours at which the feedings are to be given can be other than those suggested, so long as an appropriate interval is allowed between feedings.

Feedings should be given according to a regular schedule, arranged to meet the baby's needs and the parents' convenience.

AMOUNT OF MILK MIXTURE

The amount of milk mixture given to a baby at each feeding is small at first and is gradually increased as the baby gets older.

The baby who is fed at 4-hour intervals receives larger feedings than the one who is fed at shorter intervals. But even babies fed at the same intervals vary considerably with regard to the amount of milk mixture that they will take at a feeding. For newborn babies it is well to offer a small amount at a feeding—say 2 to 2½ ounces—and to increase the amounts as the baby wants more.

EQUIPMENT NEEDED

If a baby is to be weaned before he is old enough to drink from a cup, or if he must be fed a milk mixture from birth, it is a great help if the mother is able to have a set of utensils especially for preparing the milk mixture and to keep these utensils together and not use them for anything else. To do this will cost a few dollars extra, but if the family is able to afford the cost, the extra equipment will help to make certain that the baby's milk mixture is correctly made and clean *every* day. Besides, the mother will find that much time and trouble will be saved.

The utensils needed include (1) those needed for feeding, (2) those needed for preparation, and (3) those needed for keeping the equipment in good condition.

For Feeding

Nursing Bottles

Number and size.—When the baby's food is prepared only once every 24 hours, the mother will need as many nursing bottles as there are feedings in that time, and it may be convenient

for her to have at least two extra bottles.

The ordinary nursing bottle holds 8 ounces. A smaller size bottle, holding 4 ounces, may be convenient for giving water and orange juice and for giving small amounts of milk mixture to a young baby, although the larger bottle may be used instead. For water and orange juice, two of the smaller bottles are usually enough.

Material.—Nursing bottles made of heat-resistant glass do not break easily, but they cost more than bottles made of ordinary glass. If a baby is to be bottle fed for a long time, it is worth while to buy the more expensive bottles.

Shape.—A kind of bottle should be bought that can be cleaned thoroughly with a bottle brush; there should be no corners that are hard to clean. The neck of the bottle should gradually slope into the body, and the bottom should slope into the side without a sharp corner.

Bottle Caps

When a baby's milk mixture has been put into a nursing bottle the bottle must be kept tightly covered until it is used.

A bottle cap covers the lip of the nursing bottle and therefore protects the milk mixture much more satisfactorily than a cork.

Wax paper held in place with an elastic band may be used as a cover. It is somewhat troublesome to put on, and a bottle covered with wax paper must be kept upright to keep the milk from leaking out and from touching the wax paper, which is not sterile. Wax paper must never be used twice.

Nipples

If possible, have enough nipples for a day's use, so that they need be boiled only once a day. A day's supply of nipples includes one for each feeding, one for each drink of water, and one for each drink of orange juice. When buying nipples select the kind that can easily be turned inside out to be cleaned.

Before using a new nipple find out whether the holes are about the right size. To do this put the nipple (before it is sterilized) on a nursing bottle of water (one that is not to be given to the baby), turn it upside down, and squeeze the nipple with the fingers somewhat as the baby will suck upon it. When the nipple is squeezed in this way several fine streams should come from it.

If the holes in the nipple are too small, the baby may get tired before he gets enough milk; if they are too large, he will get all his milk before he has sucked as long as he wants to. A baby sometimes starts thumb or finger sucking because he still wants to suck after he has had all his milk.

If the holes in a nipple seem to be too small heat an ordinary sewing needle to a red-hot heat, holding it by means of a cork, and enlarge the holes by poking the red-hot needle through them.

Several small holes in a nipple are better than one large one.

For Preparing the Milk Mixture

A *saucepan* in which to mix and boil the milk mixture is usually needed. It is helpful if this saucepan has a lip, to make pouring easy.

A *funnel* is usually needed in pouring the milk mixture from the saucepan into the nursing bottles. If the saucepan has a good lip a funnel may not be necessary.

A *large measuring cup* marked to measure ounces is convenient for measuring milk and water, but a nursing bottle marked in ounces is also satisfactory.

A *tablespoon and a teaspoon* are needed for measuring sugar. Measuring spoons, which can be bought in sets of four fastened together on a ring, are inexpensive and are much more accurate than ordinary household spoons.

A *knife* should be kept for leveling spoonfuls of sugar or dried milk.

A *sirup server* that has a spring top to prevent dripping may be convenient.

Strainer.—A scum is likely to form on a fresh-milk mixture when it is boiled, and therefore a strainer is needed. If a fine-mesh strainer is bought it may be used also for straining orange juice.

Can opener.—If evaporated milk is used a can opener is needed. A can opener that makes a large three-cornered hole may be convenient. If an ice pick is used, or other opener that makes a small hole, two holes are necessary.

Egg beater.—If dried milk is used an egg beater is needed.

For Caring for Equipment

A *brush* with a long handle and with long bristles, which will thoroughly clean the inside of the nursing bottles, is needed.

A *kettle with a cover* is needed for sterilizing the bottles, bottle caps, nipples, and other utensils used in preparing the milk mixture. Baby-bottle sterilizers, which consist of a kettle and a bottle rack, can be bought.

A *wire rack* for holding bottles when they are being boiled and filled is a convenience. This rack should fit inside the large kettle used for sterilizing as it does in commercial sterilizers. A rack can be made at home by bending a piece of heavy wire with a pair of pliers.

A *long-handled spoon* is needed for removing utensils from the sterilizing kettle and for stirring the milk mixture.

Jars.—Two small wide-mouthed covered jars are needed, one for clean nipples, the other for used ones. The covers should be of glass or of a metal that does not rust. There should not be a paper top inside the cover.

STERILIZING EQUIPMENT

All the utensils that come in contact with the milk mixture after it has been boiled must be sterilized—boiled or steamed for 5 minutes; those used before the mixture is boiled need only be washed thoroughly with hot water and soap.

After the baby has finished a feeding, rinse the nursing bottle and the nipple immediately with cold water. Leave the bottle standing full of water. Put the nipple into the jar for used nipples.

Before the mother starts to prepare the milk mixture she should wash and sterilize all the bottles and other necessary utensils in the following way:

Scrub the inside of each bottle with the bottle brush, using plenty of soap and hot water. Rinse each bottle carefully.

Place each bottle upside down in the wire bottle rack, which fits inside the large covered kettle. If a rack is not used, lay the bottles on their sides in the kettle.

Wash the bottle caps and the nipples with hot water and soap, turning each nipple inside out and seeing that all the soap is removed.

Then put the bottle caps and nipples into the large kettle along with the bottles.

Put into the kettle also the funnel, strainer, long-handled spoon, jar for clean nipples and its cover, and any other utensils that will come into contact with the milk after it is boiled or with the sterilized nipples. (If there is not room for all these things in the kettle at one time, sterilize the bottles first. Then take them out of the kettle and let them stand on the table while the other equipment is being sterilized.)

After the bottles and the other utensils are in the kettle and are covered with water, put the kettle on the stove. Boil the water actively for 5 minutes.

If you have a kettle with a tight cover and also a bottle rack, the bottles can be steamed instead of boiled. An inch or two of actively boiling water in the bottom will be sufficient to fill the entire kettle with steam, which will sterilize the utensils. If you do not have a kettle with a tight cover and also a bottle rack, it will be necessary to cover the articles with water and boil them.

It takes much longer, of course, and uses more fuel, to heat to boiling a large kettle full of water than it does to form steam from an inch of water in the bottom of a covered kettle. The saving in fuel will help to pay for the cost of the tightly covered kettle and the bottle rack.

After the water has boiled for 5 minutes, the utensils are ready for use in preparing the milk mixture.

If the water in the kettle covers the utensils, pour some of it off so that the kettle and its contents will cool quickly, and you can lift out the sterilized articles without letting your fingers touch the sterile water.

Let the kettle cool until the articles inside can be lifted out without burning the fingers.

Take great care in taking the articles out of the kettle, so as not to let anything that is to come into contact with either the milk mixture or the nipples after they have been boiled touch anything that has not been sterilized. The outside of the bottles and of the jar for sterilized nipples may be touched with the fingers, but not the lip nor the inside.

Lift out the rack of bottles and let the bottles drain.

Lift out the jar for sterilized nipples. Using the long-handled spoon (touch only the handle), lift first the nipples and then the bottle caps from the kettle and put both into the jar. (Some bottle racks have a special place to hold the nipple jar. With such a rack the nipples and bottle caps can be steamed in the jar, which will be lifted out with the bottle rack.)

The remaining utensils, such as the strainer and funnel, are less likely to get germs on them if they are left in the kettle until used.

If, after the nipples and bottle caps are taken out, the long-handled spoon is put back, with its handle propped against the side, the lower part of the spoon will still be sterile so that you can use the spoon in picking up the other utensils.

Never put your fingers, nor anything not sterilized, into the water to pick up any of the sterilized articles.

PREPARING A DAY'S FEEDING

Always have a copy of the doctor's written order for the feeding fastened up in a convenient place so that you can refer to it every day.

Put a clock where you can see it while preparing the milk mixture.

Always wash your hands before beginning to prepare the milk mixture.

Using Fresh Milk

Have ready the saucepan, measuring spoon, measuring cup, sugar or sirup, and knife (if sugar is used); and also the kettle containing the nursing bottles, bottle caps, funnel, strainer, and long-handled spoon, all of which have just been boiled.

Take the bottle of milk out of the refrigerator.

Unless the bottle has a cap *that protects the lip,* clean the top of the milk bottle by holding it under fast-running water and wiping it with a fresh paper towel.

Shake the bottle to mix the cream well with the rest of the milk.

Measure into the saucepan the required amount of milk and of water, using a measuring cup or a nursing bottle marked to measure ounces.

Measure into the saucepan the required amount of sirup or sugar, using the measuring spoon. If sugar is used, level each spoonful with a knife.

Stir the mixture to disolve the sugar.

Place the saucepan on the stove and let the mixture boil (bubble) actively for 5 minutes by the clock, stirring it constantly.

Take the saucepan off the stove.

Put into each nursing bottle the milk mixture for one feeding, using the sterilized funnel and strainer.

If heat-resistant nursing bottles are used, strain the milk mixture immediately into the sterilized bottles.

If nursing bottles of ordinary glass are used, cool the mixture by placing the saucepan in a pan of cold water. Stir the mixture while it cools, using the long-handled spoon that was used for stirring it during the boiling. When the mixture is cool, strain it into the sterilized bottles, using the sterilized funnel and strainer.

Cover each bottle with a sterilized bottle cap.

Put the bottles into the refrigerator.

Using Dried Milk

Have ready the can of dried milk and the saucepan, long-handled spoon, measuring spoon, measuring cup, sugar or sirup, knife, and egg beater; and also the kettle containing the nursing bottles, bottle caps, funnel, and strainer, which have just been boiled.

Measure the required amount of cold water and pour it into the saucepan.

Measure the required amount of dried milk, using a *dry* measuring spoon and leveling each spoonful with a knife. Put the milk on top of the water.

Beat with the egg beater until the milk is well mixed with the water.

Measure into the saucepan the required amount of sirup or sugar, using the measuring spoon. If sugar is used, level each spoonful with the knife.

Stir the mixture with the long-handled spoon to dissolve the sugar.

Place the saucepan on the stove and let the mixture boil (bubble) actively for 5 minutes by the clock, stirring it constantly.

Take the saucepan off the stove.

Put into each nursing bottle the milk mixture for one feeding, using the sterilized funnel and strainer.

If heat-resistant nursing bottles are used, strain the hot milk mixture into them.

If nursing bottles of ordinary glass are used, cool the mixture by placing the saucepan in a pan of cold water. Stir the mixture while it cools, using the long-handled spoon that was used for stirring it during the boiling.

Cover each bottle with a sterilized bottle cap.

Put the bottles into the refrigerator.

Using Evaporated Milk

Have ready the can of evaporated milk and the saucepan, measuring cup, measuring spoon, sugar or sirup, and knife (if sugar is used); and also the kettle containing the nursing bottles, bottle caps, funnel, strainer, can opener or ice pick, and long-handled spoon, all of which have just been boiled

Measure the required amount of water, using the measuring cup or a nursing bottle marked in ounces, and pour it into the saucepan.

Measure the required amount of sugar or sirup and add it to the water in the saucepan, using the measuring spoon. If sugar is used, level off each spoonful with the knife.

Stir this mixture to dissolve the sugar or sirup.

Place the saucepan on the stove and allow the mixture to boil (bubble) actively for 5 minutes by the clock, stirring it constantly.

Take the saucepan off the stove.

Clean the top of the can of evaporated milk by pouring boiling water over it or holding it under fast-running hot water. Wipe it off with a fresh paper towel.

Make one large hole in the can with the sterilized can opener, or two small holes with the sterilized ice pick.

Measure the required amount of evaporated milk, using a sterilized nursing bottle, and pour it into the saucepan. Stir the mixture, using the long-handled spoon that was used to stir the sugar and water during the boiling.

Pour the mixture immediately into the sterilized nursing bottles.

Cover each bottle with a sterilized bottle cap.

Put the bottles into the refrigerator.

If you wish, the milk, sugar, and water may be boiled together just as is fresh cow's-milk mixture.

Although a can of evaporated milk does not need to be kept cold while it remains unopened, it needs to be kept cold from the time it is opened until it is used. The milk left in the can after a feeding has been prepared, can be kept for the next feeding if it is kept in a cold place. The can should be covered so that no dirt can get into the milk. A small bowl or a glass turned over may be used to cover the can, or a piece of paper towel may be fastened over it with an elastic band.

PREPARING A SINGLE FEEDING

It is sometimes necessary to prepare single feeding as when a breast fed baby is given an occasional bottle and also at the beginning of weaning.

Also, when there is no way to keep milk cold, it is better not to make up a whole day's feeding at a time, but to prepare each feeding as the baby needs it. In this case it is usually best to use evaporated milk.

When single feedings are to be prepared it is necessary to divide the day's allowance of milk, water, and sugar or sirup by the number of feedings in 24 hours so as to know just how much of each is needed for a single feeding. The doctor will be glad to make the calculation for the mother.

Preparation for a single feeding may be done in various ways. The following is one way of sterilizing the equipment and making the milk mixture for such a feeding when made with evaporated milk:

Make sure that the doctor's written order for the baby's feeding is where you can look at it.

Make sure that a clock is where you can look at it; see that it is going.

Wash your hands.

Have ready the following:

Small (6-oz.) can of evaporated milk.

Sugar or sirup.

Bottle brush.

Measuring cup, if the nursing bottle is not marked off in ounces.

Measuring spoons.

Pan in which the bottle, nipple, and spoons can be boiled. If this pan has a tight-fitting cover, the boiling can be done in less time than if an open pan is used.

Tea kettle or saucepan for boiling water.

Knife, if sugar is used.

Can opener or ice pick.

Nursing bottle, which has been rinsed after the previous feeding and left full of water.

Nipple, which has been rinsed after previous feeding.

Scrub the inside of the bottle with a bottle brush and hot soapy water.

Rinse the bottle thoroughly.

Wash the nipple with soap and water, turning it inside out.

Rinse the nipple thoroughly, seeing that all the soap is removed.

Fill the bottle with clean water.

Put the bottle and nipple, the measuring spoons, the can opener, and the measuring cup, if one is used, into a saucepan. Cover them with water, and let the water boil actively (bubble) for 5 minutes by the clock.

Remove the saucepan from the stove.

Pour off as much water as possible.

Take the bottle out of the saucepan without touching the lip of the bottle or the nipple.

If the bottle is marked off in ounces pour out enough of the water so that the amount of boiled water left in the bottle is the amount needed for the milk mixture.

If the bottle is not marked off in ounces pour the boiled water from the bottle into the boiled measuring cup, and after the bottle is empty pour back into it from the measuring cup the amount needed for the milk mixture.

Measure the required amount of sirup or sugar, using the boiled measuring spoon, and put it into the bottle.

Shake the bottle to mix the sugar or sirup and the water.

Clean the top of the can of evaporated milk by pouring boiling water over it or holding it under fast-running hot water. Wipe it with a paper towel.

Make one large hole in the can with the sterilized can opener or two small holes with the sterilized ice pick.

Pour the needed amount of evaporated milk into the bottle, measuring the amount by means of the marks on the nursing bottle. If the nursing bottle has no measuring marks, measure the milk in the boiled measuring cup and pour it into the bottle.

Take the boiled nipple out of the saucepan and put it onto the bottle, being careful not to touch any part of the nipple except the rim.

Test the temperature of the milk mixture by letting a few drops trickle from the nipple onto the inner side of your wrist. It should feel warm but not hot.

WARMING A FEEDING

When a bottle of milk mixture is taken out of the refrigerator it is necessary to warm it for the baby.

Stand the bottle of milk mixture in a small, deep saucepan of warm water. Special bottle warmers may be bought, but they are no better than the ordinary saucepan. Heat the mixture rapidly. (While the milk is warming is a good time for the mother to wash her hands in preparation for feeding the baby.)

Usually the contents of the bottle become sufficiently warm (100° F.) in a few minutes. It is not necessary to wait until the water boils. Shake the bottle several times to make sure that the milk is warmed through.

Remove the bottle cap and put on a sterile (boiled) nipple taken from the covered sterile jar. Touch only the rim of the nipple.

The temperature of the milk may be tested by letting a few drops trickle from the nipple onto the inside surface of the mother's wrist, where it should feel pleasantly warm but not hot.

Never test the temperature of the baby's milk by taking a suck at the nipple.

The part of the nipple that goes into the baby's mouth should not be touched by anyone nor come in contact with anything until it reaches the baby's mouth.

SAMPLE MILK MIXTURES

The milk mixtures shown on page 104 are examples that may assist the mother in following the doctor's instructions.

The weights shown in the table are not intended to indicate that a baby of a certain age should weigh the amount shown. The weights are given because the feeding that is suitable for a baby depends upon his weight even more than on his age. For example, a 1-month-old baby who weighs 9 pounds usually needs more to eat than one of the same age who weighs 7 or 8 pounds.

The doctor should be consulted frequently regarding the milk mixture for any baby.

SAFE, FRESH MILK

The problem of the milk supply varies greatly, depending on whether the family lives in a large city, in a small city or town, or in a village or rural district. In most cities milk is purchased from dealers who are required by law to meet certain standards. In smaller communities there is often less careful supervision of milk production, and so it is important to investigate the conditions under which milk is produced before selecting a milk supply. On the farm milk to be used on the premises or by the neighbors should be handled with the same care as is taken in the larger dairies.

In Cities

In most large cities and in many small cities and towns, laws have been passed regulating the production and care of all milk sold and establishing standards for certain grades of milk. These standards take into account the composition of the milk (especially the percentage of fat), the conditions under which it is produced, the number of bacteria in it at the time of delivery, and whether it is to be sold raw or pasteurized. Sometimes milk is sold just outside a city which cannot be sold in the city because it does not meet the city requirements. Such milk should be avoided.

Pasteurized milk should be bought in preference to raw milk, whenever it can be obtained.

Several grades of milk are on the market in cities, but the standards for a given grade are not uniform from city to city. Your health department can tell you what grades of milk sold in your community are suitable to give babies. In most cities grade A milk is milk from tuberculin-tested cows, which is produced under very good conditions and which has a low bacterial count.

"Certified milk" is milk produced under such good conditions that it meets certain special requirements of a medical milk commission. It is often sold raw. When certified milk is to be bought for a baby, buy certified milk that has been pasteurized rather than certified raw milk.

Certified milk is more expensive than other fresh milk, and it is not available in all communities.

In Small Communities

In villages and rural districts where milk is supplied from small herds or single cows, public regulation of production and care of milk is more difficult. It is as important, however, to regulate the supply of milk in small towns and rural districts as in cities. All milk-borne epidemics, whether in cities, towns, or villages, are preventable if the milk supply is properly safeguarded.

If the milk supply in your community is not well regulated, you should find out how the milk that is sold is produced and cared for. Raw milk is not a suitable food for babies unless it is handled according to the standards described in the following section.

Care and Handling of Milk on the Farm

Milk is a very perishable food and is easily contaminated with disease germs from cows or from human beings. As much care should be taken with milk which is to be used on the premises or for distribution to neighbors as is taken in the larger cities.

Milk should be taken only from healthy animals. A sick animal should be immediately isolated and its milk discarded.

Cows are very susceptible to tuberculosis, and if a cow has this disease the milk may be contaminated. If the owner is to be certain that his herd is free from tuberculosis, each cow should be examined and tested every 6 months.

Bang's disease is a contagious disease among cows, the chief symptom of which is abortion. A baby who drinks milk from a cow with Bang's disease may develop a serious illness called undulant fever. If you know that a farmer's cows are having abortions do not buy milk from him.

Goat's milk as well as cow's milk may contain the germs of tuberculosis or of undulant fever if the animal is infected.

The baby will not get either of these diseases from milk if his milk is always boiled.

To be kept healthy, cows (or goats) must be well fed and well cared for in clean, healthful surroundings. Stables that are well built, well aired, and well screened are necessary. The udder and teats of the cow should be washed and wiped dry before milking. This prevents dust and hair from dropping into the pail during the milking.

Milk should be chilled immediately after milking and should be kept clean, cold, and covered until delivery.

Milk Handlers

Milk should be handled only by perfectly healthy persons. If a milk handler has tuberculosis, septic sore throat, typhoid fever, scarlet fever, or diphtheria, he may contaminate the milk and be the cause of a severe epidemic if the milk is consumed raw. Frequent examinations of milk handlers by physicians should be required as part of the routine. The milkers should wash their hands with soap and dry them carefully before milking. Milking with wet hands is almost certain to carry impurities into the milk. A clean washable suit should always be worn while milking. The milker should be very careful not to raise dust nor permit anything to fall into the milk.

Milk Utensils

The pail, strainers, milk cans, and all other utensils should be clean and sterilized by boiling or steaming them before use.

The water used in washing the utensils and bottles, the udder of the cow, and the hands of the milker—everything touching the milk—must be clean and uncontaminated by disease-producing bacteria. Serious outbreaks of disease have been caused by use of contaminated water for washing.

Refrigeration

After milking, the milk should be cooled quickly by placing the cans in a cooler or in cold water. Milk should be kept at 50° F. or below but not frozen.

Bottles

The bottles should be thoroughly washed and sterilized daily. Clean caps should be used. The type of cap that covers the whole top of the bottle is the best, as it insures perfect cleanliness of the lips of the bottle over which the milk flows. When milk is to be used on the premises where it is produced it should be kept in sterilized, covered bottles or glass jars.

WATER FOR THE BABY TO DRINK

IF YOUR BABY doesn't seem to want water to drink, don't bother about offering it to him. Some babies don't want it—except perhaps in very hot weather or when they have a fever—because they are getting all the fluid they need in their formula.

If your baby seems to want occasional drinks of water, however, by all means give it to him—between meals of course, not just before a feeding—once a day or more often. He probably won't want as much as two ounces, probably less, if any. Don't urge it on him if he doesn't want it. It will only make him angry.

If you do give it to him, boil for about three minutes as much as you think he will need for the day and keep it in a sterilized bottle. Pour just as much as you are going to give him each time into another bottle and warm it slightly as you would a bottle of milk.

Boil all your baby's drinking water for at least a year. To be on the safe side boil his drinking water until he is two.

DIFFICULTIES OF THE BOTTLE-FED BABY

STOOLS

THE STOOLS of a bottle-fed baby are quite different from those of a breast-fed baby. They are almost always fewer in number, frequently only one in twenty-four hours. The movements are much firmer, often formed, and with slight odor. The color differs, according to the food, from lemon yellow, if cow's milk is the sole food, to dark or light brown, if malt products or starchy gruels are use. A well baby's stool should be smooth and somewhat pasty in character, showing that the food is well digested. An occasional variation in the appearance of the stool is not important. But the persistence of abnormal movements whether they be loose and green, or bulky and foul-smelling, or hard and pellet-like, indicates something wrong with digestion. Although the food itself may not be the real cause of the disturbance, changes in the formula often help to correct it.

UNDERFEEDING

Underfeeding may be caused either by not feeding enough of the right food or by feeding the wrong kind of food. The underfed infant usually sleeps for shorter periods and frets and cries before the usual feeding period. Given the bottle, he finishes it completely before becoming drowsy from a full stomach. If the baby fails to make regular gains in weight, the food either needs to be increased in quantity or properly modified to suit the baby's needs. No two infants have exactly the same ability to utilize food.

OVERFEEDING

Overfeeding is a common cause of digestive disturbances in bottle-fed babies. Usually this is due to an over-enthusiastic mother or nurse who urges her baby to eat more than he really wants. There are a few babies who will of their own accord eat more than they need. But ordinarily, with proper formulas, the baby's own appetite can be trusted to be the best guide to how much he should be given.

The infant who is overfed may cry and fret a lot because he is uncomfortable from being given more food than he can digest. He may continue to take all that is urged on him, or he may lose his appetite and leave some of his bottle. He may regurgitate ("spit up") or vomit after his feeding. He may even stop gaining weight.

SIGNS OF ERRORS IN FEEDING

Following sooner or later on a dietary error, any one of a number of symptoms or combination of symptoms may appear, such as:

1. Vomiting.
2. Gas.
3. Colic and flatulence.
4. Stools full of undigested "curds," either of fat or protein.
5. Loose stools, frequently green and sour.
6. Diarrhea.
7. Large, dry, whitish stools ("Soap stools").
8. Constipation with small stools of normal appearance.
9. No gain in weight.
10. Loss in weight.
11. Increased fretfulness and crying.
12. Disturbed sleep.

The result of a continuance of a mistake in feeding varies with the individual child and the seriousness of the error. Many infants gradually overcome digestive difficulties as they grow older and thrive in spite of them. Other children grow gradually worse and a serious condition may develop, such as:

1. Chronic weight disturbance.
2. Chronic indigestion (dyspepsia) with intolerance to fat, sugar, or starch.
3. Atrophy or chronic malnutrition.
4. Summer diarrhea.

The outcome depends on the degree of intolerance developed to the chief food constituents, the rapidity with which the cause of the condition is diagnosed, the skill with which the food of the sick child is adapted to his weakened powers, and the native vigor of the infant.

FOODS BESIDES MILK*

ALTHOUGH milk is the most important of all the foods for babies, milk by itself does not supply everything that babies need from their food. Mother's milk does this much better than cow's milk, but even breast-fed babies can be kept in better health if they are given certain other foods besides milk. Foods that babies need during their first year of life in addition to milk are: Fruit juice, cod-liver oil, cereal, eggs, vegetables, fruit, meat, and toast or dried bread.

FRUIT JUICE

Fruit juice is given to supply vitamin C. The juice of the citrus fruits such as orange, grapefruit, and lemon contains larger amounts of vitamin C than any of the other commonly used fruit juices. The juice of certain tropical fruits, such as guavas, mangoes, and papayas, is even richer in vitamin C than the juice of citrus fruits; consequently physicians in the tropics sometimes recommend them instead.

Orange juice usually may be given without sugar, but grapefruit juice and lemon juice almost always have to be sweetened. Occasionally, an especially sour orange juice will be liked better by the baby if a little sugar is added.

Tomato juice contains about half as much vitamin C as orange juice and therefore should be given in twice the quantity.

Citrus-fruit juice and tomato juice may be given either canned or fresh, as commercial canning does not destroy the vitamin C in these juices. Strained canned tomatoes may be used. Tomatoes and tomato juice canned at home are good sources of vitamin C if they are canned by the method recommended by the United States Department of Agriculture or a State college of agriculture.

Canned pineapple juice, unlike orange juice and tomato juice, does not contain as much vitamin C as the fresh juice. Canned pineapple juice must be given in such large amounts that it is not suitable as a source of vitamin C for babies.

Occasionally fruit juice may cause some digestive or skin disturbance. If it seems likely that the trouble is due to a particular fruit juice, another juice may be given. If the disturbance continues consult the doctor. If he agrees that the

fruit juice is to blame he will probably suggest a substitute for it.

Fruit juice should be started when the baby is 2 weeks old. When the mother of a breast-fed baby has been eating a liberal amount of citrus fruits and other fruits and vegetables, some doctors prefer not to give the baby fruit juice until about the end of the first month of life. Start by giving 1 teaspoonful of strained orange juice daily. The amount can be gradually increased until by the time he is 2 months old the baby is getting 3 ounces a day.

Tomato juice and other fruit juices should be kept cold after the fruit is squeezed or the can is opened, so as to prevent much loss of vitamin C.

SOURCES OF VITAMIN D

Both breast-fed and bottle-fed babies need more vitamin D than they receive in their milk. Some food or other preparation to supply this vitamin should be given the baby by the end of the second week of life and continued throughout at least the first 2 years. It is usually better to give a preparation that supplies vitamin A and vitamin D, rather than one that supplies only vitamin D.

Amount of Vitamin D Needed

The amount of vitamin D in any food or other preparation is measured in units defined in the United States Pharmacopœia; these are known as U. S. P. units. The label on every bottle or package of a preparation that supplies vitamin D should show how many U. S. P. units of the vitamin are contained in a given amount of the preparation.

Some babies need only 400 units of vitamin D daily, but many babies need more than this amount. For this reason it is desirable to give all babies and small children 800 units daily in order to allow an ample margin of safety.

In midsummer, even if your baby is getting a good deal of direct sunshine, it is better not to reduce the amount of vitamin D preparation he is getting unless your doctor advises you to do so.

Cod-Liver Oil

Cod-liver oil and some other fish-liver oils are commonly given to babies because they are rich

* From *Infant Care*, U. S. Children's Bureau Publication.

in vitamins A and D. Ask your doctor which preparation is best for your baby and how much to give.

The amount of vitamin D and vitamin A in cod liver oils is variable. If the label on a cod-liver oil bottle states that the oil contains the minimum requirement of vitamins A and D, this means that it is standard cod-liver oil. A standard cod-liver oil contains at least 85 U. S. P. units of vitamin D and 850 of vitamin A in each gram (about one-fourth teaspoonful). Many cod-liver oils contain more of the vitamins than these minimum requirements. Some may contain as much as 200 units of vitamin D and 2,500 units of vitamin A in each gram.

Some manufacturers market a cod-liver oil to which extra vitamin D has been added. This is called fortified cod-liver oil. The vitamin D in such an oil may be as high as 2,500 units per gram.

Other Fish-Liver Oils

The doctor may recommend the use of oil from the liver of some other fish, such as the percomorphum and the halibut, which contain more vitamins A and D than does cod-liver oil. The oils of several kinds of fish are sometimes mixed and sold as a blend, and some doctors recommend the use of these mixed oils. They are sold as liquids or in capsules.

Viosterol

Viosterol is vitamin D dissolved in a bland oil; it is not a concentrated fish-liver oil. It does not contain any vitamin A, and therefore viosterol alone is not a substitute for cod-liver oil.

Vitamin-D Milks

There are several varieties of milk—both fresh and evaporated—on the market that have had the vitamin D value increased by some special process. If such milk is used, enough additional vitamin D should always be given to insure that the baby gets not less than 800 units a day.

Amounts of Vitamin D in Different Preparations

How much cod-liver oil or other vitamin D preparation a baby needs will depend upon the amount of the preparation that will supply 800 U. S. P. units of vitamin D.

For cod-liver oil that just meets the U. S. P. standard of 85 units of vitamin D per gram, the amount recommended for most children under 2 years of age is 2½ teaspoonfuls a day. The following table is a rough guide to the amounts of different preparations of vitamin D needed to supply 800 U. S. P. units.

If a preparation is used that is given in comparatively large daily doses (more than 10 drops), start by giving the baby a small part of the dose. Increase the amount gradually until the recommended amount is being given by the end of the first month of life. For example, standard cod-liver oil may be begun by giving ½ teaspoonful twice daily, and gradually increased until, by the time the baby is a month old, he is getting 1¼ teaspoonfuls twice daily.

Giving Cod-Liver Oil

When a baby is very young it is difficult to feed him anything with a spoon, but it is easy to feed him cod-liver oil with a medicine dropper.

APPROXIMATE AMOUNTS OF COD-LIVER OIL AND OF OTHER PREPARATIONS NEEDED TO SUPPLY 800 U. S. P. UNITS OF VITAMIN D

If the cod-liver oil or other preparation contains in each gram the amount of vitamin D shown below—	The amount that should be given daily to supply about 800 units will be—
85 units	2½ teaspoonfuls.[1]
175 units	1¼ teaspoonfuls.
250 units	¾ teaspoonful.
400 units	½ teaspoonful.
1,000 units	40 small drops.[2]
5,000 units	8 small drops.[2]
10,000 units	4 small drops.[2]

[1] A household teaspoon holds 4 grams of cod-liver oil.
[2] This amount is approximate only. Usually a special dropper, which delivers small drops, is supplied with the preparation, and the label tells how many units of Vitamin D are contained in 1 such drop.

The oil should be gently dropped into the corner of the baby's mouth and then his lips closed until he swallows. Care must be taken not to squirt the oil far back into his mouth as this may make him choke. Some oils are put up in capsules made so that the tip can be nipped off and the oil dropped into the baby's mouth.

As the baby gets a little older it is easier to give him the oil from a spoon.

Whether the oil is given with a dropper or from a spoon, the baby should be held in a partly sitting position so that the oil will not "go down the wrong way."

A glass medicine dropper with a rubber bulb is satisfactory for giving the oil to a young baby. It must be thoroughly washed with soap and hot water immediately after each using and the glass part boiled before it is used again. The rubber bulb should not be allowed to come into contact with the oil as oil makes rubber deteriorate. A dropper that fits into the top of the bottle of a concentrated vitamin preparation need not be washed if put back into the bottle immediately.

Cod-liver oil leaves a stain on clothing or bed linen. It is, therefore, wise to have at hand a paper handkerchief with which to wipe off oil from the baby's face. Some mothers prefer to give the oil when the baby is undressed, just before the bath, so that there will be little danger of getting the oil on clothing or blanket.

By the time a baby is a few months old he generally learns to take cod-liver oil without spilling it, and then it can be given after a meal.

If the mother dislikes cod-liver oil herself, she must be careful not to let her expression or her actions show her dislike. If she does, the baby will learn to dislike it by watching his mother. Strange as it may seem to many mothers, almost all children like cod-liver oil.

Keeping Oils Containing Vitamins

Cod-liver oil and other oils containing vitamins spoil rather easily and therefore should be kept cold, covered, and clean. Always keep the bottle of oil in a cold place, and keep the cap well screwed on. Each time some oil is poured out, wipe off the lip of the bottle so that the outside does not become sticky with oil. If properly kept, the oil will remain fresh for several months after the bottle has been opened. If a cold place is not available for keeping the cod-liver oil, it is not wise to buy a bottle that holds more than a 2 months' supply.

A pint bottle holds 96 teaspoonfuls of cod-liver oil; a baby who is getting 2 teaspoonfuls of cod-liver oil a day will use a pint bottle in about a month and a half.

Frequently when a mother complains that cod-liver oil or other fish-liver oil does not agree with her baby it is found that she has been using a rancid oil. Keep vitamin-containing oils as carefully as you would butter.

CEREALS

Cereals may be started when the baby is about 4 months old. Cereals made from whole grain, such as rolled oats and water-ground corn meal, are better for the baby than refined cereals, such as white farina and bolted corn meal.

Some cereals on the market have had vitamins and minerals added to them, and the doctor may recommend some of these.

Cereals need to be cooked thoroughly, either at the factory or in the home, before being given to a baby. Some cereals have been partly cooked at the factory and do not need long cooking at home. If a quick-cooking cereals is used the label on the package will tell how long it needs to be cooked.

Certain cereals, especially prepared for babies, have been thoroughly cooked at the factory and need merely to be mixed with warm milk or water. These cost a little more than most cereals prepared at home.

The cereal that is cooked for the family may be used for the baby. For a young baby cereal with coarse fiber, such as cracked wheat, and any cereal that has lumps should be strained and it should be thin enough to run off the end of a spoon. If it is too thick it may be thinned by adding boiling water or part of the baby's milk mixture.

Begin with a teaspoonful of cooked cereal just before the 10 a.m. feeding and increase the amount gradually by a teaspoonful or two a day.

By the time the baby is about 7 months old he may be taking from 2 to 5 tablespoonfuls of cereal twice a day. It may be made thicker so that he will learn to take some solid food.

If no cereal is prepared for the family, the mother may find it convenient to cook enough at one time to last the baby 2 days. If this is done the cereal that is left over should be kept covered and cold.

As a substitute for cereal, potatoes—boiled, steamed, or baked—which have been mashed with a fork may be given several times a week after the baby is 6 months old. Cook the potatoes with the skins on and peel them after cooking.

EGGS

Egg yolk may be added to the baby's diet when he is about 4 months old. Some doctors add it in the third month or even earlier. The egg may be soft-cooked, or hard-cooked and mashed.

The first time egg yolk is given, give a very small amount (one-fourth teaspoonful or less) at the 2 p.m. feeding. Increase the amount gradually each day. When the baby is about 9 months old he may be given a whole egg.

A very few babies are made sick by eggs. If your baby seems sick after he first gets egg yolk, do not give it again until you have told the doctor about it.

VEGETABLES

Vegetables should be started when the baby is about 5 months old and given once a day at the 2 p.m. feeding. Give a green leafy vegetable such as spinach, chard, beet greens, turnip greens—any green leafy vegetable that is in season—two or three times a week. On the other days give carrots, green peas, green lima beans, asparagus, broccoli, or string beans, or any other vegetable that can be readily mashed through the strainer. Potatoes may be given occasionally in place of cereal at 10 a.m. or 6 p.m. but should not replace other vegetables. Begin by giving about a teaspoonful of mashed vegetables once a day and increase the amount fairly rapidly to 2 tablespoonfuls when the baby is 6 months old, 3 tablespoonfuls when he is 8 months old. From this time on give 4 tablespoonfuls daily. Remember that these amounts are only average ones. Some babies will take more, some less. Do not try to increase the amount of vegetable faster than the baby is willing to take it.

Vegetables should be cooked until tender in a small amount of water, with a little salt, then mashed through a sieve or strainer. If any of the cooking water is left it should be added to the strained vegetable.

The length of cooking will depend upon the kind of vegetable, but it is important to cook vegetables only long enough to make them tender and to use so little water that most of it will be taken up by the vegetables while cooking. Use an uncovered pan for cooking vegetables with a strong flavor, such as cauliflower, but for all other vegetables use a covered pan, as this makes it possible to use very little water. Start the cooking with boiling water. Usually it is not necessary to add water to greens because enough water clings to the leaves after washing. Never add soda to vegetables; soda destroys some of the vitamins.

Vegetables for the baby should not have any seasoning except a little salt.

A small amount of butter or fortified margarine may be added toward the end of the first year, if desired.

Mothers can often save time in preparing the baby's meals and give the baby a greater variety by using some of the vegetables cooked for the family table. For the baby, mash some of the cooked vegetables through a sieve or strainer. Enough mashed vegetables to last the baby for 2 days can be prepared at one time, if the part kept for the next day is kept covered and cold, preferably in a refrigerator.

Later, it is desirable to allow him to have his vegetables in a little coarser form, or mashed with a fork but not mashed through a strainer.

Canned vegetables may be used in place of fresh vegetables by mashing through a sieve or strainer. Some canned vegetables prepared especially for babies are on the market. Those prepared for young babies have been mashed through a strainer; those for older babies, cut fine. They need only be warmed. These canned vegetables are a convenience, but they are rather expensive. If only part of a can of vegetables is used at a time, the remainder may be kept in the can for the next day only if the can is covered and kept cold.

When home-canned foods are used, it is of the utmost importance to know whether nonacid vegetables (that is, all except tomatoes) have been canned in a pressure cooker with a gauge that has been tested recently and found to be reliable. If there is any doubt as to whether they have been canned by this method, nonacid vegetables should be boiled for 15 minutes after they have been removed from the can, even if they are to be served cold. Count the time after boiling has begun.

FRUITS

Apple sauce, apricot or prune pulp, and some other stewed fruits such as peaches, mashed through a sieve or strainer, may be given once a day, beginning when the baby is about 7 months old. Bananas provide sugar in a form easily digested by a baby and are also a good source of several vitamins. Only thoroughly ripened bananas that have yellow skins with spots of brown should be given to babies. The ripe banana should be peeled, the stringy material scraped off, and the soft pulp mashed and fed to the baby with a spoon. Never give a baby any of the banana that has any green in the skin. The doctor will tell you at what age the baby may have banana and how much he may have.

MEAT

By the time the baby is 7 months old he may have scraped liver or other lean meat with his 2 p.m. feeding. Scraped meat is prepared by scraping a piece of raw meat with a knife. The tough, fibrous part of the meat remains attached to the main piece, and the tender pulp is collected. The pulp should be cooked quickly in a hot pan with just enough fat to prevent sticking.

BREAD

After the baby's first teeth have come give him bread dried in the oven or zwieback after his meals. If commercial zwieback is used it is better to buy the unsweetened kind. Commercial zwieback is more expensive than dried bread.

Bread made from whole grains, and enriched bread are better for the baby than bread made from unenriched flour. The whole grains contain minerals and vitamins that are lost in the process of refining the flour. These minerals and vitamins are valuable food substances for the baby. Whole-grain bread must not be confused with cracked-wheat bread or bran bread, which are made from refined flour with coarse particles of the wheat kernel added. Cracked-wheat bread and bran bread are not suitable for a baby.

Dried bread is much better for a baby than crackers because crackers soften in the mouth and give little exercise for the jaws and teeth. It is dangerous to give a baby dried bread while he is lying down, as it may choke him.

FOODS IN ADDITION TO MILK THAT ARE GIVEN TO BABIES AT DIFFERENT AGES[1]

2 weeks old .... 1 teaspoonful orange juice; 1 teaspoonful cod-liver oil.
1 month old .... 1 ounce orange juice; 2½ teaspoonfuls cod-liver oil.
2 months old.......... 3 ounces orange juice; 2½ teaspoonfuls cod-liver oil.
3 months old.......... 3 ounces orange juice; 2½ teaspoonfuls cod-liver oil.
4 months old.......... 3 ounces orange juice; 2½ teaspoonfuls cod-liver oil; cereal; egg yolk.
5 to 6 months old...... 3 ounces orange juice; 2½ teaspoonfuls cod-liver oil; cereal; egg yolk; vegetables.
7 months old .... 3 ounces orange juice; 2½ teaspoonfuls cod-liver oil; cereal; egg yolk; vegetables;
          fruit; scraped meat.
8 to 12 months old..... 3 ounces orange juice; 2½ teaspoonfuls cod-liver oil; cereal; whole egg; vegetables;
          fruit; scraped meat; dry toast as soon as the baby has some teeth.

[1]Amounts of cod-liver oil are for standard cod-liver oil.

FEEDING THE AVERAGE BABY

THE following plan for feeding the baby is suggested only as a guide to the mother in following her doctor's instructions, not as a substitute for them. Babies vary tremendously in the way they accept new things. One may be ready for solid foods at two months and another may not take them until five months. If mothers will recognize that these differences exist and will respect and make allowances for them, both babies and mothers will have calmer lives and will be much happier.

It may be desirable to change from one formula to the next sooner or later than the schedule. If the baby is draining all of his bottles and seems to be hungry, by all means change to the next formula even if it is not the "right" time to. On the other hand, if the time comes and the baby seems to be perfectly well satisfied with the mixture he is getting, there is no need to make the change right away. Wait until the baby is ready for it.

A baby's appetite may vary from feeding to feeding too. If he wants more than is in the bottle at certain times and leaves some at other times, it is all right to fill the bottles unequally so that there is more in the one he gets when he is hungry. Usually it is safe to let the baby's appetite be the guide to how much he should eat.

SUGGESTED DAILY FEEDINGS FOR AVERAGE WELL BABIES WITH SAMPLE MILK MIXTURES FOR DIFFERENT WEIGHTS AND AGES

Either whole milk or evaporated milk may be used. The latter has slight advantages in that it does not need refrigeration until after the can has been opened, and it does not have to be boiled when the formula is made. But both are nutritious for the baby.

It is better to go by the baby's weight than by his age if one or the other does not correspond with the schedule.

At each age level, baby may be fed oftener than specified if he appears hungry.

FIRST DAY

Give no milk. Offer ½ to 2 ounces, every 4 hours, of a mixture of 10 ounces of boiled water and 1 level tablespoon of granulated sugar.*

AT THREE DAYS
(For baby weighing 7 pounds)

Whole milk....... 8 ounces
Boiled water...... 7 ounces
Granulated sugar.. 1 level tablespoon

OR

Evaporated milk... 4 ounces
Boiled water......11 ounces
Granulated sugar.. 1 level tablespoon
In 24 hours, offer 6 feedings of 2½ ounces each. (For a single feeding, use ¾ ounce evaporated milk, 1¾ ounces boiled water, ½ level teaspoon granulated sugar.)

AT TWO WEEKS
(For baby weighing 7¼ pounds)

Whole milk.......12 ounces
Boiled water...... 6 ounces
Granulated sugar.. 2 level tablespoons

OR

Evaporated milk... 6 ounces
Boiled water......12 ounces
Granulated sugar.. 2 level tablespoons
In 24 hours, offer 6 feedings of 3 ounces each. (For a single feeding, use 1 ounce evaporated milk, 2 ounces boiled water, 1 level teaspoon granulated sugar.)
In addition, baby should now have daily:
Orange juice .... 1 teaspoon
Cod liver oil† .... 1 teaspoon

* Whenever granulated sugar is specified, an equal amount of corn sirup may be substituted.
† Or Vitamin D concentrate as ordered by the doctor.

AT ONE MONTH
(For baby weighing 7¾ pounds)

Whole milk.......14 ounces
Boiled water...... 6 ounces
Granulated sugar.. 2½ level tablespoons

OR

Evaporated milk... 7 ounces
Boiled water......13 ounces
Granulated sugar.. 2½ level tablespoons
In 24 hours, offer 5 feedings of 4 ounces each. (For a single feeding, use 1½ ounces evaporated milk, 2½ ounces boiled water, 1½ level teaspoons granulated sugar.)
In addition, baby should now have daily:
Orange juice......1 ounce (which may be mixed with 1 ounce of boiled water)
Cod liver oil ....2½ teaspoons

AT THREE MONTHS
(For baby weighing 11 pounds)

Whole milk.......19 ounces
Boiled water...... 6 ounces
Granulated sugar.. 3 level tablespoons

OR

Evaporated milk... 9½ ounces
Boiled water......15½ ounces
Granulated sugar.. 3 level tablespoons
In 24 hours, offer 5 feedings of 5 ounces each. (For a single feeding, use 2 ounces evaporated milk, 3 ounces boiled water, 1¾ level teaspoons granulated sugar.)
In addition, baby should now have daily:
Orange juice...... 3 ounces
Cod liver oil...... 2½ teaspoons

AT FOUR MONTHS

(For baby weighing 12½ pounds)

Whole milk.......21½ ounces
Boiled water...... 7¼ ounces
Granulated sugar.. 3 level tablespoons

OR

Evaporated milk...10¾ ounces
Boiled water......18 ounces
Granulated sugar.. 3 level tablespoons
In 24 hours, offer 5 feedings of 5¾ ounces each. (For a single feeding, use 2¼ ounces evaporated milk, 3½ ounces boiled water, 1¾ teaspoons granulated sugar.)
In addition, baby should now have:
Orange juice...... 3 ounces daily
Cod liver oil...... 2½ teaspoons daily
Cereal, cooked or precooked...1 to 3 tablespoons once or twice a day mixed with formula
Egg yolk, hard-cooked and mashed...
¼ teaspoon at first

AT FIVE MONTHS

(For baby weighing 14 pounds)

Whole milk.......24 ounces
Boiled water...... 8½ ounces
Granulated sugar.. 3 level tablespoons

OR

Evaporated milk...12 ounces
Boiled water......20½ ounces
Granulated sugar.. 3 level tablespoons
In 24 hours, offer 5 feedings of 6½ ounces each. (For a single feeding, use 2½ ounces evaporated milk, 4 ounces boiled water, 1¾ level teaspoons granulated sugar.)
In addition, baby should now have:
Orange juice...... 3 ounces daily
Cod liver oil...... 2½ teaspoons daily
Cereal, cooked..........1 to 3 tablespoons twice a day with milk or formula
Fruit, stewed and strained. .1 to 3 tablespoons twice a day (if doctor advises)
Egg yolk, hard-cooked and mashed...
1 once a day or every other day
Vegetables, cooked and strained....
½ to 1 tablespoon once a day

AT SIX TO SEVEN MONTHS

(For baby weighing from 15 to 16½ pounds)
Whole milk.......28 ounces

Boiled water...... 4 ounces
Granulated sugar.. 1 level tablespoon

OR

Evaporated milk...13 ounces
Boiled water......19 ounces
Granulated sugar.. 1 level tablespoon
In 24 hours, offer 4 feedings of 8 ounces each. (For a single feeding, use 3½ ounces evaporated milk, 4½ ounces boiled water, 1 level teaspoon granulated sugar.)
In addition, baby should now have:
Orange juice...... 3 ounces daily
Cod liver oil...... 2½ teaspoons daily
Cereal, cooked..........2 to 4 tablespoons twice a day
Fruit, stewed and strained.....2 to 4 tablespoons twice a day
Egg yolk, hard-cooked and mashed...1 daily
Vegetables, cooked and strained
2 to 4 tablespoons once a day
Meat, lean, scraped.......1 to 3 tablespoons once a day

AT EIGHT OR NINE MONTHS
TO ONE YEAR

(For baby weighing at least 18 pounds)

Whole milk ....28 to 32 ounces

OR

Evaporated milk ....13 to 16 ounces
Boiled water ....15 to 16 ounces
In 24 hours, offer 4 feedings of 7 or 8 ounces each. (For a single feeding, use 3½ to 4 ounces evaporated milk, 3½ to 4 ounces boiled water.)
In addition, baby should now have:
Orange juice.....:3 ounces daily
Cod liver oil......2½ teaspoons daily
Cereal, cooked ....2 to 4 tablespoons twice a day
Fruit, stewed and strained.....2 to 4 tablespoons twice a day
Meat, lean, scraped......1 to 3 tablespoons once a day

OR

Egg, whole..1 ounce a day (if doctor advises)
Vegetables, cooked and mashed...
2 to 4 tablespoons once a day
Dry toast or zwieback......as soon as baby has some teeth
Potato, baked ....occasionally

CIRCUMCISION

IT VERY frequently happens that the foreskin of a little boy is too long or that the opening in it is insufficient to allow it to slip easily back and forth over the glans. This condition gives rise to many symptoms in the child, such as bed-wetting, extreme nervousness, and other bad habits.

When this opening in the foreskin is of fair size it may be stretched by the physician and the adhesions broken up; it should then be kept well greased with boric acid ointment night and morning, and the foreskin worked back and forth over the glans twice daily. By this means circumcision may be avoided. When the opening is only of pin-head size, a complete circumcision is indicated. This little operation should be done as soon as possible. It may be necessary to circumcise a baby almost as soon as it is born, and if done by a competent physician no harm results from the operation; in fact, many modern doctors agree that circumcision is desirable in any case.

WHY THE BABY CRIES

RECENT studies of the behavior of children and infants have shed new and interesting light on why babies cry. For one thing, it has been found that when a very young baby cries, it seldom means anything serious at all. All babies need to do some crying. We know now, too, that we cannot discipline an infant by ignoring his cries nor "spoil" him by giving him the attention he wants. A baby needs the sense of emotional security he gets from knowing that his mother will come and love him when he is uncomfortable or unhappy. Intelligent parents, therefore, no longer let their babies cry miserably for long periods, not because it is likely to do the babies any physical harm but because it upsets both the babies and the parents emotionally and nervously.

It is possible, of course, to "spoil" a baby if you really try to—that is, if you fuss over him contantly whether or not he needs attention. If you do that, he will probably get into the habit of fussing and crying for you whenever you leave him alone. But if your baby can depend on you to come to him and comfort him when he really needs you, he will usually be willing to accept being alone when he doesn't. A baby needs a sense of being loved and wanted. You can't "spoil" him by giving him that sense, especially when he cries.

By the time your baby is a few weeks old, you will recognize his different kinds of crying and will know what they mean.

Babies, being unable to express their needs in words, cry whenever they want something.

Discomfort

Naturally a baby will cry if he is physically uncomfortable. See whether a pin is sticking into him, whether he is lying in an uncomfortable position, whether he is suffering from insect bites, skin irritation or the discomfort of being too hot, too cold, too wet or soiled. If so, it is easy to remedy the cause of the crying.

Hunger or Thirst

Babies often cry because they are hungry. This kind of crying usually comes before feeding time. If it does, it will do the baby no harm to feed him before his regular feeding time. Hunger cries stop as soon as the baby is fed, just as cries because of thirst stop as soon as the baby is given a drink of water.

Exhaustion or Fright

Babies cry, sometimes, from exhaustion or from fear or nervous tension before they go to sleep. These may be low, moaning cries, if the baby is very tired or weak, or sharp, piercing cries if the cause is fear or edginess. In the first case the baby will usually slip off to sleep comfortably in a short while; in the second he may have to be soothed and comforted.

Indigestion, Colic, or Just Irritation

More frightening kinds of crying, especially to the mother of a first baby, are "irritable crying" and "three-month colic" crying. In the first of these a baby may cry for hours at a stretch; in the second he will scream piercingly and be in obvious pain, pulling up his legs and clenching his fists. Unlike hunger crying which comes before feeding time, the crying of colic usually comes either right after or soon after feeding.

If the crying is from simple indigestion, a change in formula usually remedies the situation—at least after the right formula has been found and tried for a few days. But irritable crying and colic crying are harder to cure, partly because pediatricians are not sure of their basic causes. In some cases, a change in the baby's formula may bring about an improvement; in others, putting the baby on his stomach and rubbing his back or giving him a warm enema may help. It is very important to get a colicky baby's bubble up after feeding. But it is possible that both prolonged irritable crying and colic crying are the result of occasional or constant tensions which the baby's undeveloped nervous system is not ready to cope with. This may be why these attacks so often occur in the late afternoon or evening, when the baby is tired out. Fortunately, crying of this kind is often found in babies who are otherwise healthy and who are gaining weight at a good rate. The chances are, in such cases, that they need less tension and more tranquility.

Illness or Pain

If the baby is losing weight or if his crying persists too long or if he has a temperature or seems otherwise sick or in pain, consult a doctor as soon as possible.

Comfort him, of course, as much as you can, but be very gentle about it. Babies who are sick or in pain are in especial need of emotional comfort; but they should be handled as little, as gently, and as calmly as possible until the doctor arrives.

Temper

A baby's crying is usually without tears except when he is in pain or in a rage. But babies don't usually yell and cry in anger until they are about a year old. Practically all babies from then on have occasional temper tantrums. If your baby has frequent crying rages, and if neither you nor the doctor can find anything physically wrong with him, he probably needs to live in a calmer atmosphere and to be given more cuddling and a greater sense of security.

Desire for Attention

Finally, there is the baby who is well and comfortable but just wants more attention from you. Try to give it to him, casually, when he wants and needs it; but do not make the mistake of fussing over him when he doesn't need it. Try not to let anything frighten him; but if he *is* frightened, give him the extra loving that he needs. Always remember that too much loving is better, in the long run, than too little, though a casual, comforting, dependable happy medium is best of all.

THE BABY'S CARETAKERS

NURSES

FULL-TIME NURSES are, in general, a fond memory of the past. Most families, today, can neither afford them nor find satisfactory ones even if they could. For the family who, however, does find it necessary and possible to employ a nurse, a few words of warning may be in order.

First of all, never employ anyone to care for your child unless she genuinely loves children, regardless of how competent she may seem to be. Love of children, understanding and patience, are the prime requisites. Experience and competence come second.

Every prospective nurse, no matter how healthy she may seem, should be carefully examined by a reputable physician.

One has only to visit the parks and streets of any city on a pleasant day, to see many instances of carelessness and neglect on the part of nurses toward the children in their charge. And it is not only in matters of physical neglect that nurses may harm children. A nurse may frighten a child so that, in later years, it is sometimes impossible to eradicate fear thus instilled in the impressionable mind and emotions of a child.

A too rigid obedience to the nurse should always be regarded with suspicion. On the other hand, there is no sense in employing a nurse who spoils the child in an effort to gain his affection. No mother can afford not to investigate thoroughly the character, experience, and disposition of anyone she engages to care for her child. Fortunately there are some who are thoroughly honest, conscientious, intelligent, and devoted.

CHILDREN AS CARETAKERS

In some families the older children are expected to take care of the baby, and many of them are quite competent to do so. But it is anything but wise to expect them to use for this purpose the time they should have for play and pleasure. Young boys and girls need time for outdoor play and recreation if they are to have a wholesome physical and emotional development. It is also worth noting that a fat baby is a heavy load for anyone to carry and that doing so too often may injure the pliant bones and muscles of a young girl. This is not to say that older children should be absolved of all responsibility for taking care of the baby. They should know how to do it for their own sakes as well as for their mother's, not to mention the baby.

BABY SITTERS

Most mothers, today, take care of their own babies if they can. This is, of course, best for baby. But even the most devoted of mothers need occasional diversion. They are less tense, less nervous, and more competent mothers if they occasionally forget about the home chores and go out and enjoy themselves. For occasional daytime excursions and for evenings spent out with husband or friends, the popular present-day solution is a "baby-sitter." Gruesome stories have been printed in newspapers and magazines about the hazards of employing young, inexperienced, and sometimes dishonest persons as baby-sitters.

Every mother would do well to consider these hazards and stay at home, even if it entails a sacrifice, rather than entrust her baby to anyone she is not entirely sure of.

If possible, it is better to have an older, more experienced person sit with the baby than a youngster, although many young girls and boys too are very competent and conscientious. The important thing is to know whom you are hiring and to be sure the person is trustworthy, experienced, and not likely to become panicky if something goes wrong.

The sitter should be well acquainted with the general rules of baby care; but if you require any particular care for your baby, it is well to leave written directions, going over them before you leave with the sitter to make sure that they are clearly understood. And of course, leave your telephone number or any other directions necessary for getting in touch with you in case of necessity.

There are, in some cities, reputable agencies where you can get reliable sitters at the prevailing wage. In small towns the available sitters are likely to be personally known to you. And of course many babies are fortunate enough to have grandmothers, aunts, or other relatives, friends, and neighbors who can be depended upon to sit with them when Mother and Father go out. If possible, always have as a sitter someone the baby knows. If this is not possible, have the sitter come some time before you go out so that the baby can become thoroughly acquainted with her, or him, before you leave. After that, try to have the same sitter next time you need one. It is not desirable to have a different sitter each time unless they are all persons with whom the baby is thoroughly familiar.

SPECIAL SUMMER RULES*

BY L. EMMETT HOLT, M.D., AND HENRY L. K. SHAW, M.D.

REVISED BY ROWLAND L. MINDLIN, M.D.

FOOD

MORE important than all else is not to overfeed, especially during very hot spells. A nursing baby should have fewer feedings and be given water freely.

---
* Reprinted from *Hygeia* by permission.

For a bottle-fed baby the food should be diluted from one-third to one-half with boiled water and water given freely between feedings.

If the bowels become loose, all food should be stopped at once, only water given, and medical advice sought. A diarrhea should never be allowed to run on for days because it is thought the baby is teething.

CLOTHING

The chief thing is to keep the baby cool and comfortable. In the middle of the day only the lightest clothing should be worn, often only a diaper is necessary. It is equally important during cool mornings and evenings that the body is well protected.

SKIN

Baby's skin is very sensitive and sunburn is quickly produced unless special care is taken to protect the body and the head from the sun's rays.

Prickly heat, one of the most annoying things of summer, may usually be prevented by having only linen or cotton next to the skin, bathing frequently, and dusting toilet powder or corn starch freely on the skin.

BATHING

Not only should the baby have his morning tub, but usually one at night also. On very hot days a third one at noon before the midday nap adds much to his comfort. A large handful of bran may be added to the bath water if there is a tendency to prickly heat.

FRESH AIR

In the hottest weather the baby is kept indoors in the middle of the day and given his airing in the early mornings and in the later afternoons and evenings. If he cannot be sent to the country he should spend as much time as possible in the park or on day excursions to the beach.

DIAPERS

Soiled diapers are a source of danger. They should be placed at once in water and washed as soon as possible.

FLIES AND INSECTS

Their bites cause much discomfort and may be a means of carrying disease, therefore the baby's crib or carriage should always be carefully protected by netting, or a few drops of a good non-irritating insect repellant applied to the exposed skin.

SUPERVISION OF A DOCTOR

Nothing is more important in keeping a baby well than to have him under the supervision of a doctor. He should be seen at least once a month during the first year and every three months during the second year. This should be the rule even if baby seems to be perfectly well. The object is to keep him well.

THE BABY'S CLOTHES *

A BABY's clothes are for the baby's comfort and should be planned with that in mind and not to satisfy the mother's longing for frills.

Clothing planned for a newborn baby will be suitable for only about half the first year. At the end of that time the baby will have outgrown many of the clothes he wore soon after birth. He will be much more active than he was when he was very young and will therefore need clothing of a somewhat different type. Besides, in most parts of the United States the temperature changes considerably in 6 months, and a baby by the time he is 6 months old usually needs clothes that are warmer or cooler than those he needed at birth. For these reasons the clothing

bought for a newborn baby should consist of as few pieces as possible.

The average baby needs the following for about the first 6 months:

Diapers ....(dozen) 3-4
Shirts (long or short sleeves, or sleeveless,
   according to climate) 3-4
Abdominal bands 3
Nightgowns (or wrappers)................. 5-6
Sweaters 2
Flannel squares or baby blankets........... 2-3
Warm hood (if climate is cold)............. 1

Other garments, such as dresses, additional sweaters, and a bunting or other wrap for cold weather, may be good to have but are not essen-

* From *Your Child From One to Six*—U. S. Children's Bureau publication.

tial. It is better to have plenty of diapers, shirts, and nightgowns so that the baby can always have plenty of clean ones.

SELECTING CLOTHES
Warmth and Coolness

To keep the baby comfortably warm, but not too warm, his clothing should be selected to suit the climate, the season, the temperature of the house, and the baby's age and condition.

In hot climates and those in which the range in temperature is nearly constant, night and day, for most of the year, it is easy to dress a baby so that he will not be too cold nor too warm. In parts of the country where seasonal and even daily variations in temperature are considerable and sudden—conditions found over the greater part of the United States—keeping a baby comfortably warm requires considerable thought and judgment.

In warm weather the baby needs to be dressed lightly; in the hottest weather only a sleeveless shirt and a diaper need be worn, or just a diaper. On hot days when a diaper is enough, care must be taken to see that the baby is not chilled by a breeze or by the drop in temperature that often comes with a rainstorm or at nightfall.

In moderate weather or in a changeable climate it is usually better to dress the baby lightly and to have an extra garment, such as a sweater or other light wrap, that can be slipped on easily when needed.

In cold weather warm clothes will be needed when the baby is outdoors, and unless the house is well heated, even indoors. Warm clothes may include various garments, according to the need for them, such as a long-sleeved shirt, warm nightgown—or for the older baby, a warm sleeping suit and a sweater.

When the baby is outdoors in cold weather be sure that his clothing is warm enough and especially that his hands, feet, and ears are warmly covered. Care should be taken, however, that he is not dressed too warmly, whether he is indoors or outdoors. If he is dressed too warmly he will perspire, and his body will become damp. If this happens while he is wearing outdoor wraps the dampness may cause him to be chilled when he comes indoors and his outdoor wraps are removed.

Very young babies and feeble ones lie still most of the time, and they need warmer clothing than older and more robust babies, who are active.

Ease in Dressing and Undressing

The baby's clothes should be so designed that they can be put on and taken off with the least possible discomfort for him.

Of course, a young baby is unable to make any moves that help in dressing and undressing him, so that it is necessary actually to put his body into his clothes. So that this can be done with the least possible amount of pulling, pushing, and turning, garments that go on and off readily should be selected.

A sweater, for example, should either open down the front or have a neck that is stretchable enough to let the baby's head go through without discomfort. All garments should have large armholes so that the baby's arms can be put into the sleeves easily.

A garment should be just roomy enough for the baby's comfort, as such a garment is easy to put on and take off. Of course, when a garment is too small for the baby, either because it has shrunk or because the baby has outgrown it, the baby should not be forced into it.

It is easier to dress a baby if the buttons and buttonholes are large enough to manage easily and if they are in places that are easy to reach. Some parents find tapes easier to manage than buttons.

Garments that open all the way down are easier to manage than those that open part way or on the shoulders.

Ease in Laundering

All the baby's clothes should be washable. Materials that must be dry-cleaned have no place in the baby's wardrobe. Garments that do not need ironing, such as creepers made of crinkle crepe, will save work.

It should be remembered that sweaters and blankets must be washed with some skill to avoid shrinkage and to keep the wool soft.

Safety

A drawstring should not be used in the neck of a baby's garment. Such a string is dangerous, for it may get pulled too tight about the baby's neck and strangle him. Long ribbons, sometimes used as trimming on babies' clothing, are undesirable for the same reason.

DIAPERS

Diapers should be soft, absorbent, light in weight, and not bulky. (Bulky diapers may interfere with good posture when the baby begins to stand or walk.) They should be made of material that absorbs moisture quickly, is easy to wash, and dries quickly. Diapers of cotton bird's-eye cloth may be pinked instead of hemmed; the diaper is less bulky and also is easier to wash.

Several types of satisfactory diapers are on the market, such as a diaper made of two layers of soft, fine-meshed, gauze-like cotton material, finished without hems and woven together at all the edges.

Many mothers put pieces of old cotton goods or absorbent paper tissue inside the diaper to catch the stool. Disposable diapers and also disposable diaper linings are on the market and may be used if the mother wishes.

The shape of the diaper depends largely upon the mother's preference. Some choose square diapers, some oblong. The size depends partly upon the size of the baby; a diaper that is too large for the baby is bunchy and uncomfortable. Many square diapers are 27 inches each way (after shrinking); others are smaller. Oblong diapers are usually 20 by 40 inches.

Putting on the Diaper

If the diaper is square, fold it triple thickness. Then fold one end back about one-third, so as to make a pad of six layers of cloth. For a girl baby this six-layer pad is to go behind the baby; for a boy baby, in front. The part that is to pass between the legs is only three layers thick.

Lay the baby on the folded diaper (the turned back flap may be either on the inside or on the outside).

Draw the other end up between the baby's legs, over the abdomen, and pin the front and back of the diaper together at each side at the waistline with safety pins, keeping your hand between the baby's body and the point of the pin.

The pins should be placed crosswise and should pass through both shirt and diaper. The back fold of the diaper should overlap the front.

Pin the front and back of the diaper together at each knee.

If the diaper is oblong, it may be folded to form a center panel of extra thickness.

To form this panel, using a 20- by 40-inch diaper, fold the diaper crosswise, bringing one end to about 8 inches from the other. The folded diaper will then be 20 by 24 inches.

Turn back the short end to about 3 inches from the fold.

Bring the other end of the diaper over to the first fold. The diaper will then be 12 by 20 inches, with a panel about 6 inches wide in the center.

It may then be pinned on like a square diaper, except that there is no flap.

Care should be taken not to hamper the free movements of the baby's body or legs by pinning the diaper too tight.

Care of Diapers

The diaper should be changed as often as it is wet or soiled. At night it should be changed when the baby is taken up to be fed. No diaper should be used a second time before being washed. Used diapers should never be left lying about the room nor dried on radiators.

Wet diapers should be placed at once in a covered pail and left until they can be washed.

Diapers soiled with stool should be held over the toilet and shaken, brushed or scraped so that as much stool as possible may be removed. If the family has a flush toilet the diaper may be held by one end inside the toilet and the toilet flushed so that the water flows over the diaper. When only a stain is left, the diaper may be put into the covered pail with the other soiled diapers.

All the diapers should be washed in very hot water with plenty of mild, unmedicated soap, with no washing powder or strong soap. They should be rinsed through four waters so that all the soap is rinsed out. Diapers should be dried in sunshine and open air whenever possible. It is not necessary to iron diapers, though they may be ironed if the mother wishes.

Sometimes the skin of the baby's buttocks and thighs become chafed. This chafing is often due to soap left in the diaper and means that greater care in rinsing the diapers must be used. Boiling diapers helps to remove soap.

Occasionally, with some babies, there is an odor of ammonia when the diaper is changed. In some cases the odor is noticed only after a night's sleep. Not only is the odor unpleasant, but the ammonia in such diapers frequently causes an irritation of the baby's buttocks and sometimes, in boys, of the end of the penis.

When ammonia diaper occurs it can be remedied by caring for the diapers as follows:

After washing and rinsing the diapers, wring

them as dry as possible and place them in a solution made by dissolving 4 level tablepoonfuls of boric acid to 1 quart of warm water. Wet the diapers thoroughly with the solution. Then wring them lightly and dry them, preferably in the open air.

If the baby has diarrhea the diapers should be boiled after they are washed and rinsed. The boiling should be done every day until the diarrhea is gone.

It is unwise to put an unboiled diaper under a baby's head, or to use it near any part of the body other than the genital region.

BABY PANTS

Pants over the baby's diaper to protect his clothes or bedding should be used only on special occasions when such protection is particularly important. Ordinarily it is better to provide extra protection by placing a rubber square and a folded diaper or a square of quilted cotton on the bed under his buttocks.

Occasionally, when it seems especially important to protect the baby's clothes or surroundings, as during a journey, pants over the diaper are very helpful.

Knit wool pants for this purpose are better than waterproof ones, as they permit more evaporation. If waterproof pants are worn they should not be so tight at the waist or knee as to leave marks on the baby's skin, and they should be made with air holes to allow for evaporation. Pants that are cut to fit the waist and thigh permit better ventilation and are therefore less heating than those in which elastic is used at these places.

When a baby wears waterproof or absorbent pants over the diaper, the mother should be especially careful to change the diaper as soon as it is wet or soiled.

ABDOMINAL BANDS

A baby's first band is usually a strip of gauze or soft flannel 4 to 5 inches wide and 18 to 20 inches long, which holds the navel dressing in place. It should never be tight enough to bind. As soon as the navel has healed the baby no longer needs an abdominal band.

SHIRTS

Under most circumstances cotton is the best material for the baby's shirts. In cold climates, if it is hard to keep the room warm, it is usually better to keep the baby warm with sweaters or other garments rather than with a wool shirt. Wool may irritate the baby's skin, and all-wool shirts shrink considerably.

Before buying a shirt that goes on over the head, see whether the neck will stretch enough to go over the baby's head easily and yet be firm enough to say in place on the shoulders. Shirts should have large armholes so that the baby's arms can be put into the sleeves easily.

A hem or a facing at the bottom of the shirt to which the diaper can be pinned will make a shirt last longer.

STOCKINGS AND SOCKS

In warm weather or in a well-heated house a baby who has not yet begun to creep will be most comfortable barelegged and barefooted; he will not need any kind of stockings nor shoes—not even bootees. In cold weather outdoors or in a house that is not well heated, his legs and feet will need to be covered. If long stockings are worn they should be fastened to the diaper in such a way that they will not bind the baby and restrict his activity. Short socks or bootees are not very satisfactory as they can be kicked off easily. One way to keep the baby's legs warm is to put a pair of long pants on him, like overalls, pajama pants, or the pants of "sleepers." These may be made with feet.

Later, when the baby needs some kind of stockings to wear with his shoes, short socks are better than long stockings since they do not need to be fastened up and so cannot pull on the other clothing. Overalls will keep his legs warm.

Socks and stockings, after washing, should be at least half an inch longer than the baby's foot. A baby's feet grow quickly, and the mother needs to watch the size of the stockings she puts on the baby to see that they are not cramping his feet.

SHOES

Shoes for the baby before he walks are for protection only, not for support. When he is creeping, especially if the floors are rough, shoes will protect his feet from being scratched. At this time soft-soled shoes such as moccasins, which permit free movement of the feet, are satisfactory.

When the baby begins to stand he needs shoes

with firmer soles, because then he puts his weight on his feet.

The sole of a baby's shoe should be shaped like the natural outline of his foot, straight along the inner line. It should be made of rough leather so as not to be slippery. It should be firm, but should not have a stiff metal shank. Heels are not advisable, as they limit the range of motion of the ankle joint.

The uppers should be made of soft, pliable material, such as kid. They should not be made of patent leather, as such leather is finished with a varnish that keeps perspiration from evaporating.

The shoe should fit snugly at the heel, and it is best if it is made with a stiff counter around the heel to keep the foot firmly in place.

Shoes should always be long enough, wide enough, and deep enough (at the toe) not to crowd the baby's toes. Shoes when bought should be about a half inch longer than the baby's foot and at least one-fourth inch wider at the toes. Notice the thickness of the baby's toes and see that the shoes provide ample space for them up and down. This is very important; sometimes shoes are correct in the shape of the sole and in length and width, but are not high enough at the toe. Check the fit of the shoe carefully and often to see that the toes are not crowding as the feet grow. As soon as the baby's toes come within one-fourth inch of the end of the shoe, longer shoes should be bought.

A baby will outgrow his shoes very rapidly in the first year of life. If he wears shoes by the time he is 8 months old, he may need a new pair almost every month; from 15 months to 2 years he will need a new pair every 2 or 3 months. Most mothers dislike to discard a pair of shoes when "there is still a lot of wear in them," but if they realized the permanent harm that outgrown shoes can do, they would make a great effort to keep the baby supplied with shoes that fit.

Parents should examine a baby's feet often to see whether there is any thickening of the skin or any pink or red place on the foot, as these may be due to pressure from shoes.

Low shoes are better for the baby's feet than high shoes because low shoes give the ankles greater freedom. If a baby gets the habit of taking off low shoes, high shoes will be necessary.

When the doctor gives the baby a health examination ask him whether the baby's shoes are the right style and size.

NIGHTGOWNS

During the first few months of life, when a baby sleeps almost all the time, he may wear nightgowns both day and night. A nightgown may be embroidered or otherwise made dainty and pretty, but it should wash easily. It should be easy to put on and take off, and be the right weight for the time of year.

Any soft material may be used for nightgowns, such as cotton or part-wool flannel, or, in warm weather, thin white-cotton goods such as batiste.

Winter nightgowns for a very young baby may be made with a drawstring through the hem at the bottom. Such a nightgown must be long enough to come well below the baby's feet so as to permit him to kick.

In hot weather a nightgown is unnecessary.

Many mothers like to use wrappers for the baby. A wrapper is easy to put on the baby when the mother wants to remove a dress or nightgown that is wet or soiled but when she is not ready to dress the baby again; or it may be used instead of a dress or nightgown. Wrappers are usually made of knitted material or outing flannel.

SUITS AND DRESSES

When the baby is at the creeping age he needs the greatest possible freedom for reaching, trying first steps, and getting around on hands and knees. If he is to have this freedom his garments should be designed, cut, and fitted so that there is extra room exactly where it is needed.

Creepers, overalls, or sun suits are less apt to get in the baby's way than dresses. Such garments should be made so that they are easy to put on and take off and so that the diaper can be changed easily. They should be made of fabrics that will stand hard wear, such as cotton broadcloth, cotton poplin, and gingham. The colors should stand much washing.

Overalls or long pants, like sleeper pants, will protect the baby's legs when he is creeping over rough surfaces.

Many mothers like to have a few dresses in the baby's wardrobe for dress-up occasions. Dresses should allow as much freedom for activity as possible, should be easy to put on and take off, and should wash easily.

No trimming should be used that can scratch or irritate the baby's tender skin.

The baby's dress can be worn without a slip, though mothers sometimes prefer to put a slip under thin, transparent dresses.

OUTER GARMENTS

In parts of the country where the weather may be cold one day and mild the next, the baby's outer clothes should be changed accordingly. It is wise to have a sweater for a light extra wrap to be worn indoors or outdoors, as it can be taken off and put on easily.

For a very young baby a square of blanketing may be used as an outdoor wrap.

An older baby may wear a woolen play suit in cold weather. A knitted suit gives more freedom for activity than a suit made of woven material; but it is not very warm, and there may be times when an extra sweater and pants are needed.

The baby may need a winter wrap, such as a bunting, of warm woolen material, with or without a thick interlining of wool.

A warm woolen cap or hood will be needed in cold weather. In mild weather no head covering is needed for warmth, but a soft muslin or silk cap may be worn if the mother wishes. On hot days the baby's head should be protected from the sun by a sunbonnet or cap.

BIBS

Toward the end of the first year, when the baby begins to help feed himself, a bib will be needed to protect his clothes. A bib should be large, for a baby just learning to eat spills food all over himself.

The baby's bib may be merely an oblong piece of cloth, fastening around his neck by means of short tapes; or it may be made something like a pinafore, tying around the waist as well as the neck.

Bibs can be made of any absorbent goods—old turkish towels, flannel, or several layers of cheese-cloth. Absorbent-gauze bibs may be purchased. Bibs made of oilcloth are sometimes used.

THE DAILY BATH

A HEALTHY baby should be bathed every day. During the first two weeks this and all the matters pertaining to the care of the baby usually are under the supervision of the doctor or nurse. The full tub bath may be given as soon as the scar where the navel cord was attached has fully healed. For some weeks a tiny baby may be bathed in a basin or bowl; after that he should have a baby tub.

The mother may find it convenient to give the bath before the mid-morning feeding, after the bowels have moved. Never bathe a baby within an hour after feeding. Sometimes it may be more convenient to give the bath at night, just before the baby's bedtime. The water for a young baby's bath should be slightly less than body heat; that is, about 95° F. As the baby gets older the temperature may be slightly lowered. A bath thermometer that floats is useful, but if none can be had the mother may test the temperature with her elbow. When the water feels neither hot nor cold it will be comfortable for the baby. It should be tested after the baby is undressed and ready to be put into the water. Never add hot water to the bath while the baby is in the tub. Never put the baby into the bath while the tub is standing on a stove or heater; he might be seriously

burned in this way. Never bathe a baby close to the kitchen stove. Never leave a young baby alone in the tub.

Before beginning to give the bath the mother should wash her hands clean and see that there are no pins or needles in her clothing to scratch the baby. The room should be comfortably warm —about 75° F.—for a young baby. It is not wise to have it so hot that the baby perspires, as there is then danger of his being chilled when taken into another room where the temperature is lower or if the room is cooled rapidly.

Take off all the baby's clothes and wash his face and scalp. Wash the face with water, but no soap, with the small soft cloth kept for this purpose. Then lay the baby on his back in your lap. It is usually more convenient to have his head to your right, and slightly lowered. Rub a little soap on the cloth and wring it out of the warm water so as to make suds. Lather the baby's head completely and quickly rinse several times in clear warm water, all without raising his head. Rub lightly and dry quickly. By this process the head is easily washed without running any risk of getting soap into the eyes. The baby is then turned about so that the mother may more conveniently use her right hand for the rest of the bath. Do not be afraid to wash the top of the baby's head thoroughly. By daily care "milk crust" or "cradle cap" may be prevented. If it forms rub in petroleum jelly or oil each night and wash the head thoroughly in the morning.

Next go over the entire body (not the head) with a soapy wash cloth; then place the baby in the tub, holding him with the left forearm under the neck and shoulders, the left hand under his arm, and lifting the feet and legs with the right hand. Go over his body with the wash cloth, this time not soaped; then lift him out and wrap him at once in a warmed towel. Dry him carefully with soft warm towels, patting the skin gently.

If the skin is carefully dried after the bath there will be little need for talcum powder, but a little powder may be used in the creases and folds of the skin, under the arms, and around the buttocks. It should be applied only after the skin is dry. After bathing girl babies do not powder between the folds of the genitals. Avoid too much powder as it may cake and cause irritation. If the baby tends to chafe or have a "diaper rash," oil is better than powder as it protects the skin from urine and stool. Mineral oil applied with absorbent cotton may be used instead of powder.

When putting the baby into his tub hold him firmly, and until he is able to sit up steadily by himself hold him all the time he is in the tub to avoid even one accidental slipping. If a baby becomes unwilling to get into the tub do not force him to do so for a day or two but let him sit by the tub and play over the side of it with the water and soap and floating toys.

Dress the baby carefully but quickly, turning him as little and as gently as possible, for a little baby may be tired by a too-prolonged toilet. Everything should be done to make the dressing simple.

Keeping the baby's finger nails short is necessary to prevent him from scratching himself.

CARE OF SPECIAL ORGANS

EYES

AFTER the first two weeks of life the baby's eyes may be washed with plain warm water and absorbent cotton. Whether the young baby is awake or asleep his eyes should always be turned away from direct light, whether sunlight or artificial light, and shielded from dust and wind. In bathing the baby take care not to allow any soapy water to enter his eyes. Swelling or redness of the eyes or any discharge should have a doctor's attention at once.

MOUTH

THE INSIDE of a baby's mouth should never be cleaned before the teeth come, unless the doctor orders it. The saliva is a cleansing fluid, intended to keep the mouth healthy. It is possible to injure the delicate membrane of the mouth by attempting to clean it with a cloth. If the membrane is injured a disease called thrush may develop. A drink of water after feeding will keep the mouth clean.

EARS

WASH the baby's ears with a soft cloth, but never attempt to put any hard instrument inside the ear to clean it. Always dry the ears and the creases behind them very carefully.

NOSE

THE BABY's nose should be cleaned as a part of the daily toilet in the same way as the ears. When the baby has a cold his nose should have special attention, and separate handkerchiefs should be provided.

GENITAL ORGANS

THE GENITAL organs in babies of both sexes should be kept scrupulously clean with as little handling as possible. Boys should be examined by a physician to see whether the penis is normal or whether circumcision is needed. Two or three times a week, at bathing time or as often as is necessary for cleanliness, the foreskin should be drawn back until the raised edge of the glans (end of the penis) is visible and the organ then cleansed. If the mother finds it difficult to draw back the foreskin she should not attempt to do it until the doctor has shown her how. The genitals of a girl baby should be washed carefully twice every day. Any swelling or redness of the parts, or a discharge, however slight, should be brought at once to the doctor's attention. Do not use talcum powder between the folds of the genitals.

SUNSHINE AND FRESH AIR*

SUNSHINE and fresh air are good for the baby. When the weather is bright and sunny and the air is balmy, or crisp and cool, nearly everyone enjoys being outdoors—babies, older children, and grownups. In such weather the baby, even the very young baby, should be outdoors as much as possible.

But extreme cold and dampness and extreme heat are not good for the baby. On cold, blustery days when there is a high wind, he is better off in a warm, well-venilated room than outdoors. In hot weather the baby needs to be in the coolest place that can be found, whether indoors or outdoors; on the hottest days the house may be cooler than outdoors.

A good rule for the mother to follow is to take the baby out when the weather is such that she herself enjoys being outdoors. In winter, even when the temperature in the shade is low, if the sun is shining it is often possible to find a sunny spot, protected from the wind, where the baby can be outdoors in comfort during the middle of the day. Of course he will need to be well wrapped up, especially his hands, feet, and ears. A baby's face should never be covered.

Being bundled up keeps a baby from kicking and playing freely. When the baby is too young to run around it may be better, therefore, in cold weather to let him sleep when he is outdoors and have his playtime in the house, where he can be freer. If, however, he is being wheeled in a carriage, or if he can watch something that interests him, he will enjoy being outdoors even though bundled up.

A very young baby should be outdoors in cold weather only if the sun is shining, if he is protected from wind, and if the temperature of the spot where he is placed is at least 65° F. Take the wall thermometer from the baby's room and find out the temperature of the place where you are putting him. The temperature in a sunny spot is often 40° to 50° higher than that in the shade.

EFFECTS OF SUNSHINE

Certain rays of the sun—the ultraviolet rays —when they reach the baby's skin produce a substance called vitamin D, which enables the baby to use his food so as to build straight bones, strong muscles, and sound teeth. Ultraviolet rays cannot pass through clothing (unless it is loosely woven or very thin) nor through ordinary window glass, and they are greatly reduced by passing through a smoky or dusty atmosphere. In order to produce vitamin D in the baby's skin sunshine should fall directly upon the baby.

In most parts of the United States babies cannot get enough sunlight throughout the year to provide them with all the vitamin D they need. It is only in the tropical and subtropical parts of the country—Puerto Rico and the extreme South and Southwest, for example—that this is possible.

In the North Temperate Zone and in the far North, the ultraviolet rays are weaker in winter and are useful only when the sun is overhead.

Even in summer, in most places it is difficult to give a baby enough sunlight, for some days are cloudy and some are so hot that the baby should not be exposed to the sun very long. Some localities are so smoky that the babies get little benefit from the sun at any time of the year. It is best, therefore, for babies to get vitamin D not only from sunshine but also from some other source.

Vitamin D can be given to babies by using a special kind of lamp that produces ultraviolet rays or it can be given them by mouth in foods or special preparations.

"Sun lamps" are of two types—mercury-vapor lamps and carbon-arc lamps. Either type may be satisfactory for supplying the baby with vitamin D, but before using a lamp it is wise to obtain expert opinion as to whether it is really efficient. It is unwise to use any sun lamp without the advice and supervision of a doctor.

When one of these lamps is used the baby's eyes must be protected by goggles, and care must be taken not to injure the baby's delicate skin through overexposure.

Sun lamps are relatively expensive, and for most babies it is easier and just as satisfactory to give vitamin D in food or special preparations.

Cod-liver oil has been for many years the principal food given to babies to supply vitamin D. Within the last few years other foods and special preparations have been made available for this purpose. In most climates every baby should have one of these daily. Your doctor will tell you which one to use for your baby and how much to give.

* From *Infant Care*, U. S. Children's Bureau Publication.

SUN BATHS

Sun baths may be given when it is warm enough for the baby to be comfortable in the sun without clothes. In starting sun baths remember that a baby's skin is delicate and burns easily. At first expose a small part of the baby's body for a short time. If your baby is fair, with thin, white skin, be especially careful. Slight reddening and tanning of the baby's skin will show that he is benefiting from the sunshine, but not all babies tan, even in the sun. Gradually both the time the baby remains in the sun and the amount of his body exposed can be increased. But it should be remembered that too much sunlight may be harmful to the skin.

The baby's eyes will not be injured by sunlight unless the rays enter his eyes directly. This happens only when the eyes are turned toward the sun and are open. If the eyelids are closed or if the face is turned away from the sun, no harm will be done. If the baby lies with his feet away from the sun and his head slightly raised, his eyes will be protected by his forehead and eyelids. A baby old enough to sit up will protect his own eyes by turning and bending his head. As the baby gets older, much of his playtime can be spent in the sunshine, with few or no clothes in summer and with suitable warm clothes in winter.

SITTING UP

THERE is no set time when babies are ready or able to sit up by themselves. Some show signs of wanting to as early as five months; some show no interest in it until they are a year old.

This ability requires watching. That is, as soon as a baby is able to roll over by himself, he should never be left unguarded for a minute unless he is strapped in or on to something. Babies can roll out of anything, once they get going, before you have time to turn around. So be especially careful to guard against accidents.

Most babies want to try sitting up before they can actually do so safely by themselves. It is all right to let them try to pull themselves up by holding on to your hands as soon as they show they want to try. But most babies are not able to sit up steadily by themselves, even after they have been helped up, until they are somewhere between seven and nine months old. It is better, in general, not to prop a baby up into a sitting position, except for fun while you are holding him, until he can sit steadily by himself. When he can do that, you will be tempted to let him sit in a high chair and have his meals with the family. But high chairs have their hazards. Flimsy ones are dangerous, and even those with a broad base are risky. Besides, baby doesn't like being strapped in. He wants freedom to thrash around. High chair accidents are far too frequent.

Better for baby, and far safer too, is a good solid low chair-table arrangement like the Babee-Tenda. The Babee-Tenda carries the baby's weight right in the center, has a self-adjusting back and an adjustable steel-braced footrest, and surrounds the baby with a big square table-top for playing or eating. It can't collapse, and the baby can't squirm out of it or tip it over. Babee-Tendas are a boon to the baby and wonderful for the mother's peace of mind. Every baby whose family can afford it should have one.

BABY'S EXERCISES

THE BABY needs exercise every day to develop his muscles. Waving his arms, kicking his legs, and crying are the means by which he gets this needed exercise.

His clothing should be loose enough so that he can toss his arms and legs about when he is awake, but there should also be every day a regular time in which he is permitted even greater freedom in using his limbs. The best time for this is immediately following his bath. Let him lie in the sun without any clothes on for half an hour. Of course, he should not be in a draft. This sun bath not only gives him the opportunity of exercising the muscles of his body, but also gives his body the benefits to be derived from sun and fresh air.

When the baby is a few months old, he will try to turn himself over. Now is the time to begin watching him very closely, because as soon as he learns to make a complete turn he is quite apt to roll himself from one place to another and if he is lying on the bed alone and unprotected, he may get a bad fall to the floor.

BEGINNING TO CRAWL

At about six months of age the baby should be put on the floor with space enough to crawl. Mothers often object to doing this because they are afraid that the baby will take cold and they know that he will get dirty on the floor. These are both good objections, but neither one is unsurmountable. In the winter-time there should always be heat in the story of the house below the room in which the baby is placed on the floor—if the nursery is on the main floor of the house, there should be heat in the cellar. Even so, a baby should not be placed on the uncovered floor. There should be a blanket or thin mattress on which to put him. As he grows stronger, he will want to crawl off the mattress or blanket. Then comes the trouble of keeping him clean.

BABY PEN

A BABY PEN will solve this problem. It is not necessary to buy an expensive one. A smooth board, 12 inches wide and 8 to 10 feet long can be used to shut off one corner of the nursery or porch. If it is summer-time, the blanket or mattress can be put on the grass in the back yard, four stakes driven into the ground at the corners, and a tennis net put around the outside of the stakes. The baby pens which can be bought readymade have two advantages: First, they can be moved from one place to another; second, the sides are made of upright pieces with no cross pieces on which the child can climb. When the

baby is about ten months old, for the mattress or blanket may be substituted a large tray of sand. Of course, the sand should be kept clean and dry. He will enjoy rolling and crawling in it and letting it trickle through his fingers.

STANDING AND WALKING

ABOUT the eighth month the baby will pull himself up on his hands and about two months later the mother will be surprised one day to find him standing on his feet holding on to the side of his crib, his pen, or a chair. At first he will not stand for many seconds, but gradually the time will lengthen and then he will begin to take a few short steps still holding tightly on to some support. Somewhere between the twelfth and fourteenth month, the average baby will take his first step alone, and after that first step it will seem no time before he is running about the house and yard. Some babies do not stand or walk as early as those ages we have just mentioned. They should not be hurried. A baby will walk when his muscles, limbs, and joints are capable of supporting him. If he is forced to stand upon his feet before he does it voluntarily, he may develop weak ankles, flat feet, bow legs, or knock knees. Just why one baby makes attempts to stand and to walk earlier than another is hard to say. We do know that if a baby has been ill, if he is overweight, if he has not been given sun baths, or if he has not been permitted to crawl on the floor, he will not begin to stand or walk at an early age.

HELPING A BABY TO EXERCISE

FATHER and mother plays have a definite value in the physical education of the child as well as in his mental development. The first plays should be pat-a-cake and telling how big he is. The baby loves them and they exercise arm and trunk muscles.

THE BABY'S DAY*

MOST BABIES can get used at an early age to eating and sleeping at regular times, and they are usually happier and eat and sleep better if habits of regularity are established.

During the early weeks of life a baby sleeps almost all the time, waking only for food. If, during the first few days, he is offered the breast (or a bottle) at regular times—every 4 hours for most babies—he is likely to form the habit of

waking up and wanting food at these times.

Though most babies fit easily into a plan of feeding every 4 hours—for example, at 6, 10, and 2 o'clock (until the 2 a.m. feeding is given up)— some gabies will need a different schedule. For some, feedings every 3 hours are better. Occasionally, as a baby gets a little older and is awake more of the time, a mother will find that at one of the feeding times the baby is usually

*From "Infant and Child Care"—U. S. Children's Bureau publication.

too sleepy to eat. By shifting the hours of feeding to a time a little earlier or a little later, she can adjust the schedule so as not to interfere with his hours of sleep. Often the whole schedule can be shifted; for example, if the baby is always sound asleep when it is time for the 2 p.m. feeding, a plan of feeding at 7, 11, 3, 7, and 11 may suit him better. But if the same baby is awake and hungry at 6 a.m., such a change will not suit him, and it may be better to change only one or two of the feeding times; for example, it may be best to give his feedings at 6, 10, 2:45, 6:15, and 10.

There are no fixed hours at which every baby should be fed. If your baby does not fit into the routine you plan for him, try to change the plan to suit his needs. After you find the best routine for him, however, try to keep to the same plan each day. Babies generally thrive on doing the same thing at the same time, day after day.

The majority of babies will fit themselves easily into the plan that you make for them, as long as it provides for regular feedings and regular hours of sleep. It is usually possible, therefore, for the mother to consider her own convenience in planning the baby's day. In some homes it is easier for the mother to start the day early, with the first feeding at 5 a.m. and the last at 9 p.m. (after the 2 a.m. feeding is given up). For others a later start, say at 7 a.m., is more convenient.

There is nothing rigid, therefore, about the feeding hours that are shown in schedules such as are given in the suggested plans that follow. It is usually best for the mother to take such a plan, shift the hours a bit one way or the other if this is more convenient for her and the household, and then follow the plan until the baby shows that some other plan would suit him better. He may show this by crying regularly half an hour or more before feeding time or by sleeping through feeding time. If the baby cries before it is time for him to waken for his feedings, it may be that he needs more food rather than a change in his schedule, and the doctor should be consulted regarding a change in his feeding.

FIRST FOUR MONTHS

6 a.m......*Feeding.* Breast or bottle feeding. Sleep or play, alone in crib.

9:30 a.m...Cod-liver oil or other source of vitamin D, and orange juice. Bath. Undress baby in time to allow for exercise and play before bath.

10 a.m.....*Feeding.* Breast or bottle feeding. Nap, out of doors if weather permits. Drink of water after nap. Put baby where he can play safely. Sun bath if weather permits. (In very hot weather give sun bath before morning bath or after afternoon nap.)

2 p.m......*Feeding.* Breast or bottle feeding. Nap, out of doors if weather permits. Cod-liver oil or other source of vitamin D, and orange juice, when the baby wakens from nap. Put baby where he can play safely. Offer water at some time during afternoon.

5:45 p.m...Prepare for night. Allow time for exercise and play.

6 p.m......*Feeding.* Breast or bottle feeding. Bed, lights out, windows adjusted for night, door shut.

10 p.m.....*Feeding.* Breast or bottle feeding.

2 a.m......*Feeding.* (Before end of second month most babies give up this feeding. Some give it up soon after birth.)

Beginning about the second or third month most babies will have a waking period in the late afternoon. This will develop into a playtime as the baby gets older. It is wise to let the baby spend part of this time by himself so that he may get used to being alone.

FIFTH AND SIXTH MONTHS

6 a.m......*Feeding.* Breast or bottle feeding. Sleep or play, alone in crib.

9:30 a.m...Cod-liver oil or other source of vitamin D, and orange juice. Bath. Undress baby in time to allow for exercise and play before bath.

10 a.m.....*Feeding.* Cereal and breast or bottle feeding. Nap, out of doors if weather permits. Drink of water after nap. Put baby where he can play safely. Sun bath if weather permits. (In very hot weather give sun bath before morning bath or after the afternoon nap.)

2 p.m......*Feeding.* Egg yolk, vegetable (after baby is 5 months old), and breast or bottle feeding. Nap, out of doors if weather permits. Cod-liver oil or other source of vitamin D, and orange juice, when baby wakens from nap. Put baby where he can play safely. Offer water at some time during afternoon.

5:45 p.m...Prepare for night. Allow time for exercise and play.

6 p.m......*Feeding.* Cereal and breast or bottle feeding.
Bed, lights out, windows adjusted for night, door shut.

10 p.m.....*Feeding.* Breast or bottle feeding. (If baby does not waken, this feeding may be omitted.)

During these months the baby usually has longer and longer periods when he is awake, especially before the 2 and 6 p.m. feedings. If he is wakeful at night it may be well to waken him a little earlier from his afternoon nap.

The baby should spend part of the time he is awake alone with a toy or two, in a place where he can play safely—in his crib or play pen, or on a pad on the floor—but part can be a playtime with the mother or father or other children.

SEVENTH, EIGHTH, AND NINTH MONTHS

6 a.m......*Feeding.* Breast or bottle feeding.
Sleep or play alone in crib.

9:30 a.m...Cod-liver oil or other source of vitamin D, and orange juice.
Bath. Undress baby in time to allow for exercise and play before bath.

10 a.m.....*Feeding.* Cereal and breast or bottle feeding.
Nap, out of doors if weather permits.
Drink of water after nap. Put baby where he can play safely.
Sun bath if weather permits. (In very hot weather give sun bath before morning bath or after the afternoon nap.)

2 p.m......*Feeding.* Egg yolk or meat, vegetable, and breast or bottle feeding.
Nap, out of doors if weather permits.
Cod-liver oil or other source of vitamin D, and orange juice, when baby wakens from nap. Put baby where he can play safely. Offer water at some time during afternoon.

5:45 p.m...Prepare for night. Allow time for exercise and play.

6 p.m......*Feeding.* Cereal, fruit, and breast or bottle feeding.
Bed, lights out, windows adjusted for night, door shut.

When the baby is 7 months old consult the doctor about weaning him.

The baby can now begin to learn to take some of his milk from a cup.

Most babies at this age will begin to shorten either the morning or the afternoon nap.

TENTH, ELEVENTH, AND TWELFTH MONTHS

About the tenth month some babies are ready for a schedule of three meals a day. Many babies are not ready for this schedule until 2 or 3 months later; these may continue on 4-hour schedules.

The three-meal-a-day plan that will best suit your baby and yourself will depend partly on the habits he has already formed, such as the time when he takes his nap, and partly on what fits into your day. One such schedule follows:

6 a.m.   (or a little later, depending upon when the baby wakens).
Orange juice.
Sleep or play, alone in crib.
Wash and dress baby before breakfast.

7:30 a.m...*Breakfast.* Cereal, toast, milk, cod-liver oil.
Play, out of doors when the weather is suitable. Let baby have some water to drink during morning.
Sun bath, if weather permits.

11:30 a.m..*Dinner.* Egg or meat, vegetables, toast, milk.
Nap. Undress baby for nap. When he wakens from nap give him a cup of milk.
Play. Offer some water during this time.

5 p.m......Bath.

5:30 p.m...*Supper.* Cereal or potato, fruit, toast, milk, cod-liver oil.

6 p.m......Bed, lights out, windows adjusted for night, door shut.

If the baby takes a long nap in the morning undress him for his nap at a regular time (usually about 10:30 or 11 a.m.) and give him a cup of milk. Give him his dinner at 1 or 1:30.

Many babies continue to take two naps at this age. The time of the noon meal for such babies will depend upon whether the long nap is taken in the morning or in the afternoon.

In some families it is more convenient to give the baby his breakfast at 6:30 or 7 and his orange juice at 9 or 9:30.

The bath may be given at any hour of the day (except shortly after meals). It is best to have a regular time for it.

HABITS AND HABIT TRAINING

FORMING GOOD HABITS *

THE HEALTH, happiness, and efficiency of the older child and of the adult depend largely on the habits formed in early childhood. The habits of the little child are begun in the first year of life, some of them directly after birth.

A baby wants to repeat the things that give him pleasure and satisfaction. He does not want to repeat the things in which he does not find pleasure or satisfaction. Therefore, to help a baby form good habits, we must see that he gets satisfaction out of doing the things we want him to do. We must also see that he does *not* get satisfaction out of doing the things we do *not* want him to do.

As babies get older they get more and more satisfaction from their parents' words and smiles of approval and from any kind of attention. If the mother gives the baby attention and approval when he is doing what she wants him to do, it will be easy to get him to do it again. This will have a better effect on his training than scolding him when he does what she does not want him to do.

When the baby does something that the parents do not wish him to do, such as throwing his cup on the floor, they must try to see that he does not enjoy their response so much that he does it again just to get the response. Sometimes when the baby throws his cup on the floor his parents laugh at him and call each other's attention to the "cute trick." Of course this makes him do it again because he enjoys being the center of the stage. Sometimes when he throws his cup on the floor, parents may scold him and call him "bad" or slap him. About all he is able to understand of the grown-up's behavior is that it is *he* that everyone is interested in, and he is likely to repeat the "trick" to get attention.

If the parents can succeed in making themselves pay little attention to the baby when he throws his cup on the floor, and if they praise him generously when he succeeds in drinking his milk without spilling it, he will act most of the time as the parents would like to have him.

It is to be expected that sometimes he will do things that are very annoying. From the baby's point of view it must be quite entertaining to watch the milk trickle onto the floor. He knows nothing about the trouble it causes. If he does not get too much satisfaction from doing such things he will not do them very often.

It is also to be expected that the mother will be cross sometimes over some of the annoying things all babies do. Mothers, like babies, are human. But a mother should try not to be cross very often.

A baby's behavior may be very annoying, but he is not willfully "bad." To be "naughty" or "bad" means that the child understands that one way of acting is right and the other is wrong and that he deliberately chooses the wrong or bad way. Babies have no conception of right and wrong. They are exploring their world, and everything within reach is usable. It is the mother's fault, not the baby's, if he happens to upset and break a treasured vase. The mother should not have left it where the baby could get hold of it.

Eventually the child will learn to behave by imitating the people about him. In the meantime the parents should provide the baby with a place where he can explore his world and still be protected from harming himself and from harming the possessions of others.

Lessons learned by imitating are fixed much more firmly as part of the child's personality than lessons learned through force and punishment. A child who learns by imitating good behavior

---

* From *Your Child from One to Six*, U. S. Children's Bureau Publication.

acts in the acceptable way because "that's the way we do." The child who learns because of fear is likely to act in the acceptable way only when he thinks somethings will happen to him if he does not. He will try to "get away with" as much as possible.

Long before he can talk, a baby can understand what is said to him. Mothers and fathers should be honest with their children from the very beginning.

For example, if a mother says, "Open wide; I have something my baby will like," it should be something that he does like—not bad-tasting medicine.

If you are leaving the baby alone in his bed or play pen, do not try to slip away while he is busy with a toy or some other interest. If you do this, the baby will lose a little of his confidence in you. But if you leave him in an open and matter-of-fact way, he can enjoy the times when you are with him without fearing that you might slip away when he is not looking.

Treating a child honestly is the only way to gain his confidence; it is the only way to teach him to be truthful. The older the child gets, the more important is his absolute trust in the truth of "what mother says."

EATING HABITS

Almost all babies enjoy eating. They learn very early in life that eating gives them pleasure. This feeling of pleasure is due not only to the relief of hunger but also to the things that go along with eating—the warmth of the mother's breast, the holding, the rocking, the human contact of being handled and cared for.

As the baby grows up and extra things he wants along with his food change. The young baby wants the warmth of his mother's breast. The older baby wants to hold his bottle, and the still older baby wants to help feed himself with a spoon. When he becomes an adult he will enjoy his food much more when he can have pleasant companions and cheerful surroundings.

Good food and pleasant surroundings are necessary for the greatest pleasure in eating, but it must not be forgotten that even more important is the need of being hungry at mealtime. In all human beings (including babies) hunger occurs at intervals, usually quite regular intervals. If we offer a baby food at regular times we usually find that he is ready for it at these times. Before we know it, he has developed good habits of eating; this in a baby merely means that he enjoys eating at regular times.

LEARNING TO EAT*

By Miriam E. Lowenberg
Iowa State College

A CHILD needs to learn to eat enough food for body needs. Then he should have a willingness to eat, to try new foods and to eat cheerfully what is offered, as a matter of course, and within a limited length of time. Finally he should eat with increasing independence.

The question is often raised: "How much time should be allowed for eating a meal?" Thirty to forty minutes have been found to be sufficient time for most young children. This, however, is an individual problem, since it is closely related to the child's inability to attend to one thing for a long period of time. If the child is eating at the family table he may become absorbed in "listening in" on adult conversation and so forget that food is to be eaten.

Often eating becomes discouraging to the child because adult social forms are demanded. The use of "please" and "thank-you," words which hold no real meaning for the young child, only makes eating more difficult. It is well to give the child time to master the spoon and other implements for eating before expecting much in the way of table manners.

A child's refusal to eat new foods may be due to lack of technique in chewing and swallowing. Merely getting the food in the mouth doesn't solve the problem, for many children even at the age of four have been known to hold food in the mouth. It seems that chewing has to be learned and is accomplished by trial and error. Hard, crisp foods stimulate chewing. Direct instruction may help this learning. A command to chew, illustrated with exaggerated chewing movements, may be used.

*From *Food for the Young Child*. By Miriam E. Lowenberg, Iowa State College, Collegiate Press, Inc.

WHEN INDEPENDENCE BEGINS

IT IS not known when a child should eat independently. The individual child and his power to manage his body must be the guide. Allow him to do what he can for himself, but at the same time do not hesitate to give some help if that makes things go better.

The way in which the child is helped with his eating is a factor in learning to eat. Assistance can be given by placing the spoon in the child's hand so that he will use large rather than fine muscles. If the hand is guided as it conveys food to the mouth, the child will make the movement which later he will make alone. The use of words which the child can use later in directing himself has been suggested as a step in this learning. "Drink" may be the direction given as the child lifts the cup of milk to his mouth. Then approval should be given for what he later will be doing on his own account.

As the child grows independent in eating, gradually withdraw supplementary help. Physical help should be removed first, then verbal directions and finally approval or praise.

EXPECT FOOD TO BE ACCEPTED

THE ATTITUDE with which food is presented to the child is an all-important factor in determining the child's acceptance of it. The over-solicitous adult who is concerned with each mouthful can create a condition in which the child senses that in order to become the center of things all he needs to do is to toy with his food. Evident unconcern on the part of the adult is one of the most profitable contributing factors in the food consumption of the young child. Serve suitable portions with the expectancy that the food will be eaten. If the meal is not eaten within a reasonable period of time the plate may be removed without comment and no food offered until the next meal. Avoid incentives or rewards of any kind to make the child eat. Even putting a premium on dessert is now considered highly questionable.

Wise guidance of the child as he is learning to eat, will be based on the child's physical condition, his developing power to control his body, to use language, to concentrate on a task, to sit still, to adapt himself and make changes. The child needs a comfortable feeling of security created by interest and understanding of those about him, and environment that is calm, peaceful and free from strain and anxiety. Interest in progress, patience and understanding are the ideal attitudes of the adult who allows the child to grow up in learning to eat.

LEARNING TO WASH AND DRESS *

By ETHEL B. WARING

Professor of Child Development and Parent Education, College of Home Economics, Cornell University.

THERE is a time when the best of adult care is none too good for the infant. His well-being is conditioned by such care. The regularity of his routine gives him a basis for predicting what is going to happen to him. An adult's handling of him, and the inflection of her voice, add assurance to his feeble predictions. After weeks of such practice, he builds confidence and security. All later learnings have a sound basis in the security of this child-adult relationship.

A baby discovers at an early period that he can do things with his arms and legs, his head and body. If the adults of his family capitalized these new activities, they can readily direct them toward caring for himself. In so doing, they enrich his discovery. While he is enjoying vigorous activity with his arm, Mother may direct it into a sleeve, and say happily, "That's right. In sleeve." He responds at first only vaguely to the whole situation as a pleasant one. When the same thing has happened several times in the course of the day, and day after day, he discovers when to make that particular movement with his arm. He now can do it, knows *when* to do it, and *likes* to do it. This is a simple but important step in learning to care of himself. Similarly with pulling off stockings or shoes. Mother may help him make all the simpler movements ,and she will commend him for making them. Gradually, he discriminates between certain situations. He notices that certain words go with certain movements. When he hears, "In sleeve," and "Stocking off," he finally

* Reprinted from *Junior Home* by permission.

learns to make the appropriate movement. When he is right, Mother approves. If he makes a mistake, she redirects him until he makes the right response.

When he begins to help with his washing, Mother will still rub his knees instead of accepting his random splashing and slapping. Gradually he learns that "Rub knees" means just that. "Rub hands" means something different. He does either whenever Mother says, "Rub knees," or "Rub hands." In time he can perform many simple acts when told, one after the other.

Perhaps you have noticed in your own routine that you tend to do one thing after the other in the same order day after day without much thinking. In dressing, for example, putting on your shoe seems to start you off on tightening the lower laces, lacing, tying, for first one and then the other shoe. Picking up your shoe starts you on this whole sequence. Finishing your shoes starts you on the next sequence in your dressing system. The influence of sequence is evident in the little beginner's early learning to care for himself. Not only can he do one act after another as directed by his mother, but he can carry well into the sequences he has practiced. Gradually he learns each of these sequences so that he can carry through with only a simple direction to start him off.

When a toddler begins to help himself with the cleaning-up process preceding dinner, he has many details to learn. He begins by participating actively with Mother in some of the details in her care of him which he has heretofore just accepted. As he learns the meanings of the words she uses in approving and directing him, he can do several of these things whenever she tells him to. As he practices them in their sequence, he learns them in that order. Sometimes he pulls out the stopper after rinsing his hands without waiting to be told. Sometimes he washes his face without being told, after squeezing the cloth.

In time, all these numerous details of getting washed and ready for dinner will come along in their learned order if Mother gives few, instead of the many, directions. "Get your towel," will bring towel, face cloth, and comb. "Wash," or "Get washed for dinner," or "Get your water," or "Wash your hands" (whichever phrase Mother habitually uses), will cover all the details of putting in the stopper, turning on and off the water, rubbing on soap, rubbing hands front ad back, rubbing arms, rinsing, and pulling out the stopper. If at this point he needs a new start, "Wash your face" will often cover refilling the bowl, wetting and squeezing the cloth, rubbing the face

with the cloth, rinsing the cloth and squeezing it again, and pulling out the stopper. Here again, he may need a new direction about drying. This one will probably suggest the hair combing if it has been practiced in that order, and may even result in the taking the comb, the cloth, and the towel back to their places. If not, the additional direction can be given at the point where the sequence breaks down.

Many a three-year-old is performing this whole routine preparatory for dinner with one general direction, "Get ready for dinner." That one direction has come to include all the groups and separate items of behavior he has learned to do in that situation.

The little children who learn to care for themselves in the manner described have adults who are good teachers. These adults are consistent in their own behavior so that the child can accurately predict what is going to happen next. They are consistent in labeling their movements in simple words for which he can discover meaning, and later use for himself. They notice and approve his every effort to participate in these routine activities. They give just enough help to make his effort succeed. They call attention only to his successes, ignoring his failures. As he learns, they give him a chance to do for himself before they start to do for him. They wait for him to do without being told before they tell him, if necessary, just what to do. They withdraw their approval for those details that he has already learned, and leave him to practice them as a matter of course. They let him go as far in any given sequence as he can, only adding direction or encouragement as the sequence breaks down. They call his attention to his progress in doing things alone and in doing without being told. Thus they make it possible for the little child to discover new capacities daily—and to achieve new learnings.

Routine is truly a realm for discovery and achievement at that age and under those conditions. Learnings not attained under these fortunate conditions become tasks unwillingly assumed by the older child whose field for discovery is in the constructive and social activities of later childhood. Learning to help himself while routine learning is ardent discovery, makes the child efficient in these daily duties by the time he wants to play all day with things and other children.

Meanwhile he has established a secure and happy relationship with his helpful hands. As a result, he can and will continue to turn to them for understanding and appreciation, for encouragement and for guidance.

TOILET HABITS*

BOWEL TRAINING

WHEN a baby can sit up by himself, when he begins to pay attention to what is said to him—usually at 8 to 10 months—is a good time to start training him to have a bowel movement when he is on a chamber or a toilet seat. It is possible to start training much earlier, but, regardless of when training is started, babies as a rule do not learn to control their bowel movements much before they are 10 to 12 months of age.

Some babies have a bowel movement at almost exactly the same time every day, so that it is possible for the mother to put the baby on the toilet when she sees he is about to have a bowel movement. This is a good thing to do if you can do it easily, as it saves having a soiled diaper to wash, but it should not be confused with real training. One mother who did this was asked whether her 5-month-old baby was trained. "No," she said, "he is not trained, but I am."

In real training the baby learns to take part in the effort and to try to wait until he is on the toilet before he has the movement. A baby cannot do this until he can control the muscles of his bowels. Usually by the time the baby is 8 to 10 months old he will begin to be able to do this. At this age, however, he will not be able to delay the bowel movement for more than a short time, nor to make a stool come ahead of the time it would come of itself.

To start training, notice at what time the baby usually has a bowel movement. (This is usually 10 to 20 minutes after a feeding—most often after breakfast.) At the time when the baby usually has a bowel movement watch him closely, and if possible put him on the toilet when he is just about to have the movement.

At first the baby will not understand what is expected of him, and you may have to put him on the toilet daily for several days before he has a movement there. When he does so, show your approval so that he will understand that this is what you want him to do. If, each time you put him on the toilet, you make certain sounds and gestures, he will learn to associate these with having a bowel movement and to understand what is expected of him. The baby should not be allowed to remain on the toilet for more than about 10 minutes.

Most babies will have at least one movement every day, but for some babies it is normal to have a movement only every second day. Many breast-fed babies have two to four bowel movements a day.

The training should be continued by placing the baby on the toilet about the same time every day.

If the training is started at a time when the baby is old enough to cooperate, he is likely to learn soon to have his bowel movement at the toilet, and probably training will be more or less complete in 4 to 6 weeks. Accidents will occur, however, from time to time for several years.

It is not necessary to use suppositories, soap sticks, or enemas to train the baby; in fact, these may actually do harm by making him expect them.

Do not start bowel training and weaning at the same time. One of these or both may be hard for the baby. Let him learn only one hard thing at a time.

BLADDER TRAINING

CONTROL of the bladder is more difficult to establish than control of the bowels and is, therefore, begun a little later. Soon after bowel-movement control is fairly well established the baby may be placed on the toilet after each feeding and often he will pass urine. Approval may be shown by the mother whenever the baby urinates into the toilet. Even after a baby has become accustomed to passing urine into the toilet after meals and after waking up from a nap, it will be some time before he learns not to wet his diaper between times.

Most babies will develop daytime control of the bladder and will learn to tell when they want to go to the toilet between the second and third birthdays, although some learn more quickly than others.

When the baby begins to walk, diapers should be discarded for pants. Many children seem to grasp more easily the idea of going to the toilet for emptying the bladder when they wear pants instead of diapers.

Children usually learn night control of the bladder between the second and third birthdays, after control during the day is well established. The mother must remember that as she is trying to establish the "dry" habit it will not help to leave the wet clothing on. If the child wets himself by accident the pants or diaper should be changed at once. He should be praised when he keeps dry. *He should not be scolded when he has an accident.*

---

*From *Infant Care*, U. S. Children's Bureau Publication.

TOILET CONVENIENCES FOR THE CHILD

THE little child should not be expected to use a toilet built for adults. Small seats that can be placed on top of the ordinary toilet are now on the market. Quite as important as a comfortable seat is a firm support for the child's feet while he is seated on either the toilet or the nursery chair. A wooden box for this purpose and for the little boy to stand on in front of the toilet should be provided. If it is necessary to use an outdoor privy, a chamber or commode should be provided indoors for the little children and should be used during very cold weather and whenever else it is convenient.

TEACHING THE CHILD TO USE THE RIGHT WORDS

IT IS important for the child to associate with the toilet chair and with elimination the correct words —"toilet," "bowel movement," and "passing urine" —and not some special words understood only by the family. Many a child who is old enough to be greatly distressed by the accident has wet his clothes because some adult has failed to grasp the idea that "wee wee" or "tinky" or some other special word means that he needs to go to the toilet. These functions are normal, and should be treated in a perfectly matter-of-fact way. However, the toilet chair should distinctly belong in the nursery or the bathroom and should not be used in the living room or the kitchen. The child should learn early that certain things are done and talked of publicly and others are not.

CONSTIPATION

CONSTIPATION is the passing of very hard material from the bowels, or the passing of a very small amount, or failure to empty the bowels daily. In young children it is much more often due to a poorly chosen diet and poor training in regular toilet habits than to any disease.

Castor oil or other cathartics should not be given except on the order of a doctor. Constipation is more often made worse by them than cured, for the diarrhea that they cause is usually followed by further constipation.

The following method may be used in handling a mild case of constipation:

1. Have a regular hour when the child is taught that his bowels are expected to move, preferably soon after breakfast.
2. Serve meals at regular hours and give a diet with a liberal allowance of laxative foods.
3. Give 3 or 4 glasses of water a day.
4. Encourage vigorous out-of-door play.
5. Do not let the child become too impressed with the importance of having a bowel movement. If he occasionally goes for a day without a movement, do not worry unless he seems sick. Leave him alone at the toilet, but do not let him sit there more than 7 or 8 minutes. If his bowels do not move, do not become anxious and do not urge or coax him. Wait until the next day before trying again. Coaxing and anxiety on the part of the mother may increase the child's unwillingness to try to make his bowels move.

Constipation that persists in spite of such treatment should be reported to the doctor,

BED WETTING

BY ROWLAND L. MINDLIN, M.D.

MANY CHILDREN wet the bed at night until three or even four years of age. This is a perfectly normal thing and should cause parents no concern. It is only after the bed wetting persists into the fifth year that some attention should be paid to it. As with other conditions that affect children, it is much more sensible to find out and eliminate the cause than it is merely to try to treat the end result.

In the case of bed wetting, the cause is very rarely found to be an organic disease of the bladder or kidneys. In most of the diseases which are accompanied by wetting at night there is also wetting during the day. Usually there is very frequent dribbling of very small amounts of urine so that the child is almost always wet. However, since there may be an occasional child who does have actual disease of the bladder or kidneys, it is well to have the doctor examine the child and his urine to be sure that is not the case.

Usually bed wetting in children past the age of three or four can be traced to some emotional disturbance. Sometimes the relationship is very direct and obvious, especially in the occasional bed wetter. A child may be dry most nights, but wet after a particularly exciting day such as a picnic, or after a change in surroundings when travelling or visiting. This type of wetting presents no very great problem.

More often the cause is not at all obvious, particularly with the chronic bed wetter who never has a dry night. This child is under continuing tension or emotional conflict which is at the root of his trouble. Just why psychological disturbances should be reflected in a disorder of the bladder muscle control is not at all understood. Perhaps it has something to do with the emphasis that has been placed on keeping dry. The child tries very hard to do what is expected of him. The harder he tries the tenser and more anxious he gets, consciously or not, and the tenser he gets the more difficult it is for him to gain control.

Sometimes bed wetting turns out to be an expression of a child's unconscious desire to go back to the easier days of early childhood when it was expected that he would be wet. This is seen particularly in the boy or girl who is under a lot of pressure to live up to a high standard set by his parents, and also in the child who, of his own accord, tries too hard to compete or to please. This excess pressure or competition may be in any part of his daily life from school work to play, or from table manners to chores. It need not have any direct connection with the actual bed wetting.

The unexpressed desire to return to early infancy is also present when the child has feelings of insecurity. Such feelings may have no foundation in actual fact, but that does not make them any less real to the child. He may be as emotionally upset from imaginary as from real fears. If a new baby arrives he may think he has lost his mother's love. If he sees and hears his parents quarrel often he may think that his home will be broken. There are many possible reasons why a child may feel insecure. And insecurity may be the emotional basis for bed wetting.

Parents of the chronic bed wetting child should, of course, be sure that there is no organic disease present. He should be seen by the doctor for a careful examination and urinalysis. If anything abnormal is found it should be corrected. Next the parents should try to put themselves in the child's place to see if they can find out what the possible sources of tension, or pressure, or of insecurity may be. Is too much expected of him in school because of his older brother's excellent record? Has there been too great emphasis on keeping dry? Does he get a reasonable display of affection and attention from his parents? Is he really leading a happy, contented life?

It sometimes helps with an older child to limit the amount of fluids he takes late in the afternoon and at supper time. But this must be done with his cooperation. It is hardly worth trying with the four-year-old because restriction will usually make him want to drink that much more. If not permitted to, he is apt to fuss and fret with resulting increase in the tension that should be eliminated.

Punishing, nagging and shaming a child never help to cure bed wetting. These things just increase the child's innter tension and his anxiety about staying dry, making it even harder for him. The child who wets his bed past the usual age feels badly enough about it without his parents increasing his emotional unrest. What he needs is kindliness and understanding.

Getting him up at night will help to keep the bed dry, and it does no harm toward an eventual cure so long as the child himself does not get too tense under the responsibility. For instance, one child may be given added self confidence if he uses his alarm clock to awaken him in the middle of the night so that by getting up he remains dry. Another child under the same conditions may get very worried and tense about hearing the alarm clock or about being already wet when it rings; he is made worse rather than better. Some children sleep too soundly for alarm clocks. For the latter few types of children, the parents had better take the initiative and the responsibility for the child's getting up. But he should be thoroughly awakened and allowed to go to the toilet by himself.

If the bed wetting continues in spite of all that parents can do to increase the child's sense of security and of self confidence, and to diminish the pressures and demands upon him, it may be that his emotional problem is a very deep-seated one. Should that be the case, professional help may be necessary to alleviate the condition and the doctor or a child guidance center should be consulted.

THUMB SUCKING

By Rowland L. Mindlin, M.D.

THUMB SUCKING is a natural thing for some young babies and should cause parents no concern. One of the basic instincts in a newborn infant is to suck, and, for many months, in doing so he derives considerable satisfaction and gratification as well as food. Just as some babies require more food than others to satisfy their physical needs, so do some require more sucking than others to satisfy this instinctive need. If those who require more do not get it while nursing, they will find some other occasion. Since a thumb is always available, and is a convenient size, it is not surprising that the baby who needs to suck will eventually get his thumb into his mouth and keep it there.

When a baby who has been satisfied begins to suck his thumb more than just once in a while, his mother should consider whether the sucking time at feedings can be increased. A breast-fed baby may be getting too much milk from both breasts and may do better given only one breast at a feeding, and allowed to suck as long as he likes. A bottle-fed baby may need new nipples for his bottles because the old ones have become too soft or the holes in them too large. If such simple measures do not eliminate the thumb sucking ,they will at least tend to diminish it. Restraints on the hands or elbows or aluminum mitts should not be used. They may prevent the actual thumb sucking, but they do not eliminate the basic need to suck, and they do positive harm by frustrating the baby in denying him the opportunity to satisfy that need. Weaning to a cup should not be started while the baby shows a great desire to suck.

The one or two-year-old child who sucks his thumb is a little different from the baby. He is usually tired or bored or unhappy. Thumb-sucking may be a sign it is time for his nap. Or he may have too little to do, the wrong kind of toy for his age, not enough companionship from his parents or from other children. Or he may have too much to do, too much stimulation from his toys or older children. For one reason or another he is seeking a certain kind of comfort and satisfaction which he gets from sucking his thumb. It is up to the parents to discover what is lacking in such a child's daily life and to supply it. A child who is still sucking his thumb past four years of age usually has a real problem in getting along with the world as it appears to him, a problem which may need a physician's help to discover and solve.

Restraints and bad tasting applications are no more desirable for the older child than for the infant. They sometimes make matters worse. Nor do constant reminding, nagging, punishing serve any good purpose. All of these things wrongly focus attention on the actual thumb sucking rather than on the conditions which have caused it. And to be permanently rid of the habit it is necessary to eliminate the cause.

There is very little danger that the amount of thumb sucking done by most children will affect the teeth or the shape of the jaws. Even in persistent cases it is usually given up before the child is five, the earliest that the permanent teeth come in. And any slight changes are likely to be taken care of naturally as the child grows older. But don't hesitate to seek professional help if the habit persists.

NAIL BITING

LIKE thumbsucking in an older child, nail biting is usually a symptom of some underlying difficulty. Any child may occasionally gnaw at a hangnail, a ragged cuticle, or a broken or nicked nail. But when the nails are well kept so that there is no local irritation, then the cause is something general. Usually it is under conditions of tension, of increased excitement, of overstimulation without the opportunity for the release of nervous energy that nail biting starts. Sitting in his seat during an exciting movie may provoke it in one child, awaiting his turn in some competition in another. Or it may be that the child's whole environment, rather than one specific event, is too much for him. Parents may expect too much of a child, and this can make him tense and anxious. Competition with older brothers and sisters or jealousy of younger members of the family are common causes of poor adjustment resulting in nail biting.

To cure nail biting ,as with thumb sucking, the underlying cause must be found. This is not always easy. There are a great many aspects to a child's life which may create emotional tension. But one thing is fairly certain. Nagging, punishing and shaming the child only increase the tension and make matters worse. It is better to ignore the act completely. Bitter medicine painted on does not help either. The nails should be kept short and smooth and the cuticle soft and well pushed back. Pride in the appearance of the nails is sometimes easily encouraged, especially in little girls who like to wear polish in imitation of mother. But the chief problem is to eliminate emotional tension.

MASTURBATION (AUTO-EROTICISM) *

MASTURBATION is found at every age level. The term is not correctly applied to children. (We understand by masturbation the conscious manipulation of the sexual organs for purposes of sexual pleasure.) There probably is some return pleasure even to a young child in the practice just as there is in thumb sucking, or he wouldn't continue it. Yet manifestly there is a great difference between childish and adult responses to such stimulation.

From the start, if we are to take care of the subject intelligently, we must set aside the idea that masturbation carries serious consequences. It is practically universal in childhood among boys and girls. Like thumb-sucking in infancy, its dangers have been greatly exaggerated and misrepresented. Like thumb sucking, too, it may arise spontaneously or as the result of situations in the environment. The job of the parents is to recognize contributing causes, remove them when possible, and without emotion co-operate with the boy or girl to bring about release from the habit.

We do not put the burden of the correction of masturbation upon the children. Instead we do everything possible to find the cause and eliminate it. It may be: a full bladder or rectum; a warm, close room; heavy bed covers, blankets, quilts; irritating clothing, tight, ill-fitting or over-warm; too little exercise with no physical fatigue

*From *New Patterns in Sex Teaching*, by FRANCES BRUCE STRAIN, Copyright. Used by permission. D. Appleton-Century Co., Inc., Publishers, New York, N. Y.

at night; a too early bedtime with too much sleep; imitation of others; curiosity; inner tension caused by insufficient freedom, too many commands, too much solitude, worry, anxiety, too much talk about sex, too much talk about masturbation, suspicions about masturbation, lack of sex knowledge.

To go about its correction, we must believe that masturbation does not result in serious impairment of health, either physical or mental. Having removed our own anxiety, we must remove any built-up fears and worries in the mind of the child we are trying to aid. Having no reason to worry about it, the child can dismiss it from his mind. With a free mind he is at liberty to become centered on something else. The something else may be a bit of good scientific introduction to human biology.

We must stop talking, stop nagging, stop watching, stop trying to assure ourselves the habit has left the child. Give him time and freedom to get a new start. Allow him plenty of freedom, plenty of outside interests, plenty of play with children of his own age. Avoid over-exactions, demand for too strict conformity to rules and regulations.

If sex subjects have been taboo let them work their way naturally to the surface.

There is no reason why we can't always meet this problem with success if we approach it properly. Children will co-operate with us, if we co-operate with them. If we believe in them, they will believe in themselves.

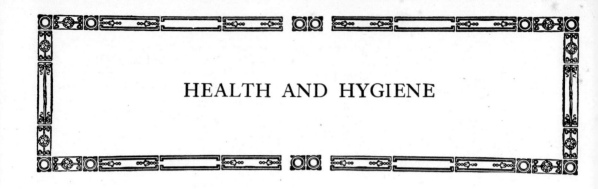

HEALTH AND HYGIENE

PRESERVING HEALTH*

THE foundation for health is laid in the first 6 years. The healthy child has the best chance of growing into the healthy adult. The child who lives a regular life and has good health habits— who eats well-planned meals at regular hours, gets plenty of sleep at regular hours, plays vigorously out of doors in the sunshine—has the best chance of laying a good foundation for future health.

Parents are learning more and more that it is wise to go to a doctor to keep their children well rather than to go to him only to cure illnesses that might have been prevented. Besides giving the child regular health examinations, the doctor will give him protection against certain diseases and will tell the parents what they can do to guard against other diseases. He will advise the parents as to the child's health habits.

The healthy child is active, alert, and interested in everything. His color is good and his eyes are bright. His skin is smooth, his muscles firm, and his body straight and strong. He is gaining in size and weight. He plays vigorously, creeping, running, jumping, climbing, according to his age. His mother may find him a strenuous companion, with his never-ending desire for activity. He is probably a bit noisy, getting pleasure out of banging and shouting and singing. But when it is bedtime he sleeps soundly. He is hungry at mealtimes and needs no coaxing to persuade him to eat. His bowels move regularly. His teeth are clean and in good condition. He does not have pains or aches.

The child who is "not really sick" is usually the same child as the one who is "not really well."

"But," says Tom's mother, "I can't think Tom is sick just because he is thin and pale. He takes after my mother. She was always thin, too."

"Mary has never seen a doctor in the 5 years since she was born, and I know she's not really sick," says her mother, "but she's always been nervous and fussy about her food."

Like many other parents, here are two mothers who are puzzled because their children do not measure up to the best standards of health, and yet they cannot believe them sick.

Too many people are satisfied with a child that is "not sick." Ill health is often excused or explained on some ground or other and considered unavoidable.

Nothing short of really healthy children should satisfy parents, for every child is entitled to the best health possible.

KEEPING THE CHILD WELL

To be healthy and learn to live a happy, useful life, a child should have—

The security of a family in which he shares in the love and affection of his parents and the family group.

A clean, well-ordered home and a room of his own, if possible.

Well-planned, adequate meals at regular times.

Plenty of sleep at night and an afternoon nap.

Enough clothes to keep him comfortable.

As much fresh air and sunshine as the weather permits.

Playmates and a place to play, indoors and out, and time to play.

A thorough examination by a physician at regular intervals.

A visit to the dentist every 6 months.

---

* From *Your Child from One to Six*, U. S. Children's Bureau Publication.

Inoculations against smallpox and dipththeria (and whooping cough and tetanus, too, if the doctor advises them).

THE DOCTOR

Soon after a baby is born, most parents select a doctor to look after the health of their child. He may be a pediatrician—a doctor who is a specialist in the care of children—or the family doctor. Or it may be that the mother has been taking her infant to a well-baby clinic (or child-health conference) and plans to continue doing so until the child is ready for school.

The things about a doctor—either a private practitioner or clinic doctor—that the mother wishes to know are—

Has he been well trained in medicine?

Has he had special training in the care of children?

Has he had experience in the care of children?

These are important things. It is, of course, also desirable to have a doctor who is kind and sympathetic and "has a way with children" besides being well trained and experienced.

Every child should be examined by a doctor at least every 4 to 6 months. At these regular examinations, if it is possible, the same doctor should see the child. In this way the child will get to know the doctor well and the doctor will be able to follow the child's progress much better. Then, too, the doctor will understand the child's condition better than if he has never seen him before.

The visit to the doctor's office, to the well-baby clinic (or the child-health conference) should be a pleasant experience. A child should be taught that the doctor is his friend. A mother who threatens to "call the doctor if you aren't good" makes a great mistake. It is next to impossible for a doctor to examine a screaming, struggling child properly. On the other hand, if a child has been told in advance that he is being taken to the doctor and what the doctor will do, he will usually be less apprehensive about the examination. He should be told that "Mummy will stay with you while the doctor looks at your eyes, teeth, arms, and legs, and listens to your heart with a big thing that looks a little like a telephone."

Prepared in this way, the child generally learns to look forward to his visit with the doctor with pleasure rather than dread.

At each visit the doctor will want to know what has happened to the child since the last visit. It will be helpful to him if the mother is prepared to answer such questions as the following:

Has the child been well? Has he had any diseases? Any accidents?

Has he been active and playful? Or listless and cross?

Whom does he play with?

Has he been eating well?

What has he been eating? Is he getting fish-liver oil or some other source of vitamin D? Is he getting orange juice or other some other source of vitamin C?

Do his bowels move regularly? How often?

Does he sleep well? How many hours?

Have any other members of the household been sick?

It will help the mother as well as the doctor if she has written down whatever she thinks she should tell him and any questions she wishes to ask, so that she will not forget them.

At the examination the child should be completely undressed. After being weighed and measured by the nurse or the doctor, the child will be examined by the doctor.

The doctor first of all will inspect the child carefully and take note of his state of development and nutrition, his skeletal structure, his posture, and the color and condition of his skin, lips, and nail beds. Then he will examine each part of the body separately, including the head, eyes, ears, nose, mouth, teeth, throat, neck, glands, chest, heart, lungs, abdomen, limbs and genitals. After this, the doctor will do any special tests he thinks necessary, such as an examination of the child's urine or his blood.

From this examination and from what the mother tells him, the doctor can judge whether or not the child is growing and developing as a healthy child should. The doctor will keep a record of his findings at each examination so that at later examinations he can compare them with previous ones. This helps him to judge how the child is progressing and to keep in mind any unusual conditions he wants to watch.

After the examination the doctor will talk to the mother about her child's health and will make suggestions about his care. He will recommend that the child be immunized against diphtheria and smallpox, if this has not already been done, and will advise her about immunizing and guarding against other diseases.

A mother should be sure, before she leaves the

doctor's office, that she understands just what he wants her to do. Since he is an expert in health, she will find it well worth her while to carry out his orders to the best of her ability.

THE DENTIST

Young children as well as older children should have their teeth examined regularly by a dentist. Many dentists nowadays make a specialty of caring for children's teeth. The "baby teeth" need home care and the dentist's care just as much as the permanent teeth do.

From the time a child is 2 years old he should be taken to the dentist every 6 months so that his teeth can be examined and cleaned and any small cavities filled or defects repaired.

A child who goes to the dentist from the age of 2 is not likely to develop fear of the dentist or of having his teeth fixed.

If the first few visits are only for inspection or cleaning, as is likely to be the case, the child will often actually enjoy going to the dentist.

If cavities or defective fissures appear in the child's teeth, they should be filled promptly.

If a small cavity or defective fissure is not filled, the tooth will decay still more, and the results of neglecting a child's teeth are familiar to us all—ugly, broken teeth and toothaches. The child with a sore tooth tries not to bite on it and may avoid coarse foods that need to be chewed or may chew on only one side of his mouth. If the cavity becomes very large, the root of the tooth is likely to become infected and the tooth may have to be pulled out. The shape of the jaw may suffer, from either lack of exercise or loss of teeth, and the permanent teeth that are being built may not have room enough to come in straight. If a child has a tooth in which decay has destroyed or exposed the nerve, he should be taken to the dentist often so that the dentist can give the necessary treatment that may save the tooth.

Perhaps the moth important teeth in childhood —and the most neglected—are the 6-year molars. These four permanent teeth, which come in sometime between the fifth and seventh birthdays, do not take the place of any baby teeth but come in directly behind them. For this reason they are often wrongly thought to be baby teeth. The 6-year molar is the sixth tooth from the front on each side; there are two in the upper jaw and two in the lower.

The 6-year molars are the first permanent teeth to come through. If they are lost, the other teeth are likely to come in crooked and the dental arch may be poorly formed. As soon as the chewing surface of each of these teeth has appeared, it should be examined by a dentist to see whether there are defective fissures. Great care should be taken of the 6-year molars.

BATHING

As the baby grows older and stronger he is not content to sit quietly in the bathtub; he wants to play and splash. He can then be given his bath in the large family tub. Bath time should be very attractive to him so that the bathing habit will become firmly established. It helps if the mother washes him quickly and thoroughly and then lets him play for a few minutes in the tub. Floating toys such as those made from celluloid or wood are enjoyed by the small child. He should not be left alone in the bathroom because his curiosity might lead him to try to turn on the faucets and he might get an unexpected shower of steaming hot water. Then too he might slip on the wet bottom of the tub and fall. He should not be allowed to stay in the tub long enough for the water to grow cold and chill his body.

Some time during the second year many children rebel at their baths. Often this is from having been frightened by slipping or actually falling in the tub, or from having a painful experience while being bathed, such as getting soap in the eyes or being put into water that was too hot. When the reason for the child's fear of the bath is obvious, it is usually enough to reassure him that "everything will be all right this time—I won't let you fall," (or whatever it is), repeating this many times while getting him and the tub ready. If in spite of this he still fights against being put into the tub it is much better to skip the bath entirely. Sometimes it is impossible to tell what it is that has made the child afraid. When this is the case, and also when the simple reassurance tried before does not work, it is best not even to try to give him a tub bath for a while but to keep him clean with sponge baths until he is ready to go back into the tub. That day will come sooner if no great issue is made over the child's behavior and if he is not forced to the tub before he is willing. When bathing is resumed, he should start again in a very small amount of water, be taken out, dried, and taken out of the bathroom before the water goes down the drain.

About the time the child reaches the school age, he has a strong desire to bathe himself. This desire should be encouraged. His mother will, of course, have to wash the back of his neck and to guide him so that he does a thorough job on the other parts of his body. As he reaches the teen age he should prepare the water for his bath and take it without assistance, but mother's watchful eye will quickly detect any overlooked spots and send him back for more thorough cleansing.

Children should be taught the great importance of clean hands. Many disease germs are undoubtedly carried to the nose and the mouth by the hands. To prevent this the hands should be washed immediately after each visit to the toilet, before eating, and before handling foodstuffs of any kind, and particularly after using the handkerchief. Because clean hands are so important it should be made easy to keep them clean by having basins, towels, cloths, brushes, and water easy of access. The table or washstand should be low enough so that a child can wash his hands without wetting his clothing. A box or stool under the washstand will save a great deal of trouble.

THE CHILD'S TEETH*

THE TEETH begin to develop about 6 months before birth and keep on developing during the entire period of childhood. Nearly all the teeth of the first set—the deciduous, or "milk," teeth—are already partly or wholly hardened at birth. As the baby grows, the teeth grow also, and some teeth begin to cut through the gums at about the sixth to the eighth month of life. From then on, new teeth appear at intervals until the baby is about 2½ years old, when, as a rule, all the 20 teeth of the first set have come through.

By the end of the first year many babies have six front teeth, although some healthy babies have only two. If a year-old baby has no teeth at all, the doctor should be consulted. The diet may be at fault, or some disease may be slowing the child's growth; racial and family traits, too, may account for delayed teething.

There is a good deal of difference in the age at which the various teeth come through the gums, but the order in which they come is the same for almost all children. First the two lower front teeth appear, then after a time, the four upper front teeth. After this, it is usually some months before more teeth come through. Then two more lower teeth appear in the front of the mouth. In a few months two teeth appear in the lower jaw—one on each side—near the back; then two in the upper jaw, opposite these.

Later four "eye teeth" come through—two upper and two lower. After awhile the four back molars come through, and then the temporary set of teeth is complete.

While a tooth is coming through the gum, the child may be irritable or fretful and may not eat well, but teeth alone rarely accounts for illness. An illness should not be attributed to teething until all other possible causes, such as a cold, an abscess in the ear, and other diseases have been ruled out by the doctor.

If the child is to have good permanent teeth—straight, strong and regular, with the upper and lower sets meeting to form a good chewing machine—his baby teeth must be kept in good condition until the permanent ones are ready to come in. The permanent teeth come in from the sixth to the twelfth year, and until then the child needs his baby teeth to chew his food and to hold the jaws in shape so that the permanent teeth will have plenty of room. If the baby teeth are to be kept in good condition as long as they are needed, they must be built of good material and they must be taken care of properly at home and by a dentist. Every effort should be made to save the baby teeth, but they should not be retained too long, for when they are, serious defects often develop in the permanent teeth.

The material of which the teeth are built depends largely upon the nourishment of the body.

* From *Your Child from One to Six*, U. S. Children's Bureau Publication.

As the formation of the temporary teeth begins to take place to a large extent before birth, the mother is the child's only source of nourishment while these teeth are being built; and, if during this time she does not receive enough outdoor sunshine and enough of the foods that supply the elements for tooth building, her own teeth may suffer and the baby's teeth may be built of poor material.

Foods that supply the elements needed for tooth building are milk, fish-liver oil, fruit—especially oranges—green leafy vegetables, raw vegetables, and egg yolk. These foods not only should be part of the diet of the mother during pregnancy and the nursing period but should be in the diet of the child also.

In preventing decay of the teeth, diet is of great importance. The same foods that build strong teeth will help greatly to prevent decay. Too much sugar and other sweets in the diet bring about conditions that may have a bad effect on the teeth. Eating too much sugar may make the child neglect other important foods.

The structure of the permanent teeth may be influenced by the child's health during the years in which they are forming, especially the first 2 years; any serious disease may cause defects in the permanent teeth. Rickets, for instance, may damage the permanent teeth that are in process of formation at this time (the 6-year molars and a number of the front teeth). Fish-liver oil and sun baths are needed for tooth building, especially during the first 2 years, the period when a child is most likely to get rickets.

CARE OF THE EYES

IMMEDIATELY after every baby is born the doctor or his assistant will sponge off the eyelids and put a couple of drops of a liquid in each eye. This is to prevent a serious infection of the newborn's eyes called "ophthalmia neonatorium" which used to cause about half of the cases of blindness in children and nearly ten per cent of the blindness of adults. Now it is being eliminated as a cause of blindness. The Credé method, which most doctors follow today, of instilling one per cent silver nitrate in the eyes at birth has been largely responsible for this. So important is this procedure that it has been made obligatory by law in many states.

During the first week of life any discharge from the baby's eyes must be called promptly to the doctor's attention. Most often it will be from chemical irritation by the silver nitrate originally used; sometimes it may be a mild infection by a germ or filterable virus that can easily be treated; and occasionally it may be the dreaded "ophthalmia neonatorum" which must be considered very dangerous and controlled with the most modern methods. The doctor will determine which and treat the baby accordingly.

As long as the eyes are healthy they need no special care. The lids can be washed with warm water and a soft cloth at bath time. The eyeball itself is constantly bathed by tears even when the baby is not crying, so no irrigations or drops should be used. If the lashes seem scaly, a little vaseline can be applied to the edges of the eyelids once a day for a few days. Very bright light should be avoided, especially in the first few months before the baby has learned how to turn his head away. This does not mean that bright lights for a very short time, or even flash bulbs for a few pictures can not be used. But it does mean that the baby should not be left with his face to the sun, and that the usual light in the nursery should not be glaring.

Usually when something is wrong with the eyes it is obvious that there is trouble. Either the lids are swollen or stuck together from a discharge, or the white part becomes pink or red, or there is pain, or objects appear blurred, or there is a squint. For any of these things the doctor should be consulted. The eye is a very delicate organ. Neglect of the early stages of some eye disorders may lead to serious permanent damage to vision.

Sometimes poor sight may not be noticed by parents. But a child who holds his books closer than usual, who cocks his head to one side to examine something minutely, who simply begins to do poorly in school, or to have headaches for no apparent reason should be seen by an oculist just as much as the child with obviously crossed eye. It may well be that both such type of children have errors in refraction that glasses or exercises can correct. Most babies appear to be cross-eyed at one time or another but as they develop they lose this tendency if the eyes are normal. If cross-eyedness persists after a year and a half, an effort should be made to correct it. Without treatment, the eye the child does not use as much will gradually lose part or all of its vision. Once gone, this vision cannot be restored. Treated soon enough, sight may be saved. This is truly a situation where an ounce of prevention is worth a pound of cure.

THE USE OF GLASSES

ORDINARILY, there is a great indisposition to wear glasses; a prejudice that is born and fostered of ignorance. Few misapprehensions are more foolish, for the proper adjustment of lenses to the improperly refracting eye is one of the greatest boons to humanity. Where glasses are needed, they should be worn, and a failure to do so usually produces much unnecessary suffering to the individual.

To those who wear glasses, a few words as to their proper use may not be inappropriate. They should not be laid carelessly on tables or stands. They should be kept clean. This may be done by rubbing them gently with a clean and soft cloth. Glasses should not be worn indefinitely. They should be changed or repaired as they become worn, nicked, cracked, and out of shape.

An important point in obtaining glasses is not only to get the lenses that have been ordered after a careful examination by a competent physician, but also to see that the frames are correctly adjusted by a competent optician. This is necessary, as there are so many varieties of facial features which require genuine skill and judgment to harmonize with lenses and frames that the proper fitting of the spectacles and glasses requires the combined skill of both the physician and the optician, and the one will be sadly crippled without the intelligent aid and co-operation of the other.

LIGHT

ONE OF the most important questions pertinent to the care of eyes is that of light.

The best light is the diffuse natural light of day, and the best artificial light is that which most nearly approaches daylight. Even daylight may be abused, or, at least, it may be improperly used, for care must be taken that it reaches the object gazed at in the right manner. The light should come from the left side, so that it may be ample and yet not shine directly in the face, and so that

it may strike the paper during the act of writing, without obstruction from the hand.

AVOIDING EYE-STRAIN

A POSSIBLE source of eye-strain is reading while the body is resting in a recumbent position. Especially is this so during convalescence following a severe illness, when the temptation is strong, but the general and ocular systems are weak and unable to stand even a limited amount of work. Even in health, owing to the fact that under such circumstances it is practically impossible to hold a book in a favorable position where the muscles of the eye will not undergo excessive strain in accommodating themselves to the abnormal posture, such a practice is injurious.*

It must never be forgotten that the eye is a delicate and exceedingly complex organ, and that, while it is long-suffering, its endurance has a limit, which, if pressed too far, will rebel and precipitate the most direful consequences. Therefore, the eye should be treated with judgment and forbearance, and not be made to perform more than a fair day's work. Such a resolution would suggest occasionally resting the eyes by looking from time to time at distant objects through a window, or by changing occupations as often as may be.

It is wise to use caution in passing suddenly from a very dark to a very light room, and to avoid looking long at any bright object.

The general system has much to do with the health of the eye. Anything that conduces to health and vigor will assist in maintaining ocular strength and vitality. Let him, therefore, who wishes to keep his eyes in a strong and useful condition, see that his digestive and eliminative functons are properly conducted; that his body is not poisoned with drugs or stimulants; that he takes an abundance of outdoor exercise; that he has plenty of refreshing sleep, and that he occasionally rests his mind and body by a relaxing vacation. In short, let him be sure that he is following sensible rules of hygiene, for by so doing not only his general health but the usefulness of his eyes will be best maintained.

*The eyes are often sensitive after illness, particularly after measles and scarlet fever, and the mother must take care that they are not used too soon or too long at a time. Care at such times, even at the cost of some trouble in providing entertainment which avoids over-use of the eyes, should not be weighed against the harm that may result from overstrain.

The child should not be allowed to form the habit of rubbing the eyes. A teaspoonful of boric acid dissolved in a pint of water is an excellent eyewash, and a child who persistently rubs his eyes may need to have them washed every day. Such treatment will doubtless do much to prevent styes and crusts on the edges of the lids, to allay inflammation, and often to avert more serious trouble. Use bits of absorbent cotton for cleaning the eyes—a fresh piece for each eye—and destroy them immediately.

CARE OF THE EARS

HEALTHY ears require little or no care beyond keeping the external portion clean. No hard article of any sort should be introduced into the ear.

Children sometimes push beads or other objects into the ears. Do not try to remove any foreign body from the ear with a wire or anything pointed. If it does not fall out when the ear is inclined downward and the head shaken, take the child to a doctor.

Do not try to swab or dig out earwax. Careful bathing each day will keep the ear passage free from such accumulations. If enough has formed to block the passage, take the child to a physician.

Do not let the child stand near a cannon or a giant firecracker which is about to explode.

Do not strike him on the ear, and teach him that he must never hit any one else there.

Never insert medicine or douches in the ears except under your physician's advice and direction.

Never pull the lobe of the ear.

DO YOUR EARS HEAR?*

By Harold Hays

MOST DEAFNESS STARTS IN CHILDHOOD

THE MAJORITY of cases of deafness start in childhood and the majority can be arrested at that time. This means that there are some cases that cannot be improved or cured. No one can do anything for a deaf-mute. Seldom can anything be done for the child who becomes deaf as the result of syphilis or meningitis. Often very little can be done for the ears of the child who has had a severe mastoid operation. But a great deal can be done for the child who has become deaf as the result of one of the contagious diseases, from repeated colds in the head, from repeated ear-aches or from blowing his nose improperly.

TRY THESE TESTS ON YOUR CHILD

THE chief tests to be used are the natural voice, the whisper test, and the watch test.

1. *The Voice Test.*—The ear not to be examined is closed off with the finger. The examiner stands at least twenty feet away in a quiet room. In a natural voice, he states numbers which he asks the child to repeat. The normal ear should hear the voice at twenty feet. The other ear is then tested in the same way.

2. *The Whisper Test.*—The examiner should stand at least ten feet away. He then whispers numbers or words, gradually approaching the child. The whispered voice should be heard six feet away without any difficulty.

*Reprinted from *Hygeia* by permission.

3. *The Watch Test.*—Any loud-ticking watch will do for the test. One should start at least ten feet from the child and gradually approach. The watch should be heard distinctly at six feet.

Of course it is almost impossible to make these tests accurately in very young children and sometimes in older ones. But a great deal can be gained from ordinary conversation. If you once obtain the confidence of the child, it is seldom that you cannot ascertain whether there is any appreciable degree of deafness.

If one finds that a child is deaf, what can be done to improve the hearing defect? This will depend on the degree of deafness and the pathological condition which is present in the ear. Moreover, it will depend on the factors which may, sometimes very remotely, cause the trouble.

The child may be deaf from a stoppage of the tube going into the ear from the throat (the Eustachian tube) because of the presence of diseased tonsils and adenoids. To improve the ear condition, the tonsils and adenoids must be removed. Otologists feel that there will be far less deafness in the future because tonsils and adenoids are being so well removed nowadays.

The child may have a running ear. This discharge from the ear must be arrested in some way. The treatment will vary considerably according to the individual case.

Or the child may be blowing his nose like a trumpet and forcing too much air into the ears with the result that the drums are blown out of position. In blowing the nose, the handkerchief should be held loosely below it or one nostril should be held at a time.

Aside from these forms of treatment, the ear specialist will be able to employ certain forms of treatment adapted to the individual case. In any event, one must consider that no treatment is disastrous, that inefficient treatment is useless, and that worth-while results can be obtained in many cases, provided there is the proper co-operation between the patient and the specialist.

THREE SUGGESTIONS FOR THE DEAF

LIP-READING is the salvation of the deaf. In the first place it stimulates the individual to a greater effort to understand, and therefore stimulates the ear mechanism. But one must remember that lip-reading is a new language and that it may take years to master it. But it also takes a long time for anyone to master the German and the French languages.

Once the art of lip-reading is cultivated, a patient's whole life is changed. He understands!

I know of deafened soldiers who have mastered the art of lip-reading in three months of intensive study and I know of one case in which the family did not learn for months that the soldier was deaf.

The wearing of a hearing device goes against the grain of the majority of deaf people. They are so afraid they will be found out—that they look conspicuous. But the only people they fool are themselves and today the wearing of hearing devices is so common that no one ever notices the person who wears one.

But the greatest salvation of the deaf is in joining one of the various leagues for the hard of hearing. The leagues have social service agencies, they have employment bureaus, they have classes in lip-reading, they indulge in suitable social activities, but better than all this is the propaganda they are spreading that deafness must be prevented and that every teacher, every parent, every physician must be made aware of this very important fact.

CARE OF THE CHILD'S HAIR

THE SCALP should have the same care that the rest of the skin requires. It should be washed sufficiently often to keep it clean and active, but not often enough to remove all the natural oil. When the child has short hair, the head may be washed two or three times a week if necessary.

The shampoo is done most conveniently at hot-bath time while the child is in the tub. Use either a jelly made of plain mild soap such as castile, dissolved in hot water and cooled, or surgeon's liquid soap, or some of father's shaving cream. First wet the hair and then rub well into the scalp some of the jellied soap, the liquid soap, or the cream, using great care that the finger-nails do not scratch the skin. Then attach the bath spray and regulate the temperature of the water through it so that it will be neither too hot nor too cold. Give the child a dry small towel or wash cloth to hold over his eyes. Then with his head tipped back over your arm so that the water runs away from his face, rinse the soap from the hair. Do this rinsing very thoroughly. The child's hair should be rubbed nearly dry with towels and, if it is

long, it should be allowed to hang loose for a time.

If the child is unfortunate enough to come into contact with some one who has head lice, and he acquires some in his own hair, it is a simple matter to get rid of the lice. Obtain from the druggist an eight-ounce mixture of alcohol and glycerine in equal parts with a little rose-water. The alcohol will kill the living lice and remove the nits, or eggs, from the hair; the glycerine will keep the alcohol from injuring the hair. The rose-water is merely to make the mixture smell better. Saturate the hair with the mixture and then comb it with a fine comb.

The selection of the comb and the brush is important. The comb should have the teeth set fairly wide apart, with the points dull and the edges rounded so that the hair cannot be caught and pulled out or broken off. The brush for the hair should have moderately stiff bristles, and the back should be made of material which will not be injured by hot water. Both brush and comb should be kept scrupulously clean. A good rule is to wash both as often as you wash your hair.

THE CARE OF THE NOSE AND THROAT

THE AIR we breathe is not fit to enter the lungs directly, and so nature has provided a complicated mechanism to prepare it properly. The nose, not the mouth, is the channel by which the air should find its entrance into the body. There is a screen of hairs at the entrance of each nostril moistened by the fluid which comes down into the nose from the eyes, through the nasal duct. The entire structure of the nose is lined with mucus membrane, moist and sticky with the mucus which it prepares. The air which comes into the nose with each breath must pass over these hairs, which catch any large particles that may be floating in it, and then over the moist mucus membrane, which will catch smaller particles.

On the inner side of each nostril are also three curious, scroll-shaped, fragile bones, the turbinates. Through their grooved passages the air is conveyed for further purification. Air in passing through this apparatus is filtered, warmed and humidified, and thus made ready for entrance into the lungs. Below and above the eye the so-called nasal accessory sinuses communicating with the nostrils probably have more or less to do with the preparation of the air supply.

Where the nose ends internally and the pharynx or throat begins is an enlargement narrowing the air passage. This is adenoid tissue. These adenoids, if they become enlarged, not only may interfere with and obstruct breathing through the nose, but they may also block the opening to the Eustachian tube which leads from the throat to the ears, thus causing possible middle ear disease and deafness.

Carefully though the air which enters the body is thus filtered and prepared, it is yet a fact that many of the diseases from which people, and especially children, suffer are conveyed by germs through this air apparatus. How much greater, then, is the danger when the air is inhaled through the mouth which has none of this mechanism for purifying it. Mouth breathing may be a serious trouble. It necessarily means dryness of the mucus membranes of the mouth and throat with much discomfort even when there is no acute disease. Children who are mouth breathers should be examined to see if they have any nasal obstructons which can be relieved.

The nose should be left alone as much as possible. Picking should be avoided. It is a bad habit and may have bad consequences. When dried mucus and dust accumulate, the nose can usually be cleared by blowing. Compress one nostril and blow into the handkerchief, and then repeat on the other side. If the dried mucus and dust does not come away with this procedure, a dab of vaseline or mineral oil can be introduced into each nostril, but only as far as the little finger will reach. This will serve to soften up the material.

A healthy throat and tonsils need have no protective gargles or other treatments. Even enlarged tonsils do not necessarily have to be removed if they are not diseased. But it is essential to remove them if they are.

CHILD POSTURE

By MILTON I. LEVINE, M.D.

ANY PERSON following a large group of children and studying them from a physical as well as an emotional point of view is certain to come to definite conclusions regarding the inter-relationship of these two factors. In the study of posture sufficient evidence has been obtained to show that improvement in posture and muscle tone is associated with an increase in alertness and a sense of well being. Professor William James, the psychologist, wrote in 1899 that he was convinced "that erect posture keeps up the spirits and tends to banish fear, despondency, and depressing thoughts; that bodily postures definitely influence the emotions."

The converse is also true. There is no question but that in a great many cases the posture of an individual is dependent largely upon his emotional state. A child who is happy, alert, and interested usually reflects it in his good muscle tone and fine body carriage. On the other hand, the disinterested, dissatisfied child, or one emotionally upset usually exhibits a poor posture and develops a poor degree of muscle tone.

Failure to recognize this relationship has undoubtedly led to a great deal of unnecessary and even detrimental procedure with many children and adults as well. Only too often is the

---

* Reprinted by permission from *Child Study Magazine*, February, 1937.

droop-shouldered child forced to wear braces, to take formalized exercises, or, worse still, to undergo constant criticism and nagging, when a little study and correction of unfortunate environmental factors would produce quicker and far greater therapeutic results.

We have frequently had the opportunity to watch children gradually adjusting themselves after having been unhappy in their home or school environment. There were children whose parents were overanxious and whose overanxiety was reflected in their children; children who for the time being felt themselves unwanted by their classmates; some who felt themselves unable to cope with their companions in the natural competition of daily life. A defeated child, or for that matter any defeated individual regardless of age, will rarely carry himself erect. But, let the same individual experience the thrill of accomplishment and the satisfaction of being looked up to by his fellow men—and an almost incredible improvement occurs in posture and carriage.

What is the most correct method of judging posture? Unfortunately, all standards are based upon the figure of the child standing still and erect. This method is grossly inaccurate, for one sees numerous children who have poor postures in standing, especially when lacking in interest—but who, in motion in some game of activity that they enjoy, become beautifully coordinated and assume excellent postures. A motion picture study of children enjoying rhythms or some game will bring this point out clearly, especially when compared with stills taken of the same children attempting to "stand up straight."

It is not to be inferred, from what has been said, that all cases of poor posture are based upon emotional difficulties. Poor posture is not infrequently due to fatigue, and then, of course, one occasionally finds children suffering from congenital physical anomlaies such as variations in the number and shape of the vertebrae and ribs, inequality in length of limbs, dislocation of hips, lack of development of certain bones in the extremities, etc.; and there are a certain number of poor postures which are the end result of disease processes, such as rickets, poliomyelitis, and tuberculosis.

Muscular fatigue as the cause of poor posture may be due to a number of factors. A child may not get sufficient rest to compensate for his degree of activity. He may go to sleep too late, or arise too early. He may be straining to keep up with children physically more capable. Under any of these circumstances, the muscles fatigue, and we find the typical picture of drooping shoulders, prominent abdomen, and occasionally low arches. Lack of sufficient physical exercise will often bring about a weakening of the muscles with a similar resultant posture. Muscular weakness is also found as the result of a general run down condition associated with certain toxic diseases (such as the infectious diseases, sinusitis, pneumonia), and any condition which forces the child to remain in bed for long periods of time.

What is good posture? Throwing the shoulders back and the chest up, drawing the abdomen in, and pulling in the chin is the common idea of good posture. It is a superficial picture, however. Really good posture implies a naturally relaxed and well coordinated body with a proper balance of all muscles and is best observed when the child is unconscious of the purpose of the observation, and especially while making active use of these muscles.

One should also remember that there are various types of body build among children, and that excellence of posture in these various types is not to be measured by any single standard. The slender, long-boned, usually high-strung child has much greater difficulty coordinating and developing a good posture than the broad-muscled, stocky, placid child.

And in this respect it is frequently forgotten that heredity plays a most important part in body build, a factor neglected in the usual standards for weight and height. If one examines both parents of a child he will often find the same postural defects that the child exhibits, especially when they are related to a particular type of body build. Bowing of legs, incurving of the back, protrusion of the abdomen ,and flatness of the feet may be among such defects.

Before discussing treatment, it should be pointed out that many temporary postural defects accompany physical development and clear up normally as long as a child gets sufficient compensation. Practically all children of two years of age or younger have flat feet. These disappear with continued use of the feet and with the development of increased muscle tone. Bow legs of early childhood, even those resulting from rickets, will usually straighten out as the child grows older if proper food is given and hygienic measures followed. The protruding abdomen, typical of the so-called infantile posture, almost always disappears with improvement in general muscle tone.

In planning the treatment of any child with a postural defect it is essential that the cause of the deftc be understood. Is it due to a structural defect, a congenital anomaly, or the end result of some disease; is it due to some habit, such as constantly carrying things in one hand, or sitting on one foot; or is it due to poor muscle tone?

If it happens to be the latter, a study should be made of the child's environment and habits, and every attempt made to obtain optimal conditions—always bearing in mind that the unhappy child and the fatigued child is more than likely to reflect these conditions in his carriage.

In cases where children need extra rest it is far preferable, from an emotional standpoint, that this be obtained at home after school— so as not to make the child appear physically inferior before his schoolmates. Children of over-anxious parents suffer greatly from this embarrassment, especially when they are kept out of physical activities at too frequent intervals. They will at times compensate in intellectual ways, believing that they will never be able to reach the physical attainments of the other children.

If exercises are necessary to correct a postural defect it is desirable that they be given in an informal way such as through games and rhythmic exercises. For instance, to develop the muscle tone of the upper extremities baseball batting, ball throwing, chopping trees, and swinging a sledge hammer are enjoyable and desirable aids in treatment. Well-regulated rhythmic exercises not only can improve coordination but if properly given can build up the muscle tone in almost every part of the body.

In the correction of specific defects much more can be accomplished if a prescribed exercise is presented in an interesting manner. For example, for flat feet the picking up of marbles with the toes is greatly enjoyed by all children; for curvature of the spine, a chinning bar hung in the doorway will prove a valuable aid; for knock-knees bicycle riding should be encouraged, whereas roller-skating should be discouraged. For general muscle and body development, swimming is unsurpassed as an ideal combination of exercise and enjoyment. For bodily poise, grace, and coordination folk dancing is ideally adapted.

In 1923 and 1924, a study was made of 1,708 elementary school children in Chelsea, Massachusetts, under the auspices of the United States Department of Labor. Of these children 961 were given postural training and 747 received the ordinary gymnastic exercises. The two groups were similar at the outset in respect to age, sex, nationality, and posture grade.

Among the valuable findings recorded were the facts that improvement in body mechanics was also associated with improvement in school work; that the rate of absence due to personal illness decreased in children who received posture training until it was considerably lower than that of untrained children; and that the improvement in deportment and scholarship was greater among the trained children than among the untrained.

It is evident, therefore, that the posture of a child and his emotional state are closely related. In a great many cases an unhappy emotional condition is the etiological factor behind a poor posture, while in many other cases poor posture due to muscular fatigue or some organic defect causes a poor emotional state.

It is our duty, therefore, to study a child from all aspects, physical as well as environmental, and if it is necessary to treat the child, to do so in as enjoyable and unobtrusive a manner as is possible.

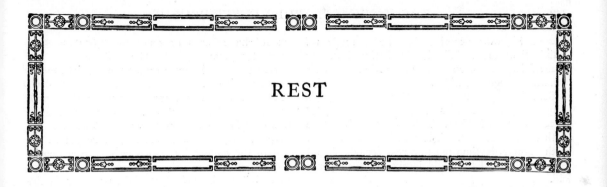

REST

SLEEP

SLEEP REQUIRED BY THE AVERAGE YOUNG CHILD

(Including daytime sleep)

At birth	At 6 months	At 1 year	2-5 years
20-22 hours	16-18 hours	14-16 hours	13-15 hours

SLEEP REQUIRED BY THE AVERAGE OLDER CHILD

6-7 years	8-10 years	11-12 years
12 hours	11 hours	10-11 hours

SLEEP REQUIRED BY THE AVERAGE YOUTH

13-15 years	16-18 years
10-12 hours	9-10 hours

THE faster a child is growing, the more sleep he needs. Adults need less sleep than children because they have stopped growing. A baby less than a year old grows very fast and sleeps most of the time. When he gets a little older he does not grow so fast and does not need so much sleep. After about a dozen years, when the child enters the adolescent stage, growth speeds up again, and sometimes this older boy or girl needs even more sleep than the child a year or two younger. Many parents do not know this and permit the older children to stay up later than the younger ones. As a result boys and girls 13 to 15 are often listless and inert. They may be sleepy and tired most of the time, and unable to concentrate on their lessons.

Steady loss of sleep is bad for a child's mental and physical development. A full allowance of unbroken hours of restful sleep helps normal bodily growth and encourages alert mentality; so be sure that your child is getting all the sleep he needs. But there are some who all through infancy and childhood seem to require less sleep than the average. These are the children who are up playing long before anyone else in the family awakens in the morning, or who do not go to sleep for an hour or more after an early bed time. Yet they are happy and active during the day. They grow and develop normally. They do well in school. They simply do not need so much sleep and there is no way to make them get it, nor is there any reason to.

Sleeping at regular hours is a habit that you should start for a new baby. If you accustom your child to a regular bedtime from infancy you not only help his chances for normal development of body and mind but also simplify your own problems of child management, for, as years pass, so long as he remains happy, secure, and well-adjusted, your child will continue to go quietly, unquestioningly to bed.

The habit of an unbroken night's sleep, from 6 or 7 p.m. to 6 or 7 a.m., can be started when the baby finally begins to sleep through his night feeding. This may be any time from the third to the eighth month. It is better to let the baby do this of his own accord, when he is ready to, rather than to "train" him by letting him cry himself back to sleep from exhaustion when he awakens hungry at night.

Sometimes you may want to change a baby's diaper or take an older child to the toilet after a few hours of sleep. This will not interfere with the night's rest. A twelve hour night sleep with regular daytime naps or rest periods should be the rule until the child is six or seven years old.

The early bedtime habit—six o'clock during infancy and not later than seven throughout early childhood—should seldom be broken. But an occasional extra half hour or hour as a special treat does no harm.

Do not keep the child up to entertain visitors, and do not allow him to stay up because he begs too. It is unwise to give in to a whining child, and permitting him to lose sleep in this way leads to a vicious circle: Loss of sleep makes him irritable and overactive, and overactivity makes him restless and wakeful, so that on following evenings it becomes harder and harder to get him to go to bed. On the other hand, a child who goes to bed tranquilly is likely to sleep well and to be happy and cheerful the next day. Clashes between parent and child are often due to the fact that the child is worn out from lack of sleep.

Your child's night rest depends largely upon how he has spent the day. An exciting day, without a nap, may leave a child literally too tired to sleep. The end of the day especially should be free from excitement. The half hour before bedtime should be devoted to quiet pleasures, without romping or exciting games and stories, or any other activities that are stimulating.

Proper rest in the daytime helps to give the child a good night's sleep. The young baby gets plenty of day and night sleep. As he grows older his waking hours are longer, and the mother should see that his main sleep is at night, and that he also gets two daytime naps, usually a long one in the morning and a short one in the early afternoon. As a rule, by the time a child is two years old he needs only one nap in the daytime— a long one, at whatever time of day is most convenient for the mother: such as 10 or 11 in the morning or after the midday meal. In winter the forenoon hour would seem best so that the child may have the midday hours for play in the sun. The nap should not last until too late in the afternoon, or it may keep the child from sleeping at night. Even if the child does not sleep he should spend the nap time in bed, undressed. He

should have books or quiet toys so that he is content to stay in bed. The daily nap or rest period should be kept up until the child is six or seven years old.

Most babies can learn to take daytime naps outdoors in the sunshine if their eyes are shaded and care is taken that the skin is not burned. On very hot days the baby should not be put in the sun in the middle hours of the day. Sleeping in the sun gives the baby the benefit of the sun's rays, but if the bright sunlight or noise in the yard keeps him awake he had better take his naps on the porch or in the house. If the baby's long nap is taken in the shade the day's program must be arranged so that he will get his sun baths when he is awake. A child past the second year should take his nap in his own bed.

If your child has the habit of staying up late it will be hard to break it, but you can do it. Ask yourself first why the child does not want to go to bed. Has bed-time pleasant associations for the child? If you put him to bed as a punishment when he is naughty, he will feel that there is something unpleasant about going to bed. If you have done this in the past it will be hard to change this idea, but you can at least give up using bed as a punishment. Do not let him feel that he is missing pleasure by going to bed. Go into his room with him and stay till he is tucked in. Then leave him alone, but do not seem in a hurry to get away. If the child is afraid of the dark, a dim light in his room does no harm. Do not expect him to sleep with his room completely dark until he has learned not to be afraid. A little light from a street lamp, or from the hall through a partly closed door, not shining in his eyes, may help. If he has other fears that make him dislike being in his room alone, stay with him and help him to conquer them.

Does the child get his daytime nap regularly? If not he may be wakeful at bedtime.

Do you always put the child to bed at a regular hour? If not, begin tonight to put him to bed at the hour that you have decided on, and make no exceptions. Treat bedtime in a matter-of-fact way; do not argue about it. Give the child warning about five minutes before bedtime, so that he can come to a stopping place in what he is doing. Do not announce bedtime too suddenly.

Do both parents try to make the half hour before the child's bedtime a time of quiet play, without exciting games or stories? Active play during the day makes children pleasantly tired, but just before bedtime it makes them wide awake so that sleep is difficult for them.

Are you firm about the child's staying in bed quietly after you leave him? If he keeps calling to you and asking for a drink of water or anything else that will get your attention, teach him that this will not work.

See that all necessities are attended to before the child finally is tucked into bed; then ignore all calls from him, unless you think there is a real emergency.

If your child goes to bed readily but stays awake or sleeps fitfull, find out the cause of his poor sleep.

Has he had enough active play during the day to tire his muscles?

Is his physical condition good? Ask the doctor about this. Enlarged or diseased adenoids or tonsils or other defects may keep a child from sleeping well.

Does the child have a bed to himself? Children in bed together may stay awake to play. Any bed that is large enough to hold two children can be replaced by two cots in which they can sleep separately. For many reasons it is important that every child should sleep alone. For a baby it is easy to make a clothes basket or a large box into a comfortable bed.

Is the room at a comfortable temperature (45° to 50° F. in winter, and as cool as possible in summer), with plenty of fresh air from open windows?

Is the bed comfortable? The spring and the mattress should be firm and flat, not sagging in the middle. If a pillow is used it should be thin and not too soft. The sheets should be large, so that the edges will stay tucked in all night; the blankets light in weight and wide enough to keep out drafts. For a child who kicks off the covers try a sleeping bag.

Are the child's nightclothes comfortable? Are they loose, so that they do not bind the child anywhere? Of course the child should be entirely undressed before his nightclothes are put on.

Is the child's supper satisfying and easily digestible, so that his sleep will not be disturbed by hunger or indigestion? Keep him from drinking much liquid at night: a full bladder may make him wakeful.

Do you try to prevent loud or sudden noises from reaching the child's room? The house need not be hushed at night, and you should train your child to sleep through ordinary talking or other minor disturbances, but his bedroom should be as far as possible from the radio. Early-morning noises should be prevented as much as possible, for sleep in the early morning is lighter than the first sleep at night.

And finally, is he a happy, well-adjusted child? Undue tensions and pressures, feelings of insecurity, unexpressed jealousies and rages may disturb his sleep just as much as a physical discomfort or a loud noise. Try to put yourself in the child's place and see if he is getting the love and affection he needs. The happy child does not usually have any long-continued disturbances of sleep.

FATIGUE AND NAUGHTINESS

MORE children get spanked for being tired than for any other one reason. And yet fatigue is certainly not a sin. It is, rather, a sign that the child needs rest.

The physical signs are not hard to detect: in babies, clenched fists held close to sleepy eyes and an irritated cry; in other children, tensity of the muscles, restless walking around, irritability, and the mood of discouragement.

With young people fatigue may be discovered not so much by symptoms as by its effects.

Fatigue interferes with the will to accomplish any vigorous action. The mind gets tired as the body does. We think it strange that our children never seem to show weariness at play, but only when they are asked to work. We forget that we seldom ask them to work until after they have become exhausted by play. I have seen a child too tired to undertake anything new, even getting off his clothes.

Fatigue makes the child unable to do any fine work. He stumbles when he walks. He spills whatever he carries. Whatever he tries to mend, breaks.

Fatigue makes the child unable to focus attention. He roams about the house because he is literally too tired to sit still. He does not notice when he is called, and he at once forgets what he is told. We know that a child is often too tired to start anything, but it is equally true that he may become too tired to stop.

The fatigued child is not easily pleased. He

teases others apparently because he enjoys discomfort. He craves an argument, and he does not intend to become convinced.

SOME CAUSES

THIS FACT suggests where to look for the cause. He has not been abused, though he thinks so. He has not failed, though he asserts he can never succeed. He is not unloved, though he is not lovable. So do not look for a mental case, but a physical one. Don't listen to his tongue, look at it.

Just now it may be the heat. It may be bad air. It may be broken sleep or rest. It may be insufficient sleep. In summer-time it is often the lack of a rest-space just after the noonday meal. It may be due to drudgery, even of play. It may be because of uneven growth.

Treat fatigue like an illness. Don't punish the child. Don't feed him. Give him rest.

REMEDIES

OFTEN the difficulty is to get a tired child to take rest, for he feels restless. Over-tired children do not welcome a nap or an early bedtime.

It is a bit discouraging to find a young person in such a state at the close of a so-called vacation. Yet school-teachers frequently testify that it takes the first month of school in the fall to help some of their pupils get over their summers.

The fatigued person usually welcomes solitude when he does not care to sleep. He is glad to have people keep away. Suppose, without any special explanation for doing so, you give your cantankerous son the spare room for a little while. Tell the "nervous" daughter that you would like to have her consider herself your "guest" the next two weeks. The seclusion will be beneficial. Trying to be considerate "company" will then do the rest.

EXERCISE

SPORTS FOR EXERCISE

By Rowland L. Mindlin, M.D.

MOST adolescents enjoy sports. Not so much for the exercise itself as for the thrill of competition and the sense of achievement do Jane and Johnny run and jump and play ball. Incidentally they do exercise, and they develop and strengthen the muscles of their growing bodies. But the driving force behind their activity is pleasure.

There is no reason this should not be indulged, so long as two basic safeguards are observed. First and foremost is the need for a brake of some sort. In the heat of a contest children will drive themselves up to the limit of their endurance or even beyond. The rules of the game should be adjusted to the capacity of the players, and the umpire should be one who knows when they are overdoing, and can call a halt if need be. Second is the need for actual protection of the body in the so-called "contact sports," such as football, basketball and boxing. If the contestants wear well-made pads and splints, the danger of real injury is minimized. No activity is completely safe, not even mere walking. You might stumble and break a leg. All that any parent can do is lessen the chances of an important accident by providing the equipment for the game and the supervision of an umpire.

The good that children get out of sports is many-sided. Most obvious is the physical. Muscles strengthen; co-ordination of movements, with themselves and with eye and ear, develops. An awkward boy or girl is sometimes helped over this difficulty by participation in games at school. Just as important is character development, to which properly conducted sports contribute. Team games depend on co-operation among the players. Here is one of the places where Bill and Mary learn to work and get along with other children. Winning and losing gracefully, both in individual and in group competition, are arts they are first introduced to in their sports. In the long run these things are even more significant than their athletic abilities themselves.

In all the aspects of children's sports their adult leadership is important. Good coaching will teach the right way to play. Along with better performance will come heightened interest and fewer accidents. Good umpiring will keep the game within the limits of the players' abilities, and accidents are reduced even more. From the adults' attitudes the children learn to be good or bad winners and losers. The "do or die for Junior High" spirit may be commendable during the game, but it is deplorable off the athletic field.

Practically any sport is suitable for the adolescent child so long as the rules and equipment are adjusted to fit the players. This is particularly important for the sports in which there is heavy bodily contact: boxing, basketball, football, hockey and wrestling. In these, the players should be separated into classes by weight so that no child is up against an opponent who is more than ten pounds heavier. In boxing the gloves should be heavy and well padded, and the rounds shortened. In football, basketball and hockey the playing field should be smaller and the periods shorter.

All children should be given an opportunity to learn some of the non-team sports which require either fewer competitors or little equipment or both. Swimming, tennis, golf, handball, bowling, horse-shoe pitching, riding and boating fall in this category. These are the games and sports in which boys and girls are more likely to participate later on, when school days and teams are only memories. The proficiency which makes for enjoyment of the game is more easily acquired by the youth than by the adult. He, and she too for that matter, is more likely to continue to play beyond school age if he learned how well before he grew up.

What about James who does not want to play in sports? Should he be forced to participate? The answer to this question is always "No." Instead, an intelligent effort should be made to find out *why* he is different from his mates. There may be something wrong with the child, poor physical condition from some unrecognized disease. Or again, he may have some emotional conflict resulting in his withdrawal from activities that can be straightened out for him. Or finally, there may be nothing wrong with the child but rather with the way the activities are conducted. But parents should also recognize that children differ one from another. Just as there are sedentary adults who never exercise except for the walking they have to do to get around during the day, so there are children who just do not enjoy sports. They have other interests. Efforts to induce them to vigorous play are fruitless. When this is the case, and when there is nothing wrong either with the child or the games, a lot of effort and aggravation can be saved if he is left to his more inactive life. He will grow up well even if he does not exercise much. And he will be a lot happier if he is not nagged about it.

DANCING FOR YOUR CHILDREN

By Lucille Marsh

DANCING is no longer considered a luxury; it is an essential part of every child's education.

Modern psychology has discovered how essential rhythm is in the normal development of every child. Dancing creates the most fundamental rhythmic responses in the every-day movements, definitely stimulating health and growth, and giving co-ordination, poise and grace.

Especially for the modern girl whom modern life requires to look as delicate as an orchid and still be in reality as strong as a horse, dancing solves the exercise problem. Too much athletic training tends to coarsen a girl, whereas dance training, emphasizing, as it does, grace of line and expressiveness of movement, develops the slender symmetrical strength that is greatly to be preferred.

For the boys, too, dancing has its value. Even the football, track and boxing coaches now use dancing to tone up an athlete's speed and finesse of movement.

When Mary cannot or will not stand erect, dancing supplies the necessary "sugar coated" corrective to strengthen weak back muscles and make Mary want to look like the Winged Victory. When John shuffles his feet and pounds down stairs like a ton of brick, the dancing school tackles the problem with tested methods. Shy little Jane and self-conscious Dick are put at ease and taught to be happy and socially at ease at a party.

It is no wonder that the dance is a time-honored medium of education. The Greeks used it to develop strength and beauty in their young men and maidens. In medieval Europe the aristocrats employed dancing masters to teach them to carry themselves with the grace and dignity befitting their station. Even in the time of our own American great-great-grandmothers, dancing teachers conducted schools of dancing in which they passed down the morals as well as the manners of the race. Today the dance is incorporated in the progressive school curriculum and is considered as important a part of a child's education as the proverbial "three R's."

The question before mothers, therefore, is not whether the children should be sent to dancing class. It is already prescribed by leading educators as a thoroughly tested heritage of the ages. The problem is where, when and what type of dancing to give the children so they will derive the greatest benefits from this ancient educational medium. Every teacher seems to have a different name for her particular brand of dancing, such as ballet, esthetic, Duncan, eurythmics, Spanish, tap, musical comedy, Greek, acrobatic, ballroom, toe, folk, modern, rhythmic and many other varieties. Each teacher claims superiority for her specialty with the most amazing but persuasive arguments. Mothers are left wondering which one is the best.

Experts in the field have now worked out a program of dance study carefully correlated with the school program and the study of the other fine arts, music, sculpture, painting, poetry and drama. This plan fits the dance instruction to the interests, abilities and needs of the various ages of childhood and adolescence, and insures the child a graded progression. It will also give him the maximum physical benefits as well as the proper mental and emotional stimulus for each age. A type of dancing that may be highly beneficial at one age may be seriously detrimental at another; for example, ballet dancing. Other types of dancing, as tap dancing, for instance, may discourage small children and make them tense and awkward in their co-ordinations, while at a later date it will fascinate them, and, at the same time, give them excellent rhythm, speed and accuracy in small foot movements. It is not sufficient to know what type of dancing our children should be taught. We must also be informed at which age they will get the most out of each particular form of dancing.

Art study should always be a joyous affair. Children should never be forced or drilled into an adult perfection. The love of the dance is the first lesson to be taught, and the joy of creative activity should always be stressed in every dancing lesson from pre-school years through college.

The all-round dancing teacher who knows her art from all its many facets of beauty is a better instructor for children than the specialist. She can give them the various types of dancing when and as they are needed without interrupting the continuity of this study. Save the famous specialist for later years when your child has the interest and ability to grasp the fine and difficult points of technique that only the specialist can give.

One of the first questions mothers always ask in regard to dancing instruction is at what age a child should start dancing. If dancing is to help strengthen and beautify the body and give co-ordination and grace to movement, then the earlier the lessons start the better. Even the ancient Greeks realized that the normal child was ready for regular physical education at the age of 3 years. To allow children to spend the first six years of their lives making bad habits of movements which will take the next six years to correct is foolish indeed. By all means, then, parents should plan to start their children in dancing classes before their fourth birthday. The class should be chosen with utmost care and the teacher with the greatest discretion.

RHYTHMIC DANCING

CHILDREN at this age should have what is called natural or rhythmic dancing, with emphasis on their joyous, rhythmic response in such natural movements as running, skipping, walking and the like. Singing games and simple folk dances are enjoyed at this age. Scarfs, balls, balloons and such properties delight the children. The dance costume should be a light little tunic over silk underwear, for much of the benefit of exercise is lost unless the air circulates freely on the skin. The feet should be bare, as they are the most restricted part of the body and often become weakened in later life because they do not get enough exercise in childhood.

At this point some mother always asks with anxiety in her voice, "Aren't you afraid such young children will catch cold dancing barefoot?" Children do not catch cold from bare feet any more than they do from bare hands. Of course, the floor should be warm and the room properly ventilated without drafts. However, since there is danger involved in going out into the cold air with damp underclothes on, the child's clothing should be changed completely after the lesson. Children susceptible to colds can be given an alcohol or witch-hazel rub after class to insure the correct skin reaction to the change of temperature outside.

The ideal dance class is conducted in a warm, sunny room with a smooth, absolutely clean floor. The class can last for forty-five minutes or one hour, but the periods of activity should be short and should not be strenuous. Young children have a short span of attention and must never be overstimulated or fatigued. The class should be happy and recreational in character. Neither mothers nor teachers should expect finished performances at a tender age. In fact, the foundation work done in the first few years is not spectacular; but if it is properly done it lays an infinitely valuable foundation for advanced forms of the dance as well as for a perfect posture and naturally graceful movement throughout life.

Classes for this work should be made up of children of practically the same age, 3, 4 and young 5-year-olds. Under no consideration should this young group be put in with older children, as it immediately gives them an unfortunate feeling of inferiority.

Besides having had a thorough training in all types of dancing under properly qualified masters, the teacher should be a cultured, well educated person of unassailed reputation to whom parents can trust the personality of their child. So often the dancing teacher becomes a sort of idol of the pupils. They copy her walk, her speech, even her facial expression and mannerisms. Be sure, then, that the dancing teacher is a worthy example for children to follow. This is particularly important in finding the right teacher for your boys. Be sure he is a worthy example of virility in the dance.

In addition to possessing the desired personal

and artistic qualifications, the teacher should be well versed in child psychology and anatomy. She should know how to make the learning process easy and delightful. She should be able to interest the pupils sufficiently in the work to make them want to go to dancing class and remember to practice for each lesson. She should be sufficiently well versed in anatomy to correct posture faults and strengthen such conditions as weak ankles, relaxed abdomen, sway back, and weak arches.

ACROBATIC DANCING

STRANGELY enough, acrobatic movements to some extent classify as natural movements. All little animals tumble, twist and somersault in their play. So do all children. Spontaneous back bends, forward and backward rolls, cartwheels and hand stands are all natural, wholesome and strengthening play. Children will try them anyway, so it is better to have a capable teacher tell them how to do various stunts correctly. The only danger in acrobatic work is that the teacher will take the attitude of a circus master instead of an educator, and drill youngsters into difficult stunts which may strain and distort their delicate little bodies. Of course there should be no forced stretching or limbering, no endurance stunts and no "showing off." If form and rhythm are stressed and the stunts are so arranged as to bring all muscles into natural co-ordination and equilibrium, acrobatic dancing can be a popular and educational form of dancing. Here again, the teacher's credentials in child anatomy will be the greatest safeguard.

TOE DANCING

TOE DANCING is now absolutely forbidden for children. The toe point, which took many generations of dancers to develop into its present virtuosity, is the last trick of technique that an adult dancer adds to her style. Not only is it far too difficult for children, but in attempting this arduous feat, immature little muscles and tendons are put under such a strain that they generally collapse, leaving the child with weak, unhealthy feet for the remainder of her life.

It must be remembered that in Europe, where the toe point was perfected, it was superimposed on many years of arduous daily training which developed the feet into veritable structures of steel. Americans, however, are temperamentally unsuited to any long systematic preparation. We apparently want everything, including toe dancing, by some speedy short cut. Conscientious teachers

know this cannot be done in toe dancing and will explain the situation to mothers. Those teachers who agree to put the child on her toes either do not know their business or do not care how much they harm the child as long as they are paid to do it.

BALLET DANCING

THE WHOLE ballet system is unsuited to children both psychologically and physically. The ballet is a mature professional system that is rich in wisdom and art for the advanced student; but to the child it is boring, artificial and thoroughly beyond comprehension. In fact, it is almost a physical impossibility for a child to do ballet movements correctly. Is it sensible to waste these precious childhood years by forcing difficult feats on immature minds and bodies, when there are so many important techniques a child can study with joy and success at this time? Parents might as well expect children to study algebra before they learn simple addition and subtraction. The study of ballet dancing must be postponed to the 'teens. Don't be worried if a European dancing master argues, "But then it will be too late ever to dance really well. Ballet dancing must be begun when the child is young."

Modern science has proved this old-world theory fallacious. If a child wants to be a toe dancer she will have a much better chance for success if she spends her youth mastering other valuable dance techniques and does not weaken her feet and develop sway back and heavy legs trying to do what her childish body and mind cannot master.

To the adolescent girl who has had fine fundamental dance training, the study of ballet dancing offers great benefits.

In the first place ballet dancing is an aristocratic system. It emphasizes control, line, delicacy, brilliance and finesse of movement. In the hands of a really capable teacher, ballet dancing can add a gracious beauty of gesture and movement that cannot be excelled.

As for boys, the ballet in the hands of a worthy man teacher has a tradition of virility and dignity that will challenge any boy's masculinity.

After several years of barefoot dancing the child's natural posture should be easily erect and the movement free, rhythmic and thoroughly graceful. The body should show a subtle, symmetrical strength and an unconscious precision and co-ordination in all its movements.

Up to the age of 6, boys and girls enjoy the dancing class together, although the boys should be given a much more masculine motivation than is given to the girls. For instance, if the class is interpreting the flight of birds, the boys may be eagles or hawks and should be urged to be vigorous and clean-cut in all their movements.

FOLK DANCING

When the boys begin to feel their masculinity too strongly they should be taught in a separate class, preferably by a man teacher. In this class they will want to do American Indian dances, Greek Pyrrhic and other classics of male dancing. However, before long they should be studying the folk dancing in connection with their school work in geography and history. The boys and girls will usually dance these together, but that will be determined by the customs and manners of the country they are studying. This study of the folk dances of the world is one of the most cultural and enjoyable parts of the dance training and should be conducted only by a teacher who has a rich and authentic background in the genuine folk dances of the nations. When children dislike folk dancing, it is because the teacher is getting cut-and-dried steps out of a book and does not teach her subject as the vital, joyous expression it is.

BALLROOM DANCING

In the fifth and sixth grades, boys and girls should be taught ballroom or social dancing. After years of experimentation, authorities have decided this is the ideal time to begin this important class. At this age children are able to accomplish easily all the necessary steps. As yet, they have no adolescent self-consciousness of the opposite sex, and they are not too young to learn the reactions which they will need on social occasions throughout life. Incidentally, mothers should not leave this important aspect of a child's dance education to pick-up methods. A bright child may be able to learn the ballroom steps without definite instruction, but the steps are so small a part of the valuable training and social contacts of the ballroom dancing class that wise mothers will include this class as an indispensable part of the young person's social education.

The modern social dancing class is conducted like a party or dance, and the children learn naturally to take part graciously in all aspects of the social occasion, including receiving lines, Paul Joneses, cotillions and elimination dances. They learn to manipulate favors, punch, refreshments and prizes; in short, they become familiar with everything they will meet in the real live party.

It is interesting that our great-grandmothers' dancing classes were advertised as practice balls because this function was to prepare the young people to acquit themselves with distinction at the real ball. This is still the function of the social or ballroom class. If the children fail to enjoy their real dances; if your daughters are wall flowers, and your sons hilarious stags, blame their dancing teacher. Besides developing both boys and girls into attractive ballroom dancers the class should teach them the responsibilities of host and guest and should cultivate in them a genuine desire to share good times. In the sixth grade of one modern school the children plan their own parties and conduct them with great skill and enthusiasm. They dance fox trots and waltzes, and they tango in the most approved style of the season, enjoying it immensely. The teacher interests herself in their outside parties, helps them with their plans and often drops in to prove her interest.

During junior high school the class should continue as a weekly social evening with general dancing after the instruction period. In senior high school it should be almost completely a social evening with an instruction period now and then to keep the students up to the minute in their steps. Contests for the best teams, trickiest original steps and most clever party are all valuable in keeping up the interest and the standards of this group.

TAP DANCING

Tap dancing is really a combination of the folk forms, known as Irish step and clog dancing, Negro shuffle and jazz. The recent fad for this type of dancing can be traced chiefly to the popularity of professional Negro dancing. As a matter of fact, tap dancing has much to recommend it in its rhythm, gaiety and speed, and the children do enjoy it. It is one of the few types of dancing that boys consider free from "sissiness." Children learn it most readily around 10 years of age, although under certain favorable circumstances they may pick it up at an earlier age. However, most children under 8 years of age find it boring and discouraging. In tap classes, too much stamping and heavy foot work should be guarded against as it is hard on the arches. The best tappers are never guilty of heaviness; they are, in fact, as light as thistledown on their feet, and their stamps have the clear click of a castanet. The greatest weakness in tap dancing as a form of good education is the objectionable repertoire of burlesque gestures it has acquired as a background for the steps.

DANCE THEMES

THIS brings us to the whole problem of dance content. It is difficult to understand how a mother can calmly allow her children to make gestures that she would blush to explain. If mothers realized to what an extent the children's dances influence their thoughts and feelings, I am sure dances would be censored much more carefully. Dances which dramatize the street urchin are certainly not elevating; neither are Apache dances which teach the gestures of the lowest dives in Paris. "Hotcha" numbers, unauthentic Hawaiian wiggles, suggestive high kicks and voluptuous oriental movements certainly cannot develop our daughters into finer, more sensitive and discriminating women.

THE DANCE RECITAL

A DISCUSSION of dancing would not be complete without mention of the dance recital, ballet or whatever the closing dancing school program is called. The modern educational attitude is one of enthusiasm for a satisfying culmination to any course of lessons. If the lessons have been properly planned and systematically mastered, something worth while should result. There is nothing so dear to a child's heart as participation in a beautiful closing program which allows him to show his accomplishments to parents and friends.

Too many teachers, however, use the closing recital not as an educational device but as an advertising project to attract more pupils for the following year. Mothers should refuse to allow their children to be relentlessly drilled and rehearsed for the sake of "putting on a good show." Long and late rehearsals in a tense, emotional atmosphere wear down a child's nervous and physical resistance to a dangerously low point. Fear of making a mistake, envy of another child's superiority, a desire for limelight and an opportunity to "show off," are all unwholesome reactions to inculcate in any child.

Another important requirement of the closing recital should be that it does not encourage the child to become stage-struck. The teacher who lures pupils into her dancing classes by guaranteeing stage careers is promising something she cannot deliver even if it were a desirable reward she was offering. A wise mother will protect her children from such a teacher if she wishes to protect their peace of mind and emotional integrity. Sometimes mothers hope to better the financial and social condition of the entire family by exploiting their children. It can be truthfully said to the credit of most American mothers, however, that their chief interest in dancing is as education and recreation to make their children healthier and happier. They realize that the art of living is the greatest of all arts and that a gorgeous human being is the greatest masterpiece.

In helping your children get the most out of their dancing lesson, there are many things parents can do.

Even before the child is sent to dancing school he can be encouraged to play the children's folk and singing games. "Looby Lou," "Here We Go Round the Mulberry Bush," and such, are a delight to children. A victrola that the children are allowed to manipulate is a splendid stimulus for creative experimentation with rhythmic movement, especially if at least some of the records are chosen for their particular interest and suitability for young people.

After you do choose a teacher, co-operate with her to the full. Arrange a time and place for your children to practice, show interest in their accomplishments and attend their recitals and performances. Help to build up their interest and self-confidence by due appreciation of their dancing but help them also to keep their mind steadily growing. Take them to see good dancing as often as possible. Allow them to arrange dancing parties and amateur performances in their homes. Above all, help them to enjoy the joy and beauty of the dance for itself. Dancing can be a valuable addition to the art of living and a real factor in the development of healthy, beautiful, happy children.

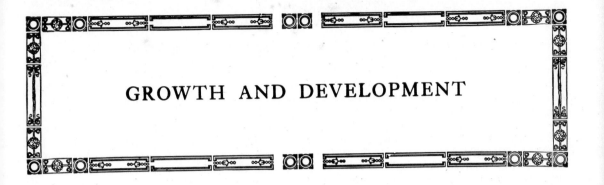

GROWTH AND DEVELOPMENT

WHAT HEIGHT–WEIGHT TABLES MEAN*

By George Truman Palmer, Ph.D.

All children do not gain at the same rate. One child may increase in weight with fair regularity. Another child will increase in spurts, with periods of stationary weight and even temporary loss of weight.

In spite of these different ways of growing heavier, each child may be perfectly healthy. Weight is influenced by many different factors. Heredity, the functioning of certain glands, diet, illness, activity, rest—all influence the gain in weight.

How much should a particular child gain? No one knows exactly. The average gain of children of the same age is a useful, general guide, but there is no reason why a particular child's increase in weight should conform exactly to the average gain. The person best fitted to say whether a child's gain is proper for him is the family physician who is acquainted with the family history, the habits, and the appearance of the child.

Average weight is the sum of the weights of a large number of children divided by the total number of children. It is customary to classify children first by sex, and age, and height, and then to find the average weight for children of the same sex, and age, and height. Tables of height, weight, age, and sex are built up in this, or an equivalent manner.

This average weight is not the prevailing weight, or the weight of the majority of children. It is a sort of mid point between the extremes of weight. Weights of children of the same height are always found to vary widely.

Under-weight means being below the average weight shown in tables for a given height, age, and sex. The amount of under-weight may be expressed in pounds, or in per cent. Jerry is

eight years old. He is forty-seven inches tall and weighs forty-five pounds. The average weight for boys of this age and height is fifty pounds. Jerry is five pounds under weight. Or we may say he is ten per cent under weight, five being ten per cent of fifty.

Naturally, when a child is under weight, it means that his weight is below the average for his age, height, and sex. It does not mean, necessarily, that the child is undernourished or in bad health. All under-weight children are not in bad health, nor are all up-to-weight children in good health. Poor nutrition and poor health will be found both sides of the average weight line just as good health will be found on both sides.

The principal reason for variation in weight either side of the average weight for height is the differing widths and depths of children's bony framework. If the pantry shelf is only four inches wide, it will hold only one row of jars of jam. If the shelf is eight inches wide, it will hold two rows. The wider and deeper a child's skeletal shelf, the more room there is for muscle and fat.

One cannot tell, then, from the height alone whether a child is usual or unusual in weight. It depends principally upon his skeletal width and depth.

Children who are under weight for their height, age, and sex may be so because of narrow and shallow skeletal framework, or because of small muscles and very little fat, or from a combination of both. Rarely, will we find under-weight children among those with wide skeletal frames.

A narrow or shallow skeletal framework is not a reliable sign of malnutrition, nor of physical unfitness. When such a body build is accompanied by muscular development that is *average for chil-*

*Reprinted from *Junior Home*, by permission.

dren of the same framework, we are not in a position to say that the child weighs less than he should. Sickly children may be under weight for their height, but sickly children may also be over weight for their height. Of course, it would be rare to find the extremely emaciated child who is not under weight. But it is not at all rare to find the child with deficient muscles and fat who is not under weight.

What we are interested in practically is the diagnostic value of weight for height in the general run of children. For ordinary purposes, weight for height, age, and sex does not serve as a useful index of nutritional status. The family physician should be relied upon for this.

It is desirable for parents to weigh the child and determine his height at intervals and make a diagram of these records to show how the child is growing and developing. Growing up is always an interesting subject. Interest in growth may be used to motivate proper health habits in the child.

Stationary weight or particularly continued loss of weight is something very proper to bring to the attention of the physician. But when one goes further and tries to make a home diagnosis by comparing a child's weight with average tables of weight for height, that is reading a significance into the tables that is unwarranted.

HOW TO USE HEIGHT AND WEIGHT TABLES

HOW TO USE HEIGHT AND WEIGHT TABLES

1. Take the Height First. Lay the baby on his back on a piece of paper, holding the knees down, and mark where the top of his head and the bottom of his heels come; then measure the distance between the marks.

For the older children, nail an accurate measure on the wall. Two yardsticks, a new tape measure, or a drawn scale will serve. Let the child stand, without shoes, flat against the wall, with heels, shoulders, and head touching the wall, and place at right angles a piece of wood (a medium-thick book will answer) firmly over his head and against the measuring scale.

2. Next, What Is the Child's Age? Take the nearest birthday.

3. Then, Consult the Chart for the Proper Weight for The Child's Age and Height. First find the height in the left column and follow across the chart to the appropriate age column. The figure so found is the average weight of boys or girls the same age and height as your child.

4. Now Weigh the Child. If you are using a regulation baby-scale, first be sure the scale is set to register zero with the basket in place. Then place the infant in the basket. If you are using a platform scale, put in the center of the platform a basket large enough to hold the baby, and note the weight of the basket before putting the baby in it. Have the older child stand in the center of the scale platform. Teach the child to weigh himself.

5. Next, the Record. Enter the weight on the weight record. This record is more interesting if kept in the form of a graph. On the pages following the tables are some picturing the growth in weight and height of an average baby.

Similar graphs should be made for the older child. An ordinary school blank-book can be ruled into squares for the purpose; or a large sheet of wrapping paper can be ruled and tacked up on the wall of the play-room so that the weight and height record may be seen at a glance.

HEIGHT AND WEIGHT TABLES

BY ROBERT MORSE WOODBURY, M.D.

Bird T. Baldwin, Ph.D., and Thomas D. Woods, M.D.

The HEIGHT AND WEIGHT TABLES which follow, like all figures based on general averages, are not to be taken too seriously. Many factors —small or large bones, family tendencies, individual idiosyncrasies of appetite, exercise, illness, etc.—may account for deviation in height or weight. Do not worry, therefore, unless there are no gains at all or the variations one way or the other are abnormally great.

AVERAGE WEIGHTS BY HEIGHT AND AGE FOR GIRLS UNDER SIX YEARS OF AGE*

By Robert Morse Woodbury, Ph.D

Height in Inches	Under 1 Month Lbs.-Ozs.	1 Month Lbs.-Ozs.	2 Months Lbs.-Ozs.	3 Months Lbs.-Ozs.	4 Months Lbs.-Ozs.	5 Months Lbs.-Ozs.	6 Months Lbs.-Ozs.	9 Months Lbs.-Ozs.	1 Year Lbs.-Ozs.	2 Years Lbs.-Ozs.	3 Years Lbs.-Ozs.	4 Years Lbs.-Ozs.	5 Years Lbs.-Ozs.	Height in Inches
20	7-14½	8-4½												20
21	8-11½	9-4½	9-10½											21
22	9-4	10-3½	10-12½	11-2	11-1½									22
23		11-3	11-10	12-1½	12-8	12-15	13-6½							23
24		11-14	12-8½	13-3½	13-10	13-14½	14-2½							24
25			13-6	13-15½	14-9	14-15½	15-6½	15-6						25
26				14-15½	15-8	15-15½	16-6½	16-14	17-12½					26
27				16-9	17-1½	17-8	17-14	18-2½						27
28							18-10½	19-½	19-3					28
29							19-7	20-3½	20-3½					29
30							20-10½	21-5½	21-4	22-4				30
31							22-3½	22	22-8	23-1½				31
32							23-6½	23-1	23-11½	23-15½	25-4			32
33									24-15	25-½	25-15½			33
34									26-1	26-6	26-7½	28-9½		34
35									27-7	27-10	27-15	28-6½		35
36									29-4	29-1	29-1½	29-9½		36
37									29-13	29-8	30-5½	30-8		37
38										31-10	31-12	31-10	31-12	38
39										32-13½	33-2	32-13	33-5	39
40										34-3	34-10	34-6½	34-10	40
41											36-7½	35-15½	35-14½	41
42											37-7	37-10	37-5½	42
43											38-8	39-3½	39-2½	43
44												40-15	40-14½	44
45												42-9½	42-8½	45
46													45-1	46
47													46-10½	47

*Heights are classified to the nearest inch: 20 inches means 19½ to 20½; 21 inches means 20½ to 21½, etc. Dr. Woodbury tabulated the results of his investigations in pounds and the decimal fraction thereof; but we have translated these fractions into ounces, as most scales

154

AVERAGE WEIGHTS BY HEIGHT AND AGE FOR BOYS UNDER SIX YEARS OF AGE*

By Robert Morse Woodbury, Ph.D

Height in Inches	Under 1 Month	1 Month	2 Months	3 Months	4 Months	5 Months	6 Months	9 Months	1 Year	2 Years	3 Years	4 Years	5 Years	Height in Inches
	Lbs.-Ozs.	Lbs.-Ozs.	Lbs.-Ozs.	Lbs.-Ozs.	Lbs.-Ozs.	Lbs.-Ozs.	Lbs.-Ozs.	Lbs.-Ozs.	Lbs.-Ozs.	Lbs.-Ozs.	Lbs.-Ozs.	Lbs.-Ozs.	Lbs.-Ozs.	
20	7-15	8-8												20
21	9-1¼	9-8	10											21
22	9-12	10-8	10-14	11-2										22
23	10-8	11-6	12-1	12-6½	12-8½									23
24		12-4	13-4	13-12	13-15	14	14-3							24
25		13-1	13-15	14-10½	15-½	15-4	15-14	16-7						25
26			14-4½	15-9½	16	16-11	16-14	17-7	17-13					26
27				16-6½	17	17-10	18-1½	18-5½	18-13					27
28						18-11	19-3	19-8½	19-10					28
29							20-5½	20-10½	20-13					29
30							21-11½	21-13½	22	22-7				30
31							22-11½	23-½	23-3½	23-12				31
32							24-2½	23-15	24-7½	24-14				32
33									25-11	26-6	27-4			33
34									26-13½	27-2	27-10			34
35									28-4	28-6	28-8	29-10		35
36									29-4½	29-10½	29-12	30-8		36
37									30-8	31-2½	31-½	31-3½		37
38										32-6½	32-7	32-7	33-5½	38
39										33-8	34	33-11½	33-14½	39
40										35-4	35-7	35-3	35-4½	40
41										36-5½	36-15½	36-12	36-15½	41
42											38-8½	38-6	38-5½	42
43											40-6	40-1	40-3	43
44												41-9½	41-11½	44
45												43-4½	43-7	45
46												45-1½	45-7½	46
47													47-4	47

are marked with pounds and ounces. These weights are net; if a child is weighed with any clothes on, due allowance for the extra weight must be made. Records of 80,263 girls and 82,721 well boys were used in making these summaries.

AVERAGE WEIGHTS BY HEIGHT AND AGE FOR GIRLS FROM SIX TO EIGHTEEN YEARS OF AGE

By Bird T. Baldwin, Ph.D., and Thomas D. Wood, M.D.

Height in Inches	6 Years	7 Years	8 Years	9 Years	10 Years	11 Years	12 Years	13 Years	14 Years	15 Years	16 Years	17 Years	18 Years	Height in Inches
38	33													38
39	34													39
40	36	36												40
41	37	37												41
42	39	39												42
43	41	41	41											43
44	42	42	42											44
45	45	45	45	45										45
46	47	47	48	48										46
47	50	50	50	50	50									47
48	52	52	52	52	53	53								48
49	54	54	55	55	56	56								49
50	56	56	57	58	59	61	62							50
51		59	60	61	61	63	65							51
52		63	64	64	64	65	67							52
53		66	67	67	68	68	69	71						53
54			69	70	70	71	71	73						54
55			72	74	74	74	75	77	78					55
56				76	78	78	79	81	83					56
57				80	82	82	82	84	88	92				57
58					84	86	86	88	93	96	101			58
59					87	90	90	92	96	100	103	104		59
60					91	95	95	97	101	105	108	109	111	60
61						99	100	101	105	108	112	113	116	61
62						104	105	106	109	113	115	117	118	62
63							110	110	112	116	117	119	120	63
64							114	115	117	119	120	122	123	64
65							118	120	121	122	123	125	126	65
66								124	124	125	128	129	130	66
67								128	130	131	133	133	135	67
68								131	133	135	136	138	138	68
69									135	137	138	140	142	69
70									136	138	140	142	144	70
71									138	140	142	144	145	71

AVERAGE WEIGHTS BY HEIGHT AND AGE FOR BOYS FROM SIX TO NINETEEN YEARS OF AGE

By Bird T. Baldwin, Ph.D., and Thomas D. Wood, M.D.

Height in Inches	6 Years	7 Years	8 Years	9 Years	10 Years	11 Years	12 Years	13 Years	14 Years	15 Years	16 Years	17 Years	18 Years	19 Years	Height in Inches
38	34														38
39	35														39
40	36														40
41	38	38													41
42	39	39	39												42
43	41	41	41												43
44	44	44	44												44
45	46	46	46	46											45
46	48	48	48	48											46
47	50	50	50	50	50										47
48	52	53	53	53	53										48
49	55	55	55	55	55	55									49
50	57	58	58	58	58	58	58								50
51		61	61	61	61	61	61								51
52		63	64	64	64	64	64	64							52
53		66	67	67	67	67	68	68							53
54			70	70	70	70	71	71							54
55			72	72	73	73	74	74	74	72					55
56			75	76	77	77	77	78	78	80					56
57				79	80	81	81	82	83	83					57
58				83	84	84	85	85	86	87					58
59				87	88	89	89	90	90	90					59
60				91	92	92	93	94	95	96					60
61					95	96	97	99	100	103	106				61
62					100	101	102	103	104	107	111	116			62
63						105	106	107	108	110	113	118	123	127	63
64							109	111	113	115	117	121	126	130	64
65							114	117	118	120	122	127	131	134	65
66								119	122	125	128	132	136	139	66
67								124	128	130	134	136	139	142	67
68									134	134	137	141	143	147	68
69									137	139	143	146	149	152	69
70									143	144	145	148	151	155	70
71									148	150	151	152	154	159	71
72										153	155	156	158	163	72
73										157	160	162	164	167	73
74										160	164	168	170	171	74

WEIGHT AND HEIGHT

Weight Chart

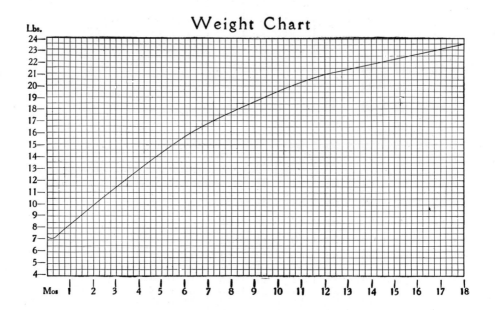

Height Chart

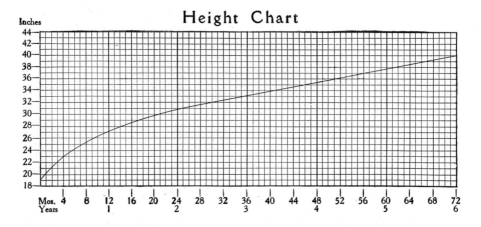

These charts show the increase in weight and height of the average baby. To use the Weight Chart: Put a dot on the line at the left at the point corresponding to the weight of your baby. Each week put a dot on the line to the right of the last one used, and draw a line to connect. Compare this curve with that of the average baby. Use the Height Chart in the same manner at month intervals.

EVERY MEMBER OF THE FAMILY
SHOULD HAVE PERIODIC HEALTH EXAMINATIONS

1. Do not guess about your health and the health of your family; be sure.

2. Do not wait for health troubles to mature; nip them in the bud.

3. When pain comes, it is often too late.

4. You can buy a new motor for your auto, your washing-machine, your ice-less refrigerator, etc., but you cannot buy a new heart, new lungs, new kidneys for a human body—and we expect our bodies to outlast mechanical contrivances several times over.

5. For each member of the family a birthday is like the sign on a railroad grade crossing:

> *STOP!*
> Not slow up, but stand still and ask yourself:
> 1. When last did I have a physician examine my heart, lungs, kidneys, blood-pressure, ears, nose, throat, etc.?
> 2. When last did I have a dentist clean my teeth and look for cavities?
> 3. When last did I have an oculist test my eyes?
> 4. In short, how certain am I that my most precious possession, my body, is properly safeguarded?

> *LOOK!*
> Through the knowledge of your physician, dentist, and oculist, look your body over.

> *LISTEN!*
> Heed their advice.

6. Birthdays come once a year; health examinations of all persons over six years of age should be made once a year; common sense directs us to make health examinations part of the routine celebration of the birthday.

REMEMBER: *An Ounce of Prevention is Worth a Pound of Cure.*

A CHILD'S GRACE

Some hae meat and canna eat,
And some wad eat that want it;
But we hae meat and we can eat,
And sae the Lord be thankit.

—*Robert Burns*

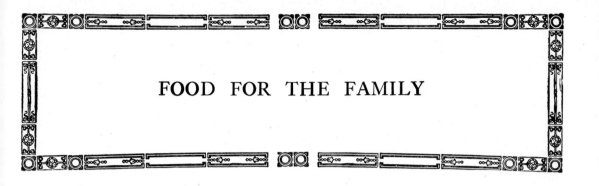

FOOD FOR THE FAMILY

NUTRITIONAL REQUIREMENTS OF GROWING CHILDREN*

By Mary E. Sweeny and Dorothy Curts Buck

As a child grows his bones become longer, his muscles increase in size, his organs become larger; every part of his body advances toward its own maturity. This growth cannot take place, normally, without the needed material being supplied in his daily food intake.

Food serves the body in many ways. Some foods are necessary for building tissue, others are valuable for the energy they yield, and still others are indispensable as body regulators. Many foods are a mixture of a number of substances and can, therefore, serve the body in several ways; other foods can be used by the body in only one way. Milk serves all three purposes, while sugar supplies only energy. The substances present in food which are necessary for the body are protein, fat, carbohydrate, minerals, vitamins, and water.

PROTEIN—ITS IMPORTANCE AND CHOICE

Protein is an important part of all living tissue, whether plant or animal. Every tissue and fluid of the body contains it. There are many kinds of protein present in the food we eat. Some are more valuable to the body than others, some will both maintain the body and promote growth, some will only maintain the body, some will neither maintain the body nor promote growth when they are the sole source of protein. Therefore, in choosing foods for children those containing protein which both maintains the body and promotes growth are essential.

Milk, cheese, eggs, meat, poultry, and fish are valuable in children's diets as foods rich in protein. Milk and eggs have been shown to be especially good for promoting growth. Some grains, such as oats and wheat, and also peas and beans, furnish tissue-building protein, but they are not so rich in the necessary protein as milk, eggs, meat, fish, and cheese, and cannot completely substitute for these foods.

HOW MUCH PROTEIN IS DESIRABLE FOR THE PRE-SCHOOL CHILD?

The amount of protein contained in one egg and one tall can of evaporated milk, or one egg and one quart of bottled milk, together with a well-chosen diet, will, so far as we know now, fulfill the daily protein requirement of the child of nursery school age.

FAT AN ENERGY-GIVING FOOD

Fat is the most concentrated form of energy-giving food which the body uses. Such fats as butter, cream, lard, oil, and suet are familiar. Some fats are more valuable to the body than others because of the vitamins which they carry in solution. Notable among these fats are butter, with vitamin A, and cod-liver oil, with vitamins A and D in solution.

Almost all foods contain some fat, and the sum of these small amounts of fat in each food may make a surprisingly large total, even when the amount of concentrated fats, such as butter, lard, and cod-liver oil, in the diet is small.

* Reprinted with permission from *How to Feed Children in Nursery Schools,* by Mary E. Sweeny and Dorothy Curts Buck. Published by The Merrill-Palmer School.

Large quantities of fat are undesirable because they upset normal digestion, cause loss of appetite and nausea, and influence the absorption of calcium.

BUTTERFAT

WHOLE milk contains cream, which is one of the valuable fats for children because it contains vitamin A, is emulsified, is evenly distributed throughout the milk, and occurs in a proportion to the rest of the food constituents which makes it easy to digest when it is taken in whole milk.

Evaporated milk, when diluted with an equal amount of water, has the same percentage of cream as bottled milk. If a child gets a quart of whole milk a day, buttered vegetables, and butter on his bread, his fat requirement will be met.

CARBOHYDRATES

POTATO, rice, flour, and sugar are some of the carbohydrates which have an important place in the child's diet. They are also some of the cheapest of energy-giving foods.

Experiments have shown that one-half of the energy required by the body may be supplied by carbohydrates, and that if the remainder of the food is wisely chosen the child will still have a well-balanced diet.

Vegetables and fruits are usually classified under carbohydrates, since they contain either starches or sugar, but they are indispensable not because of their carbohydrates, but for their minerals and vitamins.

MINERALS

MINERALS are present in every body tissue and fluid. A number of them are needed by the body and must be "nicely balanced" or trouble ensues. Many minerals are present only in traces and if a well-chosen, mixed diet is eaten, an adequate quantity of these elements will be supplied. However, calcium, phosphorus, and iron are required in comparatively large amounts and are not equally abundant in all foods and should therefore be given special attention or they will not be present in sufficient quantity in the diet.

WHY CALCIUM IS NECESSARY

IN the human body calcium is necessary for the growth and maintenance of bones and teeth, plays an important part in the beating of the heart, and in carrying of messages by the nerves, and is essential in bringing about coagulation of the blood.

Growing children need an abundant supply of calcium. It is estimated by authorities that they should have at least one gram a day.

WHY PHOSPHORUS IS NECESSARY

PHOSPHORUS, like calcium, is very important in its influence on the cells of the body, and is equally necessary in the building up and maintenace of nerve tissue, blood, bone, and teeth. Growing children require at least one gram a day.

Milk and foods made with it, and milk derivatives such as cheese or buttermilk are the only important sources of calcium and phosphorus in the diet. Calcium and phosphorus cannot be used to the best advantage in the body unless vitamin D is present.

WHY IRON IS NECESSARY

IRON is essential, also, for normal growth and plays an active part in the secretive processes of the body. The amount required by the body each day is small, but if it is not supplied in adequate amounts the child becomes pale, listless, and anemic. Opinions from the most authoritative sources indicate that from 10 to 15 milligrams of iron are necessary daily for buoyant health.

HOW TO SECURE CALCIUM, PHOSPHORUS, AND IRON

GROWING boys and girls should have a quart of milk a day, supplemented by a well-chosen diet, adequate in amount, to supply the calcium and phosphorus demands of the body.

For a long time it was thought that if food contained iron, all the iron present would be available for the body's use. Recent research tends to show that this is not entirely correct. There are marked differences in the use which the body can make of iron furnished it by various foods. The quality of the iron is significant as well as the quantity. In the light of our present knowledge egg yolks, liver, dried beans and peas, green vegetables, whole grain cereal, and certain fruits are regarded as valuable sources of iron.

IODINE

IN THE SO-CALLED "goiter belt" which includes the Great Lakes states, Minnesota and the Dakotas, there is less iodine in the soil and in the water supply than elsewhere. Unless extra iodine is provided in the diet, people in this region are more likely than others to develop goiters. If the iodine is supplied this tendency is eliminated. The extra iodine is commonly incorporated in the salt known as "iodized salt."

VITAMINS

VITAMINS occur in natural foods. Some are soluble in fats, some are soluble in water. If they are consistently absent from the daily diet, a diseased condition of the body occurs sooner or later. Laboratory experiments with animals show that no matter how adequate the ration may be in tissue-building, energy-giving, and body regulating constituents, the body cannot use it properly without the aid of vitamins. Vitamins serve the human body by regulating its processes, stimulating growth, and protecting it from certain deficiency diseases. A well-balanced diet contains adequate amounts of all the vitamins except for Vitamin D which must be added to the growing child's food in some way.

Vitamin A is present in butter, cream, whole milk, eggs, and green and yellow vegetables, and is especially concentrated in cod-liver oil and other fish oils. In human beings, as in animals, diets deficient in Vitamin A cause nightblindness and widespread disturbances of the skin and other surface tissues of the body. It is recognized that Vitamin A is an essential of children's diets because of its relation to growth and the maintenance of healthy tissues.

Vitamin B was formerly thought to be a single substance, but is now known to be a mixture of several vitamin factors. These are present in many foods, notably in whole-grain cereals, meat, especially liver, vegetables, milk, fruits, and nuts. Highly milled foods, such as white flour, white (polished) rice, and refined breakfast cereals have lost much of their value as sources of Vitamin B through the milling process. Vitamins of the B complex must be included in the diet if normal growth is to take place and are needed by the human body at all ages for proper functioning.

Vitamin C is present in oranges, lemons, and other citrus fruits, tomatoes, raw cabbage, and lettuce, and in fact most fresh vegetables and fruits. Since 1700 the disease known as scurvy and the possibility of curing it by adding lemons or raw vegetables to the diet have been recognized. Animal experiments have demonstrated that a diet lacking in this vitamin affects many tissues of the body. Most conspicuous among the effects of its deficiency are loosening of the teeth, swelling of the gums, and changes in the structure of the teeth and ribs. A diet lacking in Vitamin C affects the growth of the young unfavorably though not so conspicuously as one lacking in the other vitamins.

Lack of Vitamin D results in rickets with its misshapen chests and bent bones. Nature meant that this vitamin should be created in our bodies by the ultra-violet rays of the sun shining on us, but smoke, window glass, the walls of houses, and clothing all shut off these rays. Fortunately, it has been found that ultra-violet rays can be produced by certain types of lamps. When the body and certain foods are exposed to the ultra-violet "sunshine rays" from those lamps, Vitamin D is created in exactly the same way as by sunshine itself. Milk, our best source of calcium for bone and tooth building in children, is one of the foods which can be enriched with Vitamin D by "irradiation" with the "sunshine rays."

Cod and other fish oils are naturally rich in Vitamin D and are the source of the extra supply needed by young children.

BULK

SOME food material, such as vegetable fiber, is not digested by the body and remains as a residue in the intestinal tract. A certain amount of bulk in the food is desirable. It promotes better absorption in the small intestine and stimulates the muscles of the large intestine so that they contract and move the unused food material and such wastes as are thrown off through the intestine along the tract until they are finally expelled from the body. This insures good intestinal hygiene and prevents the stagnation and putrefaction of food in the digestive tract.

Bulk is necessary not only to move the fecal material along the intestines but also to insure tone to the intestinal muscles and the secretion of mucus which facilitates the passage of the material along the tract. Water also has an important part to play in the passage of the material.

Fruits, vegetables, and the outer coats of grains are high in residue and if eaten in sufficient quantity should supply the demands of the body for bulk.

BODY NEEDS FOR WATER

WATER occurs in every living tissue and constitutes about two-thirds of the weight of the body. It is an important regulating substance, serving the body in the following ways:

1. It is necessary for digestive fluids.
2. It dissolves the food materials so they may be absorbed and used by the tissues.
3. Since chemical reactions cannot take place unless they are in solution, it makes possible the change of food into body tissue.
4. It keeps materials in solution so they may be transported to different parts of the body by the blood and lymph.
5. It facilitates the removal of the soluble waste products.
6. It regulates body temperature by removing excess heat by evaporation of water from the surface of the body.
7. It keeps the air passages moist.

Water is excreted from the body by the kidneys in urine, by the skin in perspiration, and by the lungs in water vapor, and a certain amount is lost in the feces. The amount needed daily may be supplied to the body by drinking water, milk, which has 87 per cent water, fruit juices, which may contain up to 90 per cent water, and eating such vegetables as tomatoes, such fruits as strawberries and watermelon, and even a solid food like bread, which has 35 per cent water. There is no reason why water cannot be taken in moderate amounts with meals or before a meal. It is an aid to digestion. A reasonable quantity is needed by children in addition to that contained in their food.

BEVERAGES

THE OPTIMAL diet for the child will include one quart of milk a day. This amount of milk is easily included in the day's food if the child drinks one cup of milk at each meal, and secures the fourth in his prepared food.

Children should be encouraged to like the natural flavor of milk, and to enjoy drinking it. However, sometimes it is desirable to combine milk with other substances such as chocolate or fruit juices in order to give variety to the diet, and to increase the food value of the milk combination.

Fruit juices alone, or in combination with each other are palatable, appetizing, and well liked by children. Fruit juices add valuable minerals and vitamins to the diet. It is unnecessary to add sugar to any fruit juices except those which are sour, such as lemons, cranberries, and grapefruit.

VEGETABLES

VEGETABLES are excellent sources of minerals, vitamins and bulk, and a liberal use of them is to be encouraged.

In order to retain flavor and food value, most vegetables should be boiled in a very small quantity of water in a tightly covered pan, or they should be steamed. Any liquid left after cooking should be saved and used in soups or sauces. Such liquor is also valuable for diluting irradiated evaporated milk.

Leafy vegetables, such as spinach, need no other water for cooking than that which clings to the leaves after washing.

Strong flavored vegetables such as cabbage, cauliflower and onions require a quantity of water, but not an excessive amount.

If it is desired to retain the bright green color of certain vegetables, leave them uncovered during cooking.

Fresh vegetables should be cooked only until tender. Overcooking changes flavor, texture and color and decreases food value.

The addition of salt to the water in which the vegetables are cooked tends to withdraw the vegetable juices raises the temperature at which the water boils but gives better flavor. Allow ½ teaspoon salt to each pint of boiling water. When vegetables are to be steamed, sprinkle with salt, allowing ¼ teaspoon salt to each pound.

Left-over vegetables can be used to advantage in creamed or scalloped dishes. They may be used individually or in combination. For added nourishment and variety add ¼ cup grated cheese to each cup white sauce. In creaming vegetables use a sauce that is thick enough not to run over the plate.

EGGS

EGGS are an excellent source of protein, minerals and vitamins. A rapidly growing child should have an egg every day.

When eggs are used in combination with other foods, as in puddings, soufflés and cakes, a serving does not ordinarily contain a whole egg. Other sources of protein should be included in the meal.

An egg dish may have its protein supplemented by using cheese, such as cheese soufflé; or, protein may be supplied in another dish, such as a liver sandwich or custard sauce on fruit. Left over puréed or chopped vegetables, also meat and fish may be used to advantage in soufflé. You can be sure that soufflés are cooked sufficiently when a warm knife, inserted in the center, comes out clean.

FISH

FISH supplies protein. Owing to the characteristic odor and flavor of fish, children many times have to learn to like it. Once they acquire a liking for it, however, it becomes a popular dish.

It is well to use sea food once a week for the iodine it provides.

Fish should be boned carefully. To prepare fish flakes, tie fish in cheesecloth, drop into boiling water and boil 5 minutes. Remove bones and flake fish with a fork.

MEATS

MEATS are an excellent source of protein and phosphorus, and are relatively high in iron.

When the child has learned to chew food thoroughly, one serving of lean, tender meat a day is allowable.

In the preparation of meat for the young child, excess fat should be removed. Very tough cuts of meat may be ground, stewed or made into casserole dishes. More tender cuts may be broiled or roasted.

Coarse, stringy meat is obviously difficult for the child to chew. It has been found that diced meat in soup is usually not eaten. If the same meat is ground and served with macaroni and tomato sauce, for example, it is consumed with relish.

Bacon does not replace other meat. The small portion which should be served to a child contains little protein and a high concentration of fat, even though cooked until crisp.

Bacon adds flavor and increases the child's interest in a bland meal.

Liver (beef, calf, lamb or pork) is an excellent source of iron and copper and is rich in Vitamins A, B and G and should appear in the child's menu once a week. Other organs, such as kidney and sweetbreads, are also valuable for the same reason.

CHEESE

CHEESE is an economical, highly concentrated food, rich in protein, calcium and fat. If used in moderation it may advantageously be substituted for meat.

Mild-flavored cheese should be used.

Cottage cheese is not as high in fat and calcium as other cheese. It can be used as a substitute for meat for the child.

CEREALS

WHOLE grain cereals are valuable for their energy, minerals and vitamins.

For variety, as a substitute for potatoes, cereals such as steamed brown rice may be served occasionally.

If a cereal such as macaroni or rice is the main dish in a midday meal, it should be supplemented by a protein food. Combine the protein with the cereal, as in a macaroni and cheese dish, or serve a protein dessert, such as a baked custard.

SALADS

RAW FRUITS and vegetables should be introduced gradually into the diet of the child as he learns to chew his food.

Salads provide minerals, vitamins and bulk, and serve as appetizers. They also acquaint the child with food that is sometimes difficult to learn to like later in life.

Mildly seasoned salad dressing, made with milk and egg, or fruit juices, sometimes combined with a little oil, is desirable to serve to the young child.

SOUPS

MILK soups are very nutritious. Those made of stock depend largely upon the ingredients added to the soup for food value.

When soup is served to the child it should take the place of the main course, being accompanied by a nutritious salad or sandwich, and dessert. Meals including soup weary the child if too many other foods are served.

The consistency of soup is a factor to consider; a thick soup is more easily eaten than a thin one. The temperature of the soup is also important. Soup should not be served too hot.

Thin, crisp crackers or toast cut in cubes or strips are a pleasing complement to soup.

BREAD

EASILY chewed, light, dry breads should be served. Whole grained breads supply energy, minerals and vitamins. White bread should be "fortified" by replacement of some of the vitamins removed in refining the flour.

One can vary the usual bread and butter by serving a variety of sandwiches or crisp toast.

Quick breads are not indigestible, but their frequent serving to the young child is not considered desirable.

SANDWICHES

SANDWICHES provide variety and are a means of using eggs, meat and raw vegetables.

Vegetables which can be served unchopped, such as lettuce, spinach and cabbage, are easily eaten in sandwiches.

A salad dressing added to grated or chopped foods make a moist sandwich filling.

SAUCES

SAUCES are often rich in the nutrients necessary to round out the meal: cheese sauce, egg sauce and mushroom sauce add protein, minerals and vitamins to foods with which they are served; tomato sauce and fruit sauces contribute minerals and vitamins.

Raw, cooked or canned berries pressed through a fine sieve and sweetened to taste make excellent pudding sauces.

DESSERTS

SIMPLE frozen desserts are a wholesome addition to the diet, for they introduce fruit juices and milk in a pleasing way.

Milk sherbets are the ideal way to serve frozen food to children.

Children prefer the sherbets and ice creams not too cold or frozen too solid.

Fruit desserts or fruit-flavored desserts supply simple sugars as well as minerals, vitamins and bulk, and are popular with the children.

Puddings afford an excellent opportunity to use milk in a meal. If the main course does not include milk as one of the ingredients of the dishes served, it is well to serve a milk dessert.

Baked custard should be used as a dessert in a meal which is otherwise low in protein; for example, following a vegetable plate.

Fruit used as a sauce or garnish often adds to the attractiveness and palatability of a pudding dessert.

CAKES

SPONGE cake and angel food cake can be an interesting part of the child's menu. These cakes contain protein and carbohydrates.

Any icing on cakes is undesirable for children. It is similar to a rich candy in its composition. Powdered sugar dusted over a cake is acceptable.

The "usual" butter cakes are high in fat and sugar and undesirable for children. Plain cakes are low in fat and sugar, are very palatable and can be included in a child's menu.

Cookies are similar in food value to cake.

CONFECTIONS

HARD candies and those made from ground fruit are preferable. Candy can supply some of the energy needed by the body. It should be given at the end of meals, and not before. Candy between meals is undesirable as it may lessen the child's appetite for foods served at the regular meal periods.

PLANNING THE YOUNG CHILD'S MENU*

By MIRIAM E. LOWENBERG

CHILDREN of pre-school age may be taught to eat all foods not actually harmful to them. While the injury certain foods may do to the body is as yet somewhat in doubt, it is better to err on the side of too much rather than too little caution in allowing children to eat certain foods. All fried foods and foods prepared with a large quantity of fat or sugar are to be omitted from

the diet of children. This rule eliminates all pastries, rich cakes and puddings, rich sauces and gravies. Since condiments may have a harmful effect upon the digestive system of children, it is wise to omit all highly spiced foods.

TEXTURE, COLOR AND FLAVOR

A MENU which meets a child's needs for adequate nutrition is not always acceptable to him. At the

*From *Food for the Young Child*, by MIRIAM E. LOWEN-BERG, Iowa State College, Collegiate Press, Inc.

pre-school age, food habits and lifetime likes and dislikes are being formed. The association of one food with another is, hence, an important factor. A well-balanced meal has a nice variety of texture, flavor and color. For children, another factor is important; they should not have to encounter more than one or two foods at one time that are difficult to handle in eating.

CHILDREN FAVOR CRISP TEXTURES

SOME crisp food should be included in each menu. Mastication is difficult for some children, and more than one chewy food on the menu will slow the process of eating. On the other hand, a menu of soft, "sloppy" foods is unpopular with children. In planning meals for children it is well to consider this rule of three: in every meal serve one crisp, one soft and one chewy food.

Flavor plays an important part in the child's food. In a food-preference study with nursery school children, cream of tomato soup ranked several points higher than cream of pea soup, equally attractive in color and texture and alike in ease of eating. Although in general the flavor of children's food should be bland, meals which contain one accenting flavor, such as tomatoes, a fresh fragrant fruit or tantalizing bacon, are most popular with children. A strong-flavored vegetable needs to be combined with a bland one to give a pleasing combination of flavors. The skillful blending of strong with bland flavors, of sharp, acid flavors with mild, sweet ones is an important part of menu planning for children.

That children do observe color in foods was evidenced by the four-year-old boy who said to his mother, "Your turnips are black and I don't like them. They're white at the nursery school." Children rarely fail to comment on the food to which a tiny sprig of parsley has been added, or bits of hidden color in tomato, carrot or parsley sandwiches. Yellow is apparently a popular color with children, for they frequently remark about yellow and orange in their food. If the plate is to be interesting in color, not more than one pale or white food should be served at one time.

EASE OF MANIPULATION

WATCH a two-year-old eat a bowl of soup and you will observe how many trials he makes before finishing it. Soup on a menu usually increases young children's total time of eating about ten minutes. Pieces of carrot that slide across the plate and are too small to lie on the fork easily, or cubes of beets that must be cut into bits by tiny fingers, exhaust the patience of a three-year-old. Stringy spinach or tomatoes are a trial. Much can be done in the kitchen to make vegetables easier to eat. A whole lettuce leaf, a piece of toast and a hot vegetable which is easily handled may be used on a soup menu. No meal should include more than one food which is difficult to eat.

Vegetables should be cut in pieces large enough so that the child will recognize them. Most vegetables in dices three-fourths of an inch square are easily handled by the majority of pre-school children. Some small vegetables, such as tiny beets, are attractive to children if left whole. Small pieces of crisp, tender, raw vegetables may be used. It is highly important that these vegetables be free from coarse, tough, woody fiber and that they be grown under conditions which made their raw use safe. Children are fond of sticks of carrot, turnip and celery, or whole leaves of lettuce, because the shapes are interesting and the pieces are easily handled. Broccoli flowerettes, or the flowers of cauliflower, may be served, too. These vegetables should be crisped in ice water until they snap when broken, and it is advisable to remove the tough strings from celery which is to be served raw.

The greater part of fruit the pre-school child eats should be cooked. Oranges, bananas and small amounts of apples may be safely served raw to children.

INTRODUCING NEW FOODS

NEW FOODS should be introduced to a child during his pre-school years, for at this age he learns to like new flavors and textures more readily than later. Only one new food should be introduced at a time, and this served preferably with a favorite food. Two or three bites only are served the first time, with the amount gradually increased as the food becomes more familiar. A child's hunger is at its peak at mid-day and new foods are taken most easily at the noon meal.

Foods for children who do not chew well should be mashed or cut into very fine pieces. It is well to teach the child to chew on toast or hard bread. Small pieces of raw vegetables may be introduced gradually after the second year if the child's teeth are well formed. A stick of vegetable, carrot for instance, will teach the child to chew raw vegetables better than if the vegetable is cut into tiny cubes or grated.

FOOD SENSITIVITY (ALLERGY)

OCCASIONALLY some food behaves as a specific poison to a child. Eggs frequently are offenders, as are wheat, liver, fish, some vegetables and fruit. When a food such as eggs, which should be used in every day's meals, must be omitted, this deficiency should be compensated for as much as possible. If eggs are omitted from the diet, cheese, milk and vegetable proteins may be used to supplement the day's supply. Foods high in iron and vitamins A and D should also be used to replace the eggs.

Since the omission of such a common article of the adequate diet as eggs must necessarily limit the diet, it is well to feed minute amounts of egg until the child is desensitized, if this is possible. Such a plan for treatment should always be under the supervision of a physician.

Raw egg whites should never be served to children under eighteen to twenty-four months since raw albumin may pass, undigested, through the intestinal wall. When this protein reaches the blood stream it behaves as a poison. If the raw egg yolk is fed it should be separated from the white. Raw egg yolk rarely causes trouble.

FOOD PLAN FOR THE GROWING CHILD

WHEN the baby is past a year of age he should be getting three meals a day of foods chopped or mashed rather than strained, with one or two regular, between-meal feedings. This pattern is followed through childhood, with gradual changes in the types and amounts of food offered. The general food plan for breakfast, dinner, mid-afternoon and supper follows:

BREAKFAST
Fruit
Cereal
Egg
Bread and butter
Milk

MID–MORNING
Fruit or cracker
Milk

DINNER
Meat
Potato
Vegetable
Leafy vegetable
Bread and butter
Dessert
Milk

MID–AFTERNOON
Cracker or fruit
Milk

SUPPER
Cereal
Vegetable
Bread and butter
Milk

The most important thing about this food plan is not to take it too rigidly. It is quite true that there are certain foods that children need in certain amounts for healthy growth. But it is *not* true that a certain, definite amount of each must be taken every single day. Children's appetites vary as adults' do. On a hungry day your child may eat much more than the minimum requirement. Then he may have a day or so when he will not feel like eating much. In the long run, which is what counts, the two will tend to balance. Over a period measured in weeks rather than in days, he will get what he needs as long as he is not actually sick and as long as he is not forced, nagged or coaxed to eat. Mealtime should be pleasant and easy-going, without tensions. If the food is refused it should be taken away without comment. Dessert or candy should not be held out as a bribe for finishing vegetables. That will confirm the child's suspicion that dessert is extra desirable and vegetables are not.

The meals as outlined are too much for the child under two unless the portions are extremely small. It is better to omit one or two of the items from each meal until he is bigger and can eat more. It does not matter which food is left out at any particular meal. It can be included some other time. As a general guide, the mother should plan to serve the following:

MILK: averaging one to two pints a day as a beverage or cooked in the food

EGG: in some form at some meal three or four times a week

MEAT: or fish or poultry, several times a week

VEGETABLE: at least one vegetable besides potato, should appear on the table every day, preferably a green or a yellow one

FRUIT: one of the citrus fruits or their juice, or tomato juice once a day

When the child gets tired of cereal twice a day, soup, macaroni or potato or some other filling dish may be given instead at supper. Desserts should usually be fresh or cooked fruit, or custard or junket puddings.

As the child gets older, more foods or larger portions can be given at meals until they are more or less like the general food plan. But wait until he is ready for more. It is a mistake to load a child's plate too full. He may be overwhelmed by what seems to be an ordinary serving. It is better to let him finish a smaller amount and come back for more than to take his appetite away by heaping his plate.

The mid-morning and mid-afternoon feedings are best restricted to simple foods that do not stay in the stomach very long and so do not depress the appetite for the next meal. They should be given at fairly regular times, an hour or an hour and a half before the next meal is due. Milk and fruit or milk and a cracker with a little butter or jelly are usually enough. If this seems to interfere with eating at meals, it should be skipped.

There is no set age at which certain foods must be introduced into the diet. Some children are ready for and take to new things months before others. But always, with anything new, start gradually with only a taste or two the first few times. Fatty and fried foods, and also very sweet or rich pastries and desserts, are best avoided for as long as possible. This does not mean that occasional servings should be completely forbidden, but that they should not become regular items of the child's diet. The same applies to highly seasoned and spiced foods. Practically any cooked vegetable can be given to children past a year of age, with the exception of whole corn which they do not digest. Raw vegetables can be started by a year and a half, and many children become quite fond of them. Poultry and fish can be substituted for meat even earlier. There is no point in serving berries or cherries much before two years because children swallow them whole and do not digest them. But most other fruits, raw or cooked, can be given by one or two years of age. Melons are usually started around two and pineapple a little later. Canned fruits are usually put up with an extra large amount of sugar which is undesirable, and they should therefore not be used.

SUGGESTED MENUS FOR CHILDREN FROM TWO TO SIX
By S. Josephine Baker, M.D.

FROM TWO TO THREE

Breakfast; (1) 3 ounces orange juice or tomato juice, or 3 tablespoonfuls apple sauce, or 6 cooked prunes, or baked apple. (2) 8 ounces cooked cereal with top milk and 2 teaspoonfuls sugar. (3) 1 glassful milk. (4) 1 slice of bread and butter.

Dinner; (1) 8 ounces soup made with vegetables, chicken, beef or lamb. (2) 4 level teaspoonfuls chopped beef or lamb or broiled fish. (3) 1 small baked or boiled potato. (4) 4 tablespoonfuls green vegetables: beets, green peas, string beans, carrots, spinach or cauliflower. (5) 1 slice of bread with butter. (6) 1 cup of milk. (7) Dessert; one of the following: apple sauce, prune pulp, rice pudding, bread pudding, tapioca, blanc mange, junket or baked custard.

Supper; (1) 1 egg, poached or boiled. (2) Slice of bread with butter. (3) 1 tablespoonful jelly. (4) 1 cup of milk. (5) 4 tablespoonfuls cooked fruit or 4 tablespoonfuls pudding.

FROM THREE TO SIX

Breakfast; (1) Fresh fruit: pears, apples, orange or cooked fruit. (2) Egg: soft boiled, poached, in omelet or scrambled. (3) Cooked cereal with top milk and sugar. (4) Cup of cocoa or glass of milk. (5) Slice of bread and butter.

Dinner; (1) Soup: vegetable, beef, chicken or lamb. (2) Meat: chicken, beefsteak, roast beef, lamb chops or boiled fish. (3) vegetables: beets, spinach, carrots, string beans, peas, cauliflower, baked or boiled potatoes, macaroni, spaghetti, lettuce (without dressing). (4) Bread and butter. (5) Cup of milk. (6) All milk puddings, rice pudding, tapioca pudding, apple sauce, prunes, or ice cream.

Supper; (1) Egg, in various forms. (2) Cup of cocoa or cup of milk. (3) Jelly. (4) Cream cheese. (5) Cereal, ½ cupful. (6) Slice of bread with butter. (7) 2 pieces of fruit, or 6 tablespoonfuls of cooked fruit, or 6 tablespoonfuls of pudding.

FOOD FOR SCHOOL BOYS AND GIRLS

By Mary Swartz Rose

CARE of the diet should not cease with the first four or five years of life. The small boys and girls trooping off to school every morning have not progressed so very far along the path of growth. They have started on a climb lasting for nearly a quarter of a century, and while it is true that they triple their initial weight in a single year at the beginning of their career, it is also true that they must increase it fifteen or sixteen times more before they reach adult stature.

THE MORNING MEAL

THE first consideration in the school child's program is his breakfast. He should never be permitted to go off without it, for he has not reserves in his body to tide him over long periods without food, as an adult has. No breakfast, or a very unsuitable one, is frequently cited as a cause of undernutrition. The precise form of this meal will depend somewhat upon the age of the child. For those from five to eight years of age it may consist of the following:

1. *A mild fruit:* as orange, fresh ripe or baked apple, baked banana, stewed prunes.

2. *A well-cooked cereal:* oatmeal having the preference; Wheatena, rolled wheat, hominy grits introduced at intervals for variety; occasionally a ready-to-eat cereal, especially in the summer time. Any of these should be served with a liberal supply of milk but not with sugar, as when it is taken thus children are less likely to tire of it.

3. *Some form of dry, rather hard bread:* as toast, zwieback, whole-wheat crackers, very crusty rolls baked a second time when at least 24 hours old. These help to develop chewing habits and also to bring blood and exercise to the jaws and lay the foundations for strong teeth.

4. *Milk to drink:* this should never be very cold, and may very well be hot, especially on cold mornings. It may be flavored with a little cocoa or cereal coffee, if by such means the milk is taken more freely.

If the breakfast must be simpler than this, it will be best to give the cereal and milk and trust to getting in the other foods later in the day. For the older children, there may be more variety in fruit, the preference being given to that which is only mildly acid. Fresh fruits in season, and many kinds of dried fruits, may be used. To increase the amount of fuel, an egg or some bacon may well be added. The main changes in the meal will be in amount rather than kind. No hot breads or fried foods should be included before the age of fourteen and after that only at long intervals and in small amounts, so that they are never permitted to constitute the chief part of the meal.

A regular schedule for meals is very important as an aid to digestion. The alimentary tract may be trained to respond to the stimulus of food taken at a definite time much better than when the food is taken haphazard. The breakfast hour should be early enough to prevent any one fretting or eating hastily through fear of being late to school. Serenity promotes good nutrition; excessive emotion of any kind retards the digestive processes and sometimes actually produces acute indigestion. Whimpering over food should never be permitted; eating should be stopped till calmness is restored.

THE NOON MEAL

DINNER should be served at noon rather than at night for children under twelve, so that early slumber, also imperative for good development—especially of the nervous system—shall not be interfered with. Dinner for children from five to eight years of age will serve with little modification as luncheon or dinner for the older ones. It may consist of:

1. *A soup:* made with milk and vegetable juice or pulp; or a mild broth used as a medium for carrying vegetables or cereals.

2. *An egg:* dropped, poached, coddled, made into an omelet, or scrambled—never fried. For variety, a little bacon, a bean purée, creamed macaroni, or baked rice with a little cheese can be used.

3. *Stale bread or crackers* with butter.

4. *A green vegetable:* of mild flavor and delicate texture, mashed or finely chopped for the youngest. Much of the variety in the diet, to which children need to be trained for their future good, is obtained through careful choice and method of serving of vegetables; and a cultivation of a taste for them, not only as sources of building material in childhood but as a means of keeping the body in good running order in later life, is a duty of those who have such feeding in charge.

5. *A very simple dessert:* as junket, baked custard, blancmange, rice, or other cereal pudding. If sweets are further desired they should be in-

cluded in the dessert. A little candy (one or two pieces) may be taken at the end of a meal without harm, but should not be allowed at other times.

6. *Milk to drink:* this may be omitted if a milk soup is served.

For the older children, who have dinner at night, the luncheon should be substantial, and the above plan with more choice of hot dishes will serve very well.

THE EVENING MEAL

THE EVENING meal should be very simple indeed for children up to eight or nine years of age, and furnished not later than six o'clock. Bread and milk, milk toast, creamy egg on toast, or thick soup with bread, and mild stewed fruit, accompanied by a plain cooky or cake or by some cereal pudding, will make an adequate meal. For the older children, the evening dinner should be about as substantial as the noon meal, including a small serving of meat and a simple salad of fresh fruit or vegetables, preferably with French dressing. Stewed fruit may be substituted for the salad when desired. There should be plenty of bread and butter.

THE SCHOOL LUNCH–BOX

By MARY SWARTZ ROSE

WHEN the noon meal cannot be taken at home, the problem of a suitable school lunch must be met. If the lunch-box is carried from home, the advantage of warm food in promoting easy digestion and leaving the mind freer for action in the afternoon is lost; there is also more danger of the food being bolted than in a regular meal at a table with others. Consequently special care needs to be taken that the foods are suitable in kind and amount, and appetizing when the box is opened.

1. *Sandwiches:* which form the best staple, made of whole-wheat bread and filled with hard-cooked eggs, well but mildly seasoned; a nut paste, as peanut-butter softened with milk or cream; a dried fruit paste, made of chopped dates or figs. These kinds are all suitable for the younger children; for the older ones, chopped meat, cheese, jellies, and jams are also desirable.

2. *Fruit:* which is appetizing and carries well. The varieties mentioned for breakfast are suitable, also cooked fruit if it can be carried, as apple-sauce, stewed raisins, pears, etc. Tomatoes may often take the place of other fruit when liked.

3. *A sweet:* as baked custard, plain cookies, sponge cake.

4. *Milk or fruit juice to drink.*

For the older children, stuffed eggs mildly seasoned, nuts, sweet chocolate, baked beans, crusty rolls filled with potato or other simple salad, help to give variety.

LUNCH TIME AT SCHOOL

By MARY AGNES DAVIS

THE lunch hour at school is the one hour of the day in which no guidance is offered to the children in many schools, because no provision has been made for a school lunch. Children eat a cold lunch which has often been prepared hastily in the morning from what has been left from the previous evening meal. The school lunch should do more than give children something to eat at lunch time; it must give them the right kind of food and teach them how to choose food intelligently; it sends, through the children, information regarding food into the homes.

Many homes do not provide the right kind of food, not because they are not willing, but because they do not know what should be provided in order to obtain the best results from the amount of money spent. Through the school lunch a child learns that food has a money value.

If the menu for the following day's lunch is placed in a conspicuous place, the children will notice it and talk about it at home. This not only shows the child how much money he will need for lunch, but carries a discussion of food into the home, the very thing that the conscientious school lunch director wants.

SERVE SOMETHING HOT

THE school lunch does not have to consist of an elaborate menu; a menu that requires an unusual amount of time for preparation is unnecessary. Something hot, cocoa or soup, is a valuable addition to the sandwiches and fruit brought from home. If there has been no provision made for the preparation of a hot lunch at school, cocoa and soup can be prepared before school and reheated at lunch time.

The menu should be simple and short. Milk, eggs, cereals, vegetables and fruits should appear on every school lunch menu. It will make no difference then if a child does eat two desserts, if the desserts contain the food which he should have.

Children will learn to choose food wisely and without mistake if the choice is small. A small choice permits of a greater variety of menus and therefore less repetition of the same dishes. Children, just like grown folks, lose interest in food when it appears in the same form each day. It is true that the same foods are needed every day, in many instances, but these foods should be used in different ways.

FOOD BETWEEN MEALS

CHILDREN must eat to grow as well as to live; and as the capacity of a child's stomach is small, he needs more than the regular meals per day. Midway through the morning he should have something that is wholesome and easily digested—a piece of zwieback or dry toast, a cup of broth, a cup of gruel, some ripe fruit, or, best of all, a glass of milk.

Then again half-way between the noon and the evening meals he should have another bite or snack. Marion Brownfield tells of one clever mother who has solved this problem. In a certain place in the kitchen there are three paper plates awaiting the three children each afternoon. Often there is fruit there: a bunch of grapes, an orange, a banana, or some figs. Frequently there are a couple of crackers. Sometimes these are spread with peanut butter if they are plain crackers. Perhaps they will be of different kinds; there may be a fig bar and a graham cracker. Perhaps there will be an apple, and a walnut to crack. Even left-overs are enjoyed as a surprise; bread pudding, an ear of corn, a tomato or scraps made into an interesting sandwich sometimes greets the youngsters. As a real treat, the left-over may be cake! Because it is understood that the luncheon must be eaten "as is" with no requests for more until meal time, the plan relieves the mother of a great deal of teasing and it also prevents the temptation to dip into food prepared for a coming meal.

If these extra meals are kept as simple as the above suggestions indicate, they will not interfere with the child's desire for his "three squares per day" and there will be no trouble in eliminating them when the growing period is over.

But, some one inquires, how is a child to get even a glass of milk between breakfast and noon if he goes to school? The solution of that problem is easy. The school principal or superintendent should arrange with a local dairy to deliver to the school-house each day the same number of one-half pint bottles of milk as there are children in the school. Cups or glasses are not necessary if straws such as used at soft-drink counters are supplied to the children, as it is easy to make a hole in the cardboard cap on the bottle and insert a straw.

GOOD FOOD HABITS

By LUCY H. GILLETT

1. Meals should be at the same hours each day.
2. Plenty of water should be given between meals.

3. Children often have to be taught to like things which are good for them.
4. Children should not be forced to eat when

they are not hungry for the food that is offered them.

5. Children should be happy while eating.
6. Plenty of time should be allowed for meals.
7. Dirt is dangerous:

Children should have clean hands and faces while eating; they should sit down to a clean table and eat in an orderly manner; flies should never be allowed to alight on food.

SUMMER DRINKS FOR CHILDREN*

By ALICE IRWIN

THE QUESTION "What can I give my children to drink on hot summer days?" is asked so often that it seems that the number of mothers who find this a particularly bothersome problem is legion. Yet I suppose that the number of times each summer the average mother has to hear the petition "I want a soda" or "I want an ice-cream cone," would be an appalling figure.

The daily demand for ice-cream cones or sodas is a bad habit for several reasons. In many neighborhoods the cleanliness of the local stores may be questioned. The corner Greek candy store, which is frequently patronized, may manage to get by when municipal inspectors come to visit, but would scarcely comply with all the requirements of sanitation. From the standpoint of healthfulness, the wisdom of gulping down much ice-cold food is doubtful. And from the standpoint of cost—how few families can afford even five cents to each child daily through the summer season, for of course anything which one child in the family is permitted to have, every other child in the family must have.

I asked one mother of two children, a girl of seven and a boy of five, how she meets this particular problem. I knew that ice-cream cones cost seven cents in her neighborhood, and sodas ten, and that she would not feel that fifty cents should be allowed each of her children for this purpose weekly. I knew that she would have other objections to this practice too, and that since she lived in the same block with families who are not quite so conscientious in taking thought of what is best for their children, it must be hard for her small boy and girl to see the other children going gaily off to the corner drug store on a hot afternoon when they may not.

Her plan is to allow the children refreshment at home. She keeps a supply of lemons on hand and iced water always in the refrigerator. It is her small daughter's privilege to go into the kitchen whenever she pleases and use one lemon to make two glasses of lemonade, one for the small

brother and one for herself. She is not allowed to chip off ice, but the iced water is there for her use. It happens that this little girl has an allowance, and her mother has pointed out to her that the saving in money she makes by making her drinks at home may be added to an amount she is putting aside to buy a coveted toy.

MILK

MILK is the drink *par excellence* for children at any time of the year, and if it is possible to keep a supply of it on ice in order that the children may have it whenever they wish, the problem of summer drinks for children will be solved to a large extent. Milk served in pitchers or tall tumblers of colored crystal or with those fascinating hollow-tubed glass spoons which have bowls of colored glass may often prove more tempting than milk served in a more prosaic manner.

LEMONADE

NEXT to milk as a summer beverage for children comes lemonade. Plain lemonade may be made with the basic proportion of one lemon, one tablespoon sugar, and one glass of iced water for each portion. The average amount of juice-yield by a lemon is one-fourth cup, and although a lemon to each glass of water is the proportion given for adults, children are usually just as well pleased if a lemon is used to each two glasses of water. But the amount of sugar, one tablespoon for each glass, will probably still be wanted.

Here are some variations of the ordinary lemonade recipe, which like all standard recipes, is planned to serve six portions:

Plain Lemonade

1 cup sugar
6 cups water
6 lemons

---

* Reprinted from *Hygeia* by permission.

Heat the sugar and water to the boiling point; chill and add lemon juice.

Fruit Lemonades

For raspberry, strawberry, or blackberry lemonade, add two cups of berry juice.

For ginger ale lemonade, add two cups ginger ale.

For grape juice lemonade, add one pint grape juice.

For fruit lemonade, add two cups finely diced fruit—peaches, strawberries, oranges, grapefruit, or a mixture of fruits.

For pineapple lemonade, add two cups of pineapple juice or a No. 2 can of grated pineapple.

An imitation mint julep may be made by adding from six to twelve sprigs of mint to the hot syrup.

For prune lemonade, add two cups of prune juice.

For egg lemonade, add from four to six well-beaten eggs, mixed with one-half cup of sugar.

For the mother who has reason to try to introduce larger quantities of nourishing foods into her children's diet, an oatmeal lemonade is recommended.

Oatmeal Lemonade

1½ tablespoons fine oatmeal
A few grains salt
3 tablespoons cold water
3 pints boiling water
3 tablespoons sugar
Juice of 1½ lemons

Mix the oatmeal and salt with the cold water; add them to the boiling water and cook until reduced to a quart. Strain, add sugar, and, when chilled, add lemon juice.

ORANGEADE

ORANGEADE is made in precisely the same way as lemonade and is a popular drink with children. The addition of one lemon to each two oranges improves the flavor for adults.

Plain orange juice, if ice cold, is particularly refreshing and is of great importance in the feeding of undernourished as well as of normal children.

ICED COCOA SYRUP

ALMOST all children like the flavor of chocolate; an iced cocoa syrup may be prepared and kept on hand ready for use.

2 cups cocoa (1 pound)   ⅛ teaspoon salt
2 cups granulated sugar   2 cups lukewarm water

Mix the cocoa, sugar, and salt, and add the water slowly. Bring to boiling point and boil for ten minutes. Place the mixture in the top of the double boiler and continue cooking for thirty minutes longer. Fill hot sterilized bottles to overflowing and seal.

When the syrup is served, one-fourth cup of this mixture is added to one pint ice-cold milk or water.

BLACKBERRY SYRUP

HERE IS a recipe for blackberry syrup which may be kept ready to serve:

2 quarts berries   1 pound syrup
2 cups sugar   1 teaspoon cloves
2 inches stick cinnamon   1 teaspoon allspice

Wash the berries well, put them in a preserving pan, and heat slowly, stirring often, until the boiling point is reached. Do not add water. Strain through cheese cloth. Add sugar and spices which have been tied in a small cheese cloth bag. Boil for thirty minutes. Add one pint boiling water. Fill sterilized bottles to overflowing and seal immediately. The spices may be omitted if they are not desired.

ICE CREAM

CHILDREN enjoy ice cream so much that a moderate use of it is permissible all the year round. Ice cream for dessert for Sunday dinner is always a treat and may be especially welcome if served with fresh crushed fruit or like a chocolate or butterscotch sundae. The sauces may be made at home at about one-fourth the cost of those purchased in the stores.

Chocolate Sauce

1 cup sugar   2 cups water
2 tablespoons cornstarch   A few grains salt
6 tablespoons cocoa or   1 teaspoon vanilla
2 squares unsweetened chocolate

Mix the sugar and cornstarch; add the cocoa or melted chocolate. Add water and heat the mixture to the boiling point; boil five minutes. Add salt and, when cool, add vanilla.

Butterscotch Sauce

3 tablespoons flour   1½ cups boiling water
1 cup dark brown sugar   1½ tablespoons butter

Mix the flour and sugar; gradually add the boiling water. Bring to the boiling point and add butter. Remove from fire and cool. If desired, twelve marshmallows may be cut into halves and added to this.

Marshmallow Sauce

1 teaspoon gelatin softened in
1 tablespoon cold water   White of 1 egg
1 cup sugar   A few grains salt
⅛ cup water   ⅛ teaspoon vanilla

Put the gelatin into the cold water to soften. Heat the sugar and water until the syrup spins a thread (238° F.). Remove the syrup from the stove, add the softened gelatin, and then let stand while the white of an egg is being beaten until stiff. Pour the syrup slowly over the egg white, and beat until they are thick and creamy. Add the salt and vanilla. Should this sauce stiffen through standing, it is only necessary to put it into a bowl in a pan of hot water, and beat with a Dover egg beater until the sauce is again creamy. These sauces will keep for several days in a cool place.

TEACHING CHILDREN TO LIKE WHOLESOME FOODS*

By Lydia J. Roberts

MANY mothers already know what the child should be fed; but their all-absorbing question is, "How can I get him to eat it?" And that, one realizes, is another story and a long and important one.

HOW LIKES AND DISLIKES ORIGINATE

BEFORE coming specifically to this practical problem of how to train children in correct habits of eating, a brief consideration of how people in general form their food habits may prove highly suggestive of modes of attack.

Why, we may ask ourselves at the outset, do we all like some foods and dislike others, and why do my likes and dislikes differ from yours?

Presumably we both have the same taste organs and, if we eat the same food, the same sensation is doubtless carried to the brain of each of us. And yet to you that sensation of taste may be pleasant, to me positively disagreeable. How can it be?

It is evident that the difference lies not in the food, nor in the organs of taste, but in the mind's reaction or attitude toward the taste recorded. The whole question of how such varying mental attitudes toward the same food may develop in different individuals can be fully explained only by the psychologist. Nevertheless, certain methods by which our tastes are developed may easily be discovered by any observing person.

It is evident first of all that *we like, in general, foods to which we have been accustomed from our earliest years.*

Why do the Chinese like rice, the Italians macaroni, the Irish potatoes, and the Scotch oatmeal?

Because of an inborn preference in each for that particular form of starch? Not in the least. An Italian child brought up from birth in a Chinese home would share the typical Chinese liking for rice rather than for the Italian macaroni, and a Scotch child in an Irish home would doubtless be as fond of potatoes as any Irish lad. Each of these nationalities, in short, likes his own diet largely because it is the one to which his palate has been educated through a long period of years.

This prejudice in favor of foods with which we are familiar may be observed not only in the likings of nationalities and sectional groups, but in individuals as well. How else explain a grown man's preference for his mother's pies, or bread, or cabbage, when, to an unprejudiced observer, the pies are tough, the bread sour and heavy, and the cabbage dark in color and vile in flavor from bad cooking?

FOOD HABITS ACQUIRED BY IMITATION

WE NOT only like foods to which by long experience we have grown accustomed, but *we readily acquire likes or dislikes by imitation, conscious or unconscious, of those about us, especially of those we admire.* So common is it, indeed, for a child to duplicate exactly the tastes of an adored parent —the father perhaps in particular—that parents commonly assume such tastes to be hereditary.

"But aren't there children who can't eat certain

---

* Reprinted from *Hygeia* by permission.

foods because they have inherited an idiosyncrasy against them?" inquired a mother. "Now, I *just can't* drink milk. The thought of it nauseates me. And John has always been just like me."

Of course the correct answer to this question was that such idiosyncrasies for foods do exist. A few questions, however, clearly revealed the fact that in this instance—as in the large majority of such cases—John's dislike for milk was not an idiosyncrasy, neither was it inherited; it was merely a dislike acquired by unconscious imitation of a parent, who not only set the wrong example but talked about it continually. Had the mother but known, she might by the same method have developed a liking in her child for that same food.

"Father and I don't like tomatoes, but we do like carrots, and mother and John like tomatoes and don't like carrots. Isn't it queer?" Such is the familiar formula by which children, and often their mothers, call attention to this interesting resemblance. There is, as a matter of fact, nothing queer about it. It is merely an illustration of the well known axiom that we imitate what we admire, in food habits as well as in other matters.

Who, even of us adults, has not acquired a liking for something to which we were naturally averse—olives, artichokes, lemon in tea—in imitation of people whom we admired or because correct social usage seemed to demand it? Make it really popular—the style, if you please—to like any food, and its liking by the large majority is already assured.

FOOD LUXURIES ARE ENTICING

A FOOD *easily becomes popular and a liking for it consequently more easily acquired by most of us, if it happens to be regarded as a luxury.*

It is human nature not to want to miss any good thing which others seem to enjoy.

A little girl who claimed she had learned to like spinach was asked to tell how she did it.

"Oh," she explained, "father and mother and sister all ate it and seemed to like it so much I thought I must be missing something; so I began to eat it, too, and after a while I liked it."

A small boy of my acquaintance learned to like olives, though at first they were so distasteful that he practically swallowed them like pills, because his sister regarded them as luxuries, and was glorying in the fact that she could have more because he didn't like them.

Children beg for coffee because it is regarded as a privilege confined to and evidently enjoyed by their elders. I venture to say that if the father **each morning took his coffee with a grimace**, as

if it were a bitter dose of medicine, there would be little begging on the part of the child for tastes. And even if he did taste it the bitter flavor would be sufficiently convincing to make one dose enough for him.

Not only do we acquire tastes by conscious or unconscious imitation of those whom we admire, or because some foods being regarded as delicacies or luxuries seem especially desirable, but *to a certain extent we deliberately train ourselves to eat,* and as a rule therefore eventually to like *foods which we are convinced can benefit us in some much desired way.*

True, we may in general resent the idea of eating foods merely because we know in an indefinite way that they are good for us. Nevertheless, once convince the average person that the presence of a particular food will actually have a certain desired effect, and he will be not only willing but anxious to eat it.

EATING CRUSTS TO MAKE HAIR CURLY

SOME of us can remember having eaten onions day after day for the sake of the promised good complexion, or of having faithfully consumed bread crusts and burned toast in the earnest, even if mistaken, belief that thereby we might acquire curls.

Boys in athletic training live strictly on their prescribed diet, not because of some indefinite future good they hope it will do but because they honestly expect it will help them win the game to-morrow or next week.

"You'll never be much of an athlete," said a physical director to a freshman on completion of the boy's first physical examination. "You're too light."

"How much do I need?" promptly responded the boy.

"Put on ten or fifteen pounds and you may stand some chance," was the director's answer, to which, quick as a flash, came back the boy's eager "How'll I get it?"

TO PLAY ON THE TEAM

THE DIRECTIONS he received were followed to the letter, and the fifteen pounds gained in a surprisingly short time because the motive was a vital and urgent one.

Furnish an honest and compelling motive to any child who has reached the age of reason, and he will do the rest.

Let us then consider methods of applying these

principles specifically in the developing of right food habits in children.

This problem presents two somewhat different aspects. The first, and by far the simpler of the two, is the problem of how to develop right food tastes in a child, assuming you can have him from the very beginning before any habits are formed; the second is the more difficult task of training the older child who has already formed bad habits and has developed strong food prejudices, many of which must be uprooted.

TRAINING THE CHILD FROM BIRTH

A CHILD is born without habits. It is almost safe to say, therefore, that if one can take a child from birth he may educate that child's taste almost as he wills, provided he has his ideal in mind from the outset, understands the method of procedure, and carries it out faithfully and consistently.

Put into the form of definite rules for parents, the program of training may be given as follows:

1. Remember our strongest and most ineradicable likes are those of longest duration. *Begin early,* therefore, *to cultivate a taste for foods which are most important for a child to like.* The newer method of infant feeding makes full use of this principle. Small amounts are given at first to accustom the child to the new flavor, the amounts being increased and the kinds varied as the taste is developed.

The child thus gains a definite "food vocabulary" so naturally and gradually that by the time he is two years old he knows and likes all the common cereals, a variety of vegetables and fruits, egg, milk, potato, bacon, and all the foods which it is desirable he should have.

2. *Let the parents set the right example* if they would develop proper habits and likes in their children. The only safe way is for the parents really to like and to eat all the foods they desire their children to eat, and this they can train themselves to do by the self-same methods which they plan to use with their children.

3. *Make it an infallible rule never to talk of dislikes in the presence of children.* The safest method is to talk as little as possible about foods, but to assume that everyone likes and eats all foods served.

"We don't talk about oatmeal at our house, we just eat it," said a four-year-old from a home where this rule was observed.

If any talking must be done, let it be of likes rather than dislikes. Nothing could be more fatal to the development of healthy habits than the almost universal custom mothers have of rehears-ing their children's dislikes for the edification of their friends in the presence of the children. If they would make it a rule to boast only of a child's likes and to keep his dislikes in the background as something which should be overcome—as it is —the child would adjust his attitude accordingly with decided profit.

4. *See that the child's mental attitude is right when giving a new food,* if this is possible. Like it yourself; eat it with relish; treat it as a luxury meant for grown-ups; let the child himself first request it, if possible; give it grudgingly in small amounts, and see if the new food is not easily introduced.

5. *Be sure the foods given a child really are good,* if you expect them to be liked. Although a child may by persistence be taught to like almost any flavor, it distinctly simplifies the matter if the foods are palatable. Many of children's dislikes for milk are due to giving them milk which has turned or has absorbed flavors from the ice box or from weeds the cows have eaten; and some of the prejudices against cabbage and other vegetables are justly due to the unpleasant cooking odors or to the overcooked product with its unappetizing flavor.

6. *Keep the diet simple, limiting all highly flavored foods, particularly sweets,* if you would have a child like the foods he ought.

A dislike for spinach, cabbage, or other foods with decided flavors may merely mean a lack of training in their use; but when a distaste for milk and other mild bland foods develops, it is usually a safe guess that the child is getting far too much sweets or other foods with distinctive flavor, such as meat or coffee, or merely too much variety.

If a child who is not sick does not like plain wholesome foods, try removing all sweets and other highly flavored foods from the diet, send him out-doors to get good-and-hungry, give him three plain meals of milk, cereal, bread, vegetables, potatoes, eggs, with *nothing* between meals but water, and see if he does not shortly respond with a healthy appetite for the plain foods.

WHAT TO DO ABOUT
FINICKY CHILDREN

BUT NOT all parents are wise, neither have all children been correctly trained in eating from the beginning. Indeed, the great majority of children have been allowed to form food prejudices and are on the whole a fussy, finicky lot who don't like vegetables, who can't drink milk, and who must have candy.

When children have reached school age with

such habits, there is little likelihood that the parents unaided are going to be very successful in uprooting old habits and establishing new ones, for it means suddenly veering round and changing their whole method of conduct, forbidding things which have heretofore been allowed and insisting on things which have formerly been neglected. This is a possible but very difficult thing for parents to do, and it rarely, in fact, occurs.

In such situations, therefore, *some one outside the home—the teacher, the nutritionist, the physical-training teacher, the physician, the dentist, or the nurse—can do more than the parents to*ward *establishing better food habits, though the cooperation of the home is of course needed.* And even parents who have always insisted on the correct diet appreciate the help of the outside influence during this period.

It is nothing short of miraculous to the mother when the child suddenly comes home some day and demands a food he has formerly refused because he has learned to like it. And the comparative ease with which children's attitudes and likes may be changed by a skillful teacher seems no less marvelous to the ones who are responsible for these changes.

FIREPLACE MOTTO

The beauty of the house is order;
The blessing of the house is contentment;
The glory of the house is hospitality;
The crown of the house is godliness.

—Author unknown.

HOUSING

A HOME FOR THE CHILDREN

CHILDREN are entitled to the best home their parents can give them. This does not imply a luxurious house. On the contrary, surroundings which are over-ornate, easily destructible, or otherwise luxurious are definitely undesirable for children. They should, however, have a house that is as safe, clean, dry, sunny, spacious, uncluttered, and comfortable as possible.

If you can give your children such a house, furnished in good taste and with a genuine feeling of culture, you will be giving them a fine place to grow up in. Remember, though, that "it takes a heap o' living to make a house a home," that a poor home where love is, is far better than a rich one without love, and that, in the long run, "home is where the heart is."

THE BABY'S ROOM

WHENEVER possible a room should be given up to the exclusive use of the baby, since it is hard to give him the quiet he should have in a room that must be used also by other members of the family. A bright, sunny room should be chosen for the nursery.

TEMPERATURE

IN ORDER that the baby may be dressed properly the temperature of his room should be known. This can be done by hanging a thermometer about 3 feet from the floor.

A very young baby, or a delicate one, requires a warmer room than an older or more robust baby. For the first weeks of the baby's life the daytime temperature of the room should be kept between 65° and 70° F. At night it may be between 50° and 60° if the baby is properly dressed and protected. For older babies the day temperature may be from 65° to 68° F., and the night from 40° to 55° F. A healthy baby is much better off in a cool room. He should be protected by screens against drafts of cold air.

In winter the temperature of the room should be kept as even as possible. Oil or gas heaters may be used to give quick temporary heat, but gas heaters should not be used in a baby's room unless no other method of quick heating is available. They are likely to leak and give off poisonous fumes that are very dangerous; a slight leak day after day may make anyone exposed to it very ill. The baby's clothing should be adjusted to the temperature of the room.

In summer, when it is very hot, the baby should be kept in the coolest part of the house or porch, and he should wear only the lightest clothing, such as a band and a diaper.

VENTILATION

THE best way to ventilate the baby's room is to keep the window open. Most of the time the window may be left open at the top, or at the bottom when a window board is used. It is possible to shield the crib in such a way that no direct draft falls on the baby.

For ventilating the nursery at night in cold and windy weather tack one or more thicknesses of cheesecloth on a wooden frame like that of an ordinary wire screen and insert in the open window. The cloth breaks up the air current and distributes it in various directions, thus preventing drafts. A narrow cloth screen a few inches wide may be inserted in an opening at the top of the window, thus making it possible to keep the window open most of the time even in very cold weather.

WALLS AND FLOORS

The baby's room should be kept scrupulously clean. If the family moves into an old house, the nursery should be freshly papered and painted.

A bare floor is easily kept clean. Hardwood floors are better than soft for they do not splinter, but a softwood floor painted or varnished will do very well. If the floor is old, it may be covered with linoleum, which is easily cleaned. Heavy rugs and carpets are not suitable for a nursery, but washable rugs may be used. When the baby is old enough to sit on the floor to play, a heavy blanket folded or even a bedquilt may be used as a mat.

FURNISHINGS

Everything not actually needed for the care of the baby should be kept out of the nursery. Furnishings must be washed often with soap and water and exposed to sunshine and open air. If old furniture is used, it should be painted with washable paint—white or light colored. For cribs and play pens it is well to use paint containing no lead, as a baby may bite the railing and swallow paint, and if it contains lead he may be poisoned.

The following articles are essential:

Bed or crib, bedclothes, bureau or chest of drawers for clothing, one or two low chairs, bed or couch for nurse or mother, so that she can sleep in the same room if the baby is sick, wall thermometer, low chair for the mother to use when nursing the baby, folding or stationary dressing table on which to bathe and dress the baby; bathing equipment: tub—tin, enameled ware, or rubber—washbasin, enameled-ware tray, or a box or drawer divided into compartments in which are kept such things as—absorbent cotton, boric acid solution, safety pins (three sizes), soap (castile), squares of gauze or old linen, talcum powder, mineral oil, tube of petroleum jelly, or cold cream, soft hairbrush; six soft linen towels, six soft wash cloths, bath apron (butcher style), of outing flannel, rubber apron to wear under flannel one, bath towels for mother's lap or dressing table; toilet equipment (kept in bathroom if possible), painted nursery toilet chair for the young baby, with a cushion, small toilet seat with back and sides, which can be firmly fastened on the regular toilet, with a safety strap that goes around the baby's hips, and a foot rest for the older baby, small enameled-ware chamber, covered enameled-ware slop pail or two for diapers, covered soiled-clothes hamper.

Other useful articles are:

Clothes rack, balance scales, table to hold scales, screen, nursery ice box, bath thermometer, little chair and table, hinged gate at stairway.

THE BABY'S BED

THE FIRST requisite of a good bed is that it should enable the child to lie perfectly flat. The first bed may be a bassinet, or it may be a large flat clothes basket, or even a wooden soap box. A folded piece of table padding or several thicknesses of blanket may be used as a mattress; it must be flat and smooth. The basket or box should stand on a table or on two chairs placed with their seats together and should never be left on the floor while the baby is in it.

A larger bed will be needed as soon as the baby tries to sit up, so that it is well to start with the permanent crib and a firm mattress that does not sag in the middle. If the side of the crib lets down, the catch that holds it up should be well out of reach of the older baby or little child. The bars of the crib should be fairly close together, so that the baby cannot put his head between them. If the crib is of metal it is well to pad the ends and sides.

To make the baby's bed, cover the mattress or at least the middle section of the mattress with a piece of oilcloth or soft rubber sheeting, to each corner of which a strong tape has been sewed. Tie these tapes together under the mattress to hold the rubber cover smooth. (The rubber cover may be made like a pillowcase, covering the mattress entirely.) Over this place a cotton pad. Cover this with a small sheet, which should be tucked under the mattress on all four sides, so that the bed is perfectly smooth. If a sleeping bag is used no other covers are needed, except in cold weather, when extra blankets may be needed. For weather when sleeping bags are too warm, lightweight wool blankets should be provided. Such blankets are much warmer than heavy cotton ones. In very hot weather no covering is necessary, not even a top sheet. The bed may be finished with a dimity or seersucker spread, which is easily washed and requires no ironing. Do not use a heavy spread.

It is better not to use a pillow, as the baby will lie more nearly flat without one. A folded napkin may be placed under his head instead of a pillow.

A combination bed and play pen, with a bed spring and a mattress, may be used for a young baby. Such a bed usually is covered with wire netting on all four sides, the bottom and the top, to keep out insects. The top opens like the cover of a box. The top should have a fastening that locks automatically when it drops, so that, when the baby begins to stand up, he cannot raise it with his head and possibly injure himself. This bed may be fitted with casters or wheels so that it can be moved readily between the porch and the house or from room to room. After the baby is about a year old this kind of bed should no longer be used. He will probably need more room than it affords and a larger bed should be provided for him.

A baby carriage should not be used as a bed unless this is absolutely necessary, and then it may be used only for the little baby. There should be a flat mattress in the carriage. As the baby will soon outgrow a baby carriage, he should have a bed with space large enough to permit him to turn over, stretch his arms and legs, and kick freely.

DRESSING TABLE

A TABLE on which to change the baby's diaper and to bathe and dress him is a great help. It should have a smooth top or be covered with oilcloth so that it may be scrubbed. A soft pad should be put under the baby.

A small clothes rack, which can be removed, close to the table is convenient for use in dressing and undressing the baby.

PLAY PLACES IN THE HOUSE

By KATHERINE BEEBE

DURING the many days and hours when children cannot be told to "run out and play" they must play in the house, as a matter of necessity. Where the abode is a spacious one there is of course no problem, but a great many families nowadays live in small houses and, alas, apartments.

Time and again it has been my lot to spend visiting sessions in houses where to all intents and purposes the only play places were under the visitor's feet, on the arms and rockers of chairs and entirely in the vicinity of the grown people who were going through the vacuous form of conference or conversation. The usual apologies were always forthcoming. "The weather is so bad!" "The house is so small!" "The children are so full of life!" "They love so to be with mother!" and so on.

Now an A B C application of ordinary sense would make it plain to that mother that consideration for her guest, for her own comfort, for her children's good, demands some other play place, and a little ingenuity would make one possible.

Play is so vital a part of a child's life that a place for it, both indoors and out, is a necessity, not a luxury.

One mother whom it is my privilege to know, following the modern custom of opening windows at night, has several little beds in a row in one room—the smaller one, a larger one being reserved for the necessary bureaus, play space and playthings.

In another home the dining room is the play place, and the very fact that it must be put in order before meal times is giving one group of little folks invaluable lessons in neatness, order, consideration, and helpfulness.

But the ideal play place is the attic, and there often is one of some sort. Such a space kept reasonably clean, and having its windows protected, would solve many a household problem. The fact that the attic is cold is in its favor rather than otherwise. Indeed while the children are playing there the upper sash of the windows should be open. There is no reason why with coats, sweaters, caps, and even mittens on, the children should not be told to "run up and play" at such times as rain or cold make outdoor sport impossible. There being no occasion for putting on the despised and clumsy rubbers is also an advantage. Wise parents would see to it that such an attic contained an old mattress for "jumping on," a ladder, a clothesline, some odds and ends of discarded furniture, wooden boxes, a trestle or two, boards, hammers and nails, an old tarpaulin or other cloth for tent-making enterprises, together with such toys as the children choose to take with them when they go upstairs to play.

I have seen many porches which would make fine play places on wet days and wondered why none of them was in use. I suppose mothers consider the weather "too damp." But when I remember a neighbor's healthy brood of children who, equipped with rubber boots, coats and caps, played out of doors every day in the year, except when the thermometer was twenty below and a wind blowing, I am of the opinion that a few hours in damp fresh air would be much less fraught with dangerous possibilities than whole days in furnace-heated rooms.

THE LITTLE CHILD'S ROOM

By Ellen Creelman

Every home, if possible, should contain one room for the child's especial use. Not that he must always be confined to this one room, or denied the privileges of the entire home, but that he may have the privacy of a room in which to commence his education through play uninterrupted by the many activities that must go on constantly in the home.

The child should be required to spend a part of the time in his room. This he will gladly do without coercion, provided he has a pleasant room, suitable toys, and protection from intrusion as he attempts to develop his mind through play. There should be a sunny exposure, good ventilation and low windows protected against accident. The child enjoys pictures of the outside world as seen from the windows. The blue sky, the wind-blown clouds, rain drops, wind storms, sunbeams, flowers, trees, and birds afford him a continuous source of pleasure. In fact such pictures acted upon by his keen imagination frequently record more vital and lasting impressions upon the child's mind than those hung upon the walls.

The walls and woodwork of the child's room should be finished in soft harmonious colors, while the utmost cleanliness and neatness are necessary.

The walls may be relieved by pictures of interest to the child. There is a wide selection of suitable pictures from which to choose. But there should always be a picture of "Mother and Child," pictures of the child's near-at-hand environment, human life, plant life, animal life, natural phenomena, also pictures illustrating nursery rhymes. These should not be hung indiscriminately upon the walls, or they may destroy the beauty of the room. Many pictures may be kept in portfolios or presented through picture books.

There should be growing plants in the window boxes where bulbs and seeds are frequently planted which the child may care for. His interest in them is natural and also ought to be cherished.

The furniture should be simple, with the chairs and tables of suitable height placed correctly as regards the light. Cushions are useful upon the floor.

There should be a cabinet with low shelves and individual places for all toys and play materials, and always there should be a sand table.

The child should play as frequently as possible in the open air, and be kept away from the distractions of the street.

The child's room should be attractive for the child learns more from incidental impressions than from direct teaching. In fact the child's whole environment should aid the natural development of his mind, protecting him against undesirable impressions, guiding him happily towards the goal of education—good habits.

THE PORCH AS A PLAYGROUND

By William Byron Forbush

Are you making the best use of your home porch?

To turn it into a playground for the children does not require expensive or extensive furnishing. Of course, a hanging porch couch is a luxury, but it takes up room. A little swing is fully as pleasant to a little child. A slide is better, if a porch be on the ground floor. It acts as a substitute for the dear old cellar door. There is an adjustable one that the kindergarten houses sell, but father can make one just as well.

A simple thing that gives vent to the instinct for precarious footing is a humble 2 x 4 scantling. Fasten it to the floor of the porch, and the little children will toddle along it indefinitely and learn balancing and body control. Large oblong blocks arranged in irregular pathways are even more beguiling.

Dry-goods boxes are staples for the porch playground. A nest of different sizes will build into a staircase for climbing. The biggest is just the material out of which to build the playhouse. It is much better than one you could buy all papered and furnished and electric-lighted. With a large box for a table and small ones for stools, the children may have tea parties to their hearts' content.

Pulleys and rope give a singular variety of pleasure. Penrod used his as an elevator to gain access to his retreat in the barn. They suggest the germ of all sorts of delightful mechanical contrivances.

A modest seesaw is practicable. Ringtoss is a good porch game.

So much for the active plays. A sandbox, a box of big building blocks, and a tub to sail walnut shell boats in are the three best quiet amusements we can think of. There ought to be a portable screen, for separate "housekeeping" and for occasions when two small children wish to be ceremonious—or to quarrel. Another use for a large flat box is to serve as the stage of a toy theater.

No single plaything will give more lasting pleasure than a blackboard. It is the handiest, biggest, and most simple medium for picture writing.

If I were writing about porch housekeeping, I would speak of the baby-basket or baby-pen, varieties in comfortable porch-chairs, and how to connect the washer, the ironing board, the electric table stove, so that the whole family may live, move, and have their being outside.

If some of these things are done not only may the mother work with greater comfort during warm weather, but she may, with a few inexpensive and homely devices, keep her group of playfellows safely and happily around her.

THE GIRL'S OWN ROOM

By Allen L. Churchill

THE girl's room should be what the title implies—her own. During the most important formative period of her life—from twelve to eighteen—her room should be to the girl the most precious and sacred room in the house. It should be the heart of her own little world.

With these considerations in mind, the girl's room should be a reflection of the girl herself; her tastes, her affections, and her aspirations should be suggested by the atmosphere of her room. It should be, not only a place for sleep and rest, but a work room, a quiet corner of the house for reading and thinking and study, and a place, also, for the quiet entertainment of her friends.

The influence of a room upon children has long been recognized by students of child psychology. This influence should, of course, be at work long before the child has the ability to become conscious of it. The attention given nowadays to the location and decoration of the rooms of even very young children indicates that both parents and interior decorators are awake to the relative importance of the children's rooms, as compared with the other rooms of the house. The children's room, in the wisely planned house, is no longer located in an out-of-the-way place, and fitted up with such odds and ends of furniture as have been discarded, or are useless elsewhere. In such homes, the selection of the situation and furnishings of the children's rooms receives as much care and thought as is given to the living room or the kitchen.

When the girl is still young—under twelve years of age—it is probable that she will be satisfied to allow her mother to select the furniture, and to decide on the decorative scheme of her room. Even at this age, however, every indication of personal taste and preference on the part of the girl should be carefully studied and wisely encouraged. A little intelligent effort on the part of the mother to explain why certain combinations and effects are in good, and others in bad, taste will have a guiding effect on the daughter's mind. The girl should be urged, unobtrusively, to give her reasons for preferring a particular color for walls or special designs in furniture and decorations for the room.

Between the ages of twelve and fifteen, the girl should have developed for her room a strong feeling that it is her own special part of the house; a place set apart for herself and her belongings.

It is not to be expected that a girl of this age will have, unless she is unusual, any strongly developed æsthetic sense. Her choice of pictures for her room, for example, may reflect rather the current taste in magazine covers than the canons of art. This, however, is a passing phase, and if it is regarded with patience and tolerance by the parents, it will soon pass.

The chief physical essentials of the room of a girl of this age are that it should have an abundance of sunshine and fresh air. The furniture should be simple and comfortable. The wall covering should be carefully chosen. It should be neither too stimulating nor too depressing in color. If wall paper is used, it should be tasteful and quiet in design, and of a pattern that will not grow monotonous if it is long lived with.

In rooms with a northern exposure, which the sunlight rarely enters, bright colors for the walls are excellent. Where the exposure is southern, soft shades of green, gray, dull blue, or ivory are pleasant.

The curtains and other hangings should, of course, harmonize with the walls. There are many materials that are admirable for curtains. They come in a variety of designs and colors. The furniture for the girl's room should be light in structure and color and simple in design. A bare floor, with a few rag or woven rugs in colors harmonizing with the walls, is most desirable. The chairs should all be comfortable, and at least one that is uncommonly so. Whatever pictures are chosen should be hung on a line with her eyes and arranged as best to fill the wall spaces.

The girl's own room should, as noted above, be her own workroom, as well as her sleeping and resting room. Educators emphasize the necessity, as an aid to concentration, of a room for study, apart from the general gathering place of the family. The atmosphere of the room should be a help towards quiet concentration on work. For a certain and regular period each day, the girl should be secure from interruptions from other members of the household.

A desk of some simple and tasteful design, bookshelves, and a comfortable, but not too easy, chair, are requisite aids for a study room.

For girls of fifteen to eighteen, a separate room, to be used as a study or workroom, is the ideal arrangement. Where one room must serve as a bedroom and a workroom, a day-bed, with a slip cover and bright cushions, will be more pleasing and useful during the day than an ordinary bed, and quite as comfortable for sleeping.

The girl who is fortunate enough to have a sitting and workroom as well as a bedroom will have an opportunity to expend upon its furnishing and decoration whatever she possesses of creative taste and judgment. It can be made a delightful place of resort for her friends, and here she can learn the first and most important lesson in the art of graceful entertaining. By this time the girl should have developed her own taste in the choice of pictures and other æsthetic embellishments, and she should be given a free hand, with an occasional suggestion or word of counsel from the mother.

The atmosphere of the girl's room should at once suggest the personality of its occupant. The girl should learn that the foundation of good taste is the elimination of the unessential, and that the best things are not always, or often, the most costly. Simplicity is the keynote of beauty. With these truths in mind, the girl can make her own room the most charming, restful, and individual room in the house.

THE BOY'S OWN ROOM

By Frank H. Cheley

EBEN REXFORD, in his "Plea for Boys," says: "Every home in which there are boys growing up is surely incomplete without a place which these boys can call their own. Most boys care little how plainly a home is furnished if it is comfortable. The main thing is a room of which the boys can feel themselves the sole proprietors. The ordinary boy's room in the dwelling in which they sleep and where they keep their clothes never quite answers the purpose. Too often they are there on probation, as it were, because they have to be put somewhere, yet they are likely to be turned out of their quarters, on a moment's notice, on the appearance of some unexpected guest, under the mistaken notion that 'the boy doesn't care.'

"Now, the fact is the average boy is delighted when he can have a place all to himself, for he feels that sense of proprietorship which is flattering to human nature when he can invite his boy friends to visit him, and knows that Mother isn't worrying over the disarrangement of things which quite naturally results when boys get together to have a good time. Here he is on his own ground, and therefore feels free to act the boy nature in him without dread of hearing an inquiry sent up from below as to what's 'going on up there'?"

NOT "WHERE," BUT "HOW"

THIS does not mean by any means that to provide a boy's room necessitates the arranging of a sound-proof padded cell; far from it. It can easily be made one of the most attractive of all rooms in the house and yet serve every purpose as a boy's own room. It may even be in a well-finished basement that is warm, dry, and well-lighted, or it may be a finished-off attic, or it may be the upstairs of the garage, heated from the house or warmed in cold weather by means of a carefully constructed open grate. Nothing else can quite take the place of an open grate in a boy's room, whenever it is possible to have one. Such a feature will many times repay the cost in the spirit of sociability and chumminess that it will make possible, not only between boys themselves, but between father and son, as well as other members of the family, for that matter.

It may be a clubroom and shop combined. It may even have certain simple gymnasium features at little expense, save a bit of time and a little ingenuity.

The dominant idea of the place, however, if it is to serve its largest purpose, must be a place where the boys can feel the same sense of ownership that Mother feels in the kitchen and that Father feels in the garage or barn. If you are building a home, or expect to build in the future, be shrewd enough to work into your plans your finest conception of a room for the boys. The mere fact that modern parents do not do this very thing accounts in no small way for the difficulties they experience in keeping their boys at home.

Following are five proven fundamentals that should be given consideration in the development of a boy's room:

1. Boys will doubly appreciate and take pride in what they themselves have helped provide or make possible.

2. Thoroughly first-class and artistic furnishings and equipment are none too good and are the most economical in the long run.

3. Boys will take better care of good things than cheap things. "Put a boy in a barn and he will act accordingly."

4. It is easily possible to develop a sense of ownership which makes boys protect and preserve their own things.

5. Boys can be placed upon their honor so that things need not be made of iron nor all kept under a lock and key to insure their conservation and care.

TASTEFUL, BOYISH PICTURES

A BOY's room need not be elegant in the commonly accepted meaning of that word. It, however, should be tasteful as to color and decoration. There should be space for the boy's own books and catalogues and magazines. Generally speaking, rugs, if there are to be any, should be loose and small enough to be easily dusted.

GOOD, STURDY FURNITURE

THE FURNITURE should be straight-lined and sub-stantial. Under no circumstances let the boy feel that the old, worn-out, repaired stuff from the living room is good enough. This is a fatal error. There should be a table that can be used for study, for games, or as a desk. There should be, in addition to the straight chairs, at least one comfortable easy chair that will encourage quiet at times for both reading and thinking or friendly chat. Start with only necessary furniture and encourage the boys to build for themselves the extra pieces as they need them, such as stools, book racks, book ends, cupboards for collections, and such other odds and ends as need to be cared for; a chest for camp equipment, and a set of drawers for electrical or mechanical apparatus. Boys will greatly prize such home-made things; and because their own time and effort have been invested, will take better care of all the furnishings they have had a hand in constructing.

SENSIBLE LIGHTING

THE LIGHTING is an important feature. Get as much daylight as possible and arrange for good artificial lighting for games, reading, and shop work.

If the room is to be a combination of shop and clubroom, the shop features should be kept at one end and arranged so that all tools and litter can be completely put out of sight in a convenient cupboard for that purpose or a set of drawers under the bench. Insist upon an orderly room that is thoroughly cleaned and straightened at least once a week and by the boys themselves.

If it is also necessary for the boys to sleep as well as to keep their clothes in this room, then individual couches should be provided, equipped with stout yet attractive couch covers for use during the day, and an out-of-the-way clothes closet or wardrobe for clothing.

A boy's room, like a boy himself, should be well balanced and should radiate, at least to a certain degree, the very personalities of the boys that are to live in it. It is of greatest importance that the boys themselves have considerable to say in the planning and furnishing. It must not be a room fixed *for* them. That is where the average home and parents make a great mistake and fail to utilize a powerful element in boy nature. We continually do too much *for* boys when we should do more things *with* them. Volumes could be written of how mothers, and fathers, too, have literally saved their boys to the home and to ideals and to general usefulness in the world by paying the price of providing a boy with his very own room.

THE BACKYARD

By ALLEN L. CHURCHILL

IT MAY be too much to say that the first essential of a home is a backyard, but if there are children of any age in the family, this is little short of the truth.

Nowadays it is universally agreed that the physical and mental health of the child depends, to a large degree, on the extent to which it is possible to provide him with outdoor air and exercise. The backyard can furnish both these abundantly.

If anything relating to parents and their children were astonishing, it would be incredible that so many fathers and mothers ask helplessly how they shall provide air, exercise, and entertainment for their children when the answer to the question is visible from the back windows.

And here, as is not always the case with essential things, there are few difficulties that cannot be overcome. For small children a load of clean sand will furnish an abundance of amusement, and if a little intelligent direction is added, of instruction as well. Every child who has been to the seashore knows very wonderful things can be made from sand and a little water. And when these have been made, they can be destroyed, and equally wonderful, but different, things can be created. A sand pile is a great stimulus to developing the creative talent in many children. As the children grow they should alternate the sand-play with amusements that are a little more strenuous. These can include running, jumping, balancing, throwing at a mark, and other of the so-called kindergarten plays and games. So a grass-plot should be part of the backyard.

It is wise to have available a simple canvas or wooden screen, or shrubbery, so arranged as to be a protection from the hot sun, and from drafts and winds. A tent or summer-house will, of course, answer the same purpose and will, in addition, provide further sources for entertainment. The tent or summer-house should be open on the sides, so that the mother can see from a distance what is going on inside.

For children of six to nine years, the backyard can be made quite as fascinating and helpful as for those of an earlier age. Now, however, it will be necessary for parents or older children to exercise a little more care and ingenuity. A few simple pieces of apparatus will give a great deal of entertainment and exercise, not only in their use, but in their construction. Boys of nine (and girls, too), can build simple houses from boxes and loose lumber, but a watch-

ful eye should see that no serious accident comes in the course of the work. Minor casualties are, of course, a part of the game, and are soon forgotten.

The evolution of the backyard as a place of entertainment and instruction should continue as the children progress in years and in knowledge. When they have reached the ages of nine to twelve they can do many things for themselves. By this time there will very likely have developed among the boys a "gang," and among the girls a group. For these the backyard should be made the headquarters for games and meetings. A cage for basket-ball and other simple apparatus will provide plenty of pleasant and healthful exercise. The summer-house quite likely becomes the club-house.

Boys of this age are capable of making bird-houses, sailboats, and other things that will readily suggest themselves to their active minds. There may be available a high school boy or Boy Scout who would enjoy supervising weekly games, such as obstacle races, three-legged races, and the like. Girls of nine to thirteen who wish to play at something more distinctly feminine than the games of their brothers, will find entertainment in many ring games, such as "Lazy Mary, Will You Get Up?" "London Bridge is Falling Down," and in the beautiful old Morris and other dances.

For the adolescent boys and girls the backyard should be even more attractive than for younger children. If it is large enough for tennis, simple forms of football, and baseball, the "gang" can learn there the elements of these games, and of other forms of athletics. For the girls, in addition to games of different kinds, a sewing class might be held on certain days. Some competent and willing mother could readily teach girls to make their own dresses or to embroider.

The backyard lends itself to many uses of value and of beauty. A garden of flowers will give many happy hours, while a vegetable garden will furnish opportunities for careful and steady work, and its results, if the labor has been faithfully done, will win for the gardener the appreciation and applause of his family. The flower garden is most likely to appeal to the girls, while the boys will find in the vegetable garden plenty of exercise and excitement. The best flowers for the beginner to plant are the showy annuals: zinnias, marigolds, and morning-glories.

If there is a shady corner, a fern collection

186

can be started therein; wild flowers can be brought in from the woods for a wild garden, and a few stones and a little good earth may be combined, with the requisite amount of work, to make a rock garden.

A bird-bath is very easy to construct, and will furnish much pleasure to the children, and even more pleasure and benefit to the birds. On the hot summer days it will be used by many varieties of feathered friends, and it will give the family an excellent opportunity to study them. To make a simple but quite satisfactory bird-bath it is necessary only to make an excavation about four inches deep. This should be lined with cinders or gravel. Mix Portland cement with sand, in the proportion of one part of cement to three of sand. Put in sufficient water to make a mixture that will flow readily, and then pour this on top of the cinder or gravel foundation, so that it will be covered to a depth of about two inches. When this has hardened it will hold water, and the bath will be ready for its guests.

A tent in a backyard affords pleasure and adventure for day and night. In the daytime it can be used for many games, and as meeting place for the group or "gang." At night the boys, with a father or older friend, or the girls with a mother will find sleeping in a tent a fascinating and thrilling experience.

While in our northern states the backyard will be more readily used as a place of resort and exercise in the spring, summer, and autumn, it will have its additional joys in the winter months as well. Snow can be made into houses, forts, and men. Snowball battles, if carefully supervised, give excitement and exercise in abundance. Geography, as studied by relief maps in the snow, is transformed from work to play. Then, too, what fun it is for a boy or girl to have his or her own private slide for coasting, and how much safer Mother knows they are when they are in the backyard and not on some hill with a big crowd, or coasting on a public thoroughfare in danger of automobiles! There are many winter birds, and after a heavy snowfall they often find difficulty in getting food. Lumps of suet placed on trees or elsewhere in the backyard will bring chickadees, nuthatches, downy woodpeckers and other "winter" birds regularly to the feast prepared for them. There is joy in watching and identifying these birds, and even more in knowing that this food is keeping them from hunger, and perhaps from starvation.

One of the most important and useful opportunities afforded by a backyard is the cultivation of the spirit of civic responsibility by teaching boys and girls the duty and dignity of helping to keep clean not only the yard, but the vacant lots in the immediate neighborhood.

The backyard can go a long way toward answering the question, What shall we do with the children? Make it a place which they will prefer to any other for their exercise and recreation. Use your backyard for the benefit of your children, and for your own satisfaction, pleasure, and peace of mind. If you have no backyard do your utmost to remedy the lack as soon as you possibly can. You owe this to your children.

Is there, when the winds are singing
In the happy summer timc—
When the raptured air is ringing
With earth's music heavenward springing,
Forest chirp and village chime—
Is there, of the sounds that float
Unsighingly, a single note
Half so sweet and clear and wild
As the laughter of a child?

—Laman Blanchard

VACATIONS

THE BABY'S VACATION

By Mrs. Max West

In the summer, trains, boats, cars, and busses carry thousands of families to the seashore, the mountains, or the farms for their annual vacations from the hot and crowded cities. Whether this change from city to country life is beneficial or not depends largely upon the sort of living conditions into which the children go, the character of the milk and water supplies, and the sanitary standards of the place. The mother should select, if possible, a place where a water-closet or some other form of sanitary toilet is in use. In going to a new place, it is best to boil all the drinking water and the milk for the baby. The doors and windows, and, if possible, the porches, should be screened. If the house is not screened the mother should use a cotton netting in order that the baby's crib, at least, may be protected from insects.

TRAVELING WITH YOUNG CHILDREN

If a trip with young children is an absolute necessity it should be carefully planned. Berths and seats should be reserved in advance and accurate information as to leaving and arriving times of all the conveyances concerned should be secured. The easiest child to feed on a journey is the breast-fed baby. The bottle-fed baby presents a problem, for his milk must be boiled and the bottles sterilized. If dried or evaporated milk is to be used, enough feeding bottles to last the whole journey must be boiled and stoppered before starting. If this is not possible, arrangements must be made with the porter or steward to allow the mother to boil them daily or to have them provided. Just before each feeding time the dried or evaporated milk should be mixed with boiling water, which may be heated, if necessary, over a solid-alcohol stove on a metal tray, and the whole brought to a boil again. If an outlet for electrical attachment can be had, an electric water heater will be found safe and convenient.

For a trip no longer than 24 hours, cold boiled milk or milk mixture may be carried in a vacuum bottle (unless dried or evaporated milk is used). The vacuum bottle should be cleaned, scalded, and cooled, and the milk should be boiled and then thoroughly chilled before being put into the vacuum bottle. Milk must not be put into a vacuum bottle while it is warm, as it may sour. Milk from a vacuum bottle should not be used after 24 hours. At each feeding a nursing bottle must be filled and warmed. For warming the feeding take a utensil holding a pint, which the porter will fill with hot water from the dining car. Place the bottle in it to heat, but wait until the water has cooled somewhat, so that sudden heat will not break the bottle.

A separate bag or basket lined with rubber sheeting should be provided for the diapers, and with them may be packed a small enameled-ware chamber. For a young baby a number of inner pads of soft paper or old cloth which can be destroyed should be provided. When one of these is soiled, wrap it in newspaper and destroy it. Wet diapers may be tightly rolled and kept in the rubber bag, if necessary.

THE BABY'S SUMMER CLOTHING

In the hot summer weather, for a long journey, the older baby should be dressed only in the sleeveless gauze shirt and diaper, with one thin outer garment. A short-sleeved, low-necked slip of white nylon is cooler than cotton, sheds the dust, and can be washed out in the basin when soiled. Warmer clothing should be at hand to slip on at once if the day suddenly cools.

It is well to change the baby's clothing as soon as the journey begins, in order to have the regular outfit clean to put on when leaving the train. The little baby may go barefooted, but an older child should have barefoot sandals.

The usual règular hours for feeding the baby should be observed. Mothers sometimes give the baby cakes, candy, bananas, sweet crackers, and the like, to keep him quiet in the train. Irregular feeding with unsuitable foods, together with the fatigue and excitement of traveling, are very apt to make the baby irritable if not actually ill.

HOW TO GIVE THE CHILDREN A GOOD TIME DURING VACATION*

By Nena Wilson Badenoch

When the last hour of school has passed and the children come home jubilantly with their pile of books, many a mother has a sinking of the heart, wondering just what she is going to do to keep them busy and happy. Will she turn them loose to do as they please in the two months or more of vacation, letting them fritter away their time with a freedom which leads to lawlessness and laziness, with lax hours for food and sleep? Or will she mold this freedom in a constructive way that will bring the children to September full of vigorous health, physically and mentally alert, with awakened interest in the world about them and an increased capacity for the new ahead?

The summer is usually a period of growth and abounding health for children who are given the right kind of food, enough sleep, and plenty of outdoor occupation and play. The temptation to eat between meals, which leads to poor health, may be forestalled by regularity of meal time. Much fun and informality may be had with picnic lunches or dinners under a shady tree or in the park.

To keep the children healthy and comfortable not only requires the right foods at regular times, but also many cleansing and cooling baths with an adequate supply of fresh clothing. With a bath brush and spray even five-year old Tommy can be taught to scrub and spray his body into fresh coolness for restful sleep. Bare feet and light, clean clothing bring health to the body as sure as sun and air make leaves green.

One of the health problems during the summer months is to see that the children get enough sleep. The tendency toward irregularity in the bedtime hour is most natural when, on hot nights, the house is stifling and all of the world is awake and outdoors. But children need regular sleep and enough to keep them fresh. Some shift their hours and sleep later in the morning; others go to sleep as they speed along in the family auto. On very hot nights I have often dressed my children in nightgowns and kimonos, provided pillows and light covers, and taken them in the auto into the cool fresh air of the country. The purpose of the ride was understood at the start and it never was long until they were asleep.

Because of the general tendency toward less sleep it is especially desirable, even with older children, to insist on a rest at noon. It may not mean sleep, but at least each person should be alone, sitting or lying down, which invariably brings relaxation. I have found it necessary to provide my children with pictures or books to look over, crayons for drawing, or other attractions to quiet occupation. Often they drowse off to sleep, sometimes not, but invariably they come from their rooms, at the end of an hour or an hour and a half, refreshed and rested, ready to play happily for the rest of the day.

With the fundamentals of health provided, the children are ready for happy work and play all the day. Each day of vacation should begin, I believe, with some definite home task. It may be sweeping the porches, making the beds, gathering the vegetables, going to market, or washing the dishes. The task or tasks may be suited to the age and ability of the child, but every child should contribute something to the running of the household. I have found it important to assume that this work will be done willingly and cheerfully and as a matter of course. Never should it be made drudgery or the source of nagging. It is far better to leave it undone and let the child see the silent reminder of it all the day than to nag about it or do it for him. To make the work interesting a change of tasks may be provided each week, or a system of promotion may be instituted so that the child tries hard to do a task well enough and speedily enough to pass on to a harder one. The age between eight and twelve is said to be the golden age for the teaching of housework, and boys should have the training as well as girls, just as girls should learn to drive a nail straight or put in a screw. Any spirit of play and interest which can be introduced with the daily task helps to maintain the right attitude toward work, a point in mental hygiene that may affect the whole life and working efficiency of the individual.

For these daily tasks I never pay, as I expect the child to contribute his share to the home life. When they are done, I let the child feel that his bit is done for the day and he is free for other plans and occupations. But there is certain work

*Reprinted from *Hygeia* by permission.

about the house for which I do pay, and the child may earn the money if he likes. Our arrangements are on a purely business basis; the work has to be done satisfactorily. I make it a point to keep some small change on hand so that I can pay at once for completed work.

With the home duties happily planned and put into practice, the mother needs to talk over with the child what he would like most to accomplish during the summer months and plan for some constructive work. The mother of two active boys tried this plan: She proposed to give each one five dollars with which to finance any work he might wish to undertake for the summer. One of the boys interested in carpentry wanted to build a shack. The brother thought that if he could learn to lay bricks his happiness would be complete. So it was agreed that he should build a fireplace for the shack. This required a good deal of reading and making of plans, with figuring of lumber and bricks, consulting of price lists, and scouting for the best market. The mother was as keenly interested as the boys, but was careful to offer suggestions only when consulted. It brought a comradeship and co-operation which was even more valuable than the work done, and it provided a constructive interesting occupation for the summer, which kept the boys constantly out of doors working with hands and brains.

A nine-year-old friend of mine was eager to earn some money during his vacation. He wanted to sell something. His mother agreed to go into the candy business with him. She was to be the production department, making the candy, and he was to be sales manager. She made some fudge for samples, and he solicited orders among friends and neighbors, offering a taste of his goods. John bought all supplies, paying for the free samples out of his first profits. The profits were then divided equally between the two partners. Early in the partnership a complication arose which provided excellent opportunity for training. More than a pound of candy was on hand after orders had been filled. John was supposed to find another customer for that amount. It was a rainy day. Curled up in a big chair to read, John thought a taste of candy would be very nice for himself and brother. The result was that at dinner time only a few pieces of the pound remained. His mother questioned him, and upon learning the facts said that she would have to dissolve partnership, for that candy belonged to both of them; in it lay their profit, and, most important of all, to use partnership goods without the knowledge and consent of the second party was plain dishonesty. John was deeply distressed and begged for another chance. He paid the mother's share of profit on that pound out of his own earnings, and the offense was never repeated.

Little girls invariably like to sew for their dolls. They can gain much practical knowledge if they are allowed to buy their materials, learning the kinds and quality of textiles, cut their patterns, and use the right kind of stitches. We had a great deal of fun in a club of three little girls who wanted to sew. They met twice a week for instruction and carried home work planned for other days.

Boys always go through a certain stage when their keenest interest lies in digging a cave and cooking out of doors. If a vacant lot is near home this can be arranged, but it is important to make sure that the construction is right so that there will be no possibility for the earth to cave in. This interest makes a splendid link with the Boy Scout training of kindling fire and of camp cooking, with the baking of beans and potatoes.

For city apartment dwellers the back porch may offer the only spot for outdoor constructive occupation. The children will revel in painting it, filling window boxes, or making them, hanging curtains, and making cushions. The important point in training lies in letting them do the planning, buy the materials, with judicious supervision, and actually do the work.

For the free play of my children I have provided a neighborhood sand box in the back yard—near enough to my window so that I can see and overhear the play without intruding—and a combination play frame, with sturdy uprights and cross beams, which support a swing, a "shimmy" rope as the children call it, a ladder for climbing, and a horizontal bar. The yard has become a miniature community play-ground, for all the children in the neighborhood gather there. There are only two rules on which I insist: "take turns" and "play fair." A two-by-four scantling placed on edge provides a substitute for walking on the old picket fence and gives good training in balancing.

Every mother's chance to know her busy and developing children and to keep their comradeship lies within the vacation days. If during the weeks they are at home she plans a special outing or sightseeing trip once a week, taking them boating or bathing, to the woods or park, she will have as happy a time as they. With games about the birds they see, the kinds of trees and shrubs, the activities of the people they pass, she can do much to arouse their interest, occupy them, and sharpen their powers of observation.

SEA BATHING *

By Guy Hinsdale, M.D.

SEA baths are employed far more than any other special kind of bath, and yet they are not often used as a distinctly therapeutic measure. At Atlantic City and at Manhattan Beach as many as 100,000 may bathe in a single day at the height of the season, and at countless places on the Atlantic coast this is the principal pastime.

Yet it is rare for any one to take ocean baths under the direction or guidance of a physician. No competent person is in attendance; it is hard to keep track of the time elapsing, and few persons have any idea of the temperature of the water.

The conditions of ocean bathing are by no means constant. The temperature of the water varies almost from day to day, especially when the wind makes a notable change. Preceding or during a heavy northeast or easterly storm on the Atlantic coast, the strong winds drive the surface water toward the shore, with the result that in summer the temperature rises and there is excellent bathing. As the storm clears away and the wind blows fresh from off shore, the coast water is blown out to sea, and the colder water from greater depths takes its place. Thus there may be a fall of from 8 to 10 degrees F. in twenty-four hours.

When the wind is west or northeast, one may expect cold bathing on the north Atlantic coast. At the coast resorts of Nova Scotia and eastern Maine, the water is too cold for enjoyable bathing, except for the robust. On the westerly or southwesterly coast of Maine, and thence around the New England coast, there is excellent summer bathing at a temperature of from 60 to 70 F.

In Long Island Sound and on the south shore of Long Island, and on the New Jersey coast, higher temperatures are reached after July 15. At Manhattan Beach and Southampton, Long Island, Long Branch, Spring Lake, Atlantic City, Ocean City, Wildwood and Cape May, and at innumerable intermediate points, excellent bathing is the feature of summer life.

In winter, there is good bathing at Palm Beach and Miami, where the temperature of the water during the latter part of January and during February and March is 70 F. It is the same at Nassau during January, but rises slightly during February and March. Sea bathing is quite popular during these months.

On the Pacific coast, the water temperature at Coronado and San Diego Bay is above 70 from June 15 to September 30, and usually reaches a maximum of 74 or 75 during the latter part of July and during August, after which it rapidly falls until a minimum of 54 is reached December 15. The water is frequently warmer than the air.

Ocean bathing also varies greatly as to the force of the waves. Surf bathing in cold water calls for greater activity in meeting the onrushing waves, and the reaction is usually quickly established. For those who do not swim, the quieter bathing in protected bays devoid of surf is not so safe, because, the bather is not inclined to make proper physical effort, and hence is more quickly chilled. He fails to enjoy the bath or to get sufficient exhilarating and refreshing exercise.

OCEAN BATHING MAY BE DANGEROUS

ASIDE from the danger of being carried beyond one's depth by unknown currents, or the common danger on some parts of the New Jersey coast of getting into channels of deep water on returning shoreward, a rather frequent source of trouble, there is the danger of remaining in the water too long and of failing to react properly afterward.

On entering the water, there is a profound impression on the circulation. The temperature may be thirty or forty degrees below that of the body, and the stimulus to the nerve centers is great. The superficial vessels are immediately contracted, and the abstraction of heat from the extensive surface of the skin calls immediately for greater heat production. The momentary shiver on entering the water should promptly give place to warmth and to a sense of reaction. When the skin circulation is poor, as it commonly is in those inherently feeble or weak from illness, or in those of advanced years, sea bathing should be avoided; at least until better conditions obtain.

Great care should be exercised by persons with heart disease; but, as is well known, cold bathing, when properly used, tends to strengthen the dilated and weakened heart. Persons with cardiac lesions should have friends or attendants near, and should take no risks.

IMMERSE COMPLETELY FOR SAFETY

COMPLETE immersion is a *sine qua non* of safety;

*Reprinted from *Hygeia* by permission.

it tends to equalize the circulation and hasten reaction. Women, especially, dislike to wet their heads, as it takes so long to dry their hair; but with closely fitting rubber bathing-caps, the hair may be kept dry and the head and neck are sufficiently cooled. The modern style of bobbed hair obviates these difficulties.

Sea bathing should not be indulged in when the body is greatly overheated; but a good warmth is to be desired, and no time should be lost, lest one gets chilled by strong winds before going into the water. The chief safeguard in the water is to keep moving. A tennis ball in the surf promotes activity and adds to the pleasure of the bath. Of course, no one should bathe shortly after a meal; two hours should be allowed for digestion. One should not bathe when greatly fatigued. The bath in the quiet of one's house will then be safer and more refreshing.

I have taken ocean baths each summer for many years, and rarely have I seen ill effects in those who bathe regularly. Children who go in and out, sun themselves on the sands, and return again to the water, sometimes show bad effects; but most young people acquire a well-tanned skin in summer, and they become so accustomed to sun and water that they seem to bear these transitions with wonderful ease.

No fixed rule can be made as to the proper duration of an ocean bath. It will vary from five to twenty minutes, according to the bather's age and physical condition and to the temperature of the water. No one who has pulmonary disease or has recently had pneumonia, pleurisy, endocarditis, peritonitis, appendicitis, or acute kidney disease should bathe in the ocean. Indeed, if there is *any* reason to doubt the advisibility of sea bathing, a physician should be consulted.

DON'TS FOR BATHERS

BATHING don'ts laid down by four beach directors from Atlantic City, Ocean City, Cape May and Wildwood are as follows:

Don't go in where there is no life guard.

Don't go beyond your depth. The best swimmers get cramps.

Don't bathe less than two hours after eating.

Don't go in alone.

Don't struggle against an undertow if you are caught; go with it and call for help.

Don't wade with your hands above your head. You'll go down like a plummet in deep water.

Don't yell "Help!" unless you need it. Remember the boy who called "Wolf!"

Don't drink liquor and then go in bathing.

Don't swim with inner tubes or water wings. They are treacherous.

Don't forget you are endowed with common sense. Use it.

TAKING ADVANTAGE OF THE SUMMER CAMP FOR YOUR BOY

By FRANK H. CHELEY

THE summertime always brings the vacation problem to the home. It is in the long "do-nothing" time that boys, generally speaking, get into difficulty. Wise parents, however, instead of looking upon the vacation time as an unfortunate thing, look forward to it as a time when they will be able to supplement the regular routine of their son's school life and training by a generous amount of outdoor activity. There is hardly an available agency in the community that can so completely aid in this phase of the summer problem as the summer camp for boys. There are a hundred varieties, conducted under a score of auspices, but in general they are all built on the same fundamental principles and have the same objectives. If you never have before, consider carefully what the summer camp has to offer **your** boy this coming season.

Not many years ago the organized summer camp for boys was a new and strange idea. Some thoughtful folks looked upon it with a question, others were at once frightened by its dangers, but a few, who by training and experience knew boyhood and its needs, hailed the summer camp as a long-sought ally, and began at once to use it as a grand opportunity. It is interesting to note that today the well-conducted summer camp for boys has not only the indorsement of the doctor and the health enthusiast, but also has the support of a great many wide-awake educators, both secular and religious. Surely then there must be some element in these camps beside just "fun and sunburn," or outstanding educators by the score, as well as trained boy-leaders, would not be given such great blocks of time in discussing and teaching camp principles and methods in order to make these outdoor schools of woodcraft and citizenship even more effective and valuable.

If the summer camp for boys, as its best exponents understand it, is a principle of national significance in work with young people, then the home should also be vitally interested in its growth, expansion, and development, and take advantage for the boys of the good things it offers.

True, many camps, especially for boys, have been founded with the avowed purpose of providing, under high-class leadership, primarily a summer of fun and outing for the boy, only to discover that after the camp was once in actual operation the avowed purpose became of incidental importance, and that after all the big values lay in quite a different direction. Wide-awake men are fairly appalled by the magnificent educational opportunity that is presented to them by living in the Great Open with a group of growing boys, all entirely detached from the conventional atmosphere of artificial city life. Here all find a splendid opportunity to be quite themselves. Time and again educators have been surprised to discover how absolutely differently boys, whom they knew in more than a passing manner, impressed them under these new conditions of living together. They are constantly impressed that in the education of a boy, the important thing is not always "what does he *know*, especially of formal studies?" but "what *is* he and what will he *do* when placed in such and such a set of circumstances?" They come quickly to see with a new understanding what one of our masters of woodcraft meant when he suggested long ago, that real education should have as its prime objective the building of manhood and character and not merely the acquiring of scholarship; and to accomplish this every boy needs "something to do, something to think about, preferably in the great out-of-doors, with a view always to character-building; for manhood, not scholarship, is the first aim of education." These men have noted also that many boys who were very good scholars, but who have been accustomed to doing pretty much as they please at home, find themselves in many strange and trying circumstances when it becomes necessary for them to adjust their wishes to the somewhat imperative demands of a group. Henry van Dyke has remarked that "If you can teach boys to live together, to play together, to fish and romp together, freely and with fairness to one another, you will be able to produce for society men that can work together for a better citizenship."

Many a good student makes a poor comrade, for he is not always by any means willing to do his share of the necessary work, especially when the task in hand happens to be a mean job. The good student is not necessarily the lad that can be depended upon in an emergency, nor is he the boy who most times has the necessary initiative to undertake and bring to completion any desirable task for the mutual benefit of all.

There is hardly a conceivable circumstance that you can place a boy in that will so surely define just what he is made of as a well-conducted summer camp. Very often it reverses commonly accepted judgments of him. Boys whose mothers and aunties have declared them models, stand out in camp as striking examples of selfishness, laziness, priggishness, and hot temper, probably because in all their lives they have never been challenged to measure up and make good to the standards of a group. While on the other hand, the boy with the mischievous, troublesome reputation, the lad whose grades are not always topnotch, whose appearance is not always faultless, who is always just getting out of a scrape or perhaps just getting into another, the boy with originality and vigor of life, very often proves himself, in camp, to be essentially the better educated boy. The boy's camp becomes to the boy just what the proving ground is to a motor. It gives him an excellent chance to demonstrate exactly what he is.

The tendency of modern life is to become more and more superficial. No member of society suffers more from this aspect of things than does the growing boy. He is as yet untamed. He is seeking opportunity to express his primitive and semi-savage instincts. So much of our teaching is academic and unreal, with far too little action in it for him. It is subjective instead of objective. It is too often repression, with no opportunity for expression. It is "don't" instead of "do's." It has far too little emphasis on the fundamentals of character-building by doing. It too often leaves out of all major consideration education in the social virtues. One authority has suggested, however, that "to live one season in a real boys' camp is to acquire a liberal education in the fine art of living with others—a fine art of which a very considerable part of the human family knows but very little."

Camp directors know that most boys are tremendously responsive to high ideals while in camp. To the surprise of many folks, discipline is a very simple matter as long as a program of worth-while activities is provided. All good camps, especially for older boys, are semi- if not entirely self-governing. Democracy of the finest sort is to be found there, while hypocrisy finds very poor picking. The three vices that boys will not tolerate in camp or anywhere else are selfishness, egotism, and cowardice. Leadership rises from the ranks by virtue of its real worth. "Reputations" must be proven or forever thrown in the discard. On the other hand, the group spirit is rarely exacting, most always generous, and truly forgiving for unwise acts, if these acts are succeeded by a genuine repentance on the part of the culprit. Boys' camps that have strong leadership invariably engender in most boys present a fine spirit of co-operation, mutual understanding, and brotherly love. It is because of these conditions that it is so easy in a boys' camp to teach purposeful and unselfish living.

No doubt the great outdoors, the beautiful sunsets, the moon on the lake, the wind in the trees, and all such experiences do have their effect in mellowing the heart and making it responsive to all that is best, yet I am personally strongly inclined to believe that the reason real democracy, lived on a high plane, may be so easily and effectively taught in boys' camps is because the human relationships of one boy to another are about as normal as they can be, coupled with the fact that the intimate life together in the simple relationships offer an almost ideal, certainly a most normal place for the boy to at once give *expression* to his *impressions*. God becomes very near, because, as individual boys, they are having a chance to live godly. In the practice of ideals comes a new understanding of them. In such a boys' camp, too, there is very little to offset or even neutralize the good example.

I have known intimately hundreds of boys in summer camps and am certain that the benefits boys derive from a period spent on such an outing cannot be estimated. Communities find it desirable to support such camps in increasing numbers, confident that when the average home comes to understand their true purpose and work, they will make larger use of them than at the present time. A genuine camp experience should be a part of the training of every boy, and money invested in such an experience on the part of the home should not be looked upon as anything save a high-class investment in training and character.

Some of the larger cities are already conducting such camps for the people as a part of the educational system. It is a splendid thing to have an annual family outing, but even this cannot fully take the place in the boy's development as an outing in a first-class boy's camp.

In selecting the camp you are going to allow your boys to attend, be sure of the following matters:

1. Is the camp run for profit or for character-building?
2. Is the Camp Director a strictly first-class, trained worker with boys, or only a well-meaning novice?
3. Has the camp a satisfactory history?
4. What is the type of boys who attend?
5. Is it well located as to food and travel?
6. Is the water absolutely pure and satisfactory?

If you are satisfied on these six points, you may send your son with perfect impunity, and rest assured that he will greatly profit by the experience. If, on the other hand, there is no convenient camp to which your boys may go, gather a half dozen interested fathers of boys about yourself and create such an institution for the benefit of your community. There is a great deal of available information on the subject, and a neighboring Boy Scout man, Y. M. C. A. secretary, or representative of some other boy agency will be glad to help you get under way.

SUMMER CAMPS FOR GIRLS

By Allen L. Churchill

THE rise and development of summer camps for boys and girls are one of the most significant phenomena of the present century. Only a few years ago, such camps were unknown. Today, there are thousands, large and small, and in these are gathered, every summer, boys and girls of every age.

The growth of the summer camp idea for children has paralleled the development of the automobile as a pleasure vehicle. This resulted in a re-discovery of Nature by parents and others who had at heart the health, pleasure, and welfare of children and from this grew, logically, a desire to have boys and girls benefit physically, mentally, spiritually, and socially from the manifold blessings afforded by out-door life and freedom.

Summer camps for boys and girls are a boon no less to the parents than to the children. They have, to a large degree, answered the question: "What shall we do with the children this summer?" The alternatives were, usually, either to stay at home and devote time and energy to the difficult task of keeping the sons and daughters occupied and out of mischief, or to take the entire family to a hotel, or other resort, or on a tour. From either experiment a maximum of expense and discomfort, and a minimum of pleasure and benefit were often the only results obtained.

Now, the problem resolves itself into choosing the camp which, in all points, is the best, making the arrangements necessary, and sending off the youngsters, with the assurance that both children and parents will benefit from their temporary separation.

Summer camps for boys were the first established, and their success was so quickly assured that camps for girls speedily followed, with equally successful results.

Camps for girls, as well as for boys, are of two general kinds: Those organized and maintained by societies and organizations, and those conducted privately by individuals, or by companies formed for that purpose. Among the great bodies which conduct summer camps as a part of their work are the Girl Scouts, the Girl Pioneers, and the Camp Fire Girls. Other organizations, such as the Young Women's Christian Association (for older girls), the various denominational and fraternal societies and many schools also maintain summer camps.

The camps conducted by these organizations are usually carried on with every attention to the health, welfare, and entertainment of those who attend them. The Director of the larger camps is is chosen for his experience, and, above all, for his personality, and his assistants are selected from those who are most competent in their special departments. These assistants include a physical instructor, teacher of various handicrafts and arts, tutors, a physician, etc. College girls or teachers are often employed as councilors, which is the title usually given to those who, under the Director, have charge of the activities of the camp.

In choosing a camp of this kind, it is necessary for parents to assure themselves of the standing of the organization which conducts it, and of the suitability of its program and routine to their particular girl. When these questions have been favorably answered, the responsibility of the parents should cease, and it should be transferred to the Director of the camp and his associates. For a normal healthy girl there should be no reason for anxiety on the part of her parents for her physical, mental, or moral welfare while she is in a wisely selected camp.

The large organizations publish prospectuses and other information, which can readily be obtained. It is advisable, however, to have a personal interview, if possible, with the Director of the camp before a decision is made. However excellent a camp may be, it may not have the facilities necessary for a girl who requires special care or attention. The camps maintained by the large

organizations are usually less expensive than the privately conducted camps. They are likely, too, to have fewer "extras," or special expenses not included in the general fee.

The selection of a private camp is a much more difficult problem. These camps are of many kinds and qualities. Most are good, few are bad, and some are indifferent. The last two should, of course, be avoided. If personal knowledge of a camp cannot easily be obtained, consult the advertising pages of the reputable magazines. These list a bewildering array of camps, but it should not be difficult to select those which seem to offer the special attractions desired. Then write for full particulars and *references,* and investigate the references.

An excellent test for a camp is the length of time it has been in existence. Poorly conducted camps do not survive many seasons.

In selecting a camp, there are certain important essentials to be considered. The most important of these is the personality of the Director. Upon this depends entirely the character and conduct of the camp. The distance from home, the location, the standards of health, precautions for safety, equipment, number of councilors, and their fitness for their duties, sewage disposal, the daily program, the camp specialties—these are details that should be carefully examined before a decision is made. The same care should be taken in selecting a camp as in choosing a school.

In general, it may be said that the privately conducted camps of the higher type are better equipped to develop the individual traits of a girl. If she has pronounced gifts or tendencies, it is possible to find a camp which specializes along the lines of that tendency of gift—whether it be music, art, dancing, or any other.

The physical equipment of the private camp depends on the ideas and the resources of its conductors. Some have costly and elaborate houses, with every convenience and facility; others strive for simplicity and aim to reflect their rustic surroundings. Other things being equal, the simpler camps are better. Tents are ideal for outdoor life and if they are properly designed and put up are quite as comfortable and safe as houses. Most camps, however, provide bungalows or houses, at least for sleeping quarters.

The question of clothes for the camping girl may be easy or difficult to answer. If she is a Girl Scout, Girl Pioneer, or Camp Fire Girl, she will wear the attractive and practical uniform of her organization. In the case of a private camp the variety and quality of her clothes will be limited only by her common sense, and the family attitude and purse. The greatest amount of pleasure and benefit is obtained from the simplest apparel. There should be no "dressing up" in a camp, unless it is required by some special occasion or function.

The program and routine of the organization camps are planned to give to all the girls the greatest possible physical and mental benefit. Necessarily, the work and recreation are largely "in mass," that is, the participation is general. There are stated hours for rising, for meals, for swimming, for instruction, and for other camp activities. Ample opportunity is given, however, for individual freedom and leisure.

The camp government is, of course, under the supervision of the camp Director and his associates. A feature of the Girl Scout camps is the Council Ring, which meets daily and settles questions of camp discipline and other problems. The girls themselves compose the Ring. The Girl Scouts do all the work of the camp except the cooking. Other organizations have their special features. One of the most important aims of the girls' camps is to inculcate self-reliance and a sense of responsibility. For this reason a large measure of self-government is permitted and encouraged.

The private camps, as suggested above, have facilities for giving individual attention, when it is desired or required. This may take the form of special instruction in any of the arts or crafts, or of tutoring for school or college. Camps adaptable to almost any need can be found.

There is a considerable latitude of cost in the private camps. Embarrassment and friction may be spared by a careful inquiry into possible extra charges, in addition to the general fee. In some cases, such "extras" may equal or exceed the fee.

The success of the summer camp for girls as a social experiment is shown by the fact that children of rural families are sent, in ever increasing numbers, to these camps, not so much for physical, as for the social benefit.

The New England States still attract the largest number of girls' camps, but there are few of the other States where they are not found, and the movement is everywhere spreading yearly.

It is impossible to over-emphasize the profound influence for good that these summer camps are exerting on the generation of girls now approaching womanhood. Love of nature, self-command, self-sacrifice, responsibility, community obligation, loyalty, as well as the more obvious physical benefits, are some of the qualities inspired and developed by camp life. These are the qualities that will mark the woman of to-morrow.

CHILD AND MOTHER

O Mother-My-Love, if you'll give me your hand,
  And go where I ask you to wander,
I will lead you away to a beautiful land—
  The Dreamland that's waiting out yonder.
We'll walk in the sweet posie garden out there,
  Where moonlight and starlight are streaming,
And the flowers and the birds are filling the air
  With the fragrance and music of dreaming.

There'll be no little tired-out boy to undress,
  No questions or cares to perplex you;
There'll be no little bruises or bumps to caress,
  Nor patching of stockings to vex you.
For I'll rock you away on a silver-dew stream,
  And sing you to sleep when you're weary;
And no one shall know of our beautiful dream
  But you and your own little dearie.

And when I am tired I'll nestle my head
  In the bosom that's soothed me so often;
And the wide-awake stars shall sing in my stead
  A song which our dreaming shall soften.
So, Mother-My-Love, let me take your dear hand,
  And away through the starlight we'll wander,
Away through the mist to the beautiful land—
  The Dreamland that's waiting out yonder.

                     —Author Unknown.

HOME NURSING

SYMPTOMS OF ACUTE ILLNESS

PARENTS should know about the symptoms and signs of acute illness in their children. This is especially true for those illnesses which require prompt specialized treatment, surgical in the case of appendicitis, or medical in the case of meningitis. There are some illnesses that can be cured easily and completely, without complications, if they are caught in the early stages which may be fatal or at best complicated in their outcome if neglected.

For a little baby, the most important danger signals are *hoarseness, convulsions* and *blood in the stools.* In the presence of any one of these, the doctor should be consulted promptly. Hoarseness may be the forerunner of spasmodic croup, or of diphtheria of the larynx. A convulsion may be the first sign of any acute infection from a simple sore throat to a serious meningitis. Blood in the stools may be the result of intussusception, a condition in which the intestine has rolled up in itself and must be made to unroll as soon as possible.

In the older child there are two additional danger signals. These are *pain in the abdomen* and *stiffness of the neck or back.* The first is important if it is due to appendicitis; the second if it is from an infection of the nervous system.

For any of these five symptoms, it is much better to consult the doctor immediately and to let him have the responsibility of making the diagnosis rather than to procrastinate at the risk of endangering the child's life. The symptom may not be caused by one of the dangerous illnesses, but the untrained parent is not the one to pass on the seriousness of the condition.

Most of the illnesses that children get are acute infections. At the very onset, a good many of these will be ushered in by the same symptom or group of symptoms. Fever, loss of appetite, vomiting, diarrhea, fretfulness and drowsiness, singly or in any combination, are usually present. This is as true for an upset stomach as for an abscessed ear. In addition, many children with acute illness have a running nose, a cough, or a skin rash, or, as in measles, all three. They may complain of persistent or recurrent pain in any part of the body.

Should a mother's watchful eye detect any of these disturbances in her child's behavior, she is wise to put the child to bed and take his temperature with a clinical thermometer. The mercury should always be shaken down well below 97°, the bulb of the thermometer should be lubricated with vaseline or cold cream and, with the child lying on his side or on his belly, inserted about an inch into his rectum. The stem of the thermometer should be held, and the child should be kept quiet, for at least two minutes while the bulb is kept in place. Then the thermometer is removed, wiped off and read and the temperature written down, along with the time of day, for future reference. The thermometer should be cleaned with alcohol or with cool water and soap before being put away.

If the temperature is over 101° the doctor should be notified. So many illnesses in children start off with fever that it is foolhardy to attempt to treat just the elevated temperature without finding out what the trouble really is. And that is the doctor's job. Children in general tend to run higher fevers during acute illness than adults. Ordinarily this does no great harm unless the temperature climbs to 105° or more. When the fever does reach this level it is better to attempt to reduce it. Aspirin in a dosage of one grain for each year of age may be given once if the child has not been vomiting. A sponge of tepid water mixed with rubbing alcohol should also be given.

A convulsion is a frightening thing especially to a parent who has never seen one before. The child becomes unconscious, his eyes roll up, his muscles twitch and jerk or become very rigid and then very relaxed. He may froth at the mouth and bite his tongue, he may have involuntary evacuations from the bladder and bowel, he may turn blue. Most convulsions in children are caused by the onset of an acute infection usually outside of the nervous system. They are accompanied by high fever. They seem to be somewhat comparable to chills in sick adults. The important things for parents faced with a convulsing child are to keep calm, to prevent the child from injuring himself by biting his tongue, and to reduce his temperature if it seems to be high. Force his jaws apart and put a lead pencil, a tooth brush or a wooden spoon between his teeth. Then sponge him off repeatedly with tepid water until the fever is past its peak. A cool enema sometimes helps to accomplish this. Always have the doctor see a child who has had a convulsion.

Even if the child's temperature is not found to be over 101°, and he has not had a convulsion, the doctor should be consulted if any of the above-mentioned symptoms of acute illness persist for more than a day or two. It is not fair to the child, nor to those with whom he comes in contact, to allow symptoms of an illness which is likely to be contagious to go on without proper treatment.

CARING FOR THE SICK CHILD

By Mrs. Max West

THE mother should learn to read a clinical thermometer so that she may know whether or not her child has a fever. A thermometer may be purchased at any drug store and her doctor or the druggist will be glad to show her how to read it.

The baby's temperature normally ranges from 98.6° to 99.5° F. The temperature of a baby is much more variable than that of an adult, and a temperature higher than 99.5° F. is not unusual even in babies who are not sick. If the temperature is higher than 100° F. the doctor should be notified. A baby's temperature should always be taken in the rectum. It is wise to purchase a thermometer with a thick bulb for taking a rectal temperature. The bulb should be smeared with vaseline or oil and inserted into the rectum for at least an inch. The thermometer should be held in the rectum for at least two minutes and care taken that the baby is kept quiet so that there is no possibility of breaking the thermometer. In most cases it is just as well not to take the temperature frequently because it may cause unnecessary worry to the mother and annoyance to the baby.

Children are more likely to have fever than grown persons. A rise in temperature frequently accompanies even a slight upset in children, but a *continuous* fever, even if slight, is more important in both children and adults, than a higher temperature for a short period.

The pulse and breathing are difficult to count in infancy. A mother should note how rapid they are when the child is well so that in case of illness she may detect any difference.

The mother should also observe the normal position of the child's body, the expression of his face and his color, so that indications of discomfort, pain, or unusual irritability can be quickly noticed. The character and number of bowel movements and the amount and color of the urine should be watched. The mother should note the color of the tongue and throat and the condition of the skin.

ESSENTIALS IN CARING FOR A SICK CHILD

A YOUNG child who has any rise in temperature should be kept in bed in a cool, quiet, well-ventilated room and should be allowed to rest or sleep undisturbed as much as possible. A fussy, uncomfortable baby, or a child showing evidence of physical discomfort but without fever, should be treated in the same way.

The sick room should not be a gathering place for the family or neighbors. Even if no contagious disease is suspected, a sick child should be kept away from other children until the trouble is known. This one precaution, if observed faithfully, would do much to stop the spread of communicable disease.

The doctor should be promptly notified of the illness of a baby, and the mother should keep a written record of the temperature, rate and regularity of the pulse and respiration, cough, crying, evidence of pain, and general appearance of the child. She should note the amount and kind of food taken, amount of water, number and character of stools, amount of urine passed, vomiting, or any unusual symptom. A specimen of the stool and urine should be saved for the doctor to see.

When orders are given by the doctor, they should be carried out carefully and exactly. The mother should put down daily on a sheet of paper, or a chart, the hour at which she performed each detail, the result, and any unusual symptom noted.

If a doctor cannot be secured, the following general directions for nursing care should be observed. A child should be kept in bed as long as he has a temperature over 99.5° F. If his illness has been at all severe, he should stay in bed from three days to one week after his temperature has remained normal (98.6° to 99.5°) for twenty-four hours. The after effects of many diseases may be largely prevented by prolonging this care during convalescence.

Frequent changes in position while in bed are important not only to rest the child, but also to prevent congestion of any part of the body.

A daily sponge or tub bath should be given. A bath for fever (about 90° F.) may be given once or twice a day or oftener, if the fever is high. The temperature of the bath should be tested by a thermometer. Every precaution should be taken in bathing a sick child not to chill him by undue exposure nor to frighten or excite him. A cold compress or ice cap may be kept on the head during fever, while bathing to reduce the temperature, or while giving a warm pack. If the hands and feet are cold, hot water bottles may be used.

The amount of food should be reduced in every acute illness.

The taking of water is of the greatest importance in illness. Water should be offered at very frequent intervals, possibly every hour while the child is awake, and the amount taken in twenty-four hours should be recorded.

The bowels of a sick child should be moved daily; if necessary, an injection, or enema, of warm water may be used for the purpose. The amount of the urine should be noted, and more water should be given to drink if the amount of urine is scant.

Plenty of fresh air in a well-ventilated room, or on a porch, where the sick bed may be placed in summer, is part of the necessary treatment in any sickness. In winter, the sick room may be kept moderately warm (60°-68° F.) in the daytime while the child is awake, but may usually be kept several degrees cooler at night, or when the child is asleep.

A child that has been trained in proper health habits and has been accustomed to having the details of his toilet carefully attended to, is much easier to take care of in sickness. It is also helpful if a baby has been taught to show his tongue and throat and to allow himself to be handled. A child should never be frightened by threats of punishment.

The comfort and happiness of the baby or young child do much to hasten recovery from sickness, but strict discipline must be maintained as to nursing care and the carrying out of the doctor's orders. The way a child is managed makes the greatest difference in what can be done for him. Even a young baby is conscious of the difference between quiet, skillful handling and noisy or clumsy treatment, and responds quickly to gentle, restrained methods.

HOME NURSING

By Mary E. Carter, R.N.

(With Additions)

THERE are very few people, no matter what their station in life, who do not find themselves at some time so situated that they would be very glad to know some of the first principles of good nursing. Moreover, there are a great many who find the cost of a trained nurse a heavy tax upon a limited purse. And all would like to be able to judge of the competency of one coming into the home as a total stranger to take charge of the health and comfort of their dear ones.

RECOMMENDATIONS REGARDING THE BED AND ITS FURNISHINGS

THE FIRST thing to be considered is the bed. A firm hair mattress should always be used, with a thin blanket or covering of some kind under the lower sheet. After long service all mattresses are inclined to sink in the middle and become very uncomfortable to lie upon for any length of time. A blanket folded lengthwise and placed under the mattress, in the middle of the bed, or two flat pillows, will overcome this difficulty. When there is much fever a hair pillow will be found, though harder, much cooler than a feather one. A number of small pillows of all shapes and sizes, especially during cases of long illness, will prove of the greatest comfort. You can tuck them in odd corners, under the back and shoulders as a help to keep up the knees and thus take all the strain from the back. They form comfortable resting places for injured limbs, and support the weight of the clothes from sensitive parts of the body. Small pillows made of cotton or wool, covered with cheese-cloth or old linen, answer the purpose quite as well as more expensive ones of feathers or down.

It is much wiser to use cotton sheets in sickness instead of linen, unless in summer time, as linen is chilly and uncomfortable to a delicate person.

Three sheets are required in making the bed, also a piece of rubber sheeting to be used under the draw sheet. The rubber sheeting should be about three-quarters of a yard wide and as long as the sheet is wide. Where there is no danger of the patient soiling the mattress, the rubber sheeting may be dispensed with, as it causes unnecessary perspiration, and if it wrinkles under the patient may even lead to bed-sores.

HOW TO ARRANGE THE BED

To ARRANGE a bed for a sick person so that it will be thoroughly comfortable and free from wrinkles, the under sheet must be drawn very smoothly and well tucked in. The sheets should be three yards long and two to three yards wide— two yards wide for a single bed, two and one-half for a three-quarter width, and three yards for a full-size; sheets these sizes can be firmly tucked in. Over the under sheet and across the middle of the bed, lay the rubber sheet, and cover with the draw-sheet, which is a sheet folded to the width of the rubber, and tuck both rubber sheet and draw sheet firmly under sides of the bed. The advantage of the draw-sheet is that it may be changed as often as may be required without disturbing the patient, and it serves also to keep the under sheet clean for a much longer period.

In putting on the upper sheet leave a good margin turned over at the top to cover the blanket. Instead of a heavy white spread, place over the blanket another sheet or a thin cotton counterpane. Three points to be observed about a sick-bed are perfect cleanliness, no crumbs, and no wrinkles.

Where the supply of linen is limited a clean pillow-case can be made to do duty for a double period. Change it at night and hang it out to air until the morning, when it will be fresh for the day. The upper sheet, which is often only crushed—not really soiled, can be straightened, folded, and used for a draw sheet.

THE ADJUSTMENT OF LIGHT IN THE SICK-ROOM

SUNLIGHT is one of the necessities for a sick-room. Even should the windows have to be darkened at the commencement of an illness, as soon as your patient is convalescent plenty of sunshine will be of inestimable value, both mentally and physically, and should not be excluded except for especial reasons. If the light is too strong for the eyes, you may tone it by placing a screen between the windows and the bed.

REGULATING HEAT IN THE SICK-ROOM

IN VERY cold weather the sick-room should be kept at an even temperature. Where there is no open fireplace an electric heater or a small gas stove should be on hand in case of emergency to supplant the regular heating system.

A thermometer must hang near the middle of the room, at some distance from both the window and the heater, so as to record the exact temperature. In ordinary cases a temperature of 70° F. is the best, but where there is much fever, as in typhoid or scarlet fever, the room should not be warmer than 65° F.

In the early morning hours, between three and five o'clock, the atmosphere is colder than during any other part of the day, and as the vitality of the body is always lower at that time, care should be taken to have extra blankets on hand for the invalid, and if necessary give a hot drink and apply a hot-water bag to the feet. This is especially to be noted with elderly people and in very serious cases of illness.

VENTILATION

THE BED should stand a little out from the wall on all sides for the air to circulate around it. When the weather is very warm the bed should stand in the middle of the room. A screen protects the head from draughts.

Thorough ventilation may be had in severe weather without exposing the patient to draughts. Two windows facing each other, left open two or three inches at the top, will give a continuous current of air high enough above the bed to prevent a draught immediately upon the patient. When there is but one window in the room it should be open at the top and, if it is not near the bed, at the bottom also once in a while, but never let air blow on the bed's level. Hot air rises, cold air descends; cold air forces the impure air up and out at the window's top. Ventilation may be obtained by raising the window three or four inches from the bottom and placing a piece of strong cardboard or a strip of wood six or eight inches wide over, but an inch away from, the opening. This permits the air to enter gradually in an upward direction. The bed should invariably be protected by a screen. When ventilating is done through an adjoining room, put a screen between the bed and the door.

This last method of ventilating is done by first filling the room with fresh air and allowing it to warm gradually before opening the door into the sick-room.

CHANGING THE AIR

EVERY morning and evening the window should be opened wide for a few minutes—the number of minutes depending upon the weather. Two minutes in some weather will accomplish as much of a change in the air as twenty will in milder weather. Common sense, and not any particular time limit, should govern the duration of the ventilating period. The patient should be carefully covered with extra blankets before and during the morning and evening airing. Afterwards remove the extra coverings gradually. Never, through your carelessness, let your charge get a chill.

To dissipate an unpleasant odor, take a towel or a newspaper in each hand, and wave them to and fro with the window open. This method is efficacious in summer, as it creates a rapid circulation which freshens and cools the room.

In fever cases it is absolutely important to have a current of fresh air passing through the room all the time; when the temperature is high it is almost impossible for the patient to catch cold.

The invalid, or anyone who is constantly in the room, cannot judge the temperature or the purity of the air. By entering the room from the open air, or from some other part of the house, the difference in the atmosphere is immediately noticeable.

Even healthy people lose appetite in a close, hot room. By opening the window for a breath of fresh air before meals the patient's appetite can be stimulated.

STRICT CLEANLINESS

PERFECT cleanliness should be the inflexible rule in caring for the patient, the bed, and the room. After the daily bath the hair should be brushed, the teeth and finger-nails cleaned, the bed changed, and all soiled clothing removed. The room should be cleaned as noiselessly as possible and no dust raised.

All furniture that holds dust should be discarded. Never use a feather duster in a sick-room. It does not remove, but merely disseminates, dust.

Allow no soiled clothing to remain in the room any longer than necessary. Remove all evacuations also as quickly as possible. It is well to have somewhere outside a disinfectant—a can of chloride of lime is good. Sprinkle a little in the vessels if they have to stand anywhere before emptying. Use plenty of soap and hot water and ammonia for washing bed-pans and urinals. In fever cases they should be also rinsed off with a disinfectant solution. Never permit these vessels to stand in sight when not in use.

Flowers should not be left over night in the sick-room; they keep fresh longer if put in a cool place. Flowers can be kept fresh for some time by taking them out of the vases at night and cutting off a little piece of the stem in a slanting direction; then lay them in a pasteboard box and sprinkle them—or else pin them up in newspaper and put them outside the window.

A screen may be had with little delay and no expense by using a clothes-horse and covering it with muslin, cheese-cloth, or simply a sheet pinned securely with safety pins.

Food and drink should not be kept in the room with the patient. If he wants a glass of water near him, there should be a cover for it. One can easily be made by using one end of a large envelope or a small paper bag.

Pillows should be turned often. Never allow them to get hot and packed. They should be shaken in the open air at least twice a day. Avoid jarring patients in doing anything to promote their comfort. Do everything possible away from the bed.

If possible have two sets of pillows, one set airing and sunning while the others are in use.

Keep patients fresh and clean if you would hasten convalescence and minimize their suffering.

LIFTING A PATIENT

To RAISE a sick person while changing the pillows or to draw him up in the bed, let him clasp his arms firmly around your neck, then place one hand well under his back, and lift gently and slowly, while with the other hand you slip out one pillow and put in another.

When a patient is too weak to help himself, get assistance. With one person on each side of the bed, each clasping the other's wrists firmly under the patient's shoulders and back, you can raise or draw him up in bed without any strain or fatigue.

This should be learned by practice with a well person, before undertaking it with an invalid. Then there will be no nervousness on the part of the tyro nurse. And here let it be said that nervous, anxious people should exclude themselves from a sick-room. They do no good and often do serious harm. If very desirous to be of some service, they will find plenty to do outside of the sick-room to help the nurse without ever crossing the threshold.

Never permit your patient to be annoyed by flies or any insects. Keep the screens on doors and windows closed during insect season.

Change of position can be accomplished, when the bed is a double one, by keeping one side for the day and the other for the night. If the patient is too weak to roll over alone, you can draw him over on a sheet. With two small beds side by side the change can be made by putting a large sheet over the two beds and allowing the patient to roll over, or you can draw him over on, and with, the sheet.

CHANGING THE SHEETS

CHANGING sheets, with the patient on the bed, requires practice and should be learned with a well person on the bed until you are expert. Make no experiments with the sick one. Have the clean sheets always well aired and in cold weather warmed. Shut the door and windows while the change is being made.

First change the under sheet. Turn the patient over from you on one side, fold the soiled sheet tightly, in flat folds, close to the patient. Lay on the clean sheet smoothly, with half of it folded up against the roll of the soiled sheet, then both can be slipped under the body at once. Tuck in the clean sheet on that side of the bed, then cross to the other side, turn the patient back on the opposite side, gently pull out the soiled sheet from underneath. Afterwards draw the folds of the clean one, pull straight, and tuck firmly and neatly. By following this method the under sheet, rubber sheeting, and draw-sheet may all be changed at one time.

To change the upper sheet loosen all the bedclothes at the foot, then spread the clean sheet with blanket on top of the other bedclothes. With one hand hold the clean sheet and blanket up to the neck of your patient, with the other slip down the soiled clothes underneath right over the foot of the bed; tuck in the fresh bedclothes. An expert will do this without uncovering or fatiguing the invalid.

MAKING AND KEEPING THE PATIENT COMFORTABLE

No ONE should ever sit on the side of the bed or lean against it. No one should walk heavily across the floor of a sick-room or the floor above.

To protect any injured part of the body from the weight of bedclothes without the use of the cradles used in hospitals, two or three barrel hoops will answer the purpose, or a round bandbox large enough to slip the injured limb through. Pillows laid at each side of the bed will keep bedclothes a couple of inches above the sensitive part.

If unprovided with a bed-rest, one may be contrived from a straight-back chair with the legs turned upward on the bed. The long sloping back then forms a support for pillows piled in, one behind another, to the top. Put a small pillow under the knees to prevent the body from slipping down in the bed.

Guard carefully against bed-sores. Some people have very sensitive skins. Even during a short illness continual pressure may cause trouble. The back, elbows, knees, and heels, but especially the back, should be watched closely. The first symptoms of a bed-sore are redness of the skin with a pricking, burning sensation. Bed-sores will be found when the vitality is weakened by fever; indeed, it takes very little in the way of pressure, moisture, or continued dampness, and even wrinkles in the sheets, or crumbs, to produce these dreadful sores. It is far easier to prevent than it is to cure bed-sores. In paralytic cases, and with elderly people, they are most difficult to heal.

To prevent, as far as possible, any appearance of them, bathe the parts daily with warm water and pure soap, then rub briskly with alcohol to harden the skin, and dust on talcum or bismuth powder to remove all moisture. Guard carefully against crumbs, or wrinkles in the under sheet. Persuade the patient to turn in different positions every two or three hours, to avoid long-continued pressure on one spot.

With unconscious patients, greater watchfulness is required. When there are involuntary evacuations, the clothing must be changed immediately and the body thoroughly washed and powdered.

The first symptoms of bed-sores should be watched closely and all pressure removed from the part by a judicious use of air cushions and soft pads made from cheese-cloth filled with cotton.

Should the skin become broken, stop using alcohol and apply a little oxide-of-zinc ointment or balsam of Peru on a piece of gauze. Protect the place with a pad. If it does not heal immediately, seek special treatment from your family doctor.

VISITORS

No ONE should enter the sick-room straight from the open air on a cold or a wet day; all should wait elsewhere until their clothes lose dampness and become warm.

No matter how acceptable the visitor may be, it is necessary to guard against tiring the patient. Under no circumstances permit two people to sit, one on each side of the bed, and converse across the invalid. Visitors should occupy chairs so placed that the sick one can look at them without any effort. They should leave *before* tiring the patient.

DISINFECTING THE SICK-ROOM

AFTER a contagious illness, clean the room thoroughly. Scrub the floor, woodwork, and furniture with soap and hot water. Wipe the walls with cloths wrung from a 1-1000 bichloride solution and leave the windows wide open. Destroy toys and books; boil in soapsuds all washable bedding; send mattress and unwashable bedding to a steam disinfecting place if possible, or expose to sunlight for two or three days and beat thoroughly in the open air.

If the bathroom or any other room has been used by the nurse, it should be cleaned in the same way.

POULTICES AND THE LIKE*

By HARRY ROBERTS, M.D.

LINSEED MEAL POULTICE

LINSEED meal poultices should be made quickly, and therefore all the materials and appliances required should be got together before the process is begun. There will be required a kettle of boiling water, a basin in which the poultice is to be mixed, a spoon for stirring it, a piece of soft cotton or linen about two inches longer and wider than the size of the poultice required, and linseed meal. Some boiling water being placed in the basin, the linseed meal is to be steadily dropped from the hand into the water, the mixture being continually stirred the while. Meal is to be added until the mixture is of the consistency of thick paste. This is at once to be spread on the piece of linen, the surface smoothed by means of the spoon dipped into hot water, and the edges of the linen folded in over it about half an inch on all sides. The poultice should be, in the case of a child, about half an inch in thickness, except when placed on the chest, in which case it should not be thicker than a quarter of an inch. The linseed meal employed is either in the form of powder obtained by grinding oil cakes or it may be what is known as crushed linseed. The latter, if it can be obtained quite fresh, is the better, as it is softer and more oily, but it does not keep so well, and soon turns rancid. In order to retain the warmth as long as possible, it is well to cover the poultice with a piece of waterproof material, such as oiled silk, and outside this to arrange a layer of wadding or cotton-wool.

BREAD AND STARCH POULTICES

BREAD poultices are employed for much the same purposes as linseed poultices, but they are usually used only when a small poultice is required. Boiling water is placed in a basin and powdered stale bread-crumbs stirred into it. The basin should then be stood in another large basin of boiling water for about five minutes. The bread is then

---

* Reprinted from *Hygeia* by permission.

to be spread after the manner of a linseed poultice.

Starch Poultice.—Mix some powdered starch with cold water and then boil it for a few minutes, stirring the while, until it forms a thickish paste. Like the two previous poultices, it should then be spread upon linen, and applied directly to the skin. In all cases the heat of a poultice should be tested against the nurse's face before being applied to the patient, as serious burns are sometimes produced through neglect of this precaution.

MUSTARD POULTICE

MUSTARD poultices are sometimes employed to set up irritation on the surface of the body with a view to relieving congestion of deeper parts. Various internal inflammations and pains are certainly much relieved in this way. A mustard poultice may be made in either of two ways. In any case it consists of a linseed poultice in which a certain amount of mustard has been incorporated. One way is to make a linseed poultice as already described, and then to add the mustard and thoroughly stir it in. Another way is to mix the mustard first with a little cold water, and then to add the boiling water, adding the linseed meal to this as in making an ordinary linseed poultice. The proportion of mustard to linseed meal must vary with the age of the patient. In the case of adults, one part of mustard may be mixed with three parts of linseed meal, but in the case of babies, one part of mustard to five parts of linseed meal is quite strong enough. As a rule a mustard poultice should not be kept on for more than an hour or so.

Mustard Plaster.—Mustard plasters are much more active in their effect than mustard poultices. They are made by mixing one part dry mustard to 3 parts flour, adding a little table salt, and then spreading it to the thickness of the tenth of an inch either on clean gauze or thin, soft linen, the edges of which should be turned in to prevent the escape of the mustard at the sides. Mustard plasters as a rule should not be kept on for longer than fifteen minutes, and it is not commonly desirable that more than a small portion of the surface should be treated at one time. A plaster larger than four or five inches square should seldom be employed.

FOMENTATIONS, AND HOW TO APPLY THEM

VARIOUS forms of inflammation need the application of hot fomentations. The simplest way of preparing fomentations is to take a piece of boracic lint or flannel, fold it so that it is four thicknesses, the size of the folded piece being that of the surface which is to be covered, and lay it in the center of a clean towel. Let this towel lie across an empty basin, pour boiling water over it, and then twist the towel so as to squeeze most of the water out of the lint. The towel should then be opened and the hot lint directly applied to the patient's skin. It should be at once covered with a piece of oiled silk, and over this should be laid a thick layer of cotton-wool or wadding, the whole being kept in place by a bandage. Fomentations need to be replaced about every half-hour, as they quickly lose their heat.

TO MAKE TURPENTINE APPLICATIONS

A PIECE of flannel is taken of such a size that when folded four thick it will cover the desired surface. This folded flannel is then placed in the center of a towel, which is to be laid across a basin, boiling water is then to be poured over the flannel, and the two ends of the towel are to be twisted in opposite directions so as to squeeze out most of the water from the flannel. A little turpentine—about half a teaspoonful to the square foot—is then evenly sprinkled over the surface of the four-fold flannel, and this is at once applied to the skin. It should not remain on for more than about an hour. The action is very similar to that of a mustard poultice or plaster.

TO APPLY DRY HEAT

IN CERTAIN forms of inflammation, as well as in certain cases accompanied with pain, the application of dry heat is indicated. This is also sometimes required in cases of chill or shock. Various methods are employed. A hot-water bottle, surrounded by flannel, or a brick treated in the same way, is perhaps the simplest of these methods; but for special purposes, small bags filled with salt or sand previously heated in an oven are more convenient. In these cases, as in the case of poultices, the heat should be tested against the nurse's cheek before application to the patient.

TO APPLY COLD

IN THE treatment of pneumonia and various other diseases it is sometimes necessary to apply cold to the surface of the body, either to relieve pain, to modify the inflammatory process, or to lower the general body temperature. In some cases this is best effected by plunging the patient into a tepid bath, but this should never be done except by the direction of the doctor, the exact temperature named by him being strictly observed. Another method is to sponge the chest or the entire surface of the body with cold or tepid water. In this case, a waterproof sheet covered by a blanket should be arranged on the bed under the patient. The patient should be covered with another blanket, and this should not be removed until everything is ready for the sponging. It is generally as well to leave the patient undried for about a couple of minutes, so as to allow the temperature to be still further lowered by the evaporation of the water from the surface of the body. Instead of cold sponging, another possible method is to arrange the waterproof sheet and blanket as before and then, lifting off the top blanket, to wrap the patient entirely in a sheet which has just been wrung out in cold water. The top blanket is then again placed over the patient. The sheet may be changed in five minutes, and the process may be repeated as often as the doctor thinks necessary. Finally, the patient should be thoroughly dried, and the bed remade.

Cloths wrung out of cold water may be applied to any part of the body without dealing with the whole surface, in the manner above described. These cloths may be changed as fast as they begin to get warm. A greater degree of cold can be produced by the application of water-proof bags containing broken ice. Special rubber bags adapted to application to various parts of the body can be obtained for this purpose. The ice is best kept in a large block until required for use, and the vessel containing it should be surrounded by thick layers of flannel or wadding, in order to protect it from outside heat. The lumps are best broken up with the aid of a very fine brad-awl and a hammer. If these articles are not at hand a strong needle or an ice-pick will answer perfectly well.

USE OF ENEMAS AND SUPPOSITORIES

IT WOULD be wise for mothers to learn a few points concerning the proper method of administering enemas. The hard rubber nozzle that is usually purchased in connection with the regular enema outfit has many disadvantages. As a rule it is too wide and too hard, and it often becomes detached from the rubber tube. Every children's physician has accounted for one or more emergencies occasioned by a hard rubber nozzle becoming lodged in the rectum during the process of the administration of an enema. In a recent case the physician in attendance had great difficulty in removing the nozzle and the child's rectum was severely lacerated as a result. All this can be avoided by the use of a small thin rubber catheter (No. 12 to No. 14 French) to be attached to the hard rubber nozzle of the enema bag. The catheter can be introduced easily into the child's rectum if the tip is well oiled. There is no danger of a catheter staying within the rectum.

Another mistake that mothers usually make in administering an enema is that they hold the enema bag too high and thereby produce a flow under high pressure. This is very irritating to the child and may become very painful. Under low pressure one is able to introduce the proper amount of water or oil without discomfort. Accordingly, the bag should be hung not more than two feet above the level of the bed or table the child is on. For infants it is convenient to use a rubber ear syringe with a rubber tip. This is filled by squeezing the bulb, placing the tip under the liquid, and relaxing on the bulb so that the liquid runs in. The bulb and nozzle should be completely full so that no air is injected into the rectum. Then the tip is lubricated and inserted into the rectum and the liquid gradually pushed in.

The doctor will order the kind of liquid to be used and the amount. Usually plain water will suffice. Sometimes mild soap suds or a weak salt or bicarbonate solution are recommended. Occasionally an oil enema is desired. A baby of a few months can be given half a cupful. At a year he can take a cupful or more, and at four or five years two, or two and a half, cupfuls. After the liquid has run in and the tube removed, the buttocks should be held together for a few minutes so that it does not run out immediately.

Suppositories usually do not cleanse the rectum as well as enemas, but they are quite helpful in starting a bowel movement in some children. It is important that the suppository, whether it be made of soap or glycerin, be dipped into some kind of a lubricant such as oil or vaseline before being introduced into the rectum; also that it be introduced very slowly and retained in the rectum by means of a diaper or a piece of cotton until it has melted.

PRESCRIBING BY MAIL*

THERE is a widespread impression that medical treatment can be prescribed by mail on the basis of the description of symptoms and signs by the patient. It is not possible to do this satisfactorily. Symptoms do not make a diagnosis. Oftentimes what appears to the non-medical person to be the same symptoms and signs in two individuals may be due to quite different causes.

Moreover, the wise physician does not prescribe for a disease, he treats the person afflicted with what is best for that person at that time. This can only be determined in each instance by a thorough knowledge of the previous history and of the symptoms and physical signs present in the patient. Even in the very few diseases for which specific remedies are known (such as quinine for malaria) the dose and the frequency and method of administration must be determined for each separate patient.

Exceptionally, the physician who has been in attendance on a sick person, and is thoroughly familiar with the conditions, may by written or oral message indicate what measures can be adopted to meet temporarily a new development in the case. To attempt, however, to give anything more than the most general medical advice or treatment for any person, except on the basis of a careful personal examination, is usually dangerous and is questionable practice.

* Reprinted from *Hygeia* by permission.

CAUTION

The general reader of magazine and newspaper advertisements and the radio audience cannot be warned too often against the too free and frequent use of headache nostrums and patent medicines of all kinds.

INTRODUCTION

TO

NEW YORK STATE DEPARTMENT OF HEALTH
REQUIREMENTS FOR COMMUNICABLE DISEASES

By Ella Oppenheimer, M.D.

A CERTAIN group of diseases especially common in early childhood are often called children's diseases. The so-called infectious diseases include "acute eruptive fevers" (scarlet fever, measles, German measles, chicken pox, smallpox), whooping cough, mumps, diphtheria, infantile paralysis, and cerebrospinal meningitis. These diseases as well as all contagious diseases are spread from person to person, largely by direct contact or contact with the excretions or secretions from the person suffering with the disease. This means that contagious disease is carried because some one was ignorant or careless enough not to prevent its spread.

The younger the baby, the more serious is the disease apt to be; therefore every effort should be made to keep a baby from getting any of these diseases. Any child suffering with a contagious disease should be kept on his own premises, or at least away from other children, as long as there is any possibility of his giving the disease. In most states this quarantine or isolation of disease is compulsory by law for at least those diseases considered most dangerous. Children may have a second attack of any one of these diseases, but this is rare and not the rule. It is wise to employ a physician even in mild cases.

Every effort should be made to prevent infection and spread to other members of the household, especially other children. Parents must realize that they have a responsibility to the community as well as to the patient.

A tabulation of the most important facts concerning these diseases is given in the following four-page chart prepared by the New York State Board of Health. Write to your own State Board of Health for a copy of a similar table for your State if you do not live in New York.

1	2	3	4	QUARANTINE OF HOUSEHOLD CONTACTS		
DISEASE AND INCUBATION PERIOD	COMMON EARLY SIGNS AND SYMPTOMS	METHOD OF INFECTION	ISOLATION OF PATIENT	5 IF PATIENT AND CONTACTS ARE DOMICILED AT HOME		6 IF PATIENT GOES TO HOSPITAL OR CONTACTS LEAVE HOME
				CHILDREN	ADULTS	
CHICKENPOX Incubation Period: 11–24 days. Usually 13–16 days	In children the first symptom usually noticed is the rash which probably at that time consists of small blisters that have developed from small pimples. In a day or two crusts form which fall off in about 14 days. The eruption comes out in crops so that there may be pimples, blisters, and scabs all within a small area of the skin	Contact with a previous case. Infection believed to be contained in discharges from nose and throat and the skin lesions	Until recovery	No	No	No
DIPHTHERIA Incubation Period: Minimum, less than 1 day. Maximum, indefinite. Usually 2–5 days.	Sore throat is usually the first symptom in patients over a year old. In very young children it is apt to be croup. In the latter there may be no patches showing, but in the former they can always be found in "typical" cases either on the throat itself, the tonsils, or the palate—sometimes on all of them. Some cases look like simple tonsilitis. In nasal cases discharge from the nose occurs which usually excoriates the upper lip and may be bloody. Diphtheritic croup simply means diphtheria of the larynx. It is an exceedingly dangerous form of the disease	Contact with a previous case or carrier. Discharges from nose and throat contain infection. Milk may convey infection. Often spread through mild, unrecognized cases, or by persons harboring the germs of the disease, though giving no evidence of having had an attack of diphtheria (carriers)	Until two successive cultures each from throat and nose at least 24 hours apart, the first taken not less than one week from date of onset, contain no diphtheria bacilli; if diphtheria bacilli re present after 5 weeks from date of taking first release culture, patient may be declared a carrier	Yes Until patient is released from isolation and cultures taken from both throat and nose show no diphtheria bacilli	No *Provided* patient is properly isolated and that cultures from the nose and throat of the adults show no diphtheria bacilli and that they will not subsequently be exposed to the patient. Adults, however, are prohibited from following any vocation which involves close association with children	No *Provided* cu tures fro both throa and nos show n diphtheri bacilli.
MEASLES Incubation Period: 5 (?)–18 days. Usually 9–12 days	Begins with fever followed by symptoms like cold in the head, with running nose, sneezing, inflamed and watery eyes, and fever. The rash is usually first seen behind the ears, on forehead and face. It is blotchy and usually dusky red in color. The rash usually appears on the 3rd or 4th day but may occur on the 1st or as late as the 7th day	Contact with a previous case. Discharges from nose and mouth of a patient especially in the early days of the disease before the rash appears, convey infection	Until recovery	No	No	No
MENINGOCOCCAL MENINGITIS OR MENINGOCOCCEMIA Incubation Period: 1–5 days, possibly longer	Onset usually abrupt, with vomiting, fever, headache, and stiffness of neck	Contact with a previous case or carrier. Discharges from nose and mouth of a patient or carrier convey infection	Until end of the febrile stage	No	No	No

7 ISOLATION OR QUARANTINE OF INCIDENTAL CONTACTS	8 REMARKS	9 EXCLUSION OF PATIENT FROM SCHOOL	10 SCHOOL OBSERVATION PERIOD All school children who recently have been close contacts of the patient and are presumably not immune (but have ceased all contact with the patient) shall report for observation each school day for the period indicated below before admission to any class
No	Very contagious. A mild disease and seldom any after-effects. Important because of possible confusion with smallpox. The ong and variable period of incubation and mildness of the disease do not warrant quarantine even of susceptible contacts	Yes Until recovery—at least 8 days from onset and until all skin lesions have healed after the crusts have fallen off	For 22 days from last day of contact
No	Very dangerous, both during attack and from after-effects. When diphtheria occurs in a school all children suffering from sore throat should be excluded and the health officer notified of their names and addresses. There is great variation of type and mild cases are often not recognized unless a culture is taken or subsequent paralysis develops. Cases regarded as ordinary "sore throat" often start epidemics. Tonsilitis cases should have a certificate before returning to school CHILDREN MAY BE MADE IMMUNE AGAINST DIPHTHERIA BY TOXOID. ASK THE MEDICAL INSPECTOR OR THE HEALTH OFFICER FOR FURTHER INFORMATION ABOUT IT	Yes See column 4	For 7 days from last day of contact
No	Very contagious especially during the first few days before the rash appears. Practically every one who has not had disease is susceptible. Because of these facts measles occurs characteristically in epidemics. Efforts to cut these epidemics short through the quarantine of contacts are seldom successful and cause much inconvenience and loss of school time. The primary object should be the prevention of deaths through adequate medical and nursing care. Parents should be instructed in early symptoms and told to keep the child home if these develop. If found in school the child should be sent home and the health officer notified of name and address Measles is very dangerous to children under 3 years old. School children nearly always recover unless they are in poor physical condition or are not properly cared for during illness	Yes Until recovery—at least 7 days from onset	For 18 days from last day of contact
No	*Cultures require special apparatus and technique*	Yes See column 4	For 7 days from last day of contact

1	2	3	4	QUARANTINE OF HOUSEHOLD CONTACTS		
DISEASE AND INCUBATION PERIOD	COMMON EARLY SIGNS AND SYMPTOMS	METHOD OF INFECTION	ISOLATION OF PATIENT	5 IF PATIENT AND CONTACTS ARE DOMICILED AT HOME		6 IF PATIENT GOES TO HOSPITAL OR CONTACTS LEAVE HOM
				CHILDREN	ADULTS	
POLIOMYELITIS (INFANTILE PARALYSIS) Incubation Period: 5–21 days. Usually 8–10 days	Onset sudden, with fever, dull pain on bending neck forward, pain on being handled, headache, vomiting. Sometimes sudden development of weakness of one or more muscle groups	Virus present in nose and throat secretions and feces of cases, abortive cases, and probably carriers. Milk apparently has conveyed infection but very rarely	Until end of the febrile stage	No	No	No
SCARLET FEVER Incubation Period: 1–7 days. Usually 2–5 days	Onset usually sudden, with headache, fever, sore throat, and often vomiting. Glands (lymph nodes) of neck usually enlarged. Usually within 24 hours the rash appears as fine, evenly diffused bright red dots. The rash is seen first on the neck and upper part of chest, and lasts 24 hours to 10 days when it fades and the skin peels in scales, flakes, or even large pieces	Contact with a previous case or carrier. Discharges from nose and mouth suppurating glands or ears of a patient. Milk may convey infection. Often spreads through mild, unrecognized cases	Until the mucous membranes of the nose and throat appear normal and until all abnormal discharges from the nose, throat and ears and suppurating glands have ceased provided that such isolation shall continue for not less than 7 days and not more than 90 days from onset	Yes Until release of patient	No *Provided* patient is properly isolated and adults show no evidence of infection and will not subsequently be exposed to the patient. Adults, however, are prohibited from following any vocation which involves close association with children	Children—Yes One week from date of removal Adults—No
STREPTOCOCCAL SORE THROAT Incubation Period: Same as scarlet fever	Same as scarlet fever but without the rash	Same as carlet fever	Same as scarlet fever	Same as scarlet fever	Same as scarlet fever	Same as scarlet fever
SMALLPOX Incubation Period: 5–21 days. Usually 10–14 days	Onset sudden, usually with fever and sever backache. About third day usually upon subsidence of constitutional symptoms there develop red pimples, felt below the skin, and seen first about the face and wrists and mostly on exposed surfaces. They form small blisters and after two days more, become filled with yellowish matter. Scabs form which begin to fall off about the fourteenth day. In mild cases the pimples and blisters may closely resemble those found in chickenpox	Contact with a previous case. Discharges from nose and mouth, and contents of pustules are believed to convey infection	Until 14 days after onset and until skin has healed	See * below	See * below	See * below
WHOOPING COUGH Incubation Period. 2–14 days. Usually 5–8 days	Begins with cough which is worse at night. Symptoms may at first be very mild. Characteristic "whooping" develops in about two weeks, and the spasm of coughing sometimes ends with vomiting. If a child vomits after a hard spell of coughing he probably has whooping cough	Contact with a previous case. Discharges from nose and mouth especially in the early stages before the whoop begins	Patient restricted from associating with children or attending public assemblies until 1 week after last characteristic cough but not more than 8 weeks	No	No	No

* QUARANTINE OF SMALLPOX CONTACTS:

If (1) contact does not reside or continue to reside on same premises as the patient
  and either

(2) is successfully vaccinated within three days of first exposure
  or

(3) presents evidence satisfactory to the health officer of *previous* successful vaccination or a previous attack of smallpox *and* upon revaccination shows either an immune or accelerated reaction
  he may be released from quarantine after the vaccinia reaction has reached its height, but must be observed daily by the health officer until three weeks after last exposure
  Otherwise contact must remain under quarantine until three weeks after last exposure.

7 ISOLATION OR QUARANTINE OF INCIDENTAL CONTACTS	8 REMARKS	9 EXCLUSION OF PATIENT FROM SCHOOL	10 SCHOOL OBSERVATION PERIOD All school children who recently have been close contacts of the patient and are presumably not immune (but have ceased all contact with the patient) shall report for observation each school day for the period indicated below before admission to any class
No	Disease is probably most communicable in the early stages. After-effect usually paralysis of certain muscle groups, transitory or permanent. Death is due usually to paralysis of respiratory muscles	Yes See column 4	For 21 days from last day of contact
No	Running ears and discharging noses or suppurating glands may greatly prolong the infectious period. Slight attacks may be as infectious as severe ones. Mild cases, not diagnosed, and carriers are important in spread. When scarlet fever occurs in a school, all cases of sore throat should be sent home and health officer notified	Yes See column 4 After release by the health officer, patient may return to school at the discretion of the school physician	*School contacts*—To be observed for 7 days from last day of contact *Household contacts including teachers and other adult school employees*—Excluded from school for 7 days from the date of last exposure
No	Same as scarlet fever	Yes Same as scarlet fever	Same as scarlet **fever**
See *below	Very contagious. Cases of modified smallpox may be and often are so slight as to escape detection. Existence of disease may be concealed. A severe illness may result from exposure to a mild case	Yes See column 4	See * below While complying with requirement of daily observation by health officer in * below, individual may attend school
No	After-effects often very severe and disease causes great debility. Relapses are apt to occur. Second attack rare. Especially infectious for first week or two before the "whoop" occurs. Great variation in type of disease. Often fatal in young children, and the weak and aged. More than half the deaths are in children less than a year old and 95 per cent are in children under five years old	Yes Until 1 week after last characteristic cough—not more than 8 weeks	For 14 days from last day of contact

The following communicable diseases are not reportable to the health officer but require the exclusion of the patient from school

German measles cases excluded until recovery—at least 4 days from onset	For 21 days from last day of contact
Mumps cases excluded until after disappearance of all swelling	Nonimmune contacts who have ceased all contact with patient with mumps shall report daily for observation for 22 days from last day of contact

Children with acute conjunctivitis, impetigo, colds, sore throat, scabies, lice or ringworm shall be excluded from school until in the opinion of the school physician there is no longer danger of transmission of infection or infestation to others

THE IMPORTANCE OF QUARANTINE

"**W**HO keeps infectious disease going?" asks Dr. Hilbert W. Hill. And this is his startling answer: *"Women* in general, and chiefly the mother. Mothers propagate and keep alive and spread the infectious disease of children more than any one other body of people.

"For the first 5000 days of the years of the life of each generation, the race is fed, dressed, undressed, washed, combed, cuddled, kissed, praised, blamed, led, driven, coaxed, taught, spanked, bossed, and otherwise 'brought up' by women. It is chiefly during this time of tutelage and supervision by women that children receive their infections; it is during this time that the race runs its gauntlet, dances its little dance with death. It is women," he says, who "must learn 'the rules of the game,' and follow them, for no amount of coaching from the sidelines can do more than help."

CHILDREN DO NOT "HAVE TO HAVE CHILDREN'S DISEASES"

THE APPARENT inability to avoid contagious diseases has led to the assumption that the children must have them, and sometimes to the intentional exposure of the children, on the theory that the sooner the illness is over the better. If we would but count the child-deaths and the number of children who carry through life an affliction or a weakness left by the measles, the mumps, or the whooping-cough, we would think twice before exposing the child to any of them. Hardly one leaves the child as healthy as it was before; and weak hearts may be counted up against them. Though it seems almost impossible to avoid them, the mother should not carelessly expose a child to infectious children's diseases any more than she would to the smallpox!

The time will come when these diseases will be treated as is smallpox and they will then be as rare in their visitations. Nearly all cities now quarantine against them, and mothers should do all that is possible to aid in this direction and promptly report all cases, even very mild ones, in their homes.

The placard which the local board of health puts on a house where there is a contagious disease is not a sign that the occupants are in disgrace—it is a warning which translated means "Do not trespass under penalty of the law of health," and indicates that the citizens of that town believe they have duties toward their neighbors.

WHAT IS REAL QUARANTINE?

MODERN quarantine consists in isolating infected persons until the germs from which they are suffering leave their bodies.

It does not consist in closing the schools and leaving a lot of infected children to play together on the streets. It does not consist in the formal or partial conformity to local ordinances, which may be unjust and ignorant. It is not a temporary arrangement during a "scare," which ends as soon as business suffers. Neither is it a matter of bringing everybody to general good health or keeping everybody reasonably clean. The problem of entirely preventing contagious diseases in this country is not the problem of watching 100,-000,000 people, but is the simpler one of seeing that only the 200,000 who are sources of infection be isolated from the others.

Your share and my share in quarantine is conscientiously to isolate the infected person or persons in our own households until the germs from which they are suffering have left their bodies, and in co-operating with the health authorities to see that other households do the same.

COMMON MISAPPREHENSIONS ABOUT DISEASE

THE CARELESSNESS of even good mothers regarding quarantine is often due to certain very common misapprehensions.

One of these is that "dirt breeds disease," and hence only dirty people are likely to have disease. The inference is that our own children will be exempt. As a matter of fact dirty people are no more subject to contagious diseases than clean. What spreads such disease is one specific "dirt" (the discharges of the patient), and the dirtiest people, who guard against this specific infection, will escape, remaining as dirty as they please in other ways.

Another mistake is, supposing that good health prevents disease. The inference again is that our own children, if healthy, will escape. As a matter of fact, in the case of contagious diseases, measles, for example, almost invariably *every* child, whether strong or weak, who has not had it before, will have it if exposed to it.

A foolish idea is that mild attacks of infectious diseases are less infectious than severe ones. True, during some seasons scarlet fever may, in a given neighborhood, be showing itself generally in "a mild type," but if your child should die, after having been infected by a mild case (for he is as likely to as if infected from a very sick child), would the good fortune of other homes be of much comfort to you? If your own child is but mildly ill, ought you not to be just as conscientious as if he were sorely stricken?

COMMON NEGLECTS IN HOME QUARANTINE

WITH the best will in the world, some mothers who have, as they suppose, quarantined a child permit contacts which neutralize all the protections that they have sought for.

Some of these neglects are as follows:

1. Letting the father or the other children into the sickroom.
2. Kissing the sick child and then kissing the other children.
3. Letting a neighbor into the room while she does an errand.
4. Letting the mouth-spray of the sick child fall upon articles that are removed from sickroom.
5. Associating with the rest of the family after leaving the sickroom without changing her clothes or washing her hands.
6. Allowing the convalescent child to wander about the house before the quarantine is lifted.

RIGOROUS HOME QUARANTINE SHOULD BE ESTABLISHED

EVERY mother can help to bring about better standards as well as to safeguard her own, by establishing a rigorous quarantine in her own home. At the first indication of illness, even in the mildest form, loss of appetite, headache, or fever, the afflicted child should be separated from the other children of the household, and so kept until the disease, if any, develops. Usually the arrangement of the household will admit of such a child being put into a separate room, and the other children should be given to understand that absolute separation is necessary both for themselves and for the child who is ill. If this separation is made at the first indication of any illness, there is no reason why the other children in the household, unless they have been previously exposed to the disease, should suffer from it, and even the most contagious disease may be cared for and the isolated and unaffected children remain at home without contracting it.

HOW TO PREVENT CONTAGION

MARY L. READ, in "The Mothercraft Manual," outlines the following common-sense rules to prevent contagion:

(1) Avoid exposing the child to any one who has a contagious disease.

(2) Do not take young children (under seven, at least) into crowds, busy streets, city dust, or street cars.

(3) Household employees, especially child's nurse, cook, kitchen employee, or laundress, should be selected with regard to their health; a thorough health examination for the child's caretaker, unless personally well known or professionally trained, is the only safeguard.

(4) No one with a cold, sore throat, or other symptoms of contagious disease, should be kept with a young child or prepare his food.

(5) Keep special handkerchiefs for each child and never use any one else's for him.

(6) Teach scrupulous individual use of cups, spoons, forks, wash-cloths, towels, handkerchiefs, whistles, and not to use wash-basin for brushing teeth.

(7) Avoid pacifiers; wipe toys daily.

(8) Clean the child's finger nails daily, and always wash his hands before eating.

(9) Attendant should always wash hands before preparing food, giving medicine, caring for eyes, nose, mouth, or wounds; and after care of diapers, toilet, wounds.

(10) Milk and water supply should be carefully guarded; unless assured pure, milk must be pasteurized, water boiled.

AGAINST WHAT SHOULD WE BE IMMUNIZED?

EVERYONE is familiar with the fact that there are certain infectious diseases that people catch only once even though they may be exposed again and again. Measles is a good example of such an illness, where one attack confers a life-long immunity. There are other diseases, for instance influenza, from which people may suffer repeatedly. One attack gives immunity for only a short time. It is one of the goals of preventive medicine to enable everyone to have a lasting immunity to all of the important infectious diseases without even having the first attack of any of them. This goal has already been attained for a number of diseases. It is parents' duty to give their children the benefit of this achievement.

Vaccination against smallpox has been known the longest. At the end of the eighteenth century, before bacteriology became a science, Edward Jenner noticed that milkmaids who had had cowpox never came down with smallpox even in the most severe epidemics. He vaccinated a boy with pus from a milkmaid who was in the active stage of cowpox. Then he deliberately tried to infect the boy with pus from patients with active smallpox. But the infection did not take: the boy was immune! The experiment was repeated many times, always with the same good result. Since then the practice of vaccination against smallpox has become more and more widespread and we therefore have no large epidemics of it in this country. But there still are scattered cases of the disease in persons who have not been vaccinated.

Every baby should be vaccinated against smallpox during his first year. It will not bother him as much then as it would if it were delayed until he was older. The material the doctor uses is the same as Jenner originally used more than 150 years ago: the virus of cowpox. Only now it is prepared under very rigidly controlled conditions so that it is absolutely pure. The doctor cleans the skin, puts a drop of the cowpox virus on, pricks or scratches through the drop and wipes the material away. No dressing and no special care are necessary at this time. In about three or four days, if there is a "take," a small red bump forms. From then on the vaccination should be kept dry and the child given sponge rather than tub baths. Over the next four or five days the bump gets bigger and a blister appears on the top of it. This is the sore of the cowpox which gives immunity to smallpox. There usually is fever and tenderness when the reaction is at its height, about the eighth or ninth day. Still no dressing should be put over the blister unless the child scratches at it a lot. If he does, a very loose piece of gauze can be put over it. The celluloid vaccination shields should not be used. The blister soon dries up and becomes a brownish scab which may stay on for another two weeks. When the scab finally falls off, the site can be wet again.

The immunity from a vaccination against smallpox does not last a lifetime. Everyone should be re-vaccinated every six or seven years, and re-vaccinated *immediately* if there is a case of smallpox in the community. Every vaccination should result in some sort of a "take." An immune person will have a small red bump appear and fade in one or two days without going on to a blister. If the red bump does not develop, there was something wrong: either the vaccine was too weak or it did not penetrate the skin. If that is the case, the vaccination should be repeated until a reaction is obtained.

Sometimes it is wise to delay a routine vaccination. If a baby has eczema he should not be vaccinated until the skin has cleared up. A sickly baby or one who is frail should wait until he becomes more robust. If the baby is coming down with a cold it is better to wait too. But if there is smallpox in the neighborhood all of these considerations are outweighed, and everyone should be vaccinated immediately.

Diphtheria is another disease that used to take a great toll but is now controlled by immunization. In this case the material (called *toxoid*) that is used is the toxin secreted by the diphtheria germs, purified and treated chemically so as to make it harmless. The doctor gives two or three injections under the skin one or two months apart. These do not usually bother the baby very much except for a slightly sore arm the next day. Sometimes a lump will remain at the site of the injection for several months. The best time for the diphtheria injections is during the second half of the first year. The baby's inherited immunity has worn off and he is not yet exposed to many other children.

The immunity from these first diphtheria injections does not remain strong enough all through childhood without reinforcement. An additional "booster" injection is usually given about a year after the first series and again when the child starts school. His susceptibility to diphtheria can be tested at any time by giving him a Schick Test. But this means giving him an injection, and, if the test is positive, a booster injection anyhow. Consequently many doctors now give the reinforcing injection to all children without bothering the child with the test.

The third disease to which all babies should be immunized is whooping cough. In little babies this can be a very serious illness, often with a fatal outcome. The material that is injected to develop immunity consists of killed whooping cough germs. The doctor gives three injections of this vaccine three or four weeks apart. This injection will probably upset the baby more than the one for diphtheria does. He is likely to have some fever as well as a sore arm for the day after the injection. The best time to start the whooping cough vaccine is at 6 or 7 months of age, but any particular injection should be delayed if the child is sick, for it may have serious results.

The injections may not give the child complete immunity. He may come down with whooping cough in spite of them. But if he does, it will be a mild case compared to what it might have been. For this reason it is wise to have the injections given. And since these too require reinforcement, it is well to give the child an annual "booster" injection for three years, until he is past the age when whooping cough is dangerous.

The experiences with immunization against tetanus in the Army and Navy during World War II were so good that they are now applied to civil life. Two injections of tetanus toxoid, similar to the diphtheria toxoid, a month or more apart, with a reinforcing injection once a year, and another when in actual danger of contracting the disease, give complete protection to anyone. There is no reason this should not be given to all children. If it is so given, there will be no call to use tetanus anti-toxin which is an entirely different substance, made from horse serum.

Mixtures of diphtheria and tetanus toxoids and also of the two with whooping cough vaccine have been introduced since the war. They have the advantage of reducing the total number of injections that a child needs in order to be protected against these three diseases. If the mixtures are definitely shown to provide as good immunity as the substances injected separately they should be used as a series for all babies before a year of age, with several annual "booster" injections.

There are a number of less commonly used vaccines to protect against a variety of diseases. Injections for scarlet fever have been available for some time but are not used very much. The reactions are moderately severe and there is some question of the degree of immunity they give. Typhoid and paratyphoid fevers, typhus, cholera, plague, yellow fever and influenza all have vaccines. But injections are not given unless a person is going to travel to or through a place where these diseases are common.

An injection of an entirely different kind is used for *temporary* protection against measles. The substance is called gamma globulin and it is extracted from human blood serum. If it is given in the proper amount within the first few days of a susceptible child's exposure to measles, it will prevent that particular attack. But this immunity lasts only a few weeks. If the injection is not given until five to seven days after the exposure the child will come down with measles, but it will be a very mild case and he will then be immune. Accordingly, the best way to use this particular injection when exposure to measles is definitely known is to give it late to most children so that they get mild cases and become immune, but to give it early to babies under three years, and to any sickly or rundown children, regardless of age, whose health might be endangered by even a mild case. Of course no one who has ever had measles should have the injection.

Somewhat related to this measles serum are the anti-toxins for diphtheria and tetanus. These are extracted from the blood serum of horses that have been immunized to these diseases. In addition to use in treatment, the anti-toxins are used to give *temporary* immunity to susceptible persons who the doctor feels are in danger of contracting the disease and who have no immunity of their own from previous injections of toxoid or exposures to the disease. These anti-toxins have the disadvantage that they sensitize the recipient to horse serum.

Finally, rabies vaccine. This is a whole series of injections which must be given to any person who has been bitten by an animal with rabies. Except with severe bites around the head it is safe to wait ten days for symptoms of the disease in the animal. But if the animal is not known and cannot be watched the injections should be given. And if it was killed, the head should be examined by the Health Department for signs of the disease, because once the symptoms start in humans there is nothing that can be done; all patients with rabies die.

WHILE THE CHILDREN ARE GETTING WELL*

By Abraham Levinson, M.D.

CONVALESCENCE is the period of recuperation. It is the period between the disappearance of the active symptoms of the patient's disease and the time of his return to normal health. The length of the period of convalescence varies according to the nature of the malady, the amount of damage it has produced, and the degree of resistance of the patient after the acute symptoms have subsided.

ARE QUICK CURES POSSIBLE?

WE HEAR of rapid recoveries. One who is not informed on the subject may believe that a patient actually recovers from a severe disease like pneumonia or an operation for appendicitis in a few days. This false conception of what constitutes complete recovery is due to the mistaken idea that when a patient leaves the hospital with a normal temperature he is well. As a matter of fact, some patients just begin their convalescence when they leave the hospital; recovery is sometimes delayed for weeks or months, or, indeed, may never be complete. This is as true of children as it is of adults.

In order to understand the finer points of convalescence, one must know the changes from the normal of both disease and convalescence. We cannot, as was the custom among the older physicians, separate diseases into stages, assigning to each stage a certain change in the various organs of the body. We cannot even, properly speaking, limit the changes of a given disease to one organ.

EFFECT OF DISEASE ON EVERY ORGAN

WHILE it is true that a single organ may bear the brunt of change in certain diseases, every other organ necessarily partakes of some changes. For example, although the intestines bear the brunt of the disease in typhoid fever, every other organ in the body feels the effects; in meningitis the covering of the brain is most vitally affected, yet every other part of the body suffers concurrently. In some diseases the heart muscle suffers most, as in diphtheria; in others, the kidneys, as in severe cases of scarlet fever. In any disease in which there is much fever, with rapid pulse and breathing, the internal organs of the body are sooner or

later affected. In short, no severe disease fails to leave its imprint on every organ of the body. If actual inflammation or degeneration of the organ does not occur, there is at least a lowered resistance on the part of the more vital organs of the body, resulting in loss of their power, to some degree, to perform the normal amount of work consistent with health. This is especially true in children, in whom, because they are growing, the vital processes are more active.

With this broader conception of disease, convalescence assumes great importance from the standpoint of prophylaxis and treatment. Once it is appreciated that every disease may attack every organ in the body, we cannot make light of the period of restoration or reparation. It is necessary for every organ of the body to regenerate during convalescence, if the damage done is to be repaired and the vitality lost is to be regained. Of course, in many cases some of the damage done can never be undone. An injured heart or a badly damaged lung can never be mended. If the damage to an organ has not been very extensive, however, it is possible for regeneration to take place, provided too much strain is not put on that organ. Every convalescing patient should be under the charge of a physician who has a proper understanding of convalescence, its abnormalities, its physiology, and its inherent dangers. The management of convalescence must necessarily vary with the disease and with the patient, but some general directions may be outlined.

PHYSICAL AND MENTAL REST

IF IT is necessary to protect a child's energy during illness, it is doubly necessary to do so during convalescence, for during the actual illness the child is too sick to exert himself, but during convalescence, when he feels strength returning, he is very liable to overexert himself. This overexertion frequently brings on a dilatation of the heart. Experience has shown that the best way to prevent inflammation of the heart during disease or convalescence is not to overtax the heart. Rest in bed is obviously the best way of taking the burden off the patient's heart. Of course, it is hard to keep a well child in bed. No sooner does his temperature drop than he wants to be out of bed and at his usual activities. But the danger of

* Reprinted from *Hygeia* by permission.

overexertion on the part of the heart makes it imperative that this organ, which must be in constant action, be taxed as little as possible for a considerable period. All persons with uncomplicated cases of infectious disease should be kept in bed at least five days after the temperature has subsided to normal, and should have two to three hours' rest every afternoon for two weeks thereafter.

Just as it is necessary for the child to have a physical rest, it is important to let him have mental rest. One of the most difficult problems in connection with the convalescence of a child is how to keep him quiet in order to avoid complications. A child gets restless unless he is kept busy. A grownup person may indulge in reading. A child either does not know how to read or tires of it quickly. Some form of entertainment should therefore be selected for the child, with consideration for his physical and mental condition.

ENTERTAINMENT

ENTERTAINING a convalescing child is important, but it must be done systematically and must be suited to the patient's general condition; otherwise the patient will easily be fatigued. Permitting a convalescent child to be visited by many friends is often bad for him. A child likes to show off and may use his reserve strength in order to impress visitors with his recovery. Every convalescent child should be entertained, but the entertainment must not be exciting and should preferably be prescribed by the attending physician.

A child with St. Vitus' dance, for example, should not be given any toys that will require the use of his hands, because this interferes with the rest which is so necessary for such a patient. No matter how good the physical condition of a patient may seem to be, entertainment that requires excitement may be disastrous. The mental age of the child should also be taken into consideration. A child of five should not be given toys that are intended for a child of ten.

NECESSARY EXERCISE

IT MAY sound paradoxical, but it is true that a convalescing child needs rest on one hand and exercise on the other. The exercise, however, must be light and graduated. After some diseases the exercise needs to be passively administered by means of massage or electricity, as in cases of infantile paralysis, after the muscle pain has entirely subsided. In most diseases, however, the exercise should be active, that is, it must be carried out by the patient himself. The exercise should preferably be directed by an expert. If not, the mother may be guided by the rule, "Slow but sure."

The mother must be impressed with the danger of permitting the child to resume strenuous exercise too suddenly; at first, playing with toys while in bed is the only exercise permissible. Later, walking in the house, and still later, exercise outdoors.

SUNSHINE AND FRESH AIR

"I SUPPOSE I cannot take the baby out for another two or three weeks," is the usual wail of the mother during the child's convalescence. This same mother may have taken her baby out for an airing during the severest storms before he was ill, but after the child has had pneumonia, she insists on keeping him in, in spite of the lack of sunshine in the house and the abundance outside. A convalescent child needs sunshine and air, even to a greater degree than a healthy child. The convalescent child should be taken out on the porch in a wheel chair whenever the weather permits, and so gradually accustomed to cold air. The time to be allowed for that must naturally be guided by the patient's condition.

FOOD

PHYSICIANS go to both extremes in feeding convalescent children. Some overfeed, others underfeed them. The first group insists that the convalescent child needs strength, which he must get through an abundance of food; the other group insists that the convalescent child cannot digest even ordinary food properly.

Experience has convinced me that a convalescing child needs proportionately more food than does a healthy child. Of course, the food should be as simple and as wholesome as possible. On the other hand, if the child shows a distaste for food, there is something wrong with its digestive apparatus or he has not fully recovered from the disease. This type of child should be neither overfed nor starved, but should receive enough food to sustain him. Convalescing children are very particular about the taste and appearance of food. Pains should therefore be taken to make it as palatable as possible.

DISCIPLINE

As IMPORTANT as it is to rest and to entertain a convalescing child, it is also important not to pamper him. The average child takes advantage of his mother's sympathy and soon becomes a dictator to his mother and the rest of the family. It is important to be firm, and to make the child under- stand that he is not master of the situation. A certain amount of discipline is of prime importance both to the future of the healthy as well as of the sick child.

AMUSEMENTS FOR CONVALESCENT CHILDREN

By William Byron Forbush

CHILDREN are so active, so eager to be about in the world, so dependent upon playmates for pleasure, so interested in their school and social life, that days of *malaise* are dreary and borne by them with impatience. Sometimes recovery is post- poned by misery, homesickness, and fretting. Because of the lack of recreational resources, chil- dren when ill are usually a burden to overtaxed mothers and a trial to nurses, skilled in physical care but not in play devices. The children them- selves lose much during illness, not only by waste of time, but also by getting the habit of self-pity and of selfish demanding and by the long interval of lack of exercise of body, mind, and will.

Plays during convalescence must have obvious limitations. They should all be suited to a sitting or lying posture, they should not tax the eyes, the fingers, or the trunk muscles. They should be absorbing but not exciting. Since in case of in- fection toys must be destroyed or disinfected, many of the materials should be inexpensive and others should be capable of being sterilized. Some of the games at least should be suitable to encourage soli- tary play, others may be adapted for two players. It would be well if some could involve a serial interest, so as to be taken up with renewed pleas- ure day after day.

Plays for invalids should involve certain positive values. Some of them may offer slight physical exercise, deep breathing, arm or leg movements, or exercise of the circulation. They may be of some intellectual value, particularly in training the sense perceptions, the memory, and the apper- ceptions, and in stimulating inventiveness. They may bear at least a general relation, not too tax- ing, to school subjects. But best of all they may be used to counteract certain moral disorders of physical illness, by encouraging self-control, initia- tive, self-reliance, cheerfulness, and friendly co- operation.

These considerations have been kept in mind in preparing the following suggestions. Free play rather than organized games has been emphasized as generally better suited to the situation. No dis- tinction is made between plays suitable for the home and those for the hospital.

BABIES UP TO THREE YEARS

THE amusements used in the cradle when a baby is well are generally useful when he is ill, if they do not require him to change position too much. During the first years simple toys like large balls and rattles, and later, articles that appeal to the sense of sight, hearing, touch, and temperature are a delight. So, such common articles as smooth stones, spools, keys, bright objects, bells, tin dishes to clash together, paper suspended about the feet to induce kicking, a celluloid ball or a bell on a rubber string to induce stretching, a large rag doll that can be nestled or kicked about, rubber animals, boxes, and blocks to handle, are indi- cated.

For self-directed play, a mother who was obliged to leave her baby alone at times used to take a pasteboard shoe box and fill it with all sorts of harmless articles—a silver shoe horn, a bright card, a bit of colored worsted, an old tea strainer— things that would in turn catch and hold the baby's attention.

For a little child for whom a bath immersion is desirable, but who still dreads the water, bath- ing dolls, made of rubber, or celluloid floating animals, to be placed in the tub, are helpful in overcoming this difficulty.

CHILDREN OF THREE TO SIX YEARS

CHILDREN of this age engage largely in construc- tive play, dramatic play, and imitation of adult activities, and many playthings lend themselves to such uses in the bed or chair.

For constructive play, there are light nests of boxes, easy sectional puzzles, the larger kinder- garten tablets and mosaics, small nails to pound into soap bars, soap bubbles to blow (good for breathing) over a woolen shawl, making the bubbles bound on it, all the lighter kindergarten apparatus used in training perception of color, form, smoothness, and sound, including the letter forms and the geometric insets, etc. A peg board in which to stick wooden pegs in the form of various patterns is interesting. By taking a small, soft pine board and driving nail holes half an inch deep close together and using match sticks for pegs a home-made device may be easily prepared. A small sand box arranged to set just over the chair or bed or even a pan of sand snuggled close to a child who cannot sit up will give an almost inexhaustible pleasure. It should be furnished with spoons and small kitchen tin dishes with which to dip and mold, and clothespins, spools, buttons, and scraps of bright ribbons with which to make men and scenery.

For imitative play the doll is the standard medium in all ages. Dolls for sick children should be small and light. A Noah's ark with its animals, perhaps one filled with animal crackers or small tin soldiers, for sailing and marching over the bedclothes are agreeable expressions of the doll interest.

Children of this age, when they are well, like games of only short duration, and when they are ill, games should be extremely short and simple. A story-game in which the adult is the chief actor and tells a story while the child cooperates in some slight action, is ideal, as when he hides under the bedclothes and plays he is in the tent of which the story tells or closes his eyes and tries to guess the place or the person which his mother is describing. The stories should be happy and soothing.

To make the sick room cheerful, a prism hung in the window to make "light birds" for the children is always a joy.

CHILDREN OF SEVEN TO NINE YEARS

THE constructive interest continues and may now be expressed in more skillful ways. The mother who will put on a tray a lot of suggestive material, such as small boxes, spools, paste, paper, ribbons, yarn, or will let the child choose what he wants out of her piece-bag, will not need to suggest what to make or how to make it. Small articles fastened to the magnetized "fish" of a "magnetic fish pond," fished for with magnetic fish hooks, furnish prolonged surprises. Making doll furniture, dressing clothespins, making button dolls by pasting buttons to cardboards for heads, cutting the cardboard in the shape of the bodies and then dressing them in crepe paper, will be delightful during this period, which marks the summit of the doll interest.

Scrapbooks may be made out of old window shades, folded and sewed into booklets. Drawing may be done in bed by purchasing stencil pictures so that the child can trace with the pencil on paper placed beneath. Sewing cards are similarly used. Painting may be done in a cleanly way even in bed by placing a large blotter underneath the work which will absorb the water in case of accident, using a smaller blotter on the work itself and keeping a cloth handy to wipe the brush.

In dramatic play, dolls are still central, and a few changes of costume, a box or two for the house and some furniture cut out of a furniture catalog or made by folding paper are all that are needed for an elaborate bed-game. Mrs. Dorothy Canfield Fisher has suggested a story method which appeals to the dramatic instinct in a way to suggest calmness at the restless hour of trying to get to sleep. The child is to agree upon the names, ages, and characters of her children, whom she may take from her favorite books if she will. Then she is to carry on their adventures from night to night to herself. Of course, they must all be good children, or at least if they are bad they must be funny, and if the child is subject to night terrors, one of them may be very brave and be always summoned to watch over his mother every night. In the morning the child may be encouraged to tell the sleepy time adventures. She thus goes to bed with the sense of being in good company.

As this is the age of competitive games, particularly of those involving skill, the child would now enjoy, if they are not too exciting, anagrams and other letter games, sentence building, lotto, and the simpler card games. They keep the mind from getting stale and the joy of contest prevents a child from thinking about himself.

To a person quarantined with a child of this age who tends to become too demanding and consequently querulous and unhappy, two devices are helpful. One is a continued illustrated story of which the adult tells one or two new chapters each evening which the child illustrates in a notebook at his leisure. The other is to ask the child to play alone with certain toys until an agreed time limit, the child thus not only becoming more patient but also getting the fullest play-value out of every plaything.

CHILDREN OF TEN TO TWELVE YEARS

THERE is likely by this time to be an almost inexhaustible interest in puzzles, and the small metal and cardboard puzzles are easily handled and if not too exacting are greatly enjoyed. This is the age, too, for collections, and stamps, post cards, and post marks, etc., may be profitably arranged and studied. Jackstraws and jackstones are appropriate games, and scrapbook making becomes more of a fine art.

Craftsmanship as the child grows stronger should be more skillful than before. Stuffing and sewing dolls from patterns, beadwork and weaving interest girls, tinkering old clocks and watches and making small traps and whistles interest boys, and both boys and girls like clay modeling, braiding, and spool knitting. Coloring pictures, making fancy initials and letters and thus illustrating a favorite poem or motto or books of the Bible has proven very attractive, especially if done with others. A variety of companionship is now desirable if safe.

Ranging in price from one to twenty dollars, according to the number of pieces, and easily sterilized after use, the various construction sets will take the mind of a boy off himself for hours and, without exhausting his muscles, will leave him healthily tired and then ready for sleep.

TEACH CHILDREN THAT THE DOCTOR IS THEIR FRIEND

THE VISIT to the doctor's office or to the child-health center should be a pleasant excursion. Every child should be taught to think of the doctor as a friend. A mother who threatens to "call the doctor if you are not good" is building up fears in the child that will cause trouble when the doctor's aid is needed. A child should never be deceived about a visit to the doctor. It is foolish to tell a child, "The doctor isn't going to touch you," or "He won't make you take your clothes off."

When the doctor examines the child's heart and lungs he will be grateful to the mother who has taught her child to have no fear of him. Nothing is harder than to listen to the chest of a crying, struggling child. The signs of early trouble in the lungs, which it is of great importance to discover, often cannot be heard unless the child is quiet. If he fights and cries, three or four visits may be needed.

Many mothers find that daily inspection of teeth, ears, neck and nails helps to remind the children to scrub them well. If occasional throat inspection is added to the list it will help the doctor.

MAKE FRIENDS WITH THE DENTIST

EVERY child at 2 years should be taken to the dentist for thorough inspection and cleaning of the teeth; he may be taken before he is 2. If the first visit to the dentist is for these purposes only, the child will usually enjoy going.

Every six months the visit should be repeated. Then any small cavity will be found by the dentist soon after it appears, and it can be filled then with little discomfort for the child.

If the child is to have good permanent teeth—straight, strong, and regular, with the upper and lower sets meeting to form a good chewing machine—his baby teeth must be kept in good condition until the permanent ones are ready to come in. The permanent teeth come in from the sixth to the tenth year, and until then the child needs his baby teeth to chew his food and to hold the jaws in shape so that the permanent teeth will have plenty of room. If the baby teeth are to be kept in good condition as long as they are needed, they must be built of good material and they must be taken care of properly at home and by a dentist. Every effort should be made to retain the baby teeth as long as possible.

If a small cavity is not filled, the tooth will decay still more, and the results of this neglect are familiar to all—ugly, broken teeth, toothaches, and gumboils. The child with a sore tooth tries not to bite on it and is likely to avoid wholesome foods that need to be chewed or else to chew on one side of his mouth. If the cavity becomes very large, the root of the tooth is likely to become infected and the tooth may have to be pulled out. The shape of the jaw will suffer, from either lack of exercise or loss of teeth, and the permanent teeth that are being built may not have room enough to come in straight. The teeth are affected by whatever affects the body as a whole. Factors that bring about poor general health are likely to affect the teeth. The child whose general health is good, who has the supervision of a doctor and a dentist, who gets proper food and enough sunshine, sleep, and exercise, will probably have good teeth.

INDEX TO

DISEASES OF CHILDHOOD

By ROWLAND L. MINDLIN, M.D.

	PAGE
THE COMMON CONTAGIOUS DISEASES	225
LESS COMMON CONTAGIOUS DISEASES	231
DISEASES OF THE SKIN	236
DISEASES OF THE RESPIRATORY TRACT	238
DISEASES IN THE ABDOMEN	240
DISEASES OF THE KIDNEY	245
DISEASES DUE TO ALLERGY	246
DISEASES OF THE EYE	248
DISEASES OF NUTRITION	249
PHYSICAL INJURIES	250

(For Specific Diseases and Ailments, See alphabetically
arranged INDEX at the back of this MANUAL)

SYMPTOMS

BLOOD IN THE STOOLS

CONVULSIONS

HOARSENESS

PAIN IN THE ABDOMEN

STIFFNESS OF THE NECK OR BACK

(Any of the above may be SYMPTOMS OF ACUTE ILLNESS. See page 199)

THE DISEASES OF CHILDHOOD
By Rowland L. Mindlin, M.D.

THE COMMON CONTAGIOUS DISEASES

CHICKENPOX

CHICKENPOX is usually a very mild disease. There may be a little fever and discomfort, but ordinarily the rash is the first symptom. This comes out just as a few red pimples on the face or body which itch and may be mistaken for insect bites. But they continue to come out in crops for three or four days. Most of them go on to form whitish blisters which may be as large as a pea. These blisters gradually dry up leaving scabs or crusts. The whole cycle for any individual pock is usually about a day and a half, but then the crust may not fall off for more than two weeks. When the eruption is at its height there is usually fever, more in some children than in others. The pocks itch.

The treatment of chickenpox is very simple. The patient should stay in bed as long as new spots are coming out. If there is general discomfort, aspirin relieves it. The itching must be relieved or scratching prevented if permanent scarring is to be avoided. Calamine lotion or starch baths will help. So will keeping finger nails short and wearing cotton mittens.

The disease may not develop until as long as three weeks after exposure, but the usual incubation period is from fourteen to eighteen days. It is contagious only as long as new spots are coming out. But most children are not allowed back to school until the crusts have all fallen off, on the mistaken idea that the crusts themselves are infectious.

MEASLES

Measles is a disease that practically everyone gets before he has grown up. It is not nearly as dangerous as it used to be because the complications can now be treated with modern drugs. But it is still a serious illness for children under three or four years of age and for rundown, sickly children at any age.

The cause of measles seems to be a filterable virus, a minute germ that cannot be seen even under a powerful microscope. But in spite of this, it has been isolated from the blood and the secretions of measles patients, and it has been cultivated outside of the human body in developing chick embryos. It should not be too long now before medical science develops a vaccine to give all children permanent protection. Until that day comes, it is well to know what the disease is like, how it is spread, and what to do about it.

Measles starts off like a bad cold. For the first three or four days there is no rash. There is only a running nose, sneezing, a dry cough, sometimes a sore throat, red and watery eyes and fever. During this stage no one thinks particularly of measles unless there are other cases around. After two or three days of this, an experienced person can make a definite diagnosis of measles even though the rash still has not appeared. He does so by a very careful examination of the mouth. About two days before the rash comes out Koplik's spots show up on the inside of the cheeks. These are pin-point sized raised whitish specks surrounded by a little zone of redness. At first they are only on the cheeks opposite the molar teeth. But they may spread all over the inside of the cheeks and lips and the palate. They cause no symptoms. The child does not even know they are there; neither, frequently, does anyone else. But if they are noticed, and if they really are Koplik's spots, it is important because they are found in no other disease but measles. They usually fade by the time the rash fully comes out.

The pre-eruptive stage of measles lasts anywhere from one or two to five or six days, with all of the symptoms continuing, and the **fever** gradually mounting. Then the rash appears. It begins just behind the ears, on the neck, or on the forehead as scattered dark red spots. In the course of a day or two, there are more of them and they are all over the face. There may be a lot of swelling, especially of the eyelids. On the second or third day of the rash it spreads to the trunk and arms, from the shoulders downwards, and finally in another day or two it shows up on the legs. By this time it is already fading from the face. It fades in the same sequence that it appeared, often leaving a brownish discoloration of the skin for a week. For the first two days the rash comes out, the child is usually at his sickest, with high fever, generalized discomfort, painful eyes which are sensitive to light and a dry harassing cough. As the rash fades the temperature rapidly comes back to normal and all of the troublesome symptoms disappear in the course of two or three days. Then the skin peels in fine, branny scales wherever the rash was. Peeling lasts about a week. The scales are harmless.

What has been described is typical, uncomplicated measles. There are milder cases to be sure; the rash may come out and fade much quicker and the fever be lower. And there are also more severe cases, particularly in young infants. Most of the severe cases have some complications. In fact *any case of measles where the fever remains high after the rash has been out two or three days should be seen again by the doctor*. The usual complications are pneumonia and infection in the middle ear, together or separately. Both of these can be successfully treated with modern drugs which have no effect on the measles itself. For this reason they are not used unless the complications develop. But then they should not be withheld. When children die with measles it is always because of some of its complications.

It was mentioned before that the measles virus is found in the secretions from the nose and throat of a measles patient. This is true before the rash appears as well as after. Every sneeze and cough of the child with measles sprays the infectious material in the air. When this is breathed in by someone else, he acquires the virus, and it does not require much of an exposure to bring on the disease in someone who has never had it. Practically all measles is spread in this way. A third person does not ordinarily transmit it from one case to a new susceptible child. Nor is it usually spread through the handling of clothing or toys or furniture that have been contaminated. It usually takes nine to

sixteen days after exposure before the first cold-like symptoms develop.

The treatment of the measles patient is to make him as comfortable as possible. Cooling sponges when the temperature is high; aspirin for discomfort; a darkened room when light hurts the eyes; plenty of liquids to drink; and cough mixture to try to help the cough all should be thought of. There is no specific medicine for the measles, only time. The specific medicines are for the complications especially if the fever does not go away with the rash. Bed rest should be insisted upon for at least a day, and preferably two or three days, after the temperature has returned to normal. The child should be isolated from other children for at least a week or until there is no more discharge from the nose and throat, whichever is the longer.

Measles can be prevented or made milder by an injection of gamma globulin given at the right time between the exposure and the beginning of the illness. This is discussed in our article "Against What Should We Be Immunized?" If possible measles should be prevented in all children under three years and in any sickly child. They are the ones who develop the complications and it is the complications that cause the fatalities.

GERMAN MEASLES

German measles is a very much milder disease than measles. There may be some general discomfort and slight fever before the rash appears, but as often as not it is the first symptom. It may look just like a measles rash, or it may resemble a scarlet fever rash. Usually it starts on the face and spreads rapidly from the head downward over the body during a twenty-four hour period. The fever and discomfort are worst while the rash is out. At this time too there is usually tender swelling of the lymph nodes behind the ears and on the back of the head. Rash, fever, discomfort and swellings are usually gone in three or four days. There are practically no complications. No treatment is usually necessary except bed rest while the rash is present. Even this is hard to enforce because the symptoms are so mild.

This disease is less contagious than measles. It is spread in the same manner; children who have it are kept home from school for at least four days. It takes two to three weeks after exposure for the rash to appear in a susceptible person.

MUMPS

Mumps is a virus disease that usually involves only the parotid glands. These are two of the salivary glands, on either side of the jaw just below the ear. The symptoms are fever, pain and swelling of the gland. Only one side may be affected, or the other may become involved at the same time or as much as two or three weeks later. The pain and swelling are at their worst three days after the onset and then slowly get better. Chewing and swallowing may be painful at the same time.

The other salivary glands under the jaw may also become swollen. In boys past puberty, and in men, the testicle sometimes becomes swollen during the second or third week. This may result in atrophy of the organ if untreated.

Usually all that is necessary is rest in bed and a light diet for a few days. Hot or cold applications to the swollen glands, whichever brings comfort, may be used. The bed rest should continue until all swelling is gone. The infectious period is usually considered to be three weeks from the onset, and an attack will usually start two to three weeks after the exposure to the disease.

It is wise to have a doctor see the patient to make sure that it is really the parotid gland that is swollen. Enlarged lymph glands in the neck are often confused with mumps and treatment which should be given is therefore withheld to the patient's detriment.

ROSEOLA

Roseola is a peculiar disease that affects only children under three or four years of age. There is a sudden onset of fairly high sustained fever that lasts for two to four days. The child does not appear to be very sick and the doctor can not find any real cause for the fever. Just as abruptly the temperature falls to normal and then a measles-like rash appears on the body and a little on the face. It fades in a day or two.

There is no treatment.

SCARLET FEVER

Scarlet fever is no longer a scourge of childhood. Partly this is because the disease itself has become milder than it used to be, and partly because modern methods of treatment help to shorten its course and eliminate some of its complications.

The typical case of scarlet fever starts off with vomiting, fever and sore throat. Usually the child looks and acts sick from the beginning. At this time all there is to find on examination is a moderately inflamed throat, including the tonsils. The rash comes out one or two days later. It starts on the neck and chest, but it is most noticeable under the arms, in the groins and over the back. It is made up of tiny red points on a reddish background, so that at only a little distance it looks like a diffuse red blush. It may itch or burn. The face does not show this rash, only flushed cheeks and paleness about the mouth. The throat usually gets much worse for a day or two and the fever stays up. Then everything clears up gradually. The tongue develops the "strawberry" appearance as the fever subsides and the throat clears up. The rash fades in about three days to a week. During convalescence the peeling starts, the outer layer of the skin coming off in fairly large pieces, particularly from the fingers and toes. Sometimes this goes on for a month or even longer.

Naturally there are much milder cases, with only a little fever and not much sore throat. The rash may last only a day or two, but even so there is always peeling of the hands and feet. And also there are very severe cases where the child is prostrated and delirious and should be treated in a hospital.

There are two types of important complications of scarlet fever. The first represents a direct spread of the infection from the throat to some nearby location and there may be sinusitis or swollen glands in the neck or abscesses in the ears. When they occur, these infections usually come within the first week of the disease. They can all be treated by the new drugs the doctor has at his disposal. The second type of complication is not so well understood. Sometimes during the second or third week, even though the child has seemed perfectly well, bloody urine or swollen joints may appear. These represent nephritis (kidney disease) and arthritis or rheumatic fever, respectively. Both are serious. Both require prolonged bed rest.

The spread of scarlet fever from one person to another is just like the spread of any other respiratory disease. It is caused by a special strain of the streptococcus germ. Many people can carry this in the nose or throat without being sick at all, and others may have it as the cause of an ordinary sore throat without any rash.

The child with scarlet fever should be kept in bed for a full three weeks. This is particularly important because of the possibility of the kidney complication developing in the third week. The general measures for any sore throat should be used: increased fluids, cooling sponges, aspirin for discomfort. Any other treatment should be in the hands of the doctor who will decide whether sulfa drugs, penicillin, or serum should be used.

The quarantine period for scarlet fever is usually about three weeks so long as there are no discharges from the ears, nose or throat. But different communities vary in their requirements.

DIPHTHERIA*

By George H. Weaver, M.D.

Diphtheria is one of the best understood of human diseases. We know its essential cause, how it operates and the manner of natural recovery. We know how the disease is spread and are able, by a simple test, to determine which persons can contract it if opportunity occurs. We are able by harmless measures to protect the susceptible ones from the disease. If infection has occurred we possess a remedy which, if administered promptly, will bring about a return to former health in practically every case.

Diphtheria is caused by the diphtheria bacillus, which is a microscopic rod-shaped organism sometimes called a germ.

When a person contracts diphtheria, the bacilli usually locate on the tonsil, and as they grow there they elaborate their special poison or toxin. This poison first irritates the tonsil, and as a result redness, pain, and swelling occur.

Because of further injury to the surface of the tonsils there appear white spots, which soon unite to form a larger membrane.

As the bacilli continue to grow beneath this membrane, more toxins are produced and they enter the lymphatics and cause a swelling of the neck. They soon enter the blood and are carried to all parts of the body. In this way they reach and damage the heart, kidneys and nervous system. If the injury inflicted on these vital organs is sufficient, death results.

How the Disease Begins

Diphtheria usually has an insidious beginning. There is at first a moderate fever, slight general depression with indisposition to play, redness of the throat, and loss of appetite.

At this time the child does not usually complain

---

* Reprinted from *Hygeia* by permission.

of a sore throat, and the parents think the child has a cold or is "upset" from some cause. The soreness of the throat is not so marked as in tonsillitis or at the beginning of scarlet fever.

Soon one or both tonsils become enlarged, and on the surface there appear whitish spots which quickly enlarge and unite to form a membrane. This membrane at first is white and semitransparent, but it rapidly thickens and increases in size by extension at the edges. It soon assumes a yellow or gray or even blackish color.

This membrane soon extends from the tonsil to the adjacent soft palate, covers the uvula, the second tonsil and the back of the throat. From here it often goes upward into the nasopharynx and forward into the nose. With the extension to the nose, an irritating, bad-smelling discharge from the nostrils appears.

For this spreading, three or four days may be required. About this time the process often extends downward into the larynx, making breathing difficult, and from there to the trachea and bronchi, often terminating in pneumonia. The picture of diphtheria which we have attempted to paint represents the disease as it occurs when uninfluenced by antitoxic treatment.

Recognize Diphtheria by Cultures

Since diphtheria is always caused by diphtheria bacilli, no case is certainly known to be diphtheria unless their presence is demonstrated. The final test in the diagnosis of diphtheria is the finding of the specific bacillus in the local secretions. Bacilli are usually readily demonstrated by means of culture.

In making the culture, a little of the secretion from the tonsil or elsewhere is collected on a small sterile cotton swab. This is spread over the surface of a special culture medium in a glass test tube or tin box, which is then kept at the temperature of the body for twelve to twenty hours. On the surface of the medium the diphtheria bacilli multiply rapidly and are recognized under the microscope. When diphtheria bacilli are found, the culture is spoken of as positive; when not found, as negative.

The use of throat and nose culture has great value. It makes possible the recognition of mild cases of diphtheria which might otherwise pass for tonsillitis, and also the early identificaton of cases of diphtheria which might be mistaken for other conditions.

The making of cultures from every sore throat

at the onset is a desirable procedure. Many cases of diphtheria can be almost certainly recognized without cultures by the appearance of the throat, and every case which has a suspicious appearance should be treated as diphtheria and the administration of antitoxin not delayed.

How Diphtheria Is Spread

Every case of diphtheria has its origin in a preceding case, either directly or indirectly. From the nose or mouth of the person with diphtheria the bacilli are passed on to other persons. The mode of this passage is variable.

Sometimes small particles of infective secretion are thrown into the air by the patient in coughing or hawking. These particles may be inhaled by persons near by and lodge in the noses or throats.

More often the infectious secretions are carried by some object from the patient to others. Anything which is contaminated by the secretion of the patient may serve this purpose. Among such objects we may mention clothing, handkerchiefs, pencils, toys, eating utensils, and pet animals.

The hands of those who care for the sick may carry the infectious material to themselves and others, and may also contaminate foods and other materials which in turn convey the infection to a third person.

Direct contact by kissing has been the means of transferring diphtheria to many mothers from sick children.

Persons who are not susceptible to diphtheria may still receive the bacilli into their throats and noses and harbor them for some time, but without any sign of disease. Such persons are spoken of as "diphtheria carriers." The "diphtheria carrier" being well and perhaps never having been sick is a fruitful source of innocent spread of diphtheria.

Schick Test Tells Who Will Take Disease

It has long been known that certain persons do not contract diphtheria when abundantly exposed. Such persons are said to be immune or not susceptible. Until recently there has been no method of determining whether an individual is susceptible or immune.

This is now possible by a simple, harmless test which was devised by Dr. Bela Schick, of Vienna, and is known as the "Schick Test." It consists of the injection superficially in the skin of a minute amount of diphtheria toxin. A slight redness follows in 48 hours in the susceptible and none in the immune person. By this test it is possible to determine what persons in a group will have diphtheria if an opportunity occurs and what ones will not.

In New York City large numbers of school children have been given the Schick test. It has been found that in schools attended by the children of more well-to-do parents 50 to 70 per cent of the children gave positive reactions and were susceptible to diphtheria, while in schools in crowded sections of the city only 16 to 25 per cent gave positive reactions. In the country districts the percentage of susceptible children is very high.

Antitoxin Used in Treatment

Medical science throughout the civilized world recognizes diphtheria antitoxin as the only essential agent in the treatment of diphtheria.

It is evident that the most important thing in the treatment of diphtheria is the administration of the antidote, diphtheria antitoxin, in sufficient amount at the earliest moment. Damage to the body produced by the toxins before antitoxin is given is not undone by the antitoxin. The extent of this initial injury before sufficient antitoxin has been given determines largely whether the patient will recover promptly or after a long, tedious convalescence. Deaths multiply with each day the antitoxin treatment is delayed.

The Earlier the Treatment the Better

Given the first day of the sickness, practically every patient recovers promptly; given the second day, most patients recover; but given still later, a considerable number of patients recover only after a protracted convalescence or they die.

It is important that the amount of antitoxin given shall be enough to neutralize the toxin in the circulation quickly. The experience and judgment of the doctor enable him to estimate the dose suitable to each case. The earlier the patient comes under treatment the smaller the dose. If the subsequent course of events indicates that the initial dose was too small, more should be given after 12 to 20 hours.

No ill effects are known to follow the administration of an excess of antitoxin, and it is safer to give more than may be needed rather than just enough. The dose of antitoxin is measured in units. A moderate dose is from 5 to 10 thousand units, a full dose is from 20 to 30 thousand units. Some patients are benefited by amounts up to 100 thousand units.

To those who remember the course and treatment of diphtheria in pre-antitoxin days, the effects of antitoxin are simply marvelous. Then the throat was treated at frequent intervals with swabbings, gargles, and sprays. This was specially harrowing in children who resisted every effort. Most patients with laryngeal diphtheria died in spite of all physicians could do, and many required operations to prevent their dying from suffocation.

Now a few hours after antitoxin is given the aspect of the patient is entirely changed, and this with no local treatment at all. The swelling of the neck and throat subside, the membrane begins to peel off, color returns to the pasty cheek, the pale lips become red again and the little patient who was struggling for breath a few hours before falls into quiet sleep.

If persons have not received antitoxin early, the complications which follow must receive appropriate treatment.

Children May Be Made Immune

Immunization against diphtheria has been found most effective when instituted at the age of nine months and thereafter. For children under three years of age, two injections of toxoid are given at an interval of four weeks. For older children, this same number of injections is given, but the amount of toxoid at each injection is diminished. This has been found to be very effective in protecting children against diphtheria infection.

Ways to Avoid Diphtheria

Some of the things which seem important in overcoming the prevalence and destructiveness of diphtheria follow:

1. Examination of the child's throat whenever he is not well.

2. The immediate summoning of a doctor when a child has a sore throat, swelling of the neck, or any croupy condition with hoarseness.

3. The making of culture from the throat at the first visit of the doctor.

4. Administration of antitoxin whenever there is any condition even remotely resembling diphtheria, without waiting for the results of cultures.

5. Protection by an injection of antitoxin of children who are intimately associated with others who have diphtheria.

6. Immunization of all children over six months of age with toxoid. If the first injections are not followed after six months by a negative Schick test, the injections should be repeated.

WHOOPING COUGH

Whooping cough is one of the most serious of the contagious diseases. It causes more deaths in children under two than any other infection with the exception of penumonia and diarrhea. Most of the deaths occur in babies under one year of age. The disease is frequently complicated by inflammation of the lungs, and the violent coughing which occurs may produce a harmful dilatation of the lung tissues themselves. In rundown children tuberculosis sometimes follows; and cases have been reported of brain hemorrhages, as the result of the violent coughing, which have gone on to paralysis. The disease is caused by a small rod-shaped germ which occurs in the sputum several days before the patient begins to cough and continues there for several weeks after the whooping begins. Consequently the disease may be spread by the sputum even before the patient is known to be suffering from whooping cough. The germs are not easily found in the sputum in the latter part of the disease, but experience has shown that a patient who is nearly over it still may transmit it to someone else. Pretty intimate contact is required for this, however, so that for all practical purposes, the communicable stage is considered to extend from seven days after an exposure to an infected individual to three weeks after the onset of typical paroxysms.

The course of a disease in a case of ordinary severity may be roughly divided into three stages:

First, the catarrhal stage, presenting the symptoms of an irritant cough, without fever or vomiting, and with little expectoration. This usually lasts from one to two weeks.

Second, the paroxysmal or spasmodic stage which usually begins during the second or third week in which the cough appears in spasms and ends with a whoop. This stage may last from four to ten weeks.

Finally, the third stage, or the stage of decline, during which the symptoms correspond with those of the first stage, but are usually accompanied by greater exhaustion of the patient.

The child at first has the symptoms of an ordinary cold in the head and chest accompanied by sharp nervous coughs which have a tendency to come in a series. This gradually increases until there is a succession of violent coughs accompanied by a feeling of suffocation and flushing of the face. The child coughs until he is "black in the face." As soon as the series of coughs stops he tries to fill up his lungs again, but there is a nervous spasm of the muscles of the throat which narrows the opening through which the air must pass. The violent attempt to breathe air through this small space produces the familiar whoop from which the disease receives its name. In mild attacks the child may cough only once or twice a day. But in other cases the seizures may occur as often as every few minutes. If the child is kept quiet the paroxysms occur less often. They may be brought about by the inhalation of dust or by excitement. Laughing, crying, eating or drinking may also bring them on. Sometimes the violence of the cough may cause vomiting or the involuntary passage of urine or feces. In very severe cases there may be bleeding from the nose and into the whites of the eyes. In the early stages there is fever and the child is very restless. The eyelids are reddened and swollen and the face is puffy. There is likely to be quite a falling off in the appetite, and, this combined with the vomiting may cause loss of considerable weight. The most frequent complication of whooping cough is broncho-pneumonia. This must always be looked for when the child develops fever during the paroxysmal stage of the disease. Convulsions sometimes occur and when they do it is very serious. There also may be bleeding from the nose or bleeding into the brain. Obviously no child should be allowed to go through an attack of whooping cough without intelligent care and attention by a physician.

The outcome of the disease depends on three main conditions:

First—the nutrition of the child.

Second—the ability to get enough sleep and rest.

Third—the nature of the complications, if any.

During good weather the patient should be kept out of doors as much as possible. Fresh air, rest and sunshine are all desirable. Anything which brings on a coughing attack should be avoided. Some of these things are breathing of cold air, smoke or dust, over exertion, and sometimes the swallowing of food.

The diet should be light so that it can be easily and quickly digested. Soup, pasteurized milk, eggs and the like should be given frequently. Treatment with drugs and treatment of the complications should be left to the doctor.

Children with whooping cough should be kept isolated from other susceptible children. The germ of whooping cough is found in the sputum and during spasms of coughing this infected sputum may be thrown a considerable distance. Particularly indoors, the air will become laden with whooping cough germs, and any susceptible child who breathes it may come down with the disease. It may also be taken from clothing, linen, toys and the like which have become contaminated with the child's sputum. The vaccination against whooping cough is described in the article "Against What Should We Be Immunized?" While it may not protect completely against an attack of whooping cough it certainly makes the immunized child somewhat more resistant, so that he gets a milder case of the disease. Every baby should be immunized against whooping cough during his second six months of life.

LESS COMMON CONTAGIOUS DISEASES

INFLUENZA

INFLUENZA is also called the "grippe." It is an acute contagious disease which comes in epidemics. It starts suddenly with a moderately high fever, and generalized aching. No special symptoms develop to involve any system or organ of the body. The illness runs its own course in two to four days. Sometimes it is as long as a week. The convalescence is slow; the patient usually feels prostrated for a week or more after the temperature has returned to normal.

In one special form of the disease there may be symptoms of vomiting or diarrhea or both. This variety is called "intestinal flu."

Most cases of influenza seem to be caused by a filterable virus, but there are several different strains of this which are not identical. A couple of these strains have been isolated and used to prepare a vaccine which can be injected to give a temporary immunity lasting a few months. This influenza vaccine gives immunity only to the strains of influenza which are injected. It does not give immunity to colds. The only time to use it is when an epidemic of influenza is predicted. Influenza is not itself serious, but the pneumonia which sometimes complicates it will require special treatment.

INFANTILE PARALYSIS

Infantile paralysis is an acute contagious disease that attacks the nervous system. It is caused by a small filterable virus, but how this gets into the body is still not definitely known. It has been found in the nose and throat secretions of patients with the disease and also in their stools. Flies from the neighborhood of cases of infantile paralysis have also been found to harbor the virus. Consequently all kinds of precautions should be taken to prevent the spread of infection. This includes avoiding crowds, public places and swimming pools, screening houses, and disinfecting the secretions and excretions from patients. While a few cases of infantile paralysis are seen all year around, it usually comes in large epidemics during the summer months.

In a typical case the onset is sudden with symptoms like those of any other acute infection, namely fever, vomiting, irritability and headache. After the first day the specific nature of the disease begins to show itself and there are signs of irritation of the nervous system, stiffness of the neck and back, and pains in the muscles of the extremities. The child sits up in bed in a tripod position with his hands stretched out behind him, and he is unable to put his head down between his knees. The paralysis of the muscles, when it occurs, usually starts on the third day and usually progresses for two or three days before it stops. All of the acute symptoms, the fever, the pain in the muscles, and the headache have usually cleared up by the fifth or sixth day, but muscle paralysis remains to be treated.

There are, of course, a number of different results to infantile paralysis depending upon the part of the nervous system that has been affected. In fact there are many cases that have no paralysis at all and would not even be diagnosed as such if they did not occur in the course of an epidemic and spinal fluids were therefore examined.

There is still no treatment for infantile paralysis in the acute stage. There is no way of stopping the spread of the paralysis from one muscle to the next. But if the patient survives, the infection eventually burns itself out and the process comes to a halt. The treatment from then on should, if possible, be in the hands of a specialist in this disease. The hot packs in the Kenny method of treatment should have been started even earlier, while the soreness of the muscles was at its height; or the splinting of the paralyzed parts, if that method of treatment is to be used, should be under the spe-

cialist's direction.

Infantile paralysis never remains as extensive as it appears at the worst, and in some epidemics almost half of the paralyzed patients recover completely. In any event, the improvement in muscle function can continue to take place for many months after the acute disease has subsided. Every patient with infantile paralysis should of course be isolated. Hospital treatment is desirable and may be essential if there is a paralysis of respiration. One attack of the disease results in life-long immunity, and many adults are immune who have no recollection of ever having had it. These persons probably had unrecognized non-paralytic attacks in childhood. The disease is most common in children from two to eight years of age. A susceptible person who comes down with the disease was probably exposed to it about nine or ten days earlier.

INFECTIOUS MONONUCLEOSIS
(ALSO CALLED GLANDULAR FEVER)

Infectious mononucleosis is a disease in which the lymph glands all over the body become swollen. It usually starts suddenly, like other infections, with fever, headache, generalized discomfort, and sometimes a sore throat. Occasionally a nondescript rash will appear over the body. After a few days the characteristic enlargement of the lymph glands begins. They are found especially in the neck, under the arms, and in the groins. They are tender. The fever generally lasts about a week or less but the glandular swellings may persist for as long as three or four weeks. Once the glands have appeared a definite diagnosis can be made by various types of examination of the blood. The disease does not usually have any after-effects except a mild prostration for a while. It is not very contagious and no quarantine is necessary.

MENINGITIS

Meningitis means inflammation of the membranes covering the brain and spinal cord. It is always a very dangerous disease and should if possible be treated in a hospital. It may be caused by any one of a number of different kinds of germs. Fortunately, practically all of them can be treated with one or another of the new drugs that have been discovered during or since the war.

Meningitis usually starts off like any other acute infection with fever, vomiting, headache, and generalized discomfort. The thing that differentiates it from most other acute infections is the appearance, sooner or later, of stiffness in the neck or back, or inability to straighten out the legs if they are raised up when the child is lying flat on his back. If any of these signs should be noted, the doctor should be called at once. If he decides that they are due to a meningitis, the sooner the treatment is started the better it will be for the patient.

There is a certain type of meningitis sometimes occurring in epidemics that is also called "spotted fever" because of a characteristic rash that comes out in these cases along with the usual symptoms of fever, vomiting, headache, stiff neck and, in this disease, frequently delirium.

RHEUMATIC FEVER

The importance of rheumatic fever lies in its effect upon the heart. In certain sections of the country rheumatic heart disease makes up about 40% of all cases of heart disease and well over 90% of the heart disease in children. No two children with rheumatic fever are exactly alike. The disease is very variable. One patient may be quite sick and another child may have no symptoms at all but may have heart disease discovered at a routine examination. When a child with rheumatic fever looks and acts sick he is apt to have fever which may be quite high. There may be pains in his joints, migrating from one large joint to another, or involving the small joints in the hands and feet. Knees, ankles, wrists or elbows may become painful, red, hot, or swollen, all at one time or one after another. When there is severe heart involvement during the acute part of the disease, the child may complain of pain in his heart, and have difficulty in breathing. He may be unable to lie flat in bed. His color may be very poor, either pale or bluish. Most children are not this sick, and many complain only of some indefinite pains in the muscles or joints, and have only a low, irregular fever. They may not show any obvious signs of involvement of the heart. This does not mean that every pain in a muscle or joint is caused by a rheumatic fever, but persistent complaints should at least be looked into. They may be caused by muscle strain, by flat feet, or by poor circulation, but even so, these things should be corrected. If a child appears to be pale and listless and has occasional attacks of fever, along with the joint or muscle pain, he should have the benefit of a very careful examination and whatever laboratory tests the doctor thinks should be made.

The cause of rheumatic fever is not yet known. Sometimes it seems to have something to do with an earlier attack of a sore throat due to a streptococcus germ. Attacks are more likely to occur in the spring and fall when the streptococcus infections are more prevalent. The disease tends to run in families. It is much more common in the temperate parts of the country than in the sub-tropical.

Unfortunately rheumatic fever is a disease which tends to come again and again in the same patient. Each time he suffers from an attack he is likely to have additional damage to the heart. There is no absolutely sure way of preventing recurrences. It helps to live in a part of the country where the climate is mild. It is particularly important to avoid catching a cold or sore throat. The best way to do this is to avoid people who have them. Sometimes chilling and over exertion have been thought to bring on recurrences of rheumatic fever.

A child who has had one attack of rheumatic fever should be treated much more conservatively than another child when he has a respiratory infection. He should stay in bed for several days after the temperature has returned to normal. Preferably he should be seen by a doctor before returning to full activity. So long as a child survives his acute attacks of rheumatic fever he can get along pretty well. The main damage that the disease does in the heart is to injure a valve that separates one part of the heart from another. This results in either an obstructing valve or a "leaky valve," but so long as the heart muscle itself remains strong the child can carry on without any disability. In fact, when the infection is not active it is desirable to let him lead as completely normal a life as possible. Just because a child has a heart murmur is no reason, in the absence of infection, to make a complete invalid of him. On the other hand, a very vigorous child should not be given a completely free reign if he is the sort who drives himself to the point of exhaustion.

CHOREA (ST. VITUS' DANCE)

Chorea or *St. Vitus' dance*, is related in some way to rheumatic fever. Children who have it sometimes end up with the same kind of damage to the heart as do children who have had attacks of acute rheumatic fever. The disease usually attacks children between the ages of seven and thirteen years of age. They develop purposeless movements of any muscles of the body. These are different from tics or habit spasms. The small muscles of the hand may be affected so that there are slight twitchings of the fingers, or the large muscles of the trunk may be involved and the twitching may throw the whole body of the child to one side. In addition to the actual disturbances with the muscles, there is also a change in the child's emotional reactions. He is apt to be irritable and restless and moody, easily provoked to tears.

The condition usually comes on very gradually and the parents often are not aware that something is wrong for several weeks, thinking merely that the child has become unruly. But this is a real illness and should be treated as such. Bed rest is sometimes necessary for several months. The child should be protected from injuring himself by his own uncontrollable movements. Sedative drugs sometimes help and fever treatments are sometimes given.

If there is no damage to the heart the outlook for the child with chorea is good even though he may have several different attacks. The twitchings themselves always go away in time.

SYPHILIS

Syphilis is a disease caused by a specific germ which may infect the system before or after birth. When the infection occurs after birth, it is spoken of as "acquired syphilis." This is no different in children from acquired syphilis in an adult. There is a primary stage or chancre; a secondary stage, which is a generalized rash about two months later; and a tertiary stage with involvement of practically any part of the body coming on several years after the beginning of the disease. In adults it is usually spread by sexual contacts and the primary sore is in the region of the genitals. In infants and children it is usually spread by the kiss of an infected person. The primary sore is at the site of the kiss and may be on any part of the body.

When syphilis has been acquired before birth, it is spoken of as "congenital syphilis." It is seen only in a baby whose mother had syphilis during pregnancy. In a very severe case the baby may be born dead; when it is less severe there may be symptoms present at the time of birth; in the usual case the symptoms do not show up until about one or two months after birth. The main early symptoms are snuffles and a generalized rash all over the body with sores behind the ears, at the corners of the mouth, and in the folds of the buttocks.

Congenital syphilis can be completely prevented by the adequate treatment of the syphilitic infection of the mother. This is why a blood test from every pregnant woman is required by law in most states. If the blood test is positive, treatment should be started at once and continued right through the pregnancy. Halfhearted treatment will not prevent the disease in the baby. If the mother's syphilis has gone unrecognized, and it does appear in the baby, his treatment should be started as soon as the diagnosis is made if the best results are to be obtained.

TUBERCULOSIS

Tuberculosis may affect children at any age, but it is most likely to be a serious danger to life and to health in very young babies and in adolescents. A good many children in middle childhood pick up a mild case of the disease before adolescence, especially when they live in cities. But this form of the disease seems to do them no harm. In most cases tuberculosis is caused by another person with the disease who is spreading the germ in his sputum. For this reason whenever a child is found to have tuberculosis, everyone with whom he has much contact should be examined. Sometimes this will turn up an unsuspected case of active tuberculosis in a close associate of the child. Naturally this person too should receive treatment. He should not be allowed to expose any other children, nor even adults. Sometimes no other case of tuberculosis is found in a child's contacts. When this is so, the child has usually picked up the infection from germs in dust or on the street. The tuberculosis germ is a very resistant one and can live for long periods of time outside the human body. There is also a variety of the tuberculosis germ, slightly different from the human strain, which infects cattle. It can be transmitted to children in raw milk. This variety of the germ affects glands, bones and joints, rather than the lungs. But tuberculosis of these parts of the body is very seldom seen in this country nowadays because of the widespread practice of pasteurization of milk.

There is no standard set of symptoms of tuberculosis in children. A baby may seem to be doing very well even while an extensive infection is developing. The fever, cough, bloody expectoration and night sweats of the typical advanced case of tuberculosis in an adult usually are not seen in childhood. Any child who persistently runs an unexplained fever, who has long continued swollen glands, or who just does not seem to be doing well should be examined for tuberculosis.

In infants and children the first step in looking for a tuberculous infection is usually the tuberculin test. This is a skin test. A small amount of an extract of the tuberculosis germ is injected into the skin. A red spot at the side of the injection showing up two to four days later is a positive test. All this means is that at sometime in the past tuberculosis germs have entered the child's body. It does not necessarily mean that the infection is still active. It does mean that the child has been exposed to tuberculosis and that more studies should be made to see if the exposure has done him any harm. These studies will undoubtedly include an X-ray of the lung. There may also be X-rays of other parts of the body, blood tests, evaluation of fever, and examination of the sputum. When sputum cannot be obtained directly because the child is too young to cooperate, it can be gotten by washing out of his stomach what he has swallowed.

If a diagnosis of active tuberculosis is made, practically the only treatment is rest. It is important to break the contact with the source of the infection so that the body will not continually be receiving new tuberculosis germs. The amount of rest necessary depends upon the severity of the infection and the age of the child. A mild primary infection with tuberculosis in someone in middle childhood, say from five to ten years of age, may require only rest periods during a relatively normal day. A more severe type of infection, or one in a younger child, may be an indication that complete rest in bed for months at a time is needed. Tuberculosis of the glands, bones and joints sometimes need surgical treatment. Children who are known to have had a recent case of tuberculosis of the lungs, even though it was very mild, should have their immunity to whooping cough kept high by annual "booster" injec-

tions of whooping cough vaccine and should receive a protective injection when they are exposed to measles. These two diseases may cause a healing case of tuberculosis. Any child who was once known to have had tuberculosis should be examined and a chest X-ray made at least every few years to be sure that the disease remains quiescent.

UNDULANT FEVER

Undulant fever is a disease caused by the same germ that causes infectious abortion in cows. It is usually transmitted by drinking unpasteurized milk from an infected cow. The germ may also get into the human body through a break in the skin. The disease is usually characterized by prolonged fever, which may be steady or intermittent. There is weakness and easy fatiguing and profuse sweating. There is no special local symptom, nor is there any special treatment. The fever may last for as long as four or five months, but the children who have it, at any rate, all ultimately get better, even though they may pick up some complications along the way which may require special treatment.

TYPHOID FEVER

Typhoid fever is a preventable disease. We know the germ that causes it. We know how that germ gets into the body. We know how to increase a person's resistance to it. Because of this knowledge, the large epidemics that used to devastate an entire community have been eliminated, largely through advances in sanitation. In times of flood and other disasters when sanitary services break down, everyone is immunized with typhoid vaccine by the public health officials and the Red Cross.

Every case of typhoid fever represents a connection between the excretions of a person harboring the typhoid germ and the mouth of the person coming down with the disease. Before the days of sensible sanitation, this connection was made through the public water and milk supplies, and hundreds of people were attacked at the same time. Now the cases come mostly from two sources: *flies* which alight on food soon after crawling on typhoid-contaminated material, and *"typhoid carriers."* These are people who excrete large numbers of typhoid fever germs in their stools while they remain in perfect health. The famous "Typhoid Mary" was one such person in

New York City who delighted in getting employment as a cook. Many cases of typhoid fever were traced to her cookery.

The diagnosis and treatment of typhoid fever must be in the hands of a doctor. It should be considered whenever there is an illness with fever lasting two or three weeks without especial localizing symptoms. Frequently there is a characteristic rash over the abdomen. But a definite diagnosis can only be made through laboratory tests on the blood and stools. The disease tends to be relatively mild in infants and children, but there is still danger from two of its complications: perforation of the intestine with spreading peritonitis, and hemorrhage. When either of these occurs emergency treatment in a hospital is necessary.

SMALLPOX

Smallpox is a highly contagious, eruptive disease of high mortality. Formerly the epidemics were very much dreaded, but vaccination has proved to be a great prophylactic measure, and minimized the danger of infection.

The disease begins with chills, headache, backache, vomiting, and fever which lasts 3 or 4 days. The eruption then appears, remains for a week, and is followed by a secondary rise of temperature. The face is swollen, the eyes closed from the inflammation; a cough may be present.

Eruption appears on the third day, first on the forehead and lips; it resembles red papules, which are hard and feel like shot imbedded beneath the skin. These gradually change to vesicles and finally to pustules with a depression in the center. In severe cases hemorrhage occurs under the skin.

The patient should be put to bed, and liquid diet given. The headache is relieved by local cold application. For the fever, sponge the body with cold water, give cool drinks. Irrigate the eyes with boric acid solution if necessary. The mouth and nose should be kept clean with a solution of boric acid. To prevent the skin from pitting, scratching must be prevented. For the itching apply carbolized vaseline twice a day.

The vast predominance of world-wide evidence is that smallpox *does not* occur in successfully vaccinated individuals. Every child should be vaccinated in infancy; if the first attempt does not give a successful result, repeated trial should be made until the vaccination "takes." Repeated inoculation with smallpox virus should be made again in from seven to ten years. *Everyone* should be vaccinated or revaccinated in the event of the occurrence of the disease in the neighborhood.

DISEASES OF THE SKIN

IMPETIGO

IMPETIGO is an infection of the skin with staphylococcus or streptococcus germs. It starts off as very small blisters which enlarge quickly, filled with fluid which is at first clear but becomes cloudy and yellow. As the blisters break and the fluid dries up, the typical honey-colored crusts form. The disease usually starts on the face but it can be spread to any part of the body that the hands touch. It can also be spread to other persons by contact with clothing, towels, toys, and the like. If treated early it can usually be cleared up in a few days. A most important part of the treatment is the removal of the crusts with warm soapy water so that whatever medicine the doctor prescribes can get at the germs which grow underneath.

RINGWORM

Ringworm is an infection with a fungus, not a worm. When it involves the scalp there are round patches of scaly skin with the hairs broken off very short so that they look bald. It is very contagious among children but is seldom seen after puberty. Ringworm of the body usually shows up as round patches of rough, scaly skin with very small blisters at the edges. Ringworm of the feet is the familiar "athlete's foot" with raw skin between the toes. All types of ringworm infection should be treated promptly and vigorously by a doctor. They are sometimes very difficult to get rid of, especially in the scalp where it is often necessary to pull out the affected hairs individually or get rid of them by X-ray.

SCABIES

Scabies (The Itch) is due to the burrowing into the skin of the female itch-mite with secondary sores from scratching. The itching is worse when the body is warm, especially under blankets at night. The infection can be on any part of the body, but is most often on the hands, wrists, abdomen, and penis, and very seldom involves the face or back. Treatment consists in thorough washing, the use of an ointment or lotion to kill the mites, and care to prevent reinfection by changing and boiling bed linen and clothing. Scabies is readily contagious. Other children should not be allowed to sleep with the affected child nor to use the same towels, linen or clothing.

WARTS

Warts are little bumps of skin. They may appear singly or in bunches of a cauliflower shape. They may come on in a whole crop at one time. Usually no treatment is necessary and they will go away by themselves. If they are on the feet and painful, or if they are very unsightly, they may be burned off in a variety of ways.

ACNE (PIMPLES AND BLACKHEADS)

Acne is a disease of older children during puberty. It is characterized by numerous pimples, pustules and blackheads mostly on the face but sometimes on the shoulders and back, and occasionally on the chest. It seems to be related to excessive oiliness of the skin especially at the beginning of adolescence. It is not contagious and has no relation to venereal disease. In addition to special attention to the diet, and frequent soap and water scrubbing, various ointments and lotions are used in treatment. In severe or persistent cases, X-ray therapy may be given.

ECZEMA AND HIVES

(See Diseases due to Allergy)

HEAT RASH

Heat rash starts usually around the neck and shoulders or the groin. There are fine red bumps which may itch. Lighter clothing, frequent bathing followed by thorough drying, and free use of a corn-starch-and-boric-acid powder will help to clear it up.

BOILS AND ABSCESSES

Any collection of pus is called an abscess. If it is a small one in the skin it is called a boil. Symptoms from these conditions come from the infection and from the pressure of contained pus. There is heat, redness, swelling, and tenderness locally. There may also be fever, swollen lymph glands and general discomfort. Moist heat is best for these infections, applied as a poultice, a fomentation or a continuous wet dressing. Care should be taken not to burn the skin. If the boil does not soon point through the skin and rupture of its own accord, it should be incised and drained. Anyone who suffers from a series of boils one after another should be examined by his doctor.

CELLULITIS AND ERYSIPELAS
(St. Anthony's Fire)

These are spreading infections of the skin. There are usually general symptoms of chills, fever and discomfort. In erysipelas the involved skin is red, hot, swollen and painful with the edge sharply outlined from the surrounding skin which is normal. In cellulitis, the border is not so well defined and the inflammation is usually deeper. There may be red streaks running up the arm or leg and tender swollen glands in the axilla or groin. These are very serious infections which should be treated at once by a physician. The new sulfa drugs or penicillin are required for the treatment.

RASHES OF THE COMMON CONTAGIOUS DISEASES

Chickenpox has small, widely scattered red pimples which progress to blisters and then form scabs. All stages are present at the same time.

Measles has flat red spots starting on the forehead and behind the ears and spreading down.

German Measles also has flat red spots. It spreads more rapidly, the child is not as sick as with measles.

Scarlet Fever has a diffused red flush with pinpoint sized red lumps, most marked under the arms and in the groins, never on the face.

DISEASES OF THE RESPIRATORY TRACT

DISEASES of the respiratory system are far more common in childhood than of any other system of the body. Every child suffers at some time from the common cold. Sore throat, tonsillitis without or with swelling of the lymph glands in the neck, due to a variety of different germs, are quite common. Ear infections, laryngitis and croup also occur in children very often.

COMMON COLD

Simple, uncomplicated colds are caused by a filterable virus. They are contagious, and are transmitted from one person to another by "droplet" infection. Every sneeze and cough of a child with a cold sprays the virus into the air where it can be breathed into the nose and throat of the next person. So all children should be taught to cover their noses and mouths when sneezing and coughing. Also it is much better if the discharges from a patient with a cold can be wiped away by paper tissues and discarded, rather than in handkerchiefs and carried around.

A small baby with a cold is not apt to be bothered very much so long as it does not spread. The runniness of his nose does not seem to make him uncomfortable, but should the nose become stuffed up so that he can't breathe through it, he may become quite miserable until it becomes clear again. A small baby's first cold ordinarily lasts for a week or ten days but sometimes it may go on for three or four weeks before it clears up.

Older children with colds may start off with a high fever for the first day or so before the runny nose appears. Other children will just have a runny nose or scratchy throat without much fever at all. A child with a cold should be kept at rest. This means in bed if possible, but the children who rebel vigorously about being put to bed may be allowed to play quietly in their own rooms. The room should be at an even temperature, without drafts. The child should be dressed comfortably, not too warmly. He should not be urged to eat if he has lost his appetite for a few days.

If the discharge from the nose is troublesome it sometimes helps to humidify the air for a half hour or so, four or five times a day. This is best done by putting a kettle of boiling water in the room and letting it boil there. It should be out of reach or else someone should stay with the child.

Nose drops may be prescribed by the doctor. They may be to shrink down the swollen tissues of the nose and give the child more breathing space, or they may contain a medicine to combat the infection. Nose drops for children should always be in a watery solution. If oily nose drops are used, they may be aspirated into the child's lungs, where they can cause a great deal of harm.

The importance of the cold is not so much the cold infection itself as the fact that it lowers the body's resistance to other germs, which may cause a more serious infection. Any unexplained fever, hoarseness or pain in the ears or chest coming in the course of a cold, should be evaluated by a doctor. Also a good many of the common contagious diseases of childhood start off with symptoms resembling those of a cold.

SORE THROAT

A number of different conditions are grouped together under the classification of sore throat.

It is important to differentiate between them because some are potentially dangerous infections which may require specific treatment. Any time that white patches are seen in the throat or on the tonsils, it is particularly important that the correct diagnosis be made. These patches may be due to diphtheria. They may be caused by the germs of a Vincent's infection, which usually causes "trench mouth." They may be part of an infection called infectious mononucleosis. Most commonly they are caused by a streptococcus infection of the throat or tonsils.

Sore throat in a child may make him appear to be quite sick, yet he may not complain of the throat hurting or bothering him at all. Nevertheless, fever, generalized discomfort, headaches, vomiting, diarrhea, pain in the abdomen, stiffness of the neck, and even convulsions may be caused by infection of the throat in a susceptible child.

A mild sore throat requires no special treatment except rest in bed, and possibly small doses of aspirin to relieve discomfort. But a severe sore throat is best treated by a doctor.

There is a special form of sore throat called Quinsy, which may require emergency treatment. In this condition an abscess tends to form behind the tonsil on one side. As the condition progresses, the swelling of and behind the tonsil may become so great as to prevent the patient from opening his mouth more than a fraction of an inch and from swallowing anything. If treatment is started in time this uncomfortable situation can usually be prevented. But if a real attack of Quinsy develops, these conditions do occur, and an abscess forms which either ruptures spontaneously or must be opened by the doctor.

SWOLLEN GLANDS

The lymph glands in the neck sometimes become swollen as a result of an infection in the throat or of the tonsils. This may happen while the child is still sick and running fever, or it may come several weeks after a sore throat has gone away. Sometimes the glands are tender and become quite large and break down to form pus inside of them. When this happens an operation to drain the pus is necessary. More often the swelling is only mild or moderate, and the child may not appear bothered by it at all. They may persist this way for many months. When they do, it is wise to be sure that there is no generalized disease, such as tuberculosis, which is causing them. If not, forget about them.

CROUP

Croup is the common name for laryngitis in children. There are two kinds. One is mild; the other is severe and may jeopardize the child's life.

The mild form is simple spasmodic croup. This usually comes on during the night in a child who went to bed apparently perfectly well. He wakes up with a barking cough, hoarseness and some difficulty in breathing. This usually frightens and excites him and makes all of the symptoms worse. The two things that are most important in the immediate treatment are to calm and soothe the child, and to have him breathe warm, moist air. He should be moved to a warm room in which there is a kettle of steam going all the time. The doctor may suggest making a "steam tent" out of his crib, by draping sheets over it. This is all right so long as it does not frighten the child and so long as the steam kettle is way out of the way so that it cannot tip over and scald him. The attacks frequently come on two or three nights in a row. They seem to be caused by a combination of a susceptible child, a mild cold in the larnyx, and the breathing of cold air. Consequently, any child who has had an attack of croup one

night should sleep in a warm, moist room for the next couple of nights, until he is well over it.

The more severe type of croup is called infectious croup. In this condition, there is fever, as well as hoarseness, cough and difficulty in breathing. The symptoms persist during the day and always tend to become worse at night. The breathing may become so labored that the effort exhausts the child. An emergency operation to give him an air-way is sometimes necessary so that he does not suffocate. A child with this kind of croup should be under constant observation. Diptheria of the larynx must be considered in every case but it is not likely to be the cause if the child has previously been immunized.

EAR INFECTIONS

Ear infections are particular common in infants and children because the Eustachian tubes which lead from the middle ear to the throat are shorter than they are in the adult. It is easier for the infection to get in. Most of the time infection in the ears is a complication of a cold or a sore throat. Sometimes it may be the primary illness.

The two main symptoms are pain in the ear and discharge from the ear. An older child may or may not complain about this pain. A younger baby may pull at the hurting ear, or he may just cry. Sometimes there is little or no pain and the first thing that is noticed is a discharge from the ear.

A good many children will have some inflammation of the ears along with their colds, which may not amount to anything. But fever, pain, or discharge should always be treated. The dangerous things with ear infections are first, spread to the mastoid requiring an operation, and second, spread to the nervous system causing meningitis. With modern treatment, neither of these complications happens very often.

TONSILS AND ADENOIDS

The tonsils and adenoids are lymphoid tissues. This is the same tissue that is in the lymph glands in the neck, under the arms and in the groins. Its function in the body is to help combat infection. In doing so, it becomes swollen.

The importance of the tonsils and adenoids lies in this fact and also in their location. The adenoids are at the roof of the throat behind the nose. When they become enlarged, as a result of repeated or chronic infection, they may obstruct the nose and be one of the causes of mouth breathing. Even more important, however, is the effect of enlarged adenoids on the ears. When adenoid tissue enlarges it may get to interfere with the opening of the Eustachian tube. This tube is responsible for the proper drainage of the middle ear. Interference with its normal function results in greater susceptibility to ear infections.

The tonsils, lying on either side of the throat, may enlarge a great deal without causing any trouble because of their size. But sometimes they may become so huge as almost to meet in the mid-line, and may cause difficulty in swallowing. Tonsils may be chronically infected without being this big.

It is no longer thought necessary to remove tonsils and adenoids merely because they are there. There should be some definite reason for the operation. Adenoids should be removed if they are obstructing a child's breathing or if he is having a number of middle ear infections. Tonsils should be removed from a child who has repeated attacks of tonsillitis. This should be real tonsillitis, not merely a sore throat that does not involve the tonsils. A child who has an attack of Quinsy should have his tonsils removed. Chronically diseased tonsils should also be taken out, especially if they are associated with swollen glands in the neck. But tonsillectomy should not be considered a cure-all. It certainly eliminates future attacks of tonsillitis, but it need not cure everything else that ails a child, as it was once thought to do.

If possible, the operation should be delayed until the child is seven or eight years of age. It is easier to do then, because there is more room; and the lymphoid tissue is not as apt to grow back as it is if the operation is done earlier.

Tonsil and adenoids operations should not be done when there is infantile paralysis around. The raw area left in the nose and throat seems to make the child more susceptible to a very serious form of this disease. Nor should the operation be done until the child is well over any acute infection of the nose or throat.

BRONCHITIS

Bronchitis is apt to accompany almost any cold, or the cold may start off in the chest. The disease consists of an inflammation in the air passages in the lungs. The membranes lining these passages become somewhat swollen and pour out mucus. This mucus may rattle up and down inside the tubes with each breath causing the characteristic wheezing that is frequently heard. In a little baby whose bronchial tubes are small to begin with the swelling may be so much as to make it difficult for air to get by and the baby may have a lot of difficulty in breathing. Sometimes it even requires treatment in an oxygen tent. This seldom is true in older children with bronchitis. The inflammation and the mucus in the tubes may cause a lot of coughing. There may be fever but the seriousness of the case, especially in babies, does not necessarily go hand in hand with the fever. For any but the mildest cases it will be well to seek medical care. Modern drugs frequently help to shorten the course of the attack.

PNEUMONIA

Pneumonia is always a serious disease. It may come on after a few days of a cold, it may come in the course of whooping cough or measles, or it may come out of a clear sky in a previously healthy child. In the beginning it may be like any other acute infection with fever, vomiting or generalized discomfort and possibly even a convulsion. Typically in pneumonia there is rapid, sometimes labored and grunting breathing. There is usually a cough. Thanks to the sulfa drugs and penicillin, the mortality from pneumonia even in little babies has been reduced considerably. Many times the patients are not even sick very long and only rarely is the oxygen tent necessary. As with other acute infections, the younger the patient the more serious the case is. Pneumonia is still a dangerous disease in very young babies,

DISEASES IN THE ABDOMEN

COLIC

Colic is a condition which is not very well understood. It comes in some babies during their second and third months. Sometimes it starts earlier, but it seldom lasts much longer. The colicky baby thrives in every respect except the one which gives him the name. He is healthy and active. He gains weight well. The only trouble is that he has prolonged spells of crying. These may be a very regular occurrence. They may come about the same time every day and last for the entire interval between two feedings while the baby is perfectly comfortable for the rest of the day. Other babies may have two or three "attacks" during a day.

During a bout of colic a baby seems to have pain from cramps in his intestines. He pulls his legs up on his abdomen and cries miserably. He may quiet down a little for a few minutes, only to have the same thing happen again and again. The gurgling of gas in the intestines can sometimes be heard along with the worst crying spells. He may pass gas from the rectum.

A lot of different things are done about colic but none of them seems to do much good. For the acute discomfort it may help to pick the baby up, rock and comfort him. Usually he feels better lying on his belly either in the crib or across his mother's knees. A hot water bottle (if it is well covered to prevent any burn) to the abdomen sometimes makes him feel a little better. If the baby's misery is most severe a small enema of plain warm water will frequently help more than anything else, but this should be reserved for special occasions, not used as a routine thing.

In an effort to prevent the baby's discomfort, many different kinds of formulas are tried. This should be done only under the doctor's direction. The use of drugs too should be left to his discretion. A colicky baby is usually a lot better if he can be kept in a calm, peaceful environment. He can apparently sense it when his parents are tense or anxious about his crying, and this sometimes upsets him even more. A mother who is very upset by her baby's unrelieved crying would do well to have a nurse or a neighbor to substitute for her once in a while in the care of the infant.

JAUNDICE

This disease is also called infectious jaundice or infectious hepatitis. Both are better names for it, because it is an infection of the liver. This kind of jaundice comes in epidemics, but the germ that causes it and the way in which it is spread are still not known. The child who comes down with it usually starts with a slight fever. He is apt to be irritable and have no appetite. Then he usually complains of abdominal pains. This is usually on the right side, high up under the ribs. It is fairly steady pain and may make the child miserable.

All of these things may continue for several days before the jaundice appears. But then the whites of his eyes will be noted to be yellow and the urine very dark. The temperature usually comes down a few days after the jaundice appears, but the discoloration of the eyes and the skin may continue to get worse for as long as a week or two even though by this time the patient feels fairly comfortable except for weakness.

There is no special treatment for the condition as far as medicines are concerned. Aspirin may be given to relieve the pain. Special attention should be paid to the diet; fats such as cream, butter and fried foods should be avoided. Extra rations of carbohydrate in the form of sweet drinks and jellies can be given. When the jaundice is very intense the skin may itch. If calamine lotion does not help, a starch bath should be given. No complications are ever seen from this disease in children.

STOMACH DISORDERS

Most of the so called stomach disorders basically have nothing to do with the stomach at all. But when a child vomits, has diarrhea, or complains of abdominal pains, he is said frequently to have an "upset stomach." Some of the things which can cause these conditions will be discussed here, and the proper way to begin treatment will be decribed.

Vomiting may be caused by any acute infection from a cold to meningitis, but then it is usually accompanied by fever. Over-excitement, over-tiredness, and fatigue may cause vomiting, usually without fever. Eating some foods which disagree with him may make a child vomit. So will eating contaminated food (food poisoning). Vomiting is also seen when there is something wrong with the intestinal tract, as in appendicitis or intestinal obstruction.

Diarrhea may be caused by practically any of the things which cause vomiting. Most often it is some acute infection outside the intestines. When it is from an infection of the intestine, it may have been acquired from eating of contaminated food or it may be that the child has picked up dysentery. This being the case the stools, in addition to being loose and frequent, will also contain blood, mucus, and pus. Sometimes diarrhea is seen as a part of "intestinal flu."

Abdominal pains too may be caused by any of the conditions which will give vomiting and/or diarrhea.

The important thing is to know what to do, and especially what not to do, for a child who has vomiting or diarrhea or abdominal pains or any combination of the three. First he should be put to bed. Second his temperature should be taken. If it is over 101° a doctor should see him. Third, nothing should be given by mouth for a while. How long depends on what happens. If the vomiting continues, giving of food by mouth will only provoke it the more. Starvation except for sips of water is frequently good treatment in the beginning of a diarrhea. A cathartic should never be given unless the doctor orders it. A small enema of plain water may be given to a child with pain or vomiting as long as there is no diarrhea. Any child with a "stomach-ache" who continues to complain for more than two or three hours, any child with persistent vomiting who cannot keep anything on his stomach over a period of three or four hours, and any child with a succession of loose stools should be seen by a doctor.

Blood in the bowel movement, especially when it is intimately mixed with the stool, is also a danger signal. Small children can become desperately sick very quickly from a major loss in their body fluids. These conditions should not be neglected.

CONSTIPATION

Most people pay entirely too much attention to the frequency and regularity of bowel movements of normal, healthy children. So long as he does not complain of discomfort, no particular harm will come to a child who goes for a day or two, or even longer, without moving his bowels. Certainly no cathartic medicines should be given merely because a child has missed a bowel movement on one day. Some children develop a perfectly regular bowel habit every second day. This is just as normal and just as healthy as if it were every day. A child whose bowel movements are very hard may have pain when he passes them. When this is the case his diet needs looking into. He may not be taking enough liquids, or he may not have fruit or vegetables at his meals. Most active healthy children have no trouble with their bowels unless the parents look for trouble. Medicine should not be given except under the doctor's direction. The "cathartic habit" should not be started in childhood. Once the intestinal tract gets used to these irritants, it is very difficult to get along without them.

APPENDICITIS

Appendicitis is strictly a surgical condition. The earlier the diagnosis is made and the child brought to the hospital, and the sooner the inflamed appendix is removed, the easier the operation, and the better the chance for a complete uneventful recovery. Delay is dangerous because the inflamed appendix is like a boil. Even as a boil may burst, so may an appendix rupture and spill its pus all over the abdominal cavity. When it does this peritonitis results, and the outlook becomes very grave. The early symptoms of appendicitis may not be very spectacular. There are usually nausea, vomiting, fever, abdominal pains, but none of these may be very severe. The pain most often starts around the middle of the abdomen and later shifts to the right side below the navel. It is usually a steady pain rather than cramps. The bowels are usually normal. The child is apt to prefer lying on his back with his right leg drawn up. There is tenderness when the abdomen is pressed in the region of the appendix.

When appendicitis is suspected the child should be put to bed and kept there, given nothing to eat or drink except small sips of water. By no means should he be given a cathartic or any medicine to dull his pain. An enema will do no harm. An ice bag may be applied to the abdomen in the region of the pain. Other than these things, nothing should be done until a doctor has seen the patient. He will decide on future treatment.

INTUSSUSCEPTION

This is an emergency which occurs once in a while. It is a condition in which the intestine rolls up on itself something like the finger of a glove being turned inside out. Every time the intestine contracts, the condition gets a little worse, and with every contraction there is pain and a slight amount of bleeding. With the pain the baby cries. Between pains he is perfectly comfortable. Eventually some of the blood comes out on his diaper, mixed with his stool. When this happens the doctor should be called right away. Usually an immediate operation is necessary.

WORMS *

By PARK J. WHITE

It is remarkable how delighted—even flattered—many folks are by having certain favorite diagnoses made of their own or their beloveds'

---

* Reprinted from *Hygeia* by permission.

ills. How they thrill to the sound of "biliousness," "grippe," "ptomaine poisoning," "teething," and, alas! *"worms!"*

Now, if we except biliousness, which is scientifically beneath contempt—any of these diagnoses may be accurate enough, but they are sometimes made by doctors who are either too busy or too lazy to be painstaking, or still oftener by druggists, neighbors, or relatives who are forever impelled to make some sort of diagnosis.

Nowhere is diagnostic mythology more potent or more popular than in relation to wormy children. Even in this generation of intelligent care of the young, worms are likely to be considered guilty until or even after they have been proved innocent.

I know many grandmothers who are scornful of the doctor who ventures the suggestion that the child may not be wormy after all. For that matter, many persons devoutly believe in the influence of the quiet, kindly moon upon the activities of worms.

Child's Habits Cause Suspicion

Now, what does the poor child do to make his elders suspect or accuse him of being wormy? One might almost answer, "Anything." As a matter of fact, there are three performances on the part of the child which make it practically certain that someone in the household has at some time had serious thoughts of worms.

First there is grinding of the teeth at night. It is astonishing what a piercing, raucous noise a child can make when he does this. But let us, in all fairness to the child and to the worms, remember that there are several conditions which may produce this symptom, such as decayed teeth, infected gums or adenoids. Besides, there is a host of things that may prevent proper sleep and so lead to that state of semi-sleep during which all sorts of undesirable nervous habits are likely to be formed.

Certainly worms deserve a place in the long list of rest-preventers. To overlook them, to deny that they might be responsible for the symptoms, is at least as serious a mistake as to make a positive diagnosis of worms without proper evidence. Finally, with regard to the teeth-grinding mentioned, we must not forget that there are many children known to be infected with worms who never grind their teeth at all.

The second standard popular symptom of worms is nose-picking. The third is restlessness or twitching of any sort. Obviously, any nasal discharge or irritation can make a child start picking his nose, and such a habit once begun is very difficult to stop. Obviously again, the causes of restlessness are legion. All of them must be investigated or their eggs must actually be found before worm medicine is given, or far more harm than good will be done the child.

The list of symptoms, then, that worms do not cause is a very considerable one. What symptoms do they cause? It depends, of course, upon which worm is guilty.

Varieties of Worms

I have heard parents refer to worms in much the same vague, uncertain way that men used to refer to evil spirits. Like everything else we talk about, when we discuss worms we are likely to mean the kind of worms we are acquainted with. In the South, for example, the popular worm is affectionately known as "the hook."

In general, however, when persons speak of worms in children, they mean pinworms. When they don't mean pinworms, they mean roundworms. More rarely the remark is made that "He must have a tapeworm"; a remark which would be made less casually if the typical villainous-looking beef tapeworm were more commonly known.

Tapeworms

As far as symptoms are concerned, one would think that the tapeworm, with his twenty-odd feet of villainy, would cause more symptoms than the voracious appetite commonly ascribed to him. But it is an absolute fact that in practically every case of proven tapeworm infection, not a single symptom could reasonably be traced to the worm. Its presence was discovered only on appearance of segments of worm in the stools.

Roundworms

The same is true of the roundworms, with certain important exceptions. These beasts make up in enterprise what they lack in length. For, though they seldom do so, they may spontaneously pass out through the anus and cause tickling and all its results. Medical textbooks all present pictures of masses of roundworms obstructing intestines and even passing upward to cause choking. It should be strongly emphasized that the latter is very unusual.

It is peculiar that sometimes children who harbor any roundworms at all harbor but a single worm instead of many. I know of a boy of nine who was much alarmed one morning by finding he had passed a roundworm about eight inches long. I searched diligently and frequently for eggs and for further worms, after putting him through a course of treatment. He has never passed any more.

Hookworms

As is well known, many of the tropical worms cause severe, and some of them dangerous, symptoms. The hookworm, formerly so common in some of our own Southern States, produces laziness, apathy, anemia, and perverted appetite; fortunately these symptoms are not found in patients infected with the more familiar parasites.

Laymen—poor wretches—and patent medicine makers—rich wretches—share the idea that getting rid of the larger worms mentioned is a very simple matter, especially if you follow the directions on the bottle. Anyone with hospital experience knows how painfully false this is. The proper dietetic management of the patient, the determination of the dose of cathartics required, proof of the final passage of a tapeworm's head— these require real medical acumen, not to mention courage.

The same is true of the treatment of the individual case of hookworm. From the point of view of sanitary engineering, of sociology, of sheer medical enterprise, the task of ridding the South of hookworm infection has resounded to the everlasting credit of the men responsible, and of the Rockefeller Foundation, without whose financial aid the work could not have gone on.

The Pinworm, Her Life and Work

I have touched upon the activities and the treatment of these important parasites in order to clear the way, as it were, for a separate consideration of that tiny but mighty pest, the pinworm. She it is that 90 per cent of persons mean when they talk of worms.

The answer to the question, "Where do they come from?" has shared in the general mythology about worms. Many are convinced that they come from eating sweets; they often follow up this conviction with the dire threat, "If you don't stop eating so much candy you'll get worms." It requires but little thought to make it clear that neither sugar nor candy undergoes a magic, devilish transformation into worms inside the child. Pinworms come from pinworms, and from nothing else.

We all know how unsanitary are the habits of children, what a literally hand-to-mouth existence they lead. If to this natural tendency is added lack of household sanitation, lack of care in washing raw fruits and vegetables, lack of care in cleansing spoons, dishes, and other utensils, plus a few other infected children in the house —there you have conditions in which any family of pinworms would revel.

The fully developed female pinworm is about half an inch long and can best be seen at night, crawling about the anal region. After the eggs are ingested by mouth, the adults develop in the small intestine where breeding takes place and the males die. The females pass out of the anus at night, full of embryo-containing eggs, which are hatched out in the folds.

Now, gross and microscopic stool examination by a trained person is of the utmost importance in the diagnosis of tapeworm or roundworm infection. But the habits of the pinworm make the examination of the anal region at night of at least as great importance as the physician's examination of the stool, for the forms will probably have died by the time the stool reaches the physician. The eggs are seldom really incorporated in the stool substance but are found in scrapings from the anus.

Wrong Treatment for Worms

As far as the child's symptoms are concerned, itching of the regions involved is obvious. The casual relation between such worms and bed wetting can easily be seen. Even during sleep, the child scratches about the anus, transfers eggs and even worms to the mouth, and so constantly reinfects himself. There is no intermediate host; that is, no other animal necessary for a certain stage of development of the worm.

The reason so many mothers wail that pinworms are hard to get rid of is that the methods they use are neither proper nor thorough. I have worried along for months with a certain family, all nine of whom were afflicted. Because the children don't like the treatment, the parents lack the courage of their convictions, so the worms thrive on.

The much-advertised patent medicine, old Dr. So-and-So's Vermifuge, may be responsible for failures. Some of these concoctions may be of value because of the santonin or other really useful drugs which they contain. But this sort of treatment alone, though possibly successful in occasional cases, is likely to fail in the majority because of the necessity of taking additional precautions against reinfection.

Treatment for Pinworms

The proper treatment of pinworms consists in frequent enemas of infusion of quassia or garlic, and, in stubborn cases, the administration of santonin. To prevent reinfecton, the night clothes must be arranged whether by buttons or by drawstrings, so that the child cannot get his hands through to scratch the anus. The finger-nails must be kept short. An ointment of ammoniated mercury or other antiseptic of proper strength should be applied nightly in order to kill the embryos. The genitalia should be thoroughly searched and cleansed, lest the worms should find lodgment there.

I hope I have made it clear that there are several things which conscientious parents should remember about worms. First, they must not give the child bad treatment for worms that do not exist. Second, if the child actually has worms, it is essential to know what kind of worms they are, and then fight to a finish with the proper weapons. There is no reason why, to use the picturesque language of Job, "the worm shall feed sweetly on him."

DISEASES OF THE KIDNEY

PYELITIS

PYELITIS is a rather common infection of the kidneys in little girls. The diagnosis is made by finding pus in the urine. Children with pyelitis usually have fever. They may also have vomiting and abdominal pains. The older ones are apt to complain of painful and frequent urination. Any child who has unexplained fever for several days, especially a girl, should have the urine examined. The condition can usually be cured promptly with the sulfa drugs. Any girl who has two attacks of pyelitis and a boy who has it even once, should have special kidney X-rays made to make sure that there is nothing wrong with the structure with her or his kidneys which makes them particularly susceptible to infection.

ACUTE NEPHRITIS

Acute Nephritis is an entirely different type of inflammation of the kidneys. It usually comes on in a child who has just gotten over a streptococcal infection such as a sore throat or scarlet fever. It sometimes comes in a child who has been perfectly well. The urine may be smoky colored and scanty, or it may be grossly bloody. There is usually some puffiness of the eyes and the hands and feet. This disease may be very serious, with convulsions or heart failure coming in the course of it. Sometimes it is quite mild. The convalescence is sometimes very slow. The child should not be allowed out of bed for several weeks after the urine has cleared up completely.

NEPHROSIS

Nephrosis is an uncommon disease of the kidneys. It starts out very gradually with increasing swelling of the legs, arms and abdomen. The condition seems to be due to the fact that the albumin of the blood leaks into the urine through the kidneys. There is no satisfactory treatment for this, but these children now do much better than they used to because modern drugs can be used to clear up the secondary infections to which they are particularly susceptible.

VAGINITIS

Many little girls will develop a slight vaginal discharge at some time. This may come from lack of cleanliness especially after going to the toilet. It sometimes comes after an acute infection. Ordinarily nothing special needs to be done to clear it up other than a few extra or more thorough baths. Otherwise, the less attention paid to it the better.

A persistent discharge, especially one in which there is blood as well as pus, may come from a foreign body which the child has introduced into the vagina. This will have to be removed, preferably under anesthesia, before the discharge will stop. Once in a while a little girl will be innocently exposed to the gonorrhea germ, usually on someone's hands. This can cause a very severe infection in the immature vagina with thick creamy pus, pain and fever. Such an infection needs immediate treatment by the doctor.

DISEASES DUE TO ALLERGY

HAY FEVER

HAY FEVER is a seasonal form of allergy in the nose. The symptoms during an attack are sneezing, itching and watering of the nose; itching, burning and watering of the eyes; and sometimes itching of the ears and throat. The hay fever sufferer can be a very miserable individual. The time of year that a person has symptoms depends upon the kind of pollen that he is allergic to. Sensitivity to the pollens of trees shows up in the earlier spring, to grasses in the later spring, and to ragweed, which is the commonest of all, in August and September. Some people may have symptoms for more than one season, or even all year around. Usually this means that they are allergic to a variety of substances, at least one of which is in the air all the time.

The sufferer from allergy in the nose can frequently be helped a great deal by medical treatment. If the history is sufficiently clear-cut to incriminate one particular type of pollen, or even several different types of pollen, a course of desensitization injections, started well before the sneezing is expected, will frequently help a great deal. When the history is not so clear-cut, the doctor may do a large number of skin tests in the hope that substances which give a positive test in the skin will also be substances which irritate the nose. Then, if the things which give the positive skin tests can be avoided (for instance dog hairs by a person who owns a dog), he will suggest that they be avoided. But if it should turn out to be something that is hard to avoid, like dust or certain molds that are in the air all the time, he may give a year 'round series of injections to build up an immunity to it. This sort of treatment will also frequently help the person who "carries a cold" all the time, if his trouble turns out to be allergic rather than infectious, even if he does not do a great deal of sneezing. Most medicines taken by mouth have been of very little benefit for the hay fever sufferer, with the possible exception of ephedrine. But recently some new drugs have been developed which work on an entirely different principle, and which seem to help about one person out of four.

ASTHMA

Asthma is a condition in which there are attacks of difficulty in breathing accompanied by wheezing in the chest. The trouble is caused by a spasm of the muscles around the smaller air passages which constricts them, making it more difficult for air to get in and out of the lungs. At the same time there is usually the outpouring of a lot of sticky mucus into those same smaller air passages which cuts down still more on the air space, and also which provokes a lot of coughing. There is usually no fever with the attacks. Any individual spell of wheezing may last anywhere from half an hour to four or five days and at times the difficulty in breathing may become quite alarming. The doctor can usually terminate any individual attack with an injection of adrenalin.

Asthma is usually caused by sensitivity to something. It may be something eaten, especially in a younger child, or it may be something breathed in. In any event it is a potentially serious condition. It should be investigated by a physician before it has lasted very long or had a chance to get very severe. The doctor will take a very careful detailed history in an attempt to get a clue about what might be precipitating the attack. It may be anything from eating chicken or tomatoes, to playing with a rag doll, or sleeping on a certain pillow. In addition to the history, the doctor will probably also do a long series of skin tests. These tests are made either by scratching or injecting an extract of the suspected substance into the skin. A positive test shows by a wheal or hive, developing within a half hour at the site of the injection or scratch.

Anything that seems to have any relation to the child's asthma should be eliminated from his life. This will probably mean stripping his room to the bare essentials. The rugs, the draperies, the feather pillow, and the stuffed furniture should be eliminated. A special dust-free cover should be made for the mattress. Woolen blankets and stuffed toys should be put away. In other words anything that may catch or create dust should be removed from the room. Just as things are removed from the patient's room and thus the air he breathes, so sometimes must things be removed from his diet. If a special elimination diet is prescribed by the doctor, it should be followed very rigidly. If all these things combined should result in freedom from attacks, then the things which have been taken away can be brought back, but they should be brought back one at a time with several days in between. If the elimination diet and the "dust-free room" do not give relief from the recurring attacks of asthma, desensitization by a long series of weekly injections is sometimes helpful. There are some children, and adults as well, whose asthma attacks seem to be brought on by emotional disturbances. This may be true whether there is any precipitating factor found in the environment or not. This type of asthma is very difficult to cure except in the hands of a very understanding physician or a competent psychiatrist.

The ultimate outlook for children with asthma is very variable. Some are helped a great deal by the doctor's treatment within a very short time. Others are not helped by the treatment except to get temporary relief, but seem to outgrow the condition as they reach puberty. And still others never get anything but temporary relief from each attack or series of attacks as they come.

HIVES

Hives are whitish elevations of the skin surrounded by a pinkish area. They usually itch a lot. There may be few or many. They may be from a quarter of an inch to several inches in diameter. Usually hives are due to sensitivity (allergy) to some substance which is eaten, breathed or touched. Sometimes hives are associated with nervousness. The cause may be obvious or it may require a lot of detective work to find it out. In the meantime local treatment with calamine lotion or bicarbonate of soda dressings may relieve the itch. Sometimes the doctor can prescribe or inject a medicine which will help.

ECZEMA

Eczema begins as rough red patches of skin which are scaly. In young babies it usually starts first on the cheeks or the forehead. If it spreads it usually goes next behind the ears, on the neck, and then on the body. In older children it may start anywhere, but the commonest places are in the folds in front of the elbows and behind the knees. When the eczema is bad it gets very red and covers a large part of the body. The itching is very bad. The baby is apt to scratch himself until he bleeds. This lets the eczema ooze so that brown scabs and crusts form. It also opens the way for secondary infection with the germs of impetigo.

Eczema is an allergic disturbance in the skin. This means, as with other allergic disturbances, that there are some things to which the skin is particularly sensitive. These may be things which the skin touches, but it is more likely to be things in the diet which are brought to the skin by the blood stream, or both.

Fortunately eczema can usually be helped a great deal by medical care; and in addition the great majority of babies with eczema outgrow the tendency as they get older. But some of them come down later with hay fever or asthma.

The treatment of the baby or child with eczema can be divided into three phases. There is the general care of the baby. Usually he is fat so that nutrition is no problem, but he is generally very uncomfortable and every effort should be made to promote his comfort in every way. Yet he may have to be tied down, or have mittens put over his hands to prevent scratching. In a very severe case, he may have to be spread-eagled on a sheet of cellophane rather than cotton or linen. When this is necessary the doctor will probably also give him sedatives.

Second, there is the local care of the skin. For this there are hundreds of lotions or ointments which may or may not be helpful. Sometimes a mild case can be practically cured by treatment to the skin alone.

Usually the third phase is also necessary. This is the search for the things in the baby's diet or his environment to which he is allergic. By discovering the sequence of events, it is sometimes possible to incriminate one food or another that started the eczema going or that definitely seemed to make it worse; or it may have been the acquisition of a new toy or a change in the mother's brand of face powder. A little baby, who is not eating much anyhow, is usually put on an elimination diet right away by giving him nothing but milk; or he may be changed from fresh milk to canned milk; or the doctor may recommend boiling the milk for a long period of time. If these changes do not work, and it seems the baby is allergic to cow's milk, he may be given goat's milk or one of several artificial preparations to substitute for the milk. An older child is more likely to be skin tested by the doctor than a baby, and then given a rigid elimination diet depending upon the results of the skin tests. But if this is a diet he is going to remain on for any length of time, it must be a well-balanced one so that his nutrition will not be impaired in the long run. The term "in the long run" is used advisedly, especially in older children. A food or even an external article which provokes the eczema must be avoided for a long time. Desensitization by a series of injections such as are given for hay fever and for asthma is not used very much in eczema because it seldom does any good. Sometimes desensitization to certain foods can be carried out after the eczema is under control by giving very, very minute doses of the food by mouth and gradually building it up in strength. Unless this is a food which is hard to leave out of a diet such as milk or eggs, this is not worth while.

DISEASES OF THE EYE

STYE

A STYE is an infection that appears upon the upper or lower eyelid. It is like a small boil any other place on the skin caused by the same kind of germ. It is not very serious, but children sometimes get one right after another because they rub the infected eyelid with their fingers and spread the infecting germ. The treatment is usually hot applications if the child will permit them to be put on. These help to bring the infection to a head. It may open spontaneously, or it may have to be lanced. The doctor may prescribe an ointment to use on the eyelid. Anyone who has a number of styes in a row should have his urine examined for possible diabetes, and of course, the eyes should be looked at.

CONJUNCTIVITIS

Conjunctivitis is the medical name for "pink eye." When this condition is present the membrane covering the eyeball and lining the eyelids becomes inflamed. There may be a discharge of pus. This may make the eyelids stick together. When conjunctivitis comes in the course of a common cold, it is probably no more contagious than the cold itself, but it has also occurred in epidemics not associated with colds. Occasionally redness of the eye-covering is the forerunner of a more serious disease. The mild cases and those associated with colds usually need no treatment except frequent bathing of the eyes with warm saturated boric acid solution and the application of vaseline to the eyelid margins. The more serious inflammation should be treated by a doctor with a specific medicine which will attack the germ that is present.

FOREIGN BODIES IN THE EYE

One of the commonest of minor accidents is the lodging of a foreign body in the eye. The pain caused by even a smooth and comparatively harmless particle resting on the sensitive ball of the eye is often severe, and if the object has a sharp or cutting edges it may become embedded in the eyeball causing permanent injury.

The best way of examining the eye is to have the patient turn the eye upwards while the lower lid is pulled down with the finger. This will expose the lower half of the eyeball. If nothing is seen there, the upper half must be examined. This is more difficult to get at but it may be almost completely exposed by turning the lid back over a small piece of wood such as a match stick, while the eye is directed as far downward as possible. The corner of a handkerchief wet with boric acid solution or a cotton swab will be found effective in removing the object should it merely be lying on the surface. If the particle becomes embedded, the situation is a little more serious, and it is best to leave the treatment to a doctor. In this the removal will entail the use of a magnifying lens with which to locate the injury, and possibly the application of a local anesthetic, as the object will probably need to be actually dug out of the eyeball. When this kind of foreign body has been removed, the eye should be closed, covered with a pad, and rested for a day or two. Even when the foreign body has been easily removed from the eye, the eye solution should be used.

Certain forms of inflammation of the eyelids give the impression of grit or sand in the eye. This is due to the inflamed condition of the membranes lining the lids. Needless to say, the worst thing to do in any case of foreign body in the eye is to rub the eye even though this is the first natural impulse. This serves only to scratch the eyeball or else to embed the foreign object still more firmly in it. The eye should be half closed and allowed to water or tear in the hope that the flow of tears will wash the object away.

DISEASES OF NUTRITION

RICKETS

RICKETS is a disease in which the calcium salts are not properly laid down in the growing bone. Because of this the bones are weak. They easily become deformed under pressure, from gravity, or from muscle pull. This leads to the deformed shape of the head, the chest and the legs which come as a result of rickets. The cause is usually the lack of sufficient Vitamin D in the body. Vitamin D can be formed by the action of the ultra violet rays of sunlight on certain fatty substances in the body. But under modern conditions it is practically impossible for any baby to get enough sunlight to manufacture all the Vitamin D he needs for proper growth.

Every baby should be given extra Vitamin D in his diet in some form from the time he is about two or three weeks old. It may be given in cod liver oil, or in one of the other fish liver oils which are more concentrated, or in the synthetic Vitamin D.

Apparently the way the vitamin works is to enable the intestine to absorb properly the calcium and phosphorous from the diet. If these minerals are not present in large enough amounts in the diet rickets may develop even though abundant Vitamin D is given. Fortunately milk is an excellent source of both calcium and phosphorus. Any child who gets an adequate amount of milk will not lack for them. For all practical purposes the prevention of rickets boils down to supplying the baby with Vitamin D in some form along with his milk every day so that he may absorb his calcium properly and have good strong bones. A premature baby who is growing even more rapidly than a full term one needs even more Vitamin D than the average in order to protect him from the development of rickets.

SCURVY

Scurvy is a disease which occurs when the body lacks enough Vitamin C. This vitamin is easily destroyed by heat, and the pasteurization and boiling of the baby's formula destroys what is normally present in the milk. A breast-fed baby whose mother has fresh fruit every day never develops scurvy. The usual story is that it comes on in a baby who is bottle-fed, who has had no orange juice because it disagreed with him or was given orange juice that was boiled or mixed with boiling water.

The condition comes on gradually. The first symptom is usually that the baby is irritable when he is handled although he is perfectly all right when left alone. He may cry when his diaper is being changed or when he is picked up. Later the baby may become pale. He may not gain weight well. He may fail to move an arm or a leg, although it is not really paralyzed. He may develop swellings at the ends of his bones. All of this trouble is due to the fact that the lack of Vitamin C results in a tendency to bleed. But the bleeding at first is only small in amount, and it is around the bones where it cannot be seen. A baby who has teeth may have bleeding into his gums around them. If scurvy has developed it can easily be cured by giving a lot of Vitamin C. But it should not be allowed to develop. All babies should be given Vitamin C in some form from the time they are a few weeks old. If fresh orange juice does not agree with a baby he should get one of the synthetic vitamin preparations.

ANEMIA

Anemia shows up in paleness of the skin and mucous membrane. A child who is anemic is apt to be listless. He may have a poor appetite. He may get out of breath easily. When there is anemia the blood is deficient in hemoglobin, the red coloring matter which carries oxygen from the lungs. There are several different reasons why this condition might be present. These should be investigated by the doctor so that the correct measures can be taken to remedy them. A child may be anemic because his diet is lacking in enough iron-containing foods. These are meat, especially liver, egg yolks, the green leafy vegetables and whole-grain cereals. An anemia may develop in a young baby around three to five months of age if his mother's diet was deficient in these substances during pregnancy.

Another cause of anemia in children is an acute or chronic infection. Sometimes in the presence of infection the body does not absorb the iron that it does get. Anemia may also be caused by the loss of blood. This may have happened in one large hemorrhage as the result of an injury, or it may be a small daily loss of blood in the urine or bowel movement which may not be no-ticed. Girls at puberty sometimes become anemic after they start to menstruate. Occasionally anemia in a child is due to a rare blood disease such as leukemia.

DIABETES MELLITUS

This is a condition in which the body is not able to use starches and sugars properly because the pancreas, a large gland in the abdomen, does not manufacture enough insulin. When this hap-pens the sugar piles up in the blood and spills out in the urine. Along with it in the urine comes an extra amount of water so that the sugar will stay in solution. This makes the patient thirsty and he drinks more water. When the condition gets very bad there is also a disturbance in the body's ability to take fats, and eventually coma develops.

Diabetes is not seen very often in children, but when it is it is often severe. In the days before insulin was discovered most children who had diabetes succumbed to it. But now, with good supervision and proper insulin doses, a diabetic child can lead an almost normal life.

The insulin requirements sometimes seem to be less if the disease is treated early. It should be looked for in every child who drinks and urinates an inordinate amount, or who eats very well and yet loses weight.

CELIAC DISEASE

Babies and children with celiac disease have bulky foul-smelling bowel movements and big pot bellies. They are usually quite poorly nourished and their growth is retarded so that they are small for their age. This condition comes on be-cause the child's intestines lose, or else never did develop, the ability to digest properly either the starch or the fat in the diet. If this situation is recognized early, it can usually be handled pretty well, by adjusting the child's diet to include only those foods which he can tolerate. This should be done, of course, only under a doctor's direc-tion, so that no deficiencies of vitamins or min-erals are permitted to develop.

PHYSICAL INJURIES

CUTS AND WOUNDS

THE two important things in the treatment of cuts and wounds are—
1. The prevention of severe hemorrhage, and
2. The prevention of infection.

A little bit of bleeding from a wound does no harm. In fact it probably helps to wash out some germs which may have been carried into it. But profuse bleeding can endanger life. It should be stopped by pressure. Someone who knows about tourniquets and pressure points should use these. Otherwise firm, direct pres-sure right over the bleeding area will usually control the hemorrhage. Then a very firm tight bandage should be applied.

For the prevention of infection, soap and water is as good an agent to clean the skin with as any, and has the advantage that it does no harm. Dirt in a wound should be washed out and any soap used should finally be flushed away with plain water. If all of this is done cor-rectly, no antiseptic need be put on the skin but the cut or wound should always be com-pletely covered with a sterile dressing. This will keep germs from getting at the area once it has been cleaned and will prevent the devel-opment of secondary infection which delays heal-ing. Changes in dressing should be made using the same sterile precautions as with the original dressing.

BURNS

The best treatment for minor burns which in-volve only a small area of skin is to cover them with a sterile ointment such as vaseline or boric acid in petrolatum. Cover them completely and thoroughly with a sterile dressing and leave them completely alone. Blisters that form should not be opened deliberately. Frequently they will go away and the area will heal much quicker. If the blisters do break, the dead skin should be trimmed away with scissors that have been boiled for at least five minutes and another vaseline dressing applied.

For any extensive burn the doctor should be called right away. If there will be any delay in his seeing the patient it is wise to start for a hospital. Someone with a severe burn is apt to go into shock very soon. To transport such a patient he should first be wrapped in a clean sheet and then covered warmly with blankets.

If medical care will be gotten very soon, it is wiser not to put anything on the burned area as it may interfere with the doctor's treatment.

DOG OR OTHER ANIMAL BITES

Animal bites should receive the same emergency first aid treatment as any other cuts or wounds. They should be well washed out with soap and water. Sometimes the doctor will cauterize the area with nitric or with carbolic acid. The important thing with dog bites is to be sure of the dog. It is best to have the dog kept under observation and see if any disease develops. So long as the bite was not around the head it is permissible to wait for several days or so. Should the bite have been around the head, the wisest course is to begin anti-rabies treatment at once. For more about this see the article "Against What Should We Be Immunized?"

FROSTBITE

A frostbitten part of the body first becomes white, hard and painful. The color of the skin changes later to dark red or purple, and it is sometimes covered with blisters which rapidly change to ulcerations. If the exposure has been severe, the tissues in the discolored area will die and slough off from the rest of the body.

In the treatment of frostbite, the important thing is not to do any more damage. The frozen part should not be rubbed with snow or anything else. Nor should the frozen part be warmed up with heating pads or hot water bottles. The best thing to do is to expose it to the air in a room that is just a little above freezing temperature. As the frozen area thaws out, the outside temperature can gradually be raised. A little whiskey or brandy may be given by mouth as a stimulant and to help dilate the blood vessels in the frozen part. Other medicine may be necessary because of the severe pain. If the area does become dark red or purple, a doctor should be consulted to see if an operation will be necessary.

BITES AND STINGS

Mosquito and Flea Bites

The itching and irritation from these bites can be relieved by a lotion of carbolic acid and boric acid. It should be applied by dabbing on with a small wad of cotton, or better still, by spraying it on the surface with an atomizer. To make the lotion, add a level teaspoonful of boric acid powder and 20 drops of pure carbolic acid to a half pint of hot water. Stir well or shake until the boric acid is dissolved. Cool before using.

Other Insect Stings

The stings of bees and wasps and yellow jackets are very painful, but not dangerous to life unless the victim is attacked by a large number of the insects.

If the sting remains in the flesh, it should be pulled out and a drop or two of diluted ammonia water or a paste made by moistening bicarbonate of soda (baking soda) applied to the wound. A compress wet in cold water or cold boric acid solution will help to allay pain.

BLACK EYE

A *black eye* is merely one form of a bruise. As soon as a blow is received in this region a handkerchief wrung out in ice water should be applied. The ice water should be renewed as often as it gets warm, thus combining the effect of both cold and moisture. This treatment should be kept up an hour and may prevent discoloration from setting in.

If treatment is begun after the flesh has become black, hot water applications for half an hour, three times a day, will hasten the disappearance of the swelling and discoloration. The old-fashioned practice of applying raw beefsteak is not recommended. In all cases where a severe blow has been received in the region of the eye a physician should be consulted, as there is danger that injury may have been done to the eyeball.

BUMPS AND BRUISES

These are perhaps the commonest injuries which young children receive. A slight bruise ordinarily requires no treatment and is forgotten in a few minutes, although the discoloration of the skin may remain for some time. If the injury is more severe, cloths wrung out of very cold water, or cracked ice wrapped in a cloth, may be applied to the bruise. Either alcohol, or witch hazel, each diluted with water, may be used upon a bruise.

If the skin is broken, it should be treated as a wound.

FOREIGN BODIES IN THE NOSE

Close one of the child's nostrils (the one *not* containing the foreign body) and try to make him blow his nose. Do not try to pick out the foreign body with a pin, hairpin, etc., as you will push it farther up his nose. It is well to take all these cases to the doctor, as much harm may be done by unskillful attempts to remove the foreign body.

FOREIGN BODY IN THE EAR

When a child gets a foreign body of any kind into the ear the wisest thing is to take him at once to the doctor, as much harm may be done by those not well acquainted with the anatomy of the ear. When a doctor is not available, the best thing to do is to syringe the ear with warm water, unless the foreign substance is a pea or bean, which would at once commence to swell as the result of moisture, and would consequently cause great pain and become more difficult to remove. Should an insect get into the ear the head should be held over to the opposite side, and the ear filled with warm oil, after which the ear may be syringed with a little warm water.

FOREIGN BODIES IN THE THROAT AND STOMACH

If a child has swallowed something he should not, the services of the nearest doctor should be sought immediately, but if the foreign object fills the throat and the child is choking, slap him on the back. Hold his head down and squeeze the sides of his body together. If the patient is a child, he may be picked up by the feet and held suspended with the head downward, which may cause the object to fall out by its own weight.

Dr. Chevalier Jackson states that nearly 90 per cent of such cases are due to avoidable carelessness and he suggest the following precautions:

1. Foods for children, invalids, and aged persons should not contain such things as bones, watermelon seeds, orange seeds, lemon seeds, grape seeds, cherry, plum, prune, or peach pits, or stems of fruits.

2. Foods other than fish or birds, with small bones, should not be served, even to normal adults. Fish and birds should be eaten with the utmost care as to the bones.

3. It is careless to serve food containing fragments of nut shells, egg shells, oyster shells, crab shells, and so forth, and to permit containers and utensils to contribute to the food such fragments as of egg-beaters, chips of enamel or chinaware, splinters of wood from flour or sugar barrels, and

solder from tin cans. When a fruit jar or jelly glass breaks or chips in opening, the contents should be strained or thrown away.

4. Care should be taken when cooking or serving food to see that there are no loose pins or buttons on the clothes that could fall into the food.

5. Hasty eating and insufficient mastication should be avoided as dangerous.

6. The chewing of pencils, toothpicks, grass stalks, straw, and the like, apart from the general objections, is a cause of foreign body accidents. Pencils are filthy things to put in the mouth anyway.

7. Children should be taught not to put inedible substances smaller than a spoon in their mouths.

8. Coins are filthy things to put in the mouth and may get lodged in the throat. Teething rings are objectionable, but a coin as a "tooth-cutter" is worse.

9. It is careless to allow a child to run or jump with anything, even food, in his mouth.

10. Babies should not be put on the floor to amuse themselves until after the floor is cleared of all small objects, such as tacks, seeds, and bits of coal.

11. Children's toys should be inspected for small loose parts, such as eyes, butons, fragments of metal and wood.

12. Babies should not be allowed to play with corn (maize,) coffee berries, seeds, small marbles, jacks, and the like.

13. Children under two years of age should never be given peanuts, peanut candy, or any other kind of nut candy. They cannot chew the nuts and are liable to choke on them and aspirate them into the lungs.

14. Don't set a bad example to a baby by holding a straight pin or safety pin in your mouth.

15. Don't bend over a baby or take it in your arms without making sure that there are no pins, needles, safety pins, buttons, or jewelry in your clothing that could get into the baby's mouth.

NOSE-BLEED
(HEMORRHAGE FROM THE NOSE)

Nose-bleed is a common and usually unimportant ailment, but occasionally the amount of blood lost is of serious moment. Pressure on each side of the nostrils may help stop the hemorrhage. The nostril may be plugged by inserting a small wad of cotton. The head should be kept elevated and ice may be applied locally.

In serious cases packing the back of the nose may have to be resorted to by the physician if the bleeding is beyond reach from the front.

One, if not the chief, cause of nose-bleed is improperly blowing the nose. To clear the nostrils hold one nostril closed and blow through the other; then reverse. Never try to clear both nostrils at once by "pumping"—alternately holding shut and releasing the nasal passages while forcibly exhaling.

BASIC MEDICAL AND SICKROOM SUPPLIES FOR THE AVERAGE FAMILY

Fountain Syringe with rubber tube and assorted nozzles
Bed Pan
Rubber Sheet
Bandages of various widths from a half inch to three inches
Adhesive Tape in various sizes
Absorbent Cotton
Paper Tissues
Thermometers (2), one for taking temperatures by mouth, one for rectum
Hot Water Bag
Ice Bag
Atomizer for spraying nose and throat
Graduated Medicine Glass for measuring dosages
Scissors

Milk of Magnesia
Castor Oil
Mineral Oil
Glycerine
Vaseline
Rubbing Alcohol
Zinc Oxide Ointment
Calamine Lotion

Tincture of Iodine
Boric Acid
Hydrogen Peroxide Solution
Sodium Bicarbonate
Aspirin
Aromatic Spirits of Ammonia
Talcum Powder
Butesin Picrate (for burns)

POISONS AND THEIR ANTIDOTES

By The American Red Cross

CHILDREN sometimes eat or drink poisonous substances, and it is necessary for the mother to know what to do in such an emergency. The first thing to do is to send for the doctor. An emetic should be given at once, except when the poison swallowed belongs to the corrosive class. (See Tables II and III following.) Lukewarm water is a good emetic. Let the patient swallow all he can be induced to take. In addition, a tea-spoonful of common salt or mustard dissolved in a glass of warm water will cause vomiting in many cases, or one or two teaspoonfuls of the wine or syrup of ipecac. The tickling of the back of the patient's throat will also be found effective to induce vomiting.

Tables I, II, and III, which follow, give a list of the different classes of poisons with their antidotes.

TABLE I.—POISONS FOR WHICH AN EMETIC IS ALWAYS GIVEN FIRST

Poison	Symptoms	Treatment (besides emetic)
UNKNOWN		Stimulants; soothing liquids.
ALCOHOL: In any form—rum, gin, whisky, proof spirits, etc., also methyl alcohol.	Giddiness, swaying of body, inability to stand. Face flushed, eyes red, skin clammy, weak pulse, may be convulsions and unconsciousness.	Hot coffee or aromatic spirits of ammonia. Try to arouse, but if weak do not exhaust by making walk. Dash cold water on face and chest. When somewhat recovered, wrap warmly and put to bed.
ARSENIC: Found in rat poisons, vermin killer, Paris green, Fowler's solution. Sometimes in tinned fruits and beer.	Severe pain in stomach, purging, severe cramps in legs, vomiting, dryness of throat, cold sweats, profound shock.	Much lukewarm water. Magnesia in large quantity or dialyzed iron in ½-ounce doses, repeated. Beaten-up eggs or castor oil and stimulants. Warmth and rubbing. If rat poison has been taken, treat as for poisoning by arsenic.
LEAD: Sugar of lead, lead paint, white lead.	Throat dry, metallic taste with much thirst, colic in abdomen, cramps in legs, cold sweat; sometimes paralysis of legs and convulsions.	½ ounce Epsom salts in tumbler of water. Stimulants and soothing liquids.
OPIUM: Laudanum, morphine, paregoric, some soothing syrups and cough mixtures.	Drowsiness, finally unconsciousness; pulse full at first, then weak; breathing full and slow at first, gradually slower and shallow; pinhead pupils; face flushed, then purple.	May have difficulty in getting emetic to work; plenty of strong coffee. Try to arouse by speaking loudly and threatening, but do not exhaust by compelling to walk, etc. Stimulants and artificial respiration.
PHOSPHORUS: In matches, phosphorus paste in many rat poisons and vermin killers, often with arsenic.	Severe pain in stomach, vomiting. Skin is dark and may have odor of phosphorus. Bleeding from nose, bloody purging. Convulsions.	Epsom salts, ½ ounce in tumbler of water, or magnesia. Stimulants. Soothing liquid best. Milk. Avoid fats and oils.
PTOMAINE: Poisoning by decayed meat, fish, milk, or ice cream.	Nausea, vomiting, purging. Skin cold and clammy. Pulse weak. Severe pain in abdomen, cramps, great prostration and weakness. Often eruption on skin.	Purgative, castor oil or Epsom salts. Rest in bed; soft diet.
STRYCHNINE—NUX VOMICA: Strychnine is frequently used on meat to poison animals and in some vermin killers.	Convulsions, very severe, alternating with cramps, affecting all muscles of body. Back is bowed up by spasms of muscles. Jaws are locked. Spasm of muscles is so great that it prevents breathing, so face becomes dusky.	Absolute quiet so as not to bring on convulsions. Follow with another emetic.

TABLE II.—POISONS FOR WHICH AN EMETIC SHOULD NOT BE GIVEN FIRST

Poison	Symptoms	Treatment
MERCURY: Corrosive sublimate, antiseptic tablets. Other salts of mercury much less commonly used.	Corrosive sublimate is very irritating, so when taken turns mouth, lips, and tongue white. Mouth is swollen and tongue is shriveled; always metallic taste in mouth. Pain in abdomen. Nausea and vomiting mucus and blood, bloody purging, cold clammy skin, great prostration, and convulsions.	First, give white of egg or whole egg beaten up; flour and water, but not so good. Emetics, soothing liquids, and stimulants.
NITRATE OF SILVER: Lunar caustic.	Pain in mouth and stomach; mouth first colored white, then black; vomit first white, then turns black.	Common salt dissolved in water, or milk very frequently. Then emetic. Afterward soothing liquids and stimulants.

TABLE III.—POISONS FOR WHICH AN EMETIC SHOULD NEVER BE GIVEN

Poison	Symptoms	Treatment
Strong corrosive acids: 1. **ACETIC.** 2. **HYDROCHLORIC (spirits of salt).** 3. **NITRIC (aqua fortis).** 4. **SULPHURIC (vitriol).**	Very severe burning pain in mouth, throat, and stomach. Wherever acid touches skin or mucous membrane they are destroyed. Frequently vomiting and purging. More or less suffocation from swelling of throat, great prostration and shock.	An alkali to neutralize acid. Best, baking soda, magnesia or chalk in water, given frequently and freely. Afterwards, soothing liquids, milk, milk and egg, olive oil. Stimulants are practically always required. If acid has entered air passage, may inhale fumes of ammonia.
OXALIC ACID (salts of lemon or sorrel).	Much like corrosive acids just named, but not so much burning of lips, etc.	Magnesia, baking soda, chalk, and water or limewater to neutralize acid. Then 1 ounce of castor oil and stimulants freely.
CARBOLIC ACID (phenol): (Very commonly used in attempts at suicide.)	It is also a powerful corrosive poison which causes great pain and vomiting. Severe case: Unconsciousness very soon and early death. Usually easy to tell by odor of acid and burn, which with pure acid is white and with impure black.	Rinse mouth with pure alcohol. If grown person, should swallow 3 or 4 tablespoonfuls of alcohol mixed with an equal quantity of water. Follow this in 5 minutes with 2 tablespoonfuls of Epsom salts dissolved in a little water. Though not so good, limewater may be used to rinse mouth, several glasses of it being swallowed; 3 or 4 raw eggs may be given or castor or sweet oil. Stimulants always, and keep warm.
Strong caustic alkalies: 1. **AMMONIA: Strong ammonia, ammonia liniment, camphor liniment.** 2. **LIME: Quicklime.** 3. **POTASH: Caustic potash.** 4. **SODA: Caustic soda.**	Much like corrosive acids. Immediate severe burning, pain in mouth, throat, and stomach. Vomiting and purging. Alkali destroys tissues of mouth it has touched. Severe shock and suffocation from swelling.	An acid to neutralize alkali. Vinegar, lemon or orange juice. Tartaric or citric acid in plenty of water. Soothing liquids, stimulants. If cannot swallow, may inhale acetic acid or vinegar from a pocket handkerchief.

CAUTION: In giving any antidote do not wait for it to dissolve, but stir it up in any fluid which can be obtained, except oil, and give it at once.

POISONOUS PLANTS*

By Theodore Tieken, M.D.

Poison	Symptoms	Treatment
POISON IVY, POISON OAK, POISON SUMAC	Wherever the sticky sap of the injured plant comes in contact with the skin of susceptible persons it causes intense irritation, which begins suddenly and progresses rapidly, with a violent reaction. In many cases it begins between the fingers, on the back of the hands, or the exposed part of the face, and at first covers only the area of contact, but soon it spreads, invading the surrounding tissues, causing intense swelling, and vesicles (blisters) that often become very large. The surrounding area becomes swollen and itches intensely. The scalp and the inside surfaces of the hands are rarely affected. Besides local lesions there may be general disturbances, such as loss of appetite, coated tongue, fever, and constipation. The acute symptoms usually disappear in from six to eight days, depending on the area of skin involved and the reaction of the patient. Persons once affected seem predisposed to subsequent attacks, just as are patients with hay fever.	After the patient has developed a rash there seems to be nothing that will stop its progress. Local applications of every description have been tried, but none seems to do much good. Hot applications make some persons more comfortable, while cold applications relieve others. It makes little difference which is used. Patience seems to be most important to the victim of ivy poisoning. If itching is intense and the area involved is large, it is well to consult a physician. Good common sense, free elimination, and a light diet with plenty of fluids are the prerequisites in all cases. Susceptible persons should make every effort to avoid exposure. When they go into the woods they should carry a very strongly alkaline soap or a solution of potassium hydrate in alcohol (solution potassium hydroxide, 2 drams; alcohol, 4 ounces) or a bottle of gasoline, with which to remove the resinous exudate at once. The area touched by the poisonous substance should be washed thoroughly with soap and water. Recently attempts have been made to decrease sensitization to the poison ivy group of plants by the injection of extracts of the plant, in increasing doses, under the skin. The principle of this treatment is the same as that in hay fever.
BITTERSWEET POTATO, DEADLY NIGHTSHADE	The person affected complains of dizziness and dryness of the mouth and throat. The pupils of his eyes dilate and the muscles of the eyes become paralyzed and interfere with his sight. The skin may be dry and burning and covered by a red rash. The patient feels as if he must urinate, but he cannot. In severe cases delirium develops, and sometimes convulsions. Fortunately, few persons get enough of the poison to cause death.	As much of the poisonous material as possible should be removed at once by emptying the stomach. This may be done by carefully putting the finger into the throat in order to cause vomiting, by tickling the throat with a feather, or by drinking two or three teaspoonfuls of mustard water (a teaspoonful of ground mustard to a pint of warm water). If a physician is available, he should be called at once because the giving of the proper antidote in such cases is of vital importance. Washing out the stomach with a mild solution of iodine, which prevents the poison from spreading through the body, can be done only by a physician or trained nurse.
WATER HEMLOCK, OREGON HEMLOCK	Sometimes the first symptom is dizziness, then violent vomiting, cold, clammy skin, profuse perspiration, slow, weak pulse, unconsciousness, and finally violent convulsions, much like those of epilepsy. Usually the pupils are widely dilated and the jaw firmly set.	Recovery depends entirely upon prompt treatment, emptying the stomach and bowels and combating the pain and convulsions with suitable medicines administered by a physician. There is no known antidote for these poisons.
POISON HEMLOCK ("Stinkweed" or wild hemlock).	The symptoms of poisoning develop quickly. As a rule the patient becomes extremely weak, his skin cold and clammy, and he sees double through drooping eyelids. Later it is hard for him to breathe, and his heart beats fast and weak. Finally he sinks into collapse.	In order to save the victim of hemlock poisoning the stomach must be emptied by vomiting or by use of the stomach tube—the sooner the better chance he has. The body should be kept warm by hot pads, hot-water bottles, or whatever is to be had. The lower bowel should be flushed by injections of hot water and baking soda. Stimulants for the heart and breathing should be given, but only by a physician. No specific antidotes are known.

*Reprinted from *Hygeia* by permission.

MENTAL DEVELOPMENT

GREAT THOUGHTS ON THE VALUE OF LEARNING

"Wisdom is the principal thing; therefore get wisdom: and with all thy getting get understanding."

—Proverbs 4, 7

"Education is an ornament in prosperity and a refuge in adversity."

—Aristotle

"Perhaps the most valuable result of all education is the ability to make yourself do the thing you have to do when it ought to be done."

—Thomas Henry Huxley

"Lost, somewhere between sunrise and sunset, two golden hours each set with sixty diamond minutes. No reward is offered for they are gone forever."

—Horace Mann

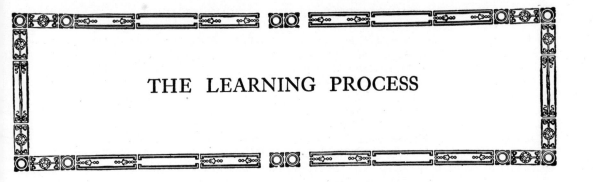

THE LEARNING PROCESS

HOW CHILDREN LEARN*

FORTUNATELY for parents, human infants learn very easily. In fact, they learn so fast that parents are hard put to it to keep one jump ahead, in order to see that their children have more opportunities for learning things that will be useful to them than for acquiring "poor" habits.

Learning goes on from the moment children are born, whether it is learning to roll over, learning to swallow solid food, or learning to know the mother's voice. Children learn as naturally as they breathe. They learn by imitating others (watching father pound a nail, for instance), by suggestions that we don't even know we give them ("No, I never could eat liver"), by trying over and over again to do something they want to do (learning to walk, to "pump" a swing, to tie their shoelaces).

Between the time they learn to walk and the time they go to school they cram in more learning than they possibly can in that amount of time later, for they are learning with every bit of their bodies. Their mouths, their ears, their noses, their eyes, their feet, and their hands are all channels for the knowledge that pours into their minds. They learn what different sounds mean, how to get feet into shoes and buttons into buttonholes; they learn to use speech, so that they can tell others about their wants and interests.

Parents can find a great deal of enjoyment in setting the stage so that their children make the most of these tremendously important years if they will keep in mind some of the rules upon which learning is based.

UNDERLYING PRINCIPLE OF ALL LEARNING

Learning is dependent upon maturation. This means the development of all parts, structures, and organs of the body until they reach maturity; it takes place by degrees.

How a child learns will depend upon the readiness of his body, especially of his brain and nervous system, for whatever it is we want him to do. Try as we might to help an 8-month-old child learn to draw a picture of a man, we would fail because he is not mature enough then to do anything more with a pencil than to scribble. But we can teach him to hold a cup to drink from it; that he is ready for.

RECOGNIZING READINESS TO LEARN

We are sure to fail if we try to teach a child something before he has developed enough to undertake it. Sometimes people try to bring about the dry habit in a baby whose nervous system has not matured enough to make control of the bladder possible. To sit quietly in church or to remain quiet at the table while grown-ups enjoy a long-drawn-out meal is very difficult for 2- and 3 year-olds because they have not developed to the point where they can bear to be inactive for so long.

If attempts are made to force a child to learn things he is not ready for, his lack of success is all too likely to make him unwilling to try to learn other new things.

Waiting until the proper stage of development

*From *Your Child From One to Six*—U. S. Children's Bureau publication.

has been reached is important, but just as important to a child's habit training as an opportunity to do things when he *is* ready. If he is not allowed to experiment and practice when he has an urge to do so, he may lose the desire to learn. This is sometimes true, for example, of a child whose mother does not take advantage of his interest in feeding himself when it appears. By continuing to feed him she gradually builds up in him a feeling of pleasure at getting this attention that is greater than the pleasure he would have in doing something for himself. This loss of desire to learn can happen in connection with playing with other children, dressing himself, or any other part of his learning experience.

PLEASURABLE REPETITION ESSENTIAL

A child, like everyone else, has to do a thing over and over again to learn to do it well. When he takes his first steps a baby's movements are clumsy and unorganized. Only after many attempts and many months does he succeed in emerging from the staggering, wavering stage of walking to the sure, confident gait of the 3-year-old.

It is the same with everything he learns; holding a spoon, building with blocks, steering his wagon—all have to be practiced over and over.

But why do some things take so much more repetition than others? Why does a baby learn the thumb sucking habit after only a few tries and yet take so long to learn to keep dry? This brings up another very important part of learning; that pleasure-giving acts become habits much more quickly than things that give no special satisfaction. Thumb sucking gives a child pleasure, but it is no fun for him to keep having his clothes taken off and to sit still on the toilet.

Because he tends to repeat what he enjoys, it is worth while for us to try to make enjoyable those things we want a child to learn. Going to bed, washing, eating desirable foods are some of the things we want the child to make habitual, so we must make them simple and pleasant. A story at bedtime helps to make going to bed enjoyable. Having the things a child needs for washing handy for him and letting him do as much as possible himself about getting clean, encourages the enjoyment of cleanliness. A small-sized fork, foods that are attractive to look at as well as to taste, a cup or glass that can be handled easily help a child to learn good eating habits. In the earlier stages, letting a baby have a spoon and try to help feed himself when the food is easily managed (like mashed potatoes) is a good plan, for he finds it pleasant to be active in satisfying his own desires. A happy atmosphere at mealtime too will encourage him to form good eating habits.

Of course, we must be equally careful to see that a child has no chance to attach unpleasant feelings to the things we want him to learn. Thus, we must see to it that he is not uncomfortable on the toilet seat when we are training him for toilet habits. We must be sure not to nag and scold him when he is learning to feed himself. We must make sure that he has interesting things to do when we are teaching him to play alone. When he is learning to play with other children, we must try to arrange it so that his first experiences are happy.

INTERFERENCES WITH LEARNING

1. If we insist too much or too frequently that a child do a certain thing over and over, we shall dull his interest and may even lead him to develop a resistant attitude. If, for example, we insist on a child's feeding himself for a whole meal while he is still very far from expert at it, we are hindering the building up of good eating habits. If we interrupt his play too frequently to put him on the toilet, we risk having him hate the whole business.

2. If a mother is too concerned about her child, she may actually slow up or interfere with his learning. Too great anxiety over whether a child eats enough, sleeps enough, learns to keep dry early enough often has the effect of making him resist learning. If she talks too much about his eating, sleeping, toilet, or other habits, she causes feelings of unpleasantness, and this is just the opposite of what she is trying to achieve.

3. If the parents are impatient at their children's slowness and fumbling in learning to do things that seem simple and easy to grown-ups, they may hinder good habit formation by making a child stubbornly refuse to try, or fearful of trying, new things. If we tried to look at things through children's eyes, and to feel things through their skin and muscles, we would be slower to criticize and correct when they make mistakes or seem clumsy.

LEARNING SELF-RELIANCE*

By Dorothy Canfield Fisher, Ph.D.

As soon as the average normal child emerges from babyhood his instinct for self-help emerges as clearly, with as much emphasis, as his instinct for getting his own way. And curiously enough he is usually forced to fight for the one as strenuously as for the other. If you will spend one day in watching a healthy child of eighteen or twenty months, you will come to the conclusion that he is straining every nerve to learn how to "do for himself" and his mother is straining every nerve to prevent him, except in certain ways, now stereotyped. With cherishing care she springs to serve him a dozen times a day, when almost any child of a year and a half can learn in five minutes how to do it for himself.

The mother painstakingly repeats over and over the word the child is trying to pronounce, and she is not discouraged by the stumbling inaccuracy of his unpracticed little tongue. The fact that he is interested enough to try it is proof positive that he will soon be able to master it. She never dreams of saying: "No, dearest baby, 'kitty' is too hard a word for baby to say. Let Mamma say it for him!" The absurdity of that is patent to her.

But she does not with equal patience show him over and over how to carry a light stool about and use it to climb up in the armchair he covets. She says: "Does baby want to get in to Papa's chair? There, Mamma lifts him in!" And then Mamma must lift him out, of course! This furnishes a delightful passage in Mamma's life, with a chance at which all of us mothers are only too eager to snatch, of hugging the sweet small body and kissing the round cheeks. It is quite a bother to show him over and over how to climb up on his stool and thereafter to watch over the first experiments, to safeguard the inevitable first upsets. But if she is looking out for the best interests of the small person under her charge, rather than for a good excuse to give him a hug, she will patiently insist upon the use of the stool whenever it is possible.

The stool, the cup, the stick, the bureau drawer, the faucet, what are they but tools devised by human ingenuity; and the use of tools is one of the most important devices for training the young human animal to self-help. Being human he has a profound interest in tools, and is willing, for instance, to bend every energy to learn to use the lever, although he may not know its name for a dozen years. Is he trying to extricate from his sand-pile a buried stone? Don't pull it out with one jerk. Give him a stick, show him how to thrust one end under the stone and put his weight on the other end. You will find him a week later using the principle to force open a door that is difficult to open.

No child is naturally passive. If we can avoid forcing him into passivity in early childhood, we need have no fears as to his capacity later to look out for himself. A little boy who does not ask to be lifted up on a sofa, but goes and gets a little stool to climb up and down, has set his feet on the path which leads surely and certainly to self-reliance. The three-year-old girl who can open and shut doors for herself, can put on and off her own wraps, and can get a clean dress out of her own bureau drawer, will not at seven ask her teacher to put her rubbers on for her. The little child who has discovered the delightful extension of his strength which comes from the use of a lever will, when the time comes, seize eagerly on the use of a hammer and saw and plane; and that means he will make things for himself, instead of asking somebody to buy them for him.

Any human being, young or old, who has once tasted the pleasure of competent activity will never lack the instinct to do for himself. There is no surer beginning for the habit of self-help than the consistent training of the capacity for it. What people know how to do well, they like to do.

*From *Self-Reliance*, by Dorothy Canfield Fisher. Used by special permission of the publishers, The Bobbs-Merrill Company.

PLAY A WAY OF LEARNING*

PLAY is the child's way of learning, of experimenting, of trying himself out, of finding out about everything in the world around him. It is full of pleasure for him, for it is full of new experiences and new combinations of past ones. Play is at the same time a serious thing to him and should be planned for seriously by his parents.

Every mother can learn a great deal about play if she will watch her child and not interfere with him. By the time he is a year old he bangs his toys to make a noise and piles blocks one on the other. He fills his pails with sand and empties them again; he points out figures or colors in his picture books, trying to repeat the word he heard when someone else pointed them out.

Gradually, as the child grows older, he becomes more skillful in his movements and can pile his blocks higher and even tries to catch a ball and later to string large beads. Things that he could not do a few months before are becoming easy. He wants toys with which he can do something. He learns to walk, and with this new accomplishment he starts the pulling and pushing kinds of play. He drags along the floor a toy dog or a box tied to a string, and shoves a chair across the room. Perhaps you have shown him how to throw a ball, and he suddenly begins to throw everything he can reach. Then, perhaps, he finds a crayon and scribbles with it on paper, on the walls, on the floor.

At 2 or 3 years he begins to play with other children of his age. If he has older brothers and sisters, they may try to make him share their games, though at first he will not know what they are driving at. To play his part, to wait his turn, to follow the rules of the game, to pay a penalty if he plays out of turn are ideas that are as yet over his head. After a while he will have grasped them and with them some of the fundamental lessons of happy living.

When a mother has thus stopped and looked at her child's play, she realizes that play is his way of learning. Through it he becomes skillful in the use of his muscles. The little child who can put the last block on top of his tall tower without upsetting it may well dance up and down with pleasure at his accomplishment. He has learned something quite as important for his age

*From *Home, Play and Play Equipment for the Preschool Child*—U. S. Children's Bureau publication.

as how to add 2 and 2 will be later. Encourage this training of senses and muscles. Give the child toys that call upon him to use new combinations of movements. Playing with a bean bag or a game of ring-toss teaches him to throw accurately; stringing beads teaches another kind of skill; drawing on a blackboard another. The big muscles of the back and abdomen are made strong by climbing, swinging, walking on all fours, and turning somersaults.

Do not try to teach a little child to use the small muscles first. Stringing large beads, drawing on large sheets of paper, tearing and cutting out large figures are much better for the young child from 2 to 5 than trying to do anything fine with the hands like sewing cards and weaving.

Perhaps the most important lesson learned through play is that of coordination, or the working together of muscles and senses. When you watch a 6-year-old girl jumping rope to the sound of her own singing, or that of her playmates, you perhaps do not realize that the working together of eye, ear, and muscles in perfect rhythm is the result of the lessons learned through play during the pre-school years. Childhood is the right time to learn this type of skill; the child who has played with vigor and freedom attains it without conscious effort.

A child needs to walk and to run, to climb, to swing, to ride, to pull, to push, to dig, to throw. He needs to have his interests always widening. Although quiet play is important, especially for the little child, at least a part of every child's play should be free and active.

It is best to have the room in which he plays indoors so arranged that he can play freely all over it (or in a fenced-off portion) and handle and touch everything within his reach. A playhouse or a porch that is fenced and screened but open to the sun is useful.

PLAYING ALONE

It is worth while for every mother to teach her child to enjoy being alone. The mother who hurries to pick up the baby as soon as she hears him cooing or talking to himself is making trouble for herself. Any child who is used to being left alone will play very happily by himself and amuse himself with a tin pan and a spoon, clothespins, blocks of wood, or other toys with which he can make or do something.

By playing alone without adult interference or help, the child learns to make his own choices, his own decisions; he learns to concentrate his attention on what he is doing; he learns some of his first lessons in independence. Do not interfere with the child's play. If he seems to you to be doing something awkwardly, do not try to do it for him. Let him learn by doing it himself. Even if the result is not up to your standards, it may be very good for one of his experience.

A little child will do the same thing over and over without tiring. He needs much practice if he is going to learn to do things well. Give him ample opportunity to practice climbing, balancing, pushing, talking, singing, sweeping, dusting, shoveling, hammering. Do not interfere in these activities. Let him learn that success comes only through trying and failing and trying again.

A play pen or a fenced-in part of the yard is a great help to the busy mother. In the pen the child who has not yet learned to climb is safe; and if it is built with a floor, which is covered with a blanket or quilt (except in hot weather), he will escape the cold and the drafts that make play on the floor uncomfortable. The pen should be large enough to allow him considerable freedom of movement, and he should have things to play with so that he will not stand hanging to the side of the pen too long.

PLAYING WITH OTHER CHILDREN

A little child also needs other children to play with. Adults or older children cannot take the place of companions of the child's own age. A little child needs to play and develop with other children who are in the same stage of learning as himself, who are his equals, as well as with those who are a little older or a little younger. The parents of an only child especially must bear this in mind. Through group play a little child learns by following the example of others, by having to consider what others want, by finding out that he can set an example which others will follow.

He learns many valuable lessons in adjusting himself to the demands and ideals of his group as he will later have to adjust himself to the demands and ideals of his community. Self-reliance, initiative, and leadership develop through group play.

Parents should know who are the companions of their child; he may be learning from them to play fair or to cheat. Be careful about letting a little child play out of your sight with children of whom you know nothing. Listen to their talk as they play, and see that no one teaches your child "not to tell your mother" or to "hide it, your father might see." There are plenty of playmates who will help you teach your child fair play, honesty, and courage. It is well for children to learn early that certain rules of the game must be observed, that no one can always win or have his way, that a good sport can lose without sulking, and that crying is unpopular.

When children are playing together, interfere as little as possible. It is usually better to let them settle their own disputes. Do not encourage tale-bearing; but if you are asked to settle a disagreement, hear both sides and help the children to make their own decision fairly. At times interference is necessary; no one should permit cruelty or dishonesty among children.

PARTIES AND CHRISTMAS

Parties for children under 6 years of age should be very simple and occur very seldom. Above all they should be small, not more than three or four children, especially for the child who is not accustomed to playing in a group. Parties should not interfere with the regular nap and meal times. Unusual foods should not be served, nor should any food be served at unusual times. Foods that would usually be served for dinner or supper may be served in special dishes or in a special manner, such as fancy shapes for cookies or oranges, or sandwiches instead of bread. The child for whom the party is being given may be allowed to choose which of the usual dishes he would like to have.

Simple table decorations may add a little extra color. The children should not be dressed up in fancy clothes that may be spoiled by play. The getting together of a few children for play is in itself sufficiently exciting and unusual to the average little child to warrant the name of a party. Simple games without undue excitement, played outdoors in a group, followed by a simple supper at the usual time, make the best kind of party for little children.

Do not overdo the Christmas festivities for children. A tree hung with apples and a few shining ornaments and festooned with strings of cranberries and popcorn and colored papers gives just as much pleasure as one elaborately trimmed. Simple toys are often those most loved by children. It is often the parents who cannot afford to spend much money at Christmas who succeed in making it the happiest time. Christmas can be made a truly happy time for the children by avoiding confusion, fatigue, too many things at once, too much excitement, upsetting of the daily routine, and unusual food. One mother lessened the confusion by having the little children get their presents at a different time from the adults and by putting away all but a few toys after a short time. She also insisted on an outdoor playtime and a long midday rest for all. The children had their dinner alone, and she made it a simple meal of the things they liked; she knew that digestions are upset very easily by excitement, and she gave them no rich and unusual food at dinner and no candy between meals.

Do not take a little child to public gatherings, such as fairs or circuses, or into crowded stores. These are always overexciting and overfatiguing and offer great risk of infection. Unless you suggest to the child that he is missing something by not going to such place, he will feel no disappointment. A child should not be expected to sit through movies or other entertainments suitable only for grown-ups.

IMITATIVE PLAY

Much of a child's play, whether he is alone or in a group, is imitation of what he has seen and heard about him. He learns to do the ordinary things of life by practicing them in his play. A child will act out the events of the household, going over and over what he sees and hears, and he sees and hears just about everything that goes on.

PRETENDING

The little child enjoys his toys because of what he can do with them; as he grows older he enjoys them also because of what he can pretend they are. He will often play in an elaborate world of make-believe, perhaps with dolls or boxes, blocks, flowers, stones, or bits of wood and china. All these things take on an importance to him that the grown-up outsider sometimes finds it hard to see. The flowers may be people, and the blocks, boats or engines. In his imagination he may turn his playroom into a wood full of wild animals or a lake with each chair a boat. He is happy so long as he is allowed to play in this way, but he may be made most unhappy by the misunderstanding adult who destroys his fairy castles. Play of this kind is used most often by a child who plays alone; less often children playing together will build up a make-believe world.

It is well for the parents to respect and enter into the spirit of such play. "Let's pretend" is a part of every life, and the imagination of the child should be helped to grow in a healthy direction; however, this make-believe life should not occupy a child's whole time. Play with real toys and real children should be a larger part of his life.

Dressing up to play parts, especially with costumes, is usually enjoyed by children playing together. This kind of play cultivates the imagination and at the same time encourages a social spirit.

TRAINING THE SENSES

Teach the child to enjoy form and color, to draw, however crudely, and to make patterns out of colored blocks. Help him to develop the sense of touch shown by the child who is letting sand run through his fingers, shaping a mud pie, or tenderly smoothing a piece of satin or velvet dropped from his mother's sewing box. Even the very young child may get great pleasure out of beautiful sounds and shapes and colors. Musical interest is keenly developed in some young children, and a piano, a phonograph, or a radio is a great source of pleasure and instruction.

Rhythmic movements to music are a great pleasure to most children—singing, marching, keeping time to music with hands or feet or bodies. Thus they learn to appreciate and respond to rhythm, to recognize and reproduce musical sounds. Such activities help to develop love of music as well as skillful use of the body. Every child who plays the singing, dancing games of childhood is getting his ear as well as his muscles trained. Ball-bouncing games and hopping games also are of the rhythmic type.

REASONING IN EARLY CHILDHOOD*

By John Dewey

THERE is not any reasoning of early childhood which is different from the reasoning of later childhood, adolescence, or adults. There is reasoning in little children, just as there may be in a grown-up man or woman, but there is not reasoning of early childhood if you mean by that "of," something which as reasoning can be marked off definitely from reasoning somewhere else.

The ends which a young child has are different from those of the grown-up; and the materials, means, and habits which he is able to fall back upon are different, but the process—one involving these three factors—*is exactly the same.*

There is a difference which needs to be mentioned because it is so important practically. Just because the child's ends are not so complex and not so remote in the future, the tendency to put every idea in immediate action is stronger with the child. His dramatic instinct or his play impulse is markedly more active, more urgent and intense. Adults use words and other symbols as the media for selection and arrangement, but words are not dramatic enough for the thinking of the child in a great many situations. He wants to reach his end with his whole body instead of doing it with the muscles of the throat and tongue alone. Adults carry on a constant physical activity of a suppressed kind; to get a remote and far-reaching end, they employ minute and invisible kinds of expression. A child wants to bring into play, in an active and overt way, his hands and arms and legs.

HOW WE DISSIPATE REASONING POWER

WHILE native rational power can hardly be improved to any great extent, if at all, it can easily be allowed to decrease. A child can be surrounded with conditions which cause the power to be dissipated and rendered ineffective. If a child is bright, the power can be drafted off in all kinds of futile and irrelevant ways which result in mind-wandering, inability to control the attention or center the mind on a topic around which the selecting and arranging of materials are to be carried on.

This dissipation may take place in three ways:
1. Plain frittering away of time. It is called frittering away of time or wasting time, but this is merely another phrase for fooling away intellectual energy. This comes from not having any purpose in view. "Amusing," in the worst sense of amusing, means that there is no *recreative* element, but only dissipation of energy. It is not enough to *catch* a child's attention; it must be *used,* and this implies an end. The mind should be carried on to something new.

2. Another thing which makes for retrogression is the amount of purely dictated work that the individual has to do. Undoubtedly the best way to train animals—horses and dogs—to do their stunts is to assign a specific thing to be done, dictate it, and give a reward when that particular thing is accomplished—and something else when it is not done. Children are animals, too. It may be that physical habits are most readily formed by a process which is largely dictation; but it must be borne in mind that in the latter case, while the physical habit will have intellectual meaning to us, to the child it will be entirely senseless.

3. The third thing which has a detrimental effect upon the child is presenting ready-made, finished formulae upon the basis of which he is to act. Since there should be reaching out for something new, the process should be more or less a process of trying this or that to see how it will work, then retaining the things that carry toward the end and dropping the other things. Conscientious parents and teachers are prone perhaps to fail here more than at any other point. They want to forestall all failures. They want to dig the little plant up by the roots to see that the roots are growing—and growing in the right direction. It is quite safe to say that no two grown persons get the same result by the same method unless the situation is an exceedingly simple one.

LET HIM GET HIS OWN RESULTS

THE orderly method is good, but it comes as a result and often comparatively late. What might seem to a grown-up person to be disorder might seem to a child's mind, order, in the way he selects and arranges things. The mere fact that a certain order of things does not fall into the adult's schedule of thinking means that a child is one person and the adult another. Yet we imagine that there is just one right way to think, and if another person does not get results in the same way we do, there is something wrong.

Perhaps the most difficult thing to get is in-

*Stenographic report of a paper presented before the Department of Kindergarten Education, Teachers College Alumnæ Conference. Used by special permission of Patty Smith Hill, head of the Department.

tellectual sympathy and intellectual insight that will enable one to provide the conditions for another person's thinking and yet allow that other person to do his thinking in his own way and not according to some scheme which we have prepared in advance.

HANDWORK AND FELLOWSHIP

THERE is one point which has not been touched —the question of the materials appropriate for the thinking of young children. This matter cannot be easily anticipated or cleared up in advance of actual contact with actual children. But we may ask what ends occupy the attention of most children. They will be found to fall under two heads:

1. The very small child has as his chief end the adjusting of one of his physical organs to another. He has to learn what the lower animals have to start with. He has to work out by practical experimentation how to make his hands and eyes work together, his ears and eyes work together, how to manage and manipulate physical materials by means of his own organs. Here we have one of the great reasons, on the physiological side, for the success of the kindergarten movement. In various ways it has secured a large opportunity for direct muscular adjusting, and for manipulation of various kinds of objects. If the young child has an end which he wants to reach and has sufficient freedom in choice and arrangement of materials *to work out for himself the end he is after,* there is sure to be a genuine keeping-going of the thinking process.

2. The other great problem for a little child is to get along with other people. He has the definite occupation of adjusting his conduct, in a real give-and-take of intercourse to that of others. He needs to make other people realities to himself, while he gets the power to make himself real to them. There is an adjustment of behavior which includes a good deal more than that of outward or muscular acts. The questions arising from the groupings of persons are the most perplexing problems of life even for grown-up people; but for the children, the problem is especially acute, owing to their dependence upon others.

Material selected then from situations of physical control and social adaptation is most appropriate in maintaining the mental acuteness, flexibility, and open-mindedness, the dominant interest in the new and in reaching ahead that are at once such marked traits of the life of childhood and such essential factors of thinking.

CURIOSITY*

By ELIZABETH J. WOODWARD

THE little child tastes, feels, listens; he watches, imitates, dramatizes, becomes; he breaks and tears; he pounds and pulls, and by the use of all his senses, tests his environment long before he shows the form of curiosity which we most easily recognize as such when it begins to prick our complacency—that is, by asking questions.

If the baby does not show response to these sensations we are anxious lest he may not be normally keen. If an older child takes the pose of "no interest," it is a reflection of the home or community of which he is a part, and an adverse comment upon it as well. If he is actually not interested to test his world, he is either repressed by the ignorance of those about him or he is mentally or physically ill. In any case, parents and teachers should bend themselves to the problem, for curiosity is a vital means of growth. It may be merely a matter of vocabulary—he may not know how to frame his question or he may fear that he will not understand your answer. A child asks what seems to be the same question over and over; occasionally, of course, this is a trick to gain time, but more often it is because he is adjusting your adult phrases to his thought.

With the naturally slow or reserved child it may well be the need of getting behind the problem or question, or of absorbing it, before he can put it into the words of his own growing personality. We do the same. We revolve a new idea in our maturer minds until we utterly reject it or until we accept it tentatively as part of our mental equipment. Not until then do most of us put our question in words, even to those whose thoughts lie close to ours. It has been and is potentially a part of our growth in individuality.

When speech finally comes to the aid of curiosity she brings a bunch of keys. They jangle a bit even in mother's ears, but *Why, What, Who, Where, How* unlock the secrets of the universe.

Grown-up defenses must then be ready to meet the onslaught of inquiry, for parental wisdom is never nearer the divine than when telling the truth to a child. "Nothing but the truth" always; "the whole truth" seldom.

The child hungers for ethics, for guidance in

*Courtesy of the Federation for Child Study.

the conduct of life, long before he knows it, and a person whose mind is not open to ethical possibilities ought not to be with children.

When the child asks, "Where did I come from?" you are strewing your path with thistles if you frame your answer, "You came down from heaven." Heaven and the sky are too nearly interchangeable in nursery parlance, in song and story, not to bring confusion in place of clarity.

"Did I come when it rained? Who caught me?"

If the child has seen the moon, or learned to watch the stars, it will not be many years before he will seek some other authority, for of course he will not believe that he is kin to a meteorite!

If we believe with Dr. Kirsopp Lake that a knowledge of facts is the basis of virtue and of religion, we must be sure of our facts, and of the order in which we think it wise to present them.

The child living in the country has the opportunity of meeting the question of the early whereabouts of the baby much more normally than children who do not know plants and animals as everyday companions. He may be shown the seeds of the plants, the pine tree which has pollen branches, and the other pine, looking like it, but bearing the crimson "blossoms" which will later become cones. He sees the bird's nest with well-guarded eggs; the hens, keeping the eggs warm until the chickens are strong enough to live without the shell; mother-cat keeping her kittens warm inside her furry "stomach"; lady-dog "married" to a father dog, and then having puppies.

It is the resulting chickens, kittens, and puppies that are of primary, wholesome interest to the child, and the preliminaries are accepted as nature's way of presenting new material. The story of human motherhood will lose none of its noble beauty because of likeness to the friendly animals.

But granting it is desirable to answer all of the child's questions—can it be done thoroughly? Heaven forbid! Thoroughness does not belong to young children; a child does not know a subject thoroughly; he thinks in points, touches a point that interests him, and the subject is his ever after; he has the key to it, though it may grow rusty by disuse.

On the floor of one of the kindergarten rooms the solar system drawn in crayon challenged the visitor as scarcely adapted to kindergarten days or ways. It was an outgrowth of the questions —not of one child but of many children. They were satisfied with the small measure of truth for which they asked, and soon their active feet danced the sketch, literally, from sight.

Though the child's knowledge cannot and should not be thorough, it should be sound—a simple, active nucleus for larger truths. The little question demands only the little answer; to give a full answer is to inflict a wrong. You must become a little child to hear and answer. If you add to your reply the tactless, "You can't understand yet," or, "I'll tell you more when you are older," or "You will know by and by," you do not answer at all, and the child knows it. Next time he will ask someone else, not you. But if you answer his little groping thought with a germ of truth and say it as if you believed it, he will accept it as final. When the idea recurs, it will have grown and he will want to know more. He will ask *you,* and with each question and answer will draw nearer to the full confidence in you and with you that will become your pride and his safeguard.

This is not a counsel of superficiality; this is not teaching self-deception; it is weaving his web of life with fine, strong threads as he sees their beauty and their strength.

Curiosity, when it is true interest, grows upward to sympathy, and it is the gateway to noble research in every field; but like other qualities, it may grow downward to the reverse of its height —to intrusive questions, inquisitiveness.

Curiosity in the adult is often curbed by the very vastness of the matter to be curious about; we select and eliminate. The child knows no limit, no scale of values, and we are unfair when we tell him not to ask questions about things he cannot understand. He doesn't know that there is anything he cannot understand! The duty of discrimination is laid upon the grown-up who must not let him see that one question is trivial and another vast.

The connection of topic of question to the present or to any recent happening you may not see, but to the child the relevancy is there, and the query must be bravely met.

Mothers must often echo Tagore's wish:

"I wish I could take a quiet corner in the heart of my baby's very own world. I know it has stars that talk to him and a sky that stoops down to his face to amuse him with its silly clouds and rainbows. . . .

"I wish I could travel by the road that crosses baby's mind, and out beyond all bound; where messengers run errands for no cause between the kingdoms of no history; where Reason makes kites of her laws and flies them, and Truth sets Fact free from its fetters."

WHEN THE CHILDREN ASK QUESTIONS

ASKING questions is the most respectable thing a child ever does. When he is practising the habit he should not face a line of retreating backs, but a group of pleased and commending relatives. A child asking questions is giving proof of a number of gratifying qualities.

In the first place, he is proving that he has a mind. Animals and imbeciles never ask questions. Human beings that have stopped growing ask no questions.

He is proving that he is hospitable to ideas. This is a rarely fine trait.

QUESTIONS ARE THE WAY TO LIFE

THE best way to understand your child is to listen to his interrogations. "A shrewd parent can learn more from a child's questions," Kirtley says, "than the child can learn from his answers." To test this, quietly note down the next ten inquiries your young hopeful makes about any given topic. Your guidance of his whole future vocation may be wrapped up in them.

WHAT TO DO WITH QUESTIONS

THE first thing to do with a child's questions is to sort them out. They fall into three classes: (1) thoughtless questions, (2) impossible questions, and (3) real questions.

There are two ways to deal with thoughtless questions. One is to regard them as the efforts of a tired or lonely child to be sociable. When a child pours out a stream of inquiries without waiting for one answer before he propounds another question, what he often wants is just a little notice or some friendly conversation. Under such circumstances it is better to engage in a pleasant chat with him or to tell him a story. Occasionally, however, the listener may note that he is getting germs of a real question, in which case he will treat them as such, by methods explained below.

Impossible questions include questions that are unintelligible and questions that nobody can answer. There are no questions unsuitable for a child to ask even if he is too immature to comprehend the answers. One should never say "hush" or act the coward before any question, but one can postpone certain answers. If the question is one that nobody can answer, boldly say, "I don't know. Nobody knows." Yet even in such a case possibly a clue can be given. A child asks, "Who made God?" Mrs. Edith Mumford, a sensible English writer, suggests approaching an answer by calling the attention of the child to the fact that just as dresses come from cloth and cloth from the warehouse and the warehouse gets it from the factory and the factory from the sheep—and men cannot "make" sheep, so always when we talk of "making" we are really only "changing" things, and by and by we get back to something that we cannot make—face to face with life and growth.

DEALING WITH REAL QUESTIONS

REAL questions should be carefully collected. Sometimes they cannot be answered at once. This is unnecessary, if the child recognizes that they are being saved for him. One mother jots inquiries down just as she does her grocery-list and keeps them for Father's return at night. Another has an answering-bee on Sunday afternoon. Still another has them talked over by the entire family at table.

The real reason we parents don't answer questions more genially is, frankly, *because we do not know the answers.* And this leads us to quote the sensible words of Dorothy Canfield Fisher as to the resources for such answers which are right at our hands, if we weren't too lazy to use them:

"Take the simplest expedient first. It is astonishing how many questions can be answered, how much information acquired, and how alertness of mind can be fostered by the use of a fairly large dictionary. And yet the average family either does not own a good dictionary, or consults it only at rare intervals, to ascertain the spelling of a difficult word. A child hears the main highway spoken of by an elderly person as the "turnpike." "Why is it called the 'turnpike,' Aunt Sarah?" Aunt Sarah doesn't know, she's sure—never thought of it before—it just *is* the turnpike. Mother doesn't know, either, but, quickly turning to good account the stirrings of intellectual curiosity of the child, reaches for the dictionary and with the child looks up the word. The result is not only an interesting bit of information acquired, but the historical sense of the little brain has been improved, and (most important of all) the habit of persistence in the search for knowledge has been strengthened and encouraged. Now notice by what simple means this was accomplished. Almost anybody, even the busiest mother, can find a few minutes in the course of the day to consult a dictionary.

HOW TO USE A REFERENCE SET

"OF COURSE, an encyclopedia is a bigger store-house of knowledge than a dictionary, and though it costs more, it seems to me that a good ency-clopedia is almost as necessary an article of fur-niture as a dining-room table in a home where children are being brought up. Indeed, it *is* a sort of dining-room table, on which is spread a bounteous feast, open to all who will give them-selves the trouble to sit down and partake. Cer-tainly an encyclopedia of some sort is more neces-sary for growing children than rugs on the floors or curtains at the windows.

"But there is only one variety of encyclopedia that will do. I mean a *used* set! Except in its first newness, a clean, fresh-looking book of ref-erence is a shame to any family. A thumbed, dog-eared encyclopedia that opens with a meek limpness and lies flat open at any page with broken-back submission is the kind I mean."

ANSWERING ONE'S OWN QUESTIONS

WHILE clear, intelligible answers are always a child's due, it is usually better to get the child to help answer his own questions. Even when you give a reply, ask the question back to see if he understands well enough to put his knowledge into words. The dictionary habit and the ency-clopedia habit are indispensable to form early, if one is to keep a questioning child.

"But," concludes Mrs. Fisher, "although books are precious mines of information, they are not the only, or even the best, educational material available for the question-answerer at home. There is much talk nowadays about 'nature-study' and the value of going straight with the child to original sources for such study. This is all true. The excellence of studying trees, flowers, and insects at first hand can scarcely be exaggerated.

"The principle of question-answering as a means of education applies to nearly all the ele-ments of everyday life. Instead of breathing a sigh of relief when a child's question can be stifled and silenced by the blanket-answer, 'Oh, that's the nature of it,' his mother ought to re-gard each query as another thread in the clue which, held firmly in his little hand, will lead him through the labyrinth of indifference and mental sloth to conquer and slay the monster, Ignorance."

OBSERVATION

By MRS. ELIZABETH HUBBARD BONSALL

SOME time ago I was talking to one of my friends who had come to live in our neighbor-hood more recently than I. In referring to the in-teresting features of the community, he remarked that in one of the fields near by was a peculiar little ridge of earth, which was all that remained of breastworks thrown up by soldiers during the Revolutionary War. Although I had passed the ridge many times, I had never noticed it. Then he spoke of a queer old stone bridge across a stream which bore the unique inscription that it was made by the donor's own hands, and was a free gift to the community. Although I had often crossed the bridge and passed the inscription, I had never noticed it. Then he mentioned the home of Benjamin West, on Chester Road, the oldest road in the state of Pennsylvania. Again I had never heard that the famous painter lived anywhere near us, or that there was anything remarkable about Chester Road. These comments and others made me realize more than ever be-fore how much I was missing in life by not ob-serving what was around me, and I resolved that my children should learn to keep their eyes and ears open to all the wonderful things about them.

LEARNING FROM THE INDIANS

THE Indians have always been noted for their keen observation. At great distances they can distinguish small differences in birds and animals. In this age of glasses, when so many of us keep our noses in books a good part of the time, and are hemmed in by four walls, it is our duty to see that our children's eyes are strengthened and not ruined while they are young.

There are various Indian methods which we have adopted—methods which the children love. We are fortunate in having a little strip of wood-land near our home, so that the background is very realistic. The first game that we played tended to develop a sense of location. I would lead my two children among the trees, over rocks, around bushes, and finally back to the place from which we started. Then Betty, my five-year-old daughter, would try to lead us over the same path again. To the casual observer trees are pretty much alike, and must be watched very closely if we are not to lose our way. We vary the game slightly by taking longer tramps and blazing a trail by marking a cross with a piece of chalk on convenient trees in our pathway, and then finding our way back. Every turn has to be carefully watched, and all the blazes must have been marked on both sides of the trees, or they will not be seen on the return trip. While the woods furnish the best background for this game of location, it can be played in the city by encouraging children to watch carefully when they are taken to unfamiliar places, and letting them lead in coming back. How many adults are helpless in a strange city, and what a lot they miss by not daring to go around by themselves. We even play this game ourselves indoors on rainy days by starting from some place, for instance the front hall, and going around in back of the stairs, through the dining-room, winding in and out among the chairs and tables, and finally arriving in the hall again. I remember distinctly my first day at school; how I lost my way in the strange building and wandered for some time in the corridors, not daring to ask where I belonged lest I should be teased. I am determined that Betty shall not have any such humiliating experience.

INDOOR GAMES

THE old-fashioned game of "Hide the Thimble" is always popular with children, and there is no better game to train the eye. With little two-year-olds the thimble should be placed in easy view, but as they grow older it can be hidden where it will take more and more skill to discover it.

Remembering names of persons to whom I am casually introduced is one of my problems, and even at this late date I am trying to improve, and at the same time prevent my children from being as unobserving as I in this respect. I pretend I am making a call, and let Betty bring down three or four of her dolls, introducing them to me. How she enjoys making up peculiar names for them—Martha Bunnyfoot, Mary Oatmeal, and Helen Window. After a few general remarks, I speak about each doll in turn, trying to recall the name, and then it will be my turn to be the hostess. It is splendid practice.

A good game for observing forms, and one that will be of service later in life, is that of putting together dissected maps. Cardboard maps may be purchased very reasonably, or can easily be made by pasting a copy of a map upon a stiff piece of cardboard and cutting it in small pieces with a sharp knife. I have had several beautiful maps sent me in booklets advertising histories, which I have pasted on cards and cut out along boundary lines as far as possible.

It is astonishing at how young an age children are interested in this sort of game. Before Betty was four years old she could put together perfectly maps of the United States and Europe, needing assistance only when she would push the edges out of place. And Baby Ann, not quite two, loves to pick out Texas, California, and Florida. We frequently play with the maps wrong side up, judging the countries or states entirely by their shape.

Copying patterns with colored papers or blocks is fascinating to my children. They are particularly partial to a set of colored cubes, with four of the faces painted in solid colors, the remaining two being divided into two triangles of different colors. Baby Ann can distinguish the blue and yellow faces, and will place them in separate groups when I ask her. The next step will be to alternate the colors, and gradually copy more difficult figures.

STATUES

THE MASTERPIECES of art furnish splendid material for indoor observation on stormy days. I have a good supply of prints of famous subjects, some of which I have bought and many others that I have cut from papers and magazines. The Greek statues are particularly interesting to use, as they are in such characteristic positions. We stand about ten of them, which I have mounted on cards, in a row along the back of the couch, and then we take turns posing as the different statues, and guessing which one we represent. Difficult costumes do not stand in our way at all; we drape ourselves with sheets, use scrap-baskets for helmets, the top of the washboiler for a shield, and the final effect is usually recognizable. And what fun it is to improvise these costumes! It is comparatively easy to have a general idea of what a certain statue looks like, but when you try to reproduce it—that is quite another thing. The position of both hands and feet must be studied, the tilt of the head, the expression of the face, and many other points. We take great delight, in a good-natured way, in finding flaws in each other's representation. Betty is so interested that she will stand for several minutes in as difficult a position as that of the Discus Thrower, or Mercury, whereas ordinarily, when I am trying to fasten her dress or put on her hair-ribbon, such quiet is an impossibility.

PICTURES

PICTURES may be studied in this way, too, especially if full of action. Millet's are particularly good, portraying the peasants at work in the fields and in their homes. Shawls, baskets, and old shoes usually supply the necessary atmosphere. Our favorites are "The Angelus," "The Gleaners," "The Sower," and "Starting for Work." In many of his pictures a baby is to be found, and little Ann is as pleased as can be when we include her, though of course she won't stay in one position for more than a moment. Of these home scenes, "Feeding Her Birds," "The First Step," and "Feeding Her Hens," we have found the most attractive to represent.

ARCHITECTURE

FEW PEOPLE have more than vague impressions concerning most of the famous cathedrals. We have a beautiful picture of York Cathedral in our living-room, and formerly nearly everyone who visited us would exclaim, "What a lovely picture of Notre Dame!" Betty and I, who have been studying my prints and comparing them, feel sure that, if they had taken more than a casual glance, they would have seen that York has no rose-window, while Notre Dame has a beautiful one, with three statues in front of it; and that York has a large central tower, while Notre Dame has only a slender spire.

Bell towers, too, are surprisingly individual in spite of their common limited purpose. Betty has discovered that the one in Florence has many beautiful windows, the one in Venice has hardly any windows but a pointed spire at the top, while the one at Pisa is cylindrical, with six rows of columns around it, besides having the unique feature of leaning, for which it is noted. One might think that children wouldn't be interested in pictures of buildings, but everything depends upon the way in which the pictures are presented. We take two pictures to compare, and the first one who notices a difference between them says, "I spy!" and then points out what has been especially seen. Next it is the other's turn, and we keep it up until one of us gives up. We look up in the dictionary some of the architectural terms: facade, flèche, buttresses, and others, so that we can describe our points more clearly. Perhaps I enter into games like this with unusual zest, for I have practically no opportunity for reading except what I do with my children, and I like to feel that I am gaining something myself each day, be it ever so little.

IMITATIVE PLAY

By ALICE CORBIN SIES

SOMEONE has said that a child builds up his personality under certain limitations, by copying the actions, temper, and emotions of those who are his companions. We mothers often see our dispositions as well as our actions reflected in the children playing about us. If rude and uncultured servants are employed in the home, it is easy to detect their habits and actions in the play of the children. I once observed a child who had been for a week continuously associated with a servant. This child had taken on certain rude actions copied from the servant. He indulged in such expressions as "Get out of my way!" "I'm in a hurry!" "Don't bother me!" when but a week earlier, "Excuse me!" and "Please let me pass!" had been commonplace remarks.

During the third year we see children imitating almost any action or event which appeals to their interest. The most familiar experiences are not always the ones first acted out, although this is likely to be the case if the commonplace experiences appeal to the active life the child leads. Before our boy entered upon his third year I saw him struggle to envelop a baby doll in a diaper. He then placed the doll on a couch and covered it up, sticking safety pins about in the bedclothes with an idea of somehow fastening the doll in. He often made a trip to the bathroom to secure a washcloth with which to wash his doll. This kind of play seemed simple, but it involved a definite plan of action and was a step in advance of such simple dramatic plays as scrubbing the floor with a brush he happened to find, or dusting the furniture when someone else was dusting.

When a two-year-old child plays at dusting, sweeping, or cleaning, he is learning something about each act he imitates. If we observe carelessly, the play may seem on about the same level for several months, but if we look more carefully, we will see how the acts change. For example, as our boy continued the play of putting his doll to bed he observed more closely the *putting-to-bed act* and learned to adjust the bedclothes and pins more nearly as I did.

One day when R. was twenty-six months old he

placed a paper plate on his head, a market-basket on his arm, and with a cane in his hand strutted about the house, chanting in a tuneless fashion at the top of his voice. He was arrayed to look like me when I start to market, with the addition of a cane, which symbolized Daddy's festive walking occasions. In some way he achieved a sense of importance by the addition of hat, cane, and basket. He did not deceive himself into believing that he was really going to market or out for a walk.

This sense of illusion or pretense seems to give children a great deal of pleasure even as early as the third year. About this time R. derived considerable pleasure in eating imaginary meals from a spoon and empty dish, knowing quite well he was not partaking of food, but enjoying the pretense, nevertheless. This enjoyment of pretense extends so far as to make even disagreeable acts pleasurable. One of R.'s favorite plays during this third year was *pretending* to go to bed, while *really* going to bed was rather a matter to be endured. When being put to bed he would sometimes say, "But I don't want to sleep so much," but *playing* bedtime was a different matter. It was a *self-planned* activity, hence it could be terminated at will.

into a play, which had started as a dramatization of a real experience.

Just after the close of the third year I noticed that the plots of dramatic plays became more true. At that time Santa Claus was the engrossing subject. The plot changed from day to day, yet never exceeded the bounds of stories and pictures connected with Santa Claus. Sometimes Santa "propelled" himself over the floor in a large pan. Again, he strutted about with a pack over his back and insisted upon my closing my eyes while he deposited toys at my feet. At another time a chair became the tiny reindeer, and, perched upon an improvised seat in a clothesbasket, R. slapped his reins and speeded on his journey o'er the snow.

One day I attempted to use the chair which had a short time before played the part of "the tiny reindeer." R. resisted with a vigorous protest, "Oh, don't! It's my reindeer!" This Santa Claus play almost dominated the boy's personality for several months. "I'm Santa Claus!" he would exclaim before he had even partaken of breakfast, and all during the day, off and on, the Santa personality dominated his actions. When people asked him his name he invariably and quite seriously replied, with no thought of being amused, "Santa Claus!"

THE DEVELOPMENT OF IMITATIVE PLAY

DURING the last part of the third year children dramatize pretty nearly everything that strikes their fancy. Shaving like father, running like horses, hopping like frogs, flying like birds, crawling to represent mice, cats, etc., barking to represent dogs, are part and parcel of the day's play. When using blocks or toys, these inanimate objects are made to perform events seen or heard of in stories. Ideas suggested through pictures are also incorporated in dramatic play. One day while R. was playing I saw a train run under a bridge and a sailor boy stand on top of the bridge, looking down upon the swift-moving train. Pretty soon a man appeared on top of one of the cars. I remembered just where R. had seen these things. But soon the play became unlike his own actual observation. A motor truck passed over the bridge with a lady doll on the seat. Suddenly a story was remembered. "I want a cat to jump on her lap," I heard R. exclaim. A wooden block became a cat and jumped into the lady's lap. Then a dog (another block) appeared and chased the cat up a tree. And so several jumbled-up facts from different stories were remembered and incorporated

THE EDUCATIONAL SIGNIFICANCE OF IMITATIVE PLAY

CONSIDERING the facts brought out in the discussion of dramatic plays, it is a commonplace to attempt to point out the educational significance of such plays. They are the very stuff of life itself. We can control the kind of play only by controlling the conditions of life. If our lives with our children abound in rich experiences which set good copies, we need have no fear of what the child will dramatize. Within certain limits parents can enrich the significance of dramatic games by playing with their children, being careful, of course, not to usurp leadership or to suggest a content to the play which is quite foreign to the child's genuine interpretation. During the third year, also, a parent can greatly enhance the content of dramatic plays by descriptive songs and stories. For this purpose I found *fact-stories* relating to animals and activities in which the boy was interested more appropriate during the third year than stories in books. During the fourth year I could use longer stories, but during the third year only Mother Goose rhymes and the simple fact-rhymes found in kindergarten song-books.

DRAMATICS IN THE HOME

MUCH the smallest use of the dramatic instinct is that which is to be made through theatricals. The main purpose here is to show in what a wide range of activities it expresses itself wholesomely in a child's life. The earliest of these is through dramatic play.

George E. Freeland watched a baby of two and a half years for a whole day and noted that he engaged in fifty-four different imaginative games. This is the time when the child imitates the acts of older people; whatever tiny implements or apparatus he can use please him. Toy furniture for the house, the sand pile for outdoors, and the doll for both, are most useful. "The doll," as Sully tells us, "takes a supreme place in this fancy-realm of play." "A good, efficient, able-bodied doll, like the American girl's," says Joseph Lee, "is at home in any situation in life, from princess to kitchen-maid, to which she may be called. And one doll in her time plays many parts. She has to, or lose her job."

"The rhymes of Mother Goose," says Alice M. Herts, "were predominatingly dramatic. A great many of them associate words, song, and action. The ordinary printed collections are misleading in this respect. The words, taken alone, are not the thing. Think of printing 'Pease porridge hot' as a separate and independent poem without the dramatic hand-play!"

The mother may help the development of this expressive instinct even in early childhood. Even a baby ought to be treated as a play*mate* not as a play*thing*. There is an old-fashioned game known as "Come to see." The little damsel with her doll, and perhaps "dressed up" in some of her mother's wardrobe, came to call on mother. Her efforts to behave exactly as a lady should were aided and guided by the mother's careful behavior as hostess. It was a training in manners. When the children played visit each other they used all the manners they had. They were practising useful lessons without knowing it.

A CHILD "PUTS HIS EYES IN HIS POCKET"

THE CHILD from four to seven is capable of a wider range of imagination. These years are regarded by psychologists as the most active imaginatively in human life. Capable of imitation of the ideas as well as the acts of adults, the child uses dolls, soldiers, Noah's arks, carts, play-houses, blocks, sand-piles, paint-boxes and stencils to act out a great variety of adult occupations.

"Nothing," says Robert Louis Stevenson, "can stagger a child's faith; he accepts the clumsiest substitutes and can swallow the most staring incongruities. The chair he has just been besieging as a castle, or valiantly cutting to the ground as a dragon, is taken away for the accommodation of a morning visitor, and he is nothing abashed; he can skirmish by the hour with a stationary coal-scuttle; in the midst of the enchanted pleasance he can see, without sensible shock, the gardener soberly digging potatoes for the day's dinner. He can make abstraction of whatever does not fit into his fable; and he puts his eyes in his pocket, just as we hold our noses in an unsavory lane."

No doubt clumsy interference by adults most often spoils imaginative enjoyment. Sully tells this: "A little girl of four was playing 'shop' with her younger sister. The elder one was shopman at the time I came into her room and kissed her. She broke out into piteous sobs; I could not understand why. At last she sobbed out: 'Mother, you never kiss the man in the shop.' I had with my kiss quite spoiled her illusion."

The child soon tires of mechanical toys, talking dolls, or elaborate doll-houses with which there is nothing he can do. The passion for destruction which often manifests itself during these years is simply the perversion of the instinct for construction. Being provided with no materials with which he can build, he takes apart his too complete toys. A pile of blocks, a sand-pile, a paint-box, dolls that must be cut out, a ruined shed that perhaps may be made into a doll-house, these are ideal materials for childish play.

INCREASING POSSIBILITIES IN THE DRAMATIC USE OF MATERIALS

BETWEEN seven and nine there is still wider possibility in the dramatic use of materials. Sliced animals and other puzzles which consist of building pictures from sections of cardboard, dolls furnished with patterns for dressing, pasteboard farms and villages, a doll's school outfit, stamped patterns of birds and animals to be sewed and stuffed—these are some of the store-made plays that are worth while. A child will, however, have equal enjoyment by making a toy village out of blocks, stones, and twigs; he can make a miniature theater out of an old kennel that will satisfy him better than the brightly colored ones which can be bought, and he can play store, train, and expressman with nothing more than some boxes and a cart. The larger skill and knowledge of the child now give more content to plays of an earlier period.

A "P'RAD OF GINRULS," INTRODUCING THE ENTIRE COMPANY

ABOUT this time the boy begins to get up original theatricals, dramatizing the stories he has read or the plays he has seen. William Byron Forbush gives an illustration from his own household: "On going upstairs in the country, the author has often been confronted by a large brown-paper poster which reads:

GREAT SHOW AND FEED

At two o'clock

Admission One Cent

"I pay my fee at the door of one of the children's chambers, and am asked by the youthful ticket-seller if I care for a reserved seat. In a stage whisper he adds, 'O Parp, do take one; if you don't we'll come out short on the refreshments.' I deposit the additional penny, and am ushered to a seat upon the bed, over which is the placard, 'First Balcony.' The rabble is seated on chairs. We receive programs, executed with the expenditure of much muscle and saliva. First, according to this program, is a 'P'rad of Ginruls,' introducing the entire company. Then follow recitations, songs, shadow-pictures, stereopticon and original plays, one of border-life and the other of conflict with crime in the city. A reminiscence of Cooper and the dime novel is traceable in these vigorously acted dramas. The manipulation of apparatus and the movements and dialogue behind the scenes are as entertaining to the spectators as the regular acts. At the close a plate of delicious plums is passed, for which the youngest must have walked two miles in the hot sun, and mortgaged all of the proceeds of the entertainment in advance."

The superior craftsmanship of the child between ten and twelve enables him to enjoy games which imitate many adult activities. The boy now enjoys some of the published games by which he can play conductor, post-office and banker, and the girl who plays house does some actual cooking and house-cleaning with equipment that really works.

DRAMATIC PARTIES

To THE mother who is at her wits' end in trying to devise something new and good for children's parties, the idea of using the dramatic instinct should come as a godsend. Nothing could possibly be more delightful than an afternoon of dramatic games, varied by more quiet story-telling. Playing statues, getting up tableaux, performing charades, and even extemporaneously acting out story-plays are all methods of entertainment which win enthusiastic response. If the foresighted mother will bring down the contents of some old trunks and whisper to the mothers of the other children to do the same, an afternoon of wholesome self-entertainment is assured.

It is a curious fact that that which is the easiest form of dramatic expression to young children is the most difficult to adolescent young people, namely, the pantomime. This is explained by the fact that little children enter so unconsciously into action without the use of speech. Of pantomime for little children, the simplest form is that of "statues," in which the children pose, either dressed all in white with powdered hair, or with no change of costume, to represent scenes from life, familiar people, common trades, forms of action, famous people and thoughts and feelings. The next dramatic step is to tableaux, in which the children are grouped at least in pairs, arranged in a frame or behind a curtain, dressed in costume. Here, as in the statues, their own inventiveness may be largely depended upon, as they pose to represent characters in story-books, characters in poems, scenes from history, people of other lands, and famous pictures. The third variety is the shadow-play, in which with even simpler properties but with more careful rehearsal, the children pose as silhouettes and employ a few dramatic gestures.

A pleasant device to encourage young children to work is to denominate them as "soldiers," "watchmen," or "little partners." The addition of a paper cap or a wooden sword or a policeman's club will carry many a small youngster through a task which would otherwise seem intolerable. If a boy or girl can only turn something into something else more to his liking, he will develop considerable industry. In one home where there were many humdrum tasks to be performed by the children the oldest won the enthusiasm of the rest by printing the names of all the tasks upon slips of paper and letting each draw lots. The uncertainty of the lot and the chance to relieve the tedium by entering for a time into the work of another made it more fun.

SPEECH AND LANGUAGE

YOUR CHILD'S SPEECH*

By James Sonnett Green, M.D.

WHILE a child's articulate speech usually begins when he is about nine months old, there is no need for the parents to worry even if the speech is delayed until the age of two years, provided only that the delay is not due to impaired hearing. As long as the child can hear, he will speak in time.

The intellectual appreciation of sounds heard apparently represents the earliest part of the speech faculty developed in the history of the race. Certainly it is the hearing center and the capacity of appreciating the messages there received that are the first indications in the child of the intelligence that produces speech.

Normally a child begins to hear and to react to sounds about the fourth day; at the end of the first month he recognizes sounds; and at the end of the third month the instinct to imitate sounds appears. The first words he picks up are, of course, gained through his hearing and his instinct of imitation; it is from hearing his mother say "ma-ma" or "dad-dee" that he learns to say it.

BABBLING COMES FIRST

ALL OF a child's first words and phrases, in fact, are of the nature of what is technically called echolalia, a term from the Greek signifying babbling; that is, mere echoing or repetition without meaning. Not allowing for this, fond parents are wont to consider the speech of the young child more intelligent than it really is; hearing the child use a certain phrase, they credit him with the intelligence necessary for the formulation of the phrase, whereas the use of the phrase is merely echolalia. Truth to tell, echolalic speech persists with some persons all through their adult years. Witness their habitual talk, with its "says he," "says she," and "they said"—no intellectual development here; merely the meaningless repetition of others' remarks.

However, the normal thing is for the child to make rapid progress during his second year in understanding the words he hears and in using the words correctly and with discrimination. At first every man to him is daddy; at length he learns that the term applies only to one.

It is in his third year that the child usually begins to fashion words into phrases and sentences under the direction of his own conscious intelligence. Who has not observed the high order of felicity often attained in the phrases of very little people? A girl child of my acquaintance, on being taken to the seashore for the first time, promptly called the surf, "noisy water," and a sail boat, "a boat with a dress on." A little later, pointing to some scurrying clouds, she said, "walking sky." Poetic expressions these, which point back to the childhood of the race, when all the objects of nature were fresh and full of meaning and wonder to man, and he struggled with his word-making faculty to give them definite names.

To the parent, the mother particularly, the development of the child's speech faculty is a source of continual joy. This joy testifies to the parent's instinctive recognition of the part played by speech in the life of man.

But in how many cases does the parent's instinctive recognition of the importance of speech become fully conscious? How often does a parent deliberately reflect that speech is pre-eminently the medium of human intercourse; that speech, rather than bread, is the staff of human life; that a child's training at school and college, his happiness in social life, his success in business all depend on it; that everyone, to get on in our human social

* Reprinted from *Hygeia* by permission.

organization, must be able to give an account of himself, must be able to sell his services and ideas, if not his goods, to others, and that this can be done effectively only through straightforward, normal, standard speech?

SPEECH DEFECTS OFTEN NOT OUTGROWN

MY EXPERIENCE, particularly as director of the National Hospital for Speech Disorders, indicates that parents who deliberately consider these things are few. Even those who otherwise exercise a highly intelligent watchfulness over their children commonly show interest in their children's speech only to the extent of seeing that it is free from bad grammar and from what are called bad words. The general idea would seem to be that straightforward, normal, standard speech is something that a child picks up just naturally, and though the child may have the worst kind of speech defect— as, for example, a bad case of stuttering—entire reliance is likely to be placed on the happy-go-lucky idea that he will outgrow it in time.

Now, in the sense that a child gradually acquires the faculty of speech through his faculty of hearing, it is strictly true that he does—naturally, as it were—pick up his speech. But this brings us to the question as to what kind of speech he is going to hear. Will it be straightforward, normal, standard speech; that is, speech preceded by definite, complete thought, and consisting of correctly and distinctly articulated words, put together in straightforward, complete, grammatical, and logical sentences, the whole being governed as to intonation, rhythm, and accent by the "innate musical ear"? Will it be speech in which the whole power of the personality is collected and concentrated, and thus made tremendously influential and moving?

Training in speech should begin as soon as the awakening intelligence of the child prompts him to struggle after speech. For training is simply a matter of substituting right habits for wrong, and it is obvious that the difficulty of overcoming a wrong habit is in exact proportion to the length of time it is permitted to exist.

It follows from this that the worst thing to talk to a baby is baby talk. What is this talk?

From his earliest years a child should be spoken to in correctly and distinctly articulated words, put together in simple but complete sentences. In the first place this will instill in the child in his most impressionable years habits leading directly to the development of straightforward, normal, standard speech, and in the second place it will tend to give the child from the beginning a good vocabulary and thus will greatly promote his mental development.

WHY AN ONLY CHILD SEEMS SUPERIOR

FREQUENTLY it has been observed that the only child of a fully mature, staid, educated couple far outruns the average child in mentality. It is not that this exceptional child has greater innate intelligence, but the explanation is that, having spent most of his time with his parents, he has acquired good speech habits and a good vocabulary; for be it remembered that mentality is essentially the power of coherent, definite thought, and that all definite, coherent thinking must be done in words. Surely we here see the folly of leaving a child mainly under the influence of some uneducated, loose-talking nurse girl, and the wisdom of guarding him from the bad speech habits of other children.

The most evil outcome of talking baby talk to babies, and particularly of imitating their omissions and substitutions of consonants because this mutilated speech sounds "so cute" is that such speech often becomes confirmed in the child as a habit, and thus remains throughout his adult years when it is far from sounding "so cute" to any one. Hardly anything could be better designed to confirm defective speech in a child than for him to hear it constantly imitated.

The very common lisping is the omission of sibilant sounds or the substitution of other sounds for the sibilant, as when "toap" is said for soap and "Mithithippi" for Mississippi.

Mutilated speech normally arises in children from lack of practice in causing the tongue and lips to assume the positions needed for the production of consonant sounds, and it may continue as a form of clumsiness in the use of tongue and lips. Or it may have a peculiar kind of mental origin.

In cases of deformities of the mouth, such as a cleft palate, or in some pathological condition of a vocal organ, the cure, of course, must be a purely medical or surgical one.

STUTTERING*

Its Causes and Cures

By Smiley Blanton, M.D.

PEOPLE speak to express their thoughts. Speech is the chief means by which we adjust ourselves to other people. But an even more important reason for speech is to express the feelings, desires, wishes, which together make up the emotions. The infant has emotions long before he has thoughts, and the first and perhaps most dominating emotion in the infant's life is fear. Babies are born with the fear of falling and rough handling, and most babies, when away from their mothers, fear strange people. The emotion of fear, as well as the emotions of anger and love, finds its expression through speech which is developed in the first years of life primarily to express emotions.

Since speech was developed to express the emotions, the speech mechanism, which includes the breathing muscles and vocal and articulatory muscles, is responsive to the slightest emotions of fear or anxiety, anger or irritation. The breathing is disturbed especially by feelings of timidity. In fact, the whole speech mechanism may be so disturbed by even slight feelings of anxiety as to cause a blocking or hesitation in the speech, which is called stuttering, or stammering. To use a very common analogy, stuttering, like headache, is only a symptom and what causes it in one person may not cause it in another. It is therefore usual to find the symptom of stuttering varying greatly in different persons and even in the same person at different times.

A student, a native German, stuttered only when speaking German. Another student stuttered only over the telephone and nowhere else. One stuttered only in school and not with his parents. Another stuttered almost entirely with his parents and never when he recited in school. A very successful teacher, curiously enough, never stuttered while she was on the platform teaching, but found it difficult to speak when she was standing on the floor talking to someone on the platform.

It must be obvious from these facts that stuttering could not be caused by any injury or disease of the nervous system, otherwise the symptoms would be more constant. Nor has it been our experience that stuttering is caused by lack of calcium in the blood, incoordination of the breathing, or by forcing left-handed children to use their right hands. However, we definitely advise that every left-handed child be allowed to use his left hand in writing and not be forced to change. Such a change may cause stuttering, but we believe it is due more to the nervous strain of forcing a child to use an unaccustomed hand than to any changes in the speech area.

The fundamental cause of stuttering is fear or timidity. This timidity is sometimes very slight. It may in some cases be buried in the subconscious mind and not perceived by the stutterer himself. This fear or timidity which causes stuttering arises during the first years of life. The infant has to be trained to give up the anti-social habits of infancy and to take on more adult habits. Parents often are too anxious that the child be perfect. In their effort to train him, they instill in him a feeling of shame, of guilt, of sin, which often disguises itself in the form of inadequacy, inferiority, insecurity, or timidity. When a child with such a fear has to meet other people and adjust to them through speech, this fear often causes a blocking or hesitation.

We believe, then, that stuttering is caused primarily by a feeling of timidity on the part of the stutterer, which causes a change in the breathing and the articulatory motions necessary for speech.

There is no dividing line between the frank stutterer who shows all the typical symptoms of blocking and hesitation, and a person who is nervous, embarrassed, and timid when the social situation calls for speech. There are many such people in high school and college who find it difficult to recite. They often cover up their embarrassment by refusing to speak. Such refusal is not infrequently interpreted by the teacher as sullenness or obstinacy.

An example which illustrates how children may develop a stutter is that of a girl of four, who was so tiny and so pretty that she looked like a doll. She was adored by her family and was constantly stopped and spoken to on the street, even by strangers. At home, her every movement and activity was noticed and commented upon. The physical and mental strain under which she was placed caused her to break down into a stutter.

The conception of speech as a means of adjustment to group-living makes more understandable the type of stuttering caused by negativism in children from whom is demanded an excessive speech response. Far too much speech response is demanded of most children and not enough spontaneous speech allowed. Nearly all children are

* Reprinted from *Junior Home* by permission.

pestered by their elders by such questions as, "How old are you?" "What did you get for Christmas?" "Speak to Auntie,—Grandmother, —Grandfather." They are asked to recite for relatives and friends rhymes and poems that they have learned at school, or to repeat words that they have heard. No wonder that under such circumstances the child balks, or becomes negative, or refuses to speak. Sometimes, however, a child instead of refusing to speak, tries to carry out the speech response demanded and in the ensuing anxiety develops a stutter.

Illustrating this condition is a little girl of four. Her parents were very proud of her capacity to talk. She was frequently taken to visit relatives and friends, and on such occasions was asked to speak for the company. She became very irritable as time went on. On one occasion, after a long and exhausting visit, her father asked her to say good-bye to all the assembled company. The child refused and began to cry. Whereupon the father said, "We won't go until you have said good-bye to everyone." The child began to stutter and continued to stutter for some time afterwards.

Sometimes we find children suffering because of an anxiety over the fact that they feel they are going to lose some of the love of their parents because of the arrival of a brother or sister. A very interesting case was that of Jack, a boy of five years of age. His father was too severe and insisted on a type of behavior far too rigid for a boy of five years. As a result of this, the mother became very tender and loving. She tried to make up to him for his father's severity. As a result of this treatment, Jack became over-attached and dependent upon his mother. When his mother went to the hospital, he seemed somewhat distressed but soon regained his composure. Twins were born, and after a few days, Jack was taken to see them. When he was shown the first baby, he looked at it and seemed rather disappointed, but watched it nurse with some interest. Then the nurse brought in the second baby, and he said, "Is that ours, too?" The nurse replied, "Yes, this is our little baby, too." Jack cried, "Oh, my goodness, I can't stand two of them. Take them away!" Soon afterwards he began to stutter. His stuttering continued for more than a year. Apparently stuttering was caused by anxiety and fear of the loss of his mother's love by the birth not only of one baby, but two babies.

It has been claimed that the emotional difficulties found in stuttering are the result of stuttering and have nothing to do with the cause. A study of the personality of stutterers, however, shows that their emotional attitudes are primary and are the cause of the speech defect. Stuttering may accentuate feelings of fear or anxiety, but it does not cause them. The essential characteristic of the temperament of the stuttering child is a marked sensitiveness to social situations. This sensitiveness is really a great virtue if properly trained and controlled. In my own experience with stutterers, I have come to feel that they have the most pleasing and delightful personalities of any group with which I have come in contact. Their quick responses to social situations, their marked sensitiveness, and their keenness of perception of social relationships give them an insight and develop a type of personality that is often pleasing and appealing. Stuttering should be thought of more as a danger signal which indicates that the stutterer requires very careful training in order that he may properly utilize a sensitive, overacting nervous system.

It is to be deplored that the stutterer is so often considered to be funny. On the stage, the stutterer is often presented as a comic figure.

Speech is a delicate recorder of the emotions, and stuttering should not be considered so much as a speech defect but rather a difficulty of the emotional life—a difficulty which can be overcome in most cases by intelligent, early treatment of the stutterer.

It is not helpful to give the young child who stutters any specific speech training. He should not have his attention called to his stuttering and he should not be made to repeat sentences or words, or told to speak slowly, or given vocal or phonetic exercises. No frontal attack can be made on the child's speech difficulty. It is his environment that must be changed. The child must be given more freedom, less pressure must be put upon him to talk, and wherever possible in such cases, the young child should be placed in a play group or a nursery school where he can play much of the day unimpeded and unhampered by adults.

One of the most helpful things is the teaching of general relaxation. Pageants and plays are excellent training, for they give the child or adult a chance to speak while being another character, and in this way some of the fear is eliminated and the stutterer is often able to speak without difficulty.

Since stuttering is caused by feelings of timidity, the treatment should be primarily directed toward overcoming this fear. We do not believe that phonetics or vocal drills should be used, for it makes the stutterer even more self-conscious about his speech. With older children and with adults, the treatment consists of helping them to understand their problems, helping them to adjust themselves more successfully to their friends and to their work, helping them to be more successful in sports, liberating their creative energies, and acting as a sympathetic friend and adviser. What is needed is to free the stutterer from his lurking fears which come from the subconscious and to help him to understand his deeper emotional nature.

TEACHING A CHILD TO TALK

By Michael Vincent O'Shea

There is something very cheerful and courageous in the setting-out of a child on a journey of speech with so small baggage and with so much confidence. He goes free, a simple adventurer.—Alice Meynell.

THE FIRST sound a child utters may be indicated by the vowel *a*. In the beginning he cannot utter any consonant sound; one can hear nothing but vowel sounds from him for several months. Why? Because the vowels are easily uttered. They require no coordination of the lips, teeth, tongue, and palate.

The first articulate word is something like *ma-ma*. The next is apt to be *pa-pa* and the next *ba-ba*. The consonants in these words are made in a simple way. The child is always uttering the *a* sound during his waking moments, and when he is feeding or indulging in voice play he unconsciously modifies the stream of *a* sound by the lips, which results in the *ma-ma* that infants repeat over and over again in voice play. Then again as the child is playing vocally in his cradle he puffs and puffs and produces something like *pa-pa* by modifying the stream of *a* sound, by blowing against the opening lips. In the same way while he is indulging in vocal gymnastics he produces a sound that resembles *ba-ba*. In due course other consonants appear and they are joined with the original *a* sound; and in time other vowels are developed; thus the range of sound combinations is continually enlarged.

By the time the average normal child is twelve months of age, he begins to imitate some of the words spoken by his father, mother, brothers, and sisters, but he never reproduces any word with complete accuracy. He mutilates every word more or less, because he avoids the more difficult sounds, either eliminating them altogether or substituting other sounds for them. Very rarely, if ever, would a twelve-months-old child say "milk," giving the full and exact sound of the *l* and the *k*. Sometimes young children will omit all consonant sounds, and "milk" will be simply *"i."* More often it is *"mi"* with the *l* and *k* omitted.

CAUSE OF SPEECH DEFECTS

A SIX-MONTHS-OLD child can not control the tips of his fingers in coordination with one another so that he can perform delicate tasks such as threading a needle. Neither can he control the tip of his tongue in relation to the teeth and the palate so that he can produce difficult consonantal sounds. This is why he mutilates words. Most children of eighteen months and even older will omit the sound of *g* on the ends of all words ending in *ing*. They will substitute other sounds for *th, fl, sp,* and so on, or omit them altogether. Thus "that" will be "dat"; "spot" will be "pot"; "flowers" will be "fowers"; "run" may be "glun" or simply "un"; "drink" may be "ding" or "dink"; "Christmas" is likely to be "ismas" or "Kismas"; "hold" may be "ho"; "let" may be "et"; "come" may be simply "cu"; "through" is likely to be "frough." The "th" in "either" will probably be changed to "v," and the word will be pronounced "eiver." A hard word like "scissors" will be likely to be simply "si." One might go on with these instances to any length.

By the time the child has reached his third birthday all these mutilations should have disappeared, if he develops normally. If he still retains his "baby talk" it is an indication that he is not gaining mastery of speech in quite the right way, and he should be given some special attention. The first thing to do is to avoid using "baby talk" in speaking to him. A parent should always prevent people from using mutilated words in talking to his child. The next thing to do is to look into the child's physical condition. Does he have adenoids? Is he tongue-tied? Does he have enlarged tonsils or enlarged glands? Is his palate properly formed? Are the nasal passages open, or are they obstructed by congested conditions or misplaced bony structures? In some cases the tongue is so thick that the child seems to be unable to use it to make the more difficult consonant sounds.

The chances are that a child who is normal physically will grow through the period of speech-mutilation, and will reproduce correctly all the sounds in the language without special instruction. But occasionally a child is found who is normal physically and mentally, but who persists in using mutilated words. With such children special instruction is desirable. These children must be taught how to place the vocal apparatus in making the sounds which give trouble. Take the *th* sound, for instance. A parent can help a normal three-year-old child by showing it how the vocal organs are placed in sounding *th* in "through," for example, or in "this" or "that." A one-year-old child can not imitate the position of the vocal apparatus in making particular sounds, but a typical three-year-old child should be able to do it successfully.

PRECISE ARTICULATION

THE SOUNDS that are made in the front of the mouth, so to speak, so that the child can see the position of the tongue, teeth, and lips, can be more easily imitated than sounds that are made in the back of the mouth; but even these latter sounds, as, for instance, *g* in "pudding," can be taught to a normal three-year-old child who habitually omits it, but can not be effectively taught simply by pronouncing it. The child must *see* the vocal organs in position and in action. If necessary, he must feel them with his fingers so that he will have something definite to imitate. A child can not imitate the mere sound of a word as readily as the movement of the vocal apparatus which he can see and feel.

The majority of children will in time articulate correctly without special training, provided they hear language spoken correctly about them. But if they hear slovenly speech they may never learn to articulate precisely, which will prove a serious handicap in life. Clear, precise articulation will prove a valuable asset to anyone.

ENLARGING THE CHILD'S VOCABULARY

By ANN ROE-ANDERSON

NUMEROUS ways are given to enlarge one's vocabulary, but as is the case in many matters, it is best, in order that the adult may know many words, to "begin with the child."

If as children we had learned, easily and naturally, a few thousand words instead of only a few hundred, we should now be able, under most circumstances, to speak without hesitation or embarrassment, and there would be no need "to enlarge our vocabulary" by setting ourselves the stint of learning each day a new list from the dictionary.

Over and over we employ the same words, trying vainly to express thoughts about our various experiences. If words were borne out by use we should soon find ourselves greatly at a loss to carry on our "every day" conversations. When we make bold to use a word now and then that is not worn threadbare, the blank look of amazement or the sly smile causes us to feel embarrassed, but if these words were inherent from childhood we should not be self-conscious in their use.

THE SYNONYM GAME

An interesting way for the child to get a large, practical vocabulary is through the Synonym Game. The child "wins" who can tell or write the greatest number of synonyms for words taken from some familiar verse, such as:

"Old Mother Hubbard
Went to the cupboard,
To get her poor dog a bone;
When she got there
The cupboard was bare,
And so the poor dog had none."

Synonyms for "went": walked, ran, hurried.
"Cupboard": kitchen-cabinet, pantry, storeroom.
"Got": (which the children should be taught not to use incorrectly) arrived, reached.
"Bare": empty, stripped.
Of course there are many others.

A verse from Stevenson may be used:

"A child should always say what's true,
And speak when he is spoken to,
And behave mannerly at table,
At least as far as he is able."

"True": honest, reliable, good.
"Speak": answer, talk, converse, chat.
"Behave": act, appear.
"Mannerly": ladylike, gentlemanly, gracious, politely.

The little ones enjoy the game and gain fluency of speech unconsciously. The older children often rule that the words which they have used must be defined, and without using a derivative of the word. A book of synonyms studied after the game is over shows other words they might have used.

LEARNING TO USE LANGUAGE*

IN LANGUAGE, the wealth of learning and aspiration of the race have been stored up, ready to be unlocked when the child has found the key of some actual experience which will give him the power to enter into his inheritance. Words are symbols; that is, they suggest and represent meanings. John Dewey says, "Words should be signs of ideas, and ideas spring from experience."

GENERAL AIMS

1. *To provide a means of communicating with others.*—The pre-school period is the one during which a child should become thoroughly grounded in colloquial, conversational English. He should gain in the ability to grasp the meaning of others as interpreted in language.

2. *To aid in the clarification of ideas; to crystallize a meaning which the child has discovered in his experiencing, so that such meaning may be used in thinking.*—As the child realizes finer distinctions in his experience, he seeks for a word that will fix his idea. If it is supplied to him or if he coins one for the situation, he can make easy reference to that situation in his later thoughts; the word gives him a new basis for discrimination.

SPECIFIC AIMS

1. *Improvement of the technique of oral expression:*—Increase of vocabulary due to wider experiences and finer distinctions.

Better grammatical construction, sentences more complete and following each other in sequence without loss of spontaneity in expression.

Clearer enunciation; correct pronunciation; pleasing, expressive tone of voice.

2. *Organization of thought:*—In striving for adequate expression of his ideas, a child learns to emphasize the more significant phases of his experience, to relate these to his former experiences, and to define them in terms of former experiences. In social intercourse he interprets the thoughts and feelings of others in the light of his own, and so enlarges and modifies his own.

3. *Freedom of expression:*—A child should be led to feel that he has something to say which is worth saying. A child should be led to feel that he has an interested listener. A child should be led to feel that he will be encouraged to communicate his ideas.

METHOD

CONVERSATION should not be limited to certain periods of the day set apart for that purpose; for in such a case it becomes formal and forced.

Throughout the day the child should have freedom of expression. He should ask questions of other children as well as of his mother; he should ask their help in work and play; he should express his opinions, and thus test his ideas by the knowledge of others who may sanction or disapprove. It is only when a situation does not provoke energetic thought that a little child's talk becomes silly.

Wrong Methods.—It is almost impossible to give model outlines for conversations because of their inherent nature. Conversation is a give and take, modified by the mental attitudes of the people taking part. It is easier to show what the so-called conversation periods should not be like.

1. Question and answer method: The mother may start by asking, "What did we talk about yesterday?" If little impression was made the previous day, no answer may be forthcoming or perhaps a random guess. "It was a tall man who carries a flag." "Yes, a soldier." "What did we say a soldier did?" This method rouses a half-hearted interest because the child gives information only.

2. Monologue method: The mother may tell the child all about some experience. The child is passive, may not be interested in the topic, and has no opportunity for expression. Children should usually gather information from some direct experience.

3. Over-organized method: The mother may say, "Yesterday we talked about where the squirrel lives; to-day we will talk about what he looks like." A little child is not ready for concentration on such minute details, pigeonholed under headings. A child must respond to a whole situation if his language is to flow freely and fully.

---

* Adapted from a report by the Committee on Curriculum of the International Kindergarten Union.

4. Poor method of using pictures: "Here is a picture; what do you see in it?" is often a way that a conversation is started. Such a question is unnecessary if the picture illustrates experiences familiar to the child. The picture itself will suggest interesting conversation. But if the picture shows objects or activities entirely foreign to the child, he may guess at its meaning, but there is little language value. The child may learn to speak the words which the mother uses in describing the picture, but as there is no content to the words, these will drop from the vocabulary.

Right methods.—1. Recall of an experience: A vivid experience, such as watching the carpenter at work, playing in the wind, planting in the garden, is a good starting-point for a general conversation. Language will become vigorous and effective when there has been reaction toward elemental things. The child himself must use correct language form. Nothing but persistent oral repetition of the correct form will overcome the habit of using incorrect, ungrammatical, and inelegant expression in daily speech. These are matters of ear-training and motor-habits as well as of knowledge.

If the child describes an experience in a desultory, disjointed way, the mother may ask a few suggestive questions and at the end may combine the child's ideas in a sequence of events, an interesting summary.

2. Experience of the child told to others: When the child's contribution is of such a nature that it is of significance for others, the mother should help the child to tell the experience. The responsibility for interesting a group because one has something worth while and interesting to say is an attitude that should be encouraged in a social situation.

3. A social situation which calls for organization of oral expression: Invitations to celebrations, letters to absent friends or other children, etc., are excellent opportunities for the formulation of ideas in written form.

4. Good method of using pictures: A question which leads to picture-interpretation complies more with the spirit of art than one that suggests picture-analysis.

The following stories were told by some five-year-old children as interpretations of Millet's "First Step":

"The father is saying to the baby, 'Come over here.' And the mother is holding the baby. 'Come over here, come over here, and I will put you on the car.'"

"Once a man was in his garden picking up wheat and putting it all in his wagon. His mother and his baby came in to see how it was in the garden, and he put out his arms to lift up the baby, and he wanted to lift the baby, too, but he had too much work; he couldn't. Then, after he was done with that, he planted some seeds. So many trees are there! All the people came from all over the country to see how nice it was. He had fences so that nobody could come in to touch his stuff. He took his wheat to the miller, who made it into flour so that we'd have something to eat."

After a few stories about a picture have been told by the child, the mother can draw attention to different parts of the picture which have been misinterpreted. For instance, the above stories show that the wheelbarrow in the "First Step" is an unfamiliar object. Conversation will then center on these unfamiliar objects in familiar surroundings. Sometimes it is the activity, the meaning of the picture, which is misinterpreted. In such cases the mother will question about the detail which gives the clue to the rightful meaning.

This method of studying a picture develops imagination and gives a unity to a picture and to the ideas about it. When questions lead to the mere naming of different parts of the picture, observation is developed, but it is not true picture-study; that is, a consideration of the idea, the underlying meaning as expressed through the relations between the various parts.

AIDS TO ORAL LANGUAGE

Aids to oral language.—Language-work is greatly aided by drawing, handwork, dramatization. Any communication of ideas is really language, because the hand and the bodily gesture have a language of their own which really carries over into verbal language and enriches it.

Dramatization, drawing, and language bear a close relation to one another. A child of pre-school age strives to fix and clarify an idea, first by dramatization, then by oral language, then by drawing. The younger child dramatizes the different parts of the experience without much regard to the sequence in which the events happened. His subsequent oral expression is still disjointed, but is more related than his actions. His drawing illustrates isolated parts of the experience. As the child grows, his ideas become better organized, his dramatization shows an attempt to relate different incidents, his oral expression contains incidents woven into an embryo story, and his drawing represents several objects in some relation. Dramatization is composition in primitive language form; drawing is composition in picture-writing form. Both should be used in conjunction with language to aid in the organization of thought.

ATTAINMENTS

No ABSOLUTE standard can be set, for home conditions exercise great influence upon the language-development of children. Training should result in increased control, power, and desire in the following directions:

1. Control over tone of voice, enunciation, pronunciation, and grammatical construction.

2. Power to put ideas into language, either in asking questions or in making simple statements of fact.

3. Ability to understand simple conversation and to respond to directions which have been stated once.

4. Desire to find proper and adequate verbal expression for vague ideas and to add to the vocabulary.

The vocabulary should include the names of the most familiar objects in the school, home, and neighborhood; also such qualities and activities of these objects as are necessary for a child to understand in order to carry on his life and play-projects, or the qualities and activities concerning which he is curious.

GOOD MANNERS

Habits of courteous response and intercourse should be developed. "Please," "Thank you," "Excuse me," "Yes, Mother," should come naturally at the appropriate time. Replying when spoken to and waiting until others have finished speaking, should be one result of training.

Education in language is not measured by the number of words which a child can pronounce, but by the clearness of his ideas about a number of selected experiences, as shown through his adaptable, usual vocabulary.

HOME OPPORTUNITIES IN ENGLISH

Is ANYTHING more important in a child's education than that he should acquire the ability to express his thoughts in his own native tongue? In no way does the home have a greater advantage over the school than in the encouragement of free oral expression among the young folks of the family.

Every one knows that normal children make remarkable progress in the mastery of their mother tongue during the pre-school period. This mastery is attained through the abundant and free use of speech. Children use language as do adults in a dynamic way—they wish to influence the behavior of others, to get things done, and to enter into more intimate social relations with other people.

TABLE-TALK OUR BEST OPPORTUNITY

In MANY modern families the longest consecutive time the members spend together is at the table. Especially in city homes, where dinner is eaten at night, the evening meal is the greatest social opportunity of the day. There is then an instinctive disposition to linger about the table, quite unlike the eager haste seen at breakfast or at lunch. Work is over for the day, everybody is tired, even the little ones who have done nothing but play. Father is ready for slippers and a comfortable chair; the children are ready and eager to recount the experiences of the day. This is the time when each should be cheered, rested, and also stimulated by just the right sort of conversation, just the right sort of amusement. But often the hours at this one meeting-place are wasted, or even worse, and instead of leaving happy memories, leave unpleasant ones.

MEALTIME IS A SOCIAL AND MORAL OPPORTUNITY

Mealtime is a unique social and moral opportunity to children. "It is not the child of six who sits at the table and listens," says Colin A. Scott, "it is a human spirit, eager, curious, and wondering, surrounded by mysteries, willingly taking in what it does not understand to-day, but which will take possession of it next year and become a torch to light it on its way. It is through association with older people that these fructifying ideas come to the child; it is through such talk that he finds the world he is to possess."

Even parents can learn from the interchange of ideas. Socrates used to clear up the minds of young people by asking them apparently simple yet ingenious questions, but it has been suggested that he got his reward in clearing up his own mind by listening to their answers. The family table is a place where the wisest can learn and where the most foolish can sometimes teach. The old adage, "Children should be seen and not heard," ought to be amended. Children should be both seen and heard. Unless they are seen by, and see, wise people, how can they become wise, and unless they can be heard, how can they have their mistaken ideas properly corrected?

THE POSSIBILITIES OF TABLE-TALK

"THERE is," says Scott, "no educational opportunity in the home more important than the talk at table. There are homes in which the very atmosphere makes for wide knowledge of life, for generous aims, for citizenship in the world, as well as in the locality in which the home stands. Teachers in schools and colleges find the widest differences in the range of information and the quality of intelligence of the boys and girls who come to them. . . . The fortunate children have grown up in association with men and women of general intelligence, have heard them talk and have lived among their books."

One of the most attractive forms of culture which comes from table-talk is the ability to talk well. Those who cannot talk are in the danger expressed by Lord Bacon's pungent phrase of "suffering their thoughts to pass in *smother*." In a household where there is some thoughtful conversation upon the topics of the day, upon the simpler facts of science, or upon the work that is being done by the children in school, good minds are being developed. It is not, as we know so well, mere memorizing which constitutes the scholar. It is solitary rumination and social intercourse. The latter is just as important as the former. There is no better place for such intercourse than about the home table, where the earnest endeavors of even the youngest to enrich the conversation are received with kindliness, and where constant practice in expressing thought is bound to be helpful.

SUCH TALK SHOULD BE LARGE AND CHEERFUL

THERE should always be a certain largeness about the family conversation. Professor Mahaffy reminds us that "the weather is almost invariably the first pawn to be moved. This method of opening the game seems, however, so stale that every sensible person should have some paradox or

heresy ready, whereby he may break through this idle skirmishing and make the people about him begin to think as soon as possible." Largeness implies, too, the avoidance of remarks and comment upon food, so constant a habit in many homes. It also implies the avoidance of personalities on the part of either children or parents, in telling tales about teachers, fellow-pupils, neighbors, or of quarrels or disagreeable contact with friends. It implies the avoidance of any unkind or thoughtless remarks about anybody.

Another ideal for table-talk is cheerfulness. Father's business troubles, details of which can have no general interest, and only indicate selfish absorption on his part, have no place at table; but the interesting and amusing incidents of the day have an important place. Mother's household worries and cares, the petty details of work and troublesomeness of children, are not to be brought to the common meal. Remarks at table about personal faults or peculiarities of those present are to be avoided. It is a good general rule that nobody is ever to be pointed out or scolded at table and that disagreeable decisions, especially as regards the pleasures of the evening, are never to be made or announced at that time.

CUSTOMS INAUGURATED IN VARIOUS HOMES

IN A certain American home, described by a writer in the *Mother's Magazine,* a pleasant custom was inaugurated by the parents while the children were young. Said the mother to them: "A day started right is good until night. Now to breakfast hereafter everyone must bring a happy thought, and after grace is said, and before eating, repeat it."

"Will you bring a happy thought, Mamma?"

"Certainly."

"And Papa?"

"Of course he will."

The children took to the idea with great glee. Their "happy" thoughts would be something to talk about, and then there was always the anticipation of what Father and Mother would have to say.

The same writer tells of an English family that has always begun each meal with a song. "I have gone to that table in a very depressed mood, and when the song was ended I have had my entire view of things changed. In this family, the children, young and grown, are remarkably cheerful. They have an optimistic way of looking at things, and I attribute much of this to the cheer that is kept uppermost at the table, from the beginning of the song to the end of the last dish."

CHILDREN ARE SELF-CENTERED

Children are naturally self-centered. Their rehearsals of the annals of the day are often tiresome to their elders. It is desirable, however, in order to retain their confidence and to develop their interest in one another, that each should be given his turn at such rehearsal. The table where this is the only line of conversation is a dreary one, and the mother or father who will lift the eyes of the children to a wider horizon, after they have recounted their individual doings, is not only making everybody happy, but is wisely educating all.

SUGGESTIONS TOWARD MATERIAL FOR CONVERSATION IN FAMILIES WITH CHILDREN

IN SOME families it has seemed wise to go so far as to adopt a weekly program for conversation, to arrange either that the talk should be led in turn on successive mornings or evenings by different members of the family, or that definite topics which individuals have asked for should be taken up in turn. The suggestions that follow are, as to possibilities in the range of topics, to be brought to the attention of a family where there are children.

THINGS SEEN—CHILDREN MAY LEARN HOW TO OBSERVE AND HOW TO RELATE

"THERE is," says Charles Dudley Warner, "no entertainment so full of quiet pleasure as hearing a lady of cultivation and refinement relate her day's experiences in her daily round of calls, charitable visits, shopping, errands of relief, and calls of condolence. I do not mean gossip by any means, or scandal. A woman of culture skims over that like a bird, never touching it with the tip of a wing. What she brings home is the freshness and brightness of life. She touches everything so daintily, she hits off a character in a sentence, she gives the pith of a dialogue without tediousness, she mimics without vulgarity; her narrative sparkles, but it does not sting. The picture of her day is full of vivacity, and it gives new value and freshness to common things."

The experiences which are brought home by the father may be even more unusual and interesting. The children also have their fresh angle upon life and soon learn to imitate their parents in habits of observation, of humorous relation, and of acute detail. In riding or walking in the streets of town or city, some of the themes which the day's observations suggest are these: Many incidents of people coming and going, pretty hats and dresses, interesting conversation, curious characters, foreigners, or distinguished people. Looking in shop windows, one sees the artistic arrangements and the new fashions. In the market, mother notices the fresh vegetables and fruits, their beauty of color, and the facts about them as told by the grocer or marketman. Father, in the office, has had a letter with a foreign postmark; in the shop he has received a new invoice of goods from a foreign country; in the factory, he has installed a wonderful new machine, or has seen a fine piece of handwork turned out. The occasional glimpse at a swift airplane or dirigible balloon, with its marvelous mechanism, opens up a wide field for intelligent conversation and speculation. In the country or the parks there are the interesting things about Nature: the migration of birds, the blooming of flowers, indications of the change of the seasons, or such special features as birds' nests, the ant-hills, the habits of birds or animals. Comment upon a single incident in nature often leads to closer observation and to special reports from time to time on changes and developments.

SAMPLE QUESTIONS TO STIMULATE OBSERVATION AND THOUGHT

IT IS a good idea to fling forth a question suggested by something that has been seen and leave it with the children to think of or look up, referring to it again a day or two later. The following sample questions immediately suggest to the reader the item of observation which called them forth:

Which is the largest star you can see to-night?
Why are two stars in the Dipper called pointers?
What color are crows' eggs?
What use are crows to farmers?
How does a dog know a stranger?
What are some of the pets kept by sailors in our navy?
Does a bird ever sail with his tail toward the wind?
How can you tell an oak tree?
Why is salt water not good for plants?
What makes us sneeze?

What is the benefit of holes in the young bark of a tree?

Why does a duck never get wet?

Another class of questions may be propounded which have no direct connection with immediate observation, but which are thought-starters. They include such as these:

What makes a bee hum?
Does a tadpole know he will lose his tail?
Where are the frog's ears?
How did a pig nearly cause a war?
How did we come to use an umbrella?
Why will a rug smother a fire?
What should you do in case of fire at our house?
How do West Point cadets do honor to the flag?

PEOPLE MET—DEVELOPING HABITS, HELPFULNESS AND HUMANITY

OFTEN in his business relations a father meets people who have something of interest to offer in the exchange of ideas; people of different nationalities; people from different parts of our own country; persons who reveal curious phases of their own history. To cultivate this sort of genial intercourse with the folks one passes by is to awaken a steady interest in people and to develop a habit of kindly helpfulness in growing boys and girls which makes for a large humanity in later years. This, too, will awaken a general interest in community life—policemen, motormen, street-cleaners, men at the railroad crossings, girls behind the counter. Often one runs across bits of rare experience and sees the picturesque background of these lives. The ability to draw out such bits of human life and to relate them give one a rich fund for thought and conversation.

SAMPLE TREATMENT OF AN INTERESTING SUBJECT

ONE SUBJECT that is fascinating to children of all ages is that of transportation. They like things that "go" and they like to go themselves. While young children are not yet interested in the mechanics or economics of transportation, there are many simpler facts that are most engrossing to children of primary years.

Take such questions as these:

What are some of the things transported in our town?

(Food, clothing, materials for shelter, tools, people, etc.)

Why are they being carried about?

What kinds of power are used to carry them?

(Mules, horses, oxen, men, electricity, gasoline, etc.)

What kinds of wagons are used?

(Carts, trucks, wheelbarrows, bicycles, motor-cycles, automobiles, etc.)

GAMES PLAYED AT TABLE

IT IS often a pleasant diversion for people to play games at table, especially toward the close of the meal. The game of "Twenty Questions" is familiar and good. Telling a story in sections, demanding that the next take it up where the first left off, and so continuing in turn, is good exercise. Guessing games, describing some familiar or famous event or scene, are instructive. Guessing riddles or conundrums is a fine diversion and sharpens wits. An original game was invented by one motherly soul to teach children good manners and to avoid the nagging habit of incessantly calling attention to the lapses of others during the meal. After dinner was over, a short time was given occasionally during which each one in turn was allowed to imitate any wrong table-manners he had observed in someone else at the table, and then the guessing to whom the fault belonged was done by the others. The caricature of one's behavior made much fun and a deep impression, and at the same time took all the sting of personal rebuke out of the situation.

SOME RESULTS OF HAPPY MEALTIME

SUCH a mealtime, at morning or at noon, sends the family out separately with merry, loving faces to meet the burdens or responsibilities of the rest of the day. If it comes at the close of the day it leads to a pleasant evening. Children who enjoy such fellowship are not likely to be strongly attracted away from home at night. Even when the members of the family are obliged to be apart, they will be together in spirit. They are creating happy memories which will always hold them together. The problem of discipline in such households will never be a difficult one, for sympathy is thus continually being reëstablished. The children of such households grow up alert, interesting, and interested, to live lives full of intelligence and charm. Truly, upon such tables shine the high lights, and at such boards is perpetually broken the Bread of Life.

WORK AND PLAY IN ENGLISH *

By EDNA E. HARRIS

LITERATURE fulfills a twofold purpose: It widens our range of experiences, setting before us ideals toward the realization of which we may aspire, and it expresses perfectly and completely that which we feel and experience but imperfectly and incompletely express. It is both a vehicle of expression and a stimulus to larger growth.

The mother or teacher who wishes to develop a real love for literature must keep these two purposes ever present in mind. They will determine her selection of material, guide her as to method, and keep her more or less conscious of correct form.

But the six-year-old child must remain blissfully unconscious of all purpose. To him "English" should be simply an opportunity for making new acquaintances and renewing old friendships; an opportunity for reliving his experiences through rhymes, stories, pictures, dramatizations, and play.

Language is the golden key that unlocks for us the world's vast treasure-house. A child should be taught to look upon a book as a dear friend who introduces him to charming people and gives him delightful experiences.

The child who has never heard of Field, Riley, and Stevenson has been cheated of his birthright, and the one who does not know dear old Mother Goose—well, that is too dreadful to think of at all.

RHYMES

THE RHYME is the most natural approach to literature. The rhythmic appeal is strong, the content is simple and satisfying, and the technique of expression lies within the ability of the very young child.

The mother is unconsciously arousing her child's literary instincts when, in its earliest infancy, she repeats some dear old nursery rhyme, accompanying the words with appropriate movements of her baby's tiny fingers and toes. "This little pig went to market" has been many a man's initial experience in the world of literature.

Unfortunately, most mothers stop here, and the child's future development is left to his own undirected efforts or to the mechanical drudgery of classroom instruction.

Few children voluntarily read or memorize poetry after their nursery days. This is most unfortunate, especially so since there is such a wealth of rhymes and simple verses strikingly appropriate to the interests and everyday experiences of child life.

That it is true is undoubtedly due to the fact that few mothers concern themselves with their children's education, and the formality of the schools kills rather than fosters literary growth.

As a result, the normal child, with his overwhelming enthusiasm for life itself, turns his attention to the more physical activities of childhood.

From this it may easily be seen that the mother has a very great responsbility, but when we consider the material at her disposal, we cannot help but feel that it is an even greater privilege.

When Robert Louis Stevenson wrote that delightful little couplet:

"The world is so full of a number of things,
I'm sure we should all be as happy as kings,"

he might easily have been thinking of the wealth of material available for the English lesson, for no other subject offers such a rich and inexhaustible supply.

Rhythm.—Mother Goose forms the connecting link between the child and poetry proper. The universality of these rhymes leads us to believe

---

*After Miss Harris had finished these inspiring suggestions, she was in a quandary as to what name to give this chapter. She had two purposes in mind in her work: one was to show us how to help young children appreciate what is beautiful and worth while in the treasures of our literature, and the other was to show us how to help children express themselves adequately and effectively by means of language. To this mingling of language and literature there has occurred to her and to us no better name than the short, though perhaps inexpressive word, "English," the name of the language we use and the literature which we inherit.

Beneath all the methods suggested, you will see that Miss Harris has constantly in mind the enrichment of the lives of our children. These play-methods and dramatic methods and the use of pictures all help develop the imagination of children. No child will ever be really poor, the beginnings of whose educational life are based on these broad and dynamic methods.—*The Editors.*

that they were originally composed in unconscious response to the child's need for greater rhythmic expression.

That this rhythmic appeal is not a negligible consideration with the adult is evidenced by the number of people who "do not like blank verse" and infinitely prefer the lyric poets to those of more irregular stanzas.

Rhythm is by no means unimportant, and the child should be allowed to express this musical quality.

Imagination.—Children revel in personification, and simple rhymes or stories that personify animals or objects are to him an endless source of delight. "Hey Diddle Diddle," from Mother Goose, is an excellent example of personification.

In personifying, certain qualities or activities common to man are often transferred to objects or animals which do not naturally possess these qualities or partake of these activities. This transference of qualities and activities is the beginning of constructive imagination. It is a natural tendency of childhood which, if allowed to develop, leads to originality and inventiveness.

Over-development of the imaginative faculty is commonly mistaken for lying. If your child seems to be telling you a fairy-story, enter into the fun, do not punish him, but do not let him think for one moment that you consider it a "really truly" story.

Direct the imagination. Do not try to suppress it.

Memory and Observation.—Modern educators are beginning to realize the importance of awakening, developing, and directing the child's memory and observation.

It is a part of common experience that poetry is easier to memorize than prose, hence simple rhymes should be memorized as an initial step in the development of memory.

This need not necessarily be memory made easy solely by rhythm, for very often the simplest Mother Goose jingles embody a closely connected series of events. "Little Fishes in the Brook" illustrates this type of verse.

> "Little fishes in the brook,
> Papa catches with a hook,
> Mamma fries them in a pan,
> Baby eats them like a man."

The sequence is very apparent. A great value of these rhymes lies in the fact that they reduce life to its simplest terms and processes to their essential stages of advancement. Such natural sequences assist memorizing by directing the child's conscious attention to certain definite and closely related facts.

A simple illustration of a sequence with social interdependence will be found in the familiar "Pat a Cake" rhyme.

The following introduces still another—the miller:

> "Blow, wind, blow! and go, mill, go!
> That the miller may grind his corn,
> That the baker may take it, and into rolls make it,
> And send us some hot in the morn."

This series is a little more extensive than the others, and leads to the consideration of the final dependence of man upon nature.

Remember it is always the essential facts that should stand forth prominently in the consciousness of the little child.

Later on these same rhymes may serve as a point of departure for the study of more complex industrial processes.

A slightly different chain of consequences is depicted in "Humpty Dumpty" and "Three Wise Men of Gotham."

The preceding rhymes lead to the consideration of natural phenomena and industrial activities; the latter to moral reflection.

Not only are these sequences an aid to the development of memory, but they draw the child's conscious attention to the law of cause and effect, leading to closer and more accurate observation of things in their existing relations.

Children often ask, "What happened then?" Teach them to "forecast the coming event" by directing their thoughts to what might naturally be expected to happen.

Ideals and Experiences.—As has been previously stated, one of the most important functions of literature is to broaden our range of experiences and fill our minds with ideals toward the realization of which we may aspire.

These need not, necessarily, be moral ideals. They may be ideal environments or ideal experiences that may eventually lift the slum child from the sordid conditions of his immediate life, or arouse and awaken the child of good but limited experiences to the possibilities of a larger way of living.

Humor.—There is a current proverb to the effect that a man may be known by the things he laughs at. This is, to a very great extent, true. A keen sense of humor is such a choice possession it would almost seem as though it were an especial gift, like genius. Nearly every one starts out in life with the precious gift, but many lose it on the way. Without it, life would be unbearable. The perverted type is worse than no humor at all.

Anything in the way of exaggeration or surprise fills the child with delight. The nonsense tale is wholesomely humorous, and it usually depicts a series of situations resulting in consequences which contain real moral value.

Ethics.—Few parents and teachers resort to literature as an aid in discipline, yet it is far more interesting than the prevailing methods and, in most cases, quite as efficacious.

Label the "smart" child "Simple Simon" and see how soon his smartness will end. The child who constantly justifies himself by "laying it on to the other fellow" has no relish for being called "Silly Jill," who tumbled simply because Jack did. The sad fate of "Humpty Dumpty," especially when personally experienced, is quite likely to arrest the reckless climber.

"A dillar, a dollar, a ten-o'clock scholar" is a pretty sure cure for lateness.

Stevenson's
  "Birdie with a yellow bill"
that
      Hopped upon the window-sill,
      Cocked his shining eye and said,
      'Ain't you 'shamed, you sleepy-head!' "

will prove a pleasanter and more effective means of awakening the "sleepyhead" than any plan ever devised by a despairing parent, and "Wee Willie Winkie" will help get the grumbler to bed in a happier mood.

Read the charming stories and verses in the "Fun and Thought for Little Folk," "Golden Stories," and "Famous Stories and Verses." The children may not yet appreciate the implied moral, it is true, but never mind.

  "A man's reach should exceed his grasp,
    Or what's a heaven for?"

We should have ideas in the mind as we have money in the bank, to prepare for the coming of "the rainy day."

It matters little whether the child really understands a poem now, so long as it is worded simply and embodies wholesome ideas which lie somewhere within the range of either real or imaginary experiences.

Ideas are like seeds which sink into the subconscious, where they germinate and grow until, in due process of time, they force their way through consciousness and make their meaning clear. They may be like Wordsworth's "Daffodils." You remember the lines:

  "For oft, when on my couch I lie
    In vacant or in pensive mood,
  They flash upon that inward eye
    Which is the bliss of solitude;
  And then my heart with pleasure fills,
    And dances with the daffodils."

Surely literature fulfills a worthy purpose if it does no more than fill our "vacant moods" with gladness.

Hero-worship. The mere memorizing of golden texts is, of course, not the best activity connected with literature for little children. The main service of books is that in them we have life speaking to life. Their best contribution is that they show us how goodness looks when it is lived. Whether the lives portrayed be those of the kindly fairies, or the mythical heroes, or the unselfish men and women of history, they all speak to the heart of the child. It is from these "Ten Commandments in action," these Beatitudes incarnate, that the child gets the impelling desire to rise up and be like them.

METHODS OF INTRODUCING VERSE TO A CHILD

As to method, I am inclined to believe the less of it the better. First get the spirit of the poem. Feel it, become thoroughly saturated with it, then repeat it over and over, again and again, to and with your child until he, too, catches its joy.

Help him to speak the lines correctly, but not too correctly, with painful emphasis on enunciation and expression. Just get the words, that is all.

A little four-year-old girl went to the window early one morning and, seeing the bright sunshine, clapped her hands and exclaimed:

      "A sunny day,
      A day to play."

Encourage your child to make up rhymes.

Help him by playing a game in which each tries to outdo the other in naming words that rhyme with a given word.

Illustration:

man	**all**
can	**ball**
fan	fall
ran	tall

If you are familiar with a musical adaptation of a rhyme, introduce it as a song.

If you have a good picture illustrating it, establish a visual association by showing the picture After the child has become familiar with a number of such pictures, show them in succession. having him repeat the rhymes which they illustrate.

THE STORY

IF EDUCATION is designed to meet the needs of life, the story should occupy a place of honor in the course of study. No other device is so irresistible in its appeal, no other includes in itself so many educational advantages, and no other is so sadly neglected. We tell stories too infrequently, and the few that we do tell are not sufficiently varied.

Were mothers and teachers to realize the benefits to be derived from story-telling, they would selfishly tell them for their own pleasure, if not for the sake of the children.

The story is the magic cloak that transforms us according to our wish; the winged slippers that carry us whithersoever we would go. Even if you are of the Philistine mind and prefer not to travel in the land of fancy, story-telling has practical advantages which none of us can afford to ignore.

The story embodies all the essential characteristics of the rhyme, the values of which have already been mentioned, but it is more flexible than the rhyme and affords greater opportunities for self-expression.

Stories stand for progress, for growth; they exist in response to a universal impulse toward development. They interpret our experience, and they answer a real need for adventure. Life demands that the individual shall transcend the narrow limits of his own experiences; it tempts him to do this by appealing to his innate curiosity. Whether his adventures be made into the land of fancy or that of fact matters little, so long as they widen his own experience and enable him to enter into a sympathetic appreciation of the lives of others.

Tell your child stories. Tell them principally to give him pleasure, but, as a secondary consideration, to enrich his imagination, stimulate him to self-expression, and develop conversational power.

The best way to tell a story is to tell it without thinking much about method. Get the spirit, familiarize yourself with the principal characters and events, then when you are quite sure of the story, tell it. Power comes through doing, and your second attempt will exceed your first far beyond your fondest expectations.

After you have told the story a few times, let your child tell it, repeating it *in his own words* with the possible exception of a few conversational phrases which have become sanctioned through long usage.

Whatever you do, *do not interrupt* to correct errors in English. Interruptions embarrass the child and tend to divert his attention. After the child has told the story, correct any erroneous impressions he may have in regard to the facts, and tactfully suggest better phrasing.

§5. PICTURES AN AID TO THE STORY

When children find difficulty in following the events, the memory may be strengthened by the use of pictures. These may be imaginary drawings made by the child himself, pictures cut from old books or magazines, or those made by tracing around cardboard patterns and filling in the outlines.

Paste the pictures on cards and arrange the cards in sequence. In this way the story may be told with the aid of several pictures. Whenever pictures are used, each picture should represent a distinct phase of the story.

WHAT STORIES TO TELL

The age and natural interests of the child should determine your selection of stories. The six-year-old child prefers those which move rapidly and naturally, each event presenting in itself a simple but distinct picture.

"The Three Bears," "The Three Pigs," "The Old Woman and Her Pig," "Red Riding Hood," "Chicken Little," "The Little Red Hen," "The Little Small Red Hen," "Peter Rabbit," and "The Gingerbread Boy," are always prime favorites.

Cumulative stories appeal to a child's love of repetition.

The transition from the rhyme to the story proper may be made by means of simple rhyme-stories like "The Old Woman and Her Pig," or stories in which rhythmic repetition occurs at more or less regular intervals.

These should be followed by the nonsense-tale, the fairy-story or wonder-tale, and nature-stories which are rich in personification. Simple myths and fables will serve as an introduction to the short story.

We are too apt to limit our story-telling to stories having educational value. It should never be forgotten that the story's first mission is to give pleasure, and the many charming stories written with no other end in view should find a ready welcome in both home and school.

DRAMATIZATION

A sigh of satisfaction follows the conclusion of the story; then—"Let's play it," suggests someone. This is a moment of opportunity, for it is only by actually participating in an experience that we are really able to comprehend. Besides, the dramatization will be the test of the child's understanding of the story and will enable you to decide just which parts you should emphasize when you tell it again.

Simply considered as a pleasure-producing resource, dramatization takes the lead, for it is here that full scope is given the imagination and self-expression has free play.

The method is practically the same as that of the reproduction-story. First, tell the story, then discuss it informally as to characters, settings, and events. When the children are familiar with it, "play it." Conversational phrases may be memorized, but the children should be permitted to work out all details for themselves.

Some other day retell the story, then discuss it again in the light of the deeper understanding gained through the previous dramatization. After this second discussion "play it" again.

In my experience I have found that many children who are indifferent to, or mildly interested in, a first dramatization become enthusiastic as time goes on. Repeated dramatizations enable them to get the spirit of the story and also develop confidence and skill.

Do not attempt to be too realistic. The living-room, nursery, or out of doors will furnish all the necessary stage accessories. As far as possible let the children use their own inventiveness; they will think of things that would never occur to the adult.

In my own classroom, "Simple Simon" fishes for his "whale" with a blackboard pointer, using the waste-paper basket for a pail, and "Boy Blue" sleeps peacefully under a cloth-covered chair while his cows wander serenely through rows of children who represent the corn.

One day when we were about to dramatize "Hey Diddle, Diddle," I was surprised to find that someone had been selected to represent the moon. I protested mildly, but was told the cow *had* to jump over the moon. She did, quite solemnly, after the manner of boys playing leap-frog; no one was amused, the children seemed to consider it quite the proper thing.

It is nearly always possible to assemble a sufficient number of children to complete a dramatization. Little neighbors will be only too glad to join in the fun. Adults may do so without injuring their dignity, but whenever this is impossible, a child will find great pleasure dramatizing a simple story or rhyme alone. Children are adepts as "quick-change-artists," and very effective dramatizations may be made by the child who plays by himself.

PANTOMIME

WE MUST not leave the subject of dramatization without mentioning the possibilities suggested by the pantomime. Either stories or simple experiences may be presented in this way. Where groups of children are playing, a number may be selected to enact the pantomime, after which the others may be requested to reproduce it in story form. This is a particularly useful exercise when the children who tell the story have had no previous knowledge of pantomime, so are obliged to depend entirely upon that which they actually see.

We will suppose that three children are playing. One should be requested to leave the room while the others decide upon a pantomime.

A decision having been made, the other child is summoned. He must watch very carefully in order to find the material for his story.

Illustration: A little girl dressed in mother's hat and shawl walks across the room. She pretends to open a door, then bows to another child who stands behind an improvised counter. The second child returns the bow. The little girl looks about as though searching for something. She finally selects an imaginary article, which she hands to the child back of the counter. The second child pretends to wrap the package, then gives it to the little girl. After paying for the package and receiving her change, she bows again and walks away. The story will be somewhat as follows:

A lady walked along the street. She came to a store and went in. She said, "Good-morning," to the storekeeper. He said, "Good-morning," too. The lady looked about for a few minutes, then she bought something. The storekeeper wrapped it up, and the lady paid for her package. Then she said, "Good-morning," and walked away.

ORIGINAL STORIES

WHILE the child has been listening to stories and dramatizing them, his thoughts have been unconsciously organizing, his ideas have been taking more definite form. He is now ready to tell his own stories. This does not mean that all attempts to express himself originally are to be discouraged until this time; it simply means that these earlier attempts should be incidental, unconscious, and undirected. Original stories may now have a regular place in the program, and they should be more or less consciously directed to real story form.

The four difficulties usually encountered by the classroom teacher are (1) limited experiences from which ideas may be drawn, (2) a meager vocabulary, (3) lack of initiative, and (4) mind-wandering. The first three belong to the school rather than the home, the last is common to both. This is one of my reasons for so constantly emphasizing the importance of simple classifications and sequences. Through these the child's ideas will become more consciously organized, his power of concentration will develop, and he will be stimulated to closer and more accurate observation.

When the first three difficulties are experienced it is simply a question of time and patience. Give a rich and varied story-experience with plenty of opportunities for reproducing the experience either in story or dramatic form.

Original stories may be based on experience or pictures, or they may be purely imaginative. The experience-story will, undoubtedly, be embellished by the child's imagination, but the main facts will probably be told very much as they actually occurred. The picture-story needs a little judicious direction, but the imaginative story should be absolutely free.

A delightful form of imaginative story is the "Dream Story." In this the child closes his eyes and pretends to sleep. When he awakens he tells what he has dreamed.

HOW TO USE PICTURE-STORIES

THERE are two ways in which the picture-story may be presented. In the first the child is given a picture and allowed to ramble on at will. The second, which I myself prefer, I call the development-method.

Using as an illustration the picture, "The Village Choir," on page 37 of vol. 4 of the BOOKSHELF, let us ask the children to study it, then tell us what they have seen. By removing the picture and having them describe it from memory, we compel them to speak in terms of the past. This simple little exercise enables us to overcome the child's natural tendency to talk only in the present tense.

The description will probably be somewhat as follows:

"I saw six little children (or three boys and three girls). They were chasing two geese down the street. They had hold of hands. There was a grandpa and a little girl watching. One boy had fallen down."

This is a good description of the picture, but it is not a story. A story must be developed by tracing backward to a probable beginning and forward to a probable ending.

Why are the children chasing the geese?
Why are the children playing in the road?
Where did the geese come from?
Will the little boy cry?
What will the geese do? etc.

This will require definite thinking, but it is an exercise well worth while. Try it with your children and see what their stories will be.

The BOOKSHELF has a host of pictures about which the children can weave their own stories. A dozen of them are:

	Vol.	Page
The Land of Nod	1	67
The Doll's Bath	1	122
My Scottie	1	143
Please Read Another Story, Grandma	1	242
The Little Gray Kitten	1	279
Breakfast	1	287
What Brilliance! What Splendor!	2	313
The Fairy of the Pond	3	148
American Indian Warrior	3	288
Can't You Talk?	4	36
Fishing	7	195
Crabbing is Fun	7	256

My own little folks always enjoy a picture of two little kittens seated under the shelter of an open umbrella while a frog watches them through the pouring rain.

The situation is simple, but it has been the source of many a heated argument. Some of the children think that the sun was shining when the kittens started out walking, and they carried the umbrella to protect them from the sun. Others declare that it doesn't belong to the kittens at all, but that someone was sitting under it and left it there. Still others are firm in the conviction that a little girl was carrying it and the wind blew it out of her hand.

The endings are just as varied. Some think that it will stop raining and the kittens will fold up the umbrella and walk away. Others, equally confident, believe that the little girl will come back for the umbrella and leave the poor kittens out in the rain.

Even the probable conversation gets its full share of discussion. Some think the kittens are inviting the frog to come under the umbrella, while others feel certain that they are saying, "Go away, you horrid thing. We're afraid of you." If the frog is invited he usually accepts the invitation, but recently one little girl assured us that what he really did say was, "No, I thank you. I like the rain."

Just as soon as a child has completed a story to his satisfaction, he claims it as his own, and woe betide any boy or girl who dares tell the same story without first giving due credit to the source from which it was derived.

This seems to me a much better method, although I must confess it is slower, and for a long time the stories are likely to be very crude.

Is it not wiser to develop power of expression rather than to impose purely arbitrary results which have implied neither effort nor intelligence on the part of the child?

OBJECT LESSONS

THE CHILD should not be limited to that in which the imagination is dominant. There are other ways by which attention must be developed, definite information must be imparted, and accurate observations must be made.

Every child manifests a natural curiosity as to the world about him. Satisfy this curiosity and through it awaken interest in other related things. If your child does not possess a natural curiosity, stimulate one by carefully worded statements or questions which will appeal directly to his imaginative sense.

The bright fire burning on the hearth—does it mean anything to the child? Make it mean something. Introduce the subject by a remark like this: "Who would ever think that a plant which lived thousands of years ago would be the means of keeping us warm to-day?" The apparent improbability of such an assertion arouses curiosity; now tell the story of a piece of coal—how thousands of years ago, long before there were any people on the earth, huge plants and gigantic trees covered its surface. Describe how these plants and trees were gradually buried beneath the soil and compressed into hard layers. Talk about the miner with his lamp, pick, and shovel; the mine, with its long dark tunnels and winding passageways. Describe the mining-cars and the cages which carry the coal to the surface. Tell how it is finally prepared for its journey to the far distant cities where it is sold.

Discuss the various uses of coal—to give us warmth, to cook our food, to make the gas which lights our houses, and to furnish the power which moves machinery, trains, and boats.

This discussion will awaken interest in other kinds of mines, as the iron mine, which supplies iron for our stoves and the horses' shoes; or the silver mine, which furnishes us with knives, forks, and spoons. Trace to its source a penny, the blade of a knife, or any other simple object that has had its origin in a mine.

Simple nursery rhymes, as "Pat a Cake" and "Blow, Wind, Blow," or "The Story of a Loaf of Bread," may be taken as the point of departure for a lesson on rye or wheat. Describe the preparation of the field, the sowing of the seeds, the action of the sun and rain, the growth from tiny green shoots, the golden grain, harvesting the wheat, threshing it, the miller, the action of the mill-wheel, the baker with his huge ovens and long baking shovel, and finally the baker's boy who brings us hot rolls "in the morn."

From this lead to the origins of other kinds of food and drinks, as sugar, butter, tea, coffee, milk etc. The story of honey never fails to delight. If you are not sure of the origins, look them up in some good encyclopedia. The encyclopedia habit is an excellent habit to form.

When we were reciting "Baa, Baa, Black Sheep" one morning, I asked the children what they supposed "the master," "the dame," and "the little boy who lived down the lane" would do with the wool. The query led to the wildest speculations, so I told them the story about wool. The children were much interested. They thought that it was very kind of the sheep to give away his coat. Some of them felt very sorry that he had to lose it, fearing that he might suffer from the cold. However, they were reassured when told that the coat would grow again.

The following topics are merely suggestive: wool, the fleecy covering of sheep; the sheep, the shepherd; washing and cleaning the sheep; shearing them; combing, spinning, and weaving the wool; uses—clothing, etc.

From wool we may proceed to silk and cotton, tracing the silk ribbon to the busy little silkworm, and the piece of cotton to the fluffy cotton boll.

From the clock we may trace back to the sundial, thence to the sun itself. The sun—the source of all light—suggests other forms of light, as the candle, the lantern, the kerosene lamp, gas, and electricity.

The object-lesson is so closely connected with the nature-lesson, it is difficult to tell just where one begins and the other ends. However, the line of demarcation is unimportant. Whether we class these lessons under "language" or "nature" matters little, so long as we really give them in such a manner that we shall awaken within the child some realization of "the miraculous interestingness" of ordinary things. And whether we call our conversations "nature" or "language," let us always begin with the objects themselves, and not with what somebody has said about them. Don't be bookish, when real things are all about you.

CLASSIFICATIONS

THE OBJECT-LESSON leads us again to a consideration of classifications, a subject that cannot be too constantly emphasized. Children are not interested in abstract classifications, but they do enjoy organizing their knowledge, just as they enjoy sorting beads, sticks, and blocks according to color, form, and size.

With little people this should not be at all formal. In fact, it should be presented as a game, usually along very broad lines. See who can name the greatest number of things coming under definite headings, or collect pictures and make charts, or arrange them in booklet-form. The following topics will probably suggest others:

Animals—barnyard, field, forest, jungle.

Birds—according to color, size, time of appearance, etc.

Clothing—man, animals, fish, birds.

Objects—according to color, form, size, uses, etc.

Trades—blacksmith, baker, printer, etc.

Stores—grocery, fruit, dry goods, etc.

Things sold in stores—sugar, salt, flour, spices, etc.

Homes—man, animals, birds, insects, fish.

School—home of educational life.

State House—home of political life.

Church—home of religious life, etc.

Charts.—Collect pictures and paste them on charts. Have each chart illustrate some definite idea. (See preceding list.)

Booklets.—Collect pictures and paste them on sheets of drawing-paper. Arrange in booklet-form. Have each booklet illustrate some definite idea. These booklets will be more interesting and more instructive if they are arranged so that they show some kind of progression, as:

Page 1. House—the child's own home.

Page 2. School—the home of the child's educational life.

Page 3. Church—the home of his religious life.

Page 4. Town Hall, Opera House, etc.—the home of his social life.

Extend by showing the homes of the various civic units, as: county courthouse, state capitol, and United States capitol. Whenever possible, actual photographs should be used. For many of these booklets "Stamp-craft" pictures or "sticky backs" may be used. Paste these on sheets of drawing-paper, and arrange in booklet form.

CORRECTION OF ERRORS

UP TO the present, the child has been unconsciously acquiring good English habits, but there comes a time when he must be made conscious of certain incorrect forms. Now the work of correction begins. This is often far more difficult than it at first appears, for he must be made conscious of his errors without being made self-conscious—I hope the distinction is perfectly clear. When children are made self-conscious they refuse to express themselves at all.

With my own little people I try to create a class-consciousness of good English. By this I mean that the class as a whole is made conscious of errors without drawing attention to the children who have made the mistakes. Certain errors are anticipated and games are devised whereby the correct form may be established in the child's mind. All errors are noted, even those which are apparently ignored. For instance, having heard a child say "ain't got," I would ignore it for the time being. A day or so later, I would probably say, "Do you know, the other day I heard a little boy say 'ain't got.' Isn't that a funny way to talk? What do you suppose he meant?" If no one knows, I tell them; then we proceed to include this word in our game of "catch." This is simply a game in which we watch out for incorrect expressions. Whenever we hear one we say, "Tom's caught!" then point out the mistake that he has made. No one wants to be caught, so everyone watches, but if anyone is caught we laugh good-naturedly, just as we would in a game of tag.

A helpful device for learning to spell and understand the meanings of words is by making nursery dictionaries. Little children are often as interested in finding and analyzing a new word as a new bug. Have ready small oblong sheets of paper with a margin of an inch at the left. Let the child print neatly at the top of one of these sheets the word which you are studying. Then, after you have found the simplest possible definition, print this yourself or have him print it beneath the word. Put these slips in alphabetical order in a special box, or fasten them with a clip inside a cardboard binder which the child made or labeled for the purpose.

An appendix may be made of common errors. Let him print at the top of each page the correct word or phrase, and beneath it in smaller letters the incorrect one which he sometimes uses.

So in the home, the mother may tactfully point out the child's errors, and the entire family may "play the game." Occasionally the older folks should use an incorrect expression so that the child may "catch" them.

"Ain't" is an ever-present enemy, not particularly easy to overcome. We had been singing Stevenson's "Birdie with a Yellow Bill," one morning, when I said, "Children, I am quite sure that little birdie never went to school. Had he gone, he would have known that ladies and gentlemen never say 'ain't.' They say 'aren't.'" A few days later a little fellow came running up to me, his eyes sparkling with the joy of discovery. This is what he said. "I know all about that 'ain't' word now. If a thing 'ain't' there, you don't say no more 'it ain't there,' you say, 'it aren't there!'"

The children had become conscious of the incorrectness of the expression, but "aren't" didn't always seem to fit. We finally disposed of the matter by calling "ain't" an ugly old word that just steps in and takes the place of several very nice little words, but the children still find it difficult to determine just which one of those "nice little words" should be used.

"Did" is a wonderful little helper when we are trying to master the past tense. Do something, then ask the child to tell you what you did. Let him do something, then you tell him what he did. Illustration: "You walked," "You skipped," "You sang," etc.

"Was" and "were" may be introduced in the same way. Do something, then ask, "What was I doing?" The child must answer in a complete statement. "You were writing" knitting, singing, or whatever your particular activity might have been.

Let the child do something, then ask, "What were you doing?" Be sure that the child gives a complete statement in reply.

Have the child perform some simple imitative activity, as a horse galloping, a rabbit hopping, a soldier marching, etc. Ask, "What were you doing?" The answer must be given in full:

"I was a little girl writing to Santa Claus."

"I was an airplane sailing through the sky."

"I was a farmer plowing" (a lady knitting, sewing, sweeping), etc.

Children delight in these simple pantomimes. They may be made still more interesting by turning them into guessing games. "Try to guess" what the child has been imitating, or do something yourself and make him guess.

"See" and "saw" may be introduced in various ways. The child may close his eyes and see some imaginary object, then tell what he has seen. He may look out of the window or he may look at an object or a picture of an object and tell what he has seen. This, too, becomes more interesting when used as a guessing game.

"See" and "saw" are combined with "go" and "went" in the journey game.

The child takes an imaginary journey. Let him harness up a chair and drive away, sail away on a rug, or travel on a "make-believe" train. When he returns ask, "Where did you go?" and "What did you see?" Introduce "bring" and "brought" by asking, "Did you bring me anything? What did you bring me?"

Let him go to a "make-believe" store. When he returns ask, "To what store did you go? What did you buy?" By asking him to name other things that he has seen, you will stimulate closer and more accurate observation and teach him to classify.

Illustration:

Mother. "To what store did you go?"
Child. "I went to a fruit-store."
Mother. "What did you buy?"
Child. "I bought some apples."
Mother. "What else did you see?"
Child. "I saw oranges, pears, bananas," etc.

Another good "make-believe" game is the "If-I-were" game. It proceeds somewhat as follows:
Question: "If I were a man, I would be a builder. What would you be if you were a man?"
Answer: "If I were a man, I would be a doctor," etc.

Other suggestions:

"If I were a lady, I would be—" etc.

"If I were a fairy" (tell what you would do).

"If I were a traveler" (tell where you would go).

"If I were a painter" (tell what you would paint).

This is particularly interesting when a group of children are playing. Follow out one line of thought with the entire group.

"It is he," "it is she," and "isn't" are emphasized in the following games:

Game 1
Child. "I am thinking of someone. Who is it?"
Mother. "Is it father?"
Child. "No, it isn't he."
Mother. "Is it grandma?"
Child. "No, it isn't she."
Mother. "Is it Cousin Lucy?"
Child. "Yes, it is she."

Game 2 (a group game).

One child closes his eyes while another leaves the room. The first child then opens his eyes and tries to guess who has gone.

Children. "Who has gone?"
Leader. "Is it Mary?"
Children. "No, it isn't she," etc.

"Is it I?" is emphasized in the following, which is another group-game.

Game 3 (a group game).

One child is blindfolded, another taps her on the shoulder. The blindfolded child proceeds to guess who it is.

Susie.   "Is it Mary?"
Margaret. "No, it is I."
Susie.   "Is it Margaret?"
Margaret. "Yes, it is I."

Margaret then takes Susie's place and the game goes on.

The following will help to overcome the expression "have got." One child hides his eyes while a button is given to some other child. The first child then opens his eyes and guesses who has the button.

Harry. "Have you the button, John?"
John. "No, I haven't it."
Harry. "Have you the button, Mary?"
Mary. "No, I haven't it."

The game may be modified by directing the question to the entire group.

Harry.   "Has Mary the button?"
Children. "No, she hasn't it," etc.

Good English is largely a matter of environment—the child speaks only that which he hears; but these little exercises will make him definitely conscious of certain incorrect expressions and teach him the correct ones to use.

While it is true that the mother cannot control her child's environment when he is away from home, she can overbalance the neighborhood environment by making the child definitely conscious of the difference between good and bad English form.

One summer I watched with great interest two boys who had been brought up in a typical New England home. Their English was delightful, a decided contrast to that of the children with whom they played. Occasionally the younger boy would lapse into the environmental English, but he was immediately brought to task by the older child, who always said, "Remember, Mother doesn't like us to talk that way." Within a few weeks the country children were making a conscious effort to imitate the little New Englanders. Surely their mother built better than she knew.

THE READING MOTHER

By STRICKLAND GILLILAN

I had a mother who read to me
Sagas of pirates who scoured the sea,
Cutlasses clutched in their yellow teeth,
"Blackbirds" stowed in the hold beneath.

I had a mother who read me lays
Of ancient and gallant and golden days;
Stories of Marmion and Ivanhoe
Which every boy has a right to know.

I had a mother who read me tales
Of Gilbert the hound of the hills of Wales,
True to his trust till his tragic death,
Faithfulness blent with his final breath.

I had a mother who read me things
That wholesome life to the boy heart brings—
Stories that stir with an upward touch.
Oh, that each mother of boys were such!

You may have tangible love untold;
Caskets of jewels and coffers of gold.
Richer than I you can never be—
I had a mother who read to me.

READING AND STORY TELLING

THE BABY'S STORY–HOUR

By Mary Adair

FOR THE first education of the baby through stories, three types are useful. These are *Lullabies, Body-Stories,* and *Egoistic Stories.* For the beginnings of story and of story-telling, one had need to rub a lamp or question the Sphinx. So elemental is the first story that it seems only a voice, a deep calling unto deep; as people who pass give the sign, and the countersign is given in return, so mother and child call to and answer each other.

The mother sings a lullaby as the earliest story, the embryo of literature, so to speak. It is the unutterable made vocal, the age-long story of love that slumbers not nor sleeps. To be sure, in the present oversophisticated moment some mothers do not croon to their babies, but happily the lapse is only for a moment; presently Nature will bestir herself, and some dear old "bye bye" will come to life again. Mother Goose is a wise old bird; she will know what's what, and when's when, for no doubt Nature senses the psychological moment better than we think.

LULLABIES

THE lullaby of my babyhood was a weird one enough:

"Hush ye, hush ye, little pet ye—
The Black Douglas will nae get ye"

but still across the span of time I hear it now as saying only, "My darling, my darling, you are a precious jewel in a golden casket within a fortified castle surrounded by a moat across which no evil may pass. So sleep, my little one."

Wherever she learned it, the Southern Mammy is the star performer in this first "story hour."

An ancient lullaby is illustrated in such melodies as "The Alabama Lullaby":

"Little Pickaninny, close yo' eyes an' go to sleep,
Moon am swingin' low and spooky shadows 'gin to creep."

BODY–STORIES

AFTER lullabies—what? The baby would say, "Oh, some story with movement and human touch, as well as sing-song." Therefore, *Body-Stories* seem to be the logical form. These are played as they are rhymed, and may be grouped into whole-body plays, riding-plays, knee-plays, foot-plays, face-plays, ear-plays, nose-plays, hand-and-finger plays.

The first of the whole-body plays is the burrowing game, in which a gentle hand or maybe a head fumbles about in the pit of baby's stomach and a growly voice says "Boo-oo," or

"See the little mousie creeping up the stair,
Looking for a warm nest—there, oh, there!"

In this game the climax occurs with the fumbling in the hollow of baby's neck. These stories always demand an encore.

RIDING–GAMES

THE THRILL enters at this stage. Well-known games are: "Ride a Cock-Horse," etc., from Mother Goose.

"The baby goes riding away and away,
Goes riding to hear what the dog has to say,"
etc.

—*From "Father and Baby Plays," by Emilie Poulsson.*

"All the pretty little horses,
  Black and brown and gray and white and bay,
All the pretty little horses
  You shall see some day, some day."

or

"Gallop and gallop and gallop away,
  See how my baby can gallop to-day."

§5. KNEE-GAMES

"What do I see? Baby's knee—
Tickily, tickily, tic, tac, tee;
One for a penny, two for a pound,
Tickily, tickily, round and round."

"One, two, three, away goes she,
Sliding down father's knee."

§6. FOOT-PLAYS

"Up, down—up, down,
  One foot up and one foot down,
  All the way to London town,
  Tra la la la la la."
          —*Mother Goose.*

"Shoe the old horse and shoe the old mare,
But let the little colt go bare. Rap-a-tap."
          —*Mother Goose.*

"Blacksmith, Blacksmith, fellow fine,
Can ye shoe this horse o' mine?" etc.
          —*Mother Goose.*

"Pitty, Patty, Polt,
Shoe the wild colt,
Here a nail, there a nail—
Pitty, Patty, Polt."
          —*Mother Goose.*

"Kick about, kick about, farmer's man,
  Thresh the corn as fast as you can;
Kick it and stick it and pick it with glee,
  And put in the barn for Tommy and me."
        —*Adapted from "Pat a Cake."*

§7. EAR-GAME

"What's here?
Baby's ear.
Click-clack,
Put it back."

§8. NOSE-GAME

"What's here? Baby's nose.
  Click, clack, on it goes."
(*Making believe to take off and hastily to put it on again.*)

§9. HAND-AND-FINGER STORIES

THESE are so numerous, it is only necessary to suggest the types. Other contributors have discussed these.

"Pat a cake, Pat a cake," etc.
          —*Mother Goose.*

"This little pig went to market."
          —*Mother Goose.*

"Thumbkin, Pointer, Middleman big,
Sillyman, Weeman, rig-a-jig-jig."

"This is mother, this is father, this is brother tall,
This is sister, gay and happy, this the baby small."

"Here's my Father's knives and forks,
Here's my Mother's table,
Here's my Sister's looking-glass,
And here's the baby's cradle."

"Here is the church, and here is the steeple,
Open the door and see all the people."

"Thicken man build the barn,
Thinnen man spool the yarn,
Longen man stir the brew,
Gowden man made a shoe,
Littlen man all for you."
          —*Old Norse Game.*

§10. FACE-PLAYS

(*Indicating the parts by a light touch*)

1. "Knock at the door, peep in,
   Lift up the latch and walk in."

2. "Here sits the Lord Mayor," etc.
          —*Mother Goose.*

3. "Forehead, eyes, nose, mouth,
   Dearest baby, North or South."
          —*Emilie Poulsson.*

These may be continued indefinitely as to sources, developing later into cat's-cradle play and object-stories.

EGOISTIC STORIES

There is a third group of baby stories of great educational importance. These are usually in prose-form and frequently incidental, the chief educational value being the emphasis upon a child's interest in himself, his name, his possessions, his comings and goings, etc.

"Click-clack, click-clack,
   Off we go on horse's back.
   Ride and ride a mile or more
   Till we come to Grandma's door.
   Whoa! now, Dobbin, dear,
   Grandma, see who's here."
                —*Emilie Poulsson.*

In "Child-Stories and Rhymes" Miss Poulsson has stories of baby's spoon, baby's pillow, and other endless possessions.

An adaptation from Tagore's "Crescent Moon" gives charming illustrations of egoistic tales. One represents the child talking—he says: "Mother, you are riding in your palanquin and I am riding beside you on my red horse (his toy-horse). You will not be afraid, Mother; I will take care of you," etc.

BEGINNINGS OF PERSONAL HISTORY TALES

These tales represent the germinal form of the biographical-autobiographical and personal-history-tales of great persons in great literature; hence their importance and the responsibility of mothers to understand the significance of beginnings.

THE USE OF MOTHER GOOSE

"No, no, my melodies will never die,
While nurses sing or babies cry."

Mother Goose was the first musical comedy. When you ask yourself why children in all ages and many lands have enjoyed these infantile rhymes, there seems to be no better reason than that given by Joseph Lee: "We like it because we are tuned to like it."

But who is Mother Goose? Since the higher criticism has destroyed the legend of an English Mrs. Vergoose or a French Mère L'Oye or even a real Mother Goose who used to sing these rhymes to her grandchildren, we have to acknowledge that this nursery classic does not trace its origin to any individual author.

What, then, is Mother Goose? A Mother Goose rhyme is a short verse with a rhythmical beat that almost, or quite, makes sense. The verses of many poets do not belong to the Mother Goose category because they are too sophisticated or too meaningful or not rhythmic enough.

THEY SATISFY THE INSTINCT OF RHYTHM

The strength of Mother Goose is that her rhymes are rhythmical. The baby's ga-a, ga-a is rhythmical and so is even his kicking. The sound is more important than the sense. "Such rhymes as 'Heigh diddle, diddle,' 'See-saw, Margery-Daw,' and 'Ding-dong bell,'" so Joseph Lee says, "give

a child the freedom of the world of rhythm, teach him the first paces of the mind, the varying gaits of thought and action—to understand, with Touchstone, who time ambles withal, who time trots withal, and who he gallops withal, and how it feels to have him do it."

These rhymes are accompanied by action. "Pat a cake" combines rhythm—the rhythm of sound —and the action of patting together the baby hands; "Swing, swong, the days are long" is a melody to which little children are tossed up and down upon the parental knee. Through action-plays the child enjoys the imaginary adventure of being chased, of traveling, or of falling. He feels as deeply as is possible all that these little melodramas enact.

RHYTHMS RUN INTO ACTION

There is almost no limit to the dramatic possibilities of Mother Goose and almost every rhyme suggests possibilities for action:

"Pitty, Patty, Polt,
   Shoe the wild colt,
   Here a nail, and there a nail—
   Pitty, Patty, Polt"

is used while the baby is being dressed.

"One, two,
Buckle my shoe,"

for the same occasion, is also serviceable to count by. "Here we go 'round the mulberry bush," is excellent for running.

"Dance to your daddy,
My little babby,"

is the earliest known encouragement to solo-dancing. "Pease Porridge Hot" and "Dance, Thumbkin, Dance," are excellent finger-plays.

"A farmer went trotting upon his gray mare,
Bumpety, bumpety, bump,"

is an enticing combination of action and humor, while "Diddle, diddle, dumpling, my son John," is an excellent soporific.

These action-plays pass inevitably into counting-out rhymes.

RHYMES THAT PLEASE THE SENSES

LITTLE children are very fond of stories that involve sense-impressions. They like tales about houses built of ginger-bread and rivers that run with milk. Mother Goose has such a lyric that appeals to the sense of taste—it is about Queen Pippin's hotel:

"The walls were of sugar, as white as the snow,
And jujube windows were placed in a row;
The columns were candy, and all very tall,
And a roof of choice cakes was spread over all."

Similarly the children enjoy rhymes that appeal to the sense of sound, particularly those that are imitative of the familiar animals, such as "Bow, wow, wow," and

"The girl in the lane that can't speak plain,
Cried, gobble, gobble, gobble."

WHAT THE BABY'S SENSE OF HUMOR IS LIKE

THIS leads us to say that a baby's sense of humor always has a physical quality. This may consist merely of an amazing conglomeration of sounds, such as the familiar quotation:

"With a rowley, powley, gammon and spinach,
Heigho, says Anthony Rowley."

Such humor may be expressed in vigorous rhyme, as the following:

"As I was going up and down,
I met a little dandy,
He pulled my nose, and with two blows
I knocked him down right handy."

Or, it may consist simply of such an incident as the following:

"Said my mother to your mother,
It's a chop-a-nose day,"

which is followed of course immediately by the appropriate action which the little child enjoys enormously.

A calmer kind of humor is expressed in the following pleasant adventure:

"Little Tommy Grace had a pain in his face,
So bad that he could not learn a letter;
When in came Dicky Long, singing such a funny
song,
Then Tommy laughed, and found his face
much better."

THE FIRST ANIMAL-STORIES

CHILDREN like action-stories of animal-adventure long before they are old enough for Uncle Remus, such as

"Dog! dog! bite pig;
Piggy won't go over the stile;
And I shan't get home to-night."

Or, again, the fox who went out in hungry plight, closing with the *dénouement* so satisfactory to the children:

"And the little ones picked the bones, O."

GRANDMOTHER-STORIES

THE OTHER kind of adventure-story familiar to Mother Goose is, strange to say, concerned with old people. The predominance of old women in these stories can be explained only, I suppose, by the loving presence of so many grandmothers who assist in carrying down these nursery traditions from generation to generation. There is Old Mother Hubbard, the Old Woman who lived in a shoe, the Old Woman who was tossed up in a basket, the Old Woman who had her skirts cut off up to her back, and Old King Cole.

In fact, all the people in Mother Goose were either very old or very young. Aside from the elderly individuals whom you chance to remember, we have Little Miss Muffet, Little Polly Flinders, Little Boy Blue, Little Johnnie Green, Jack Horner, Little Tommy Tucker, and Simple Simon. These little folk are much more real to our nursery comrades than Washington, Lincoln, and Roosevelt, and are twice as familiar as Moses, Solomon, David, and Paul.

THE UNMORALITY OF MOTHER GOOSE

I SUPPOSE one of the reasons why little children enjoy Mother Goose is that these are stories without a moral; they are, as children themselves are said to be, unmoral, rather than immoral. Aside from the occasional savagery, the tone is usually that of pleasantness:

"What are little girls made of?
    Sugar and spice and all that's nice!"

"And why may not I love Johnny,
    And why may not Johnny love me?
And why may not I love Johnny
    As well as another body?"

"'Coo!' said the little doves,
    'Coo!' said she;
And they played together kindly
    In the dark pine tree."

There is occasionally a moral situation, like the story of the kittens who

"First began to quarrel, and then to fight"
with the sequel:

"They found it was better, that stormy night,
    To lie down to sleep than to quarrel and fight."

THE GRADED USE OF MOTHER GOOSE

THE GOLDEN age for the use of Mother Goose rhymes is for the years from one to six. These rhymes are useful to babies because they indulge their sense of rhythm, give them exciting experiences at second-hand, and open to them the gates of story. They are useful to the older ones because they may be employed in their singing games, their counting-out games, and their games of running and chasing.

LITERATURE FOR PRE-SCHOOL CHILDREN *

STORIES and rhymes are the literature, the art of language, for children of pre-school age. To appreciate good literature means to enjoy one of the highest products of civilization, a product which is the result of the high development of capacities which raise man above the brute—imagination and verbal expression.

GENERAL AIMS

To give pleasure, and in giving pleasure to develop appreciation of good literature.

To arouse the imagination and the desire to create through verbal form or through dramatic representation.

SPECIFIC AIMS

To develop control of verbal expression by supplying a choice vocabulary and by giving a model of art-form.

To suggest lines of action which will appeal to the child and which he will produce dramatically, carrying his imagination over into situations which he has not actually experienced.

To promote high ideals: 1. Through stories of humorous situations. The crude or callous enjoy unusual situations even if these bring discomfort to another. The ideal humor provokes laughter by harmless surprise.

2. Through stories which interpret a child's experience. The significant in the child's own experience can be isolated and emphasized or shown in its proper relations by means of a story.

3. Through stories of moral purpose which give models for ways of acting. The moral should never be stated; if it is not indicated obviously enough for the child to interpret for himself, the story is weak.

SUBJECT-MATTER

THE REAL subject-matter of a story is the attitude toward the world which is emphasized by the activity of the characters in the story; it is the emotional response evoked in the listener. Stories may relate very directly to the mood which is to be aroused. "The Night Before Christmas" will be told at Christmas-time, because it is the interpretation of this experience given in literary

* From a special report made to the International Kindergarten Association by its Committee on Subject Matter and Method.

form. "The Old Woman and Her Pig" typifies the idea of sequence, and should be told when the children are engaged in activities which may exemplify the idea of interdependence.

Stories for older children may be classified as myths, hero-tales, fables, fairy-tales, humorous and interpretative stories. There are only a few stories for children of pre-school age that can be placed under the first three headings. A simple myth which may be told is that of "Little Red Riding Hood." The stories that serve the same purpose as the hero-tales are simple interpretative stories of good children. In only a few of the well-known fables is the meaning evident enough to make them interesting at this age; such are "The Hare and the Tortoise," "The North Wind and the Sun," and "The Lion and the Mouse."

Most of the stories told to young children may be classified under the last three headings—fairy-tales, humorous stories, and interpretative stories. The best fairy-stories should be told often. The child realizes the irresponsibility, the unreality of the characters, and he enjoys the play of the unhampered imagination. He does not take the characters as models upon which to base his ideals of right and wrong.

The humorous story generally gains its distinctive character by the unusual response of some person in a familiar situation, or perhaps by the change of tone of the story-teller. It should never involve appreciable discomfort to any one; in the "Gingerbread Boy" the predicament creates humor, because it is the little man himself who calls out, "I'm all gone!" Such stories should never be adapted to convey an ethical meaning; they are intended for pure humor.

In the stories that deal with situations of everyday life, there should be no subtle, ethical complication, but an evident struggle of right and wrong with the right always triumphant.

Stories should occasionally be read to the children. A story-teller's dramatic manner aids in holding the child's attention, but sometimes his attention should be centered directly upon the story itself. At such times the story should be read, as the personality of the reader is not felt as much as that of a story-teller. Stories that depend for much of their attraction on their peculiar phrasing can be chosen for reading, and are good for this purpose.

CHOICE OF LANGUAGE

THE LANGUAGE used in telling a story should be suitable to the theme of the story. The fable should be given in concise, terse language, the fairy-tale in beautiful, flowing language. For children of pre-school age there should be little descriptive detail; the action should be rapid. Repetition of rhythmical phrases is much enjoyed at this time.

GOOD FORM

STORIES should have a definite plot, with introduction, complication, climax, and ending. The principal characters should stand out distinctly and all the rest be merely a setting. Little children enjoy particularly the repetition of a plot showing the principal characters in contrast, as in "Little One Eye, Two Eyes, and Three Eyes."

METHODS IN STORY-TELLING

THE NUMBER of stories told will depend upon the development of the children. As a general rule, some story should be given every day, but the well-known and well-loved "best literature" stories should be repeated until the children can correct if one word is misplaced. In this way the stories are absorbed and made a vital part of the child's life, of his imagination, and his expression.

Children should be encouraged to retell the simpler stories and to reproduce others dramatically. If the children do not readily recall a story, it is better to retell it than to drag the details from the children.

Children should be encouraged to tell original stories. These may be very crude, but power to control imaginative thought and give it verbal expression comes gradually through exercise. Interpretation of pictures helps the child to develop creative power in story-telling. The following was told by a boy of four, about Millet's picture entitled "First Step":

"Once there was a papa, and mamma, and a baby. The papa worked all day, and by and by mamma said, 'Papa's coming.' Papa took baby up, and they went in the house and had dinner."

This simple tale follows the laws of good literary form.

A story-teller's manner has much to do with the interest of the story. One who expects to impress her hearers must believe that the story is worth telling, that she is giving the highest and best of the world's thought, and that it can be imparted in no other way. She must believe that she can tell it so that the listeners will get the full value of the story. She must know the story well, not just memorize the words, but visualize it clearly. She must know why she tells it, must

know the main point and how to emphasize it.
She must feel and enjoy the story so much that
she will be expressive in tone, face, and manner.

> "My mother has the prettiest tricks
> Of words and words and words.
> Her talk comes out as smooth and sleek
> As breasts of singing birds.

> "She shapes her speech all silver fine,
> Because she loves it so;
> And her own eyes begin to shine
> To hear her stories grow.

> "And if she goes to make a call,
> Or out to take a walk,
> We leave our work when she returns
> And run to hear her talk.

> "We had not dreamed that things were so
> Of sorrow or of mirth.
> Her speech is as a thousand eyes,
> Through which we see the earth."
> —*Anna Hempstead Branch.*

FAULTS TO BE AVOIDED

The full value of stories and story-telling is
lost when these faults are committed: Telling a
story in a weak, rambling form; telling so many
stories that none of them is remembered; telling
so few that a taste for them is not formed; telling
too many on the plane of everyday experience;
telling stories that are adapted to older children.

THE POETRY HABIT*

By Clara Whitehill Hunt

WHEN I was a little girl I had the good fortune to live in a city where there were no
bridges, crushes, and police-patrol gongs, barrack-
built flats and brownstone rows, to frighten away
the birds and crowd out the flowers and play-
spaces; but where fathers, even on moderate salaries, could own little houses with big piazzas and
generous yards. We boys and girls raised Jack-
o'-lantern pumpkins in those yards, and cheerful
morning-glories and downy chickens. We plucked
juicy plums and cherries and grapes from our own
trees and vines. We played in safe, shady streets
without fear of trolleys or motors; for our city
was so charmingly behind the times that the jin-
gling horse-car did not readily give place to the
clanging electric.

In Spring we tapped the maple trees in front
of our houses, smacking our lips over the few
spoonfuls of sap that dripped as musically into
our suspended pails as if this were a "truly"
maple-sugar camp in the country.

After school hours, in the rapidly gathering
dusk of short autumn days, we raked gorgeous
leaves into huge piles and danced wild Indian
dances around bonfires that blazed like beacons
up and down the length of streets unpaved with
forbidden asphalt. We made snow-forts and snow-
men and Eskimo huts, we wallowed in clean snow-
drifts, we coasted down long, hilly streets on our
brothers' "bobs."

Yet how all these pleasures of the school year
were as drab to scarlet contrasted with the radi-
ance of vacations on Grandmother's beautiful
farm!

How we hated to take off our clothes at night
for fear troublesome buttons would make us miss
something in the morning when we woke far too
early to bother poor Mother to help us dress.
How, beneath all the childish, physical delights
of wading and huckleberrying and riding atop
the loaded hay-wagon and playing "I spy" in the
shadowy barn, there flowed the deep current of
joy in the beauty of earth and sky!

When barefooted under the willows, we tugged
at heavy rocks which we perspiringly erected
into lighthouses and forts to guard our homes
along the brook—I should say the seashore—we
were only dimly conscious that the song of the
brook and the carpet of dancing light and shade
under our feet, the feel of the flower-scented
breeze on our hot little faces, the murmur and hum
of insects in the waving meadow grass over the
stone wall, the vivid blue of the sky—which an
old black crow "caw-caw'd" for us to look up and
notice—that all these beauties of Mother Earth
were a deep part of the happiness of our free
play in the outdoors, whose largeness was answering to a craving of the child-soul, that feels the
intolerable cramp of the city more than does the
adult.

---

* From *What Shall We Read to the Children?* by Clara Whitehill Hunt. Published by Houghton Mifflin Company.
Reprinted by permission of the publishers.

HOW PROSAIC THE CITY CHILD'S LIFE

To-day I watch the children at play as I walk to my office along streets of high respectable apartment-houses. How cruelly narrow the range for the imagination of the young child! The very "respectability" of a neighborhood—which exacts a rent that often eats up all country vacation money —is against the child. How can a youngster possibly have a good time if he is not allowed to muss up the front steps and get his clothes dirty? Yet it is not the physical handicap of the city child that most stirs my pity, for his health record is steadily improving. It is the little one's missing experiences in beauty, it is the robbery of his imagination, effected by paved streets, that I deplore.

There is no possible help for these children except as they shall get their experiences vicariously through Father and Mother and books. For our comfort we know how marvelously books can be made to supply what Father's salary can not. Only we need to remember how and when to apply the various books. There is a best time for introducing poetry and myth and heroes of history; and a lifelong loss may be that child's whose parents know not when to feed a certain interest.

BEGIN IN EARLIEST BABYHOOD

The baby's first taste of poetry should be given not later than a month after he alights, trailing his clouds of glory and with the music of his heavenly home attuning his ears to a delight in rhyme and rhythm, long before Mother's songs convey the word-meanings to his mind. There never was a normal baby born into this world who did not bring with him a love for poetry; and the fact that so few adults retain a trace of this most pure delight points to the need of conscious effort on the parent's part to foster the child's natural gift.

So the first book I would put into the baby's library would be a collection of the loveliest lullabies and hymns and sweet old story-songs. I know that doctors and nurses frown upon rocking the baby to sleep, but if I were a young mother I'd rock and sing to that baby after he waked up! I would sing Tennyson's "Sweet and Low," and Holland's "Rockaby, Lullaby, Bees in the Clover," and Field's "Wynken, Blynken, and Nod"; the little German slumber song—

"Sleep, baby, sleep,
The large stars are the sheep";

and the Gaelic lullaby—

"Hush, the waves are rolling in
White with foam, white with foam."

I would sing "O Little Town of Bethlehem," and "It Came Upon the Midnight Clear," and "While Shepherds Watched Their Flocks by Night." I would sing the "Crusader's Hymn," and Luther's "A Mighty Fortress Is Our God," and Newman's "Lead, Kindly Light," and Pleyel's "Children of the Heavenly King," and Baring-Gould's "Now the Day Is Over." I would sing "Annie Laurie," and "Home, Sweet Home," and "Flow Gently, Sweet Afton," and "The Suwanee River."

USE OF LULLABIES AND FINGER-PLAYS

Choosing songs so beautiful and so appealing to a child's heart, I should make sure that when the little one began to try to imitate Mother, he would sing of winds that ruffle the waves, of dew, of pleasant banks and green valleys and clear, winding rills, of the Heavenly Father's care, of the enduringness of home love. I should know that, though the words at first called up no clear mental pictures, they would spell love and beauty and happy feeling, and that life would, little by little, unfold to the child the full meanings of these lovely songs.

Before the baby is a year old he will enjoy action-rhymes like "This little pig went to market," "Pat a cake, pat a cake, baker's man." By the time he is two, he will be trying to repeat the gay Mother Goose jingles with their irresponsible nonsense and their catching rhyme and rhythm. When he is three he will be enjoying Stevenson's "I have a little shadow that goes in and out with me," and other posies from "The Child's Garden of Verse."

USE OF STORY-TELLING POEMS

Now the important thing is for the baby to acquire the poetry habit. A few years later, this child, if he has not listened to verse nearly every day of his life, may begin to be bored by the language of poetry, so dear to one who comprehends quickly, so tiresome to one who, for the lack of right preparation, must dig out the meanings, as he works at a translation from a dead language.

At first we need to repeat nursery jingles and the simplest child verses, because these are the bottom steps of the "golden staircase" to real poetry. If, however, we try to get firmly lodged in mind the fact that children enjoy an infinite number of things which they do not understand; that they understand far more than they can express; that their understanding grows by leaps and bounds if we foolish adults do not interfere —we shall stop trying to stint their active imaginations by keeping them so long on baby-rhymes.*

The child will most easily climb the staircase to real poetry by way of story-telling poems. Sentimental and martial, merry and sad, the story-interest and the music of the old English and Scotch ballads fit them exactly to the liking of children, little and big. Browning and Tennyson, Matthew Arnold and Scott and Longfellow give to the children "The Pied Piper," "The Lady of Shalott," "The Forsaken Merman," "Jock of Hazeldean," "The Bell of Atri."

CONNECTING POETRY WITH BIOGRAPHY AND HISTORY

EACH poem may be made to introduce many others, if we take advantage of the child's delight in the association of ideas he has acquired. For example, the little one has loved to hear mother sing "Annie Laurie" and "The Blue Bells of Scotland" and "The Campbells Are Comin'." He has mourned brave Sir Patrick Spens, has galloped with Lochinvar, and "wi' Wallace bled" in defense of Scotland's freedom. Scotland to him has become a land of romance, dear to his heart. One day, after he has been lustily singing "The Campbells Are Comin', Oho! Oho!" Mother tells him how the dying English, penned up in Lucknow, sprang to their feet laughing and crying with joy as they heard, faint and far away, the bagpipes playing "The Campbells Are Comin'." Now is the time to read Whittier's "The Pipes at Lucknow," as Bayard Taylor's "Song of the Camp" will touch the children after they have joined in singing "Annie Laurie." Taylor's poem, and the bit of explanation about the Crimean War which it involves, will introduce "The Charge of the Light Brigade," another stirring poem of the same war.

---

* "She read a poem to her child one day,
   And added explanations not a few,
But paused a moment at the end to say,
   'I wonder, darling, if it's clear to you.'

"But still he sighed, and slowly shook his head;
   She turned the page as if to start again,
When, drawing nearer, 'Mother, dear,' he said,
   'I'll understand it if you don't explain.' "

A whole cycle of Southern and Civil War songs and poems may follow the reading of the Uncle Remus stories—"Dixie" and "Maryland, My Maryland," "My Old Kentucky Home," "Sheridan's Ride," and "Oh, Captain, My Captain!" Somehow, the child will enter into the heart of the North and South, the soldier and the slave, and he will be a better American in this reunited country for loving the songs of both sections that gave their best for what they believed to be the right.

THE RIGHT POEM AT THE RIGHT TIME

MAKE it an unvarying practice to link poetry with the children's every happy experience, every celebration, family or national or religious. Read the "Concord Hymn" and "Paul Revere's Ride" on the Fourth of July, "The Landing of the Pilgrims" at Thanksgiving, "The Flag Goes By" and "The Commemoration Ode" on Memorial Day.

Weeks before Christmas begin to read and sing every beautiful poem and song you can find. There are so many, we have no excuse for descending to doggerel. On New Year's Eve read Tennyson's "Death of the Old Year"; on a gusty winter evening read "Old Winter Is a Sturdy One." Before taking a journey, hunt up poems of places the children will visit. After an exciting trip to the Zoo read Blake's "Tiger, Tiger, Burning Bright," and Taylor's "Night with a Wolf."

When the children have enjoyed the Norse stories, read them Longfellow's "Skeleton in Armor." After hearing the stories of Tarpeia and Cortius and other Roman legends, they will be ready for Macaulay's "Lays."

Does any father or mother think I am going too fast? Prove it by experiment! I am suggesting a poetry course, not for the "exceptional child," but for real little bread-and-butter boys and girls of happy birth and home environment. There are only three rules necessary to follow if you would delight your soul with watching your children's poetry taste grow with their growth. These are:

Begin early.

Read poetry every day.

Read the right poem at the right time.

FAIRY–TALES FOR CHILDREN

By William Byron Forbush

THE ORIGIN of fairy stories has been called "the prettiest riddle in the world."

Fairies are dwindled gods. The fairy king was once the sky and the fairy queen the earth, and Prince Charming was the sun and the Princess was the daydawn. Cinderella was originally the dawn fleeing from the Palace of Night and Little Red Riding Hood was the sunset that gets swallowed up by the wolf, the Night. Shakespeare's Oberon was simply a German-French night-god and Titania was none other than Diana, the moon-goddess, and their quarrel was only the separation of darkness from daylight.

The reason that "the first thing to which the eyes of literature opened was the fairy story" was because people believed in these stories long before men began to write books. There have always been dwarfs and tiny races of men. So these have been adopted into the fairy fold. So they say that "Picts" and "Puck" and "pygmies" and "pixies" and "bogeys" are really one. Add to this that men have had many pleasant dreams, such as of lands where animals have human speech, and paradises where there is no winter, and grottoes where there is no thirst, and forests that never cast their leaves, and you account for the familiar scenery of Fairyland.

FAIRYLANDS OF MEMORY

BY THE time the fairies crept into the nursery they went through one more transformation. They did not live in any magic world and they were not different from other people except that they had magic powers. Cinderella's godmother wears no wings. In Bluebeard the only charmed thing is the fatal key. In the Arabian Nights it is a lamp that has fairy powers. In short, we are telling our children only the wonderful things that we wanted to be when we were ourselves little. "Peter Pan" is a reminiscence of our own childhood, rather than a play for children. The nursery Fairyland is the place where things begin over, as we wish they might be.

POVERTY AND DREAMS

WORKING-PEOPLE ought to be the first to stand up for their right in fairies. For fairy-tales are a part of the poor man's charter of freedom.

Have you ever thought of it, that the countries of the poor are the chief homes of fairy-tales? "The main population of Ireland to this day consists of fairies." Then there is Arabia and the peasant part of France. England has produced few fairy-stories and as for America it has not been a fairy-tale land at all, except for the "Uncle Remus" tales of its freed-men.

Indeed fairy-tales are the dreams of the poor. They consist of fancies by which they have illumined the hard facts of life. Have you not noticed how prominent eating is in the stories about fairies? Who would ever weave dreams about food except those who had been hungry? Could Cinderella, Aladdin, and Goody Two-shoes have come out of any but a workingman's home?

The value of the fairy-tale is that it tells about the wonder of the world, the magic of living. Like the Old Woman, in Mother Goose, it "brushes the cobwebs out of the sky."

HEAVENLY STORIES WITH EARTHLY MEANINGS

IF A parable be defined as an earthly story with a heavenly meaning, Richard Le Gallienne seems to be right in saying that "a fairy-tale is a heavenly story with an earthly meaning." In such tales the child finds animals, trees, flowers, and the stars friendly. The brave child is master even of dragons. He can live like a prince in disguise, or if he be uncomely he may hope to win Beauty after he is free of his masquerade.

Almost every fairy-tale contains a test—of goodness or courage or shrewdness. Sharp distinctions are made, that require a child of parts to discern. So such stories, as Gerald Stanley Lee says, "put a nozzle on the stream of consciousness" and help "reduce the moral illiteracy."

HOW TO TELL STORIES

By MARY L. READ

FOR THE person who "can't tell a story," there is one essential: forget *yourself* and plunge in, and practice until you have gained confidence.

1. Tell something in which you and the children are interested, and keep at it repeatedly until you feel at ease.

2. Recall stories that interested you at that age.

3. Tell stories the children themselves ask for, refreshing your memory by reading up a standard version, or by asking the children to tell it to you.

4. Study Mother Goose, Aesop, and Bible stories as models of the best story-telling.

5. Live the story as you tell it—see it as pictured in your own mind. Tell it so vividly that the children can play it out afterward.

6. Use direct speech in telling conversation.

7. Make your picture vivid by a few descriptive words, especially of colors and sounds; increase your vocabulary of adjectives.

8. Beware of making it too long.

9. Use perhaps a very few natural gestures, but do not try to act it out. Most children have enough imagination to hear narrative and see action at the same time.

10. Children love the same story repeated, and they want it told *the same way*, in order to see the same pictures; therefore, have your story clear in your mind the first time you tell it.

11. If you are telling a classic or standard story, respect it as it is, just as honestly as you would an historic or scientific fact. If you do not wish to tell it that way, don't tell it at all, and don't tinker with it.

12. Do not try to memorize a story, except possibly the conversations.

13. If a story is clearly told, the child will usually absorb and discern the ethical principle involved, without any necessity on your part obtrusively to "point the moral." Sometimes a child will draw an erroneous or unexpected inference because his judgment is yet immature or his ethical experience is elementary or perverted. Under such a condition, try to tell another story that will concretely clear his thought.

GOOD TASTE NEEDS CULTIVATION*

By MARGARET ERNST

ONCE when I was very green as a children's librarian, a group of ten-year-olds came to me and demanded, in Tenth Avenue gangster voices, a murder story.

As I admit, I was green—I didn't know any better—I lost my head—and did just the wrong thing.

"Oh," said I in a shocked tone, "a murder story! We've nothing like that here. You're too young for things of that sort!"

The children looked at me with contempt mixed with pity for my soft sappiness. I doubt if my word on literary matters ever carried much weight with that particular group again.

Of course, in a theoretical way I was right. Murder isn't the perfect reading diet for ten-year-old appetites. Reading needn't stop just at the threshold of a child's own experience, or we'd rule out all imagination; but murder even vicariously tasted is a little outside a young child's emotional scope, I hope.

I learned then that you can be right but very, very wrong. You can't influence taste by setting up a concrete dam in its path—the baffled desire will flow around or over, or tunnel underground, and such subterranean seepage is dangerously akin to perversion of taste just as any emotion forced under cover is likely to become perverse.

DIVERT THE CHILD'S INTEREST

WHAT YOU can do is to divert, to point out another stream-bed attractive enough to lure the child's desire along its way. That's what I do now when children of ten ask for murder stories. I've learned never to say, "We haven't them here." I never say, "You're too young." Instead I start telling the child about a swell modern mystery story—*The Ship Without a Crew*, by Howard

* Reprinted by special permission from The National Parent-Teacher Magazine.

Pease, or Geoffrey Household's *The Spanish Cave,* for example—and most times I am successful in centering his interest on something he didn't ask for but which satisfies him equally.

A boy of twelve refused all books except those clashing with armor and red with blood. One day I sat down next to him in the library easy-chairs with Christopher Morley's *Where the Blue Begins* in my hand. I read to myself one of those delicious and tender paragraphs about the pups, Bunks and Grouper and Yelps, and I laughed a little (really almost spontaneously—I was play-acting a bit). John was interested. He looked over my shoulder. He read the passage. Soon he took the book away from me! Swords and scimitars were forgotten. The next book he read was Robert Nathan's *Enchanted Voyage.*

INFLUENCES ON A CHILD'S TASTE

IT TAKES a grown-up a long time to find out what children like in the way of books; and even longer to find out why. Perhaps children are all born with potential good taste, with a kind of protective discrimination which chooses instinctively the right book for the right ripeness of need. But this potential good taste is tinged by many influences before a child is seven and old enough to come to the library.

PICTURE BOOKS

FIRST, there are the picture books his mother or his aunts have given him. They may be simple and true in line and color, suggesting to his baby mind familiarities of everyday life in a new medium. What develops in him, although it is on a two-year-old level, is as surely discrimination as what takes place in an eleven-year-old who discovers more thrill in Masefield's *Jim Davis* than in the cheap thrillers.

THE COMIC STRIPS

THEN there are the funnies. Children seem to read them solemnly, without cracking a smile. Why? For the most part, boys and girls don't consider the comic strip comic. They tell me it is rather a continued story and half the interest lies in the day-after-day renewal of acquaintance with Benny or the weekly visit of the Katzenjammers. I felt that way once about Foxy Grandpa and Buster Brown. Educators and parents frequently condemn all funnies, without themselves discriminating between strips, on the ground of taste: slapstick drawing of grotesque figures; lan-guage from the lower levels of slang; sadism inherent in the humor (if any) found in "hitting" some one over the head—the burlesque show technique of being funny through slamming somebody with an inflated bladder.

I would condemn the funnies chiefly because they are dull and really needn't be; and the ever-increasing flock of books of comics because they are ruinous to eyesight. But I am no longer afraid of them and any permanent influence they have on children's discrimination. Boys and girls who read pages of comic strips weekly often turn out the purest and most poetic creative writing of their own.

When my own eldest child was about nine or ten, I was convinced that reading the comics would destroy her sense of reality and beauty. We solemnly and unselfishly took the comic-sectionless New York *Times* on Sunday, though I preferred the *Herald Tribune* book reviews myself, in order to guard her from the contamination of "Pa's Son-in-Law."

After a long while, I discovered that Connie spent her Sunday mornings at the corner newspaper store, working industriously sorting Sunday papers for the proprietor. Pay: she could read all the funnies in existence. I was pretty disturbed, but there seemed little I could justly do about so thoughtful and businesslike a child—I just worried.

Well, Connie is now nineteen, and her taste in literature is irreproachable.

THE MOVIES

I FEEL more certain about the lasting effect on children of movies done in poor taste. Live people move through real houses and actual scenery, and do such unreal things! There is a danger here that the young mind, trustful and unknowledgeable, may be led to expect some things from life which aren't there, and never could be.

THE RADIO

CHILDREN who listen unlimited hours at the radio have their taste impaired very definitely—temporarily, in cases where home and school have a firm standard for them to return to; perhaps permanently where this isn't the case. Not that there aren't good radio programs, but most children spend the hours between school and bedtime listening to mediocre ones.

I find a definite effect on reading of children's radio hours—more and more children, boys particularly, rejecting any book not full of the kind of staccato action heard over the radio.

Luckily, with many children the passionate absorption in radio is a passing phase. I have seen children who, at nine or ten, had to be limited by strict and worried parental ordinance to x programs a day; at twelve, they scarcely turned on the radio for weeks at a time. The easy sensationalism that had satisfied a desire for shared danger and thrills at nine seemed childish and untrue to the adolescent. Taste had matured.

Where home and school are secure in a standard for creative work, I think parents needn't worry.

SIX TESTS

THERE are six tests of a book of fiction—six questions to ask about it. First, did the author have a story to tell? Second, did he tell it well? Third, is the atmosphere and local color right? Fourth, is the book sincere; true to life? Fifth, has it an underlying sense of humor? And sixth, has it vision and ideals behind it?

Every first-rate story possesses all these qualities to some degree, generally with one or two especially prominent. If you give each story you particularly like an examination on these six points to see how high it "passes," you will know why it is a good book and perhaps appreciate a little more fully than one does thoughtlessly, just how good a book it is. And a little practice in such rating of books makes it very easy to eliminate poor books, because in too many respects they simply don't measure up to the standard.

—*Stokes Library Bulletin.*

CHILD CULTURE

By Lena E. Bliss

A PROFESSOR in one of our colleges recently said: "A child's sense of rhyme and rhythm is nearly always accurate. It shows itself in his every motion. A child's feet instinctively dance to the joy of life."

So a child's heart instinctively throbs to the joy of song, to the rhythmic pulsations of poetry, and to such a degree that a teacher finds great difficulty in eliminating the sing-song effect in a recitation of poetry by a child.

The sympathetic teaching of good poems, therefore, is one of the highest forms of child culture. Children will soon detect the difference between a good poem and a poor one, for their taste is naturally good. They are very good critics also as to the correct interpretation of a poem. Beauty as memorized in poems will prove a constant source of joy as well as uplifting of soul and character, and in many instances may be the determining factor in a good choice at some crisis of later life.

Stories, too, should be carefully chosen and well told. One of the most potent devices to-day for the good or ill-being of childhood is in the radio bedtime stories. I have found that children usually appreciate most the stories they know are true. In relating stories to a group of children I know, I often begin with:

"Once upon a time, years and years ago, when I was a little girl like you," and they will listen long past the hour.

Truth, originality, beauty—these appeal to childhood as to the maturer mind. It does not need a creative artist, but it does need an artist-soul to awaken these responses in childhood and, when awakened, they are among the highest factors in child development.

PICTURES AND DRAWING

HOW TO INTEREST CHILDREN IN PICTURES

By ESTELLE M. HURLL

I REMEMBER very well the family amusement when my small brother came home from grammar school in a state of incredulous amazement that a certain playmate had never heard of Raphael. The youngster soon learned that there were many others in the same deplorable ignorance—and this in families whose culture was not questioned. People willing to spend money freely on books are often very stingy in their purchase of pictures. Anything is good enough to cover a bare space on the wall. As well say anything is good enough to fill a vacant place on a bookshelf. Far worse, indeed, because the picture forces itself on the attention willy nilly, while a book may be left unread.

BEGIN WITH WHAT THE CHILD LIKES

IT IS too much to expect a very young child to like a picture because it is beautiful. The esthetic element is not to be reckoned with in his early picture experience. It is the subject which interests him, not the art in which it is embodied. His pleasure turns on what it is about, not on how it is treated. He has reasons of his own for his preferences, and some of them are rather hard to fathom. On the whole, however, they seem to grow out of very simple psychological principles, which we can analyze by careful observation. I recently asked a young mother what sort of pictures her little boy liked best. "Animals," was the prompt reply. I glanced around the nursery and saw a perfect menagerie of toys: horses, dogs, cats, bears, etc., in every imaginable form, from rubber and china to the most realistic skin and fur imitations. The father had begun in the child's infancy to bring home this sort of toy, and it was a natural transition from toy to picture. A girl baby's first and most common toy is the doll, and from this the most natural transition is to pictures of children.

THE CHILD'S PLEASURE IS THAT OF RECOGNIZING SOMETHING FAMILIAR

IF DADDY is fond of yachting, the boy's first toys are likely to be boats, and so he is ready for any sea pictures, even Turner's. If Mother has a fad for gardening, the little girl trained in the love of flowers will naturally like pictures of flowers. In all such cases it seems to me quite plain that the child's pleasure is largely that of recognition. He is proud and pleased to be able to identify and name the object. You secure his interest in a picture by pointing out the familiar things. The other day I dropped a bank-book which opened at a small woodcut frontispiece of the "Institution for Savings"—not much of a work of art. My four-year-old nephew fell upon it eagerly. "Oh, see the house, isn't it cunning!" he exclaimed, gazing at the picture with the rapture of a Ruskin before the cathedral of Amiens. This of course was the sheer joy of recognizing a familiar thing. The mother might well take a hint from the episode. Here was a starting-point from which one might lead a child on to an interest in great architectural monuments. It behooves us to find out, first, what sort of picture a child likes, and if possible why, and then to gratify this taste in the most beautiful and artistic forms. If the child likes animals, give him Rosa Bonheur and Barye, rather than posters and Sunday supplements. If baby pictures are in favor, supply prints of Correggio and Bellini, Van Dyck and Sir Joshua, rather than a ten-cent picture-book. If it is flowers, fruit, boats, houses, search out pictures of those objects which have genuine artistic merit.

BUILD ON THE CHILD'S CURIOSITY

As I count recognition, or identification, as one of the first elements of a child's interest in pictures, I regard curiosity as another. It is a pleasure to look at something which provokes investigation. From pictures of domestic pets, which a child identifies so quickly, he passes with awe and curiosity to pictures of strange creatures which have never come into his ken: elephants, camels, lions, and all the rest. From pictures of houses and churches, such as he sees daily, he turns with inquiring eyes to views of beautiful Old-World buildings. Let the new thing be enough like the old to seem half-way familiar, yet enough unlike it to stimulate a fresh interest. The child must begin with what he can understand, but his thirst for knowledge gives him an eager zest for something a little beyond his understanding—not so far beyond it, however, that it is in outer darkness. The universal rule of progress is by one step at a time.

NEXT WE COME TO STORY-PICTURES

As soon as the child is capable of grasping a composition of more than one object, or to put it more psychologically, of relating the various elements of a composition, he is ready for story-pictures. These may be illustrative of a text, like subjects from the life of Christ; or anecdotes in themselves, like the pictures of Sir John E. Millais. The child's imagination is now keenly alive, and affords him his finest enjoyment. The story subjects he likes best are of course drawn from his own little world. A picture of mother and babe is a familiar scene to him, and the world-old theme of the Madonna never loses its charm.

The story-pictures in which children figure are of peculiar interest, just as children's books are largely tales of children's doings. A child with an animal is a delightful combination in a picture—a subject unhappily not easy to find in good art. Velasquez's "Prince Baltasar on his Pony" is perfect. Velasquez also painted his young prince with his dogs; and other portrait painters, notably Van Dyck and Reynolds, have turned out charming compositions of children with their animal pets. Little Miss Bowles hugging her spaniel is one of the most familiar of this happy company. The child John the Baptist and the Lamb was a subject several times repeated by Murillo in some excellent pictures. By the same painter is a lovely picture, in the Madrid gallery, of the Christ-child playing with St. John and the Lamb. Murillo also drew groups of children at play directly from the scenes of the street and market—pictures full of story suggestion.

This theme of children playing together, like that of children with animals, has not been nearly so often treated as we could expect or desire.

One finds most examples perhaps in the English portrait school of the eighteenth century.

OTHER SUBJECTS

The next step, logically, is to compositions in which the child is associated with grown people. Such subjects as "St. Christopher Bearing the Christ-child," "Tobias and the Angels," "The Boy Jesus Among the Doctors," "The Presentation of the Virgin," illustrate this motive, and are all very common in the religious art of the Old Masters.

In carrying out the analogy between juvenile literature and art, we see that the child's interest is by no means limited to subjects in which children take part. Tales of love and adventure appeal strongly to the imagination and dramatic sense of boys and girls alike, and myths and legends are immensely popular with them. Happily there are good pictures of many subjects of this kind. Raphael and Carpaccio have given us "St. George and the Dragon," and Van Dyck, "St. Martin Dividing His Cloak with a Beggar." Giorgione has shown us Apollo in pursuit of Daphne, and Guido Reni has depicted the sun-god driving his chariot in the wake of Aurora. But even common, everyday affairs involving no thrilling adventures, may furnish story material to interest the child. Take Millet's works, for instance, of which children are especially fond. Many of Millet's pictures, it will be remembered, have to do with work, and children love to see things done: the seed sown, the potatoes planted, the butter churned, the hens fed, the water drawn, and the harvest garnered. Old Giotto, the first of the Italians to interpret human nature, was a born story-teller. It would certainly never have occurred to me to show his works to children, but I was much edified, at an exhibition of art photographs, when a group of little girls timidly asked me to explain the Giotto pictures, from the frescoes at Assisi and Padua. They had instinctively grasped the story quality, and with very little guidance were ready to enter intelligently into the meaning. The seventeenth-century Dutch and Flemish schools are full of pictures in a vein of homely realism which children readily appreciate. They suggest to a quick imagination all sorts of stories of everyday life: the goldsmith weighing his gold, the old market woman haggling over her fish or vegetables, the lady at her piano, and the cavalier with his lute. We look into the parlor, the chamber, the kitchen, the banquet hall, the tailor's shop, the inn, and imagine all sorts of things about their occupants.

SUMMARY

WE may summarize our suggestions as to the choice of pictures for children as follows:

Give them pictures of people in action.

Let the action suggest a story within their own experience or range of appreciation.

Use colored pictures whenever possible, if it is reasonably good color.

Ignore for the present the history of art, chronological order, reference to technical details.

For the sake of later impression choose pictures that are good if not great, honestly drawn, faithfully colored, sincerely conceived.

Avoid in the main the weakly sentimental, and postpone until adolescence explanation why a child of Murillo is greater than one of Bouguereau, why a Madonna of Raphael is finer than one of Max, why a Botticelli is more beautiful than a Landseer. All this will come better through the work in drawing in the school, where honest drawing and color and clear-cut purpose or sentiment in the actual work of creating beauty will give the child a good sound taste and the power of discriminating for himself.

PICTURES FOR CHILDREN

By EDITH RILAND CROSS

LET us give our children special training in the early years of their lives, in the knowledge of beautiful pictures. Help them to enjoy the pictures in the home.

When our children were babies, we often talked to them about our pictures. As a result, they could point out such pictures as Raeburn's "Boy and the Rabbit," Sargent's "Frieze of the Prophets," pictures of the Boy John, the Aurora, Hofmann's "Head of Christ," several of the Madonnas and Sir Galahad.

It always gave them great pleasure when they would find these pictures in other homes. It also gave them an appreciation of art, and stimulated their interest and observation.

One day, my oldest boy, age five, pointed to the picture of Burne-Jones's "Golden Stairway" and said, "Mother, did they take that picture with a kodak, or did someone paint it?" Then and there we talked together of how prints were made from great pictures, and of the galleries where the originals are kept.

While teaching kindergarten, I had bought a large plain oak picture-frame with a hinged back so that pictures could easily be changed during the years. As I recalled this, I decided that it would be a good thing to have one in the home.

So I had two such frames made. The boys are so proud to have their own framed pictures hanging by their little white beds.

And it has been interesting to see the enjoyment they take in changing the pictures, and in making their own selections.

It has resulted in a good collection of pictures which the children add to as they find those that interest them. To this I have added many of the Perry and Brown prints which I had used in my kindergarten work, and we save the covers of different magazines that depict child life and activities.

I have noticed that the children prefer colors to the black and white studies. They care for pictures of people or animals rather than for those of inanimate objects. Boys like pictures showing strength, as knights and soldiers; while girls like those portraying daintiness, beautiful children, and ideal surroundings. Both boys and girls like pictures of activities and sports and once in a while they fancy a beautiful landscape.

Of course, to be honest, I must add that the pictures sometimes found in their frames are not always the most esthetic. For I have often noticed prints of the football heroes, in their season, the attractive advertisements for Campbell's soups, and posters for a coming circus. Yet it is best to let it be the children's choice.

Another suggestion which I have found helpful in the home is to have the pictures in the children's bed rooms or play room hung on a level with their eyes. It is surprising to see how much keener is their observation when this is done. Let the children climb up or be lifted up to see those pictures which are hung higher so that they can really study them. Always take time to help them understand pictures, for you thus begin their appreciation of art.

These suggestions could be carried out in any home, for, with the present wealth of good magazines, such a collection could be easily made, and at little cost, while a very inexpensive frame would suffice.

DRAWING AND COLORING BY LITTLE CHILDREN

By Mrs. Bertha Payne Newell

ALL children go through a scribble stage in drawing. In it the enjoyment, like that of their play in blocks, sand, clay, and cuttings, is largely pleasure in their own movement. Their joy in the marks made has not much to do with picture-making. By and by it dawns upon them that the moving arm makes the trailing line go in certain different directions, round and round, back and forth, up and down.

The next step is when an *accidental* picture is made. Then he tries to get the resemblance again and again. Not very successful, nevertheless, he is started on a new road, that of *choosing certain movements to get certain results which he foresees.*

He has learned that the wonderful things that others draw for him are not the results of some mysterious hocus-pocus, but are produced by some such purposeful guidance of the pencil as he himself is now striving after. Gradually he learns to tell his ideas of things in simple outlines: a circle with two downward strokes for legs is a man, a "peaky" roof and two downright lines are a house. The four-year-old is usually in this stage of the drawing art.

Do not be afraid to exercise your own slender skill for your children. It will be a great incentive to them to try their own. Suppose you have told them the old tale of the Three Little Pigs. Draw for them the straw house, the brush house, and the brick house; or the three beds of the three bears, for which three lines each will suffice. Remember it is the story aspect of the pictures that a child delights in. Let your pencil talk, saying, for instance, "Here is a man, here is a dog following him. Here is a bone the dog finds. Now they are going over this bridge. Here is their house," etc. In this you will enlarge his power of representing what he has seen in lines, just as you improved his speech through imitation.

OTHER STEPS IN DRAWING

AFTER the simplest outline stage, the third stage in drawing is in added detail. Bodies now intervene where earlier the legs sprouted directly from the head. Buttons on coats, eyes and mouths in faces, fingers on ends of arms, hats on heads, chimneys on houses, and similar details are signs of progress.

It will be noticed that these items are all connected with *use*. Buttons fasten coats, hands are to grasp with. Steps lead up and one enters houses by them, and so on. But still we, as the children themselves, should not be too fastidious in our demands for grace or likeness in their productions.

MATERIALS FOR PRACTICE

NOTHING is so productive of freedom in the use of line as blackboard drawing. The arm swings freely across it. The eyes and fingers are not strained by too fine motions. It is easy to get a blackboard in a toy or department store. School and kindergarten supply-stores carry them, and also slated canvas to tack on the wall. A green prepared board is to be had that is much more pleasant to the eye than black. This may be bought by the square foot.

Since the free-arm movement is the easiest, and the surest, it is important to begin with it. So, Mother, give your youngster large, soft pencils and large sheets of cheap paper, or better, a blackboard, and see that he does not grip crayon or pencil with tense finger muscles.

I used to enjoy the babies of the kindergarten at play with the chalk and blackboard. Francis used to amuse himself while waiting for his mother to come for him by traveling the length of the long board, leaving "trolley-wires" in his wake. Then he drew up-and-down marks at intervals, which I interpreted to be poles; later he added more horizontal lines for tracks. So far he was partly enjoying his power of making long lines, and exercising his legs in walking back and forth. One day this ceased and he toilsomely drew an oblong on one of the lower lines and carefully traced a slanting line to connect it with the upper line. This was, of course, a trolley-car. And as his mother and I knew, this was his first piece of *real drawing.*

Encourage all such developments; talk with children about their drawings, and listen to what they tell you. *Draw for and with them.*

CUTTING PICTURES

ONE OF the constant delights of children is cutting. Just to see the scissors snip off bit after bit and to look curiously and see if by chance each piece may *mean* something, this is the main purpose at first. Then it dawns on the cutter that a turn of the wrist will make a piece of a certain shape, and the use of scissors as a picture-making tool begins. The process of drawing with the scissors is described further in the BOOKSHELF.

Cutting out pictures from the advertising pages of magazines may be made very delightful, if you will let the children make a temporary art-gallery on the nursery-door. A three-year-old nephew used to do this with a large varnish-brush and a dish of varnish as tools. I used to find the door plastered over, as high as he could reach, with the pictures that most took his fancy. Of course they peeled off by bedtime, but that did not matter. It was the *doing* that he was after and that gave him pleasure.

The cutting is of course roughly done, and for that reason it is just as well not to place them in a scrapbook permanently; meanwhile the rough cutting is a training for later, more accurate use of scissors.

The three-year-old child is lacking in the muscular control that is needed to manage water-colors with any degree of skill; but finger-painting is easy and little children love to daub with the bright colors on large sheets of paper.

The love of color is strong, and may be satisfied and trained in many ways. The rather heavy kindergarten colored papers lend themselves to cutting and pasting. Colored crayons are useful to draw with or to use in coloring printed pictures.

PAPER COLOR-FORMS

HERE is a device that I have used to good effect. Give a child a sheet of manila paper and three strips of brown or black paper, one long and two shorter of equal length. Ask him if he can lay a picture of a table with these strips. When this is done let him paste each strip in position. Give him some pieces of red, yellow, and orange paper, from which to cut apples, pears, oranges, and bananas, to put on the table.

A piece of brown wrapping-paper may be cut in the shape of a dish and the fruit cut out and pasted in it.

SELF-DISCOVERY THROUGH PAINTING AND DRAWING*

By HELMUT HUNGERLAND

DRAWING and painting possess distinct psychological values beyond their traditional function of developing special abilities. They aid the child in discovering himself and in establishing a sane relationship to his world. The reason for encouraging a child to draw and paint is not to produce "good" pictures immediately, but to assist in the whole development of the child, to help him clarify his ideas by making "right" pictures. By "right" pictures I mean the paintings appropriate to the child's phase of development and to his essential nature.

During the earliest stages of his growth, the child is confronted with many psychological difficulties, arising out of his own inherited characteristics and out of the nature of the world he touches, but they come into sharpest focus in the period of adolescence. Reality, to the adolescent is constantly changing. At one time it is dangerous; at others, hostile, attractive, repellent, etc. It may seem too narrow to permit him full growth, or too uncertain and expansive to give him a sound footing. The very sources of his existence are stirred, and he seeks to find a new measure of order and unity in the diverse elements of his existence.

I suggest the medium of art as one way by which he may work his way through this confusing reality. To offset his struggle against limitation, drawing and painting offer him complete freedom of expression, which means free abstract work with colors. But freedom is not an end in itself; the goal is the unity of personality best fitted to use real freedom. The child can find unity and new reality as he moves from complete freedom of expression to the organization of his ideas in a picture.

Painting and drawing, like other realms of creative activity such as dancing, music, and sculpture, offer means by which the child can discuss his problems with himself. He works out all his difficulties in color and line; he paints out his troubles. Three values are inherent in this method: first, because he is talking with himself, perfect discretion is possible; second, many of the difficulties slip away without his becoming conscious of their real nature; third, the self-confidence of the child is enormously strengthened because he

* Reprinted from *Progressive Education*, by permission.

succeeds by his own powers in overcoming his difficulties. Moreover, as most of the complexes originate in the area of "feelings," it is better to resolve them by a means that is related to this area. Art that springs from the field of emotion offers an avenue by which complexes may be dispelled.

Drawing and painting are merely modes of expression, just as talking and writing are. Once the child senses this fact, he will be encouraged because he is not expected to "produce art," but just to paint. Children up to the age of about twelve years are able "just to paint," and they express themselves freely. During adolescence, a strong sense of self-criticism permits them to see the disparity between their own paintings and works of art. If, at this dangerous moment, we talk about "art," or try to make the adolescent work after a traditional technique, we discourage or even destroy all chances for free expression by means of color and line. The human product of such attempts is the person who feels sure he cannot draw.

A vivid imagination is the foundation stone for creative work, and in most children it has been fettered by external causes. It is most easily released by perfectly free use of color and line without any attempt to represent nature or to make a pattern. The emotional use of color, line, and rhythm for their own sakes possesses a salutary psychological effect because the child loses his former inhibitions, his fears, and his negative attitudes.

Once the child has lost the bonds which restrict his imagination, he is ready to learn the elements of drawing and painting. He moves from free use of color and line for their own sake to a discovery of the same colors and lines and rhythms in the reality around him, and then to the representation of simple objects.

MUSIC

MUSIC AND RHYTHM

By Mrs. Bertha Payne Newell

MUSIC supplies something that nothing else can replace. It charms, rests, and invigorates. The two factors that contribute to a child's musical sense are his native impulse to croon—to invent little melodies of his own, and the impulse to imitate sounds made by others, just as he learns speech. The teaching of both singing and piano-music to-day makes use of both these impulses, invention and imitation.

We would do much to cultivate the musical sense in children if we would begin early to sing short phrases, which they can answer like an echo. Your little girl calls, "Mamma, I want you." Answer:

Yes, my dear, Here I am.

Echo:

Come to me, Come to me.

or this:

Just a mo-ment dear, I pray,
Moth-er has some work to-day,

In a jif-fy I'll be through

Then I'll come right in with you!

There are scores of these tuneful dialogues that any ordinarily musical person can invent on the spot. Frequent dropping into these melodious conversations would make musical phrases as natural a form of expression as speech alone.

In carrying out this suggestion, use the simplest scale fragments. If you will think of the octave as the body of the scale, the first, third, fifth, and eighth tones are the backbone on which the other tones depend. These make what is called the common chord when sounded together. When sounded successively they make an *arpeggio*. Emphasis on these helps to give a firm grasp of the foundation of all tunes. They are most easily heard and reproduced.

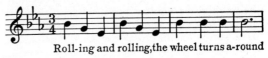

Roll-ing and rolling, the wheel turns a-round

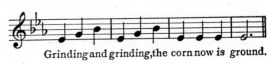

Grinding and grinding, the corn now is ground.

The scale may be broken into two fragments, each of which is a unit in itself. Practicing on these halves of the octave is good ear-training.

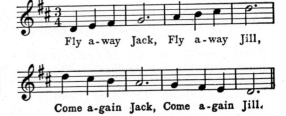

Fly a-way Jack, Fly a-way Jill,

Come a-gain Jack, Come a-gain Jill.

Now we're climb-ing   up   the   lad-der,

High-er,   high-er,   still   we   go.

Hear   the   blue-bird   in   the   tree-top,

Sing-ing,   chirp-ing,   spring   is   here.

A favorite game in some kindergartens is to sing tones in imitation of chimes. The teacher leads and the children try to imitate her exactly, using intervals similar to those given with the words above. Numbering the tones of the octave sing, 1-3-5-8—8-5-3-1. To the same succession sing "la-la-la-la-," or "lo-lo-lo-lo-."

THE CHILD-VOICE

CHILDREN'S voices have a narrow range. What is a comfortable tone for a grown person may be too high or too low for a child. The average person pitches a song too low for children. It is a strain on the vocal cords to sing out of a comfortable range. Songs that range from middle C to F above the second C are safe, provided there are no long-sustained notes at either of these extremes.

Soft singing should be insisted on at all times. Loud singing, like screaming, has a disastrous effect on the throat organs. All kinds of vocal faults show up when it is indulged in. It is painful to listen to much of the singing in day-schools and Sunday-schools. It is so harsh and tense that one is reminded of the Irishman's reply to someone who asked him if he sang by note. "Well, no," he replied, "mostly I sings by main for-rce."

EXERCISES IN RHYTHM

THERE is nothing deeper, more primitive, in the range of human instinct than the feeling for rhythm. The savage's tom-tom sways the line of dusky dancers; the mother's rocking-chair soothes both her tired self and her baby; the weary business man steps alertly when a strain of martial music drifts down the street. It is a steadying, a soothing, or an arousing force, according to the character of its pulsing. But it is as an *organizing* influence that it is valuable to a group of children.

When they have been playing together for a time, the conflict of plans begins to irritate tired brains. They find it hard to compromise and agree. Then it is a great rest to the immature little citizens to have the burden of self-government lifted from them for a space. If you hear jarring sounds growing louder and more frequent in the nursery or playground, try going to the piano and playing something in spirited march time. Then call to them to march, under the leadership of the one best fitted to be captain, round the room once or twice, out into the hall, around the dining-room, and back to you.

They may march on tiptoe, with a change of music if you can manage it; then on heels for a little way. Change to a waltz time for a running step; a two-four time will do, but the run is a little more light to three-four time.

Institute a band and let all be drummers clapping to your music. Change the time from *one*, two, three, four, to ONE, two, ONE, two. See who can clap loud on the strong beat and soft on the weak beat. Let them play imaginary bugles to a familiar song, following the tune with their voices.

Change to a soft lullaby and let them sway to the pulsation, like trees in the wind. End with "Rock-a-by, Baby, in the Tree-top." Hands may shape nests to swing at the ends of branches—and here is a good stopping-place, for by this time the current of their thoughts has been changed. And a little lesson in rhythm has been painlessly administered.

SONG-SINGING

THE IDEAL song for a little child is one of but two or four lines set to a very simple melody. Most songs are too long. Excellent examples are found in Neidlinger's "Small Songs for Small Singers," and in the Primer and First Book of both the Modern Music Series and the Eleanor Smith Series of school song-books. An unusually good collection for home use in the nursery is the one by Miss Emilie Poulsson and Miss Eleanor Smith, which is exactly what its title indicates, "Songs for a Little Child's Day."

No attempts should be made to have a child sing any song or phrase until he is quite familiar with it from hearing it sung. Most children will chime in here and there, when they have been sung to and have absorbed the musical and verbal ideas. Then it is time to take pains to have them sing with and after you. Many children cannot reproduce intonations accurately at this age, and appear to be tone-deaf, when really the perception of pitch has not been formed from lack of hearing enough simple melody. The appreciation of the "Upness and Downness" of pitch will only come through much hearing of simple songs simply and clearly sung. This is one of the most notable lacks in our American homes to-day. Children are as dependent upon their elders for musical language as they are for a grasp of the spoken word. This mastery of musical phrases will come only through imitation, just as speech came.

The pity of this scarcity of true music in the home is that it leaves children a prey to the fearfully meager common music heard on the street, at the movies often, and alas! on the phonograph at home. A revival of folk-songs and folk-singing will be the best means to introduce musical ideas and lay the foundation for good taste in the home.

An illustration from our own home shows how sensitive very little children may be to the spirit and character of the music they hear often.

I had been accustomed to put our little girl in a high-chair at the piano from the time she was eighteen months old, to keep her entertained at meal-times, as she had no nurse, and this was the most effective way of disposing of the young lady. I could watch her through the open door between the living- and dining-rooms. This was possible without harm to her musical sense or the piano either, for she never pounded and had no love of discord. The result was that she soon found pleasant little chords and melodies, and at three would repeat some of them for her own delight. I paid no attention to teaching her, merely approving when the result was especially good. At four years she noticed that she could find a harmonizing tone with the left hand in the bass. As she had seen that older people played with both hands, this gave her a feeling of being much more real in her imitative way of "playing."

One day she called me to hear what she could do. Playing grave chords with the right hand with the proper first and then fifth in the bass in a slow four-four time, she said, "Listen, Mamma, this is a church tune." Then changing to a lively "jig-a-jig-jig, and tum-a-tum-tum," she turned to me with a radiant face, saying, "Now do you know what that is? It's a Sunday-school song!"

Let me repeat, for it cannot be too strongly emphasized, if you would have your children sing, sing to them; if you would have them love the best, sing the best. And the best is often found in the old English, Irish, Scotch, and German folk-songs, such as we all ought to know. "Annie Laurie," "Robin Adair," "Comin' Thro' the Rye," "The Low-Backed Car," "The Wearin' o' the Green," are all fair examples.

MOTHERS AND PRACTICING *

By J. Lillian Vandevere

IF you look forward to the study of music as a natural part of your child's education, and are determined that he shall enjoy its wholesome influence; if you have started your child in music and find the path difficult for any one concerned, then a word on the subject may be welcomed.

SELECTING A TEACHER

THE BEST place for the mother to start is with the teacher. When you find the teacher with whom you wish to place your child, go to one of her pupils' recitals, or meet some of her patrons and ask how she has pleased them. Remember that European study does not give the music-teacher any insight into child psychology, and skilled technique is no indication of ability to create and hold the child's interest. Note her manner, and determine whether she likes children, and deals with them in a natural, wholehearted way that will win even the small boy. Find out what class of pupils she deals with most successfully. Don't send a beginner to Miss Jones or Mr. Brown because their advanced pupils play Chopin well, but select the teacher who has the happy gift of making music a vital thing and easy for little children to acquire. If possible, find one who gives her small pupils class work as well as private lessons, for the stimulus of working together and the joy of competition will cheer the first arduous steps and make progress more rapid and enjoyable. Perhaps it is not feasible for the

---

*Most mothers, no matter if they are musical, are not the best music-teachers of their own children, but this sensible article shows in how many ways a wise mother may sustain her child's enthusiasm and support the teacher's efforts to the best results. We have obtained permission to reprint this interesting article which originally appeared in *The Mothers Magazine.—The Editors.*

teacher to have class work; but the alert and progressive teacher will plan to have gatherings where the pupils will play for each other, or she will arrange for informal recitals by the children.

When you have found a teacher who fills the requirements, one who has a pleasing personality and unending patience, then remember that she may put her highest energy into every minute of the lesson, but her work will not produce the desired results unless you co-operate and supervise the home study.

THE MOTHER'S TASK

"What shall I do?" you ask. The mother's mental attitude toward the child's work is the root of the matter. If your child shows a disinclination to practice, in justice to the teacher remember that aversion to practice is not a sign of lack of musical ability on the child's part, nor is it sufficient reason for discontinuing the lessons. Voluntary practice involves mental control and powers of concentration which are not part of the equipment of the seven-year-old, and one should not look for it. The mother must make clear to the child that practice is a part of the daily routine, and then help him to perform it. As the keyboard and notes grow familiar, the child's interest increases and the practice-hour becomes more of a delight.

Always provide a footstool for the small student. The fussing about and distaste for practice is almost always due to actual physical discomfort. If little feet hang, there is pressure on nerves and blood vessels where the thigh strikes the piano stool, the circulation in the feet is stopped, and the child is not to blame when he is restless and fails to keep his mind on the work to be done.

It is not wise to insist on practice immediately after school, for the normal child who has been in school till half-past three needs time for play. If, on coming home, he is immediately put at practice, he will feel that music has robbed him of legitimate freedom.

TIME FOR PRACTICE

If there can be fifteen minutes' practice before school, and fifteen minutes after a play-time in the afternoon, that is enough for the small child. If the child is physically strong, and exceptionally talented or interested, a half-hour period may be assigned. More than thirty minutes' practice at a time should not be required of the child under eleven or twelve years, though two thirty-minute periods may be introduced whenever the child's progress warrants it.

With a small pupil, it is often wise to arrange with the teacher that she require each portion of the lesson to be gone over a given number of times a day. The practice-time is practically the same, but clock-watching is obviated, and the child who works patiently and steadily will finish with equal benefit in even less time. The mother may tell the child that at the third rendition the little tune must have fewer mistakes than at the first, or if accurately done at first, it must gain speed. A review piece should show gain in expression at each repetition. This objective raises the standard of the home work that intelligent mothers require in any line of effort.

If the mother can occasionally bring her knitting and sit within conversational reach during the practicing, and comment interestedly, it will be a help for which both the teacher and child will bless her. As the little pieces, even the tiniest ones, are well worked up, have Father listen politely and attentively some evening, or a friend who evinces real interest. Insist that one or two such numbers be always on hand, and that the child play at once when asked. From the beginning have some selections memorized, and these will be the joy of the twilight hour or of the winter evenings.

ENCOURAGING THE CHILD

Hold out continually the delightful possibilities that lie ahead of the child who works. Tell the boy what music in college and social life will mean to him. Prepare for family gatherings by having the child learn a simple Christmas carol, or an Easter or Thanksgiving hymn. Many of the old songs which are being revived have simple accompaniments which a child can learn. Let the ambitious boy or girl learn to play "America."

If the teacher assigns duets, give your child an added interest by playing with him. It is excellent discipline for the child to keep time with another, while watching his own part. If duets are not part of the child's assigned work, get one or two books of duets for home use. A little extra work of this sort will be a real delight, for the child's part will be simple, yet the combined result is unexpectedly brilliant.

As the repertoire of simple pieces grows, keep an indexed list, and ask to hear a number from it once in a while. It will aid review work, and wear off little rough places in a most gratifying way; and the child's pride, as he sees his list increasing, will spur him to continued endeavor.

When the child goes to the teacher for his

lesson, look over the assignment when he returns, and make sure that he understands definitely what is expected of him. Get him to tell you how he played his lesson for the day and to criticize his own work. It will make for attention to detail, musical understanding, and sound judgment.

Should some difference with the teacher arise, settle it by letter or telephone when the child is not about. Let the teacher who honestly does her part have the comfortable assurance of knowing that you, in the home field, are giving her your very best possible support always.

CHILDREN'S SINGING IN THE HOME

By Myrtle Douglas Keener

IF SINGING for children in the home is to mean anything in a child's development, there must be first of all the careful selection of songs. So if mothers will select songs with words of educational value and the music, real music, not meaningless jingles, the child's taste for music will grow. The music must be written neither too high nor too low. It is safer for young children to sing from middle C to D, fourth line of the staff, rarely, if ever, going higher or lower, and then only a tone farther, either up or down.

To make the songs effective select them to fit the occasion. Let the day with its experiences, its weather conditions and so on, call forth songs expressing the thoughts of the day. When it rains, sing of the rain; when you gather violets, sing of their beauty and their modesty; if a child swings, a swing song, and if playing with dolls, then a song (there are many) of the "precious family." There is a song, I believe, for every experience in a child's life; for all he loves and understands.

DUSK IS THE BEST TIME FOR SINGING IN THE HOME

MOTHERS will ask, "when and how shall I teach my children to sing? How shall they use their voices; and how can they learn words and music of so many songs? It is too ideal, and it is not possible in our busy days of practical things to find time for this singing in the home." It is *not* too ideal. Children need to have all of the beautiful, all of the ideal we can give them. And it is too important an element in a child's training to neglect. From a child's earliest conscious moment, this singing should be a daily experience and the ideal time is "between the dark and the daylight, when the night is beginning to lower." There is not, I know, in every home, "a pause in the day's occupations" at this hour, so the mother must plan for it and choose the time of day best

suited to her duties, never selecting, however, the half-hour just after meals, for it is better not to sing right after eating.

GOOD WAYS OF TEACHING CHILDREN TO SING CORRECTLY

CHILDREN naturally breathe correctly and use the voice very well. Where these natural conditions have not been lost, let the child sing easily just like the birds, never allowing shouting, for loud singing strains the voice, and besides producing anything but pretty tones, often causes serious throat troubles. Play the melodies of your songs and sing them, having the children sing, at once, gently and quietly. Children learn so quickly by imitation, it is surprising how they get tuneful songs by just singing them. If there are faults in the child's singing, of course, he must be brought back to the natural way of using his voice, and if the fault is that of incorrect breathing, that, too, must be corrected. Changing the character of the song will often produce the desired effect. For example, if the fault is straining the voice by loud singing, select quiet songs and light, dainty tunes, always using the bird as an illustration of correct singing, telling the child to observe how wide he opens his mouth and how easily he sings. It is as natural to sing as it is to talk, and children should sing with as little effort as they use in speaking. If the mother will lead her children from the beautiful lullabies that she should sing herself into the songs natural to their development, little training will be needed. They will learn to sing as easily as they talk. Children should never have lessons in so-called voice culture. Care only is required that the little voices are never forced, and that they are sweet and musical.

What is more beautiful than a burst of song from a happy child trained to express the emotion that fills him!

SINGING IMPROVES THE SPEAKING VOICE AND STRENGTHENS HOME INFLUENCE

SINGING, too, improves the speaking voice and this alone is of infinite value to a child. Who does not acknowledge the charm of a musical speaking voice, but how rarely we hear one! Mothers can cultivate this charm in the home through careful singing with their children, and we will not then be a nation with unpleasant, nasal voices.

But over and above all, singing in the home, centered as it should be around the mother, strengthens her influence. Children love to sing. I know four little children who beg for it, and they sing, and the mother's influence grows stronger as they cultivate, through her, the love of the higher things of life. I hear some one say, That is old-fashioned! Well, if it is? Give us back the old-time home influence that is passing into history; let the mothers of America restore it by singing in the home of the sacred things of life; of all that is good and true and beautiful.

MAKING MUSIC TOGETHER*

By FRANCES M. ANDREWS

PERHAPS you have already gone through the trials of saxophones, trumpets, drums, or some other musical instruments in your home. To many parents such periods must seem like strenuous struggles between the child and the instrument with neither one victorious. I remember one frantic appeal that came to me in the shape of a note from a parent. It read as follows:

"John, Irene, and William have all decided to join your Junior Orchestra. John is choosing trumpet; Irene, clarinet; and William, violin. At present we are living in the midst of ear-splitting din. Could you possibly give them some extra attention so they will get beyond the stage of producing just *noise* and thus preserve our reason?"

John, Irene, and William soon passed beyond the stage noted above. But my sympathies were very much with their parents for a month or so, and with all parents who at some time or other must be shut up in the same house with a snorting saxophone or a howling clarinet.

ARE MUSIC LESSONS WORTH THE MONEY?

"IS IT WORTH IT? How do I know that it will pay me to spend time and money on music for my child?" Every year thousands of anxious parents ask this question of some music teacher. The question is justified, because every year many children take a few painful lessons on some instrument and then beg off as rapidly as possible, leaving music lessons in the memory of their parents as only a few painful scratches and scrapes and some music books in fairly good condition to be cast off to Cousin Annie's little boy when it is

time for his attempt at music. Sometimes the fault of such failure is the teacher's, sometimes it is the parents', sometimes it is the child's. Wherever it lies, time, money, and effort have been wasted uselessly.

Uselessly? Yes, because modern educators are convinced that with the rising standards of private and public school music, the chances of your child's getting more out of music now than ever before have been tremendously multiplied. Why? Well, look at it this way. How many things does your child learn to do by himself? Play marbles? No, he has some companions of his own age playing with him. Ride a bicycle? No, some older child is always around to steady the wheel and rescue the fallen. Dress himself? No, mother, brother, or sister is always close by to take care of the button that just won't go into place. Even reading and writing most of us learn by association with a group of equally beset classmates. But music!

MAKING MUSIC FUN

UNTIL recently there has been only one conventional procedure for music. Once a week, Teacher came and gave William a concentrated dose of instruction. The other six days William, confined to a practice period by the never-moving hands of the clock, struggled in solitary confinement while all the neighborhood children whooped their loudest across the street playing Cowboy and Indian. Now almost anyone knows that if you match the glories of a scale with the glories of being Indian Chief or Tom Mix (all this at the age of eight or ten), you give the scale a terrible handicap. What happened in the end was that Mother finally **gave**

---

* Reprinted by special permission from the *National Parent-Teacher Magazine.*

up saying what a lot music would mean to little William when he was older and lessons and practice ceased, leaving music in the mind of the child only something attempted and failed.

Let's analyze the situation for a moment. To begin with, something was wrong when Mother had to say, as an incentive to practice, that music would mean a lot when you grew older. We concede that, all advertisements to the contrary, there is no royal road to learning music or anything else. But one important step toward keeping the child's interest and sense of achievement while he is *learning* has been the publication of music materials designed to meet the child's level of interest. Music formerly was a completely adult world; the procedure for the learner, no matter what age, was scales, exercise, and an occasional adult piece. Now the story is different. If you are interested, go into any music store and ask to see the piano materials for children beginning the study of piano. The copyright dates will prove to you that at long last the child is being fed the sort of thing he can understand and assimilate. Of course the standard studies go on forever, but the stress is now upon them as a means to an end, not as an end in themselves. If a child wants to play a piece with scale passages and can't do it because his fingers stumble, you'll need no more motivation to induce him to study a few scales. But this is incidental, and is subordinated to the real business of making music. How many musicians, once expert, play scales and finger exercises for an audience? Well, Johnny doesn't hear any one playing scales, either, so why should he practice them? More likely than not, Johnny wants to play jazz in as snappy a manner as the organist at the corner music palace; not scales! So we relegate scales to their proper place and Johnny swallows them unprotestingly when the time comes. Music written in a manner interesting to children has been a big step toward prevention of victims of the trial and error method.

MUSIC AT SCHOOL

BUT WHERE, you are asking, does the aforementioned school music come in? In many places. First, through giving your child a background of musical experience early in his school life. Singing appropriate songs, playing musical games, participating in a toy orchestra for the purpose of *having fun* (and incidentally developing a sense of rhythm); public school music gives all these to your child in kindergarten and first grade. The song material used is within the best tradition of music, and all in the range of child experience.

Usually after second grade there is an opportunity for the child to join an instrumental ensemble; perhaps instruction will be furnished by the school on certain of the orchestral instruments. The ideal is, of course, to have your child play in an instrumental group while taking private lessons.

ENSEMBLE PLAYING

MUSIC then becomes a natural form of recreation. In one town of which I know it is a common occurrence for a child to invite several of his friends in for an evening of ensemble playing. In the case of John, Irene, and William, mentioned before, one of the favorite family amusements is to get together for a musicale after dinner. Each of the children plays his respective instrument, Father plays the guitar and Mother the piano. Yet none of these children is regarded by his family as a musical prodigy, or given a halo to wear about the brow by virtue of his musical accomplishments. Occasionally, perhaps, but not as a rule, one of them is asked to perform for guests.

In the ideal community, should it ever be achieved, it is to be hoped that a mother would as soon urge her child to demonstrate cleaning his teeth as to show off for company by playing a little ditty. For in many cases it seems to lead a child to hate music, this showing off for company. If it is the child's idea, very well; he is sure enough of himself to gain in poise and sense of achievement by performing. But no child ever gained in anything but mortification by being dragged unwillingly to a place of prominence and forced to struggle through a half-learned piece. For the average child, this is embarrassing; for the oversensitive child of a retiring nature who may really love his music, it is sometimes agony which may soon turn to resentment toward music. Nature cannot be forced. When a child is adequately prepared and knows he will give pleasure by his performance, he will perform willingly. Until then, hands off!

High schools will offer your child advanced orchestral and vocal work in school choruses, glee clubs, bands, and orchestras. The average high school offers good training in these and in the fundamentals of music theory as well. Add appreciation of music as it is now taught, and, all in all, your child, if he wishes, may acquire a fairly adequate musical training during his school years. In the last analysis, however, probably the biggest achievement of the school has been substituting group performance for individual performance during the uncertain years of learning, thus providing a natural situation where before there was an artificial one.

CHOOSING AN INSTRUMENT

Now let us be concise. Suppose your child has announced to you a desire to study some musical instrument. To begin with, take it calmly as you would should he express a desire to learn to swim. Consult the best-qualified music teacher you can find. If your public schools employ a teacher of instrumental music or an all-round music supervisor whose work you respect, consult one of them. In teaching music or anything else the temperament of the individual child may make all the difference in approach and method, so anything you may tell your child's prospective teacher concerning his personality may greatly expedite the child's learning. One thing must be remembered in this business of selecting an instrument: never force a child to attempt an instrument he dislikes or doesn't wish to learn. I've seen it tried. Because Uncle George had a cello, Harry must learn the cello, when he really wants to play the good old trombone. *It never works.* The cello soon dies a natural death. You cannot fit your child to an instrument; the instrument must be fitted to the child. When with the advice of the teacher and the wishes of the child you have selected an instrument, don't expect genius to flare immediately. First days are days of experiment and blunder. But the average child soon finds himself in the strange ways and means of producing music, as naturally as he finds his new legs in roller skating or bicycling. Then, if he becomes associated with a group of children playing instruments, he will probably go on playing for the fun of it all through school, and often, all through life.

THE CHILD WHO "CAN'T CARRY A TUNE"

MANY persons still hold to the unfortunate idea that because a child cannot "carry a tune" he is not musical. This thing of being musical is a ticklish subject, depending entirely on the individual's interpretation of the term "musical." It used to be that the child who sang off-pitch or on a limited number of tones was told summarily not to sing. His chances for developing that musicality which many enlightened music educators hold to be the birthright of nearly every child were thus dismissed without even investigation. But many

a child who, in first grade, sings everywhere but on the right note is in perfect conformity with the group in third. What has happened? Simply and naturally his teacher has helped him find and place his singing voice. Most music educators agree that the difficulties of so-called monotones fall into the following classes, and may be remedied in one of the following ways: If the child is not aware of difference in pitch, his attention should be drawn to the difference between going up and going down, thus developing a sense of tonal or pitch direction, a process possible because more often the fault in such cases lies in unawareness rather than in actual physical defect. Or perhaps the child cannot produce a tone although he may hear it correctly. Attention, given in a casual but skilful manner by the teacher, will many times remedy this defect in coordination. Sometimes, though, the non-singing child has a physical handicap which only medical or surgical attention can remedy. Tonsils, adenoids, and aural defects come under this classification.

MOST CHILDREN ARE MUSICAL

THE PERCENTAGE of children who can't benefit by some kind of musical training is very small. If your child upon medical examination is discovered to have no actual physical defect which will interfere with his adventures in music, you are justified in allowing and encouraging him in a desire to be musical, and in the belief that he is musical. The person who loves to hear an orchestra, but does not know a clarinet from a cornet, may be just as musical as the concertmaster in the true sense of the word. One is musical in the passive sense and the other in the active; who shall say that one is more musical than the other? In our training of talents and dispositions toward music in the public schools we are glad when we find the former, but we welcome the latter as eagerly, and sometimes as much comes of it. One small boy with a desire to play the fiddle or the trumpet and only average ability may get more from such playing than may a brilliant student with a more marked talent. Many an inferiority feeling has been cured by the lusty blowing of a horn, and many a feeling of superiority has been put in its place by the necessity of playing *with*, not ahead of or behind, an orchestra or band. Psychologically speaking, the surface of music has not even been scratched as applied to the "problem" child.

NATURE STUDY

THE HERITAGE OF CHILDHOOD

By Augusta M. Swan

Love of nature is the heritage of childhood. It is a tendency in every child of every land.

All nature is akin to childhood; birds, animals, flowers, insects are all beautiful to children, even the "lovely crawly caterpillar," and the "creepy snail."

We all know how a dog will allow a child to stumble over him, recognizing the action by only an expression of long-suffering indifference; he will stand all kinds of teasing which he would not tolerate from an adult.

There seems to be a silent but mutual understanding among young animals of all kinds whether they have four legs or two.

ANIMAL FRIENDS

By Mrs. Helen Y. Campbell

The child's animal friends will find no small place in his Nature training, and no child should be without such, and especially pets, to care for and learn to love. The first instinct of the tiny child toward the lower forms of animal life is usually as fearless as it is destructive, and the discovery of a hapless insect or a weakly fly is usually the signal to "dead it," much as he tears his picture-book to pieces in the newly discovered delight of being able to use his hands.

EARLY FEARS

Toward the higher forms he feels more or less antagonistic and works experimentally, with a sense of unusualness and a certain amount of fear —the friendliest doggie or the most inoffensive puss has his hair tugged and his tail pulled unmercifully, partly from curiosity to see what he will do. Close acquaintance brings more confidence, and the suggestion that he gives pain or destroys a happy little life, a more humane attitude.

But only when the child has pets, and is thereby in touch with their daily life and needs, does he feel quite in sympathy with them, and then they are his most cherished friends. His friendly and faithful doggie, who will join him in many a romp, and eagerly accompany him in all his walks, will be his first chum. He will delight to watch the kitten's frolics, see it take its morning bath, and lap its milk; and to supply a pet bird with food and drink and daily tub; to watch the fowls run for the tidbits he scatters for them, and to search in the wake of the cackling hen for her warm, newly laid egg in the nest, and to stroke and listen to the peeping of the tiny fluffy chicks, and watch the anxious, fussy care and furtive glances of the clucking mother-hen. He will delight to watch the feeding and the munching and the milking of

> "The friendly cow, all red and white,
> I love with all my heart;
> She gives me cream with all her might
> To eat with apple-tart."

and later the child will find great pleasure in and learn much from feeding and caring for his own doves, rabbits, and guinea-pigs.

NATURE STUDY FOR YOUNG CHILDREN

By Rhoda Bacmeister

THERE seems to be almost nothing of so much interest to children as nature. They love flowers and insects, and how quickly they will desert the most charming toy for a kitten or a dog! All the little things that we take for granted or even dislike, such as caterpillars and weeds, are a genuine delight to the child's alert eyes.

VALUES FROM NATURE STUDY

IT IS very fortunate that this is true because an interest in nature is one of the most valuable possessions anyone can have. In the first place it is an unfailing source of pleasure. One may be fond of good music or pictures or drama and live where these pleasures are rarely accessible, or the styles may change so that the kind one admires disappears like last year's snow; but nature is always there and always the same although never monotonous. Each flower is new and yet a familiar old friend. For people who live in the country, in suburbs or small cities, opportunities to enjoy nature are easily available, and even those who live in big cities often have some yard space, parks, or the possibility of excursions by car. The increase of summer camps, too, is a means of giving many children their birthright of contact with natural things.

A familiar closeness to nature is almost certain to bring a fundamental sort of understanding of life. Children who grow up close to nature come to realize how everything grows through food and rest, reproduces and dies, how nothing can live without changing, how no two creatures are ever quite alike, and yet birth and death, seedtime and harvest time, lay out the inevitable pattern for it all. These are the laws of life to which we must all become adjusted, and the sooner the better. There is a breadth of sympathy and a certain steadfastness and directness about many country people which is hard to find among those who have grown up among bricks and machinery instead of field and woods.

Nature study, again, is valuable because it forces a child to think in terms of real things, rather than to learn by heart words he does not understand. When he knows which are the weeds in his garden plot and finds out what will happen if he neglects them, he has something useful and so real to him that he does not forget it as he does the capital of Uganda.

Yet many children are not getting the experiences with nature they well might have. This is chiefly for two closely related reasons. Parents often want their children to have such contacts but do not realize how easy they are to find. Or they may know that, and yet hesitate to try to teach the child because they feel so ignorant themselves. That is all a mistake.

BEGINNINGS ARE EASY

A SMALL YARD, or even a window box can provide delightful experiences with plants and insect life, and there are a number of pets which are quite simple to keep. Moreover the child does not need or want a course in botany or entomology. At first he just wants to plant a seed and see it grow, or to watch the pretty beetle on the milk-weed. Any grownup can help him do those things, and can add to his pleasure and profit by telling him the seed will need watering, and asking him what the beetle seems to be doing and how many legs he has. It really is not hard at all. You just have to throw away your prejudices and look at things as though for the first time. Then you have the key to fairyland! A rainy day is no longer a bore, but becomes a gay dance of raindrops in the puddles, with a lilting, rhythmic pitter-patter for music. Dandelions change from weeds to rosettes of crystallized sunshine, and ants become queer interesting little people out shopping for the family dinner.

It doesn't matter a bit whether you can name the particular creature under consideration. Far more important is it to teach the child, and yourself, to watch what he is *doing* as well as what he looks like. Then you will both come to realize, as most people do not seem to, that he is not just a curiosity made to amuse or annoy human beings, but an individual in his own right, out to hunt food, find a mate, take a sun bath, build a home, or lay eggs. Of course as a child grows older he will enjoy learning which caterpillar will develop into a certain butterfly and what the habits of life of the species are, but those things can be looked up when the time comes. It is amazingly true that people are so little concerned to observe things about them that there are a great many gaps in the knowledge of common species. But one can usually find out all that is wanted, and there is always the thrilling possibility that some little fact noticed by an observant child will fill a gap in the scientist's work. We all know of astronomical discoveries by amateurs and they are not uncommon in other fields, although they receive less publicity.

THE YOUNG CHILD LEARNS

BUT ALL that is for the child of ten and up. At first he needs only to see that you find birds and plants and rocks interesting, as he does, to learn to watch what the specimen is doing, and to move slowly and quietly so as not to frighten the object of his interest. A baby always wants to run toward a kitten or a robin and has to learn that thereby he loses it.

The adult must remember that a young child is not interested long in one thing, otherwise he will be sure to explain too much or to expect the child to work too long at a time at one thing. We must also provide something to do about the things the child sees or he will experiment and very likely develop cruel habits. He won't stamp on worms, for example, if he knows it hurts them and he can really have more fun by watching them crawl over things and then making them a hole in the dirt to live in.

THE CHILD'S DESIRE TO COLLECT

ANOTHER thing to recognize is the child's desire to collect. A pre-school child will do it in a very miscellaneous manner, much like a crow, and will be content to keep his treasures piled in a box. Periodic clearing out will have to be done privately by the parent to allow the family room to go on living, but it must be done on the basis of what seems to have been forgotten rather than of what seems worthless. Then it will probably never be noticed. The child should be taught that flowers are put in water if picked, and that little living things, such as toads, turtles and caterpillars, may be kept a while for the fun of watching them but must be let go again soon to find food and their way home.

Older children also will want to collect, but can usually be led to some sort of a system. At first it may be a nature museum in the attic where deserted birds' nests hobnob with scallop shells, but later everything will be classified, labelled and grouped, and the pressed flowers, perhaps, will gradually absorb most of the child's interest.

NATURE STUDY OPPORTUNITIES IN THE AVERAGE HOME

FOR OUR own purpose of discussing precisely what nature study opportunities are open in the average home, we, too, shall find it convenient to classify our material as inanimate nature, plant life, animal life, and mixed projects.

Tiny children, of course, spend a lot of time learning about the qualities of inanimate objects, such as that chairs are hard but pillows soft, concrete rough, sand trickly. Before they are through with this, however, they show interest in weather, snow, ice and rain, wind, sun and shadows. They notice sun, moon and stars, they take an interest in mud and clay and stones. Usually by six the child has passed beyond his superficial interest in geology and astronomy and it may not awaken again until about ten, or later.

In regard to plant life the situation is quite different. A baby of two loves the color and smell of flowers, and this interest, if fostered, will persist and increase. There are an amazing number of common wild flowers to be found in any vacant lot and literally hundreds if fields and woods are available.

CHILDREN'S GARDENS

So MUCH has been written about gardening for children that it seems worth while to give only a few suggestions here. The prime requisite for success is a kind of plant that will grow fast and stand considerable abuse. Lettuce, radishes, beans, corn, and peas are all good vegetables if there is space for them. One can even raise very nice radishes in a flower pot. Nasturtiums, cornflowers, zinnias, and marigolds among others are sturdy flowers. Do not make the mistake of letting the child start too large a garden, or he will tire of it, and do not let him overcrowd his space as he is certain to want to do. He will need advice and supervision on the weeding for a year or so. Otherwise let the child do as he likes. He will over water one day and forget the next, but tough plants will survive and he will learn to love his garden.

In thinking of plant life do not forget trees and shrubs as possible interests. Children often love learning the leaf and the characteristic form of various trees, and they should certainly be shown how the next year's buds are already set on when the leaves fall. Mushrooms and fungi, bulbs and house plants offer other fascinating and easily accessible experiences.

CHILDREN NEED PETS

COMMON pets and farm animals naturally form a large part of a child's introduction to animal life, but we must not forget frogs and turtles, beetles and butterflies, bunnies, birds, and chipmunks or fish and other water life.

Every child should have pets certainly, for the pleasure they give him as well as for the training he gets in kindness and responsibility and the help they are in understanding reproduction and death. Kittens are good, and one need not fear scratches from a cat that has always been kindly treated. Dogs are excellent and, if the breed is adapted to the city or country home, easy to care for. There are also the possibilities of the pet stores, birds, fish, guinea pigs, bunnies and all sorts of unusual pets,—or even better, for the country and suburban children, the lost baby chipmunk, the tame crow, the wandering turtle or adopted field mice.

AN AQUARIUM

In the same way, an aquarium stocked with plants, fish, snails, polliwogs and miscellaneous "things" from the brook or pond in the fall will be far more educational and interesting all winter than the conventional goldfish. If a screened box can be arranged near a window with such an aquarium in it together with earth and land plants a real piece of the out of doors can be studied at leisure. All sorts of insects, small turtles, salamanders, toads and frogs, even tiny snakes can live there. Cocoons will hatch, flowers will bloom, and so on.

GO AFIELD WITH OPEN EYES

But nothing, of course, will take the place of the wandering along seashore, or brook, through woods or fields with open eyes for whatever there may be to see. It is often something quite unexpected, but always interesting. You will find a pocket magnifying glass useful, and you will soon learn whether you want a few empty pill-boxes for bugs, a tin box for plants, or a number of paper bags in your pocket for this and that.

It will very likely lead gradually into a collection of some sort, and you and your children will find that you need advice about your new hobby. It is not hard to get. Go first to your school and your library—either may solve your problems. If not, your state university or agricultural college will be able to supply much free information and will be glad to encourage nature interests. The Department of Agriculture at Washington, too, publishes a great number of leaflets free or very cheap. Your congressman will be glad to get a list of them for you or you can get it by writing direct.

When we realize how valuable nature interests are to children, how easy they are to encourage, and what a bond of shared pleasures they build between parent and child, we shall no longer hesitate to start the grand adventure in some simple way.

NATURE STUDY FOR OLDER BOYS AND GIRLS

By the Hon. E. W. Butterfield

(With additions by the Editors)

There comes a time in his development when the child imitates the useful activities of adults as he sees men and women engaged in the various industries. Here identification of objects without relation to other things ceases to be sufficient. The wild flowers, trees, and common animals are so well known that other elements of interest need to be emphasized.

Home gardening being a creative process and one affording satisfaction through its results, is particularly educative. The occupations which produce food, market gardening, fruit raising, general agriculture, and canning industries, if visited and explained, are among the most valuable aids the teacher has for these boys and girls.

Growing out of these creative-constructive enterprises and hence intimately related to them are such topics as insects, plant and animal diseases and their causes, soils and their relation to plants, weather observations and forestry.

WEEDS

The common weeds should be listed and studied with methods for their eradication. For this reason they should be listed as annual, biennial or perennial.

ROCKS AND SOILS

How crude, disintegrated rock is modified by plant and animal life. How lichens, moss, brambles, ferns, saxifrage, heath, juniper, grass, and bushes are seen growing on stones, ledges, and gravel banks. How decaying vegetation accumulates in shallow ponds, stagnant rivers, forming muck. How trees and leaves fall and decay in the forest, forming leaf mold and rich soil. How earth worms eat decaying leaves and mix dark and light soils. How running water separates the fine from the coarse parts of soil. How brooks cut a way through banks, carrying the material down stream, dropping some of it in sand bars, some in fine silt in stagnant places. These and many more topics are appropriate during these years in both the fall and spring.

EXCURSIONS

Go to forests, streams, bogs, ponds, pastures, stone quarries, ledges, and walls to get specimens of vegetation growing in places where there is little soil, such as (a) on rocks and ledges, (b) on stumps and decaying logs, (c) on living trees.

Get samples of rock waste, sterile soil, pasture turf, garden loam, decaying wood, leaf mold and muck. Bring in soft and hard rock and rock which has lichens or moss growing on its surface.

The boys and girls should be taken to gravel banks, plowed fields, rocky pastures, forests, meadows, bogs, ponds, rivers, and brooks; (a) to note changed character of vegetation in different situations, (b) to see soils of different kinds and how they are being modified by frost, water, plants, animals, and man. See how earthworms, ants, woodchucks, and squirrels mix deep and surface soil.

WEATHER

Quantitative observations are now increasingly possible. With these should be studied the clouds and their meaning, storms, winds, temperature, rain, hail, and snow.

INSECTS

Study and list common, beneficial and destructive insects, with methods of extermination.

GARDENING

During these years there should be for all boys and girls home projects of good size. These projects should be made to produce food usable and salable. It should not be difficult to arouse interest in fall work in canning and preserving to salvage the surplus garden produce.

PROPAGATION

In rural schools there is a real opportunity to make nature study valuable and to improve the school ground by setting out fruit and shade trees and caring for them.

LOCAL INDUSTRIES

Go to any place where water power is used to drive machinery and see how the river is located, how dams and canals are built.

Notice how ledges are cut through by the river forming gorges, or how the water flows over rapids or undeveloped falls.

The simple industries are best to study. A sawmill or grain mill is likely to be available. Get the miller to show how corn is made into meal. Then pound dry corn or grind it in a mortar, separating the fine parts. Study the corn kernel by cutting it with a sharp knife until its different layers are seen. In a sawmill see the way logs are sawed and the grain of the wood. In paper mills get samples of pulp and try to get answers to such questions as these: Why are spruce and poplar and fir used? Why not use pine or oak? Relate the paper used in school to the tree in the forest, or the flour used in the bread to the wheat fields, or the cotton handkerchief to the cotton fields.

These are the true and interesting ways of *going from the near at hand known to the remote related unknown.*

"Oh, Painter of the fruits and flowers,
We thank Thee for Thy wise design
Whereby these human hands of ours
In nature's garden work with Thine."
—*Froebel.*

SELECTING TOYS WISELY*

PLAY is growth to the child. It is as necessary as food and sunshine. The child who is not permitted to run in the open, to climb to high places, to regulate his own ideas, to adjust to his contemporaries, is not leading a normal existence and cannot develop into a wholesome, happy child.

The routine of eating, sleeping, and elimination is controlled by adults. This is the child's work. To balance this he should have long uninterrupted periods of play, with a minimum of interference from adults.

WHERE TO PLAY

PARENTS do not realize the influence that a room of his own may have upon the development of the child. What the home is to the adult his own room should be to the child. In a family with several children this may seem impossible, yet one room where the pre-school member may play regularly and which is arranged to meet his needs is not impossible. The child should early become accustomed to a degree of solitude, to selecting his own playthings, to depending upon himself. When he is permitted to play all over the house, too often he is constantly with the mother, growing increasingly dependent upon her suggestion and approbation.

If care is taken that the furniture is such that he cannot hurt himself, he can have the run of his room from the time he begins to crawl. If a gate is put on the doorway, the mother can watch him without entering the room.

The floor should be covered with cork carpet, if possible, as this is both warm, soft, quiet and easily kept clean. The furniture should be plain and limited to the actual needs of the child. Low cupboards built in the room help in developing habits of tidiness; a low seat on which the child may sit or lie down is an attractive addition; to these may be added shelves where the first books are kept. A low table and chair will complete the furnishings. This can be accomplished in a small room with expenditure of labor rather than much money. One or two good pictures, if carefully selected, may exert an influence upon the tastes and interests of the child out of all proportion to their cost.

Outdoor play should begin with the infant who is put outside to play in a pen whenever weather conditions permit. The pre-school child should be given the run of an enclosed space. It is often difficult to get him to play alone, but by providing the right materials and persistently turning a deaf ear to all protests, it can be accomplished.

Cultivation of the ability to play alone lays the foundation for self-reliance in later life. The child who has become dependent upon adult companionship and suggestion is often at a loss when this outer support is removed; while the child of only two who has come to rely upon himself has an inner control and assurance which carries over into new situations. As the child grows older play materials are useful in encouraging children to play together as well as for developing independence when a child plays alone. Although it is within the family that the child receives his first social training, these contacts are not a substitute for play with children of his own age and play outside the home.

CARE OF PLAY MATERIALS

PART of the education which comes through play is found in the establishment of habits of order.

Few rules should be made but they should be observed. If proper cupboards have been pro-

* Courtesy of Extension Service, New Jersey State College of Agriculture.

vided, the child should be taught to keep his toys in specific places and to return them there when he has finished using them. If the child has a share in determining the arrangement, he will be more cooperative about using it. If nagging and scolding are avoided and his willingness is assumed, it often helps toward satisfactory results. It is unwise to wait until the child is overtired, and the observant mother will give the child occasional assistance to tide him over the difficult moments.

If a child flatly refuses to put a toy away or is destructive with it when he has been shown how to handle it, the toy should be removed without comment and kept until the child has shown a willingness to use it properly.

THINGS TO REMEMBER IN SELECTING PLAY MATERIALS

IN SELECTING toys we should keep in mind such points as attractiveness, safety, durability and variety of use.

Buy few but good toys. Toys which stand wear may serve to teach habits of care for playthings. Buy individual pieces rather than sets of tools, paints, or sewing equipment. A few pieces at a time as the child needs them are less confusing. A good hammer or paint brush brings better results than the cheaper articles so often found in sets. Provide toys which stimulate effort. Toys which "do it all" encourage laziness and a love of being entertained.

Beginning with the simplest toy, and giving from time to time one which is a little more complex and elaborate will help the child to get all the good possible from that type of toy over a long period of time. Between the strong composition doll of medium size with painted hair and fixed eyes suitable for the two-year-old, and the lovely, breakable, life-like and life-sized doll which can be dressed and undressed by the older child, there is a great variety of dolls—rag, felt, wooden, and composition—to be enjoyed. To give the best doll first is to rob the child of this growth and pleasure.

TOYS FOR DIFFERENT AGES

THE FOLLOWING list of toys is merely suggestive but may help to make plain the various types of toys appropriate at different age levels. From it the parent may make selections. It is not intended that a child should have all the toys listed under any particular age, or that he should be limited to those mentioned here, but he should have at least some toy of each type.

For the Baby

Sturdy bone, wood, or celluloid rattles; soft cuddly animals; soft, washable dolls; bright balls, some toy with a short cord attached, wood embroidery rings, wooden spoon, large bead doll.

For the Child from 1 to 2 Years

Stuffed animals to hold, stuffed animals to pull and ride on, nested blocks and pans, wooden scoop, cart, doll carriage, doll cradle, soft doll, large rubber ball, blocks (cubes, 2x2x2 inches) or large light-weight hollow blocks, color cone, peg board, clappers or rattle boxes, home-made drum.

For the Child from 2 to 4 Years

Physical Exercise—Express wagon, slide, climbing frame, swings, wheelbarrow, sand box, sand toys, ladder or long boards, set of steps, tricycle, garden tools, balls.

Dramatic Play—Dolls (unbreakable, washable, medium size), doll furniture, tin dishes, laundry set, dust pan, broom and mop, telephone, wooden train, dump cart, truck, wooden aeroplane.

Constructive and Creative Play—Large blocks, large crayons, clay or plasticine, blunt scissors, library paste, colored paper, large wooden beads (1 inch dimension) and laces, hammer, large headed nails, and soft wood or soap, standing easel and poster paints, wash or sash brush.

Games and Puzzles—Strip puzzles illustrating scenes on the farm, domestic animals, wood cut-out puzzles, color cone, peg board.

Music and Rhythm—Victrola records, tambourine, drum, musical dumb-bells, wooden xylophone, books of children's songs.

For the Child from 4 to 6 Years

Physical Exercise—Tricycle, wagon, broom and dust pan, strong shovel, rake, hoe, sled. To the gymnastic equipment mentioned for the child 2 to 4 years old, should be added trapeze and parallel bars.

Dramatic Play—Play houses with doors, windows, and curtains, larger doll furniture, store-keeping toys such as scales and toy money, transportation toys such as trucks, cranes, boats, toy circus, Noah's Ark, toy villages.

Constructive and Creative Play—Large floor blocks, peg blocks, carpentry bench and tools, village to build, pictures and straight line cut-outs for pasting, paper dolls to dress, easel for painting, large brushes, large paper, poster paint, modeling clay.

Games and Puzzles—Simple large puzzles, picture dominoes, animal rubber stamp sets, ring toss.
Music and Rhythm—Same as earlier age.

For the Child from 6 to 8

Physical Exercise—Ice skates, large express coaster. The gymnastic equipment commonly found on school play ground, basket ball, tricycle, garden spade.
Dramatic Play—Paper dolls, doll furniture, play suits, play house, baby dolls, water tower, submarine, electric train and accessories, chart printing outfit, concrete mixer, steam shovel.
Constructive and Creative Play—The same materials should continue to be used with more finished results. To these may be added, hand loom and cotton roving for weaving, raffia and reed, wood for bird houses, more tools, interlocking building blocks, pasteboard, pastels, oil paints, India ink, etc.
Games and Puzzles—Dissected maps, stamp book, anagrams, geographical lotto, checkers, dominoes, marbles.

For the Older Child, 8 and Beyond

Physical Exercise—Sporting equipment for football, baseball, basketball, golf, tennis, archery; fishing; bicycle; trapeze; ladder; and rings, garden tools.
Imitative Play—Play house, typesetting machine, speed boat, movie machine, magic toys, electric iron, stove, sewing machine, cooking utensils.
Constructive and Creative Play—Oil paints, arts and craft materials, knives for wood carving, wood-turning equipment, drawing kit, building materials, erector sets, stamping sets, sewing materials, typewriter.
Dramatic Play—Toy theatres, puppet shows, materials for dramatizing stories, for costuming and making scenery.
Games and Puzzles—Parlor croquet, ping pong, pool, checkers, parchesi, flinch, rummy, authors, chess, jig-saw puzzles, anagrams, maps and travel games, chemistry set, microscope, small engine, camera, globe.

TOOLS FOR DIFFERENT AGES

IN PROVIDING tools for children parents must take time to help until the children have learned how to use them properly. This is especially important for the safety of the child, the home and the tools.

A sturdy work bench or table with an edge for the vise is necessary. Plenty of soft wood should be obtained from a mill or lumber yard. The solid ends of grocer's fruit boxes may be salvaged for the youngest carpenters. Wooden axles and wooden wheels can be obtained for home-made wagons; large dowels may also be cut for wheels, and empty spools will serve for pulleys, smoke stacks, wheels, and other purposes. A child should be provided with paints and brushes (if water colors are used provide shellac for a coating) in order to make a finished product that will give him more pleasure.

Get good tools. Poor equipment will discourage a beginner. Good tools are *easier* for a child to handle and will last a lifetime. Every home needs tools for the use of the whole family. Provide a sturdy wooden box for a tool chest.

A PLAN FOR PROGRESSIVE PURCHASE OF GOOD TOOLS FOR CHILDREN

Tools for a Child of 2-4 Years

1. Vise, at least two-inch opening.
2. Hammer, light weight, with broad hammering surface and claw.
3. Nails, short, with large heads.
4. Saw, short, broad, small teeth.
   (The toddler should not be left alone with his tools.)

More Tools for a Child of 4-6 Years

5. Nails (1½ inch).
6. Drill (works like an egg beater).
7. Drill point (¼ inch).
8. Dowel sticks (¼ inch).

More Tools for a Child of 6-8 Years

9. Screw driver (small).
10. Screws (¼ inch); also hooks and eyes.
11. Pliers (small).
12. Chisel (small).
13. Flint papers (Number 1 or 2).
14. Bright paint, paint brush and shellac.

18 Tools When a Child is 8-12 Years Old

15. Saws (cross cut, keyhole, jig).
16. Carving tools (for wood or linoleum).
17. Assorted nails, screws, drill points, and flint papers.
18. Plane.

If of fine quality, and if the child is instructed in their proper use and care, many of these tools will last a lifetime.

SPECIAL REQUISITES FOR OUTDOOR PLAYTHINGS

OUT-OF-DOORS furnishings should be of a kind to encourage creative play. Playground apparatus, therefore, in addition to providing for big muscle development, should combine the following requisites:

1. Intrinsic value as a toy or plaything. The play of children on it and with it must be spontaneous.

2. Adaptability to different kinds of play and exercise. It must appeal to the imagination of the child so strongly that new forms of use must be constantly found by the child himself.

3. Adaptability to individual or group use. It should lend itself to solitary play or to use by several players at once.

Additional requisites are:

4. Safety. Its use should be attended by a minimum of danger. Suitable design, proper proportions, sound materials, and careful construction are essentials.

5. Durability. It must be made to withstand hard use and all kinds of weather. To demand a minimum of repairs means also to afford a maximum of security.

YOUR FAMILY'S LEISURE*

EVERY member of the family, from infant to breadwinner, should have time for play. Real recreation should be a change and a relief from those things that seem burdensome because they are confining, monotonous, or uninteresting to us. The need of many adults to-day is to make a careful selection of a few community activities that to them are interesting and worthwhile and through which they may make a personal contribution to the community. Too many people go into things only for what they personally can get out of them. They fail to realize that as members of a community they owe that community some service. To act as leader of a boys' or girls' club, for instance, or to become a member of some organized community group allows the individual to make a contribution. Frequently people discover that therein lies one of the most satisfying uses of their leisure time.

DISCRIMINATE!

WHILE the automobile, the radio and the moving pictures have brought their problems, they also offer opportunities for family entertainment. The extent to which they serve either to integrate the family or to disintegrate it by causing dissension and disharmony is determined by the amount of consideration given the rights of each individual.

Let us consider the radio, for instance. The children may want jazz or cheap comedians, while the adults prefer lectures or a symphony concert. Who is to determine the selection? It is largely a matter of mutual regard and consideration. In one family where the father objected strenuously to jazz, the children were found grouped about the loud speaker with the music so low that it could not be heard in the next room. In another family I know of, it is understood that if a particular program is to be listened to, those not wishing to hear it retire to some other part of the house.

AVOID OVER-STIMULATION

YOUTH is eager for novel experiences but it is neither necessary nor wise that all of its desires be gratified. There is no reason why a boy or girl should hear every radio program, see every good play, all the available works of art, every remarkable performance of any sort. A few suitable samples, a few notable experiences of each kind will suffice. Intellectual advantage does not require a full round of concerts, lectures and club activities. Nor should children be prematurely socialized by a steady succession of dancing parties, theatre parties and house parties. Such social life is essentially adult life, yet in our cities especially, boys and girls are being over-stimulated along these lines. They enjoy excitement but too frequent excitement overtaxes vitality. In denying children injurious excitements the parent need not fear that he is depriving them of rightful enjoyment provided he substitutes saner pleasures.

"But," says the parent, "all the other children are doing it. I have to let mine, too, or he will be miserable." Again we say—begin early to develop the child's own resources—help him to find satisfaction in what he can make and what he can do. Encourage him to spend his leisure in using tools, clay, paint, in drawing, in playing some instrument, in dramatizing stories. We

---

* Courtesy of Extension Service, New Jersey State College of Agriculture.

have grown away from the idea that children must have special ability along these lines to enjoy them or make them worth cultivating. To the gifted child should be given special training, but to all children may come through the use of these various mediums an appreciation and enlarged outlook that will add much to their enjoyment of life.

ADVENTURING IN HANDCRAFT

By Elizabeth Price

National Recreation Association

YOU WHO have made something with your hands do not need urging to be interested in handcraft. You will never lose that deep feeling of pleasure and satisfaction that came with creating a thing of beauty, whether it was a dress, a toy, a bookcase or a quick sketch. But it is well to remind ourselves of the satisfactions in making things, lest in the busy daily round we forget to pass this experience on to the children or neglect it for ourselves.

WHY HANDCRAFT?

THE CASE for handcraft for children (and adults) is a strong one. Because through it the child finds a way of expressing his thoughts and experiences creatively, even before he can express himself articulately in words, it is essential that he be given opportunities in it. As an older child and as an adult handcraft continues to satisfy a basic human need for creative self-expression. For the adult caught in a non-creative job, it may be his only means for satisfying this basic need. A varied handcraft program for children develops skills which will make living a little easier. There will come a time when a woman needs to hammer a nail, a man to sew a seam, put up shelves or make the children's toys. It is helpful to have these and other skills among one's accomplishments. There is also pleasure in ability to use one's hands adeptly. Interest in handcraft can develop patience, control, appreciation of high standards of craftsmanship and beauty. It calls on the creative ingenuity and inventiveness of the child— and one may sometimes discover or develop rare gifts or talents through it. It is an activity which lends itself in almost any aspect to a life-long hobby.

MEASURING STICKS

THERE are ways and ways of doing handcraft— good ways and poor. Suggestions fill whole books on the proper way—but they boil down to a few basic principles which may be used as measuring sticks for our program. We must take care lest handcraft activities degenerate into "busy work"; handcraft should be thought of as a creative experience, not something to keep idle hands busy. Our aim is to raise handcraft to a high level of workmanship and creative possibilities. This we can do by stressing creative activities—keeping away as much as possible from patterns to color, cut or trace which limit the development of creative self-expression out of which comes personality, growth and happiness. We can use simple materials such as clay, wood, metal, cloth, and paper and use them as they are intended, not making tin flowers or imitation leather objects our goal, but original drawings and paintings, wood carving, pottery, leather work, and suitably applied original designs on metal and cloth—things of which any craftsman may be proud, for a craftsman uses his materials appropriately. We can encourage good quality of workmanship.

ADAPTING TO AGE

HANDCRAFT skills are progressive, and the materials we provide and the results we may expect must, therefore, be adapted to the age of the child. The small child's handcraft experience is largely of an exploratory nature. He learns to handle materials such as clay, wood, paper, cloth and paints; learns what he can or cannot do with them, and develops skill in manipulation. He makes endless sand patties and clay balls, pounds nails haphazardly into boards, scrawls on paper, and sews in huge stitches. All of it seems meaningless to the adult, yet to the child it is important and a basic step for later skills. We must provide him with all kinds of simple materials to explore and develop skill in handling. During this period particularly, and in the first part of the next period the child must be given large things to handle, for his skill in manipulation is limited. His interest span is short, so objects to make should be suggested which can be finished quickly.

The older child handles his materials more comprehensively. The blot on the paper, he says, is a boat; it may not be quite the adult idea of a boat, but it is his symbol for a boat. He is representing things by symbols—a natural stage. Later he will grow into a more naturalistic representation, but forced or urged over these natural steps, the child loses spontaneity and creative ability through self-consciousness.

With the child in the later grades and high school, more complicated crafts and techniques may be explored. Loom weaving, leather, metal work, block printing and pottery, and practically all aspects of handcraft may be carried on increasingly higher levels of craftsmanship.

HELPING THE CHILD

We can provide various media for self-expression for the child so that he may develop skills as a part of his natural growth—easily and unself-consciously. The older child or adult without skills naturally developed has difficulty in expressing himself spontaneously and creatively. He is self-conscious, too self-critical and liable to stop at the first difficulty he meets.

The child must make whatever he tries by himself to gain full pleasure and satisfaction from it. If we rush to his rescue when a problem arises and solve it ourselves, the child no longer feels the object is truly his. Better to explain carefully or demonstrate how he may solve his problem and let him do it himself.

By taking the child to museums and galleries, through craft shops and industries, to talk to craftsmen, and by reading aloud and conversation, we can open the child's eyes to the many ways of making things, arouse an appreciation of beauty and standards of workmanship and deepen his interest in handcraft. We can show appreciation of the child's efforts and try to judge his work from his stage of development, not by adult standards for adults.

HANDCRAFT ACTIVITIES

Following are a few of the many possibilities in the handcraft field. A glance at them will bring many more to your mind.

Sketching and drawing	Stilts
Painting	Clothing
Clay modeling	Embroidery
Pottery	Toys
Wood carving	Games

Weaving baskets, rugs, etc.	Kites
Marionettes	Furniture
Aquaria	Bird houses
Terraria	Batik
Model boats airplanes	Knitting
Metal work	Basketry
Block printing	Scrap books
Sand modeling	Decorated boxes
Tie dying	Doll houses
	Scooters
	Crocheting

SPECIAL USES FOR HANDCRAFT

While the child's chief development and joy lies in the actual creating of an object, there are a number of uses or purposes to which these objects may be put which are important. The child who makes birthday and Christmas presents for his family gives more than any store gift he might purchase. Christmas cards, party favors and decorations made by the child add much to the significance of the occasion. Decorative drawings, wall hangings, book ends, shelves, pottery animals and objects of furniture made by members of the family make a home more "homey." Handcraft may be combined with other family hobbies or activities. Making a puppet stage for the puppet plays, building the backyard playground or furnishing the remodeled basement playroom will enlist the ingenuity and skill of every member of the family.

SOURCES OF MATERIALS

Handcraft materials may cost much or little as you wish. Silver is expensive, but German silver is not, and it is quite satisfactory for even advanced craftsmen. Wood may be brought from the mill or obtained from boxes and odd boards. Cloth may be purchased by the yard or a rag bag may be explored. Paper for scrap books or drawing may be wrapping paper rather than expensive art paper. Many more such substitutions can be made. Keep a scrap box as well as a scrap bag and put in it materials the child or you can use for handcraft. Store away old cardboard boxes, magazines, wall paper, cloth and oil cloth, wood from boxes, half-used cans of paint, glass jars, and old silk stockings (for weaving). Add to this box materials you may have for the asking— old inner tubes (garage), cigar boxes (cigar store), cardboard boxes (department stores), cloth scraps (friend's scrap bags), battleship linoleum (scraps from department stores), wood (lumber yards or boxes from stores).

Some things you will need to buy—but you can do it cheaply. Cold water powder paints are obtainable at hardware or paint stores for painting on paper or wood and are less expensive than oil or enamel paints. Nut picks (ten cent store) make excellent leather tools. Many people use a razor or pen knife for linoleum blocks. Miracles can be worked with a hammer, saw, coping saw and sandpaper. These tools cost little and you probably have some of them already. With balsa wood or white pine and a jackknife a child can find rich creative experience in simple carving or whittling. Plasticine is a good substitute for professional modeling clay, more expensive, yet cleaner to use with small children. Books in the library will give you "free instruction" in all manner of handcraft activities.

THE HANDCRAFT CORNER

IN ORDER to carry out a handcraft project, the child needs an appropriate place to work. A corner of his room, a basement, attic, garage or barn workshop will do much toward encouraging the child with his projects. Good lighting, shelves, stools, and tables of appropriate height are essential. Planning, decorating and furnishing this handcraft corner or room makes a splendid family project and may lead the whole family to making a hobby of handcraft.

HOBBIES

By ELIZABETH PRICE

National Recreation Association

IF YOU are searching for happiness for yourself or your children, pause a moment and consider the way marked "Hobbies." It is only one of the many ways leading to happiness, but it is one of the most traveled, and, according to those who have explored it, leads swiftly and directly to the goal.

A hobby is not a mysterious or a new road to happiness. It is merely an "intense interest" or a "favorite activity" to which one repeatedly returns when work or school is done. It might be tinkering at a work bench, collecting rocks, making marionettes, gardening, reading or a thousand other things. Simple? Yes. But there is a key to happiness in a hobby. Look at the people about you. There is a man wholly happy in his work. He is indeed fortunate, for his work and his hobby are one. Here is another whose work is purely mechanical drudgery. He does not like it, yet he seems to be happy enough. He finds his happiness in gardening. This woman takes real pride and satisfaction in her piece-work hobby. How forlorn that person is there, forced to slow down in the midst of life, complaining of nothing to do, of life a burden and a bore. She has no hobby.

Even the people whose work seems exciting and glamorous and time-consuming to us find need and place and time for hobbies.

The children, too, show the effects of "intense interest" in some play-time activity. Mary and Bob are absorbed in a stamp collection and the making of puppets, and for them the days are not nearly long enough. John, however, lacking a hobby interest, continually complains, "What can I do now?"

HOW HOBBIES WORK

WE CAN SEE that hobbies and happiness often go hand in hand, but we must ask the questions "How?" and "Why?" more specifically before we start our children or ourselves on the road marked "hobbies."

In his hobby the child (or adult) finds his own avenue of self-expression. He finds happiness and emotional release in pursuing it, laying plans and carrying them out. He learns patience and control, gains new experience, skills, information, assurance and poise. He is interesting because he is interested, and, because he is absorbed in doing things, he maintains his mental health through the inevitable impulses and desires of the teen years.

A child's hobbies often tend to change as he grows up. There are years or months when he is absorbed in turn in music, drama, nature, games, making and collecting things. In fostering and assisting him in his various hobby urges as they appear, we help him to develop skills in a number of fields at a time when he learns easily and unself-consciously as part of his natural growth. These skills prove invaluable to him as an adult, for he continues with or returns to some activity in which he has had experience as a child for his adult recreational or hobby activity. Without basic skills in an activity the adult is apt to draw back, saying, "I can't" or "I never did," or, as a result of over-self-consciousness, eye his attempt with scorn and never try again.

Hobbies tend to draw members of a family together. A new bond of unity and understanding is introduced when all the members work together on a stamp collection; when Dad helps the boy to use his workshop tools; when Mother reads aloud or when each member, through possession of his own hobby, sympathizes more fully with the interests of the others. A happily busy child is not often a naughty one, and freedom from need for continual parental discipline makes for harmony in the home.

HOBBIES MAY BE VOCATIONAL LEADS

THROUGH hobbies the child sometimes discovers or develops a skill and interest which leads him to make a life work of his hobby. George Eastman's hobby as a boy was photography; the Wright brothers' hobby was flying, while they made a living in a bicycle shop. Not all of us will make a life work of our hobbies, but the development of abilities and interests through hobbies is nonetheless worth while.

GUIDING IN HOBBIES

THERE is much that adults can do toward fostering hobbies in children. It is a difficult and delicate task and yet a challenging and rewarding one.

By giving the child opportunity to have experience in a number of different activities—music, drama, handcraft, nature—the adult can give the child a wider field for choice for his hobbies. The child will develop a hobby from things he experiences; no one can choose it for him, but how many boys take to wood work because Dad had it for a hobby, like good books because Mother reads aloud, and turn to nature because of family picnics? Many, I warrant.

By refraining from harsh criticism and even good-natured ridicule, by respecting and encouraging a child's efforts, the child's reaching out for means of self-expression will continue. We must remember to judge his efforts on standards for children, not for adults, to take him from where he is, and by tactful suggestion, guide him to better interests or efforts if we do not approve those he has. One father subscribed to and read a movie magazine so that he might better help his daughter in and through her consuming interest

in this subject. Having a hobby ourselves does much to give the necessary understanding.

HOBBIES MEET DIFFERENT NEEDS

BY ANALYZING each child's specific needs and offering experiences which will best satisfy them, we can guide his development. Some hobbies are social; some solitary. The retiring child needs to be drawn out in social activities such as dramatics, while the too easily over-stimulated child might profit best by quiet, solitary hobbies such as craft, scrapbooks and nature. Girls tend to drop physical activity hobbies when they still need them for their development. Coupled with social activities, interest in these activities persists longer. The unmusical child may need music experience more than the musical one to develop his skills or interest in this field.

By using hobbies as special events, interest in them can be increased. A family hobby show, with each member exhibiting, will deepen interest. A family show may lead to a neighborhood or community hobby show, drawing the members of the group closer together through sharing of personal interests and enthusiasms. Hobbies may be used as party entertainment. Boys interested in magic delight in putting on a show; the hobby cook may give a supper party and the child interested in Indian lore may entertain with Indian games and music and dances.

Providing material and space and time for the development of hobbies, the adult can help the child to a more profound interest in his hobby and better standards of workmanship.

SPACE AND MATERIAL FOR HOBBIES

HOBBIES, as a rule, take space. If a child must be continually nagged to move his "treasures" out of the way, to clean up litter or be quiet about his work, his interest will be short-lived. But a basement or attic room for hobbies—even a tool shed, corner of the porch or his room fitted up with shelves, boxes, work bench or whatever the hobby requires will increase the child's interest in the activity. Each member of the family from Johnny at nine to grandfather at ninety should have a respected and suitable place for his hobby.

Hobby materials are not difficult to obtain. Keep a scrap box for use for possible hobbies. Scraps of cloth, string, ribbon, wall paper ends, magazines, wooden and cardboard boxes, linoleum, cans of paint and such will provide the materials needed for many hobbies. Ten-cent stores yield nature, poetry and music books within the reach of almost any purse. The radio and victrola can be used to provide musical experiences. The library will lend you books on all hobby fields and there are a number of inexpensive hobby magazines on the market.

KINDS OF HOBBIES

STRICTLY speaking, any intense interest or favorite activity in leisure time may be a hobby, but *Making Things* and *Collecting Things* are most commonly thought of as hobby activities. *Making Things* yields, perhaps, the richest returns because of the deep feeling of satisfaction that creative self-expression brings. Making things may involve block prints, drawings, clay modeling, puppets, jewelry, scrapbooks, baskets, models of any or all kinds, embroidery, poems, or anything of which you can think. *Collecting Things* may include poetry, pictures, rocks or leaves, coins, stamps, samplers, pottery—again, anything under the sun that happened to catch and hold the interest of the collector.

Then there are *Doing Things* hobbies, such as magic or dramatics, gardening, hiking, tennis or golf, puzzles and games, cycling and so on, and for many adults and a number of children, *Learning Things* or studying is a hobby. Studying history, drama, novels or music are examples. Practically any activity in the world may be enjoyed in a hobby way—the way that makes for happiness.

"Young man, get a hobby; preferably get two, one for indoors and one for out; get a pair of hobby-horses that can safely be ridden in opposite directions."
—*A. Edward Newton*

For further suggestions on Hobbies, Collections, etc, see Volume 5, **Things to Make and Things to Do.** For more on Nature, see Volume 7, **Nature, Recreation, and Physical Development.**

HOME AND SCHOOL

WILL YOU SEND YOUR CHILD TO A NURSERY SCHOOL?*

By WINIFRED E. BAIN, Ph.D.

IF CHILDREN are suffering from poor home conditions it is obvious that the sooner they are put into a good school the better. But what about the child in the comfortable home? Should he leave home to enter school at the age of two or three? If I were the parent I should look twice at the school to see what it could do for my child before deciding this important question.

VALUES TO CHILDREN

AMONG the physical advantages, a good nursery school offers space in which children can play. This is often difficult to procure in the modern home. Large apparatus which is cumbersome and expensive for average home equipment is made available in a nursery school where it can be shared with an entire community. Space and apparatus allow children to run, climb, pull, push and explore just at the age when they are becoming so troublesome at home. Children need to exercise their growing bodies and practice simple motor skills, and maybe the nursery school will provide the best place for doing this.

REGULAR PHYSICAL ROUTINE

BUT THE two-year-old doesn't need to run and play all the time. He needs frequent periods of rest, often more frequent periods than busy parents realize. The nursery teacher's time is protected from too many household interruptions; so she goes through the day regulating the routines of eating, sleeping and toileting, and does it for the whole neighborhood.

"Surely it is better for a child to eat at home," you say. Well, maybe it is; but perhaps the teacher or nutritionist at the nursery school has a knowledge of the dietary needs of children and can help if your John isn't eating well or isn't gaining, at the same time that she helps your neighbor whose Mary is getting too fat or whose Sam is suffering from constipation.

HEALTH

IT WOULDN'T be worthwhile to send a baby to school for these things, however, if he were going to catch diseases from the other children. But if the nursery school provides a morning inspection before children come in contact with each other, and if teachers are alert to watch during the day for symptoms such as flushed cheeks and running noses, it may be safer to send the child there than to keep him home. The nursery school may also give your child a physical examination and possibly repeated check-up. You may get some excellent advice about how to build resistance to disease and how to keep the little body growing in a normal way. If so, it is better to put money into nursery school than into doctor's bills.

SOCIAL GROWTH

PHYSICAL growth and health are, however, not the only considerations. There remains the question of social growth. It is a good thing for children to come to know others of their own age, even as early as two years or before. They enjoy being with other toddlers even though they know nothing about real social cooperation. One child of three who bit another child asked naively, "What makes Jackie cry?" Just such social lessons each child has to learn. If the nursery school offers an opportunity for children to play together naturally and wholesomely, under the guidance of a teacher who can lead them little by little toward good social habits and understandings, then it is a boon to a parent who cannot ordinarily have the house overrun with the neighbors' babies in order to provide social contacts. On the other hand, if the school under consideration is one where children of this age are made to assume too much social responsibility, it would be better not to send your child to it. And again, a child might be better off at home than in a school where all his thinking is done for him or where he is forced to learn such social usages as "thank you," "excuse me" and "if you please" until he becomes worried, confused and frustrated.

BEHAVIOR PROBLEMS

THEN, too, a good nursery school will probably be able to help with behavior problems which have already grown up in the first two or three years of life. Often those outside the home have a better opportunity to help a child overcome difficulties than those who are close to him day in and day out. The baby should learn to trust and like many people. The nursery school may be just the opportunity you are looking for to accomplish this.

VALUES TO PARENTS

PARENTS as well as children may learn a great deal at a good nursery school. If the school provides for parent conferences, as it usually does, there is opportunity to talk over the puzzling problems which arise in the care and education of your child with people prepared especially to deal with the many types of problems which occur when children are in this early stage of growth.

Besides consultations, the observations of teachers at work in the nursery school are also helpful to parents. It helps not only to know what should be done but also to see how other people do it. It also helps to see other children doing the same things your child is doing.

Some nursery schools are organized so that parents may work in them a certain number of hours a week. Other nursery schools offer home service as well as consultation. The staff members will not only advise parents what to do, but they will go into the home and assist the parents. The amount of service which parents receive from their nursery school depends in part on their needs and largely on the staff which they are able to afford for the little institution. Such community sharing in a nursery school provides also a common meeting place where parents of young children can get together to talk over mutual problems and establish neighborhood policies.

THE NURSERY SCHOOL PROGRAM

NURSERY schools usually open about eight-thirty or nine in the morning. The hour of beginning is quite generally a flexible one so that the two and three year olds are not introduced to the meaning of being "late to school." If any home difficulties are experienced and there have been upsets in the home regime these should be reported to the teacher so she may take them into consideration in the work of the day.

On arrival the child's nose, throat, eyes and skin are examined and in cases where there is question a temperature is taken by the nurse. After inspection the child goes to the playroom where other children are assembling, announces himself to the teacher, and retires to the locker room. If he has not worn his play suit from home, he finds it there in his locker and with some help from the teacher in charge proceeds to change. Then he goes to the toilet where toileting is made easy by fixtures his own size, washes and goes to the playroom for orange or tomato juice and a period of play.

He doesn't stay indoors long, however. Large muscles need exercise with big materials suitable for out-of-door use. When weather is nice, the children stay out all forenoon.

Music and picture books find their way to the playground, too. A few minutes of rest usually break the long forenoon of active play and dinner is served between eleven-thirty and twelve o'clock. Little children fatigue easily and must have protection from over-exhaustion. Naps come directly after dinner. Sometimes children remove their clothes, but more often only the outer garments. An informal lunch of milk and crackers follows as soon as the children get up from their hour or hour-and-a-half naps and about four o'clock parents call to take them home.

Thus through the nursery school days the toddler grows and matures. He learns many large muscle skills which contribute to his motor coordination. There is much cause for gratification in his social progress, too. He learns much about the rights and feelings of others, how to take turns and the advantages of give and take.

GROWTH IN INDEPENDENCE

A NURSERY school child becomes much more steady

and sure of himself, too. He learns to be more independent of his parents and his home surroundings. He feels a sense of confidence in his ability to get along with other people as he discovers how to deal with the thwartings which are imposed on him by the other children. Thus gradually his emotional adjustment to the world becomes more steady.

Living in an extended environment gives nursery school children many ideas and skills. They learn to sing wee bits of song and to enjoy more music than they are able to sing. With sureness of locomotion come definite rhythmic patterns in their bodily activities such as were never possible when they entered. Rhythmic patterns also make their appearance as the child gains mastery of speech.

With the coming of speech techniques comes the power to express thought, and with expression follows the clarification of ideas. In part this progress of the child between his second and fourth birthdays comes because he is naturally a growing individual. The nursery school recognizes these natural tendencies for growth and builds its program in order to make the most of them, to extend and unify the child's development in natural ways and in as rapid and wholesome a course as is possible for each child.

WILL YOU SEND YOUR CHILD TO A KINDERGARTEN?*

By WINIFRED E. BAIN, Ph.D.

THERE isn't usually so much question in these days about sending a child to kindergarten as about putting him in a nursery school. He is older now, and less of a baby, and probably his parents began their own school careers in kindergartens. But modern kindergartens are much different from the first institutions of that name, where children built queer little forms from tiny blocks, traced intricate patterns on cardboard with needle and thread, formed a circle with toes to the line for every conceivable purpose, singing, dancing, stories or just talk.

The modern kindergarten program is better adapted to little children than the one of former years. It begins the day as soon as the children arrive with the same kind of active play in which they engage at home. There are many toys in the room which attract your child as soon as he enters, and without any ceremony he finds one of these and begins to play.

THE FOUR-YEAR-OLDS

THE FOUR-YEAR-OLD children, like those in the nursery school, spend much of their morning out of doors. Not only do they need the fresh air and sunshine but also the space which will enable them to keep out of each other's way. They are not social enough yet to cooperate in very closely knit play. It isn't long, however, before they play in small groups of three or four, but the play isn't very highly organized. Sometimes the teacher plays with them, and perhaps she may make a suggestion. Seeing that one child has a tendency to dominate the others she helps him to assert himself without being a despot. Another child, she sees, takes all thwarting as a catastrophe and rages and storms to the others. Still another shrinks back into submission when things do not go his way. Each one she helps according to his needs so that he may meet his difficulties courageously and take his place in the little loosely organized groups which are characteristic of early days in kindergarten.

THE FIVE-YEAR-OLDS

BY THE TIME the children are five and still in kindergarten they have learned many techniques for getting along with other children so that they are able to organize themselves into larger groups. They are interested in more detail, and before they enter the first grade at six they will band together day after day in playing boat, train or fire department. Thus growth takes place in techniques of doing, in social organization and in continuity of purpose.

Excursions often need to be taken so that children may see such things as how switch tracks are built and how signals are operated. The four-year-olds do not go far, but before they enter the first grade at six, they investigate many things —animals, plants, minerals, water supply, magnets, electric wiring, weather, farming, carpentry, transportation, etc. The great wealth of ideas thus obtained gradually becomes sorted and re-

* From *Parents Look at Modern Education*, by Winifred E. Bain, Ph.D., Copyright—Used by permission of D. Appleton-Century Company, Inc., Publishers, New York, N. Y.

lated so as to give children as they grow older and more mature the larger meanings of the social sciences and the natural sciences.

PLAY MATERIALS

IN A MODERN kindergarten many materials are provided with which children may express themselves. Blocks are important because they can be quickly and easily put together in building. Work benches, saws, hammers and nails have a place in the kindergarten. The first bits of construction are accidental but later the five-year-olds make crude things they need in their play.

Painting is easier. Children love to wield a brush, and in early days of nursery school they are as content to paint with water as with colors. Four-year-olds delight to experiment with pigments. At first they are usually given only the primary colors, red, blue and yellow. On large news sheets they splash color with big brushes to their hearts' content. Other colors are added to the original supply. The first pictures are more or less accidental and the "artist" tells the other children what they are; later they know without being told that the arrangement of head, arms, and legs on the paper is a picture of daddy, and the combination of head, skirt and feet is mother. It will be some time before the picture tells a story, but by and by that time comes and one tells it to the teacher so that she may write it on the back of the sheet for mother and daddy to read when it is taken home.

STORY-TELLING

STORY-TELLING is very popular in the kindergarten. It always has been common practice for teachers to tell stories to children, but nowadays children are encouraged to tell little stories, too. Now that speech as well as ideas is growing rapidly, the teacher knows that the children need the chance to express themselves about many things, not just in telling stories. She knows, too, that if ever stuttering or other speech difficulties are to develop it is likely to be at this age. Consequently, she gives considerable attention to the matter and many times prevents speech disorder by her careful guidance. Again she will secure a speech specialist if the matter gets out of hand.

MUSIC AND RHYTHM

EVEN though the children do not read there are many books in the kindergarten. Some of them have pictures and stories; some of them have rhymes and poems which sound very beautiful when the teacher reads; they look very beautiful when the children handle them for themselves. The children say beautiful little bits in rhyme almost as lovely as the poems in the books.

The teacher sometimes puts these little rhythmical expressions to a tune and often gives the children music to go by in their active play. Before they have been in kindergarten very long she finds that children like to get together in small groups to sing and dance to the rhythm of music. They learn more about tones and sequences, simple musical form and the joy of spontaneous bodily rhythm of different types than about elaborate and cooperative dance forms, such as the folk dances and singing games of the old kindergarten which proved to be too complex for their social development and too taxing to their physical powers.

Sometimes they experiment with instruments, too. At times even in kindergarten there are children who learn enough of the vocabulary of music so that they can put it together into simple little songs which they compose themselves.

OUTDOOR PLAY

PART of these many activities go on out of doors and part of them in the kindergarten room. The five-year-olds usually spend more time inside than the fours, partly because of their increased physical maturity and partly because of their ability to organize their endeavors better within four walls. But they go out of doors for part of the morning when weather is favorable. Both the fours and the fives have a chance to climb, swing and jump on the playground apparatus.

REST PERIOD

ABOUT the middle of the morning the children have a rest period during which they lie on cots or rugs, not to nap but to relax completely from the activities of a busy day. After the rest there is usually a lunch which varies in content in different communities. Some children who need it may have milk; others may have orange or tomato juice; still others may have only a cup of water with a wafer. All depends on the nutritional status of the child and the balance of his home meals.

MEDICAL SUPERVISION

MEDICAL supervision varies considerably in different kindergartens, since the kindergarten is generally the child of the public school system where this service is an uncertain provision. In many schools, however, there is a medical examination by a physician on entrance as in nursery school practice. Schools which have adopted this system have found it of great value since it gives the service when parents greatly need it. It offers opportunity for supervision of health practices and correction of difficulties at any early age before the days of the elementary school begin. Often there are school nurses who aid parents in following up the findings of the physical examination.

The kindergarten day usually ends at noon. Sometimes the younger children, the four-year-olds, come to school in the morning and go home for dinner and naps; while the older ones, the five-year-olds, come after dinner and go home later, perhaps at three or four o'clock.

KINDERGARTEN AIDS ACHIEVEMENT

AT TIMES parents have asked whether children get along any better in school for having had kindergarten work. Research workers have taken such tests as we have of school progress and have shown in certain studies that children who have had kindergarten experiences progress faster in the grades; that they make higher scores on certain mental and achievement tests than do non-kindergarten children; that they show a lower percentage of failures in the grades; that they receive better ratings on social traits than non-kindergarten children, and further, that children who have had a year and one-half of kindergarten obtain better rating on social traits than those who have had only one year or half a year of kindergarten experience.

YOUR CHILD'S PROGRESS IN THE ELEMENTARY SCHOOL*

By WINIFRED E. BAIN, Ph.D.

IT IS a well-recognized practice to send a child to school when he gets to be six unless there are unusual circumstances which prevent his going. So common is it to look upon six as the age of school entrance that many parents are amazed to discover that by this time some children who enrolled in nursery school at the age of two may already have been in school four years! Given a child at this age what kind of school shall there be for him?

THE TRADITIONAL SCHOOL

THE NAME "traditional school" sounds as if the institution were out of date. As a matter of fact some of these schools are. The emphasis of the traditional school is on the subject matter which has been developed through the history of the race. They have written courses of study which tell how the contents of textbooks in reading, mathematics, geography, history, civics, and so on, may be mastered by the children and at what times in the school career a child should learn different things. If the assumption is correct that all knowledge which has been found of worth in the past has been thus systematically assembled, then it may also be assumed that in the course of school years children will have mastered what

they need to know if living in the future is to be like past experience.

If your child is in a traditional school you may have witnessed him "boning" on dates in history, the rivers of Africa, or the names of the members of the president's cabinet. Tucked away in the heads of each member of a good traditional school is the lore of the ages as well as certain mental skills which can be called forth automatically on demand of the teacher.

"But," you ask, "is there no chance for application of these skills and knowledges?" Applications are likely to be theoretical. The day is a busy one of study and recitation. The primary teacher, who can depend for support on very few books, is the busiest of all, since it is she who, by this method or that, must see that children learn to read, write, cipher and spell. If she fails in this the whole machinery of the later school is thrown out of gear.

DISCIPLINE

THE DISCIPLINE of such schools depends largely on the personality of the teacher. Rules and regulations are quite necessary. The conscientious believers in the traditional school feel that such obedience to law is one of the great lessons of life.

---

* From *Parents Look at Modern Education*, by Winifred E. Bain, Ph.D., Copyright—Used by permission of D. Appleton-Century Company, Inc., Publishers, New York, N. Y.

Granting this generalization, doesn't one still need to consider that not all laws are necessary, and that the governed should have a voice in determining which ones are needed?

The supporters of the traditional school also believe that the discipline of the mind will carry over into life. They believe that the content which children master through long years of childhood will find application to the problems of adult life. To drill in a systematic way on arithmetic will, they think, enable a person to drill in a systematic way on another job. "But," say the opponents, "this will not be the case unless the job is similar to arithmetic." They maintain that unless there is application of what one learns to problems as they come along in life day by day, that practical way of doing will not be learned and cannot be expected to burst upon the man unless it has been practiced by him as a child. Then, too, they point out, the traditional schools without real life in them are too drab, too colorless. They would not appeal to children.

THE MOTIVATED SCHOOL

EARLY exponents of change in the school attempted to put interest into the work. They thought that if children were interested they would work harder and learn more. Many a parent who has witnessed his child being motivated by a sugar-coating to the bitter pill of learning has wondered if perhaps the sugar didn't dilute the strength. Sometimes the motivation was a reward. Usually there was competition. One's name appeared in the paper for merit or one had a half-day off from school. Lessons were made more interesting through concrete illustration. Children drew pictures of what they were learning. They made booklets and illustrated notebooks on various subjects. Every conceivable device was used to make the lessons more interesting, but they were otherwise the very same lessons as those of the traditional school.

A further attempt was made to relate knowledge and skills. In making a sand table representation of Holland, for instance, one needs to read about the life in that country, not just its history but its geography, government and customs. Then there is need to know how to use materials for constructing the miniature objects, windmills, dikes, boys and girls in native dress. What more natural than that the project should be made complete with songs about Holland and a Dutch dance? This method of putting things together is known as correlation. Each subject of the curriculum, reading, writing, history, geography, was woven about a central theme thought to be interesting to the children.

The motivated school had little to recommend it. Its objective was exactly the same as that of the traditional school—to teach the subject matter of textbooks. But its way of doing this was artificial and misleading. The motivated school did not deal with realities any more than the traditional school; it dealt with representations or imitations of the real thing.

It is difficult to know in what tense to describe the motivated school. Its theories are not generally in good repute, yet some of its practices are still to be found. Historically speaking, it is probably a transition to the more recent developments, variously known as the new school, the modern school, the activity school, or the progressive school.

THE PROGRESSIVE SCHOOL

THE PROGRESSIVE school has forsaken the system of the textbook for a more varied assortment of materials. Firsthand experiences with life furnish the basic content. Children take excursions to see life as it actually is. They go to museums to get realistic pictures of the life of other countries, Holland perhaps. Where there are no museums they resort to pictures. Many different books are used and sometimes discrepancies in accounts found in one and another are noted. The community furnishes much of the material of the school and a realistic type of living in the community constitutes the procedures.

"Then surely this must be a hit-or-miss type of school," you think. It could be were there not some guide, some chart, to show the way. This guide is contained in a written curriculum of a flexible sort. Instead of being based on an orderly arrangement of subject matter in such fields as geography, history or science, as is the course of study in the traditional school, the curriculum of the progressive school is organized around those issues or problems which one needs to solve for happy and effective living in a world made up of various social groups.

The work on such curricula involves the co-operation of economists, sociologists, politicians, artists, musicians, engineers, and poets, since life is full of problems which need the contribution from all these various fields for their solutions.

Care has to be taken to avoid giving children too large doses and too biased a point of view. The modern curriculum maker and the modern teacher lay great stress on the fact that children should understand their experiences. They believe that to develop ways of understanding how to deal with the problems of life is the important task of education. These meanings do not develop to their full size in a moment. It takes many years of experience to round them out, and for most of us even in a lifetime they are still incomplete.

LEARNING THE MEANINGS OF THINGS

THUS it is that progressive education places more value on the meanings of things than upon facts. And so it is that the curriculum of the progressive school sets forth, besides the big problems or issues of life, lists of the understandings necessary for living; but it is largely left to the individual teacher to carry forward the specific work of the school according to the immediate interests of the children at any given time.

It is a difficult job to teach in a progressive school for one needs to have the wisdom of the ages and to be able to bring it gradually to the lives of children in varying stages of maturity. It is a delightful task, however, since it permits—yes, requires—that children live naturally and without strain through days of wholesome, varied, and stimulating experiences. Much is known now about the natural ways of children that was not known even a few years ago. It is known now that children are harmed by being inactive; that their natural activity will help them to learn more things and learn them faster than could be done by the regime of passive compliance to a rule of quiet unoffensiveness. It is now recognized that the physical body needs exercise for growth, and that it is as important for a child to grow in physical power as in mental and indeed that the one may be related to the other. The way a child feels about doing his work is recognized as important. It is only as he learns to want to do things that we can be sure that he will continue to do them when authority is removed. Students of childhood have

found, too, that children profit as much, yes more, by learning to take responsibility for themselves, even though they sometimes make mistakes, than by learning from books by a system which dictates logically step by step and safeguards them from errors.

COOPERATION WITH PARENTS

PROGRESSIVE schools work actively with parents and seek by every means to coordinate the two educational agencies—the home and the school. The system in both institutions lies in the manner in which the choices of activities are guided. If wisely guided, they lead the children to an understanding of how to live richly, fully and colorfully, and the richness, fullness and colorfulness will of course differ for different children at different ages.

CRITICISM OF PROGRESSIVE SCHOOLS

CRITICS of the progressive schools have pointed out that many of them are superficial. They maintain that the flexible program of social activity which supplants the studious system of the traditional school gives children the opportunity to cultivate habits of getting by easily rather than those of real integrity. These criticisms have been stimulated by the procedure of some schools which have abandoned the irksomeness of the old without taking on the full responsibilities of the new.

Prediction about the future is uncertain. Will the schools get back to where they were? Will they be different than they ever were before, because of a new interest in the education and protection of the next generation, and a new vision of public service? The thing which gives optimism to the uncertain picture is the increased consciousness of educational values and problems on the part of the American people.

HOW THE HOME CAN COOPERATE WITH THE SCHOOL

THE SUCCESSFUL man of business selects a person whom he believes capable of doing a certain task, and then does he stand one side and do nothing, or does he constantly interfere with suggestions and criticisms? No, he follows neither of these courses of action, because he realizes that either one would lessen the value of the results which his employee is expected to obtain. So he asks these questions: Is the material which I am giving you satisfactory? Are the

conditions under which I am expecting you to work all that they should be? Is there any other thing I can do to insure the success of your task? In brief, he knows that although he has given the responsibility for the accomplishment of the task to his employee, he cannot shake off his own shoulders the greater responsibility of his own cooperation.

So it is with the parents' job—training children. While we have transferred to the school the responsibility of teaching our children how to live, we have not and can not shift our responsibility for cooperation in the task.

PHYSICAL LIFE

IT IS the home's duty to see to it that children go to bed at a reasonable time and have good physical conditions for growth, eat nourishing foods, and make the proper gains in weight which result from that.

Parents can, if the state or city doesn't, see to it that the child's physical being is in condition— clean, strong, vigorous—for school work. They can particularly see to it that sense organs— eyes, ears, nose, etc.—are efficient tools. Parents should be informed about quarantine laws and medical inspection and obey them.

HABITS

EACH CHILD of school age needs a definite schedule. He should have regular hours of sleep, regular time for meals, and an uninterrupted period of study in a quiet place. He should have wholesome recreation and leisure-time activities. Parents can best cooperate with the schools by seeing that the pupil's home life is as carefully supervised as his school life.

In at least nine cases out of ten the home rather than the school determines whether or not a child shall *use* "good English." Like the Indian who goes back from the government-school to the Reservation the child almost inevitably conforms to the usages which he hears first and most frequently.

In a similar way and in about the same percentage of cases the home determines whether or not the child shall have sound health habits, whether he shall be industrious or lazy, reliable or uncertain, self-centered or public-spirited and generous.

Over and over again a teacher has worked earnestly and skillfully to develop an appreciation of good books, good pictures, or good music only to find her efforts wasted because there is not and never has been any home influence in the same direction.

SYMPATHETIC UNDERSTANDING

THE GREATEST thing the home can do is to get into sympathy with, and assist in creating an *atmosphere* in the home conducive to study and love for school tasks. Let the boy climb up on Dad's lap and be told a bear story; let parents, even

though they cannot always comprehend the problems brought home by the children, evince a sympathizing attitude toward their efforts, suggesting and supplementing, and sometimes studying with them instead of taking in theatre parties or other social affairs, and we will have gone a long way toward solving the problem of cooperation. Parents must get *acquainted* with their children; and to know them *well* means to *live with them* at home.

A SPECIAL PLACE AND TIME TO STUDY

LET EACH home set aside what might be called a study hour during which time each member of the family, if possible, and the children without exception, are required to do some real studying. The parents should see to it that the purpose of this hour is not violated. There is nothing quite equal to the effect of a good example on the part of the parents in this matter of study. Children unconsciously acquire the attitude of the parents in this matter as well as in others. There should be a light, comfortable, quiet place for home study.

REGULARITY IN ATTENDANCE

HAVE the child cleanly and neatly clothed and in his place at *nine o'clock* every day unless the child himself is physically unfit.

CHARACTER

CHILDREN being naturally imitative, every influence which surrounds them is really part of their education; therefore, it becomes our duty and opportunity to make their home-life a guide to right living in all its relations.

The home can teach a child obedience, self-control, confidence; to put things he uses in their proper places when he is through with them; to think of the right and privileges of the *other fellow*—respect and consideration for other people; to honor his family too much to do a mean, dishonorable thing; to love his family, his community, his school, his country, his God.

BACK UP THE TEACHER AND SCHOOL

BACK up school demands; parents are too prone to place the whole responsibility and the enforcement of school rules on the shoulders of the teachers. The parents should take an active, wide-awake interest in all school activities, and thereby encourage their children to do the same thing.

Parents should be informed about the curriculum, rules of the school, etc. In case of misunderstandings between teachers and pupil, the home can help by reserving judgment until the matter has been talked over amicably with the teacher.

SHOW INTEREST IN SCHOOL PROGRESS

Inquire from the school teacher concerning the progress of the student and do not wait for the teacher to send home reports. This inquiry is far better if made in a personal interview. Parents should express occasionally their appreciation of the teacher's work; the same may also be said with regard to appreciation of the student's work; a deserved compliment will yield fully one hundred per cent. on the investment.

COMPLAINTS AGAINST TEACHERS AND SCHOOLS

The home can cooperate with the school by not believing every wild tale brought home from school by the children. Most children are truthful; yet by great stretches of imagination are able to tell at home many tales which have little foundation. If a child makes a complaint at home of ill treatment by a teacher, go at once or as soon as possible to the teacher herself or to the principal of the school and find out just what the teacher said and just what happened. You may and you probably will have your opinions entirely changed by meeting the teacher and by finding out the sort of man or woman who has charge of your children. Do not go to the Superintendent at first. He can examine the case, but can only talk with you in regard to it from second-hand facts. If you are dissatisfied with what you find out at school, then see the Superintendent and lay the case before him. Discourage trifling complaints from the child and withhold judgment upon more serious matters until the teacher's viewpoint has been presented.

VISIT THE SCHOOL

Teachers ought in every way possible to keep parents informed of school activities, but in addition to this parents ought to visit schools and make inquiry about the progress of their children. The plea of "no time" isn't satisfactory. Most mothers have time for clubs and other outside meetings and fathers have time for all sorts of community meetings, neighborhood visiting, long lunch hours in cities and other activities which consume time. In most instances a little thinking and planning beforehand will solve the question and leave enough time for genuine business engagements and the necessary home duties. For example, thousands of men in cities eat lunch downtown every day. Lunch is served in nearly every junior and senior high school and in many elementary schools. Arrangements could easily be made for fathers to meet their sons and daughters in school a little before noon. Together they could attend classes and become acquainted with the different activities, with the teachers and the principal. Lunch might then be had with the pupils at school, after which the fathers could return to their work.

CHILD STUDY CLUBS

The home can best help the school by working with it through parent-teacher associations and similar organizations; so that parents will know better the conditions in the school and help to improve them, will realize more fully the need of parental cooperation, and just where that cooperation is needed to brace weak points in the system. Through this medium the teachers may gain appreciative understanding of home conditions and the parents may obtain appreciative understanding of the problems of the class-room. The effectiveness of such cooperation depends greatly upon the interest which both parties show in this common medium of exchange of ideas, experience, and interest. The success of any organization, of course, depends upon its leadership and the vision which this leadership possesses.

There is a psychological effect of parent and teacher working together, knowing each other, that has a splendid influence on the child.

HOW TO MAKE THE SCHOOLS BETTER

Parents should see to it that teachers are paid salaries commensurate with the services rendered by them in order to retain in the profession men and women of the greatest ability. The social status of the teacher should be made the equal of the best in order that the highest types of manhood and womanhood will be made to enjoy the dignity of their positions and the high esteem of their patrons. Parents can safely look upon the school-tax money as the best spent of all their earnings. They can well afford to make sacrifice, if sacrifice be necessary, to see to it that pupils are provided with books and necessary material with which to work.

After all is said and done, let us remember:
A child's task is to learn how to live; the school's task is to teach a child how to live; and the parents' task is to see that both the child and the school do their jobs in a thorough and efficient manner.

WHO SHALL GO TO COLLEGE?*

By MAX McCONN

Dean of Lehigh University, Bethlehem, Pennsylvania

OUR COLLEGES, as they *are,* are by no means good places for every boy and girl. They are very fine places for some boys and girls, but for a considerable majority they are very bad places. They offer to one particular type of young man and woman quite worthwhile opportunities for mental and moral development; to all other types they offer virtually nothing, and much worse than nothing, namely, frustration and discouragement.

I shall attempt to specify certain criteria and tests which any parents can apply to their own child and by means of which they can determine, with reasonable assurance in most cases, whether that child is or is not what college faculties call "college material"—that is, the kind of human material for which the colleges are at present willing and able to provide.

I shall begin with three major criteria. The boy or girl who is to go to college should possess: (1) A fairly high degree of bookish aptitude. (2) An awakened intellectual interest in something. (3) A fairly high degree of self-mastery or capacity for self-direction.

BOOKISH APTITUDE

BY BOOKISH aptitude I mean merely a capacity or knack for learning quickly and effectively out of books—by the perusal of printed pages. That is only one way of learning; it is not even the best way; the best way is undoubtedly by living and doing. And the second-best way is probably by talking with those who have lived and done.

But the existing college method of learning is almost exclusively bookish. Consequently, the fact that a particular youngster seems alert and keen in practical matters, quick to understand what is said to him and to respond appropriately in word and action, does not necessarily mean that he is "college material." For that he should be also in some fair degree definitely bookish.

SPECIAL TALENTS: ART, MUSIC, ACTING

IT SHOULD be noted that bookish aptitude is only one among many valuable kinds of special aptitude or ability. Three of the other kinds are widely recognized; namely, musical ability, "artistic" ability, meaning aptitude for the graphic arts, and histrionic ability. It is quite commonly understood that these are special talents, and that they either may or may not be associated with bookish ability in the same individual. But there are almost certainly other special talents which have not yet been so definitely identified, and which may not be associated with the kind of aptitude that is needed for success with book studies in college.

MECHANICAL APTITUDE

ONE of these is the special knack which we call "mechanical"—the gift displayed by the boy who, without instruction in physics, builds complicated radio sets and picks up London or Melbourne, or takes the car to pieces and puts it together again so that it runs better than it did when it came from the factory. Many parents assume that the possession of this mechanical gift means that the boy is an embryo engineer and will infallibly succeed in a college of engineering. Alas, that does not follow. For success even in an engineering college, the most essential aptitude is bookish—in this case an aptitude for mathematics and the exact sciences dependent on mathematics, including physics, chemistry and mechanics. The mechanical knack is a valuable thing for an engineer to have, and combined with a flair for mathematics it affords a valuable prognosis of success as an engineer. But merely by itself it affords a prognosis only of success as a mechanician—an electrician, a plumber, a garage mechanic, or the like.

* Reprinted by permission from *Our Children,* Edited by Sidonie M. Gruenberg and Dorothy Canfield Fisher, Published by Viking Press.

PERSONAL-RELATIONS APTITUDE

THERE is one other particular aptitude which I want to describe, though I do so with some hesitation because I have never seen it treated by any psychologist as a special talent; but from my own long experience with young people I am almost sure it is practically that. I shall call it, for lack of a better term, personal-relations aptitude—the kind of charm and tact which enable certain attractive youngsters to make friends with everyone, to be instantly *en rapport* with every person they meet, and hence to deal with and manage and lead other people with striking success. This is, of course, one of the most valuable gifts the gods can bestow. It is priceless in personal relationships and in any profession; and in business, under the existing economic system, it is worth more in dollars and cents than the highest intelligence, even genius, of any other kind. But, according to my experience, it has no clear correlation, either positive or negative, with bookish ability. Many who have it are good also at books; but some who have it in high degree are no good at all at books; and, conversely, some who are excellent at books have little or none of this gift. I stress this point because these youngsters always impress other people as highly "intelligent," and it is almost invariably assumed that they are good candidates for college; but scores of young men and women of just this type are "dropped" from colleges every February and June for hopeless ineptitude at bookish tasks.

With this point well hammered home, I turn to the practical question as to how bookish aptitude of the degree necessary for success in college can be identified. How can parents determine with respect to a particular child whether he has this thing or does not have it?

TESTS OF BOOKISH APTITUDE

IN ANSWER to this question I shall list half a dozen tests which any parent can apply. But, before naming these tests, I must insert a large CAUTION: *No one of them is dependable by itself.* Each of them is subject to numerous qualifications and sources of error, but a consensus of results of four or five of them is probably trustworthy.

(1) Our first resort will naturally be to the so-called mental tests, which are available nowadays for many children who have come up through fairly progressive school systems. That these successfully measure "general intelligence" (whatever that is), many people doubt, and I am one of the doubters; but I do believe they usually gauge pretty well the much more limited thing we happen to be concerned with here, namely, bookish aptitude. In order to be definite—and warning my readers that I am taking, and am inflicting upon them, the serious risks of definiteness—I will say that in my opinion an Intelligence Quotient of 120 on the Binet-Stanford Test, or a comparable rating on other standard tests, is one indication of probable success in college. On the other hand, an I Q of much below 120 at least raises a question as to whether the boy or girl is likely to profit by existing college courses.

(2) Next we may consider the student's rank in his high school or preparatory school class. To be definite again: a student who ranks in the top third or the top two-fifths of his class in a reasonably good secondary school can probably do college work, but if the student regularly ranks below the second fifth of his class in the high school, there is some real danger that he may not be able to meet even the minimum standard in college.

(3) Is the student at least up with his agegrade?—that is, is he graduating from the senior high school at eighteen? Educational statisticians have repeatedly found a high positive correlation between youthfulness at entrance to college and success in college (as measured by marks). According to these studies a boy or girl who finishes the high school at eighteen is a fair college risk, one who finishes at seventeen is an excellent risk, and one who finishes at sixteen is a very superior risk—will probably win honors. Conversely, the student who does not complete the secondary school course until he is nineteen is a slightly dubious risk, and the one who does not finish until twenty or later is much more doubtful. (In applying this test in an individual case, consideration should, of course, be given to protracted or major interruptions of school life on account of illness, travel, the removal of parents from one city to another, or similar circumstances.)

(4) Reading speed. Rapidity in reading has an obvious direct bearing on success in college work, because of the large amount of reading which must be covered in nearly all college courses. But it is probably also a direct measure of the special kind of aptitude which I am calling bookish, because rapidity of reading usually correlates with comprehension and retention. Generally speaking, the more rapidly a reader reads, the more effectively he grasps and retains. The median reading speed of college freshmen has been found to be around 250 words a minute on ordinary

reading matter, and a student who reads more slowly than that will certainly have difficulty in completing his college tasks within reasonable study periods. To be a really good college risk under this criterion one should readily and habitually cover not fewer than 300 words a minute on ordinary reading matter.

(5) Vocabulary. The possession of a full and accurate vocabulary for recognition and for use is one of the best indications of bookish aptitude. I do not know of any definite form in this matter that can be cited for the use of parents; but I will suggest one rough test that any parent can use: A young man or woman of eighteen who is thoroughly good college material should be able to read aloud a non-technical article in such a magazine as *Harper's* or The *Atlantic Monthly* with practically no stumbling over the pronunciation or meaning of words.

(6) Does the prospective college student show some predilection for the use of dictionaries, encyclopedias, gazetteers, maps, and the like? In other words, does he or she evince some appetite for precise information, with the habit of going to the recognized sources of such information? I am not prepared to say that the absence of this predilection and habit is significant; but its presence can be scored as an excellent indication of bookish aptitude.

The second and third major criteria suggested at the beginning of this chapter probably need only brief elaboration.

AWAKENED INTELLECTUAL INTEREST

THE SECOND one was—it may be remembered—an awakened intellectual interest in something. Under modern conditions all children must become literate and must therefore attend the elementary school. Perhaps all, or as many as possible, should go into the secondary schools, whether they take any interest in book learning or not—though of this I am far from sure. But in any case there seems to be no good reason why any young man or woman should proceed with advanced studies at the college level unless there is at least one subject he or she has enjoyed studying and really wants to go on studying. To me this seems axiomatic.

There is a fair number of young men and women of eighteen or thereabouts who have numerous intellectual interests—who sincerely want to learn more about many things. From the standpoint of this criterion these are ideal candidates for college. Then there is a larger number

of young people who display no great enthusiasm for most subjects of instruction, but are genuinely keen in some one field of intellectual interests, whether poetry or anthropology or psychology or banking or international relations or mathematics or geology or biology or chemistry or electrical engineering or forestry or interior decoration or counterpoint or what else. I would say that if there is any subject whatever that is taught in college which a young man or woman has definitely enjoyed studying and really wants to go on studying, then that young person qualifies for college under this heading. But if no such subject can be discovered, then I should not send that student to college—at least not yet.

SELF-MASTERY

MY THIRD major criterion—a fairly high degree of self-mastery—is not intellectual, like the first two, but moral. Its importance arises from the fact that the colleges—whether they should do so or not—throw their students almost wholly upon their own responsibility for their personal living and even for their attention to studies.

How can parents tell in advance whether a particular boy, let us say, meets this criterion? That is comparatively easy. They have only to give truthful answers to some such questions as the following: Does he get up in the morning by his own alarm clock, or does some one have to call him repeatedly? Does he manage his small weekly allowance with some discretion—make it last through the week and occasionally save some of it for some major purchase? Or is it all spent within the first day or two for trifling indulgences? Does he, on the whole, choose his friends wisely, or do Mother and Dad have to pry him loose every little while from associates whom he should have been able himself to recognize as undesirable? And especially, when he has "home work" to do, does he get at it himself and stay with it till it is done, or does some one have to watch to see that he does not let it go and slip out in the car or to the movies? If the answers to most of the foregoing questions are favorable, the boy is probably ready for college on the score of sufficient self-mastery. If the answer to a good many of them must be unfavorable, there is grave danger that he will encounter disaster in college, and if he were my boy I should not send him, irrespective of his intellectual brilliance—not yet.

IF NOT COLLEGE—WHAT?

THERE remains the difficult question as to what

should be done with the boy or girl of college age who under the criteria presented above does not measure up to the college standard.

The answer depends, of course, upon which one or several of these criteria the youngster fails to meet. If the deficiency is in bookish aptitude, the college road should be definitely and permanently avoided. It can lead only to failure, discouragement, inferiority complexes, and personality maladjustments. In cases of special talent for music, art, or acting, not conjoined with bookish aptitude, I would strongly recommend one or more years in a conservatory, a school of art or design, or a school of dramatic art; this recommendation is based on the strictly educational consideration that, quite irrespective of whether the youngster finally makes a career of his talent, he will get in such a school much more real education and development, general as well as special, than he would in college. In other cases, where the parents can afford it—and it will cost no more in money than a year of failure in college—a trip abroad or around the world or a year on a Western ranch is an educationally excellent temporary alternative. But in most cases, the alternative, immediately or shortly, is a job, in choosing which—even under economic stress—every effort should be made to see that it is in accordance with the boy's or girl's best aptitude, whatever that may be. For example, the boy with mechanical aptitude, but without the mathematical ability necessary for the profession of engineering, may well be encouraged to take a job in a garage or an electrical supply store, with a view to working up to the management of his own automobile or electrical business. And the boy with personal-relations aptitude, but without bookish ability, should certainly go directly into business, in which his success is as nearly certain as any success can be.

If the disqualifying deficiency is not in bookish aptitude but in intellectual interest or in self-mastery, the same answers hold good, except that in these cases they should be regarded as possibly temporary—not necessarily final. A year or two of additional maturity and practical experience will often see the emergence of one or more genuine intellectual interests. Even more frequently the discipline of a job for a year or two will develop an adequate degree of self-mastery. After such a flowering of genuine interest in studies, or such an attainment of capacity for self-direction, a young man or woman who would previously have entered upon an apathetic and profitless—or a highly checkered and equally profitless—four years, may then enter college with the prospect of real success.

HE WHO SERVES

He has not served who gathers gold,
Nor has he served, whose life is told
In selfish battles he has won,
In deeds of skill that he has done,
But he has served who now and then
Has helped along his fellow-men.

The world needs many men today;
Red-blooded men along life's way,
With cheerful smiles and helping hands,
And with the faith that understands
The beauty of the simple deed
Which serves another's hour of need.

Strong men to stand beside the weak,
Kind men to hear what others speak,
True men to keep our country's laws
And guard its honor and its cause;
Men who will bravely play life's game,
Nor ask rewards of gold or fame.

Teach me to do the best I can
To help and cheer our fellow-man;
Teach me to lose my selfish need
And glory in the larger deed
Which smooths the road and lights the day
For all who chance to come my way.
                                —*Edgar A. Guest.*

VOCATIONAL GUIDANCE

VOCATIONAL GUIDANCE IN HOME AND SCHOOL

By Fred C. Smith

THE DAY has passed when parents took it for granted that their children would drift easily into suitable occupations. Every conscientious father today is disturbed by the economic uncertainty facing the coming generation, and is wondering how he can best equip his son to find security and happiness.

If parents needed only to select the careers and to prepare their children for them the problems would be difficult enough, but the procedure is complicated by the fact that each individual must think through his own problems and make his own choice. A superimposed decision will not bring a satisfying life. Vocational guidance should be a process of *self*-examination and *self*-realization resulting in the individual's choice of his own occupation. The part of the parent or counselor, then, is the more difficult one of guiding and assisting. He must impress upon the child the importance of preparing for adult life, and he must lead the child gradually to understand himself, to know something about occupations, and to realize what training and what character traits are necessary to carry him toward his goal.

GUIDANCE PROGRAMS

IN MANY localities the public-school system takes over a large part of this responsibility, but, where no such organized help is available, groups of parents can always combine to study their common problems. Good guidance programs can be put on by Parent-Teachers' Associations. The important thing is that parents understand the philosophy underlying vocational guidance and realize the importance of some continuous program. The public school will probably concentrate on guidance during the Junior High School

years. The home program, however, can begin much earlier to prepare the child to make intelligent decisions.

If a youth realizes that a problem exists and is making a serious effort to find his own best place in the occupational world, we need not worry because he is slow in making a decision or because he changes his mind. If he recognizes opportunities and continues to grow, his choice may well evolve through a period of years. One per cent of the men listed in *Who's Who in America* changed their occupations to more successful ones after they were sixty years of age.

SELF-ANALYSIS OF INTERESTS AND CAPABILITIES

VOCATIONAL guidance is approached from two standpoints, study of the individual and study of occupations. The child should be led to analyze his own interests and capabilities as revealed by a study of the following seven points:

(1) *Mental capacity.* This can be measured objectively by tests and is best done by the school. A person should not undertake difficult professional training unless his mental test score justifies the effort. These tests, however, do not predict success in life, which often depends far more on the person's ability to make the best use of all the talents he does possess.

(2) *Mechanical aptitude.* Some people are mechanical, some are awkward, and these traits seem to have little connection with intelligence or inheritance. This gift can be measured to some extent by existing tests or by practical tryout experiences and should be considered when an occupation is chosen.

(3) *Interests.* One man likes to work with people, another with figures, another with en-

gines. One likes a crowd, one wants to be alone. Contentment in a vocation depends largely upon doing what you genuinely enjoy.

(4) *Home background.* Early training and surroundings influence one's social customs and viewpoints. Unless a person can make satisfactory readjustments he should keep to a familiar environment.

(5) *Physical condition.* Occupations vary greatly in their demands upon strength and health. The parent knows better than anyone else whether there is any physical weakness or handicap which must be considered in planning for the child's future.

(6) *Economic status.* Financial resources must sometimes determine the extent of training a student undertakes. However, industry and determination can often overcome such lack.

(7) *Social understanding.* "Job intelligence" is in many cases more important than any special training in skills. In many fields the man who advances is the one who can get along with people and who is able to recognize and overcome his own shortcomings.

STUDY OF OCCUPATIONS

FOR A HELPFUL guidance program this study of the individual must be supplemented by a study of occupations. All available information should be obtained and analyzed. Occupational maladjustment often is the result of a misunderstanding as to just what the occupation really is. Childhood games always show an interest in adult activities and a shrewd mother might guide that interest into a habit of analyzing different types of work. If the school does not offer a definite program of job exploration, a group of fathers can accomplish much in a community project. Industries and business houses may be visited, business and professional men interviewed. Public-spirited citizens will always cooperate with an earnest father and son group intelligently seeking information. The local librarian can supply books describing many professions and trades. Inexpensive government bulletins offer some help. Young people should be encouraged to investigate, read, and think, and to report the results of their studies in some organized way. Teachers can cooperate by correlating this work with school lessons, especially in English classes.

EIGHT POINTS TO CONSIDER

EIGHT points are suggested for consideration in examining any occupation:

1. *Importance of the occupation in the community.* How many people does this work employ? Is there a steady demand for its product? Will the need for it probably continue? What opportunities does it offer for beginners either at home or in near-by communities? The United States census report of your city will be of some help on this subject and good bulletins are issued by the State and the United States Department of Labor.

2. *Description of work actually done.* The visiting, interviewing, and reading mentioned above will help the student to determine what people really do on the job—what is expected of them hour by hour. The showy and exciting phase of an occupation is usually obvious but behind the scene there may be a price in tedious drudgery which the youth would not be willing to pay.

3. *Advantages of being connected with this occupation.* Each vocation carries its own advantages. Is wealth of greatest importance to this person, or social standing, or service to humanity? Will this employment leave time for satisfactory home life, will it mean opportunities for travel, will one rule or be ruled?

4. *Disadvantages of the occupation.* Before a final choice is made a person should consider the disadvantages of that occupation. A doctor, for example, must put in long and irregular hours. He must go to his patients in the night if he is needed and must care for them though they be maimed or dying. The person to whom these would be disadvantages should consider carefully before entering this profession.

5. *Preparation necessary for entrance upon this occupation.* In almost all of the trades and professions certain training requirements have become standard. An ambitious young person should plan for adequate preparation before he undertakes to compete with others in his chosen field.

6. *Special qualifications required.* In general, the three requirements for occupations are manipulative skill, technical knowledge and occupational understanding. These vary in importance in different fields. A worker may have great skill and yet fail because he lacks technical knowledge. A stenographer, for example, who is an expert typist may lose her job because she cannot spell. Both skill and technical knowledge may fail if suitable occupational understanding or attitude is lacking. The stenographer again may be unsatisfactory because she is untidy, discourteous or dishonest. Each occupation requires special traits which must be carefully considered.

7. *Financial income.* Financial returns are im-

portant to most of us, although they should never constitute the sole basis of choice. It is usually possible to determine the average salary of beginners, the possibilities as to future, and the provisions for retirement which accompany an occupation.

8. *Effect upon the worker.* The daily task leaves its imprint upon the worker. It can develop his character, ruin or improve his health, control his social or political outlook. The young person should try to look ahead and see himself as he will become.

TRYING OUT A JOB

ONE OF THE best ways to learn about an occupation is to work at it, and here again the father may guide his son into valuable experiences. A summer's job will often tell a boy whether certain work would interest him permanently. Much of the foregoing information can be collected during vacation and odd time jobs, especially if he watches not only his own tasks but the duties of those above him, to whose positions he might aspire. Much can be said for the old-time apprentice system.

As all of this information is obtained, each youth should be encouraged to sort out the occupations and to try to fit himself into the general scheme.

The counselor has both the privilege and the duty of helping the youth to fit these patterns together and to discover what groups of occupations call for his particular qualifications and what further efforts he must make if he would succeed. Many schools hire trained counselors, but in their absence great help can be rendered by the parent, teacher, Sunday-school teacher, or club leader who is willing to study the subject seriously.

IMPORTANCE OF CHARACTER AND ATTITUDES

AFTER all of this analyzing and selecting and preparing is done, the real progress of the individual in his chosen field will depend largely upon certain traits of character and attitude. An investigation made by Doctor Brewer of Harvard University revealed that sixty-six per cent of persons losing their jobs do so for such reasons as insubordination, unreliability, laziness, or dishonesty. The average employer of today is more concerned about the attitude of his employee than about his knowledge and skills. The latter can be acquired as the need arises, but attitudes are largely fixed during the early years. It is the function of the school to develop skills and to impart knowledge, but attitudes are more often developed in the home. Here then is the parents' greatest opportunity to contribute to the child's adult life. Parents should train their children during their formative years to character traits which will become assets. Children given no responsibilities or definite tasks become lazy; if shielded from the consequences of their mistakes they do not develop reliability or judgment. The child who accomplishes his own ends by having a tantrum has a rude awakening when he learns that the same tactics in adult life lead to failure rather than success. A mother who thinks indulgence is kindness and allows her child to consider his own desires without respect for other people's rights does not foresee his bewildered unhappiness when he realizes that his associates dislike him.

ADJUSTABILITY AND VERSATILITY

ONE TRAIT which is peculiarly valuable in today's world is adjustability. Unemployment itself is scarcely a greater problem than that created by the constant shifting of occupations. New fields are opening while erstwhile important industries disappear. The man who can adapt himself recognizes new opportunities. Occupations should be classified in a general way by the skill and knowledge they require so that workers can intelligently transfer their abilities from one field to another. Each job should teach something which can be carried on. It has been said that fifty per cent of the people in America could make an average success in fifty per cent of the occupations. Surely adjustability and versatility are at a premium today.

As a final word to parents we would urge that they not allow their own pride and ambition to force a child into a career for which he is unfitted. A few occupations call for brilliant students. Others, equally important to the world, depend more upon personality and ability than upon a scholarly mind. Let each person find a place in which he can progress and where he can be happy. Then will the world's work be leading toward a better social and economic order.

HOW TO RECOGNIZE YOUR CHILD'S SPECIAL ABILITY

By Clarence C. Robinson

IF THERE is any one problem where a parent more often bungles the job than in this matter of special ability, we have failed to locate it. Not even in matters of the heart, where parents have a reputation for doing irreparable harm in the lives of young people, do we more often make mistakes than in our superficial judgments about talent.

Within a week, an exceedingly capable worker in social and religious lines told me that he had been for years striving to overcome the early effects of his father's lack of confidence in him, in relation not to integrity, but to ability. In this particular case, the boy had been doubly distressed because of frequent comparison with his brother who, the father was sure, was destined to be a great man. As it turned out, both are able and useful men, but the father ran a serious risk by starting what might have been a dangerous sense of inferiority on the part of one of his boys.

The mother who thought her little son certainly was going to be a druggist because he so delighted in playing with bottles containing different colored liquids is only more obviously foolish than most of us. Consider, if you will, with what powerful forces we are dealing, how intricate are the possibilities in any one boy, and how far below the surface may rest the things that are really fundamental in his life.

SIGNIFICANCE OF SPECIAL ABILITY

IN THE first place, we may as well realize that the boy has a fixed heredity. It may be capable of great development in this direction or that, but nature has given him, because of the contribution from his mother's and his father's lines, a certain set of unit characters. A boy is like a ship sailing out of harbor with no ports of call before its final destination. The ship has a certain kind of hull, it is well built or poorly built, it is propelled by steam or by sailing apparatus, according to its nature; it has a certain amount of machinery for hoisting, for fire control, and the like. The ship is provided with stores of food and water, and it carries a certain cargo which is presumably of some use to the life of the world.

HEREDITARY EQUIPMENT

TO BE SURE, accidents may happen and if the engine gives out makeshift sails may be hoisted, but that is merely a way of limping into port, and

does not represent the proper functioning of that ship. Peculiarly enough, a boy is much like a ship. He is built a certain way, fat or slim, strong or weak, he is a speedy runner, a fine jumper or slow and heavy in his movements. He possesses certain talents, and though they are not evident and catalogable at the time of birth, they are there just the same and it is only our lack of ability to understand and analyze human nature that prevents our being able to sit down and write out for a boy just what is represented in his ship, cargoes, and stores. However, we need not chide ourselves as parents for not being able to do this cataloguing job well, inasmuch as one of our leading scientists declares that considering the varied hereditary elements that come from father and mother, and their fathers and mothers, back for a few thousand years, the youngster has the chance at birth of something like 1,048,576 different hereditary possibilities or combinations. Of course he will not have this enormous number of characteristics, but if nature has this many chances for the individual, no wonder we are different from each other and distinctly hard to understand.

DEVELOPMENTAL POSSIBILITY

WHEREAS the particular capacities, interests, and tendencies in the life of a boy are fixed by nature, they are only fixed in the sense that certain deposits have been made in the boy, and these, when properly nurtured, are capable of utilization and development in the human animal to an extraordinary degree. So true is this developmental possibility in human nature, that we have made the grievous mistake of thinking that we could do almost anything if we wanted to badly enough. Fortunately for ourselves and the boy, we are learning that a short, chubby-legged boy cannot possibly run as fast as a tall, lithe boy and no amount of training or will power will enable him to do so.

However, we do find that almost any normal boy can do something in the line of games and athletics, if he is encouraged and given some sort of adequate training in a phase of physical activity for which he is adapted.

The ship or the athletic analogy could be carried out to a remarkable degree, but in a brief study like this we must turn our attention quickly to other matters.

WAYS OF DETERMINING SPECIAL ABILITY

IF THE parent, teacher, or worker with boys is ruled by pride or prejudice, he will waste time reading these paragraphs. Approaching a boy with preconceived notions, or with a particular emotional desire to have the boy become a minister, a business man, or a farmer, will spoil the whole effort.

UNOBTRUSIVE OBSERVATION

OF COURSE happiness and usefulness are to be considered as well as money, but where the pride of either the parents or the boy is keeping a boy from undertaking that for which he is fitted, or that which is not overcrowded, money will sometimes attract quicker attention than the needs of the world.

For those who really want to know what the boy can do, we suggest among other processes the following: In the early years, say four to ten, perhaps there is nothing more useful than *unobtrusive observation,* and we mean exactly what the words indicate. We must not expect an interest which absorbs the boy at eight years of age to be good for a life run. It may be and it may not. The ardent interest in toy construction sets or building huts in the backyard, may represent a mechanical or a construction tendency of some kind, or may merely mean that an active brain is feeling about in the world, testing everything to find out what is interesting and worth while. Stamp collecting may mean an intense interest in world travel, a desire for contact with strange peoples and places which may be significant in the boy's life-work choice, but it may, however, merely mean the functioning of an acquisitive instinct, and the next day he may turn his attention to collecting bugs, or to gathering rope and old iron to sell to the junk-man.

Through such observation, which does not interfere with the boy, unless he is getting into real danger of some kind, one may learn much about a boy, especially if we try to distinguish between this boyish experimentation with anything he can lay his hands on and that persistent, increasingly intelligent interest in some one or more definite activities that marks special ability.

THE TEST OF EXPERIENCE

FOLLOWING observation, it is possible to use *various kinds of tests.* The test of experience, for instance, is an important one. A boy's life around the home, church, school, Y. M. C. A., scout troop, and the like, gives the boy opportunity for experiences of various kinds—work, play, leadership, organization, service, and the big out-of-doors; all these experiences begin to reveal, in the years twelve to fifteen, in what directions the boy's capacities may lie. There ought, of course, to be some way for various adults who touch the life of a single boy, to confer with reference to their concept of the boy's capacities and interests, based on their observation and experience with him. Many a boy has revealed clearly to his associates by the time he has reached the middle teens certain evident characteristics which mean special ability.

SCIENTIFIC TESTS

COMING to more exact measurement, we have more or less *scientific tests.* These are of two kinds: (a) for general intelligence, and (b) for special ability.

SELF-ANALYSIS, RE-ANALYSIS AND COUNSELLING

As THE boy grows older, *self-analysis* may be undertaken by simple and practical methods, combined with a *re-analysis* of his own study by someone familiar with such work, *counselling* with exceptionally well-informed men, either on the general problem of life work, or with men engaged in the trades, business, or professions in which the boy's analysis and experience may indicate that he has some ability. All these combined make it much more possible to-day than ever before to help a boy distinguish between that which is superficial or momentary, and that which is fundamental and constant in his character and individual abilities.

LEAVE THE FINAL DECISION TO THE CHILD

A SAFETY valve in all this is found in the principle of letting the boy finally decide so far as vocation is concerned. None of us have a right to take that into our own hands, for the boy has a right to live his own life and to make his own decisions. Personally, in contacts with boys in every State in the Union, I am amazed to find how modest, how open-minded, and how willing boys are to spend time and effort to find out what God has really put in them, and how they ought to use it for their own satisfaction and for the benefit of the world.

VOCATIONAL APTITUDES THAT AFFECT SCHOOL SUCCESS*

By Johnson O'Connor

A DISCREPANCY always exists between actual accomplishment and inherent ability; few persons ever reach the goal within their power. In school and college the hiatus is least for average boys and girls. They encounter fewer obstacles in classroom assignments; they complete more satisfactorily every course which they undertake; for each class sets its own pace, one suited to its average member. It is the exception whose grades fall short of what a knowledge of his capabilities leads one to anticipate, for, whether sluggish or brilliant, he who departs from normal finds the rate too fast or too slow.

One expects the dull boy to lag, and until recently it has been assumed that slowness in school evinced lack of intelligence. But during the last two decades a technique has been developed by means of which it is possible to measure capacity independent of its manifestation in the classroom. The original aim was to isolate the characteristics requisite to achievement in each occupation and profession and so guide boys and girls; successful surgeons, for instance, differ radically in their inherent characteristics from successful salesmen, and this difference can now be measured. Then the technique was turned to the study of retarded pupils with the aim of determining that characteristic which was wanting and examining it scientifically.

Poor students are of two types. Some lack ability, as might be expected; others possess too much. From the standpoint of the school they are indistinguishable, for both fail. Only painstaking measurements sort the one kind from the other.

Even parents do not always recognize ability in their own children. The Human Engineering Laboratory at Stevens Institute of Technology and in Boston purposes to diagnose educational and vocational problems and so to assist in solving them intelligently. To this Laboratory a white-haired grandmother brought not long ago a nineteen-year-old grandson. His parents, both brilliantly successful, had given him up as hopeless. He had failed and been asked to leave a well-known preparatory school. The Laboratory staff were all but told that he was a hopeless moron. Only the grandmother had courage enough to hope that some hidden ability might be discovered. When measured, the boy excelled in every characteristic. The larger the number of aptitudes inherent in an individual, the greater should be his chance of success. But one as abnormally gifted as this boy, one who scores high over too wide a range, instead of ranking at the top in scholarship as he should, frequently falls to the foot of his class and often leaves school or college under the duress of some deficiency.

The boy with too many aptitudes is restless. He dabbles in many fields; he meanders, hoping to discover something absorbing, abetted by finding everything so easy that an obstacle causes merely a change in direction. Even when he graduates from college his first position seldom demands the full gamut of his endowments and he continues to stray aimlessly in search of an ideal niche.

The multi-aptitude student knows his ability, feels his own superiority to most of those counseling him. He needs not advice, but data on which to base his own conclusions.

The second step is the conscious utilization of each aptitude which can be measured; and then, as life progresses, the integration of the aptitudes into a complete pattern. Ninety-two chemical elements are recognized by the analytical chemist. Only eight mental elements, facets of the human mind, can be measured by the Human Engineering Laboratory with sufficient accuracy to identify them in the boy or girl of school age. Two more such mental elements certainly exist; and six or seven additional ones are already anticipated. The total may exceed a hundred, for the mind probably surpasses the material world in complexity, but the conscious use of even eight is a step in the right direction.

ENGINEERING APTITUDE

ENGINEERING aptitude, which seems to be an inherent gift for visualizing three-dimensional structures, is measured by the time consumed in solving four simple but carefully designed mechanical puzzles presented under controlled conditions. These puzzles are solved more rapidly by surgeons than by physicians; the work of the surgeon demands that he visualize structures with speed and absolute surety. They are solved by architects, who must picture a building solidly in three dimensions before it is built. They are

* Reprinted with the permission of the author and *The Atlantic Monthly*.

solved more rapidly by sculptors than by painters, for sculptors work with solid forms. They are solved by engineers, but rarely by bankers, accountants, and men in the advertising and merchandising fields. Surgeons, architects, sculptors, and engineers, although different in many ways, have one common factor: all deal with solid forms.

With boys engineering aptitude develops much as does physical height. With girls it is almost nonexistent, for only three in one hundred possess it to any great extent. It is dynamic and demands employment. Men who measure high in the trait and who are in work which does not utilize it seem restless and less successful than the Laboratory would expect them to be in the light of their other qualities.

The pupil with engineering aptitude has one of the characteristics of the successful architect, the successful engineer, and the successful surgeon, but may, because of this, find difficulty with school work. Not until he reaches the last year of high school does he ordinarily have an opportunity to use the gift. Until then he tries to visualize Latin and French in three dimensions, as he will later picture constructions in solid geometry and problems in physics. He seeks the whys and wherefores of language, but rebels at learning vocabulary and grammar rules by rote. Vaguely aware of a strength not recognized, he feels dissatisfied and experiences the same sensations as the mature engineer who is drawn by circumstances into a non-engineering occupation.

The remedy must give the boy a feeling of success in school; inspire him with confidence in his own capacity to do school work; and assure his teachers that he has ability, for too often the boy who measures extremely high in engineering aptitude is thought of as slow-witted, partly because of his language difficulties, partly because he insists on thinking through each problem in his own manner. Tinkering with an automobile, building a radio, and doing manual training utilize the ability, but are too far removed from the academic to be satisfactory remedies.

TONAL MEMORY

TONAL memory, as measured by one of Dr. Carl E. Seashore's musical tests, is another aptitude, a gift for carrying musical themes in mind. It is possessed by those who play by ear, and approximates what is ordinarily thought of as musical ability. It is essential to a musical conductor and probably also to one who plays with an orchestra. Not every boy should be driven to practise the piano or the violin. For one who scores low in tonal memory, hours of drill may not only waste valuable time, but may be extremely discouraging. But for one who scores high, no matter what occupation or profession he enters, music gives a sense of accomplishment, another means of self-expression, and the satisfaction of using one more aptitude.

CREATIVE INSPIRATION

CREATIVE imagination is a third aptitude which if not used leads one astray. Actual accomplishments, which require work, materialize so slowly that one with an excessive creative imagination finds it easier to imagine a thing done than to do it. The solution is not to stifle imagination, as is the temptation, but to use it constructively. It plays a part in writing, in advertising, in creative work in music and art, and in original work in science and engineering.

ACCOUNTING APTITUDE

A FOURTH aptitude, accounting aptitude, is requisite to school success. It is fundamental to accuracy in arithmetic, and plays a part in the solving of all mathematical problems; it is relied upon in the copying of themes and in the construction of neat papers in every subject. Unlike other aptitudes, its employment need not be consciously sought, for it is essential almost from the first day of school.

Only half the time does a multiplicity of gifts include accounting aptitude; and the boy who possesses a wide range but lacks this has not only the school difficulties attendant upon restlessness, but the additional handicap of being without the one characteristic upon which schools call more than upon any other. The boy whose instinctive tendencies make him a poor clerk finds speed and accuracy hard to attain, for the discrepancy between his swift thinking, engendered by other aptitudes, and his tardy recording leads him into ever-recurrent lapses. In copying a theme his thoughts fly ahead of his place on the paper. He races on in his imagination, oblivious of having written only a single line. In solving an algebraic problem he sees the answer before reaching it and fails to record the intervening steps; or, conscious of this tendency, he wonders continually if he has slipped and reviews his work. Even though he finds no mistake he often errs in starting again where he stopped.

Accounting aptitude, which grows irrespective of environment as do other aptitudes, reaches maturity with boys at the age of 18 or 19, and with girls three years earlier, at 15 or 16. Even at maturity boys average lower than girls in this respect, although the difference is not great; but prior to this, between the ages of 12 and 18, the sexes differ strikingly.

Boys, as a group, never equal the level which girls reach as early as 15, and, in addition, boys of this age are still three years short of their own maximum. Between the ages of 12 and 18, boys are ordinarily outstripped by their feminine classmates, who, because of higher accounting aptitude, do their homework more easily and quickly and arrange it more neatly. In this period the boy who is naturally low in this characteristic, who will be low even when adult, is at a disadvantage if compared with girls. If in a coeducational school, he often becomes unreasonably discouraged. Sometimes he gives up all thought of continuing and, disdaining physical labor, turns to a minor clerical job with a forlorn expectation of advancement. Sometimes he plods on with a sense of inferiority which he may never overcome, for low accounting aptitude often causes a boy to be considered mentally slow. Actually it means little more than a slowness in routine clerical work. Outside the clerical field its lack is unimportant; but this is difficult to explain to the discouraged boy of this age.

There are many reasons both for and against coeducation. Each parent must make the final decision. But, so far as this one characteristic is concerned, the multi-aptitude boy, with low accounting aptitude, belongs in a boys' school. In these ages a classroom comparison with girls exaggerates too dishearteningly this weak spot of the boy.

REMEDIAL STEPS

When accounting aptitude is sufficiently low to cause serious school difficulties, four remedial steps may be taken. They are briefly: correction of eyesight, separation of thinking from its recording, greater speed, and intelligent selection of courses.

Psychological tests have not yet reached the stage at which they invariably measure the desired characteristic, but, except for entirely uncorrected eye difficulties, the test for accounting aptitude ordinarily discloses an aptitude in the true sense of the word. The records of the Laboratory show that several times in the last few years the school marks of a low-accounting-aptitude boy improved strikingly after an eye examination and correction by proper glasses. Occasionally a re-examination and a change of glasses achieved a similar result.

The second remedial step for the boy whose clerical aptitude is low in comparison with his other characteristics is the separation of his thinking from its recording. He should deliberately lay his pencil aside, think through to the end of the theme or the algebra problem, determine upon the procedure without the burden of paper or pencil. Then he should perform the clerical manipulation rapidly and with unquestioning confidence.

The third remedial step comprises the deliberate acceleration of clerical operations. "Slow but sure" sounds true. The phrase carries conviction by alliteration. Unfortunately, however, its truth evaporates under scientific scrutiny.

Just how rapidly can work be done accurately? The time expended in comparing two parallel columns of numbers has been recorded for many individuals and the errors made by each counted. The shorter the time, the fewer the errors. The fastest individuals prove the surest. Exceptions turn up; an occasional person rushes through oblivious of mistakes, and another plods cautiously without them. But, *en masse,* quick workers are accurate, sluggish ones inaccurate. Lapses inevitably inspire the caution, "Slow down; be more careful"; and yet, if the laws which have been found in the Laboratory hold in the classroom, such directions mislead and hinder. The corrective is not time, not even care, but speed. A boy must drive his pencil to keep pace with his mind; not, as so often happens, slow down his thinking to his pencil rate.

The last step is an intelligent avoidance of certain school courses. Although all school work demands accounting aptitude, some phases employ it more than others. Success in typing, stenography, bookkeeping, and accounting rests primarily upon it, and courses in these subjects should ordinarily be avoided by one whose weakest spot is clerical accuracy. Although they are often ideal for one who excels in accounting aptitude, for one deficient in this characteristic they are discouraging; they do not alter his inherent ability, and ordinarily do not develop facility rapidly enough to warrant the time which they consume.

COMBINATIONS OF APTITUDES

Thus one might review in turn the eight aptitudes which can be measured, showing some of the uses to which each may be put. Then one should discuss each combination. Creative imagination and engineering aptitude are the characteristics of the inventor; and the schoolboy who scores high in these two should be given an opportunity to use his inventive ability perhaps in the solution of original problems in solid geometry and physics, perhaps in constructing new laboratory apparatus, perhaps in rediscovering for himself some of the scientific discoveries of the past. Creative imagination and inductive reasoning are the characteristics of the writer, and the boy or girl who scores high in these should be encouraged to write not only for his or her classes but for the school paper. Tonal memory is a characteristic of the musician, but low accounting aptitude may make it difficult to learn to read music. One who scores high in tonal memory but low in accounting aptitude should sing or choose an instrument to play which has only a single clef.

Eight independent aptitudes combine in several hundred different ways. Each of these combinations probably fits an individual ideally for some particular type of work. About a hundred combinations have been studied sufficiently to give an idea of their significance, and research is under way on others. Ultimately each combination will be understood and it will be possible to guide everyone toward a field which will use each aptitude but overtax none. In the meantime, the too widely gifted pupil must be recognized early in his school career and a higher standard set for him, one more apt to require all of his gifts, for lack of early incentive to work is one of the difficulties. During grammar school years a pupil progresses necessarily on the strength of inherent ability. Without factual background, he places himself by quickness of wit and by the ease with which he grasps new concepts. As a result, the multi-sided youngster hears only praise during his formative years. Without exertion on his part he obtains good grades and various rewards of merit.

As the years pass, the lower-ability classmates fall back or shift to special schools, and drop out altogether in high school. Before the first semester of college the student body, originally a heterogeneous assortment, has become selected. No longer do any few rise markedly above the group. In consequence, the basis of faculty judgment shifts from ability to attainment. A boy receives little credit for his innate gifts, but survives solely because of the completed work which he turns in. One whose limitations made it difficult for him to enter college continues under the new conditions. One at the top in aptitudes, with no previous challenge to develop sound habits of work, almost certainly fails when weighed by the altered criteria.

§8. ENGLISH VOCABULARY TEST

ALTHOUGH the Laboratory aims to seek the natural propensities of an individual, it has found a simple measure of pure knowledge, an English vocabulary test, convenient in showing the contrast between inborn qualities, won without labor, and grasp of facts achieved by study. A youngster, just twelve, recently excelled in all aptitudes, a brilliant boy. As he tried the aptitude-measuring devices and found himself transcending others of his age, he accepted his position at the top without comment. Not until he reached the English vocabulary did he fall to the bottom, possibly already too far below in accumulated knowledge to overtake the average person. In school he had always done reasonably well, ingratiating himself by intrinsic worth. Only the sharp isolation of his factual acquirements from his inherent ability demonstrated the scantiness of his achievements.

The answer is more work rather than less. Such a boy must be challenged, not usually by skipping a grade, not by pushing him into advanced work so rapidly that he misses fundamental principles, but by giving him more difficult illustrative problems, problems which show the simple principle but which tax his ingenuity to solve them. The many-aptitude boy too often sees at a glance the answer to the ordinary classroom problem and never learns to use fundamental laws as tools. As a result, when later in life he encounters problems which cannot be solved at sight he has no technique for attacking them and he gives up without effort. In the last years of high school and in college, a teacher needs courage to heap sufficient work on a boy already failing to compass his success. But success ensues often enough to warrant the procedure if the diagnosis is more than a chimerical impression of brilliance. In one case, a daring headmaster outlined a program whereby a boy who had already been dismissed from two preparatory schools could complete in a year nearly two years' work, enough to enable him to enter college, and could carry at the same time heavy responsibilities in extracurricular activities, an impossible task for a normal person. Yet this boy finished the year triumphantly.

The piling on of additional assignments is not always a panacea for low school marks. A prudent selection of courses obviates some, alleviation of clerical chores obviates others; the stiffening of standards meets only the one impediment, a multiplicity of aptitudes. The efficacy of so drastic a therapeutic measure hangs on the accuracy of the diagnosis. Under such carefully controlled conditions as obtain in the Laboratory, scientific instruments disclose the presence or absence of these isolated aptitudes as early as at ten years of age. At this stage a few schools now assign more difficult problems to the exceptional boy and so instill normal work habits early in life before their lack conduces to serious misadventure.

TRAINING THE EXCEPTIONAL CHILD

THE READER, with a son in distress, unfairly criticizes some teacher or perhaps the entire educational system, not realizing that, while a school may cater each year to one or two extreme cases, the process cannot be carried far without handicapping the larger, normal group. The exceptional boy must train himself to hold his own standards sufficiently high. He may abate his instability by creating a use for every aptitude. He may aim to head his class; but it is irksome to plod through a mass of work which for him is uninspiring. A more effective solution involves an altered attitude, a new philosophy. He should, early in his school career, discover and prepare himself to solve some difficult problem, perhaps some tangled social question, perhaps some knotty scientific difficulty, perhaps some abstruse mental puzzle.

A spectacular bridge completed, a great dam finished, a new vehicular tunnel opened, may for a moment give the impression that any goal can be achieved. But there are more unsolved and as yet unsolvable problems to-day than perhaps ever before. Highly gifted boys and girls fail for lack of setting themselves sufficiently difficult tasks early in life before the necessities of job hunting and holding engross the attention. Since both school work and the first minor task at which one must start are unsatisfactory incentives, the highly gifted youth should tackle a social, scientific, or educational problem serious enough to tax every ability which he can marshal to its better understanding.

This research into the measurement of aptitudes was undertaken with the purpose of discovering the characteristics of successful men and women. But even to-day the Laboratory cannot define success. It can tell a boy or a girl his or her relative chances of earning a living in a number of different types of work. It can tell the chances of sticking to each type of work for a period of five years. It cannot tell the chances of finding real happiness in the work, which, after all, is true success.

Yet, whenever the Human Engineering Laboratory has an opportunity to measure an adult who seems in some intangible way truly successful, who seems to have found real happiness in work, it is always someone who has discovered a use for every aptitude which he possesses, who makes use of his entire range of abilities, who lives life to the full; and the Laboratory has taken a first step, a scientific step, toward helping each boy and girl toward this particular type of happiness.

SOCIAL AND EMOTIONAL
DEVELOPMENT

Marguerite Sayer.

HOME

"Home's not merely four square walls,
  Though with pictures hung and gilded;
Home is where affection calls,
  Filled with shrines the heart hath builded."
                    —*Charles Swain*

This above all: "Home is where the heart is."

The most valuable thing any home can give a child is love.

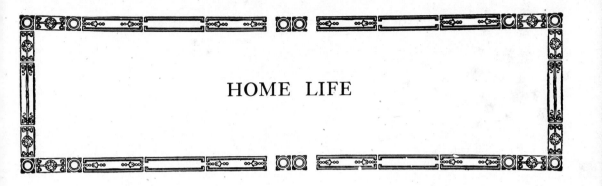

HOME LIFE

A HAPPY FAMILY—IF *

Don't mourn the breakdown of old-time discipline
until you've tried democracy in the home

By Dr. Mary Fisher Langmuir

Professor of Child Study, Vassar College

I AM GOING to draw for you a rough picture of an average modern family. It's an important family because it is the soil in which many American children grow up to face an increasingly complex adult world. It may seem at first glance a mere deterioration of the old-time family, but, as we shall see, it can provide roots as healthy as any child could need.

This modern family believes in earning more money as a matter of necessity—or as a step on the road to social success. To earn more money many fathers are forced to spend more and more time away from home. Hence many children have only a week-end acquaintance with their fathers—and even then only at those times when schedules happen to coincide.

The result is something that can be called only a one-parent home. In this one-parent home the mother is bound to become more child-centered than her grandmother was. The children too often tend to become the only focus of the mother's life. They are precious objects to be scheduled, manipulated, coaxed, and somehow maneuvered through a prolonged childhood and a lingering adolescence.

The wife will see her husband off to his work; shepherd the children to school; meet them after school and escort a reluctant John to the dentist and a not much less reluctant Susie to the music teacher; whip about town doing the shopping; and then rush home to be on hand when Daddy and the evening paper arrive. Between these fixed points in her busy schedule, mother is privileged —unless there's a baby at home—to be alone. Alone with the housework. Alone with the soap operas.

The effect of this is hardly healthy. Too many women say they feel more like stage managers and taxi drivers than like individual human beings, or even wives and mothers. Or they cock an envious eye at their menfolks' world, and consider it so much more interesting, more important, and more sociable. They are filled with an uneasy sense that they and their husbands seem to have few experiences in common and to enjoy little of a shared life.

Along the road of our boasted progress a certain kind of family unity and solidarity has in the past 50 or 75 years been lost. Why? How?

What was it like, the old-fashioned American home, the home of Grandmother's day?

We like to think of it as filled with a large family, with father playing a masterful and dominating role, with mother in the house working hard to see to it that everybody was happy and comfortable and well-nourished. As for the children, they knew their place. They had all the virtues that grownups admire in young people: they were polite, industrious, and never got under one's feet.

Such a home was part of a less complex society than ours. Its rules were simpler, more definite. The children had to conform to the respectability-pattern—or light out. Black sheep wandered west or ran away to sea. No compulsory school attendance or need for working papers forced those with an itch to see the world to stay home and face problems. There was less help, less social security, less community responsibility, true; but there seems to have been more individual freedom. And along with that went a greater sense of individual responsibility.

Keeping a large family warm, fed, clothed, and, above all, respectable was a full-time job. It required many skills, a kind of realistic competence, a practical pair of hands, and a stout back. As the home moved closer to the frontier more work was was required. *But it was required of everyone.* The older children minded the younger. In rural areas the boys helped the fathers with the heavier work and, long before progressive education, learned by doing. Girls worked side by side with their mothers and were proud of their skills. Women were as essential as men. Husbands and wives were equal in responsibility and productiveness. They needed each other, they needed the family, the family needed them.

Togetherness and *being essential;* there you have the warp and woof of the old family pattern. It was a pattern that created a definite kind of conduct. Standards of behavior and competence were not vague and subjective. The do's and don't's of life did not depend so largely on mother's wishes or her hurt feelings, or on father's pet ideas of how children should behave.

When things were at their best in these Currier and Ives homes, mothers and fathers loved and liked, as well as depended on, each other. Children were the gift of God and were accepted without much question. This shared life at its best was rich and varied and interesting. And even where the parents did not love each other, there was often a sustaining mutual respect.

On the other hand, we must not take too wistful a view of our grandparents. Judged by modern standards, discipline was authoritarian, undemocratic, arbitrary. Not all husbands and wives liked or even respected each other. Uncounted men and women resented their lot in life and the drudgery which cemented them together. Many more children were born than survived. For large groups in the population, life was too hard to be rich or varied or interesting. The standard of living was too low for many groups to achieve any measure of decency or dignity.

No, we don't want to go back to it. We are done with the days of the frontier period or even of *Life With Father.* We all accept and are proud of the fact that technology has developed as rapidly as it has and that cities have multiplied. Looked at fairly, our rising standard of living can be considered genuine progress in terms of human as well as material values.

Nevertheless, in any time of stock-taking, we begin to see that we have lost something, too, since Grandmother's day. What we have lost— and are beginning to refind—are certain values which were a natural part of the earlier patterns of family living. The typical American family of 1947, in contrast to that of 1897, is smaller, lives in a smaller home, has more conveniences and more service, moves around more, leaves home for its recreation and much of its food, provides for its old people and sick members in hospitals or institutions—*and is more self-conscious and unsure about what to do with its children.* Gain? Loss? Perhaps both.

The gain is linked with the loss. We point with pride to the commercial and social agencies which have taken over some responsibilities from the home. We easily buy things which formerly had to be made with difficulty by the members of the family. But we forget that in Grandmother's time the making of these things created a common core of shared and essential tasks, and with the disappearance of these tasks that core has vanished.

Many suburban fathers and mothers are able to provide expensive educations, cultural advantages, and physical care unknown in earlier times. But as a consequence the children all too often get a feeling that life centers in them and their wishes. Gain—and loss.

The very fact of smaller families increases this danger of overconcern and overprotection. In many groups in our country children are no longer taken for granted or considered God-given. Husbands and wives try to decide, wisely and consciously, when to start their families and whether to have one or two children—or none at all. Some of them even try to space their children so that Johnny can be spared the ordeal of sibling rivalry, which is supposed to be most acute in the preschool years. Others deliberately limit their families to one child. Still others have no children because the experiences of their own parents leave them frightened at the thought of being burdened or limited by a young brood.

Children of parents who are in doubt or in conflict about parenthood have a hard time getting well started. Children of parents who have one child "in order to give him every advantage" carry heavy burdens. Both groups are less free to develop properly than children who are welcomed as a natural consequence of marriage.

Children are like plants. And we know now that the old-fashioned soil of family relationship, rich with the nourishment of togetherness, held certain elements good for growing children.

How can we restore this soil?

In the last three decades enough children have come out of small child-centered families of adequate incomes for us to evaluate the results. We know now why it is not wise to make every effort to give children completely carefree childhoods. Gratifying every whim does not strengthen the roots of character. It is not enough for children to be able only to receive and to enjoy. Their emotional roots must be sturdy enough and deep enough to help them withstand the winds of change and the periods of drought or storm that come to all lives.

Many of the experiences and responsibilities which used to help build stamina are no longer normally a part of everyday living. We must now consciously recreate them. Parents today want to know what experiences, what qualities in family living give children strong roots for growing. Fortunately we are learning that a good home is not to be judged primarily by the size of the income, or even the evidences of culture and taste. Wherever it may be, a good home for children has certain unmistakable characteristics: The members of the family respect and like each other; they enjoy being together and working together; they help each other out; and they feel reasonably free to be themselves.

It is in this psychological freedom "to be themselves" that modern families can develop a new source of strength. The areas in which life can be shared by parents and children have been multiplied by greater freedom of movement, greater freedom from want, and broader education. The "togetherness" of the old-fashioned family can be reinstated in new and more democratic ways. It is already happening in hundreds of thousands of homes. In them the modern democratic family is taking shape.

THE DEMOCRATIC FAMILY—IF

AMERICAN PARENTS no longer need to be unsure about what children need. They can believe and trust that their home will be a *good* home for a child *if* . . . he is loved and wanted—and knows it; *if* he is helped to grow up by not having too much or too little done for him; *if* he has some time and some space of his own; *if* he is part of the family, has fun with the family, and belongs; *if* his early mistakes and "badness" are understood as a normal part of growing up and he is corrected without being hurt, shamed or confused; *if* his growing skills—walking, talking, reading, making things—are enjoyed and respected; *if* he plans with the family and is given real ways to help and feel needed throughout childhood; *if* he has freedom that fits his needs and responsibilities that fit his age and abilities; *if* he can say what he feels without being afraid or ashamed; *if* he can learn through mistakes as well as successes; *if* he knows his parents are doing the best they can, and they know the same about him; *if* he feels his parents care as much about him as they do about his brothers and sisters; *if he is moderately and consistently disciplined from infancy, has limits set for his behavior, and is helped to take increasing responsibility for his own actions; if* he has something to believe in because his parents have lived their ideals and religious faith.

Such good homes for children to grow in are much more common than we realize. Their traditions and beliefs rest soundly on the best of our democratic heritage. They will be perpetuated through the children they are rearing soundly and well. The soil of American family life is reclaimable. It can—and must—make strong roots possible.

THE HOME ATMOSPHERE—ITS EFFECT ON CHILDREN*

IN THIS world the important thing is not what happens to us but how we take it. Whether a person is an optimist or a pessimist depends upon his way of looking at life. His outlook is determined in large measure by the influences to which he is exposed in childhood. Some of the most potent influences are found in the relationships which exist within his own family group.

What kind of home atmosphere should be created by parents in order that a child shall develop a desirable outlook on life, an outlook that will help him to face difficulties and attack whatever comes with courage and the spirit of adventure? There are, of course, many factors that go to make up a home atmosphere that is desirable and satisfying, but four are undoubtedly essential to every happy and successful home.

DEVELOPING CONTENTMENT

THE FIRST essential is happy, contented parents. Parents who are unhappy and dissatisfied with life cannot fail to project upon their children their own outlook. Marriage is a disappointment to many people. Its demands are complex; "men and women have many interests and the serious failure to achieve any one of these may become a sufficient cause of trouble to spoil completely the marriage relationship." People enter marriage with their attitudes toward life already formed. It is frequently true that what to one is essentially satisfying in the marriage relationship is to the other of small importance. Happy, contented parents seem, however, to have been able to discover certain fundamental attitudes upon which to establish a relationship that is not only satisfying emotionally but that is at the same time a true partnership in the best sense of the word.

There is no question in such a partnership of either parent's having superior rights, for each should enjoy certain unique privileges and each has his own contribution to make to the maintenance and operation of the home. This relationship helps to eliminate petty jealousies and strivings for domination over each other or the children. In such a partnership one finds joint planning of the family income, with a spirit of equality in all money matters, because happiness and contentment cannot reach high levels if the father or mother alone holds the purse strings.

Equally important is the satisfactory division of labor in the home, for the over-fatigued mother is not likely to be a contented one. When there are many tasks to be done, with inevitable interruptions occurring every day, mothers often despair of ever getting any time for themselves. This is particularly true in homes where there is more than one child under six years of age.

If our grandmothers enjoyed being slaves to their families the present generation of young mothers does not. Parents should and can be helped to find those deeper satisfactions for which they are searching. Perhaps this help should come from the home economists rather than from any other group since they have always considered homemaking their business. Some people think that the economic changes are going to turn us back to a simpler mode of living. Perhaps it will. We need help in reorganizing our home life along simpler lines. We need help in working out better balanced plans for meeting the requirements of each member of the family. We need to give more consideration to father's place in homemaking. Too often his only responsibility is fitting in where mother dictates and he is made to look upon his job solely as that of the breadwinner. We need to study our homes to discover what educational opportunities they offer to the child. The child who does the dusting week-in and week-out or who washes the dishes three times a day may be relieving her mother from certain routine work, but after she reaches a certain degree of facility in the performance of these tasks the mere repetition is of little value in acquiring manual skill. Educationally speaking, she should pass on to other tasks that offer opportunities for acquiring new skills.

No standard rules for the budgeting of time are possible since each home situation must be considered on the basis of the number of members in the family, their living conditions and their aims and purposes. But the young mother who fails to make time for relaxation and refreshment, whether found in reading, playing with her children or listening to a concert, is being unfair to herself and to her family. Then, let me repeat that the first factor in a wholesome home atmosphere is happy, contented parents.

CREATING CONFIDENCE

THE SECOND essential is confidence. If a child is to develop a wholesome outlook on life, it is essential that he should grow up with complete trust in his parents provided that trust is deserved.

---

* Courtesy of Extension Service, New Jersey State College of Agriculture.

Sincerity in all our dealings with children is the basis for this attitude of confidence. Children begin life with this belief and trust in their parents. Why do they change? Are they too often deceived?

When you threaten a child with punishment, when you tell him that the policeman will get him, perhaps you do not intend to deceive him. You may, perhaps, only want to get him out of a dangerous street. But he soon learns that what you say is not true and his faith in you is shaken. When your adolescent daughter shocks you by doing something of which you do not approve and you tell her that you never did that when you were her age, you only want to impress her with the undesirability of her behavior. But she may feel that you are not strictly honest because if you didn't do that particular thing you probably did something just as bad in the eyes of your parents. Or she may think that you are priggish and then decide to keep still about her escapades in the future.

It is often the fear of the over-anxious parent that prevents the loosening of the apron strings as the child grows older. Such warnings as "Helen, don't forget your rubbers, you may catch cold," or "Billy, have you done your homework?" indicate a lack of faith on your part in your child's ability to remember. This the children resent and they show it oftentimes by taking their confidence elsewhere.

Children should feel at all stages of their development that there is someone in whom they may confide. Of course, a child's confidence cannot be forced by insisting that he tell everything, but by respecting his reticences and by being ready to listen when he wants to tell something, the channel of communication between you and your child can be kept open.

CULTIVATING A SENSE OF HUMOR

THE THIRD essential in developing a wholesome outlook on life is a sense of humor, provided it is considerate. Humor is an asset in any home. Seeing the funny side of a difficult situation and taking it good humoredly, reduces tension and helps to maintain pleasant family relationships.

Humor such as this should be distinguished from fun at the expense of children. Have you seen parents repeat to guests the amusing mistakes of their children? Have you seen them laugh at children's confidences, read their letters and joke about them, or make fun of their "puppy loves"? Doing these things not only teaches the child a lack of consideration for others but makes him resentful and self-conscious.

While it is true that ideas of what is funny differ with children and adults, there are many experiences which they can share. Some people have the happy faculty of radiating good humor and of giving others a sense of relief and freedom from strain as soon as they enter a room.

Begin to develop this attitude by helping your child to take his bumps with a laugh instead of a tear. If, later he can learn to take good-humoredly disappointments and accidents as well as jokes on himself, he has acquired an important asset in the development of healthy personality. We adults know how much energy we waste through useless worry, irritability over things we cannot control, and conflicts of one sort or another that leave us exhausted and ashamed.

PRACTISING CONSIDERATION

THE FOURTH and last essential in a wholesome home is consideration for each other among the members of the family. Professor Groves says: "Perhaps the most commonly forgotten need in marriage is justice. It is so easy for one to take what belongs to the other, especially if the husband or the wife is more inclined to sacrifice for the sake of the other's happiness. Justice in matrimony requires that there be on the part of both partners a genuine respect for the personality and the rights of the other." The same holds true with reference to consideration in the treatment of children. This does not mean doing things for the child, nor does it mean giving things to him, but rather treating him as a person, with the same courtesy that you would show to any adult.

In this everyday matter of living there is probably no one factor that helps more to keep the home machinery running smoothly than consideration. There is no more important lesson for any child to learn than respect for the rights of others. There is no better place for him to learn that lesson than in his own home.

AN ADEQUATE HOME

DR. MIRIAM VAN WATERS gives this definition of an adequate home: "Within the adequate home there should be tolerance, flexibility, a scope for new departures. Life should be viewed as a perpetual conflict; a spiritual and biological venture that deserves our utmost. Child and adult go together up the same trail. One departs a little sooner than the other. There should not be strife between them."

THE COOPERATIVE FAMILY*

PARENTS are beginning to see the home not as a place in which to get tasks done but a place in which education is going on. Wherever you have education you have change, you have development, you have growth. This does not mean growth for the children alone; it means growth for the parents, too. Something is happening to every member of the family each day as the result of this group living.

Whether this experience is to lead on to something more complete, something richer, something more satisfying as the years progress or whether it is to become disintegrated, colorless and commonplace is dependent upon the way it is used.

Are you running your home as an autocracy in which the parents do all the planning, issuing orders to the other members of the family which it is their business to carry out? If you are, your home is not an educational center for your children.

Are you running your home as a democracy in which each member has a voice in the planning as well as in the executing of the activities?

GROUP PLANNING

REAL group planning is a process in which each member of the group is a participator. Although every participator must be willing to work for a solution of the situation, each must recognize that he will probably approach the problem from an angle dominated by his own desires and interests. Differences of approach cause conflict and the success of any plan evolved will depend upon the degree to which each participant is willing to subordinate his own personal interests to the interest of the whole. This is the situation with the world powers. If individual nations go to a conference determined to get all they can for their own country a successful outcome is jeopardized. If, on the other hand, they are more anxious for the permanent peace of the world than for any material gain for themselves, there is hope of attaining the desired end.

THE FAMILY COUNCIL

THE children in the family must be given an opportunity to discuss their hopes, fears, and problems with an understanding group, to air their differences and grievances, and to be guided by parental advice in seeing wherein they are selfish and wherein they are unwise, if they are to develop the ability to direct their own thinking. There is probably no better medium for providing this opportunity than a family council, of which each child, together with the parents, is a member. In such a council all the cards are laid on the table—the work to be done, the money to be spent, the pleasures to be sought, and the standards to be maintained. "It becomes an hour for mutually solving the problems of living together," says one father in describing his experience with this method. "The child gladly assumes responsibility as a member of a group in which everyone is on equal footing. A keener sense of honor, a greater family loyalty, and a fine, democratic way of life become part of the child's experience."

Such a plan requires that adults as well as children take the matter seriously. It is important that parents maintain a practice of allowing every case to be presented and of reserving judgment until all the facts are in. Each person must agree, also, to concede his opinion if the majority rules against him. Sometimes emergencies have to be met with a temporary plan, the final decision being made after more discussion has taken place. There are many ways of handling such a discussion but the important factor is the desire of the whole group to be fair to each member and to arrive at a decision which will be not necessarily what the parents wish but what, in the light of all the evidence, will make for the happiness of the entire family.

Under this plan children become more tolerant and are less ready to jump at conclusions or to misinterpret the motives of others. They have practice in seeing all sides of a question as well as in developing the power to express their ideas and to present them in a forceful manner.

A child who is free to work out his own ideas, who can plan his own life, and feels secure in the affection and sympathetic appreciation and guidance of his parents, will grow into a happy, well-adjusted adult, able to face life with courage and reasonable success. In ways such as this family life may become a true educational experience for both parents and children.

* Courtesy of Extension Service, New Jersey State College of Agriculture.

TRAINING IN HOUSEHOLD TASKS

By Mrs. Bertha Payne Newell

LITTLE children like to feel that they are sharing the occupations of grown folk. Often it would be easier to dispense with the help, but the children would be the losers. Every kind of work has its charm, but cooking, with its delightful odors, surreptitious tastes of sweets, and chance for making messes, is chief in attraction.

There were occasions when Helen was only three years old and Mother had to play nurse and cook at the same time. Perched on a high stool she beat the eggs, sifted flour, and creamed the butter for cake. When the mixing was done she had a bit of dough for her own. These impromptu cooking-lessons acquainted her with many qualities and processes. Think, for instance, of the transformation of an egg: the breaking of the frail, brittle shell, the pouring out of the translucent white, the globular yellow, the gradual blending of the two in a foamy mass. Could there be a better lesson in colors, forms, and textures?

The flour has its qualities to be tested with all the senses: squeezed in pudgy palms, dusted over the board, sifted through the wire mesh. How good its wheaty odor is, how sweet its taste to the tongue, and how it flies about! This all changes when it is wet. Now it is sticky, clinging to fingers and pan, but with more flour it becomes soft; elastic when squeezed and pinched. How many of us, I wonder, ever think of the sense-training in such experiences as these?

Quite as desirable is the training in deftness gained in handling the dishes, sifter, and egg-beater, and the dish-mop and pan during the washing up that follows. The soap and water make shimmering bubbles, just as lovely as though not made in the course of necessary work. There is more to be noticed and felt and done, neatly and deftly. The mixing-bowl is heavy, demanding all the strength in arms and wrists to lift and turn it. The wooden rolling-pin is not so smooth nor as heavy. The egg-beater makes one wonder what makes it turn so regularly, and the cogwheels seem somehow concerned in the motion.

Helen seemed to think that if she took a pinch of this and a spoonful of that, something good would come from the mixture. She would not take my word for it that cocoa, salt, flour, and sand would not make a delectable mess. So I let her try a few of her own mixtures until she was ready to take my advice.

Then I let her measure the ingredients for sweet muffins, in doing which she learned to measure in cupful, half cupful, tablespoonful, teaspoonful, as well as the difference between *level* and *heaping*. It was not cooking in the real sense, just play, but she was learning, too.

REGULAR DUTIES

MOTHERS find it hard to train children in household tasks where they keep servants who do not want children fussing around. One of the compensations for the difficulty in obtaining domestic help is in the occasion it furnishes for children to have regular duties. It was one of the sources of education in the old-fashioned home that "all were needed by each one."

What can children under five years do? They can wash silver and the smaller dishes, dry and put them away on low shelves. They can dust and polish furniture. Setting the table is another task within their capacity. When our cook left I put the dishes used most often on a low shelf so that Helen could reach them easily.

Then there are errands. How many errands they can do in the house and out of it!

No work should be too long continued and it is good to change work occasionally. In all this the charm will wear off when the novelty is gone and the lesson then is one of "standing to" and learning the moral lesson of responsibility.

HABITS OF ORDER

IT IS usually easier to pick up toys and clothes than to see that children do it for themselves. But it is one of the things in which we should be firm with ourselves and hard-hearted with the children. It is one of the disagreeable necessities of civilized life, and the sooner we make it habitual in children, the easier it will be for them and us. Just *once* disregarding the rule, and the mischief is to pay. For the secret hope is born in a child's soul that the omission may occur again. Then he will have to be followed up.

Miss Elizabeth Harrison told a story of a boy who for a time came to the table repeatedly with unwashed hands, and was as often sent away to wash them. At length his mother said, "Why do you persist in coming without washing—you know I never let you stay?" "Oh, yes, you did *once!*" the young hopeful replied. "When?" asked she. It turned out to have been a week before.

SHARING THE LIFE OF THE FAMILY CIRCLE

By Mrs. V. Oma Grace Oliver

CHILDREN must not be shut off in one part of the house to remain aloof until a certain age, but ought to be a part of the family circle, sharing its joys, work, and minor sorrows. I do not mean that children should be pushed before visitors, have all their meals at the family table, or remain up till their elders retire; but there are times and places when it is the children's right and privilege really to be members of the family.

Even when they are very young children can assume responsibility for certain light tasks about the house, and as their age and strength increase, more and more duties should be added. The great American idea has been to remove all responsibility from the child and to give him a care-free childhood. I would not take one second of joy away from any child, but I would make it a joy for him to feel that the home is his and that he, too, helps in the making of it by performing certain duties that need to be done for the comfort of all. The child of two can pick up toys, put away dishes and silver, help set the table, dust low furniture and run many errands upstairs and down, and he loves to feel that he is "mother's helper" like the little boy in the following verse:

> He brings his daddy's slippers,
> He picks up baby's toys,
> He shuts the door for grandma,
> Without a bit of noise.
> On errands for his mother
> He scampers up and down,
> She vows she would not change him
> For all the boys in town.*

Then the child can help prepare for the great festival days, birthday, Thanksgiving and Christmas, those joyous days which bring the family very close together, and we can let him share not only in the preparation but in the joy of the day itself and here very clearly he gains a presentiment of the love and spirit of service that make home, and an ideal of the home that he will some day found.

As we would let the child share the labor and the festivals, so we must permit him to share the great family secrets and home joys. Let him know that he must never divulge anything that concerns only the family and I know that a child properly trained will never tell his playmates what he is told is a family secret.

So we begin very early to train him to keep his word and the sanctity of the home. When he has been thus prepared he is ready to share with the mother and father that greatest family secret, the coming of the new baby, and this confidence will bind the little one closer than anything else to the very heart of the home.

Children are so open-hearted and ready, and respond so sweetly and quickly to faith and trust that we often miss great happiness by not sharing our hopes and joys more freely with them.

If we keep the bond very close our home will become the great meeting place of all children, and this love and companionship between parents and children will be like a powerful magnet whose attraction the children cannot resist. So from these beginnings the home tie will be so strengthened that we need never fear that the allurements of the world can draw our children from us, but can rest assured that they will always return to the "center of deep repose."

THE CHILD NEEDS SOLITUDE

PERHAPS the most important thing in the strengthening of a child's nerves is to be let alone. A very well-brought-up small boy, when asked what he would like for Christmas, replied: "A half hour to myself."

Nearly all children who have a too carefully supervised daily schedule are nervous. Their salvation lies in long, uninterrupted play, as well as in long, uninterrupted sleep.

What the race needs is wise mothers with well-

*Song for A Little Child's Day, by Emilie Poulsson and Eleanor Smith.

trained nerves who will feed their children well and educate them so that no nerve force is wasted in performing the necessary bodily and social functions, so that there is no external expression of fear, worry, haste, excitement over trivial and avoidable happenings, and so that there is leisure and quiet for the child to develop in his play the nerve-energy that will pass over into his lifework.

Just as aseptics give a wound a chance to heal, so the isolation of solitude and silence affords opportunity for moral healing. Give the child a chance to think over his problems.

FAMILY DIFFERENCES*

Parents frequently say, "I can't understand why my children are so different," as though they expected them to be alike because they are brought up in the same home. Differences between human beings are due to a variety of influences, but the first, most fundamental, or original differences are due to the determiners, or genes, found in the egg-cell from which every individual develops. Because our inheritance is double, one half coming from each side of the family, the results are often a surprise. It is very important to remember, however, that an individual may inherit the basis for a characteristic and still may not develop it.

The fact that these rather loosely organized tendencies or potentialities constitute the make-up of human beings is of significance to all of us because it makes possible a far greater development for the child, provided the environment is favorable, than would be possible were his equipment more fixed at birth as is the case in animal life.

Often parents are inclined to place at the door of heredity the weaknesses and defects they find both in themselves and in their children. Such an inclination is only a means of protection against criticism and an excuse for failure. To say that Mary inherits a bad temper from her father's side of the house is likely to mean that her temper is accepted as inevitable and something about which nothing can be done. It is true that it does not lie within your power to add one iota to your child's original equipment, but who knows the extent of that equipment? It is true also that many factors often attributed to heredity are the result of training and not of inheritance at all.

The significant point to realize is that each child enters the world with an equipment of his own, different in some respects from that of every other human being under the sun, and that only when he is permitted to set goals for his life which are in harmony with this equipment will he be able to achieve success and happiness. Sometimes even before a child is born, but frequently while he is still in the period of early childhood, a parent begins to dream of what this child may become, never realizing that perhaps in so doing some unsatisfied desire of the parent himself is being gratified.

Have you ever heard a father say, "My son is going to be a lawyer," or perhaps "a minister" or "a doctor"? Think of the heartaches and possibly the tragedy ahead for such a boy if his interest and ability lie in some other direction. Growing up under the shadow of his father's ambition, he may reach adulthood feeling a strong sense of his obligation to please his father, thereby ruining his own chances for success and happiness.

To plan a college education for a child before you are sure that the child can make the college grade often results in developing a sense of inferiority in the child when some substitute for college must be accepted. Later success is dependent upon the success with which the things from day to day are done.

Let us now consider some of the differences in children which should be recognized in the training given in the home.

PHYSICAL DIFFERENCES

Do you allow for the individual differences of your children in the care and supervision you give with reference to food, sleep, elimination, amount of clothing and recreation?

If you have one child who is more easily fatigued than another by excitement or anything that results from a change in the ordinary routine, you may have to deny that child the privileges accorded some of his brothers or sisters.

"Why can't I go to the movies? You let Carl go." A child speaking in this manner must be helped to realize that it is part of his responsibility to the family group to keep well and reasonably agreeable. If by going to the movies once a week he becomes too excited, loses sleep, is cross and irritable the next day and is not fit to live with, he must take his entertainment in a less stimulating form.

Although these are not easy situations to handle, parents find that children usually fall in with necessary adjustments provided they are based upon discriminations that are fair. Children can learn that fairness consists not in treating every one exactly alike but in treating each person with consideration for his individual needs.

MENTAL DIFFERENCES

When we come to differences in mental capacity, we find that here the members of the same family may differ from each other as much as they do in physical respects. One child may fail to make his promotion in spite of long hours of patient study while another secures high marks with no apparent effort.

* Courtesy of Extension Service, New Jersey State College of Agriculture.

Some children require much more time than others in order to acquire certain simple habits. Some will learn words and phrases by hearing them only once or twice whereas others may need to have them repeated many times.

Some parents find it difficult to accept a child as he is, particularly if he is not able to measure up in some respect to a neighbor's child or to an older child in the family. This situation is probably due in part to the fact that the child's success in school is closely tied up with one's own self-esteem, but it is also the outcome of a rather unsound and inconsistent emphasis upon equality.

We tell a child that if only he will put forth more effort he will be able to pass Latin, to master the piano, or to become the best speller in the class. We do this on the assumption that it is possible for everyone to arrive at the same goal and that the difference in result is due only to a difference in effort; whereas, if we are willing to face the facts, we must admit that John is not capable of mastering Latin, that Helen is not musical, and that Frederick is rather slow in spelling.

What is the effect of this practice upon the children? A child may struggle doggedly, at the same time feeling baffled and perplexed, if not depressed, by the futility of his efforts. He may be developing a lasting sense of inadequacy and inferiority. On the other hand he may turn around and belittle what he is forced to attempt, with a "sour grapes" attitude. "Who wants to know anything about Latin, anyway? It isn't worth knowing," he says. This is an unfortunate attitude, since happiness and success in life are in part dependent upon one's ability to enjoy the success of others while still recognizing one's own personal limitations.

Rivalry is bound to exist among children. It is a natural means of testing their powers. But there is a wide difference between self-chosen competition and that instigated by parents to satisfy their own ambitions. When children in the same family are pitted against each other, it frequently happens that one child is expected to excel beyond his power to achieve in the class room because a brother or sister has been on the honor roll. The progressive school is emphasizing more and more the importance of providing an opportunity for children to compete with their own records. To secure satisfaction from improving one's own achievement and at the same time to accept one's place in the group with equanimity is an essential factor in the development of a healthy personality.

It is a common practice on the part of parents under such circumstances to show their disappointment freely, to nag and criticize a child for laziness and by continual comparison with the records of the other children in the family to destroy the self-confidence of the child who is failing, and develop a feeling of egotism and conceit in the more successful children. It is small wonder if we find that as time goes on the children develop personality traits that interfere both with their outlook on life and their chances for happiness.

The family can do much that will be helpful by providing for the development of a variety of interests among its members. Parents who study their children find that every child has interests worth cultivating. These interests may not lead directly to any one vocation, and they may not carry the child far enough for him to acquire marked skill or mastery of a technique. But they will serve as resources to guide him in a constructive and satisfying use of his leisure time and they will aid in giving him a wider understanding of the interests of other people—factors which are as essential to a happy and successful life as the learning of a vocation.

EMOTIONAL DIFFERENCES

When we come to consider emotional differences we find ourselves in a still more difficult realm as far as knowing where the responsibility of training lies. Sometimes one finds the friendly, responsive child who enjoys meeting new playmates and having new experiences in the same family with another who is shy and timid, and for whom it is an agonizing experience even to move from one grade to the next because of the adjustment that must be made to a new teacher and new surroundings. How much of this behavior is due to inherited individual differences and how much to the training to which the children have been exposed, is difficult to determine.

In recognizing the individual differences of your children you do not assume that every child has important talents hidden away, but rather that it is possible for the mass of people to adjust themselves to happy group living when they are granted sufficient freedom to develop their own interests in ways which are satisfying to them and which, at the same time, do not interfere with the interests of others.

"In the home," says Dr. Benjamin C. Gruenberg, "the recognition of individual differences should mean a redistribution of our approvals and appreciations in terms that have greater significance for all concerned. It should mean an avoidance of invidious comparisons, and an increase in tolerance leading to a broadening of appreciations. The unseemly processions of the large crowd trying to keep up with the Joneses indicate a vast number of people who do not know what is worth doing, what is worth striving for, what direction is worth following.

"It is to the home that we have to look primarily for cultivating those attitudes and values that will make it possible for the individual to attain sufficient self-respect, and sufficient regard for other personalities, to accept differences without false modesty or false pride."

Since no two individuals are born exactly alike you will find among children of the same family not only physical differences, but mental and emotional differences as well.

These differences call for wisdom and skill on the parents' part since in the successful training of children one must adjust one's practices and methods to the various needs of all members of the family.

Let us recognize the fact that children are not all alike and rejoice in it. Let us endeavor not to bring all to the same standard but to capitalize to the fullest extent possible the particular talents with which each has been endowed. We should realize that by so doing we shall afford each one the best opportunity not only for accomplishing his own happiness and success but for making the greatest contribution to society of which he is capable.

THE FAMILY LODGE
A Plan for Family "Get-Togethers"

To our way of thinking, one of the healthiest principles of modern child psychology is the returning importance of the home and the family as the center of a child's life.

This return to what seems to some of us an old-fashioned situation is actually a step forward.

In the old days—say three generations ago—the home and the family were the accepted center of life chiefly because it was not so easy then as it is today to get away. Transportation was difficult and diversions were less specialized. Whatever entertainments, meetings, and other outside interests there were, were meant, for the most part, for the whole family. And, on the whole, they were no more alluring than the jolly good times families had together at home: charades and other games, taffy-pulls, picnics in the summer, reading aloud, Sunday School and church and the big, home-cooked Sunday dinner, singing around the piano, hobbies and other pleasures enjoyed by young and old, with occasional friends and neighbors to join in the fun.

The chores were a family affair too, with the children doing their part as an accepted part of the family's daily routine.

The result was that children so reared felt secure in the love of their parents, accepted as a part of the family by their brothers and sisters, and so grew up with a comparatively healthy attitude toward life and a sense of their own responsibility toward it.

It wasn't perfect in some ways. We have learned a great deal of value since then about child psychology and the emotional sources of human behavior, especially children's behavior. But it had something very important—a stability and a sense of belonging together which a later generation sadly lacks.

For a while all sorts of forces seemed designed for the purpose of pulling families apart: boy's clubs, girls' clubs, women's clubs, men's clubs; movies, theatres, even churches and schools. Pretty soon the family was almost never at home together —or out together either, for that matter. Johnny was shooting marbles with the boys down the street, sister was at the movies with her friends, father was at his lodge meeting, and mother had her afternoon bridge parties.

For a while the members of the family scarcely saw one another except at meals and not always then. Even when they were together in person, their thoughts and interests were very different— and generally kept to themselves. "You wouldn't understand," is a phrase they often threw around at each other. They seemed always to be getting ready to go out—alone, in different directions.

The result was bad. Complexes and neuroses appeared and multiplied like rabbits. All kinds of hostilities developed—from war among nations right down to private wars among members of the family.

Something had to be done, and it was done.

To the credit of progressive educators, psychiatrists, and child psychologists be it said that they found many of the world's troubles caused by the breakup of the home and the family. Without that as the nucleus of our children's lives, they agreed, there could be no health in us—or in them.

So today the cry is "Back to the home!" We know today that to get a good start in life a child, from earliest infancy, must feel emotionally secure in his parents' love for him and for each other—he must feel that he belongs in his own home, that he is wanted and cherished there.

Realizing this, it is comparatively easy for the mother of a new baby to surround the child with this kind of love and security. It is when the children begin to grow up that the difficulty usually begins. It is then that the home and the family are challenged by the competition of outside interests, and it is then that the home has got to make itself sufficiently interesting to meet that challenge.

There are many ways of doing this, depending upon the circumstances, tastes, and interests of different families and their various members. Chief among them is a genuine interest—not prying curiosity but genuine interest—on the part of each member of the family in the special preoccupations, hobbies, etc. of the other members. If this is established and enthusiastically manifested, the rest is likely to follow fairly naturally.

Of course one cannot expect the interests of persons varying greatly in age or sex to be similar; but if there is a genuine respect on everybody's part for others' peculiarities and even eccentricities, and if there are enough general family interests in which everybody can and does share, and if family get-togethers are taken as a matter of course and conducted with casualness and humor and tolerance, they are pretty certain to be enjoyed by all the members. Even the persniketty ones generally come around when they see how much fun everybody else is having.

As we have said, this family spirit should be so spontaneous as to be the rule whenever the family is together. But in order to get it going, it has often been found useful, as well as enjoyable, to have a family council of some sort, say once a week, at a stated hour when everybody in the family can conveniently devote some time and attention to it.

As an example of this, we have worked out a program which has proved popular with many families, has been enjoyed by parents and young folks alike, and has resulted in a healthy improvement in the behavior, understanding, and tolerance of all concerned.

We call our program The Family Lodge. It is a very flexible program that can be modified or adapted to the needs and interests of almost any family.

Families with religious inclinations—those who follow the beautiful custom of saying grace before meals, for example—sometimes begin with a brief and simple devotional, perhaps with appropriate music by some member of the family who can play or a hymn sung by the whole family.

Other families, less religiously inclined, omit this ritual and plunge right in.

So-called unfinished business may come first—a round-up of what may have been left pending since the last meeting.

Next, each member notes all the constructive and pleasant and helpful things that other members have achieved since the last meeting. These are wholeheartedly praised, appreciation and encouragement expressed.

Infractions of rules and regulations adopted by the Lodge are then confessed, or, if necessary, complaints are made. This should never be done in a tattle-tale spirit or sarcastically. On the contrary, a mutual desire to be helpful should animate these discussions. Members should be encouraged to defend themselves. There should be debate and rebuttal. This can be both stimulating and helpful if the parents cooperate by being as willing to take criticism as they are to give it. After all, this kind of thing—the spirit of the Town Meeting—is the very essence of democracy, and where is a better place to learn to live democratically than in our own homes?

Finally, there is the entertainment. This is, of course, the "dessert," so to speak, and may indeed be actually accompanied or followed by ice cream and cake or some other family favorite. The entertainment, if indoors, may consist of games, stories, puzzles, conundrums, charades, music, or any other simple entertainment which the whole family enjoys.

An occasional outing for the whole family to a theatre, movie, community meeting, or projects in which the whole family can share—painting, building, photographing, or constructing something, to mention a few—these can be thoroughly enjoyed if they are undertaken in a spirit not of competition but of cooperation.

In summer, when outdoor entertainment is feasible, family get-togethers can be even more varied and enjoyable. There are picnics and outings of all kinds, even vacations to be undertaken together. And there are endless craft projects, such as can be found in Volume 5 of this Bookshelf.

It must not be thought that a program such as that suggested by The Family Lodge, if given only lip-service or merely the outward form of interest, can accomplish much. The program must be entered into wholeheartedly and with enthusiasm by everybody to be a real success. Whether or not this can be achieved depends largely upon Mother and Dad. If they enter into it in the right spirit—that of good fellowship, tolerance, patience, sympathy, and enthusiasm—it is pretty sure that the children will do the same—perhaps even outdo them in time.

Such a program, if successfully carried out, bringing the family together in the home, is the best possible background for the building of character, security, happiness, and achievement for our children, the citizens of the future.

SPECIAL NOTE TO FATHERS

THERE is one point concerning children's welfare on which all the experts are agreed: *When both father and mother take an active part in bringing up their children, providing them with a wholesome, cooperative family life, the children are invariably better off for it.*

This has become increasingly clear during recent years when so many children, deprived of normal family life, have suffered a variety of personality disturbances in consequence.

Every child needs to have a warm, friendly, easy-going relationship with *both* his parents. It helps the child to develop more normally into a well-balanced human being. It helps not only to give him a feeling of security while he is growing up but also makes it easier for him, when he *has* grown up, to feel more at ease with both men and women.

Every child feels most secure with whomever has cared for him in direct, personal ways when he was a baby. That is why it is so important for fathers, as well as mothers, to love and cuddle their babies often and to bathe, feed, and diaper them at least occasionally. It makes the babies used to them and familiar with them from the beginning. In a family like that, if ever the mother is ill or away or otherwise unable to tend the baby, the father can take over over and the baby will enjoy it. An aloof or inexperienced father, on the other hand, will inevitably upset the baby's routine or his digestion or his nervous system—not to mention the father's own nervous system! To give a child the best possible start in life,

it is not necessary for him to be born with a silver spoon in his mouth. On the contrary, too many material advantages often tend to obscure an appreciation of life's more important spiritual and emotional values.

But even parents whose means are of the slimmest can give their children that most precious of all advantages—a family life in which both mother and father whole-heartedly participate on a partnership basis. All the money in the world cannot buy for a child the benefits that being born into such a family gives him.

The first step toward giving a child this priceless gift is for both parents to make their baby feel warmly welcome from the moment of his birth on. The second step is for them to plan on *sharing* the responsibilities of parenthood as well as its joys.

Unfortunately, this doesn't always happen. Sometimes it is because the mother insists she is the only one capable of tending the baby. More often it is because the father thinks baby-tending is exclusively the mother's job.

Too many fathers think this way. They are all but strangers to their children during infancy, and then, as the months and years go on, these same fathers wonder why their children are strange or shy with them — why mother is the one to whom they turn with their problems and affection.

Many a father has forfeited his daughter's confidence or his son's companionship because he failed to get on terms of sufficient intimacy with that son or that daughter during the child's early years. Many another has fallen down because he felt he was too busy being the family bread-winner, failing to realize that it was equally important to contribute enough time and patience and understanding to be a genuine father to his children.

If you are a father, determine to be a real one. Get in some practical spadework while your child is still a baby. Let him get to know you so well that he will coo and smile at you just as familiarly as he does at his mother. It will pay you handsomely in dividends when he is older—for many reasons, one of the most gratifying of which is that you will then be in a fine position to be his hero.

It is wonderfully good for a growing boy to feel that his father is his pal. So be companionable with your boy. Instead of being critical and demanding, be friendly with him. Don't force him to live up to your ambitions for him, but encourage him to live up to his own. Treat him as man to man. Go on excursions with him occasionally—fishing or hiking. Don't be above pitching a ball with him now and then. Get together with him on home chores as well as outside projects, especially on games, activities, and undertakings that *he* enjoys. Show him that you are interested in his occupations and that you take pleasure in his company—and occasionally in the company of his friends as well.

If your child is a girl, she needs your friendship too. She may or may not want to go with you on hikes and fishing trips or to baseball games, but she will be thrilled and flattered if you sometimes ask her out to a restaurant for lunch or to a movie or just for a walk in the park. She needs your approval quite as much as her brother does. Indeed, the relationship you establish with her will strongly influence her relationship with boys as she grows up and will doubtless be an important factor in determining the kind of man she will choose to marry.

Just as any venture works better when there is a true partnership among the managers, so is it with parenthood. And isn't parenthood the most important of all ventures in life, the one entailing the most personal and most interesting of all responsibilities?

Neither mothers nor fathers are perfect, nor are children. But, in general, the more genuine cooperation mothers get from fathers, the better the children are likely to turn out. So do your share—not only by trying to provide for your family financially but also by assuming equal responsibility with your children's mother in every important matter concerning their welfare. Join in helping solve their problems as well as in creating good times for them. Be their pal. Don't give them any reason to be afraid of you and certainly never let them down. Be the kind of father they can have fun with and of whom they will say with a glow of pride, "That's my father!"

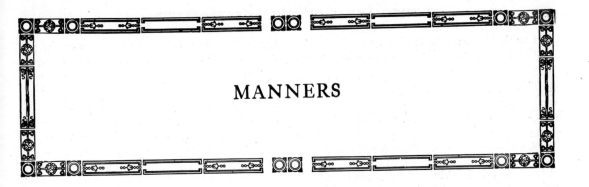

MANNERS

MANNERS RIGHT FROM THE START*

By Eva von B. Hansl

W E ALL want our children to have "nice manners"; but do we ever stop to think what we mean by that phrase? Surely we are agreed that we want them to use "please" and "thank you" and "excuse me" as common coin, to be neither shy nor bold, to have poise but not pose, to make others comfortable in their presence, to be friendly and pleasant-spoken and considerate—in short, to hold their own socially, whether among strangers, relatives, or friends.

But why do we want them to have nice manners? Partly, of course, to advertise ourselves! Since a child reflects his home environment, we want him to reflect credit on us. But to a child this is of little or no importance, unless he is old enough to have a sense of "noblesse oblige."

First of all, *manners must have meaning to a child for himself as a person.* They must mean an inner sense of self-assurance which makes him feel at ease with all sorts of people in any circumstances. If they do not, he is likely to be not only conspicuous for his awkwardness (or his forwardness) but inwardly so unhappy as to cause personality difficulties which may hamper him in his school work and his business career as well as in his social life. The importance of a right start cannot be overemphasized. A child is born into a world of people. Whether he regards them as friends or potential enemies, whether he becomes confident of their good intentions or suspicious of their motives, depends much more upon his upbringing than it does upon his native "disposition."

Manners are compounded of two things—attitudes, or the feeling underlying our social behavior, and the outward form in which we express our behavior.

"He has such a pleasant manner," we say of someone who makes us feel comfortable in his presence.

"He has such nice manners," we say of one who goes the long way round instead of crossing in front of us, who doffs his hat with a courtly bow.

Two men may rise when you enter the room; one makes you feel like a queen; the other like an intruder. They both go through the same outward form, but one infuses it with good will, the other with selfish irritation. Their skill is the same; their attitudes differ. In other words, "manners," as such, are merely the tools of behavior. To be effective, they must go hand in hand with the right attitude or "manner."

How can they be made to do so?

Attitudes and skills develop side by side and both are closely linked with a child's growing physical and mental powers. From the moment a child is born, it begins to develop attitudes. The skills come later as the body develops and the muscles, nerves, and brain cells all work together. The parent who expects a two-year-old to greet strangers with an outstretched hand is as unreasonable as the parent who lets a nine-year-old go visiting when she hasn't learned to cut her own meat. Expecting too much of a child at one stage and too little at another results in a nice mess of behavior problems; and that means bad manners of some sort.

"When can my child be expected to do what?" is therefore the first question for which to seek an answer.

There can be no time table for this, any more than for teething and learning to walk or talk. One can only say, "Watch for the first symptoms of a child's desire to try something new, give him his chance, and then exercise his new powers." That is to say, when he wants to wash his own

* Reprinted by courtesy of *Pictorial Review* and the author.

face or tie his own bib, let him try it—don't keep everlastingly doing it for him because it is easier, quicker, and neater.

The people who have the most to do with little children, such as the teachers in nursery schools, seem to expect the least of them. They know what the limitations are, at different age levels, from having watched many hundreds, year after year, go through the same process of learning to be members of a social group. They have devised a sort of curriculum similar to that of the primary school, which lays down "expectations of learning" for each grade. Most of us parents, especially those of us whose experience with children dates from the birth of our first baby, seem to expect them to come into the world with a full set of nice manners in their system, like their two sets of teeth.

What a shock it sometimes is to discover that we have brought a little savage into the world!

TEACHING MANNERS AS GOOD HABITS

TEACHING manners is a part of character-building and must therefore be a constructive process, with more "do's" than "don'ts" in it.

Since a child "learns" good manners as he acquires good habits of any kind, it behooves us to find out what a child does in the process of learning and what part the parent plays in it. In brief, this is about the way it goes:

The child, driven by his ego, seeks to get out of life what he wants on the best terms for himself. He meets a new situation—new food, a new person, a new tool to use in eating, let us say —and tries out different ways of meeting it. If he likes the result, he will do that again. If he did *not* like the result, he will avoid this response to the situation the next time it arises and try another way of meeting it or quit trying altogether. One of the chief responses he is working for is adult approval.

This is called the "trial and error" method of learning. Eventually it leads to a realization of cause and effect: "If I do this, that will happen."

To play an effective part in a child's learning process, the parents must know in their own minds what their policies and objectives are. What is important enough to "go to the mat" about? What is not to be tolerated? What might be condoned? For instance, is it more important what a child eats than how he eats? Is it better that he bring home undesirable children than no children at all? Would you be content if your daughter remembered to say "I had a very nice time" to her hostess, even if she had sulked in a corner and refused to play games all during the party?

Parents must give a child confidence and make him feel that they *know* what is right. They should anticipate a new situation—that is, prepare the child, whenever possible, for what is coming. "Tomorrow you are going to have tomatoes for the first time; won't that be fun?" or "Aunt Maribelle is coming next week; I am sure you will love her!" and so on. To help in the preparations for a guest leads to a welcoming attitude, provided, of course, the preparations do not cut into the child's own plans too much. How much more effective it is to let your daughter share in the excitement of having a guest than to say, "Run away, now, don't bother me. I have to get Aunt Maribelle's room ready for her—and she's so fussy!"

Although it is well to let a child experiment with new situations, parents must find out when is the time to teach a short-cut method, to develop a new technique. Then they must provide exercise and practice in the performance of that new technique and gradually increase the difficulty of the performance required. So is progress made. Once the "forms" are established, they must be adhered to—bib or napkin in place before one eats and folded after the meal is completed; a request to be excused if one wishes to leave before the hostess (Mother); chair pushed back to the table before leaving the room.

Try to find cause for praise rather than censure; to expect better behavior the next time instead of giving up hope with some such remark as, "You always do that so clumsily!" For there is much in what is called "the psychology of expectancy." You get back measure for measure what you give—desperation for hopelessness, improvement for faith and confidence.

Sometimes it is well to "play" at tea parties, introductions, telephone conversations and the like, by way of practice. I know one mother who, pretending she was a smart young man, carried on imaginary conversations with a shy daughter who professed she had no "line" and became tongue-tied in the presence of the opposite sex.

Maintain a kind, cheerful tone. (Yes, easier said than done, but it's worth everything to keep on trying for it!)

Speak for the child until he wants to speak for himself, instead of ordering, commanding or suggesting that he do it. For instance, when a friend brings Bobby a new toy, instead of saying, "What do you say to the kind lady, Bobby?" suppose you try this: While Bobby is quietly admiring his new plaything, say, "Oh, Bobby is going to have such fun with that new boat—aren't you, Bobby?" When Bobby looks up and smiles his beamingest and you add, "We're so grateful to you for thinking of him!" won't she feel as richly rewarded as if Bobby had had a thank-you wrung out of him before he had had time to find out whether he liked his new toy or not? It won't be long before Bobby will begin to say his own thank-you's—and he'll have a more varied vocabulary than if he had been taught to use that one expression to meet every occasion for appreciation. It's a longer way round, perhaps, but a far more secure road; and you make better time in the end, you know, by going the safest way.

Be always firm and consistent. Remember that we parents are our children's models in everything we do or say—worse luck! Some day they in turn will be parents, too; and if we have shown them how to be good ones, their task will be that much easier.

This is the method of precept; the other is of command.

MANNERS AS TRICKS

You can put a child through a course in manners as you would a dog through a set of tricks. This is called "training" and the process is something like this:

The parent gives a command.

The child does as told.

The parent gives approval (anything from a kind word to a gift).

or—

The parent gives a command.

The child does *not* do as told.

The parent withholds approval or metes out punishment.

Then, when the trick (or manner) is learned, the child has to show it off to all the admiring guests and relatives.

This method is quicker in results than the other; but are the results as good and as lasting?

When the approval or the punishment is withheld, what becomes of the manners?

When the situation is varied, will the child know how to apply the original formula? Will the forms he has learned stand him in good stead in an emergency? Is the child using his manners to oblige his elders or because he feels gratitude, consideration, or friendliness toward the people to whom he is being polite?

Knowing that the manners he has learned get him what he wants, may it be that he will use the form as a cover for getting away with savagery?

There's the child on the playground—we all know him—who grabs the ball, trips up another player, runs out of turn, and thinks to undo the effects of all these evidences of bad sportsmanship by emitting a curt "Sorry" after each offense; but playmates are not so indulgent as mamas.

MANNERS HAPPILY TAUGHT

"MANNERS," said Emerson, "are the happy ways of doing things." And they can be happily taught. That means, without nagging! Did nagging ever really produce the desired results? Does it ever really do more than get one's back up in defense against the constant admonition, seal one's ears to the eternal reminder?

Then why do mothers and fathers keep everlastingly at it, especially at the table?

Wouldn't they themselves get a great deal more out of living with their children if they stopped nagging them? It all comes out of the desire, so eternally parental, to be forever perfecting their beloved ones. If the same amount of energy that goes into the "constant reminding" process could be used to find out what a child *is,* how it learns, and what it can do at different stages of its development; to formulate a consistent plan of developing good habits and right social attitudes, wouldn't the well-being and happiness of the entire family be vastly increased?

Children absorb much more from the atmosphere in which they are brought up than from any amount of preaching, training, correcting. Since what we do speaks so much louder than what we say, even our undercurrents of feeling and emotion have an incalculable effect. Children are much more aware of the subconscious than we are because so much of their living is done on that level. The sweetly sugared voice covering up rancor does not fool them. Nor are they frightened by the bluff exterior worn over a warm heart. They know!

But we parents, what do we know?

Do we know what agony it costs to be forced to hold out a hand in greeting to a person who threatens to monopolize Mother? Do we fool ourselves into thinking that it does the child any good, or really makes amends, to wring an apology out of him? Do we ever stop to think what we are doing to children's honest little souls by foisting our social hypocrisies upon them? How often we punish them for being honest because we want them to be polite, instead!

A while ago, when I visited a nursery school, the teacher placed me behind a heavily screened door, inside the house, so that I could look out at the children playing in the courtyard without distracting their attention. We both thought I was invisible. But the children sensed my presence. One little boy tried to engage me in conversation, found me an unresponsive lump, and turned away in disgust, calling out over his back, "You're a crazy lady!"

Of course I was crazy, from his standpoint. I was unfriendly. I was inexplicable. I didn't behave like anyone he knew. I see that now; but at the time, I must confess, I did resent his telling me so! And, had this happened at his home and had his mother heard him, she would undoubtedly have felt constrained to reprove him for his "rudeness."

But would he have understood *why* he was told to apologize? And where did he get that phrase "You're crazy!"? Did anyone apologize for flinging it at him?

Then there was Polly, the cutest, fattest little roly-poly you could ever hope to see. Her admirers were many, and what they probably said to her one can guess when she patted the knee of her dowager aunt and remarked, "Nice little fat legs!" The dowager aunt, of course, complained of the child's impertinence. Who had reproved the elders who commented on Polly's chubby charms?

Even as children appropriate the swear words and the slang they hear, so they absorb the vocabulary of politeness, probably just as quickly and just as well; only we don't notice it because it doesn't shock us into recognition!

TABLE MANNERS, TAUGHT AND CAUGHT

FORTUNATELY, children want to imitate their heroes—and heroes parents always are, until they prove themselves not to be.

Table manners begin when the bottle is substituted for the breast. The same patient weaning process is called for when the child changes from the bottle to the cup; from the bowl with retaining walls, so to speak, to the flat plate. All these changes, and more, a child is expected to make within the first two years of his life. So be patient. Isolate your offspring on an island of oilcloth; inure yourself to splashings and spillings. The important thing is that the food gets inside the child; not so much how it gets there. That will come in time, when he wants to sit with the family and is told he may when he knows how to eat tidily, "like Daddy."

Meanwhile, you can sow the right sort of seed by substituting a crust of bread for the outmoded pusher; also by providing a short, flat-handled beginners' spoon from the first, instead of the old-fashioned kind with a curved handle. Do this, and your child need never unlearn the "circular grip."

If you don't pay any attention to him while he is eating, he will get through his meal much more expeditiously than if you fuss. For children adore being fussed over—it means they are getting a lot of special attention, and if dawdling gets attention they'll dawdle for all they're worth. The child who comes to the family table because he has earned his place there will make no disturbance, unless he finds that some one of the others is getting more attention from Mother than he. Much of the tension at family meals grows out of an undercurrent of rivalry; it is therefore wise to keep the table conversation as impersonal as possible, saving praise and criticism for private discussion.

A matter-of-fact objectiveness creates the best atmosphere: 'Too bad you don't like cabbage! Neither do I, but I eat it." . . . "No vegetables? You'll change your mind, won't you, when you know we're to have ice cream?" . . . "Suppose you tell us about the game after you've finished your plate. We'd like to hear, but the rest of us are ready for dessert, and you're rather holding us up!"

Try to have everything ready, and keep things moving. Long waits make for mischief.

Don't expect more of your child than he can do; conversely, let him do anything he possibly can—butter his bread, cut his meat, clear his place, or help set the table.

Know when to wink an eye; sometimes to see nothing. But be ever alert to scotch an insidious sloppiness of manner, an accumulating carelessness. Pounce on it like a hawk and jack it up to standard.

Make out a list of what you consider to be the minimum essentials in table manners. If your children are old enough, let them contribute their ideas; in any case, it will be interesting to find out how nearly you and your husband are agreed. Here is a suggested list:

1. Clean hands and face; hair combed; coats for boys and men (save in summer, when clean shirts will do).
2. Wait until others are served; see that others have everything they want.
3. No comments about food; no sniffing it.
4. Mouth closed while eating!
5. Use elbows only to lift the hand to the face; not to lean on.
6. Don't reach; ask your neighbor if he would

like what you want; usually he will take the hint.

7. Take part in the conversation, but do not monopolize it or interrupt.
8. Napkins to be used, and folded after use.
9. Ask to be excused, if leaving before hostess (which means Mother).

Now, then, what will you parents give in return? Will you do your part toward making mealtimes happy and gay, and not occasions for moralizing and pointing out defects to various members of the household—exclusive of yourselves? Will you refrain even from reproving looks and give the digestion a chance to work?

Will you uphold your end of it, or will you expect more of your child than of yourself?

THE MINIMUM ESSENTIALS

WHAT are minimum essentials in manners, other than of eating?

There is the matter of greeting and good-by. To teach a child phrases, like a parrot, is to run the risk of having your little girl say to the hostess, as little Jennie Smith did when she arrived at Susie Smedley's birthday party, "Thank you for a very good time. I'm glad I came!"

Phrases, clichés, are merely crutches. They're all right to lean on, at first, but your child should learn to get along without them. There are many ways of saying you're glad to see a person or you've enjoyed his company or you're grateful or sorry—*if* you feel that way about them, that is. If not, you can be like my honest but tactful Quaker friend. When one of her guests had been misbehaving she could not bring herself to say, "I am so glad you could be here this evening." So without a trace of sarcasm in her voice, she deftly put it so: "I hope you had a pleasant evening?" She had carefully maintained her integrity.

Introductions are becoming more informal all the time, but even with front names only, they are still being made. If you want your children to introduce their friends to you, remember to introduce them to your friends. Many grown-ups who ignore a child standing right beside them would doubtless be the first to censure similar rudeness in the child if the situation were reversed.

Promptness is politeness; laziness, rudeness.

Now as to conversations.

The radio has done much to make us thoughtlessly rude. If we don't like what someone is saying whose voice alone is present in our home, we can tune him out, refuse to listen to him.

The greatest courtesy anyone can pay us is to listen to our every word as if it were a pearl of wisdom. No one is more popular than the good listener.

We grown-ups do an inordinate amount of interrupting. We interrupt children talking to one another, we disturb them in their play to come to meals (don't you think we might give them at least five minutes' warning that dinner is ready?). They are torn from a book to run errands, to come meet our friends—and how often do we apologize for our rudeness?

The old dictum that "children should not speak until spoken to" seems as outmoded as pantalets. We have found out long since that to restrain a child from talking does not keep him from thinking and wishing and breaking out elsewhere with speech! So what to do? Parents must discriminate between the conversation that is pertinent to the situation at hand, that which is manufactured to divert attention, and that which is intended to get attention—and treat it accordingly. Furthermore, since reciprocity is the essence of conversation, isn't this a matter of taking turns? If you stay respectfully in the background when they and their friends are talking over childhood affairs, will they not, of their own accord, give you and your friends a chance to talk about the things that interest you?

SHARING AND TAKING TURNS

OUR YOUNG savage is in a fair way to becoming tamed when he has learned to share and to take turns—two of the hardest of all lessons to learn.

Between the ages of two and three, when the ego has its first ripe blooming, what is *mine* is of prime importance; it must be guarded at all costs, defended against all comers. To convert this intense possessiveness into cooperation is a task requiring the patience of saints, the persistence of fanatics, and the ingenuity of genius. But it is worth while beyond all others, for teamwork and cooperation are the keys to social development.

When a gang of ruffians invaded the vacant lot next to Sally's house, crowding out the little children who were coasting there, her father threatened to call the police. But Sally, who went to a school where all group activity involved sharing—of goods, of responsibility, of opportunity—had a better idea. Accordingly, one Sunday afternoon, her father called the boys into the house, her mother served hot chocolate and cookies, and Sally and the boys worked out a fair compromise.

To take turns is akin to sharing. But until a

child is three, that seems almost too much to expect; for before that time he has not learned to project his mind into the future.

"He has it. I want it. Right now. I can't wait!" is how he feels when he sees another child using the only express wagon in the yard.

I watched a group of children between three and five years old playing on a slide at a public playground a while ago. The attendant lined them all up in an orderly queue—which remained a queue no longer than six children could step out of place at once. Pushing, shoving, they got themselves scrambled into knots so that you couldn't tell who was first, second, or last. So, writing their names down in order, the attendant began to sing out:

"Now it's Johnny's turn! . . . No, it isn't your turn yet, George. First comes Mary, and next it will be Jimmy's turn; and then, if you're a good boy, it will be yours." And so on, down the line.

As each child returned from the slide, did he go to the end of the line, to wait while five others took their turn? He did not! He tried to squeeze in where he didn't belong. Each time a firm, restraining hand had to put him in his place.

"It takes a whole season to get that into their heads," said the attendant. "And just when I think they've learned to take turns by themselves, some little bully will begin pushing ahead of the others again!"

THE QUESTION OF DISCIPLINE

A WORD about the disciplines involved in the teaching of manners: A child, in seeking to get what he wants, will try at the same time to keep on your right side; for he aims to please, and thus win approval. So he learns to conform. "If I do thus and so, they praise me, or at least leave me alone," he would say if he could formulate his reasoning. "If I don't do as they want, they bother me until I do. So I guess I'll do it!"

The giving and withholding of approval, therefore, are among our chief weapons of control. But these are such potent weapons that no word of warning against their misuse can be issued too loudly. So *don't ever* give your child cause to think that love is dependent on behavior. It is Cardinal Sin Number One to say, in dealing with your children, "If you do this, I won't love you." Or, "If you love me, you won't do that!" Love must be bigger than that. It must be above bargaining.

So, too, banishing the child from the group for disturbing its peace can be seriously overdone.

This weapon, also, cuts both ways. The child who feels himself to be a pariah may never again find comfort in a group of people. Be ever mindful of his sensitiveness. Braggadocio usually is a cover for a breaking heart.

Because of their very desire to please, little children are likely to be more amenable to direction, more polite, in fact, than youngsters of the "between stage" who have begun to "gang up" against the authority of their elders. In the trying years when happiness can almost be measured in terms of dirt and noise, wise parents soft-pedal insistence on etiquette. As hands clean on the inside may be all you'll get at the end of a struggle, anyhow, it might be just as well to overlook the space behind the ears.

Provided they have had the right start, boys and girls will come back to the amenities just as soon as they begin to cast their eyes in the direction of the opposite sex. Suddenly, one fine day, your little gangster will be taking the rest of the family to task for "the way you look" and "the way you behave!" Then is the time for *you* to watch your P's and Q's.

WHY MANNERS?

THIS is an age of debunking. The younger generation no longer accept tradition as the reason for doing a thing. They want to know what good it is, what use to them. "Why have manners at all? Why not just be natural?"

When your children ask that inevitable question, I hope the answer walks into the front door, as it did at our house! It was in the form of a mongrel police dog which the Pound had sent us in the hopes of replacing our beloved Boots— a monarch among dogs, impeccable in his manners, aristocratic to the tip of his long, bushy tail.

But not so the newcomer. He was a stray indeed, a poor wayside waif who had evidently had little or no proper upbringing. As we didn't know his name, we couldn't call him; as he was huge and ungainly, we couldn't budge him. He answered no whistle, heard no command. He barged right into the sitting room, upset a table holding a vase of flowers, brought down the andirons with a snoop of his long nose, and then made straight for the steak on the dining-room table. We ate a vegetable dinner that night. Finally we lured him into the auto and back to the Pound; but in spite of all the damage he wrought, my husband and I were always grateful for his visit.

For whenever anyone asked, "Why manners?" we had only to say, "You remember the tramp dog, don't you? And you remember Boots? Which one did we want to have live with us?"

Stories and story-books afford excellent illustrative material from which children will gladly draw their own conclusions. The indirect method of pointing a moral is so much more pleasant than the direct attack!

MATURITY AND INDEPENDENCE IN MANNERS

FINALLY, there is this to remember: that the end and aim of all learning should be maturity and independence. Independence, in the matter of manners, means that the child no longer has to be reminded what to do. In maturity the individual has learned control of his emotions and no longer uses the infantile weapons of temper, hysteria, pouting, or other petty tyrannies to get what he wants. He has learned to subordinate the desires of the individual to the good of the whole group.

The other day I was in a day-coach crowded with college students returning home for the holidays. Every seat was filled, if not with themselves, then with their bags, their books, their overcoats. At the first stop, four pretty young women boarded the train; at the second, three older women got on. All seven were allowed to stand in the aisle until the third stop, when some of the men left the train.

Now, every one of those boys knew better. Had any of their parents, or even the college dean, been in that car, they would have provided seats for the women. But, unreminded and unwatched, they thought only of their own comfort. Not one had the conviction of his manners.

There was in them none of what Lord Moulton, writing in the *Atlantic Monthly* a few years ago, called "obedience to the unenforceable"—those elements of good taste, fitness, sympathy, and graciousness which cannot be taught.

If the ultimate aim of all manners is consideration for others, it is understandably the last to be learned. What is so difficult as to project your imagination into the needs of others? How to give children the "understanding heart"? Constant association with a thoughtful mother helps to cultivate it, but only by practice in doing for others will one find out what pleasure may be derived from it.

The child who finds out that consideration for others and good manners are their own rewards will reap a rich harvest of good will from his fellow men. Are you giving your child that opportunity?

FRIENDS

'Twould never do for God
   To live across the street,
Or in the house next door,
   Where we should daily meet,
So in His Wisdom and His Love,
   He sometimes sends
His angels kind to walk with us—
   We call them "friends."

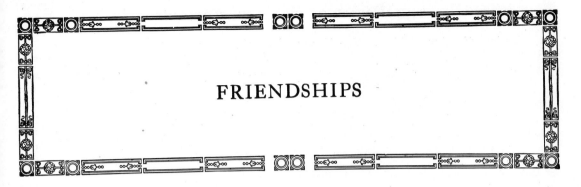

FRIENDSHIPS

LEARNING SOCIAL BEHAVIOR*

By Marguerite Wilker

Perhaps you have wondered about the social behavior of adults more than about the social traits of children. You have noticed the charm, frankness, honesty, and subtlety of some of your friends, and the timidity, lack of control, or strained inhibitions of others. If you have become sufficiently interested to wonder how such traits have developed and have investigated literature on the subject, your study has shown you that many social traits are well developed in early life long before you are aware of it. Many desirable, as well as undesirable, social traits develop within the first few years and go with the individual throughout life. All psychologists are agreed that we can trace back into our early histories and discover much concerning the influences which made us as we are. We may study our own childhood to get light on our own social tendencies, or we may study young children around us to see social behavior in the making.

Charlotte Bühler, who has studied this type of behavior, tells us that infants of six to ten months, if put together, will try to communicate with each other by interfering, by touching, by pushing, by pulling, or by exchanging toys. She has noted individual differences at this early age—some infants apparently desiring more contact, while others seem inhibited. She has observed that within the first year of life, the infant is able to keep up an actual contact with only one person at a time; then a group of two seems sufficient until three years of age; and thereafter the group increases with age. Groups of three- and four-year-olds exist for only a short time, perhaps as long as twenty minutes.

A number of nursery schools have been established in connection with institutions of higher learning to bring young children together where they can be well provided for, and where they can be studied to discover actual needs. All nur-

sery-school people are agreed that the young child should have regular companionship on his own age level, beginning not later than two years. Recommendations are being made to parents, since nursery schools are not available to many communities, to organize small play groups which meet daily for a period of several hours.

BEHAVIOR OF YOUNG CHILDREN IN A GROUP

When a small group of children come together for the first time, there is much interesting behavior to observe. Each child plays alone with material which he chooses and manipulates to his own satisfaction. While playing alone, he is, however, playing near other children his own age. This may be considered his first step in social learning. He is aware of the presence of others, and he learns to be comfortable in such a situation. He observes and watches to see what others are doing. Then, gradually he begins to make more tangible contacts. He finds some one to whom he is attracted, and the first attempt at making a contact may often be very clumsy. Sometimes he strikes, or kicks, or spits. He may know no better way of getting along. He has not had previous experience, and he must be given the helpful opportunity for learning all the principles involved in complex social relationships. When he kicks or strikes, it may be fortunate for him if an adult is not around, or, if near, is occupied.

Here is an excellent opportunity for him to learn to make decisions for himself. After a number of such experiences, and usually only a few are sufficient, this socially inclined child finds out definite facts; namely, that other children when slapped or kicked, tend to run away, to cry, or to fight back. This, in itself, is not exactly what our social initiate wants. He really wants the

* Reprinted from *Junior Home Magazine* by permission.

companionship of other children. So, if you watch closely, you will see that he will try other modes of approach. Sometimes he will try kissing and hugging, but he very soon finds out that other children object to such huddles. They remonstrate, or they get away. And gradually, but surely, he discovers that his companions stay with him, work with him, and give him much satisfaction when he shares toy material, when he talks to them, when he asks for what he wants or awaits his turn with a toy, and when he listens to them and cooperates with them. All this he learns for himself in a very dynamic way, and since he has actually lived through the experience, he can understand the meanings far better than he could if some adult were constantly interfering or attempting too many explanations.

ADULT SUPERVISION

OF COURSE this does not mean that children should be unsupervised. An adult should be nearby, peacefully oblivious to the harmless scrapping and slow, clumsy learning. This adult can be helpful in many ways. She can provide materials which encourage playing together, and when necessary give a few direct suggestions. There should be a great array of climbing and building materials in the back yard, large drygoods boxes, small boxes, boards to serve as walking beams or climbing beams, ladders, kegs, ropes, wagons, tricycles, sand, and sand toys.

OUTDOOR PLAY HAPPIEST

SOME studies have shown that children get on more happily together out of doors than in the house. We may suspect that this is due to ample space, air, sunshine, and adequate materials for investigation and manipulation. Young children who have playmates their own age are willing to stay out of doors long hours every day, say from nine to eleven-fifteen every morning, as they do in nursery schools, and from two to four in the afternoon. A child who can run, jump, climb, build, pound, pour, dig, and engage in all the other activities which a young, growing body needs, will come into the house somewhat relieved of excess energy and ready for more quiet activities.

OMIT INDOOR PLAY

WHEN the child comes in, he and his companions should be encouraged by the various centers of interest arranged for him to engage in play of a different type—constructive and dramatic play. There should be a low table and chair for this toddler, in a corner of his own, and there should be shelves or a cupboard near by where he can find paper, crayons, scissors, and clay. This material will occupy him for only a short time—fifteen minutes at the most and then he may turn to his books with pictures of familiar things, such as trains, automobiles, airplanes, familiar animals, and familiar people—the postman, the grocer, and the policeman. The pictures should be simple in outline, true in form and color, without confusing background or too much detail.

When books have satisfied him, his pets may attract him. He may watch the goldfish, the turtle, or the canary for many minutes, and then there may be some block-building with large blocks which make bridges to walk on, towers, barns, houses, and pens to live in. A housekeeping set-up with dolls, dishes, and broom will keep him busy in fine dramatic and imaginative play. He should thus be encouraged by an environment rich in materials to spend much time alone, depending upon himself, entertaining himself, and learning. But he is entitled to some exclusive attention from adults, and will look forward to a story, some music, or conversation. Children who have been given wise attention from adults, learn to take care of themselves for the greater share of the day, expecting only legitimate time and attention.

INFLUENCE OF ADULT SOCIAL BEHAVIOR

A FINAL word should be said about the influence of adult social behavior on young children. Companions, materials, time, suggestions, and opportunity for learning desirable social behavior are great aids, but the example of the adult behavior is, no doubt, one, if not the most powerful, of all influences. We may suspect that the boy whose parents find it easy to encourage desirable behavior and wisely approve his gains, no matter how small, will grow up to be the man who can recognize signs of achievement in himself and in others. The boy, on the other hand, whose parents emphasize the undesirable, fails often, because of this unwise emphasis, to see the many desirable and worth-while events going on around him.

The child's social attitudes develop at a great rate under the intangible, informal stimulation from adults. The child reflects his environment. Social behavior, then, is the result of many influences—the kind and number of companions, the age at which companions are provided, the kinds and amount of materials, and the direct guidance of adults.

THE LITTLE CHILD NEEDS FRIENDS

By Mrs. Alice Corbin Sies

EVERY child inherits naturally a desire for companionship with children his own age, as well as with grown-ups. Both are necessary. Companionship with children gives one kind of social training; companionship with adults gives yet another end.

In observing the difference in the result when our boy played constantly with me, and when he enjoyed the companionship of children his own age, I stumbled upon some interesting facts. First, I noticed that he became elated and that his personality seemed expanded when he was playing with children his own age. There was not perhaps the swift and sure flow of sympathy and ready speech that I noticed when with me. But his personality became different; he developed new attitudes and new ways of doing things. It seemed quite evident that he was changing in ways I was powerless to make him change because of the fact that I was adult. One day I heard him beg a little neighbor to come over and play in his sand-pile. His beseeching tones made no impression upon the little lady, who busied herself in her garden without any sign of interest except to answer "No!" R. looked heartbroken, and running to me for sympathy, cried out, "Mother, she won't come over!" As he hid his face against mine I realized that what he craved and needed was another little personality feeling as he felt, acting as he acted, and even at times behaving in quite new and unexpected ways. And I, his mother, although I had spent years in companionship with children, could not hope fully to supply this need of a friendly, socially inclined small boy.

LIMITATIONS IN ADULT COMPANIONSHIP

IT WAS at one time possible for me to observe daily, for a considerable period, the behavior of an only child who had been alone a great deal with her mother. Because of the refinement of her mother's personality, this child appeared superior and more attractive than children usually do. Yet, placed with children her own age, she appeared at a disadvantage. She did not know how to defend herself against their aggressions, nor was she trained to cooperate with them in their play. She had not developed the social weapons of defense and offense necessary in group play.

CHILDREN LEARN HOW TO ACT BY THE WAY THEIR ACTS ARE RECEIVED

OUR BOY learned, early in his third year, that little friends went home if he pushed them about or monopolized the toys. It was in play with other children that he found it did not pay to hit or strike. The early appearance of this tendency had troubled me not a little. I tried holding his hands after such acts, taking him away from the group, and other forms of discipline. Finally I instructed a child two years older to hit him back. I shall never forget the look on his face when this particular playmate did hit back. And I saw at once the effectiveness of this swift, just, sudden judgment. Not long afterwards, when I was dressing R. he struck at me playfully with considerable force. I devised a hand-tagging game which interested for awhile. Still the impulse persisted, returning again and again. Remembering the effect of the child's return blow I paused and said quietly, "It hurts; I'll show you how it feels!" And I administered one swift blow, smiling and saying, "Do *you* like it?" He looked surprised and put both arms about my neck, dropping his head on my shoulder. Somehow I had assisted him to see the social result of this purely playful yet socially harmful act. Even during the third year he would start to strike, so strong was the natural tendency in this particular child, then hold his hand suspended in the air as reason told him to stop.

We mothers are often too protective in our attitude toward our children. Because we believe them to be immature we shield them from the consequences of their mistakes and often make it impossible for them to learn by experience. Play with other children is invaluable in showing up these prime necessities of behavior.

I once saw a fond parent playing "Pussy-wants-a-corner" with his little daughter and three or four other children. He schemed to give his little daughter unfair advantages, and thus helped her to change places successfully. If limited to his companionship, what chance had this little girl to learn through play how to be fair, and to win honestly the points of the game?

ADULT INTERFERENCE IN CHILDREN'S PLAY

DURING the third year I found that my supervision was very necessary if play with other children was to prove profitable. Not that I needed to interfere constantly, but I found it best to be near enough to see that sudden conflicts in the possession of the toys did not lead to throwing toys and blocks about promiscuously. A child of this age is too young to be told to count ten before he acts, as we adults sometimes do. In childhood many instincts pull for different kinds of behavior. A child usually acts in the direction toward which the strongest and quickest instinct pulls him. Often we mothers can attract a child's attention away from the object of his wrath and thus give him a chance to get himself under control before he wreaks vengeance on property and playmates. This does not mean that we should protect our children from the effects of their misdemeanors. Nothing could be more harmful than to prevent them from learning by experience. Where neither property nor life is threatened it seems safest to let our children act naturally, and learn by their little mistakes how to act differently. Sometimes a warning is sufficient.

When I saw our boy monopolizing a treasured toy I sometimes suggested that his little friend would go home if he kept the toy to himself, then left him free to decide what to do. And he soon learned that it *paid* to be *generous* and to *cooperate in play*. When I played with him I demanded my turn and fair play. R. soon learned that I expected this kind of treatment and gave it. He would often offer me a treasured iron engine as an inducement to play, keeping a less highly prized wooden engine for his own use.

In conclusion, it was the result of my own observations that if I wished our boy to have a happy, all-around development, he must play with other children. I therefore decided to accept the inevitable drawbacks seen in certain undesirable habits copied from other children, as well as to accept the advantages such play afforded.

FINDING FRIENDS FOR THE PRESCHOOL CHILD

By Mrs. Preston F. Gass

VERY little children of two and three years require the companionship of other children in work and play as much as those of recognized kindergarten age. The child of two is intensely interested in the activities of children four, five, and six years old, and is able to imitate, enlarge his knowledge and experience, and even share in their activities. The activities of the adults about him, while they can be imitated and in some measure shared by him, cannot have the same value in his mental or physical development.

When Daddy saws a large board with a large saw, the two-year-old is interested; but when the four-year-old saws a small board with a small saw, possibly making some toy that will be used by the little one, he is more than interested—he saws wood as soon as he can. Watch an adult try to amuse this two-year-old with a new box of blocks. Invariably the blocks are piled high for steps, towers, arches, and so forth, and the little child finds great delight in sending the blocks tumbling with a crash to the floor. He takes no particular pleasure in the building of one block upon another, and we think he has not yet reached the age for building. Now the group of older children making structures with these same blocks do not pile them one upon another, but lay them side by side, to form the walls of a house for the doll or a barn for the woolly dog. And immediately the little one is interested—not in tumbling the blocks down, however, but in laying them beside each other, one after another.

Many mothers realize this need of their children to have group activity, but know of no way in which to bring the group together until they are ready for the regular kindergarten. It can be accomplished in almost any home, however, if the mother is willing to devote a few hours a day to working and playing with the children in the immediate neighborhood under school age, or those at home for the long summer vacation.

Whenever the weather will permit, activities are best carried on out of doors and very little equipment is necessary; a sand-pile if possible, an unused kitchen table, or wide board laid on any available foundation, with boxes for seats or the little chairs which each child may bring from home. The materials already on hand for use by the children in the home, such as balls, bean-bags, blocks, Mother Goose and other story books, will serve the whole group. The other mothers of the neighborhood are sure to be willing to contribute, for the use of all, materials which their own children possess, and each child can bring some of his pennies for the purchase of paper, paste, crayons, and so forth.

OUR HOME NEIGHBORHOOD NURSERY

PERHAPS an account of our experiment will serve best to show how the nursery school can be carried on in an ordinary home. We lived in a sparsely settled suburb of a large city, and the only available kindergarten for the children immediately about us was situated at such a distance that none of the mothers would permit them to attend. Our group consisted of our own boy of two years, another child of the same age, three children of four years, two of five, and two of six.

Fortunately, when we built our six-room bungalow, we provided a nursery for our little ones, a large practical room with fireplace and built-in shelves, so that our group found space for all indoor activities there. Any room not needed for other purposes at the time of the school session might be used equally well.

As a center for outdoor work and play we had a sand-pile under the trees. This had been left by the builders, and to close it in, the children dug trenches on four sides, into which we inserted planks.

Two of the mothers had old kitchen tables not in use. The legs we cut off at the right height for children to work at, and several children contributed their little chairs. A trip to a lumber mill near by provided us with all the soft-wood boards needed for making things with little saws and hammers, some of them being cut up into building blocks to supplement those we already had.

For pets we had goldfish, a mother bunny with little ones, and our own tiny baby of three months. The baby served as a center for many of our doings; many times our songs were sung to him, our houses of blocks made for him, our table constructed for him. The children watched him grow through the months, and he was the real main-spring of our group-life.

THE ADVANTAGES OF SUCH A NURSERY-SCHOOL

SINCE the group was made up of children of varying ages, each younger child depended on an older for leadership, assistance, and consideration. The five- and six-year-olds learned to lend a hand to the four-year-olds and to be patient and kind with the littlest ones.

Having a neighborhood nursery-school has a tremendous advantage for the busy mother who has difficulty in finding time for uninterrupted work and play with her own child. Children will play contentedly together for long hours, especially if they are provided with a few materials to work with. And as the hours of the nursery-school become known in the vicinity, the children confine their visits more and more to this time. The whole routine of housework is accomplished more quickly and in better spirits when at the same time the mind is occupied with the learning of stories, finger-plays, songs, games, and so forth, and on the planning of the next day's work for the children.

The neighborhood nursery-school not only affords the busy mother in the ordinary home a means of giving the right kind of training to her own child, but it provides the opportunity for knowing in an intimate and unusually happy relationship the children who are to be his playmates for a number of years.

IMAGINARY COMPANIONS*

A DEVELOPMENT to be avoided in the child who has few or unsatisfactory associates, is the invention of imaginary playmates which may lead him away from a desire for real playmates. It is natural and desirable for children during their strongly imaginative period to enjoy the companionship of make-believe children. But the parent whose child is dependent altogether on these fictitious playmates is allowing a condition to arise which will make the child less and less confident in his real contacts. The best companionship is found in children of his own age. Children need this companionship if they are to be happy and to develop normally. To be accepted by a group of their peers is absolutely essential to their happiness.

The child who cannot get on with other children, who is picked upon and excluded by the group, who prefers grown-ups to children for companionship, the child who prefers staying in the house at all times and playing in a solitary fashion to getting out with the "gang," needs readjusting if he is to avoid becoming an isolated and lonely adult.

Many parents quite unconsciously place a child in a position where normal contacts are impossible. Charles is a case in point. He was a child of divorced parents; he lived with grandparents

* Courtesy of Extension Service, New Jersey State College of Agriculture.

whose rigid, old-time standards left no room for the enthusiasms of youth. The boy was only average in intelligence and to succeed in school, which he was anxious to do for love of his mother, it was necessary for him to study night and day.

His associates were all adults, who expected Charles to be an adult too. His ready tears and nail-biting were the chief outward signs of inward conflict in this fifteen-year-old, and he was criticized and scolded for being a baby.

WHEN FRIENDS SEEM TO BE DOING HARM

SOMETIMES normal contacts are misguided. Edward, a boy of twelve years, had begun to steal things. Part-time school sessions, combined with poor companions, were responsible. A normal outlet for his desire for excitement and adventure was found in a boys' club and gymnasium. Through this avenue it was possible to redeem not only Edward, but his whole gang. It is neither necessary nor desirable to break up a gang, but rather to direct its outbursts of adventure and activity.

Sometimes in this fear of the influence of "gangs" of undesirable playmates, parents put too much emphasis on the selection of their children's friends. But quite as dangerous as the roughness which the child may learn from un-selected playmates, is the snobbery and false standards which he may acquire from those children who appear to be "nice" children but with whom the values emphasized are superficial and shallow.

We cannot hold our children by the hand throughout life. The most difficult thing for the parent to face is the fact that he must prepare against the time when his child will no longer look to him for guidance. How can we better prepare for that time than by allowing the child freedom in accordance with his years! If we ourselves make all his decisions, pick and choose his activities, carefully cull his companions, we are neglecting a possible growth of judgment and discrimination which is the outcome of choices not foisted upon one, but made by one's self.

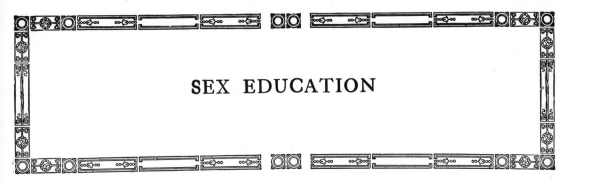

SEX EDUCATION

BEGINNING SEX EDUCATION*

By Edith D. Dixon

Extension Specialist in Child Training and Parent Education

MANY parents are puzzled by the startling remarks made by their offspring at the tender ages of 3 and 4 years. But remarks would not be so startling if parents were prepared for them. Too often we give the matter no thought until the question is sprung, then our hesitancy and embarrassment create in the child's mind a feeling that he has offended in some way. As a result, we have the beginning of worries and fears as well as attempts to satisfy legitimate curiosity in unwholesome ways.

One of the chief reasons for the reluctance on the part of parents to discuss these matters with their children lies in the nature of their own early training. The reticence with reference to sex which existed in the childhood homes of the present generation of parents made discussion impossible. To-day many parents are preparing themselves by reading and discussion to meet the questions of their children and by so doing are emancipating themselves from early traditions and developing a more wholesome attitude toward sex.

HOW TO TELL THE CHILD

IN considering the needs of the child we should remember first that sex instruction is not sex education. Sex instruction is the telling of facts about sex. Many people give a few such facts to children and think they have done their duty. Sex education, like all other education, is a developing process, and the child must grow and mature both in his ideas of sex and in his attitudes toward it.

When only 3 years old many children have asked that question, "Where does the baby come from?" To the child this is not a sexual question. He asks it as he would ask, "Where does the wind or rain come from?" and the answer should be direct and as free as possible from all emotional coloring. He should be told that the baby comes from the mother's body; that it starts "from the union of two cells, one that grows in the body of the mother and one that comes from the father and is placed by him in the mother's body." For most children this is enough to start with. The importance of answering any question when it is asked lies not wholly in the information given but quite as much in the assurance to the child that he may expect satisfying replies from the parent, and that things will not be misrepresented to him. There is no more occasion for sentimentalism, for whispering, or for an air of secrecy than there is in the teaching of spelling or tooth brushing. Matters of fact should be stated in a matter-of-fact manner.

By introducing the idea of two cells, one in the body of the mother and one in the body of the father, the foundation is laid for the explanation to follow when the child wishes to know what share the father has in the being of the child. The answer should still be truthful and direct: "The cell of the mother cannot grow unless it is fertilized by the cell of the father." The young child is not likely to follow up this point, but is more interested in where the baby grows, how it is cared for, and how it gets out of the mother's body. He should be told that the baby grows in a special place prepared for the purpose inside the mother's body, called the "uterus"; that the baby is fed from the mother's body; that when he is

* Courtesy of Extension Service, New Jersey State College of Agriculture.

large enough he comes out through an opening in the center of the mother's body between her thighs. This information, however, should in every case be prompted by the child's own questions.

The tendency of many parents who have prepared themselves for this situation is to hurry the child into too much information. The important thing is to preserve the questioning attitude by answering truthfully and directly. The child will then seek information when he needs it. It is desirable that he feel free to discuss such questions with *both* parents. Since the matter in hand pertains to the existence of a family and is essentially a family affair, the responsibility should be shared by both parents. Some parents are deterred from telling their children the truth by the fear of criticism from neighbors and friends who have not instructed their children. This difficulty may be met by suggesting to the child, without conveying any idea of secrecy, that other parents will tell their children what they wish them to know about sex. He may be led to see that, like the family income, this subject is of a sufficiently personal nature to be kept within the privacy of the family circle.

WHAT THE CHILD SHOULD KNOW

An important factor in giving sex information is the vocabulary. Very early, while the child is still a baby, opportunity is offered to teach him about the parts of his body. We do not hesitate to name the fingers and toes, the parts of the face, and often use little finger plays in connection with them. The following vocabulary is considered necessary by the time the child enters school, in order to protect him against unwholesome associations with the meaning of the words:

Pertaining to parts of the body: breast, nipple, navel, abdomen, rectum, anus, foreskin, penis, testicles, vulva, vagina.

Pertaining to functions: emptying bowels, emptying bladder, urinate, defecate, constipated, loose bowels, diarrhea, pregnant.

The vocabulary should be acquired as most information is acquired by the young child, incidental to the happenings of his daily life, and tied up with the teaching of health habits, cleanliness, control of appetite, and regularity of bodily functions.

BEGIN EARLY

Since we would agree that all questions bearing on sex life should take their coloring from persons with clean and fine attitudes, it is important in order to set up the right standard, that we begin our teaching early.

Very often parents say of a child of 10 or 12 years, "Oh, but my child is entirely innocent of such things. She has never asked a question." Is there any reason to think that a child who asks questions about everything else under the sun is going to close his mind to as universal an interest as this? It is far more likely that the parent has failed in answering some of the child's earlier questions, thereby setting up a barrier and closing the path to further information.

An opportunity for giving sex information should be created if one has not arisen by the time the child goes to school. Such opportunities come with the arrival of a new baby in the family or in the home of a friend or playmate. The birth of a batch of kittens or a litter of pups may stimulate the questions in the child or may suggest to the mother the need of giving instruction. If the child has pets and is curious about their sex behavior his questions should be answered briefly and *often*. This sometimes gives a less personal approach to the matter than to begin with babies. If he sees animals in copulation he should be told the meaning of what he sees, the suggestion of anything shameful or disgusting in the spectacle being carefully avoided. If a hen is being cleaned, eggs can often be shown in various stages of maturity. This will give the child an inkling of development before birth. A father took his small son on a fishing expedition and then allowed him to help in cleaning the catch. This offered an opportunity to answer the questions which arise as a result of the child's own observation.

To many parents the more impersonal approach is attained through the garden. As soon as a child can be interested in flowers and vegetables he can learn how plants come from seeds. A child who has been encouraged to observe growing things is prompted to ask questions about reproduction. It is only one step farther to information concerning the mating of human beings, but be sure to take that step. Many parents stop in the realm of natural objects, leaving the child in confusion with reference to human reproduction. Like the little girl who, after having had a satisfactory conversation with a friend on human reproduction, exclaimed, "Isn't that beautiful? Now why didn't my mother tell me that when I asked her? She said it was a terrible secret and that I mustn't talk about it to any one else but her, and then she told me about flowers and pollen and bees, and I got all mixed up. I couldn't see that bees had anything to do with babies except to sting them."

By the time a child can read he is wanting more definite information than can be obtained from conversation. A book with illustrations will do much to satisfy his interest in the mechanism of reproduction.

SEX DIFFERENCES

CHILDREN are often criticized and punished for playing "doctor games" or "peeping Tom," when they are prompted by no other motive than that of a natural curiosity to know what the opposite sex is like. If the child is early accustomed to differences in the sexes through seeing his parents in the bath or being present in the dressing room, he need never be conscious of any curiosity concerning these differences.

Opportunity for romping and playing during dressing and bathing periods while children are small, causes them to absorb in a natural way the necessary information. Some parents fear that such free relations in childhood will interfere with the proper development of modesty and respect for privacy. This, however, does not seem to be the case. As the child grows to be 10 or 11 years old he or she begins to withdraw and if such desire is respected, the transition occurs naturally. Too much emphasis on privacy at an early age is likely to create false modesty in the child.

If only one sex is represented in the children of a family an occasion should be made to let a child see a baby of the opposite sex having a bath. This relieves curiosity and gives the mother an opportunity to answer any questions that may arise. If, however, a child is found examining another child it is desirable to treat the matter casually, saying, "Now you have discovered what you want to know, it will not be necessary to interfere with any other child." Avoid appearing shocked and do not refer to the matter unless it is repeated, when it would be necessary to plan an occasion such as has been suggested where the child could have sufficient opportunity to observe and satisfy his curiosity.

THINGS TO BE REMEMBERED

FREE yourself from ignorance and self-consciousness, through reading and discussion.

Meet the child's first questions honestly, and if he doesn't ask any, make an opportunity for them before he goes to school.

Maintain a matter-of-fact attitude.

Use the correct vocabulary, and base your answers on biological truth.

PREPARING FOR MATURITY*

By FRANCES BRUCE STRAIN

IN THE pre-adolescent age, sex instruction emphasizes anatomical structure and physiological functioning—how things are made and how things work. One can go into a good deal of detail at this age safely if one proceeds impersonally, objectively, and knows one's stuff.

There are two or three explanations that must be accomplished before adolescence begins. This age between ten and the teens, when the children are just rounding the corner from childhood, is a good time to accomplish them, if they have not been accomplished before: menstruation in girls, seminal emissions in boys, and, when advisable, the venereal diseases and masturbation. The first two are normal functions and so are an essential part of every child's sex instruction. The last two can be omitted in childhood if a parent wishes to omit them; though parents should be prepared to explain them when necessary.

MENSTRUATION

EXPLANATIONS of the physical changes that are to take place accomplish many things. They prepare children for their future development, set the children's minds at rest and stop worrisome speculation, as well as make possible checking on their sexual development so that one may provide intelligently when the time comes for their health and comfort. One is careful to mention that menstruation is a normal function, that it is not an ailment or a sickness.

It is only too well known that girls reflect the mother-image. The hysterical, nervous, sick-headache mother is likely to produce the same kind of daughter. Much of the menstrual distress of young girls is psychic.

Suppose your eleven-year-old asks, "Mother, what is menstruation?" She may have seen the

* From *New Patterns in Sex Teaching.* Copyright—used by permission of D. Appleton-Century Co., Inc., Publishers, New York, N. Y.

word or heard it. (Like similar words of this nature, it is easiest to get used to an accepted term if it is established early. Some of the names that menstruation travels under—"curse," "sickness," etc., deserve discouragement.) Tell her, "You know that babies grow in their mothers. This monthly discharge is chiefly of blood. It accumulates in the part of the body where the baby grows. It is sent there for the purpose of making ready for a little baby embryo if there were one. But when there isn't one there, and of course much of the time there isn't, especially in the case of young girls like you, then the extra supply of blood isn't needed. It is just expelled from the body. It is perfectly good blood. It just isn't needed when there is no baby in the mother. In some girls when menstruation first starts there is more or less pain. Every girl doesn't have pain, just some girls, and many times the pain is not necessary and could be avoided.

Boys as well as girls are entitled to this instruction.

SEMINAL EMISSIONS

When you are explaining menstruation to your ten or eleven-year-old son, suppose you say, "You know, boys have a discharge, too, when they begin to grow up. It is called a seminal emission. You may hear some one use a crude expression, 'a wet dream.'" (Horrible term!) "I use it in order that you may know what it is when you hear it. Like menstruation in girls, when the seminal emission appears, it is a sign that a boy has begun to mature, that he is beginning to grow up. His voice will change, his beard will begin to grow so that he will have to shave. These things all start when a boy is about fourteen or fifteen. The fluid is discharged at night now and then at irregular intervals. It is perfectly normal for all boys.

"What is the discharge for? It is the fluid that bears the sperm cells—the little cells that are made to unite with the egg cell and fertilize it. They are so tiny and so delicate they need a medium, something to carry them, and protect them from the acids of the body, also to provide nourishment. This seminal fluid does all of these things. The cells swim in it and look like tiny tadpoles."

Many mothers have asked, "If we explain a girl's physical changes to our boys, shall we explain his changes to her?" I don't see any reason for omitting them. Girls at thirteen or fourteen very frequently ask whether boys have anything like menstruation. The explanation is not equally urgent because the boy's function is much less conspicuous. It doesn't interfere with his social life as menstruation frequently does with a girl's. But it is necessary to an understanding of fertilization and is much more impersonally accepted at this age than it is at adolescence, when the sex emotions are more readily stirred.

THE QUESTION OF PETTING

By Max J. Exner, M.D.

Director of the Department of Educational Measures of the American Social Hygiene Association.

IN THE general trend in recent years toward freedom, there has been manifested among young people the impulse to taste life in all its phases, and in no respect more frankly than in their social relationship; so much so, that there has developed what some believe to be the chief diversion among young people—the promiscuous play-at-love, popularly known as petting. And with youth's exasperating way of asking embarrassing questions they have faced the protests of their elders with "What's the harm?" The question being met mostly with conventional taboo and evasion, the young people have kept on petting. The challenge is fair, and if we have no answer that can inspire youth to convinced personal choice, we may not appropriately reprove or condemn.

While, on the one hand, there is no need to attribute to young people the reckless frivolity that many do, on the other hand, the matter is not to be passed off so lightly as others are inclined to do, for essentially we are dealing with the supreme source of human happiness—love. On the cultivation of the affections in adolescent years depends, more than on anything else, the development of the permanent personality, happiness, and social reactions of the individual. Does petting enhance or hinder a fine culture of the affectional life?

Let me first say a word by way of encouragement of friendships and companionships between the sexes. Attraction toward the other sex and craving for their companionship are among the most deep-seated native impulses of every normal individual. They, above all else, give life flavor, meaning, and inspiration. Each is to the other the complement, the "unsatisfied valence," without which life cannot reach its fullest realization, no matter what may be its other compensations. Can any more ennobling, more inspiring influence come into the life of young people than well-chosen and finely nurtured friendships with the opposite sex? In my opinion the principle of co-education is thoroughly sound.

Sex companionship is necessary for normal growth of the personality. When of the right sort, it is the most effective aid to a wise control and refinement of the sex urge. Separation of the sexes does not minimize these impulses; it renders them more insistent—and more subtly so. The last war strikingly revealed this fact. When we took great masses of men out of their normal setting and placed them in military camps, away from wholesome companionship with women, sex tension among the men was greatly increased. In the moral conservation program which was developed in the army no measure proved more fruitful than the service of fine women among the troops. The testimony of the extent to which their presence helped men to hold on to their ideals and resist the pull toward savagery is striking.

It is important that young people should have many companionships among the opposite sex rather than that they confine themselves too closely to single friendships. No two personalities are alike. The stimulus, the educative and refining influence, and the satisfaction of natural social needs which come from companionships with a variety of well-chosen persons, contribute generously toward a well-rounded personality. Such diversity in friendships will tend to bring to the affectional life an intellectual quality, one of fine discrimination, and will lessen the chances of being swayed by a blind, muddling infatuation—often mistaken for love. Young people whose range of companionship with the opposite sex has been too greatly restricted are seriously handicapped in the most vital of all life's choices—the choice of a mate.

Young men and young women need not be prudish in their friendships. They need not be afraid of one another. Many well-meaning parents and teachers seek to discourage sex-companionships among young people on the assumption that each sex is a danger to the other. This is a great mistake. Much in the present tendency among young people toward greater freedom in their sex-social life is wholesome. The only danger in freedom is the misuse of it. Such freedom as is consistent with full respect for the personality of the companion is desirable. Without having tested mutual responsiveness with a variety of persons of the other sex, how can a young man or woman be expected to make an intelligent choice of a mate? Moreover, the question may well be raised as to whether a limited degree of physical intimacy between young people, especially those who are engaged, when guided by a quality of character that stops short of the danger point, may not serve to release sex tensions and sublimate the whole relationship.

Such tensions are a price of civilization. Animals and man on the savage and barbarian levels do not experience these tensions. When the sex urge periodically arises, it is gratified like any routine want. With the advance of civilization came a more gradual approach to, and progressive postponement of, marriage and sex relations. With this postponement of physical culmination came also the growth of courtship, of the finer psychic qualities of love, the considerate restraints, the uplifting substitutes, and thereby the delicate social graces, ideals, and virtues which raise love-life infinitely above the animal and savage levels and give it high esthetic and spiritual meaning. But these higher types of affection and of social life are bought at the price of self-discipline, of conscious postponement of satisfaction of natural desires. It means tensions and strains which create for youth no light problem of self-control. It may be that greater freedom in sex-social relations of young people than has been sanctioned in the repressive training of young people in the past may serve to give a degree of wholesome release to sex tension and to render companionships more wholesomely social. It brings the fight for self-mastery into the open, as a definite, intelligent repression of recognized desires for equally recognized and tremendously rewarding goals. To win in such a fight is the highest possible use of the new freedom.

But the testing of love's responses between a young man and a young woman does not call for a full abandonment to physical impulses such as petters are inclined to indulge in. Love's impulses lie close to the surface. It does not require abandonment to physical expression to reveal hidden fires, to sense the magnetism of the personality, and to discover natures that are attuned to one another. Indeed it is such abandonment that tends at first to blind one against discrimination in the higher personal values and in the end to bring disillusionment and misery to both. Intelligent choice of a mate must look not only to mutual physical attraction but more so to harmony of tastes, feelings, desires, aspirations, appreciations, and of temperament. It must weigh spiritual more than physical values. The sheer physical gratifications require none of the individuality needed for true mating. Physical gratification can be given and received, as a rule, by anybody and everybody. The life-mate, however, must possess characteristics more individualized than the capacity to gratify physical hunger. But this consideration is likely to be swept aside when the merely physical urges are over-stimulated. The best marriages are not begun because of physical attraction alone. But many marriages that end

in failure do begin in just this poorer way. Petting is likely to lead to such mismating by over-stimulating the merely physical urges and blinding one to the more essential personal qualities and the more subtle harmonies which are required for a lifelong companionship and enduring happiness. These necessary gifts of discrimination and appreciation are not inborn. They must be cultivated and developed in friendships and companionships in the years of the teens, when love is developing from bud to bloom. And they are not to be cultivated by promiscuous petting.

Young people often seek to justify petting by the simple statement, "It is natural," implying that what is natural is right and good. They are supported in this by a group of present-day writers who are seeking to develop a philosophy and ethics of naturalness. They insist upon freedom from repression and social restraints for the individual, and advocate full and free expression and satisfaction of natural impulses.

Obviously the course of civilization has been one of progressive departure from the natural to the artificial. Hunger for food is one of the most powerful natural urges. Nature provides the materials for satisfying that urge. The natural way to satisfy it is to eat food raw as nature has served it. Yet man has learned to cook it, to combine its varieties, to blend its flavors, and to decorate it in numberless ways to tease the appetite and enhance the pleasure of eating. Man has learned to make food not only good but beautiful.

Again, the "natural" way to eat is to grab one's bone, away from others if necessary, and run into a corner or on top of a rock to devour it with all speed until it is safely down. That is the normal response to the natural urge, and it gives full satisfaction *on that level*. But man has learned to enhance the pleasure of eating by exercising self-restraint and eating socially. He has added to the mere satisfaction of physical hunger the pleasure of social intercourse, of companionship, of sharing with others, until to-day the act of eating has come to be the central feature of our sociability. By departing from nature, and in this sense becoming artificial, man has gained in eating a greater, richer, more enduring satisfaction *on a higher level of life*.

The sex urge, which is the basis of love, is another powerful human hunger. Its *natural* satisfaction is found in the savage, in whom sex expression takes the shortest route between desire and satisfaction on a physical plane, unembellished by the artifices of love. It is the way of the animal. But in this, too, man has learned to increase his satisfactions by the art of courtship, by long-circuiting sex expression through the whole wide range of esthetic, affectional, and social appeal of which he has become capable. By self-restraint, by delay, and by limiting sex satisfaction on the animal level he has gained an infinitely richer and more lasting satisfaction of his natural impulses.

In his departure from the natural to the artificial, man has in one direction developed perversions which tend to make him more beastly; in another direction he has developed lust into love. Even so all that we boast of in civilization as an advance over the life of the savage has been achieved by passing from natural to artificial modes of life.

Is then the petter's reply, "It is natural," a valid justification? Does it not rather imply an acceptance of the lesser for the greater gift?

Petting is, as I have said, play at love. It is mock love. It stimulates the intimacies of genuine love which in marriage normally find their culmination in the rarest of all intimacies—the full physical and spiritual union of two personalities.

Love on high levels is characterized by a fine balance between its physical and spiritual elements, and also by freedom from promiscuity, because love is the most definitely personal of all human relationships.

The object of love is full identification of one's self with another personality. To this there is no satiety, no end of progress, no imposition, no regrets. This is the acid test of its genuineness. When love shifts its objective from a personality to a variety of casual and shallow experiences it becomes a mockery. Love's symbols and intimacies lose their psychic and spiritual meaning and minister mainly to the animal sense. Necessarily then, mock love tends to limit the development of the most precious elements and capacities of the personality, and often becomes the beginning of disillusionment and cynical disregard of honor. In genuine love the deepest physical intimacies may serve love's highest spiritual ends. There need be no limit to such intimacies so long as they serve the spiritual enrichment of life. Indeed, it is the failure to cultivate and utilize these love capacities of mates in marriage to the full, the failure to cultivate "the art of love," that renders many marriages beyond the honeymoon stage dull and progressively unsatisfying. Anything which enhances the vividness of love's expression and enriches life is legitimate and fine.

No intimacy which serves these ends, even though simulated by those who have perverted love to base and commercial purposes, need offend the esthetic sense of lover mates. It is not that the lover has borrowed from the prostitute; rather that all those who make such mockery of of love have prostituted the art of the lover to serve primitive passion on a plane lower than that of the animals. But the physical intimacies which in genuine love become esthetic and spiritual to the highest degree and which serve to reveal to lovers the wealth of love's resources, become unlovely, vulgar, and degrading when employed in the promiscuous travesty of love. They lose love's meaning. It is because of this that young men and women should be prepared by education both to seek with singleness of purpose the highest uses of love, and to shun the casual indulgences which inevitably shut out the best.

Love's intimacies are, then, neither good nor bad in themselves. It is the conditions under which, and the ends for which, they are employed that determine their personal value and their ethics.

The drifting tendency of petting seems to head steadily toward a rather careless promiscuity. Physical thrills are the object sought, not the interplay of the whole of two personalities. Love made thus casual, and hence impersonal, is robbed of any lofty or permanent meaning. For young people who are disposed to consider these matters thoughtfully it is also important to realize that all love expressed on a physical plane alone is self-limiting. It can never satisfy the higher psychic longings and needs. It is subject to the law of diminishing returns. Is this not likely a reason why petters seek a variety of experiences?

This impersonality which is found in promiscuous petting must mean in the end that one person comes to exploit another for purely selfish conquest regardless of the consequences to that person. This is, of course, particularly true of prostitution, and it is one of the principal reasons why prostitution is so degrading to the individual and so destructive to society. But do we not have very much of the same element of exploitation in petting? Real love seeks to give, and finds its supreme satisfaction in the giving. It seeks the happiness and the good of the object of love, and it suffers at an injury to the person loved. The real lover aspires to personal development and perfection in order that he may the more richly contribute to the happiness of his mate in love. The petter seeks chiefly his own pleasure and uses other persons to that end as he would use a thing, each to be cast aside when it has served its purpose. Such exploitation of others must necessarily be destructive to the personal character of an exploiter. Being essentially selfish it must in a measure lower self-respect. And we recognize self-respect as a first requisite to a soundly integrated personality.

Of course, there would probably be in most cases a mutual loss of respect for, naturally, each assigns to the other the same selfish motives which actuate him or her. One is bound to lose respect for the partner he exploits.

Many times, when in discussing these matters with college men who have sought to rationalize their petting experiences, I have said something like this:

"You realize, do you not, that these girls with whom you engage in petting do as a rule pet also with other men?" "Yes, of course."

"Is this the sort of girl you expect to marry?"

Usually the impulsive answer is, "Well, I should say Not!" and the answer is followed by confusion and embarrassment when they realize how they have exposed their ignoble motives and the selfishness of their position. They are willing to make a plaything of the girl who will permit it, but when it comes to choosing a love mate, they set for their choice a higher, more discriminating ideal. Whether or not we admit such an attitude to be altogether sound, it is, nevertheless, significant that men very largely take this attitude.

Even more serious than these effects is the possible irreparable damage to marriage that may result from this casual expression of the affections. Is it not a degrading of the marriage ideal? The most important factor in the development of human personality and character is the cultivation of tastes. The quality of the tastes which the individual cultivates will measure the level and quality of his life and his happiness, and none so much as his tastes in love. These are cultivated and determined during the years of the teens. Petting means the cultivation of low tastes and ideals in love. He whose musical tastes have been fed on jazz is not likely to rise to a full appreciation or rendering of a masterful symphony. Young people whose affectional capacities are cultivated by the mock-love of promiscuous petting and who thereby come to identify it with married love, are training for an order of marital life that tends to follow an ill-fated course through an exciting honeymoon, disillusionment, growing distaste, disharmony, maladjustment, and divorce. *The essential harm of petting lies in the fact that it is a cultivation of a low order of love.*

Another important consideration is the fact that petting is playing with fire. We humans are so constituted that one cannot indulge in intimate physical contact with one of the opposite sex toward whom he has a natural attraction without arousing deep responses over which he has but partial control. This is especially true in the developing years of adolescence when sex impulses are strong and the powers of self-control still immature. In petting each is assuming responsibility for creating for the other as well as for himself a serious problem in self-control. The great majority of departures from chastity do not occur with deliberate intent, but result from loss of self-control under the spell of imperious forces aroused by unwise intimacies.

As I have already intimated, deliberately to forego an immediate, limited satisfaction for the sake of reaching a fuller, more lasting one on a higher plane of life is the essence of human progress. It is the way to self-realization. It is the way to the fullness of life. Petting offers the immediate reaping of love thrills on a physical plane that are undeniably pleasurable and fascinating. But are they worth the price? And what is the price? The progressive limitation of power to carry life to the high altitudes of love's experience. Anyone who fritters away his emotional capacities in the cheap and limited adventures of promiscuous petting, who cultivates the love capacities on a cheap emotional level is never likely to know the ecstasy, the richness, the expanding, compelling power of love at its best, such love as alone can give to life its fullest meaning. As Luther Gulick said: "The deepest love and passion is so engrossing that there is no room for the many. The man who rushes up each little ascent will never get the great all-inclusive view. The mountaintop is reserved for those who give themselves to it with single heart and utter devotion."

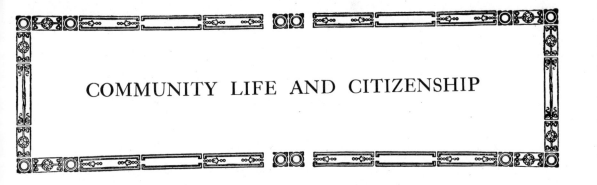

COMMUNITY LIFE AND CITIZENSHIP

PREPARING OUR CHILDREN FOR CITIZENSHIP

MANY schools do a fine job of preparing our children to be good citizens. But no school, no matter how dedicated to this task, can accomplish the job alone. Parents must cooperate to the fullest possible extent. Indeed, the real preparation for good and responsible citizenship must be begun in the home, by the parents' precept and example, before the child goes to school at all.

To give our children the background they need for good citizenship in a democracy they should be sure that we ourselves understand the system behind the democratic way of life and know why it is good. We must realize that, as the Greek philosopher, Aristotle, said centuries ago, "If liberty and equality are chiefly to be found in democracy . . . they will be best attained when all persons alike share in the government to the utmost."

To share in the government intelligently, we must understand its functions and operations and we must have an appreciation of our privileges as well as our obligations in helping to run it. We must realize that in return for our rights to protection by our government we owe it our loyalty and, when necessary, our service.

Schools teach our children by means of courses in Civics, how our government is run, how it serves us, what we have a right to expect of it, and how best improve it and make our influence felt in high places.

To be free to do this is a privilege which is not universal by any means. But it is the essence of the American way of life. Unfortunately, it is sometimes abused by individuals who try to "lobby" for special interests. The privilege of being an American citizen should carry with it the obligation to be well-informed on the functions, inter-relationships, and services of our local, state, and national governments.

Naturally these are matters which a pre-school child cannot understand. But even the youngest child can be *prepared* to understand them by being made aware of the democratic way of life in the home. The child who has autocratic parents—who is expected to obey rules blindly without a chance to express himself regarding them is likely to abuse the privileges of democracy when he grows older. Anyone who knows only the roles of master and slave (as so many children brought up in previous generations did, especially in countries like Germany) are totally unprepared for self-government. They do not value freedom because they do not understand it.

In a democracy, therefore, we must begin early, in the home, to let our children do for themselves whatever they can. We must train them to be independent, to think for themselves and to be responsible for their own actions as soon as they are emotionally and mentally ready to assume such responsibility.

Later, when they are of school age, we must cooperate in every possible way, with our children's teachers who try to instruct them in the ideals of fair play, cooperation, mutual understanding, and appreciation of democratic attitudes.

We must keep *ourselves* well informed on current events and issues. And above all, we must realize that the essence of democracy is *change*—change by vote and voice of the people, to ever greater conformity to the changing needs and interests of the citizens.

Such an attitude on *our* part will surely inspire our young people to carry on fearlessly and progressively on their own.

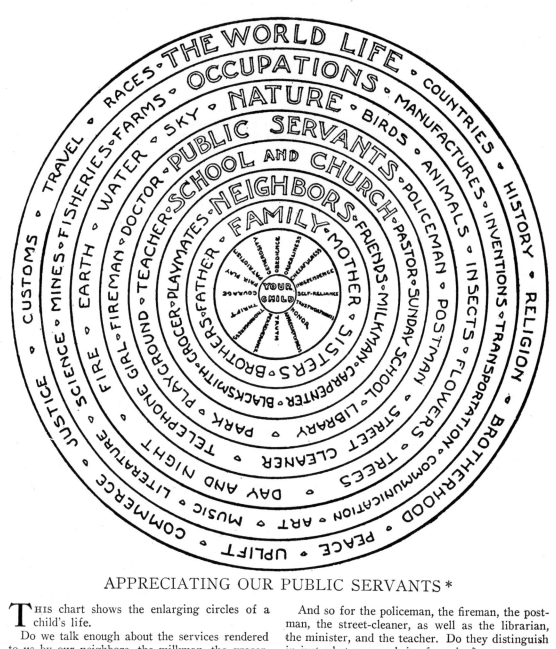

APPRECIATING OUR PUBLIC SERVANTS *

THIS chart shows the enlarging circles of a child's life.

Do we talk enough about the services rendered to us by our neighbors, the milkman, the grocer, electrician and the carpenter? Have the children seen these men actually at work? Do they realize how much care and skill and preparation go into their services? Do they understand how much their own comfort depends upon them?

And so for the policeman, the fireman, the postman, the street-cleaner, as well as the librarian, the minister, and the teacher. Do they distinguish in just what way each is of service?

To talk about these servants of the common good is not enough, but it is something. Table-talk might be one of the most effective opportunities of the day, and it is so often wasted. Take time to impress this on your children.

* Modified from a circular in the *Young American Readers* of J. B. Lippincott.

CHILDREN AND THE WORLD TODAY

By FLORENCE BREWER BOECKEL

Education Director
National Council for Prevention of War

WE ARE citizens of the world and do not know it. That, it has been said, is the tragedy of our times. And it is in just this field that parents face one of their most difficult problems. The world which lies ahead and which we must prepare our children to live in is not the one which is pictured in our minds or which, because of our own upbringing, serves as a basis for our thinking. To give our children the knowledge of the world today that they will require for useful and successful lives calls for a planned and deliberate effort on our part. It is not knowledge which they will naturally absorb from us for we have not absorbed it ourselves.

WHAT PARENTS CAN DO

THE SCHOOLS and individual teachers are facing this responsibility more and more. But what can parents do? Their greatest influence, of course, will be through talks with their children and the direction that they give to their reading. The important thing is for parents to acquire, themselves, the basic facts and ideas which will enable them to give their children a true picture of the world as it is.

In the first place, because much of our knowledge and many of the conditions under which we live are new, it is inevitable that many of our institutions and our traditional standards and principles are not in line with them. This inconsistency, it is easy to see, may do great moral damage to children. To protect them against that damage, it is of the greatest importance to make them aware that they have been born into a rapidly changing world. If they recognize this, it will increase their sense of life as an heroic adventure and inspire them to play their full part in making the adjustments which will mean a more intelligent and better world.

ALL MOTHERS BOUND CLOSELY TOGETHER

IT IS only within the last hundred years or so that scientific discoveries and inventions have broken down the great barriers of space that separated different parts of the world and different groups of men. Suddenly, we have found the daily life of the peoples of all nations bound closely together. This means that the solution of many problems which face us all and the chance for progress and advancement depend upon all peoples working together. Somehow, we must bring our ways of living into harmony with this fact. The great effort of the world today to abolish war is due to this necessity. War is now the next great barrier which must be removed if we are to work together and progress.

THE STORY OF MANKIND

IT IS also only in recent years, because of actual excavations and the studies of historians and anthropologists, that we have come to know that the story of mankind's life on earth is really one story, that the differences in races are superficial differences, that all men have been busy with the same tasks of securing food and shelter, and have sought the same things, happiness, beauty, God. They have done these things in different ways because of the different conditions they have had to meet, and thereby have enriched the total life of mankind.

This is one conception which we should try to give our children. In almost any library, there are many children's books which describe as one story the effort of humanity to turn the earth into a home, such as Kummer's *Early Days of Man,* and the histories of such things as transportation, communication, the use of tools, the development of light, the production of food and clothing. Although many of the books about other nations and the children of other nations emphasize peculiarities and differences, there are a few which do the more important thing of bringing out the similarities and show how much the daily life of the children of other countries is like the life of our own children at home, such as *Spending the Day in China, Japan and the Philippines,* by Sally Lucas Jean and Grace Hallock.

One way in which this sense of likeness with the children of other parts of the world can be gained is through games, for everywhere children play much the same games under different names and have the same toys though they are made of different materials. Against a background of similarity, the differences will lead to interest rather than to antagonism. Books of games of other countries can also be found in almost any library.

WHERE THE THINGS WE USE COME FROM

IN addition to this sense of likeness with other peoples, it is important for children to realize how all people actually depend upon the work and products of each other. Any breakfast or dinner table offers a chance to start a conversation along this line. Our foods come from every region of the earth. Once the hunt has begun for where what we use every day comes from, it can be carried on in connection with the household furnishings, or with the clothes a child wears. Someone has said that a pair of shoes is a League of Nations, since the materials that go into the tanning of the leather, and so on, come from twenty-six different countries. And there is the automobile, which requires materials from many lands. Back of the materials lies the labor and life of other peoples and a sense that our lives are bound up with theirs. There is plenty of material along these lines in libraries or in pamphlets issued by manufacturing concerns or distribution agencies. There are two good books by William C. Redfield, *Dependent America,* and a child's book, *We and the World.*

MAKE A WORLD MAP

MORE important, perhaps, than the fact that the things we eat and use come from all parts of the world is the fact that our jobs and incomes depend in two ways on this exchange of materials from one country to another. In many cities, children have visited the local manufacturing plants and found out from what countries the materials used are brought and in what countries the products are sold, and then on an outline map of the world have drawn lines to show with what countries their town is connected. In any single home, a child might be encouraged to make his own "world map" based on the things he uses, or could with a little help get the information needed to make a world map of his town.

Besides maps, or better a globe of the earth, there are photographs and posters which bring out the fact of world unity, for instance, of the beautiful statue of the Universal Postal Union at Berne, Switzerland. The statue shows a globe of the earth with five figures representing the five continents relaying a letter around it. It is also possible to obtain posters of children of other nations or those made by children of other nations, or to put up on a child's walls reproductions of famous paintings by artists of different countries. Children can be encouraged, too, to start collections of things that come from different countries.

PROTECT CHILDREN AGAINST PREJUDICES

BUT MOST important from the point of view of parents is the need of developing in children the qualities of character called for by the present close relationships of all human beings. If they are to be equipped for the life that lies ahead of them, our children must realize the importance in a changing world of keeping an open mind, of protecting oneself against prejudices, of knowing how to distinguish between fact and opinion. Children should be encouraged to study things for themselves, to form their own opinions, and be ready to change these opinions if they gain new knowledge. If they express an ill-found opinion, particularly one derogatory to some other people or race, help them to trace it back to what, if anything, it is based upon. If they quote someone else have them consider whether what they have been told is a fact that can be proved or merely someone else's opinion.

TEACH CHILDREN TO BE DISCRIMINATING READERS

THIS sort of training will be of the greatest possible advantage in teaching them to be intelligent and careful readers of newspapers, from which, as they go through life, they will get the great body of their information about the world. The more information that can be given children as to how the news in newspapers is actually gathered, the various hands through which it passes, from the reporter to the news association, the local editor, and so on, and what factors play a part in determining the kind of news a paper publishes, the owners, the advertisers, the public to which it caters, the better it will be for their later understanding of world affairs.

In an interdependent world, all relationships, from those of individuals to those of nations, must be worked out on a basis of reason and not of violence. Where there is interdependence, violence can lead only to loss or destruction for both sides.

In addition to what parents can themselves do to give their children a true and useful picture of the world today, they should lend all possible support to the efforts of the schools and of individual teachers to see that the children are equipped with the correct knowledge of present-day world life.

BOYS' CLUBS AS A HELP TO THE HOME

WHILE it is very desirable that the boy should be "tied up" as tightly to the home and its interests as possible, we must not forget that, after all, the great task of the home is to produce a high-class, intelligent citizenship. To do this will take more than facts about self-government, but also practice in self-government. It is because this is a fundamental that boys' clubs have always thrived and always will. It is as natural for a boy to belong to a half dozen clubs as it is for him to eat, make a noise, and get dirty. The wise parent understands this fact and so encourages a reasonable amount of club-life for the boy, conscious that such clubs are the elementary schools of democracy and citizenship. They are the place where normal boys are socialized. They stimulate wider interests and are an invaluable help in giving birth to generous altruism in a boy's development. Too often parents have endeavored to keep their boys clean and good by total isolation instead of by a program of directed and supervised association, with the result that when the boy finally does slip out from under the family thumb, he is an infant, unprepared and undeveloped for social living.

Dr. Allan Hoben, in his discussion of "Training for Citizenship through Boys' and Girls' Clubs" in *Religious Education,* has well said: "It is a recognized fact that among boys the gang is the first expression of citizenship and that a boys' club is only the gang turned to good account. The impulse to get together and do things by joint effort, underlies citizenship and government, and this desire is dominant in most boys from the age of ten to twelve and upward. This social impulse, which cannot be fully satisfied in even the best home, is not only the beginning of democracy, but the natural school in which progressive training in government and social control is carried on. Through this experience, rightly directed, the boy becomes measurably a citizen—a constituent member of a group seeking a common as distinct from an individualistic end.

"The fact also that the club is not a club unless officers are elected and organization is effected through expression of the common will means that the members must learn citizenship by the practice of its cardinal requirements, rather than by submitting themselves as targets for such civic instruction as may be fired at them. To think in terms of the common weal, to express one's opinion on matters having to do with taxing (or dues) or with the aim and undertakings of the group, and to abide loyally by the action and policy of the club, is good primary training for civic duty in a republic. Thus the first and inalienable civic value of the club consists in the fact that by its very existence the members have training in the art of self-government.

"On the other hand, if voluntary organizations of boys are left to run wild and do not have the friendship and counsel of a responsible adult, they constitute a civic menace, since they usually find expression in violation of peace and property and in lively opposition to government, especially as it is embodied in the policeman.

"There is a great deal of crookedness and cynicism among our youth, and especially among those who have been most pampered and who know how their own fathers and other prominent business men 'got there.' The club which will cultivate honor and is not ashamed of idealism, which makes public service a sacred obligation and a glorious opportunity, is the kind of club needed, for we probably have plenty of clubs bent only on pleasure and fripperies, and are altogether too easy with the rising generation. We need clubs which will produce clusters of great men, and we cannot have them by stupidly ignoring the profound appeal which should be made to youth. For this reason the club-life should be made rich in association with the great public servants of the past and present, and clubs should be addressed from time to time by representative statemen of sterling worth. And we may count on the ability of youth to respond to the least priggish of all forms of altruism, namely, good citizenship."

There are innumerable kinds of clubs for boys, with as many different interests as boy-life itself; clubs for athletic purposes; clubs for the pursuit of the hundred and one hobbies; clubs for debating and public speaking, electrical clubs, hiking clubs, kodak clubs, stamp clubs, religious clubs, Scout clubs, Y. M. C. A. clubs, woodcraft clubs, and so on. There is a club for every need for every boy. Use these clubs. Have them meet in your home. Give them your enthusiastic support. Keep close enough to them so that you can get the most of values from them for your boy, but do not try to dominate them or "boss." If you do, they will fade into thin air, and you as well as the boy will be the loser. Do not be afraid of boys' clubs. They can be made the greatest supplementary aid to your boy's largest growth and development in rounding out his character.

BOY SCOUTS

By the Editorial Board of the Boy Scouts of America

THE Boy Scout Movement is dedicated to making healthier, happier, better boys and potentially healthier, happier, better men. It is a sort of first-aid to parents by supplying a wholesome, interesting, developing set of activities which occupy his out-of-school hours and divert his fearful and wonderful energies to constructive courses.

As every parent knows, the early teen age is a difficult one to manage and beset with strange pitfalls. By the time a boy is twelve he is already feeling the tug of the world outside home walls. He wants to be off with the crowd. He wants to do things, find out things for himself.

And Scouting comes in here opportunely with its program ready worked out, based on sound pedagogy and sure knowledge of boy nature. It gives the boy that "something to do" which he craves, something that is fun and in which he delights for its own sake, but something which is also worth doing, something which will help him to grow all around—physically, mentally, morally.

For boys over ten and not yet of Scout age (12 years), the Cub Pack provides group activities. Many Cub Packs are supervised by active mothers.

It utilizes the gang instinct. With his troop or his patrol the boy gets that delightful sense of comradeship which is the germ of every gang. But the Scout gang is organized, directed, purposeful, not a matter of chance or idle drifting. Together, Scouts learn knot-tying, signaling, first-aid work, swimming, nature study, campcraft, and hundreds of other fascinating pursuits. Together they hike and camp and together they carry on city clean-ups, anti-mosquito campaigns, fire drills, Red Cross work, and all the rest of the community Good Turns which are some of the most important phases of Scouting.

While he is off with his fellow Scouts, not even the most timid mother need worry about her son, for every Scout is taught to look after himself and others, to take no foolhardy risks, to be "prepared" for any and all emergencies. Moreover, no Scout hike or Scout camp is conducted without adult leadership. There is always the right kind of a man to help your boy have the right kind of a good time.

Every parent of a real Scout can testify that Scouting makes the boy pleasanter in the home, more cheerful, more obedient, more helpful, more reliable. The Scout Law has a way of sinking unobtrusively but surely into his system. The daily Good Turn, which every Scout must perform, tends to crystallize the habit of cheerful service which is invaluable in the Home. "A Scout is Trustworthy," runs the Law. He must do "exactly" a given task. He is helpful, and helpfulness means "sharing the home duties." "A Scout is Cheerful. His obedience to orders is prompt and cheery. He never shirks nor grumbles at hardship." All this is in his Law, an obligation he has voluntarily taken upon himself and which he well knows he has to live up to if he is to be a real Scout, and not a sham one who wears the uniform but not the true spirit of Scouting.

The Scout Oath, too, is well worth careful consideration of every parent. On entering the Scout Movement a Boy Scout takes his pledge:

"On my honor I will do my best—
1. To do my duty to God and my country, and to obey the Scout Law;
2. To help other people at all times;
3. To keep myself physically strong, mentally awake, and morally straight."

That last phrase alone should recommend the whole movement to parents. For what parents are not anxious to have their sons "physically strong, mentally awake, and morally straight"? And what parents would neglect to investigate a movement which can give their sons a recreation-education program which has proved sheer delight and all-round benefit to thousands and thousands of boys the world over?

Remember that Scouting isn't trying to supersede your influence or teaching. It aims merely to reinforce what you are doing yourself to make your boy into the right kind of a man.

Remember, too, that there is a place in Scouting for every man who has a boy or who loves boys. As Scoutmaster, troop committeeman, local council member, examiner, such a man can stand side by side with his boy and others helping to make the Scout Movement the biggest boy's movement in the world.

GIRL SCOUTS

By Mrs. Jane Deeter Rippin
Former National Director, Girl Scouts

THE Girl Scouts were organized in Savannah, Ga., in 1912, and incorporated under the laws of the District of Columbia, in June, 1915.

PURPOSE AND POLICY

THE PURPOSE of this organization is to help girls to realize the ideals of womanhood, as a preparation for their responsibilities in the home and service to the community. Its aim is to give girls through natural wholesome pleasures those habits of mind and body which will make them useful, responsible women.

This corporation favors no creed, party or sect, but cheerfully co-operates with any organization which shares its views for good which may be exercised by women in the home and in religious, social, and civic affairs.

PROGRAM AND METHODS

THE PROGRAM follows the lines of women's activities, adapted to the capacities and interests of girls. Emphasis is placed on methods of training to develop initiative, self-control, self-reliance, and service to others, and in general the qualities of character of most worth in adult life.

The unit of organization is the patrol of eight Girl Scouts. One or more patrols form a troop and they are grouped, whenever possible, according to age and congeniality. The activities of the troop are developed through the Patrol System. The girls themselves appoint a Patrol Leader from among their own group, who soon discovers that she must be a leader, not only in name but in fact and in act. She develops, through initiative, the power of command to hold and lead those under her. As a member of the troop, she has learned how to restrain herself, thus developing her own sense of responsibility. Above all, the Patrol System means for each individual the development of character.

It teaches group responsibility, and that the real aim in life is to "play the game" for the good of all, and not the individual, for the Girl Scout is trained at every turn to think of others, becoming unconscious of herself. Thus girls are taught unselfishness, simplicity, and freedom from self-consciousness, and gain a beauty which can never be developed in an individual who is self-centered. The Girl Scout does a good turn every day with a conscious desire to help others, and with no thought of self. To "look out and not in" is her constant practice.

Girl Scouting is founded on the principles and plans so ably developed by Sir Robert Baden-Powell for England which took shape in the Boy Scout program. This program has become the inheritance of boys and girls alike throughout twenty-seven great countries of the world. It has different names in different countries, and is somewhat modified to meet various conditions. In most countries the names for the boys and girls are identical, as in France, where they are merely the masculine and feminine forms of the same word. In England they are called Girl Guides.

However, the plan for Girl Scouting is not a copy of the Boy Scout program; it is a development of the Girl Guide program which was also founded by Sir Robert Baden-Powell to meet the needs of the girls. The program used by the Girl Scouts, Inc., has been changed and adapted to meet the needs of the girls of our country.

The basic principles of Girl Scouting are found in the Promise and Laws. The Promise helps to develop loyalty toward God and Country, and Laws serve as a simple code which every girl can put into practice in her daily life.

PROMISE

On my honor I will Try:
To do my duty to God and my Country
To help other people at all times
To obey the Scout Laws

LAWS

I. A Girl Scout's Honor is to be Trusted
II. A Girl Scout is Loyal
III. A Girl Scout's Duty is to be Useful and to Help Others
IV. A Girl Scout is a Friend to All, and a Sister to every other Girl Scout
V. A Girl Scout is Courteous
VI. A Girl Scout is a Friend to Animals
VII. A Girl Scout Obeys Orders
VIII. A Girl Scout is Cheerful
IX. A Girl Scout is Thrifty
X. A Girl Scout is Clean in Thought, Word and Deed

CAMP FIRE GIRLS

By Rowe Wright
Editor-in-Chief, Department of Publications

UNDER the summer starlight a circle of girls gather around a blazing camp fire. In soft robes of brown they are, decked with gaily colored beads, and about the head of each a bright band of curious design. As the firelight throws its ruddy light on eager faces, the girls chant slowly, musically, in harmony with the whispering breeze and the voice of the fire, The Firemaker's Desire:

> As Fuel is brought to the fire,
> So I purpose to bring
> My strength
> My ambition
> My heart's desire
> My joy
> And my sorrow
> To the fire
> Of Humankind,
> For I will tend,
> As my fathers have tended
> And my fathers' fathers
> Since time began,
> The fire that is called
> The love of man for man,
> The love of man for God.

The voices float away on the wind. The fire flickers lower. The Council Fire of the Camp Fire Girls is over.

But the play and work and fellowship of Camp Fire Girls are by no means over. For the Council Fire but represents the formal and most solemn function of this organization which now numbers 170,000 girls in every state of the Union—and in eleven different countries all over the world. Camp Fire itself enters into the daily life of its members, in their homes and schools, at play with their friends—for it is founded on a program of things to *do,* to do every day and in every place the Camp Fire Girls may be.

On March 17, 1911, the Camp Fire organization was started. A group of people, headed by Dr. and Mrs. Luther Halsey Gulick, conceived the idea of an organization for girls—much needed, they felt—which would foster in the girls of to-day all that their mothers had most loved and cherished, and which would also build sturdy, self-reliant women to face the many new problems in this fast-changing age.

Having camped and worked and played with girls for many years, they knew that the way to make such an organization of any value would be to base their program, not on coercion, but on the aspirations and enthusiasms and desires of the girls themselves. They knew that almost all girls in their early teens were romantic, that the lure of adventure and the love of beauty were deep in their hearts, however demure they might look and seem. They knew that most girls were eager to try their sprouting wings to do things for themselves, interesting things, original things —not the mere tasks dictated by their parents and teachers.

And so the Camp Fire program was made up of things *to do*—things which would tempt each girl's ability and ambition. And secondly, it was based on an honor system, whereby awards, carrying certain distinction in Camp Fire circles, were given each girl for achievements in carrying out the Camp Fire program. And finally, Camp Fire appealed to romance by interweaving with its program of activities and its system of awards, a code of *symbols*. Each girl on entering Camp Fire was to choose for herself a symbol, which she believed most nearly expressed what deep in her heart she felt was *herself*. And the organization itself had a symbol, and certain national and special honors to be awarded had symbols.

The symbol for Camp Fire Girls organization was the crossed logs and flame—the age-old symbol for the hearth, the center of the home. In this symbol was an appeal for every girl, no matter what her disposition and temperament.

And Home Craft is the first of the activities of Camp Fire Girls. For such household tasks as cooking, planning the family menu, taking care of the children, cleaning and dusting, marketing and the like, flame-colored wooden beads are awarded. Each task—explicitly set down in the Camp Fire manual—must be well done and show a real proficiency before the honor is given.

Next to the Home Craft come the Health Craft honors. These are bestowed on the girls achieving certain accomplishments in outdoor games and sports, in first aid, and in keeping health records. The color of the Health honor beads is red.

Brown beads are awarded for Camp Craft. These include adventurous things, like pitching tents, building fires in the rain, trail making, making fire without matches. There is not a Camp Fire Girl who is not proficient in at least one of these exciting feats.

Hand Craft honors are closely related to Home

Craft, but also give opportunity for the artistically inclined girl to show her skill. Sewing, weaving, painting, carpentry, dyeing, designing and decoration come under this head. Inasmuch as each Camp Fire Girl must design her own symbol, and her own head band, and must, on attaining the second rank of the organization, that of Fire Maker, decorate her own ceremonial robe, Hand Craft honors play a very important part in Camp Fire life.

Yellow beads are won for proficiency in business. Keeping of personal and group accounts, budgeting, living on an allowance, are some of the ways in which even girls in their teens can win honors in this quite adult craft.

Finally, there are the red, white, and blue beads, given for Citizenship Craft, a craft which represents the very essence of the Camp Fire spirit. For, while the development of each individual Camp Fire Girl is one object of the organization, the bigger goal is the realization of the individual's relation to all those about her, and the subordination of her own desires and ambitions to the good of the group and the good of all those in her community. So, the red, white, and blue honors, for co-operation in civic and religious and philanthropic activities of her town, are among the proudest honors Camp Fire Girls may win.

In this program of the seven crafts ample opportunity is given for every girl to excel in some way and for all girls to round out their personalities by at least a slight familiarity with activities "not just in her line." To give fullest opportunity, however, certain national and special honors are awarded for accomplishments not set down among the regular honors. The writing of a poem or story or article, musical performance, artistic photography, are some of the achievements that win these special honors.

The Camp Fire Girls are divided into ranks. First are the Novices, those who have just joined the organization; next the Woodgatherers; then the Fire Makers; and finally the Torchbearers, highest of rank. Nothing but a girl's standing in the Camp Fire organization and her proficiency in carrying out the program determine her rank. The shy and the self-confident, the rich and the poor, the brilliant and the plodding—all alike have equal chance.

For with all its spirit of service, or because of it, Camp Fire aims to make life happier and fuller for all of its 170,000 members. In the comradeship and the good times of Camp Fire, the shy girl loses her self-consciousness; the bold girl learns that aggressiveness and arrogance are detrimental to camp spirit; the timid girl discovers that there are things in which she can excel; and the clever girl finds that being a "good sport" is a real achievement.

The activities of each Camp Fire group depend on the girls themselves. All of them have their weekly meetings, at which parties and hikes and co-operation in some community service are planned. In these plans the outdoor activities always play a large part. For the Camp Fire girl must be healthy and strong and happy in the great out-of-doors. Hikes, which are sometimes two and three days long, camping trips in summer, winter sports, are the regular custom in Camp Fire. All sorts of entertainments and plays occupy the girls during the winter months, in addition to their outdoor frolics. Whatever the ingenuity of a Camp Fire girl can devise, that she does.

A Camp Fire group may be formed of any six girls of eleven or over who wish to follow the Camp Fire program whose watchword is Service and whose slogan is WOHELO—standing for Work, Health, Love—and whose Law is

> Seek Beauty
> Give Service
> Pursue Knowledge
> Be Trustworthy
> Hold on to Health
> Glorify Work
> Be Happy

Each group must have a Guardian, over 18 years of age, who acts as leader and sponsor. A Camp Fire manual and all instructions for organizing a group may be had by writing to the Camp Fire headquarters at 16 East Forty-eighth Street, New York 17, N. Y.

THE YOUNG MEN'S AND YOUNG WOMEN'S
CHRISTIAN ASSOCIATIONS

THE Y.M.C.A. and Y.W.C.A. appreciate the primary place of the home, the church, the school, and recognized authority, as operative in the life of the boy or girl. They came into being to supplement these fundamental agencies in ways that may prove agreeable and practical.

Their primary object is not to build up a great independent institution, but to serve these fundamental agencies. They do not propose to take the place of the home in a young person's life, but are desirous of placing at the disposal of the home certain valuable helps in the way of trained leadership, program, and equipment that the home cannot of itself supply.

They are children of the church, called into being to provide for boys and girls certain features that the individual churches in the community cannot hope to provide. Their leadership, program, and equipment are available to the Church for the enrichment of *its* program. Their leadership is available for the training of church leaders of boys. They are an agency made possible by the churches, to bring a character-building program to all boys and girls of a city, using such ways and means as have proven acceptable and productive.

The Christian Associations are an agency to stimulate better school work on the part of boys and girls, and to aid with the moral and religious problems of the school. Through vital contacts with boys and girls, they help them in school, and provide supplementary education to thousands who work. The Associations are increasingly bringing a great moral and spiritual uplift to the school boy and girl.

The Christian Associations are servants of the community, endeavoring, in co-operation with the home, church, and school, to keep a community conscious of the presence of its child-life and the problems of childhood which should have their best attention, constantly stimulating the development of various ways whereby boys and girls are led out into service tasks to individuals, the community, the State, the Nation, and to God.

The Christian Citizenship Training Program has been developed from the many years of experience of the Associations working with boys and girls in these fundamental relationships. It is a graded, minimum program of activity, covering a wide range of interests under mental, physical, devotional, and service development. It emphasizes to the young the worth of home, church, school, industry, the world about them, as well as recognized authority in their lives, and leads them into a service attitude toward each of these relationships through their effort in its required and elective tests. Any leader of a group, or any agency or organization working with young people is privileged to use the program and to have the aid of the Association's equipment and organization as an ally and partner in work with young people.

The Christian Associations are a world-wide fraternity of men and boys and women and girls interested in promulgating an all-round type of Christian manhood and womanhood by means of directed and purposeful activity. Wherever available they can be made a wonderful ally of the home in serving the boy and girl in innumerable ways through their wide range of clubs, classes, camps, conferences, and so forth. They never knowingly compete with the home, church, or school for the boy's or girl's time or interests. They are more interested in seeing every boy and girl in the community provided with a four-square program than they are in tying up the individual youth to themselves, and are rendering a great variety of helpful services to hundreds of thousands of young people the country over. The boy or girl who will get the most worth-while and lasting benefits from contacts with an active Christian Association will be the boy or girl whose parents help him to select wisely a certain activity for himself out of the widely variable programs offered or who is able to select such activities without help.

THE JEWISH CENTER

THE Jewish Community Center is the institution created by the Jewish community to provide for its leisure time Jewish cultural, general recreational and health needs as a Jewish group. Born of experiences and desires common to all American Jews, the Jewish Community Center is a unique organizational contribution of American Jewry to Jewish life and to the general American community. Its goal is to foster democratic and creative Jewish living within the framework and in the spirit of American democratic traditions.

The essence of the Jewish Community Center's program is to provide the Jew with an enriching experience which makes him a better Jew and a better citizen and therefore a more useful and happier individual.

Membership in the Jewish Community Center is open to all Jews regardless of age, sex, economic status, social affiliation, religious belief, organizational ties or country of origin. Seeking to reach and enlist the active participation of every member of the community in order to fulfill its function as the center of Jewish life, the Jewish Community Center's membership is a representative cross section of the community it serves.

People of all ages join the Jewish Center. They join for a variety of reasons. Children belong because they want a place to play—a game room or gym during the year or in the Center's home camp or country camp in the summer time. But the Center does more than provide a "place to play." It provides trained leadership and interested adult volunteer service to give direction and purpose to the child's participation, thereby increasing the child's enjoyment and benefit derived from the activity. Children are encouraged to express themselves creatively—in the arts and crafts workshop, in the dramatic group, in interpretive dancing, in every way that develops their latent talents and responds to their real interests.

Children, being normal, like to be among friends and engage in group activities. Hence the Center emphasizes club work, or, as it is now known more generally—group work. A good group, under a good leader, has the greatest possibilities for personality development of its members. In the group they learn to get along with each other, to work together on all kinds of programs and projects, to shed shyness and to submerge aggressiveness and desire for domination. They make friends, sometimes for life. They come under the subtle but very real influence of a leader who helps shape their behavior, their ideas and their ideals. They learn from the content of the club or group program. Their Jewish knowledge is enlarged and they join with other groups in learning about Jewish customs, ceremonies, holidays and great Jewish personalities.

The program lasts the year around, in town and in the country. Where there is a Hebrew School or Sunday School in the Center, the group activities and gym classes are arranged to supplement the formal Jewish education. Thus Jewish education becomes attractive and normal in the life of the child.

Not all children in a community can come readily to the Center, because of distances. This does not mean that they cannot benefit from the Center because in most cities, where such a situation exists, Centers have organized extension activities, carrying the program into the various neighborhoods or into suburbs of the larger cities and utilizing existing facilities, especially of synagogues, for group and mass activities. The Center no longer limits its program to the four walls of a building but looks upon itself as a *community*-wide organization, available to serve the entire community, as needed.

The Jewish Center appeals very strongly to the youth and young adults of both sexes. For them it is a "clubhouse," a social center, a recreation center, a gymnasium, an educational institution, a center of Jewish activity. It is their leisure time home, offering opportunities for meeting friends, for wholesome enjoyment, for useful participation in activities, for discussions of current problems, for reading books and periodicals of special interest, for listening to recordings or to the radio or to a lecture.

Young adults constitute the largest group among the users of the gymnasium and swimming pool. The Center encourages them to maintain health and bodily vigor through a well directed program of sports and exercise. Health examinations are given and the advice of trained instructors is always available. Those who have aptitude for sports join teams and engage in intra-mural and extra-mural amateur competition.

Young people are interested in their future. They are concerned about vocations and get advice and direction in selecting and preparing for their careers. They are guided into Center activities that will develop their abilities and talents or overcome personality difficulties. They are, as a group, interested in the current American scene—in political, social, economic issues. They follow closely the developments in international relationships. They are vitally interested, as Jews, in the fate of European Jewry and in the future of Palestine. They are naturally idealistic, eager to understand the meaning of events and to express themselves in discussions, debates and in affiliations with like minded groups and individuals. The Center provides these opportunities through forums, clubs, councils of clubs and community councils in which other youth groups join. Staff members work directly with youth and young adults in this vital field of their interests.

Young people have a natural desire for social activity. The program of the Center includes many opportunities for socializing — the game rooms, the attractive lounges, youth canteens or refreshment counters, the many parties and dances, celebrations of Jewish and national holidays, out-ings and picnics in the summer—all under supervision but of the unobtrusive kind that allows for the maximum of initiative in planning and conduct of the activity by the young people themselves.

There is also encouragement to young people to develop special interests—hobbies in crafts, photography, dramatics, singing or playing in the orchestra, Jewish studies and other cultural courses, working on the Center periodical or a club newspaper and many other activities that respond to the needs of young people for self-improvement. A number of young men and young women also develop qualities of leadership, serving on committees and leading clubs, Scout troops and other groups. Indeed, the Center is one of the principal sources for the training of leadership for Jewish and civic activities and many present day leaders in the community are the products of this process.

COLUMBIAN SQUIRES

THE GREATEST problem that confronts society is the proper upbringing of youth. Time was when home and church adequately met this obligation, but with the development of a highly cultural civilization, need was felt of a third agency to take part in the training of the young, and thus came forth the school. Now, however, in the midst of the changed conditions of present-day society, one phase of which is a great increase in leisure time as a result of the invention and perfection of labor-saving machinery, there is pressing upon us the demand for a fourth agency to help hand over to the young their enriched social heritage, this agency to be called, perhaps, "The Free-Time Guidance of Youth."

In the case of the boy, the need for such a guiding influence is particularly pressing. The industrial revolution of the past century has driven industry from the home to the factory and the father has followed after. An age of specialization now compels professional and business men to herd together in the marts of commerce and trade and the ambitious father finds little time to give to his boy at home. Even the school, in its present developments, with its teaching staff drawn largely from the ranks of women, has contributed to this process of robbing the boy of his natural right to constant contact with a man as his inspiration and model. Definite steps, therefore, must be taken to put the man back into the boy's life. This is the true significance of all programs planned for the free-time guidance of youth.

For a considerable period now, organizations have been conducting such programs in an admirable way. Support has not been lacking to them when they appealed to the public, because they have been functioning efficiently. They get results. Not only that—in many cases a large percentage of their clientèle has been made up of Catholic boys. Few, indeed, have been the places under Catholic auspices where our boys could find recreation and amusement. Little wonder then that they took advantage of such opportunities wherever available. It was to meet such a situation that the Holy Father called upon the Knights of Columbus to begin their recreational work in Rome, and he has given his hearty endorsement to the project of initiating similar free-time work wherever the Knights are established. The Hierarchy of the United States and Canada have likewise been generous in their approval of the project of the Knights of Columbus to undertake boy work as their major contribution to the country and the Church in the way of service.

The Knights seem peculiarly fitted to enter upon this work. They constitute the largest body of organized Catholic men in the United States and Canada. Their resources are in proportion. They know no bounds of race or nationality. Catholic boyhood of America will indeed be fortunate to be the object of their special solicitude. The response of the Supreme Body to the appeal of the Hierarchy of America, as well as to that of the Holy Father, has been both prompt and generous.

Assembled in Convention in Atlantic City, in 1922, a committee was appointed to be known as the Committee on Boy Life. This committee, after conferring with experts, reported to the Convention of 1923, in Montreal, and a Boy Life Bureau was established, to head-up all boy work as entered upon. Chief among the activities to be conducted was the creation and supervision of a junior order to be known as the Columbian Squires.

ULTIMATE AIM AND IMMEDIATE OBJECTIVES

EDUCATION is now recognized as co-extensive with life. Any activity worth while in itself has educative value, if properly directed. At the outset, it is to be recognized that the program of the Columbian Squires is educative in character. Its general purpose is to lead Catholic youth into the "kingly constitution of their bodies, minds, and souls." In other words, character building through supervised free-time activity. In common, then, with all other educational agencies, its first task is to determine definitely its specific objectives. Only when this has been achieved can the second task be approached, that is the selection of materials for the program of activities, the carrying on of which, it is hoped, will achieve these objectives. Catholic philosophy of education well distinguises between the ultimate aim of all education and immediate objectives. The worth of the latter is measured by their contribution to the achievement of the former. The immediate objectives, having for their specific purpose a definite contribution to this ultimate aim thus formulated, may well be distinguished as five. With the boy as the crude material with which we work, we wish to form—first (in the order in which these ends most obviously appear), a healthy human being; second, a worthy home member and a worthy citizen; third, a cultured gentleman; fourth, a person with a life-purpose preparing himself to be a self-supporting member of society; and fifth, a man of Christian character. The Program of Activities aims to contribute towards all these objectives. But just as one objective, for example, Christian character, is

especially the task of the Church, or cultural education is that of the non-technical and non-professionalized school, so, too, the Columbian Squires, as a free-time program, appropriates one of these objectives as peculiarly its own, namely, worthy home membership and worthy citizenship.

The Columbian Squires is distinctly an older boy program. It is planned for this purpose, limited to boys who have attained their fifteenth birthday, and having for its specific purpose the promoting of the ultimate aim of Christian education as described above, "the transforming of the child of the flesh into a child of God," particularly as this can be done by a Program of Activities with major emphasis on the social-civic objective. It is first and foremost a school of citizenship. The qualities of citizenship it would inculcate are those preserved and developed in the Christian Catholic culture of the ages, interpreted in the light of American ideals of freedom and democracy. It may make its first appeal to the heart of the boy through organized athletics, but its primary aim, worthy home membership and worthy citizenship, must be kept constantly in mind to prevent its degeneration into an organization purely atletic in purpose. Character building is always first, not muscle making.

The supreme purpose of the organization of the Columbian Squires is character building. A Program of Activities, fivefold in nature, is pursued throughout an extended period to prepare the young Squires for Knighthood. The following outline sketches these activities in brief:

PROGRAM OF ACTIVITIES

THE IDEA of the founders is to develop the members completely; therefore, there will be a fivefold program:

Religious—Inculcation of fidelity to prayer, Mass, Sacraments and the Study of Christian Doctrine.

Cultural—Supplementary Reading, Art, Music, Public Speaking, Drama, Debates, Nature Study, Craftsmanship.

Educational — School subjects; Educational Guidance Health Study, Arts and Crafts, Collections, Attendance.

Physical—Physical Training, Apparatus Work, Camp Craft, Team Games, Group Games, Aquatics.

Social-Civic — Home Duties, Social Accomplishments, Duties of Citizenship, Community Service, Boy Council, Boy Parliament.

THE AMERICAN YOUTH FOUNDATION

By JOHN L. ALEXANDER

Director of the American Youth Foundation

THE American Youth Foundation is incorporated under the laws of the State of Missouri as a non-profit "Pro forma Decree" institution for a period of fifty years.

The American Youth Foundation is committed to the discovery of personality in young people and their training for Christian leadership in Community Life through vocational, home, school, church, social, and municipal institutions. Service in the ideal of the American Youth Foundation is the doing of the everyday task so Christianly that the total of everyday living, including working, is a contribution to the Kingdom of God. It places whole-time Christian service in the home, factory, school, store, office, bank, church, and any place of Christian business life above the old idea of marginal, voluntary, or spare time service. All of life's activities should be Kingdom-service instead of merely the residue activity—the left-over time after making a living. The American Youth Foundation seeks to inculcate the idea of Christian Service among youth and the more effectively to carry on its assistance to youth to personalize this view of Christian Service. The American Youth Foundation offers the services of its staff to any organization whose primary interest is in the development of youth. The American Youth Foundation is a service car that may be attached to any train. It has no geographic, auxiliary organizations and offers its services in the Cause of Youth wherever there is need and opportunity. By research, literature, experiment, conferences, platform addresses, and personal contacts, it seeks to enrich the activities of established institutions and organizations for the religious education of youth.

The American Youth Foundation operates summer camps in various sections of the country and conducts Older Boys' and Older Girls' Camp Conferences, Institutes for the Leaders of Youth, and Younger Boys' and Younger Girls' Recreational Camps. Special attention is invited to the Older Boys' and Older Girls' Camp-Conferences conducted at Camp Kiniwanca, Shelby, Michigan, and at Camp Merrowvista, Mountain View, New Hampshire. Particulars will be sent on request.

The American Youth Foundation has no official relationship with any organization. It is non-sectarian in its purpose and management and is dedicated to the religious educational welfare of American youth everywhere. Through it a group of specialists offer the experience of a lifetime working with youth to organizations whose interest is in youth—and to youth itself. It seeks friendly contacts with all Christian organizations.

A DEED AND A WORD

A little stream had lost its way
  Amid the grass and fern;
A passing stranger scooped a well,
  Where weary men might turn;
He walled it in, and hung with care
  A ladle at the brink;
He thought not of the deed he did,
  But judged that all might drink.
He passed again, and lo! the well,
  By Summer never dried,
Had cooled ten thousand parching tongues
  And saved a life beside.

A nameless man, amid a crowd
  That thronged the daily mart,
Let fall a word of hope and love,
  Unstudied, from the heart;
A whisper on the tumult thrown,
  A transitory breath—
It raised a brother from the dust,
  It saved a soul from death.
O germ! O fount! O word of love!
  O thought at random cast!
Ye were but little at the first,
  But mighty at the last.

          —*Charles Mackay.*

MORAL AND SPIRITUAL DEVELOPMENT

Marguerite Geyer

THE BROTHERHOOD OF MAN *

By HENRY F. COPE, D.D.

Goodness is as contagious as badness. Children catch the spirit of social love and idealism in the family. Where men and women are deeply concerned with all that makes the world better for people, better for babies and mothers, for workers, and, above all, for the values of the spirit gained through leisure, opportunities, and higher incentives; where the family is more concerned with folks than with furniture; where habitually it thinks of people as the objects most of all worth seeking, worth investing in, there children will receive direction, habituation, and motivation for the life that binds them in glad love to the service of their fellows, and makes them think of all their life as the one great opportunity to serve, to make a better world, and to bring closer together God's great family.

*From *Religious Education in the Family*, published by The University of Chicago Press; used by permission of the author and the publishers.

DISCIPLINE

WHEN PUNISHMENT IS NECESSARY

By Helen K. Champlin

Must we punish our children? How should we do it?

The modern, up-to-date parent is not so interested in ways of punishing his children as he is in methods of training that will make punishments unnecessary.

Modern parents want their children to grow up as their friends and companions. They hope to achieve a pleasant and wholesome parent-child relationship. They know that it is the parent who is experienced and the child who is inexperienced and that, therefore, while young, the child needs constant guidance.

CHILDREN ARE NOT NATURALLY BAD

A few generations ago people held the false belief that children are naturally bad until the badness is punished out of them. Many of our unfortunate ideas about punishment grew out of this false belief. We have discarded the false belief. The old-fashioned ideas about punishing children must also be discarded.

It was once thought necessary to repress much of the natural activity of childhood, to make children humble and obedient and to fill them with a fear of parental authority. Such an attitude is no longer held by well-informed parents. Instead of emphasizing authority, we now emphasize *growth in self-reliance.*

GROWTH IN SELF-RELIANCE

We have come to realize that children must grow gradually in independence and must learn to think for themselves. They must be prepared for the time when parental authority is no longer there. So blind obedience to parents is no longer thought

the virtue it once was. We do not repress today's child. Neither do we permit him to express his every whim in an unbridled manner. We have come to realize that children are born neither good nor bad but are merely untrained to the ways of the world. When they make mistakes, they are not so likely to need punishment as helpful *guidance.*

PUNISHMENT SITUATIONS ARISE FROM PARENTAL MISTAKES

In child training, there is a problem of punishment largely because of the mistakes of parents. A good many punishment-situations should never have occurred. They come about because the parent is careless in training the child, or ignorant of the child's make-up, or unsympathetic toward the child and his problems.

For children are constantly facing problems. In gradually getting acquainted with the world of adults, they have to learn a good many things by trial and error. If they make mistakes, it is because they are not yet mature, or because they have not been properly prepared for the new situations they must face, or because poor training has made them uncooperative and hostile.

TEMPER TANTRUMS

If three-year-old Mary stages a temper tantrum because she can't have the toy she wants, more than likely she has been made combative through a long series of faulty relationships with her parents or she has learned from experience that temper tantrums pay!

If four-year-old Jack refuses to share his blocks, someone responsible for his social training has not succeeded in helping him grow cooperative.

In either case, there is far greater need for constructive training than for mere punishment.

FREQUENT PUNISHMENTS ARE SYMPTOMS OF FAULTY TRAINING

Unpleasant as the fact may be, parents have to admit that the more punishment-situations arise in a home the poorer the job of parenting has been done in that home. Frequent punishments are a symptom of faulty training. The parent who finds himself constantly scolding and punishing may as well face the truth and blame himself. He brought Jack and Mary up! If they are not the right kind of children, he did a poor job!

What are some of the chief causes of punishment-situations?

THE CHILD MAY FAIL TO UNDERSTAND THE SITUATION

Children fall easily into error. New, untried situations present real problems. Children learn only by a very gradual process what kinds of behavior adults think right and what kinds wrong. What adults say is not always clear. It takes a good many years to learn the exact meanings of the many words that adults use so freely when they give directions to children.

LACK OF SKILL

Some situations require skill. A lot of practice is needed to learn to handle growing muscles with skill, and a lot of experience must be had with articles about the house before they can be lifted and carried and used with safety and ease. Injury done to objects is not always because of destructiveness on the part of the child. Children are not born appreciating the market value of radios or upholstered chairs. They have to be taught. Neither do children sense the sentimental value that adults attach to favorite dishes or books. They don't know, until they are taught, where it is proper to scribble and where it is not. They have a proper respect for books and toys and house furnishings only when trained, by example and explanation, how to handle them with care.

IMMATURITY

Because of immaturity, children make many mistakes. They fail to come home when told to come because they lack anything like an accurate sense of time. They take what is not theirs because property right is something that has to be ex-

plained over and over. Small children tell untruths because the difference between fact and fancy is difficult to see without considerable help. Honesty grows with careful, friendly cultivation and, like other virtues, cannot be pounded into children!

The modern parent realizes that, in most cases, the mistakes of children point out the need for help and guidance rather than for punishment.

PARENTS OFTEN FAIL TO UNDERSTAND THE CHILD

Parents too often punish children when no wrong has been intended by the child. Examine the motives that prompt the act before hastening into punishment. Unless the parent takes time to search out the motives, it is perfectly possible to punish a child for doing something that was altogether good from the child's point of view. Mrs. Jones came into the kitchen and found it in heartbreaking disorder. Her sudden fury brought only confusion, disappointment and resentment to the two little girls who had happily decided to clean house and surprise her. Robert took a toy from his little sister and was promptly—and impolitely—slapped for selfishness. A belated investigation disclosed that the toy had developed a sharp edge on which Robert feared his sister might be hurt. His fine protectiveness would not soon be repeated.

LEARN WHAT TO EXPECT AT DIFFERENT AGES

Study the development of the child. Learn what can be expected of him at different ages. There is no fairness in punishing a child for spilling his milk when what he needs is help in learning to keep his attention on the task in hand. Children are not born with grown-up powers of controlling their attention. Or, the child may be so young that his muscles have not yet learned sufficient coordination to handle the glass with skill. The muscles fail to work together properly and the glass falls. He needs a lighter glass, practice in manipulating objects, encouragement in directing attention and praise for success.

CHILDREN NEED TO EXPERIMENT

Certainly the child should not be punished for the process of growing up. But many parents do just this. The child needs to experiment and explore. He needs to try out his ideas. He is put together in such a way that the most natural thing in the world is for him to wiggle and squirm. He needs endless activity and plenty of opportunity for taking things apart and putting them together. When the parent supplies plenty of suitable occupation, there is little or no question of punishment.

PHYSICAL CONDITION

ANOTHER cause for punishment-situations is to be found in the physical condition of either parent or child.

Family tempests in tea-pots grow out of the taut nerves and over-tired bodies. Where children are brought up with scheduled naps, regularity in bed-time and sufficient family fun and relaxation, the problems of discipline are likely to be few. Mothers and fathers who neglect their own recreation become snappy and irritable. They are likely to be unreasonable and unfair and very poor companions for growing young people. Discipline begins to take on huge proportions and punishments are many. The parent-child relationship soon becomes antagonistic and strained. The chance for appealing to the child on any higher plane than punishment is lost.

It is well to avoid getting into disciplinary complications just before bed-time, just after a disappointment or bad news or over-work, and at times when the presence of company alters the usual routine of the household. It is at times like these that unreasonable, unnecessary punishments are too often meted out.

HASTY COMMANDS

PUNISHMENT-SITUATIONS may come about because a parent gives hasty commands. He does not prepare the child for what is coming next. If it will soon be bed-time or dinner-time or time to put away the toys, a little helpful warning sets the stage for cooperation. It isn't hard to do a thing when we are ready to do it. But it may be "against the grain" if the idea is sprung on us too suddenly. Children are like that too. "In a few minutes it will be time for bed." "Get ready to put things away, for when the clock hand comes to this spot (pointing) it will be time to wash hands for supper." "Soon it will be time to come in." Such warnings help avoid irritations and help build more friendly and cooperative relationships.

FAILURE TO PROVIDE SUFFICIENT DESIRABLE ACTIVITY

MANY punishment-situations occur because parents tell children what not to do but fail to tell them what to do. The child who lacks desirable means of activity finds undesirable ones. He must do something. He must be busy. He was made that way. He is not necessarily getting into mischief intentionally. He is occupying a normally active nervous system and a developing mind. Keep him sufficiently busy with the things you like to have him do and he will not need punishment.

PUNISHMENT SHOULD BE ONLY A LAST RESORT

IF THE time comes when you feel incapable of dealing with the situation except by punishing, you face the problem of what sort of punishment is best. It is not true that any sort of punishment that suddenly occurs to you will do. To have any constructive value, a punishment must follow certain principles:

1. It must be related to the offense, and the child must be made to see the connection between the two. Generally the easiest punishment to connect with an offense is that of taking away a privilege.
2. It must follow the offense as early as possible.
3. It must be followed up. That is, training can be constructive only when it is consistent. It will not do to punish lightly and then allow the offense to be repeated unnoticed when the punishment is over.
4. It must be given without anger and vindictiveness and must not make the child feel that he is bad. The offense is bad; the child is not. The child must see the difference.
5. It must help the child build future power to avoid like offenses.

CORPORAL PUNISHMENT USUALLY VALUELESS

PUNISHING the child physically will seldom, if ever, be in line with principles of constructive punishment. Spanking, slapping, pulling ears, pushing and shoving and overpowering a child are the lowest kinds of appeal. Humiliating him before company or companions or even before the other members of the family can be more damaging to his personality than helpful to his character. Such modes of appeal are so evidently impolite that they have little to defend them.

FIRMNESS IS RESPECTED

GUIDING a developing child points to understanding, kindness, justice and a friendly person-to-person relationship. There need be nothing soft and sugar-coated in this constructive kind of parent-child relationship. Firmness is needed wherever guidance is to be given. And firmness on the part of a parent is highly respected when it is found in company with justice and affection.

When parents accept the responsibility for preparing children for new experiences and for helping them understand the *reasons* for certain conduct, few punishment-situations arise. Rather than punish the wrong, it is far better to help the child avoid the wrong.

WHAT ARE GOOD CHARACTER HABITS AND HOW ARE THEY DEVELOPED?

By Corinna Marsh

THE whole subject of habit training and its relation to good character has had a thorough overhauling in recent years by our most eminent child psychologists. Fortunately for the future of our children, we now have a new and far sounder approach to character development than any of the older theories ever produced.

We know now that children do things which are considered bad behavior by adult standards but which are entirely normal, natural, and necessary for healthy development in childhood. We know that merely correcting a child for so-called wrongdoing is often worse than useless and merely setting a good example is not enough either.

There are times when a young child's "wrongdoing" must be curbed, usually by quick, on-the-spot action, for the child's own protecton.

But any successful long-range program of character-building must be based on an understanding of two important factors which are new to many mothers. One is the child's ability or readiness to understand correction, and the other is his feeling toward the person who is doing the correcting and the example-setting.

In habit-training, as in every other phase of a child's development, we can neither hasten nor retard nature, except at the child's peril. We must be constantly aware that every child develops at his own pace and in his own rhythm. Trying to train him before he is physically, mentally, and emotionally ready to *train himself* will inevitably do more harm than good.

In the matter of setting a good example, the important thing to realize is that a child will learn only from someone he loves and admires and wants to imitate. Many a child has been eternally set against a good habit or a good characteristic because he did not wholly trust or genuinely admire the person who recommended it.

What you do for your child is usually less important than when you do it and how. If you do **whatever you do for your child at the time when** he is ready for it and with genuine consideration, affection, understanding, and tact, you will be pretty sure of doing the right thing. Good old-fashioned mother-love is coming into its own again and is now thought by the most modern child psychologists to do more for a baby's health, happiness, and character than any scientifically administered punishment or reward.

The really important thing in character-building, then, is how you *feel* about your child and how he *feels* about you—in other words, how well the emotional relationship between you and your child is developing.

These may be rather startling concepts to parents still addicted to the "spare the rod and spoil the child" school of thought. They are, furthermore, not nearly so easy to practice as the cut-and-dried "do this and don't do that" type of instruction. But in the light of experience and understanding there is no denyng their validity.

Let us ask ourselves what, after all, we are trying to accomplish by "habit-training." We want our children to know the difference between right and wrong—of course. But we want them to understand that difference not only in words but as standards and principles by which they themselves will want to be guided. We must therefore give them a chance to discover those differences for themselves — when they are ready. Naturally we can and should help them when they stumble or seem confused; but we must understand that our help will be accepted by them only if our relationship with them is what it should be—that is, if we not only love them but make them feel that they can always depend on our love.

Besides wanting them to know the difference between right and wrong—and acting on what is right—we want them also to behave in a way which is socially acceptable, to outgrow their childish "naughtiness," and to become human beings willing and able to assume responsibility for their own motives, decisions, and acts. To achieve these ends we must not "discipline" our children or train them in habits but rather teach them, through our affection and our dependability, to discipline themselves.

This, as we have noted before, is not always simple. It requires constant self-restraint on our part, constant searching for the causes which lie behind what we think of as bad habits. Obeying that impulse to pull the baby's thumb out of his mouth is so much easier than trying to find out why he is sucking it and getting at the cause!

We are greatly tempted by the impulse to nip in the bud all kinds of evidences of misconduct lest they become "bad habits." But we must hold fast to the knowledge that children almost always outgrow these childish habits *if left alone until they are mature enough,* whereas constant nagging or frequent correcting *before* they are mature enough may leave them with psychological and emotional scars for the rest of their lives.

Too often we inject our own anxieties into our dealings with children. We fuss over this or that bad habit because Uncle Harry or Aunt Emma had the same thing, and look what happened to *them!* But this is exactly the kind of tense worrisome behavior on the part of parents which will set children to imitating Uncle Harry or Aunt Emma rather than doing what mother suggests. The children will not have *inherited* Uncle Harry's or Aunt Emma's habits; they will have developed them because their mother made too much of a fuss over her own anxiety.

Children's motives for doing what they do are often rooted in emotions which are sometimes hard to discover because they may be deeply hidden in a child's subconscious. Thus a child may have temper tantrums because he is jealous of a new baby; he may kick and scream because he feels that is the only way he can gain the attention he craves; he may suck his thumb for comfort because he is lonely and unhappy, or bite his nails because he is worried, or refuse to eat because his mother nags him or bores him or tyrannizes over him about his meals.

These are all matters which bear looking into, all situations which need clearing up before any attempt at correction can have more than superficial or temporary success.

Even in adulthood emotions are far more potent factors in governing what and how we learn than used to be understood. In childhood they are far more so. Therefore, if you want your child to value honesty, kindness, courtesy, and all the other fine traits of character, be assured that trying to teach them to him as "habits" will be teaching him only the outward forms at best. To develop them as truly inward graces he needs to grow up in a family whose members not only believe in and practice these traits but seem to the child to be admirable and dependable people who love him and whom he loves.

The child who feels that his parents are glad they have him and are genuinely interested in him will usually flourish even if the parents make mistakes in some of the rules and regulations which, after all, can never take the place of that sense of affection and security on which a child's whole emotional well-being depends.

See, then, first of all to your relationship with your child. Make is as warm, as loving, as tranquil, as secure, as naturally courteous and as mutually satisfying as you can. Second, let his character develop, in a good and happy family environment, at his own speed and in his own way with only tactful guidance from you.

Once you have accepted these two important concepts of habit-training and character-building, and if your own character is the best you can make it, you can, by and large, let nature take its course. Be your child's guide and friend, and you will be delighted to find how naturally and beautifully his character will develop of its own accord.

MOTIVES TO WHICH YOUTH RESPONDS*

By HENRY NEUMANN, PH.D.

HERE are some of the normal desires of the young which we can harness in the interests of moral growth:

1. Desire for strength: For example, a boy may not quit smoking for other reasons, but he may do so when convinced that the habit will interfere with his athletic achievements.

2. Desire to earn a living: This is bound up

*From "The Child," edited by M. V. O'Shea. By permission of The Children's Foundation, Valparaiso, Ind., publishers.

with the self-respect and pride in self-reliance to which many an appeal must be made.

3. Hero worship: The child's first heroes are the people who perform the striking, dramatic, physical exploits. Their admiration for firemen, policemen, chauffeurs, baseball stars, can be used in the interests of courage, persistence, self-control. As they grow older, we must enrich their acquaintance with admirable types in worth-while biographies. At every stage, however, the strongest influence will be exerted by the living examples of friends, parents, teachers. It is well for parents to have frequently as their guests at home men and women of many different careers in order that the children may the better be able to choose their own careers and personalities.

4. Desire for fellowship: Jane Addams tells how a group of boys had infected one another with the drug habit. At the institution to which they were sent, it was at first proposed that the lads be segregated from one another; but a wiser counsel was followed, and the group spirit which had led them astray was enlisted to encourage them to work together for their cure. The love of fellowship is intertwined with many other desires. It shows itself, for example, in family pride, which may lead to the conceit of caste, or, on the other hand, to a strong incentive to make good for the honor of the family name. School spirit is a familiar resource which every wise teacher employs. It should in time widen out into community spirit and into patriotism. The sacrifices which people are willing to make for their country indicate how useful a contribution to moral nurture can be reaped from the social impulses.

5. Desire for distinction and independence: Along with the desire to be a member of a group like all other members, there is also the wish to stand out and to be one's own master. The athlete not only wants his school to excel, but he desires to be known as the one to make this possible. Individual praise is a familiar enough incentive. So is the wish to be master of one's own life. Our cue is to get the child to understand as early as possible that if we allow him freedom, it is with the expectation that he can be trusted to guide himself wisely. Teachers of history and civics have a splendid opportunity to bring home to young people the thought that freedom is good only to the extent that people use it to liberate in themselves what is most deserving of such freedom. The best kind of liberty for any one of us is that which encourages and promotes the liberation of the highest life in our fellow-beings.

6. Desire for leadership: This is closely related to the preceding. It is good to gratify it by such methods as having the children take turns in leading games, occupying executive positions in the school-government or in otherwise directing their groups. The timid gain self-confidence; and the aggressive get the chance to work off their bullying tendencies constructively.

7. The will to power: Every game is at bottom a setting up of artificial obstacles for the sheer fun of getting the better of them, as we see in the working out of puzzles or in tennis. This propensity to make a game out of difficulties can be used to get children to do useful things that would otherwise be distasteful. It has long been used in the kindergarten. Experience there has shown that wisely directed play is the best beginning for serious study. In recent years the principle has been extended into the grades.

We must beware, however, of misapplying this modern educational doctrine of interest. It is good to have children make a game of the things they dislike to do. This does not mean, however, that they should do only the easy tasks or drop the harder ones the moment the latter become distasteful. Instead, we should use every possible means to have children go at the hard things with a hearty desire not to let the difficulty frighten them, but on the contrary, to let it serve as a challenge to the will to power. Otherwise, we shall run the danger of having them grow up morally flabby.

We have already seen how the will to power shows itself in the desire for leadership. Children can understand that to deserve to be leaders, they must train themselves.

The "combative instinct"—another expression of this tendency—should be directed into siding with causes which are just but which are as yet unpopular.

8. Desire for justice: Most people are willing to observe fair play when once they see clearly enough wherein it consists. Here, too, the earliest beginnings are laid in children's games. Normally, they appreciate readily enough what it means not to take an advantage denied to others. It is our part to cultivate still finer practices and finer understandings of just dealing. Pupil participation in the government of the school, for example, is an indispensable resource for civic training.

9. Benevolent impulses: Few people are born without desires to show kindness and mercy. It is good practice to get the children to begin young with the habit of considering the needs of those less fortunate than themselves. To make sure that their charities represent a genuine feeling, the objects must be people whom the children actually know to be in want. We must be on our guard against arousing these feelings too frequently

without giving the children a chance to express them in acts of honest helpfulness. Otherwise we shall run the danger of encouraging sentimentalism.

10. Sex impulses: Capable of doing endless mischief, these are also capable, when rightly trained and directed, of contributing much to the development of character. Chivalry is a single instance. The subject is dealt with elsewhere in this volume.

11. Religious impulses: Where the religious beliefs of the parents and the teachers are sincere, there can be no question of the stimulus they offer to worthy conduct. The same is true of the children. Search deeply enough, and at the roots of every strong character we find reverence. Whether, however, religious instruction should be given in public schools is another matter. Private institutions are free to do as they wish. But in our public schools it would seem wiser to avoid reviving the sectarian antagonisms which are likely to be aroused whenever questions of religon are broached. It is better to have all the best influences in school and community unite upon those moral teachings to which all our citizenship can subscribe with whole-hearted, unified effectiveness. The churches can make their offerings through the home, because there they are free to emphasize to the full whatever beliefs and practices they regard as most distinctive and precious. They can also reach the child through the inspiration they afford to the teachers and through their efforts, as power-houses of idealism, to encourage every spiritual influence at work in the community anywhere. The church can contribute largely in this way to worthy conduct.

WHAT ARE OUR RESOURCES?

What resources from without can we bring to aid in the development of these inner tendencies?

Our leading help must be the providing of opportunities for practice. The chief influence in the forming of character is what the children themselves do. The way to learn perseverance, regularity, promptness, justice, kindness, team-spirit, initiative, responsibility, is to begin early to practice these essentials.

Fathers and mothers know that one of the most promising moments in a child's life comes when he begs to be permitted to go on a far errand and pleads that he can be trusted. Parents find also that a steady allowance of spending money with the responsibility for its use vested in the boys and girls themselves is a better training in self-mastery than for father or mother to decide at every step whether they should buy things or not.

Along with the training in free self-direction, there must be practice team-work. The best preparation for the character required for democratic citizenship is that which trains the child to take a free and real share in the responsibilities of the groups to which he belongs. This is why participation in the government of the school should be encouraged as far as possible. Even more valuable in some respects are the opportunities offered in collective enterprises whose success or failure depends entirely (as the running of the school does not) upon the children themselves. The best way to learn responsibility as a member of a group is to share in an enterprise which may go to pieces entirely unless all the members do their part.

THE FEAR-PUNISHMENT

By Edith Lochridge Reid

"You'd better behave for that policeman's looking at you—he grabs little boys that cry." So spoke Donald's mother when her small son was making a scene because she didn't have a penny to let him get some candy from the slot machine while they were waiting for the street car at the corner. Less than a month later Donald got separated from his mother when they were watching a street parade. A blue-coated officer attempted to help the child locate his home and parents but Donald was so terrified to have the policeman touch him that he almost had a spasm. The nervous shock of feeling he was in the power of the man he had been taught to fear left him half sick.

One only needs to walk the streets of any city for a day to hear similar remarks by parents. "The conductor will throw you off the car," or, "See that man watching you—he'll chase you with his cane," these are typical expressions to quiet children because the parent is too weak in discipline to control them in any other way.

Recently a doctor remarked confidentially in describing the trouble he had encountered with a frightened child, "Some one ought to wake up mothers to the fact that it is very serious to have a child fear the doctor. This child to-day had been taught that I carry terrible things in my black bag for children that coax for rich desserts and fall out of trees because they disobey.

She raised her temperature several degrees fighting me off."

And this case is only one of many. I heard a mother say to a child that was impatient about staying in bed for the necessary time after an attack of measles, "If you don't mind I'll send you to the hospital and the nurse will come along and strap you right in bed and not give you any dinner."

How much better to have read to the restless tot or planned surprises for her or to have played a new record on the victrola. She should have willingly stayed in bed because she loved her mother and had been taught to respect authority rather than through fear of being sent to the hospital.

A threat to a child always denotes a weakness in the tie that binds that child to respectful authority.

Why does a mother need to tell a child a big black bear will get him if he doesn't shut his eyes and go to sleep? Probably because she has managed his bedtime very erratically. Perhaps one night he went at seven and the next night if the family wanted to go to a movie he trailed along and was put to bed at nine or later. Now, tonight, because there are guests and Son must be disposed of summarily, he is told he must go right to sleep or—then follow the penalties that will come if he disobeys, all of which instill fear into his heart that lasts until he is old enough to become disillusioned.

Can't we aim to have our children do right because it is right, and not because they fear doctors, hospitals, officers, and bears? Let us develop caution and judgment but not senseless fear.

THE FAMILY OF JUDGES

By E. M. Megraw

EIGHT of them sat at table and each had a fling at Dickie—grandparents and parents, sister and brother—and their missiles, though only of words, were sharp and stinging and Dickie grew "madder" every minute.

He seemed a tough little proposition, it is true. He had pitched greedily into the feeding process as soon as he had noisily and rudely taken possession of his chair.

Grandfather and Grandmother looked frowningly at him. Their projectiles began with "In my day—"

"Look at those hands!" big sister demanded of the company in general. "I'd be afraid to eat the bread they touched, but Dick seems to thrive on a germ diet."

Big brother's ammunition required a big gun. He raised his voice for the mention of some "perfectly awful" thing Dickie had done that day, and Dickie's shortcomings, which were generally very short indeed, were resurrected and hammered at one after another.

Father looked as fierce as a South Sea Islander as he said, "I'll 'tend to you later."

Mother wound up by saying, "I can't do a thing in the world with him," her voice a despairing plaint.

There was no such ugly trouble in the family near by, though it included a boy of Dickie's age and proclivities. For fault in the presence of the family, a quiet "Go to your room, Tommy," from his mother was sufficient to end the incident.

Dickie's mother visiting Tommy's mother on one of these occasions, appreciated the even flow of cheerful conversation that continued uninterrupted by Tommy's defection. It was so different from the general squabble in her own home that followed misbehavior by Dickie.

When Tommy's mother reappeared, and her son had dashed out of doors to his play, the less successful mother put her plea:

"Please tell me how you settle things so easily. I can't do anything with Dickie. I believe he takes pride in his successful rebellions."

"I make it a rule never to correct Tommy in the presence of others," her friend answered quietly. "Notice that tree," she continued, pointing through the window to a fine, straight little beauty. "A few months after it was planted it began to lean. I set the gardener to work. He drove a strong stake, the top pointing as directly to the sky as if a plummet had been hung as a guide from the cloud above it, and to it he fastened the young, growing thing. Not with flimsy strings that would break in a day—as inefficient as intermittent discipline—nor did he pull it violently into place allowing others to join in the rough treatment. No, alone he tied it with strong bands neither harsh nor confining, leaving it room to grow true to the guide, upright. My dear, a mother may be the strength that will keep the child growing straight, bound and protected by bands that will not break—truth, affection, respect. The child respects the mother who shows respect for him. One of the ways of doing this is by recognizing his one, inviolable right—correction in private."

USE PRAISE INSTEAD OF BLAME

By Helen K. Champlin

CHILDREN thrive on the same sort of friendly treatment that adults find pleasant and helpful.

You bake a good pie, prepare a good dinner, plant a promising garden or succeed in repairing the family car. No one notices it. You feel decidedly "let down." Or, suppose someone does notice it. Suppose you get a smile of appreciation or a word of approval or a pat on the back. The whole day goes better and you welcome the next task with a feeling of courage and assurance. You have a sense of having "made good."

"NOTHING SUCCEEDS LIKE SUCCESS"

THIS sense of having "made good" is one of the most worth while experiences a growing, developing boy or girl can possibly have. To a very large extent, it may be the deciding factor in his keeping on making good. We are accustomed to saying that "nothing succeeds like success." Success does, in truth, become almost a habit. It comes from an increasing confidence in ones ability to meet problems, and confidence comes from the knowledge that people whom you respect recognize that you have done a worthy piece of work.

EVERY CHILD CAN DO SOMETHING WELL

SUCCEEDING in doing something well is so important an experience that it is actually part of every parent's duty as a parent to see that his children experience it. Every child can do something well. His success may be a very simple one. But he must receive enough praise so that he knows that, in the eyes of those whom he respects and loves, he has succeeded. He may have made a neat drawing, swept the porch well, straightened his room properly, put his toys away where they belong, helped a playmate over an obstacle, written a good letter, brought peace to a quarrelsome group, washed the car well, made a bed properly, received an improved grade in a school subject or overcome a bad habit. There are countless ways in which every child can meet with real success according to his abilities.

These may seem like simple things. But they are part of a child's life. And if he feels success in these simple undertakings he is far more likely to succeed in greater. We can be certain that he will have the benefit of a feeling of success only if we give him proper recognition and praise when he succeeds.

THE VALUE OF PRAISE

WE ALL know that praise is especially valuable if the task we set out to do is a difficult one. And the task of the boy and girl in growing into a fine adulthood is indeed a complex and difficult one. It is full of problems and possibilities for error. Encouragement is needed all along the way.

We grown-ups have made some rather hard and fast rules for the game of living together. We expect boys and girls to learn them. We say that one kind of conduct is right and another is wrong. We even say that a thing is right to do in one instance and that the same thing is wrong in another instance. We have standards of politeness. We permit some words to be used and not others. This is all very confusing to young children. We expect them to acquire information and skills and attitudes and ideals. We have made a very complicated world in which they must learn to live.

Try to remember some occasion on which you found yourself suddenly set down in an altogether strange environment. You didn't know just what was going on and you didn't know just what would be expected of you. You were among others who seemed to know the rules of the game. But you yourself were a stranger to them. You will recall your state of confusion. You were very grateful if someone came along and assured you that you were doing the right thing in the right way. You felt a strong foundation of self-assurance and security bolstering you up. You could feel new power grow. With such encouragement, the new experience turned out to be a pleasant and a profitable one.

Now suppose that, instead of letting you know that your conduct in the new environment was right, someone had kept telling you of all the things you were doing that were wrong. You tried this and you tried that, but you kept making mistakes, and every time you made a new mistake someone scolded or punished you. Soon you would be ready to cry out in desperation, "How do you expect me ever to learn what is right to do if you tell me only what is wrong?"

Is it fair to expect a child to know when he is doing things to suit adult standards if we notice him only when he is doing something not acceptable?

GOOD TRAINING PUTS EMPHASIS ON PRAISE

GOOD training puts a lot of emphasis on giving praise for success. It has been found out, by means of experiments carried out in laboratories, that children actually do learn faster when we praise them for doing things right than when we scold them for their mistakes. It is a good thing to point out the mistakes in a patient, friendly way if we can give clear suggestions about how the mistakes can be corrected. But it is very important, if we want the child to learn fast and well, to let him know just where and how he did the thing right and to give him a feeling of pride in his improvement when he does improve.

It is not enough to tell a learner that his performance is "good" or "satisfactory" or "excellent." He should be told just what makes it good, why it is satisfactory and in exactly what way further improvement can be made.

NOTICE IMPROVEMENT

IMPROVEMENT is the thing to praise. In most efforts, success does not come suddenly. It comes by slow degrees. So each tiny improvement is one step further toward success. Every time we encourage a child for making even the slightest improvement we are making it more probable that his good act will be repeated and in time become a habit.

John is not sufficiently polite. It will not be worth much to punish him for impoliteness. Neither will it be of much help to keep telling him to be polite. You will have to be more specific. Politeness is a complex matter made up of many little details. It will be necessary to say, "You did right in walking *behind* Mrs. Smith's chair." "Good, you remembered this time to take off your hat." "It is more polite for you to let others get into the car first." Pointing out the right things to do and then praising for success is good child training.

Mary is not very careful about picking up the things in her room. You may scold her time after time and she doesn't seem to care very much about improving. But suppose some day you see her make one single step toward putting things away. That is the moment to catch. "Good girl, you are making things look better. I think you will soon have a neat room." You have given her a feeling of pleasure and you have touched her pride. If

you keep patiently on with this method it will bring results—not sudden results, but certain improvement and gradual success. That is training.

Sara's school report showed a D grade in arithmetic. Her father scolded her soundly. Sara tried hard to improve and was very happy the next month to bring home a C grade. But her father scowled and told her that there was nothing to be happy about until she had an A grade or at least a B. Sara's grade slipped back to a D in another month, but her father would not believe that his failure to praise the improvement she had made was undoubtedly one main cause of her slipping back.

PRAISE IS A STIMULANT

IT IS a fact that praise and the feeling of success that follows it actually changes the physical condition of the body. When a person is happy and successful, certain glands of the body tend to pour out into the blood stream a chemical that strengthens the tone of the muscles and increases vitality and energy. On the other hand, the person who is constantly being nagged and who meets with one failure after another is being physically depressed because of the decreased activity of these glands. The happy, encouraged, appreciated child is actually a stronger child—more likely to meet with success and readier to take up a challenging task and do it well. So there is a real physical reason for that old saying that nothing succeeds like success!

BLAME AND PUNISHMENT HAVE DEPRESSING EFFECTS

BLAME and punishment have an accumulative effect on a child. He becomes easily fatigued, readily discouraged and increasingly nervous. On the other hand, the accumulative effect of praise and encouragement is a child with increased initiative, a happy outlook and a sense of personal worth. For that reason, success in school comes more easily to the child who is guided at home with constructive praise where it is deserved.

The most significant effect of recognizing proper conduct with a word of praise is seen in the child's personality. Repeated blame deadens personality. The child grows insecure and self-conscious. He becomes so accustomed to doing the wrong thing that he *expects* to be wrong at every move. Consequently, he is backward socially, shy about expressing himself and develops an uninteresting, negative personality. Properly chosen and directed praise has the opposite effect. The child is not confused about what is expected of him. A friendly, cooperative relationship develops between him and his parents. He has a sense of security in expressing himself. He does right things and *expects* to be right. The result is proper initiative, self-respect, a growing independence and an interesting, positive personality.

GOOD CHILDREN TOO OFTEN IGNORED

A PARENT, like a teacher, has to be on guard or he may neglect the good, well-behaved child. When we are annoyed by a child's misbehavior, we have a tendency to do or say something about it almost at once. When the child's behavior is quiet or unobtrusive or correct we have such a sense of satisfaction that it is easy to fail to acknowledge the fact with a fitting look or word or smile. When their attention is called to it, parents are often surprised to discover how sadly they ignore their children when they are being good. Commend good conduct and there is every chance that it will be repeated. Ignore good conduct and you have wasted one of the finest opportunities for fruitful child training.

If children are noticed only when they are doing something undesirable, they soon learn to misbehave just for the sake of being noticed. They will be like neglected babies who soon learn that the best way to get attention is to make a lot of disagreeable noise. Children, like adults, sometimes need an audience!

Some parents wonder whether there is a chance that praise will make a child bold and "stuck-up" and conceited. There will be no danger of such a result if the praise is directed as it should be, if it is not overdone and if it is sincere.

PRAISE THE ACT, NOT THE CHILD

PRAISE should not be directed toward the child himself. Praise what the child *does,* not the child himself. The child is neither good nor bad. What he *does* is right or wrong. What he *makes* is well made or needs guided improvement. What he *says* is well said or can be corrected. When it is the product and not the child himself that receives the praise, the child's attention is directed toward the value of what he is doing rather than toward any virtue in himself.

Guard against over praise. Children are very sensitive to exaggeration and insincerity. They sense it when we are really pleased, and they sense it when we are covering up disappointment or lack of interest with flattery and sentimental slush. A quiet word or look of genuine appreciation is much more valuable than any amount of sentimental flattery.

DON'T USE BRIBES OR PAY FOR GOOD BEHAVIOR

GENUINE approval is more valuable in training children than pay or prizes or material rewards. There is no question about it being a good practice to pay children for certain tasks. This offers a good opportunity for them to learn the value of earned money. But pay is not a right incentive for good conduct. If a child is paid to be good or given a prize for doing only what he should do without reward, you can scarcely expect him to learn to do these things just for the sake of knowing that he is right.

Approval and disapproval are a higher plane of appeal than material rewards and physical punishments. Praise or blame from highly respected parents can become much more significant to children than prizes for success and punishments for wrong behavior.

A deserved compliment is a spur to progress. Children develop more rapidly when we let them feel the happiness of achievement that is recognized.

HOW TO TELL STORIES FOR CHARACTER-BUILDING

By WILLIAM BYRON FORBUSH

A FEW special instructions as to story-telling for moral ends may be suggested. In the first place, we must always be sure that what we intend to give is a story. Yet if a story is really to be effective, it must be a *story*, and not a *sermon*. Let us never call it "an anecdote"; never in story-telling use the word "character," "will-power," "virtue," or any of the names which go with a book of ethical lessons. A child should go away from our story not feeling "instructed," "improved" or depressed, but joyous, affectionate, and courageous.

Let us use at least the tact of a Pueblo Indian in our choice of a time for story-telling. In a quiet moment before going to sleep, in the leisure of Sunday, during the confidential half-hours which come frequently, though unexpectedly, the skillful mother will present her story.

The manner of moral story-telling is of considerable importance. Though preaching, we are not to adopt the preacher's tone. We are to avoid the "high pulpit manner." The story is to be told with evident enjoyment, if possible with a touch of humor.

DO NOT OVER-EMPHASIZE THE "MORAL"

"Do NOT take the moral plum out of the fairy-tale pudding," says Dr. Felix Adler, "but let the child enjoy it as a whole. Do not make the story taper toward a single point, the moral point. You will squeeze all the juice out of it if you try.

Do not subordinate the purely fanciful and naturalistic elements of the story, such as the love of mystery, the passion for roving, the sense of fellowship with the animal world, in order to fix attention solely on the moral element. On the contrary, you will gain the best moral effect by proceeding in exactly the opposite way. Treat the moral element as an incident; emphasize it, indeed, but incidentally. Pluck it as a wayside flower."

And when it has been told—let it alone. For that reason it is usually well for the story-teller to depart suddenly after he has winged his arrow to the mark. May we be delivered from the temptation of what Emerson once termed, to "pound on an incident."

SHOW SYMPATHY WITH THE SUBJECT AND THE HERO

IN OUR manner the finest virtue will be sympathy. Sympathy with our subject and our hero. To quote Emerson again, his highest praise of Plutarch, the greatest purposive story-teller of all time, was that "he never lost his admiration," or, as he put it in another place, "He had that universal sympathy with genius *which makes all its victories his own.*" Sympathy, too, with the child. The vice of the teacher is contempt of his pupil. It is hard to tell a child an improving story without looking down upon him. But if Dr. Norton said that the worst book is the one that makes life seem less interesting, he might have added that the worst story is the one that makes the child feel inferior.

And yet, with all our caution about preachiness, we do want our children really to get the application of the story. Nathan's tremendous parable to King David did not satisfy the prophet until he was sure that the king received into his heart the words, "Thou art the man." Especially perhaps in the Bible stories, are children likely to feel content that what we tell took place a long time ago and related to the sins of somebody else. The child, we have said, tends to personalize himself as the hero of each, but he may not do so unless the story is effectively told.

INDIRECT APPLICATION—THE CHOICE OF SUBJECTS

ONE MOTHER of our acquaintance used to be sure of her application by making it a point on Sunday to tell, under the name of another child character, of dispositions and incidents which she had noticed in her own children's lives during the week. She did this so skillfully that they would, in surprise, tell her that they had been in the same case. The application was not difficult. It is possible to carry along from time to time incidents concerning an imaginary "Grumpy," or "Lazy Lawrence," or "Mary, Quite Contrary," and promise to call some child by such a title of reproach if he deserves it, or, still better, to tell of the exploits of a hero and encourage the children to incarnate him.

Tales are the natural soul-food of children, their native breath and vital air; but our children are too often either story-starved or charged with ill-chosen or ill-adapted twaddle tales. Good tales, well told, perform the moral choices of adult life aright. Many Bible stories are among the best, but there are not enough, and there are not enough of them adapted to any age, so we should go outside, and draw on other sources.

In the choice of stories for moral needs, one aim is to be remembered above all others. Such stories must answer questions which are already being raised by the children, which refer to experiences or acts of their own. The parent who is a physician of the soul will apply his medicines as they are needed and reiterate stories which bear upon certain truths until the children begin to live them—until right paths are worn. In early adolescence, the method of telling stories should be that of biography, and moral instruction may be based upon incidents in the lives of men in fiction passing through moral experiences as real as if they had actually lived. When we try to teach morals by mere words, the pupil gets words; but when we do so through lives he gets images and ideas.

PERSONALITY PROBLEMS

HOW PERSONALITY GROWS*

By Mandel Sherman, Ph.D.

The behavior of a child must be analyzed carefully before an estimate of his personality can be made. There are no tests for personality, similar to those for intelligence, and as a result, information must be obtained from various sources. Valuable information may be obtained, for example, by observing the everyday activities of the child; his method of meeting obstacles, his manner of making friends, his reaction to frustrations of all kinds, his intellectual and emotional interests.

Each new condition which a child meets requires a change in his behavior—old ways must be re-shaped into new ways. Thus the personality is constantly fashioned and refashioned, always changing and enlarging. This growth and change continue until long after the individual reaches adulthood, if indeed it can be said that personality ever ceases to change.

THE DEVELOPMENT OF PERSONALITY

Personality develops in the process of learning new ways to adapt to environment. The young child tries one way and another and finally adopts what appears to be the most successful. Traits such as initiative and independence, often considered inherent in the make-up of the child, are determined by the environment. The situations in which nursery school children are placed demand independence and initiative. As a result they develop these traits. Many nursery school children at first lack independence and initiative to undress themselves for the afternoon nap and to dress after the nap, whereas others are independent of the help of adults. Investigation of their back-ground shows that the parents of the dependent children were responsible for their behavior, having insisted on helping them on all occasions and having given them little opportunity to learn to be independent.

HOW PHYSIQUE AFFECTS PERSONALITY

A relationship is often observed between physical and mental traits, but no one has shown conclusively that heredity is the only factor in the relationship. The healthy, robust individual, for example, has a more optimistic viewpoint than the sickly person. He can be friendly to his fellow-men because he feels that he is their equal. On the other hand, the individual who suffers from some defect is likely to develop an antagonistic attitude towards others because he feels in some way inferior to them.

Sometimes a slight physical defect causes a serious personality abnormality, as Dr. Alfred Adler has shown. The existence of an unusual bodily development, deformed teeth, or other defect of little physical importance, can cause a child to develop a deep feeling of inferiority if attention is called to his defect in an unfavorable way.

On the other hand, circumstances may favor the development of very useful characteristics as a result of the physical defect. A child who finds himself unable to compete physically with other children, for example, may apply himself industriously to his school work and do better than he otherwise might have done. Charles P. Steinmetz (hunchback), noted electrical engineer, is a typical example of great mental development as a result of a physical defect.

* Reprinted by permission from *Mental Hygiene and Education*. Published by Longmans, Green & Co.

HOW INTELLIGENCE AFFECTS PERSONALITY

THE INTELLIGENCE of a child also influences the characteristic traits he develops. Intelligence is usually more important in this respect than physique. Understanding of the environment and insight into one's conduct have a profound influence upon character. An intellectually retarded child may develop many undesirable traits because he does not have sufficient insight into his behavior.

Conflicts develop as soon as a child begins to comprehend the necessity for adaptation to other people. Conflicts do not affect the personality of the pre-school child greatly because he is sheltered from difficult social problems by his parents and his wants are attended to promptly. When the child enters school, however, he must use his own resources. For the first time he feels keenly the frustrations of life. The more he is indulged and protected the more difficulty he has in the process of adjusting to other people. If he is concerned about his inability to match the strength of other children he begins to develop aggressiveness. In time he may be characterized by others as a bully. But if his training has made him timid and in addition he meets strong opposition from other children he is likely to become abnormally timid.

Curiously, many very intelligent children develop feelings of inferiority which often affect their personalities permanently. There are many seemingly backward children who are not at all intellectually inferior but are so shy and timid that they do not express themselves with sufficient force to make an impression on their teachers.

THE CLASSIFICATION OF PERSONALITY FACTORS

MANY psychologists have proposed classifications of personality factors, that is, the breaking up of personality into its parts for study and for the purpose of therapy. For example, the moral part of personality is important because of its influence upon the total personality and upon behavior. We might also consider character as another part, that is, the honesty, trustworthiness, reliability and stability of the individual.

The difficulty with most classifications is due to the artificiality of the process of classification.

Studies by many child psychologists have shown that personality traits can be moulded easily by appropriate training during early childhood and that they group themselves according to the mechanism of adjustment which the individual adopts.

ADAPTATION OF PERSONALITY TO THE ENVIRONMENT

SINCE personality traits develop as a method of adapting to the environment, it may be seen that every normal person modifies his behavior in adjusting to his environment. Thus the personality which characterizes an individual at one time may not describe him at another. A person may be retiring in one environment but aggressive in another. Only the mentally abnormal person does not vary his conduct according to the environment. The normal person does not have any trait which dominates his personality at all times.

CRITICAL PERIODS IN THE GROWTH OF PERSONALITY

THERE are a number of critical periods in the young individual's life which seem to determine the development of definite traits. These critical periods are due for the most part to the necessity of adjusting to new groups of social problems. Naturally, these periods vary with the individual, but in general, psychologists recognize a few periods that have special significance.

1. *The period between the ages of two and three.* At this time the child has developed an understanding of language and has begun to react to other people through the medium of speech. This is the time when he must be guided carefully, since the traits he develops during this period are of utmost importance in determining his future personality.

2. *The school period,* when the child enters nursery school, kindergarten or first grade. Many children are guarded so closely by their parents during early childhood that they are not able to modify their behavior readily in order to adjust to a wider social order than their home affords. Many traits which serve to adjust them at home are inadequate in a group of children of their own age. They find themselves in situations requiring give and take and are frequently confused by the behavior of teachers and fellow-pupils which they interpret as antagonistic.

3. *The adolescent period.* This is a period of social emergence during which the individual must readjust himself to an adult level of behavior. The adolescent is expected to be mature in his attitudes and behavior but at the same time is not supposed to think and act too independently. His desire to explore and take part in new experiences is frus-

trated by the domination of his parents. He is likely to become confused by his interests in a variety of new problems—social, educational, vocational, and the relation between the sexes.

WAYS OF MEETING PERSONAL DIFFICULTIES

1. *The compensatory mechanism.* Dr. Alfred Adler believes that every individual sooner or later senses his inferiorities, real or imagined, and begins to compensate for them. Some persons are able to compensate in desirable and others in socially undesirable ways. The degree of compensatory behavior depends upon the intensity of basic conflicts and upon the ability to find expression in activities which bring satisfaction and social recognition. The compensatory mechanism is seen clearly in neurotic and insane patients. Compensation is a major factor in the efforts of man to attain social prestige and personal satisfactions.

2. *The evasion (escape) mechanism.* Just as some psychologists hold to the theory that the compensatory mechanism forms the central drive in man's behavior, so others believe that an individual behavior centers about the evasion mechanism. If one had no frustrations in life, he would not need to evade reality. Nevertheless it is evident that from earliest childhood reality becomes more and more difficult to face unless training has been directed properly.

Numerous examples can be given of simpler methods of evasion employed by children. Temper tantrums, sulkiness, neurotic pains and even some fears are utilized by children in their efforts to evade unpleasant tasks. The older child and the adult use more complicated methods of evasion of personal difficulties.

Psychologists have shown how some forms of forgetting are means of evasion. The individual instructed to perform some task unpleasant to him "forgets" the directions. Hysterical attacks are often the means of evading unpleasant realities. Some people utilize sleep as a method of evasion. Some neurotics, for example, spend the major part of their time in sleep.

3. *The defense mechanism.* We see individuals whose personality is characterized by a defense mechanism, easily observed even by friends and acquaintances. Very few psychologists maintain, however, that the defense mechanism in normal behavior can be separated completely from the compensatory mechanism. Neurotic and mentally abnormal individuals utilize defenses more extensively than normal persons in their attempts to adjust to their difficulties. A very common method of defense is a critical attitude toward others. By taking the initiative in criticising others, the individual thus prevents criticism of himself. Intense interests and hobbies may also function as defenses.

THE TIMID CHILD*

By Mandel Sherman, Ph.D.

THE TIMID child is often overlooked as a problem because he is not anti-social and does not interfere with others. He is, nevertheless, a social problem or becomes one as he grows up, and is an educational problem as well. Because of his timidity he lacks the robust assertiveness necessary for success. He is likely to waste his time on undue attention to detail. He makes strenuous efforts to attain success, nearly always at the expense of his emotional energy. He is likely to be a plodder—successful scholastically—but lacking the initiative necessary for creative work. Realizing his lack of proper social outlets, he may attempt to overcome his failures in various ways detrimental to normal personality growth. A common substitute for actual experience is excessive reading. Another common substitute is daydreaming. In his daydreams all his wishes are granted and he casts aside his feelings of inadequacy. Daydreams are normal to a limited extent and are utilized by every child. But when they become excessive the child has increasing difficulty in adjusting to everyday reality, for his habit of retreat from actuality grows stronger.

THE CAUSES OF TIMIDITY

A CHILD develops a timid personality when he is unable to adjust to conditions which affect him emotionally. Simple fears may lead to timidity. When a child develops a large number of fears he becomes restless and anxious. He is subject to fright and shock, and conditions which have little effect upon the normal child excite him

* Reprinted by permission from *Mental Hygiene and Education.* Published by Longmans, Green & Co.

unduly. He is unable to assert himself because of his lack of self-confidence. He remains socially backward, although he may not be actively or consciously asocial.

Undue authority of parents or teachers makes cowards of many children. If the child does not become rebellious, as most children do under such circumstances, he accepts the world about him without outward struggle.

THE FOUNDATION OF FUTURE DELINQUENCY

When a child develops a rebellious attitude toward authority the foundation is laid for future delinquent behavior. He may not rebel outwardly at first—as long as the discipline is so strict that he finds no successful means for combating it. But all the time he may be planning ways of freeing himself from restraint. The child who feels keenly the restraining effect of authority may even be planning ways of getting back at those who thwart

him. We are startled when the good child becomes delinquent, not realizing that undue authority may have been responsible for his anti-social attitudes.

Over-protection by parents is another common cause of the development of feelings of inferiority. Unfortunately, parents sometimes continue to treat their children as though they were still babies. They take undue responsibility for them, worry unnecessarily about their school attainment and about their health. Their own neurotic behavior is transmitted to their children.

HOW TO HELP THE TIMID CHILD

The timid child needs encouragement but not undue sympathy. Frank discussion with him of his worries and fears may bring his basic problems to the foreground. He should be placed in a situation in keeping with his special interests and where he is likely to succeed and thus gain confidence.

THE HYSTERICAL CHILD*

By Mandel Sherman, Ph.D.

Sigmund Freud was the first to show that unpleasant experiences tend to be relegated to the (so-called) subconscious. As time passes and the child fails to reconcile his (real or imagined) difficulties with existing conditions he becomes restless and begins to seek a solution for his problems. In many cases he seeks some form of escape from his difficulties, although he is usually not aware of the process of his escape mechanism.

Some children solve their difficulties at least in an outwardly successful way. If they have feelings of inferiority they may develop attitudes of superiority. They "talk themselves out of" their inferiority by dwelling on their successes; they develop an aggressiveness beyond their capacity. Others develop a retiring attitude and take no part in activities in which they believe they would not be successful. A few develop physical and mental incapacities which force them out of the activities from which they feel the urge to escape. This type forms the group of hysterical-like children. They are not aware of the function of their symptoms and thus avoid a sense of guilt.

Headaches, bodily pains, confused states and

paralyses are some of the hysterical-like conditions frequently found in children whose difficulties revolve about the school situation. We are often uncharitable to the child who tries to evade school by developing a stomach-ache, and make the error of forcing him to attend school before investigating the possibility that his pain may be due to personal problems and not malingering. Even the most flagrant malingerer, the child who develops physical symptoms in a premeditated fashion, must have some unsolved difficulties which have produced that behavior. Forcing these children back to the routine of school can solve the problem only temporarily, and usually aggravates the condition. The life history of adolescents and youths with nervous breakdowns nearly always contains incidents showing that their fundamental difficulties developed early in their school years.

The causes of hysterical behavior are numerous. Only a painstaking analysis of previous events— method of treatment at home, attitude towards other children, first reactions to school and particularly to the teachers, and so on—can furnish clues to a child's fundamental difficulties. A child who has been over-protected by his parents, for

* Reprinted by permission from *Mental Hygiene and Education*, Published by Longmans, Green & Co.

example, is more likely to develop a hysterical personality than one who has tried to solve his difficulties with only as much help as he needs. A child who is given responsibilities at an ap-propriate age and who is taught to face his problems realistically meets his difficulties with less emotion than one who has always relied on his parents to solve them for him.

THE SELF-CENTERED CHILD *

By Mandel Sherman, Ph.D.

THE SELF-CENTERED (egocentric) child pre-sents many difficult problems, for he con-tinually seeks attention and his methods of attaining dominance are annoying to others. He may be successful in his school work but fre-quently becomes maladjusted because of his in-ability to adapt to the teacher and other children. The egocentric personality manifests itself early in life. The three- or four-year-old of this type constantly wants new playthings. He demands the toys of his brothers or sisters, wants to show off his abilities, and annoys everyone around him by wanting attention. He makes demands upon others in the family and is forever dissatisfied with his possessions and attainments.

THE CAUSES OF EGOCENTRICITY

THERE are many reasons for the development of egocentricity. One is over-indulgence by parents, which leads the child to assume that his demands should always receive immediate attention. Ego-centric behavior often results from an attempt to overcome a feeling of inferiority. The child adopts the compensatory mechanism and the longer he employs this mechanism the less control he is able to exercise over it. In consequence, he overcompensates, resulting in the establishment of egocentric traits which maladjust him further.

The difficulties of the egocentric child increase as he approaches adolescence. The attempt of the adolescent to gain attention and his efforts to lib-erate himself from the authority of adults some-times tend to intensify his egocentric behavior with unfortunate results. The feeling, in a child, that he cannot rely on his parents when he needs them may produce even more serious egotism.

The egocentric child, unless properly treated, may develop paranoid ideas, that is, ideas that others are persecuting him. If he does so, he. and perhaps his parents too, may need psychiatric help.

THE "CROSS" CHILD

By Michael Vincent O'Shea

JUDGING from one's correspondence, most par-ents who have children must sooner or later deal with the problem of the "cross" child. And as our American life becomes more complex, the problem of cross children will become increas-ingly difficult. And why? First, because children in many homes are overtaxed nervously much of the time. Often in the homes of the well-to-do there is so much excitement, in all of which the children participate, that they become tense and irritable. In the homes of the poor, where a large number of individuals are crowded together in small space, the children are liable to be nerv-ously unstrung. Children who have to live on the street, and are excessively stimulated by cease-less noises and moving objects, can hardly avoid becoming cross.

What does it mean for one to be cross? It means that he has lost his nervous balance, or control, or poise. Anyone, young or old, who loses his self-control will be likely to become cross or even ugly. Our fundamental instincts lead us to snap at people who deny us what we want in any way. Now, if we get into such a condition that we cannot control these instincts, then we will probably become irritable and dis-agreeable, or cross. Doubtless every reader of these lines can remember periods in his own

---

* Reprinted by permission from *Mental Hygiene and Education*, Published by Longmans, Green & Co.

life when he was "off his base," as the phrase goes, and he probably said and did things at such times that he would never think of doing on other occasions when he had himself well in hand.

Sometimes children are cross who are apparently not overstimulated either in the home or outside. In such cases, the chances are that there is some error in their diet or in their habits of living.

Again, a child three years of age or over is likely to become irritable and disagreeable if kept in the house continually, because he will not have exercise enough so that he can eliminate irritating elements from his system. Often cross children of this type become amiable and affectionate when they take up a life out of doors, working in sand or climbing trees or playing competitive games with other children, provided they do not become overtaxed or unduly excited.

THE CONTRARY CHILD*

WHEN contrariness begins to make its appearance in a young child of two and one-half or three years we need to recognize that it is a natural thing at that stage of his development. At this age children are beginning to realize that they have personalities and want to test them out in various ways.

If John runs away when you try to take his hand while crossing the street, he is only making use of his new-found independence. If you are wise you will give him a chance to run down the block alone after showing him some mark of safety such as a tree or the curb at which he must stop.

Constant interference and attempts to direct the child in every detail often result in arguments over everything that has to be done. The child will early learn that he can successfully refuse to do many of the things that are demanded of him and he comes to enjoy the commotion and concern his refusals cause his thoughtless, indulgent parents.

Some parents practice the plan of suggesting the opposite of what they want. This is not good procedure since it serves as an example of the very thing they want the child to avoid. Other parents attempt "to break the child's will" by forcing submission. This only stimulates the child to fight and sets up resistance to all authority.

You may avoid inviting the child's refusals by making only reasonable demands and few of them and by selecting the strategic moment for making requests. If a child is in a state of contrariness for a day or even longer, it may be wise to ignore refusals and center on a few things which can be carried through to success. Repeatedly reproving a child for his contrariness will only make him worse.

"Let the child off the leash and it will cease to strain and chafe and oppose."

THE CHILD WHO SULKS*

"HOW CAN I best help my seven-year-old son to overcome an inclination to sulk or cry when things do not go his way, or when he is denied something?" asks a perplexed parent. "Ignoring him has not brought success. . . ."

Ignoring a child when he misbehaves is useful when one feels that the child is playing for attention, but it is of no particular help when the child needs guidance in discovering ways of meeting a disappointing situation. Life is full of disappointments and it is desirable that a child begin early to develop a resourcefulness in finding satisfying substitutes.

What happens when the child sulks? Isn't it true that he nurses his disappointment, which grows until it reaches large proportions in his own eyes? He then begins to feel injured and abused and to look about for someone upon whom to pin the blame for his unhappiness.

We need to help the child to constructive ways of thinking and planning if he is going to grow out of a habit of sulking. If with the denial of a request we can add a suggestion for something that can be permitted it often helps. Making those denials as few as possible will result in less sulking. If we can guide a child in the planning of his leisure time so that he always has many things ahead to do, it will not be so hard to find a substitute.

By helping children to accept the inevitable,

---

* Courtesy of Extension Service, New Jersey State College of Agriculture.

such as plans spoiled by changes in weather, with a philosophical attitude we may induce them to carry this attitude over into other situations that vex him.

It is important that example be set children by the adult members of the family in these matters. We know that "crying over spilt milk" gets us nowhere and yet many adults hash and rehash their disappointments in the presence of children, who are likely to absorb the practice. In the home where everyone accepts the inevitable cheerfully, makes the best of it, and turns to the doing of something else there is an optimistic atmosphere and no room for sulking.

THE CHILD WHO HAS TEMPER TANTRUMS*

WHAT mother has not been disturbed by having her child at some time or other throw a temper tantrum? Perhaps it was in a public place where, under the eyes of strangers, she suffered chagrin and confusion, not knowing whether to carry the kicking, screaming child from the scene or to punish him then and there, unable to ignore him because of the noise and commotion he was making.

PHYSICAL CAUSES

A CHILD who is subject to temper tantrums is an unhealthy child and we need to look first for physical causes of such behavior.

Has he any unremedied defects, such as poor eyesight, enlarged tonsils, or faulty teeth? Is his diet properly balanced and his elimination regular? Is he getting abundant sleep and rest? Fatigue from trips to shops or movies, where excitement, bad air, and crowded conditions disturb sleeping and eating habits, often causes a child to be irritable and hard to please. Is he getting enough play in the open air with playmates of his own age? When too much in the company of grown-ups children are apt to be fussy, whiney, or cross.

Perhaps you yourself are the cause. If you give him his own way, if you bribe him with promises or sweets, if you tell others of his tantrums, he is gaining something by keeping on with them.

Perhaps you are setting him an example by losing your own temper. If you relieve your feelings by shouting or angry retorts, you only irritate him the more.

Perhaps the things you ask of him are unreasonable and you punish him without explanation. We need to make it easy for children to be agreeable by keeping them physically fit, providing adequate play equipment and then interfering with them as little as possible.

If the cause lies in a conflict of wills between parent and child then the parent must decide to ignore a good deal but enforce a few well thought out rules. It is important to avoid arousing the child to anger since the practice of temper displays fixes the habit. This can be done by making requests positive, using more do's and fewer don'ts; by leaving the child alone as much as possible, giving him sufficient warning when things must be done, and praising him for his efforts to do what is asked.

ANGER NEEDS AN OUTLET

WHILE it is important to avoid arousing anger, it is necessary to realize that when it is aroused, it must have an outlet and cannot be successfully repressed. People who are able to control anger have not learned to repress it but have found legitimate ways of using the energy aroused. Some vigorous physical activity is often a relief, and the child may be taught to use this method by finding such outlets as hammering nails, running across the yard or riding a kiddie car.

THE QUARRELSOME CHILD*

PARENTS are deeply concerned about the quarreling and bickering that goes on among children in the same family. They do not realize that a certain amount of conflict is bound to arise among the young during the process of getting adjusted to each other.

Conflict may be stimulating to growth. The disagreement between individuals should progress

---

* Courtesy of Extension Service, New Jersey State College of Agriculture.

from quarreling based upon selfish motives to discussion with a desire to get the other person's point of view; in other words, from war to arbitration. The problem for parents is not how to stop quarreling but how to direct it into healthy channels.

We need to define what we mean by fighting. Many children when they appear to be fighting are, like young puppies, only wrestling. A child who can carry on good natured wrestling, and takes his medicine when he meets a superior opponent, is learning good sportsmanship. Wrestling is good exercise and doing it well is an asset. It is desirable for children to be taught to wrestle according to the rules of the game. The desire to compete, to test one's strength against that of another, is natural, and with the exercise of it comes a certain feeling of security in one's ability to take care of one's self. This is essential in the development of the child.

SCHOOLBOY FIGHTS

WITH children from four onward through school age, striking with the fists and calling names are the favorite methods of expressing anger against others. During a large part of school life, fighting seems to be a habit as much as an expression of passion. Quarreling at this age is a kind of game; squabbling as an expression of bravery is a daily custom, and two brothers or two chums fight with fully as much pleasure as wrath.

Much fighting grows out of the normal human desire to prove one's power. If every child is taught to excel in something so that he has a contribution to make to the group, this will help him to build self-confidence, the lack of which lies at the bottom of both over-timidity and over-aggressiveness. Some strife may be relieved also by recognizing that the position of each child in the family group carries with it certain privileges and certain responsibilities.

SHOULD PARENTS INTERFERE?

THE QUESTION of the extent to which a parent should interfere in the quarrels of children is often a disturbing one to many mothers.

If they become quarrelsome over a particular toy and it is impossible for the mother to know who had the toy first, it may be wise to remove the toy, the source of dissension, if the situation is serious enough to warrant intervention by an adult.

One mother states that her policy of separating the children when they are quarreling, without trying to find out the facts of the matter, meets the problem for her most satisfactorily. She realizes that when she is not present at the beginning of the quarrel she cannot know the facts at first hand, and it is, therefore, wiser for her to avoid discussing the whole affair. If this practice is consistently followed by the parents, the children's desire for companionship is likely to be strong enough to outweigh their tendency to quarrel. But it should be recognized that such a plan makes no provision for teaching children the technique of settling disputes.

Too often the parent is emotionally aroused over what she thinks is injustice to her child, and it requires considerable self-control to maintain an open-minded attitude until she has heard the whole story. But, unless one can maintain such an attitude, she had better stay out of the picture, for, as the defender of her own child, she is no help to him or to the situation.

LEARNING TO SETTLE THEIR OWN DIFFERENCES

THE ONLY way that children learn to settle their own difficulties is by settling them. When a real difference of opinion occurs on such questions as the building of a block house or the method of playing a particular game, an opportunity should be given the children to explain their differences in the presence of an impartial judge, probably the mother, who will help them to arrive at a compromise, one excellent way in which children can progress from belligerent to peaceful methods of settling their disputes.

Sometimes when children have been shut up in the house for a period of time due to illness or bad weather, they become irritable and peevish. A discussion of their quarrels under such circumstances only makes matters worse.

When the parent interferes it should be on rare occasions and then as an arbitrator, entering the fray with an open mind, hearing both sides of the argument and helping the children to make their own decision in favor of justice.

Children should never be told not to fight. They should not pick quarrels but they should be encouraged to stand up for themselves, even to the point of being taught how to box. The boy who is not allowed to fight or who won't fight, probably does not lack the desire, but is likely to exhibit it in less wholesome ways. He is likely to be underhanded, to win by fraud, or treachery, to egg others on to "lick" his enemies, or to curry favor by bribes.

THE CHILD WHO TEASES*

TEASING is often an indication of a need on the part of the teaser. Sometimes a younger child teases an older one because he resents the ability of the older child to do things which he cannot do. Under such circumstances the need should be met by planning opportunities for the teaser to accomplish on the basis of his own ability, giving him due recognition when he makes an effort.

More frequently it is the older child who teases. A mother writes:

"My boy of nine is continually teasing his five-year-old sister. He likes to annoy her, then laugh when she whines or cries. What is the motive?"

There are many possible motives, but let us consider a very general one.

Is this boy getting his satisfaction from feeling his power over his sister?

If she whines and cries she is admitting that he can make her uncomfortable. Is it a legitimate desire, this wishing to feel superior? The psychologists tell us that we are born with it, so there is no use in trying to eradicate it. In fact, it is valuable and necessary since it is the drive which stimulates us to do our best. But we would agree that this desire when exercised at the expense of others, is not legitimate.

What this boy needs to realize is that there are better ways of feeling superior to his sister than by making her uncomfortable. He needs to be aroused to a more grown-up attitude toward her by protecting her when taking her out, by making or doing things for her which she cannot do for herself; and to be helped to see that by teasing her he is cowardly and unmanly.

But in any quarrelling situation one child is never entirely to blame. Is the sister bringing the teasing upon herself in order to get attention and affection from the parents and bring criticism upon her brother? This would help her to feel superior to him in the eyes of the parents. Should the boy by any chance feel that his sister stands higher than he in the affection of the parents, he would be likely to tease and bully her as the only way in which he could bolster up his self-esteem.

If we want children in the same family to have affection for each other, we must help them to face their motives frankly, not through criticism and scolding but through friendly and sympathetic discussion. By talking over with them their difficulties and assuming that they wish to do the right thing and cooperate in making a happy home atmosphere, we can build up between parent and child the confidence necessary to improve the situation.

Parents cannot be too careful, however, in treating a situation involving the children of the family, to preserve the integrity of each child's personality by showing no favoritism, considering each child honestly in the light of his assets as well as his liabilities.

THE IMPUDENT CHILD

By William Byron Forbush

IMPUDENCE has two reasons. One is the quickness of the emotions of the child, who expresses his feelings before he has time to restrain or choose his words. The other is the increased comradeship of modern parents and children. The child who expresses his love and joy freely to his parents is likely to be almost as free with his wrath and disappointment. "Old-fashioned" children were just as impudent at heart as children are nowadays, but they did not dare to so express themselves.

Two suggestions may be made. The more important one is that the problem in every case of impudence is not the personal affront to ourselves but the child's own lack of self-control. Difficult as it is for us, especially if we are quick-tempered, we endure the aggravating remarks of our children, we let the affront pass, if we can cure the child.

The other suggestion is, that it is better to consider impudence as a danger to the family organization than as an indignity to ourselves. Most impudence from children is public, it is in the presence of the other children or the maid, and it is wiser to protect the clan than to be too anxious for our own dignity. As a matter of fact, if we take this viewpoint, and line up the clan against the offender, we really take care of the personal offense.

This second suggestion takes care of most un-

* Courtesy of Extension Service, New Jersey State College of Agriculture.

pleasant outbreaks. If the child, at table, starts a contentious discussion, or a disagreeable series of comments, or a boresome, self-confident statement, we can refer it to the others, whether this is interesting enough to let him continue. In other words, the clan decides, not whether the bumptious one is right, but whether he is interesting. He must, as a result, either find somebody who wishes to hear him or, if he persists, leave the table.

It is usually dangerous to allow arguments when a child has an immediate personal interest. He is too passionate and unpoised to understand. Protests at such a juncture do him as little good as they do you.

Most impudence is unconscious. In such a case it is necessary to take the child aside and show him kindly and lovingly how to put himself in the place of another and to realize that he would not like to hear the words he has just been uttering, if applied to himself.

Further, the child has some right to his own "day in court." Nobody likes to be told "where to get off," to receive an order without explanation or qualification. There is a difference between reasoning together and indulging in impudence. While a child ought not to ask questions concerning customary commands, it is helpful to him to have some reason and incentive for unaccustomed ones. This does not mean that, after a considered injunction, we may perhaps be talked or scared into a reversal. Listen to him, but do not necessarily reply. Listen with respect and attention. Or, if the thing is too urgent to be fully and fairly discussed at that time, say, "Tom, I am afraid I shall have to ask you to do this for me now, and then, just as soon as you have done it, come to me and we will talk it over more fully, and I will tell you more carefully why I think this is the best thing to do, and I will listen to all you have to say." Your attitude is that there is something bigger than either yourself or himself—namely, the imperative Duty, before which all must bow.

THE FORGETFUL CHILD

By Michael Vincent O'Shea

A MOTHER asks how she should discipline her children when they do not keep their agreements in respect to coming home on time. She gives them permission to play for a half-hour at a neighbor's house, but they may not come back for two hours. They are playing on the lawn; she calls them and says to them, "Your supper will be ready in ten minutes, and I don't want to have to call you again. Be very sure to be here in ten minutes." They promise to be on time. But a half-hour passes, and they are still playing, and they often will not come until she calls them again. She thinks they are careless and indifferent and ought to be punished in some way, so as to make them more considerate.

Let the readers of these lines test themselves to see whether they can measure a half-hour accurately without a timepiece. How many readers could be depended upon to come to supper in fifteen minutes if they were playing an interesting game of golf, for instance, or reading a captivating book, or even sitting out under a tree enjoying Nature? As a matter of fact, many well-meaning adults are constantly late at meals because they cannot estimate the flight of time. A woman will call out to her household, "Dinner will be ready in ten minutes, and I want everyone here on time." The adults in the family are about as likely as are the children to have to be called again, not because they are inattentive but because they are quite unable to judge when ten minutes have passed with any degree of accuracy.

Young children have a weak time-sense. Fifteen minutes or an hour means nothing definite to a six, seven, or eight-year-old child. If he be engaged in play, he is oblivious to the flight of time, as he should be. One who is deeply absorbed in any undertaking, as a child usually is in his play, cannot be sensitive to the passing of minutes. It is precisely as though he were sound asleep; there is no time for him. Psychologists show in their experiments that it is a very subtle and difficult thing to learn to judge of the passage of time. One's organic sensations, or the changing light in the sky, or semi-consciousness of the coming and going of people or of things—experiences of this sort convey the idea that time is passing, but if one is so immersed in any interesting business that he is not aware of these happenings, then time does simply not exist for him.

It is a rather foolish proceeding to call out to a group of young children who are playing, "You may play fifteen minutes longer, and then I want every one of you to be in here, or I will never let you go out again." There is constant trouble in some homes because parents or older brothers and sisters give orders of this sort. Not once in a hundred cases will such commands turn out well. The majority of adults would score low in a test of this kind.

Often children are late at school, though they wish to be on time. But on the way they get interested in some object or are attracted by some happening, and they are unaware that time is passing. Teachers give children permission to leave the room if they will be "back in five minutes." They may not come back for fifteen minutes or a half-hour. An experienced teacher should know that children cannot be trusted to return to a classroom on time unless there is some signal given which will remind them that the period of freedom is up. Observing teachers always mark the termination of a period of freedom by some symbol or signal which will attract the pupil's attention and remind him that he must return to his duties.

A wise parent would say to his children, "When you hear the whistle blow, or the church bells ring, or when you see Mr. So-and-So returning from this business (if he is regular in his habits) come running to the house for your supper." This will impress upon children the importance of reacting to a signal, and they will soon learn to respond if privileges are withdrawn when they do not respond. But it is utterly unreasonable to ask a child to keep track of time when he has no signals or signs to help him. No amount of scolding can develop an accurate time-sense in a young child.

How much strain and stress there is in many households because parents cannot get their children out of bed on time! They call them and say, "You may stay in bed fifteen minutes longer, and then you must jump up or you will lose your breakfast." A half-hour passes and there has been no jumping up. An hour or two may pass, and still the children remain in bed. Two hours or three hours are as fifteen minutes to a sleepy child, especially if the room is darkened and he cannot see the sun ascending, or if he cannot hear the increasing activity on the street. The mother who is preparing the breakfast may be very sensitive to the passage of time. She can tell within a few seconds when fifteen minutes have passed, because she is performing actions which she has performed in the past, and she knows from experience how long it takes her to set the table, or cook the eggs, or whatever else she is doing. But in a certain sense there is no time for the boy who is lying in bed, and he cannot be expected to "jump up" when his period of grace has expired. If the mother could rig up any device which, at the end of fifteen minutes, would give a signal, it will not take him long to learn that when a given signal occurs he is to react in the appropriate manner without delay.

THE LAZY CHILD *

By Sidonie Matsner Gruenberg

WE HAVE used the word "lazy" to cover up a heap of ignorance about human nature, and it is the easiest thing in the world to resort to this adjective—certainly much easier than trying to understand people, and especially children.

Those who have given most attention to the problem of child nature are pretty well agreed that is is impossible for a healthy boy or girl to be lazy. It is a contradiction of terms to say that a young human being would prefer to do nothing. Indeed, it is the irresistible impulse to be up and doing that makes the healthy child so much of a nuisance to people who wish to have everything quiet and "orderly." The first thing to do, when a child shows symptoms of "laziness," is to have him thoroughly examined by a competent physician.

LAZINESS BECAUSE OF ILLNESS

Now THIS sounds as though we considered laziness a disease. And several years ago, when Dr. Stiles of the United States Public Health Service announced his discoveries in regard to the hookworm, it was quite the fashion for respectable people (who have a great deal of contempt for lazy folks) and for the newspapers to think up jokes about the "laziness germ." But seriously,

---

*From "Sons and Daughters," by Sidonie Matsner Gruenberg, published by Henry Holt & Company, New York. Used by permission of the publishers.

laziness is very commonly an indication of impaired health, if not of actual disease. This is especially true when it occurs in young children. When a child sits or lies about, without caring to do anything, without even getting into mischief, there is generally something wrong.

LAZINESS FROM BEING BORED

BUT PERHAPS we all know older children who are "pictures of health" and at the same time lazy enough to exasperate their parents and teachers. When we have made sure that the picture of health is not a deceptive appearance, it is time to look for other causes, and not till then. Judging from the experience of the schools, there are lazy children who have good health. But the usual attitude toward indifference to work is hardly effective in making children get over it. To scold and to drive may help in getting a particular task finished, but they have not been very helpful in establishing habits of industry. And that is the whole problem in most cases—how to establish habits of industry.

By nature the child adapts himself very readily to the establishment of such habits. In the first place there are the instincts for activity, the native curiosity and the imitativeness. And in the next place, there is the ease with which repeated acts become organized into habit. Could anything be easier than making a child get into the habit of doing something all of his waking time? But children do certainly grow up "lazy"; so what can be the trouble? We are quite sure that it cannot be anything wrong with his muscles, for example, because the amount of energy that a child puts into his play after he is tired out by his "work" is enough to do the work several times over. That ought to give us a clew. The energy that is expended in play has meaning to the child; too often the energy required of him in work—whether it is home work or school work or work that earns money—has no meaning to him whatever. In other words, where there is interest and enthusiasm there is effort and exertion; when there is indifference or repugnance there is lethargy and indolence. Children will acquire the habits of industry only where they have practice in exerting themselves with purpose and enthusiasm.

But we cannot let the children play all the time; it is necessary to study sometimes, and to do other things that are not very pleasant in themselves. Indeed that is true. But it has been found possible to organize study and other necessary work in such a way as to get the children to do it cheerfully and effectively, and so to get the habit of doing what needs to be done without shirking and without complaining. To most older people this would seem to be demoralizing; but experience shows that work done under conditions that arouse interest is at least as valuable for "discipline" as work done under compulsion. For children can certainly learn the various processes involved in the handling of tools, for example, by making things in which they are interested; and they can as easily acquire skill in such work as in monotonous work. But the "moral" habit of application to the disagreeable, for the purpose of carrying out a more remote end, which is the essential thing in what we call our "discipline," has been successfully developed by parents and teachers who have known how to use interest in leading children from play to work.

It is the children who have been driven to do the unpleasant things that have no meaning for them who resort to "laziness" as the only escape from the disagreeable tasks. They have never learned to be interested either in the work itself, or in the work as a means to something desirable, that should crown all labor. They have acquired laziness because their impulses to activity have been thwarted by association with stupid, monotonous, fatiguing effort.

LAZINESS FROM BEING IRRESPONSIBLE OR DREAMY

AND THIS suggests a third type of laziness. In spite of the beautiful poems and the stirring orations on the "dignity of labor," the children do not have to be very shrewd to discover that society honors many of its members in inverse proportion to the amount of useful work they do. It is a short step to acquire a contempt for real, honest work, since the workers that the child sees about him receive anything but respect from "the better classes." If a clever girl or boy half-unconsciously makes up his mind that it does not pay to work, if he adopts the attitude expressed by the cant phrase, "Let George do it," we must look seriously to the conditions that make for laziness in our own habits and views of life.

Finally, there are a few children who naturally take to the contemplative life—they are dreamers, poets, philosophers. They have their uses even if they do not do "useful work."

THE CHILD WHO IS JEALOUS

By Minerva Hunter

"Frederick is a terror," young Mrs. Allen told her mother. "I cannot understand the change in him. From tiny babyhood he was always so sweet and friendly with strangers. He attracted attention everywhere we went and our walks in the park brought numerous compliments. Now when we go walking and any one stops to say something about the twins he kicks their carriage and screams at the top of his voice. Every airing ends in punishing him. What can truly be the matter?"

"You told what is the matter without realizing it," her mother laughed. "Frederick wants the attention he used to get and now the twins get."

"That must be the trouble, but how am I to help it? Twins are sure to attract attention."

"The help should be in making Frederick able to adjust himself to the new conditions. We must try to help him."

When Frederick woke up from his nap he was delighted to find his grandmother visiting him. It was her first visit since the arrival of the twins. Frederick embraced her, collected his Christmas toys for her inspection, got into her lap and talked to her, but not once did he mention the babies. When he went into the yard to find his dog, Mrs. Allen confided to her mother that she feared Frederick really disliked his little brothers.

"We must make him proud of them," the grandmother answered.

A little later, when one of the babies woke up and cried, Frederick could no longer keep their presence a secret. "Twin babies; two of 'em," he told his grandmother.

"Whose are they?" his grandmother asked.

"Mother's."

"And yours, your own little brothers."

Frederick looked indifferent.

"Howard Green across the street has only one brother," grandmother reasoned, "but you have two. Do you know any one else who has twin brothers?"

"No," Frederick acknowledged after thinking.

"You are fortunate to be the only boy on this street to have twin brothers."

Frederick smiled.

"Other boys have horns and drums and blocks and sleds, but twin brothers are wonderful!"

"Come and look at 'em," Frederick invited.

Grandmother went. Not once did she mention that she had hugged and admired them while Frederick took his nap. As she stood and looked at them now, her hugs were for Frederick. "Aren't you glad you have twin brothers all your own?" she asked.

The idea took effect. Next time the mother went walking with her trio Frederick announced, "I'll show the babies. They are my twin brothers."

The mother wisely consented. Now Frederick is so interested in exhibiting the charms of his two brothers that he hardly notices the words and looks of admiration directed toward himself.

THE CHILD WHO LIES*

All children tell tales which adults call untruthful, yet a parent experiences a distinct shock when, for the first time, he discovers his child in a falsehood. We seem to expect children to be born truthful, yet a habit of truthfulness must be acquired, like any other habit.

A father who recently discovered his eleven-year-old in the act of smoking, described his experience as follows: "I smelled cigarette smoke as I entered the tool shed. I looked about and discovered two cigarette stubs. With these as evidence I went in search of Harold and his young playmate. When I accused them of smoking in the tool shed they denied it and when I showed them the stubs, they insisted that they had been left by a carpenter who had been working there in the morning. I knew they were not telling the truth both because of their guilty expression and because I happened to know that this particular carpenter did not smoke. I didn't care so much about the smoking but the fact that Harold would lie to me made me furious."

Most parents feel this way about it. It is humiliating to a parent to realize that the child's respect for him is not sufficient to prevent deception. But we have to realize that self-preservation is a strong impulse, and when a child senses danger, he is going to escape if he can. Too often we make it very difficult by our accusing tone of voice, by threats, and by punishments administered

* Courtesy of Extension Service, New Jersey State College of Agriculture.

when the child has owned up to doing a thing. He comes to feel that it pays to take a chance on escape through lying.

The habit of truthfulness must be cultivated like any other habit, in the process of which the child makes many mistakes. These mistakes should be looked upon as opportunities for teaching truth rather than evidences of moral depravity in the child. Much of the early imagining of children is branded as lying when it is not lying at all. A little boy who passed through a grove every morning on his way to kindergarten told most wonderful stories of wild animals, "money mines," huge butterflies and mysterious happenings. On one occasion his mother went through the grove with him. He pointed out a large stone which he said was the top of the "money mine." In explanation he said the money that gets lost has to go somewhere. "I think it is all together in a deep hole under that stone; but no one can get it because the wild animals will come at you." When asked whether he had ever seen these wild animals, he replied, "only their shadows." This boy had heard his father talk of money lost by himself and others in a certain business venture. He was simply trying to find an explanation. As adults we often fail to realize how much that is commonplace, every-day knowledge to us is unknown to the child and must be made a part of his experience.

"But," asks the parent, "when can we expect the child to begin to distinguish between fact and fancy?" Generally by the time the child is five years old we begin to find other motives at work in the stories he tells.

He may be playing for attention. Charles Darwin states in his autobiography: "I confess that as a little boy I was much given to inventing deliberate falsehoods and this was always done for the sake of causing excitement. For instance, I once gathered much valuable fruit from my father's trees and hid it in the shrubbery and then ran in breathless haste to spread the news that I had discovered a hoard of stolen fruit."

Ignoring it is often the best treatment for this type of lying as many children prefer being punished to being ignored. Children may also be taught to see that "make-believe" stories are a legitimate form of entertainment, provided they are recognized as such with no attempt to pass them off for truth.

We cannot teach children the importance of telling the truth by talking about it. Neither can we help them to realize it by punishing them when they tell lies. Too often that kind of treatment frightens children into greater deception.

Each time a child is found in a falsehood we should try to discover what the motive is. If it is fear, resulting from our accusing tone or too persistent questioning, then we must be more gentle and use a more casual tone, saying, "Come, let us talk over the whole affair and you tell mother just what happened; then we can decide together what to do about it." If the child is in a state of excitement or fear after a wrong has been committed, it is better to seem to overlook it rather than to accuse the child directly of the fault. At a later date the experience should be recalled and talked over calmly. The child will be in a more receptive mood as a result of the consideration shown.

Perhaps the child, seeking the approval of her playmates, boasts of having things that she doesn't really possess. In that case she can be made to see that people who are most respected are genuine and sincere, and that honesty and sincerity are better ways of proving superiority than are material possessions.

If the child's desire to do something is very keen, she may misrepresent the facts in order to gain her end. She may say, for example, that she was invited to tea by the mother of her playmate, when actually the mother had only happened to come into the room at the time the playmate issued the invitation.

Children can have many motives in telling untruths, and, if we are going to teach them the importance of truthfulness, we must help them to discover their motives in each instance. Teach them to see that in the long run it pays to hold to the facts, since that is the only way to gain the confidence and respect of others.

It is natural for children to try to protect themselves against disagreeable or painful experiences. The little girl who empties the contents of the medicine bottle down the sink and then declares she knows nothing about it, needs to be helped through patient understanding to meet disagreeable situations with courage.

The worst kind of lies are those which are motivated by selfishness or the desire to gain at the expense of another. These, if allowed to grow, are apt to lead to unscrupulousness and dishonesty. Children are sometimes trained to this kind of lying by bribes and rewards. The parent who offers to give presents or sums of money to the child if he receives high marks at school is tempting the child to secure them by dishonest methods.

The most important essential in developing a habit of truth-telling in children is a home where truth is not only told but loved and lived. If we fail in our promises to the child, if we misrepresent the facts in order to make ourselves appear better before our friends and family, if we invent reasons that are not true in order to avoid doing or having the child do something we do not wish, all such situations confuse the child with reference to truth and set him an example quite contrary to the precepts we are laying down.

THE VAIN CHILD

By Christine Terhune Herrick

ARE SMALL children born with vanity, do they achieve it, or is it thrust upon them by injudicious parents, relatives, and friends? "I don't know what to do with my little girl," said a mother, "she is only five years old, but her chief thoughts are given to clothes. She is always watching the clothes of other children and comparing them with her own, and at home she spends much of her time posturing in front of a mirror."

Her vanity could hardly have attained such dimensions if it had not been fostered by praise of her looks, or by talk in her presence which gave an undue importance to dress.

RIGHT AND WRONG WAYS OF CORRECTION

"Don't tell me that vanity is confined to girls!" laughed another mother. "My small boy of three has a long white coat with a blue collar and cuffs made like a German dress uniform, and he wears a little blue visorless cap with it. The other day I found him admiring his reflection in the cheval glass. 'Aren't I stunning?' he said complacently."

"What did you tell him?" I asked.

"Not at all," I said. "You are a very plain little boy and no one would look at you a second time!"

This does not seem to me quite the way in which to correct vanity. The boy may have been disconcerted for the moment, but as he was really a pretty child, he could hardly escape more or less frequent compliments, and in a short time he would probably be called upon to decide whether it was his mother or a number of other persons who were in the right about his appearance.

More than this, mortification is not the best method to cure a child of vanity. In many cases it drives them from satisfied self-consciousness to unhappy self-consciousness.

"Much of my childhood was darkened by my conviction of my surpassing unattractiveness," confessed a woman, who although not beautiful, could never have been really ugly. "Again and again I was told, 'Put as much as you can inside of your head, for no one will ever care to look at the outside!' I had a predisposition to morbidness, and I dwelt upon the idea of my ugliness until I dreaded to meet strangers, because I felt that their first thought would be of my unattractiveness. The admonitions did have the effect of making me devote myself to study, but I think the same result might have been won by means which would have been less painful."

Often vanity is entirely unconscious and children may outgrow it naturally. I have a clear recollection of a small girl of my acquaintance, who, having heard or read of hair which was brown in the shadow and golden in the sunlight, used to take a great deal of innocent pleasure in standing on a chair in front of the bureau and studying in the mirror the effect of her own hair when the sun was upon it. Undoubtedly there were golden gleams in the brown locks, and the fact gave her a happiness and comfort which brought content to her and did her no harm.

I do not believe that unwholesome vanity exists in the majority of children unless it has been cultivated—perhaps ignorantly—by vain or thoughtless adults. If a mother bestows undue time and thought upon clothes, talking of those she wears and those worn by other people, placing dress in a position of false importance, her children will naturally follow her example.

THE CHILD WHO STEALS

"**M**Y SON has been taking money from my pocketbook," a distracted mother wrote us not long ago. "I can't bear the thought that my boy is a thief. What can I do?"

Many parents are confronted with this problem at one time or another. The mother facing it must look into the various factors contributing to it and must, first of all, find out what is causing it before she can hope to solve it.

When a very young child takes things which belong to someone else, he is not doing what adults think of as stealing because he has not yet learned to distinguish between "thine" and "mine." Nor can you make him understand the difference before he is mentally mature enough to do so. You can merely take the toy or whatever it is away from him and give it back to its rightful owner. If possible it is wise to give your child another one, or a similar one to take its place. Above all, don't *in any way* try to make him feel that he has done something wicked. That will only frighten him and will do no good because he won't understand what is wrong.

When an older child takes something that does not belong to him—a child over five or six—the problem is somewhat different. By the time he is that age he knows that he is doing something he shouldn't. He is likely to hide whatever it is he has stolen, showing that he is well aware he has done something wrong.

Most childhood stealing is done by children around seven or eight and again in early adolescence. These are the two ages when children try hardest to gain a measure of independence from their parents. This would seem to indicate, therefore, that these are the two ages when children feel most at a loss, most isolated, most at sea, being not yet quite ready for the independence they are seeking and perhaps not quite comfortable in their old relationships. This theory is reinforced by the noticeable fact that many children who steal at these ages steal money which they use to "buy friendship," so to speak, in one form or another. They may want to appear generous by treating their companions to sodas or by giving them presents or in similar generous ways. They may do this not only because they are themselves drawing away from their parents but, possibly more often, because their parents, exasperated by their trying behavior, have made them feel unwanted or otherwise isolated, whether consciously or not.

The first thing to do, then, if your child is stealing, is to find out *why* he is doing it. Is he lonely, unhappy, not getting along well with his family or his friends? Ask yourself whether you are showing him too little affection at this time instead of the added rations he needs and wants, whether he admits it or not.

Scolding or shaming such a child will only make him more unhappy—quite possibly to the point of desperation. If he stops stealing, which is unlikely in such cases, his despair will only manifest itself in some other way. Or he may use still subtler or more devious methods of stealing if he feels that he has to satisfy his needs in that way.

Of course the stealing should be discussed with the child—seriously but sympathetically, calmly and unemotionally, with an effort to understand the underlying motives. The stolen money or articles, or their equivalents, should be returned by the child if possible, to their owners, with an apology or explanation or a plea for understanding, as the occasion demands.

If the child seems to be lacking something he very much wants, whether it is something tangible or some emotional lack, every effort should be made on the part of his parents to supply that lack, to give the child the satisfaction he craves and needs in order that he feel no necessity to steal or to commit other offenses of a similar nature.

If you feel that you *have* got at what seems to be the cause of your child's stealing and have done everything you can to correct it, and if he still continues to steal, you may have to enlist psychiatric help because the child's motives may be too deeply hidden for you to fathom, or his maladjustment may stem from conditions beyond your ability to correct.

It is possible that your adolescent child may have the misfortune to get in with a gang of boys who think stealing is a sign of manly daring—who are actually proud of what they can "get away with." If your child *has* fallen in with such a group, he should be spoken to about it by someone he respects — his mother or father, teacher, preacher, Scout leader, or whoever it may be. He should be shown that stealing is not considered manly or in any other way smart in the adult world, that it is, indeed, a crime punishable by heavy penalties, and that it does not "pay."

Of course the entire gang should be so informed, not only your child. By and large, stealing will be prevented only when the urge to steal has been eliminated on both the economic and the psychological levels.

PERSONALITY IN THE MAKING*

BY LOUISE P. WOODCOCK
Author of "Life and Ways of the Two-Year-Old"

**Psychologists trace both the ability and the inability to live
and work happily with others to early childhood experiences.**

IF FAIRY GODMOTHERS still, as of old, were bestowing gifts on each newborn child, not the least among gifts that parents would choose for their children would be likable personalities. Again and again, mothers say, "I don't care so much if she isn't really beautiful but I do want her to be liked." "He needn't be a genius, but I want him to get along well with people." Parents think perhaps of their own shyness or of difficulties some persons have when they try to work with others and they don't want their children to suffer from such handicaps. Can they do anything, while they are still very young, to begin building personalities that will be comfortable for the possessors and acceptable to their fellows? Fortunately there are a number of things they can do.

Let us look at the ingredients that usually go into the making of the likable, interesting, satisfactory personality. Some that come readily to mind are courage and self-reliance, sympathy and responsiveness toward other people, vitality and good humor, adaptability, intellectual aliveness, and personal integrity. Some of these derive from deep emotional sources and their foundations are laid in a baby's earliest experiences. Others are relatively less deeply grounded, but all of them can be nurtured from the beginning by thoughtful, caring parents.

If I were trying to help a little child grow to be a person whom almost everyone liked and accepted and who could work and play successfully with almost everyone, I should attack the problem on a broad front. I should first of all try to help him lay down the deep, secure emotional foundation that he needs to become a person unafraid in his world. Then I should do a number of concrete things to help him cultivate an attractive personality.

Courage and the expectation of good are desirable character traits. The really timid person, who is always uncertain as to how things are going to turn out, is not happy himself nor apt to be very satisfactory to other people, for most of us need our courage rather than our fears

reinforced by the attitudes of others. That is why you should give your child the greatest possible assurance, from his first hours, that he has come into a good world. And, since the baby's first feelings of whether he has come into a beneficent or an unkind world depend on the physical comfort or discomfort he finds there, see to it that he has, above all else, plenty of food and food often enough. For the baby's physical needs outweigh all others; if food comes, all is well; if it does not, he suffers acutely.

If most of the time he is warm and dry and well-fed, he is learning a lesson of contented assurance; if he recurrently suffers long minutes of hunger pangs or other discomforts he is learning to distrust what he can expect. The baby who has plenty of food and physical comfort gets off to the best start.

The specific lesson here is that mothers should make sure that their babies' schedules for feedings are adapted to the needs of the individual baby, and that the baby is not made to adjust, whether he likes it or not, to a book-made schedule. No baby should experience recurrently, before each feeding, prolonged minutes of hungry waiting for the clock to bring relief.

Next, with the same intent to give the baby a generally assured feeling about life, see that he gets a really adequate amount of physical contact —cuddling, caressing, closeness—while this gestural language of love is the only one he can understand. All that he knows of the world of human society, the tiny baby learns from the hands that tend him, the voices that address him, the faces that smile above his crib, the arms that carry him about. In the gentleness of the hands, the calm strength and security of the supporting arms, the intangible assurance in loving voices and smiles, he gains a sense of protection, of being safe in a place where he belongs. It is difficult to find any complete substitute later on for these basic reassurances.

A concrete suggestion here is that the bottle-fed baby should be held just as lovingly and protectingly during his feeding as the baby who nurses. He should not be left in lonely state with his bottle propped up on a pillow. Human close-

* Reprinted from *"The Parents' Magazine."*

ness speaks a language that brings profound comfort to the little baby.

Having laid the best foundation for confidence that one can, the next step is to help the baby retain it as he grows into young childhood. Perhaps in most homes where a baby has been welcomed, there is a general feeling that before he is about two years old, he can do no wrong. Not very much is asked of him and his relative immobility in crib or play pen prevents him from any great ventures into crime! But from two years on, his active legs, exploring hands, his newly learned "no," his growing sense of his own power to choose and, what's more, follow his own course of action lead him repeatedly into situations that are apt to bring disapproval.

The reason for a relaxed, mild attitude on the part of parents at this crucial period is that at this age a child is forming a conscious picture of himself as an entity, separate from but in close relation to other human beings. He is building up, out of what happens to him, a picture of himself either as a nice, comfortable, safe, loved person or a not-surely-loved person who may at any minute become less loved, depending on whether or not his grownups like the last thing he has done. Because he is building up this self-portrait that will have a marked effect on his personality makeup, he needs the fullest possible support and trust from the people at home. The feeling that people trust and value him has a more positive worth, in terms of personality, than the discovery that grown-ups are smart enough always to find out his little sins.

Parents should keep the learning aspect of the situation in mind rather than concentrating on a baby's small misdemeanors. They should also be quicker to redirect his activity, when it is unacceptable, than to spend much time in expressing disapproval. "Bad" and "naughty" are terms that could well be omitted entirely when talking to children—and very good riddance, for when an adult tells a child he is bad, the child unfortunately believes it, just as he believes that this is a boat in his picture book, that his sweater is red, that he will be three years old tomorrow, all because a grownup has told him so.

Worse even than being told he is bad, is the threat that he won't be loved. "I won't love you if you do that," is a terrifying consequence for a little child to contemplate when some imps in his fingers have irresistibly forced him into taking something out of mother's bureau drawer. The fear of losing love and support is the direst fear of all for little children. No child should ever under any circumstances have to face that.

The child whose home-learned picture of himself is a happy one can usually, with a little help, make contacts with other children without putting up those defenses that make the play go wrong in childhood and other human relations go wrong in adult years. Because first experiences make so strong an impression and have such important results, protect carefully a child's first relations with other children. Do not expect those social virtues of generosity, consideration, tact, which many of us never master completely, to burst full-blown from this new little member of human society.

Do not expect your child to give up his best loved playthings, at first, to another child, either guest or casual playmate, neither should you condone, for the sake of politeness, another child's abuse of him or his possessions; and do not blame him or shame him for repulsing, at first, with whatever weapons he can muster, the undesired encroachment of others upon his business —though, of course, you will protect the aggressor from damage, set forth his case (his need for a block, his interest in the way the derrick works, and so forth) and suggest peaceful ways of settling affairs. I should try, however.

The same general principle—that growth for social living is slow—can hold a child's relations with his brothers and sisters, though here the problems become more constant, insistent, and complicated by the conflicting ties of love, dependence, rivalry, and so forth. Basically, however, the child must have the support and good opinion of the people who are closest to him if he is to develop a personality that has strength and fiber. He needs sympathy and not too much hurrying and a pattern of great fairness on the part of the adults toward himself and the other children in the family. A specific danger that should be watched is possible persecution, bossing, or undermining of budding self-confidence on the part of the youngest by the older children.

One of the chief reasons, in terms of personality, for protecting a child's first relations with others, outside his home, is that early setbacks may have one or the other of two undesirable effects. A child may become frightened and reluctant to try more ventures, so that he fails to gain enough experience to learn how to get along. Or he may develop, by degrees, some type of defensive technique: it may be an aggressive "I'll hit him first" approach, or a wary "I'll wait and see if they're going to be nice to me," or some other variety of behavior that, acting as an arc in a vicious circle, makes him less likely to be well accepted by others and hence prone to become more defensive still. Generally speaking, the child who has never felt the need of being defensive does not develop the unattractive techniques of defensiveness, and his personality expresses a natural, free-flowing impulse toward other people that goes a long way toward making him liked.

If a *fundamental inner feeling of security* and an attitude of friendliness toward people have been established, many of the externals that go into the making of attractive and satisfactory personalities will follow of themselves. It is true, however, that *there are many people who seem inwardly secure enough and outwardly friendly enough without much by way of charm or interest* to offer to their social group. Could they have been helped to develop more positive qualities? There are certainly some things parents can do toward this end.

For instance, the healthy child is more likely to show the positive qualities of eager enthusiasm, gaiety, vigor and good humor than the less sturdy one. For this reason and because good health goes so far toward making or enhancing physical attractiveness, try to keep your child healthy with plenty of the right foods, adequate sleep, sunshine and vigorous play. The immediate value lies in his being a lively active companion at a time when these dynamic qualities are a greater contribution to play than the more contemplative ones of later years. *The future value of a good start in health has both personal and social aspects.*

Another factor, related though not dependent on health alone, that contributes in its own special way to a child's personality development is *good muscular coordination.* The child who knows he can compete successfully with other children in their play because of his well-integrated body, his legs that can run fast in a game of tag, arms and legs that carry him safely and easily up ladders and trees, hands that can place blocks accurately where he wants them, is free of one more cause for timidity in a social group. The child, too, who has faith in his muscular set-up is not likely to become the unhappy adolescent who stumbles over the doorsill as he enters a roomful of people mainly because he is sure he is going to do so, or who fails to learn to dance or play tennis because he is so slow or clumsy in learning that he gives up, if, indeed, he has had the courage to start.

While muscular coordination is determined partly by one's physical inheritance, *parents can help their children gain the poise that comes from quick, skilled muscles, agility, steadiness on heights, and the other rewards of physical activity.* It may mean planning such equipment and play incentive at home as will encourage and abet the children's natural desire for climbing and jumping and pulling and balancing; it may mean playing ball with an only child or follow-the-leader with the occasional child of sedentary disposition or helping a shy child to learn to skip at home so she can join in rhythms at school.

Just as good coordination serves to increase a child's self-confidence, which we later call poise, so does the ability to use language easily. In this verbal world of ours, the person who can express himself easily in words has usually the advantage, other things being equal, over the person who is slow and halting of tongue. *Parents can help by encouraging a child to express himself freely so that he can say what he thinks,* clear up confusions when they arise, and avoid the frustrations and embarrassments of the inarticulate. This does not mean that parents should try to make a child a verbal prodigy nor should they encourage, unduly, the youngster who is always too prone to substitute words for action. It means, rather, making sure that a child has enough experience in the give-and-take of conversation to express himself easily and well and so to feel socially at ease. *Children need frequent, casual, unforced conversations with their elders on topics that concern and interest them.*

Parents can help a child to build an interesting personality and to have a contribution to make to his group by encouraging his hobbies and explorations. Specifically, this means tolerance and living space for all the bug, stamp, and even match-folder collections that he needs in his business of making contact with the real world. It means providing the raw materials he needs to express his mechanical bent and his artistic soul. It means being his companion to the degree he wants one to be.

Then there are the attitudes and their resulting patterns of behavior that become part of a child's personality *not wholly but largely from example.* Parents can take a very active and deliberate part here.

There is virtue, for instance, in the simple habit of contentment and this is often a reflection of the family pattern. To be in the habit of liking the food one is offered, the books that are available, the people who are around, the entertainment that is offered, makes for contentment and helps one to be a desirable guest or companion.

The habit of gaiety is one that adds charm to a personality. I should laugh often with my child and very, very seldom repress his high spirits.

Adaptability that keeps one from being entirely upset by changes in plans or situations, sudden new responsibilities, or lack of accustomed equipment, tools or comforts can be learned partly from example. "All the doors are locked and the windows fastened and I haven't my key. Well, well! Let's see if we can get down the chimney," is an attitude that makes one a reassuring companion.

The habit of speaking well of other people, of accepting their weaknesses and faults and foibles with good humor is an excellent one. Unless a child has some deep personal conflict within himself he will readily adopt such an attitude if it is the usual one at home, and people will like him because they will feel sure of his good will.

A happy child who sees and hears those about him being courteous to each other and to him can hardly fail to follow suit, in good time, because he feels that this is the natural way to speak and act. *The unhappy child will resist politeness as he will resist food or any part of the procedure he is asked to go through.* The common forms of politeness offer no particular hurdle to children who have *the inner spirit of courtesy*—the impulse to friendliness. But, *at first, they should merely be exposed to them and not forced beyond the limits of their shyness and timidity.*

Personal integrity was included in our partial list of good personality traits. This is a rather intangible quality, perhaps, but its presence or absence is readily felt. It gives tone and dignity to the most humble and depth and fiber to the most vivid and outstanding personality. A recipe for its nurture by parents would include such factors as *constant, unfailing trust in a child's best self; more ready laughter with him—not at him—over his mistakes than censure because of them; respect always for his dignity and his abilities; scrupulous honesty with him and about his concerns, and ever and always the example of deep integrity in the parents' own lives.*

There is no escaping the responsibility for one's own impression on one's children. One just has to be the very best kind of person he knows how to be, for *nothing is so likely to make nice children as having nice parents.*

RELIGIOUS TRAINING

IMPORTANCE OF RELIGIOUS TRAINING

By Mary Collins Terry

No LITTLE child should be without religious training, for it is as essential to the balance and beautiful growth of his character as the proper food is to his body. This training can be given in the home and in the Sunday School. Both are excellent means, and should supplement each other, for it is when these two institutions work together that the child receives the highest benefit.

Because of the ease with which the child learns, and the capacity to retain even unto old age what was learned in childhood, religious training should begin early. Do not say, "Oh, when my boy is old enough to decide for himself I will let him choose his church." You do not leave his manners until then, so why his morals? High ideals and a good moral code are most easily formed in his plastic years.

The child is naturally an imitator and hero worshipper. The stirring stories of Bible heroes and the application of the truths of the great old Bible stories go far toward helping him formulate the rules which are to govern his own actions now and in later life.

The parents in the home are the ones whose high privilege it is to begin their children's religious training. It is a pity that so many, through thoughtlessness or neglect or a false sense of unfitness, neglect this sweet duty. The Sunday School next should take up and help to broaden and develop the child's religious experience.

There are several ways in which the Sunday School does its work a little better than the same work can be done at home. In the first place children are drawn to other children. They naturally tend to work or play in groups; to be with other children, imitating or joining in their activities, gives incentive to Sunday School work.

The Sunday School carries on a regular and systematic course of Bible study, adapted to the ages of children, and presenting the most suitable Bible material in an attractive form.

A visit to the live modern Sunday School in the average church would be a means of enlightenment and surprise to many. Hand work, simple songs, and rhythm for little children; and home work, class competition, and even dramatics and pageantry for the older ones, have been the means of making Bible study delightful, attractive, and absolutely indispensable to our children.

There are ways in which we parents can and ought to co-operate with the Sunday School. Our children can learn to be punctual and regular. We should show our interest in their progress and experiences. How proud they would be if father or mother would also go to Sunday School, perhaps to the adult Bible class . . . "A little child shall lead them." Then let us have faith in the old Bible promise:

"Train up a child in the way he should go: and when he is old he will not depart from it."

THE BEGINNINGS OF RELIGIOUS TRAINING

By Mary E. Rankin

HOW TO MEET RELIGIOUS IMPULSES AND IDEAS, AND HOW TO STIMULATE AND DEVELOP THEM

THE PROBLEM of religious training is a difficult one. Often we hear parents say, "I want my child to have religious influence and religious training, but I do not know when to begin or what to do." The traditional religious training of little children does not stand the test of modern child psychology and child study, and so many of us are at a loss to know "when to begin" and "what to do." Nor do we feel that the traditional type of Sunday School is the one to which we want to send our children for the same reason.

But where does religious training begin? Surely it begins in the home as soon as a baby begins to live. The religious impulse manifests itself in this way in child nature. The mother or nurse begins the work of training the moral and religious nature by her regular response to the infant's physical needs. Here begins the revelation of love, human and divine, and the meaning of life, and of law and order as the method of love. The baby soon discovers that his wants are supplied by persons, and his sense of dependence on them is the religious impulse in its earliest stage. This, then, is the beginning of religious life.

Does not our difficulty as parents and teachers lie in the fact that we do not recognize the beginnings? They are so humble and are so far from what we, as adults, are apt to think of as religion. But a little child's religion and the religion of an adult are very different. Much of the "religious training" of children is far beyond their experience and development, something superficial and meaningless as far as the children themselves are concerned. Surely we must have vision enough to see the goal, but at the same time we must realize that the goal can only be attained by building on a sure foundation. And the beginnings of religious training are not the less important because they seem so remote from the goal.

WE MAY BEGIN FROM THE WRONG STANDPOINT

WE ARE so eager to give our children information about God and Jesus, to tell them Bible stories, and send them to Sunday School as soon as they are old enough. But in all of this, unless we know what the mind and spirit of a little child is ready for, there is danger of only adding perplexing problems, and problems that should come later, because the experiences and materials which we are providing are too mature for a little child. The following illustration of the point is, I think, not an unusual one: Betty was five years old, and up to this time her mother said there had been no religious training. At Easter time she read to Betty from the Bible the story of the Crucifixion and the story of the Resurrection. Betty was a very nervous, highstrung little girl and was thrown into an agony of mind. She cried bitterly for some time, so that her mother was quite distressed and said that she felt helpless as well. But when Betty wanted to go to a Good Friday service with her mother, she was taken. The clergyman read the same passages from the Bible, and Betty clutched her mother and said, "He is reading that awful story again. Let's go home." This is not extreme, but typical of many children's experiences, because mothers do not know what to do, what the nature of a little child's religious experience is, or when it begins. Betty's mother was trying to give her an idea of religion entirely from an adult point of view, an idea far beyond a little girl's experience, and far beyond her ability to comprehend.

On the other hand, take the case of Jane, in whose home there has been a conscious and constant religious influence since her babyhood, to which Jane has responded very naturally and wholeheartedly. Before she was able to talk, the family worship and the service among members of her home group had its influence in her baby life. When she was able to talk, the idea of prayer was accepted as a matter of course. She was eager and interested to talk to a Heavenly Father. She wanted to help Mother in various little duties about the home and was encouraged to do so. Her contribution to service in the home was accepted as valuable and necessary, never discounted or discouraged.

After a visit to a friend one cold day, where she had seen a very wonderful doll-house, this was her prayer in the evening: "Thank you, God, that we have a warm, comfortable house, and thank you for many things, and thank you that we've got you. Thank you that we could go to E., and thank you that we could see the wonderful doll's house. How pleasant it must be for some good little girl like me. And I don't want any burglars to get in at night when I'm asleep. And help me to be good to Mother and not give her any trouble, and help me to be the bestest girl in the whole world.—Amen."

Jane has been wisely taught to express gratitude in her prayers and to ask not for material things, but for help to meet her little everyday problems, and this she did with unquestioned sincerity.

The little child is born into an environment of home and family. There his life and interests cente. with Father and Mother. They must, therefore, be largely responsible for his religious education. For religious education aims to influence thoughts, feelings, and conduct in his human relations in the family, school, playground, etc., so that he will begin to know himself as a member of God's family. The beginnings of training in worship, training in service, and instruction must come during those early years. The responsibility rests on the home, and cannot be put off on the Sunday School or any other agency, for they can, after all, only build on and supplement training begun in the home. It may be said also that the Sunday School needs the fullest co-operation of parents in order to make its work effective.

WHAT CHILDREN BRING INTO THE WORLD

IT MAY not be out of place to go back now and consider briefly what children bring into the world with them as a foundation for religious training. Since religion is not just a part of life or a phase of life, but includes the whole of life, every thought, feeling, and act, it begins as soon as a baby begins to live. It may be said very simply that a baby brings into the world with him certain tendencies to "respond." He is like a little sensitive plant that takes in impressions, and soon he responds to them in some way, either showing satisfaction or dissatisfaction. At first practically everything he does is instinctive or mechanical. It is not a matter of thinking or control until experience and knowledge make it possible for a child to be responsible for what he does. Because a child's nervous system is plastic, experience does soon play a part. But it is important for parents to realize that, until it does, no responsibility attaches to the baby's actions. Recently a mother of a baby a few months old said, "No, no. Peter naughty boy," when the baby did something she thought he shouldn't. But a wise old Chinese nurse said, "No say Peter naughty boy, Peter not naughty, just take his hand away, Peter soon forget, Peter not *know*." And so it was. Peter did soon forget, because of Amah's training.

THE FAMILY THE CHILD'S FIRST RELIGIOUS WORLD

THE FAMILY at first is the child's moral and religious life and world. He absorbs religion by suggestion and by imitation. The home environment, by which nervous impulses are controlled; which is free from hurry, worry, and anxiety; where the outlook on life is a happy one, and where harmony among the members of the family prevails, furnishes an atmosphere where children naturally grow into a religious faith.

It is so necessary to get a child's point of view when he seems provoking and irritable. And, too, it is well to let him share in the family's problems and perplexities as soon as he is able to, always letting him settle as many of his own problems, and make as many decisions for himself, as possible. And if we could only be consistent in all of our relations with children!

Consistency is a most necessary and stabilizing influence. The child feels his mother's religion through her love and care and devotion, and with this sort of training he comes to a realization of right and wrong for himself. A child's religion begins and ends in his associations with persons, for religion can not thrive away from life as a whole. A child's sense of dependence is directed first to parents rather than to nature or imaginative beings, and is definitely the beginning of religious life, long before formal instruction and training can take place.

WHAT ARE SOME OF THE CHILD'S FIRST RELIGIOUS PROBLEMS?

MAY A little child be conscious of the need for rule and law in life, for human sympathy, for dependence on others? Most surely he may be and is. Does a child consciously face problems day after day, and does he have temptations? Does he not have to learn self-control, to obey, to be kind, to share and to serve, to have joy in giving, to learn to be appreciative, to be courteous, to be thankful, to be brave and truthful, to play with other children and to respect the rights of others? The acquiring of these virtues creates the religious problems of his everyday life. Right in the child's realization of and efforts to meet these problems, and to overcome and conquer them, lies the surest foundation on which we can build Christian character.

Do children glory in overcoming? Indeed they do, and how often we hear them pray for help. This was Teddy's prayer after he had had his bobbed hair cut and felt very grown-up: "Dear Lord, when I fall on the kitchen floor and bump my head, help me not to cry, but just say 'Ouch'." He had been in the habit of crying frequently and very easily when hurt. And Katherine, a little girl who thought many things out for herself, and was deeply conscious of her faults, though not morbidly so, prayed that God would forgive her for "telling on" a little cousin and getting her in trouble. The next morning she prayed again to be helped to be kind and not cross all day. At night she said to her aunt, "I haven't thought about my prayer all day, but God must have helped me, for I haven't been cross or told tales once." Such is a child's faith.

RELIGIOUS BEGINNINGS ARE IN HOME LOYALTIES

WHAT, then, are the beginnings of religious growth? The beginnings of religious growth come with the feeling of love, loyalty, and service in the home group, love for mother, father, brother, and sister. An illustration absolutely to the point is that of a four-year-old boy. When Mother said to him, "Ask your father if he will do an errand for me." The father's reply was, "Tell your mother that I will if she will be good." Whereupon Bradford wheeled around and looked his father straight in the eye and said, "Mothers don't have to be good, they *are* good." A very perfect tribute and well deserved by that mother. A little child's feeling of love and loyalty to his family is very beautiful. It is so absolutely genuine and unquestioning. Would that we could always be worthy of it! Our responsibility is to see that a child's loyalty and love in the family circle reach out to ever-widening circles with interest, sympathy, and service.

How do children get their idea of God? It may be through hearsay or it may be through instruction. Children accept the idea of God just as they accept fairies and Santa Claus, and they believe what they are told about Him. Gloria, aged four, had had her first ideas of God from an old-fashioned Sunday-school, where little children and adults shared the same lesson material. Her impression of God was of someone to be feared, or at any rate the ideas gained were not pleasant ones to her. So Santa Claus was her God. She preferred to talk to him at night, and it was always Santa Claus who took care of her.

HOW CHILDREN GET THEIR FIRST IDEA OF GOD

Dr. Coe says that it is because of the child's impulse to nurture and protect that he comes to appreciate a Heavenly Father who cares for and protects His children. "We love God by taking His point of view." And so we bring to the children the idea of God as a loving father, the father of each child, and the child's response, very naturally, is to love and trust Him. "They struggle to obey Him; they desire to help Him in His work; they are grateful for His gifts. This is Christian experience."

This we must always remember, that "God can mean vastly more to a child who has experienced justice and love than to a child to whom justice and love are foreign."

Not all children respond to the idea of God in the same way. Many children talk about God and to God as they would to any person they know, and we all have had many expressions of these ideas, such as Carolyn's when left alone in bed in a strange room. Her mother told her that she was quite safe, for God was taking care of her; to which Carolyn replied, "No, He isn't, for this is God's night out."

Dorothy did not like to think of dying and going to heaven before her mother did, for "God won't be able to fasten my buttons any more than Daddy can." And Elsie who when put to bed did not want to stay alone said, "I don't want a man to stay with me, Mother, I want you. I want a woman."

SOME CHILDISH INTERPRETATIONS OF GOD

On the other hand, there are children whose interpretation is quite different. Faith and Jean, aged six and five, had no religious training at home until they went to Sunday-school. These were some of the conversations their mother overheard at different times at home, after they had been to Sunday-school for some time. Faith, looking out of the window: "It doesn't seem as though God could be inside and outside both at the same time with the window closed, does it? But He can, because He's a spirit." Jean: "What's a spirit?" Faith: "A spirit's someone who *seems* like a real person but isn't. Fairies are spirits." Faith, looking at her mother and Jean: "It seems sometimes as though I didn't really know you and Jean—as if you were both just spirits. I can't tell what you are thinking about." Mother: "You must know what sort of things Jean thinks about, because she's just a little girl like you." Faith: "I don't know what she is thinking about now." Then much later in the Winter this was overheard: Faith: "You know, Jean, everything that's alive is some kind of a spirit. Even rabbits are spirits. Chickens and hens are not much of a spirit, because they don't know much." Then at still another time—Faith: "Mother, do you believe there are *real* fairies in heaven? *I* do, and I surely believe there are real angels, for they would have to take our thoughts up to heaven when we die." Jean: "God doesn't look like a person in the world, does He, but in heaven He will look like one."

Another child who lived quite by herself, and who seldom saw or played with other children, worked out a large community, using many small china dolls for people. Over this community she ruled, pretending that she was God. This play was carried on for a long time, and in telling about it when she was grown she said that she remembered distinctly how the responsibility that she felt for her little play community raised the standard of her work and play. She must make the best houses possible for them and she must sew as well as she could when making dresses for them.

Children are so individual that no two of them ever can be trained the same way. To some children lacking in imagination the idea of God makes no appeal until later. But normal children, brought up in homes where they are wisely loved and cared for, usually respond in a natural, whole-hearted way to the idea of God as a loving, Heavenly Father, when the idea is rightly given them. The problem of answering their many questions is a difficult one, but our only way is to answer them in the spirit in which they are asked, as sincerely and wisely as possible. Always remember that to keep a child's confidence is all-important. Make him feel that he can always come to you with his questions, and that they will always be answered with interest and sympathy.

II. HOW RELIGIOUS FEELING MAY BE AWAKENED IN THE HOME

THE PROBLEM of religious training is more difficult in homes where there is only one child, and of those homes there are, unfortunately, many. It is the temptation to lavish everything on the one child and to expect no response except, perhaps, the reward of childish pleasure and comfort. It is also much easier to help children dress and to care for them than to let them try to do it. For their efforts, unaided, are clumsy and slow and often it is difficult to wait patiently for them. However, a little child of three or younger begins to try to put on his own shoes and stockings and tries to do many things for himself and that is the time to encourage it. Let him be independent in caring for himself as soon as possible. Later comes a time when children are not at all eager to help themselves, and the habit should be formed before this time comes, at about five years of age. For the humble beginning of the Christian life lies in just such things as these. Develop the spirit of co-operation and helpfulness whether there is one child or whether there are a dozen. It is much easier when there are several, because then there is more frequent opportunity to share and for "give and take" in a group. But in any case, the sooner each child is responsible for himself as far as possible and can have some little responsibility for others in the house, the sooner he will feel that he belongs to the home and that the home is really his. The first daily tasks may be such simple ones as emptying scrap-baskets, bringing in milk bottles, filling the wood box, getting the evening paper, and bringing Father's slippers every night. A baby less than three years old made himself responsible for that act every night. The point is that the child is to feel that these things are not to be done spasmodically, when he feels like it, but that, if he does joyfully his little part each day, life in the family moves more smoothly and comfortably.

PROBLEMS DUE TO MODERN HOUSEKEEPING

ONE SOMETIMES hears mothers say, "Yes, my little girl does want to help me and help herself, but I employ a maid, and it did not seem wise to have the children do these things." But the spirit of helpfulness and co-operation does not come spontaneously later on. It must be a matter of training from the beginning.

One realizes, too, that the difficulties are very great, for modern life, with its hurry and rush each day prevent a little child from participating in many home activities, and from knowing many processes that were known and experienced by children, as a matter of course, in olden days. So much greater is the need to give children the birthright that is theirs.

Life is so complicated and crowded, physically and mentally, and so expensive, that in many homes there seems to be no place for children. But never before in the history of the world have children been as precious as they are now, consequently the greater need to give them the best possible start in life.

Someone has said that in the home lies the possibility for the most perfect democracy, when each member of the family does his part.

The opportunities for co-operation in the home group bring up all of the child problems that are going to develop character—the problem of self-control, of willingness to share, of being grateful, of being brave and cheerful, etc.

OPPORTUNITIES FOR CONSIDERATION AND COURTESY

WITH the training in responsibility and service, come the training in politeness and courtesy in the family group, so sadly lacking in many American homes. Little acts of courtesy and politeness must be practiced daily in order to become habitual and to persist when children go out into life. This thoughtfulness and courtesy should early be extended to include not only people in the home group, but other people—the milkman, the grocer, the postman, the garbage man, etc.—whose service contributes to their welfare and comfort. A child should be helped to understand the large part in life that their service plays and should be taught to treat them with consideration and sympathy. Besides playmates these are probably the first persons that a child comes in contact with outside of his home. Here is a first opportunity to develop a social imagination and an appreciation of other lives closely related to his own. A child's attitude toward the tradespeople and others who serve the family is absolutely dependent on the attitude of the adults in the family. Children are such little imitators! They reflect in their lives just what they see people about them thinking, feeling, and doing.

The beginnings of the religious life and growth, then, lie in the beginnings of worship, of service and co-operation in the home group, and in other human contacts and experiences which touch little children's lives. Ideal relationships in the home and family life are the foundation for ideal relationships in the larger family of God.

NATURE EXPERIMENTS

NEXT to the revealing of God through mother and father love, comes the consciousness of God through Nature. Everything in the out-of-door world is interesting to a little child. I have recently been watching a very intelligent baby less than a year old. His first Spring out of doors is perfectly enchanting to him. He smiles, gurgles, and points at the moving leaves, the singing birds, the animals, and I am sure that he is storing up many questions that will come out as soon as he is able to talk.

Our part is to give our children all of the nature experiences possible. Give them an opportunity to experiment in their nature plays, and an opportunity to garden. Nothing equals the satisfaction of planting seeds and watching them grow. Every child should have a small piece of ground in which to plant a few seeds, and a city child should at least have a window-box. Helping to feed the birds and pets develops the nurturing and protecting impulse Young children can not have the full responsibility of caring for pets, but in helping to care for plants and animals they are beginning to help care for God's world. Jean said one time, "This is God's world." "No, it isn't," said Faith. "He gave it to us, and it's ours now."

An appreciation of the beauty of Nature comes early to some children and late to others. But it is well to call their attention to beautiful things and to walk with them as often as possible where the world is beautiful. Love of the beautiful contributes largely to the growth of the spirit.

BEGINNING OF PRAYER-LIFE

MOST children enjoy praying, "talking to God," and do it as easily as they speak to a human friend. They accept the feeling of a personal relationship as a matter of course. Consequently their prayers are at first very personal and very crude. These we should accept quite as seriously as they do. Never should we show any amusement or allow outsiders to hear the children's prayers. We can lead them to more dignity of form later on. It seems better to lead children to express gratitude in their prayers, rather than to ask for things. Even a little child's prayers may express gratitude, good will, loyalty, reverence, and faith, in simple form, but gratitude most of all. A little child's first prayer may be simply, "Thank you, God, for my happy day, Bless Mother, Father, etc." Usually a child wants to pray for everyone he knows.

The danger lies in not allowing him to pray as he likes at first, but in teaching a formal, meaningless prayer like "Now I lay me," on the one hand, or in not having a suitable prayer ready when he is no longer satisfied with his own efforts.

It is not easy to give prayers for little children to use, for prayer is a matter of experience, and is personal with children as well as with grown-ups. A simple prayer* used by many children is,

> "Father of all, in heaven above,
> I thank Thee for Thy love.
> My food, my home, and all I wear
> Tell of Thy loving care.
>   Amen."

This may be said, however: it is the spirit of the prayer that counts. "If we in our prayers have expressed gratitude for all that has been given, rather than a desire for more; if we in our prayers have expressed our willingness to fall in line with God's purpose, rather than a wish to change it in accordance with our own desires; if we have sought to live as nearly as may be as we have prayed, then the child will, in his turn, approach his Father in the attitude of one who listens, rather than one who begs.

Even a child of five may learn the Lord's Prayer. It may have meaning for him as soon as he has had the experience of "father" and "bread." The meaning will grow with him, and there is no need to try to give more than a partial explanation of it.

But the children's feeling of the power and meaning of prayer in their lives will grow as they come to realize its formality and that they need not pray at stated times, but that the great, unseen force whom they call the Heavenly Father

*Adapted from "Song Stories for the Kindergarten," by Mildred J. and Patty S. Hill.

is to be a source of comfort and strength to them at any time.

FAMILY TRADITIONS AND CEREMONIALS

It is possible for children to share in all family traditions and ceremonials. They are always eager to contribute their part and should be allowed to. For instance, even a child of five may be able to say grace at table. He may take his part in family prayers by singing a little hymn he has learned, or by repeating a Bible verse.

At all the holiday celebrations the youngest members of the family should be made to feel that they are not simply the recipients, for they should be allowed to make birthday and Christmas gifts for others, or earn the money to buy them. Having a part in decorating the Christmas-tree brings much more of the Christmas spirit to them than if they are simply onlookers when the tree is ready. The sooner children know the joy of sharing and giving on all the great family occasions, the sooner will they know the real joy of living.

OTHER WAYS OF BROADENING CHILDREN

One important way is through stories. Oh, the magic appeal of a story to all children! In it they may see other lives, different yet like their own. There are realistic stories and there are idealistic stories. Both make a strong appeal to the little child. For the most part, myths, fables, and folk tales are beyond the younger children, but oh, the joy of the fairy-tale! And has not the fairy-tale a religious value?

Mrs. Mumford says that there is no risk in using fairy-tales to draw the child nearer to the thought of God "if, as we tell them, we are ourselves conscious of the deep, underlying truth of fairy lore. In early childhood the abstract must needs be clothed in the concrete, and gradually, if we do not misinterpret, if we have told such stories in the right way, the children will cast off the husk containing the kernel—and still will understand. The romance of fairies, gnomes, and sprites is full of spiritual truth. Can the Spirit of Love, of Beauty, of Power, embodied in the world, be more fitly expressed for the child than in the undergrowth of tiny helpful creatures—creatures real enough, although to human eyes invisible?"

The right kind of a story, be it a realistic story or fairy-tale, appeals to both mind and heart. How intensely a child thinks and feels his stories! He wants to hear them over and over, and their teaching value is greater than we know. Each story well chosen and well told broadens a child's vision of life, and should, and does, many times lead to action on his part. Stories help children to form purposes and to carry them out more than we realize. Therefore, the great necessity of choosing wisely our story-books—there is so much literature for children that is not worthy of the name. Poor stories, poorly told, badly illustrated, stories that are over-stimulating or those that are silly—these we should always pass by.

A little child's mind gradually filled with the best that children's literature has to offer will become a storehouse that will make his life richer as the years go on. Not too many stories should be used at first, and they should be short and simply told, increasing in number and length as increasing experience and maturity may demand. Never add a moral to any story. Let the story stand for itself, and the child will make his own interpretation of its meaning.

With regard to the use of the Bible with younger children, it may be said that the Bible was not written for little children. There are, however, some stories and verses for them, and they may begin to know and love the book which is to contain much untold treasure for them later on.

PLAYING THE STORIES

Children always enjoy playing the stories when they are familiar with them. Often the whole family is called upon to represent the different characters. No stage properties are at all necessary, for imaginary things will suffice or anything at hand may be used. By playing the stories and being the characters, the children make not only the stories but the ideals they embody much more a part of themselves.

The opportunity of a bed-time story hour is very great, for both Father and Mother may participate in it. The children's part in telling stories is important, too, and they should be encouraged to tell the stories they know. I have seen children six years of age hold a group of children for ten or fifteen minutes as well as an adult could, and the group was absorbed in the story from beginning to end.

III. HOW TO CARRY RELIGIOUS IDEAS AND FEELINGS INTO ACTION

A LITTLE CHILD'S RELIGION IN THE WORK-LIFE AND PLAY-LIFE

A CHILD's real world is his play world. In it he lives his own life to the fullest possible extent. There he may have full control of every situation and go as far as his imagination takes him, and fortunate is the child who is not over-stimulated with too many ready-made, mechanical toys, but, rather, is given the use of materials (cloth, wood, sand, clay, etc.) and allowed to make some of his own toys, or make adaptations of materials to meet his play needs.

The play situation is ideal when there are other children, children of different ages preferably, play space, and the things to play with, for then they meet equals, superiors, and younger children. There is the opportunity for the sharing of ideas and ideals as well as of playthings; learning to co-operate, to work out the rules of the game, in a way impossible when working and playing with older people or alone.

A wide experience with informal playgrounds for young children has convinced me of the necessity for supervision of play and for frequent suggestion and guidance. But the planning, working out, choosing, and making many decisions as to ways and means, may be safely left to the children themselves. It is wonderful to see how resourceful they become, and to see shy and unsocial children learning to adjust themselves to the group and take part in the play life.

Children are very democratic in their play and are perfectly willing to take anyone in, black or white, brown or yellow, so long as he "plays the game" with them. It is not, for many reasons, always possible for us to let our children take other children in whenever they want to. But we can always stimulate an interested and sympathetic attitude, especially toward little foreigners, the newcomers to the country. It is possible for even the youngest members of society to have a community interest and even a world interest in these days of so much travel, and when knowledge of children in all lands is so readily obtained in magazines and books.

For children there is no difference between work and play. They work hardest when they play, and play hardest when they work. Our part is to help them to preserve their joy in doing—joy in doing things worth while. For that, after all, is the spirit of religion.

FAMILY PRAYERS AND SAYING GRACE

By Mary Collins Terry

ALL over the country there is a movement to re-establish these customs which were observed by our Pilgrim Fathers whose characters and accomplishments speak for their sterling worth.

How many children of the present generation have had the unforgettable experience of "seeing Daddy pray"? It is a sorry thing that, with the omission of the children of ministers' families, there are not many. Yet there is no one thing which makes such a lasting impression and is such an influence for good on the plastic mind of a child.

It seems as if time is so limited in our average American home, business and family routine so pressing that we fail to find a suitable time to observe with our children those things which we ourselves know to be wise and best. Consider first "Saying Grace." Even in the busiest of homes, surely there is time for bowed heads and a few words of thanks to the Giver of our food, a simple prayer which can be understood even by the young members of the family. The children love it and when accustomed to the little ceremony feel something is seriously missing when it is omitted. Danny, our little son, scarcely more than a year old, will come toddling from his play as we sit down to a meal and hold up his arms to be taken. He will sit quietly in his mother's lap and look wonderingly about the table, impressed by the bowed heads and his grandfather's voice "Saying Grace."

Is not wonder said to be the first awakening of religion in a little child's heart?

Virginia, who is five and has just started to kindergarten, lost her father in a recent "flu" epidemic. The mother, though interested in her children's welfare, is too busy providing food for three hungry mouths to take time for what we might call the finer things of life. When the little girl learned the "Thank You Prayer" at Kindergarten, she came home to ask if she might not say it at their table, and now the little home is touched by something which makes the commonplace seem brighter and the daily struggle less irksome than before.

The old custom of "Family Prayers" and Bible reading has been greatly crowded out of our homes because of the unavoidable rush in which we live. But every mother and father who wish their children to become acquainted with the greatest of classics and have a foundation for a last-ing religious faith will, if they are wise, make a place for just this thing. Fascinating stories of Bible heroes read at bedtime, the Lord's Prayer repeated together, perhaps at breakfast or at some other suitable time, the talking over with Mother or Daddy the little misdemeanors or failures of the day and the asking "Our Father's" help to overcome them; all these things serve to form a sweet and unbreakable bond of sympathy between the parent and child.

SOME SIMPLE PRAYERS

A GRACE AT TABLE

Lord Jesus, be our Holy Guest,
Our morning Joy, our evening Rest;
And with our daily bread impart
Thy love and peace to every heart.

THE WAWAYANDA GRACE*

By Frank F. Gray

Morning

Gracious Giver of all good,
Thee we thank for rest and food,
Grant that all we do or say
In Thy service be this day.

Noon

Father, for this noonday meal
We would speak the praise we feel,
Health and strength we have from Thee.
Thankful help us, Lord, to be.

Night

Safety, food, and health this day
From Thy bounty blessed our way.
While we thank Thee, we request
Care continued, pardon, rest.

MORNING PRAYER

God, our Father, hear me.
Keep me safe all day,
Let me grow like Jesus,
In the narrow way.

Make me good and gentle,
Kind and loving, too,
Pleasing God in all things
That I say or do.

All that makes me happy
Comes from God above;
So I thank Thee, Father,
For Thy care and love.

MORNING PRAYER

Now the shades of night are gone;
Now the morning light is come;
Lord, may I be thine to-day;
Drive the shades of sin away.

Fill my soul with heavenly light,
Banish doubt, and clear my sight;
In thy service, Lord, to-day,
May I labor, watch, and pray.

FOR EVERY DAY

Father, we thank thee for the night,
And for the pleasant morning light;
For rest and food and loving care,
And all that makes the day so fair.

Help us to do the things we should,
To be to others kind and good;
In all we do in work or play
To grow more loving every day.

MORNING PRAYER

Father in heaven, help thy little children
To love and serve thee throughout this day.
Help us to be truthful, help us to be kindly,
That we may please thee in all we do or say.

*Used by permission of the author and of the State Committee of the New Jersey Y. M. C. A.

Dear Lord, we pray thee, keep thy little children
   From doing wrong throughout this happy day.
Hear our morning promises. Father, help us keep
   them,
   That we may please thee in all we do or say.

MORNING PRAYER

I thank thee, Lord, for quiet rest,
   And for thy care of me;
Oh, let us through this day be blest
   And kept from harm, by thee.
Oh, let me thank thee, kind thou art
   To children such as I,
Give me a gentle, loving heart;
   Be thou my friend on high.

THANKS FOR GOD'S GOODNESS

Dear Lord, we thank thee for thy care,
   And all thy mercy sends;
For food we eat, the clothes we wear,
   Our health and home and friends.

EVENING PRAYER

Glory to thee, my God, this night,
   For all the blessings of the light;
Keep me, O keep me, King of kings,
   Under thine own almighty wings.

EVENING PRAYER

Now I lay me down to sleep,
I pray thee, Lord, my soul to keep.
When in the morning light I wake,
Help me the path of love to take,
And keep the same for thy dear sake.

EVENING PRAYER

Be beside me in the light,
Close beside me all the night.
Make me gentle, kind, and true,
Do what mother bids me do,
Help and cheer me when I fret,
And forgive when I forget.

THE RELIGIOUS EDUCATION OF A CATHOLIC CHILD *

By Josephine Brownson

As the twig is bent so the tree will grow" is a saying as familiar as it is full of truth. Unless, then, we wish to rear a race of agnostics, how dare we shoulder the responsibility of neglecting to make the child's religious impressions its strongest and earliest?

I know of a boy who when five years of age could discuss an airplane with considerable intelligence, and yet his mother had not then taught him the "Our Father." She said that he was too young to understand such things. Now, as a matter of fact, small children have a natural aptitude for spiritual truths which is woefully lacking in some maturer minds.

If a child of five years is unable to speak, how anxious his parents are! Should they not be equally anxious if at that age he is unable to speak to his Heavenly Father?

EARLY OPPORTUNITIES FOR MEMORIZING

Let us see to it that religious training keeps pace with the training in other matters. Thus when we teach words, let the first be the holy names of Jesus and Mary; when we teach the child to wave and clap its hands, let us teach the Sign of the Cross; when we teach the repetition of a number of words, let us teach gradually the words of the Our Father and of the Hail Mary; when we sing lullabies, let us sing hymns to the Infant Jesus; when we show pictures of flowers and birds and call them by their names, let us show pictures of our Lord, the Blessed Virgin, St. Joseph, and the Angels, and call them by their names; when we would read Mother Goose, let us read Catholic nursery-rhymes; when we would read fairy-tales, let us read Bible stories.

I remember hearing a little boy, two and a half years old, recite at a Christmas party the whole of the rhyme, " 'Twas the Night Before Christmas." Is it too much to expect a child of the same age to be able to make the Sign of the Cross and say the Our Father and the Hail Mary?

Then let us teach the child to kneel and with

folded hands say its prayers morning and evening. It will readily assume the attitude of prayer if it has watched its mother reverently pray. It is the living lesson of the mother's example that must precede the effort to train the child. Gradually, we can add these words addressed to its guardian angel:

"Angel of God, my guardian dear,
To whom His love commits me here,
Ever this day be at my side
To light and guard, to rule and guide."

The next prayer might well be the Morning Offering. We can teach it in some such simple form as, "Dear Jesus, I give Thee everything I shall think or say or do or suffer to-day." Perhaps we can do the child no greater good than to form in it the habit of transforming its daily actions into prayers. This the Morning Offering does, and we can frequently renew it by saying aloud little aspirations which the child will readily repeat. Teach it to say in all the events of its small life such as a bruise on the head or a cut on the finger, "All for Thee, my Jesus." Then, not only for a brief moment morning and evening, will its childish thought go heavenward, but its whole life will be made radiant and kept innocent by being lived in the presence of God.

Another beautiful practice for the children to learn is the pausing a moment every time the clock strikes in order to whisper, "Agonizing Heart of Jesus, have mercy on the dying and the dead. May the souls of the faithful departed, through the mercy of God, rest in peace. Amen."

§3. THE FIRST SACRED OBSERVANCES

ALL these little practices are powerful helps for the child to lead a life of faith. Thus the lighting of a blessed candle and the frequent making of the Sign of the Cross during times of special peril teach the child to seek God's help in danger.

When the child awakes in the morning let us teach it to look at some pictures of the Infant Jesus we have placed over its bed and to say, "Good-morning, dear Jesus!" Again, at night, let its last words be, "Good-night, dear Jesus, good-night!"

In the sixth year, we can begin to teach the Apostle's Creed and the Act of Contrition. The Acts of Faith, Hope, and Love can follow.

The smallest child can wear a blessed medal, and when it is old enough to understand, we can explain how the scapular stands for the uniform of our Blessed Mother and that if one wears it

faithfully through life, she will bless and care for him as her special child.

And how proud a little child will be to have a gayly colored rosary all his own. He can hang it on his bed, carry it to church and, little by little, learn to use it. During certain seasons of the church year we can gather the children for additional prayer and reciting the rosary aloud, and thus teach them the beautiful mysteries of the life of Christ.

FOLLOW THE PATHWAY OF THE CHURCH YEAR

THE Church fills the life of the smallest child as well as the life of the greatest philosopher. What better than to have the children follow her through the various seasons of her year. Thus during Advent, we can tell them of the coming of the little King, teach them to prepare His crib by acts of self-denial, and to long for Him by frequently saying, "Come, Lord Jesus, and do not delay!" Then January is the month of the Holy Childhood. Give them a desire to imitate the obedience and truthfulness of the Infant Jesus, a Child like them.

Lent usually begins in February. We can speak of the Passion, take them to church to make the Way of the Cross, teach them to give up candy and make other small acts of self-conquest, to be kind and gentle, and to put some of their pennies in the poor-box. During Holy Week, let us show them the church draped in mourning because of grief over the death of Christ. Then the glory of the Easter, the altar decked in gold and white, the Paschal candle, which will be kept near the high altar for forty days, until the day Christ will go back to His Heavenly Father.

Nor should we forget dear St. Joseph during March, when we can teach the children to say some little prayer in his honor every day and to beg of him the grace of a happy death.

Then the beautiful month of May, when the children can gather flowers for our Blessed Mother's altar and recite together the rosary and sing a hymn in her honor.

June follows with its lesson of love for the Sacred Heart of Christ that loves us so much.

July comes with its devotion to the Precious Blood. August and September take up the wonderful miracle of Christ's public life.

October is beautiful with its devotion to the holy angels. Let us speak to the children of their Guardian Angels and teach each to look upon his angel as his strongest, best, and dearest life-long friend and companion. Let us speak of the purity and beauty of the angels and of the great care they take of us.

November is sad in its devotion to the Poor Souls in Purgatory. It will be easy to enlist the sympathy of the children and to arouse their longing to send some poor soul onward to Heaven by their prayers and little sacrifices.

SACRED SYMBOLS IN THE HOME

LET us not forget the power of music. Children quickly pick up the songs they hear, and we all know how snatches of song learned in babyhood cling to one through life. Why not have a little selection of hymns that we can sing to them?

A great stimulus to devotion is the building and care of a little altar in the home. To attach a shelf or box to the wall and drape it with cheesecloth is a simple matter. Have on the altar one or two pictures and, if possible, a statue of the Sacred Heart, or Our Lady, or of the Blessed Mother holding the divine Infant.

When flowers are in season, the children will delight in arranging them on the altar. Let them also keep a little light burning, at least on Fridays, in memory of Christ's death and on Saturdays in honor of Our Lady, and on great feast days. Have near the altar a receptacle for holy water and teach them how to go to church and get holy water when the supply gives out.

Gather the children about the altar for morning and night prayers.

At Christmas, have a miniature Bethlehem. In a corner of a room, or in an open fireplace, make rocks of coarse brown paper and sprinkle them with sparkling snow from the ten-cent store. Form a cave and place in it a manger holding the Infant Jesus, and arrange the figures of the Blessed Virgin, St. Joseph, the Shepherds, etc. Let the children save their pennies and buy their own set of figures.

TEACH REVERENCE IN GOD'S HOUSE

THE child cannot be too young to be taken to church for short visits to the Blessed Sacrament. Even if he cannot yet take notice, the blessing of Christ will be upon him. When two or three years old, we can show him where Jesus lives, speak of the sanctuary lamp, etc.

Children will learn reverence for God and holy things from the carefulness with which we teach them to make the Sign of the Cross with holy water before entering the church and to genuflect before the altar; from the reverence of our attitude in prayer; from the fact that they must not turn around or speak in church. We can give them a love for going to church by letting them visit the different shrines and there telling them a word about the saint each one honors, by letting them walk slowly along the Way of the Cross while we answer the questions they will surely propound. They will delight in the music and incense of Benediction and in watching processions through the church.

And when the child is old enough to go to Mass, his curiosity will find food for many questions. He will be impressed by the lighted candles, the altar-boys, the pouring into the chalice of the water and the wine, the vestments of the priest, and the different colors that are used, according to the feast or spirit of the Church.

And then, above all, we can tell of the great miracle that takes place upon the altar.

The child will learn reverence also (and if we do not teach him reverence, all our religious instruction is in vain) from our manner of speaking of holy things. Are not many of the remarks of children, which are repeated by their elders as marvelous examples of originality and intelligence, deplorably lacking in reverence? And is not the offhand, careless manner in which holy things have been explained to them the cause? We say they are so young that no irreverence can be meant. True, but then all unconsciously they are learning irreverence instead of reverence.

By these various means our children will grow up in an atmosphere which is as necessary for their spiritual growth as is air for their physical growth. And without ever having heard of a Catechism, their hearts will be prepared to receive the fuller and more definite knowledge of their faith which will come with riper years.

DRAMATIC PLAY AND NURSERY RHYMES

THE children will show great ingenuity, too, in dramatizing the Bible stories we read, or better still, in telling them. How they will enjoy playing David meeting the giant, Judith slaying Holofernes, Daniel discovering footprints in the ashes, the messengers bringing to Job word of his losses, etc. And they can form tableaux of Abraham about to sacrifice Isaac, and of Joseph telling Pharaoh the meaning of his dreams, etc.

A valuable asset to the nursery will be a finely illustrated book of Catholic nursery rhymes. Thus a mere baby can learn of God and of His creation and of the birth of Christ, etc., by little jingles. A single quotation will suffice:

"One cold, starry night,
  A long time ago,
From Heaven above
  To the earth below,
Came little Lord Jesus
  And laid Himself down
On straw in a manger
  In Bethlehem town.

"And Mary, His Mother
  Did kneel by His side,
And Joseph was there
  To guard and to guide;
And angels bowed low
  And wondered to see
The great God of Heaven,
  A child so like me!"

THE USE OF SACRED PICTURES IN THE HOME

NOTHING makes a stronger appeal to children than pictures. Have in the nursery pictures of our Lord, the Blessed Virgin, St. Joseph, and the Guardian Angel. Have a wall set apart for these. To place them next to profane pictures leads to irreverence.

The Brown or Perry penny-pictures are very beautiful and can be easily mounted and framed. The Birth of Christ, Jesus Blessing Little Children, a Madonna and the Crucifixion will attract. Children three years of age, looking at a crucifix, have expressed love and sympathy we ourselves could envy. It is a mistake of the present day to keep away from them all suggestion of pain and sorrow. This makes for weakness and selfishness. And as nothing can be more beautiful than a child's grief over the sufferings of Christ, so nothing can be more potent in beautifying its character. There is no danger of a normal child's becoming over-sympathetic.

The silent lesson of the crucifixion on the wall is a strong factor in the child's religious training.

These pictures can be used in various ways. The children may buy them with their own pennies and make with them valuable scrapbooks. I have found a loose-leaf cover that holds the set nicely. The pictures are clamped in, which is preferable to punching holes. If Father or Mother explains each night one of these pictures to the children, the latter will never forget the lessons so pleasantly given; neither will there be need for distinct Catechism lessons until the children are older. All they need to know the pictures can be made to tell.

Again, these pictures can be used in a radiopticon, requiring an electric bulb but no curtain, if the wall is light. The radiopticon can be used as a treat, say on the first Friday of the month. We can show the pictures we have already spoken about and call on the children to give the story. Or, at each lesson, we can keep on the screen the entire time the picture illustrating the story we are telling. Even though we use these devices for the older children, the smaller ones will gain as much as though we appealed directly to them. We all know how surprisingly little children absorb what they see and hear. I remember going to a house to prepare a grown person for Baptism. A tiny, sickly child stayed quietly in the room. Later, her mother told me how she had overheard her teaching her doll the lessons I had given.

THE RELIGIOUS EDUCATION OF A JEWISH CHILD *

By MRS. ROSE BARLOW WEINMAN

THE poet has said,
  "Trailing clouds of glory, do we come
From God, who is our home,"
and we Jews would extend the glorious line by saying, "To God, who is our home," for from the moment the babe opens his eyes he looks upon a God-permeated world, or, as one of our sages of old put it, "In the beginning, God."

The birth of a child is not only an event of great happiness, but one linked closely with religion. For this blessing prayers of gratitude are uttered, and with gifts the poor and the Synagogue are remembered. Also, as is well known, a religious ceremony of profound significance, the rite of circumcision, accompanies the bestowal of a sacred name upon the baby boy. Keenly yet with great rejoicing do the parents feel the holy trust, and the Jewish mother, like Hannah of old, would gladly dedicate her child to the service of God.

The bud unfolds, and as the little one develops in health and strength the watchful parents indulge in the thought that he will one day be a fearless fighter for God; and the mother, as she guides the first unsteady, tottering footsteps, thrills with joy, cherishing the hope that the

*How rich and delightful is the treasury of Jewish traditions and festivals, and how useful for the religious training of children, will be a surprise to many who read this paper by an unusually intelligent Jewish mother.

Heavenly Father may lead her child in the paths of righteousness for His Name's sake.

Before ever the babe can prattle he knows about God.

"See the pretty flowers! God made all the flowers, and the birds, and the trees. He made the water, the sun and the moon, the rain, the lightning and the thunder, too. God made everything," we tell him.

A young Jewish mother once related this incident to me:

"We were enjoying our daily walk along a shady path," she said, "my baby boy (not quite two years old), the nursemaid, and I, when the maid, in telling about a little girl of her acquaintance, exclaimed, 'But she does ask so many questions! Why, the other day she asked her mother who made God.' 'Nellie,' I remonstrated, somewhat startled, 'I wish you had not spoken in that way in the presence of Baby.' But Baby, perhaps in defense of his beloved nurse, or was it desire to answer the great question, piped out, 'God made herself.' To be sure we were amused and surprised, but can you doubt that I was indeed happy to know that at his tender age he had begun to realize the power of God?"

"Out of the mouths of babes come wondrous truths," I answered. "If we could but hear them, or hearing them, deal with our children in accordance with the grand simplicity of their receptive minds."

"Muvver," one baby lisped, "when you came up to Heaven how did you know to pick me out?"

Another little boy whom I knew intimately, like most children, thrived on rhyme and fairy-stories, taking great delight in hearing them told and retold, even incorporating them in his own conduct and experience.

"A big bear came in my garden and played with me to-day," he said.

"You dear little boy, are you sure?" I asked.

"Well, not to-day, but when I were a lady he did."

From the age of three until after his sixth birthday, the child's frequent use of that expression caused much wonderment, and although at times we were sorely puzzled, we never once questioned that his words, "When I were a lady," indicated certain unusual or imagined experiences.

But one day we told him how Adam and Eve were sent from the Garden of Eden, and that while an angel guarded the tree of life he showed the way that they should go.

"He," cried the child in wide-eyed wonder, "He! Oh, I thought all angels were ladies." And he hid his face in shame.

These little ones in their direct and simple way arrange a world all of their own, and view that world, to be sure, with their own eyes. To the Jewish child all the world is Jewish, and no effort is made or required to connect the God idea with that of the child's Jewish origin; for they seem to be inextricably interwoven.

"This thing happened simply of itself,
Just as the night is created when the day goes."

Like a chameleon, he takes the color of his surroundings; now he is the bird in the song, hopping, flying, singing praises to his God on high; now a fairy, or a lion, or a giant. To-day he is Noah leading the animals into the ark. Sometimes the animals are naughty and will not walk in a straight line. Or he may be Jacob sleeping in the desert on his pillow of stone. Oh, the wonderful ladder reaching from earth to Heaven with the beautiful fairy angels on it! He would like to play with them.

His mother has told him the story with a sense of loving ownership, even as it was told to her. Father also paints the heroes of Israel in glowing colors. Does he never weary of relating the battle between David and Goliath—the victory of Israel over the Philistines? Or the story of Moses as he led the children of Israel over dry land in the midst of the Red Sea?

"Jew," "Israel," "God!" These are familiar words to the Jewish child, words heightened and colored by love, pride, and a subtle sense of belonging.

God is near. He loves good little boys and girls, and Jewish boys and girls should try to be good, try to obey Father and Mother, to love Brother and Sister, to be gentle in their speech, to permit their friends to share their toys, to be kind to animals; in fact, to endeavor to please God in every way. He loves all children, for they belong to Him. All the world belongs to God.

THE JEWISH HOME IS A SHRINE

WITH such impressions promptly registering themselves, a Jewish consciousness is slowly but surely developing in the child mind, and the little one, with implicit faith in the words and acts of his beloved parents, takes much for granted. Then, too, in their religious life the members of a Jewish family act in unison, even the little one soon rejoices in the fact that he is a part of the whole.

Seated with the family at meals, he hears his father day after day utter the words, "Blessed art Thou, O Lord our God, King of the Universe, who causest the earth to yield food for all."

Words, mere words, are they for several years, yet so frequently is he wont to hear them, that they become a needful accompaniment to every meal, and as time goes on, their meaning is engraved upon his heart.

Is not this home the child's first shrine, the first altar where, with Father and Mother, he may worship? He, too, holds communion with God; for in the evening, as the mother tenderly folds him to rest with loving words and quieting thoughts, he feels a beautiful something within him and is encouraged in his desire to speak to God. This is one child's first prayer: "Dear God, I love you, and I love my Daddy and my Mamma. Good-night."

THE MOTHER TALKS WITH HER LITTLE ONES

AND now, in the daily contact with her child, through means of his duties and his play, his pets and toys, the morning strolls, the loveliness of Nature, through the beauty of favorite stories, of pictures and verses, and countless other golden opportunities, through every benign and beautiful influence which environs him, the thoughtful mother attempts to satisfy the yearning, outreaching tendency of his child nature.

She speaks to him of the goodness of God. No, we can not see God's face, but we know Him through His love and kindness. Because God is kind, mother is kind. Because mother loves her little boy she does everything in her power for his good. "I love you, Mother," the child exclaims again and again, and in her wisdom she tries to have him translate that declaration into action and conduct, for love must be meaningful. And when we tell God that we love Him, we must show our love by our deeds; we must do our very best for Him; because He cares for us and watches over us day and night.

"By slow degrees, by more and more" these thoughts are given to the child, until he is ready and eager for this simple prayer:

"I thank Thee, O God, for the blessings of this day. Thou art my Shepherd; I shall not want. Thou dost neither sleep nor slumber, and wilt protect me all the night. In peace I lay me down to sleep. Bless my home and all who are dear to me. Hear, O Israel, the Lord our God, the Lord is one. I am in Thy care, O God, when I sleep and when I wake. Amen."

THE SABBATH IN THE JEWISH HOME

EVERY pious Jewish family hails with delight the celebration of the Sabbath, and the very young children, too, are impressed by this day, if only in respect to its unlikeness to other days; for the ways of the household are changed. All activity has ceased, even the "man-servant and the maid-servant" do no work. And though peace and quiet prevail, the children are happy and expectant.

On Friday, preceding the evening meal, the Sabbath is ushered in with a religious service called the *Kiddush,* or sanctification. The ceremony is begun by the kindling of the Sabbath lights and by a fervent prayer to God that the home may be consecrated by His light, which signifies love and truth, peace and good will. The Sabbath is welcomed as a messenger of joy and praise, and while workday thoughts are put aside, a calm, serene spirit of divine love hovers over all.

In praise of the good housewife and mother, the father of the family reads from the thirty-first chapter of the Book of Proverbs that glorious tribute to the good woman "whose price is far above rubies, in whom the heart of her husband trusteth, who bringeth her bread from afar and riseth also while it is yet night, and giveth food to her household. Give her of the fruit of her hands and let her works praise her in the gates." The father now lifts the cup of wine as a symbol of joy, and renders thanks to his God for the blessings of the past week, for life and the light of love, for home and friendship, for strength to work and for the Sabbath day of rest. With these thoughts the cup of wine is passed around the table and each one in turn drinks from it. Then they partake of bread dipped in salt. The beautiful service concludes as the father lays his hand upon the head of each child in silent blessing.

At the meal good cheer abounds, each endeavoring to please the other, and all waiting and attending on the guest in their midst.

To suggest that the little child participates in these ceremonies with more than vague, unformed impressions were indeed error; for only as the words and acts and symbols touch him in his association of ideas, in his daily experience, in his environment, can they come to be a part of his thought and feeling, and in time this comes to pass—a knowledge and feeling of Judaism, which is a vital thing throughout the years. Often, indeed, we have heard men in their old age declare that from the dim past they ever see the glimmer of the Sabbath lights, and feel their father's hand in blessing upon their head.

THE JEWISH PASSOVER

NOT only is the Sabbath day thus set aside for

worship and prayer, but there are many appointed days of the year when the members of the family are united by the bonds of worship and of love, days devoted to thanksgiving and praise to God, to quiet enjoyment and to acts of charity and kindness.

Especially does the great Feast of Passover appeal to the children. It is unique. It gives full play to all the poetry and heroism of their nature. How wonderful is the unleavened bread which they eat and the thoughts it calls to their minds!

There is the little baby alone among the bulrushes! Will no one ever come to the rescue? What joy they feel when his own mother clasps him in her arms! And then to think of his life in the palace with the Egyptian princess. Was it a fairy palace? But on learning more of Egypt and her cruelty to the children of Israel, their hearts are filled with pity.

The scene changes, and Moses, their hero, is a shepherd in the land of Midian. How tenderly he carries the little lamb back to the flock. And then the strange beauty of the burning bush, out of which sounds the voice of God!

For many years the bush is a real bush and the voice a real voice, just as they should be; nor does aught of their divine power pass from them when the Jew comes to feel that the fire is a fire of holy purpose to save and to serve, and similarly that the beautiful ceremonials of the Passover are but object lessons used to tell of God's mercy and providence, of the return of Spring, the urge of new life, the birth of freedom and liberty.

As the week of the Passover approaches, the inmates of the home of the pious orthodox Jew industriously prepare for its coming. All leaven must be removed and special china and utensils for cookery brought out. Each child in the family proffers his help, with a kindness persistent though impeding.

Passover eve arrives, the evening which ushers in the feast of Unleavened Bread, ever observed as a memorial of God's deliverance of the Israelites from Egyptian bondage. This festival of Freedom is celebrated by a beautiful and impressive home ceremonial called the Seder service, one in which the child participates with real joy. The Seder forms a bond of union not only among the members of one family, but between every Jew and his brother Jew throughout the world, for do not its prayers, its songs, and its traditions tell of joys and sorrows common to all Israel.

On this night of the feast, the head of the household, or one invited to act for him, conducts the service, reading in both Hebrew and the vernacular.

The table presents an unusual appearance, for not only is it in holiday dress, with flowers, sparkling glass and silver, but upon it appear the articles peculiar to the Seder. There are pieces of unleavened bread, or *matzah*, as it is called, a roasted bone of lamb, an egg, also roasted, a dish of bitter herbs (horseradish), some parsley or watercress, wine (an unfermented concoction of raisins), and *charoseth*, a mixture of minced almonds, apples, and raisins.

"With song and praise, and with the beautiful symbols of our feast, let us renew the memories of our wonderful past, and take to heart its stirring lessons," says the father. They drink of the festive cup and sing their songs of gladness.

All are given a bit of parsley or watercress, and they partake of it saying, "Blessed art Thou, O Lord, Creator of the fruit of the earth."

The reader raises the plate of unleavened bread: "Lo, this is the Bread of Affliction, and though God's providence has freed us, may we ever be mindful of those who are not free, and endeavor to aid all who are oppressed. Let those who are hungry come and eat, those who are poor, share with us our Passover."

It was written, "And thou shalt tell thy son in that day," therefore the Seder Service includes an explanation to the children of the festival and its celebration.

THE EXPLANATION TO THE CHILDREN

"WHY IS this night different from all other nights?" asks the young child, as he views the strange objects on the table.

"This night is God's watch-night over the children of Israel. He watched over our forefathers in Egypt and delivered them from slavery. He guards us continually, and to-night we praise and thank Him for His protecting care. He was our Redeemer and Deliverer, so that we may be His messengers unto all the peoples of the earth."

"What is the meaning of the Pesach?" another child inquires, and he is told that the word signifies Passover; that God passed over and spared the House of Israel not only in dark Egypt, but again and again has He saved His people from destruction.

"And the lamb bone?" calls out another.

"Ah, the Paschal Lamb reminds us of God's command to Moses to sacrifice a lamb before the departure from Egypt. The lamb was sacred to the Egyptians, and when the Israelites obeyed the words of Moses, they struck the blow for freedom."

"What is the meaning of unleavened bread?"

"The *matzah,* or bread of affliction, is the symbol of divine help. When our ancestors were driven from Egypt and forced to depart in haste, they carried no food but the unleavened dough in their kneading troughs. They did not starve, however, for this dough dried into unleavened bread. Seven days we eat of the unleavened bread as a sign of God's loving care and of His power to save.

"The salt water, the bitter herbs, and the *charoseth*—all are tokens of the hardships endured by the Israelites before their deliverance."

"But the *charoseth* is sweet," the children say, and to their minds no hardship, until they are informed that its appearance suggests the clay and bits of straw used in the making of bricks by our forefathers when they toiled in Egypt.

"And the egg?"

"The egg speaks of life and faith in immortal life."

FUN AT PASSOVER TIME

AT THE conclusion of the first part of the service, the table is laid and a delicious meal is served, which is welcomed and keenly relished by all, for has not the appetite been whetted by waiting, and has not the wife and mother devoted much time, thought, and effort to its preparation? Psalms, poems, quaint folk-songs, and refrains intersperse the entire service. What a lilt has this old nursery rhyme:

CHAD GADYA (A KID, A KID)

"A kid, a kid, my father bought
For two pieces of money—
A kid, a kid.

"Then came the cat and ate the kid
That my father bought
For two pieces of money.
Then came the dog and bit the cat,
That ate the kid,
That my father bought,
For two pieces of money, etc.

. . . .

"Then came the Holy One, blessed be He, and
killed the Angel of Death,
That killed the butcher,
That slew the ox,
That drank the water,
That quenched the fire,
That burned the staff,
That beat the dog,
That bit the cat,

That ate the kid,
That my father bought
For two pieces of money."

"It is just like 'The House that Jack Built,' or 'The Old Woman and Her Pig,'" whisper the children, one to the other, as with friendly recognition they join in the refrain.

These young commentators are in agreement with the learned ones who designate it a Jewish nursery rhyme modeled after an old French song. Others there are who affirm it to be a legend showing how Israel (the one only kid) was oppressed by the other nations of the ancient world, and how the Holy One came to his rescue.

I shall quote in part from another folk-song which is written in riddle form. The riddle, as undoubtedly many recall, was employed as a means of entertainment at the table of Jewish families. This song shares popularity with the "Chad Gadya."

"Who knows One?
I know One—
One is the God of the World.

"Who knows Two?
I know Two—
Two are the Tables of the Covenant.
Two Tables of the Covenant—
One God of the World."

This form is continued through the number thirteen. It is considered appropriate for the Seder, as it lays stress upon the fundamental truth in Judaism, "God is One."

"Who knows Thirteen?
I know Thirteen—
There are Thirteen Attributes of God (Ex. 34:6,7)
Thirteen Attributes;
Twelve Tribes;
Eleven Stars (Joseph's Dream);
Ten Commandments;
Nine Festivals;
Eight Lights of *Hanukah;*
Seven days of the week;
Six days of Creation;
Five Books of Moses;
Four Mothers of Israel;
Three Patriarchs;
Two Tables of the Covenant—
One God of the World."

"And it Came to Pass at Midnight" is the name of a hymn recounting instances of divine deliverance from the early days of Abraham to the great deliverance in the future. The poet Heine found inspiration in this song:

"Unto God let praise be brought
For the wonders He hath wrought
(Response)   At the solemn hour of midnight.

"All the Earth was sunk in night
When God said, 'Let there be light'
(Response)   Thus the day was formed from midnight.

"To the Patriarch God revealed
The true faith so long concealed
(Response)   By the darkness of the midnight.

"But this truth was long obscured
By the slavery endured
(Response)   In the black Egyptian midnight,"
etc.

The meal concludes with a bit of pleasantry. One-half of a bit of *matzah,* which has been reserved for the *Aphikomon,* a Greek word meaning "after-meal," or dessert, has been slyly drawn away by one of the children and concealed from view, the leader all the while feigning ignorance. Finally, he notes the loss, and not until he promises a gift, however trifling, does the offender bring forth the missing cake. "A game of paying forfeits," you will say.

In this brief account of the Seder service much has been omitted, but the Jewish child is sure to cry out, "Remember Elijah!" Many years will elapse before he can understand that Elijah, the prophet, the hero of the Passover, represents the protector of the home, the lover of parents and children, the messenger of redemption; but for the present he awaits the taking of the fourth cup of wine, and the opening of the door by his brother. Yes, when he is older, perhaps, he may be allowed to rise and open the door with the hope that Elijah may come in. Should a stranger or a friend enter the room at that time. it is needless to say that his place at the table awaits him and that he is most hospitably received. Little wonder that many a poem has been inspired, many a beautiful tale told, because the door of hope, of love, of religious fervor, is opened to freedom and to justice that April night.

The Passover! It is a joyful feast, a week devoted to memories of the past, praise and thanksgiving for the present and for the future. Each day does the house resound with songs, hymns or psalms:

"O, give thanks unto the Lord, for He is good;
For His mercy endureth forever,"

or this festival-song with its stirring traditional air:

"God of might, God of right,
Thee we give all glory;
Thine all praise in these days
As in ages hoary,
When we hear, year by year,
Freedom's wondrous story."

All this the little one receives, and were an observer to discover an added sense in the Jewish child, he would find that one to be the sense of religion.

THE JEWISH HARVEST FESTIVAL

IN THE religious experience of the Jews, history and Nature unite to form the background of the great festivals. Just as the Passover developed from the commemoration of the exodus from Egypt, and the ripening of the early barley crop in the land of Canaan into a festival of freedom and of springtime, so a reminder of the years when the children of Israel dwelt in booths in the wilderness, together with gratitude for the latter harvest in the conquered land, gave rise to the Feast of Tabernacles, Feast of the Ingathering, a festival of Autumn.

Can we doubt that the little child glows with interest and pleasure when, in celebration of these events, he may spend some time each day with his dear ones in a leafy arbor or booth (*succah*), which is erected as an adjoining room to their home? In this frail structure with its partly open roof the people of the household take their meals, study, and receive their friends. Here, with song and prayer, they give thanks to God for His wondrous providence. How supremely happy the little one feels to sit in this bower of green, red, and yellow leaves, with clusters of grapes and shining apples here and there! Upon seeing the dark sky and twinkling stars through the roof he asks, "Are the holes in the top so God can hear our prayers better?"

Some day a thousand meanings for this leafy tent will come to him: his own frailty, his dependence upon God, the openness that life should spell, the open hand, the open heart, the open mind, the upward look, the reverent dismantling of the structure with a fervent desire to move on and on, to follow the "cloud by day and the fire by night." But now he needs to know only that the loving Father has blessed him with all good things, and that he in turn should be helpful and kind to others.

> "Little hands be free in giving,
> Little hearts be glad to serve,"

thus is he taught to sing in gratitude to Him "whose kindness endureth forever."

We have seen that though we are concerned with the commemoration of very significant events, their observance never fails to create a place for the little child. "Thou shalt teach them diligently unto thy children," uttered back in the dim ages, still sounds a clear, insistent note in the hearts and homes of Israel's people; so we dare to hope that the celebration of the Sabbath, the Passover, the Feast of Booths, leaves a marked effect upon the character of our children, and that *Hanukah,* a feast of "mirth and joy," holds a high place in their hearts.

THE FEAST OF LIGHTS

WHAT is the meaning of *Hanukah,* do you ask?

It is the feast of Dedication and of Light. Dedication, because it commemorates the victory of the Hasmoneans over the Syrians, and a re-dedication of the Temple at Jerusalem (165 B.C.) by Judah Maccabee, that brave warrior and loyal Jew; a feast of Light because of a tradition surrounding the conquering hero, although, like Christmas and the Brumalia of the Romans, and the Yule-tide feast of the Norse people, it had its origin in Nature as a feast of the winter solstice; as it were, a feast of the birth of light.

The elements of Nature, history, and tradition, like strands of brilliant colors, are woven into a design of surpassing beauty, and we have Hanukah, the Festival of Lights, different from the other days, as the events which it commemorates happened later than those recorded in the Bible. They are told in the Apocrypha in the first and second books of the Maccabees.

The little child knows nothing of the origin, the history, or the literature connected with this holiday; but the story, the lights, the songs and the games, these he finds a never-ending source of joy.

While the young, eager faces are upturned to hers, Mother tells the story very simply, how the Syrians (Greeks) through their cruel king, Antiochus Epiphanes, tried to force their idol worship upon the Jews. But the people of Israel, faithful to God, held true to the religion of their fathers. She tells them of the good old man, Mattathias, who, with his five brave sons, raised a small army and went out to battle against the

enemy; and that when his strength left him, he bade his sons fight on and conquer. "As for Judah Maccabee, he hath been mighty and strong even from his youth up; let him be your captain and fight the battle of the people," he said.

They put themselves in God's care, inscribing upon their banner, "Who, O Lord, is like unto Thee among the mighty?" and Judah led them and gave them courage to strike for their religion and their land. After three years of war he led them into their beloved city and their Temple at Jerusalem.

"Oh, they must have been happy," said one of the children. "What did they do then?" asked our little one.

"Of course," continues the mother, "they wished to enter the Temple and worship, to thank God for His help and protection, but to their sorrow the holy place was deserted and the altar profaned. Why, they found the gates burnt up and shrubs growing in the courts as in a forest. How sad the people were! 'They rent their clothes and wept aloud.'

"But Judah gave them hope and courage. While some of the men at his command were building a new altar others were intent upon cleansing the sanctuary. At last all was purified. The grateful people were eager to re-dedicate God's house. But where was the oil for the sacred lamp?

"Someone has said that after long searching a little boy found a tiny cruse of oil and with great joy gave it to the hero, to Judah, to the tall, strong, fine, brave, loving Judah."

"I wish I was that little boy."

"You may be, dear. When you are older you will understand.

"When the oil was poured into the lamp, it was feared that there was not enough for one day's use, but wonder of wonders! the light continued to burn for eight days. These were the days of re-dedication, and so in memory of them and of God's wondrous power to help those who trust in Him, we burn the *Hanukah* lights in our home for eight successive nights. Do you remember, children, one candle the first night, two the second night, three the third night, four the fourth night, until, on the eighth evening, eight lovely tapers are burning?

> " 'Kindle the taper like the steadfast star
> Ablaze on evening's forehead o'er the earth,
> And add each night a luster, till afar
> An eightfold splendor shines above the
> hearth.' "

"Don't forget the *Shammus,* Mother."

"What is the *Shammus?*" asks the littlest boy.

"Mother will tell you, dear. The *Shammus* is the taper which kindles all the others. It is the 'Servant of the Lights.' We say it is Israel carrying God's word to all the people in the world."

"I like the *Shammus,* Mother."

"I am happy to know that. Remember the little boy who found the cruse of oil.

"Children, are you sure that you know the old, old *Hanukah* song?"

They begin to sing:

> "Rock of Ages, let our song
> Praise Thy saving power," etc.

Then the older children talk about the *Hanukah* play to be given at the synagogue, and of the beautiful pageant of lights that will be shown, where "Light," a lovely girl, will represent the light of day, of the stars, of love, of truth and righteousness, the light of knowledge, of the home, of charity, patriotism, law, and lastly, Israel, or the light of faith.

And besides, their kind mother is preparing a splendid entertainment for them, a real *Hanu-kah* party, to which they may invite their friends She will teach them some of the old games like *trendele,* that funny little square top with a letter on each side.

Does our little one understand all that he sees and hears? We know that he does not; but we conclude that the joy, the mystery, and the poetry of the events of his religious year creep into the young heart and mind, and there slowly but surely form an armor of pride in race, a true Jewish consciousness.

Soon the parents will place their little boy in the Religious School, and the kindergartner may attempt to share that sweet fellowship which has so closely linked mother and child. Will hers be a sympathetic understanding? Will she deepen in the little one the impressions begun in the home? The mother will yield her treasure to the school, hoping that the foundation for the love of Judaism has been well laid, and that her boy may grow "from strength to strength" under the guidance of those dedicated to the sacred task.

MAKING THE BIBLE REAL TO THE CHILD*

By Rev. Theodore G. Soares

UNDERSTANDING THE BIBLE AS A CHILD'S BOOK

Of course, we understand that the Bible was written by adults for adults. It was not written for boys. It has throughout an adult religious interest. Much of it, however, belongs to a very simple stage of religious development, not far removed from that of the boy himself; and much of adult religious experience, after all, is not strikingly different from that of youth. It is on these two grounds and to the extent that they hold, that the Bible is real to the boy.

A most important consideration, however, is to recognize that we have not to do with a book but with a literature, and a literature of very many strata. Our task is to appreciate the difference between those strata, and to determine in which of them the boy can live a real life.

It does not need much discussion to determine what kind of literature the boy needs for his religious development. It must be such literature as will capture his imagination, will help him to see where greatness lies, will stir him to feel that there have been mighty movements in the world towards great achievement—movements which continue and of which he is to be a part. The material that we offer to him must touch his experience vitally. It must seem utterly real to him; it must ring true according to his sense of reality. To such the boy will respond. He needs also what will develop reverence. Before what is high, and true, and at the same time simple, he bends with respect.

THE ELEMENTAL MORAL VALUE OF THE BIBLE

What, then, is there in the Bible for the boy? It is easy, of course, to make a case against the Bible. We may say that it is a Semitic literature; its language, its figures, its background, are different from ours. It is a book of miracles. In the Bible, God is always in the marvelous.

---

*Editors' Note.—This is the first simple paper, in the editors' knowledge, in which recognition is made of the fact that some parts of the Bible are more interesting, and therefore more valuable, than others to young people. The writer not only states this fact, but tells just what those parts are, and suggests what is a sensible attitude toward the Bible for the parent to assume who would teach it to his children. The article was originally intended to apply to boys, but its statements are generally true of girls, also.

The question is asked whether the boy shall learn that God is only in the wonderful and that difficulty is to be overcome by miracle. These are the objections that are easily made against the Bible, and some of them, of course, have weight. Yet it is a marvelously human book. Much of it seems as if it might have been written yesterday. We open its pages and read of those conditions so alien sometimes to our modern interest, and then, of a sudden, we come upon tales that stir our hearts, for they speak to our elemental needs—needs that have not changed with the centuries. And these points of contact are not only for adults. Boys find them also. But boys are impatient, their highest encomium upon book or play or enterprise is, "There is something doing every minute." The material that is in the Bible for them must not be separated by material which is foreign to their interest. They must have that which has continuous interest.

ECCLESIASTICAL MATTER OF LITTLE INTEREST TO CHILDREN

LET US begin with the Old Testament. A large part of the first seventeen books of the Bible is story material. We have here the stories of the beginnings. We have the tales of the heroes as they were handed down from generation to generation. We have the old stories of the movements of the peoples from the days of the nomad to the times of national settlement. Besides these older strands of narrative, we have the stories of the kingdoms of Israel, and the stories of the later Jewish community. The first three elements in this narrative material, contained in the books of the Hexateuch, Genesis to Joshua, came down for centuries by oral tradition. We have them now in our Bible in three forms. In the latest, the form in which the stories were told by the priests, the interest is ecclesiastical. Everything in the old history is of concern to the priests, as it has to do with the origins of the ritual and priestly service.

Here is the long story of the covenant of circumcision, the elaborate details of the institution of the Passover, the extended enumeration of the ecclesiastical arrangements of David, the many chapters devoted to the preparation of the material for the temple. None of this is of interest to a boy. In a scheme of religious education, it belongs very late; it belongs to the subject of the history of religion. It cannot be made real to a boy. We shall spoil both the boy and the material if we make the endeavor. But these stories that were told later by the priests were told earlier by the prophets. In the South

Kingdom some great prophetic souls, with literary skill of extraordinary fineness, gathered up the old folk tales and told them again with moral purpose and religious feeling. In the North Kingdom a similar process was carried out.

NARRATIVES AND BIOGRAPHIES THE YOUNG FOLKS WILL ENJOY

WE HAVE to-day in the Bible the interwoven stories of these two prophetic narratives. Sometimes they are duplicates and a little confusing to a boy. Sometimes there are differences of statements difficult for him to reconcile. But when we take one of these prophetic stories or the other, or, so far as they are complementary, both of them combined, we have a rich, vivacious narrative of great men, living their simple life on a great stage, meeting their moral problems often with victory, sometimes with defeat, displaying on the whole a magnanimity that stirs the imagination and captures the admiration. A normal boy will respond in altogether healthy fashion to such great tales.

A critic of our religious educational system wrote me some years ago, when I was engaged in the preparation of a book on the heroes of Israel, suggesting that it would be well to substitute modern heroes for the bigoted old Jews. Well, Jewish bigotry came later than the time of most of the heroes, but that may pass. There is, of course, everything to be said for the study of modern heroes, but who has written epic stories with the charm and power of the prophets of Israel? It is much to be wished that we could secure modern biography as brilliantly executed as that of Joseph, of David, of Elijah. But even if we could have all our heroes pictured in such fascinating fashion, our boys would still find a unique inspiration and delight, and therefore a reality, in the stories of the great men of Israel.

INTEREST OF THE JEWISH HISTORY

THE STORIES of the Hebrew kingdoms and of the Jewish community belong to the later boyhood of the high school age. Studied at the time of historic interest and in connection with the historic studies of the day school, the significant drama that was played upon the stage of Palestine will be very real to boys. It is probable, moreover that the material of the first chapters of Genesis would better be presented at this age, when it may be studied in comparison with the cosmogonic material of the other Semitic people. The Jewish history should not stop with Nehemiah, but should extend through the interesting four centuries that have been so inappropriately styled the Four Centuries of Silence. It should especially include the brilliant story of the Maccabees.

ARE THE PROPHETS FOR YOUNG PEOPLE?

A LARGE section of the Old Testament consists of the sermons and orations of the Hebrew prophets, intensely practical, concerned with the immediate social and political condition of their day. These orators, statesmen, reformers, have left us material of the highest moral and religious significance. In the later high school age the political and social situation, which is the background of the prophecies, might be made very real to a boy, and the essential message of the prophets might be understood. But the prophecies as we have them in the Bible are not adapted to boys. They are altogether too difficult reading. Their very brilliancy and poetic beauty, their fine Oriental figures of speech, the rapid transition of sentiment, make them exceedingly difficult to follow, except by the trained literary student. If the prophets are to be made real to the boy, their stories must be retold, with a culling from the prophecies of those fine passages which are within his literary appreciation.

THE LAW AND THE RITUALS DO NOT ATTRACT CHILDREN

RETURNING to the first six books of the Bible, we find there, in addition to the stories already discussed, the great common law system of the Hebrews. That body of legislation is the ancient Semitic customs revised and lifted into larger significance by Moses, edited again by later prophets and adapted to the needs of the simple agriculturists of Palestine. With the exception of the great Decalogue and some few simple moral and charitable commandments, this material is away from the interest of the boy. It belongs in the studies of national customs and comparative jurisprudence, very much later than the age of boyhood. It is altogether an adult interest. The simple facts of the introduction and significance of the laws are all of this material that is necessary for the boy's understanding of the history.

In these same six books, and also in the books of Chronicles and Ezekiel, we have the complicated ecclesiastical and ritual system of the Hebrew temple. As already suggested regarding the priestly material in the stories, this belongs to the history of religion, a recondite subject, one for advanced students, and not at all for a boy. Just enough understanding of the temple and sacrifice and priesthood to orient him in the reading of the stories that interest him is all of this class of material that can be made real to him.

ADAPT THE PSALMS TO THE BOY'S EXPERIENCE

THE OLD Testament contains, mostly in the Book of Psalms, but also elsewhere, the songs of the temple. It is the anthology of Hebrew sacred poetry. Lyric poets have never sung sweeter than the psalmists of Israel. There is that in a boy's nature—that strain of sentiment, which he will not confess, and upon which one must not intrude —which will respond to lyric poetry when it is within his experience. The fine psalms of praise, the simple songs of faith, the hymns that breathe the great hope of good times coming—these may be made real to the boy. It is well to remember that the psalms were written during the long period of tyranny and oppression, when the "enemy" was a very real factor in the Hebrew life. He was not a personal enemy, he was the social enemy, the rich tyrant of the poor; he was the national enemy—the braggart and bully, who tortured the people of God. The cry of the oppressed people is reëchoed in the psalms. Perhaps we are not anxious to make this real to the boy. It would be better to wait until the social passion shall make him feel the clash of right and wrong, and thus appreciate the cry of vengeance of the psalmist. A prepared edition of these psalms, that will leave out the execrations, will be more real and religious for our boys.

And then there are songs that speak out of an experience of gloom and struggle that is deeper than a boy knows. It would be healthier if he did not learn those songs until the harder struggles of later years make them more significant.

Eliminating, then, the psalms unadapted to boyhood, and editing those that are within his experience, we might have a boys' song book containing half a hundred of the beautiful, rhythmic songs of Israel's greatest poets, and these should be a permanent possession in the memory of our boys.

SOME OF THE PROVERBS APPEAL STRONGLY TO THE YOUNG

THERE were three classes of teachers in Israel, the priests, the prophets and the wise men. We have already suggested that the priestly material is not adapted to boys. We have further suggested that the prophetic sermons, though difficult in their present form, may yet be made real to boys. What, then, of the teachings of the wise men? These are found in the Bible in two forms: first, practical; second, philosophical. The practical teaching of the wise men is for the most part in the Book of Proverbs. These short, polished, brilliant sayings, in which the wisdom of the shrewd Hebrew sages has come down, appeal very strongly to the practical sense of the boy. The picture of the sluggard turning over for a little more sleep while his vineyard goes to ruin, will take hold of the youthful imagination. The excuse of the laggard, who was afraid to go out lest he might meet a lion, can be made very real to the modern master of excuse-making.

But not all of the proverbs are available for boys. The poetic imagery is not always simple enough. The moral problem is not always such as they will meet. The book ought to be edited, eliminating the proverbs that are obscure or unsuitable, bringing together those of similar meaning, and arranging the whole for easy reading. A boys' Book of Proverbs that would be perhaps about half of the present collection would be an admirable text-book.

THE PHILOSOPHICAL AND APOCALYPTIC WRITINGS NEED ADAPTING

THE PHILOSOPHICAL writings of the wise men are altogether beyond the boy's experience. The problem of suffering in the Book of Job might be made real to him, but it is scarcely worth while. He had better wait for that. And the splendid poetry of the book will mean more to him when he has arrived at a more advanced literary appreciation. The problem of skepticism in the Book of Ecclesiastes is altogether foreign to the boy's need. The poetical picture of old age in the last chapter might be learned as a poem, but its connection with the argument of the book had better wait for adult years.

There remains to consider the Book of Daniel. The stories of the first chapters belong to boyhood, but what of the complex imagery of the latter part? It is quite clear that in its present form it is too difficult for the boy to read. But a simple explanation of a literature that pictures great conquering nations as savage beasts, the beautiful faith in the coming of a kingdom to be symbolized not by a beast, but by a man, might easily help to a finer understanding of a real, if simple, philosophy of history by the high school student. This means that the apocalyptic material must be retold, to become thus real.

SOME OF THE GOSPELS HAVE A LARGE PLACE IN CHILDREN'S LIVES

LET US pass to a consideration of the New Testament: We have first the synoptic gospels—the story of the words and deeds of Jesus. It is a significant fact that to many boys Jesus is not a real hero. He seems almost a negative character to them. They think of Him as one who suffers rather than as one who dares, and conquers, and achieves. They do not understand Him as a teacher. Much of His teaching is beyond their appreciation. The synoptic gospels are not easy reading for young boys. The discourse material is especially difficult. We have evidently been misled by the simple beauty of the parables and their picturesqueness of illustration into the supposition that they are really material for that age of childhood which loves illustration. This is to lose sight of the very important fact that a parable is an analogy, and an analogy is a somewhat developed form of reasoning. We ought to give to young boys the stories of Jesus as the one "who went about doing good," to use the fine expression of the boy-like Peter. For young boys, therefore, a story of Jesus made up from the three gospels, with some narrative material from the fourth, should present the great Hero, whom they would admire and love. For the high school age, the three gospels are great religious material, but the emphasis should still be on the loving service and loyalty of Jesus rather than on the teaching of sacrifice.

The fourth gospel, which to many a Christian of experience is the choicest piece of writing in the world, is not a boys' book. It is too contemplative. The long discourses, so wonderfully revelatory of Christ, are too difficult for him to understand. The Gospel of John may add its contribution to the history of Jesus for the high school boy, but its profoundly spiritual teachings had better remain for a later time. This is not to say, of course, that some of the noble and beautiful expressions will not become a part of that permanent acquisition which the boy preserves in memory.

NEW TESTAMENT HISTORY INTERESTS THOSE OF HIGH SCHOOL AGE

THE FIRST part of the Book of Acts is the story of the Church. It has often been included in the hero material because several of the apostles play an important part, but in point of fact it is not boy heroism which they accomplish. The writer of the Book of Acts used his material to show the development of the early Church, and as such it is useful to us. It will belong, then, to the later high school age, in which we have placed the historical material of the Bible.

The same thing may be said of the second half of the Book of Acts, so far as the history in which Paul plays the prominent part is concerned. But this is other than ordinary history, because the writer of the Book of Acts was a friend and companion of Paul. He was an eye-witness who could describe with extraordinary vivacity the stirring deeds that he saw. There is, therefore, a story of Paul the Hero. The tireless traveler, the conqueror of crowds, the winner of friends, the orator before tribunals, the hero of a shipwreck, may be made very real to a boy. The man Paul who fought a good fight, finished his course, kept the faith, ought to be one of the boy's heroes.

THE REST OF THE NEW TESTAMENT

THE LETTERS of Paul are not material for a boy. A representative of a publishing house, largely interested in a special system of religious education, asked me some time ago rather pathetically whether I did not think the letters of Paul could be made interesting to a boy. The form of the question is almost sufficient answer. We do not want to *make* things interesting. We want them to *be* interesting. Paul is concerned in his letters with the doctrine and disciplinary matters that belong to a very much later stage of religious interest. A boy ought to understand something about Paul as a letter-writer, something about a few of the great problems that he met; and he ought to be acquainted with a few of the splendid passages like the thirteenth chapter of First Corinthians, and the description of the Christian panoply in Ephesians. He ought to read and appreciate the letter to Philemon. But it would be better to wait until the college years to appreciate the wonderful interpretation of Christ that Paul has given us in his correspondence with the Churches.

What has been said of Paul's letters applies even more strongly to the general letters. They have not even the definite historical situation which makes it easier to understand Paul's letters. We can use a few great passages, of course, as gems of spiritual expression, but the letters as such are not real to a boy.

What has been said of the apocalyptic books in the Old Testament applies equally to the Book of Revelation. Most of it is altogether too difficult for a boy to read. But if the story of its origin and character be told and some of the great descriptions of the Roman oppressor be inserted in the narrative, and then the wonders of the New Jerusalem be shown to be words of comfort to the martyrs under persecution, the book may be exceedingly real to a boy's imagination.

MORAL DIFFICULTIES IN THE BIBLE AND HOW TO MEET THEM

THE QUESTION will arise whether we are to include in our boy's Bible the stories that are on a lower scale of morality than that on which we live. Shall we admit the narrative of Abraham's denial of his wife, of Jacob's deception of Laban, of Samuel's slaughter of Agag, of Esther's bloody revenge? Shall we include in the New Testament the stories of the cursing of the fig tree, and of the death of Ananias and Sapphira, both of which are at least difficult to explain to a boy? Probably wise discrimination ought to be used. Such stories on a lower plane of morality as lead easily to expressions of right moral judgment may be exceedingly useful. It may be a good thing for the boy to see the pettiness of the magnanimous Abraham, when he denied his relationship with his wife, and he may learn that we cannot judge well of a man by a single deed.

Narratives of deception and revenge may help us to explain the growth of moral conception, and the boy, seeing that he belongs to a later stage of ethical development, may realize his greater obligation. Those stories which create a moral difficulty, either because the requisite moral distinctions are not evident in the text, or because it imposes too great a tax upon the teacher to make the adult point of view clear to the boy, should be vigorously omitted. For example, the grounds upon which Samuel fell out with Saul cannot be made clear on the basis of our present narratives, and we would do much better to summarize the facts.

OUR OWN ATTITUDE TOWARD THE BIBLE

ABOVE all, the frankest possible attitude must be assumed. If a boy does not think a thing right he must be free to say so. The biblical authority must never be imposed upon him. The Bible can only be real to a boy if it appeals to his own moral judgment. Narratives which would confuse his judgment, although perfectly ciear to an adult, are not good religious material for him. Especially must we avoid allowing the boy to come to the conclusion that God can do things because He is God which would not be right for a man.

Another question that is fundamental concerns the miracles. Of course, they occasion difficulty. The elaborate explanations which the adult may understand are beyond the appreciation of the boy. Yet the miracles are interwoven in our biblical narratives. They supply much of the vividness and picturesqueness of those beautiful stories. We should emasculate our Bible if we should remove the miraculous. The great desideratum is again that there shall be perfect frankness. There is no necessity for a leader of boys to raise skeptical objections. Often the vivid imagination which the boy has brought over from childhood makes him revel in tales of the wonderful. A careful teacher ventured to suggest that Samson possibly did not slay quite a thousand men with the jawbone of an ass, but the class resented the limitation of their hero. "Oh, I guess he could kill a thousand," said one boy. The young mind is often in that same naïve stage in which the primitive Hebrew stories arose, and the two then come naturally together.

But there must be no strain upon the boy's credulity. He must be free to say what he thinks about any narrative. A lad came home from Sunday-school and asked his father if he had to believe a certain story. The wise father answered him: "You don't *have* to believe anything. You believe with all your might those things that you know are true, the things that appeal to your heart and make you feel that you must believe them. Then you should understand that these

beautiful old stories have been told to us by very imaginative people and have come to us from the long ago. We take them just for beautiful stories that help us to understand our duty." A wise use of the miracles of the Bible with boys may remove hereafter the possibility of that cheap skepticism which is so unfortunate a characteristic of superficial manhood.

An important question relates to the language that is to be used. Shall we use the classic form of the King James version as it is still preserved in our modern revision, or shall we translate it anew into twentieth-century English? I feel the force of the argument for the latter method, and yet I plead for the classic form. I believe in the beauty of the English style. The boy has much of the poet in his nature. Occasionally an obsolete word or an obscure expression might be changed, but I believe a boy can read this simple classic language. And it will prepare him for his larger use of the Bible in maturer life. I should hope that all this rearrangement of biblical material would only prepare for a later appreciation of the Bible as we older Christians know it and love it.

In summary, then, I believe that the Bible will become real to the boys as they feel the significance of the great lives, the great deeds, the great devotion and the great hopes which the heroes of the faith present to us; and to the older boys as they appreciate the history full of movement and meaning that has led to the formation of the Christian Church. And if we give them wisely a boys' Bible that comes within their experience, they will later come to feel the reality of that larger Bible which we elders find to be the lamp to our feet and the light to our path.

THE AIM OF RELIGIOUS EDUCATION

By George R. Dodson

EDUCATION is of two kinds, that which supplies information and trains and develops the powers of body and mind, and that which shapes admirations and nourishes ideals. The one gives power and equipment, while the other, by determining the life-purpose, decides upon the end for which they shall be used. What boys *can* do depends upon what they *know;* what they *will* do depends upon what they *admire.* It is knowledge that gives power, but it is the ideal that determines the direction of life. The aim of intellectual education is clear, accurate, and adequate ideas; that of

moral and religious education is such an appreciation of values that the best things are prized most and other things estimated at their relative worth. Neither alone is sufficient, and we need a clearer appreciation of the fact that, however important it is that children should acquire a knowledge of the objects and processes of nature and of the events of history, it is still more important that they should become reverent, impartial, and devoted seekers after truth. The aim of moral and religious education is not to acquaint young people with certain ideas and doctrines to be henceforth

"Held as an infant's hand
Holds purposeless what is placed therein."

It is rather to develop in them the love of truth and to impledge them to the spirit of progress, so that with their greater opportunities they shall go far beyond our achievements, that they may always walk in the direction of the world's progress and take their places in the front lines of the world's work. Moral education aims to inspire loyalty to ideals which shall keep the young in the path of progress when they have passed beyond our love and care. It strives to bias them in the direction of the true, the noble, and the good, and to save them from vulgarity by developing in them good habits, high tastes, and a love of the best.

EDUCATION THROUGH ADMIRATION

AND THIS moral education becomes religious when young people are made to feel that loyalty to the beautiful ideals of a noble life, to the best self, is loyalty to God, to the divine life which wells up within our consciousness, when they are taught to realize that their native love of the true, the beautiful, and the good, and their sense that they are made for a life guided by these ideals, is simply the impulse of growth become conscious. To be religious means to appreciate the significance of moral aspiration, to understand that our striving after perfection is the presence in us of the power which has lifted us above the animal realm and made us to be men, and which is now urging us to further heights. It is simply to conceive of our own life in the highest way; to know in our hearts that the divine is only another name for the ideally, perfectly human. The religious life, therefore, far from being something unnatural, is our natural life in its higher ranges, in the development and exercise of its noblest and finest powers. And irreligion, in this view, means arrested development, incompleteness, a falling short of our full humanity.

These conceptions should guide the educational work of thoughtful fathers and mothers. They realize that the possession of health, wealth, and intelligence is by no means sufficient to insure success and happiness. Countless young people who have these things make shipwreck of their careers because they admire the wrong things, because they cherish a false conception of life, because they are without a noble purpose and a high ideal. Now, to nourish the ideals which ennoble human lives, which are indispensable to real happiness and success, is precisely the function of the Sunday school and Church. They cannot do this work alone; but, if properly supported and adequately conducted, they can greatly assist the home, which must always remain the main source of all that is best and noblest, finest, sweetest, and most ideal in this world.

"CHARACTER IS CAUGHT, NOT TAUGHT"

As TO methods of instruction, it is generally well understood that ideals spread by contagion from life to life, and not by talking about them or by moralizing. The main thing is the attitude and spirit of the teacher. If the one who instructs boys is filled with the spirit of good will, of love, of truth, of admiration for the beautiful and noble, these high enthusiasms will pass over into the young lives, whatever be the content of the lesson. If the teacher is without them, he may convey knowledge of facts, but he cannot teach religion. For religion, which is a spirit of reverence, of trust, of hope, and love, is "catching" and is never transmitted in any other way.

There are no facts the mere knowledge of which develops that devotion to high purposes and ideal aims which is called here religion. Young people might conceivably know as much about the Bible and about Christian doctrines and history as a whole divinity faculty, and not necessarily be morally better for such encyclopedic knowledge. Religion is not a matter of knowledge of fact; it is a question of attitude, of the individual's sense of values, of the ideals that give direction to his life.

On the other hand, just as knowledge without ideals is insufficient, so noble purposes need illumination. They are likely to succeed best in living the good life who have rational conceptions of what the good life is, whose ideals of morality, of the Bible and the Church, have been purified from superstition. In a good Sunday school, therefore, instruction is given on all these subjects. The chief reason for teaching the Bible is that it is not only a good medium of religious instruction, in the sense that in dealing with it the teacher's love of truth and admiration for heroic and beautiful lives may be expressed as well as in treating any other subject, but also that it has played so great a part in the life of civilized peoples that it cannot be ignored, and it is not being adequately taught elsewhere. For boys either to be ignorant of this great literature, to scoff at it, to make an idol of it, or to regard it in a mystical or superstitious way, is a misfortune.

APPEAL TO THE YOUTH'S REASON

THE AIM should be to give them a rational notion

of it as the literary expression of the religious development of the Hebrew people through more than a thousand years. The older classes, especially, should become familiar with the main outlines of the growth of the great religious ideas of our race. They may learn to trace the development of moral ideas and of the idea of God from the time of the Book of Judges, when He was regarded as a tribal or national deity with a local habitation and a name, up through more civilized times when the prophets taught their people to think of Him as the God of righteousness, to the culmination in Jesus' thought of God as Good Will, whose service consists in purity of heart, in hunger and thirst after righteousness, in struggle toward the ideals of perfection, and in human helpfulness and love.

Studying this ancient literature as an evolution, the children learn that the literary deposit of each age necessarily reflects the stage of moral development which that age has reached. And, while they appreciate the fact that they must reserve their admiration for the purified ideals of truth and goodness which are the fruit of the whole past life of our race, they yet have a sympathetic appreciation of the earlier stages of religious progress and a sense of fellowship with the upward-lookers of all ages.

An effort should also be made to show the advance that has been taking place since the New Testament was closed, the growth in tolerance, charity, and the sense of fellowship and kinship, and to make clear the historical significance of the ideals for which the Church ventures to stand, and of its attempt to combine the moral and religious life of aspiration with perfect intellectual freedom. And then, having taught the best the world now knows, we point to the future, assuring the children that our present ideas will be corrected, expanded, and supplemented as knowledge grows from more to more.

Besides the Bible, there is much other noble literature which may be made to serve the same purpose. "Father," said a little boy, "when I read that story, my cheeks just burned." The story was one of heroism, of splendid courage, and unselfishness. And the father was glad, because he knew that there is a deep law of our nature in virtue of which we tend to be transformed into the likeness of that which we admire. Next to inspiring teachers and companions, the best way to bring out and make dominant the best in a child is to supply him with literature which sets forth in all its beauty and attractiveness the highest human ideals. In this way the young mind is enabled to live imaginatively in the presence of the best.

TEACH RELIGION AS FULLNESS OF LIFE

FURTHERMORE, one main purpose of modern educational work is to correct the traditional ideas of morality and the good life. The notion lingers that religion summons men to self-suppression, to asceticism, and an interest in the unworldly and unreal. Its call is, therefore, unwelcome, since our deepest craving is for self-expression, for greater fullness of life. Now, it should be our endeavor to foster a more rational conception, to make it perfectly clear that the most complete self-expression is precisely the aim of all education, whether intellectual, moral, or religious. In this view the moral life is simply the organized life, the life in which our native impulses are not denied their rights, but in which they are ordered, the highest ideals in control at the top, and all other tendencies active in their proper places, including the fundamental animal needs at the bottom. The ideal is that of a graded life in which all natural functions occupy in the scale the position their relative importance demands. Discipline does not, therefore, mean asceticism or a narrow life, but rather escape from inner disorder, from the riot of insubordinate impulse. Out of the chaos of instincts, tendencies, and needs with which life begins, our constructive moral task is to build a personality, to organize the passional forces of human nature, to create an ordered inner life, which Plato calls "the city within."

We should do our utmost to make our young people understand that real goodness is just the most complete living, and that the bad man is not bad because he is strong, but because he is not large enough and has not insight enough to see the precious things that are injured by his willful actions. What is called selfishness is really a lack, a failure to appreciate the situation, to become social and human, and to live the life of the race. It has been truly said that "The egotist is not more than a man, but less than a man." So, too, the unselfishness to which we call our young people is really the result of an expanded self, of a life that is not blind to all but a few interests. We urge upon them the conception that the right is at bottom the rational, is that which, all things considered and all interests regarded, is the wisest and best thing to do, is that which, when we know our own hearts and when our whole nature expresses itself, we ourselves most want to do.

Such, then, should be the aim of moral and religious education—to teach rational ideas of the Bible, and of the nature of human nature, to make it clear that the right is not the arbitrary, but the rational, and that goodness is simply another name for the amplest expression of human life, and above all to lead our young people to reverence and trust, to hope, to love and service, to the attitude that gives to our human existence dignity, beauty and joy, serenity and peace.

RELIGIOUS TRAINING OF OLDER CHILDREN

By Frank H. Cheley

It is probably best, for our purposes, that we conveniently divide a youth's religious training activity into the following main groups:

Religious Instruction
Worship
Church Responsibility
Service to Others
An Appreciation of the Beautiful

Let us discuss each of these briefly.

RELIGIOUS INSTRUCTION*

"It is the duty of the church, in conjunction with the home, to provide food for intelligent religious thinking and to guide the minds of its boys in their religious growth and development. The aim of such instruction, in both the home and the church, should be to lead them to assume a filial and reverent attitude toward God and His world, and to live in unselfish relations of love and helpfulness among their fellowmen. To this end the home and the church should make children thoroughly familiar with the revelation of God as found in the Bible and in nature, acquaint them with the main facts in the history of the early church and of the great mission enterprise, helping them to appreciate religious customs, religious needs of other people, and inform them concerning the history and distinctive characteristics of their own denomination as well as concerning the social and missionary enterprises in which it is now engaged. Such a course of study, properly assembled and arranged in appropriate sequence, and taught by trained teachers in the church in close co-operation with the parents, should be the program of religious instruction of every growing youth.

"This is the ideal toward which the Sunday school at large is pushing, and it merits the genuine help and enthusiasm of every parent.

WORSHIP*

"It is natural for religious feeling to express itself in worship. The church and the home, however, should train boys to worship spontaneously and intelligently. To do this, boys need to become acquainted with the forms and language of worship, both private and public; but these forms which are employed by the home and church in the training of boys should be suited to the experience of the worshiper. Boys, for example, require very simple forms, while adults may properly make use of those which are more complex. Moreover, the material of worship may be so related to the material of instruction as to serve as a medium for expressing the feelings and enthusiasm aroused by the plan of religious instruction.

"Boys, generally speaking, need tactful guidance and comradeship in worship. Worship can easily be made the most powerful of all personal helps to the boy in his fight for character. The habit of drawing very near to a personal God in a reverential and worshipful attitude adds tremendously to a boy's moral reserve and is a factor that should be carefully considered by the father."

CHURCH RESPONSIBILITY

Young people invariably get out of things just about what they put into them, whether in the realm of play, study, or work. So it is with religious growth and development. One must put his best in, in the way of little responsibilities, if he is to take away anything of permanent value. Teach the child to understand and respond to reasonable church demands. A parent can himself set a working example in this particular that will prove worth much advice.

There is a vast variety of worthwhile, direct, and indirect church responsibility in which young people may be profitably interested. Missions are the result of the church. Organized charity is the result of the church. Christian colleges are the result of the church. Every one of these great tasks needs a constantly increasing number of men to share its responsibilities and burdens. The work of all such agencies could be tremendously augmented if a whole generation of young people were to be deliberately trained for these jobs.

*Based on "A Program of Religious Instruction and Training in the Local Church"; copyrighted, Pilgrim Press. and used by special permission.

SERVICE TO OTHERS*

THE ULTIMATE aim of all religious training is to reach the will and lead it to express itself in suitable action—through exercise the will grows strong. In order that youths may grow up to be efficient as well as intelligently religious beings, their wills need to be trained, through practice, to the point of vigorous action. To provide opportunity for moral practice there should be in any program of training a definite place given to definite service to others, suited, of course, to the varying powers of the growing life and including not only such simple duties as pertain to the home and to the immediate neighborhood, but more complex forms of community and social service, as well as participation in the foreign mission enterprise.

Daniel Webster once said that the most important thought he ever conceived was his sense of responsibility. In the American family, with its steam heat, regular water supply, with the milk brought to its very door, it would seem that life is sometimes made too easy for boys, and they are apt to take it for granted that the world was made chiefly for them.

In so far as it is practical or possible, these acts of service should be related to the scheme of religious instruction in order that the gist of such lessons may habitually find expression in conduct.

It should be constantly remembered by the parent that a considerable per cent. of the permanent value of the whole scheme of religious instruction will depend on how largely these service elements find practical channels for expression. Religious impression, stifled and confined, often ferments into strange doubts and disbeliefs. Let the youth "work out" his salvation.

APPRECIATION OF THE BEAUTIFUL

A REAL appreciation of the beautiful things in the world, whether it be the song of a bird, a mountain sunset, a budding flower, a beautiful painting, or the lines of a skyscraper, should be a part of every child's education. The beauty in the world is one of God's ways of expressing Himself to men so that they can catch a glimpse of His real self. We live in a materialistic age when most things are valued with a money value, and it is so easy to completely leave out of our training everything that cannot be "cashed." Henry F. Cope said:

"We must not allow our mad rush for things convenient to blind us to the greater importance of things beautiful, lovely, character-determining. Life is larger than making a living. To love some things of beauty is better than to possess all things. Pity the children born into a world of things; all their lives trained to think in terms of making a few cents or a million dollars; robbed of joy, play, imagination, and any hope beyond the slavery of the money-mill."

Nature study and music and poetry, working with flowers, visiting wonderful scenery, attracting the wild birds, and all such activity can easily be made to help develop a real appreciation of the lovely things about us. Some have objected that such training inclines toward the effeminate, but such a conception is a great error, for our greatest men through all time, including Christ Himself, have given a large place in their lives to the beautiful aspects of everything.

"To appreciate the splendor of the autumnal foliage attests the possession of artistic sense as much as does admiration of a cathedral or a sculptured masterpiece. There is beauty everywhere, in such familiar things as field and forest and orchard, as well as in art galleries, whose walls are adorned with masterpieces. It has been said that 'beauty exists in the eye of the beholder,' but it must also exist in the soul; therefore, cultivate deep in the heart of every boy a sensitiveness to color, sound, and line that is inspiring and beautiful."

"The study of the beautiful in nature and in art will help to lift a boy above petty cares and disappointments."

"A boy was born 'mid little things,
　　Between a little world and sky—
And dreamed not of the cosmic rings
　　Round which the circling planets fly.

"He lived in little works and thoughts,
　　Where little ventures grow and plod,
And paced and plowed his little plots,
　　And prayed unto his little God.

"But as the mighty system grew,
　　His faith grew faint with many scars;
The Cosmos widened in his view,
　　But God was lost among His stars.

"Another boy in lowly days,
　　As he, to little things was born,
But gathered lore in woodland ways,
　　And from the glory of the morn.

*Based on "A Program of Religious Instruction and Training in the Local Church"; copyrighted, Pilgrim Press, and used by special permission.

"As wider skies broke on his view,
　　God greatened in his growing mind;
Each year he dreamed his God anew,
　　And left his older God behind.

"He saw the boundless scheme dilate,
　　In star and blossom, sky and clod;
And, as the universe grew great,
　　He dreamed for it a greater God."

SUNDAY IN THE HOME

THE problem of Sunday observance is an important, yet a difficult, one in the lives of many growing children. It is important because we recognize Sunday as our great day of privilege, the day for joy, recreation, and compensation. The difficulty is to make it such to lively youngsters without causing it to cease to be such to their parents and to the neighborhood. In general, we shall be more successful if we emphasize the privileges and joy of the Sabbath rather than deal with it negatively. It is a day of freedom rather than a day for repression. There are perhaps three elements in a good Sabbath for children—change, rest, and uplift.

One of the most sensible ways to make a Sunday change is in the way of food. Even the saints are described in the New Testament as sitting at a table in Paradise. A change of play is a happy resource on Sunday. The recognition of the presence of children in the Hebrew family is not more beautifully seen than in the Old Testament laws, the tenor of which is that man must not work but may play on the Sabbath. In order to give particular relish to the things provided for Sunday we should reserve them for this one day of the week. If there is anything new in the home let it make its first appearance on Sunday: the new phonograph record, the new dress, the new piece of music the daughter has memorized, the new joke the son has heard, a fresh blossom on some household plant, the just-completed handiwork. Another agreeable Sunday change is for the family to do things together. In our modern busy households mealtime is the longest consecutive period when the whole family is together, except on Sunday. One, therefore, feels like recommending for the Sabbath certain tasks which can be wrought out by Father and the children around the fireplace.

Parents are probably in more need of rest on Sunday than are their children, yet children, too, grow weary, especially after Saturday play. The only point is that they take their rest in a different fashion from their elders. Rest for the youngster does not consist exclusively in lying down. What rests a child is not the attempt to stop the machinery of life but the turning of the vital force into new channels. Nobody seems to have much to say about what boys can do on

Sunday. Their interest in Bible puzzles is apt to wane after a time, and any use of the day which keeps Mother busy in furnishing entertainment is as bad for the boy as it is for the mother. One good plan, especially for winter time, is to let the boys "fix up" their rooms on Sunday. I say "fix up" rather than "clean up" for obvious reasons. This is a good time also for collections and for quiet hospitality in the children's rooms. It will not tire the boys and it will rest their mothers if they form the regular habit of preparing and serving the Sunday evening meal.

As to the problem of uplift on Sunday for boys, we get perhaps the best definition of the religious purpose of the day from that line of Burns': "They tune their hearts, by far the noblest aim." But how can we tune the hearts of boys to better things on Sundays? The first question that arises is that of Sunday church-going. Sunday school is a poor substitute for church service. In the church of the modern spirit the church service is not in such contrast with nature that church-going seems to the children like imprisonment. The service is dramatic and is enlivened by the singing of children's choirs and by a sermon or story to the young people. Children of the age which we are discussing in this chapter seldom rebel against this habit if it is established early.

The best method of keeping Sunday on a high level is that of companionship with parents. In the household where Sunday is regarded primarily as a clan day, a household day, and is so observed from early childhood, with the familiar and resourceful co-operation of all, the young people later are less likely to show disloyalty to their clan either by deserting them or putting them to shame on Sunday. Sunday is certainly Father's Day. It is the day when a generous-spirited father recognizes his privilege in giving his wife a chance for some rest and solitude and in which he steps forward and learns to know his children. The Sunday afternoon walk with Father might almost be regarded as an American institution. In many families there is a club, of which Father or Mother is the president, which meets every Sunday afternoon, perhaps in the attic where "Sunday best" toys and books are laid away for the purpose, or around the piano, where an entertainment is furnished to which each contributes at least one item.

The best opportunity for creating a religious atmosphere in the home on Sunday is that which comes through service to others. If Sunday afternoon is given to a walk in which a visit is made on a sick or lonely friend, it certainly furnishes more wholesome inspiration than does even the formal religious exercises, and any day so spent is more pleasing to the God who loves mercy and not sacrifice.

"Then," says Dr. Hodges, "if the day close with singing of hymns and the benediction of quiet music, it ends well."

HOW TO KEEP THE POISON OF RACIAL AND RELIGIOUS PREJUDICE FROM OUR CHILDREN

By Corinna Marsh

WHEREVER else certain children may later learn about racial or religious prejudice— on the playgrounds, in the schools, in some churches, or in certain communities—the fact remains that the *home* is where it is primarily either fostered or combatted.

If we truly want our children to grow up to be decent, honorable, democratic citizens, not only saying that they believe in the brotherhood of man but actually living that belief, we must look inward at ourselves. We must be sure first that we genuinely *want* our children to be free of prejudice, and second that we are genuinely free of it ourselves.

Unless we ourselves are truly convinced in our minds and our hearts that we are all equal in the sight of God, we cannot hope that our children will not reflect our attitudes. Whatever we may teach them, however sternly we may tell them how to behave in public, they are bound to betray what we ourselves really feel, for, as it has now amply been demonstrated, our prejudices begin to tell on children from the time they are about seven months old. It isn't only that they absorb what we *say* on the subect; they catch meanings in our very tone of voice, the expression on our faces—in short, they absorb our attitudes.

We do not always realize what our own attitudes are, and to hold prejudices of which we are ourselves unaware is unfortunate indeed. Some parents will admit, with varying degrees of reluctance, that they are prejudiced "only" against certain foreigners, colors, religions or creeds. Some—and let us hope their numbers are decreasing—will actually be proud of the fact that they feel themselves superior to some group or hostile to another.

They rationalize their attitude through assumptions of their own racial or religious superiority, not realizing that such assumptions may sometimes indicate a hidden sense of *insecurity*, rather than security, in themselves.

The really big person, the person who is at peace with himself and with his God, has no need to feel superior or—inferior either. Intolerance bespeaks not only insecurity but poverty and smallness of spirit. Tolerance and love, on the other hand, can do such beneficent things to the soul that were we all to practice them habitually and sincerely, we would soon find ourselves blessedly free of the need to feel prejudiced.

Getting down to the practical side of the matter, let us frankly examine our own attitudes.

It is, perhaps, inherent in all of us instinctively to dread what we do not understand. People who seem "different" from ourselves may be, we think, somehow dangerous to us. We try to avoid close contact with such people. They seem, in some vague way, to be a threat to us. However pleasantly we may behave toward them when we meet them, we are not at our best with them— and neither are they with us. Feelings of hostility or dislike or distrust sometimes stem from fear, sometimes from envy, and both these qualities make people behave in a number of unpleasant ways.

What, in such cases, are we afraid of? What do we envy? These are questions for each of us to ask ourselves. If we answer them honestly, we are very likely to reveal "reasons" of which we would have to be ashamed. Of course it is perfectly proper to have individual preferences for certain people on grounds of personality, community of interests, congeniality, etc. But if we either choose or reject people solely on the grounds of their race or religion, we are holding attitudes which bode ill for our children and for the true democracy we profess to believe in.

All you have to do is to find yourself in a hospital ward or on a battlefield or in any common danger with your fellowmen and all your petty prejudices will melt away like ice in July.

Emotional experiences shared, whether they be a common danger, a common illness, the presence of death or birth or any of the other great experiences common to all mankind, immediately dissolve prejudices of one group for another and show them up as the artificial, foolish, falsely self-glorifying feelings they are.

The next step is to embark on a positive attitude of "live and let live," of tolerance for others' differences, of respect for their good qualities, and of a wholesome realization that we are all God's children. In the last analysis, we all have the fundamentals of life in common—black and white, Christian and Jew, Oriental and Occidental, Catholic and Protestant, rich and poor. It is only in the nonessentials—the accidents of our birth and and our "conditioning" in life—that we differ. In the great essentials we are pitifully—or perhaps gloriously—alike.

Let us realize this, then, not only with our minds but in our lives. Let us not reveal false attitudes in our speech. Let us not put accents of distaste on such words as "foreigner," "Jew," "Catholic, "Protestant," "Negro," or any other word used in a belittling sense indicating a kind of person we may dislike for inhuman or irrational reasons. Let us not say, "He's *only* a this or that," or "They're all alike" or any such phrases of contempt. And let us refrain from uttering them not only because it is ill-mannered and wrong, not only because it is undemocratic and unjust, not only because we don't approve of teaching our children such attitudes, but because they are essentially *untrue*—untrue in fact and mean in spirit.

If we ourselves truly believe in the brotherhood of man, if our children's *home* environment is one of true tolerance, we need have little fear of the prejudices they may encounter outside the home. Outside influences will not affect a child's true feelings, for those will have been formed where all these essential attitudes are formed—in his own home, by his own people.

"He prayeth best who loveth best
All things both great and small,
For the dear God who loveth us
He made and loveth all."
        —Samuel Taylor Coleridge

ADOLESCENCE

Drawing by Sally Michel for *U. S. Children's Bureau*

A SPECIAL SECTION DEVOTED TO THE PROBLEMS OF ADOLESCENCE

(Introduction by the Editors of THE BOOKSHELF)

ADOLESCENCE, coming as it does between childhood and adulthood, presents many special problems which are often startling to parents as well as to the adolescents themselves.

It is a difficult period for all concerned. It is difficult for parents because they are required to give up the reins of control and management at just the time when their children, floundering to find themselves, seem most in need of control. It is difficult for the adolescents because they are struggling to free themselves from a dependency which they still feel on occasion and at the same time trying to attain an independence for which they are not entirely equipped.

It is not easy for a parent to refrain from warning a child against falling into pitfalls, especially pitfalls of his own making. But adolescence is the time when a child must learn largely by his own mistakes and grow up by his own efforts.

This is not to say that parents should step out of the picture entirely when their children reach adolescence. On the contrary. They must be more than ever ready with understanding, sympathy, and moral support. But even these qualities must be tendered, in general, only when they are openly or tacitly requested.

To have one's children suddenly blow hot one minute and cold the next, to find them alternately sulky and defiant, ecstatic and desperate, and full of vague moods and touchiness all the time is indeed a problem. It requires wisdom, understanding, infinite patience, and a sense of humor. (Do not, however, expect your adolescent to share your views of what is and what is not funny!)

Since adolescence presents many new and special problems for parents, we feel that many readers of this Manual will welcome a section devoted exclusively to these problems. Toward this end we have reprinted here, in the pages which follow, a large part of a publication of the U. S. Children's Bureau, GUIDING THE ADOLESCENT.

This excellent publication, recently brought completely up to date so as to include the best present-day thought on the problems of adolescence, is, in our opinion, the most practical and helpful discussion of the subject available in compact and easily understandable form. We feel that it is an exceedingly useful addition to our Manual, not only for parents of children who are already adolescent but also, on the theory that it is always well to be intelligently prepared for what lies ahead, for parents of pre-adolescents.

It is earnestly hoped that the articles which follow will help parents better to understand their adolescent boys and girls and more intelligently to guide them to healthy-minded, independent adulthood.

ADOLESCENCE *

WHAT IS ADOLESCENCE?

ADOLESCENCE is the period of growing up that comes between childhood and adulthood. It may be thought of either as the actual growing-up process or as the time during which this process takes place. In either case it is regarded as covering the years from 12 to 20, or the "teen" age. . . .

It is necessary for the child of today to become not only physiologically mature but also intellectually, emotionally, and socially mature ; and, as these various forms of growing up may not all take place at the same time, adolescence stretches out over an increasingly longer period. A girl who reaches puberty at the age of 12 or 13 years may find herself at a loss for a time because her intimate associates are still immature, while she is experiencing feelings that make her seek wider social contacts; or a boy, growing up with adults and spending much of his time in reading and adult conversation, may reach 16 with an intellectual maturity far beyond that of the average adult, while physically and emotionally he is still immature. . . .

PHYSICAL GROWTH AND DEVELOPMENT

General Physical Growth

A SUDDEN and perhaps surprising increase in height and weight, and in the size of arms, legs, hands, feet, and any other part of the anatomy is typical at the onset of adolescence. Within 1 year the child may gain 25 or 30 pounds in weight and 4 or 5 inches in height. This period of rapid growth usually occurs anywhere between the ages of 8 and 14 in girls and between 11 and 16 in boys. On the average 12-year-old girls are going through their most rapid period of growth, while for boys the year between 14 and 15 will frequently be the one in which the greatest spurt in height takes place.

This sudden increase, however, rarely changes the nature of the child's physique. In other words, both the short child and the tall child grow noticeably during adolescence, the short child growing into a short adult, and the tall child into a tall adult. A short child may outstrip a taller one for awhile, if the latter happens to be a late-maturing individual. If puberty takes place early, the full growth is also likely to be reached early.

There are, of course, exceptions; a child who has had long and serious illness interfering with normal growth before adolescence may, on recovery, suddenly make up for this during adolescence; and a child suffering from a glandular disturbance may have an abnormal rate of growth. For the average child, however, nothing but continuous growth should be expected.

Girls grow much more slowly after 14 years and usually stop growing entirely before they are 20. Boys may continue to grow slightly until they are 22 or even 23 years of age, but their rate of growth is slower after the fifteenth or the sixteenth year. Strength also increases rapidly from the seventh year on, and more rapidly during the early teens.

Maturing of the Reproductive System

The most outstanding physiological development during adolescence is the maturing of the

* From *Guiding the Adolescent*, U. S. Children's Bureau Publication.

reproductive organs. When these organs become capable of functioning as in the adult—when the ovaries in the girl begin to release the egg cells, or ova, essential to child-bearing and the testicles in the boy begin to release the sperm cells essential to fertilization—puberty has been reached.

It is not easy to know just when the reproductive organs begin to function. A girl is said to be "mature" when she has had her first menstrual flow, or "monthly period." Although there is no similar process in the boy, the discharge of semen during sleep, known as a "nocturnal emission," is often considered evidence that he is approaching maturity. It may be some time, however, before the maturing of egg cells in the case of the girl and of spermatozoa in the case of the boy, make reproduction possible.

The age at which these signs of maturity occur varies considerably. In this country puberty is likely to occur between the ages of 12 and 15 years in girls and a year or two later in boys. But race, climate, living conditions and the child's own physical condition all play a part in the maturing process and make even further variations in age possible.

Accompanying and preceding puberty itself, noticeable physical changes take place in the child. There is a growth of hair in the armpits and pubic regions, and further development of the genitals; the voice becomes fuller and, in the boy, is likely to "break" as it changes from a childish to a more masculine pitch. As the girl's breasts develop and her hips broaden, her body begins to appear womanly, while the boy, with his broadening shoulders and the growth of hair on his face, begins to take on a more manly aspect.

Physical Hygiene

With all these changes taking place in the child's body, some thought must be given to his physical hygiene. Rapid growth is likely to cause either a tremendous increase in the child's appetite, or, particularly in the girl, a tendency to finickiness with loss of appetite at some times and strong, special cravings—as, for example, for particularly sweet or sour dishes—at other times. Attention must therefore be given not only to the child's diet but also to his eating habits. Sudden increase in the rate of growth is likely to cause fatigue, making long hours of sleep essential. Rapid growth of the larger muscles, gain in strength, and the possible awakening of a disturbing sex-consciousness make out-of-door exercise highly desirable. As all the increased body activi-

ties are likely to increase the body wastes, good habits of elimination, including freedom from constipation without the use of drugs, and a healthy, active skin condition are of primary importance.

In other words, the rules for the adolescent are much the same as those for the younger child. Parents scarcely need to be reminded that an abundance of milk, wholegrain bread and cereals, and fresh fruits and vegetables are essential; that a diet too rich in pastries, sweets, and other carbohydrates is undesirable; and that tea ond coffee are unsuitable. They know from experience that regular meals and a minimum of eating between meals keep the small child's digestive system in good order; and that plenty of out-of-door play, regular toilet habits, and a clean body are essential to keeping him comfortable, healthy, and cheerful. By the time adolescence is reached, they should be able to depend on their boys and girls to follow a hygienic routine with little assistance.

Certain modifications may have to be introduced; e.g., increase in the amounts of food, gradual decrease in the hours of sleep, changes in the type of out-of-door activity, and perhaps greater conscientiousness about internal and external body cleanliness. But there are no special rules for the hygiene of the adolescent; puberty is, after all, but the continuation of a development which began before birth and for which the normal human being is as well equipped as he is for any other natural physical change. The parent who has helped his child establish good habits of eating, sleeping, elimination, cleanliness, posture and exercise in early childhood needs only to impress upon the adolescent the importance of continuing to observe the fundamental principles of physical hygiene in order to maintain a healthy and efficient body during this or any other period of his life.

The old attitude that the menstruating girl was "sick" or "unwell," that she could not bathe, that she must never get wet feet, that she must not eat certain foods, and that all her activities should be modified, is scorned by the modern girl who goes to coeducational schools and lets nothing interfere with the interests and activities she shares with boys; and it is necessarily scorned by the girl who enters industry or business and is obliged to ignore all minor ills and discomforts. Physical build, the position and stage of development of the reproductive organs, the functioning of the glands of internal secretion, and the general physical condition of individual girls vary so greatly that although one girl may safely indulge in sea bathing during her menstrual period, another may be obliged to cut down her activity during menstruation. Although the effects of menstruation on physical and mental activities have been studied by numerous investigators, these studies have usually been made on women and girls in whom the function was already well established; their findings would not necessarily apply, therefore, to the maturing girl who is not yet fully grown and whose periods are often still somewhat irregular.

For these reasons parents can be advised only in a general way, that they themselves regard menstruation as a normal process, neither looking upon the girl as "sick" nor letting her regard herself so. They may encourage her to continue her usual activities in the usual manner, warning, however, against overexertion and undue exposure. If she seems to be experiencing unusual discomfort or pain, they should refer her to a physician both for advice on hygiene in the particular case and for correction of the cause of the difficulty if possible.

Problems Incidental to Physical Growth and Development

Much of the behavior which parents consider unusual, disturbing, irritating, or alarming is actually but a normal reaction to the process of physical development and the general business of growing up. One of the trying difficulties for both parents and child may be the self-consciousness that comes to a child who has his attention constantly called to his rapid growth. He may become diffident and sensitive, developing an awkwardness that is the result of a feeling of social ineptness rather than of growth changes in themselves. So, too, the self-consciousness and unhappiness resulting from the poor complexion with which many adolescents are afflicted may lead to such lack of self-confidence that the boy or girl prefers solitude to participation in activities with others, and may wander about friendless and forlorn. One of the things an adolescent fears most is to be considered different from others. This makes him more aware of changes in his body and more sensitive to criticism and comparison with others. . . .

The importance of good posture habits in maintaining the various organs of the body in their proper position and in enabling them to work to the best advantage has been so much stressed by physicians in recent years that posture charts, posture exercises, and posture clinics have been made available for great numbers of children. Posture training, however, is something which should be begun in early childhood and under the supervision of someone familiar with the anatomy and "mechanics" of the human body, and therefore no attempt will be made to outline its principles here. The subject is called to the attention of parents, in this connection, for two reasons only: (1) That rapidly growing children may have difficulty in learning how to carry themselves or may feel tired and inclined to slump, so that special attention to posture is advisable at this time; and (2) that many adolescents, particularly girls, assume unhealthy posture because of self-consciousness over their sudden growth. The former may need more rest, other forms of exercise, and possibly the advice of the physician, but the latter need chiefly a change of mental attitude.

Round-shoulderedness is not an easy habit to overcome. Although it is difficult to convince the 12- or 13-year-old girl that she will come to be proud of her height and her good figure as she grows older, it is far easier to prevent poor posture habits than to correct them, once they are formed.

Parents can accomplish a great deal in this direction merely by helping the girl choose clothes suitable to her type, and, so far as possible, sufficiently attractive to make her confident that she looks well. They can also help greatly by softening some of the inevitable jibes of thoughtless brothers and sisters (or, indeed, by encouraging these members of the family to be more considerate) and, most of all, by helping the girl to see her good points and gain enough self-confidence not only to take criticism good-naturedly but to make the best of her figure as it is.

Self-consciousness over an unhealthy and unsightly complexion is even more likely to give parents cause for anxiety. Skin eruptions are fairly common during early adolescence. The small ducts through which oil is carried to the skin apparently do not grow fast enough to take care of the increased activity of the glands supplying this secretion, and, as a result, they become stopped up and a comedo, or "blackhead," forms at the opening of the duct. As the glands continue to function even though drainage is blocked, the ducts become overfilled and little raised places, or "pimples," begin to appear on the surface of the skin.

It is unfortunate that just at the time when the growing child's skin is perhaps in need of a little added care he is most tempted by chocolates, candy bars, cookies, ice-cream sundaes, and soda-fountain drinks, and possibly most careless about keeping his digestive system in healthy order. Skin specialists have found that proper attention to the fundamental principles of physical hygiene already referred to, wholesome diet, free elimination, plenty of sunshine and out-of-door exercise, and thorough daily or twice-daily washing with warm water and soap (which is not nearly so harmful to the complexion as many adolescents believe) will keep most young complexions in good condition. When the skin fails to respond well to this routine, more specific measures under the direction of a physician are advisable. It is well known, however, that proper attention to the skin in the early stages of these afflictions can prevent development of the unsightly later stages for which medical treatment may be necessary.

But in spite of our best efforts we cannot eliminate all the sources of unhappy self-consciousness during adolescence, and therefore we might well spend some of our effort in helping young people acquire a philosophy of life which will make their burdens bearable. . . .

There are always some who, being insecure themselves, seek reassurance by pointing out directly or indirectly the physical, mental, or social imperfections and inferiorities of others. To meet these attacks requires courage and a greater indifference to pain than most adolescents possess. For it is through the experience of pain that individuals develop a philosophy of life which permits them to endure suffering, and in early adolescence most boys and girls have not yet had sufficient experience to endure pain easily.

Discoursing on the injustices of life adds little sweetness to the adolescent's own suffering. Perhaps the most that can be done to help him is to encourage him to see his strong points and build his philosophy of life around these rather than around his weaknesses; and then to help him gain a little perspective, so that even though the tribulations of today loom largest, he will not completely lose sight of the fact that to-morrow and the next day and the next still hold promise of brightness. . . .

ATTITUDES TOWARD SEX

IT IS NOW generally recognized that the methods in vogue a half of a century back, which attempted to prevent undesirable sex conduct by keeping young people in ignorance and subjecting them to rigid disciplinary measures, were neither wise nor effective and that the results of such methods were more harmful than the indiscretions which they were intended to prevent. In other words, more real harm may come from the worry, anxiety, fear, and feelings of guilt and inferiority caused by unwise efforts on the part of the parent to prevent or stop an undesirable sex practice than from the practice itself. This does not mean that the subject should be ignored and that indulgences of this kind should be permitted to go on without parental intervention. It does indicate, however, that sex instruction should be frank, honest, and in keeping with the facts. No attempt should be made to bolster up good, sound advice with statements of dangers which, in the first place, may not exist and, in the second place, serve no other purpose than the creation of unreasonable fears that actually harm the individual at the time and may well become handicaps to him later in life.

Sex Instruction

Just as training in the habits of physical hygiene for adolescence should be a continuation of the training of early childhood, so instruction in the nature and function of the reproductive organs and the part that sex plays in the life of the growing human being should be a continuation of earlier sex instruction. In other words, the parent should not think of adolescence as the time for a campaign in physical hygiene and sex instruction. For just as habits of physical hygiene, either good or bad, are formed long before adolescence, so sex information, either good or bad, is picked up by most children before puberty. The parent who thinks that the child who does not discuss these things is ignorant of them should be warned that the child's very silence may indicate a greater knowledge than he cares to share with his parent.

Nowadays, parents try from the early years to build wholesome attitudes toward sex, as well as to give clear, frank answers suited to the child's intelligence and development on all questions of sex. When this practice is followed, it may well happen that by the time a child reaches adolescence, particularly if he is brought up intimately with older children, he has asked for all the information he needs. But the parents should by no means feel obliged to wait for the child's questions when they see that rapid development is taking place. They can easily notice the body changes already described and remind or point out to the child that these are signs that he is passing from childhood to adulthood.

The father can, perhaps, discuss these matters most helpfully with the boy. He should prepare him to expect an occasional discharge of semen, likely to occur during sleep, explaining that this is nature's way of taking care of his sex activity until he should be physically, economically, and socially ready to assume the responsibility of mating, and assuring him that these nocturnal emissions, as well as the involuntary erections he may experience either in sleep or in sexually exciting situations, are perfectly natural occurrences about which he should feel no alarm. He should also advise the boy that he is less likely to be disturbed by these experiences if he leads a vigorous life, finding pleasure and perhaps a certain pride in hard work and play, cool and regular sleep, cold baths, and wholesome interests.

The mother's instruction should prepare the girl for the occurrence of menstruation, explaining its purpose in relation to child-bearing and advising her how to care for herself during her monthly periods. The girl should also be given some understanding of her sex reactions. She should be reassured, for instance, regarding the vaginal discharge she may experience in situations that are in some way sexually stimulating to her. She should also have an understanding of the sex tension and urge which, although less obvious and less clearly recognized than in the boy, may, nevertheless, be disturbing. She has a right to know that her days of excessive irritability or restlessness or emotional instability are due, not so much to the minor annoyances of everyday life or to any inherent disagreeableness or crossness, as to the periodic physiological tension which is a part of every mature and normal woman's sex life. Once they are recognized, she can learn to relieve her feelings of pent-up emotion and energy by entering into suitable activities. Instead of battling blindly with something she does not understand, she will be able to seek deliberately for a satisfactory means of expression. Her outlet may be in tennis, or swimming, or cleaning the porches, or mowing the lawn; she may crave doing something physically strenuous and should be helped to find it; or she may have need for a purely emotional outlet and may find it best in music, in dramatics, or in writing. When she finds a satisfactory outlet, she should be allowed to make the most of it, regardless of how skillful she may be. It is more important that she find an enjoyable and helpful means of expression than that she become a good performer. As time goes on, she will find new outlets; happy companionship with a group of young people, engrossing work, intensive study, and service for others will all help her to satisfy her growing emotional and physical tension until she is ready to enter into a mature sex relation and assume the responsibilities of wifehood and motherhood.

Both the boy and the girl should be told not only about the organs and processes of reproduction in their own sex, but also about those in the other sex. Above all, they should be made to feel free to ask any questions or consult their parents about any feelings or experiences which they find puzzling or disturbing.

Parents who feel that they do not know enough about these matters to explain them to their children may find it well to discuss them first with each other and with their family physician. They may also get help from various books describing the physiology of reproduction and suggesting ways in which parents can explain it to their children. If for some reason they still feel unable to tackle the subject, they should arrange to have the school or family-guidance counselor or the family physician confer with the child or recommend something to be read by the child himself. Although by this method they will probably lose the rather precious experiences that come to the parent who is on an intimate, confidential level with his child, they will at least not fail the child as they would by neglecting this matter entirely.

Some parents are inclined to feel that the importance of sex instruction—and, indeed, of all aspects of child care and guidance—is greatly exaggerated. They believe that they, and many of their friends, grew up to be competent men and women without any so-called habit training or careful sex instruction. But even if they can recall no anxieties, doubts, shocks, or unhappy experiences which they might have been spared with wise guidance, they will surely be able to see that the very changes which they and their generation have made in the world are creating the need for changing methods of bringing up the next generation. . . .

Sex Talk and Reading

Parents, as well as teachers and recreation leaders, are frequently alarmed at the sexual preʀociousness shown in the conversations of some of their worldly-wise children, or concerned, and possibly offended, by what they consider "smutty" or "dirty" talk. Their concern increases when they discover that these conversations are traveling far and wide and that indignant parents are complaining of having their children contaminated.

The child's motive in such talk may be merely a response to a lively, healthy curiosity and a desire for information. If he is already well supplied with information and has not been made to feel that it is particularly private or personal, he may have a generous inclination to pass it along or to show off his superior knowledge to companions who are less well informed. Children will often use vulgar words or phrases in each other's company. Characteristically they mention the word or phrase and then giggle or nervously laugh. Every normal child experiments with these words or phrases which are taboo. Parents who recognize this, and who don't censure a child when they overhear such talk, will be helping to prevent unhealthy feelings of guilt. . . .

The method of handling these problems depends on the type of individual concerned. It is useless in any case to appear shocked and horrified, or to resort to tears or anger. It is far better to let the immature youngster know that we understand just what this activity means to him and why he is seeking to gain recognition in this particular way. The fact that people in general consider this line of conversation vulgar and offensive, just as they would bad manners, may be pointed out to him, and at the same time other ways of getting recognition may be suggested. With the younger group a frank talk on the subject of sex, making it interesting and unemotional, does more good than anything else. It gives them a new and more responsible attitude toward keeping the whole subject of sex clean.

Most children do pass through this phase of using more or less obscene language, just as they pass through phases of making grimaces or tiresome noises. It requires considerable patience to live through all these various phases with equanimity, but even a period of obscenity should not call forth parental excitement. An unemotional attitude and a certain amount of understanding of what the child is driving at are more helpful than either wrath or sorrow.

Much of the discussion concerning sex talk applies also to the reading of erotic literature. The danger in this type of lurid literature lies in the fact that much of it portrays situations which are overdrawn and not actually representative of reality as these boys and girls will experience it. There is always a sufficient amount of literature available which serves the purpose of diverting sex interests into other channels without stimulating sex phantasies and creating further problems, and both the schools and the public libraries should offer every assistance to parents and to the adolescents themselves in finding books that are worth while. . . .

Masturbation

The practice of masturbation is encountered so frequently in normal, healthy boys and girls from the preschool age through adolescence that there is no logical reason why everything possible should not be done to help the parent understand its occurrence. The real harm results from the treatment of the habit which is likely to be instituted when parents become emotionally upset. The parent is likely to think only in terms of the possible dire physical effects the habit may have upon the human organism, quite unmindful that the real danger lies in making the child feel self-conscious and inferior, and in leading him to turn all his thoughts upon his supposed wickedness and abnormality. This tendency to introspective self-examination and self-condemnation in turn affects his attitude toward the world at large; he avoids mingling with others, feeling unworthy of their society and perhaps fearing lest they suspect and discover his weakness. In this way the child's normal, healthy outlook on life may become distorted.

There is probably no surer way of perpetuating such a habit than that of making the individual feel that he is sinful, different, queer, and wicked, or will become physically degenerate, an object to be avoided, and a candidate for a mental hospital through his indiscretions. What he needs is relief from anxiety, not more anxiety; a feeling of strength and superiority, not of weakness and inferiority; truth, not lies. The adolescent already feels that he is a victim of an undesirable habit. He knows that any habit which makes him think less well of himself is something to be fought and mastered. He is already carrying a heavy burden. A panicky parent should not add to it by injecting fears which have no basis in fact merely because this seems to be the easiest way to meet the situation.

Undesirable sex behavior need not be either ignored or condemned. When it comes to the parents' attention as a problem of one of their own children, they should seize the opportunity for a frank discussion of the whole subject of sex and the varied healthy activities that may be utilized as substitutes for this immature sex behavior. If the parents cannot approach the subject in this intellectual and unemotional way, they should delegate the task to the family physician, a wise teacher, a friend, or some other suitable person who will help rather than hinder the adolescent in his attempt to get a mature outlook on sex conduct. This is not the time for evasion, prudery, or deceit; it is the time for frank, honest approach to one of the most common problems adolescents have to face. . . .

It is unwise for parents to pry into the sex activity of their children and get confessions of these secret indulgences. The whole sex problem can be discussed quite as frankly in an impersonal way and often more helpfully than the individual problem. It is wise for parents to let children appreciate that these situations are common to practically everyone, that most boys have to meet them, and that it is everyone's responsibility to learn to control them. At the same time they do well to stress the fact that solitary preoccupation with one's own body for the purpose of obtaining pleasurable sensations is an immature form of behavior, that immature sex habits tend to interfere with one's normal adjustment to other people, and that any habit which tends to lessen one's self-esteem should be discarded. Then ways and means of meeting the situation can be outlined, and there will be a much better chance of the plan being carried through by the boy whose self-esteem has been restored than by the boy who is in the grip of fear. . . .

In the end the sex behavior of the adolescent boy and girl is determined to a large extent by their whole adjustment to life. If their relations with their parents and their friends are satisfactory and happy, and they have adequate outlets for their various energies and interests, they are likely to meet their maturing sex drives adequately. It is the emotionally starved boy or girl or the adolescent without adequate interests who is most likely to plunge into experimentation with sex for the satisfaction which he has failed to find in ways more in keeping with his stage of development. . . .

ADOLESCENCE AND MENTAL DEVELOPMENT

MIND IS THOUGHT OF in terms of processes and activities, and it is naturally less easy to measure these than to measure body stature. Moreover, the various mental processes and activities become manifest at different times and in different degrees. It has been found that while many activities increase during adolescence, some remain about the same and some actually decrease. Mental development goes on unceasingly throughout life as the individual adds to his experience, knowledge, and insight.

Although the most important period of the individual's mental growth is past at adolescence, many parents first become interested in the mental development of their boys and girls at this time. Adolescents, too, begin to consider seriously their plans for the future. They begin to consider how far they can go in school and to what advantage; what their special capacities and special disabilities are. Obviously these are questions that can be answered only after careful study of the individual boy or girl. But for those lay readers who would like a better understanding of some of the factors involved in such a study the following discussion may be of some value.

Measurement of Intelligence

Within the last 30 years a large number and variety of so-called tests for the measurement of various mental processes have been devised. There are tests of memory, perception, attention, motor coordination, comprehension, suggestibility, judgment, imagination, range of emotional response, learning ability, initiative, and so on. . . .

An intelligence test should be considered only as a point of departure to be supplemented by a child's medical history, consideration of his environmental limitations and opportunities, a history of his actual school achievement and his social adjustment, and further study of such particular aptitudes or handicaps as he may manifest.

It is of greatest importance that parents understand the nature of this type of intelligence test. The interesting publicity given to various kinds of mental testing has had the unfortunate effect of confusing and misleading lay readers regarding the purpose of psychological examination before they ever had a chance to understand what it was all about. . . . ,

Parents sometimes ask whether the intelligence tests given to their children are not the same as those used to determine whether or not a child is feeble-minded. They forget that there is only one kind of scale for measuring weight, and that it is no disgrace to be found of normal weight on the same scale which showed someone else to be overweight or underweight. . . .

The Slow Mind

The problems of the mentally slow child, are often not recognized until he reaches the upper grades. . . .

There are three important principles to be observed by parents and teachers in planning for the boy or girl with a slow mind: (1) The necessity of giving frank and early recognition to whatever handicap he may have; (2) the importance of placing him properly in school so that he will not have to struggle beyond his capacity, or constantly experience a sense of discouragement and failure; (3) the wisdom of planning for the child's greatest satisfaction and happiness rather than for the fulfillment of parental ambition.

The Average Mind

. . . The principles to be observed in guiding the adolescent with average ability are but variations of those to be observed in planning for the child with the slow mind: (1) The necessity of recognizing the child's ability for what it is; (2) the importance of placing him properly in school so that his powers will be developed to their maximum fulfillment and yet not subjected to competition that would lead only to failure; and (3) the wisdom of guiding the child toward his own satisfaction and happiness rather than toward the goal set by parental ambition.

The Superior Mind

That the mentally superior child may perplex his parents and become a problem to himself is a not uncommon assumption. People have innumerable theories about the vagaries of children with superior endowment. They may be convinced that brilliant children are usually poor specimens so far as physical development is concerned; or that they are inclined to be introspective, absentminded bookworms with no sense about practical matters; or that they are selfish, egocentric individuals who are ever greedy for more learning

and more college degrees regardless of the economic cost to their parents or the necessary sacrifice of the aspirations of brothers and sisters; or that gifted children turn out to be dull adults; or that highly intellectual boys and girls make poor social adjustments and later become the crochety, cantankerous, neurotic, or psychotic members of society. Although everyone knows men and women whom the above descriptions would seem to fit perfectly, the conclusion that their maladjustments, their faults, and their failures are due to, or necessarily connected with, intellectual superiority is fallacious.

Thorough and long-continued studies of intellectually superior children all tend to show that true intellectual superiority is usually accompanied by superiority in other respects, as, for example, physical health and social adaptability. If certain of these boys and girls later turn out to be lopsided, topheavy, or otherwise unbalanced individuals, does the fault lie in their intellectual superiority in itself? Does it not rather lie in the fact that they have been encouraged by ambitious parents and eager teachers to spend all their time and energy in developing their intellects to the exclusion of their other faculties?

In some cases poverty may have made it necessary for them to be self-supporting while receiving their education, so that all the time not spent in class or at study has been spent at work, and little, if any, time was left for leisurely companionship with fellow students, or for participation in sports, in group activities, or in any other form of play and recreation. Others may have come from families whose social background was markedly inferior to that of their intellectual equals, so that they have always felt unable to enjoy the intimate companionship of the very people with whom they might otherwise have had most in common. All these factors, and more, have undoubtedly contributed to the maladjustments of some highly endowed individuals. . . .

Modern American educators and psychologists seem to agree that it is far wiser to enrich the course of the superior child than to push him ahead. . . .

The same three principles apply in dealing with the superior child: (1) The necessity for recognizing the superior ability for what it is, meanwhile taking stock of the physical development and personality traits that go with it; (2) the importance of placing the child properly in school, with reference not only to his mental age but also to his size and his general level of maturity; and

(3) the wisdom of guiding the adolescent toward becoming a well-adjusted and happy individual rather than merely an efficient set of brain cells.

Special Abilities and Disabilities

Certain special abilities and disabilities, talents, and intellectual handicaps or defects occur not uncommonly. Examples of individuals remarkable for such special abilities and disabilities are known to everyone; there are individuals with extraordinary visual memories enabling them to visualize a printed page and thus recall to memory names and dates as if they were reading them; there are individuals with extraordinary auditory memories who can recite a poem or retain the tune of a song after hearing it but once; there are some individuals who earn a livelihood by showing off their ability as lightning calculators; and in contrast to all of these, there are the students who have "a wretched memory," "no ear for a tune," or "no head for figures."

Special abilities or disabilities may be a part of the intellectual equipment of the feebleminded, the average, or the superior individual. It is, therefore, not sufficient to recognize the special ability or disability without also recognizing the general level of intelligence that goes with it. The father who said, "My son can draw well and could make a good cartoonist, but he has no ideas," showed good insight into the relation between a special ability and general intelligence, and also a good appreciation of his son's equipment. He realized that his son had superior ability in drawing but that his general level of intelligence was low.

This does not indicate that the special ability should be neglected or even that it should not be cultivated. The danger lies in building the young person's entire life around his one strong point regardless of his possible inability to bring the rest of his life up to this peak. One would not think of trying to make a tennis champion out of a boy merely because he had a good stroke and a good eye for his ball, without considering the condition of his heart and his general physical reaction to exercise; yet the mere fact that he is not up to the strenuous practice and the excitement of a professional tournament need not debar him from enjoying amateur games.

It is even more disastrous, however, to build the young person's life around a disability and to say, for example, that there is no point in continuing his education because he can never learn to spell, or to classify him once and for all as stupid and dull because he has a poor visual memory or difficulty in reading. Reading disabilities although they often go unrecognized, are relatively common and sometimes cause serious problems. In recent years much experimental work has been done in an effort to discover ways and means of helping individuals to overcome or compensate for such special disabilities. Special instruction, once a disability is recognized, will often help greatly in overcoming it. But even where it is not possible to provide such remedial assistance, it is still possible to prevent young people from looking upon a particular handicap as the stumbling block in the way of happiness regardless of the road pursued.

Naturally, the special ability has certain advantages over the disability, for it can often be capitalized with appreciable success. A good memory can be capitalized in dozens of ways and may completely conceal from the general public an otherwise inferior mind; but a poor memory—of what possible advantage can it be save to serve as a convenient excuse for failure?

Although the psychologists and their intelligence tests have contributed to an appreciative understanding of these deviations of the human mind, and although it may be necessary to turn to them for an expert opinion or a final word of advice when in doubt about the best plan for an individual child, there is no reason why parents and teachers should not be able to recognize some of these things from their own observation and take such steps as seem wise to overcome the handicap. . . .

THE INDIVIDUAL AS A WHOLE

HOW FREQUENTLY we hear a remark like this: "Why is it that John never really accomplished anything in life: He comes from a good family, was well educated, and never had any real sickness. He works hard, has clean habits, and is perfectly straight, yet he has never gone very far in business. He doesn't make friends easily, and he seems to be getting so little out of life. John has never quite fitted into the scheme of things socially, and he realizes it quite as well as his neighbors, but nobody knows why this is so." . . .

The world is full of Johns—individuals who are failing to make life as full as they should either for themselves or for those with whom they come in contact. The twists in personality which account for failure and unhappiness are not introduced into the life of the individual suddenly and unexpectedly; invariably they are the result of a very slow, insidious process, being the effect of the environment over a long period of years. One does not have to wait until the child reaches the adolescent age to determine the evidence of impending danger. All his habits and personality traits are in the process of development from birth, and it is fortunate indeed that the efficiency of an individual at any given age level can be measured with a fair degree of success.

People are inclined to think of maturity as a definite state to be reached much as if it were the end of a journey. It would be better to think of it as an ever-receding goal toward which we begin to march at birth and go on to the end of life. We can check up at any given point and find out whether or not we are on time, so to speak, or have covered the allotted distance for any given period. In other words, there is a fairly well recognized standard for maturity at 3 years of age just as there is at 13, and the adequacy with which the individual's total personality is progressing can always be measured in terms of his maturity for any given age. The 3-year-old who wets the bed, refuses to eat unless fed, and demands that his parents rock him to sleep is immature. The 8-year-old boy who needs constant supervision for his leisure time, who needs help in dressing and undressing, who sets up a howl when his parents go away, leaving him well cared for while they take a short vacation, is immature. The 14-year-old boy who is irresponsible about his school work and chores, who is given to chronic grouches if he cannot have his own way, who must have someone tell him what clothes to wear, who needs to have all his activities planned for him, is also immature. So is the adult immature who cannot stand authority, who is extremely selfish, who meets all difficulties by running away, who uses alcohol as a retreat or illness as an excuse.

The immaturity of the child during the preadolescent years is primarily a matter of concern to his parents, but early in adolescence other people, particularly those of the same age group, begin to impose certain very definite standards upon youth, holding them more rigidly accountable for their conduct during this period. The adolescent himself becomes more and more aware at this time of his own maturity or immaturity.

He is inclined to compare himself with others of his own age and social setting and feels inferior if he does not measure up to them.

The standards mentioned for maturity at adolescence are not so well defined as those for the preschool years, for as the child grows up his reactions to life become more and more affected by his past experiences and these experiences are never the same for any two individuals. There are, however, certain types of reaction which are definitely immature and therefore are not acceptable to the group to which he logically belongs. . . .

People become mature by assuming obligations and responsibilities and by having to do things for themselves and others. If a mother continues to dress her little boy until he is 8 years of age, the boy will be considered immature for being unable to dress himself, even though his mother is responsible for this immaturity. So the parents who indulge their adolescents, letting them think of life as their happy playground, are themselves responsible for the immaturity which may manifest itself as a superficial outlook on life.

Often enough the growing boy and girl are ready for more responsibility and independence than their parents are willing to give them. They resent being "babied" and begin to struggle for more freedom. They may feel, for instance, that they are old enough to know when to go to bed without being told, or that they should not have to ask permission every time they wish to go out of the house, or that it is humiliating to ask separately for each cent of spending money. . . .

One of the specific ways in which the parent can help the adolescent to become independent is in connection with the spending of money. The problem of training in the use and value of money is not one which belongs to the adolescent years. The child who reaches this period of his social development without some very definite and well-thought-out ideas about the earning, saving, and giving of money and, in a more general way, the budgeting of his income regardless of the source from which it may be derived, has missed something very important that has much to contribute to the efficiency with which he will meet many of the practical problems; of living later on. . . .

When he reaches that stage of mental and physical maturity at which he has something definite to contribute in the way of labor that has money value, he should be given the opportunity of finding out for himself just how much time and effort has to be spent in order that he may receive a well-earned nickel or dime. The wise parent will teach the child to distinguish between money given to him in order that he may meet his daily obligations and learn how to manage his finances, and money that represents payment for service of real value.

There is a marked difference between compensation for a job well done and a bribe that is given to induce the child to perform some task which he should have performed because it was the right thing to do. . . . Children should learn at an early age that there is pleasure in work and that they are entitled to the rewards of their efforts. Rewards in the form of money earned by honest toil, especially when they entail the giving up of playtime or a holiday, or acquired through some other sacrifice, will be less likely to be squandered foolishly than will be the unexpected gift or even the taken-for-granted allowance.

Most boys and girls in their teens do not enjoy asking their parents for every dime to be spent on carfare, every quarter for lunch, and every half-dollar for a haircut. If they are working on a part-time job, they may be earning enough to take care of these small needs, but whether the money comes from their own earnings or from their parents' pockets, they should undoubtedly have something definite in the way of an allowance and they should be given a certain latitude in spending it.

Sometimes the resentment of authority and the rebelliousness against close supervision is manifested as a personal dislike and even hatred of the child for his parents. . . .

During adolescence the individual becomes more keenly aware of his thoughts as personal possessions. Not only can he keep them to himself, but he can think in opposition to his parents. Fiction and biography both contain innumerable descriptions of adolescents who suddenly find that there are nice people whose views on questions of religion, economics, politics, education, science, personal relations, and conduct are diametrically opposed to those entertained by their parents. Often enough the adolescent finds that these people are not so bad nor so stupid as he has been led to believe. Perhaps, on the contrary, their outlook on life seems more intelligent and more agreeable than that of the parents.

This discovery and the adolescent's consequent refusal to adhere any longer to the point of view of his parents very often resolves itself into as much of a struggle as the adolescent's refusal to return home at the hour set, or to obey some other parental command. Frequently the struggle resolves itself into some individual issue: The adolescent insists on going to college despite his father's conviction that higher education unfits young people for meeting the practical demands of life; or he chooses for his close associates or brings to his home boys and girls who are unacceptable to his parents. . . .

The desire for personal independence and more control over one's own activities or thoughts is so normal an aspect of adolescence that the boy or girl who clings to his parents and fears to take any step that might possibly lead him further away from the security and protection of childhood is considered overdependent or immature. . . .

Often a mother glories in such a relation with her children, finding pleasure in the fact that they cannot get along without her. Such a mother is too selfish to realize that she is crippling her child emotionally. She forgets that in the natural course of events her child is likely to outlive her and if he has become completely dependent upon her, he will be lost without her. She fails to see that she is preventing the child from finding his own place in the world of other people. . . .

SOME EDUCATIONAL PITFALLS

As might be expected of all the adolescent problems those concerning educational progress are the most common. Practically every child, regardless of his mental or physical development and his social or economic status is confronted with the task of acquiring knowledge of the world in which he lives. As he advances in years competition becomes more keen, and failures in academic work become more common. . . .

Parents who fail to appreciate the increased intellectual demands that are made on children as they advance up this intellectual ladder may be quite unjust in their criticisms of those who fail. Many a parent complains that Johnny could do the work in high school if he only tried; that he never had any trouble in grammar school, where he worked hard and was interested. This may be true, but many of these children are carrying intellectual loads which are beyond their ability, and they just naturally lag behind and slacken in their efforts when nothing of real interest suited to their abilities is provided. It must be remembered, too, that on the physical side some have only a 6-hour capacity for standardized work, while others can carry on for 8 or 10 hours unimpaired by fatigue.

It is not hard to understand why parents who are but little concerned about the emotional life of the child, perhaps being quite oblivious to such personality traits as shyness, jealousy, or feelings of inferiority, and those who are rather casual about physical growth and development, take this problem of school failure so seriously. They seem to feel that such failure indicates actual inferiority, and, either consciously or unconsciously, they blame themselves. Teachers are prone to view failure as a reflection upon their ability to teach, and they, too, frequently join with the parents in pushing and prodding and generally harassing this unfortunate group of children.

It is therefore important to keep in mind that there is a fairly large number of boys and girls well developed physically, capable of fitting into the varied social situations in life quite adequately, who require a broader type of instruction to meet their particular needs. In attempting to help them, one should think in terms of breadth, rather than height; that is, the boy or girl who reaches a mental age of 13 or 14 is intellectually capable of acquiring a more useful and practical grasp of those essentials pertaining to the social, economic, and industrial aspects of the world in which he lives than many students have at the end of a college course. It all depends upon the wisdom with which these individuals are guided and directed, and the degree to which schools are willing to accept their responsibility for providing wider opportunities.

There is another group of adolescents who run into scholastic difficulties, not on account of mediocre or relatively poor intellectual equipment, but rather on account of poor preparation. Many situations encountered by the child during the school years contribute to this particular difficulty. In some cities many children enter school before they are mentally ready to do first-grade work. Such children would do well to repeat the first grade; but in the natural course of events, there is a new line of children waiting and as the number of places in the first grade is limited, they must move on. Consequently, each year children are pushed ahead from grade to grade unfitted by their previous experience to meet the task at hand. These children cannot be held back

in any large numbers because actual space in the schoolroom is not available. But their inadequate preparation in early years, unless recognized and corrected, will obviously lead to serious difficulties later.

Children who are prevented from attending school regularly on account of illness or some chronic physical handicap must also be considered. They, too, are pushed along—sometimes at the instigation of an ambitious parent, sometimes because of misdirected sympathy on the part of a teacher, and then again to make a place for someone else.

There are also a certain number of students whose continuity in school work is interrupted, sometimes unavoidably, by having to change schools when their families move. It is no small portion of the population that must seek employment wherever it is available. This problem arises in various social and economic levels and may affect the minister or the teacher or the millworker. These periodic interruptions in school work may be definite factors contributing to failure. . . .

Then there are those parents who build their lives entirely around their own pleasures with an utter disregard for the welfare of the child, so that children are taken out of school because parents want to travel, move to another neighborhood, or follow some other whim.

However, frequent removals are not necessarily a handicap. Some children develop an extraordinary ability to fit easily into different social situations and to make friends quickly, their adjustment being furthered by practice in adapting to change and new scenes. Such children speak volumes for the essential security their parents have been able to provide in spite of not being able to give them a permanent home.

Inability to concentrate is often given as a cause of failure to acquire satisfactory passing marks. The ability to concentrate is a gradual acquisition, and parents should make an effort to see that they do not themselves interfere with its development by creating a program that is altogether too active. Extracurricular activities are of real educational value in giving the young boy or girl greater opportunity for finding out what life has to offer and what he can contribute, but such activities may be overdone. It may be that special interests for which the child shows some talent are permitted to assume an importance which they do not deserve. Too much parental interest can be demonstrated in building radios and airplanes, in sketching, in music and dancing lessons, to the discouragement of any concentrated effort on the school work to be done.

Athletics, dramatics. and even the otherwise harmless associations with those of the opposite sex, may all become so diverting that the real purpose of school attendance is entirely overlooked. There are those individuals who seem to be capable of absorbing all these varied interests and still maintaining a satisfactory average in their school work. Most students, however, need considerable guidance lest they spread their interests and energies so thin that none of their activities receives adequate attention. . . .

Occasionally one finds failure in academic work to be due to lack of interest in the subject matter. This being true, the adolescent will often seek for his intellectual satisfactions in outside reading or other diversions which may in themselves be educational but which do not contribute to his progress through the school. This may mean that a change in the curriculum is advisable; or, if the student has a definite objective, such as college entrance, it will necessitate his grasping the fact that certain subjects which he is required to learn in school must be studied because they are a means to an end, even though they hold no interest for him as an end in themselves.

On account of the lack of interest in the course of study, a student may develop the idea that the work is too hard, that it is over his head, and that, regardless of how much he might study, he would inevitably fail. Here one may do much to overcome this feeling of inferiority by arranging for him to have a psychological examination. It is reassuring to the student to know that he has a good set of mental tools with which to work, that the subject matter which they are tackling is well within his grasp, and that failure is due not to inferior intellectual equipment but to the way he happens to be using his equipment.

Often emotional situations present obstacles to the child's ability to measure up to his group in school. Disturbed emotional attitudes toward life are probably far more common as a cause for failure than all other causes put together; and, although the situation may appear relatively unimportant in the beginning, the conflict over the failure itself complicates the emotional attitude toward the situation. Thus young people, who have never had an opportunity to grow up and actually become independent, may meet fairly well the situations to which they have been trained as

a matter of routine but will find themselves totally at sea when it comes to utilizing their time and ability without strict supervsion. This, again, is a matter of training.

Parents, in their eagerness to contribute to the happiness of their children and to protect them from even the minor hardships of life, are frequently inclined to believe that their own experiences, their own unhappiness and failures, can be utilized to save the child the pangs of humiliation that are brought about by failure and disappointment. They are always modifying the ordinary, everyday situations so that their children can meet them without even for the moment endangering their happiness. In other words, these parents never allow the child to meet life and all its complex problems as it actually exists. They fail to appreciate that experience is the most trustworthy weapon and that knowledge is the best armor for those who are about to step out of the home and battle with the world at large....

Overambitious parents must also be mentioned as a factor in creating emotional situations leading to school failures. In their desire to have children succeed and excel in their school work, they are likely to place too high a premium on marks and stress scholastic attainment to the exclusion of everything else. To desire success for one's children is laudable, but to demand scholastic honors of the child for the sake of gratifying personal pride is downright selfish.

The student himself may set his standard so high and become so concerned in competing for high marks that he misses much of the pleasure and satisfaction of school life. Friendships, athletics, dramatics, and the general welfare of the school are sometimes sacrificed in this keen competition; and if he fails to attain success in this scholastic striving, all is lost. This is an attitude that should not be encouraged either by teachers or by parents. . . .

One must keep in mind that many of the individuals who fail to make a place for themselves in either school or college meet the more concrete and practical situations of life successfully. Many individuals who are not what is termed "intellectual" are very intelligent; and life in its everyday contacts is met successfully only with intelligence. The emotional conflicts which have been considered may lead to behavior that brings the individual into conflict not only with the family and society at large but with himself. These behavior problems are invariably the result of an environmental situation due to a multiplicity of conditions and circumstances; and the success of parents and teachers in handling these problems depends upon their ability to understand how these complex situations create emotional atti-'udes which affect the conduct of the adolescent.

THE QUESTION OF WORK

IT IS IMPORTANT for every individual to learn to work and to derive all the possible benefits from experience with employment. Work provides a valuable opportunity for finding one's self in relation to the rest of the working world, for becoming more independent, for learning more about people and social conditions, for discovering one's own vocational aptitudes and inclinations, and for finding a valid outlet for surplus energies and emotions.

The part that work occupies in the life of the average adolescent varies widely. Each year thousands of boys and girls leave school at 14, 15, or 16 to enter regular, gainful employment, while others look forward to many more years of education and training for future usefulness. In rural districts the work of many young people ranges all the way from doing chores on the family farm outside school hours or during vacations to full-time employment in agriculture on a commercial basis. In the cities the work of adolescents may be confined to cooperation in a few simple household duties, or it may involve any of the full-time or part-time jobs open to young people in industry and commerce. . . .

Economic need is often a controlling motive in entering employment, though by no means all or even most of the adolescents who leave school early to go to work do so for this reason. The attitude of parents in many cases is a determining factor. Some parents encourage their children to find jobs as soon as they reach the legal school-leaving age, because they are eager for the additional income which the child's earnings can provide even though they may not really need it. In other cases the child himself may insist on leaving school to go to work either because he is dissatisfied with school or because his parents have failed to develop in him the proper understanding of the value of education to his adult life and are unable to cope with his impatient desire for immediate independence.

Nevertheless, in many instances, economic necessity is an important factor in determining whether or not the individual boy or girl seeks a job. The income of one family may be so low that the daughter spends all her after-school and Saturday hours working in a store for a few dollars a week when she really needs rest, fresh air, sunshine, and exercise. On the other hand, a family which has never known financial need may discourage a healthy and energetic boy from taking a job that would provide an outlet for his energy and striving for independence and would give him valuable training and experience without harming him physically. In the girl's case the loss of earnings might make it impossible for her to buy the necessary clothes and books and to provide the carfare to enable her to attend high school. In the boy's case, accepting an after-school job as mail boy in an office or shelf boy in a library might mean depriving some boy in real financial need of an opportunity to earn money. But the psychological need of the one may be as great as the financial need of the other. To advise this girl to give up her job without making some plan for a scholarship or attempting to arrange a part-time school program for her would be unreasonable. To advise the boy would involve careful consideration of whether, for the sake of his mental health, he needs the exhilaration of having a job. Obviously each case must be decided for itself. . . .

It is of the utmost importance that parents give earnest thought to the kind of work which their children undertake. Obviously, all types of work are not equally suitable, and some are distinctly harmful. A newspaper route may provide a certain amount of business training and develop habits of regularity, while a job as newsboy selling papers on a crowded street or late at night cannot be recommended. Taking subscriptions for reputable magazines may be a relatively pleasant way of earning a few extra dollars, even though it may not provide much training; but when selling on commission involves teaching boys and girls and even very young children to tell pathetic stories in order to dispose of their wares, it is an occupation in which no right-minded parent would want to see children engaged.

Aside entirely from the question of economic pressure, a certain amount of work is desirable in the adolescent's program. Not only does work of the right type and right amount encourage habits of industry and develop responsibility, but it gives the individual a sense of his place in the scheme of things. Father works to supply the income which supports the family. Mother works to make a home for father and the children. It is no more than fair to let children share in this scheme and feel themselves active participants in the producing as well as the consuming aspects of family life. If children have been accustomed from an early age to assume responsibility for a few simple but definite household tasks, in keeping with their years and skill, they will be better able and more willing to undertake more difficult and useful work later on.

There is much talk about the value of work in character training, and yet the fact is often overlooked that the simplest household tasks offer excellent opportunities for just such training. If Don understands that it is his job and his alone to clean the family automobile, that he has assumed the responsibility of cleaning it well and is under obligation to finish his job on time, if his family expresses pleasure in the result and satisfaction in being able to depend upon him, he will take pride in his task and consider it worth doing well. But this will not be true if father stands on the back porch watching every step with a critical eye or exclaiming in impatience over the length of time it takes the boy.

If Ruth realizes that everything from planning to serving the meal is her responsibility, that she is relieving mother of a real share of her own household obligations, and that her efforts are appreciated by her family, she, too, will take pride, satisfaction, and pleasure in performing this task as well as possible. Children may have to be trained to do a special job; but once they are trained, they should be put "on their own." Much of our satisfaction in work comes from the feeling that it has been our task to do and we have done it to the best of our ability. If there are certain duties for which a child seems temperamentally unsuited—if, for instance, a boy's phlegmatic ways make an endless performance of mowing the lawn—family peace and comfort may necessitate transferring him to some other activity, and yet training in persistent application to the task in hand may be the very best thing for such an adolescent.

There is also much in the old Tom Sawyer stunt of having such a good time painting the fence that everyone begs for a chance to help. Parents who themselves make drudgery of their work cannot expect their children to feel inspired to help them. . . .

If work at home has value in giving young people a sense of sharing in the productive aspects of family life, work outside the home gives them a clearer conception of the employer-employee relation. At home, if Donald wants to go to the ball game, probably his chores can be postponed or done by some other member of the family. If Ruth is going to a party, her mother may excuse her from washing the dishes after the evening meal. Or, if parents insist that the work be done as usual, Donald and Ruth may say that mother and dad are "mean" and "hard" and that they even deprive their own children of a good time. Outside the home Donald and Ruth realize that the newspapers must be delivered promptly regardless of ball games and the library must have its attendant regardless of parties. They may feel aggrieved that this is so, but they learn to expect little mercy from the powers that be in the newspaper business or the public library, and console themselves with the philosophical reflection that "life is like that."

At home, when father and mother request that things be done in a certain way—for example, that the paint brushes be left in turpentine after being used, or that the kitchen towels be rinsed out after each meal—Donald and Ruth may feel that their parents are fussy and set in their ways. They may become irritable, sulky, or resentful when reminded to do things; and if their parents also feel annoyed and irritated at constantly having to point out these oversights, the home atmosphere becomes somewhat unpleasant, and the bonds of sympathy between parents and children are heavily taxed. Outside the home Donald may consider Mr. Cash-and-Carry an old grouch for insisting that groceries must be displayed in his own particular way, and Ruth may wish that her customers could be obliged to return to the racks the dresses they have tried on but not purchased; but they are likely to accept their trials as the inevitable hardships of work instead of regarding them as personal afflictions.

If work at home has the advantage of providing the adolescent with an opportunity for sharing the business of maintaining family life, work outside the home should give him an opportunity for feeling himself a unit in the larger working world. This is important, for it is during adolescence that the individual is likely to feel most uncertain where he really fits in. He needs the security of family life, and yet he wants to escape from it; he needs to feel that he has a place of his own in the world, and at the same time he wants to feel free to explore all kinds of other places. Having a job—an after-school or a Saturday job or a summer-vacation job—provides him with at least a slight degree of the feeling of confidence and security, the assurance of having at least some place he can fill which he so much needs, and yet, at the same time, it provides him with an opportunity for exploring life outside the home.

It is in work outside the home that a young person begins to see his own identity emerge. He is no longer a mere member of a family; in fact his employer and fellow employees may not know a thing about his family. He stands and falls by his own ability and by his own accomplishments. He is paid quite impersonally, on a purely commercial basis. He begins to enjoy the relative economic independence which his earnings may give him, and with this comes a gratifying sense of independence in general. Through his work he begins to gain a new understanding of human nature and to learn to know people as congenial or cantankerous to work for. The principles of honesty and generosity which his parents or his Sunday-school teacher may have taught him take on a new meaning when he sees them practiced in his own contacts and experience with people.

Clearly, the choice of a job for the adolescent, even a temporary, part-time job, should not be left to chance if the boy or the girl is to be benefited rather than harmed by the experience as a wage earner. Such jobs if carefully selected may also provide material for vocational guidance. Employment as office boy in a lawyer's office may settle once and for all John's question whether he really wants to study law. Saturdays spent doing odd jobs around father's place of business may help to determine for both father and son whether or not this boy is a good candidate for a future junior partnership. Two hours a day spent in caring for Mrs. Jones' pre-school children may convince Sarah that she has neither the patience nor the imagination to enjoy kindergarten work. Work in a library may reveal to another girl that her real interest is not in the books but in the people who read them and that she might find future satisfaction in some kind of group-influencing activity such as social work.

Work during adolescence under proper conditions is a means of keeping boys and girls wholesomely occupied, helping them to use up some of the abundant energy that is constantly seeking an outlet, and teaching them that work itself is an excellent antidote for many kinds of dissatisfactions and tribulations.

It must always be kept in mind, however, that boys and girls in their teens are still growing and that the growing process uses up much of their reserve energy. The human machine is not always adjusted to its maximum efficiency during adolescence, and it may sometimes be wiser from the point of view of health to keep a growing boy or girl off the job entirely for a summer or discourage doing more than required school work during the school year. Parents often fail to understand the problems of their children. Clinton's father speaks sarcastically about his big, strapping 15-year-old who lounges around the house, too lazy to do anything and too awkward, when he does try to do anything, to do it well. Stanley's mother is somewhat more sympathetic and also more observant when she remarks, "You can tell that Stanley is growing; he lolls about and seems not to have strength enough to move a muscle. Then all of a sudden he will have a spurt of energy that will send him off to play tennis for 3 hours at a stretch in the glaring sun, and nothing can stop him."

This lack of capacity for long-sustained physical effort is a strong argument against the employment of immature boys and girls in jobs in which such effort is required of them. To combine school life and some daily job requires planning if the young person's time for home study, recreation, and exercise is not to be lost or unduly curtailed and if he is not to lose needed hours of sleep, thus jeopardizing his success in school or his health. A daily job should not be too taxing nor continue too many hours. Saturday jobs, in many cases, would be better.

It is important to learn to work, but it is equally important for youth to learn to play and to derive all the benefits possible from experiences with the wise use of leisure. Indeed, in the present stage of our social progress, in this machine age, training for leisure has assumed new importance. Those who grow up unable to use leisure without breaking the law, unable to seek pleasure in any but forbidden pastimes, unable to find enjoyment without expending large sums of money, or, perhaps, unable to play under any circumstances, present just as much of a social problem as those who never learn to work.

LEARNING TO USE LEISURE
Present Complaints

THE IDEA that "nowadays" young people do not know how to make intelligent use of their leisure time is constantly dinned into our ears. . . .

Men or women who have spent a lifetime working with boys and girls, watching them at work and in their recreation, and helping them through their troubles, will point out the courage, generosity, seriousness, unselfishness, and readiness to take responsibility that lie beneath the surface of the bright lipstick and cigarette smoke about which other adults are busy complaining. But parents all too seldom have a chance to talk over Mary's or John's habits with such men and women. They are dealing with day-to-day problems, and have little opportunity to step off and see their children's behavior in perspective.

What are some of the complaints that are made against the modern adolescent's use of leisure time?

First there are the complaints about leisure time spent at home: Tom is always on the go . . . Grace comes home just long enough to change her clothes and go out again . . . When they do stay home they don't know what to do with themselves, and they hang around until one almost wishes they would go out again . . . They always tune in for the loud, snappy music without the slightest regard for the tastes of the rest of the family, and they appropriate dad's favorite chair and make a mess of the evening paper . . . When they bring in their friends, mother and dad can stay in the kitchen.

Now let us see some of the complaints about spending leisure time away from home: When John goes out, the family car goes with him and mother and dad may either walk or stay at home . . . Jane must see every motion picture and some of them more than once . . . There's no use trying to suggest the time for coming home; both boys and girls are always late, and they always have some excuse—there was a flat tire, or the party lasted until 2, or someone had to be driven to the other end of town, or nobody realized how late it was getting to be . . . We've talked again and again with the children about the dangers of parking along the roadside and the cheapening effect of petting; but we don't know what they are up to when they are away, and you can't get a word out of them when they get back.

But perhaps most puzzling of all is the fact that young people nowadays don't seem to enjoy the things that young people used to enjoy; they . . . want to go "tearing around," and they prefer the entertainment offered by commercial places of amusement to anything they might provide for themselves.

But after all, the adolescents of today are merely accepting life as they find it when they make use of commercial amusements. They are not responsible for the opening of motion-picture theaters; they neither invented nor purchased the first automobiles; they are not running the dine-and-dance restaurants or the roadhouses. If, as parents, we object to our own adolescents spending their leisure unintelligently, why don't we train them to find enjoyment in activities which we consider more worth while? If, as public-spirited citizens, we object to the exploitation of youth which is practiced on adolescents in general by the worst of commercialized recreation, why don't we clean up our communities and promote the development of adequate and wholesome public recreational facilities?

There is another point to be made in defense of the modern adolescent's use of leisure; namely, that his parents probably do not use their leisure to much better advantage. . . .

A society that is only a few years away from frontier life, as ours is, has not devoted much attention to the problems involved in training for good use of leisure time. Relatively few people have had much leisure until fairly recently. In the past, too, play was looked upon as unimportant, even a waste of time, and the idea of the uses of recreation in renewing vitality, of fun as necessary to mental health, is a recent development. People were in the habit of working so hard and so long that they did not know what to do when they were not working. To learn to relax, to plan one's own time, to have inner resources fairly independent of money or location, need to be taught, like any other skills. . . .

Education In the Use of Leisure

Although leisure is a term that scarcely seems applicable before adolescence, education in the use of leisure begins long before. It begins when father and mother first set aside a Sunday or a holiday for an expedition to the zoo or a picnic in the woods, and the children realize that this outing is considered sufficiently entertaining and worth while for their parents to be willing to devote some of their precious leisure time to it. The child who never has such an experience and, on the contrary, comes to realize that his father prefers to spend all his leisure away from home and that his mother considers it impossible to have a good time with the family, is not likely to plan to have his own good time within the family circle. Many fathers and mothers would like to have good times with their children but somehow never do. Some of them think they cannot afford the expense involved; some of them think they have not sufficient time; some of them find children too nerve-racking; some of them do not know what in the world to do with children; and some of them are always intending to do something but never get around to it. The fathers often think this should be mother's job, and the mothers may think they spend enough time with the children day by day without planning special outings.

But raising children is a 2-parent job; and if training in the wise use of leisure is to be a part of child rearing, this, too, is a 2-parent job. Even busy people can plan to set aside a few hours a week for things they really want to do, and it would be just as easy to plan for a little time for activities with the family. Lack of money is not a major obstacle to family good times. As for interesting things to do, the following suggestions may offer some help to parents groping in the dark.

Beginning when the children are still quite small, short trips can be made great occasions. Both in the country and in the city there are nearby points of interest that are worth excursions. There are colorful flower gardens to be seen and fascinating fountains; the zoo must be visited and the aquarium; or there is the river to fish in, the town where the paper mill is located to visit. A tradition of family swimming parties and picnic suppers can be started at an early age and continued for years—if, as time goes on, the children's friends are included. If the baby is too small to go along and nobody can be found to look after him, let father and mother take turns going out with the children for that particular year. Family habits are established as definitely as individual habits; and if the family once gets into the habit of always letting the baby stand in the way of family companionship, there will be some other excuse when the baby gets older.

Riding to the "end of the line" has a great attraction for many children. Even a busy father can sometimes be induced to take his boys for a bus or car ride for an hour or two on a Sunday morning between Sunday school and dinner time. This has the advantages of satisfying the child's curiosity about "where the car goes" and enabling him to see something of the city, and at the same time giving his mother a bit of respite at the time when it is often most needed. For the country child a trip to town with father may be one of the rare occasions when he can chat with his father alone. For while country children see more of their fathers than city children do, leisurely companionship is often quite as infrequent. It is the quality, not the quantity of association that counts.

As the children's curiosity about everyday living increases, father can take them to visit a local fire station, or arrange to have them see the inside of a railroad locomotive. If they are near a harbor, he can take them down to see boats come in and out and load or unload; perhaps they can arrange to see the engine room, or perhaps there are drydocks where boat building may be seen at first hand. If they live near a Coast Guard station, they may see a lighthouse and lifeboats; when they are near an airport or a landing field, they can go down to see airplanes at close range.

Watching how things are made is so fascinating a pastime to adults that almost every large construction project has its audience of interested and critical adults explaining to one another what is going on and expressing admiration of the work or doubts about the feasibility of the plan. If this is interesting to adults, it is even more worth while to the children, particularly if father is able to explain how things work and what the outcome will be. Excavations for buildings, dredging, road and bridge construction, stone quarrying, projects for raising or moving a building from its foundation, steel construction work—all these will provide profitable and yet inexpensive entertainment for short periods of leisure. Visits may be made to a large market, a local newspaper press, a sawmill, a large bakery, a dairy, an ice-cream factory, and similar local industries. Sometimes it is possible for a group of parents to get together and plan to take turns taking their children on such expeditions. This may add to the fun for the children and may help the individual parent to enter into the thing with more confidence and enthusiasm.

City families do well to make trips to the country to provide their children with opportunities for some first-hand observations of horses, pigs, cows, and chickens. Families living in the country can offer their children an equally profitable opportunity by arranging for a day in the city, where even the sidewalks are exciting.

Then there are the places of historical interest to be visited; an old fort, battle scenes, monuments, birthplaces of famous people, Indian mounds, the State capitol, and the historical society. Some communities are far richer than others in such resources; and yet in the most unexpected places one may happen upon a real, old-fashioned blacksmith shop with a ringing anvil, or a primitive mill, which may have interesting associations in addition to being good examples of how the world's work was done in days gone by.

There still remain innumerable special things, such as the flower show, the pet show, the automobile show, the sportsmen's show, the State and county fairs and all kinds of exhibits. As the individual interests and talents of the children develop, parents will also doubtless wish to foster an appreciative interest in art and music by taking them to concerts and to art galleries.

Most of the things mentioned so far have been things to see rather than things to do, and it may be argued that there is little value for the future in training children to go around looking at things. Even though the objection may be met with the answer that the children are learning to find a satisfying interest in the real activities of life rather than in made-to-order entertainment, it is nevertheless desirable to introduce into a program for leisure time some activities in which they can partcipate.

Here again parents must take thought early if they look forward to seeing their adolescents enjoying leisure hours at home and in the family. If the children want to play grocery store in the family pantry, shoe store in the family bedrooms, or barber shop in the bathoom; if they want to get out old clothes and dress up; if they want to rearrange the furniture in order to play train, or church, or school; if they want to have a tea party on the porch or make a hut in the back yard, what do we do about it? Do we give them a dime and tell them to run along and not bother us? Do we tell them that we can't have them all over the house and send them out to play in May's yard or on the school playground, or to someone else's house. Do we tell them to stay in their own playroom where they belong with their own toys?

If Tommy invites us to hear him preach his first sermon from a high-chair pulpit, or Helen tries to sell us tickets to the greatest back-yard circus in the world, or Peter wishes us to attend the special performance of the junior dramatic society, are we too busy to go?

Of course we cannot be at the constant beck and call of youngsters at play, and we certainly cannot have them carrying our shoes and groceries all over the house or playing with father's shaving brush. But children are quick to learn the rules of any game, and they will play fair if they are well taught. There can be rules about which shoes to use and how not to play with them just as there are rules about checkers; there can be days when the chairs cannot be made into trains just as there are days when the roller skates are not to be taken out. And as for putting things back where they were found and straightening up afterward—that is a vital part of the philosophy of family living; pajamas are hung up in the morning and soiled clothes put with the laundry; the bathroom is left neat and clean for the next person; and toys that have been taken out are put away when the play hour is over. These things become established customs, and there is no more need for a disordered house or cross words and harassed looks in relation to habits of play than there would be in relation to habits of eating, sleeping, or the toilet.

Adolescents at Leisure

No matter how pleasant the family life and how much the children enjoy their leisure-time activities with their parents, the normal adolescent, as he grows older, will want to spend more and more time doing things with the boys and girls of his own age and less with his family. This is something which parents should be prepared to welcome as a sign that their growing son and daughter are developing in an entirely normal way and making a good adjustment to life. Instead of making all the plans themselves and participating in the activities with their children, parents will now gradually withdraw. The club and the group logically become more important than the family in leisure time. There may still be special occasions when a party with the family and their relatives will be greatly enjoyed, but even on such occasions the adolescent is likely to look around for some other young person of his own age with whom he can remain a little aloof from both grown-ups and children.

Parents should make sure that their children are not obliged to have all their social contacts away from home through lack of any privacy from an interested family. A boy who has a room of his own to which to bring his friends will spend a lot of time there; the girl who knows that her parents may be depended on not to attach themselves like limpets to the living-room chairs when she brings "the gang" home with her will spend less time joy-riding.

The adolescent may continue to enjoy many of the interests stimulated and cultivated at home; but instead of "playing show" with the neighborhood youngsters, he will want to join a dramatic club. He will wish to substitute class picnics and Scout hikes for some of the family picnics and walks. Practice with the school band or school orchestra and a real conductor will take precedence over practice at home, unless he is encouraged to bring the group to *his* house to practice. In fact, in everything from straight athletics to social dancing the adolescent boy and girl are likely to seek companionship in their own age group. They are beginning to be aware of themselves as individuals and to realize that although they must be part of the family group, they must also be themselves. Moreover, they suspect that they can be themselves more effectively in solitude or in the company of other adolescents than in the presence of a domineering, inquisitive, and critical family. Of course, even nice families sometimes seem domineering, inquisitive, and critical when one is just beginning to grow up.

There may be a rule—or perhaps a tactful understanding—about the hour for coming home, and parents should certainly know where and with whom their adolescents are spending their time. But they will do well to limit their inquiries as well as their criticisms and corrections to important issues, leaving as many minor decisions as possible in the hands of the adolescents themselves in the hope that their past training and maturing judgment will ultimately win the day.

This is a difficult role for many parents to assume, particularly if they have been counting on more rather than less companionship at this time. Fathers find it hard if they have constantly postponed the day when they would "get acquainted" with their sons, or if they have been looking forward to adolescence as the time when they would begin to make a "pal" of the oldest boy. Mothers find it hard if they have been hoping to relive the experiences of youth through keeping in close touch with their daughters. But unless they face the situation and the needs of their children frankly, and refrain from becoming

dependent on them for entertainment and companionship, they must either meet with constant disappointment or gratify their ambitions at a sacrifice of the normal development of their children. . . .

It is in our leisure time that we can be most freely and frankly ourselves, for when we are at leisure, we may exercise a choice in our activities. During adolescence more than at any other time, the individual needs the opportunity to exercise this choice, for one of his main objectives is to be himself, to reveal his own identity as distinguished from that of his family. If his parents are always wishing to determine his activities or seeking to enjoy them with him or even for him, his efforts to find himself are frustrated. The mother who bubbles over with enthusiasm over her daughter's parties and the father who gets his "biggest kick" out of his son's touchdown must be careful lest in their mature enjoyment and excitement they seem to make their daughters' parties their own parties, and their sons' touchdowns their own touchdowns, leaving the adolescents with nothing for themselves.

Thus the adolescent's need to share experiences with those of his own age, to become independent of his parents and lead his own life, and to protect the evolution of his own personality and individuality seems to require that parents expect less and less companionship and make fewer demands as the children grow older. Education in the use of leisure must be given in childhood. Adolescence is the time when companionship and confidence may be sought by the child or invited by the parent, but it is too late for the parent to force it, nor should he risk making a boy or girl feel guilty because he is growing out of his earlier intimacy with and dependence upon his parents.

ASOCIAL CONDUCT

IN ANY discussion with parents of the subject of delinquency, it is important first of all to stress the fact that the subject under consideration is not the confirmed delinquent who has been a more or less constant offender against law and order for a period of years and who has had court records and commitments to institutions. Our concern is rather with that fairly large group of young people who for some reason or other, in their endeavor to get out of life that something in the way of personal satisfaction for which everyone is striving, have introduced into their scheme of living tendencies of a delinquent nature, which, if continued, will eventually bring them into conflict with society.

In dealing with human behavior, whether good or bad, it is essential to appreciate and understand that conduct is always motivated by some inner force. Some environmental factor may be the precipitating cause, but it is the state of mind that determines whether or not trivial and inconsequential events will result in conduct of a disrupting character. The purpose of this section is to indicate in a general way the soil in which delinquent careers are most likely to develop and the particular situations in life that are most likely to act as the spurts which frequently result in disastrous explosions. . . . Delinquency may be a problem even in the most respected families. The background is but one of the factors that need consideration in the effort to understand conduct. . . . Besides the family background of the child, one must also consider certain inadequacies and handicaps of the child himself which would tend to make for difficulties in meeting the ordinary demands of life. Illness, mental inadequacy, physical handicaps—such as defects of hearing and vision, residuals of infantile paralysis, a chronic heart condition, and the like—are all particular obstacles which certain individuals have to overcome before they can fit into the social scheme of things successfully. These must be considered carefully in any effort to understand both the contributing and the precipitating factors leading to asocial activity.

It is the method by which these early delinquent trends are handled, rather than the trends themselves, however, that determine whether they are eradicated or perpetuated. Relatively few children reach the age of adolescence without having had some experiences that were very definitely of a delinquent type. These isolated, temporary deviations from the straight and narrow path need not be regarded as occasions for alarm, and yet they require wise handling if they are not to be repeated.

There is no one well-defined technique that will work out to the best advantage in all situations. Nor is there any one method of insuring success. The economic situation of the parents is of considerable importance, but neither poverty nor affluence is a determining factor with reference to managing a delinquent wisely. . . .

A tendency that leads distinctly away from the wise handling of undesirable conduct but that is nevertheless common among many parents is an unwillingness to face fairly and squarely a situation as it actually exists. This leads to the use of artificially produced excuses. Mary's mother explains that her daughter would not have stayed out at night and played about with undesirable company if she had not been led astray by her friend who was older and wiser. Tom's father complains in indignation that the school teacher who expelled his son for cheating had never given the boy a fair deal. Another father attempts to protect his son who has been apprehended for taking an automobile by explaining that it was a boyish prank and that the youngsters had just been out for a lark. A very solicitous mother finds an excuse for the truancy and mild indiscretions of her 13-year-old boy in the fact that he had always been ill and had never had a good time.

It is quite natural for the youth in trouble to accept as a means of protecting himself from criticism these excuses which the self-deceived parent offers; and although he may not accept them as the true reasons for his misdeeds, he nevertheless appreciates that they serve the purpose of letting him off without punishment or reprimand. Notwithstanding that there is a constant and progressive innate tendency leading toward the socialization of the individual, and that asocial activity can be looked upon, in a general way, as self-eliminating, this is not likely to work out in the individual case unless the youth is permitted to learn from his own experiences that his asocial activity does not pay. If, on the contrary, he finds in his delinquencies ways and means of overcoming all the difficulties and hardships in life and of acquiring those things which, for the moment at least, bring pleasure and satisfaction, without having to meet the responsibilities that actually attach themselves to such conduct, it is but to be expected that asocial trends will continue.

It must be kept in mind, however, that it is the motive behind the conduct rather than the conduct itself which really matters, and the motives are not always evident upon superficial examination. One of the fundamental and best-known principles of modern psychology is that much conduct, social or asocial, is dominated by motives that lie below the level of consciousness. Conduct is but a striving toward emotional satisfactions— a certain release of energy which, if pent up, leads to tension and a general feeling of discomfort and which can be released only by activity, either physical or mental. There may be several ways of attaining emotional satisfaction through activity. One boy may satisfy his sense of power through bullying, while another would attain the same satisfaction through protecting. It happens that one way is looked upon as being asocial and undesirable and is frowned upon by the group, while the other is approved and applauded. We, therefore, try to eradicate one method and perpetuate the other.

In brief, the effort to eradicate delinquent and asocial trends must include a plan whereby the emotional strivings of the individual will be satisfied in a way that is compatible with the social standards of the group in which he is living. This training and the accompanying experience are among the most important acquisitions of adolescence. With many of the adolescents it is not difficult to interpret the problems of their age in terms of their inadequate preparation for it. The intensity of their emotions plus the limitations of their experience makes this particular phase of life more trying than any other, and all too frequently the habits and personality traits which were fairly adequate in the protected environment of the home lead to nothing but failure of the most pathetic sort when the child is called upon to meet the broader issues of life.

Stealing

The story of 12-year-old Neal, who had gotten into rather severe difficulties on account of stealing, is a good example of how involved the underlying motives may be in what appears to be a very simple, commonplace situation. This lad's difficulties begin during his preschool years and were due, in part at least, to the fact that he had never been taught by his parents to differentiate between what was his own and what belonged to others. The fact that he took pennies and food from home and toys from other children made little impression upon his parents and at that time was overlooked because of his immature age. It was also overlooked, or at least given little attention, that he was not well trained in the fundamental habits of life—eating, sleeping, and elimination; that he did not get along well with other children, never entering into competition with them and invariably seeking companions who were younger; and that even at an early age he resorted to masturbation when out of harmony with his environment. Later on the movies and mystery stories were his chief retreats from the realities of life.

As Neal advanced in years, he broadened his field of activities so far as stealing was concerned. He went from the home to his playmates; later on, to stores; and finally he developed and carried out well-laid plans to enter the homes in the neighborhood, taking money in the form of petty cash from pocketbooks, toy savings banks, and so forth. It was while on one of these pilfering escapades that he was apprehended. He admitted a long series of delinquencies to his mother; and after a family conference, he was given a series of daily lectures by his father, meanwhile being completely ostracized from his family and having all his meals in his room. The boy was completely bewildered and confused, as well as frightened, by this method of punishment; and although both parents unflinchingly carried out the measures which they thought were best suited to eradicate the "criminal tendencies" in their son, they were depressed and discouraged. . . .

It had not taken Neal long to find out that human contacts with others of his own age and a little social recognition from those whom he admired could be purchased, for the time being at least, by this asocial activity. Had the boy's problem been frankly met and adequately dealt with—that is, had he been assisted in finding more suitable means of gaining recognition in a socially approved way through games, social contacts, friendships, development of habits and intellectual achievements that were all within his grasp—the prognosis would have been much better and both boy and family much happier. Even as the situation existed, the same plan of educating both parents and boy to meet life on a more mature level was followed, but the advice in this case had to come from outside the home rather than from the parents themselves.

The important aspect of the whole situation is the fact that stealing in this particular case was not an end in itself, but simply a means of satisfying one of the instinctive strivings common to all, whether children or adults; namely, the desire for recognition. In the process of growing up, the well-trained child develops a variety of tools which are admirably suited to this purpose, and he does not have to resort to asocial conduct to gain attention. . . .

It is not uncommon to see superior and well-trained boys, coming from good homes, with intelligent parents, occasionally getting into serious difficulties through participation in gang life. As one studies these situations, one is struck by the fact that many of these lads suffer from feelings of inferiority. They have a tendency to drift to a lower social and economic level, where they can make friends and perhaps assume some leadership with a minimum amount of effort. They feel the necessity of demonstrating to themselves, as well as to others, that they are not inadequate, and one way of doing this is by assuming a "hardboiled" attitude. They have a fear of being called "yellow." They want to demonstrate their leadership by something that is spectacular and will demand attention. The asocial activity of this particular group of boys needs most careful consideration, as such boys are likely to become the tools later on for those more cunning and shrewd individuals who dominate gang life. Often these youngsters are actually terrified after their escapades. They eat poorly, their nights are sleepless, they are constantly worried and agitated, and they are much relieved when they get up courage enough to confide in friend or parent or even when they have been detected. Parents who are on intimate terms with their children can recognize the early symptoms of these feelings of inferiority in their children and make every attempt to find ways and means of substituting activities that will offer opportunities for achieving legitimate success.

Stealing is undoubtedly less common with girls than with boys. Girls have less demand upon them for money during the adolescent period, their contacts are less likely to be of the type which would present opportunities for stealing, and gang life, as we understand it, is a less important aspect of the girl's life than of the boy's. However, stealing occurs among girls with sufficient frequency to be worthy of serious consideration.

The desire for self-adornment and for appearing well dressed is oftentimes the motivating force behind much of the petty thieving that occurs among girls in boarding schools and colleges, and the stealing itself is oftentimes characterized by an impulsiveness which is less common in boys. . . .

A girl was taken to court on a charge of breaking and entering. Investigation showed that on three occasions she had gone to the house of her best friend and stolen wearing apparel, skates, and a ring, all of which she had carefully hidden away and made no attempt to use or sell. A rather long, detailed study of the case revealed the fact that, in spite of her extreme fondness for her friend, she had times when she became intensely jealous of her, especially when the other girl appeared in new clothes which her own parents could not afford to buy. It was after such periods of jealousy that she committed the thefts.

Incorrigibility

There is a group of adolescents who, in spite of good intellectual equipment, excellent health, and what appears to be a satisfactory environment, have a mental make-up that is characterized by a sense of resentment of authority, irresponsibility, cruelty, and pugnacity. These individuals are invariably unstable emotionally, and with their sudden changes in mood and conduct, they are very difficult individuals to deal with successfully. The court looks upon them as being incorrigible, meaning that they do not respond to the ordinary methods of correction. The psychiatrists call them psychopathic personalities, constitutional inferiors, psychopaths, and various other names that add little to understanding of the forces tending to produce conduct so bizarre and purposeless. Despite their unhappy mental attitude toward life, these individuals frequently resent any effort on the part of parents or outsiders to help them. There is a gulf between their ambitions and their achievements. They are anxious to grow up all at once and often regard being "hard-boiled" as evidence of manhood. In spite of their bullying, bragging, and egotism, they are lacking in self-confidence and self-assurance; yet they assume the attitude that they are right and the world is wrong, and they utilize every conceivable method they can in getting even with their unjust world.

Invariably the parents become the victims of these moods. This is quite naturally so, as these individuals have learned from experience that parents are more tolerant than the general public and therefore safer to defy. Through fear or ignorance parents may then neglect to take a firm stand and so continue to be humiliated and persecuted. They present the most difficult cases to deal with—cases in which parents arouse antagonism and resentment in those whom they are trying to help. Regardless of how sincere their intentions may be, such parents are apt to be hurt and crushed. It is for one outside the family, free from passion and prejudice, to deal with these situations. But more important and less difficult than treatment is prevention.

Adolescent reactions of this type are not developed overnight. They begin fairly early in life, and it is not difficult for parents to see the early evidences of dissatisfaction. The child who begins to build up petty grievances, who is always complaining of not getting a square deal at school, not being liked by the children, being slighted at parties, being discriminated against by parents, who is always calling himself down and in a general way taking a critical view of life, is manifesting the early symptoms of a state of mind that is likely to become more and more a fixed part of his personality make-up as he advances in years.

As parents, we must keep in mind that defiance and sullenness cannot be overcome by force and disciplinary measures. Neither does moralizing serve any useful purpose when the child's attitude toward life is twisted and warped by his confusion and dissatisfaction. This situation calls for supreme patience on the part of the parents. They must think in terms, for the moment at least, of making the child happy rather than either obedient or efficient. This can best be done by helping the child regain his self-confidence, restore his self-esteem, and overcome his tendency toward developing ideas of inadequacy. It is essential that parents take account of the child's assets, placing him, as much as possible, in situations where these assets can be used to best advantage. It is well, too, for them to attempt to eliminate sources of friction and to withdraw, so far as it is compatible with the child's safety, much of their parental authority. All too frequently these rebellious youngsters need at least a momentary freedom in order that they may demonstrate to themselves that freedom is only a means to an end and not an end in itself.

It is striking that this particular group of unhappy, resentful adolescents invariably react worst in the home situation. For this reason, they impress their elders painfully with their ingratitude, selfishness, and oftentimes cruelty. This is particularly true when the parents happen to be the type of individuals who interpret everything that happens in an environment in terms of how it affects themselves. . . .

No permanent improvement in such a family situation will result until both parent and child can somehow change their conceptions of one another. This can be accomplished by bringing the problem to a stable, tolerant, impartial third party. A psychiatrist is usually best trained to help in situations like this.

In order to solve the conduct disorders of youth one must be sufficiently interested to take time to determine what these asocial activities really mean to the child Most of this type of behavior can be modified to the advantage of all concerned as soon as the conduct is thought of as a symptom which has its basis in an unsatisfactory adjustment between the child and his environment. The rebellious, delinquent, poorly adjusted child is invariably an unhappy child.

EVADING REALITY

MANY OF THE manifestations of an evasion of reality are found in individuals who have failed to grow up, who have been inadequately prepared through training and experience to meet life on the level which their chronological age would indicate. It is therefore important that in the process of training children parents beware of the subtle techniques which children utilize at an early age to avoid meeting the difficult situations in life.

The child who in early life has learned to use temper tantrums as a way of gaining his own end, who avoids an unpleasant school situation by vomiting or having stomachaches, who always has the ever-convenient headache when called upon to assume some responsibility, is manifesting the first evidences of such tendencies.

Parents who are intimately acquainted with their children, who are familiar with their habitual reactions to life, should be the first to notice any unusual deviation from the normal which would be the first indication that the adolescent is in need of help. The tendency to evade reality may take various forms, such as romancing, daydreaming, cheating, running away, drinking, and similar manifestations which frequently give concern to parents of adolescent boys and girls.

Daydreaming and Romancing

Both daydreaming and romancing are common methods used by adolescents to evade unsatisfactory situations through a retreat into the world of phantasy.

Daydreaming is indulged in at some time or other by almost everybody and need not be a dangerous pastime for the adolescent unless he prefers his daydreams to normal contacts with other young people or seeks in them a means of escape from minor conflicts and feelings of inadequacy. Romancing, which is but daydreaming aloud, may be defined as an attempt on the part of the individual to bolster up his self-regard and the esteem in which he desires to be held by others by fabricating tales which enhance his prestige, add influence or distinction to his family background, and in general exaggerate his own importance. Romancing is a less dangerous method than daydreaming of compensating for feelings of inadequacy, because it has the advantage of being detectable before it becomes too deeply rooted in the personality make-up of the individual.

The adolescent who makes excursions into the land of unreality may be less annoying to his elders than the one who indulges in temper tantrums or other types of vexatious behavior, but such practices may be fundamentally more harmful to healthy mental development. Boys and girls should be helped to realize that they can win the recognition they desire through active effort in some given field rather than through such unsatisfactory methods as romancing and daydreaming.

Cheating

The habit of cheating and the tendency toward evasion are utilized by children, adolescents, and adults in attempting to attain certain objectives in life without making the necessary effort; they are found in those individuals who are constantly seeking "short cuts to prosperity." Such conduct is not uncommonly found in schools and colleges with reference to examinations. One child may cheat in order to get passing marks, while another individual will cheat in order to stand at the head of the class. There are those who are always seeking the opportunity to "put it over" the person who happens to be in authority, whether it is the parent, the teacher, the counselor, or the employer.

The love of winning or the inability to lose gracefully—that attitude called poor sportsmanship—may lead to difficulties in this direction; so will an exaggerated desire for power and recognition and for freedom. The inability that many individuals have to meet any situation frankly, that is, just as it exists, also leads to cheating, evasiveness, and lying. Cheating is an individual's attempt to obtain under false pretenses something which he fears he could not get by more honest methods.

The tendency to practice evasion is seen in most children at some time or other. It is unfortunate that parents are inclined to look upon this tendency lightly, calling these attempts cute tricks and bolstering up their own fears with the idea that the tendency will soon be outgrown. The parent who allows the child to evade carrying out his part of a contract, whether it be doing certain chores about the house, accepting praise

for something he has not accomplished, or keeping the change that he should return after doing an errand, is permitting that child to entertain false ideas with reference to his obligations and responsibilities to others. It should also be remembered that one can be quite as dishonest in dealing with time as in dealing with money or examinations.

It is important to inculcate a sense of fair play at an early age in order that the child may develop the habit of looking at life frankly and honestly, sizing up the prospective difficulties and pitfalls and planning how to meet them. It is not difficult for even very young children to learn that the practice of deception rarely works out to their advantage. It is perfectly true that certain individuals may be confronted with a situation where cheating represents an unrepeated incident in their lives; but by the time the child reaches the adolescent age, these isolated experiences which bear little relation to the best moral standards of the individual are rare. They are more likely to occur in those individuals who suddenly and unexpectedly are confronted with keen competition and resort to this unfair method as a way of "putting themselves across."

In games and sports there are also various ways of cheating. One of the more subtle was observed in Gilbert, a 14-year-old lad who was a fairly good athlete but a poor sport. He excelled in tennis; but on several occasions when he was threatened with defeat, he would refuse to continue a match on the ground that his eyes were bothering him. Repeated examinations by a specialist indicated that the affected eyesight was but a way of avoiding actual defeat.

It is tremendously important for children to learn how to meet failure as well as success in early life. There is a tendency on the part of those interested in children to stress the value of success, and this is important. But the child who has never learned how to meet defeat and disappointment is poorly equipped to battle with life.

Truancy

Pushed by the spirit of the "wanderlust," many of the more venturesome children seek adventure and new experiences outside their immediate environment. These individuals are less concerned about their security than the average boy or girl. They seem to have an inherent hunger to investigate all that is strange and new. Their homes may be good, their parents just, and they themselves without any deep underlying conflict. Truancy in these cases is but the response to a deep under-lying urge to satisfy something that is closely allied to curiosity. On the other hand, a certain number of truant individuals are not running to something but away from something, and in this group truancy and delinquency often go hand in hand. Truancy in these situations is but the re-sult of conflict between the individual and his environment. When the home atmosphere is un-happy because of constant friction and emotional tension or when punishment is severe and unjust or when failure in school with its accompanying humiliation is inevitable, or when the individual is in the grip of a feeling of inadequacy, truancy may be an escape closely allied to alcohol, illness, and other similar types of escape utilized later in life.

It is the state of mind that activates truancy rather than the truancy itself which must be looked upon as the vital and dangerous aspect of the situation. . . .

It is not infrequent to find parents, either habitually or in desperation, meeting anger with anger and deception with more deception. Such a plan may work out for the moment, but it will not ultimately be successful. Frankness may make for temporary rebellion, but it never destroys the confidence and respect which are essential for the happy relation between the adult and the ado-lescent.

Drinking

If the adolescent is introduced to alcohol, it is invariably through his social activities, and his continued use of it is likely to be a symptom of some inadequacy and instability. For the less courageous, those who feel inferior, it is the most dangerous weapon with which they can play, as it temporarily bolsters up their courage, gives them a transient sense of well-being and a false sense of importance, and relieves them of certain painful inhibitions only to leave them pitifully weak and helpless without it.

Rarely can the problem be adequately met by disciplinary measures, deprivation of freedom, or moralizing tactics. The best safeguard that par-ents can throw about the adolescent to prevent indiscretion in the use of alcohol is education, and the best method of education is good example.

One of life's earliest, most difficult, and most painful lessons is that we cannot indulge without

discrimination the varied impulses and desires that are constantly being aroused and seeking avenues of expression without getting into trouble with society or creating conflicts within ourselves. Long before we appreciate just why we should not pull the covers off the table, hurl the orna-ments about the room, pinch, squeeze, and annoy younger members of the family, run blindly out into the crowded street, take candy, food, or money which does not belong to us, or do in-numerable other things, we learn that such be-havior brings swift and painful punishment or in some way or other works out to our disadvantage.

The great masses of the boys and girls of this country, with a newly acquired freedom, with un-bounded opportunity for liberty and license, asso-ciated with a realization of the force that they are capable of exerting upon the community, have taken their newly acquired privileges, all of them laden with the stuff that just naturally leads to revolt, and have managed themselves with wisdom that should demand more respect and less criti-cism from adults, whose criticism is, after all, bred of fear of what is going to happen next.

THE ADOLESCENT AND HIS COMPANIONS

The Importance of Friends

THERE IS NO phase in the individual's life in which friends count more than during the adolescent period. As has been pointed out, this stage of development in the child's life is charac-terized by intensity of feeling in combination with lack of experience to guide and direct these intense emotions with the wisdom of more mature years. There can be many substitutes for inti-mate friendships during childhood—brothers and sisters, parents, and the innumerable individuals whom the child meets in the daily routine; like-wise in adulthood, one's family, business, and other interests, or one's philosophy of life may make intimate friendships unnecessary. It is extremely difficult, however, for the adolescent to accept anything in place of his chum, his pal, his buddy, or whatever else he may call that individual in whom he can confide with absolute assurance of receiving a sympathetic hearing and being un-derstood.

The need for intimate associations with those of one's own age is greater during this period, because adolescents are apt to entertain the idea that they are but little understood by the adult world. Thus the boy or girl who in the process of development has not acquired those personal characteristics which are essential to making friends is a pathetic figure. He represents one of the real catastrophes of life, and his situation is one of the most difficult to face, for although he appreciates his own needs he may fail entirely to understand why he does not measure up.

It is unfortunate indeed that those traits or lack of traits in one's personality make-up which are essential in building up the close personal contacts which we look upon as friendships, are very often dependent upon environmental situations over which the individual has no control until the damage has been done. Yet. as one sees children during their early life, one may be easily aware of the fact that there are also inherent traits which apparently allow one group of children to be responsive to attention and to react with pleasure, while the other group tends to withdraw, reject, and be offended by quite the same overtures. The fact that these responses to life are exaggerated by the environment—that is, that attention is invariably given where it is appreciated—is obvious to all who are concerned with the behavior of children.

Certain mental characteristics, or personality traits, are found sufficiently often, however, in these friendless, lonesome individuals to make it seem only fair to assume that these traits in themselves represent the barrier between the child and the social group with whom he is brought in contact. There is, for example, the shy, diffident, reserved youngster who is inclined to be very introspective, who is extremely sensitive not only to the impressions that he makes upon the world but to the impressions that the world makes upon him. Everything seems to register, and everything that registers must necessarily be analyzed; it is in the process of examining and tearing these ordinary, everyday situations apart that the individual becomes more and more self-centered. Later in life he develops feelings of inferiority and inadequacy; he is prone to be unduly critical about himself, not infrequently setting his standards for himself so high that failure is inevitable.

The question arises: What are the environmental situations that are likely to produce this state of mind in the child when he is called upon to confront life during the adolescent period? As has been stated, the family may be substituted for friends during early life; but it is not uncommon for parents to put such a value on family life and to derive so much pleasure and satisfaction from their children that they very selfishly hold them too close to the family circle. Home life may be made so pleasant and attractive and in subtle ways

so easy during the early years of life that there is little incentive for the child to reach out and make intimate contacts with the outside world. Then, too, the child may be cut off from outside contact at a very important period in life because of some accident or illness which makes a temporary invalid of him, so that after recovery he may find it difficult to pick up the thread of social relations where it was dropped. The fact that parents move about and that the place of residence is frequently changed, or possibly changed at a rather critical time in the child's life, is another factor worthy of consideration. . . .

In some homes neighborliness and intimate contacts are frowned upon. Parents do not encourage their children to visit other children or to bring other children home, fearing that such visiting may involve some social obligation to the parents of these other boys and girls. There is a lack of cordiality in such a home that cannot but affect certain children in their early relations with others. In other homes there is a critical attitude toward the neighbors' children and toward the neighbors themselves that is also restraining. For example, Johnny may be told that the children of one family are too dirty and rough or too indecent in their language to play with, other children are to be avoided because their families are economically or socially inferior, and another group may be undesirable because of racial or religious differences. . . .

Personal cleanliness and fastidiousness are indeed important in helping the individual to get on with people. A report of a school for truant boys contains the sad record of a lad who had run away from his school because the offensive odor from a catarrhal condition had made him subject to the persecution of his classmates. Such problems doubtless stand in the way of the adolescent's social adjustment more frequently than parents realize. They are things to be watched for, and appropriate suggestions and advice should be offered. But the ability to make and keep friends is not solely dependent on good habits of health, cleanliness, and grammar; some people make friends in spite of lacking such good habits, whereas others fail in spite of having them. Let us by all means encourage good hygiene and personal fastidiousness, but let us also encourage individual personality development through intelligent, sympathetic, and unselfish guidance.

"Crushes"

While some adolescents need help in learning to make friends at all, others need help in learning to maintain a sense of balance in their friendships. They must learn to keep their interest open in many people instead of centering all their attention, affection, admiration, and devotion in one person of their own sex.

Adolescent crushes are very common and can usually be looked upon as a normal phase of development. There are, however, a certain number of these intimate relations between individuals of the same sex that either because of their intensity or because of their duration require serious consideration. Parents and teachers ofttimes need to use great care and judgment in handling these situations in order that they may be most helpful to those who quite innocently become involved in some alliance which might become quite disastrous to the parties involved.

Crushes that continue are of significance not because of any undesirable activity but because of their interference with the natural, normal, healthy development of broad social contacts which are of special importance during this period in life. These intense emotional reactions between those of the same sex, more commonly seen in girls than in boys, are all-absorbing and in most cases leave no time or interest for other social contacts. At best, when one of those involved gets a more mature outlook on life and seeks a broader field for personal relations with both boys and girls, the other is invariably hurt.

While the crush is on, any attempt to break it up or interfere in any way is met with open rebellion. Any criticism directed by friends or family is resented. The parties to the experience glory in their loyalty toward each other. Invariably they entertain the idea that this relation is something given to them alone, that no one has ever before experienced the joy of such a friendship, and that, therefore, no one else is capable of understanding it. Quite rightly they resent any intimation that there is anything wrong or bad about this relation. To those caught emotionally in this snare, it symbolizes all that is good and worth while. Helping these young people to get a proper perspective of this particular problem in relation to the entire life situation is therefore a delicate task.

Fortunately when the fires burn so intensely, they do not last long, and most of these crush situations are self-eliminating. If managed wisely, they do no harm. It is not so much the crush itself that needs careful consideration as the individuals participating in it. . . . It requires all the skill and ingenuity of the adults who are trying to help them to find ways and means of developing new interests which may serve as a diversion while these young people are finding themselves.

The family must be tolerant and not give the impression by word or by deed that they are persecuting either party. They may judiciously introduce other young people of interest into the home life or arrange for a visit that would temporarily separate the two young people. Plans for a summer at camp might be considered, depending upon the situation and the extent to which the affair has developed. Whatever may be the plan, it will require nice judgment and much toleration and patience, but it will be worth the effort. The future happiness of these adolescents may depend upon establishing their lives on a more satisfactory basis than one which is narrow and emotional. . . .

These emotional situations must never be looked upon as occasions which necessitate trying to make young people good through fear of consequences. They represent just another opportunity for the parents and the child to get together and discuss the whole situation and all its implications in an unemotional way. The task of passing through that immature stage where autoerotic tendencies and crushes play an important part in life confronts every adolescent and is a difficult one for many of these young people. They fear to take the next step forward, oftentimes being filled with a feeling that they are unable to meet it adequately.

But they are very quick to grasp any real understanding which their elders may have of the problem and to reach out for help when they have reason to believe that it is available.

Many of the doubts and misgivings these young people have with reference to taking the next step in their social development are due to the fact that their early experiences in their own homes have prejudiced them against marriage. A mother whose marital life has been unhappy and whose dissatisfactions have been an ever-present example to her children, who presents marriage, particularly the sex aspect of it, as something to be avoided, is a tremendous obstacle to the normal, healthy development of her sons and daughters. Such childhood experiences are the most common factors leading to social immaturity in these unhappy children. The development of a normal, happy, well-adjusted sex life in young people is more dependent upon the examples they have before them than on all the instruction one can give.

Boy and Girl Relations

With the introduction of coeducation and the discovery that taking part in athletics would not incapacitate girls for childbearing, a more normal and natural everyday relation between boys and girls began to prevail. Seeing each other under the prosaic circumstances of 8 o'clock classes, playing at the same games, working side by side whether on class plays or on school annuals, studying the same subjects, boys and girls came to a clearer understanding of each other. . . .

This closer acquaintance between boys and girls has everything to recommend it. In the world of today men and women must work and play side by side. How will they learn to do this, if they spend their entire youth carefully isolated from each other, fed on mysterious illusions of differences that may not exist? The element of romance with which young people wish to endow each other in their love relations, need not be lacking because of the better acquaintance between boys and girls; on the contrary, being adequately protected against endowing all girls or all boys with glamor, they should be better able to discriminate in their choice of the particular partner they seek.

Friendships between boy and girl, as between girl and girl, generally prove of greater value and greater happiness in the plural than in the singular during adolescence. It takes real ingenuity, however, to deal with fads of the moment, such as that demanding that each boy or girl have a "steady," and date only with that one person.

We shall probably all agree that there is nothing particularly new about the practice of petting, excepting for the fact that it is now practiced more generally among those who are considered nice people, that it has become more of a pastime and perhaps less well defined as a step leading to matrimony, and finally that it is no longer a practice reserved for the subdued lights of the family parlor, the country wayside, or other secluded spots. In the automobile, on the beach, in the village green, in the city park, on the dance floor, on the public street, in cars and buses, and one might say wherever adolescents as a group can be seen, petting may be witnessed. There appears to be a casual indifference with many young people to what those about see or say regarding their activities in public. These observations can be made by anyone at any time, and almost anywhere.

It's difficult to account for what appears to be a decided change in the attitude of adolescents toward petting, and it is equally difficult to evaluate what it all means in terms of promiscuous sex activity. Certainly there is no reason to believe that the sex urge is more demanding at the present time than it has been in years past. Perhaps constant exposure to love-making in the movies has made such endearments appear more casual and commonplace. Probably time will reveal that more young people of all types are indulging in these activities and that they have not changed materially in degree and intensity. The fact that young people feel free to carry on petting in public is an indication of the less cramped and inhibited feelings about the whole subject of sex that are the result of widespread efforts toward revamping attitudes toward this part of life.

There has grown a more healthy comradeship among young people of both sexes, an effort to find in the one individual those varied satisfactions which it is but human to desire. This need not mean that actual sex relations are more commonly practiced. Petting is perhaps being utilized more and more as a sublimation.

The essential contribution that a parent has to make to this particular adolescent situation is that petting is very definitely a sex experience; that naturally and normally, under happy marital relations, it precedes sexual intercourse, which in the unmarried state is as dangerous in its social implications as it ever was, in loss of social approbation, mental conflict, venereal disease and pregnancy.

Sex as one of the important factors of human development should be regarded and discussed by parents as they would approach health. The girl who overeats, who allows herself to get constipated, who fails to look after her skin, and who fails to follow other hygienic regulations gets fat and develops a poor complexion, never feels right, and is likely to become physically unattractive and socially handicapped. The girl who permits promiscuous petting with unlimited privileges gets the reputation of being "easy" and "common." As a social asset, she is less valuable and soon finds that she is left out of much that would contribute to her happiness. This may be a rather low level of adjustment from a purely moral point of view, but young people can and do understand when we talk to them about what type of conduct will actually work out to their advantage. We can tell young people that we understand all the urges that quite naturally prompt them to seek the thrills of life in this particular way, yet at the same time show them by the innumerable examples always available that it actually pays to postpone these gratifications and help them find other emotional outlets.

It is well to keep before these young people that the various activities which are generally covered by the term petting all too frequently fail to give the parties involved the satisfactions they are after. Frequently these experiences are difficult to digest. Even so, they may become habits after an appetite has been created for this particular type of emotional stimulation. The early indulgences are often brought about by the desire to test out life, to try a new experience, to indulge in some new thrill. In the case of girls particularly, such behavior is often a sincere response to what seems a great need for demonstration of affection. A desire for popularity, attention, and the participation in social activity which they feel would otherwise be denied them is the motivating factor in many instances.

In dealing with this whole subject we need to remind ourselves that the high proportion of frigidity in women, and their failure ever to make a complete response in the sex relation, are almost surely the result of inhibitions and prohibitions set up early in life. That our cultural demands set up a great barrier to the development of normal sex attitudes should not be overlooked by parents.

These are all factors which should be discussed frankly with the adolescent, and, again, the discussion may well be carried on as a subject of interest and practical importance, rather than as a personal problem. It should be kept in mind that this problem of sex is but one aspect of life for the adolescent and that many pitfalls and conflicts may arise in his effort to solve this one particular problem. The adolescent will make his own adjustment to life adequately only when he does it without being harmful to others. The adult who is in a position to gain the confidence and respect of the adolescent holds the strategic position. This can come about only when the adolescent is sure that he is dealing with someone who has a clear idea what youth's problems really are and a practical plan or philosophy of life that will meet his daily needs.

THE NEEDS OF THE PARENT

MUCH THAT has had to do with the relation between parent and child, particularly that aspect of this relation which has worked out to the disadvantage of both child and parent, has been stressed in the previous sections. One cannot understand childhood behavior without carefully investigating the effects that other people in the environment have upon the child, and of course the people who influence the conduct of children the most are the parents. . . .

Let us therefore turn to some of the more constructive aspects of the parent-child relation. This relation has changed so markedly during the past decades that it is not surprising that parents find themselves a bit confused about just what their obligations and responsibilities toward their children are in this modern world. Moreover, many children would consider it but a relic of the past if their obligations to their parents were brought up for consideration. For generations in practically all countries, civilized and uncivilized, children have been bidden to respect, honor, and obey parents. In the laws of the ancients there were no exceptions and no extenuating circumstances for any lack of respect on the part of children toward their parents. Time itself has introduced social factors which necessarily must affect the child's attitude toward his parents. As civilization has advanced and the interests of man have extended beyond hunting, fishing, fighting, and the interests of woman beyond childbearing and housekeeping, and as various trades and professions and occupations have developed, children have had increased opportunity for becoming intimately associated with a varied group of people. Under these conditions parents obviously become less dominant factors in the lives of their children.

The foregoing is simply mentioned in order that parents may grasp the idea that their children are less dependent upon them than they were upon their parents. One must understand and appreciate how efficiently and with how limited an amount of turmoil and confusion young people have taken this recent step toward developing their own independence. What this sudden transition in the attitude of adolescents toward their elders actually means is that if parents are going to continue to stand out in the social scheme of things as being the dominant influence in the lives of their children, this influence must take root at an early age and not be postponed simply to suit the convenience of the parents until the child is fairly well advanced toward adolescence. The idea which was so firmly fixed in the minds of children a few generations ago that all parents were endowed with wisdom, that they were all worthy of respect, that their achievements entitled them to admiration, and that their understanding of human nature was unfailing, no longer exists. This does not mean that children no longer love, respect, and admire their parents, but it does mean that children view their parents more critically; and if the latter are weighed and found wanting, they are not endowed, merely because they are parents, with virtues which they do not possess.

There is, on the other hand, a large group of parents who do not wish for obedience and respect from their adolescents; on the contrary, they wish to be the companions and friends of their adolescent sons and daughters, desiring only to be close to them and intimate with them. But they, too, are destined to disappointment, for, as has been pointed out, young people seek intimacy and companionship with those of their own age. . . .

Parents frequently become much distressed over the strange behavior of sons and daughters who seem abnormally modest in dressing in the presence of their parents; who never report on various phases of their physiological development; who seem embarrassed, indifferent, or annoyed when parents discuss sex with them; who keep private diaries; who never have anything to relate after attending a party or being out for an evening. Such parents are unaware first of all of the gulf that exists between any two generations merely because of the difference in age regardless of how modern the point of view or how youthful the manners of the individual mother. Teachers and recreation leaders make this same mistake when they try to bridge this gulf with some such statement as "Let's all be boys together" or "We're just a bunch of girls talking things over frankly." It is far wiser to be a parent—or a teacher or a recreation leader or other adult—in manner and attitude as well as in actuality, and to say whatever one has to say frankly, sincerely, and with dignity, and then to let young people be young.

Although we may remember how we looked when we were 15, our present 15-year-olds see us only as the aging adults we are, no longer lithe and sparkling, but increasingly stolid, wrinkled, heavy, and growing gray or bald. The very idea of our being on the same level with them and sharing experience as equals is preposterous and even absurd to them. We may try to use adolescent colloquialisms and hope to establish a relation of intimacy and mutual confidence by talking of social, emotional, or physiological experiences in the popular terms of our own day without realizing that popular vocabularies change with the fashions and that in such attempts to reach the adolescent level we meet with as little success as we should by dressing in the clothes of our youth. It is useless, for example, to talk to the adolescent about the undesirability of spooning; for the adolescent of today does not spoon. Although yesterday's necking may be today's petting our very word stamps us as belonging to another generation. The adolescent at once concludes that we speak another language and have no understanding of his problems.

Our attitudes date us quite as definitely as our vocabularies. One generation contemplates the phenomenon of birth with an attitude of romantic sentimentality, while another considers it but an incident; one generation approaches the female sex with an attitude of awe and adoration, while in another generation women themselves claim the right to be regarded as equals; one generation considers sex relations a profane mystery, while another endows them with spiritual significance, and other dismisses them as one of the natural and normal animal phases of life. There are always some individuals who are in advance of their generation and some who are behind and some who must be at war with existing conditions whatever they are. But each generation has its trends, and each new generation feels the urge to depart from these trends.

There is a second obstacle to the relation of intimate equality which some parents desire with their children, and that is the fundamental difference in personality that may exist between parents and their children despite all ties of blood. . . .

And the third obstacle to an intimate identification between the parent and his adolescent child is the adolescent's need to live his own life. . . .

The most important contribution which the parent can make to the child is that of preparing him to assume the obligations and responsibilities which are associated with independence. If it be true that children are, as a group, throwing off the parental shackles at an earlier date than they have done heretofore, it means that parents must see that they are adequately equipped with habits and personality traits and mental attitudes toward life that will work out to their advantage. The child's dependence upon the parent may result, later on, in the parent's pitiful emotional dependence upon the child. There are those parents who have built their lives so intimately around their children that they become extremely unhappy when they appreciate that the parent no longer serves the same purpose to the adolescent as he did to the younger child. It cannot be denied that this attitude of the parent toward the child is fundamentally selfish and not infrequently results unhappily for all concerned, especially if the child has not quite grown up himself. . . .

Many a parent with this selfish, demanding, emotional attitude toward his children has built up barriers which have prevented a happy parental relation in later years. Many an over-solicitous, selfish mother has wrecked the marital happiness of her son, and many a father has rendered himself miserable and unhappy and has developed feelings of being misunderstood and neglected, simply because their children did not retain in adolescent life the immature, dependent, emotional attitude which had meant so much to these solicitous parents in the years gone by. So it is well to point out that parents must prepare themselves to deal wisely with that phase of life when their children are no longer to be dependent upon them. Mothers are very much more likely to be affected by this situation than fathers because in the natural course of events men still continue to be preoccupied with the task of providing for the family. Their time is spent at the office, shop, or factory, and they come in contact with many people and many problems. The mother's big job, however, has been that of rearing the children; and unless she has provided herself with some other interests, she will feel the vacuum created when they are no longer demanding all her time.

Much has been said about the parents' responsibility toward the child, and during early years it is the parent who must supply the initiative, judgment, and patience which this task entails. But it must be kept in mind that as the child advances in years he, too, will have more and more to contribute toward the happiness and satisfaction of family life. Essentially the relation between parent and child should be maintained by a mutual effort to acquire a better understanding of each other's personality, each others' interests, problems and pleasures—both parent and child endeavoring on the one hand to appreciate the various factors contributing to their respective health, efficiency, and happiness, and on the other hand to gain a clearer conception of the influences leading to dissatisfaction, failure, and defeat.

But it must be repeated that this mutual interest in the affairs of parents and child must start at an early age, so that when the child reaches adolescence he will not be confronted suddenly with responsibilities that he will very likely resent. It is desirable to develop in him that attitude which will just naturally make him reach out and do his part of the job, for unless it is done in this spirit and not forced upon him, there is great danger that it will not be done at all.

But all these attitudes, habits, and personality traits must be regarded as only the tools with which the individual makes a place for himself in the social scheme of things—implements which he utilizes in the process of creating relations that will be satisfactory and happy not only for himself but also for all those with whom he comes in contact. In the process of development he must ever be ready to discard those tools which, although perhaps useful in one period of life, have become inadequate for the present need. Fortunately, we are well endowed with a plasticity which enables us to modify our ideas and conduct, whether as adolescents discarding infantile behavior patterns or as parents discarding adolescent behavior patterns.

There is no time when life presents so many doubts and indecisions as during the adolescent years. To many young persons life becomes a very perplexing problem as their earlier hopes and aspirations turn out to be daydreams and illusions, and there is a tendency for them to be overwhelmed with the futility of effort. The child who has had the advantage of living in a home with a religious background—that type of religion which is practiced as well as preached and which teaches the individual to think in terms of others than himself—finds that something very fundamental and important has been woven into the moral fabric of his personality. Religions helps to give to the boy or girl that sense of security and worthwhileness about life both present and future that the maturing individual needs.

GRADED AND CLASSIFIED INDEX

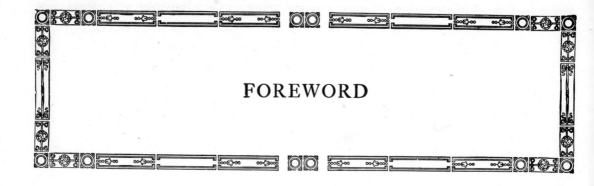

FOREWORD

PURPOSE

THE purpose of this GRADED AND CLASSIFIED INDEX is to make instantly available to you the material contained in The BOOKSHELF which is especially suited to the needs of your child.

When wisdom and love found expression in placing at your child's command a set of books like The BOOKSHELF, you had the right to ask that the gift should count for the most in the development of life and character. It is with the expectation of helping you bring this to pass that the INDEX has been made in this form.

The BOOKSHELF has been classified with unusual care, yet further organization of the vast amount of material was necessary so that with the least effort and the smallest intrusion upon your busy life you may know how to get at what is in these books, and how to give to childhood according to its needs.

This index has cost us considerable labor and care. Thus care and labor have been saved for you.

THE PLAN OF THIS INDEX

The gradation followed is:

GRADE 1—INFANCY:
From birth to three years of age.

GRADE 2—EARLY CHILDHOOD:
From three to six years of age.

GRADE 3—MIDDLE CHILDHOOD:
From six to nine years of age.

GRADE 4—LATE CHILDHOOD:
Nine years of age and beyond.

These ages are only approximate, and vary as between boys and girls, and even as between individuals, but the divisions are convenient, and, in a large sense, accurate.

The divisions, named alphabetically, are as follows:

ART
BIOGRAPHY AND HISTORY
FABLES
FAIRY TALES AND FOLK-LORE
HANDICRAFT
HEALTH
MUSIC
MYTHS AND LEGENDS
NATURE
NURSERY CLASSICS
PICTURE-STORIES
PLAY—INDOOR
PLAY—OUTDOOR
POETRY
THE SCIENCES
STORIES
TRAVEL AND ADVENTURE

HOW TO USE THIS INDEX

There are two ways in which you will find this INDEX constantly useful. When you are in search of material that will interest *your individual child*, you turn to the *graded section*, which tells all that the BOOKSHELF has for his or her age. (For example, if four years old, you go to the heading, "EARLY CHILDHOOD: Ages from Three to Six Years," and find what will help, underneath.) When you are in search of material *of a particular kind*, you turn to that *classification* in the graded section. (For example, if you want stories for this same child, you turn to the headings, "Nursery Classics," "Fairy Tales and Folk-Lore," and "Stories," under "EARLY CHILDHOOD," and find just what you want. The classifications are there printed in alphabetical order.) This you can usually do much more quickly than to trace down the titles in the Tables of Contents of each separate volume.

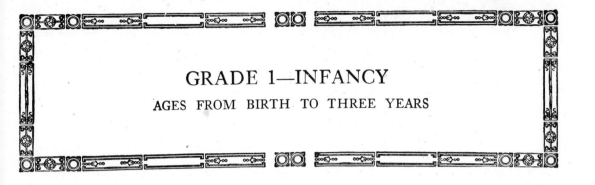

GRADE 1—INFANCY

AGES FROM BIRTH TO THREE YEARS

Most of the material included in this grade is, of course, for the mother herself to read and use with her child. It includes many plays and action-rhymes and songs. There are stories told so simply that the mother can read them even to a three-year-old, and there are many pictures around which she and baby can make up their own stories. A good deal can be done during this period to help the child understand what illustrations in a book mean, and to fix simple stories in his memory. These references will help the mother solve the problem of "What can I do next, Mother?" and bring the child into an interested and intelligent relation with his environment.

LULLABIES

	VOL.	PAGE
Little Baby	1	2
Winky Blinky	1	2
Baby Sleep	1	3
Lullaby	1	3
German Lullaby	1	4
Bye, Baby, Night Is Come	1	5
I See a Dear Baby	1	5
A Mother's Song	1	5

SLEEPY-TIME STORIES

	VOL.	PAGE
Little Bear Takes His Nap	1	8
Story of a Little White Teddy Bear Who Did Not Want to Go to Bed	1	12
Susie's Sleepy Time	1	16
Little Cat That Could Not Sleep	1	18

BABY GAMES AND FINGER PLAYS

	VOL.	PAGE
Baby's Face Plays	1	22
Baby's Nose	1	22
Brow Bender	1	22
Burrowing Game, A	1	22
Baby's Finger and Hand Plays	1	23
Bee-Hive, The	1	23
Pat-a-Cake	1	23
Church, The	1	24
Home, The	1	24
Family, The	1	25
Naming the Fingers	1	26
Little Window, The	1	27
This Is the Way My Fingers Stand	1	27
Baby's Foot Plays	1	28
This Little Pig	1	29
Baby's Riding Games	1	30
Farmer Went Trotting, A	1	30

	VOL.	PAGE
Ride Away	1	30
Dance to Your Daddy	1	31
Riding Song	1	31
To Market, To Market	1	31
Around	1	32
Dance, Little Baby	1	32
Ride a Cock-Horse	1	32
Hey Diddle Diddle	1	40
Deedle, Deedle, Dumpling	1	63

HUMOR

	VOL.	PAGE
Hickory, Dickory, Dock	1	36
Humpty Dumpty	1	38
Little Jack Horner	1	39
Little Tommy Tucker	1	39
Jack Sprat	1	41
Old King Cole	1	54
Mary, Mary	1	56
See-Saw	1	56
Ring-a-Ring-a-Roses	1	64

MOTHER GOOSE RHYMES

	VOL.	PAGE
Little Bo-Peep	1	34
Little Boy Blue	1	35
Dame Trot and Her Cat	1	41
Ding, Dong, Bell	1	42
Jack and Jill	1	42
Polly and Sukey	1	46
Rain, Rain, Go Away	1	49
Curly Locks	1	50
Bye Baby Bunting	1	51
I Had a Little Doggy	1	53
I Had a Little Pony	1	53
Baa, Baa, Black Sheep	1	55
Once I Saw a Little Bird	1	61

NURSERY STORIES

House That Jack Built, The	1	70
Gingerbread Boy, The	1	73
Henny Penny	1	80
Three Little Kittens	1	82
Luke and His Little Wagon	1	216
Lots of Places to Sit	1	218
Here Comes Daddy	1	220

SONGS

Cradle Song	4	225
Gaelic Lullaby	4	226
French Cradle Song	4	227
Sweet and Low	4	228
Now the Day Is Over	4	229
Hush, My Babe	4	230
Winkum, Winkum	4	231
Baa! Baa! Black Sheep	4	232
Sing a Song of Sixpence	4	234
Dickory Dock	4	239
Hey, Diddle, Diddle	4	243
There Was a Little Boy and a Little Girl	4	247
Little Jack Horner	4	249
Pussy Cat, Pussy Cat	4	252
Cock-a-doodle-doo	4	253
Baby Bunting	4	253
Twinkle, Twinkle, Little Star	4	260
The Swing	4	284
Blow, Wind, Blow	4	294
Going to London	4	303

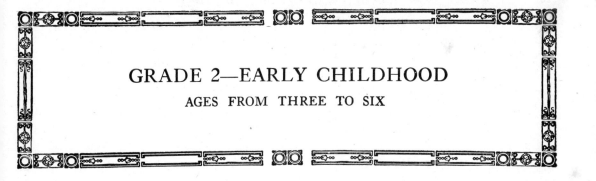

GRADE 2—EARLY CHILDHOOD
AGES FROM THREE TO SIX

THIS is the nursery school and kindergarten age. The material here will help the mother to furnish the stories and poems, the games and projects suitable for home-education during these charming years when the child is still largely in the mother's care.

FAIRY TALES AND FOLK-LORE

	VOL.	PAGE
The Three Bears	1	67
The House That Jack Built	1	70
The Gingerbread Boy	1	73
Little Red Riding Hood	1	77
Henny Penny	1	80
The Little Red Hen and the Grain of Wheat	1	84
The Three Billy Goats Gruff	1	86
The Three Little Pigs	1	89
The Old Woman and Her Pig	1	95
The Lambikin	1	322
Why the Bear Has a Stumpy Tail	1	330
The Fox and the Little Red Hen	1	333

NATURE

	VOL.	PAGE
The Tale of Peter Rabbit	1	97
The Bear Who Wanted to Be a Bird	1	102
Who Likes the Rain?	1	112
How to Get Breakfast	1	114
The Barnyard	1	126
What Robin Told	1	180
The Wind	1	182
The Wind and the Leaves	1	183
Who Has Seen the Wind?	1	183
The Little Turtle	1	198
The Squirrel	1	199
Snowflakes	1	200
Little Jack Frost	1	201
The Dandelion	1	202
How Creatures Move	1	202
Little Wind	1	202
Nature's Sewing	1	202
I'm Glad	1	203
Mud	1	203
The Snowman	1	205
Daisies	1	208
The Secret	1	210
Cobwebs	1	211
The First Song-Sparrow	1	211

STORIES

	VOL.	PAGE
The Bear Who Wanted to Be a Bird	1	102
Timid Timothy	1	104
The Story of a Little Gray Mouse	1	107
The Shy Little Horse	1	110
Peppi and the Custard	1	113
Watch Me!	1	115
There Was Tammie!	1	118
Why Jimmy Skunk Wears Stripes	1	122
The Cat Who Thought He Was a Mouse	1	127
The Horse Who Lived Upstairs	1	132
How Spot Found a Home	1	141
The Story of a Little White Dog	1	144
The Train That Would Not Stay on the Track	1	148
A Garage for Gabriel	1	150
Sneezer	1	154
Corkie	1	156
Mike Mulligan and His Steam Shovel	1	160
The Little Red Lighthouse and the Great Gray Bridge	1	165
Number 9, The Little Fire Engine	1	172
Susan and the Rain	1	214
Luke and His Little Wagon	1	216
Lots of Places to Sit	1	218
Here Comes Daddy	1	220
The Blowaway Hat	1	224
New Clothes	1	229
The Good Little Bad Little Pig	1	233
Mary Ellen's Birthday Party	1	239
P-Penny and His Little Red Cart	1	243

NURSERY RHYMES

	VOL.	PAGE
A Diller, A Dollar	1	35
The Bells of London	1	36
Hickory Dickory Dock	1	36
Mary Had a Little Lamb	1	37
Humpty Dumpty	1	38
The King of France	1	38
Hot Cross Buns	1	39

	VOL.	PAGE
Jack, Be Nimble	1	39
Hey Diddle Diddle	1	40
How Many Strawberries	1	40
Jack Sprat	1	41
If All the World Were Apple-Pie	1	43
The Queen of Hearts	1	44
The Little Nut Tree	1	45
Pussy Cat, Pussy Cat	1	45
Pease Porridge	1	46
Bobby Shaftoe	1	47
Where Are You Going, My Pretty Maid?	1	47
Tom Was a Piper's Son	1	48
One Misty Moisty Morning	1	49
Dr. Foster	1	49
Little Miss Muffet	1	50
Bossy-Cow	1	51
I Saw a Ship A-Sailing	1	52
Old King Cole	1	54
Lady-Bug	1	55
See-Saw	1	56
Donkey, Donkey	1	57
If All Were One	1	59
Deedle Deedle Dumpling	1	63
Wee Willie Winkie	1	63
My Shadow	1	88
Old Mother Hubbard	1	92
The Owl and the Pussy Cat	1	94
Star Light	1	255
Engine, Engine, Number Nine	1	265
One Two, Buckle My Shoe	1	265
Over in the Meadow	1	266

POETRY

	VOL.	PAGE
Wynken, Blynken, and Nod	1	6
The Rock-a-By Lady	1	11
When Mother Reads Aloud	1	178
Good Morning, World!	1	179
The Cow	1	180
Rain	1	181
Singing	1	181
Happy Thought	1	184
Playgrounds	1	184
Bread and Milk	1	185
The Cupboard	1	185
Thanksgiving Day	1	187
The Postman	1	188
How Doth the Little Busy Bee	1	192
Bed in Summer	1	195
Twinkle, Twinkle, Little Star	1	196
To My Valentine	1	197
Only One Mother	1	197
The Mitten Song	1	205
At the Seaside	1	207
I Never Hear	1	208
Boats Sail on the River	1	209
Time to Rise	1	210
After a Bath	1	219
Before a Bath	1	219

	VOL.	PAGE
Animal Crackers	1	223
Hiding	1	227
Feet	1	228
Haircut	1	232
Awful Mornings	1	236
Fourth of July Night	1	237
The Ice-Cream Man	1	238
Five Years Old	1	241
Growing Up	1	241
First Day at School	1	248

HUMOR

	VOL.	PAGE
Elephant in the Sky	1	29
Peter, Peter, Pumpkin Eater	1	43
Simple Simon	1	57
Sing a Song of Sixpence	1	58
There Was an Old Woman Who Lived in a Shoe	1	60
The Cuckoo	1	61
Tweedle-Dum and Tweedle-Dee	1	62
Moother Goose Riddles	1	66
The Owl and the Pussy Cat	1	94
Calico Pie	1	275
A Frog He Would A-Wooing Go	1	282a
The Elephant's Child	1	286
Mrs. Goose's Rubbers	1	294
Mrs. Goose's Bicycle Trip	1	297

TRAVEL AND ADVENTURE

	VOL.	PAGE
The Train That Would Not Stay on the Track	1	148
A Garage for Gabriel	1	150
The Airplane	1	153
Sneezer	1	154
Corkie	1	156
Ferry-Boats	1	159
Mike Mulligan and His Steam Shovel	1	160
The Little Red Lighthouse and the Great Gray Bridge	1	165
Trains	1	170
Taxis	1	171
Number 9, the Little Fire Engine	1	172
The Blowaway Hat	1	224
P-Penny and the Little Red Cart	1	243

PRAYERS AND GRACES

	VOL.	PAGE
Morning Song	1	376
Morning Prayer	1	376
Evening Song	1	376
Evening Prayer	1	376
Child's Grace	1	377
To God, the Giver of All Things	1	378
Dear Father	1	378
Father in Heaven, We Thank Thee	1	378
Nature Handicraft	7	228
Nature Playthings	7	230
A Child's Letter to God	1	379
For Things That Grow	1	379

	VOL.	PAGE
Heavenly Father, Hear Our Prayer	1	379
God's Helpers	1	380
Prayer for Children Everywhere	1	380
Let Our Home Be a Friendly Home	1	380
God Bless	1	380
All Things Bright and Beautiful	1	382
He Prayeth Well Who Loveth Well	1	383
A Child's Prayer	1	383
The Golden Rule	1	383
Do You Know How Many Stars?	1	384

PLAY

	VOL.	PAGE
Sing a Song of Sixpence	4	234
See-Saw	4	254
The Swing	4	284
The Hobby Horse	4	293
London Bridge	4	304
Lucy Locket	4	306
Miss Jennia Jones	4	307
Here We Go Round the Mulberry Bush	4	309
I'm Very, Very Tall	4	315
My Dolly	4	316
Games With the Button Bag	5	115
Boats of Walnut Shells	5	116
The Easter-egg Hunt	5	117
Dressing-up	5	119
Paper Chase	5	125
The Magnet	5	129
Peanut Hunt	5	137
Cat	7	259
Hunt the Ring	7	260
Bubble-blowing	7	262
Games with Bean-bags	7	264
Pigs and Donkeys	7	266

SONGS

	VOL.	PAGE
Cradle Song	4	225
Gaelic Lullaby	4	226
French Cradle Song	4	227
Sweet and Low	4	228
Hush, My Babe	4	230
Baa! Baa! Black Sheep	4	232
Ding, Dong, Bell	4	233
Sing a Song of Sixpence	4	234
Pop Goes the Weasel	4	235
Humpty Dumpty	4	236
Jack and Jill	4	237
Old King Cole	4	238
Dickory Dock	4	239
Tom, the Piper's Son	4	240
Hey, Diddle, Diddle	4	243
Polly, Put the Kettle On	4	244
Little Boy Blue	4	245
Apples Ripe	4	246
Mistress Mary	4	246
Little Jack Horner	4	249
Three Blind Mice	4	250
Little Miss Muffitt	4	252
Pussy Cat, Pussy Cat	4	252
Cock-a-Doodle-Doo	4	253

	VOL.	PAGE
Baby Bunting	4	253
See-Saw	4	254
Good Morning, Merry Sunshine	4	255
Soldiers Marching	4	256
The Child and the Star	4	258
Little Drops of Water	4	258
Which Way Does the Wind Blow	4	259
Twinkle, Twinkle, Little Star	4	260
Balloons	4	261
Baby Bye, Here's a Fly	4	262
Flying Kites	4	264
Little Robin Redbreast	4	270
My Kiddie-car	4	271
Singing	4	272
The Cow	4	276
The North Wind Doth Blow	4	278
Playing Store	4	279
The Swing	4	284
The Stars Are Tiny Daisies High	4	286
Blow, Wind, Blow	4	294
The Carousel	4	296
Animal Crackers	4	297
Going to London	4	303
London Bridge	4	304
Miss Jennia Jones	4	307
Here We Go Round the Mulberry Bush	4	309
I'm Very, Very Tall	4	315

HANDICRAFT

	VOL.	PAGE
Pictures and Painting	5	27
Modeling	5	31
Color-Design-Drawing	5	33
To Make a Butterfly Kite	5	56
Simple Soap Sculpture	5	70
Modeling Small Sculptures	5	75
Making Things Out of Paper	5	81
Things to Make Out of Newspapers	5	85
Making Doll-Furniture	5	86
Pattern for a Dainty Basket	5	89
More Paper-Folding	5	90
Wonderful Uses of Colored Papers	5	92
An Alphabet to be Cut from Paper	5	96
Bead-Stringing	5	99
Hammer and Nails	5	100
Weaving	5	102
Fun Making and Dressing Paper Dolls	5	110
Scrap-books	5	114
Boats of Walnut Shells	5	116
Corn-cob Houses	5	117
Burdock Burr Toys	5	126
Paper Chains	5	126
Toys Made of Candy Boxes and Clothespins	5	129
Pin-wheels	5	130
Lima Bean Pod Animals	5	140
Toys Made of Green Peas and Toothpicks	5	141
Handwork for the Holidays	5	186
Nature Handicraft	7	228
Nature Playthings	7	230

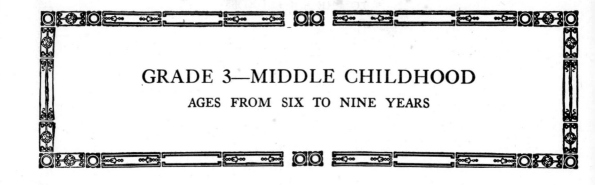

GRADE 3—MIDDLE CHILDHOOD
AGES FROM SIX TO NINE YEARS

Now the child is really in school, in a larger world than ever before. In some instances it is only necessary for the mother to support and emphasize the work of the intelligent and well-equipped teacher in handwork, nature-study, and story-telling. But there are still schools where little more than the "three R's" are provided. In such a case the mother will turn to the BOOKSHELF with particular gratitude for its wealth of material to nourish the child's development, widen his horizons, and enrich his imagination.

BIOGRAPHY AND HISTORY

	VOL.	PAGE
The Boyhood of Sir Walter Raleigh	4	18
Alexander the Great Visits Diogenes	4	162
The Wandering Minstrel	4	164
Gutenberg, the Inventor of Printing	4	165
Boadicea Leading Her Army	4	166
Joan of Arc	4	167
The Story of "The Marseillaise"	4	168
The Liberty Bell	4	169
A Florentine Poet	4	170
The Poet Shakespeare at Stratford	4	171
Sir Walter Raleigh	4	175
The Story of Columbus	4	178
Washington and His Mother	4	186
"With Malice Toward None, With Charity for All"	4	187
Daniel Webster	4	188
John Burroughs Feeding a Robin	4	189
James Watt, the Famous Inventor	4	190
The Great Pyramid of Gizeh	4	196
Beethoven and Mozart	4	199
Cyrus of Persia	8	349
The Boyhood of a Story-teller	9	1
A Nurse's Girlhood	9	6
An Inventor's Boyhood	9	10
The Boy Who Was Helped	9	13
The Boyhood of a Patriot	9	15
The Boyhood of a Statesman	9	19
Bits of Wisdom	9	22
The Boyhood of a Sculptor	9	23
The Child of Urbino	9	27
The Boyhood of an English Painter	9	39
The Boyhood of a French Painter	9	44
The Boyhood of a Musician	9	48
The Girlhood of a Singer	9	50
The Boyhood of a President	9	56
The Army of Two	9	119

	VOL.	PAGE
The Story of the Boston Tea Party	9	121
Israel Putnam	9	123
The Story of Nathan Hale	9	126
How a Woman Saved an Army	9	130
The Story of Molly Pitcher	9	133
Johnny Appleseed	9	136
The Origin of the Flag	9	146
The Pilgrims and the Puritans	9	157

FABLES

	VOL.	PAGE
The Fox and the Crow	2	2
The Ant and the Grasshopper	2	3
The Country Maid and Her Milk Pail	2	4
The Wind and the Sun	2	5
Belling the Cat	2	6
The Miller, His Son, and Their Donkey	2	7
The Fox and the Stork	2	9
The Goose That Laid the Golden Egg	2	10
The City Mouse and the Country Mouse	2	12
The Lion and the Mouse	2	13
The Hare and the Tortoise	2	15
The Dog in the Manger	2	16
The Fox and the Grapes	2	17
The Wolf in Sheep's Clothing	2	18
The Bundle of Sticks	2	19
The Shepherd Boy Who Cried "Wolf!"	2	20
The Camel and the Pig	2	21
The Oak and the Reed	2	23
The Council of Animals	2	23
The Advantage of Knowledge	2	24
The Lion and the Goat	2	25
The Rooster and the Sun	2	26

FAIRY TALES AND FOLK-LORE
All of Volume III

	VOL.	PAGE
The Water-Babies	6	41
Pinocchio	6	55

	VOL.	PAGE
The King of the Golden River . . .	6	62
The Story of Peter Pan	6	70

HANDICRAFT

	VOL.	PAGE
Pictures and Painting	5	27
Modeling	5	31
Color-Design-Drawing	5	33
To Make a Butterfly Kite	5	56
Simple Soap Sculpture	5	70
Modeling Small Sculptures	5	75
Making Things Out of Paper	5	81
Things to Make Out of Newspapers .	5	85
Making Doll-furniture	5	86
More Paper-folding	5	90
The Pattern for a Dainty Little Basket	5	89
Bead-stringing	5	90
The Wonderful Uses of Colored Papers	5	92
Hammer and Nails	5	100
Weaving	5	102
Scrap-books	5	114
Games With the Button Bag	5	115
Corn-cob Houses	5	117
Corn-cob Dolls	5	118
Toys of Cork and Matches	5	118
Paper Necklaces	5	119
Dressing Up	5	119
Quoits	5	120
Clothespin Dolls.	5	121
Potato Toys	5	121
A Dandy Plaything	5	123
Burdock Burr Toys	5	126
Paper Chains	5	126
Trumpet Vine Dolls	5	127
Dolls Made of Spools	5	129
Toys Made of Candy Boxes and Clothespins	5	129
Pinwheels	5	130
How to Build a Toy Boat	5	131
Pussy Willows	5	133
Spool Knitting	5	135
Flower Chains	5	138
A Toy Fountain	5	139
Making Furniture Out of Match Boxes	5	140
Toys Made of Green Peas and Toothpicks	5	141
Paper Lanterns	5	142
Florentine Braid	5	144
Handwork for the Holidays . . .	5	186
Shoe-scraper	5	193
Scratch My Back	5	194
Mother's Cooking School	5	195
Bookmark	5	212
The Little Mother's Work Basket . .	5	212
Nature Handicraft	7	228
Nature Playthings	7	230
Kites	5	305

HUMOR

	VOL.	PAGE
How Cats Came to Purr	2	28
Seven Little Tigers	2	34
Mr. Scrunch	2	36
A Legend of Lake Okeefinokee . . .	2	41
No Room	2	42
The Duck and the Kangaroo . . .	2	52
Nonsense Limericks	2	59
The Happy Cure	2	60
The Animal's Fair	2	63
The Monkeys and the Crocodile . .	2	64
The Skunk in Tante Odette's Oven . .	2	65
The Pobble Who Has No Toes . . .	2	73
How Many Donkeys?	2	74
Never Worked and Never Will . . .	2	76
Mrs. Snipkin and Mrs. Wobblechin . .	2	78
The Peterkin Papers	2	180
The Baker's Daughter	2	192
Mr. A. and Mr. P.	2	196
The Doughnuts	2	201
The 500 Hats of Barthelomew Cubbins	2	210
The Middle Bear	2	223
The Teacup Whale	2	232
Oscar, The Trained Seal	2	238
To Your Good Health	3	212
The Magic Fishbone	3	242
How the Good Gifts Were Used By Two	3	282
The Dragon's Story	3	290
Woman's Wit	3	294
How Pecos Bill Won and Lost His Bouncing Bride	3	357
Uncle Remus Stories	3	359
Paul Bunyan Stories	3	372

NATURE

	VOL.	PAGE
Marjorie's Almanac	2	81
Around the Year	2	82
The Months	2	83
Queen Anne's Lace	2	86
Little Rain	2	88
Autumn	2	89
October's Party	2	89
Karoo, the Kangaroo	2	119

CHRISTMAS IN VERSE AND STORY

	VOL.	PAGE
Christmas Everywhere	2	332
The Gift	2	332
The Christmas Apple	2	333
Song for Christmas	2	338
Surprise	2	340
A Miserable Merry Christmas. . . .	2	346
Mother Makes Christmas	2	352
The Stork and the Holy Babe . . .	2	360
The Friendly Beasts	3	361
Young Lucretia	2	362
Christmas Every Day	2	370
When the Mail Came Through . . .	2	376
To a Christmas Tree	2	383

	VOL.	PAGE
We Will Sing a New Song	2	384
When Christmas is Over	2	384

NATURE

	VOL.	PAGE
Before the Rain	6	314
The Planting of the Apple Tree	6	314
The Eagle	6	316
The Whitethroat	6	316
Robert of Lincoln	6	316
A Song of Seasons	6	318
What Is So Rare as a Day in June?	6	319
Rain in Summer	6	320
What the Winds Bring	6	322
When the Frost Is on the Punkin	6	323
A Visit to a Picture-zoo	7	1
How Many Birds Do You Know?	7	13
Animal Stories for Children	7	46
The Bluebird	7	56
The Sandpiper	7	57
The Story of the Plants	7	115
Stories of the Seasons	7	147

PICTURE-STORIES

	VOL.	PAGE
The Gleaners	4	6
Autumn Oaks	4	7
The Balloon	4	11
Carnation Lily, Lily Rose	4	14
Lost	4	21
Saved	4	24
The Close of Day	4	30
The Helping Hand	4	33
The Doctor	4	35
The Village Choir	4	37
The Children of the Shell	4	43
Going to Meet Father	4	45
The Blessing	4	80
Carrying Home the Calf	4	133
A Frugal Meal	4	139
Alexander the Great Visits Diogenes	4	162
The Wandering Minstrel	4	164
Gutenberg, the Inventor of Printing	4	165
The Story of "The Marseillaise"	4	168
A Florentine Poet	4	170
The Poet Shakespeare	4	171
Sir Walter Raleigh	4	175
A Hungarian Village	4	180
Washington and His Mother	4	186
"With Malice Toward None, With Charity for All"	4	187
James Watt	4	190
Try Again	4	191

PLAY

	VOL.	PAGE
Games With the Button Bag	5	115
The Easter-egg Hunt	5	117
Dressing Up	5	119
Quoits	5	120
The Blackboard Fence	5	122

	VOL.	PAGE
Paper Chase	5	125
The Magnet	5	129
Cat	7	259
The Farmyard	7	259
Hunt the Ring	7	260
Hiss and Clap	7	260
Buzz	7	261
The Game of Shadows	7	261
The Jolly Miller	7	261
Bubble-blowing	7	262
Games with Bean-bags	7	264
The Garden Gate	7	265
Ring-toss	7	265
Pigs and Donkeys	7	266
A Guessing Social	7	266
Blindfold Games	7	266
Going to Jerusalem	7	268
Three in a Row	7	269
Animated Serpent	7	271
Shovelboard	7	272
Ring the Nail	7	273
Magic Flute	7	272
The Mocking Call	7	272
Riddles, Charades, and Conundrums	7	275
A Very Interesting Stunt	7	280
Bible Curiosities and Memory-tests	7	323

POETRY

	VOL.	PAGE
Where Do All the Daisies Go?	1	197
Wonderful World	1	203
The Sun's Travel	1	207
Windy Nights	1	207
Where Go the Boats?	1	209
The Woodpecker	1	210
Poetry	2	80
Seven Times One	2	84
An Arbor Day Tree	2	85
What Do We Plant When We Plant a Tree?	2	85
Hurt No Living Thing	2	86
The Sandpiper	2	87
Song	2	90
Little Fox Lost	2	91
Ring Around the World	2	93
The Lamb	2	92
Color	2	94
Morning	2	94
Stopping by Woods on a Snowy Evening	2	95
The Sugar Plum Tree	2	96
Kentucky Birthday	2	97
Theme in Yellow	2	98
Silver	2	99
Answer to a Child's Question	2	100
The Animal Store	2	102

THE SCIENCES

	VOL.	PAGE
The Magnet	5	129
Interesting Facts about Astronomy	7	89
The Sun	7	99

	VOL.	PAGE
The Stars	7	103
How Plants Eat and Drink	7	115
The Leaves of Plants	7	117
The Roots of Plants	7	119
How Plants Work	7	122
How Plants Sleep	7	125
How Plants Are Protected	7	128
The Different Parts of a Flower and Their Uses	7	131
The Wind and the Flowers	7	135
Seed Nurseries	7	137
How the Plant Seeds Are Sent Out into the World	7	139
The Growth of a Young Plant	7	142
Robber Plants	7	144
Spring	7	147
Summer	7	152
Autumn	7	160
Winter	7	164
About the Air	7	187
Sunshine and Shadow	7	190
Clouds in the Sky	7	191
Clouds and Rain	7	191
The Wind and the Weather	7	192
Things that Grow in the Ground	7	192
Through Marsh and Woodland	7	194
Something about Milk	7	194
Bees	7	196
A Lump of Coal	7	198

SINGING GAMES

	VOL.	PAGE
Cradle Song	4	225
Gaelic Lullaby	4	226
French Cradle Song	4	227
Sweet and Low	4	228
Now the Day Is Over	4	229
Hush, My Babe	4	230
Winkum, Winkum	4	231
Jack and Jill	4	237
I Love Little Pussy	4	240
Hey, Diddle, Diddle	4	243
Apples Ripe	4	246
Mistress Mary	4	246
Little Rose-bud	4	248
Little Jack Horner	4	249
Three Blind Mice	4	250
Little Miss Muffitt	4	252
Pussy Cat, Pussy Cat	4	252
Cock-a-Doodle-Doo	4	253
See-Saw	4	254
Good-Morning, Merry Sunshine	4	255
Soldiers Marching	4	256
The Child and the Star	4	258
Little Drops of Water	4	258
Which Way Does the Wind Blow	4	259
Twinkle Twinkle, Little Star	4	260
Balloons	4	261
Flying Kites	4	264
Little Robin Redbreast	4	270
My Kiddie Car	4	271

	VOL.	PAGE
Singing	4	272
The Train	4	274
The Cow	4	276
A Funny Fiddler	4	282
The Snow Man	4	283
The Swing	4	284
The Stars Are Tiny Daisies High	4	286
Grandma's Garden	4	287
The Wind	4	290
The Hobby Horse	4	293
Blow, Wind, Blow	4	294
A Million Little Diamonds	4	295
The Carousel	4	296
Animal Crackers	4	297
Jolly Old St. Nicholas	4	300
Lady Moon	4	301
Looby Loo	4	302
Merrily Form a Ring	4	302
Going to London	4	303
London Bridge	4	304
The Farmer	4	304
Lucy Locket	4	306
The Muffin Man	4	306
The Farmer in the Dell	4	308
Here We Go Round the Mulberry Bush	4	309
Soldier Boy	4	310
We'll All Go A-singing	4	311
Oats, Peas, Beans, and Barley Grow	4	312
Uncle John Is Very Sick	4	313
Soldier, Soldier, Will You Marry Me	4	314
I'm Very, Very Tall	4	315
My Dolly	4	316
Children's Polka	4	318
English Harvesters' Dance	4	320
German Clap Dance	4	322
Swedish Clap Dance	4	323
I See You	4	324
The Carrousel	4	326
Windmill Dance	4	328

STORIES

	VOL.	PAGE
The Seventh Pup	2	103
Pino and Paint	2	109
The Dog Who Chose a Prince	2	114
The Horse That Came from Heaven	2	125
All Mutt	2	129
Such a Kind World	2	137
Champion Fire 'n Feather	2	142
His First Bronc	2	155
Almost an Ambush	2	158
The Black Stallion and the Red Mare	2	165
Pony Penning Day	2	171
Waukewa's Eagle	2	244
The Big Green Umbrella	2	249
Caleb's Luck	2	257
Katie Meets Buffalo Bill	2	263
The Family Who Had Never Had Roller Skates	2	271
Indians in the House	2	274
Blue Rocking Chair Tells a Story	2	280

	VOL.	PAGE
A Tree of Apples	2	284
Barnum's First Circus	2	290
Fung's Fourth	2	298
Willie's Good Recess	2	301
Elizabeth Ann Fails in an Examination	2	304
High Water in Arkansas	2	319
Rococo Skates	2	314
Space Ship to the Moon	2	325
The Pied Piper	6	52
Pinocchio	6	39
The Water-Babies	6	41
The King of the Golden River	6	62
The Story of Peter Pan	6	70
Gulliver's Travels	6	77
Robinson Crusoe	6	89
The Legend of Sleepy Hollow	6	93
A Mad Tea-Party	6	110
The Romance of the Swan's Nest	6	117
Paul Revere's Ride	6	291
Barbara Frietchie	6	294

TRAVEL AND ADVENTURE

	VOL.	PAGE
Roman Girl at the Fountain	4	2
Interior of a Cottage	4	4
Grandmother's Treasure	4	5
The Gleaners	4	6
The Balloon	4	11
The Boyhood of Sir Walter Raleigh	4	18
Beaching the Boat	4	19
The Village Choir	4	37
An English Mail Coach	4	172
Admiral Sir Francis Drake	4	174
Sir Walter Raleigh	4	175
A Regatta on the Grand Canal, Venice	4	176
Feeding the Doves, Venice	4	177
The Story of Columbus	4	178
A Hungarian Village	4	180
Jacques Cartier	4	182
Perils of the Puritans	4	183
Indian Children at Play	4	184
An Elk Ranch	4	185
A Japanese Family at Dinner	4	192
Japanese Children at Play	4	193
Isis, the Egyptian Goddess	4	194
A "Stenographer" in North Africa	4	195
The Great Pyramid of Gizeh	4	196
Children of Volendam	4	197

	VOL.	PAGE
A Flood in Holland	4	198
Filipino Rapid Transit	4	200
A Bus in Agra	4	201
A Family in the Land of Von Winkelreid	4	202
The White House	4	203
In Jamaica	4	204
The Waterworks of Curaçao	4	205
The Washington Monument	4	208
How Peggy Saw Holland	8	1
Peggy Visits Morocco	8	6
Peggy in Persia	8	10
A Trip to Egypt	8	12
Peggy Looks for Diamonds in South Africa	8	17
A Trip to the South Sea Islands	8	20
Peggy Visits New Zealand	8	23
A Trip through Italy	8	25
Babies in China	8	31
Babies in Greece	8	33
Babies in the Great Tents	8	35
Babies in Kafirland	8	40
Babies in Spain	8	42
Houses	8	45
Life in the Big City	8	51
Policemen and Postmen of Many Lands	8	55
Traveling in Many Countries	8	59
Schools in Many Countries	8	66
Playtime in Many Countries	8	72
Shopping in Many Countries	8	77
Life Among the Red People	8	82
John of England	8	87
Running Rabbit, Little Indian	8	88
Suzanne of France	8	92
Maisanguaq, "Frosty Eskimo"	8	94
O Hana San of Japan	8	99
Ismail of the Upside Down Land	8	104
Mang'anda of Central Africa	8	108
Felipe and Serafina of Spain	8	113
David of the Holy Land	8	118
Hugh of India	8	122
Marietta of Italy	8	125
Games and Feasts in Japan	8	128
What They Play in Africa	8	132
Games and Festivals in China	8	136
The River Holiday in India	8	143
A Picnic in the Australian Bush	8	146
The Boyhood of a Patriot	9	15

GRADE 4—LATE CHILDHOOD

AGES NINE AND BEYOND

A<small>T THIS</small> age a passion for reading often seizes the child who has been brought up in the atmosphere of books. The B<small>OOKSHELF</small>, from now on, is more than a text used by the mother to help her child. The child now uses it almost daily himself, reading the stories with delight, getting suggestions for projects which interest him, finding out how to interpret nature, learning how to make the appliances he wants for his games and collections, enriching his mind with art, music, and poetry.

The broader range of the child's interest is recognized in the maturer and more varied contents of the B<small>OOKSHELF</small> presented here.

ART AND PICTURE STORIES

	VOL.	PAGE
The Pied Piper of Hamelin	4	1
Roman Girl at a Fountain	4	2
The Horse Fair	4	3
Interior of a Cottage	4	4
Grandmother's Treasure	4	5
The Gleaners	4	6
Autumn Oaks	4	7
How Comical	4	9
The Broken Pitcher	4	10
The Balloon	4	11
Carnation Lady, Lily Rose	4	14
Madame LeBrun and Her Daughter	4	15
The Madonna of the Chair	4	16
The Bread-Winner	4	17
The Boyhood of Sir Walter Raleigh	4	18
Beaching the Boat	4	19
The Shepherd and His Flock	4	20
Lost	4	21
The Rainbow	4	22
May Day	4	23
Saved	4	24
The Horseshoer	4	25
The Maids of Honor	4	26
The Cloth Merchants	4	27
Happy Family	4	28
Three Members of a Temperance Society	4	29
The Close of Day	4	30
Hope	4	31
The Angelus	4	32
The Helping Hand	4	33
Grandmother's Birthday	4	34
The Doctor	4	35
Atalanta's Race	4	38

	VOL.	PAGE
The Daughters of the Artist	4	40
Marie de' Medici	4	41
The Buttery Door	4	42
The Children of the Shell	4	43
Going to Meet Father	4	45
A Dutch Baby and Her Nurse	4	46
A Spanish Flower Girl	4	49
The Melon Eaters	4	48
The Boy Falconer	4	51
Rubens' Two Sons	4	50
The Blue Boy	4	50
At the Spinet	4	56
The Strawberry Girl	4	58
Don Balthazar Carlos	4	63
A Spanish Boy	4	65
Alice	4	66
The Princes in the Tower	4	68
In the Garden	4	71
The Madonna of the Rocks	4	73
Mother and Children	4	77
Madonna	4	77
The Blessing	4	80
Angels' Heads	4	82
Joan of Arc	4	83
St. Barbara	4	84
The Delphic Sibyl	4	86
Don Balthazar Carlos	4	93
William II of Orange	4	94
Prince Charles of England	4	95
The Distrest Poet	4	99
The Round Table of King Arthur	4	101
The Castle of the Maidens	4	103
The Loving Cup	4	106
Adoration	4	107
Hercules Wrestling with Death	4	108

	VOL.	PAGE
Listening to the Sphinx	4	109
The Rider on the White Horse	4	111
The Trousseau	4	112
Pallas and the Centaur	4	118
The Laughing Cavalier	4	121
Thomas Carlyle	4	124
Giovanna Tornabuoni and the Three Graces	4	129
Giovanna Tornabuoni	4	130
Carrying Home the Calf	4	132
The Song of the Lark	4	135
Spring	4	137
Plowing in the Nivernais	4	136
A Shepherdess	4	146
A Frugal Meal	4	139
Ploughing in Acadia	4	143
The Coming Storm	4	145
The Harp of the Winds	4	144
The Hymn of the Earth to the Sun	4	141
Moses	4	151
The Winged Victory of Samothrace	4	153
Abraham Lincoln	4	154
Madonna and Baby Jesus	4	158
Her Son	4	154
Memory	4	158
The Adoration of the Child Jesus	4	159
The Two Natures	4	160
A Grecian Potter	4	163
The Wandering Minstrel	4	164
Joan of Arc	4	164
A Florentine Poet	4	170
Swift and Stella	4	173
Washington and His Mother	4	186
A Family in the Land of Von Winkelried	4	202
King Arthur	6	265
The Mill on the River Teign	6	287
The Deacon's One-Hoss Shay	6	345
A Typical Landscape in Holland	8	5
May Festival in Spain	8	44
John Alden and Priscilla Mullens	8	191
The Return of the Mayflower	8	193
Donald B. MacMillan	8	210
A Reading from Homer	8	235
The Bard	8	239
Theseus Returning to Ariadne	8	258
Ruy Diaz of Bivar, the Cid Campeador	8	333
Young Handel	9	49
Cromwell's Visit to Milton	9	77
Napoleon at Brienne	9	81
Elizabeth Signing the Death Warrant of Mary Queen of Scots	9	91
Joan of Arc	9	93
Joan of Arc Listening to the Voices	9	94
Queen Victoria as a Young Woman	9	101
Madame Curie	9	109
Mount Rushmore National Memorial	9	118
Retreat of the British from Concord	9	120
Drilling Recruits for the Army	9	125
Betsy Ross Making the U. S. Flag	9	147

	VOL.	PAGE
West Point Cadets on Parade	9	151
The Stars and Stripes	9	155
Pilgrims Going to Church	9	160
Penn's Treaty	9	180
Drafting the Declaration of Independence	9	183
Signing the Declaration of Independence	9	186
Washington at Valley Forge	9	193
Lafayette	9	209
Paul Jones	9	216
Oliver H. Perry	9	223
Daniel Boone	9	227
Treating With the Indians	9	228
Dolly Madison	9	230
Westward Ho!	9	241
Abraham Lincoln	9	245
Lincoln and His Cabinet	9	247
Return of the Battle Flags	9	249
Oliver Wendell Holmes	9	280
Wendell L. Willkie	9	287

BIOGRAPHY AND HISTORY

	VOL.	PAGE
The Boyhood of Sir Walter Raleigh	4	18
Portrait of Carlyle	4	123
Joanna of Aragon	4	126
William II of Orange and Mary Stuart	4	127
Alexander the Great Visits Diogenes	4	162
The Wandering Minstrel	4	164
Gutenberg, the Inventor of Printing	4	165
Boadicea Leading Her Army	4	166
Joan of Arc	4	167
The Story of "The Marseillaise"	4	168
The Liberty Bell	4	169
A Florentine Poet	4	170
The Poet Shakespeare at Stratford	4	171
Swift and Stella	4	173
Admiral Sir Francis Drake	4	174
Sir Walter Raleigh	4	175
The Story of Columbus	4	178
Jacques Cartier	4	182
Perils of the Puritans	4	183
Washington and His Mother	4	186
Daniel Webster	4	188
John Burroughs Feeding a Robin	4	189
James Watt, the Famous Inventor	4	190
The Great Pyramid of Gizeh	4	196
Beethoven and Mozart	4	199
Milton Dictating "Paradise Lost"	4	206
Tennyson Calls on Carlyle	4	207
Cyrus of Persia	8	349
The Story of Pindar	8	350
The Spartans	8	351
The Iliad of Homer	8	353
The March of the Ten Thousand	8	363
Cato the Younger	8	365
Edwin and the King of the North	8	366
The Boyhood of a Great Saint	8	368
The Story of Bede	8	369
The Story of Alfred	8	370

	VOL.	PAGE
Brian, King of Erin	8	370
Olaf the Brave	8	372
The First Crusaders	8	374
The Troubadours	8	377
Richard the Lion-hearted	8	379
William Wallace	8	383
Robert the Bruce	8	385
Bonnie Prince Charlie	8	389
Sir Philip Sidney	8	395
The Boyhood of a Story-teller	9	1
A Nurse's Girlhood	9	6
An Inventor's Boyhood	9	10
The Boy Who Was Helped	9	13
The Boyhood of a Patriot	9	15
The Boyhood of a Statesman	9	19
The Boyhood of a Sculptor	9	23
The Child of Urbino	9	27
The Boyhood of an English Painter	9	39
The Boyhood of a French Painter	9	44
The Boyhood of a Musician	9	48
The Girlhood of a Singer	9	50
The Boyhood of a President	9	56
The Boy Who Braved the Duke of Wellington	9	76
The Young Days of John Milton	9	76
King Louis XIV of France	9	78
King Charles XII of Sweden	9	78
The Boyhood of Napoleon	9	80
The Story of Garibaldi's Boyhood	9	82
Some Girls Who Wore Ruffs	9	83
Joan of Arc, the Maid of Orleans	9	93
Victoria of England	9	100
Susan B. Anthony	9	102
Madame Curie	9	107
Helen Keller	9	110
The Army of Two	9	119
The Story of the Boston Tea Party	9	121
Israel Putnam	9	123
The Story of Nathan Hale	9	129
Nathan Hale	9	126
How a Woman Saved an Army	9	130
Molly Pitcher	9	133
Johnny Appleseed	9	136
A Pig That Nearly Caused a War	9	139
The Walking Purchase	9	142
The Origin of Our Flag	9	146
Honors to the Flag	9	150
The Pilgrims and the Puritans	9	157
How People Lived in Colonial New England	9	162
Wolfe and Montcalm at Quebec	9	166
Patrick Henry	9	170
William Penn	9	178
The Signers of the Declaration of Independence	9	181
George Washington	9	191
Privations at Valley Forge	9	196
Benjamin Franklin	9	198
Lafayette	9	209
John Paul Jones	9	213

	VOL.	PAGE
Thomas Jefferson	9	217
How We Bought Louisiana	9	220
Perry and Lawrence	9	222
Daniel Boone	9	226
The Wife Who Taught Her Husband to Be President	9	229
Andrew Jackson	9	230
The Adventures of Lewis and Clark	9	234
Marcus Whitman's Ride	9	238
The Western Pioneer	9	240
Abraham Lincoln	9	244
Robert E. Lee	9	250
U. S. Grant	9	255
A Man Like a Stone Wall	9	260
Dewey	9	264
Theodore Roosevelt	9	268
Woodrow Wilson	9	277
Oliver Wendell Holmes	9	279
The Mayo Brothers	9	282
Alfred E. Smith	9	284
Queen Elizabeth	9	295
Sir Walter Raleigh	9	297
When Cromwell Was a Boy	9	300
Lord Nelson	9	304
Twelve National Heroes	9	307
Strange Colonization Ventures	9	313
The Adventures of Jacques Cartier	9	315
Marguerite de Roberval	9	320
Radisson, "The Canadian Ulysses"	9	323
The Story of Madeleine de Verchères	9	325
The Thermopylæ of Canada	9	328
Mackenzie	9	330
The United Empire Loyalists	9	332
Sir Isaac Brock	9	334
A Black-Robed Voyageur	9	336
The Story of Laura Secord	9	339
Sir John MacDonald	9	342
Joseph Howe of Nova Scotia	9	345
Sir Wilfred Laurier	9	348
The Royal Northwest Mounted Police	9	353

HANDICRAFT

	VOL.	PAGE
Modeling	5	31
Color—Design—Drawing	5	33
Modeling Small Sculptures	5	75
Making Doll-furniture	5	86
The Wonderful Uses of Colored Paper	5	92
Dolls in Costume	5	104
Scrap Books	5	114
Paper Necklaces	5	119
Quoits	5	120
Clothespin Dolls	5	121
Potato Toys	5	121
Cork-and-Glue Dolls	5	124
The Band-box House	5	124
Paper Chains	5	126
Trumpet Vine Dolls	5	127
How to Build a Toy Boat	5	131

	VOL.	PAGE
Transformation Scrap-books	5	132
Pussy Willows	5	133
Spool Knitting	5	135
Flower Chains	5	138
Making Furniture Out of Match Boxes	5	140
Florentine Braid	5	144
Handwork for the Holidays	5	186
Shoe Scraper	5	193
Scratch My Back	5	194
Mother's Cooking School	5	195
Bookmark	5	212
The Little Mother's Work-basket	5	212
Raffia Work	5	252
Tatting	5	256
Basketry	5	259
Wood-bench	5	278
Animal Toys	5	281
Water-wheels	5	294
Peg Tops and Noise Makers	5	299
Carts and Wagons	5	303
Wind and Weather Gauges	5	304
Kites	5	305
Some More Toys	5	307
Water-pumps	5	315
Sun Dials	5	313
Steam Engines	5	316
A Derrick	5	322
Pushmobile	5	324
Book-Holders	5	325
Airplane Model	5	327
Toys and Toy Games	7	271

MYTHS AND LEGENDS

	VOL.	PAGE
The Round Table of King Arthur	4	100
The Castle of the Maidens	4	104
St. Elizabeth	4	105
The Legend of Sleepy Hollow	6	93
King Arthur and His Knights	6	265
When Man Found Fire	7	72
Man's Early Dreams	7	84
Perseus	8	221
The Wanderings of Odysseus	8	229
The Argonauts	8	241
Theseus	8	252
Hercules	8	259
The Perilous Voyage of Æneas	8	266
How Cincinnatus Saved Rome	8	271
Beowulf	8	273
Childe Horne	8	278
Robin Hood	8	282
A Jest of Little John	8	290
Allen-a-Dale	8	295
Robin Hood and Allen-a-Dale	8	295
The Story of Frithiof	8	297
The Vikings	8	303
Siegfried	8	308

	VOL.	PAGE
Roland	8	319
The Cid	8	329
William Tell	8	335
Sohrab and Rustam	8	345
The Iliad of Homer	8	353

NATURE

	VOL.	PAGE
Two Skies	6	308
Song of the Chattahoochee	6	308
The Little Winds	6	309
Sea Fever	6	309
Song of the Brook	6	309
Out in the Fields with God	6	310
Day	6	312
The Cloud	6	312
Under the Greenwood Tree	6	313
Canadian Camping Song	6	313
Daffodils	6	313
The Primeval Forest	6	313
Before the Rain	6	314
The Planting of the Apple Tree	6	314
To a Mountain Daisy	6	315
The Voice of the Grass	6	315
Song: On May Morning	6	316
The Eagle	6	316
The Whitethroat	6	316
Robert of Lincoln	6	316
To a Waterfowl	6	317
The Cataract of Lodore	6	317
A Song of Seasons	6	318
The Voice of the Heavens	6	319
What Is So Rare as a Day in June?	6	319
Rain in Summer	6	320
The Death of the Flowers	6	322
What the Winds Bring	6	322
When the Frost is on the Punkin	6	323
A Visit to a Picture Zoo	7	1
How Many Birds Do You Know?	7	13
The Round Robin	7	51
The Bluebird	7	56
The Sandpiper	7	57
Interesting Facts About Astronomy	7	89
The Sun	7	99
The Stars	7	103
The Story of the Plants	7	115
Stories of the Seasons	7	147
Learning to Look About You	7	169
Little Nature Talks	7	187
Great Rivers	7	200
Great Waterfalls and Cataracts	7	207
In Rainbow-land	7	211
Great Caves and Natural Bridges	7	216
Deserts and Plateaus	7	218
The World's Notable Ice-sheets and Glaciers	7	220
A Visit to a Colorado Glacier	7	224
Nature Study	7	232

PLAY

	VOL.	PAGE
Quoits	5	120
The Blackboard Fence	5	122
Paper Chase	5	125
A Toy Fountain	5	139
Shadow Pictures	5	150
What's Wrong?	5	159
Cross-Word Puzzles	5	171
The Wheelbarrow Race	7	241
The Cat Tiggy	7	241
Bull in the Ring	7	241
Egg-cap	7	242
Here Goes Up for Monday	7	242
Tag	7	242
The Three-legged Race	7	243
The Menagerie Man	7	243
The Peg-gathering Race	7	243
I Spy	7	243
Widdy-widdy Way	7	244
Hare and Hounds	7	244
Snow Games	7	244
Jack, Jack, the Bread Burns	7	244
Buck, Buck, How Many Fingers Do I Hold Up?	7	246
The Sergeant	7	246
Aunt Sally	7	246
Hide-and-Seek	7	246
Fives	7	246
Marbles	7	246
Leap-frog	7	249
Fly	7	249
Tom Tiddler's Ground	7	250
Top Games	7	250
Shadow Tag	7	251
Snatch the Bean Bag	7	251
Fox and Gander	7	251
All-up Relay	7	252
Animal Blindman's Buff	7	252
A Garden Obstacle Race	7	252
How to Play Flags	7	254
Crazy Croquet	7	255
Cat	7	259
Kaleidoscope	7	259
Consequences	7	259
Who Is He?	7	259
The Farmyard	7	259
Hunt the Ring	7	260
Throwing Light	7	260
Hiss and Clap	7	260
Word-making	7	260
Bridge-board	7	260
The Minister's Cat	7	261
Ten-word Telegrams	7	261
Twenty Questions	7	261
Buzz	7	261
The Game of Shadows	7	261
The Jolly Miller	7	261
Bubble-blowing	7	262
Checkers	7	262
Dominoes	7	263

	VOL.	PAGE
Games with Bean-Bags	7	264
Batchelor's Kitchen	7	264
An Exchange Party	7	265
A Guessing-contest	7	265
The Garden Gate	7	265
Ring-Toss	7	265
Lost and Found	7	265
Pigs and Donkeys	7	266
A Guessing Social	7	266
The Magician of Morocco	7	266
Blindfold Games	7	266
The Adventurers	7	267
Games for Partners	7	267
Going to Jerusalem	7	268
My Lady's Toilet	7	268
Three in a Row	7	269
Artistic Reflections	7	269
Outlines	7	269
Tit, Tat, Toe	7	270
Patchwork	7	270
An Aeolian Harp	7	271
The Dancing Highlanders	7	271
Shovelboard	7	272
Magic Flute	7	272
The Mocking Call	7	272
Riddles, Charades and Conundrums	7	275
A Very Interesting Stunt	7	280
Riddles and Puzzles, Tricks and Stunts	7	297
Spellingtown	7	321
Bible Curiosities and Memory Tests	7	323

POETRY

	VOL.	PAGE
The Village Blacksmith	6	96
The Fairies of Caldon Low	6	285
A Song of Sherwood	6	286
I Remember	6	288
The Bells	6	288
The Night Wind	6	289
The American Flag	6	291
Landing of the Pilgrim Fathers	6	291
Paul Revere's Ride	6	291
The Ship of State	6	293
Warren's Address	6	293
The Charge of the Light Brigade	6	294
Barbara Frietchie	6	294
Sheridan's Ride	6	295
O Captain! My Captain	6	296
The Bivouac of the Dead	6	296
The Recessional	6	297
Old Ironsides	6	297
In Flanders Fields	6	298
The New Patriotism	6	299
Christmas Snow	6	319
O Little Town of Bethlehem	6	302
A Christmas Hymn	6	302
Abraham Lincoln	6	303
Concord Hymn	6	303
The Flag Goes By	6	304
The Blue and the Gray	6	305

	VOL.	PAGE
The First Thanksgiving Day	6	305
Jest 'Fore Christmas	6	307
Two Skies	6	308
Song of the Chattahoochee	6	308
The Little Winds	6	309
Sea Fever	6	309
Song of the Brook	6	309
Out in the Fields with God	6	310
Day	6	312
Under the Greenwood Tree	6	313
Canadian Camping Song	6	313
Daffodils	6	313
The Primeval Forest	6	313
Before the Rain	6	314
The Planting of the Apple Tree	6	314
To a Mountian Daisy	6	315
The Voice of the Grass	6	315
Song: On May Morning	6	316
The Eagle	6	316
The Whitethroat	6	316
Robert of Lincoln	6	316
To a Waterfowl	6	317
The Cataract of Lodore	6	317
A Song of Seasons	6	318
The Voice of the Heavens	6	319
What Is So Rare as a Day in June?	6	320
Rain in Summer	6	320
The Death of the Flowers	6	322
What the Winds Bring	6	322
When the Frost Is on the Punkin	6	323
Friends Out of Doors	6	323
Be Strong	6	325
A Farewell	6	325
The Arrow and the Song	6	325
Old Grimes	6	325
For A' That and A' That	6	326
One by One	6	326
A Psalm of Life	6	326
Labor	6	327
Gradatim	6	327
The Lost Sheep	6	328
Lead, Kindly Light	6	328
Burial of Moses	6	329
The Angels' Song	6	329
To My Son	6	330
Abou Ben Adhem	6	330
Work	6	330
The New Year	6	330
Maidenhood	6	331
A Wayfaring Song	6	332
How Did You Die?	6	332
The Day Is Done	6	332
Crossing the Bar	6	333
L'Envoi	6	333
In School Days	6	334
Little Moccasins	6	334
The Last Leaf	6	335
The Barefoot Boy	6	335
Clancy of the Mounted Police	6	338
Casabianca	6	340

	VOL.	PAGE
Fair Ines	6	341
Maud Muller	6	341
An Old Sweetheart of Mine	6	343
Seein' Things	6	345
The One-Hoss Shay	6	345
The Modern Hiawatha	6	348
The Invisible Bridge	6	348

THE SCIENCES

	VOL.	PAGE
Mother's Cooking School	5	195
Water-wheels	5	294
Sun Dials	5	315
Steam-engines	5	316
Airplane Model	5	327
Mechanical Movements Made Clear	5	357
Experiments with Static Electricity	5	367
The General Elementary Principles of Electricity	5	369
An Interesting Experiment with Electricity	5	371
Electric Bells and Buzzers	5	371

STORIES

	VOL.	PAGE
Aladdin and the Wonderful Lamp	6	5
The Enchanted Horse	6	11
Ali Baba and the Forty Thieves	6	14
The Wishing Carpet	6	19
Sindbad the Sailor	6	21
The Barber's Fifth Brother	6	26
The Barmecide's Feast	6	26
The History of the Fisherman	6	27
At the Back of the North Wind	6	33
Jan of the Windmill	6	38
The Story of Pippa	6	74
The Village Blacksmith	6	96
Don Quixote	6	96
Undine	6	105
The Great Stone Face	6	105
Horatius at the Bridge	6	107
A Dissertation upon Roast Pig	6	114
Goblin Market	6	116
Una and the Lion	6	118
The Story of the Blue Bird	6	122
The Tempest	6	128
The Pilgrim's Progress	6	134
Canterbury Tales	6	150
Christmas Carol	6	165
Wee Willie Winkie	6	179
Rip van Winkle	6	185
Black Beauty	6	193
Hans Brinker	6	202
The Man Without a Country	6	216
Tartarin of Tarascon	6	226
The Porcelain Stove	6	237
The Rose and the Ring	6	242
Where Love Is, God Is	6	262
King Arthur and His Knights	6	265

	VOL.	PAGE
Prince Gareth	6	277
The Story of Cuchulain	6	279

TRAVEL AND ADVENTURE

	VOL.	PAGE
Great Rivers	7	200
Great Waterfalls and Cataracts . . .	7	207
In Rainbow-Land	7	211
Great Caves and Natural Bridges . .	7	216
Deserts and Plateaus	7	218
The World's Notable Ice-Sheets and Glaciers	7	220
A Visit to a Colorado Glacier . . .	7	224
How Peggy Saw Holland	8	1
Peggy Visits Morocco	8	6
Peggy in Persia	8	10
A Trip to Egypt	8	12
Peggy Looks for Diamonds in South Africa	8	17
A Trip to the South Sea Islands . .	8	20
Peggy Visits New Zealand	8	23
A Trip through Italy	8	25
Babies in China	8	31
Babies in Greece	8	33
Babies of the Great Tents	8	35
Babies of Kafirland	8	40
Babies in Spain	8	42
Houses	8	45
Life in the Big City	8	51
Policemen and Postmen of Many Lands	8	55
Traveling in Many Countries . . .	8	59
School in Many Countries	8	66
Playtime in Many Countries . . .	8	72
Shopping in Many Countries . . .	8	77
Life Among the Red People	8	82
John of England	8	87
Running Rabbit, Little Indian . . .	8	88
Suzanne of France	8	92
Maisanguaq, "Frosty Eskimo" . . .	8	94
O Hana San of Japan	8	99
Ismail of the Upside Down Land . .	8	104
Mang'anda of Central Africa . . .	8	108

	VOL.	PAGE
Filipe and Serafina of Spain	8	113
David of the Holy Land	8	118
Hugh in India	8	122
Marietta of Italy	8	125
Games and Feasts in Japan	8	128
What They Play in Africa	8	132
Games and Festivals in China . . .	8	136
The River Holiday in India	8	143
A Picnic in the Australian Bush . .	8	146
The Fable of the Frogs	8	151
The Cities of the River Land	8	152
The Secret of the Nile	8	153
The Land of the Pharaohs	8	154
The Land of the Palms	8	156
Italy	8	158
Norway	8	159
Tibet	8	159
Australia	8	160
Persia	8	162
Morocco	8	162
South America	8	163
China	8	165
France	8	165
The First Adventurers	8	167
The New World	8	170
The Swineherd Who Wanted a Castle .	8	175
The Beautiful City of the Floating Islands	8	179
Round the World with Drake . . .	8	181
How DeSoto Came to the Father of Waters	8	183
The Little Red Princess of the Forest .	8	186
The Story of Myles Standish	8	190
The Englishman Who Sailed for the Dutch	8	195
A Little Dutch Boy and Girl of Old New York	8	198
Champlain, Explorer of the St. Lawrence	8	203
The Friends of the Indians	8	206
Peary, Discoverer of the North Pole .	8	210
Amundsen, Discoverer of the South Pole	8	213

GENERAL INDEX
of Subjects, Titles, and Authors
for the
MANUAL OF CHILD DEVELOPMENT

The general subjects covered in this Manual, as well as specific titles of articles and their authors, are alphabetically listed in this Index, with page references for each. In order to make it as easy as possible for the reader to find all the information desired on any subject, we have cross-indexed some titles. For example, you will find under Diseases of Childhood, a page reference to that subject in general as well as to such divisions of that subject as Common Contagious Diseases, Diseases in the Abdomen, Diseases of the Respiratory Tract, etc. These in turn are each separately listed in their proper alphabetical order, and so are all the specific diseases, such as Diphtheria, Whooping Cough, Measles, etc., with a page reference for each. Page references in Roman numbers refer to the material at the front of the Manual, including the Chart of Child Development.

A

Abdomen, Diseases in the, 240
Abdomen, Pain in the (*See* Symptoms of Acute Illness, 199)
Abilities and Disabilities, Special, in Adolescence, 493
Ability, How to Recognize in a Child, 358
Abscesses (*See* Boils, 237)
Accidents (*See* Physical Injuries, 250)
Accuracy, 3
Acetic Acid Poisoning, 255
Acne, 237
Acute Nephritis, 245
ADAIR, MARY: The Baby's Story-Hour, 297
Adaptability and Adjustability, 4
Adenoids (*See* Tonsils, 239)
Adjustability (*See* Adaptability and Adjustability, 4)
ADOLESCENCE, 485-516
Adolescence, Mental Development in, 491
Adolescence, What Is?, 485
Adolescent and His Companions, 510
Adolescents at Leisure, 503
Adventuring in Handcraft, 335
Affection and Love, 5
Against What Should We Be Immunized?, 215

Age-Levels (*See* CHART OF CHILD DEVELOPMENT, XIX-CII)
Airing (*See* Sunshine and Fresh Air, 116)
Alcohol Poisoning, 254
Alertness and Attentiveness, 6
ALEXANDER, JOHN L.: The American Youth Foundation, 416
Allergy, Diseases Due to, 246
Ambition (*See* Initiative and Ambition, 34)
American Youth Foundation, The, 416
Ammonia Poisoning, 255
Amusements for Convalescent Children, 220
ANDREWS, FRANCES M.: Making Music Together, 322
Anemia, 249
Animal Bites (*See* Dog Bites, 251)
Animal Friends, 325
Antidotes for Poisons (*See* Poisons and Their Antidotes, 254)
Anti-toxins (*See* Against What Should We Be Immunized?, 215)
Appendicitis, 242
Appetite (*See* Good Food Habits, 172; Teaching Children to Like Wholesome Foods, 175)
Application and Concentration, 7
Appreciation and Gratitude, 8
Aptitudes That Affect School Success, 360

Arsenic Poisoning, 254
Aspiration, 9
Asthma, 246
Attentiveness (*See* Alertness and Attentiveness, 6)
Attitudes Toward Sex in Adolescence, 488
Average Mind, The, 492

B

Baby Care and Feeding, 71-118
Baby Pen (*See* Baby's Exercises, 117)
Baby's Caretakers, 107
Baby's Clothes, 109
Baby's Day, 118
Baby's Exercises, 117
Baby's Room, 179
Baby's Story-Hour, 297
Baby's Vacation, 189
Backward Child (*See* Slow Mind, 492)
Backyard, The, 186
BACMEISTER, RHODA W.: Nature Study for Young Children, 326
BADENOCH, NENA WILSON: How to Give the Children a Good Time During Vacation, 190
BAIN, WINIFRED E., Ph.D.: Will You Send Your Child to a Nursery School?, 341; Will You Send Your Child to a Kindergarten?, 343; Your Child's Progress in the Elementary School, 345
BAKER, S. JOSEPHINE, M.D.: Suggested Menus for Children from Two to Six, 169
BALDWIN, BIRD T.: Average Weights by Height and Age for Girls and Boys, 153
Basic Medical and Sickroom Supplies, 253
Bath, The Daily, 114 (*See also* The Baby's Day, 118)
Bathing, 132 (*See also* Sea Bathing, 192)
Bed Wetting, 126
BEEBE, KATHERINE: Play Places in the House, 181
Behavior (*See* Traits to Be Discouraged, Corrected, or Left to Be Outgrown, CXI; Essentials of Good Character and Personality, 1-67; Forming Good Habits, 121; Fatigue and Naughtiness, 143; Home Life, 367-378; Manners, 381; Learning Social Behavior, 389; When Friends Seem to Be Doing Harm, 394; The Question of Petting, 399; Discipline, 419-429; Personality Problems, 431-450; Asocial Conduct in Adolescence, 504
Beginning Sex Education, 395
Beverages (*See* Nutritional Requirements, 161; Summer Drinks, 173)
Bible, Making Real to the Child, 470

Bibliography (Books and Pamphlets Consulted), XX
Birth Registration, 76
Bites and Stings, 251
Bittersweet Potato Poisoning, 256
Black Eye, 251
Blackheads (*See* Acne, 237)
Bladder Control (*See* Toilet Habits, 125)
Bleeding (*See* Symptoms, 199; Cuts and Wounds, 250)
BLANTON, SMILEY, M.D.: Stuttering, 277
BLISS, LENA E.: Child Culture, 309
Blood in the Stools (*See* Symptoms of Acute Illness, 199)
BOEKEL, FLORENCE BREWER: Children and the World Today, 405
Boils and Abscesses, 237
BONSALL, ELIZABETH HUBBARD: Observation, 269
Books (*See* Reading and Story-Telling, 297-309)
Bottle-Feeding (*See* Choice of Milk, 88; Milk Mixture, 104)
Bottle-Fed Baby, Difficulties of the, 98
Bowel Control (*See* Toilet Habits, 125)
Bowel Irregularities (*See* Difficulties of the Bottle-Fed Baby, 98; Stomach Disorders, 241)
Boy and Girl Relationships in Adolescence, 512
Boy Scouts, 408
Boys' Clubs as a Help to the Home, 407
Boy's Own Room, The, 184
Breakfast (*See under* Food and Menus)
Breast-Feeding (*See* Mother's Milk Best for Baby, 77; Hygiene of the Nursing Mother, 77; Difficulties of the Nursing Period, 85; Weaning, 87)
Bronchitis, 240
Brotherhood of Man, The, 418
Bruises (*See* Bumps and Bruises, 251)
Bumps and Bruises, 251
Burns, 251
BUTTERFIELD, HON. E. W.: Nature Study for Older Boys and Girls, 328

C

Calcium (*See* Nutritional Requirements, 161)
CAMPBELL, HELEN Y.: Animal Friends, 325
Camp Fire Girls, 410
Carbohydrates (*See* Nutritional Requirements of Growing Children, 161)
Carbolic Acid Poisoning, 255
Care of Special Organs, 115
CARTER, MARY E., R.N.: Home Nursing, 201
Catholic Child, Religious Education of, 460
Caustic Potash Poisoning, 255
Caustic Soda Poisoning, 255

Caution, 208

Caution and Prudence, 10

Celiac Disease, 250

Cellulitis and Erysipelas, 237

Cereals (*See* Foods Besides Milk, 99; Feeding the Average Baby, 103; Nutritional Requirements of Growing Children, 161)

CHAMPLIN, HELEN K.: When Punishment Is Necessary, 419; Use Praise Instead of Blame, 427

Character and Character-Building (*See* ESSENTIALS OF GOOD CHARACTER AND PERSONALITY, 1-67; How to Tell Stories for Character-Building, 429; What Are Good Character Habits and How Are They Developed?, 422)

CHARACTER AND PERSONALITY, ESSENTIALS OF GOOD, 1-67

Character Habits, 422 (*See also* A Happy Family —If, 367; How Personality Grows, 431; Personality in the Making, 447)

CHART OF CHILD DEVELOPMENT, XIX-CII
From Birth to One Year, XXII
From One Year to Two Years, XXVIII
From Two to Three Years, XXXIV
From Three to Six Years, XLII
From Six to Nine Years, LIV
From Nine Years Through Pre-Adolescence, LXXII
From Puberty Through Adolescence (The Teens), LXXXVIII

Cheating (*See* Honesty and Honor, 28; Discipline, 419-430; Personality Problems, 431-450; Cheating in Adolescence, 509)

Cheerfulness and Optimism, 11

CHELEY, FRANK H.: The Boy's Own Room, 184; Taking Advantage of the Summer Camp for Your Boy, 193; Religious Training of Older Children, 478

Chickenpox, 225

Child Culture, 309

Children and the World Today, 405

Children's Singing in the Home, 321

Child Who Is Jealous, 443

Child Who Lies, 443

Child Who Steals, 446

Child Who Sulks, 436

Child Who Teases, 439

Chorea, 233

Christian Associations (YMCA and YWCA), 412

Church (*See* Religious Training, 451-482)

CHURCHILL, ALLEN L.: The Girl's Own Room, 183; The Backyard, 186; Summer Camps for Girls, 195

Circumcision, 106

Citizenship, Community Life and, 403-416

Citizenship, Preparing Our Children for, 403

Civic Responsibility (*See* Patriotism and Civic Responsibility, 45)

Cleanliness and Health, 12 (*See also* Housing, 179-188; Strict Cleanliness, 203; The Importance of Quarantine, 214)

Clothing (*See* Baby's Clothes, 109; Learning to Wash and Dress, 123)

Clubs as a Help to the Home, 407-416

Cod Liver Oil (*See* Foods Besides Milk, 99; Feeding the Average Baby, 103)

Cold, The Common, 238

Colic, 240

Collections (*See* Hobbies, 337)

College, Who Shall Go to?, 350

Coloring (*See* Coloring and Drawing by Little Children, 314)

Columbian Squires, 414

Comic Strips, The, 308

Common Cold, The, 238

Community Life and Citizenship, 403-416

Companions, Imaginary, 393

Complaints in Adolescence, 500

Concentration (*See* Application and Concentration, 7)

Conduct (*See under* Behavior)

Conduct, Asocial, 504

Confidence, 13

Conjunctivitis, 248

Conscience, 14

Consideration for Others (*See* Sympathy and Consideration for Others, 57)

Constipation, 242

Contagious Diseases, The Common, 225

Contagious Diseases, The Less Common, 231

Contentment, 15

Contrary Child, The, 436

Convalescence (*See* While the Children Are Getting Well, 218; Amusements for Convalescent Children, 220)

Convulsions (*See* Symptoms of Acute Illness, 199)

Cooperation and Teamwork, 16

Courage, 17

Courtesy, Politeness and Manners, 18

Crawling (*See* Baby's Exercises, 117)

Crayons (*See* Coloring and Drawing by Little Children, 314)

CREELMAN, ELLEN: The Little Child's Room, 182

Cross Child, The, 435

CROSS, EDITH RILAND: Pictures for Children, 313

Croup, 239

"Crushes" in Adolescence, 511

Crying (*See* Why the Baby Cries, 106)

Curiosity, 266

Cuts and Wounds, 250

D

Daily Feedings for Average Well Babies, 104
Dancing for Your Children, 146
Daydreaming and Romancing in Adolescence, 508
Deadly Nightshade Poisoning, 256
Decision (*See* Investigation, Judgment and Decision, 35)
Democratic Spirit, 19
DAVIS, MARY AGNES: Lunch Time at School, 171
Delinquency, 504
Dentist, 132; Make Friends with the, 222
Dependability (*See* Trustworthiness and Dependability, 64)
Desserts (*See* Nutritional Requirements, 161)
Determination (*See* Will Power and Determination, 67)
DEWEY, JOHN: Reasoning in Early Childhood, 265
Diabetes Mellitus, 250
Diapers (*See* So You're Expecting a Baby, 71; Baby's Clothes, 110)
Diarrhea (*See* Stomach Disorders, 241)
Diet (*See under* Food)
Differences of Opinion in This Manual, Concerning, IX
Difficulties of Nursing Period, 85; of Bottle-Fed Baby, 98
Digestion (*See under* Indigestion)
Dignity and Reserve, 20
Diphtheria, 228
Diligence (*See* Industry and Diligence, 33)
Discipline, 419-430 (*See also under* Behavior)
Disabilities, 493
Diseases of Childhood, 223 (*See* Contagious Diseases, Common, 225; Contagious Diseases, Less Common, 231; Skin, Diseases of, 236; Respiratory Tract, Diseases of, 238; Abdomen, Diseases in, 240; Kidney, Diseases of, 245; Allergy, Diseases Due to, 246; Eye, Diseases of, 248; Nutrition, Diseases of, 249; Physical Injuries, 250; Symptoms of Acute Illness, 199; Department of Health Requirements, 210; Home Nursing, 201)
Diseases of Childhood, Index to, 223
DIXON, EDITH D.: Beginning Sex Education, 395
Doctor—Teach Children That Doctor Is Their Friend, 222 (*See also* Diseases of Childhood, 223-256; Symptoms of Acute Illness, 199)
DODSON, GEORGE R.: The Aim of Religious Education, 475
Dog or Other Animal Bites, 251
Dogs as Pets (See Animal Friends, 325; Children Need Pets, 327)
Do Your Ears Hear?, 136
Dramatics in the Home, 273

Drawing (*See* Self-Discovery Through Painting and Drawing, 315)
Drawing and Coloring by Little Children, 314
Drinking by Adolescents, 510
Drinks for Children (*See under* Beverages)

E

Ear, Foreign Bodies in, 252
Ear Infections, 239
Ears, Care of, 136
Eating (*See under* Food)
Eczema, 247
Editorial Board of MANUAL OF CHILD DEVELOPMENT, III
Education (*See* The Learning Process, 259-274; Speech and Language, 275-295; Reading and Story-Telling, 297-309; Pictures and Drawings, 311-315; Music, 317-323; Nature, 325-330; Home and School, 341-354; Vocational Guidance, 355-365; Adolescence and Mental Development, 491)
Educational Pitfalls for Adolescents, 495
Education in the Use of Leisure for Adolescents, 501
Efficiency (*See* System and Efficiency, 58)
Eggs (*See* Foods Besides Milk, 99; Feeding the Average Baby, 103; Nutritional Requirements, 161)
EMOTIONAL DEVELOPMENT (*See* SOCIAL AND EMOTIONAL DEVELOPMENT, 367-416)
Emotional Maturity and Stability, 21
Emotional Problems (*See* Personality Problems, 431-450)
Enemas and Suppositories, Use of, 208
English, Home Opportunities in, 283 (*See also* Reading and Story-Telling, 297-309)
English, Work and Play in, 287
ERNST, MARGARET: Good Taste Needs Cultivation, 307
Erysipelas (*See* Cellulitis, 237)
ESSENTIALS OF GOOD CHARACTER AND PERSONALITY, 1-67
Evading Reality in Adolescence, 508
Exercise for Baby (*See* Baby's Exercises, 117)
Exercise for Children, 145-150
Exercise, Sports for, 145
EXNER, MAX J., M.D.: The Question of Petting, 399
Extravagance (*See* Thrift, 62; The Child Who Steals, 446)
Expecting a Baby, 71
Eye, Diseases of the, 248-251
Eyeglasses (*See* Eyes, Care of, 134)
Eyes, Care of, 134

F

Fairness and Justice, 22
Fairy Tales for Children, 306
Faith (*See* Respect, Reverence and Faith, 48; Religious Training, 451-482)
Falsehood (*See under* Lying)
Family, A Happy—If, 367
Family Circle, Sharing the Life of the, 350
Family, Cooperative, 372
Family Differences, 375
Family's Leisure, Your, 334
Family Lodge, The, 377
Family of Judges, The, 426
Family Prayers and Saying Grace, 458
Fathers, Special Note to, 379
Fatigue and Naughtiness, 143
Fats (*See* Nutritional Requirements of Growing Children, 161)
Fear-Punishment, The, 425
Feeding the Average Baby, 103
Feet (*See* Shoes, Socks, Stockings, 112; Child Posture, 138)
Fever (*See* Caring for the Sick Child, 200)
Finding Friends for the Pre-School Child, 392
Finger-Plays for Babies, 297
Fish (*See* Nutritional Requirements, 161)
FISHER, DOROTHY CANFIELD: Learning Self-Reliance, 261
Food (*See* Baby Care and Feeding, 6-119; Learning to Eat, 122; Food for the Family, 161-178)
Food Between Meals, 172
Food for School Boys and Girls, 170
Food Habits, Good, 172
Food Plan for the Growing Child, 168
Food Properties (*See* Nutritional Requirements, 161)
Foods Besides Milk, 99
Foods, Teaching Children to Like Wholesome, 175
Foot (*See under* Feet)
FORBUSH, WILLIAM BYRON: The Porch as a Playground, 182; Amusements for Convalescent Children, 220; The Impudent Child, 439; Fairy Tales for Children, 306
Foreign Bodies in the Eye, 248
Foreign Bodies in the Nose, 251
Foreign Bodies in the Throat and Stomach, 252
Foreign Body in the Ear, 252
Forgetful Child, The, 440
Forming Good Habits, 121
Formula, Milk (*See* Milk Mixtures, 104)
Fresh Air (*See* Sunshine and Fresh Air, 116)
Friendliness, 23
Friends and Friendships (*See* Friendliness, 23; Learning Social Behavior, 389; Little Child

Need Friends, 391; Finding Friends for the Pre-School Child, 392; When Friends Seem to Be Doing Harm, 394; Imaginary Companions, 393; Friends, The Importance of in Adolescence, 510; The Adolescent and His Companions, 510)
Friendships, 389-394
Friends, The Importance of, in Adolescence, 510
Frostbite, 251
Fruits and Fruit Juices (*See* Foods Besides Milk, 99; Nutritional Requirements, 161; Planning the Young Child's Menu, 166; Summer Drinks for Children, 173)
Furniture (*See under* Room)

G

Games: For Babies, 297; for Children, 283, 296; for Sunday, 480; as Sports for Exercise, 145
GASS, MRS. PRESTON F.: Finding Friends for the Pre-school Child, 392
Generosity, 24
Genital Organs, Care of, 115
German Measles, 226
GILLETT, LUCY H.: Good Food Habits, 172
Girl Scouts, 409
Girl's Own Room, The, 183
Glandular Fever (*See* Infectious Mononucleosis, 231)
God (*See* Religious Training, 451-482)
Good Food Habits, 172
Good Sportsmanship, 25
Good Taste needs Cultivation, 307
Good Temper, 26
Grace, Saying (*See* Family Prayers and Saying Grace, 458)
GRADED INDEX, 517
Gratitude (*See* Appreciation and Gratitude, 8)
GRAY, FRANK F.: The Waywayanda Grace, 459
GREEN, JAMES SONNETT, M.D.: Your Child's Speech, 275
Grippe (*See* Influenza, 231)
Growth and Development in Adolescents, 485-490
Growth and Development in Children, 151-159
GRUENBERG, SIDONIE MATSNER: The Lazy Child, 441

H

Habits and Habit Training, 121-129
Hair, Care of Child's, 137
Handcraft, Adventuring in, 335
Handicaps (*See* Abilities and Disabilities, 493)
HANSL, EVA VON B.: Manners Right from the Start, 381

Happy Family—If, 367

HARRIS, EDNA E.: Work and Play in English, 287

Hay Fever, 246

HAYS, HAROLD: Do Your Ears Hear?, 136

Health (*See* Cleanliness and Health, 12)

Health and Hygiene, 130-138

Health Examinations, 159

Health Requirements, N. Y. State, Department of Health, 210 (*See also* Introduction to, 209)

Heat Rash, 237

Height and Weight Tables, 153

Height and Weight Tables, How to Use, 152

Height Chart, 158

Helpfulness, 27

Heritage of Childhood, 325

HERRICK, CHRISTINE TERHUNE: The Vain Child, 445

HINSDALE, GUY, M.D.: Sea Bathing, 192

Hives, 247

Hoarseness (*See* Symptoms, 199)

Hobbies, 337

HOLT, L. EMMETT, M.D.: Special Summer Rules, 108

Home and School, 341-354

Home Atmosphere, 370

Home for the Children, A, 179

Home, How It Can Cooperate with the School, 347

Home Life, 367-380

Home Nursing, 199-222

Home Opportunities in English, 283

Homework (*See* Home and School, 341-354)

Honesty and Honor, 28

Honor (*See* Honesty and Honor, 28)

Household Tasks, Training in, 373

Housing, 179-188

How Children Learn, 259

How Personality Grows, 431

How to Tell Stories for Character-Building, 429

Humor, Sense of, 55

HUNGERLAND, HELMUT: Self-Discovery Through Painting and Drawing, 315

HUNT, CLARA WHITEHILL: The Poetry Habit, 303

HUNTER, MINERVA: The Child Who Is Jealous, 443

HURLL, ESTELLE M.: How to Interest Children in Pictures, 311

Hydrochloric Acid Poisoning, 255

Hygiene (*See* Health and Hygiene, 130-138)

Hygiene of the Nursing Mother, 77

Hygiene, Physical, in Adolescence, 486

Hysterical Child, The, 434

I

Idealism and Life Purpose, 29

Illness (*See* Home Nursing, 199-222; Diseases of Childhood, 223-250)

Imagination, 30 (*See also under* Make-Believe)

Imaginary Companions, 393

Imitative Play, 271

Immaturity (*See* Individual as a Whole, 493)

Immunization (*See* Against What Should We Be Immunized?, 215)

Impetigo, 236

Important Note for Mothers of Children of Any Age, XXI

Impudent Child, The, 439

Incorrigibility in Adolescents, 507

Independence, Self-Reliance and Self Help, 31; 494

Indigestion (*See* Difficulties of the Nursing Period, 85; Difficulties of the Bottle-Fed Baby, 98; Why Baby Cries, 106; Stomach Disorders, 241)

Individual as a Whole, 493

Individuality and Originality, 32

Industry and Diligence, 33

Infant (*See under* Baby)

Infantile Paralysis, 231

Infections (*See* Symptoms, 199; Diseases of Childhood, 223-250)

Infectious Mononucleosis, 232

Influenza, 231

Ingenuity (*See* Resourcefulness and Ingenuity, 49)

Initiative and Ambition, 34

Injuries, Physical, 250

Inoculations (*See* Against What Should We Be Immunized?, 215)

Insect Bites and Stings (*See* Bites and Stings, 251)

Intelligence Quotient or I. Q. (*See* Measurement of Intelligence, 491)

Introduction to ESSENTIALS OF GOOD CHARACTER AND PERSONALITY, 1

Introduction to TRAITS TO BE DISCOURAGED, CORRECTED OR LEFT TO BE OUTGROWN, CX

Intussusception, 242

Investigation, Judgment and Decision, 35

Iron, Need for, in Diet (*See* Nutritional Requirements of Growing Children, 161)

IRWIN, ALICE: Summer Drinks for Children, 173

Itch (*See* Diseases of the Skin, 236)

Ivy Poisoning, 256

J

Jaundice, 241

Jealous Child (See Child Who Is Jealous, 443)

Jewish Center, The, 388

Jewish Child, Religious Education of, 463

Judgment (*See* Investigation, Judgment and Decision, 35)

Justice (*See* Fairness and Justice, 22)

K

KEENER, MYRTLE DOUGLAS: Children's Singing in the Home, 321

Kidney, Diseases of the, 245

Kindergarten, Will You Send Your Child to?, 343

Kindness, 36

L

LANGMUIR, MARY FISHER, Ph.D.: A Happy Family—If, 367

Language (*See* Speech and Language, 275-295)

Language, Learning to Use, 281

Lazy Child, The, 441

Lead Poisoning, 254

Leadership, 37

Learning Process, The, 259-274

Learning Social Behavior, 389

Learning to Eat, 122

Learning to Use Leisure in Adolescence, 500

Learning to Wash and Dress, 123

Leisure Time Activities, 331-340 (*See also* Learning to Use Leisure in Adolescence, 500)

LEVINE, MILTON I., M.D.: Child Posture, 138

LEVINSON, ABRAHAM, M.D.: While the Children Are Getting Well, 218

Lies (*See* Child Who Lies, 443)

Life Purpose (*See* Idealism and Life Purpose, 29)

Lime Poisoning, 255

Literature for Pre-School Children, 301

Little Child Needs Friends, The, 391

Little Child's Room, The, 182

Love (*See* Affection and Love, 5)

LOWENBERG, MIRIAM E.: Learning to Eat, 122; Planning the Young Child's Menu, 166

Loyalty, 38

Lunch-Box (*See* School Lunch-Box, 171)

Lunch Time at School, 171

Lying (*See* Imagination, 30; Truthfulness, 65; Child Who Lies, 443)

M

McCONN, MAX: Who Shall Go to College?, 350

MACKAY, CHARLES: A Deed and a Word (verse), 416

Make-Believe (*See* Imagination, 30; Truthfulness, 65; Play a Way of Learning, 262 Dramatics in the Home, 273; Reading and Story-Telling, 297-307; The Child Who Lies, 443)

Making Music Together, 322

Malnutrition (*See* Nutritional Requirements, 161)

Manners (*See* Courtesy, Politeness and Manners, 18; Right from the Start, 381)

MARSH, CORINNA: What Are Good Character Habits and How Are They Developed?, 422; How to Keep Racial and Religious Prejudice from Our Children, 481

MARSH, LUCILLE: Dancing for Your Children, 146

Masturbation, 129; in Adolescence, 490

Maturity, 21; Preparing for, 397; 493

Meals (*See under* Food)

Meals, 225

Measurement of Intelligence, 491

Meats (*See* Foods Besides Milk, 99; Nutritional Requirements, 161; Planning the Young Child's Menu, 166)

Medical Supplies, Basic, 253

Medicines (*See* Diseases of Childhood, 223-250)

MEGRAW, E. M.: The Family of Judges, 426

Meningitis, 232

MENTAL DEVELOPMENT, 257-364

Menus (*See* Foods Besides Milk, 99; Milk Mixtures, 104; Nutritional Requirements, 161; Planning the Young Child's Menu, 166; Menus for Children from Two to Six, 169; Food for School Boys and Girls, 170; The School Lunch-Box, 171)

Mercury Poisoning, 255

Milk, Choice of, 88

Milk Mixtures (Formulas) for Babies of Different Weights and Ages, 104

Mind (*See* MENTAL DEVELOPMENT, 257-364)

Mind in Adolescence (*See* Slow Mind, 492; Average Mind, 492; Superior Mind, 492)

MINDLIN, ROWLAND L., M.D.: Bed Wetting, 126; Thumb Sucking, 128; Sports for Exercise, 145; Diseases of Childhood, 223-250

Minerals (*See* Nutritional Requirements of Growing Children, 161)

Miscarriage, 75

Modesty and Simplicity, 39

Money (*See* Thrift, 62; The Child Who Steals, 446; The Question of Work, 498)

MORAL AND SPIRITUAL DEVELOPMENT, 417-482

Mother (*See* CHART OF CHILD DEVELOPMENT, XIX-CII; SUGGESTED READING GUIDE, CIII)

Mother Goose, Use of, 299

Mother's Milk the Best Food for Baby, 77

Motives to Which Youth Responds, 423

Movies, The, 308; Leisure in Adolescence, 500
Mumps, 227
Music, 317-323

N

Nail Biting, 128
Naturalness and Unaffectedness, 40
Nature, 325-329
Nature Study for Older Boys and Girls, 328
Nature Study for Young Children, 326
Naughtiness (*See* Fatigue and Naughtiness, 143; *See also under* Behavior)
Neatness (*See* Orderliness and Neatness, 43)
Needs of the Parent, 514
Nephrosis, 245
NEUMANN, HENRY, Ph.D.: Motives to Which Youth Responds, 423
NEWELL, BERTHA PAYNE: Drawing and Coloring by Little Children, 314; Music and Rhythm, 316; Training in Household Tasks, 373
Nitrate of Silver Poisoning, 255
Nitric Acid Poisoning, 255
Nose and Throat, Care of, 138
Nose-Bleed, 252
Nose, Foreign Bodies in, 251
Nursery School, Will You Send Your Child to, 341
Nurses (*See* Wet Nurses, 88; Baby's Caretakers, 107)
Nursing at Home, 201
Nursing Mother (*See under* Breast-Feeding)
Nursing Period, Difficulties of the, 85
Nursing the Sick Child, 199-256
Nutrition (*See under* Food)
Nutritional Requirements of Growing Children, 161
Nutrition, Diseases of, 249
Nux Vomica Poisoning, 254

O

Obedience, 41
Observation, 269
O'CONNOR, JOHNSON: Vocational Aptitudes That Affect School Success, 360
OLIVER, MRS. V. OMA GRACE: Sharing the Life of the Family Circle, 374
Open-Mindedness and Reasonableness, 42
Opium Poisoning, 254
Optimism (*See* Cheerfulness and Optimism, 11)
Orange Juice (*See* Foods Besides Milk, 99; Feeding the Average Baby, 103; Nutritional Requirements of Growing Children, 161)
Orderliness and Neatness, 43

Oregon Hemlock Poisoning, 256
Originality (*See* Individuality and Originality, 32)
O'SHEA, MICHAEL VINCENT: Teaching a Child to Talk, 279; The Cross Child, 435; The Forgetful Child, 440
Outdoor Playthings, Requisites for, 334
Overstimulation (*See* Fatigue and Naughtiness, 143)
Oxalic Acid Poisoning, 255

P

Pain in the Abdomen (*See* Symptoms of Acute Illness, 199; Diseases in the Abdomen, 240; Stomach Disorders, 241)
Painting and Drawing (*See* Self-Discovery Through Painting and Drawing, 315)
PALMER, GEORGE TRUMAN, Ph.D.: What Height and Weight Tables Mean, 151
Parent, Needs of the, 514
Patience, 44
Patriotism and Civic Responsibility, 45
Periodic Health Examinations, 159
Peritonitis (*See* Appendicitis, 242)
Perseverance and Persistence, 46
Personality (*See* ESSENTIALS OF GOOD CHARACTER AND PERSONALITY, 1-67; Personality in the Making, 447; How Personality Grows, 431; Personality Problems, 431-450)
Pets (*See* Animal Friends, 325; Children Need Pets, 327)
Petting, The Question of, 399
Phosphorous Poisoning, 254
PHYSICAL DEVELOPMENT, 69-256
Physical Growth and Development in Adolescence, 485
Physical Hygiene in Adolescence, 486
Physical Injuries, 250
Physician (*See under* Doctor)
Piano Playing (*See* Mothers and Practicing, 319)
Pictures and Drawing, 311-315
Pictures for Children, 313
Pictures, How to Interest Children in, 313
Pimples (*See* Acne, 237)
Pink Eye (*See* Eye, Diseases of, 248)
Planning the Young Child's Menu, 166
Play and Playthings (*See* Play a Way of Learning, 262; Imitative Play, 271; Selecting Toys Wisely, 331; Play-Places in the House, 181; Porch as a Playground, 182; Backyard, The, 186; Outdoor Playthings, 334; Amusements for Convalescent Children, 220)
Playmates (*See* Friends)
Play Pen (*See* Baby's Exercises, 117)

Pneumonia, 240

Poetry (*See* Work and Play in English, 287; Baby's Story Hour, 297; Use of Mother Goose, 299; Poetry Habit, 303)

Poison Hemlock Poisoning, 256

Poison Ivy, 256

Poison Oak, 256

Poisonous Plants, 256

Poison Sumac, 256

Poisons and Their Antidotes, 254

Politeness (*See* Courtesy, Politeness and Manners, 18; Manners Right from the Start, 381)

Porch as a Playground, The, 182

Posture, Child, 138

Potash Poisoning, 255

Poultices and the Like, 205

Practicing, Mothers and, 319

Praise Instead of Blame, 427

Prayers and Saying Grace, 458

Prayers, Some Simple, 459

Pregnancy (*See* So You're Expecting a Baby, 71)

Prejudice, Racial and Religious, 481

Preparing for Maturity, 397

Prescribing by Mail, 207

Preserving Health, 130

Premature, Small or Delicate Baby, 79

PRICE, ELIZABETH: Adventuring in Handcraft, 335; Hobbies, 337

Problems Incidental to Physical Growth and Development in Adolescence, 487

Problems of Personality, 431-450

Progress, Your Child's in Elementary School, 345

Promptness (*See* Punctuality and Promptness. 47)

Protein (*See* Nutritional Requirements of Growing Children, 161

Prudence (*See* Caution and Prudence, 10)

Ptomaine Poisoning, 254

Public Servants, Appreciating Our, 404

Punctuality and Promptness, 47

Punishment (*See* under Behavior)

Pyelitis, 245

Q

Quarantine, The Importance of, 214

Quarrelsome Child, The, 437

Questions, When the Children Ask, 268

Quicklime Poisoning, 255

Quinsy (*See* Sore Throat, 238)

R

Rabies (*See* Against What Should We Be Immunized? 215; Dog or Other Animal Bites, 251)

Radio, The, 308

RANKIN, MARY E.: The Beginning of Religious Training, 451

Rash (*See* Skin, Diseases of the, 236)

READ, MARY L.: How To Tell Stories, 307

Reading and Story Telling, 297-309

Reading Difficulties in Adolescence, 493

Reading Guide, CIII

Reasonableness (*See* Openmindedness and Reasonableness, 42)

Reasoning (*See* Thinking and Reasoning, 60)

Reasoning in Early Childhood, 265

Recreation (*See* Leisure-Time Activities, 331-340)

REID, EDITH LOCHRIDGE: The Fear-Punishment, 425

Relationships, Boy and Girl in Adolescence, 512

Religion (*See* under Religious Training)

Religious Education, Aim of, 475

Religious Education of a Catholic Child, 460

Religious Education of a Jewish Child, 463

Religious Training, 451-482

Religious Training, Beginnings of, 451

Religious Training, Importance of, 451

Religious Training of Older Children, 478

Reproductive System (*See* Preparing for Maturity, 397; Maturing of the Reproductive System in Adolescence, 485)

Reserve (*See* Dignity and Reserve, 20)

Resourcefulness and Ingenuity, 49

Respect, Reverence and Faith, 48 (*See also* Religious Training, 451-482)

Respiratory Tract, Diseases of, 238

Responsibility, 50

Rest, 141-143

Reverence (*See* Respect, Reverence and Faith, 48; Religious Training, 451-482)

Rheumatic Fever, 233

Rhyme (*See* under Poetry)

Rhythm (*See* Work and Play in English, 287; Baby's Story-Hour, 297; Use of Mother Goose, 299; Music and Rhythm, 316)

Ringworm, 236

RIPPIN, JANE DEETER: The Girl Scouts, 409

ROBERTS, HARRY, M. D.: Poultices and the Like, 205

ROBERTS, LYDIA J.: Teaching Children to Like Wholesome Foods, 175

ROBINSON, CLARENCE C.: How to Recognize Your Child's Special Ability, 358

ROE-ANDERSON, ANN: Enlarging the Child's Vocabulary, 280

Room (*See* Baby's Room, 179; Little Child's Room, 182; Girl's Own Room, 182; Boy's Own Room, 184)

Rose, Mary Swartz: Food for School Boys and Girls, 170; The School Lunch-Box, 171

Roseola, 227

Round-Shoulderedness (*See* Child Posture, 138)

S

Safety (*See* Caution and Prudence, 10; Sea Bathing, 192; Importance of Quarantine, 214; Against What Should We Be Immunized?, 215)

St. Anthony's Fire (*See* Cellulitis, 237)

St. Vitus' Dance (*See* Chorea, 233)

Scabies, 236

Scarlet Fever, 227

School (*See* Home and School, 341-354; Vocational Guidance, 355-366)

School Lunch-Box, 171

Scouts (*See* Boy Scouts, 408; Girl Scouts, 409)

Scurvy, 249

Sea Bathing, 192

Selecting Toys Wisely, 331

Self-Amusement and Self-Direction, 51

Self-Centered Child, The, 435

Self-Control, 52

Self-Direction (*See* Self-Amusement and Self-Direction, 51)

Self-Discovery Through Painting and Drawing, 315

Self-Help (*See* Independence, Self-Reliance and Self-Help, 31)

Self-Reliance (*See* Independence, Self-Reliance and Self-Help, 31)

Self-Reliance, Learning, 261

Self-Respect, 53

Self-Sacrifice and Service to Others, 54

Sense of Humor, 55

Service to Others (*See* Self-Sacrifice and Service to Others, 54)

Sex (*See* Beginning Sex Education, 395; Preparing for Maturity, 397; The Question of Petting, 399; Attitudes Toward Sex in Adolescence, 488; Sex Instruction in Adolescence, 488; Sex Talk and Reading, 489)

Sex, Education, 395-402; In Adolescence, 488

Shaw, Henry L. K., M.D.: Special Summer Rules, 108

Sherman, Mandel, Ph.D.: How Personality Grows, 431; The Timid Child, 433; The Hysterical Child, 434; The Self-Centered Child, 435

Shoes (*See under* Feet)

Sick Child, Caring for, 200

Sickroom (*See* Home Nursing, 201)

Sickroom Supplies (*See* Basic Medical and Sickroom Supplies, 253)

Sies, Alice Corbin: Imitative Play, 271; The Little Child Needs Friends, 391

Signs of Illness (*See* Symptoms, 199)

Simplicity (*See* Modesty and Simplicity, 39)

Sincerity, 56

Singing in the Home, Children's, 321

Sitters (*See* Baby's Caretakers, 107)

Sitting Up, 117

Six Tests for Books, 309

Skin, Diseases of the, 236

Sleep, 141

Slow Mind, The, 492

Smallpox, 236

Smith, Fred C.: Vocational Guidance in Home and School, 355

Soares, Theodore G., Rev.: Making the Bible Real to the Child, 470

SOCIAL AND EMOTIONAL DEVELOPMENT, 367-416

Social Behavior, Learning, 389

Socks (*See* Baby's Clothes, 109)

Soda Poisoning, 255

Solitude, The Child Needs, 374

Some Simple Prayers, 459

Sore Throat, 238

Special Note to Fathers, 379

Speech and Language, 275-296

Speech, Your Child's, 275

SPIRITUAL DEVELOPMENT (*See* MORAL AND SPIRITUAL DEVELOPMENT, 417-482)

Sports for Exercise, 145

Stability (*See* Emotional Maturity and Stability, 21)

Standing (*See* Baby's Exercises, 117; Child Posture, 138)

Stealing (*See* The Child Who Steals, 446; Stealing in Adolescence, 506)

Stiffness of Neck or Back (*See* Symptoms of Acute Illness, 199)

Stinkweed Poisoning, 256

Stockings (*See* Baby's Clothes, 109)

Stomach Disorders, 241

Stomach, Foreign Bodies in, 252

Stories, How to Tell, 307; How to Tell for Character Building, 429

Story Telling, Reading and, 297-310

Strain, Frances Bruce: Preparing for Maturity, 397

Strychnine Poisoning, 254

Study (*See* Home and School, 341-354)

Stuttering, 277

Stye, 248

Sulphuric Acid Poisoning, 255

Summer Camp for Your Boy, 193

Summer Camps for Girls, 195

Summer Drinks for Children, 173

Summer Rules, 108

Sunday in the Home, 480

Sunday School (*See* Importance of Religious Training, 451)

Sunshine and Fresh Air, 116

Superior Mind, The, 492

Supper (*See under* Food and Menus)

Suppositories, Use of Enemas and, 208

Swan, Augusta M.: The Heritage of Childhood, 325

Sweeny, Mary E.: The Nutritional Requirements of Growing Children, 161

Swimming (*See* Sports for Exercise, 145; Sea Bathing, 192)

Swollen Glands, 239

Sympathy and Consideration for Others, 57

Symptoms of Acute Illness, 199

Syphilis, 234

System and Efficiency, 58

T

Table Manners (*See* Manners, 381)

Tact, 59

Talented Child (*See* Individuality and Originality, 32; How to Recognize Special Ability, 358-493)

Talking (*See* Speech and Language, 275-295)

Teaching a Child to Talk, 279

Teaching Children to Like Wholesome Foods, 175

Teamwork (*See* Cooperation and Teamwork, 16)

Teasing Child (*See* Child Who Teases, 439)

Teeth, the Child's, 133 (*See also* Why the Baby Cries, 106; The Dentist, 132)

Temperature (*See* Symptoms, 199; Caring for the Sick Child, 200)

Temper Tantrums, Child Who Has, 437

Terry, Mary Collins: Family Prayers and Saying Grace, 458; The Importance of Religious Training, 451

Tests Against Disease (*See* Against What Should We Be Immunized? 215)

Tests, Intelligence and Personality (*See* Measurement of Intelligence, 491)

Tests, Six, for Books, 309

Thermometer (*See* Caring for the Sick Child, 200)

Thinking and Reasoning, 60

Thoroughness, 61

Thrift, 62

Throat, Sore, 238; Foreign Bodies in, 252

Thumb Sucking, 128

Timid Child, 433

Toilet Habits, 125

Tolerance, 63

Tonsillitis (*See* Tonsils and Adenoids, 239)

Tonsils and Adenoids, 239

Toys, Selecting Wisely, 331

Training (*See* Essentials of Good Character and Personality, 1-67; Habits and Habit Training, 121-129; How to Develop Good Character Habits, 422; Personality in the Making, 447)

Training in Household Tasks, 373

Traits to Be Discouraged, Corrected, or Left to Be Outgrown, CXI

Traits of Character and Personality to Be Encouraged, 1-67

Truancy in Adolescence, 509

Trustworthiness and Dependability, 64

Truthfulness, 65

Tuberculosis, 234

Typhoid Fever, 235

U

Unaffectedness (*See* Naturalness and Unaffectedness, 40)

Underwear (*See* Baby's Clothes, 109)

Undulant Fever, 235

Unselfishness, 66

Upset Stomach (*See* Stomach Disorders, 241)

Use Praise Instead of Blame, 427

V

Vacations, 189-198; How to Give Children a Good Time During, 190

Vaccination (*See* Against What Should We Be Immunized? 215)

Vaginitis, 245

Vain Child, The, 445

Vandevere, J. Lillian: Mothers and Practicing, 319

Vegetables (*See* Foods Besides Milk, 99; Nutritional Requirements, 161; Teaching Children to Like Wholesome Foods, 175)

Ventilation (*See* Baby's Room, 179; Little Child's Room, 152; Home Nursing, 199)

Verse (*See under* Poetry)

Vision (*See* Eyes, Care of, 134)

Vitamins (*See* Foods Besides Milk, 99; Nutritional Requirements, 161)

Vitriol Poisoning, 255

Vocabulary, Enlarging the Child's, 280

Vocational Aptitudes That Affect School Success, 360

Vocational Guidance, 355-365; in Home and School, 355

Vomiting (*See* Symptoms, 199; Stomach Disorders, 241)

W

Walking (*See* Baby's Exercises, 117; Child Posture, 138)

WARING, ETHEL B.: Learning to Wash and Dress, 123

Warts, 237

Water for the Baby to Drink, 97

Water Hemlock Poisoning, 256

Weaning, 87

Weight Chart, 158

WEINMAN, ROSE BARLOW: Religious Education of a Jewish Child, 463

WEST, MRS. MAX: The Baby's Vacation, 189; Caring for the Sick Child, 200

Wet Nurses, 88

What Are Good Character Habits and How Developed? 422

What Height and Weight Tables Mean, 151

When the Children Ask Questions, 268 (*See also* Curiosity, 266)

When Friends Seem to Be Doing Harm, 394

When Punishment Is Necessary, 419

While the Children Are Getting Well, 218

WHITE, PARK J.: Worms, 242

Why the Baby Cries, 106

Whooping Cough, 230

WILKER, MARGUERITE: Learning Social Behavior, 389

Will Power and Determination, 67

WOOD, THOMAS D., M.D.: Average Weights by Height and Age for Girls and Boys, 153

WOODBURY, ROBERT MORSE, M.D.: Height and Weight Tables, 153

WOODCOCK, LOUISE P.: Personality in the Making, 447

Words (*See* Speech and Language, 275-295)

Work (*See* Accuracy, 3; Application and Concentration, 7; Honesty and Honor, 28; Independence, Self-Reliance and Self-Help, 31; Industry and Diligence, 33; Initiative and Ambition, 34; Perseverance and Persistence, 46; System and Efficiency, 58; Thinking and Reasoning, 60; Trustworthiness and Dependability, 64; Will Power and Determination, 67; Home and School, 341-347; Vocational Guidance, 355-365; The Lazy Child, 441; The Question of Work in Adolescence, 498)

Worms, 242

Wounds (*See* Cuts and Wounds, 250)

WRIGHT, ROWE: Camp Fire Girls, 410

X, Y, Z

YMCA and YWCA, 412